THEORIES OF COGNITIVE CONSISTENCY:
A SOURCEBOOK

Theories of Cognitive Consistency:
A Sourcebook

Edited by
Robert P. Abelson
Elliot Aronson
William J. McGuire
Theodore M. Newcomb
Milton J. Rosenberg
Percy H. Tannenbaum

Rand McNally and Company, Chicago

PREFACE

The history of *Theories of Cognitive Consistency* goes back to 1961 or 1962, when the six editors more or less independently reached the conclusion that it would be worthwhile to gather together many of the streams of effort in the psychology of cognitive consistency, to compare and contrast the ideas traveling under the banners of 'dissonance theory,' 'balance theory,' 'the congruity principle,' etc., and generally to bring order out of chaos. After considerable discussion, the pursuit of these goals took the form of a proposal to the National Science Foundation to support a coordinated effort to explore these issues. Such support was forthcoming in the form of NSF Grant GS-1005 to the Center for Advanced Study in the Behavioral Sciences, largely to finance Fellowships to the Center so that we could be freed for a year from other responsibilities.

As it developed, only three of the six Fellows were able to spend the entire year 1965-1966 at the Center, and the other three undertook periodic trips to Palo Alto for a series of work conferences. During the course of these conferences, our hope for developing a theoretical synthesis gradually became converted into the desire to clarify much more fully what it was that we thought we were trying to synthesize. The issues involved in 'cognitive consistency' turned out to be much deeper and broader than we had imagined. Therefore, we invited a large number of researchers who have been working in relevant subareas to contribute 'think pieces' reviewing their own work in relation to larger theoretical issues. A gratifying number of individuals took on their requested assignments, and this volume owes a great deal to the excellent cooperation we received from our contributors.

We divided the editorial tasks according to our mutual interests and wishes. The six editors are listed alphabetically on the title page—an equitable basis reflecting the sharing of various editorial responsibilities. The order is, however, especially fortuitous in the case of Abelson, who deserves top billing for more substantial reasons than alphabetic primacy (maintained by careful avoidance of collaboration with anyone named Abbott, Aaron, or Aardvark). It was he who functioned as an editorial den leader, and who carried the chief editorial load. He is primarily responsible for creating a more or less integrated volume out of these many separate contributions, as well as sharing equally in the other editing chores.

To initiate our exploration of the consistency domain, each of us has written a chapter for Section I expressing his individual views. In the remaining sections, we have endeavored to organize the contributions into coherent packages, and then to unwrap each package and examine its contents in an interpretative summary. In the course of bringing the interrelation of the many themes into focus, many of the separate contributions underwent substantial rewriting and revision. As a result, we hope, the present volume is more carefully integrated than might be expected for a work with so many authors. Some critical issues have been joined, and a number of ideas are now on the table that used to be hidden up the sleeves of social psychologists. The book does not, of course, resolve all questions; indeed, most are still wide open—hopefully to stimulate new research.

The help we received from the Center for Advanced Studies in the Behavioral Sciences was unique in character and inestimable in value. Director Ralph Tyler, who has since retired from the Center but continues to pursue as busy a schedule as ever, gave us crucial support and encouragement in our early struggles to initiate our joint efforts. The Center staff, headed by Preston Cutler and Jane Kielsmeier, maintained us through the many tangles and trying administrative problems of this large undertaking. It is a small measure of our gratitude to dedicate this book to the Center and the enlightened manner of its operation, and to assign to CASBS any royalties which may accrue from the sales.

We are also grateful to Rand McNally & Company for the generous provisions of their contract, enabling us to cope with the many extra expenses of the project. Marianne Clark and Sheila Welch helped pave the way with their competent editorial assistance. James M. Jones of Yale University performed the indexing.

The extraordinary secretarial efforts and skills of Julie Raventos in Palo Alto, and of Martha Ascari and Laura Cooper at central control in New Haven, are noted with gratitude. Other such assistance was contributed by Judith Hilton, Juanita Salvador, and Elaine Laiken, among others. Finally, we thank our friends, colleagues, and families for their understanding and forebearance during our extended tribulations.

Robert P. Abelson
Elliot Aronson
William J. McGuire
Theodore M. Newcomb
Milton J. Rosenberg
Percy H. Tannenbaum

TABLE OF CONTENTS

PREFACE

INTRODUCTION

THEODORE M. NEWCOMB

SECTION I CONSISTENCY THEORIES: SIX POSITIONS

Editorial Introduction   3

1. Dissonance Theory: Progress and Problems   5
   ELLIOT ARONSON

2. Interpersonal Balance   28
   THEODORE M. NEWCOMB

3. The Congruity Principle: Retrospective
   Reflections and Recent Research   52
   PERCY H. TANNENBAUM

4. Hedonism, Inauthenticity, and Other Goads
   Toward Expansion of a Consistency Theory   73
   MILTON J. ROSENBERG

5. Psychological Implication   112
   ROBERT P. ABELSON

6. Theory of the Structure of Human Thought   140
   WILLIAM J. McGUIRE

SECTION II INTERSECTIONS OF CONSISTENCY THEORIES WITH
OTHER PSYCHOLOGICAL THEORIES

Editorial Introduction   165

7. Cognitive Balance as an Aspect of Heider's
   Cognitive Psychology   169
   NEHEMIAH JORDAN

8. Consistency for What? The Functional Approach   179
   DANIEL KATZ

9. Psychoanalytic Theory and Cognitive Dissonance   192
IRVING SARNOFF

10. Role Theory and Consistency Theory   201
VERNON L. ALLEN

11. Cognitive Consistency and the Psychology of Judgment   210
HARRY S. UPSHAW

12. Activation Theory   218
HELEN PEAK

13. Behavior Theory   240
BARRY E. COLLINS

14. Dissonance Reduction in the Behaviorist   246
DARYL J. BEM

15. The Motivational Significance of Collative Variables and Conflict   257
D. E. BERLYNE

16. The Pursuit of Consistency and Variety   267
SALVATORE R. MADDI

17. Résumé and Response from the Consistency Theory Viewpoint   275
WILLIAM J. McGUIRE

SECTION· III THE STATE OF INCONSISTENCY: PRECONDITIONS AND PROPERTIES

A. INCONSISTENCY AS A MOTIVATIONAL CONSTRUCT

Editorial Introduction   301

18. The Motivational Status of Cognitive Consistency Theorizing   303
LEONARD BERKOWITZ

19. Equilibrium as Motivation: Between Pleasure and Enjoyment   311
KURT W. BACK

20. The Problem of Motivation in Consistency Models   319
ALBERT PEPITONE

21. Needs, Wants, and Consistency   327
KEITH E. DAVIS

22. Inconsistency as a Psychological Signal   331
HERBERT C. KELMAN AND REUBEN M. BARON

23. Consistency as a Stimulus Processing Mechanism   337
JEROME E. SINGER

24. Summary: Is Anything Special about Consistency?   341
PERCY H. TANNENBAUM

B. SELF AND THE CONSISTENCY PROCESS

Editorial Introduction   347

25. Consistency Theory and Self-Referent Behavior   349
    PAUL F. SECORD

26. Dissonance, Expectation, and the Self   355
    DANA BRAMEL

27. The Self and Cognitive Consistency   366
    M. BREWSTER SMITH

28. A Cognitive Model of Attitudinal Involvement   373
    THOMAS M. OSTROM AND TIMOTHY C. BROCK

29. Discussion: The Concept of Self   384
    MILTON J. ROSENBERG

C. INCONSISTENCY AND PSYCHOLOGICAL STRESS

Editorial Introduction   391

30. The Bothersomeness of Inconsistency   393
    JEROME E. SINGER

31. On the Discomfort of Cognitive Inconsistency   400
    LEONARD BERKOWITZ

32. Dissonance Without Awareness   408
    TIMOTHY C. BROCK

33. Verbal Indices of Psychological Stress   415
    ELEANOR L. NORRIS

34. Experimental Investigations of Mediational Events   425
    HAROLD B. GERARD

35. Comment: Models of the Role of Stress   432
    PERCY H. TANNENBAUM

D. COMMITMENT AS A MEDIATING VARIABLE

Editorial Introduction   437

36. Cognitive Dissonance and the Control of
    Human Motivation   439
    PHILIP G. ZIMBARDO

37. Commitment   448
    CHARLES A. KIESLER

38. Basic Features of Commitment   456
    HAROLD B. GERARD

39. Discussion: Commitments about Commitment   464
    ELLIOT ARONSON

E. DISCONFIRMED EXPECTANCIES AND
BAD DECISIONS

Editorial Introduction 467

40. Predictability and Pleasure: Reactions to the
Disconfirmation of Expectancies 469
WILLIAM A. WATTS

41. Expectancy Disconfirmation and the Choice of
Negative Alternatives: Dissonance Avoidance or
Situational Demands? 479
IRWIN SILVERMAN

42. Bad Decisions and Dissonance: Nobody's Perfect 485
J. MERRILL CARLSMITH AND JONATHAN L. FREEDMAN

43. Discussion: Expectancy vs. Other Motives 491
ELLIOT ARONSON

F. ASSUMPTIONS ABOUT COGNITIVE STRUCTURE

Editorial Introduction 495

44. How Important Is Cognitive Consistency? 497
JONATHAN L. FREEDMAN

45. Conceptual Good Figures 504
CLINTON DE SOTO AND FRANK ALBRECHT

46. Processes of Ramification Among Cognitive Links 512
KARL E. WEICK

47. A Programmable Theory of Cognition and Affect
in Individual Personal Belief Systems 520
KENNETH MARK COLBY

48. Discussion: Minimalist vs. Maximalist Positions on
Cognitive Structure 526
ROBERT P. ABELSON

G. SOCIAL AND HISTORICAL PERSPECTIVES
ON CONSISTENCY

Editorial Introduction 529

49. Cognition and Social Orderings 531
CLINTON DE SOTO AND FRANK ALBRECHT

50. Consistency, Creativity, and Modernization 539
SEYMOUR J. MANDELBAUM

51. Social Structures and Cognitive Structures 544
JAMES A. DAVIS

52. Ethnocentrism and Intergroup Relations 551
DONALD T. CAMPBELL AND ROBERT A. LEVINE

53. Comment: Parallels Between Individual and
Collective Tendencies 565
THEODORE M. NEWCOMB

SECTION IV RESPONSES AND CONSEQUENCES

A. THE TEMPORAL COURSE OF INCONSISTENCY REDUCTION

Editorial Introduction   569

54. Conflict and Dissonance: A Time of Decision   571
JON D. JECKER

55. Stages in the Decision-Making Process   577
IRVING L. JANIS

56. As Time Goes By   589
NORMAN MILLER

57. The Effects of Time on Cognitive Consistency   599
ELAINE WALSTER AND ELLEN BERSCHEID

58. Comment: Time—Past, Present, and Future   609
ELLIOT ARONSON

B. INDIVIDUAL DIFFERENCES IN REACTIONS TO INCONSISTENCY

Editorial Introduction   613

59. Individual Differences and the Resolution of Cognitive Inconsistencies   615
DAVID G. GLASS

60. Individual Differences and Tolerance for Inconsistency   624
GERALD R. MILLER AND MILTON ROKEACH

61. Cognitive Complexity and Judgment of Inconsistent Information   633
JAMES BIERI

62. Responses to Inconsistency   641
IVAN D. STEINER

63. Comment: Uncooperative Personality Variables   648
ROBERT P. ABELSON

C. MODES OF RESOLUTION

Editorial Introduction   653

64. A Framework for the Study of Modes of Resolving Inconsistency   655
J. STACY ADAMS

65. Developmental Analysis of Modes of Resolution   661
BERNARD KAPLAN AND WALTER H. CROCKETT

66. Determinants of Modes of Resolving Inconsistency Dilemmas: A Functional Analysis   670
HERBERT C. KELMAN AND REUBEN M. BARON

67. A Modest Modish Model for Dissonance Reduction   684
    JANE ALLYN HARDYCK AND MARCELLE KARDUSH

68. Depth, Centrality, and Tolerance in Cognitive
    Consistency   693
    MARC PILISUK

69. Modes of Resolution and Reasoning in Attitude
    Change Experiments   700
    WALTER WEISS

70. The Panglossian World of Self-Justification   706
    KARL E. WEICK

71. A Summary of Hypotheses on Modes of Resolution   716
    ROBERT P. ABELSON

D. RESPONSES TO HETEROGENEOUS STIMULUS
   AGGREGATES
    Editorial Introduction   721

72. Some Cross-Cultural Studies of Cognitive
    Consistency   723
    HARRY C. TRIANDIS

73. A Simple Model for Information Integration   731
    NORMAN H. ANDERSON

74. What Do You Think of a *Cruel, Wise* Man? The
    Integrative Response to a Stimulus Manifold   744
    SHEL FELDMAN

75. Whither Pooling Models? Some Additional
    Variables   756
    MILTON E. ROSENBAUM AND CHARLES F. SCHMIDT

76. Discussion: Impression Processing and the
    Evaluation of New and Old Objects   763
    MILTON J. ROSENBERG

E. SELECTIVE EXPOSURE TO INFORMATION
    Editorial Introduction   769

77. Interest in Supporting and Discrepant Information   771
    JUDSON MILLS

78. The Paradox of De Facto Selective Exposure
    Without Preferences for Supportive Information   777
    DAVID O. SEARS

79. On Reopening the Question of Selectivity in
    Exposure to Mass Communications   788
    ELIHU KATZ

80. Selective Exposure: A Summing Up   797
    WILLIAM J. McGUIRE

F. COUNTERATTITUDINAL BEHAVIOR AND ATTITUDE CHANGE

Editorial Introduction   801

81. Varieties of Counterattitudinal Behavior   803
    J. MERRILL CARLSMITH

82. Attitude Change via Role Playing   810
    IRVING L. JANIS

83. The Mediation of Change Due to
    Counterattitudinal Behavior   819
    BARRY E. COLLINS

84. Discussion: On Reducing the Inconsistency
    Between Consistency Theories   827
    MILTON J. ROSENBERG

BIBLIOGRAPHY   835

NAME INDEX 879

INTRODUCTION

Theodore M. Newcomb

The family name *consistency* has been chosen for the set of problems considered in the following chapters. The classification will readily be recognized as belonging to the many-branched order *psychologia*, but its identification as a distinguishable family is very recent. Indeed, some of the problems had, as lately as a couple of decades ago, scarcely been formulated. We editors therefore owe it to our readers to indicate some of the characteristics that the family members have in common, and how it happens that the parvenus have recently achieved some prominence.

Often in the history of science, when the time is ripe, a large number of similar theories are put forward contemporaneously by researchers who have little if any direct contact with one another. So it was a decade or so ago when at least a half dozen of what we shall call 'cognitive consistency' theories appeared more or less independently in the psychological literature. They were proposed under various names, such as balance, congruity, symmetry, dissonance, but all had in common the notion that the person behaves in a way that maximizes the internal consistency of his cognitive system; and, by extension, that groups behave in ways that maximize the internal consistency of their interpersonal relations.

But why the presumed ripeness of the time? (Once something has occurred one assumes, post hoc, that its time has come.) A glance at some historical backgrounds of the present issues will at least present them in context, though it cannot really answer the question. As Ebbinghaus (1908) said of psychology as a whole at the turn of the century, the currently lively theoretical notion of cognitive consistency has "a long past but a short history." There is a justifiable suspicion of descent from the medieval notion of logical man or the notions of rational man and economic man, so popular as a guiding postulate for explaining human behavior in the early days of the dismal science. Yet these notions were themselves ambiguously used. Rational man was used to refer sometimes to reality orientation, sometimes to internal logical consistency. The latter is closer to the current meaning of cognitive consistency, but currently we use 'consistency' in the sense of operating in accord with the rules of psycho-logic (Abelson & Rosenberg, 1958) rather than of logic.

In an important sense, history began with Heider's paper (1944) entitled "Social perception and phenomenal causality," soon followed by "Attitudes and cognitive organization" (1946). His more complete and systematic treatise, *The psychology of interpersonal relations* (1958), describes in detail the conditions of balance both for "dyads" (one person as related to two objects or two aspects of the same object) and for "triads" (relations between a person and two objects of his sentiments, one or both of which may be another person). Virtually all subsequent developments owe something to Heider and some of them very much indeed—particularly to his basic assumption that an imbalanced set of cognitions is associated with 'tension' and the arousal of forces which tend to restore or to attain states of balance.

Meanwhile Heider (and later, others) were drawing, implicitly at least, upon other sources, particularly two that dealt with the nature of psychological conflict. As early as 1935 Lewin, with reference to human behavior, distinguished three kinds of conflict. In 1944 Miller, using laboratory animals as subjects, made the same distinctions, applying the terms *approach-approach*, *avoidance-avoidance*, and *approach-avoidance conflict*. As Brown (1965) has shown, all of these can be 'mapped' in terms of a "balance model." For example, in the approach-avoidance state of conflict, we have a state in which "a positive bond between objects of unlike sign is a condition of imbalance" (p. 605).

Another kind of stirring was also beginning during the late 1940's and early 1950's, signalized by the appearance of *The authoritarian personality* (Adorno et al., 1950), although an earlier and incomplete report had previously been published by Else Frenkel-Brunswik (1948). In a section of the 1950 book entitled "Cognitive personality organization" the concept of tolerance of ambiguity is discussed. The similarity of this notion to that of tolerance for inconsistency seems apparent, though there are few supporting studies (cf. Newcomb, 1961). In any case, problems of the structure of personality were beginning to impinge upon those of cognitive structuring.

One other set of historical circumstances almost certainly helped to determine the ripeness of the time. During the 1950's perception and cognition were coming to be understood in terms of information processing. One of the memorable contributions to this development was G. A. Miller's paper, "The magical number seven, plus or minus two: some limits on our capacity for processing information" (1956). He wrote:

> By organizing the stimulus output simultaneously into several dimensions and successively into a sequence of chunks, we manage to break (or at least stretch) the informational bottleneck....the process of recoding ... deserves much more explicit attention than it has received.... Recoding procedures are a constant concern to clinicians, social psychologists, linguists, and anthropologists...I anticipate that we will find a very orderly set of relations describing what now seems an uncharted wilderness of individual differences (pp. 95–96)

Perhaps the problems to which this volume is devoted represent one kind of attempt to validate his prediction.

It is an interesting fact that problems of consistency (by whatever label) have typically been regarded as part of social psychology. Of the seminal pioneers in the field, Heider titled his magnum opus *The psychology of interpersonal relations*. Another is Festinger, whose work on dissonance was foreshadowed by "Theory and experiment in social communication" (1950) and by "A theory of social comparison processes" (1954). Similarly, Osgood's interests can be traced to concerns with human communication processes. Of the 54 contributors to this volume, not less than two-thirds have major interests in one or more aspects of social psychology, according to their entries in the 1966 Directory of the American Psychological Association. (A considerable number of the contributors list some aspect of personality—not surprisingly, since social and personality psychology have traditionally been close cousins.) It is not inevitable that this should be so: after all, cognitive structures and the dynamics of cognitive organization are not in any a priori sense distinctively concerned with social phenomena.

Perhaps, however, there are good reasons why the *inconsistent* aspects of cognitive structuring should be of special interest to students of social psychology and personality. If so, this could be a consequence of the relative complexity of persons as objects of cognition, their diversity, and their salience in the lives of all of us. The more complex an entity (particularly if complexity is exacerbated by inconstancies) the greater the likelihood that it will present inconsistencies. And the more important it is to understand and to predict its characteristics, the more probable it is that those inconsistencies will become objects of study. (It is surely no accident that work on cognitive complexity [cf. Bieri, 1961] has paralleled that on cognitive inconsistency.)

Regardless of precise timing and historical roots within psychology, the formulation of problems of inconsistency had a certain inevitability. There is a general direction of movement in science, from the study of discrete elements to that of relationships among them. (See Lewin [1947], citing Cassirer [1923].) Sooner or later constancies among these relationships become objects of study. If, since the days of Titchener, psychologists have moved in this direction, the present volume will point to some of the features that have been encountered along this particular path—obstacles, detours, and partial successes.

The volume is divided into four sections. In Section I, each of the six editors reviews and expands upon a particular body of work in the consistency family. These extended personal statements give each editor the opportunity to develop the particular perspective by which he views some portion of the wide terrain which the volume covers. Section II is devoted to other theories bearing relationships to consistency theories. These alternative orientations, as revealed by the ten invited contributors, range from cozy compatibility through potential coexistence through flat contradiction with the consistency viewpoints. Following these two broad overview sections, a series of detailed probes are extended into specialized topic areas by many contributors. In seven subsections, Section III deals with "preconditions and properties of the state of inconsistency" and, in six-fold division, Section IV attacks "responses and consequences."

Each of these thirteen detailed subsections is presented within an 'editorial sandwich'—an introduction followed by a summary discussion. Section II, the long theoretical review, is similarly handled. It is hoped that in this way we can place many benchmarks beside the long research road that winds through our chosen territory.

I

Consistency Theories: Six Positions

CONSISTENCY THEORIES: SIX POSITIONS

This volume appropriately begins with six chapters describing somewhat diverse consistency theories by individuals who played a leading role in their development. While it must be granted that other approaches and other representatives of the consistency area might be included in such an introduction, most will agree that the six chapters presented here faithfully depict the current spectrum of consistency formulations, representing a full range of such approaches.

The first two chapters, by Aronson on dissonance theory and Newcomb on balance theory, represent the broader, perhaps more ambitious, consistency approaches as compared to the latter four. These two apply not just to intrapersonal cognition processes, but also to relationships between cognition and behavior and even to interpersonal relationships, paying for their broader applicability to many areas with less specific focus on any one area.

In the first chapter, Aronson presents an appraisal of the current status of dissonance theory, the formulation which up until this point has probably stimulated as much research activity as all the other approaches combined. Dissonance theory received explicit formulation and research attention in the early 1950's and its first detailed published exposition in Festinger's 1957 volume. More than any other of the approaches, it stresses the tendency towards consistency between the individual's belief system and his overt behavior, though it does have relevance to consistency strictly within the belief system. In addition to providing a current assessment, Aronson suggests the beginnings of a reformulation of dissonance theory aimed at eliminating much of the ambiguity currently associated with it.

Newcomb's version of balance theory, described in Chapter 2, is even broader in its scope in that it, more than any of the other five theories presented here, deals with interpersonal as well as intrapersonal processes. Newcomb has, at least as early as his 1953 paper, been developing the formulation that the individual has to work out some balance among the often conflicting demands of the actual environment, his interpersonal relations, and his own self-needs. The complexities of this tripartite demand system are partly compensated for by their offering multiple intra- and interpersonal adjustments that would bring about the needed balance.

The remaining four chapters deal more with consistency as an intrapersonal phenomenon. All treat the operation of a consistency tendency among the individual's beliefs, and between his beliefs and his affects. The first two of these, presented in chapters by Tannenbaum and by Rosenberg, focus upon how the force for consistency works itself out within the belief and attitude system once it arises. The last two chapters, by Abelson and by McGuire, address themselves somewhat more to the question of what the belief system itself is like and how inconsistencies arise there in the first place. The difference between these two pairs of approaches is, however, more a matter of emphasis than of exclusive preoccupation with the aspect cited.

In Chapter 3, Tannenbaum presents an assessment of the current status of congruity theory, which has generated considerable interest since the publication of the 1955 Osgood and Tannenbaum paper, at about the same time as the work on the semantic differential technique began to receive wide attention. This approach has been concerned especially with the consequences of incongruent evaluations that may result when communication messages upset the person's evaluations of two concepts or his perception of the relationship between them. Tannenbaum's recent work has reopened the study of source-concept linkages in such communication situations, particularly in terms of the generalization of attitude change among evaluatively related objects.

Rosenberg's theory of cognitive-affective consistency presented in Chapter 4 received its first partial formulation in 1953 and was more fully elaborated in articles published in 1956 and 1960. It has been most concerned with treating the attitude change process as a resolution of induced discrepancy between affective and cognitive elements. In his more recent work, Rosenberg has extended the theory to deal with problems of inconsistency intolerance thresholds, content factors, public opinion assessment, counterattitudinal advocacy affects, and other such attitudinal phenomena.

The final two theories focus more on the structure of the cognitive system which underlies consistency phenomena. In Chapter 5, Abelson focuses on a description of the cognitive structures by means of which the person receives and processes information. Here he recounts the initial theorizing found in his 1958 paper with Rosenberg, and traces the subsequent developments and diverging conceptualizations, reflected in his 1959 paper on cognitive implication and resolution and in his papers on computer simulation of thought processes. In general, the recent activity has focused on describing the structure of thought so as to account for how one belief has psychological consequences for others.

Likewise, McGuire, in Chapter 6, utilizes the consistency need more as a probe by which to explore the structure of thought than as a motivation to be studied in its own right. He describes the current state of his thinking, along the lines first published in his 1960 papers, regarding the nature and extent of the interconnectedness and internal coherence of human cognitive processes. In so doing, he tends to focus on the common and critical situations where both logical and emotional factors must be accommodated to account for emerging cognitive relationships and changes.

CHAPTER 1

Dissonance Theory: Progress and Problems

Elliot Aronson
University of Texas

As a formal statement, Festinger's theory of cognitive dissonance (1957) is quite primitive; it lacks the elegance and precision commonly associated with scientific theorizing. Yet its impact has been great. As McGuire has observed in his recent survey in the *Annual Review of Psychology* (1966a, p. 492), "Over the past three years, dissonance theory continued to generate more research and more hostility than any other one approach." I will allude to the "hostility" part of this statement from time to time throughout this chapter; but first let us discuss the research.

The research has been as diverse as it has been plentiful; its range extends from maze running in rats (Lawrence & Festinger, 1962), to the development of values in children (Aronson & Carlsmith, 1963); from the hunger of college sophomores (Brehm, Back, & Bogdonoff, 1964), to the proselytizing behavior of religious zealots (Festinger, Riecken, & Schachter, 1956). For descriptive summaries of dissonance experiments, the reader is referred to Festinger, 1957; Festinger and Aronson, 1960; Brehm and Cohen, 1962; Festinger and Bramel, 1962; Festinger and Freedman, 1964.

The proliferation of research testing and extending dissonance theory is due for the most part to the generality and simplicity of the theory. Although it has been applied primarily in social psychological settings, it is not limited to social psychological phenomena such as interpersonal relations or feelings toward a communicator and his communication. Rather, its domain is in the widest of places: the skull of an individual organism.[1]

The core notion of the theory is extremely simple: Dissonance is a negative drive state which occurs whenever an individual simultaneously holds two cognitions (ideas, beliefs, opinions) which are psychologically

This chapter was prepared while the author's research was being supported by grants from the National Science Foundation (NSF GS 750) and the National Institutes of Mental Health (MH 12357), which he gratefully acknowledges.

[1] An additional reason for the great number of experiments on dissonance theory is completely *ad hominem:* Leon Festinger has an unmatched genius for translating interesting hypotheses into workable experimental operations and for inspiring others to do so. He has produced a great deal of research irrespective of any particular theoretical approach.

inconsistent. Stated differently, two cognitions are dissonant if, considering these two cognitions alone, the opposite of one follows from the other. Since the occurrence of dissonance is presumed to be unpleasant, individuals strive to reduce it by adding 'consonant' cognitions or by changing one or both cognitions to make them 'fit together' better—i.e., so that they become more consonant with each other.[2] To use Festinger's time-worn (but still cogent) example, if a person believes that cigarette smoking causes cancer and simultaneously knows that he himself smokes cigarettes, he experiences dissonance. Assuming that the person would rather not have cancer, his cognition "I smoke cigarettes" is psychologically inconsistent with his cognition "cigarette smoking produces cancer." Perhaps the most efficient way to reduce dissonance in such a situation is to stop smoking. But, as many of us have discovered, this is by no means easy. Thus, a person will usually work on the other cognition. There are several ways in which a person can make cigarette smoking seem less absurd. He might belittle the evidence linking cigarette smoking to cancer ("Most of the data are clinical rather than experimental"); or he might associate with other cigarette smokers ("If Sam, Jack, and Harry smoke, then it can't be very dangerous"); or he might smoke filter-tipped cigarettes and delude himself that the filter traps the cancer-producing materials; or he might convince himself that smoking is an important and highly pleasurable activity ("I'd rather have a shorter but more enjoyable life than a longer, unenjoyable one"); or he might actually make a virtue out of smoking by developing a romantic, devil-may-care image of himself, flaunting danger by smoking. All of these behaviors reduce dissonance, in effect, by reducing the absurdity involved in going out of one's way to contract cancer. Thus, dissonance theory does not rest upon the assumption that man is a *rational* animal; rather, it suggests that man is a rational*izing* animal—that he attempts to appear rational, both to others and to himself. To clarify the theoretical statement and to illustrate the kind of research generated by the theory, I will briefly describe a few experiments.

Dissonance Following a Decision

One of the earliest experiments testing derivations from dissonance theory was performed by Brehm (1956). Brehm gave individuals their choice between two appliances which they had previously evaluated. He found that following the decision, when the subjects reevaluated the alternatives, they enhanced their liking for the chosen appliance and downgraded their evaluation of the unchosen one. The derivation is clear. After making a difficult choice, people experience dissonance; cognitions about any negative attributes of the preferred object are dissonant with having chosen it; cognitions about positive attributes of the unchosen object are dissonant with *not* having chosen it. To reduce dissonance, people emphasize the positive aspects and deemphasize the negative aspects of the chosen objects while emphasizing the negative and deemphasizing the positive aspects of the unchosen object (see also Festinger, 1964b).

---

[2] Although dissonance theory is an incredibly simple statement, it is not quite as simple as a reading of this chapter will indicate. Many aspects of the theory (for example, the propositions relevant to the magnitude of dissonance) will not be discussed here because they are peripheral to the major focus of this chapter.

Dissonance Resulting from Effort

Aronson and Mills (1959) reasoned that, if people undergo a great deal of trouble in order to gain admission to a group which turns out to be dull and uninteresting, they will experience dissonance. The cognition that they worked hard in order to become members of the group is dissonant with cognitions concerning the negative aspects of the group. One does not work hard for nothing. To reduce dissonance, they will distort their perception of the group in a positive direction. In the Aronson-Mills experiment, college women underwent an initiation in order to become a member of a group discussion on the psychology of sex. For some of the girls the initiation was very embarrassing—it consisted of reciting a list of obscene words in the presence of the male experimenter. For others the initiation was a mild one. For still others there was no initiation at all. All of the subjects then listened to the same tape-recording of a discussion being held by the group they had just joined. As predicted, the girls in the Severe Initiation condition rated the discussion much more favorably than did those in the other two conditions (see also Aronson, 1961; Zimbardo, 1965; Lewis, 1964; Gerard & Mathewson, 1966).

Insufficient Justification

Aronson and Carlsmith (1963) predicted that if threats are used to prevent people from performing a desired activity, the *smaller* the threat, the greater will be the tendency for people to derogate the activity. If an individual refrains from performing a desired activity, he experiences dissonance: The cognition that he likes the activity is dissonant with the cognition that he is not performing it. One way to reduce dissonance is by derogating the activity—in that way he can justify the fact that he is not performing it. However, any threat provides cognitions that are consonant with not performing the activity; and the more severe the threat, the greater the consonance. In short, a severe threat provides ample justification for not performing the activity; a mild threat provides less justification, leading the individual to add justifications of his own in the form of convincing himself that he *doesn't like* to perform the activity. In their experiment, Aronson and Carlsmith found that children who were threatened with *mild* punishment for playing with a desired toy *decreased* their liking for the toy to a greater extent than did children who were severely threatened (see also Turner & Wright, 1965; Freedman, 1965b).

WHAT IS PSYCHOLOGICAL INCONSISTENCY?

The very simplicity of the core of the theory is at once its greatest strength and its most serious weakness. We have already discussed the heuristic value of its simplicity. It should be emphasized that many of the hypotheses which are obvious derivations from the theory are *unique* to that theory—i.e., they could not be derived from any other theory. This increases our confidence in dissonance theory as an explanation of an important aspect of human behavior. The weakness occurs primarily in the difficulty involved with defining the limits of the theoretical statement. While at the 'center' of the theory it is relatively easy to generate hypotheses that are clear and direct, at its 'fringes' it is not always clear whether or not a prediction can be made from the theory and, if so, exactly what that prediction will be.[3] Although investigators who have had experience working with the theory seem to have little difficulty intuiting its boundary conditions, they have had considerable difficulty communicating this to other people; indeed, a situation has evolved which can best be described by the statement: "If you want to be sure, ask Leon." This has proved to be both a source of embarrassment for the proponents of the theory as well as a source of annoyance and exasperation to its critics.

Why is it so difficult to make a more precise theoretical statement? Perhaps the most basic reason has to do with the nature of the inconsistency involved in the core definition of dissonance theory. It would be easy to specify dissonant situations if the theory were limited to *logical* inconsistencies. There exist relatively unequivocal rules of logic which can be applied without ambiguity or fear of contradiction. But recall that the inconsistency that produces dissonance, although it can be logical inconsistency, is not necessarily logical. Rather, it is *psychological* inconsistency. While this aspect of the theory increases its power, range, and degree of interest, at the same time it also causes some serious problems. Thus, returning to our friend the cigarette smoker, the cognition regarding smoking cigarettes is not logically inconsistent with the cognition linking cigarette smoking to cancer; i.e., strictly speaking, having information that cigarette smoking causes cancer does not make it illogical to smoke cigarettes. But these cognitions do produce dissonance because, taken together, they do not make sense psychologically. Assuming that the smoker does not want cancer, the knowledge that cigarettes cause cancer should lead to *not* smoking cigarettes. Similarly, none of the research examples mentioned above deals with logical inconsistency; e.g., it is not illogical to go through hell and high water to gain admission to a dull discussion group; it is not illogical to choose to own an appliance that one considers slightly more attractive than the unchosen alternative; it is not illogical to refrain from playing with a toy at the request of an adult.

Festinger (1957) lists four kinds of situations in which dissonance can arise: (1) logical inconsistency, (2) inconsistency with cultural mores, (3) inconsistency between one cognition and a more general, more encompassing cognition, (4) past experience.

1. Logical inconsistency: Suppose a person believed that all men are mortal but also held the belief that he, as a man, would live forever. These two cognitions are dissonant because they are logically inconsistent. The contrary of one follows from the other on strict logical grounds.

2. Cultural mores: If a college professor loses his patience with one of his students and shouts at him angrily, his knowledge of what he is doing is dissonant with his idea about what is the proper, acceptable behavior of a professor toward his students—in our culture. In some other cultures this might be appropriate behavior and, therefore, would not arouse dissonance.

3. Inconsistency between one cognition and a more encompassing cognition: In a given election, if a person who has always considered himself

---

[3] Further along in this chapter some attempt will be made to specify exactly what we mean by 'center' and 'fringes.'

to be a Democrat votes for the Republican candidate, he should experience dissonance. The concept "I am a Democrat" encompasses the concept "I vote for Democratic candidates."

4. Past experience: If a person stepped on a tack while barefoot and felt no pain, he would experience dissonance because he knows from experience that pain follows from stepping on tacks. If he had never had experience with tacks or other sharp objects, he would *not* experience dissonance.

The illustrations presented above are clear examples of dissonance. Similarly, the situations investigated in the experiments I have described above are clearly dissonant. But there *are* situations where for all practical purposes it is not perfectly clear whether two cognitions are dissonant or merely irrelevant. Because dissonance is *not* limited to logical inconsistencies, it is occasionally difficult to specify a priori whether or not a cultural more is being violated, whether or not an event is markedly different from past experience, or whether or not it is different from a more general cognition. Recall the basic theoretical statement: Two cognitions are dissonant if, considering these two cognitions alone, the opposite of one follows from the other. The major source of conceptual ambiguity rests upon the fact that Festinger has not clarified the meaning of the words "follows from."

For example, if I learn that my favorite novelist beats his wife, does this arouse dissonance? It is difficult to be certain. Strictly speaking, being a wife-beater is not incompatable with being a great novelist.[4] However, there may be a sense in which the term "great novelist" implies that such a person is wise, sensitive, empathic, and compassionate—and wise, sensitive, empathic, and compassionate people do not go around beating their wives. This is not a logical inconsistency; nor is it a clear violation of a cultural more; moreover, it may have nothing to do with past experience—and it is not *necessarily* imbedded in a more general cognition. Thus, a knowledge of the kinds of situations in which dissonance *can* occur is not always useful in determining whether dissonance *does* occur.

A rule of thumb which I have found useful is to state the situation in terms of the violation of an expectancy. For example, one might issue the following instructions: "Consider Thurgood Marshall. I'm going to tell you something about his beliefs about the native I.Q. of Negroes relative to that of Caucasians. What do you expect these beliefs to be?" I imagine that most people would have a firm expectancy that Justice Marshall would have said that there are no innate differences. Consequently, one could then conclude that if individuals were exposed to a statement by Justice Marshall to the effect that Negroes were innately stupider than Caucasians, most would experience dissonance. Let us try our difficult example: Suppose we confronted a large number of people with the following proposition: "Consider the great novelist X. I am about to tell you something about whether or not he beats his wife. What do you expect me to say?" My guess is that most people would shrug; i.e., they would not have a strong expectancy (but, again, this is an empirical question; I am not

---

[4] If *I* had beaten my wife I might experience dissonance because of *my* violation of a cultural more. But since I know that many people beat their wives, discovering that a particular person beats his wife is not necessarily inconsistent with my cognition about the world and human nature. More will be said about this later.

certain that it would come out this way). If this occurred, one could conclude that X's wife-beating behavior is irrelevant to his status as a novelist. An empirical rule of thumb may be of practical utility but is, of course, no substitute for a clearer, less ambiguous, more precise theoretical statement. Near the end of this chapter we will elaborate upon this rule of thumb and indicate how it might be used conceptually.

METHODOLOGICAL PROBLEMS

Some critics have pointed to the ambiguities inherent in the theoretical statement and have concluded that they make the theory impossible to disprove and, consequently, worthless. As I have stated above, some conceptual ambiguities do exist, and I will elaborate on these shortly. But first, I should make it clear that these conceptual ambiguities exist in a very small part of the domain in which the theory has continued to make clear and precise predictions; these predictions have been validated a number of times in a number of different ways. Why, then, does the theory inspire what McGuire (1966a) referred to as "...more hostility than any other one approach"? I feel that a good deal of the hostility is misdirected—stemming from a confusion between conceptual and methodological ambiguities. Much of the difficulty in disproving dissonance theory arises from weaknesses in the methodology of social psychological experimentation. These weaknesses are hardly the fault of the theory. Moreover, these methodological problems are not peculiar to dissonance theory but are shared by research on all theories that predict social psychological phenomena. They tend to have been associated with dissonance theory precisely because of the great quantity of research generated (and, therefore, of methodological problems unearthed) by the theory. The major methodological problems stem from the lack of tried and true, standardized techniques for operationalizing conceptual variables in social psychology. Consequently, any single failure can be attributed to a failure in the experimental operations rather than an error of conceptualization. At the same time, repeated failures across a wide variety of techniques would spell the end of dissonance theory or any theory.

The lack of a standardized methodology in social psychology has contributed to another major difficulty with research in this area: it is frequently possible to come up with alternative explanations for empirical results. Thus, like experiments testing other theories in social psychology, many of the experiments testing dissonance theory are subject to alternative explanations. If some of the data can be explained without recourse to dissonance theory, our confidence in the theory is weakened. At the same time, dissonance theory does provide the most parsimonious explanation for the data taken as a whole—as McGuire has argued: "The whole set of dissonance studies would require accepting a tremendous variety of alternative explanations, whereas dissonance theory alone explains a large subset of them" (1966a, p. 493). Although this is some recommendation, it is not wholly sufficient. One still wants to be able to determine which explanation is more nearly correct. The best way to distinguish among plausible alternative explanations is through a series of well-controlled systematic experiments which are essentially conceptual replications using markedly different sets of operations to test the same hypothesis. This technique has been referred to as "purification"; the necessity for such procedures as well as a fuller description is provided elsewhere (Aronson & Carlsmith, 1968).

Let us take, as an illustration, the initiation experiment by Aronson and Mills (1959). Recall that the investigators predicted the results on the basis of dissonance theory; specifically, the cognition that one has gone through an unpleasant and embarrassing initiation in order to get into a group was dissonant with the cognition that the discussion group was dull and dreary. In order to reduce dissonance, subjects in the Severe Initiation condition (but not in the Mild Initiation condition) convinced themselves that the dull group was really quite exciting. In order to maximize credibility and impact, the investigators constructed a rather novel method for operationalizing unpleasant effort; they had the girls in the Severe Initiation condition recite a list of obscene words and some lurid passages from contemporary novels in the presence of a male experimenter. This procedure made sense in terms of the overall scenario of the experiment, thus effectively masking the true purpose of the experiment and reducing the possibility of suspicion. It also seemed to be effective in the sense that the girls appeared to be embarrassed—they tended to hesitate, blush, cast their eyes downward, etc. Nevertheless, the use of sexually related material opened the door for at least two plausible alternative explanations, both offered by Chapanis and Chapanis (1964). One is that while reciting the material the girls did not become embarrassed, but, rather, became sexually aroused; this could have produced pleasure or expectation of pleasure which supposedly would increase the attractiveness of the discussion group. The second is quite the reverse: The subjects in the Severe Initiation condition felt relief (from sexual anxiety?) when they found the group discussion banal instead of embarrassing. Supposedly, this could lead them to rate the discussion as not banal at all.

Whether these explanations are more or less plausible than the dissonance explanation is not important. The important point is that they are at least possible. In order to distinguish between the dissonance explanation and these alternative explanations, the same hypothesis should be tested using an operational definition of "unpleasant effort" which has nothing to do with the pleasantness of sexual arousal or relief from sexual anxiety. Such an experiment has recently been performed by Gerard and Mathewson (1966), who replicated the Aronson-Mills (1959) experiment using electric shock instead of obscene words as the initiation procedure and pallid group discussions about cheating on exams rather than discussions about sex. The results paralleled those of Aronson and Mills and confirmed the prediction from dissonance theory: Those subjects who underwent a series of severe electric shocks in order to gain admission to a dull discussion group came to rate that group more favorably than those who gained admission after having undergone mild electric shocks.

This single procedure, of course, does not eliminate all alternative explanations. Let us return to the critique of the Aronson-Mills (1959) experiment. To quote Chapanis and Chapanis: "It is interesting to speculate what would have happened if the girls had been 'initiated' into the group by the use of a more generally accepted painful procedure, such as using electric shock. Somehow it seems doubtful that this group would appreciate the group discussion more than the control group, unless—and here is the crucial point—the conditions were so manipulated that Ss experienced a feeling of successful accomplishment in overcoming the painful obstacle. It seems to us that if there is anything to the relationship between severity of initiation and liking for the group, it lies in this feeling of successful accomplishment. The more severe the test, the stronger is the pleasurable feeling of success in overcoming the obstacle. There is no need to postulate a drive due to dissonance if a *pleasure principle* can account for the results quite successfully" (1964, p. 5).

Thus, while Chapanis and Chapanis would appear to have been wrong in their conviction that the effect demonstrated by Aronson and Mills would *not* replicate if electric shock had been used, they have apparently left themselves an escape hatch. Fortunately, however, there are some data on this issue also. According to Chapanis and Chapanis, the more painful the situation one overcomes, the greater the feeling of successful accomplishment. Although they do not explain how this feeling of pleasure would make subjects like the discussion group better, one assumes that they are using a rather simple contiguity model: If a person feels good, contiguous stimuli (e.g., the discussion group) look and feel good. Dissonance theory, of course, does not make use of such a contiguity explanation; i.e., the group discussion looks good *not* because it is contiguous with pain reduction (dissonance reduction)—rather, it comes to look good as a *means* of reducing dissonance. The crucial aspect of dissonance arousal in this situation is that getting into a group was contingent upon going through a severe initiation. That is, it was an initiation, not simply a stimulus that was contiguous with a pleasant feeling. Consequently, if one simply hears a group discussion after having successfully undergone a severe shock, dissonance theory would make no prediction regarding the attractiveness of the group. It would make a prediction only if the person had experienced dissonance; i.e., if the person had undergone a severe initiation *in order to* get into a dull group.

Thus, a test between the Chapanis and Chapanis "successful accomplishment" explanation and the dissonance explanation can be arranged simply by comparing an initiation (i.e., an "in order to" situation) with a contiguous situation. Such a test was built into the Gerard-Mathewson (1966) study. In this experiment some subjects underwent a severe shock in order to get into a group (Initiation condition), while other subjects simply underwent severe shock (No Initiation condition). If a feeling of success is aroused by getting through the shock situation, both groups had it. All subjects were then exposed to a taped group discussion. Thus, for subjects in both conditions the discussion was contiguous with feelings of "successful accomplishment"; but only those in the Initiation condition experienced dissonance. The results clearly support dissonance theory. Those who went through severe electric shock in order to get into a dull group rated the taped group discussion as more attractive than a "mild shock" Control condition. Those who went through a severe shock (without dissonance) and then listened to the same tape rated the discussion as less attractive than those in the Initiation condition—indeed, they tended to rate the taped discussion as *less* attractive than subjects in the parallel (No Initiation) condition who underwent mild electric shock. This latter finding suggests that even in the absence of dissonance, "a feeling of successful accomplishment" does not operate—but something else does; we will make more of this in a moment. Before leaving the Gerard-Mathewson study it should be noted that one additional piece of data is of relevance. Half of the subjects in the Initiation condition were told they passed the test and one-half were not told. The "told-not told" manipulation did not interact with the severity of shock. This provides further evidence against the "successful accomplishment" explanation.

To sum up this point, I should make it clear that neither the receipt of electric shock nor the recitation of obscene words is a perfect empirical realization of the conception "unpleasant effort." Neither, by itself, is free of alternative explanations. The recitation of obscene words is open to alternative explanations involving sexual matters—electrical shock is open to alternative explanations involving pain, fear, pain reduction, and fear reduction. But taken together, they eliminate most possible alternative explanations. Accordingly, many of the results supporting dissonance theory have been and can continue to be strengthened by eliminating alternative explanations through the purification of operations afforded by conceptual replications. As this process continues, our confidence in the validity and viability of the theory increases—in spite of its simplicity and inelegance as a conceptual statement.[5]

Of course, as I have indicated, not all of dissonance theory's problems are methodological. Several additional conceptual problems will be discussed in a moment.

THE "NOTHING BUT" CRITIQUE

Scientists tend to be conservative, parsimonious creatures. This is generally a healthy attitude which most frequently manifests itself in a reluctance to accept a new theory or a novel explanation for a phenomenon if the phenomenon can be squeezed (even with great difficulty) into an existing approach. In this regard, dissonance theory has been referred to as nothing but a new name for an old phenomenon. This has been most persistently stated in regard to that aspect of the theory related to decision making. In this context dissonance theory has been referred to as nothing but another name for conflict theory.

In fact, there are several differences. Conflict occurs before a decision is made, dissonance occurs after the decision. During conflict it is assumed that an individual will devote his energies to a careful, dispassionate, and sensible evaluation and judgment of the alternatives. He will gather all of the information, pro and con, about all of the alternatives in order to make a reasonable decision. Following the decision, a person is in a state of dissonance—all negative aspects of X are dissonant with having chosen X; all

[5] I have made the point that in struggling toward greater methodological sophistication, investigators working with dissonance theory face the same problems as other experimental social psychologists. Thus, the major critical review of dissonance theory to date (Chapanis & Chapanis, 1964) is largely a methodological critique. Although many of the points made in this review involve reasonable methodological criticisms, the unfortunate illusion is created that, somehow, 'dissonance theorists' commit more methodological blunders than the rest of us. In articulating this point, Chapanis and Chapanis attempt to cite examples of good (meaning nondissonance) methodology in this area. Their principal example of good methodology is an experiment where the subjects were allowed to assign *themselves* to experimental conditions (p. 19), thus negating the major defining characteristic of an experiment!

positive aspects of Y are dissonant with *not* having chosen Y. Far from evaluating the alternatives impartially (as in conflict), the individual experiencing dissonance will seek biased information and evaluations designed to make his decision appear more reasonable. As in Brehm's (1956) experiment, he will seek to spread the alternatives apart. The more difficulty a person had making a decision, the greater the tendency toward this kind of behavior as a means of justifying his decision.

But how can we be certain that the spreading apart of the alternatives in Brehm's experiment occurred after the decision? Could it not have occurred during the conflict stage? That is, it is conceivable that, in order to make their decision easier, subjects in Brehm's experiment began to reevaluate the appliances in a biased manner *before* the decision. If this were the case, then there is no essential difference between predecisional and postdecisional processes; if so, this behavior can be considered part of conflict—and there is, indeed, no need to complicate matters by bringing in additional terminology.

Brehm's experiment does not allow us to determine whether the evaluation of chosen and unchosen alternatives was spread apart before or after the decision. Recent experiments by Davidson and Kiesler (1964) and by Jecker (1964a) serve to clarify this issue (see Chapter 54). In Jecker's experiment, subjects were offered their choice between two phonograph records. In three conditions there was *low conflict;* i.e., subjects were told that there was a very good chance that they would receive *both* records no matter which they chose. In three other conditions, *high conflict* was produced by telling them that the probability was high that they would be given only the record that they chose. All of the subjects rated the records before the instructions; in each of the conflict conditions subjects rerated the records either (a) after they discovered that they received both records, (b) after they discovered that they received only the one record they chose, or (c) before they were certain whether they would get one or both. The results are quite clear: No spreading apart occurred when there was no dissonance; i.e., when the subject actually received both records or when he was not certain whether he would receive one or both he did *not* reevaluate the alternatives systematically. Where dissonance did occur there was a systematic reevaluation; i.e., subjects spread their evaluation of the alternatives when they received only one record—this occurred independently of the degree of conflict. This experiment provides clear evidence that conflict and dissonance are different processes; whatever else dissonance theory might be, it is *not* "nothing but conflict theory."

THE MULTIPLE MODE PROBLEM

As indicated earlier, several problems are central to the theoretical statement. One of the knottiest and most interesting conceptual problems in dissonance theory involves the fact that, in a given situation, there is usually more than one way for a person to reduce dissonance. For example, the cigarette smoker has several techniques at his disposal. He may use any one, or several simultaneously. Experimentally, this problem can be eliminated by the simple device of blocking alternative techniques of dissonance reduction. This is part of the definition of experimental control; any experimenter worth his salt will attempt to control the environment so that the behavior elicited by his independent variable will occur in a manner which is measurable and at a time and place where the measuring instruments have been set up. To illustrate: In a typical communication-persuasion experiment, if a highly credible communicator states a position which is discrepant from the position of the recipient, the recipient experiences dissonance. He can reduce dissonance in one of four ways: (1) he can change his opinion to make it coincide with the communicator's; (2) he can attempt to change the communicator's opinion; (3) he can seek social support from other members of the audience; (4) he can derogate the communicator. If one is interested in measuring opinion change (No. 1), one can eliminate No. 2 and No. 3 by making it impossible for the subject to interact either with the communicator or his fellow subjects. Furthermore, one can reduce the subject's ability to derogate the communicator by assigning the latter high enough prestige so that he becomes virtually nonderogatable. Thus, if these four techniques exhaust the universe, the only way that a subject can reduce dissonance is by changing his attitude on the issue. The prudent experimenter will have built his experiment to make it appear reasonable to measure the subject's attitudes after the communication and he will use the most sensitive measuring instrument he can construct.

Thus, if the question one asks is "Does dissonance occur in such a situation and does it get reduced?" the answer can be easily determined experimentally. But we may have a different question in mind: "In a given situation, how do people generally reduce dissonance?" And the answer to this question may be strikingly different from the mode found in the laboratory experiment. Thus, in the above example, most people might prefer to argue with the communicator rather than change their opinion.

The above argument suggests that the results from carefully controlled laboratory experiments, on occasion, may be somewhat misleading. For example, suppose a young Ph.D. is being considered for a teaching position in a major department at a prestigious Ivy League university. What happens if the members of that department decide not to hire him? If he feels that he is a good and worthy scholar, he will experience cognitive dissonance: His cognition that he is a good scholar is dissonant with his cognition that he was rejected by members of a good department. As I see it, he can reduce dissonance in at least two ways: (a) he can convince himself that his rejectors are, in reality, stupid, defensive, unprofessional, and/or senile people who cannot or will not recognize a good man when they see one; (b) he can convince himself that if they can reject him (as good as he is), then their standards must be astronomically high and therefore they are a fine group of nonsenile professionals. Both of these techniques succeed in reducing dissonance; moreover, they both protect the individual's ego—he leaves for his job at East Podunk State Teacher's College with the conviction that he is a good scholar. But note that the results of his dissonance-reducing behavior can leave him with totally opposite opinions about the members of the staff at the Ivy League university. Thus, if one wanted to arouse dissonance in an individual for the specific purpose of enhancing his impressions of the people at Ivy University, one had better be careful. The same dissonance-producing situation can result in quite the opposite dissonance-reducing behavior.

This is a serious conceptual problem. One way that it can be solved is by coming up with a set of specific propositions that can lead one to state the conditions under which one mode or the other is more likely to occur (see Section IV C). I have previously outlined a possible solution in a specific situation. The situation I was concerned with involved alternative modes of dissonance reduction following the unsuccessful expenditure of effort. If a person struggles to reach a goal and fails, he experiences dissonance. His cognition that he exerted effort to attain the goal is dissonant with his cognition that he did not reach it. He could reduce dissonance by convincing himself that the goal was not worth it anyway; recall that this was the way that Aesop's fox reduced dissonance in the fable of the sour grapes. There is another reasonable way to reduce dissonance: by the person's finding something else in the situation to which he can attach value in order to justify his expenditure of effort without achieving his avowed goal. Thus, the fox might convince himself that he got some much-needed exercise while leaping for the grapes—and that even though he failed to get those luscious, sweet grapes, it was worth the effort because of the muscles he developed while trying.

Under what conditions will an individual take one path rather than the other? In my paper (Aronson, 1961) I suggested that the first solution is probably easier—but only in a situation where the effort expended is of short duration. But if the situation consists of a long and repeated expenditure of effort, it becomes a less viable solution. To use our previous illustration, if the fox made a few leaps at the grapes and failed, he could convince himself that they were probably sour anyway; but if he spent the entire afternoon struggling to reach the grapes, it would not effectively reduce dissonance to maintain that the grapes were sour—for if that were the case, why in the world did he try to reach them over and over and over again? The data from my experiment indicate that, after the repeated expenditure of effort, people *do* attach value to an incidental stimulus; however, the definitive factorial experiment remains to be done.

It is encouraging to note that experimenters are beginning to focus their efforts on this kind of problem. A good example of this trend is described in a very recent article by Walster, Berscheid, and Barclay (1967), who hypothesize that individuals will choose that mode of dissonance reduction which is least likely to be challenged by future events. In their experiment, children were given their choice between two toys. In a situation like this, individuals can reduce dissonance in two ways: by cognitively increasing the attractiveness of the chosen alternative and/or by cognitively decreasing the attractiveness of the unchosen alternative. One-half of the children were led to expect that they would subsequently hear objective information about the toy they chose; one-half of the children were led to expect that they would hear objective information about the rejected toy. The investigators found, as predicted, that individuals reduced dissonance by distorting the attractiveness of that toy which they were not going to hear information about. That is, they opted to reduce dissonance in a manner which was less likely to run up against objective reality.

In order to be of maximum use, such specific solutions should be restated into more general propositions, where possible, and incorporated into the theory. An important step in this direction was taken by Brehm and Cohen (1962) in emphasizing the importance of commitment and volition in determining not only the strength of the dissonance involved, but, perhaps more important, the nature of the dissonance and, hence, the kind of mechanism needed to reduce dissonance. Whether or not a high degree of volition is present can often change the nature of the prediction. For example, as part of one study, Aronson, Turner, and Carlsmith (1963) reasoned that disagreement with a highly credible source produces more dissonance than disagreement with a source having low credibility. The cognition that a highly sentient person believes X is dissonant with the cognition that I believe *not*-X. The higher the credibility of the source, the greater the dissonance—because the less sense it makes to be in disagreement with him. This should lead to greater attitude change in the Highly Credible condition—to reduce dissonance. The results were consistent with this reasoning. On the other hand, Zimbardo (1960) and Brehm and Cohen (1962) reasoned that under certain conditions a source having low credibility would produce *greater* attitude change than one having high credibility. Specifically, if a person had chosen of his own volition to go to hear a speech by a low credibility source, he would experience dissonance. The cognition involving volition and commitment is dissonant with the cognition that the credibility of the communicator is low; after all, it is absurd to choose to go out of one's way to hear a low prestige source make a speech which is discrepant with one's own opinion. In order to reduce dissonance, one might convince oneself that there was no essential discrepancy—that one always held the position espoused by the low credibility source. Thus, both Zimbardo and Brehm and Cohen suggested that under conditions of high commitment one might get greater agreement with a low credibility source than with a high credibility source. This prediction made by Zimbardo and by Brehm and Cohen is consistent with other data involving choice and commitment. For example, Smith (1961) found that soldiers who volunteered to eat grasshoppers when induced by an unpleasant leader, came to like the grasshoppers better than did those who volunteered to eat them when induced by an affable leader. Similar results are reported by Zimbardo (1964a).

It should be clear that the prediction made by Aronson, Turner, and Carlsmith and that made by Zimbardo and by Brehm and Cohen are not mutually exclusive; rather, they apply to a crucially different set of circumstances. Although both predictions are derived from dissonance theory, they involve different aspects of the theory; the crucial distinction is whether or not a high degree of volition is present. Nonetheless, to avoid confusion, these distinctions should be stated with even greater clarity.

To sum up this section, dissonance theory, as originally stated, *does* have some areas of conceptual fuzziness. In my opinion, much of this fuzziness can be eliminated by empirical research. Again, this research should be focused on the conditions and variables which maximize and minimize the occurrence of dissonance and dissonance reduction as well as the conditions which lead to one or another mode of dissonance reduction. This position will be elaborated upon in a moment.

DISSONANCE THEORY AND REWARD-INCENTIVE THEORY

One of the intriguing aspects of dissonance theory is that it frequently leads to predictions which stand in apparent contradiction to those made by other theoretical approaches—most notably, to a general reward-incentive theory. The words "stand in apparent contradiction" were carefully chosen, for as we shall see, these theories are not mutually exclusive on a conceptual level. No advocate of dissonance theory would take issue with the fact that people frequently perform actions in order to obtain rewards or that activities associated with rewards tend to be repeated. What they would suggest is that under certain carefully prescribed conditions, cognitive events are set in motion which result in behaviors quite different from what one would expect from reward-incentive theories. Moreover, they might also suggest that such situations are not rare and, therefore, such behaviors are not flukey. Rather, they are quite common; one reason that they seem strange or 'uncommonsensical' to us is that total reliance on other theoretical approaches (explicitly or implicitly) has blinded us to alternative possibilities or has made us disinclined to look beyond the obvious events generated by reward-reinforcement theories. The much discussed 'nonobvious' predictions generated by dissonance theory are only nonobvious in an apparent sense; they become obvious and make sense—once we gain an understanding of the dissonance-reducing process.

In the previous section, when discussing alternative ways of reducing dissonance, I tried to make the point that it is not very fruitful to ask what the mode of dissonance reduction is; rather, it is far more meaningful and instructive to isolate the various modes of reducing dissonance and to ask what the optimum conditions are for each. Similarly, rather than ask whether dissonance theory or reward-incentive theory is the more valid, one should attempt to determine the optimal conditions for the occurrence of processes and behaviors predicted by each theory.

One example of this approach has already been discussed. Recall that in Gerard and Mathewson's (1966) conceptual replication of the Aronson-Mills (1959) experiment, they found that when dissonance was eliminated from the experimental situation (in the No Initiation condition), subjects tended to rate the group discussion as being less attractive if it followed severe electric shock. Recall also that this is opposite to the "feelings of accomplishment" interpretation proposed by Chapanis and Chapanis (1964); rather, it can be considered as consistent with a general reward theory—i.e., stimuli contiguous with severe shock are considered to be unattractive. Similar findings relevant to reward theory are reported by Aronson (1961).

Another example of this approach can be found in an experiment by Freedman (1963), who had subjects perform a dull task after first informing them that either (a) the data would definitely be of no value to the experimenter—since his experiment was already complete, or (b) the data would be of *great* value to the experimenter. According to dissonance theory, performing a dull task is dissonant with the fact that it is not very valuable; in order to reduce dissonance, subjects should attempt to convince themselves that they actually enjoyed performing the task for its own sake. However, if the data are valuable, there is little dissonance, hence little need to convince oneself that the task was enjoyable. Freedman's results confirmed his prediction: Subjects in the "No-Value" condition enjoyed the task to a greater extent than did subjects in the "High-Value" condition. In addition, he ran a parallel set of conditions except that he withheld information about how valuable the task performance was for the experimenter until *after* the subjects had completed the task. With this modification he found the opposite effect: Those who were told the task was valuable enjoyed it more than those who were told it was useless. A moment's reflection should indicate that there is little or no dissonance in the above situation (see Chapter 42). No subject can have any reason to suspect that an experimenter is running him for no reason at all. If the subject performed the task in good faith, he had no way of knowing his data would not be used by the experimenter. That is, experimenters do not generally collect data that they have no intention of using. Accordingly, the subject does not need to seek justification for performing the task—the fact that his performance turned out to be futile was nothing that he could have possibly foreseen. On the other hand, if, in advance, he had some reason for believing that his efforts might be futile (as in the previous condition), he *does* need additional justification—he must convince himself that he chose to do it for its own sake. The point I want to stress here is that where little or no dissonance exists, an incentive effect emerges: The more valuable the task, the 'better' it is; the 'better' it is, the more the subjects enjoyed doing it. This experiment clearly demonstrates that dissonance effects and incentive effects can exist side by side. Moreover, it helps define some of the limiting conditions of each.

In a similar vein, a recent experiment by Carlsmith, Collins, and Helmreich (1966) has taken us a long way toward an understanding of the conditions optimal for the emergence of incentive and dissonance phenomena following counterattitudinal advocacy (see Section IV F). According to dissonance theory, if a person says something he feels is untrue, he experiences dissonance: The cognition "I said X" is dissonant with the cognition "I believe *not-X*." In order to reduce dissonance, he might attempt to convince himself that what he said was not so very untrue. Thus, dissonance theory suggests that advocating an opposite position increases one's tendency to believe in that position. However, if one is provided with a great deal of justification for advocating an opposite position (for example, if one is paid a great deal of money for telling a lie), one experiences less dissonance. That is, if I told a small lie for $53,000, I would have ample justification for having lied: The cognition that I received $53,000 is consonant with having lied. Consequently, I would have less need to justify my action by convincing myself that I really believed what I said than if I had been paid a mere 53 cents for lying. This type of prediction has been confirmed by several experiments (e.g., Festinger & Carlsmith, 1959; Cohen, 1962; Nuttin, 1964; Lependorf, 1964). These experiments have shown greater attitude change for less reward across a wide range of topics; moreover, it has been confirmed across a wide range of rewards, from $20.00 (high) and $1.00 (low) in the Festinger-Carlsmith experiment, to 50 cents (relatively high) and 5 cents (relatively low) in the Lependorf experiment. Thus, it would appear that this is a sturdy finding. On the other hand, there is some evidence that, under certain conditions, the opposite effect might emerge (Janis & Gilmore, 1965; Elms & Janis, 1965; Rosenberg, 1965d).[6] Briefly, under certain conditions, offering a high incentive for advocating a given position may lead to a better performance—i.e., thinking up more and

---

[6] For a more detailed critical analysis of all of these experiments, see Aronson, 1966c.

better arguments. This could lead to greater attitude change; i.e., a person changes his attitude *because* he has exposed himself to more arguments *because* he has looked harder *because* he was paid more money.

But what are these conditions? Or, better still, what conditions are optimal for the dissonance effect and what conditions are optimal for the incentive effect? The experiment by Carlsmith, Collins, and Helmreich (1966) provides us with a solid clue. In their experiment subjects were put through a dull task and were then asked to describe the task as interesting. The dependent variable was the extent to which the subjects convinced themselves that the task really was interesting. The results showed a dissonance effect (the smaller the reward, the greater the opinion change) only under conditions where subjects lied to another person in a highly committing face-to-face situation. In other conditions, subjects wrote an essay, were assured complete anonymity, and were told that only bits and pieces of their argument would be used. Here an incentive effect emerged: The greater the reward, the greater the opinion change. In the early experiments (e.g., Festinger & Carlsmith, 1959) the importance of the face-to-face situation was not fully appreciated by the investigators because this variable was not systematically manipulated. In a recent analysis of this area (Aronson, 1966c) I suggested that the important distinction between the above conditions is "degree of commitment." That is, in the face-to-face situation, the subject was saying things to a person which he himself believed were untrue. As I see it, this situation involves much more commitment and, hence, arouses much more dissonance than the writing of an anonymous essay which the subject had been told would not be used in its original form.

At the same time, it should be noted that the complexity of the experimental operations employed by Carlsmith, Collins, and Helmreich (1966) allows for alternative explanations. One of the most serious of these alternative explanations is in terms of the complexity of the counterattitudinal task involved. Rosenberg (1966) has argued that dissonance theory may be limited to situations where not much cognitive elaboration is required; he contends that where the task is more complex, incentive effects might occur. In analyzing the Carlsmith, Collins, and Helmreich study, Rosenberg makes the reasonable point that writing an essay and telling a lie not only differ in degree of commitment, but also may differ in the degree of cognitive complexity required. Consequently, this experiment cannot be taken as offering unambiguous support for my suggestion that degree of commitment is the decisive factor.

Two very recent experiments shed some additional light on this problem. In one, Linder, Cooper, and Jones (1967) were careful to hold the complexity of the task constant. The task was a complex one in all conditions—college students were asked to write an essay favoring more stringent paternalistic supervision of students by the college administration. The experimenters varied (a) the degree of commitment (in terms of whether or not the subjects were allowed to feel that they had a clear choice as to whether or not to write the essay) and (b) the magnitude of monetary incentive for writing the essay. The results are quite clear: When commitment was high there was a dissonance effect; i.e., the smaller the incentive, the greater the opinion change. When commitment was relatively low there was an incentive effect. A different experiment (Helmreich & Collins, 1968, in press) produced similar clear results. Here the task was also held constant, but instead of being complex (as in the Linder, Cooper, & Jones study), it was a simple one. Subjects were asked to record a statement which would be played to a large classroom of other students. In two relatively high-commitment conditions the subject's simple statement was put on *video* tape along with his name, class, major, and hometown. In a low-commitment condition the subjects made statements anonymously on *audio* tape. The results paralleled those obtained by Linder, Cooper, and Jones. In the high-commitment conditions the smaller the incentive, the greater the opinion change (dissonance effect); in the low-commitment condition the greater the incentive, the greater the opinion change (incentive effect).

THE 'UNDERLYING COGNITION' PROBLEM

The importance of commitment emerges most clearly when we scrutinize the phenomenon of the white lie more thoroughly. Clearly, every time we say something that we do not believe, we do *not* experience dissonance. Under certain conditions there are some underlying cognitions which serve to prevent the occurrence of dissonance. For example, if we stated a counter-attitudinal position in the context of a formal debate, we would not experience dissonance (see Scott, 1957, 1959; Aronson, 1966c). It is clearly understood both by the speaker and the audience that a debator's own personal views have nothing to do with the opinions he expresses. The rules of the game of debating provide an underlying cognition which prevents the occurrence of dissonance. Similarly, as teachers we frequently are exposed to a great many stupid ideas from our students. I think that unless we know the student well—know that he is capable of better ideas and know that he is capable of 'taking it'—most teachers refrain from tearing the idea to pieces. Instead, we tend to give the student our attention, nod and smile, and suggest that it is not such a bad idea. We do this because we have a general underlying cognition that we should not discourage students early in their careers and that it is wrong to be unkind to people who are relatively powerless to fight back. It would be ludicrous to suggest that teachers begin to believe that a student's poor idea is really a pretty good one simply because the teacher had said "pretty good idea" to the student. The underlying cognition prevents the occurrence of dissonance. But observe how commitment can make it a dissonant situation: If, on the basis of the teacher's statement, the student had decided to read his paper at the state psychological convention, the teacher might begin to convince himself that it was not such a bad idea—because the teacher has now been committed—he has misled the student into taking some action. This increases the teacher's commitment to the situation and is probably more powerful than the underlying consonant cognition "this is how we treat students." The teacher now seeks additional justification for having misled the student, perhaps by convincing himself that it was not such a bad idea after all.

The general point to be made here is an important one. Inconsistency is said to arise between two cognitive elements if, "considering these two alone, the [opposite] of one element follows from the other" (Festinger, 1957, pp. 260–261). But we know that in most situations two cognitions are almost never taken by themselves. Occasionally, two cognitions which in the abstract would appear to be dissonant fail to arouse dissonance because of the existence of a neutralizing underlying cognition. For example, suppose I know a brilliant fellow who is married to an incredibly stupid woman. These cognitions are inconsistent but I would contend that they do not necessarily produce dissonance. I can tolerate this inconsistency—it does not cause me pain, it does not necessarily lead me to change my opinion about the brilliant fellow or his wife, I do not conclude that he is dumber than I thought or that she is smarter. Why? Because I have a general, underlying, pervasive cognition that there are a multitude of factors which determine mate selection—similarities of intelligence being only one of them. Moreover, I know that it is extremely rare for all of these to be matched in a marital relationship. Therefore, although taken by themselves the above two cognitions are incompatible, I simply do not ever take them by themselves.

  Festinger suggests that one way to reduce dissonance is to martial consonant cognitions—thus, he might say that the above reasoning is one way of reducing dissonance. But it is a moot and important point whether I martialed the above cognitions as a result of the inconsistency, or whether I walked around with these cognitions about mate selection before the fact. If the latter is the case, then it can hardly be said that I dredged up this overriding cognition as a means of reducing dissonance. For example, let us look at the finding (Aronson & Carlsmith, 1963; Turner & Wright, 1965; Freedman, 1965b) that children threatened with mild punishment for playing with a toy tend to derogate that toy after refraining from playing with it. Suppose that many children entered the situation with the strong feeling that adults must be obeyed always, even when commands are arbitrary and threats are nonexistent ("My mother, right or wrong!"). Put another way (which will become important in a moment), suppose that part of the self concept of these children was "obedience to adult authority." If this were the case there would have been no dissonance—even though, *taken by itself*, the cognition "I like that toy" is dissonant with the cognition "I'm not playing with it." If this were *not* already a part of the person's self concept, it might have become one as a function of the experiment—i.e., developing a belief in the importance of obedience is one way of reducing dissonance in the above situation. But if it were already there—there would have been no dissonance to begin with.

This added complexity should not lead us to throw our hands up in despair. Rather, it should lead us to a more careful analysis of the situations we are dealing with and perhaps even to a greater concern with individual differences.

THE IMPORTANCE OF THE SELF CONCEPT AND OTHER EXPECTANCIES

In discussing the difficulties in making precise predictions from dissonance theory in some situations, we have purposely tiptoed around the problem of individual differences. The fact that all people are not the same presents intriguing problems for dissonance theory as it does for all general motivational theories. Of course, one man's 'problem' is another man's primary datum; i.e., psychologists who are interested in personality regard individual differences as being of great interest. For those who are primarily interested in establishing nomothetic laws, individual differences usually constitute nothing more than an annoying source of error variance. Nevertheless, whether or not we are interested in individual differences *per se*, an understanding of the way people differ in dissonant situations can be an important means to clarify and strengthen the theory. Basically, there are three ways that individuals differ which should be of concern to people investigating dissonance theory:

1. People differ in their ability to tolerate dissonance. It seems reasonable to assume that some people are simply better than others at shrugging off dissonance; i.e., it may take a greater *amount* of dissonance to bring about dissonance-reducing behavior in some people than in others.

2. People probably differ in their preferred mode of dissonance reduction. E.g., some people may find it easier to derogate the source of a communication than to change their own opinion. Others may find the reverse resolution easier.

3. What is dissonant for one person may be consonant for someone else; i.e., people may be so different that certain events are regarded as dissonant for some but not for others.

The first two are covered in Section IV B. I shall not dwell on them here save to say that, earlier in this chapter, I underscored the difficulty of ascertaining the proper conditions for establishing whether or not dissonance exists for *most people* and the conditions for determining which mode of dissonance reduction *most people* will use; the existence of individual differences complicates matters further by adding another important dimension which should eventually be specified. The third case (mentioned also in Section IV B) will be discussed here because it is of great relevance for the general theory. Furthermore, I regard it as prior to the other two, for before one can determine (a) whether an individual is experiencing *enough* dissonance to reduce it or (b) *how* he will reduce it, we must first determine whether the events are indeed dissonant, consonant, or irrelevant to him.

Dissonant or consonant with what? Recall the earlier discussion wherein I described a rule of thumb based upon an expectancy (e.g., the Thurgood Marshall and wife-beating novelist illustrations). In my judgment, dissonance theory makes a clear prediction when a firm expectancy is involved as one of the cognitions in question. Thus, our cognition about Thurgood Marshall's *behavior* can be dissonant with our expectancy about how Justice Marshall *will* behave. Dissonance theory is clearer still when that firm expectancy involves the individual's self concept, for—almost by definition—our expectancies about our own behavior are firmer than our expectancies about the behavior of another person. Thus, at the very heart of dissonance theory, where it makes its clearest and neatest prediction, we are not dealing with just any two cognitions; rather, we are usually dealing with the self concept and cognitions about some behavior. If dissonance exists it is because the individual's behavior is inconsistent with his self concept.

As I pointed out several years ago (Aronson, 1960), this point has been elusive because most of the experiments testing dissonance theory have made predictions based upon the tacit assumption that people have a high self concept. Why do people who buy new cars selectively expose themselves to ads about their own make of car (Ehrlich, Guttman, Schoenbach, & Mills, 1957) and try to convince themselves that they made the right choice? Because the knowledge that one has bought a junky car is dissonant with a high self concept. But suppose a person had a low self concept? Then, the cognition that he bought a junky car would *not* be dissonant. Indeed, if the theory holds, such a person should engage in all kinds of 'bizarre' behavior like exposing himself to ads about other cars, hearing squeaks and rattles that are not even there, and saying, in effect, "'Just my luck, I bought a lemon— these things are always happening to me." In short, if a person conceives of himself as a 'schnook,' he will expect to behave like a schnook; consequently, wise, reasonable, successful, un-schnooky behavior on his part should arouse dissonance. One of the advantages of this kind of statement is that it allows us to separate the effects of dissonance from other hedonic effects. That is, people with *high* self concepts who fail *do* experience dissonance; but they experience many other negative feelings as well—due simply to the fact that failure is unpleasant. No one can deny that success brings pleasant consequences for people with high and low self concepts alike. That is, regardless of a person's self concept, successful achievement is often accompanied by such pleasant things as acclaim, money, fame, admiration, popularity, etc. But dissonance theory allows us to predict that, for people with low self concepts, the 'good feelings' aroused by the products of success will be tempered by the discomfort caused by dissonance—the dissonance between a low self concept and cognitions about high performance. Several experiments have demonstrated that people who expect failure are somewhat discomforted by success (Aronson & Carlsmith, 1962; Cottrell, 1965; Brock *et al.*, 1965), but the data are by no means unequivocal [see Section III E].

Thus, although we may not have been fully aware of it at the time, in the clearest experiments performed to test dissonance theory, the dissonance involved was between a self concept and cognitions about a behavior that violated this self concept. In the experiments on counterattitudinal advocacy, for example, I would suggest that it is incorrect to say that dissonance existed between the cognition "I believe the task is dull" and "I told someone that the task was interesting." This is not dissonant for a psychopathic liar—indeed, it is perfectly consonant. What is dissonant is the cognition "I am a decent, truthful human being" and the cognition "I have misled a person; I have conned him into believing something which just isn't true; he thinks that I really believe it and I cannot set him straight because I probably won't see him again." (A similar point is implied in a related analysis by Abelson, Chapter 5, p. 130. In the initiation experiments, I would maintain that dissonance does not exist between the cognition "I worked hard to get into a group" and the cognition "The group is dull and stupid." Recall that for a 'schnook' these cognitions are not at all dissonant. What is dissonant in this situation is the cognition "I am a reasonable and intelligent person" and the cognition "I have worked hard for nothing." Reasonable, intelligent people usually get a fair return for their investment— they usually do not buy a pig in a poke (unless there is some reasonably implicit guarantee, as in Freedman's [1963] experiment discussed above).

As an empirical refinement this self concept notion is probably trivial. The experimenters who made the tacit assumption that people have high self concepts achieved positive results—which indicates that this assumption is valid for most people in these situations. But it may constitute a valuable and interesting *theoretical* refinement. A theory becomes infinitely more meaningful when its domain is clearly demarcated; i.e., when it states clearly where it does not apply. If it is the case that dissonance theory makes unequivocal predictions only when the self concept or another strong expectancy is involved, then an important set of boundary conditions has been drawn. What I described earlier as a rule of thumb may actually be a conceptual clarification.

I stated early in this chapter that "at the 'center' of the theory" predictions are unequivocal, but at the 'fringes' they are somewhat fuzzy. At this point, we can say that 'at the center' means situations in which the self concept or other firm expectancies are involved—and in which most people share the same self concepts or other firm expectancies. Thus, most people have self concepts about being truthful and honest so that we can make clear predictions intuitively, as in the Carlsmith, Collins, and Helmreich (1966) experiment. Most people have self concepts involving making reasonable and wise decisions so that we can intuit clear predictions, as in the Brehm (1956) or Jecker (1964a) experiments. Also, most people have firm expectancies about what Thurgood Marshall would say about Negro intelligence, so that a dissonance theory prediction makes sense and can be made clearly, even though a self concept is not involved. The prediction about the great novelist who beats his wife gives the theory trouble precisely because people differ tremendously with regard to whether or not they expect a particular novelist to be a gentle and considerate man. In a specific instance, the knowledge of whether or not individual X has this expectancy would increase the accuracy of the prediction. I do not regard this of great importance. What I do regard as important is merely the recognition of the fact that dissonance theory may be best suited for making general predictions in situations where expectancies are firm and nearly universal.

Several years ago, Zajonc (1960a) raised a very interesting and reasonable question: If dissonance is bothersome, why do we enjoy magicians? That is, magicians can be thought of as people who arouse dissonance. Should we not experience pain and discomfort when we see rabbits pulled from hats, women sawed in half, or dimes turned into quarters? Perhaps the reason why we are not upset by magicians is because the behavior of a magician is consonant with our expectancy regarding magicians. That is, since we know in advance that magicians use tricks and sleight-of-hand techniques to produce interesting illusions, why should we experience dissonance when we see him do these things? Is this not akin to the schnook who expects to purchase an inferior car?

Before the reader dismisses this as mere sophistry, let me hasten to say that this is an empirical question. What I am suggesting is that we enjoy magicians *only* when they are billed as magicians. If they were not billed as magicians, they would cause quite a bit of discomfort. If the fellow sitting next to us at the bar suddenly 'became' a fat woman, this would be very upsetting—unless the bartender had forewarned us that we were sitting next to a professional quick-change artist known as "Slippery Sam, the man of a thousand faces." If he then 'became' a fat woman, we would be thrilled and delighted. It is interesting to note that the bartender could have produced a similar result if he had forewarned us that he had placed some LSD in our drink. In short, either being told a man is a magician or being told we were fed a hallucinogen is consistent with seeing a man 'become' a fat woman!

Empirically, this can be tested by finding some young children or some people from a different culture who have never seen or heard of magicians.

My guess is that without the expectancy regarding magicians that Zajonc and I share, these subjects would be quite upset by the goings on.

MAN CANNOT LIVE BY CONSONANCE ALONE

The implication of this essay is that dissonant situations are ubiquitous and that man expends a good deal of time and energy attempting to reduce dissonance. It should be obvious that man does many other things as well. Festinger never intended dissonance theory to be imperial or monolithic. In 1957, he clearly recognized the fact that dissonance reduction is only one of many motives and can be counteracted by more powerful drives. We have already discussed how dissonance effects and reward-incentive effects can both occur in the same experimental design. Even more basic is the confrontation that occurs when consonance needs meet utility needs head-on. An extremely high drive to reduce dissonance would lead man to weave a cocoon about himself, never admitting his mistakes and distorting reality to make it compatible with his behavior. But if a person is ever going to grow, improve, and avoid repeating the same errors, he must sooner or later learn to profit from past mistakes. One cannot profit from one's mistakes without first admitting that one has *made* a mistake. And yet, the admission of error almost always arouses some dissonance. The fact is, people frequently *do* profit from their mistakes; thus, people occasionally do not avoid or reduce dissonance.

To illustrate, if a man spends $50,000 for a home, dissonance theory would suggest that he may be the last to notice that, during the rainy season, there is water in the basement. Noticing water would arouse dissonance by making his purchase appear to have been a mistake. But to notice the water has great utility—for he must notice it in order to repair it, prepare for the flood, or check the basement of the next house he buys. Thus, dissonance and utility are in constant tension by virtue of the fact that under certain conditions dissonant information may be extremely useful, and, conversely, useful information can arouse dissonance. Mills, Aronson, and Robinson (1959) suggested that one reason that people frequently do not avoid dissonant information is that it often has great utility. In their experiment, they found that many subjects who had recently committed themselves to taking essay exams as opposed to multiple-choice exams opted to read articles explaining why essay exams were more difficult, anxiety-provoking, etc. In this situation, apparently, the utility of the information was considered worth the price to be paid in dissonance. More recent experiments by Canon (1964) and Aronson and Ross (1966) have begun to indicate the requisite conditions for these effects: Basically, as utility increases and dissonance becomes weaker, individuals begin to show a preference for dissonance-arousing but useful information. But as dissonance increases (i.e., immediately after a decision or when commitment is high, etc.), individuals tend to manifest dissonance-reducing behavior in spite of the fact that the future consequences of such behavior tend to be unpleasant.

EPILOGUE

The theory of cognitive dissonance is much more complicated than it was thought to be ten years ago. A good deal of research has been done since

1957. Many of the problems which were specified early have been solved; many new problems have been unearthed, some of which remain to be solved. Hopefully, future research will lead to the emergence of still new problems, which will lead to still more research, which will continue to yield an increased understanding of human behavior. I guess that is what science is all about. In their critique of five years of dissonance theory, Chapanis and Chapanis concluded with the pronouncement "Not proven." Happily, after ten years, it is still not proven; all the theory ever does is generate research!

CHAPTER 2

Interpersonal Balance

Theodore M. Newcomb
The University of Michigan

The human condition, as I have come to view it in social-psychological terms, is such that individuals continually face a three-pronged problem of adaptation. Each of us must somehow come to terms, simultaneously, with the other individuals and groups in our interpersonal environment, with the world that we have in common with those persons and groups, and with our own, intrapersonal demands and preferences.

We face, in each of the three directions, forces that are ineluctable. We ignore properties of the 'real' world at our peril. Stones will bruise, and fire will burn—these things we learn by direct, sensory experience, aided by the teaching of others. So far, there is no problem in confronting the interpersonal world and the world of common objects, although a future problem is in the making. As we find that our own experience and the testimony of persons whom we trust are mutually supportive, we tend to rely on the latter—it short-circuits trial and error, enables us to avoid painful experiences, often leads to direct satisfaction. And so their testimony, too, is ignored at our peril. But the time comes when the two sources of evidence do not support each other, but yield conflicting evidence: our senses, or our own inferences therefrom, tell us one thing and our associates another. Or—especially when direct sensory experience is limited, or inaccessible—two trusted human sources give different testimony. How then shall we know the 'real' nature of things? It is out of such a history—presumably universal to all humans, and perhaps unique to them—that intrapersonal demands for adaptation arise. The world is at odds if one's own sources of belief are contravened by those whom one is accustomed to trust—or, indeed, must trust, *faute de mieux*.

Professor Fritz Heider (1958, especially) has proposed, among other consistency-like models, one that is appropriate to this view. He posits a psychological tendency toward organizing cognitions about things and about other persons who also have cognitions about them in "harmonious" ways. His label for this preferred way of organizing such cognitive elements is "balance," which may be considered as a special case of consistency. It is with this form of psychological adaptation that the present paper deals.

Somewhat more specifically, I am here concerned with the psychological processes that occur when a person, *P*, simultaneously experiences cognitions about some entity, *X* (an object, a person, or an idea, for example), and about some other person, *O*, whose cognitions about *X* are of interest to *P*. I shall argue that the phenomena of this special problem are sufficiently distinctive from others in Heider's family of related ones that no single set of rules can apply to all of them. If so, then the psychological processes involved in *POX* situations are, in some manner or degree, unique.

THEORETICAL BACKGROUND:
HEIDER'S GENERAL PRINCIPLES OF BALANCE

Heider, as noted by Jordan (Chapter 7), was the first systematic formulator of the principles of experiencing "separate entities" together in terms of balance (1944, 1946). "The concept of balanced state," he wrote in 1958, "designates a situation in which the perceived units [entities experienced as belonging together] and the experienced sentiments [attitudes, in the more common usage] co-exist without stress; there is thus no pressure toward change, either in the cognitive organization or in the sentiment" (p. 176). All subsequent treatments, including my own, have adopted this general position.

Heider distinguishes two kinds of relations characterizing any of the three pairs of cognitive elements. The *sentiment* relation "refers to a person's evaluation of something, as when *P* likes or admires *O*, or *P* approves of *X*, or *P* rejects or condemns *X*....[1]" In addition, there is a *unit* relation. "Persons and objects are the units that first come to mind; the parts of such units are perceived as belonging together in a specially close way. But also two (or more) separate entities can form a unit. The two entities may be related through similarity, causality, ownership, or other unit-forming characteristics. U denotes the cognitive unit between two entities and not-U the fact that the two units are segregated" (pp. 200–1). Both the sentiment relation and the unit relation may be either positive or negative (e.g., like vs. dislike and associated vs. segregated). Heider's illustrative triads most commonly include two sentiment relations and one unit relation, the latter usually referring to *O/X*.

Heider's formal statements of the conditions of balance include the following: "A triad is balanced when all three of the relations [*P/O*, *P/X*, and *X/O*] are positive or when two of the relations are negative and one is positive. Imbalance occurs when two of the relations are positive and one is negative. The case of the three negative relations is somewhat ambiguous...." (pp. 202–3). It has become common practice (in spite of Heider's misgivings about the all-negative triad) to phrase his formula as follows: The triad is balanced if the algebraic product of the three signs is positive, and imbalanced if the product is negative.

Much subsequent research on *POX* triads, however, has made little use of Heider's unit relation, so labeled. This is principally because "*O*'s attitude toward *X*" has typically been used instead of a unit relation between *O* and *X*. This is sometimes the case in work to which Heider applies his own

---

[1] *P*, *O*, and *X* refer respectively to "person" (as subject), "other" person, and some third entity, in Heider's usage, which I have followed except for the use of upper-case letters. The slash between two letters means "has a relation to."

formula—e.g., a study by Kogan and Tagiuri (1957) in which "only affective relations (like-dislike) were taken into account" (p. 204). At any rate this particular form of unit relation, which introduces the parameter of agreement or disagreement between P and O, and which constitutes a triad of three attitudes (three sentiment relations, in Heider's terms) is the one which has been most frequently studied. It is, of course, a form to which Heider considers his own formula applicable, as suggested by the following: "... a sentiment relation may induce a unit relation and vice versa. Thus I want to like what I own, to dispose of what I dislike, etc." (p. 206). And the reverse is also commonly true: I want to own what I like. Thus a unit relation often implies a sentiment relation of the same sign.

There is another justification, too, for the now common practice of substituting a third attitude for the single unit relation. The experimenter's usual assumption is that, sheerly by reason of confronting the subject with a set of cognitive elements, the subject is forced, for the moment at least, to assume some sort of belonging-relation among them. Even if (as in a type of experiment that Heider discusses on pages 205–7) the subject is presented with only two relations within a POX triad and asked to fill in the missing one—say O/X—he is being invited to consider that O has some sort of relation, positive or negative, with X. This might be called experimental or manipulative induction of the unit relation.

Although empirical findings provide a good deal of support for the substitution of attitudinal for unit relations, as shown below (pp. 33–34), such a modification may seem, at first glance, to entail a serious cost. One of the ways, carefully noted by Heider, in which imbalance may be reduced is that of breaking up a unit relation. For example, if P comes to the con-clusion that an admired O is not really responsible for a despicable act (X) that he has committed, then the unit relation O/X becomes negative; since P/O is positive and P/X negative, the triad[2] contains two negative relations and is therefore balanced, according to Heider. But this situation can also be handled in terms of a three-attitude triad: "O is not really responsible for X" becomes "O does not really approve of that act," with the result that the triad contains two negative attitudes and one that is positive. This 'translation' appears to be appropriate in a very large number of cases.

Heider's formulation of the conditions of balance includes a range of sets of cognitive relations that is broader, in more than one way, than my limited concern with POX situations. He gives considerable attention to cognitive dyads, with which I shall not here deal at all. Here is one of his "Examples" (p. 203):

5. p is dissatisfied with the lecture: (p dislikes x) is a negative relation.
   p delivered it: (p and x have a unit relation) is a positive relation.
   Conclusion: The dyad has one positive and one negative relation,
   and is therefore unbalanced.

Thus Heider is interested in simple pairs of cognitions on the part of a single person, without reference to cognitions of any other person—as I

---

[2] A given set of POX relations is variously referred to in the literature as a triad, a situation, or a structure. I have in general retained the usage of the authors whose work is being cited, occasionally adopting the term "pattern" for purposes of comparing dif-ferent arrangements of signs.

am not. In this and in certain other respects Heider's systematic theory of relations among multiple cognitions of a single person is far more inclusive than anything I shall attempt.

But my problem is also one of his problems, and in respects other than those I have mentioned my assumptions and my questions are closely parallel to his—and often borrowed from him. Specifically, the following are of importance. (a) Imbalanced sets of cognitive elements are characterized by relatively great stress toward changing one or more of the elements, and balanced sets by relatively little stress. (b) Such sets of cognitive elements as are susceptible to forces toward balance are subject to an equifinality; that is, insofar as they are in balance at a given moment they tend to remain as they are, and insofar as they are not they tend to change toward balance. (c) Different combinations of signs among a given set of cognitive elements can be either balanced or imbalanced by varying arrangements of signs; thus there are alternative paths toward balance.

THE PSYCHOLOGICAL NATURE OF BALANCE AND IMBALANCE

Balance, as a structural property of a set of cognitive elements, has to do with psychological relationships among them. As such, it should itself be understood in psychological terms, quite apart from its definability in formal (psychologically contentless) terms. I have found it less fruitful to begin with a psychological description of balance than of imbalance. I regard a set of cognitions as imbalanced insofar as it instigates the cognizer toward *modification* of one or more relationships within the set. A cognitive set may fail to be clearly imbalanced in either of two ways. First, because it is unobjectionable as it stands, thus instigating *acceptance;* such a set is clearly balanced. Or, second, because it clearly invites *neither modification nor acceptance*—whether by reason of indifference, uncertainty, or ambivalence. This latter kind of set, neither clearly balanced nor clearly imbalanced, I shall label *nonbalanced;* changes in one of its constituent relations might result in balance, imbalance, or continuing nonbalance. The former alternative to imbalance, representing balance, is such that a change in any one of its constituent relations would result either in imbalance or in nonbalance.

Thus I am postulating three rather than two distinguishable states of balance in *POX* triads. Before inquiring into the sign-patterns that identify each of them, it will be useful to examine the psychological processes presumably associated with each of the three relations within the triad.

1. *P/O.* Ignoring, for the moment, the question of what are the bases for *P*'s attitude of attraction or aversion toward *O* (cf. Newcomb, 1960), the *P/O* relation differs from the others in two important ways. First, *P* (by definition, in this context) regards *O* as having a certain relationship to *X*—namely, that of having an attitude toward *X*. Whatever the other contexts in which *P* views *O*, the *POX* paradigm requires this assumption: *O* is not only an object of *P*'s attitude but also a source of attitude toward *X*.

Second, *O* is typically[3] someone with whom *P* has reciprocal acquaint-

---

[3] The most obvious class of exceptions is that in which *O* is some public figure who has no knowledge of *P*—e.g., "*P* admires President Johnson (*O*) who is assumed to support the war in Viet Nam (*X*) which *P* also approves of."

ance, so that P's assumptions about O/P are included in his psychological processes. Various studies (e.g., Jones, 1966; Newcomb, 1961; Price, Harburg, & Newcomb, 1966) have shown that P/O tends to maintain a close relationship with assumed O/P, if P/O is clearly positive; if P/O is negative, however, there is typically much uncertainty in P's judgments of O/P. In either case, P's view of the total situation is influenced by his assumptions about O/P. Thus P/O is not directly comparable with any relation within the POX triad except O/P, information about which is not included in the simple POX paradigm.

2. P/X. This relation is the least complicated of the three, provided that the X in question is not such that it could be considered a second O (presumably a person). If so, P's psychological processes include his assumptions about X/P, and perhaps also about X/O. If not, P/X refers simply to a single attitude. In any case, the P/X relation is directly comparable only with O/X—though different, in that the former is a first-hand report of P's own attitude and the latter P's attribution of an attitude to O.

3. O/X. As just indicated, this relation is unique. It stands for secondary rather than primary information; it is provided by P about O as the source of the attitude. Otherwise, O/X is directly comparable with P/X. In fact, the comparison is altogether likely to be made by P; and this comparison, revealing similarity or difference between P/X and O/X, is, as I shall soon try to show, often crucial for P's state of balance.

In sum, the three psychological states of balance, imbalance, and nonbalance represent experiences of preferring to accept a set of cognitive elements as they are, to modify it, or to be relatively indifferent as between its acceptance or its modification. Each of the component attitudes is unique, as is the relationship within each pair of attitudes (P/O and P/X, P/O and O/X, P/X and O/X). It is therefore not to be expected that, psychologically, a shift in sign of any one of them is equivalent to the same sign-shift in any other.

This point of view hardly squares with Heider's operational definition of balance, based solely on numbers of plus and minus signs, regardless of where they appear. It therefore behooves me to provide operational definitions for my proposed distinctions between balance, imbalance, and nonbalance.

The psychological state aroused by a nonbalanced POX situation, I have suggested, is characterized by lack of clear preference for accepting or modifying the set of relations. The most common single source of such a state lies in the presence of a negative P/O relation. This stems in part from the fact that, within the simple POX paradigm, we are dealing only with the algebraic signs of P/O, P/X, and O/X, and (in the absence of information about intensity of these relations) only the first of these implies anything about the cognizer's concern for balance or imbalance. That is, P may be equally ready to accept or to change P/X or O/X regardless of its sign, but this is often not the case for P/O, because O is both object of P's attitude and source of his own attitude. The consequence of this is that a negative P/O may imply "Since I dislike O (or do not respect him, or trust him) I have no interest in his attitude toward X." (The extreme case is that of amused unconcern at pronouncements of the village idiot.) Another unique aspect of the P/O relation, already noted, is P's uncertainty about O/P when P/O is negative, resulting in indecisiveness about preferring to accept or to change the existing POX relation.

The concept of "engagement" has been proposed by Price, Harburg, and Newcomb (1966) as a polar opposite of indifference, uncertainty, or ambivalence. Lack of engagement does not necessarily imply noninvolvement in any of the POX relations, but only a state of little or no preference for balance or imbalance within the total set of relations. The notion of indifference, as opposed to engagement, applies to the total set of POX relations, not to any particular one of them. My assumption is that engagement in a POX situation cannot be stronger than its weakest link, and that a negative P/O relation is usually on the side of weakness. Even though—to mention an apparent exception—a disliked O might be a serious threat to a valued X, P's engagement in the balance properties of the set of cognitions may be minimal. (Various parameters of engagement are considered later in this chapter.)

At any rate, my operational definition is simply that any POX situation in which P/O is negative is a nonbalanced one, often though not invariably associated with low engagement. In other respects, my definitions are like Heider's: positive P/O together with like-signed P/X and O/X represents balance (which I shall label 'positive balance,' to distinguish it from Heider's more inclusive definition), and positive P/O together with unlike-signed O/X and P/X represents imbalance (as distinguished from Heider's more inclusive "unbalance."). Table 4 (page 38) compares the two category systems in visual form.

One difference between the two category systems involves the situations $(- - -$ and $- + +)$. They differ from the two situations $(+ + -$ and $+ - +)$ in that the latter involve positive P/O with P/X and O/X of unlike signs, while the former are exactly reversed (negative P/O with like-signed P/X and O/X). I regard the former as merely nonbalanced and the latter as imbalanced, while Heider regards all of them as unbalanced.

A more important difference between the two category systems involves the two situations $(- - +$ and $- + -)$ that, for Heider, are balanced; this assumption corresponds to the common-sense notion that "if I dislike him I prefer to disagree with him," or, conversely, "if he disagrees with me I dislike him." This tendency is analogous to that which I have elsewhere labeled the "negative reference group" phenomenon (Newcomb, 1952), several illustrations of which I offered in that study. I am not, of course, denying that the phenomenon occurs, but only hypothesizing that it is a less dependable one than that of indifference when P/O is negative. The rationale for this assumption[4] is basically that negative P/O engenders its own tension, which is independent of the kind of tension that is intrinsic to the notion of balance, as defined by Heider and by others who have followed him.

Predictions from my hypothesis are that, according to various measures of psychological balance, the four possible POX situation in which P/O is negative (a) will resemble each other more closely than they resemble

---

[4] For supporting positions, compare later references to Zajonc (p. 42 and to Rodrigues (p. 43).

other situations, and (b) will be intermediate between positively balanced and imbalanced situations. There follow some reports of relevant empirical studies.

EMPIRICAL STUDIES: I. ATTITUDE AND UNIT RELATIONS[5]

Ratings of Pleasantness

The prototype experiment, in more than one respect, is that of Jordan (1953), then a student of Heider. His subjects indicated their degrees of subjective unpleasantness along a 90mm. line, responses ranging from 10 to 99, with the mid-point at 55. His 208 Ss, among them, responded to all of the 64 possible combinations of liking, disliking, unit relation, and no unit relation; each of the triads was rated by 36 Ss. The triads represented "social situations comprising the self, p, another person, o, and an impersonal entity, x." A sample of these somewhat abstract stimulus situations is "I like o; I like x; o has no bond or relationship with x."

Jordan's data are analyzed below (pp. 35–36) from the point of view of balance; here I shall consider only the distinction between unit and sentiment (or attitude) relations. Table 1 presents a summary of mean ratings by Jordan's Ss and, for purposes of comparison, ratings obtained by another investigator whose procedures were almost identical except that all three relations were attitudinal (e.g., "You like o, o likes x, you like x"). This table shows that the principal effect of increasing the proportion of unit relations is to decrease the extremeness of the ratings: for seven of the eight sign patterns, ratings are more extreme when all relations are attitudinal than when none of them are (first vs. fourth columns).

Apart from this distinction, Jordan's subjects' ratings of unpleasantness show no systematic variation with the proportions of attitudinal and unit relations. The average of the six correlations among the four columns of Table 1 is .85, and even that between all-attitudinal and all-unit relations (first and third columns) is .82—in spite of the small range of scores for the last six sign-patterns.

Jordan's mean overall ratings, moreover, show close agreement with those of Rodrigues in absolute values—though the latter were obtained years later in a different setting, from different subjects, and represented attitudinal relations exclusively. The rank-order correlation between the last two columns in Table 1 is .61 (correlations between Rodrigues's scores and those of columns 1–4, taken separately, do not differ significantly).

All in all, judging from these analyses, the now common practice of obtaining responses in terms of attitudes only, rather than in terms of a combination of attitudinal and unit relations, seems justified. The former, in fact, seem to have the additional advantage—important for the purposes of this paper—of eliciting a wider range of distinctive responses to the several sign patterns than do the latter. Composite cognitions of the kind represented by these eight sign-patterns, as indexed by ratings of unpleasantness,

---

[5] The research studies reported here and elsewhere in this paper are selected as bearing upon the limited issues with which it deals. The research literature is now very extensive: Zajonc's list of references (1968) includes well over 100 citations of empirical studies (nearly all published later than 1957) of problems dealing with cognitive balance—apart from those cited in his sections on "dissonance" and "the congruity principle."

TABLE 1

Means[1] of Unpleasantness Ratings
(Jordan, 1953, and Rodrigues, 1967)

Sign Pattern[2]	N of Sentiment Relations[3] in Triad (Jordan)				Eight Triads (Jordan)	Single Triads (Rodrigues)[4]
	3	2	1	0		
+++	22	24	28	32	26	20
+--	34	40	39	42	39	35
-+-	64	58	52	48	55	54
--+	71	65	60	52	62	60
-++	59	58	54	50	56	67
---	70	60	56	50	59	65
++-	64	60	53	50	57	61
+-+	67	60	53	57	58	65
Range	49	41	32	25	36	47

[1] Rounded to nearest integer
[2] The algebraic signs refer to *PIO, PIX,* and *OIX,* in that order. The first four sign-patterns are considered balanced by Heider, and the latter four unbalanced (including the − − − triad, according to Jordan).
[3] The corresponding *N*s of unit relations in the four columns are 0, 1, 2, 3.
[4] See p. 37 for report of this experiment.

vary in about the same ways regardless of whether the relations are presented in terms of unit relations or of attitudes.[6]

EMPIRICAL STUDIES: II. CATEGORIES OF BALANCE[7]

I have argued that, in terms of psychological processes, there are important differences between *POX* triads that include positive and negative *P/O* relations; hence my distinctions among three categories—balanced, imbalanced, and nonbalanced. My rationale includes the assumption that *P/X–O/X* agreement and disagreement affect the composite cognition differently with opposed signs of *P/O*.

Ratings of Unpleasantness

Jordan's 1953 study is, again, the first to be examined, but now with this problem in mind rather than that of unit relations. As summarized by Heider (p. 204), Jordan's results "showed a statistically significant tendency for harmonious relations to be rated [less unpleasantly] than unbalanced ones." But, as shown in Table 1, the data also reveal higher ratings of unpleasantness for Heider-balanced triads in which *P/O* is negative than for similarly balanced ones in which *P/O* is positive; and the former, though balanced from Heider's point of view, are no more pleasant than those considered unbalanced by Heider. The only triads that are consistently

---

[6] Professor Robert B. Zajonc has reached similar conclusions. In one publication (1968) he summarizes the issue as follows: "For all practical purposes, L- and U- relations are substitutable." His paper, which reached me when this chapter had been virtually completed, has, in some respects at least, made my own almost unnecessary.

[7] The studies in this section include all that I have found which compare responses to all (in a few cases only four) of the eight sign patterns and that seem to me instructive. After this section was completed, I discovered that the studies analyzed by Zajonc (1968) in his table entitled "A comparison of balance, agreement, and friendship effects" are exactly the same ones as those that follow.

rated as pleasant are the first two, characterized by positive P/O together with agreement—and the only two that, according to my formulation, are positively balanced. The remaining six situations are undistinguishable in terms of mean ratings, as shown by inspection. Their "odd-even reliability" (summed ratings for first, third, fifth, and seventh against the other four of Jordan's eight combinations of liking and unit relations) is $+.09$. And (though perhaps only by chance) the single sign pattern of these six that is rated most unpleasant $(--+)$ is considered balanced by Heider.

Thus Jordan's data support my distinction between positive balance and nonbalance under conditions that Heider considers balanced (either two negative relations or none) but not otherwise (one or three negative relations). I shall later consider this (to me) anomaly.

I now turn to a study by Price, Harburg, and Newcomb (1966), designed to test my own hypotheses. Each of 156 Ss (following Jordan's procedure) indicated, by checking a position on a 90mm. line, his degree of "pleasant" or "uneasy" feelings about each of the eight possible combinations of signs (positive or negative for each of P/O, P/X, and O/X). P was the subject himself; O was a person known to S and chosen by him either as strongly liked or disliked; X was a second person (and hence labeled Q) chosen by S in the same fashion. Mean scores are summarized in Table 2; as in subsequent tables, the situations are so classified as to permit comparisons of Heider's two categories of balance and the three categories that I have proposed.

These responses are in striking support of Heider's predictions when P/O is positive, but not when P/O is negative. According to my own distinction, the latter are neither clearly balanced nor clearly imbalanced. Responses to these situations, as compared with those that are clearly balanced or imbalanced (both by Heider and by me), show not only far less unanimity but also more frequent "neutral" responses and larger differences between the two situations in each category—exactly as to be expected if nonbalanced situations differ from both balanced and imbalanced ones.

Steiner and Spaulding (1966), in essentially similar ways, obtained ratings of pleasantness from 164 Ss to each of four triadic situations (selected

TABLE 2

Summary of Pleasantness Ratings
(Price, Harburg, Newcomb)

All Situations in Which . . .	Uneasy	Range[1] of Percentage of All Scores	Pleasant
		Neutral[2]	
P/O Positive			
balanced[3]	5–6%	6–7%	87–89%
imbalanced[3]	84–89%	0–8%	8–11%
P/O Negative			
balanced[3]	28–43%	22–39%	33–35%
imbalanced[3]	17–65%	15–38%	22–45%

[1] Two situations of each type were rated.
[2] Scores within 2 mm. of the midpoint (about 4 per cent) were considered neutral.
[3] According to Heider's formula.

from the eight possible ones). Subjects were told that for each situation P did or did not like O; that P liked X; and that O did or did not like X, a specified object or activity (algebra, motorcycles, skating, horror movies, science courses, folk music, swimming, or formal parties). These were hypothetical situations in which P and O were represented by common first names.

Their findings fairly closely resemble those of Price, Harburg, and Newcomb (Table 2) for the first two situations; combining responses from four different populations, they obtained 98 per cent and 26 per cent, respectively, of "pleasant" responses, using the same criteria. For the other two situations, however (nonbalanced, in my terms), their data tend to support Heider's rather than my predictions. Though the distributions of responses to the fourth situation in Table 2 are much alike in the two studies, Steiner and Spaulding report more pleasant (66 per cent) and fewer neutral (6 per cent) responses than does the other study to the third situation. Nevertheless, their 66 per cent of pleasant responses is clearly intermediate between their 98 per cent for the situation that I consider positively balanced and their 26 per cent for the one that, to me, is positively imbalanced. Thus both Heider's and my predictions find some support from this experiment, certain procedural aspects of which I shall later return to.

Rodrigues has reported two studies similar to the preceding ones. In the first of them (1967) he obtained responses from 44 Ss to all of the eight possible patterns of signs. His instructions included the following: "The two persons are you and another person, O. The X is not specified, and may be anything at all toward which you and O have a positive or negative feeling." Table 3 summarizes his findings, in terms of the 90mm. scale ranging from 10 (labeled "best" in terms of pleasantness) to 99 through "neutral" to "worst."

Rodrigues's second study (1966) differed from the first only in the following respects. He introduced two additional variables: intensity of P's feeling for O, and O as "peer" vs. O as "expert" (the two conditions were given to separate groups of Ss); and O was, under all conditions, someone actually known to each S, as in the study by Price, Harburg, and Newcomb. Table 3 includes findings only for the "strong" P/O relation when O is a peer, in order to be maximally comparable with the latters' study.[8]

These findings, more clearly than those of Steiner and Spaulding, show

TABLE 3

Ranges of Mean Scores of Unpleasantness
(Rodrigues)

	First Study[1]	Second Study[1]
P/O Positive		
balanced[2]	20.2–34.7	17.9–27.1
imbalanced[2]	61.4–64.6	73.1–73.1
P/O Negative		
balanced[2]	54.2–59.7	63.7–65.3
imbalanced[2]	64.6–66.1	53.1–55.7

[1] Two situations of each type were included.
[2] According to Heider's formula.

[8] Other aspects of this second study are discussed on pages 39 and 45.

a sharp distinction between Heider-balanced and unbalanced situations when P/O is positive but not when it is negative. And, as in all of the other studies cited, the Heider-balanced situations when P/O is negative resemble the Heider-unbalanced ones more closely than they resemble the other balanced situations.

Because Rodrigues studied all eight of the possible sign patterns (as Steiner and Spaulding did not) it becomes possible to compare Heider's two with my three categories of balance, by noting the spread or differentiation in mean scores between balanced and imbalanced categories, as shown in Table 4.

The lesser differentiation according to Heider's category system stems entirely, according to this set of data, from the large differences in scores between his two subcategories of balance (positive and negative P/O). The modified system, by assigning these to distinctive categories, greatly increases the balanced-imbalanced range. The latter also has the advantage of reducing the spread of within-category values—from 39.5 and 5.2 for Heider's system to 14.5, 12.4, and 3.2 (See p. 40 for a similar comparison of the two category systems, according to a different subjective index.)

TABLE 4

Mean Pleasantness Scores for Two
Category Systems of Balance
(Rodrigues*)

Heider's Category		Triad Pattern	Mean Score	Modified Category	
label	mean			mean	label
		+++	20.2	27.4	positive
balanced	42.2	+－－	34.7		balance
		－－+	59.7		
difference		－+－	54.2	61.3	nonbalance difference
22.1		－－－	64.6		35.6
		－++	66.6		
unbalanced	64.3	++－	61.4	63.0	imbalance
		+－+	64.6		

* These values are from his first study only; those from the second study differ only slightly.

From all these data on responses of pleasantness one might conclude that Heider-like balance and unbalance are clearly distinguished, subjectively, only when P/O is positive. All of the studies indicate that balance in the positive P/O situations is preferred, by large margins, and that the other three categories appearing in Tables 2 and 3 are not sharply distinguished. Balance with negative P/O is sometimes, though not always, slightly preferred to all Heider-unbalanced situations. Thus, according to the index of ratings of pleasantness, Heider-balanced situations with negative P/O are more clearly distinguished from other Heider-balanced ones than from Heider-unbalanced ones. But nonbalanced situations (negative P/O) do not consistently show marked differences from those that are imbalanced by my definition, as predicted. Thus my three-fold distinction is only partially supported by the data so far presented.

Preferences for Changed Relations

Rodrigues, in the two studies already described (p. 37), proposes that "tension" (one of Heider's terms, along with "stress" and "pressure toward change") also be measured by subjects' preferences for changes within triads presented to them. Subjects checked a preferred point on a 90mm. scale anchored by the phrases "none at all," "neutral," and "very much" to indicate "how much you would want to see changes [in P/O, P/X, or O/X] take place."[9] Otherwise, experimental conditions were like those described on p. 37. Changes presumably referred to reversals of sign (positive to negative feeling, or vice versa). Findings are summarized in Table 5, which shows not only his first experiment but also those comparable parts of his second one, described on p. 37.

TABLE 5

Summary of Change Scores
(Rodrigues)

	Range		Mean	
	1st study	2nd study	1st study	2nd study
P/O Positive				
balanced*	21.4–30.1	15.6–19.1	25.8	17.3
imbalanced*	47.1–47.4	45.8–45.9	47.2	45.0
P/O Negative				
balanced*	36.5–38.4	28.5–35.0	37.5	31.7
imbalanced*	40.4–44.5	33.8–39.7	42.4	36.7

* According to Heider's formula.

The order of preference is exactly that reported by Price, Harburg, and Newcomb, although the differences between the two nonbalanced categories in that study are less consistent. The findings of Rodrigues, in short, give very substantial support to my three-category distinction.

These "change" scores, like those of Rodrigues for unpleasantness, place unbalanced situations between positively balanced and imbalanced ones. As shown in Table 6 (comparable in this respect to Table 4) the three mean scores of willingness to change are more evenly spaced than in the case of unpleasantness ratings; and, like the latter, the balanced and imbalanced categories show more difference according to my categories than according to Heider's.[10]

Rodrigues reasons as follows concerning the relative advantages of his two indices of interpersonal balance. "The assessment of tension through the measurement of experienced unpleasantness does not seem quite appropriate. The measurement is too sensitive to a host of factors other than a desire to change a situation." Certainly the question "How much do you

---

[9] An additional kind of change, which I have not considered, was "a change of P/O only in regard to this particular situation and not otherwise." This was intended to tap the alternative, noted by Heider, of differentiating O in general from O as source of this particular attitude.

[10] These comparisons, as well as those in the following paragraph, are from Rodrigues's first study solely; the second study differs only slightly.

TABLE 6

Mean Scores of Willingness to Change,
According to Two Category Systems
(Rodrigues)

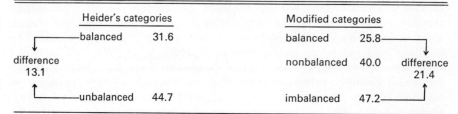

	Heider's categories		Modified categories	
	balanced	31.6	balanced	25.8
difference 13.1			nonbalanced	40.0
	unbalanced	44.7	imbalanced	47.2

want to change the relations in this triad?" has more direct face validity, in terms of balance theory, than "How unpleasant do you feel?" At any rate, responses to the former question appear to yield strong support to my predictions.

A Note on "Ease of Learning" Procedures

Zajonc and Burnstein (1965a, 1965b) have reported two experimental tests of balance-related hypotheses, the first based on six of the eight *POX* triads and the other on six selected *POXY* structures (i.e., two persons and two objects of their attitudes). Following De Soto's procedures (1960) with minor changes, they used the number of *Ss*' errors, before learning the signs of all relationships in each structure, as the dependent variable. The three (or four) within-structure relations were all attitudinal (like-dislike or approval-disapproval), and the 18 (or 36) relations were presented singly, in random order. *P* and *O* were two hypothetical men, both of each pair of names beginning with the same letter in each structure. The issues were Integration and *Newsweek* in the first and Integration and Birth Control in the second experiment.

Both sets of findings support Heider's rather than my predictions, as shown in Table 7, on the assumption that difficulty of learning a total structure is an index of its imbalance. While it can be argued that persistence in reporting the wrong sign of a given relation is a behavioral indication of preference to change it, the Zajonc-Burnstein procedure raises certain questions of index validity. As Rodrigues comments about reports of subjec-

TABLE 7

Sums of Mean Error Scores
(Zajonc and Burnstein)

	Range	Mean
P/O Positive		
balanced[1]	—	5.6[2]
imbalanced[1]	7.3–8.2	7.7
P/O Negative		
balanced[1]	4.5–6.6	5.5
imbalanced[1]	—	9.2[2]

[1] According to Heider's formula.
[2] Only one structure of this kind included.

tive pleasantness, perhaps their index is "too sensitive to ... factors other than a desire to change a situation." I shall examine this possibility.

Subjects in these experiments, as they were presented with randomly assorted P/O, P/X, and O/X relations (also O/P, P/Y, and O/Y, in one experiment), must have been searching for possible cues, perhaps trying out a succession of hypotheses. One of these (in the first experiment) was agreement—i.e., same-signed P/X and O/X—as evidenced by the fact that P/X and O/X were almost invariably learned with the same number of errors when they were same-signed, but not when opposite-signed. Another hypothesis, in this experiment, appears to have been that "all relations are positive." A single negative relation in an otherwise all-positive structure, was, by large margins, the most difficult of all single relations to learn. Since this combination occurs only in Heider-unbalanced structures, this source of difficulty in learning accounts for most of the subjects' relative ease in learning Heider-balanced structures. Such a finding, of course, is precisely as Heider would have it (for him any triad including a single negative is unbalanced), but it is interesting that by Zajonc and Burnstein's procedures, but not by ratings of unpleasantness or willingness to change, Heider-balanced triads with negative P/O resemble those with positive P/O while remaining distinctive from all Heider-unbalanced ones. This study, in short, is one of the few I have found that supports Heider's predictions in all four categories.[11]

In their second, *POXY*, experiment the same sorts of hypothesis-testing occur, *mutatis mutandis*. In addition, a tendency to look for lateral symmetry (that is, P's two attitudes as well as both of O's are like-signed) is readily detected: the numbers of lateral symmetries in the six structures are almost perfectly correlated with the total error scores for the entire structures. Since, according to Cartwright and Harary's definition (1956) of semicycle balance, the Heider-balanced structures were more readily learned than the unbalanced ones, the following question arises: If such possibly irrelevant hypotheses as lateral symmetry account for so much of the variance in error scores, how does it also happen that there are significant differences in error scores between Heider-balanced and unbalanced structures? One answer is that there is probably an artifactual consequence of the experimenters' particular selection of the 6 *POXY* structures from the 64 that are possible. It 'happens' that there was only one instance of lateral symmetry (among six possibilities) in the three Heider-unbalanced structures, as compared with three out of six in the Heider-balanced ones. By chance (following a computation of the numbers of same-signed lateral pairs in all of the 64 possible combinations) the proportions of them in structures balanced at 1.00 or .50 (according to semicycle values) is almost exactly the same as for those balanced at .33. Thus there is no artifactual necessity that balanced structures (by the semicycle index of 0.50 or above) contain more lateral symmetries than unbalanced ones. Hence the 'accident' that Zajonc and Burnstein's balanced figures contained three times as many laterally symmetric pairs as did their unbalanced ones may have contributed

---

[11] An interesting experiment by Morrissette (1958) also supports Heider's predictions in one situation of each of the four categories, according to a revision of Cartwright and Harary's methods of counting cycles. But the same results, analyzed in the simpler form appearing in the preceding tables of this chapter, are indecisive for purposes of comparing the two category systems.

something to their finding that balanced structures are more quickly learned than unbalanced ones.

In sum, Zajonc and Burnstein's ease-of-learning procedure seems to have led subjects to introduce hypotheses and cue-searching related to single relations or pairs of relations rather than to entire structures. The finding of their more rapid learning of Heider-balanced than of unbalanced structures stems partly from the subjects' use of these hypotheses, in ways not intrinsically related to balance or imbalance. It is possible that, apart from these considerations, the data would have provided little support for balance-relevant predictions. In any case, misgivings remain concerning the appropriateness of error scores in learning (by this procedure at least) as indices of preference for balanced configurations.

Engagement as Induced by Experimental Procedures

The available evidence suggests to me that when subjects are most fully engaged in the situations to which they are responding, they are most likely to make distinctions between imbalance and nonbalance. Zajonc (1968) notes that Ss who are asked to identify with P (citing Herskowitz, Jordan, Morrissette, Price-Harburg-Newcomb, and Rodrigues) "show a clear balance effect" only when P/O is positive, as contrasted with studies by Steiner and Spaulding and by Zajonc and Burnstein, in which the S "deals with hypothetical situations not involving him"; under these conditions balance effects are obtained regardless of whether P/O is positive or negative. He points out that when P/O is negative

> identifying with P necessarily brings about negative affect toward the situation. ... Negative P/O implies negative O/P, and being disliked is not pleasant. ... When the subject judges the pleasantness of some situation involving an hypothetical Dick and an hypothetical Harry who dislike one another ... the above factor ... does not enter.

Zajonc goes on to say, "But to satisfy the requirements of Heider's theory the subject must take the point of view of P," and offers this contradiction as an example of "the vulnerability of the balance principle." The present findings, he adds, "call for a refinement of the definition of balance."

Agreement and Positivity

Nearly all investigators have reported preferences for agreement (same signs for P/X and O/X) and for positivity of P/O, P/X, and O/X signs. Almost invariably, however, these tendencies are more pronounced under some conditions than others, so that an examination of such conditions is required.

The most detailed set of relevant data that I know is from Rodrigues's first experiment, in which subjects indicated the degree of their willingness to change each of the three relations in each of the eight structures. Mean ratings are shown in Table 8, categorized according to sign of each relation, balance, and P/X–O/X agreement, as each structure was presented. The virtue of these data is that they show not only general tendencies toward positivity and agreement, but also exact sources of those tendencies.

The table shows a clear preference for positivity, stemming about equally from P/O and P/X relations, but hardly at all from O/X. (Willingness to change O/X is generally high, since this is the one relation that does

TABLE 8

Mean Scores of Willingness to Change Signs of Intra-Structure Relations (Rodrigues)

Structural Properties	Sign Pattern	Positive Sign Presented			Negative Sign Presented			Mean for Sign Pattern
		P/O	P/X	O/X	P/O	P/X	O/X	
Heider-bal. positively bal.*	+++	21.8	20.6	21.7				25.1
P/X—O/X agree	+−−	24.2				35.8	26.3	
Heider-bal. nonbal.*	−−+			37.7	39.7	34.3		38.0
P/X—O/X disagree	−+−		22.7		43.4		50.5	
Heider-unbal. nonbal.*	−−−				48.7	38.4	33.2	40.7
P/X—O/X agree	−++		27.6	42.4	54.1			
Heider-unbal. positively imbal.*	++−	35.4	31.3				71.5	47.0
P/X—O/X disagree	+−+	32.7		59.6		51.6		
Mean		28.5	25.5	40.3	46.5	40.0	45.4	

* According to my modified category system.

not represent P's own attitude.) Strong preference for positive P/O is indicated both by lack of willingness to change it, especially in positively balanced structures, and by relatively high willingness to change negative P/O in nonbalanced ones; in positively imbalanced structures there is more willingness to change positive P/O than in positively balanced ones. Only when positive P/O is associated with agreement is there strong preference to keep it positive.[12]

Preference for positive P/X is found in all four types of structures, but is most pronounced when P/O is positive—that is, in positively balanced or imbalanced structures. The preference is only moderate for nonbalanced structures, and it is not associated with agreement.

P/O–O/X agreement, as such, is also related to satisfaction with existing structures; mean change scores are 32.9 for all structures characterized by agreement, and 42.5 for those characterized by disagreement. But virtually all of this difference stems from positive P/O structures; that is, positively balanced and imbalanced ones differ greatly (25.1 and 47.0, respectively) while nonbalanced ones differ hardly at all (38.0 and 40.7). Thus it is not agreement per se, but agreement together with positive or negative P/O that is related to subjective balance.

Altogether, there is little evidence that either positivity or agreement, by itself, systematically influences the relative acceptability of different POX structures. The effects of either of them are observable only in

---

[12] Other studies which do not report data in terms of the eight sign-patterns substantiate this finding. Wiest (1965), applying an interesting spatial model to sociometric responses of children, found a high correlation between strength of P/O and agreement between P and O when P/O is positive but not when it is negative. Newcomb (1961) obtained quite similar results, both for actual and for estimated agreement.

certain combinations with the other. These combinations are not random. With only minor exceptions, they are precisely those that correspond to positive balance, nonbalance, and positive imbalance. And these, I have argued, represent essential differences in the psychological processes involved in confronting other persons and objects of common interest.

These several studies, viewed together, support the following conclusions. (Those of Zajonc and Burnstein are excluded, for reasons already noted.)

1. The two subcategories of Heider-balanced situations ($+ + +$ and $+ - -$ vs. $- - +$ and $- + -$) are clearly and consistently distinguished in all of the studies. Acceptance of situations as presented varies directly with in the sign of P/O, being much *greater* when P/O is positive, though all are alike in having an even number of negative signs.

2. The two subcategories of Heider-unbalanced situations ($- - -$ and $- + +$ vs. $+ + -$ and $+ - +$) are less consistently distinguished. All studies show differences that are either trivial or that reveal much *lesser* acceptance of situations where P/O is positive than when it is negative, even though all of them include an odd number of negative signs.

3. All studies except that of Jordan show that nonbalanced situations, viewed as a single category, are intermediate in acceptability between positively balanced and imbalanced ones. The predicted differences emerge most clearly when subjects' engagement is presumably greatest (as in experiments by Price, Harburg, and Newcomb, and by Rodrigues when P/O attraction is very strong). All in all, nonbalanced situations are more clearly distinguished from positively balanced than from positively imbalanced ones.

4. In terms of within-category ranges of scores, (a) the Heider-balanced situations are far less homogeneous than the positively balanced ones. The differences are too great to be accounted for by the fact that the former include four and the latter only two discrete situations. (b) Similarly, the Heider-unbalanced situations show a wider range of scores than the positively imbalanced ones; the differences are less marked than for the two definitions of balance. (c) In every case, the nonbalanced situations show less range of acceptability than the Heider-balanced situations, and about the same range as Heider-unbalanced ones. Thus the three-category system yields greater intracategory homogeneity of response than the two-category system.

The difference between Heider's category system and my proposed modification of it is based upon hypothetically distinctive meanings of P/X and P/O agreement or disagreement when P/O is positive and when it is negative. Insofar as the available evidence justifies this distinction, it would appear to support the notion that the psychological processes involved in adapting to a given POX situation are too complex to warrant the assumption that the signs of the three relations in any POX structure are interchangeable, from the point of view of psychological balance.

SOME CONDITIONS OF PREFERENCE FOR BALANCE

The principles of interpersonal balance can hardly be expected to apply with equal appropriateness in every conceivable circumstance when P simultaneously confronts an O and an X. The following problem thus arises: Under what conditions do an individual's cognitions about another person and some third entity become interdependent? In the language of an earlier paper (Newcomb, 1953), *P*'s coorientation to a given *O* and a given *X* is a precondition for his becoming engaged in a *POX* system. Once such a coorienting event has occurred, my assumption is that forces arise toward composite cognition that are likely to eventuate in psychological states of balance, imbalance, or nonbalance. These forces, I further assume, may be of any degree of strength, but the interesting cases are those in which they are strong enough to have observable effects.

Valence of O and X for P

Other things being equal, the more important an object of any kind for *P*, in the sense of valuing it, the greater the likelihood that cognitions about it will intersect with cognitions about other objects. And, given a coorienting event, the greater the valence of either *O* or *X* for *P*, the stronger the forces that result in psychological balance, imbalance, or nonbalance. It should follow that, in the presence of a given *POX* coorientation, the greater the valence for *P* of either *O* or *X*, the more pronounced his tendencies toward balance, imbalance, or nonbalance. There follow some tests of this prediction.

Tables 9 and 10 present comparisons of responses to different valences of *O* and of *X*, respectively. The data from Rodrigues are from his second experiment (see pp. 37 and 39). They show that when *P/O* is strong the difference in pleasantness between positively balanced and imbalanced triads is much greater than when *P/O* is weak, and always in the predicted direction, thus serving to enhance the expected findings. No consistent differences appear, however, for nonbalanced triads (negative *P/O*). Thus, according to these data, the effects of the valence of *P/O* are pronounced only when *P/O* is positive.

Hershkowitz's experiment (1966) is an unusual one. His "master table" includes 120 mean ratings, all of the following being controlled: strength of *P/X* and of *O/X*; *P/O* as "friends," "neutrals," and "enemies"; and *Xs* both as "objects" and as "values." Table 10 reports data only for "objects"; for "values" results are in general similar, with a single conspicuous exception—disagreement about "values" is considered more unpleasant than

TABLE 9

Mean Ratings of Dissatisfaction Under Varying
Conditions of *P*'s Attraction Toward *O*
(Rodrigues)

	Unpleasantness		Willingness to Change	
	weak	strong	weak	strong
P/O Positive				
balanced*	34.3	22.5	30.7	17.3
imbalanced*	61.5	73.1	47.8	45.8
differences	−27.2	−50.6	−17.1	−28.5
P/O Negative				
balanced*	58.9	64.5	43.6	31.7
imbalanced*	45.5	54.4	31.8	36.7
differences	+13.4	+10.1	+12.2	−5.0

* According to Heider's formula.

TABLE 10

Mean Ratings of Unpleasantness under Varying
Conditions of Strength of *P/O* and of *P/X*
(Hershkowitz)

Relation Varied *P/X* *O/X*	strong strong	strong weak	weak strong	weak weak	Range
P/O Positive					
balanced*	7.6	33.7	35.7	19.0	28.1
imbalanced*	69.7	59.3	59.2	54.1	15.6
difference	−62.1	−25.6	−23.5	−35.1	
P/O Negative					
balanced*	60.2	54.3	59.4	50.9	9.3
imbalanced*	57.7	56.0	53.6	54.9	4.1
difference	+2.5	−1.7	+5.8	−4.0	

* According to Heider's formula

about "objects" (when P/O is strong and positive, the mean rating is 81.8, the highest I have ever seen). Three general findings emerge from Table 10. (a) None of the variables listed above has noticeable effects (with the partial exception of the object-value distinction) on ratings *when P/O is negative*—that is, under conditions of nonbalance. (b) When P/O is positive, the effects of P/X and O/X valence are not noticeable except in the positively balanced condition and in the strong-strong condition. (c) When P/O is positive, and when the valence of P/X is strong while that of O/X is weak or vice versa, the pleasantness of the positively balanced situations is not only less than under the strong-strong condition (as expected) but also less than under the weak-weak condition. This may mean that the conflict between forces toward and against engagement, when P/X is strongly valenced and O/X is not, or vice versa, reduces felt satisfaction. If so, since such conflict is irrelevant to forces toward or against balance, the finding would provide support for Rodrigues's assumption (p. 39) that ratings of pleasantness are "too sensitive to . . . factors other than a desire to change a situation."

Thus Hershkowitz's and Rodrigues's data are remarkably consistent. Both indicate that the effects of strength of P/O and/or P/X are negligible except when P/O is positive (implying relatively high engagement) and that—particularly when P/O and/or P/X are both strong—these variables have their primary effects in distinguishing positive from negative P/O relations.

It is possible to conclude, therefore, that conditions of low engagement—whether by reason of low attraction toward O or of low valence for X—evoke the relative indifference that is characteristic of nonbalance. Both theoretical considerations and the comparisons in Tables 9 and 10 support this interpretation.

Joint Relevance of X for P and O

I have previously noted (1959, 1961) that P must assume that X has some common relevance for himself and for O if he is to become engaged in that *POX* system. The essential notion here is that the nature of *X* is such as to have some presumed effects for both of them; it is not unlike that of 'common fate.' For example, if one of two men on a raft in mid-ocean assumes that both of them regard the raft as essential to survival, then for him the raft has high joint-relevance. At the other extreme, a person who likes his coffee very sweet knows that a friend prefers his unsweetened; if each of them is free to sweeten his own cup or not, independently of the other, then there are no common consequences of what either of them does, and the object "sweet coffee" is not perceived as having common relevance. If, on the other hand, it is known that the common pot of coffee is sweetened before individual portions are served, then the same object will have common relevance.

This parameter is not, of course, the same as that of *X*'s valence for *P* or *O*, since strong valence may be associated with no joint relevance. While conceptually related to Heider's unit-formation, it is nevertheless different: it is a kind of second-order unit-formation. That is, it refers not just to a single relation (*P/O*, *P/X*, or *O/X*) in a triad, but rather to the system as a whole—specifically, to a *P/O* relationship that is also dependent upon both *P/X* and *O/X*. If *X* is to have joint relevance for *P* and *O*, *P* must perceive a special kind of unit-relation with *O*, according to which both of them are affected by *X*. If not, *P* will have little or no engagement in that *POX* system.

*X*s that preclude engagement for such reasons include matters not only of sheer taste but also those which, by habituation, *P* has come to regard as private, affecting no one but himself or some clearly limited category of other persons—one's own family, for example. If *P* regards some particular *X* as none of a particular *O*'s business, he will not readily become engaged in that *POX* system.

These matters may seem self-evident, but not all of the empirical studies have taken account of them. Some experimenters have left it to their subjects to fill in their own *X*s (e.g., Jordan, Rodrigues), probably with the consequence that the parameter of joint relevance varied in unknown manner. Some of Steiner and Spaulding's *X*s were such that the best of friends might have been indifferent to each other's feelings (algebra, for example, or motorcycles). This fact may have contributed to the relatively small differentiation in mean responses to situations other than positively balanced ones.

In one of my own studies (1961) a preliminary attempt was made to control for joint relevance. In the two populations studied (groups of 17 students, selected as strangers, who lived together for several months) we found that the following hierarchy of *X*s, in increasing order, elicited positively balanced responses:

1. taste items (e.g., sweet coffee, rare steaks)
2. single attitudinal issues (e.g., House policies, University policies, political preferences, religious affiliation)
3. general values (e.g., six Spranger values, ten life goals).

The first of these categories elicited only a random relationship between attraction and perceived agreement (+ + + or + − −). The second of them rarely yielded significant differences in agreement between attractive and unattractive *O*s. The third of them (measured by rank-ordering of the values for self and for each *O*) showed strong preferences for positively balanced triads. As to the second of these categories, both inspection of data and interview follow-ups indicated that no single one of these met the criteria both of strong valence and of joint relevance for enough pairs of subjects to elicit statistically significant responses for the groups as a whole. That is, many subjects made such comments as "Sure, he's my closest pal, but that just isn't one of our common interests," or "He could be a Hottentot or a Hindu and I'd still like him; what difference does it make?" For such reasons, when all members of a small population were considered, comparatively few of our Xs yielded significant differences with respect to the second category. The more general values, however, were considered by nearly all subjects to be of such concern to all members of the group that clear preferences for positive balance emerged at significant levels for the group as a whole.

Differential Impact of X upon P and O

If two men are courting the same girl, does preference for positive balance mean that the stronger their attraction toward each other the more surely each of them will prefer that they will both want to marry her? Or, conversely, that the more convinced each of them is that both want to marry her, the greater their mutual attraction? An analysis of these absurdities will illustrate a necessary extension of the principle of joint relevance.

If the X in this situation is taken to be simply "the girl as a person," the triad is balanced for each of them if P/O is positive and if P assumes that both he and his good friend admire her. So far, no contradiction between theory and everyday observation. But each of the men views her not merely as a person who might make a lovely wife for someone, but rather as "potential wife for me." So construed, the two men face different triadic situations. For John, as P, the important triad includes Jim-as-competitor (O) and the girl-as-wife-for-John; whereas for Jim, as P, it includes John-as-competitor (O) and the girl-as-wife-for-Jim. If X now represents, for both men, "the girl as wife for P" then the situation is balanced if both of them favor it, but imbalanced if P favors it and O opposes it and if P/O and O/P remain positive. So viewed, predictions from POX theory and from common sense are identical. The apparent contradiction between theory and fact stems from the assumption that "an X is an X," whereas in instances like this one there are both aspects of the X that induce balance (the girl's attractive qualities) and other aspects that induce imbalance (X as wife for P and the same X as wife for O are mutual exclusives).

Thus joint relevance, as a criterion for the engagement of P in a POX system, requires more than P's assumption that X has an impact both upon himself and upon O. We must also ask whether the common impact is valenced in the same way by both of them. In short, it is not an undifferentiated X that matters, but a specified impact of that X. Propositions derived from interpersonal balance theory must take account of whatever distinctions are in fact made as an individual compares his own with another's cognitions about the same object.

Role distinctions, as in the foregoing illustration, often lead to differential impact of the same X upon P and O. If X is a person, then P will not necessarily assume that he and O are viewing him in the same role. Whether or not he does may have decisive consequences for the joint relevance of that X. Similar problems also arise from the role relationships of P and O. If their role relationships have put them in competitive positions (as in zero-sum games), success on the part of one of them has an impact just the opposite of the impact on the other. Again it is necessary to distinguish between X_1 (success for P) and other Xs that do not have opposed impacts for P and O. It is this distinction that determines whether or not the situation is psychologically balanced.

If, as I am implying, it may often be necessary to think in terms of the coexistence, simultaneously, of multiple substructures involving the same P, O, and X, there are interesting consequences for research. It might be helpful, for example, to present a given POX structure without supplying signs, while eliciting responses in the manner of a probing interview. As many statements of differing impacts of X should be elicited as the subject is able to offer; these, together with a subjectively weighted response of overall acceptance of any particular pattern of signs, should help to reduce some of the ambiguities that appear in the existing research literature. So, too, might the use of concrete rather than hypothetical stimulus situations. It now seems probable that such ambiguities are particularly associated with variations in the parameters noted in this section, as well as with negative P/O.

Individual Differences

Considerations relevant to individual variations in preference for interpersonal balance are discussed elsewhere in this volume. I shall therefore note only one factor, a very general one, that on theoretical grounds seems relevant. Some people appear to have adapted more than others to the fact of life according to which a great many POX situations are not in fact balanced. Such differences might be verbalized by such phrases as "Just because he's a good pal of mine is no reason why we should have the same ideas about things," and "I'm always a bit shocked to find that people whom I like or admire differ from me on important questions."

The former position could mean either that a person has learned to live with psychological imbalance or that he is simply not susceptible to forces toward balance. Tolerance of imbalance is presumably facilitated by the valuing of autonomy, which could stem either from habits of accurately assessing O/X or from a need to be different, in spite of preference for balance. Immunity to forces toward balance may have such roots as low need for affiliation and sheer indifference to the attitudes of others when such information is not of immediate, utilitarian value.

I have found even in a small (17-man) population the following patterns of preference for positive balance, using various Xs (1961): (a) Increasing accuracy in judgments of others' attitudes, often at the cost of balance. The two men who most clearly showed this pattern were very low in authoritarianism (F scale), and well liked by peers. They were obviously sensitive to pressures toward balance, as shown by the fact that they gradually developed stable friendship groups with others accurately judged as agreeing with them on important Xs. They were concerned about reality in judging others and about their own autonomy, as well as about balance. (b) Almost total failure to increase in accuracy of judging others' attitudes, together with no indication of preference for other men judged to be in agreement with them. Two men of this kind had high F scores and were highly unpopular, being considered "crude" and "thoughtless" by their peers. These characteristics suggest indifference to forces toward balance.

Such findings are consistant with the conclusions that failure to express consistent preferences for interpersonal balance sometimes does and sometimes does not imply absence of susceptibility to forces toward balance; and that the degree of such susceptibility varies with social habits and skills that are commonly referred to as aspects of personality.

SUMMARY

Individuals must often deal, simultaneously, with cognitions of another person, of some entity other than that person, and of that person's cognitions of that entity. Varying with the degree to which his cognitions are valenced, and with certain other parameters, he finds certain patterns of positive and negative valencing more acceptable than others. This chapter deals with the psychological processes governing the acceptability of different combinations of valenced cognitions, as a special case of consistency.

I have argued that the nature of the special problem that an individual confronts in this particular form of composite cognition requires some modification of the more general rules that have been developed to distinguish between more and less preferred combinations of cognitions. A priori considerations suggest that an individual's most salient concern, in dealing with such multiple cognitions, is the suitability of the other person as a source of information, or support, or of influence concerning the object cognized by each of them. Insofar as the other person is devalued in this context, he will be indifferent to the latter's cognitions, and will be minimally engaged in the set of cognitions as a composite. Under these conditions strong preferences either to accept or to reject a given set of cognitions are not to be expected. Such sitautions, characterized by in difference, I have labeled *nonbalanced*. Insofar as the other person is valued, in this context, to agree with him about the common object is preferable to disagreeing with him. Diverging in part from previous practice, I have labeled situations in which the other person is positively valued as *positively balanced* in the case of agreement about the object, and *positively imbalanced* in the case of disagreement.

Empirical findings in general support these expectations, in spite of varying experimental procedures and different indices of preference for the several three-signed patterns. Positively balanced situations are preferred to all others, according to all investigations, and positively imbalanced ones are always low in preference. These two categories, moreover, are clearly distinguished in preference level, while all investigations show considerable overlap in preference scores if the common practice is followed of considering all situations as either balanced or unbalanced, as determined solely by the numbers of plus and minus signs. Under conditions of low engagement, nonbalanced situations show little differentiation from positively imbalanced ones. In general, preference levels for nonbalanced situations, as compared with positively balanced or imbalanced ones, show considerable fluctuation with varying experimental procedures.

My central theme has been that problems of consistency that involve both one's own and another person's cognitions of some common object are psychologically different from those involving one's own cognitions of two objects. The former set of cognitions typically includes the other person as a source of attitudes, and this introduces the possibility of his agreement or disagreement with oneself.

I have, at any rate, assumed that the study of interpersonal balance requires attention to such matters, in ways that other phenomena of psychological consistency do not. If so, then it is to be expected that standard categories of balance and imbalance will need to be adapted for that special purpose. That has been the purpose of this essay.

CHAPTER 3

The Congruity Principle:
Retrospective Reflections and Recent Research

Percy H. Tannenbaum
University of Pennsylvania

Despite their fundamental characteristics in common—all the more impressive considering the essential independence of their development—the various consistency theory formulations have their respective idiosyncracies and areas of emphasis. In particular, the congruity principle has been cited as being the most precise of the models, in the sense that it includes quantification of the variables and relationships involved and hence of the magnitude of the adjustment to an inconsistency. It has also been classified as being among the narrowest of the models in that, initially at least, it was restricted to situations accounting for attitude change resulting from rather specific communication conditions. Neither of these distinctions, if that is what they are, is accidental since both derive from the factors and circumstances that prompted the theoretical development to begin with. For this and other reasons, it may be instructive to reexamine some of the bases and origins of the congruity formulation before proceeding to more recent developments and considerations.

A RETROSPECTIVE LOOK

Looking back over a period of some 10 to 15 years, I now have the impression that it may be more appropriate to speak of at least two kinds of congruity models rather than a single generalized principle. The initial presentation of the theory (Osgood & Tannenbaum, 1955) was clearly in terms of a model for attitude change, as such, with no particular intention to relate it to other cognitive phenomena. Indeed, as we stated at the time: "No attempt has been made to integrate this particular theoretical model with more general psychological theory, and we feel no urge at this time to attempt such detailed translations" (Osgood & Tannenbaum, 1955, p. 55).

That urge did develop shortly afterwards, however. This was partly in response to the usual demands for parsimony, especially so given the availability of such a general and powerful system as that supplied by Osgood's mediation theory (Osgood, 1952; Osgood, 1953; Osgood, Suci, & Tannenbaum, 1957). Another reason stemmed from other empirical work some of us were engaged in at the time dealing with factors governing the judgment of composite meaningful stimulus units such as adjective-noun combinations. Reasoning similar to that involved in formulating the attitude change principle appeared to lend itself, with relatively little variation, to such problems. While the two models—one for attitude change, the other for the prediction of the judgment of complex stimuli from their individual components—can be treated as special cases of a more general theoretical model of cognitive interaction (cf. Osgood, 1960; Osgood, *et al.*, 1957) they are not identical, and one may be entertained quite apart from the other.

The Attitude Change Model

In the early 1950's, when this work originated, Charlie Osgood had initiated and was conducting a pioneering program of research in experimental semantics at the University of Illinois. His was, and is, a most fertile and inventive mind, and it served to inspire a wide range of experimental and methodological studies, mostly centered on the development and application of the semantic differential technique as a measure of connotative meaning (Osgood *et al.*, 1957). Of the variety of psychological phenomena this activity touched upon, a principal focus of interest was the area of attitude theory and measurement. Some of us entered this program with such an interest already established. It was further stimulated by the results of the early factor analytic work with the semantic differential, designed to determine the dimensionality of an individual's 'semantic space.' The one factor appearing the most commonly across a variety of such studies, and the one almost invariably accounting for the most variance, was defined as an *evaluative* factor which appeared to bear a close resemblance to the basic attitudinal continuum.

This identification of the evaluative component of connotative meaning with attitude had a number of implications. One of these was that the same set of scales could be used to allocate a number of different objects of judgment on the same evaluative continuum, and to do so with a substantial degree of sensitivity. This, in effect, amounted to a generalized attitude scale, one that could be applied uniformly across a variety of objects of judgment and thus allow for more direct comparability between them.

At about the same time, I was contemplating a problem for my doctoral dissertation. Along with many others, I had been very impressed with the experimental work of Carl Hovland and his colleagues in the very active Yale attitude change research program. I did, however, have some misgivings about the seemingly unconnected, one-variable-at-a-time nature of many of their early studies, and felt more theoretical progress might be made by considering the effects of combinations of such variables, and particularly of the interaction between them.

I was especially impressed by the Hovland and Weiss (1951) study of the effects of varying source credibility on a message's persuasive inducements, but felt that perhaps it had not gone far enough. It seemed reasonable that not only could the degree of attitude change toward the concept or object of the communication be affected by existing sentiments about the source, but also that attitude toward the source could change as a result of similar pressures in the same situation. That is, of course, how our attitudes towards many potential sources are often initially formed and developed—e.g., an unknown politician emerges on the scene, and by virtue of the position he takes on a number of issues, we develop an opinion about him which after a while can become quite intense, in one direction or the other. The net result was the notion that, as a function of the attitudes that the subject brings with him into the communication situation to begin with, attitudes towards *both* concept and source of a message can be modified. This rather primitive formulation, coupled with the semantic differential measurement procedure allowing for reasonably refined and simultaneous assessment of source and concept attitudes on the same continuum, sets the stage for the more formal model development and testing.

In actuality, the testing of the model did not await its complete development and formalization. For example, while the research for my dissertation (Tannenbaum, 1953) did demonstrate a significant effect due to the interaction between initial attitude toward the source and toward the concept, and while it did demonstrate systematic changes toward both source and concept, it remained for the formal model to specify the precise nature of the expected interactions and of the relative magnitudes of change on both objects of judgment to be expected in specific situations. Such formalization and refinement activity proceeded while the data were being gathered and processed and was actually completed a short time afterwards.

I (and I am sure Osgood even more so) have often been asked why so formal and detailed a model was attempted to begin with. This can largely be attributed to Osgood's *modus operandi*, and is characteristic of the rigor and precision with which he pursues both theoretical and methodological issues. It was his conviction of an underlying explanatory structure that provided the main motivation to mold a number of seemingly isolated observations and findings into a coherent conceptual framework based on a set of simple postulates. Towards the latter states of the model's development, after I presumably had the benefit of a summer of training in mathematics for social scientists, I added some of the 'mathematical' embellishments, which, I now feel, give it an overly formalized appearance. For the main part, however, the model developed on its own. As in other such efforts, one begins with some apparent, possibly intuitive, notions, and attempts to structure them in some specific formal manner. After that, the sheer logic of the formulation takes over and leads onward from there. As a result, we were led to predictions which we had never really anticipated, some of which seemed not only nonobvious but intuitively incorrect. Such nonexpectancies provide insufficient reason to reject a model at such an early stage of development; if anything, they may serve to whet the appetite even more to see if research data support or refute such unanticipated predictions.

The postulates and derivations of the congruity model for attitude change have been thoroughly described before (cf. the comprehensive treatments by Brown, 1962, 1965, as well as the original by Osgood & Tannenbaum, 1955), and I will avoid going into the complete step-by-step details here. The model addresses itself to the simple and common communications situation in which an identifiable source makes an assertion for or against a particular object or concept. Prior to being exposed to such a message, the individual can maintain any type of attitude toward any number of potential sources and concepts, as long as these are not linked to one another. The consistency question arises with the assertion of the message, when that particular source and that particular concept become associated by virtue of the former assuming a position favorable or unfavorable toward the latter. Under certain such conditions—e.g., when the preexposure attitude toward source and concept are both favorable and the direction of the assertion is also favorable—there is essentially no incongruity and, according to the theory, there is little or no pressure for change. Under other circumstances —e.g., when an initially favorable source makes a negative assertion about an equally favorable concept—incongruity is said to obtain. It is this state of incongruity which generates a pressure for change in attitude toward either the source or the concept, or both, always in the direction making for a newly congruous situation.

Unlike other attitude change models, the congruity formulation dealt with specific degrees of intensity or polarization of favorable or unfavorable attitudes—a degree of refinement made possible and encouraged by the use of the seven-step semantic differential scales, which can yield an attitude score ranging from extreme favorability ($+3$), through neutrality, to extreme unfavorability (-3). One consequence of such an attempt at precision was that a pressure toward change was postulated whenever different degrees of polarization of attitudes obtained, not only for grossly favorable or unfavorable sentiments. This, in turn, led to some seemingly awkward predictions—e.g., if a more polarized ($+2$) source favored a less polarized concept ($+1$), the model predicted a drop in favorability toward the concept—but that, as has already been indicated, is part and parcel of such model-building.

By such procedures, the model specified conditions under which incongruity does or does not exist, and, accordingly, when pressures towards change are generated. Furthermore, by specifying the conditions under which a congruous situation would obtain if one or the other object of judgment would change, it also allowed for the computation of the magnitude of the total available pressure towards change. At this point, we found it necessary to invoke the fairly well-founded empirical generalization that more intense attitudes are less susceptible to change than less intense ones (i.e., merely as a function of their relative intensity as such). This led to the additional postulate that distributed the total available pressure towards change between the source and concept in inverse proportion to their respective degrees of polarization. It was then a short step for the model to generate specific formulae for the prediction of both the direction and amount of attitude change to be expected for both the source and the concept. The basic variables involved in such equations are the initial preexposure attitudes towards the source and concept, as indexed on the same evaluative continuum reflecting attitudinal direction and intensity, and whether the bond between them is associative (i.e., the source favoring the concept) or dissociative (the source opposing the concept).

As one might expect, a number of qualifying conditions and corrective factors had to be applied to these predictive formulae. For one thing, it was recognized that some specific source-concept combinations would not only be incongruous but incredible as well. In the interest of generality, we again attempted to formalize such an effect by postulating (and defining the distribution of) a 'correction for incredulity' that could be applied under prescribed conditions of attitudes towards any source and concept, not only to the more obvious cases. In addition, we found it necessary to introduce an 'assertion constant' to accommodate the fact that in communication messages of the type being dealt with it was the concept rather than the source that absorbed the major portion of the assertion's arguments.

While the design of my dissertation study (Tannenbaum, 1953) was perhaps not sensitive enough to fully accommodate the detailed predictions of such a precise model, it did allow for a reasonable assessment of the basic trends in expected attitude change toward concept and source. Substantial support for the model was forthcoming in the form of a high correlation ($r = .91$) between predicted and obtained scores. Additionally, some support was found in the data for several of the corollaries that were readily derived from the basic congruity model, including some of the less obvious predictions (cf. Osgood & Tannenbaum, 1955). To be sure, there were instances of rather substantial discrepancies in absolute magnitude between predicted and obtained results. This could be chalked up to the fact that the model "did not pretend to take account of all variables relating to attitude change," but it was not a wholly satisfactory explanation. Still in all, the data did show a surprisingly good fit to the model's expectations, and we felt encouraged that we had something quite fundamental and exciting within our reach, possibly to account for cognitive phenomena other than attitude change.

The Model for Semantic Combinations

Meanwhile, work was continuing apace on a variety of problems relating to the role of connotative meaning in human behavior, including some which involved the judgment of semantic combinations. A critical issue here was whether the judgment of the combination could be predicted from knowledge of the judgments of the component parts—e.g., an early study involved the meaning of various adjectives and nouns in isolation and then in combination to determine if some systematic relationship existed. Meaning and judgment, in this case, involved allocation of either the component or the combination along each of the dimensions of the semantic space—usually, the activity and potency factors in addition to the main evaluative dimension isolated by factor analysis. Since these factors are regarded as being mutually independent, analysis is usually conducted separately for each of the factors.

In thinking about such problems, it seemed that the congruity model could be adopted from the attitude change area and adapted to such more general cognitive issues with relatively little difficulty. The essence of the principle, as expressed at the time, was that "when two cognitive events are simultaneously elicited, each exerts a modifying pressure on the other, in proportion to its own degree of polarization and in the direction of the other's position of perfect congruence" (Osgood *et al.*, 1957, p. 277). In the context of attitude change through communication, the two cognitive events were the evaluative reactions elicited by the source and concept of the message; in the word combination situation, they could be the meanings elicited by the particular adjectives and nouns. We can readily discern here not only an adaptation of the principle from one situation to another, but the makings of a more general 'law' governing any kind of cognitive interaction.

There were, to be sure, some special considerations involved in making such a transition. A major point of difference was that while the attitude change model usually involved the modification of *both* cognitive elements to resolve an apparent incongruity, here the resolution involved the formation of a *single* composite score. This was accommodated by translating the notion of a differential susceptibility to change as a function of degree of intensity of the attitude into the corresponding notion of a differential *contribution* of more or less intensely polarized elements to the composite judgment. That is, whereas the more polarized of the elements changes less in the attitude change model, it contributes relatively more in terms of the resolution of disparate elements into a single aggregate judgment. An additional important consideration is that for all such combinations the bond between the component parts is always assumed to represent a positive linkage, akin to the communication situation where the source always favors the concept. In terms of the adjective-noun combinations, then, it is assumed that the noun is being positively associated with the particular adjectival characteristic and hence only the rules for associative (i.e., favorable) assertions apply.

These factors were readily accommodated in the development of a formula for obtaining the judgment of the composite on a single semantic factor, given the judgments of the components on the same factor (cf. Osgood *et al.*, p. 278)—now, of course, only a single formula since only a single judgment is called for. It should be noted that the resulting equation always predicts a score for the aggregate that represents a compromise between the two (or more) components, i.e., the combined score must be in between the two component scores on a given factor. This, then, is tantamount to an 'averaging' model of cognitive interaction—actually, a *weighted average* in that the different components can contribute different degrees to the composite in direct proportion to their respective degrees of polarization. Such a formulation accordingly assumes more than passing interest in Section IV D, where several such competing models for responses to stimulus complexes are given the fuller treatment they deserve.

In the first major study of the model in this new setting, eight adjectives and eight nouns were each independently rated on a set of semantic differential scales representing the three major factors of evaluation, activity, and potency. At a later time, the 64 possible combinations were rated by eight subgroups in a Latin Square design. Noteworthy support for the predictive model was obtained in the form of high correlations (above .85 in each case) between predicted and obtained results on all three semantic dimensions. But there were some notable shortcomings as well: On the evaluative factor, the obtained ratings were consistently and inexplicably less favorable than the predicted scores, no matter what kind of combination appeared. In general, the predictions were better supported on the nonevaluative factors. There was also an inordinate effect due to the adjectival component—*qua* adjective, and apart from its degree of polarization—so that obtained judgments were generally skewed in the direction of the qualifier. Another flaw that cropped up on some combinations was that the composite score was more intense than either of the components, rather than being between them as the model would hold. Not least, differences in magnitude between predicted and obtained scores left a substantial part of the variance still unaccounted for.

Despite such limitations, the data were reasonably impressive, especially since this represented a first attempt to apply the adapted model. Such an initial flush of enthusiasm grew progressively deeper as the model, in essentially the same form, came to be applied to a larger number and a wider variety of cognitive interaction situations. For example, a study of the blending of diverse facial expressions provided further support for the basic model, again in the form of high correlations between predicted and expected composite scores; in addition, the expected dominance of the more polarized element was confirmed (cf. Osgood, 1960, p. 362). While I had some personal reservations about the semantic combination model—principally because I felt it to be too simple to account for such complex phenomena and could intuitively think of too many exceptions (of course, many others shared this position)—I was quite impressed when it worked as well as it did on some of my own data. For example, I found it to predict with reasonable accuracy—at least better than other attempted models—in the judgment of combinations of randomly-generated two-dimensional shapes appearing in various colors.

Even more convincing was its demonstration in the prediction of the meaning of a variety of color stimuli selected on the basis of the Ostwald scheme for color allocation. In this case, a double weighting procedure was possible: Using the Ostwald system made it possible to define a given color stimulus in terms of the relative proportion of its pure hue, black, and white components. Semantic differential ratings were obtained from these three components in themselves, and the predictive equations were then generated to accommodate both the weightings reflecting the relative amount of each component in the stimulus complex and the weightings due to the degree of polarization of the semantic judgments. Utilizing such a double-weighting scheme proved to be significantly more sensitive than just using the basic formula, which only incorporates the degree of polarization factor. This suggests, among other things, that the predictive power of the basic model might be enhanced if one could somehow add in a correction factor corresponding to the relative proportion of each component in the composite —e.g., as if there were intrinsically different contributions for adjectives and nouns. In a sense, this is analogous to the 'assertion constant' factor introduced earlier into the attitude change model in that more emphasis is given to one component than another, apart from degree of intensity as such. However, this is only an analogy at best, since the reasoning underlying the two cases stems from somewhat different considerations.

Not all such applications of the model worked out so well. For example, when Kerrick (1959) applied it to the problem of combinations of photographs and captions, an interesting interaction effect was noted. In cases where picture and caption had opposite meanings—i.e., were on opposite sides of the zero-point on a given semantic factor—the model generally held quite well. However, if the two components were on the same side, their effects appeared to be additive in combination, rather than averaging—e.g., a slightly passive caption added to an already passive photo made for an even more passive impression. Such a summation effect has been noted in other semantic combination studies as well, and has become a particular bone of contention for someone like Fishbein who pits his additivity model for cognitive interaction (Fishbein, 1961; Triandis & Fishbein, 1963; Fishbein & Hunter, 1964) against an averaging model such as suggested by the congruity formulation on precisely this issue. Rokeach has also entered this fray with his principle of 'belief congruence' (Rokeach & Rothman, 1965) which likewise predicts such summative effects. A lively controversy has developed around this and related issues as such models get to be extended to a wide variety of cognitive phenomena and complex social stimuli including personality impression formation (cf. Feldman, 1966c; Willis, 1960; Podell & Podell, 1963; Manis, Gleason, & Dawes, 1966; Anderson, 1965a).

This controversy, and its attendant methodological and theoretical issues, is treated in fuller detail in Section IV D, where the model derived from congruity theory considerations emerges as only one of a number of such possible formulations that can be reasonably entertained to account for the judgment of complex stimulus aggregates. Whatever the merits or demerits of the other models, it is clear that there are some serious shortcomings in the congruity model. In general, the data fit leaves something to be desired in terms of closeness of correspondence, and there are too many instances where the particular weighted averaging suggested by the theory is refuted by the data. Such discrepancies cannot be ignored. They imply that the model is, at best, incomplete, and that either it should be altered to accommodate such empirical facts of life, or it should be drastically reformulated, if not entirely rejected in favor of a quite different general model such as that offered by Anderson (cf. Chapter 73).

General Theoretical Considerations

We have already noted that the initial formulation and presentation of the congruity model for attitude change (Osgood & Tannenbaum, 1955) was relatively free of ties to a more fundamental psychological theory. While linking it with the semantic differential technique and the results of the factor analytic research in this area did introduce certain theoretical considerations, the model stood more or less on its own in terms of its basic postulates. Some 'underlying assumptions' were noted at the time, but these were quite unrelated to Osgood's mediation theory which provides the foundation for so much of the semantic differential work (Osgood et al., 1957).

Instead, we referred more to a least effort principle—a presumed tendency of the organism to maintain his attitudes in the simplest patterns—as a prelude to the introduction of the congruity model itself. Thus, it was assumed that "since extreme 'all-or-nothing' judgments are simpler than finely discriminated judgments of degree" (p. 43) there would be a fairly constant pressure to allocate different objects of judgment toward one or the other end of the evaluative continuum. Similarly, it was assumed that it is more simple for the individual to accept the equivalence of similarly evaluated objects than to maintain and store fine nuances of distinction. The result of such speculations should thus be "the simplest of attitudinal structures"—a tight cluster of undifferentiated favorable concepts opposed by an equally tight, undifferentiated cluster of unfavorable concepts, or what general semanticists and others have referred to as a "two-valued orientation." Such simple structures are presumably maintained by strong associative bonds between the elements within each cluster and by strong dissociative bonds between the clusters. Tendencies of this sort were assumed to be more characteristic of less sophisticated thinking and accordingly provide for a predisposition toward the consistency that is supposed to be 'the hobgoblin of little minds.' The same sort of consistency can apply, as Osgood (1960) aptly noted, to "big minds as well ... in high places."

This premise of a tendency toward simple, psychologically consistent structures provided part of the underlying theoretical base. The derivation of the congruity principle itself goes well beyond such primitive assumptions, and makes distinctive (both intuitive and empirical) assumptions of its own. This was true enough for the attitude change model per se. It was even more so for the semantic combination model where, though the simple structure principle is not incompatible with the logic involved, it offers no direct explanation for the expected behavior.

It remained for Osgood's general mediation theory to be applied to such combinational phenomena, and thus set the stage for the development of a general congruity model of cognitive interaction. We need not go into the details of the mediational theory system here (cf. Osgood, 1952, 1953, 1957; Osgood et al., 1957). Suffice it to say that under such a conceptualization any sign stimulus presented by itself elicits its own characteristic representational mediation process. An interesting question arises as to what occurs when two such signs are presented simultaneously and elicit somewhat different mediational processes. Under such circumstances, it is assumed that the presence of one mediational response tendency would tend to inhibit the occurrence of the other. It was further postulated that such reciprocal inhibition is inversely proportional to the respective habit strengths (e.g., as indexed by the degree of polarization on a semantic differential factor) of the two mediational responses. Thus, given the near-simultaneous presentation of two somewhat opposing sign stimuli—even more to the point, when such elements are not only presented together but are also directly associated and interact with one another—the expectation is for only a *single* response to occur, one that provides for some resolution between the disparate response tendencies. If we assume that such a tug-of-war is not settled on a winner-take-all basis, then we would expect the resolution to proceed on a *compromise* basis—a reasonable if not totally justified (at least as a generalized phenomenon) expectation.

Even if one wanted to, it was difficult to resist the compelling appeal of such a parsimonious theoretical rationale. It stemmed directly from the general theory which motivated the work in experimental semantics to begin with, thus providing an attractive unity to the overall program. It also served as a basis from which a wide number of interesting and diverse phenomena could be 'derived'— or, perhaps more appropriately, it provided a single umbrella under which many different phenomena could be incorporated—including, of course, the attitude change and semantic combination models.

It is possible, however, that in the enthusiasm to structure such a general theoretical model there was not enough specific theoretical reasoning. It was a simple (perhaps too simple) matter to transfer the features of a model which appeared to have relevance in one cognitive domain to another area, and, given the ready availability of a robust theoretical and measurement system, the deliberate development of a generalized model to apply to any and all cognitive phenomena is an understandable, even obvious, step. But, as is noted elsewhere in this volume (principally in the various contributions to Section III A), such unitary formulations are apt to be premature and misleading. While the search for parsimony is a most worthwhile goal, there are also important theoretical considerations involved in defining the limiting conditions of a given model. Detailed attention to the specific conditions and circumstances of individual areas of application is often called for.

It is quite possible, even likely, that different phenomena may prescribe different kinds of models.

My particular point of contention is that the so-called congruity principle to account for attitude change through communication and the so-called congruity model to account for such phenomena as word combinations and the like should not be confused one with the other. In retrospect, I see them as having some distinctive differences, and treating them as special cases within a more general system only serves to obscure such differences.

For one thing, there is the question of just how much of the essence of the original congruity/incongruity notion is retained in the cognitive interaction model. Feldman (1966c) has recently pointed out that while one can derive the congruity hypothesis from general mediation theory, the congruity model "seems to use little of the motivational apparatus of the larger theory." Referring particularly to the composite stimulus situation, he argues that the theorized source of the motivation does not stem from the incongruity, as such, but from "the person's internal demands or those of the situation" (Feldman, 1966c, p. 87).

A crucial point here is that there is nothing inherent in the congruity principle itself that insists that only a single response occur. Rather, it is an induced requirement of the experimental conditions involved in the semantic combination studies that only a *single* response be made. The conditions of such studies do not tolerate multiple responses or no response at all (unless the subject disobeys the instructions and his ratings are disregarded) and thus demand a single response, the only choice for the subject being what the individual rating should be. Accordingly, the single response characteristic of the cognitive interaction model, which is so central to the mediation theory application to this situation, may be primarily an artifact of the particular testing conditions.

It is important to recognize that there are no such demand characteristics in the context of the communication situation posed by the attitude change model. In fact, it is the very essence of the congruity principle reasoning in this case that *both* of the elements being brought into interaction, the concept and the message source, undergo change in order to resolve the apparent inconsistency. (The only exception is the case where one of the elements is completely neutral to begin with; according to the model, it absorbs all of the pressure to change, with the other element showing no modification at all.) To be sure, the subject is required to rate both the source and the concept in such experimental situations, but he can exhibit change on only one object, or the other, or both, or neither, for that matter.

There is also some ambiguity between the two types of congruity models in terms of the 'compromise' nature of the reaction postulated by the general theory. The attitude change model does involve adjustments that could be called compromises in that the expected changes are always relative to one another and the resolution is a joint one. Actually, the model allows for reactions other than the movement of each object toward the other suggested by such a compromise notion—depending on the particular conditions, only one element may change, or they may both change in the same direction, etc. By virtue of being limited to positive associations between elements and of disallowing the possibility of incredibility to exist, the semantic combination model is restricted to the simple averaging type of compromise—a situation which may be excessively and unrealistically restrictive.

A case in point is represented by certain instances where a summation rather than averaging result is noted in a word combination study, e.g., CRUEL NURSE may be judged as being worse than CRUEL by itself. There is an inherent incongruity in such a combination and the model is forced to make its prediction of a compromise judgment—i.e., a CRUEL NURSE being not quite as bad as CRUEL and something less favorable than NURSE. However, when the very personification of kindness and consideration is positively associated with cruelty in any form, the combination may be regarded as incredible as well. It is not unreasonable to anticipate that the subject, being forced to make some judgment, will resolve his dilemma by 'punishing the transgressor,' as it were: A nurse that can so violate expected norms by being cruel must be a real she-devil, and becomes, literally, more cruel than cruel itself.

In this connection, it is worth noting that the congruity predictions in cognitive interaction studies are generally supported least (i.e., there is a greater discrepancy between predicted and obtained scores) on the evaluative, as compared to the activity and potency, factor. In terms of the factor analysis of semantic differential judgments, these three factors have consistently emerged as independent dimensions of the semantic space, and they have accordingly been treated in the same manner, as if the same sets of rules applied to each. This was, again, a reasonable and parsimonious expectation (although there is no specific reason in the theory that it be so), but it may not be the case in reality. One suggestion (and it is only a tentative suggestion) from the above findings is that *the same rules do not apply to all dimensions*. Thus, it may be that the cognitive interaction model is more relevant to the activity and potency dimensions, while the evaluative dimension is governed by a separate congruity model for attitude change.

Other support for such a division is available from some of my research dealing with the connotative meanings of various nonverbal code stimuli such as colors, two-dimensional shapes, etc. (Tannenbaum, 1966b). A major focus of this activity was to determine if there was any systematic correspondence between the objective physical characteristics of such stimuli and the nature of the semantic reaction to them. In general, highly consistent relationships, bordering on apparent isomorphisms, have been found for the nonevaluative dimensions—e.g., the hue dimension of color being in close correspondence to ratings on the activity factor, with the potency factor reflecting the brightness component—but with few such consistencies apparent on the evaluative factor. It is as if the activity and potency judgments were predetermined to a substantial degree in that they are closely linked to actual physical and perceptual attributes of the objects of judgment. On the other hand, the attitudinal judgments appear to be more subjectively bound to the individual's experience and preferences, subject more to individual freedom and choice. Again, the reasoning is that such different relationships reflect different processes, and that the same general model does not apply equally to both processes.

One last bit of somewhat fanciful speculation: In our work in this area, we have tended to equate 'cognition' with 'meaning,' as it is indexed with the semantic differential technique. Thus, each dimension of meaning, including the evaluative or attitudinal factor, is taken as an integral part of cognition and is presumably subject to the same general 'cognitive laws.' However, other consistency formulations (e.g., those of Rosenberg, 1960a; Rosenberg & Abelson, 1960) have found it useful to distinguish between affective and cognitive relations. The suggestion here is for a similar utility to accrue from the division between the evaluative (affective?) and non-evaluative (cognitive?) components, with somewhat separate sets of rules, and hence somewhat separate types of models, governing the two domains.

RECENT APPLICATIONS IN ATTITUDE CHANGE RESEARCH

Having made this distinction, we will direct our attention to the attitude change area as such, where the congruity principle had its origin and where it has its most direct relevance. Actually, relatively little research has been conducted in this area since its introduction more than a decade ago. A number of applications are scattered throughout the literature, and except for some attempts to define some of the limiting conditions—e.g., such as the notions of pertinence and salience suggested by Carter (1965) or the corresponding notions of relevance and importance (cf. Pepitone, 1966)—the model remains essentially unchanged.

Recently, my interest in the model has been renewed in an attempt to apply some of the reasoning of the congruity formulation to a number of contemporary problems in the general area of persuasion. While it is more than likely that somewhat the same kind of reasoning and predictions could be derived from the other consistency theories, this work was motivated and guided by the congruity principle and should accordingly be considered in that context. In a sense, these applications provide 'tests' of congruity theory —of the theory itself, and, in some cases, in contrast to other formulations. In none of these studies have the actual predictive formulae been employed— partly because such fineness of prediction is not germane to the problems at hand, and partly because I still regard the available formulae to be incomplete estimates at best (a possible reason being that such apparent limiting variables as importance of the issue, relevance, strength of the assertion, etc., are not fully accommodated in the equations).

Generalization of Attitude Change

Implicit in the congruity formulation and in other consistency models is the notion of structures or constellations of attitudinal items. At a given point in time and space, these attitudes are assumed to exist in some state of equilibrium to one another. If some of the elements of the structure are altered in some way, an inconsistency is introduced into the prevailing structure. One of the main means of accommodating such an inconsistency is for modifications to occur in attitudes toward the other elements, changes in accord with the maintenance of a new state of equilibrium. It is not inappropriate to refer to such phenomena as cases of generalization of attitude change in that change in one attitudinal object induces change in another object without any direct manipulation of the attitude toward that second object as such (see Chapter 6). It is important to note, however, that in terms of a consistency theory approach, the changes in the two objects can be in the same or in the opposite direction, depending on the nature of the linkage between them and upon the direction of the change in the first object.

From concept to source. In a sense, the basic communication situation used in the initial congruity experimentation represented such a case of generalization of persuasion. Communication messages were used in which an identifiable source made an assertion for or against a given concept. The bulk of the argumentation inherent in the assertion was directed at the concept, with the source being merely mentioned and not specifically manipulated. The theory holds, and the results indicated, that in addition to the expected attitude change toward the concept there should occur appropriate modifications in attitude toward the source. The original experiments, however, do not represent a thorough test of such a generalization paradigm, basically because the two main cognitive operations involved in this paradigm—the establishment of a directed relationship between the source and concept, and the manipulation of the attitude toward the concept—were jointly accommodated within the same message. As a consequence, it was impossible to have the two operations in contrast—e.g., the source could not be against the concept and still have the concept attitude manipulated in a favorable direction—and it is precisely in such contrasting situations that the more critical tests of the congruity predictions obtain.

These two steps were treated in the necessary independent manner in a recent study (Tannenbaum & Gengel, 1966). The source-concept linkage was first established, and then the concept attitude was altered without any reference to the source, the main dependent variable being the change in attitude toward the source. On the basis of pretesting, three possible sources were selected as being essentially neutral in initial attitude. Each of these was then linked with a neutral concept (Teaching Machines), one source being in favor of the concept $(S+)$, another adopting an unfavorable position $(S-)$, and the third being in a neutral relationship (S_o). A separate message was subsequently administered—half the subjects getting information designed to create a favorable attitude toward Teaching Machines, the other half getting negative information—in both cases without any mention of the sources. Attitude measures were obtained on four semantic differential scales before and after the messages.

Predictions for change in attitude for the respective sources can be readily derived from congruity theory. Where the induced concept changes are positive, we would expect $S+$ to then also change in a favorable direction, but $S-$ to change negatively. Conversely, when the concept shifts unfavorably, $S+$ should change negatively but $S-$ in a positive direction. In both cases, S_o should not change appreciably one way or the other.

The actual results were not entirely as predicted, but they did tend to conform to the congruity principle expectations. One discrepancy was that none of the expected negative changes materialized, with all changes, including the neutral S_o condition, being in a favorable direction. We tend to attribute this to a general halo effect accruing to all three sources who were identified in the linking message as "leading psychological authorities" appearing at an APA symposium. However, the relative degrees of change were in the expected directions. That is, when the concept was manipulated favorably, $S+$ did show significantly more positive change than did $S-$, with the situation being reversed when the concept manipulation was in the negative direction. These findings are more vividly supportive of the congruity predictions when the analysis is restricted only to those subjects who actually did exhibit the appropriate positive or negative change toward the concept as intended by the manipulation, a necessary precondition for any subsequent shift in the source attitude to occur.

Mediated generalization. Given the general support indicated in the above study, I then undertook to extend the same congruity principle reasonings to a more advanced level (Tannenbaum, 1966a), and in so doing may have subjected such a consistency model for attitude change to a much more critical test. It was another case of pursuing the theoretical model to its own suggested consequences.

Such an extension of the congruity model for the generalization of persuasion is apparent if we assume, as seems perfectly reasonable, that a source may be evaluatively linked to more than one concept at a time. Each such source-concept linkage constitutes a directed relationship, and change in attitude toward one concept influences that particular relationship, resulting, as we have seen, in attitude change toward the source in order to put or maintain that relationship on a congruous basis. But this modification in the source now introduces an incongruity in its relationship with a second concept (even though that concept is not specifically manipulated) and attitude toward the second concept should now change in order to resolve that new incongruity. Thus, generalization of persuasion from one concept to another may be effected in the absence of any direct linkage between the two concepts, but mediated through their association with a common source.

Pretesting allowed for the selection of two initially neutral concepts—Teaching Machines (TM) and "Spence Learning Theory" (LT)—and a single neutral source. All subjects were first exposed to a message in which the source's position on both concepts was established. There were four such conditions established: one with the source being positive on both concepts (*pp* condition); another with the source favoring TM but negative to LT (*pn* condition); a third with the source against TM but in favor of LT (*np* condition), and the fourth with the source being against both concepts (*nn* condition). After a half-hour interval of irrelevant activity, all subjects were exposed to a message designed to manipulate the attitude toward only the TM concept, without any mention at all of either the source or the LT concept. Half the subjects in each linkage condition received a message favorable to TM (*P* treatment), the other half an attack against TM (*N* treatment). Attitudes were again assessed (with semantic differential evaluative factor scales) before and after the exposures, the analysis being conducted on the appropriate change scores.

By tracing the expected patterns—from the manipulated TM change, to corresponding change in the source attitude, and hence to LT change—one could test the detailed congruity theory predictions for each of the eight cells in the design. For example, in the *Pnp* condition, the experimental manipulation (*P*) should lead to a favorable TM attitude. Since here the source was originally against (*n*) what is now a positive object, the source attitude should change negatively. Now the second relationship involves the neutral LT concept being favored (*p*) by a negative source. According to the theory, this created condition should produce an LT shift in an unfavorable direction. Using similar three-stage step-by-step reasoning, one can apply the congruity principle to predict favorable LT changes in the *Ppp*, *Nnp*, *Npn*, and *Pnn* conditions, and unfavorable LT changes in the *Ppn*,

Nnn, Npp, and *Pnp* conditions. It is the contrasts involved between corresponding treatments in such a design that makes this a rather stringent test of the model.

The results (cf. Tannenbaum, 1966a, 1967) showed that the model met the challenge remarkably well. All eight cells, without exception, changed as predicted. The four cells in which a positive LT change was predicted all changed in that direction, with the difference among them being nonsignificant, and similarly, for the four predicted negative changes. Within a given linkage condition, the differences between the matched pairs of expected positive and negative changes were all highly significant.

These results achieve even more significance when they are contrasted with those to be expected if direct transfer of persuasion from concept would occur, without the influence of the mediating source (which is, of course, where the congruity model derives its unique predictions). Such direct transfer expectations are suggested by demonstrations of attitude formation by classical conditioning procedures (Staats, Staats, & Heard, 1959; Das & Nanda, 1963) or by instances of generalization as a function of sheer affective similarity (cf. Tannenbaum, 1967). If this were the case, we would expect the LT changes to be in the same direction as the induced TM changes. The critical contrasts between the two theories occur, then, in the *Ppn* and *Pnp* conditions where congruity predicts negative shifts rather than positive change expected from direct transference, and in the *Npn* and *Nnp* conditions where the reverse prediction patterns exist. In all four crucial cases, the results emphatically confirm the congruity predictions.

These findings provide impressive support for the consistency formulations, in general, and for the congruity model for attitude change, in particular. It is difficult to account for such detailed results by a model other than the kind of cognitive, or at least affective, homeostatic system that such formulations suggest—either that, or the data are highly artifactual for reasons of experimental expectancy (Rosenthal, 1966) and/or demand characteristics of the experiment (Orne, 1962). Barring such possible intrusions, the implication is for a structured system of interrelated attitudes held together in a state of equilibrium by established bonds. When one of the attitudinal units is altered as a result of some outside force, other elements related to it can also undergo modification so as to restore congruity and preserve the original bond. In further keeping with the homeostatic model, there is some evidence from this and other studies (through the form of postexperimental questioning) that these adjustments are made without apparent awareness, i.e., subjects do not report deliberately processing the available and incoming information and of following the reasoning sequence indicated above.

Congruity vs. Informational Persuasion Processes

A model for the induction of attitude change through communication which can be contrasted with the consistency type of model represented by the congruity principle is one which focuses on the inherent informational content of the message. Given positive information, the attitude should change favorably, and given negative information it should change unfavorably. Such a viewpoint is implicit in a 'learning theory' approach to attitudes (cf. Doob, 1947; Hovland, Janis, & Kelley, 1953). It is also apparent when Katz (1960) refers to attitude change occurring when an individual "finds his old attitudes in conflict with new information and new experiences, and proceeds to modify his beliefs," and in numerous other such conceptualizations. While the validity of a given theoretical position is not dependent on how well it fares when pitted against another formulation, such comparisons are of obvious interest, especially in cases where the two theories lead to quite different predictions.

The basic dichotomy posed here is somewhat of an over-simplification, and is reminiscent of earlier efforts in this field to differentiate between so-called 'rational vs. emotional' appeals. Largely because of a lack of sufficient clarity intrinsic in such gross distinctions and because of other weaknesses in design, the evidence in this area is divided and ambiguous. Possible contaminating variables have not been fully controlled and it is more than likely that relative susceptibility to such influences varies with personality and situational factors (McGuire, 1968b). The comparison becomes meaningful only when such external factors can be controlled, and when it is made to apply to a specific persuasion situation and not to contrast generalized 'grand strategies.' We have recently tried to accomplish such specificity in two studies in which the question is directed at the mutual compatibility between two messages on the same topic and on the extent of their combined effect.

Message uniformity. Given an initial message emanating from a favorable source $(S+)$ and with information favorable to a neutral concept $(I+)$ the tendency would be for a favorable attitude to develop toward the concept. Now, if a second message on the same topic were to arrive from another, this time unfavorable source $(S-)$, two interesting possibilities would exist depending on what position the second source would advocate. If he were to present a message featuring negative information about the concept $(I-)$, that would be consistent with the first message from a congruity point of view—a negative source being against a concept is in keeping with a positive source favoring it, since both messages make for a concept shift in a favorable direction. However, from a purely informational point of view, i.e., leaving the source out of it entirely, the two messages contradict one another. If it was the information alone that was the dominant producer of change, we would expect only a slight shift one way or the other, depending on which of the opposing informational materials carried more impact.

The opposite, of course, would hold if the second message had the negative source favoring the concept. Here the information, as such, would be consistent with that in the first message, and on that basis alone we should expect a strong positive shift in concept attitude. However, from a strictly congruity standpoint, the two messages would be mutually inconsistent and should tend to cancel each other out. Actually, since the congruity principle does allow for the effect of an 'assertion constant' it could predict a moderate positive attitude movement, certainly not as strong in that direction as in the first instance described above.

The study design included four such combinations of two messages. In two conditions $(S+I+$ coupled with $S-I-$, and when $S+I-$ was paired with $S-I+$) the message pairs were compatible in the congruity sense but not in the informational. If the congruity reasoning is correct, the former should yield a highly favorable shift in concept attitude, the second a highly negative shift. If the information, as such, were responsible for inducing change, there should be only minimal change in either direction in each case. The other two conditions represented the reverse situations. In the case of $S+I+$ being matched with $S-I+$, we have seen where congruity would predict a moderate positive shift at most, but the informational approach a decidedly more favorable change. In the case of $S+I-$ being coupled with $S-I-$, congruity would predict a moderate negative shift instead of the very strong negative change expected on the basis of the informational content alone.

The results (see Table VI in Tannenbaum, 1967) completely supported the congruity predictions in each case. Whatever slight informational effect did exist was swamped by the expected congruity effect.

Source or content redundancy. Additional support was forthcoming from a second study using a similar two-message paradigm. In this case, two separate messages were constructed as attacks against the use of X-rays for the detection of tuberculosis. One message merely supported the contention that X-rays were unnecessary (A_a) while the second argued that X-rays were downright damaging to a person's health (A_b). Two different sources, both judged highly favorable on pretests, were employed—one a professor of radiology (S_x), the other the Surgeon General's Office (S_y).

The design involved four basic experimental groups, each receiving two message exposures. All groups were first exposed to the A_a attack, from either S_x or S_y, the four groups varying in terms of the relative redundancy of the second message to the first. For Group I, the situation was totally redundant, i.e., the same source issued essentially the same statement in the second message as in the first. For Group II, the second message was also identified as coming from the same source, but contained new information in the form of the A_b attack. For Group III, the situation was reversed, with a different source issuing the same A_a attack. Group IV had both sources and information nonredundant, with a different source issuing a different attack.

Our interest here is in the relative amounts of negative change (since this is what all the messages advocate) in the belief in X-rays compared across the four conditions, and in determining whether the nonredundancy of sources (as congruity theory would tend to maintain) or the nonredundancy of content (as the information approach would predict) would produce the more change. The results (see Table V in Tannenbaum, 1967) indicated that both mechanisms were effective in their own right, but with somewhat more efficacy for the congruity strategy.

Both theories predict that the least overall change would occur in the totally redundant (Group I) condition and the largest change in the totally nonredundant (Group IV) condition, and this was clearly confirmed by the data. The new information, redundant source condition (Group II) was superior to the Group I control, as expected from the information processing approach. However, the main congruity strategy reflected in Group III (redundant information, different sources) produced significantly more change than the corresponding Group II mean, and was, further, not significantly less than the maximum Group IV mean. Thus, while there is evidence that both treatments—varying the information content or varying the identified sources—produce significant increments of persuasion, the latter procedure was relatively more effective.

Again, then, we find support for the congruity principle as a model for attitude change through communication. It provides the most parsimonious explanation for the data from these studies (it is also quite possible that similar predictions would be derived from most of the consistency models which could address themselves to such a communication situation). While these investigations are not all that crucial to the attitude change model—in a way, by focusing on how two different messages are jointly accommodated to effect a single concept change, they are somewhat reminiscent of the semantic combination situation—they do contribute to the confidence in such an approach. It is again of some interest to note that subjects in these studies generally cannot report undergoing change nor the reasons for such change. In fact, when subjects in another study employing similar persuasion techniques were made aware of their change in belief and of the type of inducement strategy to which they were most susceptible, they exhibited resistance to change to a subsequent message (on another issue) with a similar persuasive strategy. If anything, this suggests that awareness is not present in such situations to begin with, and that if it were present there would be less actual change (see Chapters 32 and 35).

Reduction of Persuasion

A given theory to account for certain conditions involved in the induction of attitude change also has implications for conditions in the reduction of attitude change. In recent years, there has been a good deal of attention directed at this problem area, including several applications of principles derived from consistency theory considerations (cf. McGuire, 1964; Tannenbaum, 1967). The most systematic and viable approach is represented by McGuire's 'inoculation theory' (McGuire, 1964) which, though it has some roots in the selective exposure premise of dissonance theory (see Section IV E), represents an integrated theoretical formulation of its own.

The congruity model represents a somewhat different approach in the study of attitude formation and change and accordingly provides a somewhat different theoretical rationale for investigating resistance to persuasion. The basic reason can be stated quite succinctly: if attitude change, in a given communication situation, stems directly from the degree of incongruity in that situation, then any means of reducing the incongruity should lead to a reduction in the degree of attitude change. The particular communication situation selected for this work is that in which the favorable source makes a strong negative assertion against a highly favorable concept. This is an obviously incongruous relationship and, among other things, should generate a negative shift in attitude toward that concept. The problem posed, then, is to provide some means—administered either prior to exposure to this belief attack or afterwards—that would diminish the amount of unfavorable attitude change toward the concept.

Individual strategies. Applying the congruity principle to the communication situation suggested four distinct treatments to diminish unfavorable attitude change by reducing the degree of incongruity inherent in the situation: (a) Since the issue of incongruity arises only when the source and concept are brought into a directed relationship, any procedure which would serve to sever this link should accordingly reduce the degree of incongruity. In our studies this was accomplished by having the source issue a *denial* of having made the statement being attributed to him and, in our most recent investigations, also indicating that he actually favors the concept. (b) Given a negative assertion toward a favorable concept, a more congruous situation would obtain if the source were negatively evaluated. Another indicated strategy, then, is to derogate and *attack the source* of the main message. (c) The congruity principle also recognizes the effect of the assertion itself, the impact of the facts and arguments being directed against the concept. Thus, if we could weaken the assertion, and attack the validity of its arguments, there should be less pressure for the concept to change negatively. This was accomplished by a specific point-by-point *refutation* of the position taken in the main message. (d) Another attitude change principle incorporated within congruity theory is that more intense attitudes are less susceptible to change. Accordingly, a strengthening or *boost* of the concept attitude, as such, to a more positively polarized position would make it more resistant to change.

Using a number of generally accepted health beliefs (similar to those employed by McGuire) as the concepts and either a respected government agency or a (fictitious) professor of medicine as a source, the four indicated strategies were investigated as reducers of persuasion, with several replications available for each strategy. The results provided strong, if differential, support for each of the treatments considered separately (cf. Tannenbaum, Macaulay, & Norris, 1966; Tannenbaum, 1967, for the particular details).

Combined strategies. What would be the effect of various combinations of two of these strategies at a time? If the two particular treatments were independent in their effect—i.e., if they served to reduce the degree of change by mutually exclusive means—then we would expect their combined effect to be greater than either considered individually; in fact, an additive effect, with no interaction between the two strategies, would be indicated. It is clear from the congruity principle used to generate these strategies that the source-attack and refutation treatments represent such an independent pair. When tested across a variety of permutations of this basic combination—e.g., both treatments before or both treatments after the main attack, or one before and the other after, etc.—it was indeed found that the combination was significantly more effective than either of the components in reducing the amount of belief change (cf. Tannenbaum & Norris, 1965). Further, while a fully adequate test of the additivity hypothesis was not possible, the available data did support such a prediction. By similar reasoning, based on the congruity model derivations for each of the strategies, three additional pairings should exhibit such independence—coupling the refutation with the denial treatments, the source attack with the concept boost, and the denial with the concept boost. Again, when tested under appropriate conditions, the expected superior effects of the combinations over their respective components were confirmed (Tannenbaum, 1967). Two combinatorial treatments remain, each of which represents a nonindependent pairing, again according to the congruity reasoning behind each. It can be argued (Tannenbaum, 1967) that the refutation and boost treatments function as immunizers against persuasion by somewhat similar means in that both may result in a strengthening of the concept attitude, although the refutation has additional persuasion-reduction potential. Again, the expected results obtained—there was some redundancy in the combined effect, with it being superior to the boost treatment alone, but not to the refutation. In the case of pairing the denial and source derogation, the expectation is not only for a redundancy in effect, but even that one may contradict the other. Here too the experimental results were in accord with the theoretical predictions (Tannenbaum, 1967).

Such results constitute consistent, if somewhat circumstantial, evidence in support of the congruity model. Strategies derived from the model were shown to operate in expected ways, as did the particular combinations of such strategies. Results of this type may not prove a theory, but they help make for greater confidence in its premises and its underlying rationale. On this point, it is worth noting that while McGuire's inoculation theory and the present formulation both point to the refutation treatment as an important strategy, they suggest different mechanisms for its operation in inducing resistance to persuasion. For inoculation theory, it is the key treatment in that it embodies the essential defense characteristics required by this formulation, by alerting the individual to the vulnerability of his belief, and thus it provides the threat that motivates him to muster the necessary defenses. In terms of the congruity reasoning, the refutation treatment works mainly by blunting the force of the attack on the belief. Tannenbaum (1967) reports data from a number of studies bearing on this issue and concludes that both the posited mechanisms are tenable. Since the two theories are not inherently inconsistent, such a conclusion does not necessarily call for a major modification of either.

SUMMARY

In this paper, I have adopted the somewhat revisionist position that it is possible and fruitful to entertain a theory of attitude change based on the congruity principle separate from a more general model of cognitive interaction. The two are not necessarily incompatible, but neither are they identical.

In proposing such a separation between the two types of congruity models, the intention is not to belittle either. The general model for cognitive interaction does have its points and merits attention on its own. Similarly, its application to the judgment of complex social stimuli, where it seems the most directly relevant, deserves consideration and experimental testing. But the fact that the results of such testing have found the model to be somewhat wanting does not necessarily affect the validity of the congruity model for attitude change through communication. Nor, of course, do the results of any testing of the attitude change model prove or disprove anything about the cognitive interaction model. The distinction merely suggests that each model should be treated and assessed on its own terms.

The subsequent assessment of the attitude change model has been directed more at exploring its implications in a variety of persuasion situations than in evaluating the precision of its predictive formulae. The fact that these implications have generally been confirmed—in some instances, under rather demanding conditions—suggests that there is a reasonable basis for the fundamental line of reasoning involved in the congruity formulation. It also suggests a considerable range of generality for such theorizing. It is important to note, however, that testing is still restricted to particular types of communications situations, and that generalization beyond those situations is a rather tenuous procedure.

This still leaves the congruity principle without a base in or relationship to a more general and fundamental psychological theory. I am far from certain that such a base is required—at least not at this stage of the game.

There may well be a fundamental consistency formulation that cuts across and supersedes any of the specific theories subsumed in this volume, with the congruity model being a special manifestation of this more general principle. I believe there is some merit to this approach—at least, in not treating each theory as distinctive from the others—although I do feel that there are rules that govern purely affective relationships that may not apply to all cognitive processes. Some of the data reported here are in accord with such speculations. But speculations they remain, albeit with a heightened degree of confidence.

CHAPTER 4

Hedonism, Inauthenticity, and Other Goads Toward Expansion of a Consistency Theory

Milton J. Rosenberg
University of Chicago

How does one *test* a theory? The obvious and conventional answer is: by deriving from it predictions that can be confirmed or disconfirmed through experiments. What is thereby tested is the theorist's right to stake a claim on some circumscribed terrain of his own choosing. But the robustness of a theory, its larger relevance and utility, is tested in other ways. The most important test in this latter sense is how the theory responds, or can be made to respond, to challenges. Such challenges may come from competing theories that claim the same terrain; or they may take the form of inexplicable phenomena that haunt the margins of that terrain and impel the theorist toward exploratory forays beyond the befogged border; or, while the theorist peers into the contiguous murk, the ground may shift underfoot as, due to the influence of new data or closer logical analysis, old theoretical certainties are transformed into new ambiguities.

All of the consistency models and theories have faced such challenges over the last decade. The main burden of this chapter is to recount some of the particular challenges confronted by one of these theories, and to give some account of what that theory has done with the challenges and what they have done to it.

The theory in question has been variably labelled. I have most often referred to it as the "affective-cognitive consistency theory," and this designation seems to have been employed by most others who have commented on it (e.g., Brown, 1963; Doby, 1966; Insko, 1967; Secord & Backman, 1964). Properly it is perhaps more model than theory and it might better be designated as a radial structure model of intraattitudinal balancing. However designated, its core propositions are rather easily stated and the data that support them can be readily summarized. In what follows I turn first to this necessary prologue and then to four challenges that have, in recent years, forced themselves upon my grudging attention, and to the further work, both theoretical and experimental, that has eventuated. In recounting these developments I shall try to eschew the imperalist stance; it is not my intention to build toward a climatic pronouncement that the model examined and extended in these pages has general superiority over its neighbors and relatives. My more modest ambition, though it may still bespeak a hubristic lapse, is to show that a quite simple conceptual model of attitude dynamics can take on some fairly complicated issues, and that in so doing it yields certain findings and further theoretical conceptualizations that may be useful in the ultimate construction of a truly adequate theory of social attitudinal processes. The latter, as I see it, is a consummation that, as yet, is as unattained as it is devoutly wished.

THE ORIGINAL MODEL

The basis for the affective-cognitive consistency approach to attitude dynamics lies in a common relationship that has often been confirmed in research reported by contemporary investigators. This is the relationship of *consistency* between a comparatively stable affective or evaluative orientation toward some object and the person's beliefs about how that object is related to other objects of affective significance. Thus, persons, policies, or institutions that are favored are usually cognized as serving the attainment of desirable conditions and impeding the attainment of undesirable ones, as having attributes that are admired or cherished, as grouped with other attractive persons, policies, or institutions, and as standing separate from unattractive ones. On the other hand, persons, policies, or institutions that are disfavored are usually cognized in opposite terms: they are seen as impeding access to desirable states and fostering the actualization of undesirable ones, as possessing unattractive attributes, as grouped with other unattractive persons, policies, or institutions.

Easily derived from this proposition is the predictive hypothesis that the sign and extremity of attitudinal affect toward some object will be correlated with the overall positive or negative affective import of those other objects that are cognized as related to the object in question. Confirmations of this sort of prediction were already available in published reports by Cartwright (1949), Smith (1949), Woodruff and DiVesta (1948), and others when I set my hand, some years ago, to constructing a more precise theoretical formulation of intraattitudinal affective-cognitive consistency and a more precise empirical demonstration of it.

Focusing upon cognitions concerning the value-attaining and value-blocking instrumentality of objects in the class of advocated changes in public policy, I formulated the following main hypothesis:

> The degree and sign of affect aroused in an individual by an object (as reflected by the position he chooses on an attitude scale) vary as a function of the algebraic sum of the products obtained by multiplying the rated importance of each value associated with that object by the rated potency of the object for achieving or blocking the realization of that value (Rosenberg, 1956).

To test this hypothesis and some related ones, the attitudinal affects of a large number of college students were measured with regard to two separate issues (housing desegregation and free speech for avowed Communists). Three to five weeks later each subject went through an individually administered card-sorting procedure. Thirty-five 'value items' (we may think of these as other objects of possible affective import) were rated both for "the degree of satisfaction or dissatisfaction that this would give me" (value importance) and for the likelihood that the represented value state would be "blocked" or "attained" if "Negroes were allowed to move into white neighborhoods" and, separately, if "members of the Communist party were allowed to address the public" (object-value instrumentality). A positively valued condition (say a rating of +7 for the item "All human beings having equal rights") when perceived to be instrumentally fostered by "Negroes moving into white neighborhoods" (say a rating of +4 on instrumentality) contributed a product (of +28) to a total cognitive index computed by algebraic summation of all of the importance-instrumentality products.

Typically, many of the 35 value conditions were perceived to be instrumentally affected by the attitude objects under study. And, as I have reported elsewhere:

> By testing the relationship between this cognitive index (Σvi; i.e. the algebraic sum of the value importance-instrumentality products) and the independent measure of attitudinal affect it was shown that stable positive affect toward an attitude object is associated with beliefs relating that object to the attainment of positive values and the blocking of negative values, while stable negative affect toward an attitude object is associated with beliefs relating it to the attainment of negative values and the blocking of positive values. It was also confirmed that moderate attitudinal affects, as compared to extreme ones, are associated with beliefs that relate the attitude object to less imporant values, or if to important values then with less confidence as to the existence of clear-cut instrumental relationships between the attitude object and the values in question. Data from this study also indicated that variation in attitudinal affect is separately correlated with at least two aspects of the person's set of attitudinal cognitions. The first of these is the over-all believed potency of the attitude object for achieving or blocking the realization of his values; the second is the over-all felt importance of those values (Rosenberg, 1960c).

From this and similar demonstrations of the prevalence of intraattitudinal, affective-cognitive consistency it seemed possible to move toward a more dynamic conception of the attitude-change process. The fundamental principle was simply that attitude change is due to a sort of homeostatic process in which the production of affective-cognitive inconsistency arouses further symbolic activity leading toward restoration of inner consistency.

Stated in terms of a simple propositional sequence the basic theoretical view as originally propounded was this:

1. When the affective and cognitive components of an attitude are mutually consistent, the attitude is in a stable state.
2. When these components are mutually inconsistent, to a degree that exceeds the individual's "tolerance limit" for such inconsistency, the attitude is in an unstable state.
3. In such an unstable state the attitude will undergo reorganizing activity until one of three possible outcomes is achieved. These outcomes are: (a) rejection of the communications, or other forces, that engendered the original inconsistency between affect and cognition and thus rendered the attitude unstable, i.e. restoration of the original stable and consistent attitude; (b) "fragmentation" of the attitude through the isolation from each other of the mutually inconsistent affective and cognitive components; (c) accommoda-

tion to the original inconsistency-producing change so that a new attitude, consistent with that change, is now stabilized, i.e. attitude change (Rosenberg, 1960c).

This theoretical view is clearly a rudimentary one. It lacks specifity in two important areas: while assuming that affective-cognitive inconsistency must transcend some "tolerance limit" for attitude reorganization to occur, it does not specify the variables which will affect the operative level or 'height' of such a threshold; while positing at least three outcomes through which suprathreshold inconsistency may be reduced, it does not specify the conditions under which one or the other of these outcomes is likely to occur. Regarding these conditions, in early statements of the theoretical approach (Rosenberg, 1960b, c) I did offer the idea that rejection of the inconsistency-generating communications would usually be the first expedient attempted; and that where that failed, 'fragmentation' might obtain for an attitude in which the person had extremely strong ego-investment, while true attitude change would be more likely to occur with the usual run of attitudes that had been disrupted by the generation of internal inconsistency.

But clearly the theory required extension and elaboration in both these areas. This has since been attempted and I shall return to these matters later on, particularly in the third and fourth sections of this chapter.

A more compelling task in the early stages was to test two basic predictions, both of which would need confirmation before the general theoretical view outlined above could be accepted as a useful one. The first prediction was that the production of 'irreversible' changes in beliefs about an attitude object should produce corresponding, consistency-restoring change in affect toward that object. The second was the converse: the production of irreversible change in affect toward an object should generate consistency-restoring change in beliefs about that object.[1]

Actually, considerable confirmation of the first of these predictions was already available in the results of research undertaken for other purposes (e.g. Cartwright, 1949; Deutsch & Collins, 1951; F. T. Smith, 1943) and in some studies more directly pointed toward the hypothesis that cognitive modification generates related affective shifts (Carlson, 1956; Peak, 1960).

The second prediction received its basic experimental test and confirmation in two studies in which I attempted to produce direct modification of attitudinal affect through the technique of posthypnotic suggestion. As has been reported in past publications (Rosenberg, 1956, 1960a, b; Rosenberg & Gardner, 1958) the clear consequence of such manipulated affect change is an alteration of the person's beliefs about the attitude object. If, for example, he was previously in favor of "the United States giving economic aid to foreign nations" and has been given the posthypnotic instruction that he will feel strongly opposed to this policy, he shows not only a basic change in evaluation of that policy but also changes in many

---

[1] In anticipation of a more molecular theoretical restatement offered later in this section, the following should be noted here: Both patterns of change can be viewed as mediated by the induction of inconsistency within specific 'attitudinal cognitions' made up of believed relations (positive or negative) between affectively significant (positive or negative) objects. The distinction between the two types of change reduces, then, to the distinction between the original induction of change in the perceived relations between such objects or in the affective sign of one of these objects.

of his relevant original beliefs. Thus, a typical subject before hypnotic manipulation of affect believes that abandoning foreign aid would defeat such positive goals as "the maintenance of economic prosperity" and would serve such negative goals as "America losing its international prestige." After the hypnotic manipulation of affect he asserts, and argues for, the beliefs that abandonment of foreign aid would *foster* the former positive goal and would defeat the latter negative one. Indeed, most subjects show changes of this sort in a large number of their attitudinal cognitions.

As compared with the performances of control groups, and as probed by close postexperimental inquiry, it seemed clear that a quite significant pattern of postmanipulation cognitive reorganization was achieved by virtually all subjects and that this was not done in a role-playing way. Rather, the cognitive changes were usually internalized ones and remained so until posthypnotic amnesia was removed and the experiment fully explained.

Later studies using hypnotic (Stachowiak & Moss, 1965) and non-hypnotic (Axelrod, 1959) methods of affect manipulation have produced quite similar results.

In general, then, the relevant data seemed to lend rather strong support to the theoretical view of attitude change which I have summarized here. The most detailed statement of that view (as held before I proceeded into the further experimental studies and theoretical speculations with which the rest of this chapter is concerned) is found, I think, in a lengthy statement from an earlier publication. In that statement I attempted to lay out the full theoretical implications of the research I have described in this section. I present it here, in a slightly abridged version, as the basic foundation for a fair portion of my later work in this realm.

> It is proposed that all types of attitude acquisition and attitude change may be understood as the result of the person's having under-gone one (or a blend) of two discriminably distinct sequences. It is not contended that attitude change is an inevitable result of the arousal of affective-cognitive inconsistency; but rather that, when attitudes do change, they change through the operation of either one or both of these sequences.
>
> *The sequence originating in modification of cognitive response.* Either through direct encounter with an object or with communications about that object a person acquires one or more beliefs, each of which links the object to some "locus of affect" (i.e. some other "object," state, or condition with which a stable positive or negative affective response is regularly associated). In proportion to the strength, number, and mutual consistency of these new beliefs there will be generated a similar, but tentative, affective disposition toward the object in question. When the object formerly elicited no stable affective response and was not believed to be related to any affect locus (i.e. when no previous attitude existed) the newly generated affective disposition will become stabilized as the person's attitudinal affect toward that object. When a previous and opposite attitude *did* exist, and when the new beliefs replace the old ones or predominate over them, then the discrepancy between these new beliefs and the original affective disposition will be resolved by that disposition giving way (at least to a degree that reduces over-all affective-cognitive inconsistency to a magnitude below the intolerance threshold for the attitude) to the newly generated and opposite affective disposition.
>
> *The sequence originating in modification of affective response.*

Either through reinforcement in association with an object or through reinforcement for the imitative or trial-and-error "rehearsal" of an affective response to an object, a person acquires an affective disposition toward it. The strength of this disposition varies with the intensity, timing, frequency, and consistency of the reinforcement received. In proportion to the strength of the affective disposition the person will tentatively adopt and/or invent beliefs that are consistent with it and that relate its object to other affect loci. When no previous attitude existed these beliefs will become stabilized as the person's attitudinal cognitions. When a previous and opposite attitude did exist, and when the new affective disposition replaces or predominates over the old one, then the discrepancy between this new disposition and the original beliefs will be resolved by those beliefs giving way (at least to a degree that reduces over-all affective-cognitive inconsistency to a magnitude below the individual's intolerance threshold or for the attitude) to the new and opposite beliefs.

These two sequences are assumed to operate (1) only when the degree of affective-cognitive inconsistency exceeds the individual's present tolerance for such inconsistency; and (2) only when the original alteration of either the affective or cognitive component has been sufficiently compelling, and is strongly enough maintained, to be irreversible. Where the last-mentioned condition is not met, it may be assumed that the least effortful response to the experience of an intolerable degree of affective-cognitive inconsistency is to undo the original inconsistency-establishing change, e.g. to reject the change-inducing communication (Rosenberg, 1960a).

Before I report some of the turns this theory has taken in more recent work, I should like to examine the relations between it and kindred approaches. Obviously it is a member of the family of consistency theories. But within families one may find incompatibilities as well as sibling closeness and lines of generational descent.

The affective-cognitive consistency approach is comparatively distinct from dissonance theory, and at least so far as concerns the study of counter-attitudinal advocacy effects, the theories are partially incompatible for they tend to generate opposite predictions. In the last section of this chapter I shall discuss some experiments designed to test these predictions.

The present theory has somewhat more compatibility with the congruity model of Osgood and Tannenbaum (1955). This is largely because both approaches take as their molar unit the cognitive entity comprised of a perceived relation between two affect-eliciting objects. Otherwise the theories differ in what they assume about inconsistency processing and the likely loci of sign changes, and in the kinds of belief structures which they find typical or interesting.

The relations between the present approach and the 'balance' branch of the consistency dynasty are more truly consanguinous. While the affective-cognitive consistency theory was originally formulated without any particular influence from (or even awareness of) the work of Fritz Heider, it is in many aspects compatible with his theoretical analysis of balance processes. However, it is far less ambitious. It is a theory of attitude acquisition and change and has little utility in the direct analysis of other perceptual processes; nor can it be easily employed to bring systematic meaning to the study of interpersonal relations.

Yet the present theory, some years after its original formulation, converged with Heider's theory and with Abelson's approach to problems of multidimensional scaling to generate the rather ambitious and quite formal "symbolic psycho-logic" approach (Abelson & Rosenberg, 1958). The scene and occasion of that convergence was an extended dialogue that Abelson and I held for about a year before we plunged into the "Fenwick studies" (Rosenberg & Abelson, 1960) and other unpublished ones in which we attempted to test our new model through some rather innovative role-playing procedures.

The relationship between the affective-cognitive consistency model and the symbolic psycho-logic treatment of cognitive balancing is best described by saying that the latter incorporates the former, so that where they address the same problems they come out with identical answers. However, the symbolic psycho-logic casts a wider referential net; it is better suited to an examination of interattitudinal balancing over extended complex structures. Correspondingly, the affective-cognitive consistency approach seems to me to have a more immediate utility; it appears to be more readily applicable in cases where one wishes to focus upon a particular attitude or attitude area. In a sense, it is a model closely suited to the needs of the investigator who is interested in the content and inner structure of a particular attitude because he hopes to induce change in that attitude. And it has this particular value because it offers a heuristically effective simplification in the sort of cognitive map that it generates.

The best way I know to demonstrate this, as well as to clarify where the parent model and its offspring are identical and where they differ, is to revert to a fanciful metaphor that I have often used in lecture presentation.

Let us imagine a finite but vast space called the 'attitudinal cognitorium.' Within it are located hundreds (thousands?) of object-concepts, each of these being a verbal (or other symbolic) representation of a person, institution, policy, place, event, value standard, or other 'thing' which, when psychologically encountered, elicits some fairly stable magnitude of either positive or negative evaluative affect. Represent each of these object-concepts as a little metal disk. Between these disks run strings which tie them together, two at a time. Red strings indicate a negative or 'disjunctive' relationship of the sort that might be conveyed by the terms 'opposes,' 'prevents,' 'dislikes,' 'stays away from,' etc. Green strings indicate a positive or 'conjunctive' relationship of the sort conveyed by terms such as 'supports,' 'facilitates,' 'likes,' 'helps,' 'is part of,' etc.

Any given object disk is tied by red strings to some, and by green strings to other, object disks. But it is not directly connected to all other disks in the attitudinal cognitorium. For example, in my own repertoire of evaluative responses at the moment are the objects 'air pollution,' 'Chicago Blackhawks,' 'the romantic tradition,' 'the Vietnam war,' 'bituminous coal,' 'Gustav Mahler,' 'Senator Fulbright,' and 'my son.' No matter how earnestly I scan I find neither a red nor a green string between Senator Fulbright and either Gustav Mahler or the Chicago Blackhawks. But the object disk 'Fulbright' (which is marked by a large plus indicating positive evaluation) has a clear red string running from it to the negatively labelled object 'Vietnam war' and a thinner red string (indicating less certainty of belief in the relation) leading to 'air pollution.' However, between 'air pollution' (an affectively negative object) and 'bituminous coal' (also affectively negative) there is a thick green string (which has been spun around a Chicago fact of life; much of this city's air pollution problem is traceable, according to expert opinion, to an excessive reliance upon bituminous coal for domestic heating plants).

Consider now the object 'my son,' which elicits considerable positive affect. To it there come red strings from 'air pollution' and the 'Vietnam war.' Both, as I see it, threaten him, though the latter in a more complex way than the former. Between him and the 'Chicago Blackhawks' is a thick green string, the hockey team being one of the objects that I know him to have invested with considerable positive affect.

Compound such a structure a few hundredfold (or many thousand-fold if one takes into account all the possible combinatorial variations in object connectedness) and one has an analog representation of an individual's attitudinal cognitorium. Now lay out all the disks, with the connecting strings, on some vast floor. Peering from above at the total array or at some sector of it, we note that green strings connect like-signed objects and red strings connect opposite-signed objects (consistency by Heiderian or psycho-logic definition!) far more often than do green strings connect opposite-signed objects or red strings same-signed objects (inconsistency).

We note also that for any given object the number of others to which it is directly connected is fewer than the number to which it is connected only through other intermediate object links. 'My son' is directly connected to 'air pollution' but only indirectly to 'Senator Fulbright' by virtue of the opposition to air pollution that I have imputed to the Senator. And if 'my son' is at all connected to 'Gustav Mahler'—who, I confess, elicits ambivalent affect—this is only because I believe Mahler to represent the spirit of the late 'romantic tradition' which, in turn, I believe to be one of the cultural developments that reinforced 'adventurism in international politics,' which general style I take to be one of the background factors that has led to the misapplication of the containment strategy and thus to an unprofitable and unwise 'involvement in Vietnam.'

Where in the vast disk and string complex that is now spread over the two-dimensional space of the giant floor can we locate attitudes? I would say that each disk is the *center* of an attitude, but that to get at the full attitude one must lean over, grab the particular disk, and pull it up into the third dimension. The other disks that come off the floor shortly thereafter, because they are directly attached by red or green strings to the object that has been made central by our pulling it, are the other objects that, together with the central one, comprise an intraattitudinal structure.

Thus if I pull the object 'my son' just high enough into the third dimension to elevate also those objects that are directly tied to it (and this is as far as we usually go either in the complex measurement of an attitude or in the conscious examination of our own attitudes) I will also bring into closer scrutiny 'air pollution,' 'Chicago Blackhawks,' and a number of other objects that I have not heretofore mentioned (e.g., 'progressive education,' 'interest in books,' 'my wife,' 'trips to the Museum of Science and Industry,' etc.). Neither 'Senator Fulbright' nor the 'romantic tradition' will be brought into focus, though as objects they are distantly connected to the presently central one.

What is the purpose of all this metaphorical gamboling across the vast object-laden floor of the attitudinal cognitorium? It enables a further clarification of the identities and intended differences between the affective-cognitive and symbolic psycho-logic consistency models. By focussing, for any particular object, upon its relations with other objects that are pulled off the floor with it, the affective-cognitive approach circumscribes the task of attitude analysis in a helpful way. Attitude description, the induction of intraattitudinal inconsistency, and the testing of predictions about modes and methods of consistency restoration can all be pursued within the sort of closely bound radial structures delineated by this theoretical approach. It is within such radial structures that the assumed intolerance for inconsistency plays a strong, organizing role. For, as Abelson and I have argued earlier (Rosenberg & Abelson, 1960), a precondition for doing something about potential inconsistency is that one encounters it and thinks about it. Objects that are directly related to one another will be more closely scanned for the possibility that those relations are inconsistent; and where inconsistency is encountered within such radial structures it will be less easily evaded—'stopping thinking' will be a less available expedient than where the relations between objects are only indirect and distant. Thus the sorts of radial structures upon which the affective-cognitive model focusses represent a way of drawing a meaningfully integrated sample of object elements out of the total attitudinal cognitive space.

Instead of eliciting radial structure samples, the symbolic psycho-logic focusses upon larger blocks of attitudinal cognitive space. When one employs this theoretical scheme, no single object need be delineated as the central one in an artificially isolated substructure. Instead, one focusses upon some sizeable section of the total space, a section characterized by high to moderate interaction (or 'relatedness') between objects. This is demarked as a "conceptual arena" (Abelson & Rosenberg, 1958). Within such a conceptual arena one scans all existing relations between, say, 'getting A's,' 'getting C's,' 'being able to study,' 'good fellowship,' 'having coeds at Yale,' 'preserving old traditions,' 'dining at Morey's,' etc. Thus, going from the affective-cognitive model to the psycho-logic one, interest shifts away from the organization and achievement of further consistency within a structure organized around a single object concept such as 'having coeds at Yale'; instead, interest is now focussed upon the general inner coherence of the block of attitudinal space that contains and gives equal prominence to all these concepts. Also, with no central object delineated, the direct and mediated relations between all objects become equally relevant. In a sense one remains a wanderer (but one who knows what he is looking for) on a two-dimensional plane.

The affective-cognitive consistency approach, then, seems best suited to mapping, manipulating, and interpreting the inner consistency dynamics of the person's attitudes toward presently salient issues. The symbolic psycho-logic approach seems far better suited to tracing the ways in which inconsistencies are induced, discovered, reduced, or avoided in broader sectors of the total attitudinal cognitorium.

Also, as illustrated in the "Fenwick" studies (Rosenberg & Abelson, 1960), this latter approach is particularly effective in another way. It highlights the fact that new cognized relationships, even when they possess potential inconsistency-reducing value, may yet be rejected because they stir up other inconsistencies in contiguous areas that would not usually be represented in a simple radial mapping.

Despite these differences the later theoretical system is an extension of the earlier one. Although in this chapter I shall hew basically to the affective-cognitive formulation, most of the newer theoretical constructions and research studies that are presented are ones which could be fitted into the symbolic psycho-logic view of attitudinal cognitive processes.

To the foregoing discussion I must add one important reportorial point. I have characterized the symbolic psycho-logic approach as well suited to analyzing and predicting inconsistency reduction in nonradial complex structures. This was the sort of use to which Abelson and I put that approach when we first developed it. Appreciative commentators such as Brown (1965) and Smith (1968) have seen this as one of its major values. But in practice both Abelson and I, in our continuing separate work with this approach, have often turned away from its potential broad applicability, and toward the more molecular psychological events which mediate the kinds of cognitive balancing that the theory delineates. Particularly, Abelson has given considerable attention to the "microprocesses" (Rosenberg & Abelson, 1960; Abelson, 1963) by which imbalance avoidance and balance restoration are actually accomplished (see also Chapter 5). My own work on "hedonism" and "personal-general reference," as described in the third section of this chapter, is also a sort of lingering over some microprocess details that were left unclear in our original articles.

THE DETECTION OF ATTITUDINAL VACUITY

When is an 'attitude' not an attitude? The question is considerably more than academic. Confronted by a questionnaire or an interviewer, subjects and respondents who lack any real interest in a particular issue, who have little information on it, and who are unstable in their affective orientation toward it will nevertheless often report themselves as "strongly in favor" or "strongly opposed."

Some subjects and respondents will take such unfounded positions on personality-based grounds and across the broad range of issues toward which they feel intrinsic indifference. Others will give invalid evidence of attitudinal extremity and commitment only for certain particular issues or in certain special situations. The effect is probably mediated by embarrassment or "evaluation apprehension" (Rosenberg, 1965d) over revealing oneself to be apathetic and anomically withdrawn.

When some such process of false attitudinal representation occurs the person's self-reports are likely to be influenced by the implicit and inadvertent "demand characteristics" (Orne, 1962) that often bedevil attitude change experiments. Or, when the person is playing the role of a respondent being interviewed by a pollster, he is likely to evade the revelation of apathy toward some public issue by deflecting his attitudinal self-reports toward the 'perceived consensus' that he attributes to the total national public or to some important reference group (Rosenberg, 1965a).

What I have just stated assertively is, actually, a set of *suspicions* rather than of clearly demonstrated facts. These suspicions are increasingly voiced by specialists in attitude measurement and surveying as they scan the record of easy malleability that is revealed in week-to-week shifts of public opinion; or as they ponder the fact that many persons will readily offer ostensibly strong attitudinal judgments on nonexistent issues or toward nonexistent groups if those issues or groups are presented as stimuli by interviewers.

If more reliable attitude survey data is to be obtained, if more uncontaminated experimental research on attitude change is to be conducted, better criteria must be developed for delineating just what kinds of evaluative responses do, and what kinds do not, index the existence of an attitude.

One direct way to approach this problem is to take as a validating criterion the common element in virtually all definitions of the attitude concept: namely, comparative stability over time. It then becomes possible, whether on theoretical grounds or solely through blind empiricism, to determine what patterns of original response, as elicited by attitude measures, are associated with test-retest stability and what patterns are not.

A simple derivation from the affective-cognitive theory is that intra-attitudinal consistency will reduce the likelihood that judgments of the 'attitude object' will be easily influenced by mood changes, situational variables, and persuasion attempts. Or, to delineate the complementary hypothesis, it could be predicted that where a stated affective judgment of an object is not imbedded in a set of supporting, largely consistent cognitions, that judgment, as originally given, is more a product of situational forces than the expression of a dispositional characteristic of the person; by the defining criterion of stability over time it is a quasi-attitudinal response rather than an attitude.

A number of simple empirical tests of this view were executed.[2] In the first of these we administered to a group of undergraduate males both affective and cognitive measures pertaining to the issue "the United States expressing support of French policy in Algeria." (This was during the time that the French were still attempting to put down the Algerian revolt.) On the affective measure the subjects were required to indicate 1 of 16 positions ranging from "extreme approval" to "extreme disapproval." On the cognitive measure subjects were required to indicate how each of a number of value conditions (which they first rated for the degree to which they were positive or negative value states) would, as they saw it, be affected if the United States were to support French policy (i.e., the scale ranged from "the value would be completely achieved" through various stages of "moderately achieved" and "moderately blocked" to "completely blocked"). For each subject the index of cognitive structure was computed by summing the products obtained by multiplying the "value importance" rating of each item by its "perceived instrumentality" rating.

For the total population we then rank ordered the distributions of affective and cognitive scores, respectively. Thus for each subject it could be determined, with reference to a parameter generated by the total population distribution, how close or discrepant were his affective response

---

[2] In these previously unpublished studies I received valuable assistance from Philip Oltman.

and his overall pattern of beliefs about the value-attaining and value-blocking potential of the attitude object. In effect the computed discrepancy between the person's ranks on the affective and cognitive measures serves as a comparative index of the degree of intraattitudinal, affective-cognitive consistency that he has achieved either prior to, or on the occasion of, the administration of the measures.

To test whether the subjects who were higher on affective-cognitive consistency also showed greater affective stability over time, we simply readministered the affective measure two weeks later. The results are clear and as expected. For the group of subjects who showed no change in affective response over the two-week interval, the median affective-cognitive rank difference score, based upon the data collected at the first session, was 2.5. For the subjects who showed significant change in affect over the two-week interval the comparable median is 7.5. The overall difference in original affective-cognitive discrepancy between the "changer" and "nonchanger" groups has a Chi Square value of 8.4 ($p < .01$).

A comparable analysis was undertaken with another issue: the proposal that Yale University become coeducational, as viewed by a sample of male undergraduates at that institution. Here we used a more stringent criterion of change and stability. Subjects took both affective and cognitive measures on this issue and then were retested with the same instruments three weeks later. The distributions for both affective and cognitive change were compiled. Subjects who were in the lower halves of the distributions for *both* affective and cognitive change were designated as the Low Change group. Subjects who were in the higher halves on either affective or cognitive change or both were designated as the High Change group. Comparing the members of the two groups on the rank differences between the affective and cognitive scores obtained from them on the first administration of these measures, we find far greater initial affective-cognitive inconsistency in the High Change group. ($\chi^2 = 11.66$, $p < .001$). The median rank difference between affect and cognition scores is 2.25 for the Low Change group and 8.5 for the High Change group.

These and similar findings on other issues seem then to confirm the following simple hypothesis: When an elicited self-report of attitudinal affect is experienced (or presented) in a context of consistent cognitions, that stated affect will be more truly reflective of a dispositional orientation toward that object than when consistent cognitive supports are lacking.

An important clarification is required. By 'consistent cognitive supports' I do not necessarily mean a totally univalent structure in which all the component beliefs relate the positive attitude object to other positive affective standards and the negative one to other negative standards. This is the type of consistent cognitive support which one would expect to find (and which we did find in the aforementioned studies) for stable and extreme affective orientations.

But where a moderate positive or negative affective orientation is stably held the supporting pattern of cognitions may well have some few negative or positive elements, respectively; also some of the component beliefs are likely to be held at low levels of intensity. Again such expectations are confirmed by the data from the studies I have been reviewing here.

To the general hypothesis that affective-cognitive consistency is the hallmark of stable affective orientations (i.e., of true 'attitudes' as distinguished from situationally determined responses to an affective measure) one may add an obvious auxiliary prediction. A person who, when tested, reveals a lack of affective-cognitive consistency toward some social object should be far more easily influenced by persuasive communications concerning that object. Data collected by Scott (1959), and interpreted by him in other terms, seem to confirm this prediction; and in a study conducted by myself and Mrs. Lila Lowenherz similar evidence was obtained.

In this latter study female college students took our standardized affective and cognitive measures with reference to a then current proposal for an important change in New York state law. The majority of the subjects indicated that they were opposed (i.e., they chose negative positions on the affect scale) to the advocated change. A few weeks later they read persuasive material that summarized evidence indicating that in their own reference group (i.e., students at their college) a large majority favored the proposed new law. Then the affective and cognitive measures were readministered.

The experimental subjects had been divided into three treatment groups. In one of these they had been given a communication urging them to take a stance of 'open mindedness' to new information about other people's attitudes. In this group of 25 subjects, 11 showed change on the affect scale in the propagandized direction, while the remaining 14 showed no change. Comparing the changers to the nonchangers, we find that in their original affective and cognitive responses, as tested in the premanipulation phase, the former group had a median affect-cognition rank discrepancy of 5.5 and the latter of 2.5. This difference between the groups has a chance probability of .02. A comparable analysis based upon division of the population into those who show low and high change in their beliefs about the advocated new law produces similar findings, the high changers being those who originally showed higher affective-cognitive inconsistency ($p < .002$).

Thus the data seem to show that whether through the sheer lapse of time or in response to persuasive communication, affective responses that are not backed by, or integrated with, a set of consistent cognitive supports will show high variability. Ought one to argue from this that internally consistent attitudes are stable and that comparatively inconsistent ones are always unstable? I think not. As I have already suggested, an internally inconsistent attitude, if it does not transcend the individual's tolerance limit, will usually remain stable; and if that limit is transcended it will undergo reorganization that will render it more consistent. To be sure, when a subject answers attitude inquiries of the sort presented by the affective and cognitive measures employed in these studies, he may be forced to an examination of previously implicit, suprathreshold inconsistency—and this may account for the further affective or cognitive changes observed at a later date.

This may well have occurred with some of the High Change subjects in these studies. But what seems even more likely, given the comparatively low salience of the issues used, is the possibility that many of the High Change subjects experienced the sort of motivational pattern that I have already suggested to be a common, if usually unsuspected, feature of the attitude measurement situation: i.e., the need to cover up indifference and confusion when one is being questioned about one's attitudes. The subject who knows little and cares less about federal medical insurance, the Algerian situation, or some new legal proposal has two basic alternatives when he is confronted by an interview or questionnaire probing his 'attitudes' on such issues. He can directly confess his neutrality and further acknowledge his emptiness of mind on the issue; or he can attempt to improvise a response pattern by relying on cues from the interviewer or questionnaire, or by referring to general value standards which are real to him and toward which he will try to draw the social issue so as to give it at least temporary evaluation. Or perhaps he will simply process the decision that is being forced on him by asking himself "how do (or should) people like me judge matters like this one?"

Any one or a combination of these tactics will suffice to provide some basis for emitting a nonneutral (but also *invalid*) self-characterization regarding one's supposedly accustomed affective orientation toward an object. But when asked to go further and display his *beliefs* about the object under consideration, the individual will be comparatively barren of associative material. Some self-correcting tendency toward honesty may then influence him to rate his proffered 'cognitions' as uncertainly held; or the comparatively greater complexity of the cognitive self-report task may set him to resonating cognitive considerations that serve to undermine as well as support his stated affective orientation. Or, given his comparatively low past exposure to arguments bearing upon the issue and his inadequate rehearsal of such arguments, he may simply fail in the attempt to summon up a repertoire of convincing (i.e., consistent) cognitive supports for his stated affective judgment of the object.

The likely consequence will be that such a subject or respondent, though motivated to represent himself as having a stable and organized attitudinal orientation, will, in his attempted cognitive elaboration of it, produce a pattern of cognitive responses that is either somewhat or grossly inconsistent with his stated affective position. Behind such a show of internally inconsistent attitudinal responsiveness, then, there may lie a vacuity, or 'emptiness of mind' at least on the particular attitude issue in question.

This then is one way of accounting for the research finding that instability of attitudinal response over time is associated with initial affective-cognitive inconsistency. It stands alongside the other possibility that I have already indicated: i.e., that the encounter with intraattitudinal inconsistency (an encounter often forced by having to respond to a searching attitude measure), if it is of suprathreshold magnitude, will set in motion a process of attitude reorganization which often leads to attitude change.

I would guess that the present data demonstrating the relation between initial affective-cognitive response inconsistency and subsequent change in affective responding reflects both these processes, though each is operating in separate subjects. With the measurement techniques employed in these studies there is no fully trustworthy way of distinguishing between 'attitude change' and attitude change, i.e., we cannot readily discriminate between the kind of shifting with the social wind that is the hallmark of attitudinal vacuity and the sort of more validly-indexed change that occurs when intra-attitudinal inconsistency has reached a motivating level. Extensive interview inquiry will, I think, often make this discrimination more feasible.

At any rate, though both of these posited processes are encompassed in the general theoretical view that I have been working with, there are reasons for focussing on the vacuity interpretation here. One such reason is that at least two of the three actual issues used in the present studies were not (as, in both public opinion and experimental attitude research, they often are not) extremely salient and central ones; and where issues are peripheral but an investigator requires us to respond to them, the press toward disguising our indifference and confusion by the emission of pseudoattitudinal responses will probably play an important role. A second reason for focussing on the vacuity interpretation is, simply, that it is a counterweight to the ready tendency on the part of many researchers to reify their measurement instruments; to expect that any responses elicited by an attitude scale are thereby and necessarily indices of attitudes.

I shall therefore linger a bit longer over the vacuity problem by offering a few points in summary of the general view that I have been working toward; and from this summary I shall attempt to derive at least one important prescriptive recommendation.

To recapitulate, then, I would suggest that the following points (offered assertively though, to be sure, they require further verification) are worth serious consideration: Vacuity (i.e., indifference and lack of stable affective-cognitive orientation) toward social objects and issues is rather common. Both because of situational pressures, and because of self-imposed demands for appearing committed and responsive, persons who are vacuously disoriented on particular issues will often veil this fact from others, and sometimes from themselves, by improvising a set of pseudoattitudinal responses. Over even quite short spans of time, and also upon receipt of "persuasive communications," persons with originally vacuous orientations will show considerable shifting in their responses to attitude measures. Where such shifts are unhesitatingly interpreted as true attitudinal change, or where the initial responses are interpreted as accurate indices of attitudinal orientation, the likelihood increases that investigators will draw incorrect conclusions. These conclusions may concern the content of public opinion or change in patterns of public opinion; they may also concern the validity or invalidity of hypotheses tested in controlled attitude change experiments.

The demonstration, through studies reported here, that inconsistency between self-reports of affect and cognition, respectively, predicts the instability of both affective and cognitive responses, suggests the possibility of an important methodological corrective to this set of problems. It is simply that in attitude research one should spend considerable effort in eliciting the subjects' cognitions about the relations between the attitude object and other objects; and that where evidence of sizeable affective-cognitive inconsistency is observed one should take seriously the possibility that the subject's self-reports are invalid—that he may be covering over an essentially vacuous, nonattitudinal orientation.

Further tests of this diagnosis are, of course, possible once it has been formulated. For example, in the survey interview, one could readily apply slight pressure toward change. (E.g., if the respondent cannot offer any arguments in support of his stated attitude or offers very inconsistent ones, the interviewer can be instructed to say: "Did I misunderstand your

view on this issue? It's so different from what most people seem to feel."
A quick and facile shift by the respondent would add weight to the
vacuity diagnosis.)

I am, of course, aware that in the foregoing comments I have simplified
some quite complicated matters. At least two possible caveats must now
be examined, even if they are not submitted to close discussion. First in
importance, I think, is the fact that the present view seems to rest on the
assumption that *all* true attitudes must have cognitive as well as affective
content. Though this is by now a rather widely shared view, as evidenced
by the popularity of attitude definitions which stress a tripartite integration
of affective, cognitive, and behavioral components, it is challenged by the
argument that certain classes of stable affective orientations (e.g., 'phobias')
seem to lack detailed and supportive cognitive content. Katz and Stotland
(1959) go somewhat further in suggesting that some kinds of social attitudes
are cognition laden while others are not. My own best guess on this matter
is that it may be in the nature of man (and, even more clearly, it is in
the nature of *socialized* man) that he holds himself to the standard of
being able to justify or argue for his affective commitments in the social
realm. Those affective commitments need not always be generated by the
prior development of beliefs about the object of affect; such beliefs may
be elaborated or learned only after normative induction, social reinforcement, or inner conflict have generated a comparatively stable affective
commitment. This very distinction is the one that I attempted to codify
through the conceptualization (see pp. 77–78) of two basic attitude dynamic
sequences. Also we must acknowledge that different individuals, and
different attitude objects for the same individual, will show richer and
poorer cognitive content. But for any particular social issue or object as
confronted by a sample drawn from some fairly uniform sector of the
population (e.g., college students recruited for attitude change experiments,
or survey respondents recruited from some particular sector of the total
national population) one can reasonably expect that those who show less
intraattitudinal consistency are, on the average, less invested in the issue
and less likely to have a presently stable orientation toward it. It is
possible then to circumvent the more difficult theoretical question of
whether truly cognitionless affective dispositions can ever exist (I remain
persuaded that they cannot), and yet find support for the present approach
as a relevant aid in finding a way out of the measurement and interpretation dilemmas that continue to burden attitude research.

A second, and more narrowly technical, question needs to be confronted
here. Of the simple studies highlighted in this section one must ask: may
not the affective response shifts found in the subjects merely be an instance
of test-retest regression toward the mean? This, in fact, seems quite unlikely.
If it were the case we would expect such regressive change to occur just
as often with those who showed high initial affective-cognitive consistency
as with those who did not. The data are clearly otherwise. Further we
would expect those who showed affect change in the simple test-retest
studies to more often move toward neutral than toward extreme positions on
the affect scale. Excluding those who initially gave extreme affective responses (since they can only move toward or beyond the neutral point) we
find as much response change going toward greater extremity as toward
neutrality.

What I have attempted to show in this section is that the affective-cognitive consistency theory does have some promise for clarifying the relation between inner consistency in a pattern of attitudinal responses and the stability of those responses over time. Working from data that reflect a consistency-stability relationship, I have elaborated the view (still conjectural and requiring further empirical investigation) that vacuity masquerading as attitudinal commitment is a common basis for the observed relationship; and I have tried to show that this, in turn, has important consequences for rectifying some current inadequacies in attitude measurement techniques. The most important practical recommendation is that in attitude measurement we should, wherever and however possible, elicit the cognitive, rather than just the affective, content of the person's attitude; and that by so doing we put ourselves in a far better position to decide whether he has any attitude at all.

HEDONISM AND INCONSISTENCY TOLERANCE

All consistency theories, having put forth the axiomatic proposition that inconsistency is motivating, then go on to acknowledge that it is often nothing of the sort. The artfulness and adequacy of each of the consistency theories may well depend upon how it conceptualizes the variables that will render an encountered inconsistency tolerable or intolerable.

In my efforts at developing a general statement of the affective-cognitive consistency approach (Rosenberg, 1960a, c) and simultaneously in a collaborative effort with Carl Hovland (Hovland & Rosenberg, 1960), I employed the concept of a threshold of intolerance for inconsistency. The height of this assumed threshold was conceived to vary as a function of general personality attributes, situational factors, and attributes of the attitude itself. By the latter I meant, particularly, aspects of its structure (e.g., the number and intensity of its cognitive components) and its functional importance to the attitude holder.

The significance of yet another class of attitude content variables was suggested by the results of some studies I have already referred to: namely, the "Fenwick" experiments (Rosenberg & Abelson, 1960). As Abelson and I generalized from the relevant findings:

> ... subjects seek not only the attainment of cognitive balance and consistency but they seek also to alter their beliefs and evaluations in ways that will maximize expected gain and minimize expected loss; when both forces converge so that they may be gratified through the same change or changes a formally "balanced" outcome will be achieved; when these forces diverge the typical outcome will not meet the requirements of a simple formal definition of cognitive balance (page 145).

When we spoke of the cognitive tendency "to maximize expected gain and minimize expected loss" we laid the groundwork for a distinction that I later attempted to elaborate in terms of "hedonic" and "antihedonic" attitudinal cognitions, with each type capable of being either internally consistent or inconsistent.

In what follows I shall explicate these concepts, state some theoretically derived predictions employing them, present some research findings supporting those predictions, and then sketch certain more general propositions which were suggested by these findings and which serve to extend the affective-cognitive consistency theory. In doing this I shall rely heavily upon an earlier paper (Rosenberg, 1965c) borrowing both from its wording and its argument at a number of points.

Some initial definitions are required. We focus now not upon a total affective cognitive structure but upon the molar unit of such structures, the *attitudinal cognition*. By this I mean the perceived relationship between two affectively significant objects (e.g., "Senator Fulbright has condemned air pollution" or "The distinguished firm of Schlag and Sons has marketed a completely worthless sphygmomanometer"). Attitudinal cognitions, then, are nothing more or less than the object-relation-object units that comprise a radial affective-cognitive structure or that fill the broader sectors of the attitudinal cognitorium. In the extended metaphor I employed earlier the attitudinal cognition was represented by the two affectively signed disks connected by a red or green string.

If each of the three judgments incorporated in such a unit (the affective judgments elicited by two respective objects and the judgment of the relation between them) is given simple binary representation, the number of possible types is simply the cube value of two.

Four of these are generally acknowledged to be consistent (i.e., psychologically 'balanced' or, if one ignores the magnitude variability problem, 'congruous'). They are: + − − ("The admirable Holmes attempts to punish the evil Dr. Moriarty"); − − + ("The evil Dr. Moriarty tries to assassinate the admirable Holmes"); + + + ("The admirable Holmes is fond of loyal old Dr. Watson"); − + − ("The evil Dr. Moriarty has committed an unspeakable crime"). The remaining four are generally taken to be inconsistent and thus less tolerable, more motivating: + + − ("The admirable Holmes is a dope addict"); + − + ("The admirable Holmes is churlish toward loyal old Dr. Watson"); − + + ("The evil Dr. Moriarty has saved the life of Dr. Watson"); − − − ("The evil Dr. Moriarty condemns all detractors of noble Queen Victoria").

Though the last four cognitions are all internally inconsistent (i.e., they feature either a negative relationship between same signed objects or a positive one between opposite signed objects), the first two of these are antihedonic in import while the remaining two carry an hedonic implication. By this I mean that + + − and + − +, given their present illustrative content or any other, convey (or, with other types of content, could 'predict') some state of loss or frustration. What renders them inconsistent is, of course, the fact that the source of the imposed loss or frustration is an object (say "the admirable Holmes") that is held in positive affective regard.

On the other hand, − + + and − − − achieve inconsistency by the opposite route: a negatively regarded object is the source of some present or predicted gain or need reduction. Clearly, hedonic or antihedonic implication is present only where such directionality is built into the attitudinal cognition. Also it should be obvious that the cognition is hedonic when its second and third signs multiply to a positive product and antihedonic when the product is negative. (A similar distinction is made by Newcomb in Chapter 2 in his analysis of *POX* triads.)

The relevance of these points for the problem of specifying thresholds of intolerance for inconsistency lies in the idea that among the forces that may compete with the arousal of intolerance for inconsistency is the individual's need to so construct 'reality' as to emphasize hopeful prospects. Where need reduction or generally benign and supportive events are observed or expected, the fact that these are 'wrapped in a paradox' may well render the paradox more acceptable than it would be otherwise. Thus, the psychological leaning toward wish fulfillment may interfere with the inconsistency arousal—consistency restoration dynamic.

On the basis of this sort of reasoning I propounded the following hypothesis: *intolerance for inconsistency will be of lesser intensity (and thus less likely to motivate cognitive reorganization) if the attitudinal cognition conveys a hedonic assertion or promise of gain and of greater intensity (and thus more likely to motivate cognitive reorganization) if it conveys an antihedonic assertion or promise of loss.* To return to the illustrative content borrowed from Conan Doyle, one should be less bothered by the inconsistency involved in Moriarty doing good than in Holmes doing evil; and, in consequence, cognitions of the latter type should be less stable (more prone to reinterpretations such as "Holmes only seemed churlish to Watson; in fact he was protecting him from the invisible assailant") than the former.

However, are any of these cognitions, in the particular illustrative forms I have employed, intolerably inconsistent? That would depend, I suppose, on how closely one stood to Holmes and Moriarty, how much they figured in one's personal welfare. Surely the discovery of Holmes doing evil or Moriarty doing good would generate intolerable inconsistency for Dr. Watson or, perhaps, even for a member of "The Baker Street Irregulars," an organized group of Holmes enthusiasts whose playful literary celebrations and extensions of Conan Doyle's melodrama have rendered the characters more real than they are to most of us.

However, the ordinary, distant reader might well be able to tolerate "The admirable Holmes was churlish to loyal old Dr. Watson." But would he remain unmotivated to reduce such an encountered inconsistency as: "The admirable and wise psychologist Plimsol has just written a completely negative review of my new book"? Both cognitions are of the inconsistent and antihedonic form $+ - +$, but the former has general (or impersonal) reference while the latter is personal in the sense that it imposes loss or frustration directly upon the cognizer.

From this distinction we can readily derive an hypothesis parallel to the earlier one: *intolerance for inconsistency will be of lesser intensity (and thus less likely to motivate cognitive reorganization) if the attitudinal cognition is of general content, and of greater intensity if it is of personal content.*

A first test of these hypotheses (Rosenberg, 1965c) focussed upon the directly derivable predictions that, when persons were required to rate hypothetical cognitions they would report themselves more 'bothered' by inconsistency within antihedonic as compared to hedonic cognitions, and by inconsistency within personal as compared to general cognitions. Also it was predicted that these two content variables would be found to interact in a significant way.

Two different groups of subjects were administered a 16-item questionnaire. Each item presented a hypothetical inconsistent attitudinal cognition which the subject was to rate on a scale from 0 to 10 for the "degree to which the illogical nature of this situation bothers me." The instructions laid very heavy stress upon the point that the cognitions were to be judged for the extent to which their inconsistency (rather than their content) was bothersome. A control condition was employed to check upon the possibility that the subjects, despite this clear and strong directive, might rate the items for their pleasant or unpleasant content rather than for the pleasantness or unpleasantness of the inconsistency they aroused. The control data seemed to establish that this was not the case and thus added some further presumptive validity to the questionnaire used with the main groups of subjects.[3]

The items that comprised the main questionnaire fall into four distinctive groups: hedonic-personal, hedonic-general, antihedonic-personal, and antihedonic-general. Each of these groups contained two types of inconsistent cognitions: $- + +$ and $- - -$ for both the personal and general hedonic groups; and $+ - +$ and $+ + -$ for both the personal and general antihedonic groups. In turn each of these four basic types was represented by two separate items. Furthermore, the content of the hedonic-personal and antihedonic-personal items was held parallel and the same was true as between the hedonic-general and the antihedonic-general items. Eight of the 16 items are reproduced below to give a clearer idea of the content and structure of the questionnaire (Rosenberg, 1965c).

Hedonic-personal	Antihedonic-personal
G.L. is a fellow student (same sex as you) toward whom you have long felt extreme dislike. You learn on reliable authority that G.L. feels strong and sincere admiration and respect for you. $(- + +)$	J.T. is a fellow student (same sex as you) toward whom you have long felt great admiration and respect. You learn on reliable authority that J.T. feels strong and sincere dislike for you. $(+ - +)$
The graduate student assistant in a course you have been taking is a person whom you and all your classmates consider, with good reason, to be a loathsome and despicable person. At the end of the semester the professor who conducts the course	The graduate student assistant in a course you have been taking is a person whom you and all your classmates consider, with good reason, to be an admirable and inspiring person. At the end of the semester the professor who conducts the course

[3] The basic procedure followed with the separate group of 87 control subjects (both male and female) was to present them with a questionnaire composed of eight inconsistent items and eight other parallel but consistent ones, the placement of the items in each pair having been randomized. Within each pair, both items were either hedonic or antihedonic and either personal or general in content. But one was inconsistent and the other consistent (by virtue of a reversal of the affective sign of its first object). Instructed to rate such items for "botherment at inconsistency," the control subjects rated the inconsistent item in each pair significantly more bothersome than the consistent one. If, despite their instructions, they had been rating the items basically for their hedonic pleasantness or antihedonic unpleasantness, the significant mean differences within each item pair would not have been obtained.

is about to give you a failing grade. You learn on reliable authority that the assistant has interceded and that after great effort has dissuaded the professor from giving you a failing grade. (— — —)

is about to give you a passing grade. You learn on reliable authority that the assistant has interceded and that after great effort has persuaded the professor to give you a failing grade. (+ + —)

Hedonic-general

You have a strong dislike for political dictators. You regard a certain Latin-American dictator as a particularly unsavory type. You read a highly reliable series of articles showing that this same dictator has achieved wonders in improving the standard of living in his country since coming to power. (— + +)

Unless a large sum of money can soon be found a small but very distinguished private museum will have to close down and its wonderful and unique collection be sold to pay off debts. A large and wealthy corportion that knowledgeable people rightly consider to be quite socially irresponsible and highly insensitive to public welfare is approached as a last expedient. That corporation contributes all the necessary funds with no strings attached and this prevents the closing of the museum. (— — —)

Antihedonic-general

You have a great liking for the president of a certain Latin-American country. You read a highly reliable series of articles showing that this same president since being elected has consistently opposed and blocked programs which would have vastly improved the standard of living in his country. (+ — +)

Unless a large sum of money can soon be found a small but very distinguished private museum will have to close down and its wonderful and unique collection be sold to pay off debts. A large and wealthy corporation that knowledgeable people rightly consider to be quite socially responsible and highly sensitive to public welfare is approached as a last expedient. That corporation refuses to donate any money; because of this action the museum is forced to close down. (+ + —)

Separate administration of the questionnaire and separate analyses of variance were conducted for a group of 32 male and 104 female college students, respectively.

In both multivariate analyses the hedonic-antihedonic variable controls a significant proportion of the total variance in the "botherment at inconsistency" ratings ($p < .001$ for the male sample; $p < .001$ for the female sample). The effect, as predicted, is that the subjects report greater tension over inconsistency for the antihedonic than for the hedonic items. For the males the mean botherment ratings for the eight antihedonic and the eight hedonic items are 5.90 and 3.48, respectively. For the females the comparable means are 6.30 and 3.59. Similarly, with each matched pair of items, and with both males and females, the hedonic form arouses less reported tension than the antihedonic one.

The personal-general variable is also found to control a significant proportion of the total variance, and again the F values for each of the two groups respectively have a probability of less than .001. As predicted, the eight general items arouse less botherment at inconsistency than do the eight personal items. For the males the means for the general and personal items, respectively, are 3.80 and 5.60. For the females the comparable means are 3.20 and 5.71.

Inspection of the item means reveals the same ordering in each subject group. For both males and females the greatest tension over inconsistency was reported for the antihedonic-personal items and then, in descending order, for the items that were: antihedonic-general; hedonic-personal; hedonic-general.

Analysis of variance also discloses a significant interaction between the two content variables ($p < .01$ for the male group; $p < .001$ for the females). This interaction effect can best be understood as reflecting this fact: the difference between the means for hedonic and antihedonic items is greater when they are of personal import (e.g., for the male group this difference is 2.96 scale points) than when they are of general import (e.g., for the males this difference is 1.88 scale points).

The psychological meaning of these last interaction findings may well be that we are bothered by inconsistencies both in cognitions affecting our own welfare and also in others that do not affect our welfare; and that, typically, the former type of encounter with inconsistency is more upsetting, or that we respond to it at lower threshold levels than the latter. However, alternatively, it should be noted that issues of 'general' reference are probably often identified with, and are often cathected as objects relevant to one's personal interests or to the maintenance and expressive externalization of one's values and ideals. Perhaps when issues are truly and totally impersonal in their implications we would not be capable of any degree of tension over inconsistent cognitions bearing upon those issues. The question lies beyond the present data, but my conjecture would be against this possibility; for I think it reasonable to speculate that inconsistency in itself, whether its content is purely general or purely hedonic or both, stirs some sense, however slight and temporary, of the non-fitness of things and arouses some prompting toward cognitive rectification. However, such promptings are readily put aside and the sense of 'non-fitness' is easily consigned to the category of the 'bearable.'

The problem that faces all of the consistency models is to delineate the variables that tend to render the encounter with inconsistency more or less bearable—and particulary to delineate how such variables are likely to affect the acceptance of inconsistent cognitions into a previously stabilized structure and how they will further influence the processing of such inconsistent cognitions once they have been accepted as veridical. It is to the implications of the present data for certain aspects of this problem that I shall now turn.

In recapitulating the main propositions of the affective-cognitive consistency approach I earlier described two basic sequences of attitude change. The more commonly observed of these is the one in which the establishment of inconsistent cognitions about the attitude object fosters a consistency-restoring shift in the affective response that it elicits.

The theory, as originally propounded, takes note of the obvious fact that rejection of inconsistency-generating cognitions is the first line of defense, but that nevertheless such new cognitions may get through the defensive barrier. This will depend, of course, upon how compelling the supporting evidence is, how expert or authoritative the source, and also how important the original attitude is in the maintenance of the person's identity. But, assuming a constant level for these and other variables that are likely to affect the person's openness to inconsistent attitudinal cognitions, will the *content* of those cognitions have any bearing upon their acceptability? The data and hypotheses that have been reviewed in this section have seemed to me to suggest that a positive answer is required, at least as regards the hedonic-antihedonic and personal-general dimensions of content variability. And by a fairly straightforward deductive route this leads us toward a rather surprising proposition which can be added onto the original ones that comprise the affective-cognitive theory.

The proposition is that *the production, through persuasive communication, of intraattitudinal inconsistency will be easier in the case of originally negative attitudes than in the case of originally positive ones.* This is because in the case of a negative attitude the new inconsistency-generating cognitions that one would attempt to establish would have to be hedonic in import; for any antihedonic assertion would merely link the negatively evaluated object with a state of loss or frustration, and this would be consistent with that negative evaluation. Inconsistency will be created in the structure organized around the object "the evil Dr. Moriarty" if one comes to believe that he "saved the life of Dr. Watson," but not if one learns that he "attempted to assassinate Holmes." On the same grounds, only antihedonic cognitive assertions will generate inconsistency in the case of a positive attitude.

Now as we have hypothesized and apparently demonstrated, antihedonic inconsistency creates greater tension than hedonic inconsistency. On this basis we would have to expect that the new cognitions required to produce inconsistency in a positive attitude would be more difficult to establish, would be less readily 'introjected' and more readily rejected than those required in the case of a negative attitude. What this suggests, then, is that when two attitudes are opposite in sign (but equal in intensity and in personal or general reference) it will take more effort and skill, or more intrinsically persuasive communications, to produce some degree of internal inconsistency in the positive attitude than in the negative one.

In turn it might seem to follow that negative attitudes are more readily changed through inconsistency arousal than are positive ones. But this would seem to be a mistaken conclusion. To establish inconsistent cognitions within a previously stable structure does not necessarily produce overall attitude change. As I have pointed out, the affective-cognitive consistency view assumes (and much evidence confirms) that introjected inconsistent attitudinal cognitions need to accumulate in number and increase in intensity until some threshold of intolerance is transgressed; and only then will overall attitude change become likely. If we grant that antihedonic inconsistent cognitions are more tension-arousing than hedonic ones, then the likelihood that reorganizing change will occur within an affective-cognitive radial structure would be greater for the positive attitude (in which the introjected inconsistent cognitions are, of necessity, antihedonic) than for the negative attitude (in which they are necessarily hedonic).

Thus a second proposition emerges: *When equal degrees of internal inconsistency have been generated, the originally positive attitude is more likely to change toward the negative than will the originally negative one change toward the positive.* However, this proposition would only apply when, as the original theory suggests, the new inconsistent cognitions are 'irreversible' ones; otherwise consistency-restoring attitude reorganization can be more economically achieved by expelling the new cognitive elements from the affective-cognitive structure and restoring it to its initial stable state.

Crudely restated, the import of these two propositions is that, with initially equal intensity, negative attitudes are more 'penetrable' but, in final terms, less readily changeable than positive ones. Two further propositions of identical form could be formulated for the case of personal as opposed to general attitudes, when these are equal in intensity and affective sign. Since personal inconsistent cognitions arouse more tension than general ones, attitudes toward objects of personal significance could be expected to be less readily penetrated, but, if penetrated, more readily changed, than attitudes toward general objects.

These propositions do seem to be loosely confirmed by certain common impressions. For example, people do *seem* somewhat more ready to believe that there is "good in the worst of us" than that there is "bad in the best of us." But when they have become irreversibly persuaded that persons they once cherished or admired are characterized by evil, harmful, or morally unacceptable attributes they often *seem* to undergo more extreme affective shifts than when they have come to believe that a disfavored person has some important positive attributes. Or do they really? These new propositions must be submitted to close experimental test before they can be offered as more than informed conjectures. This testing will be difficult because it requires careful control of both initial intensity and structural complexity of the attitudes and also a matching of the intrinsic persuasiveness of communications designed to implant both hedonic and antihedonic, and personal and general, inconsistent attitudinal cognitions. However, the potential gain seems worth the effort and I hope that I, or others, will be able to carry this effort forward.

NONLINEARITY AND THE TRANSGRESSION OF INTOLERANCE THRESHOLDS

Toward the end of the last section I drew the distinction between the 'penetration' of an affective cognitive structure and its reorganization. Linear models of the additive sort profferred by Fishbein (1963; Fishbein & Hunter, 1964) or of the averaging variety represented by the work of Anderson (see Chapter 73) implicitly deny this distinction. The acceptance of any new favorable or unfavorable cognition about an 'attitude object' will, according to these models and the data offered in support of them, produce some proportionate and usually slight change in the 'evaluation' of the object.

In my discussion of these models in Chapter 76 I suggest that they may be applicable only for the kinds of objects and situations with which they have actually been tested; i.e., with 'new' rather than 'old' objects, and in a context in which the subject believes that he is expected to shift his judgments in accordance with the information that he is given.

By new objects I mean, simply, nonattitudinal ones which have heretofore been of indifferent interest (in the usual linear model studies they are hypothetical persons); and by old objects, I mean, of course, ones which are centrally located in some already existing and comparatively stable affective-cognitive structure.

My basic theoretical view of the nature of such structures is that they resist change, which is not to say that they cannot be changed. But, as I have already suggested, the consistency theories have been rather neglectful of two basic questions about the attitude change process: They have not been particularly clear in specifying *when* attitudes will change in response to inconsistency arousal; nor have they said enough about *how* attitudes will change once inconsistency arousal has become motivating.

The early articles presenting the affective-cognitive consistency theory (Rosenberg, 1956, 1960a) shared in this general deficiency. To be sure, in one publication (Rosenberg, 1960c) from which I have already quoted (see page 75) I did suggest that the encounter with a motivating degree of affective-cognitive inconsistency will lead either to "rejection of the [inconsistency-generating] communications ...; fragmentation of the attitude ...; or accommodation to the original inconsistency-producing change so that a new attitude, consistent with that change, is now stabilized." A further implication was that defense against intraattitudinal inconsistency begins with rejection, and, where this fails, proceeds to the rather rare strategem of fragmentation or to the more common one of 'attitude change.'

But greater theoretical clarity is required on the question of alternative modes of response to inconsistency. Thus my aspiration in this section is to move toward the delineation, in more precise theoretical terms, of some basic relationships between initial attitude structure and significance on the one hand, and, on the other, the type of inconsistency reduction that is most likely to obtain.

My treatment of this problem will be comparatively brief because the main propositions I shall present are easily stated, are partially continuous with ones presented earlier, and have not yet been put to direct experimental test. Also in what follows I am restricting myself to the Sequence 1 type of attitude dynamic: that in which the initial acceptance of inconsistency-generating cognitions leads (or fails to lead) to a consistency-restoring change in affect toward the attitude object.

At a number of points so far I have invoked the idea that affective-cognitive inconsistency is often tolerable and that it does not motivate consistency-restoring activity unless or until it becomes intolerable. Thus, in the last section I presented data showing that hedonic inconsistency is more tolerable than antihedonic and that inconsistent cognitions of general import are more tolerable than those of personal import. Also I have introduced the concept of a threshold of intolerance for intraattitudinal inconsistency. As Hovland and I (Hovland & Rosenberg, 1960) suggested, the height of this threshold (i.e., the amount of affective-cognitive inconsistency required to energize attitude reorganizing symbolic activity) will probably vary as a function of the person, the attitude, and the situation.

Some persons will probably be generally tolerant of sizeable inconsistency while others will be extremely vigilant against it. Evidence supportive of this view is to be found in the related work on intolerance for ambiguity (Adorno *et al.*, 1950) and in Rokeach's (1960) studies on dogmatism. At the same time it seems reasonable to assume that *within* a given individual the intolerance threshold will vary from attitude to attitude. Those attitudes that are held with extremity, or that are imporant in the maintenance of the person's self concept or of his significant group loyalties, will probably be characterized by lower intolerance threshold levels; because they render significant service in the individual's adaptive functioning, they tend to be defended against the inner disruption that would be generated by even partial inconsistency.

These last speculations may seem to have paradoxical consequences; they could be interpreted to suggest that with dogmatic, cognitively rigid persons or with particularly important attitudes (both of these having been characterized as featuring low thresholds of intolerance for inconsistency) attitude change would be particularly common. But both research data and everyday experience appear to confirm the opposite relationship: such persons and such attitudes are usually quite resistant to change. The paradox dissolves when we recall that attitude change (in the sense, for example, of affect shifting toward coordination with previously established, inconsistency-generating cognitions) is by no means the only way in which the person responds to intraattitudinal inconsistency. Fragmentation of affective-cognitive structures can occur (for example, the main finding in the study reported by Ostrom and Brock in Chapter 28 could be interpreted as a reflection of this process). Even more likely is the ultimate rejection of the new beliefs or new affective assertions whose temporary internalization generated the motivating patterns of inconsistency.

With these considerations in mind, and neglecting the fragmentation alternative, I should like to pose the following simple and, I think, quite useful proposition: *Consistency restoration through reestablishment of the original affective-cognitive structure will be more likely when a low rather than high intolerance for inconsistency threshold has been transgressed; consistency restoration through 'attitude change' will be more likely when a high rather than low intolerance threshold has been transgressed.*[4]

This proposition accords with the observation that nondogmatic persons are more likely to show attitude change. Indeed, it comes close to being a theoretical elaboration of that observation. It also accords with the common observation that peripheral attitudes, ones not anchored in the self concept and ones possessing little ego defensive utility, are comparatively easy to change.

The distinction between high and low threshold attitudes and the ways in which they are typically processed is, of course, a reduction to simplified ideal types. This is merely an expository tactic used to characterize an assumed continuum of threshold values over which continuum the probability of one pattern of response to suprathreshold inconsistency would increase as the probability of the other decreased.

Filling out this two-type view are certain related propositions about the initial 'penetrability' of low threshold and high threshold attitudes. In the case of attitudes with low intolerance thresholds one would expect to find very close and stable affective-cognitive coordination and also, in some cases, a rather simple set of strong cognitive supports. Vigilance against inconsistency-generating inputs will usually be quite thoroughgoing and

---

[4] It should be added that these propositions do not imply that true attitude change cannot occur in low threshold, egocentral attitude areas. To the contrary, though such change is less frequent than in high threshold attitude areas, when it does occur it often seems to be quite pervasive and profound. Some further considerations accounting for this fact are developed later in this section.

constant—and most communications or experiences capable of generating inconsistency will either be rejected out of hand or, if temporarily accepted, will be likely to be rejected once the intolerance threshold has been transgressed and the work of consistency restoration has begun.

Yet it does often happen that some such new elements have been *irreversibly* introjected by virtue of their having been compellingly and continuously reinforced by aspects of the person's informational or social environment. Under such circumstances the low intolerance level of the attitude will foster early and insistent efforts at affective-cognitive reorganization; and, assuming that the discrepant elements remain incapable of rejection or of evasion through affective-cognitive fragmentation, the outcome is likely to be rather decisive and thoroughgoing attitude change—for in a low threshold attitude realm a satisfying (subthreshold) restoration of consistency will not be achieved until something close to inner univalent order has been reestablished.

To illustrate these points let us consider a long time member of the White Knights of the Rumpled Sheet, one whose intense anti-Negro attitude is normatively grounded and features high internal consistency. If drafted and sent into battle with brave Negro companions one of whom sacrifices his life to save that of our bigoted protagonist (or if our protagonist is loyally religious and is suddenly confronted with a new fundamentalist preacher who argues constantly and forcefully that Christ enjoins the white to love his Negro brother) the unrelieved presence of such inconsistency-generating content will activate his intolerance for inconsistency (the threshold being vigilantly low) and the overall result may well be 'conversion' to a deeply altered anti-anti-Negro attitude pattern.

On the other hand, when the intolerance threshold is high (and, thus when the attitude is usually at least somewhat peripheral and of less than major importance in the person's ego defensive system) inconsistency-generating inputs will be more readily accepted and will lead less readily to early consistency restoring efforts than in the former case. Yet even high intolerance thresholds can be transgressed; and when this occurs recourse to attitude change (i.e., shifting of affect toward consistency with the new cognitions) will be rather common and comparatively uneffortful.

To illustrate this type let us consider again our hypothetical member of the White Knights of the Rumpled Sheet. Apart from his intense and central attitude toward Negroes he also has a moderately negative attitude toward Yazoo City, Mississippi, which he tends to think is too large, confusing, and cramping a place for a simple country boy like himself. Friends and neighbors who have made the hundred-mile journey to that metropolis more often than he has speak of its many virtues and as they do he accepts their assurances that the women are pretty, the tavern-life joyful, and that the mill jobs pay well and there is a lovely park to sit in on warm evenings. He may believe all this and still dislike Yazoo City and not be bothered to a motivating degree by the resulting inconsistency. If he now learns that a new stock car racing track has been established there by the city fathers themselves, this may be just the increment of additional inconsistency-generating information required to produce a transgression of his intolerance threshold. He should then rather easily shift to positive affect toward Yazoo City and he may begin to visit it more often.

The illustrations I have offered here are loose and probably too simple, and the propositions they have been meant to clarify do clearly err in the direction of tautology, though in this they reflect, I think, a tautology that exists in psychological nature. Nevertheless, I do think that they may have considerable value in illuminating the ways in which variations in tolerance for inconsistency are bound up both with the reception that inconsistent informational and assertive inputs receive and with the ways in which they are processed when, having been accepted as credible, they generate inconsistency.

In Chapter 76 I have implicitly employed the propositions developed here. Also in that chapter I have discussed more fully the bases and consequences of the assertion that the processing of affective-cognitive inconsistency concerning 'old' objects proceeds not with linear continuity but rather in spasm-like jumps. As a point of connection between the present treatment and what has been suggested in the later chapter I should like to draw out one further consideration, though I risk redundancy in doing so. I have suggested that the spasms of reorganization that follow transgression of low intolerance thresholds may be hypothesized as culminating in restoration of near perfect affective-cognitive consistency. However, the spasms that follow transgression of high thresholds are of less intense nature, and it may be hypothesized that typically they culminate not in restoration of total affective-cognitive consistency but merely in a tolerable pattern of overall consistency in which residual inconsistent attitudinal cognitions tend to persist. (Our friend 'country boy' will probably not become a fanatic enthusiast for Yazoo City. By shifting his affect in the positive direction he has reduced inconsistency to a tolerable level—and for such a high threshold attitude a fair degree of lingering inconsistency, in the form of some retained anti-Yazoo beliefs, will still be tolerable.)

The research implications of this whole discussion are, I think, rather clear. Experiments need to be undertaken in which estimates are made (by methods yet to be perfected) of the mean intolerance levels for particular persons and of the specific intolerance levels that characterize their particular attitudes. We could then proceed to test the prediction that greater initial rejection of inconsistent inputs will occur in low threshold than in high threshold attitude realms. Similarly we can then also test the two other major predictions that I have dwelt upon here: namely, that with suprathreshold inconsistency established in both low and high threshold attitudes the former, when compared to the latter, will more often undergo restoration to the original structure and will less often show reorganization culminating in a new, stabilized affective-cognitive structure; but that when such reorganization *does* occur in a low threshold attitude area, the attitude change will be more thoroughgoing and will lead to a more fully consistent intraattitudinal structure than when a high threshold area is involved.

There are also a number of variables whose manipulation might produce elevation or depression of the intolerance threshold. Some of these are: the public vs. private performance variable; increase or decrease in the salience of the normative standard favoring consistency; the increase or decrease in a need that is partially served by the holding of the original attitude. Manipulation of such variables would enable further testing of hypotheses concerning the influence of the threshold level upon responsiveness to inconsistency-generating communication, as well as its influence upon the processing of aroused inconsistency. And, through application of the 'construct validity' logic, confirmations of such hypotheses would also provide further substantiation for the theoretic legitimacy of the intolerance threshold concept itself.

Though research of this sort is bound to pose difficult problems of measurement, manipulation, and control, it would probably contribute much toward the demystifying of all the separate consistency theories; for, as I have suggested, so far all of them have foundered over the twin problems posed by variability in the intolerance for inconsistency and in the choice between modes of inconsistency reduction.

INAUTHENTICITY AND AFFECTIVE-COGNITIVE STRUCTURE

By now it should be apparent that the consistency theories, like all other theories, have their inadequacies. One particular defect is shared by each of the consistency theories excepting dissonance though it, to be sure, is thought by some critics (Brown, 1965; Chapanis & Chapanis, 1964) to have rather unique deficiencies of its own.

The authors and proponents of most of the other consistency theories pay ready lip service to the definition of attitude as an internally consistent structure of affective, cognitive, and behavioral components. But, in practice, the last of these components is usually slighted. Behavior (in the sense of externally visible, overt action) toward the attitude object is usually relegated to the status of a dependent variable; implicitly it is assumed that the person will simply act toward an attitude object in a manner consistent with his coordinated affective-cognitive orientation toward that object.

Yet it is very much in the nature of our time, and perhaps in the nature of all social systems featuring complex role differentiation, that persons are often impelled toward 'inauthentic' behavior; that is, toward overt action which violates their loyalties as well as their perceptions of where truth and value actually lie.

It is to the confusion and disturbance generated by this type of experience that dissonance theory speaks. And this, quite apart from any assessment of its scientific merit, probably accounts for the large vogue that the theory has enjoyed beyond the narrow precincts of the social psychological profession.

At the same time, within social psychology, dissonance theory has had at least this quite salutary effect: it has forced the other consistency approaches toward the examination of how individuals process and reduce behaviorally generated inconsistency; it has forced them, in other words, toward a closer research and theoretical examination of the influence of overt behavior, as an independent variable, upon the dependent variables of attitudinal affect and cognition.

My own approach to this challenge began with a consciously chosen conservative stance. It seemed to me that the early major *experiments* offered in support of the dissonance view of attitude change[5] were both admirably ingenious in their designs and prone to inducing considerable

---

[5] In this discussion I am concerned with dissonance only as a theory of attitude dynamics. The relevance of the theory for the comprehension and prediction of decisional processes and for certain motivational anomalies will not be treated here.

systematic bias in dependent variable data. In fact the latter defect seemed often to be due to the former virtue.

Thus, as concerns such important experiments as those of Festinger and Carlsmith (1959) or Cohen's New Haven police experiment (as reported in Brehm & Cohen, 1962), it seemed to me that one could discern a possible confounding process that had not been suspected by the original investigators.

In both of these experiments subjects were led to commit an overt action (role-playing in the Festinger and Carlsmith study and essay-writing in the Cohen study) in which they took a position opposite to their own private attitudes. With those subjects who undertook the counterattitudinal performance for low monetary reward (and thus for 'low justification') the magnitude of dissonance, and thus the resultant degree of attitude change, were expected to be greater than with those who performed for larger monetary reward.

The results of these studies, as is well known, were as dissonance theory predicted. But if one ponders the question of how the naive subjects might have *experienced* the rather startling experimental situations in which they were placed, a whole class of alternative, and possibly more parsimonious, interpretations comes to mind. Under the High Reward condition, subjects might feel suspicious about the experimenter's unrevealed purposes; or they might come to feel guilty about accepting excessive payment; or they might come to reason that if they showed subsequent attitude change they would be revealing themselves as lacking autonomy in the face of a bribe-like lure. On the basis of any or all of these assumed intervening states, and thus on grounds quite unrelated to dissonance theory, one could predict that visible attitude change would be inversely related to the degree of monetary, or other, justification that had been employed to elicit counterattitudinal performance.

Going one step further, it could be reasoned from the affective-cognitive consistency approach that, with the suspicion or "evaluation apprehension" (Rosenberg, 1963, 1965d) artifacts removed, the opposite finding would be obtained; i.e., counterattitudinal performance, particularly if it involved detailed advocacy of the counterattitudinal position, would lead to greater attitude change when it was carried out under high, rather than low, reward conditions.

The basis for this prediction would be that the greater the incentive energizing the counterattitudinal advocacy the more truly self-persuasive would be the counterattitudinal arguments developed by the subject. This greater persuasiveness would be due either to the evocation of a richer style of argumentation or to a higher assessment of the worth of one's own arguments, or to both of these processes.

In effect then, from the point of view of affective-cognitive consistency theory, counterattitudinal advocacy can be understood as a variant of Sequence 1 (see page 77); that is, it can be understood as producing attitude change not simply because it is a *behavior* inconsistent with the affective-cognitive structure to which it refers, but rather because it alters the cognitive content of the attitude and thus generates affective-cognitive inconsistency. And it could be hypothesized further that the generation of a degree of affective-cognitive inconsistency sufficient to produce affective change would be more likely when the incentive for the counterattitudinal cognitive improvisation was a strong rather than a weak one.

A test of such a prediction would have to replicate the usual styling of dissonance experiments, but also it would have to be designed so as to reduce the possibility that artifactual processes would work upon the High Reward subjects, inhibiting them from revealing that attitude change had occurred after they had engaged in counterattitudinal advocacy.

This was the logic behind an experiment I reported a few years ago (Rosenberg, 1965d). Because its design and rationale were thoroughly described in the earlier publication I shall not deal with them here except for the following few points: The experiment was basically an altered replication of the one performed earlier by Cohen (reported in Brehm & Cohen, 1962). An apparently effective two-experiment disguise was used to separate the writing of a 'dissonant' essay (the subjects were Ohio State undergraduates who wrote against the participation of their university football team in the Rose Bowl contest) from the later assessment of attitudinal affect toward the issue. The purpose of this disguise was to eliminate or reduce the influence of the processes which were assumed to have confounded the earlier dissonance studies. Subjects were promised either $.50, $1.00, or $5.00 for writing the essays and, unlike the procedure in the earlier studies, were given the promised sums and allowed to retain them.

The findings from this study clearly supported the original predictions based upon the affective-cognitive consistency approach and thus were opposite to what seemed to be the proper dissonance-derived prediction. Thus, while the $.50 and $1.00 groups did not differ markedly from one another, each of them did show significantly more positive affect toward the ban on Rose Bowl participation than did a base-line control group who had not engaged in counterattitudinal essay writing ($p < .05$). More important to the point at issue between the two relevant theories was the finding that the $5.00 group showed significantly greater positive affect toward the Rose Bowl ban than did either the $.50 or $1.00 groups (in each case $p < .05$). The distance between the means of the Control and $5.00 groups was impressively large, with the latter some two gross points higher (more positive) on the seven-point affect scale that was employed ($p < .0001$). A similar positive relationship between the size of the monetary incentive for counterattitudinal advocacy and the degree of subsequent attitude change was obtained on a related scale concerned with another 'antiathletic' proposal, thus showing some generalization of the induced change.

Blind ratings of the essays by two independent judges revealed something about the mediation of the overall effect. The essays written by the $5.00 subjects were, on the average, more persuasive (though not more lengthy) than those written by the members of the Low Pay experimental groups. This last finding seemed to support the original theoretical prediction that the induction of affect change through attitude discrepant advocacy was mediated through the strength of the cognitive alterations (and thus through the resultant affective-cognitive inconsistency) generated by that advocacy.

In the same journal issue in which this study first appeared there was also published a study by Janis and Gilmore (1965; see also Chapter 82) in which Janis's incentive theory, a conceptualization quite compatible with the present one, was supported while contrasting predictions based upon a dissonance interpretation were apparently disconfirmed.

These two studies, taken together with a related one by Elms and Janis (1965) and with the earlier critical review of the dissonance literature by Chapanis and Chapanis (1964), constituted, I suppose, a challenge to which the advocates of dissonance theory could be expected to reply with their accustomed vigor. Brehm (1965) and Aronson (1966c) put forth some usefully challenging reinterpretations designed to show that these experiments were either inadequately designed or that their findings could somehow be fitted into a dissonance framework. In Belgium, Joseph Nuttin, Jr., conducted an altered replication of my Rose Bowl study (Nuttin, 1964) whose results he interpreted as supporting the dissonance view. But, as I subsequently pointed out (Rosenberg, 1966), his version of the two-experiment disguise technique was rather clearly penetrable and thus defective and, even less arguable, his highest dissonance group (those who wrote counterattitudinal essays for no financial inducement) showed less attitude change than his Low Dissonance groups.

Lurking somewhere in the thicket of controversy that sprang up at this time were some important variables waiting to be unconfounded. The location of these variables was aided by the important study conducted by Carlsmith, Collins, and Helmreich (1966). That study, as reviewed elsewhere in this volume (see Chapters 81 through 84) consisted of an expanded and altered replication of the original study by Festinger and Carlsmith (1959). After participation in a dull experimental task each subject was led, by either low or comparatively high financial inducement, into a counterattitudinal performance in which he asserted that the original experimental task had actually been interesting and enjoyable. Half of the subjects did this in a 'face-to-face' spoken role-play, the other face being that of a disingenuous confederate presented as "the next subject." The remaining subjects, instead of undertaking this sort of counterattitudinal performance, wrote counterattitudinal essays which, they were told, were to be used later on in the composition of an effective persuasive communication.

The main result was one of those provocative interaction effects upon which modern experimental social psychology dotes and grows fat: with the role-playing subjects the dissonance prediction was confirmed, in that the Low Reward subjects showed greater attitude change (i.e., liking for the dull experimental task) than did the High Reward subjects; with the essay-writing subjects the opposite finding was obtained, with High Reward subjects showing greater attitude change than Low Reward subjects. This latter half of the experiment, then, replicated the design and confirmed the findings of my earlier Rose Bowl study (Rosenberg, 1965d). An especially interesting fact needs to be noted here, though I shall defer for a few pages the interpretation that I would place upon it: The average and maximum performance times for each of the two respective forms of counterattitudinal activity were grossly different. Thus the maximum time spent in the role-playing performance was 2 minutes; while for the essay writing it was 16 minutes.

By means of a narrative account of one line of research I have reached the point at which it now becomes possible to raise some further theoretical perspectives and possibilities. But first a general stance must be defined.

I am unabashedly fond enough of my own line of theorizing and research (and enough persuaded that dissonance experiments are often marred by unintended confounding due to the private interpretations and anxieties that they rouse in 'high dissonance' subjects) to conclude that the work done in this area in the last five years summates to this required judgment: counterattitudinal behavior often affects subsequent attitude change in ways that contradict the *original* claims of dissonance theory. Indeed I am heartened to find that something of this sort has been partially conceded, though in other and more prodissonance terms, by such writers as Aronson (1966c; also Chapter 1) and Carlsmith (Chapter 81).

Yet I am not persuaded that dissonance theory is simply 'wrong' or that the affective-cognitive consistency theory or any other balance approach is universally correct. Instead I think that dissonance theory in its original formulation was too overgeneralized and, as Brown suggests (1965), too loosely stated. Brehm and Cohen (1962) initiated a process of reexamination and reformulation that is still continuing and Festinger himself (1964) has advanced this effort in the related realm of the dissonance approach to decisional processes.

A conciliatory perspective and method are required. And, as I have suggested elsewhere (Rosenberg, 1966), these are readily available if, at the present stage in the development of consistency theory, one works toward *differentiation* rather than toward premature synthesis and unification. One needs to render unto dissonance theory that which is its proper, demonstrable possession, and unto affective-cognitive consistency theory (and the related balance approaches) that which it may properly claim and parsimoniously incorporate.

The most accessible route toward such a division lies, I think, in specifying additional variables which seem to influence whether counterattitudinal behavior leads to affect change in direct or inverse relation to the amount of justification for such behavior. This is tantamount to specifying the conditions under which dissonance theory and affective-cognitive consistency theory may be respectively applied in the realm of counterattitudinal effects.

The studies that I have reviewed here and others mentioned in this volume (see Chapters 82, 83) seem to me to highlight some of these variables. In brief compass I have discussed a number of them, and some of their conceivable interrelationships, in Chapter 84. Here it will suffice to mention only two that seem particularly tenable in the light of recent research. The first is the distinction between simple, unelaborated counterattitudinal assertion and more complex counterattitudinal advocacy. The second concerns the difference between the 'self-exploratory' and 'duplicity' sets as aspects of the subjects' definition of the counterattitudinal performance situation.

In the ensuing comments I shall deal largely with the first of these since it leads me toward an account of one recent and still unpublished major experiment; however, I shall have a few comments about the second in due course.

So far in this section I have used such terms as 'inauthenticity', 'counterattitudinal action', and 'counterattitudinal advocacy' without always drawing clear distinctions between them. In fact I am convinced that a basic distinction must be drawn between two types of counterattitudinal performance, and that the failure to employ this distinction is the main source of that sense of gently reeling confusion that dissonance theory and portions of its related experimental literature sometimes induce in interested observers. The necessary distinction, as I have already suggested, is simply that between a limited and rather concrete *counterattitudinal assertion* and a richer, more cognitively and argumentatively detailed pattern of *counterattitudinal advocacy*.

This contrast is not drawn now for the first time in this chapter. In my earlier article reporting the Rose Bowl study I conjectured that:

> ...the kind of counter-attitudinal performance that best fits the dissonance paradigm is a simple overt act that directly violates one's private attitude (for example, eating or agreeing to eat a disliked food; expressing approval of a disliked proposal or candidate; merely *committing* oneself to develop counter-attitudinal arguments; etc.). But when a person actually does elaborate a set of arguments opposite to his own attitude the dissonance he experiences ... encompasses considerably more than merely realizing that he has argued against his own position. The broader pattern of inconsistency that he encounters is that between the content and apparent plausibility, on the one hand, of the new arguments that he has developed and, on the other hand, his original affective judgment of the object (Rosenberg, 1965d, p. 39).

At the same time Janis and Gilmore (1965) made a rather similar point and also offered some data in partial, though indirect, support of it. The study by Carlsmith, Collins, and Helmreich (1966) seemed to open the way toward further experimental pursuit of this important distinction.

As I have already noted, these experimenters obtained the dissonance effect with the role-playing subjects and the incentive effect with their essay-writing subjects. Aronson (1966c) has interpreted these findings as due to a difference in 'commitment,' i.e., the role-playing subjects were publicly committed to an inauthentic position in the sense that each of these subjects thought the 'next subject' really believed him when he represented himself as having found the dull experimental task actually interesting and enjoyable. The essay-writing subjects, however, had only low or no commitment, in that they knew that the experimenter knew that the counterattitudinal arguments given in their essays were not ones which the subjects actually believed. By interpreting the situation featuring 'commitment' as one in which true dissonance is experienced and the 'noncommitment' situation as one in which dissonance is not actually aroused, Aronson is able to reconcile the available data by concluding that "... dissonance effects and reinforcement effects are not mutually exclusive; reinforcement effects will emerge when cognitive dissonance has been minimized in the experimental operations."

My own interpretation of the Carlsmith, Collins, and Helmreich data was of a different order. The fact that took on figural prominence was one to which I have already alluded: the design or the subjects were such that role-playing took a maximum of 2 minutes and essay-writing a maximum of 16 minutes. We are entitled to assume that richer counterattitudinal advocacy, and fuller internal rehearsal of its content, will be associated with greater time spent at the performance of counterattitudinal advocacy. Indeed it seems unlikely that when a subject merely spends a minute or two doing a counterattitudinal role-play he will get much further than merely asserting the counterattitudinal position (i.e., in the Festinger and Carlsmith or the Carlsmith, Collins, and Helmreich studies he will probably do little more than announce that he found the experimental task interesting and enjoyable; he will not have the time or occasion to argue for these assertions, to document or ponder them).

Thus the 'commitment' and 'simple assertion vs. complex advocacy' variables were confounded in the Carlsmith, Collins, and Helmreich experiment. In an attempt to unconfound them Jonathan Finkelstein and I undertook a further experiment. This was essentially an expanded replication of the role-playing portion of the original study by Carlsmith, Collins, and Helmreich, though we used a different, but apparently equally effective, procedure to disguise the postmanipulation measurement of attitudinal affect.

As in the original experiment, our subjects spent a long period (50 minutes in this study) circling 2's and 6's on closely printed sheets of random numbers. They were then recruited to assist us by telling the 'next subject' that the experiment seemed 'interesting,' 'enjoyable,' and 'scientifically useful.' For this they were offered either $.50 or $2.50 (the availability of this amount of payment having been first mentioned even before the counterattitudinal task was described), and their decisions were made only after the amount of payment had been clearly specified. The situation was so arranged that the subject would necessarily believe that the 'next subject' perceived him as speaking his true mind when he represented the dull experimental task as an attractive one. In our instructions to all these subjects we stressed that, in persuading the 'next subject,' they should first describe the task accurately and then "use any arguments you can think of to leave the next subject with a positive impression of the task." Thus, while persuasive intent was stressed, there was no direct suggestion that the subject engage in sheer duplicity.

The main independent variable was a contrast between simple and complex counterattitudinal performance. In one group the subjects were told that they would have about two minutes before the experimenter returned to end the persuasion period. In another group they were told they would have about five minutes.[6] The first group was actually given a minute and a half and the second was given six minutes before their counterattitudinal performances were halted. These performances were tape recorded without

---

[6] With yet another group of subjects the counterattitudinal performance was restricted to simply checking, on a large graphic scale displayed on a blackboard, the position indicating a highly favorable evaluation of the number-circling task. This was done, of course, in the presence of the 'next subject' and for either a $.50 or $2.50 incentive. The results from this experimental condition are inconclusive. On all of the major dependent variables the $.50 and $2.50 groups do not significantly differ, though some weak trends in the dissonance and incentive directions are found with separate dependent variables. For this reason and also because the experimental manipulation provided for no verbal interaction between the subject and confederate, and thus was not comparable with the other two conditions, this portion of the experiment will not receive further discussion here. However it should be noted in passing that in this special experimental condition the counterattitudinal performance is yet another type of simple counterattitudinal act. The fact that it does not lead to the type of outcome that dissonance theory requires (i.e., greater attitude change for the $.50 than for the $2.50 group—or at least a consistent trend in this direction on all of the major dependent variables) can be taken in two ways. Either it can be viewed as disconfirming the dissonance theory prediction or as reflecting a possible weakness in the experimental manipulation itself. The latter would, of course, be the more parsimonious interpretation.

the subjects' knowledge. Following the performance the subject reported to the central office of the Psychology Department and filled out a questionnaire, given him by the departmental secretary, which elicited his evaluation of the original number-circling experimental task in a non-suspicion-arousing way. The questionnaire was disguised as a standard one used with all subjects after their participation in any Psychology Department study. Close postexperimental interviews conducted both before and after debriefing seemed to provide strong evidence that the various necessary deceptions had not been penetrated by the subjects.

The dependent variable measure elicited from the subjects' judgments as to how 'interesting,' 'enjoyable,' 'pleasant,' and 'worthwhile' they had found the original number-circling experimental task. In addition to these measures, all similar to one that had been used by Carlsmith, Collins, and Helmreich, we also had the subjects assess the experimental task on various other dimensions. A multivariate analysis, based upon the four ratings mentioned above and also upon a measure of 'willingness to do the same sort of experiment again,' revealed a significant interaction between size of monetary incentive and amount of time spent at counterattitudinal performance ($p < .03$). This significant interaction reflected the fact that in the 6 minute (complex counterattitudinal advocacy) condition the $2.50 subjects showed greater positive regard for the original number-circling task than did the $.50 subjects, while the reverse was the case in the 1½ minute condition. This analysis was based upon a population from which there had been excluded 17 out of the original 59 experimental subjects. These 17 were subjects who, on a postexperimental questionnaire, had reported that they had not felt clearly free to refuse the request to undertake the counterattitudinal performance. However, when these subjects are included in the analysis the results are not altered.

When the same sort of analysis of variance is repeated for individual dependent variable items we obtain significant interaction effects with both the 'pleasantness' ($p < .03$) and 'interest' ($p < .06$) ratings and borderline ones with most of the other ratings. Thus within the 6 minute group the means for rated pleasantness of the number-circling task are $-.95$ for the subjects paid $.50 and $+1.25$ for the subjects paid $2.50. (The rating scale employed for this and the other dependent variables extended from -5 to $+5$.) In contrast, within the 1½ minute group the means are $+.75$ for the $.50 subjects and $-.40$ for the $2.50 subjects.[7]

Comparing the various experimental groups to a control group that merely did the number-circling task but engaged in no counterattitudinal performance, we find that on most of the dependent variable dimensions the 6 minute, $2.50 group deviates most in the positive attitudinal direction. By t-test comparison the differences between these two groups are significant at

---

[7] Apart from the assessment of interaction effects, these data were also analyzed by t test for the differences between the $.50 and $2.50 groups within both the 1½ and 6 minute conditions. For the four major dependent variables (the ratings of 'interesting,' 'enjoyable,' 'pleasant,' and 'worthwhile') two of the comparisons within the 6 minute group attain, and the other two approach, significance. All of these differences are in the 'incentive' direction; i.e., more positive ratings from the $2.50 group. In the 1½ minute condition the separate comparisons do not attain significance, but the trends are in the 'dissonance' direction and thus contribute to the interaction effects reported above.

$p < .005$ for 'pleasantness,' $p < .01$ for 'interest,' and $p < .05$ for 'worth-while.'[8] Thus in a condition for which the conventional dissonance approach would have to predict low attitude change, we find the greatest degree of attitude change obtained after counterattitudinal performance.

My argument is, of course, that for this group the comparatively high incentive of $2.50 (for advocacy rather than for mere counterattitudinal assertion) energized a richer, more self-persuasive, and probably more adequately rehearsed and retained set of arguments supportive of counterattitudinal cognitions; and that this in turn created a motivating degree of affective-cognitive inconsistency; and, finally, that this suprathreshold inconsistency was reduced by shifting the originally negative affective orientation to the number-circling task a significant distance in the positive direction.

Evidence in direct support of this interpretation is available from a content analysis of the protocols of the subjects' counterattitudinal performances. Three independent judges, working blind and with no knowledge of the experimental design or of the variables that were employed, rated the transcripts of the tape recordings by tabulating the total number of positive statements (i.e., arguments supporting the endorsement of the dull task as interesting, enjoyable, etc.) and the total number of nonrepetitive positive statements. The inter-judge reliability for the two indices, as computed by an analysis of variance technique suggested by Winer (1962, pp. 124–132), was very high ($r_3 = .96$ and $r_3 = .93$, respectively). Among the findings supportive of the interpretation drawn above were these: The 6 minute subjects produce more positive arguments and characterizations concerning the dull experimental task than do the $1\frac{1}{2}$ minute group ($p < .001$). Within the 6 minute group the $2.50 subjects produce a larger number of positive statements than do the $.50 subjects ($p < .05$). When the total 6 minute group is split into higher and lower halves on amount of positive statements made during counterattitudinal advocacy, the high group is found to exceed the low group both on their ratings of how pleasant ($p < .025$) and how worthwhile ($p < .025$) the experimental task was. The comparisons for most of the other dependent variable scales reveal a similar trend but either at borderline or insignificant levels of probability.

A closer analysis of these and other data must be reserved for later publication. But the foregoing summary is sufficient ground for the claim I wish to enter here: namely, that this experiment, added to others upon which it has drawn, is rather strong evidence that complex counterattitudinal advocacy (performed under the commitment conditions that dissonance theorists would require) induces change in attitudinal affect through the prior establishment of inconsistency-generating cognitions, and that such cognitions are more fully established (and thus greater affect change results) under high rather than low incentive conditions. Thus the affective-cognitive consistency theory, or at least one of its advocates, is in a position to reclaim part of the terrain upon which the dissonance theory flag had been raised.

However, this claim must immediately be tempered by acknowledging that the matter at issue is probably more complicated than has so far been

---

[8] These and other t-test probabilities reported here are 1-tailed, since the hypotheses tested were all directional ones.

suggested. One such further complication has already been noted. It concerns the set or task orientation with which the person enters into counterattitudinal advocacy.

A plausible hypothesis that I have already proferred and argued for (Rosenberg, 1966) is that the positive relationship between reward for counterattitudinal advocacy and degree of postadvocacy attitude change will be facilitated when the subject defines his task as a kind of 'self-exploration' (i.e., an examination of thoughts and percepts he has in his own repertoire); and that it will be impeded when he defines his task as 'deceiving' or 'cynically' persuading another of something that he (the subject) does not himself believe.

Such an hypothesis is consistent with data from the Carlsmith, Collins, and Helmreich experiment (1966) but, again, an inevitable confounding of some manipulated and intervening variables in that experiment prevents the use of its data as a direct test of this interpretation. Later studies by Collins (personal communication, 1966) seem to lend further plausibility to this assumed relationship, but complex interaction effects prevent our drawing a clear conclusion on this matter. In research that I am currently planning, I hope to put this hypothesis to an unambiguous experimental test.

I hasten to add that the basis for the hypothesis is not merely the presence of some data that suggest it. Rather it follows from this theoretical consideration: In counterattitudinal advocacy situations, the new and potentially inconsistency-generating cognitions (whose strength and number have developed in some monotonic relationship with the strength of the incentive) will not necessarily be internalized by the person who has performed the counterattitudinal advocacy. If he can find some clear basis for rejecting the new cognitions he probably will do so, particularly if the attitude realm is one that is characterized by a low intolerance threshold. Being able to code these cognitions as 'lies' is only one of many conceivable bases for restoring consistency through the reestablishment of the original affective-cognitive structure.[9]

Many other conditions will tend to impede, and others will tend to facilitate, the introjection of the new cognitive considerations improvised through counterattitudinal advocacy. In Chapter 82 Janis has proposed a number of such variables and in Chapter 84 I have attempted to discuss further the ways and contexts in which they operate.

In summary of the foregoing research findings and theoretical considerations I would reiterate the following conclusions: that in the case of

---

[9] It is worth noting here that in the counterattitudinal study reported earlier (a study in which our instructions urged neither the duplicity or self-exploratory task sets) a post-experimental questionnaire showed that most of the subjects perceived themselves as not having lied to the 'next subject.' Thus, without direct manipulation of this variable, the experimental situation seems not to have elicited the kind of task definition which might have provided the subjects in the 6 minute group with a way of evading the persuasive import of their own counterattitudinal arguments. It could be predicted that if the instructions had actually stressed self-exploration as the basis for counterattitudinal advocacy (e.g., "in persuading the next subject just try to put before him all the positive aspects of the task that really occur to you now that you have the time to think about it") the difference between the two reward groups in the 6 minute condition would have been even greater. Such a variation will probably be attempted in a future experiment.

complex counterattitudinal advocacy strong incentives produce more attitude change than weak ones; and that the overt 'dissonant' behavior of performing counterattitudinal advocacy seems to achieve its effects not through the direct incompatibility between the original affective orientation and the fact that advocacy has been performed, but rather through the cognitive changes that advocacy induces, and through the resulting affective-cognitive inconsistency that is thereby generated.

As regards simple counterattitudinal action, I see no clear data that disconfirm the dissonance prediction in this realm. However, I would hazard the guess that there is a further consequence associated with the kind of affect change that is induced by simple and poorly justified inauthentic acts; namely, I would suggest that such change is followed by cognitive reorganization which works to restore or consolidate intraattitudinal consistency. In other words, I am hypothesizing that the final phase of the dissonance reduction dynamic is rather like the process contemplated in my earlier description of the second basic attitude change sequence (see p. 78).

Dissonance theory has been a wonderfully stimulating goad in the development of the consistency approach to attitude dynamics. Extremely apposite to certain disturbing aspects of modern experience, it has driven the study of attitudinal dynamics toward greater human pertinence. However, in so doing, it has sometimes obscured, rather than illuminated, the important details of mediating psychological processes. In what I have said about it, here and elsewhere, and in suggesting that some of the terrain it has claimed might better be restored to the possession of other theories (or, at least to codominion), I have tried to remain sensitive to the debt we owe it and its advocates.

My main purpose in this chapter has been to provide an overview of the affective-cognitive consistency theory and then to show how it has been modified and extended in the face of certain challenges that have confronted not only that theory but the whole general enterprise now commonly designated as the consistency approach.

The integration of the separate theories representing that approach is not yet at hand and must, I think, be deferred while separate gardens are assiduously cultivated. However, I shall close with the disarmingly predictable confession that, as I see it, some of the general propositions and conceptual strategies advanced in this chapter will require inclusion in that *grand theory* of consistency processes that may yet be constructed by some coming, synthesizing genius. He, in turn, will have to be highly intolerant of those intertheory inconsistencies that the authors in this section have learned to live with and enjoy.

CHAPTER 5

Psychological Implication

Robert P. Abelson

Yale University

Viewed in grand perspective, the question of consistency is really the question of the nature of Reason. Implicit in the several present consistency theories is a resolution of the presumed apposition between the logical and illogical poles of Man's nature, a compromise characterization which might be referred to as 'subjective rationality.' This term implies two different departures from objective rationality: the use of reasoning capacity upon a personally distorted picture of reality; or alternatively, the application of predictable mental processing rules which happen not to correspond to the rules of formal logic. These two intrusions of personal calculus into the cognitive realm might also co-occur: predictable but not necessarily fully logical rules might be applied by the individual to a specifiable but not necessarily accurate picture of the world. This is a view which is essentially shared by dissonance theory and the balance theories. Both presume a high degree of cognitive order according to as yet only dimly understood principles of what might be called "psycho-logic" (Abelson & Rosenberg, 1958).

The conceptual appeal of the consistency theories, then, is due to their potentially very satisfying account of an extremely difficult theoretical problem. (In addition, dissonance theory in particular has made a novel *empirical* contribution, as is clear from Chapter 1 and many other chapters in this volume.) The danger in the easy conceptual appeal of consistency theories, however, is that systems of psycho-logic have not usually been specified in enough detail to render the subjective rationalist position potentially refutable.

At least one system of psycho-logic which is specific enough to be shown false is the system devised by Abelson and Rosenberg (1958) which extrapolated Rosenberg's (1956) earlier work, the core ideas of Heider (1946, 1958), and the systematic mathematical suggestions of Cartwright and Harary (1956) into a larger basic system. In this chapter I will review this earlier system and certain criticisms of it. Thence I will sketch the direction my own work has taken since then and the relations I now see (or think I see) between balance and dissonance formulations. Finally, I will outline an improved system synthesizing several theoretical trends into a newer psycho-logic which is hopefully better able to survive empirical difficulties than its predecessors.

Before launching into this enterprise, I should make clear that I will be primarily concerned here with cognition rather than with motivation or with behavior. As the reader will discover later in this volume, the question of whether the presence of cognitive inconsistency is usefully regarded as a drive state is moot. Sharp challenges to this assumption occur in several chapters (e.g., Chapters 14 and 23), and the upshot of Section III A on "Inconsistency as a Motivational Construct" is that the present path to greatest progress in the areas covered by this volume probably lies elsewhere than in the analysis of traditional motivational constructs (see Chapter 24). The question of behavior is quite another matter, however. My own work and that of many others interested in belief systems as intrinsically interesting objects of study has tended to neglect the analysis of action, and this deficiency is very much in need of remedy. The dissonance theorists have in general done much better with action concepts than balance theorists, although for them, too, there is not a firm theoretical bridge joining cognition and behavior, but rather a breathtaking predictive leap across the gulf between (cf. Chapter 36). I will briefly mention these problems, although the reader stands warned that in presenting what will amount to a blend of Gestaltist and information-processing ideas, my version of Everyman will make him seem much more a Thinker than a Doer.

THE ABELSON-ROSENBERG "PSYCHO-LOGIC"

In the original system (Abelson & Rosenberg, 1958), attitudinal cognitive structures were assumed to consist of sets of cognitive elements, A, B, C... (one of which was always the element 'Ego'), each ordered pair of elements being connected in a sentence by a perceived relation, r, which could be classified as either positive (p), negative (n), ambivalent (a), or null (o). The class of positive relations included the positive "sentiment relations" (e.g., 'likes') and "unit relations" (e.g., 'is responsible for') of Heider's (1946) system, and the negative class included Heider's negative sentiment relations (e.g., 'dislikes'). Additionally, various other relations were considered to belong to the positive or negative classes. A broader classificatory terminology of relations into "associative" vs. "dissociative" had independently been used in a little-known but intriguing content analysis technique called "Evaluative Assertion Analysis" devised by Osgood, Saporta, and Nunnally (1956). These authors had found that people could, with prior explanation, reliably judge whether (and to what quantitative degree) a particular action verb could be considered "associative" vs. "dissociative." Thus certain actions such as 'advocates' or 'hinders' which cannot unambiguously be said to belong to Heider's sentiment or unit categories could be included in our respective positive and negative categories. The ambivalent relation was defined as the conjunction of positive and negative relations, and the null relation was defined as the absence of any semantic relation at all or the presence of empty information (e.g., 'is indifferent to').

We were aware at the time (*op. cit.*, p. 3) that certain types of relations had been omitted from our categories. In retrospect, the most important of those omissions was that of the dominance relation (e.g., 'is more powerful

than'), which among other things can give rise to the linear orderings referred to by DeSoto and Albrecht in Chapter 45 as a "seductive and coercive" principle of cognitive organization. In any case, we regarded the
relational system, crude as it was, as broad and powerful.

The total cognitive system pertaining to a given attitude object could
thus be represented, we proposed, in a square *structure matrix* with the elements specifying the rows and corresponding columns, and the individual
entries the appropriate relations p, n, a, or o. (This representation is mathematically isomorphic to the alternative graph theoretic type of representation
discussed by Cartwright and Harary [1956], and several of our results had
counterparts in that alternative representation.) We proposed two kinds of
things that were possible for the theorist to do with the structure matrix,
one *diagnostic*, the other *predictive*. There has been some confusion about
the relevant principles in recent articles, therefore it may pay to try to
restate them here.

The diagnostic technique was a set of 'rules,' each of which specified
that a chain of relations would tend to educe a further relation, i.e., that a
relation between A and B and a relation between B and C would 'imply' a
relation between A and C when the individual thought about the topic.
These triangle implications were postulated in accordance with the general
definition of balanced triangles (see Chapter 2); for example, A positively
related to B (ApB) and B negatively related to C (BnC) imply A negatively
related to C (AnC). Our intended meaning of the term 'imply' was 'initiate
cognitive processes tending over time to produce the consequent sentence.'
Thus we were restating the Heiderian proposition (1958, p. 206) that cognitive triads tend toward balanced completions, a result which (cf. Morrissette,
1958) has been partially demonstrated by questionnaire methods involving
hypothetical social situations (e.g., 'You like Harry; Harry dislikes Bill.
Not having met him yet, do you think you will like Bill or dislike Bill?').

Our psycho-logical rules have elicited a smattering of mathematical
commentary (Mitra, 1962; Flament, 1963). Most critically, some students of
logic (Lambert, 1966; Giese, 1967) have raised sharp objections to our set of
rules, stemming apparently from the misapprehension that the rules were
meant to be *axioms* and that implication was to be interpreted in its strict
logical sense. These authors thus betray a view of cognitive systems as giant
static truth-tables in which all sentences contemplable by the individual at
any given moment obey some parsimonious axiom set yielding 100 per cent
perfect classification into those which are believed and those which are dis-
believed. While such a view is not necessarily incorrect for all individuals,
it is gratuitous in assuming instantaneous and total cognitive apprehension,
and it is certainly not what we had in mind for the dynamics of psycho-logic.
'Implication' was conceived by us as a mildly effortful cognitive process, not
as a statement of the objective logical necessity of cognitive co-occurrence
of certain beliefs. We pictured an earnest but not notably bright thinker
saying to himself (if he ever were motivated to think about the topic, which
he might well not be), such things as "If person A does action B, and action
B blocks goal C, that implies or suggests that person A is opposed to goal C.
But I always thought he was for it, so that leaves me confused." This
thinking activity might or might not be as overt as the phrase "saying to
himself" suggests, and it might occur extremely rapidly, but in any case we
would construe it to be a process taking time, and allowing possible contradiction between sentences considered true at a given moment and those

imputed later. These potential inconsistencies, *if discovered,* would create ambivalence for the individual, and thus the 'rules' of our system were simply diagnostic devices for predicting whether trouble might arise in any given system; i.e., whether it was imbalanced.

Incidentally, if despite all the above protestations anyone still insists on trying to axiomatize our simple original psycho-logic process rules, the article by Runkel and Peizer (1968) can be recommended as the clearest effort in this direction.

The predictive principle was a method for identifying from the structure matrix the relations most likely to change if imbalance were discovered (assuming change of relations to be the preferred mode to redress imbalance in the given situation). The crucial psychological assumption enabling predictions to be made was the *least effort principle:* that the minimal set of relations which could be changed to yield a balanced structure matrix would in fact be the set that would change. For some structures, the least effort or minimum change principle yields a unique prediction of which relation(s) should change, but in other cases, more than one minimal set is possible, as in the original six-element example (Abelson and Rosenberg, 1958, p. 7).

With only three elements (as in the standard *P-O-X* triads of Chapter 2), the prediction cannot be unique, but with four elements, it is easy to conceive structures with the property that one particular relation change is the only single change that can bring about total balance. A set of such structures constituted the core materials for a subsequent experiment (Rosenberg & Abelson, 1960) designed to test the least effort principle.

In this experiment, the subjects were instructed to imagine themselves in the role of a department store owner interested in maximizing sales in his store. Each of three groups of subjects was then presented with a slightly different initial attitude structure concerning a perplexing situation which had begun to develop in the store because Fenwick, the astute and professionally excellent manager of the rug department, was reportedly planning to mount a modern art display in his department, while information independently available to the owner strongly suggested that modern art displays tended to reduce department store sales sharply. The three groups differed as follows: in Group I, the store owner was said personally to admire both the personality of Fenwick and the aesthetics of modern art; in Group II, Fenwick was presented as likeable, but modern art as loathsome; and in Group III, Fenwick was said to be obnoxious and modern art loathsome. These various configurations for the three groups are shown in the Figure.

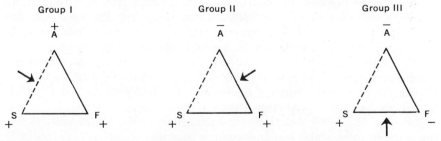

FIGURE.   Three Imbalanced Structures. *S* denotes the concept 'sales'; *A,* 'modern art display'; and *F,* 'Fenwick.' Signs attached to these symbols indicate the initial valuations of the concepts by subjects assigned to the three structure groups. Dotted lines indicate negative relations between concepts; solid lines, positive relations. Arrows indicate imbalanced bands.

Then all subjects were presented with the same three written communications, each challenging a different aspect of the information originally given to the owner. (These communications were presented as summary transcripts of remarks made by three of the store's Vice Presidents during a conference in which the rug department situation was discussed.) One communication argued that modern art displays really helped sales rather than hurt them (in view of the rapidity of change of public tastes, etc.). In a second communication it was maintained that Fenwick really could be talked out of his plan to display modern art, while the third communication purported to reveal that Fenwick's management of the rug department had not been shrewd at all, but rather poor when evaluated by general criteria for department managers in an expanding market.

The experimental hypothesis was that Groups I, II, and III, each needing a different single relation change to balance their cognitive structures, would be differentially susceptible to these three communications, because each could provide a respective group with the changed relation it needed, as indicated in the Figure. Thus if Group I were to accept the argument that modern art really helps sales (but reject the other two arguments), they could end with the balanced conclusion that shrewd and likeable Fenwick planned an aesthetic art display which would help sales. Group II, by accepting only the argument that Fenwick would indeed not post the display, could reach closure by believing that shrewd and likeable Fenwick would reject involvement with an ugly display which would hurt sales. Finally, Group III, if it behaved according to the hypothesis of structural balancing by least effort, would accept the communication impugning Fenwick's record and conclude that incompetent and obnoxious Fenwick was indeed planning an ugly art show ruinous for store sales.

The predictions about differential *communication acceptance* for the three groups were strongly supported, and these results have since been cited (Brown, 1965; Insko, 1967) as fairly clear evidence that a minimum change principle can make accurate predictions in situations involving moderately complicated cognitive structures. However, an unanticipated theoretical difficulty revealed by the study was that following exposure to the three communications, the conclusions reached by the subjects about the total structure on a post-questionnaire were frequently not the balanced configurations prescribed by the least effort hypothesis. This was not a problem with Group I, whose subjects both accepted the argument about the good effect of a potential art display on sales and maintained the happy vision of good Fenwick doing this good thing. However, in Group II, although most subjects were initially willing to accept the argument that Fenwick would not pursue his plan, a number of subjects apparently changed their minds and slipped into the happy final resolution pattern of Group I. With Group III, the final versions of the dilemma were heterogeneous and usually unresolved. The formal prediction had been that the subjects would resolve the perplexing situation by blaming the bad plan on bad Fenwick, but by hindsight this prediction clearly ignores the obvious fact that a bad action by a bad actor may leave disequilibrium in the victim not because the action is inexplicable but because it is painful.

These irregularities in the data led us (Rosenberg & Abelson, 1960, pp.

143 ff.) to recognize a "dual-motive" approach by individuals to attitude structures: on the one hand, the achievement of balance, and on the other, hedonic satisfaction through the maximization of gain and/or the minimization of loss. This theoretical recognition could hardly be regarded as a blinding insight, since it is quite in accord with common sense, and many others have made related points before or since. (A similar apposition between consistency maintenance and self-enhancement motives occurs often in the dissonance theory literature. Cf. Sections III E and IV F. Nevertheless, it helped to promote a healthful antidote to total reliance on a single formal balance rule for the prediction of changes in attitude structures.

Among the most recent studies promoting a broadened view of structural change principles is that of Burnstein (1967), who found that in addition to a minimal effort balancing principle, support could also be found for a "positivity" principle, by which more relations were changed from negative to positive than from positive to negative. His structural examples involved interpersonal liking and attitudes toward the 1964 Presidential candidates, thus a "preference for positivity" in his study specifically meant that his college subjects tended to prefer to perceive people as liking, not disliking each other, and supporting, not opposing candidates. The positivity principle is rather similar to our hedonic principle and we, too, found a preference for positive over negative relations (e.g., "Modern art *helps* sales"). However, the two principles are not necessarily identical, since some individuals might regard the negative actions involved in opposition to an evil cause as more satisfying than the positive actions performed in support of a good cause. (Indeed, there exists some journalistic lore that voting behavior is more often 'ornery' than supportive.) In any case, we do not presently have good evidence distinguishing these two principles. Perhaps in the quiet world of university questionnaire studies of hypothetical situations, there is more of a tendency to idealize the potential for the occurrence of goodness than there might be in field studies of behavior.

Among other tendencies supported in the Burnstein study was that toward *reciprocity:* if an observer thinks Joe likes Bill, then he will also think that Bill will come to like Joe. In the original Abelson-Rosenberg (1958) psycho-logic, the reciprocity principle was conveniently assumed theoretically, rather than being left open to empirical test. We simply asserted, "Relations are considered to be symmetric, i.e., if ArB, then BrA" (p. 4). Obviously, cognitions about unrequited social relationships are possible, and it is reasonable to inquire whether perceived social asymmetries tend toward symmetry. (The word 'perceived' is crucial here, since we are dealing with cognitive structures. The tendencies toward change of *actual* social relations are discussed in Chapters 51–53). But in the attitude arenas with which we were mainly concerned, the question of relational reciprocity did not arise so sharply because often a reversal of sentence subject and object produced no new semantic possibilities. For example, the only meaningful reversal of "Action A serves Goal B" seems to be the redundant "Goal B is served by Action A," in this case removing reciprocity from the empirical to the definitional realm. In still other examples not involving mutual sentiments between Actors, however, meaningful asymmetries are certainly possible; e.g., "Mr. X loves Heavy Drinking" and "Heavy Drinking harms

Mr. X." Thus the whole question of relational asymmetry is very much an open matter.

A much more detailed analysis of studies involving ratings of *P-O-X* situations is given by Newcomb in Chapter 2. I used the Burnstein (1967) study in particular here because it reflected directly on several of the factors emerging from our "Fenwick" study. I will next turn to newer directions toward which the study of psycho-logic has led me in travelling a path somewhat distinct from the route described by Rosenberg in Chapter 4. First, however, it will be helpful to interpolate a commentary on certain criticisms of the earlier psycho-logic.

Criticisms of Psycho-Logic

The most usual criticism of the psycho-logic based on the structure matrix is that the classification of relations merely into broad positive and negative categories is (among other possible defects) quantitatively quite crude (cf. McGuire, 1966b; Kiesler, Collins, & Miller, 1968, Ch. 4). Lacking quantitative specifications, any predictive device such as the least-effort principle must make use of the obviously unrealistic assumption that the effort involved in changing any single relation is the same as that involved in changing any other. Thus attempts at quantification seem to offer attractive possibilities for improvement of the system.

Later in this volume (Section IV C), a variety of propositions concerning relative determinants of structure change will be given. Included is one explicitly requiring quantification along the dimension of "value-centrality," which might be regarded as the strength of the positive relation between the self-element and the element in question. It is easy to imagine a simple scale quantifying value-centrality. In fact, Rosenberg (1956) has long used such a scale. It is likewise not difficult to produce relative ratings of the degree to which different relation verbs (with or without adverbs) express strengths of relation between elements. As noted previously, Osgood, Saporta, and Nunnally (1956) have had judges perform just such a task. Thus it is tempting to suppose that one might readily fill in an entire structure matrix with quantitative values and apply some kind of generalized least-effort principle to the problem of structural change.

There are at least two immediate problems associated with such a conceivable attempt. The most sticky problem seems to be that there is no available way to calibrate the *strengths of evaluations of objects* by the self with the *strengths of relations between objects*. The two necessary kinds of scaling operations do not have common units. The kind of question which in effect would have to be posed to subjects (either directly or through some subtle chain of mediated inferences) would be, for example, "Do you fear lung cancer to a degree greater or less than the degree to which cigarette smoking causes lung cancer?" The comparison between (say) intensity of fear and intensity of causation is a perplexing 'apples vs. oranges' question which does not seem to have a ready answer, although I would not wish to claim that it is insoluble.

The second problem concerns how one might manipulate a quantitative structure matrix even if one had it. Here some clues may arise by considering an analogy with factor analytic procedures, although the details have not really been worked out. The essential insight is that a totally balanced structure matrix (with + 1's and − 1's representing positive and negative relations, respectively) has the formal appearance of a correlation matrix arising from a single bipolar factor. Thus if a quantitative structure matrix (with some clever choice of diagonal entries) were factored, the relative size of the first matrix root might be a good measure of the degree of balance. (This idea has been independently proposed by Phillips [1967] and by Abelson [1967b].) But more interesting for present purposes is the notion that the largest absolute entries in the residual matrix after extraction of the first factor would identify the relations most discrepant from balance and therefore under the greatest presumed strain to change. This idea is probably worth some modest exploration.

A more telling criticism of the psycho-logic is that it gives too little scope to the possibilities of human thought, even as practiced by mediocre thinkers, and, on the other side of the same coin, that it imputes the drawing of certain supposedly balanced conclusions which are manifestly absurd by any standard. In short, it is too rigid and too monolithic a system, incapable of even the simplest nuance, and guilty of ignoring a number of very important semantic distinctions between types of elements and relations. One need not necessarily adopt the point of view of what McGuire in Chapter 17 calls the "complexity theories," in which stimulation, variety, novelty, and cognitive challenge are seen as welcomed by the individual to feel that the simplest form of psycho-logic is just simply too simple. (But see Chapters 15 and 16 for this other point of view, and Zajonc [1960a] for an early criticism of the excessive cognitive trivialization specified in balance-type formulations.)

BEYOND PSYCHO-LOGIC

Modes of Inconsistency Resolution

The original psycho-logic allowed changes of evaluations or of perceived relations as the only modes of imbalance resolution. Nevertheless, it had long been apparent that other possibilities were available, including such devices difficult to pin down as 'differentiation' and 'rationalization.' Accordingly, I attempted two theoretical analyses of some of these other possibilities, one within the balance tradition, the other somewhat independent of it.

In the first attempt (Abelson, 1959) paraphrased here, four modes were named: denial, bolstering, differentiation, and transcendence. Given two valued elements imbalanced by a relational connection, 'denial' referred to "a direct attack upon one or both of the cognitive elements or the relation between them" (p. 344). Thus denial encompasses exactly the sorts of changes already discussed: evaluation change and relation change. Included in the category of relation change is not only the 'incredulity reaction' (Osgood & Tannenbaum, 1955) to highly incongruous assertions ("The Pope endorses LSD?—Ridiculous!"), but also the delayed exercise of disbelief following a deliberate cognitive effort to support the contrary assertion ("The Pope would oppose LSD. After all, the Church disapproves of unnatural interference with normal bodily processes."). Moreover, denial was meant to be applicable to all signed relations, not just assertions by sources. ("Does tough U.S. military policy *discourage* Communist expansion? No, on the contrary, it *encourages* such expansion by creating sympathy for the underdog.")

The cognitive mechanism by which denial was said usually to be attempted by the individual (although this was perhaps not clearly stated in the original article) was through the *search for and emphasis on relevant sentences supporting the denial attempt.* By 'sentences' are meant the familiar *ArB* constructions of psycho-logic. Using the example given above, let *A* denote 'the Church,' *n* the negative relation 'disapproves of,' and *B* the element 'unnatural interference with normal bodily processes.' The sentence *AnB* may then be said to support the denial of the assertion "The Pope endorses LSD." Establishing the precise meaning here of *support* constitutes a conceptual problem to be addressed below. In any case, denial was viewed as a process rather than as simply a possibility.

'Bolstering' was also conceived as a *search-and-salience* process. In the situation where no sentences could be found to deny either one of the two evaluations or the relation creating the imbalance, the individual could try to find sentences tending to increase the evaluative polarity of the strongest of the two initial evaluations. This would 'bolster' the element by diluting the disturbing impact of the original imbalanced assertion. Many good acts of the Pope might be remembered and rehearsed to offset a single inexplicable denigrating pronouncement. This mechanism would be considered a temporary expedient rather than a genuine mode of imbalance resolution.

In some contrast to these two modes, 'differentiation' involved something more than search and new emphasis. It posited the *splitting* of an element *into two parts,* a 'good' part and a 'bad' part. One of these parts having stood in imbalanced relation with a second element, the other part would necessarily stand in balanced relation. For example, if the concept of LSD had some good aspects for our hypothetical individual (say, medical use in certain appropriate cases), then it would be balanced for him to believe that the Pope perhaps endorsed these good aspects, but certainly not the other bad aspects. (Abelson [1959] and Heider [1958, p. 209] have given several other illustrative examples.) Note that the defining aspects for the parts must still come from available information retrieved and reconstituted by the individual, much as in denial and bolstering. The unique feature intrinsic to differentiation is that an element previously manifesting internal conceptual unity must afterwards withstand the tension of disunity, else the resolution collapse. Presumably there would be tension to the extent that the various aspects of the element necessarily possessed contiguity or common fate and could not easily be separated. While with remote objects such as Popes and Drugs such tension might be minimal, much more differentiational difficulty would obtain with proximal objects such as Mothers-in-law, who bring their good and bad aspects in a single visit, or Pending Decisions, which when made will effectuate some good and some bad consequences simultaneously. It would be straining to say to oneself, "The non-totally-satisfactory car I just purchased is really two cars: the good one that I actually bought and the lemon that I didn't really buy." (The two mechanisms dissonance theory predicts in this situation are bolstering [dwelling on the good features of the car] and denial [putting down the bad features], with converse use of these same two mechanisms on any appealing unchosen alternative car. But differentiation as such is not predicted.)

Any resolution of the paradox of a particular unified entity containing affectively competitive subparts would constitute the basis for the mechanism of 'transcendence.' This mechanism was in my original article presumed to be difficult, and to necessitate invoking a superordinate concept explaining the contradictory unity. Various institutionalized supports for transcendence appear to exist (proverbs: "Every rose has its thorns"; role prescriptions: "You have to accept that kind of difficulty in this kind of job"; religious teaching: "God has His reasons"; etc.).

Despite the manifest emphasis on modes of resolution, the main thrust of my 1959 paper was in the direction of more detailed specification of exactly what was supposed to be happening in the accomplishment of changes in the elements or relations of a belief structure. These 'happenings' were subsequently labeled cognitive *microprocesses* (Rosenberg & Abelson, 1960, pp. 148 ff.). Neither the psycho-logic nor indeed any other consistency formulation had treated the 'how' of cognitive changes.

In my next attempt (Abelson, 1963), a further mode of resolution, *rationalization*, was detailed. In this mode, some two-link chain of relations with special properties was said to be constructed (following a search for possibly appropriate sentences, as with the previous modes). Taking as a prototypic imbalanced sentence "A Good Actor engaging in a Bad Action," three subvarieties of rationalization were postulated: (a) "Reinterpret final goal," (b) "Accidental by-product," and (c) "Find the prime mover." The three differ in the location in a chain at which new material is added. In (a), the Bad Action is seen to lead ultimately to a Good Goal, thus yielding a construction in which the Good Actor is pursuing a Good Goal. In (b), the Bad Action is seen as the accidental result of a Good Action, yielding a construction in which the Good Actor has had bad luck while pursuing a Good Action. In (c), a Bad Actor is viewed as controlling the Good Actor, with the upshot that the Bad Actor is really responsible for the Bad Action. Roughly the same three varieties of rationalization are available (and sensible) for the case of the initial imbalanced sentence, "A Bad Actor engaging in a Good Action," except of course for appropriate reversals of signs in the ingredients used in the rationalization.

This description of rationalization was embedded in a discussion of a computer program which would realize the various microprocesses by exercising them within a simulated cognitive system. The nature of such an enterprise is described in detail below, but first it will be worthwhile to take stock briefly, and ask ourselves a nettlesome question.

The microprocesses for the modes of resolution sketched above are largely concerned with the retrieval of sentences satisfying certain relational properties. But what is the process by which evaluative change is postulated to take place? Consider the mechanism of bolstering, in which sentences are sought which will tend to increase the evaluative polarity of an element enmeshed in an awkward imbalanced sentence. How exactly is evaluative polarity supposed to increase itself once the sought sentence is found? Does evaluation 'rub off' from one cognitive element onto another?

The Hypothesis of Evaluative Induction

In the article described above (Abelson, 1963), it is asserted, "When a sentence is present in thought, the affect aroused by each of the two elements [in the sentence] tends to become attached to the other element" (p. 285). The name given to this process was "evaluative transfer," and in an earlier treatment, "induction of charge" (Rosenberg & Abelson, 1960, p. 150). Unfortunately, the statement of this hypothesis has been regarded as somewhat obscure (for example, by Anderson in Chapter 73 of this volume), and is probably deserving of a clearer statement, which can be given as follows (here we finally settle on the term 'evaluative induction'):

1. Throughout the time interval when two elements, *A* and *B*, are connected by an associative relation in a sentence in thought, 'direct evaluative induction' will occur between these elements; when the relation is dissociative, 'reversed evaluative induction' will occur.

2. In direct evaluative induction, the direction of change of evaluation of each element is given by the sign of the evaluation of the other element; in reversed evaluative induction, the direction of change of each element is given by the reversed sign of the evaluation of the other element.

3. The amount of change of evaluation of element *A* is a direct function of the extremity of evaluation of element *B*, an inverse function of the extremity of evaluation of element *A*, and a direct function of the strength of the bond from *B* to *A*; the converse statements apply for the amount of change of evaluation of element *B*.

The essentials of these points appeared in the earlier articles. What has been added here is the crucial notion of sign reversal with dissociative relations (intended all along but somehow omitted from previous statements).

Certain ambiguous terms remain in the present formulation (*viz.*, "a sentence in thought," and "strength of bond"), but this slight degree of vagueness is deliberate in order to leave some flexibility in what is at present an untested hypothesis.

This evaluative induction hypothesis serves several theoretical intents simultaneously. Originally it was devised to incorporate the established effects (Osgood & Tannenbaum, 1955) from the congruity principle for source assertions about concepts without suffering the theoretical disadvantages involved in a completely literal interpretation of this principle. (I do not refer here to the use of the congruity principle in the context of 'word mixtures'—see Chapter 3 for Tannenbaum's comments on that separate problem area—but only in its application to communication assertions.) Overzealous application of a congruity prediction for source-concept linkages leads to too much regression of evaluations toward neutrality. If a moderately favorable ($+ 2$) source incongruously endorses a moderately unfavorable ($- 2$) concept, for example, the pure congruity prediction is that an equilibrium is reached in which both source and concept receive neutral (0) evaluations. Other cases in which a source endorses an oppositely valenced concept yield predictions comparably distressing to the intuition.

The supporting data from Tannenbaum's original study (Osgood & Tannenbaum, 1955) happily did not offend common sense. Evaluations of sources and concepts moved *only a fraction of the distance toward the predicted equilibria*: about one-third of the way, according to rough estimate (*ibid.*, Table 6). The evaluative induction principle says, in effect, that evaluative changes of the elements in imbalanced sentences come in small doses through gradual affective erosion *as long as the imbalanced sentence remains 'in thought.'* But since modes of imbalance resolution altering the sentence will be rapidly sought, the process of evaluative change will ordinarily be soon interrupted and evaluative inductions will be slight, much as the data indicate. If a liberal Californian is told, "Shirley Temple praises

Berkeley," he may be momentarily inclined to think slightly better of Shirley Temple and slightly worse of Berkeley than originally, but he will probably soon manage a denial ("Really, she loathes Berkeley") or a rationalization ("She only said that to mollify the alumni") or a differentiation ("She's only praising the prestige educational aspects, not the student activists"). Any of these resolutions would halt the process of induction of favorable affect toward Shirley Temple and unfavorable affect toward Berkeley.

The case of associative connection between two elements with different degrees of the same evaluative sign is interesting and critical. Say I am confronted with, "The BBC ($+$ 2) recommends isometric exercises ($+$ 1)." According to the congruity principle, this sentence embodies an incongruity because the evaluations of source and concept are not numerically identical. But there is no imbalance, since two positive elements are positively linked. The congruity principle predicts that both evaluations will move toward an intermediary equilibrium point ($+$ 1.67). Balance theory, as such, predicts nothing about evaluative change, regarding the sentence to be stable and therefore quiescent. Nonetheless, the evaluative induction hypothesis predicts that each element would induce *positive evaluation onto the other*, thus that both positive evaluations would increase rather than regress toward compromise. This effect, however, would in all likelihood be of small magnitude, because the sentence would present no problem of imbalance, and, lacking interest, would not long remain 'in thought.'

Nevertheless, we have a differential prediction here. In this situation the congruity principle predicts that the evaluation of the more polarized of the two elements moves (slightly) toward neutrality, while the evaluative induction principle predicts that it moves (slightly) farther away from neutrality. Tannenbaum's original data, at least in their aggregated published form, were not sufficiently addressed nor sensitive to the distinction between these two alternatives. The reader will, however, recognize overtones of the 'adding vs. averaging' controversy which has fairly recently invaded the impression formation literature. This topic is aired extensively in Section IV D, and it suffices to make two points here. First of all, one must be careful not simply to identify assertions about concepts by sources with the stimuli typically used in studies of how subjects form impressions of persons (e.g., adjective lists). Caution is a useful watchword in view also of the many experimental variables that affect impression-formation studies (cf. Chapter 75, among others). Still, it is interesting that the evaluative induction principle, arising from a balance theory tradition, makes an additive rather than an averaging type of prediction when like-signed entities are dynamically conjoined. This state of affairs stands in contradiction to Fishbein's (1967) unjustified belief that consistency theories must of necessity make averaging predictions. A very careful examination of solid experimental results in the face of subtly differing predictions would be extremely worthwhile.

The evaluative induction hypothesis serves still other theoretical purposes. One of these is to 'explain' how bolstering might 'work.' When the evaluation of a cognitive element is called into question ("Your friend Jones is rude to secretaries"), the bolstering mechanism requires that new sentences be found consistent with the threatened evaluation. ("Yes, but he works very hard for the organization. Besides, he can tell a lot of funny stories.") Now, what is the function of these new sentences? Presumably they serve to re-store the positive affect toward the element (Jones) which the imbalanced sentence tends to take away. And these events labeled 'restore' or 'take away' are precisely the affective changes prescribed by evaluative induction. By the hypothesis, a negative sentence (while 'in thought') about a positive element induces negative change in the evaluation of the element; the new positive sentences (while 'in thought') about the same element induce posi-tive change, thus tending to return the evaluation to its original value (or conceivably even overshooting so that the element momentarily becomes more highly valued than before).

Coordinate with this explanation of bolstering is a particular suggestion of what it is that might be considered aversive about imbalance: namely, that *all imbalanced sentences* (in thought) *induce negative affect onto positive elements and/or positive affect onto negative elements.* (See also Chapter 7.) If one supposes a basic motive to maintain *the direction* of affective orientation toward objects, then any change of evaluation toward the orienta-tion of opposite sign would be unwelcome. Thus in conjunction with the evaluative induction hypothesis, the balance principle requires that Man continue to love his Loves and hate his Hates, else he pass through trouble.

Pursuing this theoretical regress for a moment, one might ask what function is served by the maintenance of the direction of affective orienta-tion toward objects. At least one of the answers which has been suggested (for example, by Collins in Chapter 13 and K. Davis in Chapter 21) is that unequivocal *behavioral* orientation toward important objects is crucial for organismic adjustment or even survival. To the extent that stable affective positions prepare and predispose toward such unequivocal behavioral orien-tations, then they, too, become crucial.

A final and perhaps most interesting theoretical application of the evaluative induction hypothesis lies in understanding attitude change. In my second modes of resolution paper (Abelson, 1963) I used the expression "default of resistance" (p. 288) as a metaphoric account of what may typi-cally happen in cases of reversal of affects toward objects. Suppose an im-balanced sentence presents a cognitive problem that admits of no ready mode by which its aversive implications may be resisted. Because the prob-lem is unsolved, the individual continues to think about it; the more he thinks about it, the more evaluative induction takes place between the op-posed elements. Finally, the originally less polarized element crosses the neutral point of evaluation, and the problem has been solved not by a resolu-tion mode, but by attitude change in 'default of resistance.'

As a hypothetical example of this sequence, consider an individual hearing incontrovertible news that the mayor of his town, Mr. Marvelous ($+2$), is under the complete control of the Cosa Nostra (-3). Immediately the Mayor seems worse (Evaluative induction). Perhaps it is not true (At-tempted denial). But the facts cannot be denied (Fails). Maybe the Cosa Nostra isn't all bad (Evaluative induction). Hmph. Can the Mayor have an ulterior purpose? (Attempted rationalization). Hardly likely (Fails). It's terrible for the Mayor to be mixed up in this (More evaluative induc-tion). He *has* done some good things for the city (Bolstering). But nothing that would excuse gangsterism (Fails). Can you imagine? Mr. Marvelous, a gangster! (Attitude change).

There is apparently another type of attitude change in which the individual deliberately, rather than reluctantly, changes his evaluation of an object. This is the way in which attitude change is typically treated in dissonance theory discourse. If, for an insufficient reward, the individual commits himself to saying X when he believes *not-X* (Festinger & Carlsmith, 1959), high dissonance is created such that (under suitable experimental precautions) "one way ... the dissonance can be reduced is for the person to change his opinion" (p. 204). Or suppose an individual undergoes a psychologically painful initiation to join a supposedly interesting group which then turns out to be dull (Aronson & Mills, 1959). The dissonance here is said to be reducible if the individual can "find the group [to be] more attractive" (p. 177). Again, the process is seen as self-conscious and under volitional control. A great many other examples of this kind exist in the dissonance literature, and the attitude change is almost always characterized like a spigot to be turned on when need requires. One way this 'volitional attitude change' can be understood in terms of the modes of resolution above is as a variant of bolstering. The evaluation of a negative element is 'shoved' toward or across the neutral point by a search for supportive cognitive materials. If this be the appropriate theoretical account, then evaluative induction (or something very much like it) would again be the basic dynamic principle involved. (I do not necessarily assert that this *is* the proper account, but at any rate it is certainly a possibility).

The evaluative induction principle is so theoretically rich that it certainly deserves extensive experimental test. The paramount difficulty is that the predictions depend upon the specification that the sentence be 'in thought.' Since we have no direct way of knowing when a *particular sentence* is in thought (though perhaps there are reliable indicators of *general* symbolic mental activity—eye movements, frowning, EEG patterns, etc.), the predictions seem forever subject to an ambiguous escape clause. One potential solution to this difficulty, however, would seem to be just what it is for other unobservable constructs—namely, that independent variables be specified which theoretically should lead to more or less 'thinking about a sentence,' and predictions made and tested accordingly. The other potential approach, the one I have recently been following, is to use the much more indirect strategy of computer simulation.

WHAT ABOUT DISSONANCE?

All of the foregoing has been concerned with cognitive inconsistencies arising from affective imbalances. It may well be asked, where does dissonance fit into the picture—or does it require an entirely separate theoretical framework?

In dissonance theory, the crucial relationship between cognitive elements is the relationship 'follows from,' and the critical sentences are of the form '*X* follows from *Y*.' The state of dissonance can be defined by the 'triad': Ego cognizes *Y*; *X* follows from *Y*; Ego cognizes *not-X*. There appears to be a tantalizing formal similarity between this triad and certain examples of Heiderian imbalances, and one suspects (or at any rate hopes) that there may exist a general set of schemata incorporating both imbalances and dissonances.

Imbalances vs. Dissonances: Comparative Examples

The differences between the two systems seem perplexing. The cases in which X follows from Y in the dissonance view (see Chapter 1, pp. 6-10) do not include large classes of 'implications' of the psycho-logic (p. 114 above). Although the issue has not been adequately aired in the literature, dissonance theorists typically contend in private discussion that if, say, Joe likes Harry and Harry dislikes Bill, it does not necessarily 'follow' that Joe dislikes Bill. To the question "Why not?" the curt answer by the dissonance theorist is "Why should it?" and the polite answer is usually something like, "Maybe Joe can like both Bill and Harry even though there is antagonism between the two of them. The world is full of examples like that. After all, I wouldn't automatically dislike someone that a friend of mine disliked. Nor would I expect that if I disliked someone, all my friends would uniformly dislike him. You can find personality clashes or affinities for all sorts of different reasons for different pairs of people."

Aronson's notion of the 'underlying cognition' (p. 21) is relevant to the above example. Many people might have an underlying cognition of friendships as idiosyncratic dyads obeying no particular triadic laws. Now, it might be argued that such an overview would represent a successful resolution (transcendence?) of prior imbalances. Still, it would be unrealistic to insist upon a general psychological law that the perception of formally imbalanced sociometric situations should set dynamic balancing forces in motion, if many or most individuals accepted such situations as normal and commonplace and were quite unmoved to reorder their cognitions in any pertinent way.

This point immediately raises two other considerations. First, there is the issue of individual differences in these 'underlying cognitions'; and second, granting such differences, how would one assess them? Some individuals might indeed consider it normal and natural that, e.g., an enemy of a friend is necessarily an enemy. Their underlying cognition might be, for example, that the struggle for survival in a hostile environment requires decisive classification of every person as either a friend admissible to the in-group gang or as a common enemy belonging to an out-group gang. A dissonance theorist should grant that for a person with this world-view it *would* follow from 'Joe likes Harry' and 'Harry dislikes Bill' that 'Joe dislikes Bill.' Given the other two premises, it would be dissonant to know that 'Joe likes Bill,' as this would be a recognition of the possibility of positive affective bonds across hostile gang boundaries, a possibility as absurd (for our hypothetical individual) as any a perceptual dissonance such as snow during a heat wave.

The conceptual possibility is thus very clear that for some individuals, an affective imbalance based on sentiment relations would also be a dissonance, whereas for others, dissonance would be absent. The operational question of how to distinguish the one type of individual from the other is treated in a later section. The reason that dissonance theorists have not included imbalances among sentiment relations in their catalogue of dissonances is, I suspect, that they do not believe that the underlying cognition requiring balanced sentiments is sufficiently widespread.

But consider a second example of a possible implication from the psycho-logic: Joe uses (throws) a fire-bomb, and a fire-bomb causes destruction in a target area. Would a dissonance theorist say that it 'follows' that Joe wants destruction in the target area? I think that the answer is now 'yes.' The 'underlying cognition' in this case is: *What a person's knowing actions will cause, he desires.*

Although one may wish to introduce qualifications and subtleties into this straightforward statement of the naive notion of intention, even as it stands it has such a strong intuitive appeal that it is difficult to imagine a serious alternative. That people act purposefully, everyone knows, or certainly assumes. It is both imbalanced and dissonant that a person would freely carry out an action he knew would produce something he did not want.

Note that even though balance and dissonance theory both encompass this important case of intentional action, the natural 'follows from' statement of dissonance theory is more specific than the statement made by psycho-logic. If person *A* carries out action *B* (*ApB*), and *B* causes consequence *C* (*BpC*), one may educe *ApC* from the rules of psycho-logic, but no specific interpretation of this final positive relation *p* is specified. 'Person *A is responsible for* consequence *C*' is a sensible albeit not very daring eduction. More to the point is *A wants C*, the defining sentence of the intention paradigm. However, certain other positive relations when inserted in *ApC* yield conclusions which, although balanced, are vapid or irrelevant: for example, *A recommends C* or *A owns C*. By contrast with this relational indeterminacy of psycho-logic, the dissonance paradigm would presumably be confined to the relevant case, *A wants C*.

Let us consider still another case, one in which balance and dissonance interpretations part company quite sharply. This is the case of a Romantic Triangle: Joe loves Ann; Ann loves Harry. . . . Does it 'follow' that Joe likes Harry, as psycho-logic would have it? This is an evidently awkward example, since intuition and experience clearly suggest that under these circumstances Joe would not like Harry. In some reviews of balance theory (e.g., by Newcomb in Chapter 2) this situation has been reinterpreted to try to remove the paradox. Joe, it is said, wants to possess his love object, Ann; but Harry, by alienating Ann's affections, opposes Joe in his plan; therefore Joe hates Harry, as both balance theory and common sense require. In this reinterpretation, the prototypic distinction is made between the *coorientation* of the two men toward *Ann the person*, and their *contraorientation* toward the behavioral outcome, *sole possession of Ann*. To the extent that they both share a favorable opinion of Ann, the two men should like or at least respect each other as individuals of comparable good taste; but to the extent that they both compete for the unsharable commodity of sole possession of Ann with neither the clear winner, they should dislike or hate each other.

This more refined view of the Romantic Triangle yields the not unrealistic analysis that the two men may simultaneously respect and hate each other. However, the reinterpretation requires certain seemingly arbitrary semantic contortions in order to make matters come out right. A dissonance analysis, by contrast, would probably consist of a no-nonsense appeal to the well understood concept of romantic rivalry. It follows directly from 'Joe loves Ann' and 'Ann loves Harry' that 'Joe hates Harry' because of the underlying cognition, 'Men hate their rivals.' This derivation avoids the nuance and nuisance of the balance principle type of formalism, and appeals directly to a 'rivalry principle.' There is of course nothing in balance theory that demands that no other cognitive principles ever be operative. Thus if there were such a thing as a 'rivalry principle,' for example, it could coexist with the balance principle and others defining a cognitive system. The possibility of factors additional to balance was recognized, in fact urged, by Heider (1958, p. 210).

It may rightly be objected, however, that the rivalry principle statement is not a 'derivation' at all: it seems to beg the question by jumping directly to the conclusion demanded by common sense. Something follows because it follows, and the critic would say that this kind of dissonance theoretical reasoning is either gratuitous or perhaps altogether wrong (cf. Pepitone, Chapter 20, p. 324).

We have arrived at a critical theoretical juncture. Taking stock of some of the possible relationships between balanced-based implications from psycho-logic and dissonance style interpretations of 'follows from,' we have noted three possibilities: (a) implications based on sentiment relations among peers seem plausibly handled by the balance treatment but largely ignored by dissonance theory (although perhaps they need not be); (b) implications based on the commonly held model of intentional action are well handled both by psycho-logic and dissonance formulations; (c) implications in romantic rivalry situations seem well handled by a dissonance style of statement but become tangled in the balance system (although perhaps they need not be). There are of course many other cognitive scenarios that could be comparatively analyzed, but these three will suffice for our present purposes. In the course of our analysis, we noted the problems of individual differences in implicative structures because of differences in underlying cognitions, and above all the desideratum that 'follows from' be given some unambiguous definition.

Operationalizing Psychological Implication

The particular operation I propose for defining the content of psychological implications I shall call the Naive Question Game. The procedure is suitable for individual respondents, thus capable of revealing individual differences in implicative structures.

With respect to any given situation X, the individual is asked the simple question: "Here is X. How come?" For example, "Here are these two fellows, Joe and Bill, and Joe dislikes Bill. How come?" There may be any number of reasonable answers, such as "Bill dislikes Joe," "Bill is obnoxious," "Bill offended Joe," etc. Each one of these specifies a possible implication, e.g., 'Bill is obnoxious implies Joe dislikes Bill'; or, worded alternatively, 'It follows from Bill's obnoxiousness that Joe dislikes him.' In general, if the answer to "How come X?" is, "Because Y," then we may say that psychologically, 'Y implies X' or that 'X follows from Y.'

One evident feature of the above example about Joe and Bill is the great variety of possible answers, none of which stand out as much more compelling than the others. This apparent absence of a prepotent causal implication toward a stated sentiment relation is in my view coordinate with the dissonance theorist's reluctance to include sentiment triangles in his situational catalogue. A conceivable answer to "How come Joe dislikes Bill?" is, "Because a friend of Joe's dislikes Bill." This does not seem off-hand to be an answer that would very commonly occur, but recall our hypothetical individual oriented toward the sociometry of gangs. Imagine, just to sharpen the example a bit, that the respondent is a Negro militant whose answer is, "Joe dislikes Bill because Joe is black and Bill is white." For this respondent we infer the strong cognitive model, 'Racial difference implies enmity.'

Notice that the rivalry principle of our previous section was also stated as a strong model, albeit one which is almost universal rather than one specially requiring ethnocentricity. To the question, "Here are Joe, Ann, and Harry who all know each other. Joe hates Harry. How come?" the answer leaps out, "They are rivals for Ann's affection." That a common affection can in certain circumstances imply enmity, a state of affairs (at least superficially) contrary to balance theory, is very quickly revealed by the Naive Question Game.

Now let us return to the second of the three examples of the previous section. "Here is Joe who threw a fire-bomb. How come?" The answer (in some variant) that immediately comes to mind is, "Because he wanted to cause destruction." Intuitively, this intention model is a clear and prepotent source of psychological implications. It follows from wanting to achieve certain ends that one will act so as to try to produce them. Here the psycho-logic and dissonance points of view were clearly in confluence, and the Naive Question Game has helped support our intuition that the intention paradigm is such a strong source of psychological implication as to have necessitated representation in both theoretical systems.

Interestingly, Aronson in Chapter 1 (pp. 9-10) suggests a related questioning technique for determining what 'follows from' what. He proposes to tell subjects, "Situation Y obtains, and now I'm going to tell you something about X. What do you expect this fact to be?" One of his examples concerns a great novelist who either does or does not beat his wife. The respondents would be asked their expectations about this pertinent datum. (Brown [1965, p. 597] phrases the relevant question similarly: "Given A, would you say that B or not-B is the more probable?")

There are two differences between Aronson's suggestion and my own. He proposes to state to the subject the antecedent element Y and ask what consequent X follows from it. I propose to give the consequent element X and ask what antecedent Y it followed from. The reason for my preference is that since dissonance is defined via the presence of not-X, the contrary of the consequent, it is X that one wishes to specify, rather than Y. Aronson gets around this by giving the subject a forced choice between X and not-X after fixing Y. But turned around, the question may be entirely open-ended, with X fixed and the choice of Y left completely free to the subjects. If many different Y's occur (as in the example of Joe disliking Bill) this suggests a weak implicational bond between any particular Y and the given X, and conversely. This extra information would seem valuable, but perhaps it is offset by the trouble in coding open-ended responses. This Y-to-X vs. Y-from-X difference may not be of central importance, and both directions should no doubt be tried.

The more crucial difference is between Aronson's reliance on the concept of *expectation* and mine on perceived *cause-and-effect*. I confess that the issues here seem somewhat unclear, but expectation strikes me as an incomplete basis for psychological implication. If I 'expected' that the weather would be sunny for our annual Psychology Department Picnic because luck had been with us for each of the previous ten years, and then it happened to rain, I would not consider that a dissonant event in and of itself. (See Chapter 42 for a similar argument.) However, if I believed it to have been sunny on past picnic days because of a magical omnipotent ceremony of mine, and then it rained after I had performed the usual ceremony, it would seem dissonant. On the other hand, perhaps cause-and-effect is also incomplete as a defining characteristic of psychological implication, since cooccurrence or belongingness of Y with X might sometimes serve as the psychological equivalent of a 'follow from' relation even though a direct perception of causality were absent. Further clarification is necessary here.

Either of these two methodologies for operationalizing psychological implication could provide a very interesting accompaniment to any of the standard dissonance experiments* by building individual differences in implicative systems directly into the design. To illustrate (with my particular question technique), let us consider the Festinger and Carlsmith (1959) prototype situation in which a subject is paid to misrepresent to another person the enjoyability of the task the other person is about to perform. The crucial high dissonance condition is the one in which the pay to the subject is really insufficient to justify the discomfiture he must undergo for lying. The implication underlying the dissonance is presumably something like, 'Holding an opinion implies telling it to an interested party.' Now suppose that in a session independent of the experimental context, we play the Naive Question Game with all of the experimental subjects. Hidden among many filler items is the crucial question: "Here is this fellow who tells someone that a certain task is enjoyable. How come?" We now divide the subjects into two groups: (a) The Sincere Group—those who answer (in effect), "Because that's his opinion"; (b) The Insincere Group—those who give other answers such as, "Because he's kidding them" or "Because it's his job." For the Sincere Group, the implicative structure of the experimental situation is as specified by the dissonance analysis, and for them, therefore, the misrepresentation required in the experiment should indeed be dissonant, and they should maximally

---

* A complete reanalysis of all the situations typically accounted as dissonant is beyond the scope of this chapter. Nevertheless, it is interesting that in at least one case of a supposed dissonance, neither of the two presently proposed operational rules appear to be satisfied. Consider a person who holds opinion Y and is then exposed to a speaker advocating the opposed point of view. Following Festinger (1957, p. 178), dissonance theorists have always considered social disagreement to be dissonance-arousing. Yet suppose we say to our person, 'You are now going to hear a speech relevant to opinion Y. Do you expect the speaker to agree with you or disagree with you?' A strong expectation of agreement does not seem necessarily reasonable, given the frequency of encounter most adults have had with disagreement in matters of opinion, with both high and low credibility sources. Thus we cannot on this basis generally claim that "Speaker says Y follows from Person believes Y.' The cause-and-effect analysis also seems to fail. To the question, 'Speaker says Y. How come?' the answer 'Because I believe Y' seems rather bizarre. The answer might be, 'Because Y is true,' but then we would be dealing with perceived *facts*, not opinions. (Interestingly, Festinger's initial illustration of the assumption that social disagreement is dissonant concerned a fact rather than an opinion, but he freely and without hesitation generalized to opinions.) Therefore, in the absence of empirical evidence to the contrary, the net result of the present Question Game analysis is that for most people under ordinary circumstances, *opinion disagreement per se is not dissonant.*

obey the dissonance prediction (changing their own opinion about the task to conform to what they have told the other party). On the other hand, for the members of the Insincere Group, the experimental situation provides very little dissonance. For them, *offering an opinion does not follow primarily from holding that opinion*, but from other characteristics of the situation such as role requirements or the opportunity for gamesmanship. Thus they are comfortable with holding one opinion about the task while expressing another, and the dissonance prediction (of opinion change) should tend to fail for them.

This particular type of two-group experiment has not yet been tried (although a study by Epstein [1966] on High and Low Machiavellians might well be interpreted as consistent with the prediction that 'insincere' people are less susceptible to opinion change following counterattitudinal advocacy—see footnote 1 in Chapter 62). However, one dissonance experiment arising as an outgrowth of my theoretical concern with the role of psychological implication has recently been completed. If an implicative structure indeed underlies the dissonance which mediates some presumed dissonance-reduction mechanism, then any manipulation which somehow 'activates' this implicative structure (without making the subject self-conscious about his cognitive processes) ought to increase the dissonance-reduction effect.

For the relevant study conducted by Carlsmith, Abelson, and Aronson (unpublished at the time of writing of this chapter), the reasoning was as follows. Elements Y and $not\text{-}X$ are dissonant when X follows from Y. But presumably 'X follows from Y' for subjects who would answer the question 'How come X?' with 'Because Y.' Now suppose that in the presence of Y and $not\text{-}X$ (the dissonant state), all subjects are asked 'How come $not\text{-}X$?' The question has no sensible answer, and is calculated to aggravate dissonance by directly forcing cognitive activity into the inescapable trap defined by the dissonance-producing experimental situation. In the customary case of the dissonance experiment, the relevant cognitive activity is presumed to occur despite the freedom of the subject to think any thoughts whatever during the experimental situation. There well may be experimental subjects, however, who for reasons of irrelevant distraction or relevant self-protection do not 'work on' the materials of the cognitive dissonance. The key question, 'How come $not\text{-}X$?' inserted naturalistically into the ongoing dissonant situation, is designed to control against accidental or deliberate avoidance of the dissonance. (I would prefer not to confound the present interpretation with the difficult issue of 'awareness' of dissonance. In particular, it is contended by Brock in Chapter 32 that dissonance can occur without awareness. Whether or not this is so—and I do not prejudge it one way or the other—there is really no overlap with the present variable, the *amount of cognitive activity* related to the dissonance. 'Cognitive activity' can take place with or without 'awareness.')

The chosen experimental scenario was one for which dissonance effects have been repeatedly found: the 'prohibited toy' situation, in which young children given *mild* threats not to play with an attractive toy are found following a temptation-resistance period to devalue the toy more than a parallel group of children given *severe* threats (Aronson & Carlsmith, 1961; Freedman, 1965; Pepitone, McCauley, & Hammond, 1967). The key elements of this situation are Y, the attractiveness of the toy, and X, playing with the toy. For the child, it follows from the attractiveness of the toy that he would play with it. (Operationally, if we ask a child, "There is a toy that a child plays with. How come?" most assuredly he will reply, "Because he likes it" or "Because it is nice," etc.) The function of the mild vs. severe threats is to vary the amount of justification the child has for not playing with the toy, thus altering the magnitude of dissonance, but this variable will not concern us further here.

The standard experimental script for this situation requires the experimenter to leave the child alone with the tempting toy for a few minutes after administering the threat. In our study, a 'janitor' entered the experimental room during this critical period. In the Cognitive Activation condition, the 'janitor' very casually and with mere off-hand curiosity said to the child, "Hey, kid, how come you're not playing with that toy there?" (Formally, this is the key question: 'How come *not-X?*') In the No Activation condition, the janitor also made a brief chatty remark, but it was completely unrelated to the toy.

The results demonstrated at a strong statistical level that children in the Cognitive Activation condition devalued the attractive toy more than did children in the No Activation condition. This is precisely the result that we had predicted under the assumptions that an increase in dissonance-relevant cognitive activity could be produced by a 'How Come' question, and that such increased activation would result in the increased dissonance effect of devaluation of the toy.

I look forward to the increased employment of experiments of this kind. By 'this kind' I mean experiments in which the manipulations of the independent variables include attempts to stimulate varying amounts and kinds of cognitive activity. Here I am emphasizing again the line of suggestion put forward previously (p. 125). Technically speaking, 'thinking' is a 'mere' hypothetical construct, but in building cognitive theories we surely believe that this construct has substance and importance, and we ought to be busy developing its theoretical properties and trying to validate them experimentally by the best means available to us. Now, it may turn out that in most circumstances most people do not engage in thought very much of the time, and its degree of control over behavior may be limited. Indeed, that is the approximate position adopted by Freedman in Chapter 44, and I myself have argued along similar lines in a discussion of public opinion tendencies (Abelson, 1967a). But if this were so, it would not at all mean that the construct were useless, but only that the laws of its applicability would require careful circumscription.

A THEORETICAL REFORMULATION

Scattered throughout the past three sections of this chapter have been a number of psychological implicational principles. Starting with a review of the balance-based implications of the Abelson and Rosenberg psychologic, the treatment gradually branched out in a great many other directions. A gathering of these several themes into a summary theoretical statement seems now in order.

One invariant theme runs implicitly throughout all of the foregoing discussion. It is that the basic principles by which human beings manipulate the symbols they cognize are few in number and structurally rather simple, although the nature of things cognized can be of enormous variety. This is essentially a Gestaltist position. It seems evident that a mechanism such as the human brain with huge information storage capacity but limited channel capacity for the moment-to-moment processing of information (cf. Broadbent, 1965) should work in this way, with a few simple rules operating upon many contents. However, even though the rules might be simple, quite complex cognitive products could be produced through repeated application of a few permutations of the rules. Language has this aspect of complex combinatorial propensity, as does much of mathematics. (Devotees of the Oriental board game, *Go*, will recognize it as another excellent example of a simple rule system which can lead to patterns of incredible complexity.)

The function of cognitive rules is presumably to organize the information stored by the individual in a way that is likely to be useful to him, directly or indirectly, for affective or behavioral purposes. (If one wants simply to call such activity the "search for meaning" in its own right, that seems quite unobjectionable, at least from the standpoint of a cognitive theorist willing to leave the motivational analysis to someone else.) There is a great deal of information continually impinging upon an individual, both in the form of new stimuli and of self-retrieved older stimulus images or more highly encoded symbolic cognitions, and there is not enough time or energy available for him to process all of it, by whatever rules. (See Chapter 23 for a similar point.) Cognitive processing is often apt to be harried and incomplete, and many individuals may live with a lot of cognitively 'undigested' material, i.e., stimulus images which have not been recoded into verbal or other symbolic form. Behavior may or may not involve cognitive mediation—that is, some intervention between stimulus *S* and response *R*, utilizing previously cognized stimuli and cognitive implication rules, and eventuating in a behavioral response different from the one which would have been made 'without thinking.' When behavior *does* involve cognitive mediation, however, it is theoretically important for psychology that these mediational principles be understood, else the explanation of human behavior languish within the overly narrow constraints of *S-R* theory.

Implicational Molecules

Since it is very difficult for an individual to process large amounts of cognitive material simultaneously, it is tempting to suppose that cognitive elements are typically processed within little symbolic packages which I shall call *implicational molecules*. An implicational molecule is a self-contained set of statements which, taken together, are psychologically self-consistent according to a particular implicational principle. It is a "conceptual good figure" (Chapter 45). 'Joe loves Ann; Ann loves Harry; Joe hates Harry' is an example of such a molecule, with 'romantic rivalry' as the implicational principle which binds the sentences together. This example is 'self-contained' because we need know nothing more to 'understand' the situation.

Now consider an example of an incompletely stated molecule: 'Jim sent flowers to Amy; Amy was pleased.' In this example (and others like it) there is a *tendency to complete the molecule* by inferring new sentences strongly implied by the givens. A natural additional sentence here would be 'Jim wanted to please Amy,' implied by the intention principle, although further embellishments could also be added.

Beyond the tendency to complete implicational molecules, one would also expect the sentences of a molecule to be *more easily learned and stored in long-term memory* than a parallel set of sentences of comparable individual difficulty which are not bound together implicationally. Several empirical results supporting this hypothesis have already appeared in the literature (see the summary by Zajonc, 1968), almost all using the balance principle as the basis of molecule formation. Quite possibly certain other implicational principles would yield results even stronger than those already found.

Two further effects one would theoretically expect are that *sentences tending to prevent molecular completion create surprise and* (usually) *aversion;* and that *completed molecules resist change.* Here, finally, is where the themes of inconsistency and consistency reenter our account. As defined above, molecules are self-consistent structures, and thus by 'sentences tending to prevent molecular completion' we mean, approximately, 'dissonances.' If a subject were presented with the set of statements: 'Jim wanted to please Amy; Jim loathed Amy; Jim sent flowers to Amy; Amy was pleased,' we conjecture that he would find the second sentence surprising and bothersome. It is dissonant: it does not follow from loathing someone that one wants to please them. Presumably the subject will operate upon the single nonfitting sentence in order to arrive at and preserve a completed molecule. In addition to the mechanisms previously discussed for resolving inconsistencies, there is also the possibility of distortion of the stimulus input; in the example given above, there might be a tendency for the subject to misread 'loathed' as 'loved,' as this small change would fill the molecule quite satisfactorily. When once a molecule is completed, new sentences which do not fit within it will tend to be rejected or appropriately transformed. This is the inconsistency avoidance side of the inconsistency resolution coin.

In sum, it is postulated that 'implicational molecules,' governed by particular implicational principles, demonstrate (at least) five effects: tendency toward completion; ease of learning; ease of long-term retention; inconsistency resolution; and maintenance against disruption. To be sure, particular implicational principles should be specified in order to get the most empirical mileage out of these postulates. Several principles have already been stated in this chapter, certain others are introduced below, and still others appear in Chapters 20, 45, and 47 of this volume. It still remains as a major task, however, to compile collections of implicational principles which will function coherently together in models of cognitive systems.

Before turning our attention to this systemic problem, it is important to emphasize that individuals certainly differ in the cognitive rules they apply and in the complexity of the molecules they are typically capable of constructing. Therefore one should not expect to find a universal set of implicational principles, though a few particular ones such as the intention principle would appear to be ubiquitous. Furthermore, although it was asserted above that implicational principles are 'rather simple' (p. 133), this does not mean that they must be utterly trite.

One might indeed contemplate molecules built upon principles that anticipate superficial inconsistency and intrinsically provide for it, e.g., the *compulsion principle*: 'Person does X; he did not want to do X; he was forced to do X.' That is, certain 'rationalizations' and 'transcendances' might be immediately apprehended by the individual such that he would not pass through a phase of experiencing configurations as inconsistencies ('Person does X; he did not want to do X') and then resolving them ('He was forced to do X'). The latter sentence in this example is in the nature of a molecule completion rather than a resolution. This theoretical notion is similar to what Aronson refers to with his idea of the 'underlying cognition' (p. 21), and overcomes some of the banality which many writers (cf. Chapters 16 and 19) feel infests the consistency framework.

Another manner in which implicational molecules may be out of the ordinary is via the use of subtle psychological principles. This category may perhaps be illustrated best by certain psychiatric rules of implication: 'Person says he fears X; unconsciously he wishes for X.' Or again, 'Person vehemently denies fact F; fact F would imply person has motive M, person cannot accept motive M in himself.'

Hopefully these examples make clear that cognitive consistency in the sense of the orderly use of subjective rules and resistance to the acceptance of apparent violations of those rules is not to be equated with mindlessness. Perhaps an overemphasis on the homeostatic features of cognitive balance has proved misleading in this regard (and certainly the earlier psycho-logic was guilty of this overemphasis). In the present reformulation, however, we have arrived at a position which I believe to be very close to that which Heider (1944, 1946, 1958) was aiming for in his analysis of 'naive psychology,' a position much broader (see Chapter 7) than that expressed in the balance principle alone. As happens in the history of ideas, profound thinkers are often victims of popular trivialization of their writings, and it takes a long time for others to rediscover their true original intentions.

Systems of Implicational Principles

There are many combinations of principles that might mesh into coherent systems. The complex end of the combinatorial continuum is well beyond the scope of this chapter, but at the simplest end would be found *simplistic ideologies*, wherein a very small set of principles could be applied rigidly to a large set of facts. Each new fact would be either fitted immediately into a waiting molecule, or discarded entirely as irrelevant to the concerns of the system, rather in the manner of a mechanical gin rummy player looking only toward the completion of fixed sets of card holdings.

Consider the following set of implicational principles:

1. *The Saints and Sinners postulate:* Good actors have good intentions; bad actors have bad intentions.

2. *The duplicity principle:* Bad actors can exercise duplicity; duplicity causes good intentions not to be exercised and/or good results to appear to be caused by the bad actor.

3. *The determination principle:* Good actors can exercise determination; determination causes good intentions to lead to good results and/or bad intentions not to be exercised; determination overcomes duplicity; in the absence of determination, bad intentions lead to bad results.

These three principles may be said to form the basis for a simple cognitive system, but they cannot be said to define a complete system (even a very rudimentary one) without further definitions of certain terms. We must say what is meant by the phrases 'appear to be caused' and 'can exercise,' in particular, and we must also specify what concepts are to be included under 'good actors,' 'good results,' 'bad actors,' etc. The special phrases may create theoretical difficulties necessitating further principles, and it is hard to tell just what may be needed unless one tries to simulate the system (as explained below). However, the specification problem of what is to be included under what concepts can readily be solved by a concrete listing operation of all the instances of each concept. For any particular realization of a cognitive system obeying these principles, the particular actors it considers 'good' can be enumerated, etc. By this means, the *content* of a cognitive system may be conceptualized separately from its principles or *process*.

If the listing operation is to be useful, however, a further principle is really required:

4. *The concretization principle:* Any instance of any concept may be substituted for the concept without altering the applicability of any principle.

To illustrate very simply, if Red China is a 'bad actor' for the system, then since 'bad actors can exercise duplicity,' it follows that 'Red China can exercise duplicity.' Although this further principle seems innocent on the face of it, whether the free substitution of instances for concepts might sometimes lead the system into indeterminacy or absurdity is a matter that one would want to examine very carefully. Trouble might arise if 'intentions,' results,' etc., were not identified at all with particular actors, or not coordinately identified. One does not want the system to believe that 'Red China has James Hoffa's bad intentions,' etc. This problem is not at all insurmountable, but the point is that verbally stated principles of implication easily can have 'bugs' in them which may remain undiscovered unless the theoretical system is exercised by accepting inputs and producing outputs. This is the strategy of *simulation*.

I have elsewhere detailed a somewhat elaborate plan for a computer program that would assess the credibility and balance of sentences attributed to particular sources, and would apply the mechanisms of denial or rationalization to imbalanced cases (Abelson & Carroll, 1965). Practical limitations were encountered in the course of writing this program, and it was replaced by a simpler scheme. In retrospect, the replacement may have been salutary, since I have been moving in the direction of considering rationalizations as proper for direct inclusion in molecules rather than exclusively as resolutions for imbalance.

The simpler program is based on just about the minimum imaginable set of principles, two in number. The program is operational, and in one version, the content (which is separable from the principles) consists of a set of paraphrased foreign policy statements taken from the pre-1963 writings of Barry Goldwater. (Other political figures of differing ideologies could also have been chosen to serve the same purposes.) In this version, 'The Goldwater Machine,' the attempt was not made to incorporate principles such as 1, 2, 3 above. Rather, a set of some 500 abbreviated actual belief sentences were simply stored in the memory of the system. It turns out that this corpus of sentences probably does obey such simple implicational principles, and that some of the explicit storage could be replaced by giving the system facility to 'compute' most of its beliefs from a few stored core sentences.

At any rate, the two principles actually provided were a version of a *concretization principle*: any instance of any concept or any predicate may be substituted in any concept-predicate sentence without changing its truth value; and its inverse, an *abstraction principle*: any concept or any predicate for which the concept or predicate of the sentence is an instance may be freely substituted in the sentence without changing its truth value. The Machine is set to respond to input sentences by giving (if possible) an assessment of their subjective truth or falsity, using only the concretization and abstraction principles and the beliefs stored in its memory. Certain stereotyped phrases also were dubbed into the output for realism, although no strict attention was paid to grammatical niceties.

Some of the responses of the Machine are theoretically instructive. Consider the following, where S denotes the input statement and R the response:

S: LIBERAL REPUBLICANS WANTS WORLD GOVERNMENT....

R: THE SIMPLE TRUTH THAT LIBERAL REPUBLICANS WANTS WORLD GOVERNMENT IS ALL PART OF THE PATTERN WHERE LIBERALS WANTS WORLD GOVERNMENT. I NEED NOT REMIND YOU THAT LIBERAL ATTEMPTS TO HAVE U.S. POLICIES DETERMINED BY THE U.N. FOR SOME TIME NOW.

In this response, the mechanized 'Goldwater' imputes truth to the input by implication backwards from a stored sentence, 'Liberals attempt to have U.S. policies determined by the U.N.' The predicate, 'attempt to have U.S. policies determined by the U.N.,' is an instance (stored in this content system) of 'wants world government.' Therefore this replacement is freely made. Secondly, since 'liberal Republicans' is a concrete exemplification of 'liberals,' this substitution is also made. The free path from what is stored to what is asked establishes the 'truth' of the input assertion. This particular response of the system seems fairly plausible as an imitative Goldwaterism.

But now consider another response:

S: NKRUMAH INFLUENCES DE GAULLE....

R: THE SIMPLE TRUTH THAT NKRUMAH INFLUENCES DE GAULLE IS ALL PART OF THE PATTERN WHERE NKRUMAH CONTROLS THE WORLD. I NEED NOT REMIND YOU THAT NKRUMAH CONTROLS GHANA FOR SOME TIME NOW.

Here the backward 'reasoning' is formally almost identical to that of the previous example. The predicate, 'controls the world,' being more abstract than 'controls Ghana,' is freely substituted. Secondly, since 'influences De Gaulle' is an exemplification of 'controls the world,' this replacement occurs, and the 'truth' of the input is established. But in this case the response is not only a bad imitation, it is a semantic disaster. Why is this?

There may be several reasons for the peculiarity of this example, but one clear intuitive hint is that the leap from 'controls Ghana' to 'controls the world' is vastly overextravagant. If the leap were from 'threatens Ghana' to 'threatens the world,' that would still be a large jump, but subjectively not quite so ridiculous. There is something in the nature of the verb 'controls' that sharply limits the freedom of the abstraction principle. If you control a small part of something, you do not very likely control all of it, whereas if you (say) threaten a small part of something, you may conceivably threaten all of it.

In a series of studies (Gilson & Abelson, 1965; Abelson & Kanouse, 1966; Kanouse & Abelson, 1967), my students and I have explored the effects of verbs on the degree of empirical transfer of truth value from one sentence to a second sentence in which one concept is either more concrete or more abstract than the corresponding concept in the original. These effects are quite dramatically different from one verb to the next, and there is a strong tendency for verbs which permit ready abstraction not to permit ready concretization, and vice versa. (This negative correlation is well exemplified with the verb 'controls.' Whereas abstraction was hard, concretization is easy. If you control all of something then you very likely control a small part of it.) The reader is referred to the accounts of these studies for fuller details, but suffice it to say that in the study of cognitive implication, the semantics of different action verbs must be closely scrutinized, as they have very different implicative properties.

Returning to the Goldwater Machine, one of its surprising features is that though it often fails to respond to questions, or falls into semantic confusion, it *very rarely gives an imbalanced response, even though no balance principle is built into it!* The reason for this is that since almost all of its stored sentences are balanced, it has no real access to imbalance. (The reader who may remember Goldwater's statements as often self-contradictory should note that the content of the Goldwater Machine is at an ideological, not a policy level, and at that level Goldwater was very self-consistent.) Thus balance, which seems to be a motive principle, can be largely reproduced by strictly cognitive means, i.e., without any such motive process operating in the system at all. I am certain that this is true for other 'motivated' cognitive constructions as well—that a cognitive system can 'act as if it is motivated' solely by virtue of the contents of its beliefs, whether or not the relevant motive force is presently operative in the system. An example is provided by the individual whose casual conversation contains stereotyped anti-Negro remarks. From the remarks alone, one often cannot tell whether a real motive function is being served by the beliefs, or whether they are bits of coagulated cognitive flotsam picked up uncritically from others.

A final example from the Goldwater simulation will indicate, however, that a balance principle or something comparable cannot be completely dispensed with:

S: LIBERALS OPPOSE LIBERALS.

R: THE SIMPLE TRUTH THAT LIBERALS OPPOSE LIBERALS IS ALL PART OF THE PATTERN WHERE AMERICANS OPPOSE LIBERALS. I NEED NOT REMIND YOU THAT CONSERVATIVES OPPOSE LIBERALS FOR SOME TIME NOW.

Here the problem lies in the storage of both 'liberals' and 'conservatives' as instances of 'Americans.' The implicative chain races merrily from 'conservatives' up to 'Americans' and back down to 'liberals' without realizing that it has passed through an evaluative change of sign. Some warning or test is necessary to prevent this type of unrealistic and aberrant response.

Among present activities in the cognitive consistency area, perhaps the most crucial are the construction of more complete implicative models which can be tested experimentally with live subjects or via the strategy of simulation so briefly sketched above, or both. It seems to me that the pay-off in the cognitive consistency area lies in the detailed specification of a variety of implicative principles and molecules and their synthesis into larger systems, rather than in excessive reliance any single master principle.

CHAPTER 6

Theory of the Structure of Human Thought

William J. McGuire

University of California, San Diego

INTRODUCTION: A MAXIMAL CONSISTENCY POSITION

The initial and abiding interest which drew me into what I later called the cognitive consistency area was the hope that people operate under a strong need for internal consistency among their beliefs, such that the consistency tendency would provide a convenient tool for mapping the structure and functioning of human thought processes. There were several guiding assumptions behind this aspiration. I assumed that the conceptual system at any moment was highly interconnected and also in a state of internal harmony that might reasonably be called 'consistency.' I assumed further that there was a strong tendency to conserve both the connectedness and the internal consistency of the conceptual system. Hence, receipt of any new and especially any discrepant information would produce considerable conceptual activity, involving a great deal of internal readjustment, until the information was absorbed into the system with the least loss in internal consistency and the greatest gain in connectedness.

To the extent that all of these assumptions are valid, the consistency tendency would be a highly useful tool in mapping the human cognitive system, leading to new insights regarding its structure and functioning and providing a test of these hypotheses about thought processes. A tightly knit system with a strong need for conservation of internal consistency would permit the study of human thought processes by introducing discrepant information and tracing its impact through the system. Analogous physiological methods that come readily to mind involve such procedures as introducing radioactive compounds and following their dissemination through the organism in order to determine the structure and functioning of some aspects of the metabolic system. In my general strategy, the need for consistency was taken for granted, as a means rather than an end of the study. The end was a description of how people think in the broadest sense of the term. By using the assumed psychological necessity for maintaining a highly structured, highly consistent belief system, I hoped to do no less than construct and test a psychology of inference, that is, a depiction of the manner and extent to which one idea leads to another psychologically.

With such an initial aspiration, I have obviously been rather disappointed and regretful about the main directions which consistency theory has taken during the past 15 years. It seems that most of the consistency research during that period has been in pursuit of another goal and has sidestepped this major enterprise which drew me on. In the later work, the consistency need has become more of an end to be studied in its own right, rather than as a means for throwing light on thought processes. Where I would have taken the need consistency for granted and used it to map the cognitive system, the subsequent work has largely taken the cognitive system for granted, and tried to clarify the need for consistency. It has sidestepped the cognitive structure question, the subtleties of what leads to what psychologically, by various methodological tactics. For example, in much of the work the experimenter elects to use a flagrant inconsistency, such as the person's saying one thing for a rather trivial reason, when actually he believes the opposite. In these cases the inconsistency tends to be so clear that the reader is not inclined to quibble too much about the nature of the cognitive structure in order to determine whether the incident does indeed involve some kind of an inconsistency. Or alternatively, the cognitive structure in a given situation might be determined on an ad hoc basis, by a preliminary procedure in which a subject is asked to indicate "what goes with what" without an explicit attempt at teasing out the general principles involved. Or again, the inconsistency might be created on an ad hoc basis by techniques like hypnotic suggestion or role-playing. Admittedly, so much of the area is unexplored that any feasible research enterprise must sidestep major areas of uncertainty. That the major thrust of the consistency research has sidestepped the problem that I thought most deserving of attention is something which I consider regrettable, while recognizing that in the long run the advancement of knowledge will probably profit most from allowing each researcher to listen to his own drummer in guiding his steps to where the action lies.

There are several reasons why one can hardly complain if the consistency research during the past 15 years has largely ignored this area of conceptual structure and functioning where its most useful contribution may lie. In the first place, I have set a very poor example myself. After my early work from 1953–1955, I discontinued active research in the area, except for the 1959 revision of my papers for Volume III of the Yale Series on attitude organization and change. Secondly, while the consistency theorists neglected the area of conceptual structure and functioning, other lines of research did pay some slight attention to these problems. One would include here work under such rubrics as concept formation, information processing, and computer simulation of cognitive processes. And finally, the consistency researchers did not completely neglect this area. Heider's volume providing a fuller treatment of his balance theory and Abelson and Rosenberg's sketch of the laws of "psycho-logic" did grapple to some extent with the problem that I had felt deserved attention. The analyses by Cartwright and Harary contain useful graph theoretical paradigms, provided one is willing to analogize their social model applications to cognitive models instead. But while the neglect has not been complete and while I have no right to resent the lack of interest, I do feel regretful that this mapping potential of the consistency notions, which initially attracted me to the area, was not exploited more vigorously. I still believe that the potential exists and in this résumé of my thinking in the consistency area, I shall try to call attention to this promise.

In the second section of this chapter, I shall outline the thinking about cognitive structure and functioning which lay behind my 1953 work in the area. The third section deals with the empirical work which was done to test and refine my thinking about these conceptual processes. In section four I shall outline some further methodological possibilities which now might be regarded as attractive possibilities for those who do have an interest in mapping cognitive processes. The fifth and final section of the chapter will be devoted to second thoughts regarding whether the person's belief system is really as highly interconnected and as internally consistent as I chose to assume back in 1953.

INITIAL THEORY OF PSYCHOLOGICAL IMPLICATION

Basic Assumptions: Interconnectedness and Coherence

Behind my 1953 empirical work lay the extremist assumption regarding the internal consistency of the belief system which Abelson (Chapter 48) has since termed the "maximalist" position. I took as a working assumption that peoples' conceptions are highly interconnected and that people maintain a high degree of internal coherence within this structure. Even then I would probably have hedged, arguing that this assumption was a methodological one adopted for tactical purposes, like Descartes' universal methodical doubt, rather than something to be firmly believed. I hoped that assumption would turn out at least partly true, since the enterprise of mapping out the structure of human thought and the psychology of implication was interesting only to the extent that such structure was pervasive. If one's psychological conceptualizations are at all interconnected, then there would be some justification for the study. If one's conceptualizations are totally interconnected, then the interest would be enormous. I hoped for total interconnectedness, but would settle for any at all.

It should be noted that in my terminology so far I have been explicitly distinguishing two aspects of human thought: its connectedness and its internal coherence. There is some confusion in the area due to insufficiently explicit distinction between these two. The initial requirement for the discussion to arise at all is that the person's conceptualizations be interconnected. Given that they are interconnected, the further question arises as to what qualities (such as internal consistency, self-esteem maximization, goal attainment, etc.) tend to be conserved and maximized within that system. Some of those who have retreated from or never accepted the consistency theory point of view demurred because they doubt that the cognitive system manifests this second characteristic of internal consistency. Many theorists (some of whom have contributed chapters to Section II of this volume) would grant that people's cognitions are indeed interconnected but feel that the system strives to maintain and maximize characteristics other than internal coherence (e.g., self-esteem maximization).

More radical objectors have demurred on the first point of whether there exists any appreciable degree of interconnection among the cognitions at all. These theorists (including some of those who have contributed chapters to Section III F of this volume) seem to regard the human cognitive system as having all of the fine infrastructure of a bowl of oatmeal or an urn of marbles. The seemingly random constellations of stands on public issues that one finds in individuals' responses on opinion polls have led these theorists to conclude reluctantly that the average person sees so few connections among the issues of the day that he can maintain just about any set of beliefs on them without experiencing embarrassment or the need for justification. These 'minimalists,' by calling into question not only the nature of the internal coherence within the system, but the very existence of any system in the first place, raise the most serious doubts as to whether it is worthwhile to embark on the enterprise of mapping the cognitive system. If the minimalist position is correct, such an enterprise would become, at best, an 'as if' enterprise in the philosophy of science rather than an exercise in empirical psychology.

In the discussion that follows, I show more willingness to compromise with critics of the first variety, who argue that the characteristic which people try to maximize in their cognitive arena is something other than what is aptly called 'consistency'; but I show little disposition to compromise with the more radical critics of the second type who argue that there is little connectedness of any type among cognitions. It is clarifying to point out this distinction in advance and also to indicate that some critics have misclassified themselves. Later sections of this chapter show at least token tendencies to accommodate to critics such as Katz, Jordan, Collins, Sarnoff, etc., who argue that the person is trying to maintain and maximize something other than consistency among his beliefs and thoughts. I will not show even this tokenism toward the more radical critics who abandon the methodological assumption that there is some kind of structure in the belief system. These more radical critics are often fallen-away consistency theorists, for whom frustration at detecting consistency in empirically elicited belief constellations has finally led to the conclusion that there is little connectedness of any kind among cognitions.

I myself have kept the faith, clinging desperately to the assumption that people feel that certain of their beliefs have a bearing on others, and that they can be embarrassed by discovering that they hold an incompatible set. I even cling to the position that people maximize, not only the consistency, but also the interconnectedness of the system. That is, given a new piece of information they not only check cursorily to see if they must admit it is related to other cognitions, and if so, bring it into congruence with them; but more than this, they make a deliberate effort to tie in the new information with as many other cognitions as they possibly can (which admittedly raises the specter of increasing inconsistency) and then endeavor to maximize the internal coherence of this new more elaborate system. Hence, my position is so extreme as to assume that people do not simply minimize inconsistency but that they maximize consistency, this latter implying that they also seek maximum interconnectedness in their belief system. I admit that this belligerent stance is taken more because it is heuristically provocative and motivating to labor than because I have deep conviction or convincing evidence.

The Specific Model: Logic, with a Mental Reservation

Components of the cognitive system—the proposition. My basic assumption, that people tend to have highly interconnected and highly coherent belief systems, constitutes only the prolegomenon to a testable theory of psychological implication or the structure of thought. More specific postulates regarding the purported connectedness and coherence are needed. I proceeded to such specifics by positing that human thought can be adequately represented by means of verbal propositions, thus following the convention of limiting the scope of my investigation to the conscious manifestations of thought processes and further identifying the conscious with the verbalizable. (Though I do not study them, I do not deny that there are nonverbalizable processes that also deserve to be called thought. Further evidence of permissiveness will be noted in my choice of the term 'verbalizable' rather than 'verbalized,' since all that I asked was that the subject be able to verbalize the given thought when called upon to do so. In fact, it was required only that he be able to recognize a verbalized manifestation of the thought when it was presented to him.)

The *proposition*, which I took to be the verbal representation of thought, was defined as a statement which placed an object of judgment somewhere along a dimension of perceptible variation. By an object of judgment I referred to a describable stimulus situation, however simple or complex, to which people could make discriminating responses. For example, an object of judgment might be: the moon, or man's reaching the moon, or the cost of man's reaching the moon, etc. By a dimension of perceptual variation I had in mind any set of categories, at least nominally scaled, to which people could assign objects of judgment in a fairly reliable way. For example, such dimensions might include a color spectrum consisting of at least two hues and a residual category; probability of occurrence would be another dimension; desirability of occurrence, still another. Human thought is thus defined as consisting of propositions assigning objects of judgment to positions on dimensions of variability. The statement positing a certain hue for the moon would be one such proposition; a statement assigning some likelihood of occurrence to man's reaching the moon by 1975 would be another such proposition; a third would be a statement giving some desirability value to man's reaching his natural satellite at that time.

The next step in defining the components of the cognitive system in order to make this formulation empirically testable traded range for manageability. In principle, I could have accepted as the components of the cognitive system any proposition generated by the subjects. In the interest of eliciting more manageable data, I cast the subjects into a more passive role than proposition generation, confining them to responses to propositions presented to them. Specifically, I cited objects of judgment (such as water pollution at the local beaches) and cited also the dimensions on which these events were to be placed (for example, the likelihood of this event's occurring, or the desirability of its occurring). Within these constraints, the subject would indicate the propositional content of his belief system by generating numbers which, for example, assigned a subjective probability value to the veridicality of propositions such as "the beaches of our city are becoming unusably polluted." It would have been more interesting, and in principle possible, to allow the subject complete freedom in generating the propositions which constituted his belief system and to allow him to formulate these propositions more in his own terms. In the fourth section of this chapter we shall return to a consideration of the possibility of such freer procedures. Those who have had to process masses of free association data will perhaps sympathize with the placement of the above constraints on the subjects in the initial experimental work.

Laws of the cognitive system: logic in a world it never made. Having designated propositions as the components of the belief system, I had then to postulate what laws obtained among propositions in the conduct of human thought. That is, what 'rules' the thinker uses to decide in effect whether his holding certain propositions implies that he ought also to hold certain other propositions. I nominated the principles of formal logic, particularly in the commonsense classical formulation of Aristotle, as part of this body of laws. (Within this framework, my empirical work has largely concentrated on the syllogism, allowing me conveniently to predict, for example, that if the person's belief system includes two propositions which together make up the premises of a well-formed syllogism, then the person's belief system should also contain the conclusion logically to be drawn from them or else he experiences embarrassment and a detectable flurry of cognitive processing in the area represented by this conclusion. The restriction of the empirical work to the syllogism was, of course, a tactical convenience rather than a limitation of the formulation. I could in principle have dealt equally well with more complex propositional structures such as those studied by Thistlethwaite or by Moore and Anderson.)

The components of a cognitive system, as defined above, consisted of propositional statements which assigned objects of judgment to positions on dimensions of variability. Such propositions could be interconnected in any of several ways. Most obviously and easily managed by formal logic, they could be interconnected by virtue of the fact that they assigned several objects of judgment to positions on the same dimension of variability and also specified relationships among these objects of judgment. For example, the propositions might all deal with the veridicality dimension and assign to positions (such as 'true' or 'false') on this dimension such objects of judgment as: pollution at the city beaches having reached the health hazard level; the illegalizing of any recreational swimming which constituted a serious health hazard; and an impending prohibition of swimming at the local beaches. By using some rather pedantically worded phraseology, these propositions could be made into a syllogism such that anyone who believed it to be true that pollution at the beaches was reaching the health menace stage and that the city fathers would prohibit any recreational activities which did constitute a health menace, would then find it psychologically compelling to grant also that the prohibition of recreational swimming at the public beaches was imminent.

But psychological interconnections among such propositions could arise also in ways less obvious to the formal logician, for example, when the propositions assigned the same object of judgment to several dimensions among which interesting relationships were psychologically recognized. For example, the propositions could assign pollution at the city beaches to both the likelihood and the desirability dimensions. If our Panglossian rationalizer tended to feel that this was the best of all possible worlds, then his belief in the likelihood of pollution at the city beach should compel him to accept also the proposition that pollution was a good thing, or otherwise suffer psychological *angoise*.

The complexities involved in the foregoing analysis should suffice to show that in the present formulation the believer is confronted with an application of logic that is much more complex than that facing the conventional logical man. My thinking man can be considered as existing in a multi-dimensional conceptual world as compared to the logical man's unidimensional domain. Any given dimension of variability (for example, the probability of events occurring) could constitute a basis on which the various objects of judgment could become interconnected by means of propositions. There would result a system whose internal coherence could be assessed fairly simply by the application of formal logic. But there would be other dimensions (for example, that of desirability) on which these same objects of judgment could become interconnected, with additional coherence demands resulting. Such additional demands can arise when there are additional propositions in one's belief system that psychologically interrelate the several dimensions, such as, in the example, the likelihood and the desirability of events. Clearly the thinker is beset with a formidable problem in maintaining the internal consistency of his belief system as I have represented it. He must keep his belief about the probability of occurrence of a given event (for example, the continued legality of swimming at the local beach) in line with his beliefs regarding the probability of occurrence of related events. He must also keep his belief in the probability of occurrence of that given event in line with his belief about the desirability of this event and the desirability of the related events.

Still another complexity must be introduced over and above those in formal logic in order to apply this system with any great plausibility to actual thought processes. While almost all of formal logic is two-valued, it seems clear that humans show somewhat more finely graded responses in assigning objects of judgment to dimensions of variability. The experimenter can usually constrain the subject to grant that it is either true or false that an event will occur or confine himself to two values on a dimension (for example, true vs. false or good vs. bad), but actually the person is usually able to discriminate a number of gradations along such dimensions of likelihood or desirability. Many would argue that he cannot discriminate more than seven gradations (plus or minus two), but almost everyone would admit that he can and does use more than two categories reliably. Hence, in my formulation, I felt it necessary to allow the person to make a graded response in the interest of a priori plausibility. Allowing a graded response scale might seem simply an advance in the direction of quantitative precision, but it actually can lead to qualitatively different formulations of what is psychologically implied. For example, take the three propositions: The beaches are becoming terribly polluted. If they are polluted, the city fathers will forbid swimming there. The city fathers will prohibit swimming at the public beaches. The subject might believe that each of the first two propositions is, so to speak, 60 per cent true while the third is 40 per cent true. If forced to use a two-valued logic system with .50 as the plausible cutoff point between true and false, then he would report the first two propositions as true and the third as false; such a constellation of beliefs would be defined as illogical in a two-valued logical system. However, when probabilistically graded responses are allowed, this constellation of beliefs would be quite permissible. With each of the independent premises judged to have a .60 probability of being true, the conclusion which they logically imply could have any probability value above their joint probability of .36 and still be consistent with them. Hence the decision to combine probability theory with formal logic represents a qualitative as well as quantitative change in the model over that represented by a more conventional two-valued logic. I did not introduce this degree of quantification in order to frighten the sun worshippers away from grappling with the intricacies of my formulations, though regrettably this has been one of its effects. Rather, I resorted to the somewhat formidable and forbidding quantitative apparatus in that 1953 model in order to make my formulation of the laws of thought more empirically plausible.

The equilibrium point of the cognitive system: a least-square solution. The thinker I have depicted here has every right to look as puzzled as Rodin represented him. He is juggling many balls in many dimensions. The internal coherence which he must keep among the propositions involves not only a number of objects of judgment placed on a given dimension of variability (the hypothetical logical man's usual problem), but also a number of other psychologically related dimensions at the same time. As described above, not only must he keep his belief about the likelihood of a given event in line with his beliefs about the likelihood of related events, but he must keep his belief about its likelihood aligned with his belief in its desirability (and the desirability of the related events), while at the same time maintaining his belief in the relationship between the desirability and likelihood of events.

What is the optimal internal coherence solution toward which the believer tends? In my formulation the thinker was regarded as a harassed individual, functioning as an honest broker in trying to come to some 'least-square' solution among all of these contending pulls. Moreover, beset by constantly varying internal needs and external realities, he must be a wheeler and dealer in arriving at momentary least-square solutions since, as the relative salience of different consideration varies, the optimal equilibrium point shifts about somewhat. This instability of the least-square solution will be attractive rather than horrifying to the empirically oriented psychologist, since it immediately suggests interesting interaction effects and manipulations by which the equilibrium solution can be predictably varied and experimentally tested. It might seem presumptuously precise to have posited specifically a least-square solution as the minimization of logical discrepancies to which the person tends in his thought system. This definition is admittedly somewhat arbitrary. I would almost as readily settle for a postulate that the person tended to minimize the sum of the discrepancies rather than the sum of their squares. However, following a useful psychological tradition, I posited that a least-square criterion is applied, thus picturing the believer as scurrying about minimizing the discrepancies among his beliefs with particular attention to any that seemed to be getting particularly far out of line.

One additional postulate revises in a subtle but radical way my assumption regarding the nature of the coherence which the thinker tries to bring about in his belief system. In the previous paragraphs I have been phrasing this as a tendency to minimize discrepancies. More precisely, my intuition is that he tries to maximize the fit rather than minimize the discrepancies. Behind this reformulation is the consideration that there is a very simple way of minimizing discrepancies: one could simply refuse to see anything as related to anything else, thus vacuously balancing the cognitive system. If nothing implied anything else, nothing could be out of line with anything else. But as stated from the outset, I am taking the strong position that the belief system is organized so as to maximize connectedness as well as coherence. I will advert further to my reasons for tending to this strong position in the final section of this chapter.

Leaving aside for the moment why I wish to define the goal state of the cognitive system in this way, let me clarify that in fact I do postulate that the person tries to maximize the fit between his actual set of beliefs and the hypothetical state of the set if it were in maximum internal coherence as described by the laws of logic applied in the way suggested above. By this consistency maximizing (rather than inconsistency minimizing) definition, the person would gain his greatest gratification from a state of affairs in which there were many required interrelations among his various beliefs and his actual beliefs coincided rather closely with the optimal structure among them.

EMPIRICAL WORK ON THE 1953 MODEL

In this third section of the chapter I shall comment on some of the empirical realizations of the above formulation, thus clarifying its details and providing a test for its derivations. In order of increasing complexity, four different aspects of this work shall be presented. The first set of data bear on the initial state of the belief system, illustrating the extent to which the thinker does act as the honest broker in arriving at a compromise that prevents any one belief from getting too far out of line with any of the conflicting demands for congruence with other beliefs. Next I shall deal with the effect on the initially elicited set of beliefs which is produced by the altered salience effected merely by questioning the person about his beliefs, or what may be called the 'Socratic method' of producing opinion change. The third set of results deals with how persuasive communications which argue about specific issues produce remote effects on unmentioned issues which are related to the explicit one. The final results on which I shall comment bear on temporal factors and suggest differences between the short-term and long-term types of equilibrium towards which the belief system tends. More details of this work are reported elsewhere (McGuire, 1960a, b, c).

Initial State of the Belief System

The formulation discussed above has the believer cast in the role of a harassed honest broker striving to find a place for each belief so as to maximize the fit of the whole set to a maximally balanced system. In the empirical work, I focused on propositions which placed logically interrelated objects of judgment on two different dimensions of variability, their likelihood of occurrence and their desirability. Specifically, I took triads of related propositions which made up categorical or conditional syllogisms, for example: any city which is easily reached by air from the European continent will probably be destroyed by atomic bombs if another world war breaks out; our city is easily reached by air from the European continent; our city is likely to be destroyed by a bomb in the event of another world war. The subjects were asked to assign a probability of truth value to each of these propositions. These probability responses placed each of the three objects of judgment on the veridicality dimension, thus specifying three logically interrelated beliefs in the person's cognitive system. When formal logic and probability theory are applied, it can be specified that one's acceptance of the conclusion (representing belief that the city in which he lives will in fact be destroyed by a bomb in the event of another world war) must equal or exceed the product of the probabilities of the two premises. The conclusion's probability can exceed this product because it might also follow from other sets of premises besides the two stated here. For example, some of the subjective probability that one's city will be destroyed by nuclear bombs in case of war might derive from thoughts that a nuclear bomb could be placed by saboteurs or delivered by submarine or that such destruction could occur through accidental detonation of one's own weaponry. Since my experimentation involved no effort to measure exhaustively the person's beliefs on all possible premises leading to any conclusion, I was able to state only the limiting condition that the conclusion's probability must be at least as great as the product of the probabilities of the two given premises.

I also investigated the complicating problem that the events with which I was dealing lay on other dimensions besides likelihood of occurrence. Specifically, the events also had a desirability value. Hence, the subject, besides being asked to rate each proposition as regards its veridicality, was asked also to rate each one as regards its desirability. In my formulation, postulating a wishful thinking tendency, one expects correspondence between the likelihood and the desirability beliefs, since it would be incongruent to believe a state of affairs to be highly undesirable if its occurrence was believed to be very probable. It will be noted that this real-life thinker has a much more difficult task than the logical man. In the usual formulations of logic, one considers the truth value of propositions without having to consider in any way their desirabilities. The harassed honest broker in my formulation must juggle all of these additional elements simultaneously and in several dimensions in order to find the nearest to ideally congruent set of stands on interrelated propositions in the face of these conflicting demands.

The bearing of the data on the formulation developed here will probably be clearest if one thinks of the experimentation as focusing on the person's belief about the likelihood of occurrence of the state of affairs depicted in the conclusion. In the case of the example cited above, this focus of interest would be the person's probability rating that his city would indeed be destroyed by nuclear weapons in the case of a world war. The formulation views the thinker as maintaining a belief on this issue which is maximally in line with at least two other types of consideration. In the first place, he has to consider beliefs regarding the probability of occurrence of related events from which the conclusion's event would logically follow. Secondly, he must consider the desirabilities of each of these events, keeping his expectations in line with his desires. Hence even within the narrow empirical realization of the general formulation, the thinker is seen to reach a fairly complicated two-dimensional solution that maximizes the fit between his actual beliefs and an ideally congruent set of beliefs. In the terminology of my earlier papers, the believer has at least to compromise the demands of logical thinking and wishful thinking in arriving at his congruence-maximizing solution.

The details of the methodology and the results can be read elsewhere (McGuire, 1960a, b, c). It will suffice here to say that evidence was found for both logical and wishful thinking. As regards the former, there was a correlation of .48 between the judged probabilities of the conclusions and the products of the probabilities of the premises from which they followed when we used group mean data for 16 syllogisms. There are a number of serious uncontrolled factors (also described in the original papers) which would limit the magnitude of this correlation coefficient even given that the subjects were thinking perfectly logically. Hence the obtained positive value of .48 can be taken as some indication that the person places an object of judgment on a given dimension consistent with where he places logically related objects of judgment on that dimension. Evidence was also found for the other aspect of the postulated congruence, wishful thinking, indicating that the person's placement of the object of judgment on a given dimension is kept in alignment with his placement of the same object of judgment on other, psychologically related dimensions. It was found that for the 48 events that constituted the 16 syllogisms, a correlation coefficient of .40 was found between the rated desirabilities of the events and their rated probability of occurrence.

In line with the postulated complexity of the psychological problem, the person's beliefs in the likelihood of occurrence of the events cited in the conclusions can be even more adequately accounted for if both these logical and wishful thinking considerations are taken into account simultaneously. Evidence for this comes from the finding that for the 16 syllogisms a partial correlation of $+ .85$ was found between the probability of occurrence of the conclusions and the product of the probabilities of the premises when the rated desirability of these various events were partialled out. This correlation is admittedly somewhat inflated by being based on group means rather than the individual raw scores. It still accounts for an interesting portion of the total variance, considering that (as mentioned above and described more fully in the original papers) I left uncontrolled a number of factors which in my total formulation one would expect to affect the belief measures considerably. For example, the empirical work did not take into account the extent to which premises other than the two that happened to appear in the syllogisms would also bear upon the conclusions under study. Admittedly though, avoidance of this particular source of variance was not accidental but rather, as pointed out in the original papers, reflects a rather difficult problem in the empirical testing of this formulation. The problem can be solved only to the extent that the person's belief system is completely mapped out (a problem on which I touch more fully in the fourth section of this chapter), though some tactical expedients for avoiding the issue are discussed in the previous papers (see particularly McGuire, 1960c).

The Socratic Method of Changing Beliefs by Merely Asking Questions

The second set of data bearing upon the general formulation is reported here with some ambivalence since subsequent studies have failed to confirm them at statistically significant levels (Dillehay, Insko, & Smith, 1966). I do choose to present them because their exposition helps depict the flavor of the theoretical formulation regarding human thought processes. On the basis of the formulation sketched out above, I predicted that it should be possible to persuade people by the Socratic method of simply asking questions. Use of the procedure is illustrated by the classical example of Socrates' convincing the geometrically unsophisticated slave of Meno, merely by asking him questions, that doubling the side of a triangle does not double its area. The general notion is that the person's belief system includes sets of nonsalient propositions related to any given area, and that by making him sufficiently sensitive to these related beliefs, one can move him to take a more congruent stand on the issue in question. Because of the pervasive interconnections among beliefs and the limited momentary information-handling capacity of man, only a small subset of the relevant belief system is brought to bear upon any area at a given time. By the simple device of asking selected questions, thus making the individual aware of his beliefs on some subset of related issues, one can increase their momentary salience and bring him to a belief on the given issue which is more closely congruent with those about which we question him. This method of persuasion involves, not presenting the believer with any new arguments from the outside, but eliciting and increasing the momentary salience of certain beliefs which he already holds and which bear on the issue in question.

In testing the validity of this line of reasoning, I again focused on the propositions which indicated the person's belief about the likelihood of the events cited in the conclusions (for example, the probability that his city would indeed be destroyed in the case of a world war). It was assumed that the desirability of any event is to a large extent spontaneously salient when the person is questioned about the likelihood of occurrence of this event. On the other hand, it was assumed that the likelihood of the related events dealt with in the premises is much less spontaneously salient to the person when he is asked to rate the likelihood of the conclusions. Hence, the first experimental session in which these premises were presented to him would constitute a significant manipulation of the relative salience of the various related beliefs involved. The contiguous elicitation of the syllogistically related triads of beliefs would leave the subject sensitized to any discrepancies that existed among likelihood beliefs, thus shifting the congruence solution so as to leave these related expectancies in a more congruent state than they were found in the first session. I predicted, therefore, that when the same beliefs were elicited in a second session soon after, the later equilibrium would be more tailored to logical thinking at the expense of wishful thinking.

Only mild support for this prediction has been reported. On the basis of the data obtained in the first session, the 16 syllogisms were partitioned into those whose conclusions were relatively more desirable than the premises and those whose conclusions were less desirable. In keeping with the assumption of wishful thinking, the probability of the more desirable conclusions not surprisingly exceeded the product of the probability of the premises by a greater amount than was found in the case of the less desirable conclusions. The Socratic Effect prediction was that this differential regarding the probabilities of the two sets of conclusions, partitioned by desirability, would become smaller on the second session reelicitation. Evidence that reached the conventional level of significance was found for this prediction in one study (McGuire, 1960a), albeit reported with fear and trembling because of a possibly contaminating regression artifact; but the trend did not reach the conventional level of significance in two other studies (Dillehay, Insko, & Smith, 1966). This ratio of confirmation does not quite remove all remaining doubt about the validity of the prediction. Perhaps I can be extended some tolerance if I argue that confirmation would tend to be very precarious, even were the basic theory to be true. It will be recalled that the theory is being tested by a type of experimentation with which the field has little experience, and many auxiliary assumptions must be made, the unreliability of the quantitative scores is probably great, and large areas of the related beliefs in the system are left unexplored.

Remote Logical Ramifications of Persuasive Communications

There is less need to be apologetic about the confirmation ratio of the next set of predictions, which deal with the remote impact of changes introduced in the belief system by means of persuasive communications. According to the general formulation, a persuasive communication aimed at one of the premises of the syllogistically related triads and successful in introducing a change in it should produce changes likewise in the conclusion, even when neither the conclusion nor the other necessary premise for its derivation was mentioned even vaguely in the persuasive message. To use the same example as above, a persuasive message which successfully argued that his city was really more accessible by air from Europe than the person had at first believed should produce a change of belief not only on the directly relevant proposition regarding accessibility, but also in the proposition regarding the likelihood of the city's being destroyed by bombing. These remote effects should occur even when the message regarding accessibility is couched in the most peaceable terms without the slightest explicit reference to war or atomic bombs. In earlier papers on this topic, it was pointed out that the logically required change on the implicit conclusion is only a fraction of the change on the explicit premise, a fraction roughly represented by the initial probability of the other, unmentioned premise. It should be noted that in giving the equation for logically required amount of change on the conclusion (equation [3] in McGuire, 1960a), I inadvertently omitted a factor equal to "$1 - p(k)$," as Seymour Rosenberg (1968) has usefully and graciously pointed out. This correction in the equation makes only a small quantitative change in the prediction and so does not alter my original conclusions in important ways.

The empirical work bears out the predictions regarding remote logical ramifications of the changes induced by persuasive communications (McGuire, 1960a, b, c; Dillehay, Insko, & Smith, 1966). Induced changes on the explicit premises are communicated to the remote logical conclusions, even when neither it nor the other premise has been mentioned. The effect is rather small, but logically it should be small. McGuire (1960b) reports that the immediate impact on the conclusion is significant, though smaller than the small logically required amount. However, by the time a week has passed, the remote impact on the conclusion catches up with the logically required amount when one takes into account the temporal decay of the direct impact. Dillehay, Insko, and Smith (1966) in one of their experiments find that even immediately the impact is approximately that which is logically required; while in another experiment they found, as I did, an immediate impact that was somewhat short of the logically required amount but which tended to catch up with the logically required amount after the passage of a week. This temporal lag in the system is in accord with an additional assumption of cognitive inertia in my original formulation. This inertia assumption grants that the human conceptual arena may be highly interconnected and internally consistent but that there is a temporal lag before an induced change is communicated throughout the system. I grant that the human information processing mills may grind exceedingly slowly, but I continue to maintain that they grind out their logically required results quite well.

Adding a Time Dimension to the Formulation

The final aspect of the empirical work that I shall report here bears on the temporal aspects of the formulation regarding the structure of thought. It will be noted, however, that even the results reported in the previous sections have frequently adverted to the time dimension. The Socratic method of inducing belief change by merely asking questions about interrelated beliefs assumes that some time must pass before the forces toward change aroused by such a procedure would be manifested in the form of readjustments among the contiguously elicited beliefs. Also, it was left rather vague just how contiguous the elicitation had to be. In connection with the remote ramifications of opinion change induced by persuasive communications, I postulated an inertia such that these remote impacts were detectable only after time passage. In testing for this gradual seepage of the induced belief change over the cognitive system, I had further to make allowance for the temporal decay of induced opinion change.

All of these temporal considerations introduce a great deal of difficulty in setting up a test of the formulation which is at once 'fair' and also definitive. The time parameters are completely undefined and have been investigated only to a vanishing extent. For delayed effects, the only time interval that has been studied so far is one week. This was the interval used to test both the Socratic effect and the delayed remote impact of induced change. Whether this interval (selected simply because it fitted conveniently into the academic cycle) was fortunate or unfortunate as regards finding the effect at a particularly prominent time is not known. The matter is made even more complex by the fact that nonmonotonic functions of time for many of the effects must be predicted. For example, as regards the remote impact of a persuasive communication on an issue which was unmentioned in the message but logically related to the explicit target issue, I would expect this impact to show a nonmonotonic relationship to time elapsing since message receipt. Underlying the temporal trend in remote impact are two opposed mediating influences: one is the inertia of the system so that the logical seepage of the induced change occurs only gradually with the passage of time; the other is the temporal decay of the induced opinion change on the explicit target issue. Thus as time passes the pressure for the remote change due to seepage from the direct effect increases, but meanwhile the direct effect itself is decreasing through decay. The result of two such counteracting underlying processes is to produce an overall nonmonotonic effect. Hence, I feel that results of experimentation on this formulation are not definitive unless a wide range of parametric values are used as regards the time variable. I must admit that we consistency theorists have traditionally proved somewhat slippery when allowed to appeal to time considerations, as the reader of Section IV A of this volume will readily appreciate. The empirical status of the temporal predictions already cited remains unclear due to the rather mixed experimental results.

One further body of data regarding temporal effects deserves mention here as clarifying some aspects of the formulation. With the 'honest broker' notion of the thinker as engaged in arranging the best temporary compromise from moment to moment in a rapidly changing situation, one can make some predictions regarding the persistence of induced belief changes. The formulation leads to the assumption that the initial set of beliefs which the subject reports at the outset of an experimental situation represents a temporary congruence equilibrium in the very complex field of forces, only a portion of which can be salient at any moment. In the experimental situation, the salience of certain considerations relative to others is manipulated. It seems reasonable to assume, for example, that the experimental situations which have been used to test this formulation stress logical thinking relative to wishful thinking, more than does the subject's natural environment. Such procedures as presenting series of syllogistically related propositions (admittedly widely scattered throughout a questionnaire) and having the subjects rate their likelihood of truth on a probability basis which is explained in terms of betting odds does seem to stress the demands for rationality rather than autistic wish fulfillment. Hence, I would expect the subjects to move during the experiment toward a solution which takes into account logical thinking discrepancies more than does his natural environment. Once he leaves the experimental situation to return to his more complex natural environment in which logical thinking needs are less salient, those induced changes which were most in the direction of increased rationality will show the most rapid postexperimental decay, as the equilibrium shifts back to take more account of wishful thinking demands. Some evidence in support of this prediction is found in the data (McGuire, 1960b) which indicate that induced increases in the subjective likelihood of occurrence of undesirable events decay more rapidly than induced increases in the likelihood of desirable events.

In the studies cited, a number of additional hypotheses were tested with informative results that I shall not report here. However, even considering that this summary of the empirical work is incomplete, it will perhaps be obvious that the amount of experimental work done on this formulation is distressingly meager. While it is not surprising to find me arguing so, others also have pointed out that the empirical potential of this formulation has been sadly neglected (Insko, 1967). The door to the vineyard beckons; but where are the laborers?

FURTHER EMPIRICAL TECHNIQUES FOR COGNITIVE MAPPING

My empirical research on the formulation outlined here was discontinued in 1955 as situational and personal factors drew my interest into other areas. If I returned to the endeavor represented by the theoretical and empirical work discussed above, I would cast a somewhat broader methodological net in order to map out more adequately the full complexities of the cognitive system. In this fourth section I shall sketch a number of techniques that now seem to offer some promise for bringing to light the nature of the interrelations that exist among thoughts, or at least for testing hypotheses one has already formulated regarding these connections. These techniques have promise both on the creative, hypothesis-formulating side of the scientific endeavor and on the critical, hypothesis-testing side. The dialogue between theory and data is sufficiently complex so that the two processes are existentially interwoven even if conceptually distinct.

As pointed out in the first section, the general research strategy was to put the subject in a rather structured, passive stance regarding the generation of his belief system. While the flavor of my formulation might have suggested use of the strategy of giving the person an initial belief and then asking him to generate others, instead the tactical convenience was adopted of presenting him with entire sets of beliefs on which the research would focus and having him react to these possible beliefs so as to indicate whether or not he did indeed adhere to them. Changes were then introduced experimentally at preselected points in this a priori system, and the resulting ramifications to other points in the system were traced.

In this section alternative less restrictive procedures will be mentioned which seem to offer additional possibilities for teasing out the interrelatedness among cognitions. More use might be made of free association and other productive thinking procedures by the subjects. The subject could, for example, be given certain propositions and asked to generate other propositions that he feels are related to the given one. Or he could be given pairs of cognitions and asked to fill in how a thinker could proceed from one of these beliefs to the other. A study of these subject-generated propositions might suggest the rules of inference which he is following, and would also provide a demanding but convincing test of a priori hypotheses regarding the psychology of inference.

The use of sorting procedures has proved useful from the early work of Vigotsky through the current research by Sherif on the "own categories" procedures. In this tradition, one might present the subject with a large body of propositions and ask him to sort them into categories, with varying degrees of restrictions as to what categories he could use. The nature of his sorts would give some insight into his way of thinking about "what goes with what." Again, this method would also provide a technique for testing hypotheses on this point that one might draw from a priori theory. Recent methodological advances in multivariate analysis epitomized by the work of Shepard and suggestive clinical procedures such as George Kelly's Rep have some applicability for analyzing the structure of thought. Along these lines the subjects might be provided with pairs, triads, etc., of propositions and asked to make a similarity judgment. Various restrictions might be imposed as regards dimensions to be used in making these judgments. Or the materials might be presented in such a way as to yield a confusion matrix. Whatever tactics were employed in these regards, the resulting similarity judgments could be subjected to multivariate analysis which might reveal the number and nature of the dimensions used in psychological inference.

More use might be made of cognitive search procedures, techniques which attempt to trace the strategy used by humans in perception, thinking, etc., by providing some information or some problem and then tracing the subject's information-seeking behavior in coping with the situation. Perhaps the study of eye movements began this line of work. A recent example would be the "Judas-priest" experiments of Bruner and O'Connell on the search procedures used by people who have to determine what a partially hidden picture represents. By analogy here, the person might be presented with a proposition and the problem of determining whether or not it is true, while allowed to seek whatever information he wishes in order to arrive at an evaluation. An analysis of his questions might suggest or test hypotheses regarding his actual modes of inference.

Other methods will undoubtedly occur to the reader as they have to me since my original empirical work. Those I have mentioned here seem to offer some promise for extending the rather circumscribed methodology used in testing my 1953 formulation so as to reveal more adequately the totality of the belief system and its rules of operation. Rather than extend this discussion of advances in methodology, I shall turn, in the fifth section of the chapter which follows, to a discussion of the more basic problem of revisions in the 1953 formulation itself, rather than just in the method used to test it. Fifteen years of occasional further thought has suggested that some changes in the theoretical formulation itself are necessary.

THE LOGICALITY OF HUMAN THOUGHT: A REAPPRAISAL

At the outset of this chapter I took a rather extreme stance as regards the structure of human thought. I attributed to it such a degree of internal connectedness and coherence as to put myself outside of the mainstream of current theorizing on this issue. I am quite willing to grant on an informal, off-the-record basis that I have perhaps over-intellectualized the degree of connectedness in human thought, having committed the pathetic fallacy of judging others to be too much like myself. In formal theorizing in this area, however, I still adhere stubbornly to the initial assumption made regarding the high degree of interconnectedness in the belief system.

I am much more willing to make concessions regarding the degree (or at least type) of the internal coherence that obtains within this highly interconnected system. In view of the use of syllogistic materials, logical symbols, and probability axioms in the published versions of this formulation, it is quite understandable that some people familiar with my work seem to have the impression that I visualize the thinker as more logical than I actually do. Admittedly I did claim that formal logic provides a partial model for psychological thought processes, but it should also be noted that even in the initial formulations it was postulated that the internal coherence towards which the thinker tends includes also other forces (such as wishful thinking) and numerous limitations (such as cognitive inertia) all of which would cause actual thought to deviate considerably from a strictly logical model.

In this final section of the chapter, I shall present more explicitly my notion of the adequacy of a formal logical model for describing actual human thinking. Let us first turn to the adequacy of formal logic as a 'product simulation' of human thought, asking how well formal logic serves to describe the end product of thought—the belief system produced by human information processing and other forces. Then let us examine more briefly the adequacy of formal logic as a 'process simulation' of human thought, considering there the adequacy with which formal logic procedures describe the processes followed in human thinking as it arrives at its end product in the form of a belief system.

Formal Logic as a Product Simulation of Human Thought

I continue here to take for granted the postulate that the human belief system is highly interconnected. That is, the person tends to feel that his taking certain positions on given issues implies that he really ought to take specifiable positions on a wide variety of other issues as well; when he finds himself without such a congruent set of positions he shows signs of distress and of increased cogitation which tends to improve the congruence. At issue in the present discussion is the extent to which this congruent end product to which the belief system tends is coincident with the end product that would be generated by the application of formal logic to the same material. Left to the later section is the further question of how similar the 'laws' by which actual thought arrives at the final belief system are to the laws and processes of formal logic.

My position is that formal logic provides the first approximation of a product simulation but that by itself it provides a most inadequate model. In the preceding sections of this chapter and in my earlier writings on this topic, I have stressed sufficiently the positive aspect of formal logic as a useful part of the model. Here I shall stress its shortcomings by considering a half dozen additional factors which affect the maximum congruence solution toward which the belief system tends and which, therefore, limit the extent to which formal logic can provide an adequate product simulation.

The multi-valued nature of human assent. Formal logic, from the classical period to the present, has developed largely as a two-valued system. Admittedly, this is not an intrinsic limitation; multi-valued systems can and indeed have been suggested. But the almost universal presentation of formal logic as a two-valued system makes it essential to clarify that I consider human thinking to involve multi-leveled response categories. An application of a two-valued system of formal logic, failing to take into account that people do not consider propositions to be simply true or false but to have different gradations of assent, would provide an inadequate model for human thought. Such two-valued models would lead to invalid conclusions about the nature of belief congruence and would also create false problems for the theorists.

In the second section of this chapter I sketched some examples of how a two-valued system, when imposed on human thinking, could make it appear that the person was being inconsistent when actually his constellation of beliefs was quite permissible. I might point out additionally here, more in criticism of consistency theorists than of formal logicians, that most of the consistency theorists have unfortunately adopted the two-valued limitation of the formal logic work while neglecting the attractive and powerful aspects of formal logic. One result has been the appearance of unnecessary problems within their theories, which must be met with additional ad hoc assumptions. For example, such widely varied consistency theories as those of Heider, Newcomb, Cartwright and Harary, Festinger, Abelson and Rosenberg, etc., have all imposed upon themselves the two-valued limitation. In these theories, a person either likes another or he does not; one cognition either implies another or it does not. (There is no need to discuss here the question of whether the contradictory or the contrary of a thought is its negation.) No provision is made for gradations in the liking or other unit relationships. Thus if I like George and George likes Harry, it is supposed to be psychologically compelling for me to like Harry also. But when one considers that the liking bond probably has values other than $+ 1$, 0, and $- 1$, I might not find it too painful to contemplate that George, whom I like a bit, is rather partial to modern art, for which I do not care too much. If an allowance is made for the gradations in liking (for example, by the probability index of assent which I used in my empirical work) then problems of this type would not arise nor would the theorists be confronted with the necessity for elaborate adjustments, such as those suggested by Cartwright and Harary, to adjust the imbalance score for the length of a cycle in the structure. (In Chapter 5, Abelson acknowledges and briefly discusses these problems, pp. 118 ff.)

The problem of cognitive inertia. As indicated in the third section of this chapter in reporting the empirical work, my formulation postulated a certain degree of cognitive inertia. I would add more explicitly at this point that the inertia is both temporal and spatial. On the temporal side, it was postulated that the organism tends to accumulate a certain amount of discrepant information in his immediate conceptual reservoir, and works out the implications for this material through the rest of the cognitive system only gradually. Hence, it takes time for introduced discrepancies to seep through the system and manifest their remote impacts.

The notion of a spatial inertia enters through my assumption that there is a certain amount of give in the conceptual apparatus. The belief system is not a rigid structure; rather there is a certain amount of slack in the chain which ties one concept to another. A certain amount of discrepancy can build up before the incongruent belief exercises any appreciable force for change on related beliefs. Since this slack would be accumulative as one traces the implications of a belief change throughout the belief system, the waves created by a discrepant piece of information would tend gradually to die out. I prefer this notion of a certain amount of 'give' in the cognitive apparatus in order to maintain my basic assumption of pervasive interconnectedness. In this way I can picture the belief system as being almost completely interconnected, without having to demonstrate that the change in any one belief causes changes in almost all the other beliefs and, indeed, probably results in a completely unstable situation. Instead, I can maintain the postulate of high interconnectedness by assuming that remote impacts are felt with progressively less force as one proceeds through the system and, after a certain number of steps, no further force is exerted.

Capacity limitations. The computer analogues used in some of the models of human information processing and thought depict ideal intellectual slaves, experiencing practically no time lag, no loss of memory, and no reluctance to consider all of the available evidence. The humans to whom our formulations are meant to apply do unfortunately experience considerable limitations in these regards. A person's scope of attention and effective momentary recall seems so limited that he can bring to bear on a problem only a small portion of his total conceptual system. Laziness and absolute limitations of information handling seem to prevent him from making full use of his total body of information at any one moment. In the classic paper on positive and negative instances in concept formation where Hovland and Weiss (1953) pointed out that humans do not exploit the information potential of negative instances as thoroughly as that of positive instances (where the potential was defined in terms of a perfect information processing system), they also noted that one possible difference was that the human does not have the machine's absolute memory and attention span capacity to keep equally well in mind the many negative instances and the few positive ones which contain the same amount of information.

In the more complicated situations which are dealt with in the present formulation, where the person has to find a solution that is equitable to so many diverse considerations, such limitations of memory and attention come even more obviously into play. Hence the momentary congruence solution at which a person arrives in a given situation will depend on his momentary internal state and situational factors that enhance the salience of one or another subset of the total body of relevant beliefs. The data reported above suggest that the typical solution with which the individual enters the laboratory stresses logical thinking tendencies somewhat less than the solution at which he arrives by the end of the experimental situation, which makes these rational considerations more salient than they are in the natural environment. Consequently, when he returns to the real world, on reentering the laboratory certain specifiable shifts in his solution reflecting differential persistence of the laboratory-induced changes can be expected.

Nonrational needs. The extent to which the conventional formal logic model is adequate for depicting human thought is further limited in my formulation by the assumption that the congruence towards which the belief system tends must take into account nonrational as well as rational needs. For example, the believer must make his expectations on a given issue correspond not only to his expectations on logically related issues; he must also accommodate the demands of wishful thinking and bring his expectations on that issue in line with his desires. As the functional theorists have pointed out (see Katz's discussion in Chapter 8) our beliefs must satisfy needs other than correspondence to the objective world and logical consistency. The methodologies which I suggested in the previous section of this chapter would hopefully throw light on the nature of these other demands. The workings of the wishful thinking tendency, specifically, were demonstrated in the description of the empirical data in the third section of this chapter.

The problem of insufficient evidence. Formal logic was developed to handle complete information systems while the person is in almost every decision situation confronted with the necessity of drawing a conclusion from insufficient evidence. Whether in life or in the laboratory, the person is expected to give an answer, or indicate a belief, or take an action, even though his information for choosing among alternatives is seldom univocal or compelling. In such situations, formal logic typically runs scared. If the evidence is not sufficient to warrant any conclusion, none is drawn. Or alternatively, the equally arbitrary and useless strategy is imposed that, unless the premises compel the contradictory of the proposition, then the proposition is valid.

The human in the natural world is faced with the problem of arriving at some conclusion and one that seems most in accord with the admittedly inadequate evidence. It seems to me that any organism wired so that, unless he had compelling basis for a response he would make none, would have been left near the post in the evolutionary race for survival. Perhaps the rule of the jungle, the savage environment in which man's thought processes were shaped by evolution, is better typified by the opposite ultimate tactical rule taught at the Infantry School at Fort Benning: in case of doubt, do anything; but do something. The situational and personal compulsions to take a stand and to act are such that the cautionary rules of formal logic would not suffice for a vast area of human decision making. It was partly to handle this problem that the graded assent and the probability axioms were introduced into my formulation.

But these quantitative additions are not sufficient to allow formal logic alone to provide the person with adequately definitive rules for action. One must add to the formulation additional heuristics which the person seems to use in situations of insufficient evidence, after formal logic and the probabilistic addenda have carried him as far as they can. I suspect that these further additions would be typified by, for example, a 'fail-safe' rule. One might divide situations for action into approach to a desired goal or avoidance of a deleterious one. Human thought processes may have been shaped so that we overdraw conclusions in each of these situations. For example, if the individual is motivated by hunger needs and has some slight information that an area might contain food, human thought processes may tend to overdraw the conclusion that one should approach and thus one enters the area even on insufficient evidence. Analogously, the individual motivated by fear and suspecting that an area contains a danger may typically overdraw an avoidance conclusion, thus staying out of the area more than would be logically required. Perhaps hypotheses of this sort regarding metalogical heuristics could be investigated in probability learning situations more efficiently than in the attitudinal area usually studied by cognitive consistency theorists.

Homo ludens. In the commentary so far it has been taken for granted that the thinker is playing the harassed, honest broker role to the limit, faithfully trying to come to the best possible congruence solution in an impossible situation. Perhaps in a formulation of the type I am trying to develop here I should limit my conception of man to this framework. However, perhaps such a framework excludes certain diametrically opposed aspects of the human personality. The congruence towards which it has been assumed the belief system tends may be far removed from a completely rational solution in accord with the principles of formal logic, but it deals exclusively with the tendency toward some kind of congruence.

Hence, the formulation as depicted here ignores completely the possibility that the incongruent does have some appeal for the human mind. It is an interesting incident for the sociologist of science, as I have pointed out elsewhere (McGuire, 1966b), that at the same time that the consistency theorists have been stressing the tendency towards balance and the predictable in man, there have coexisted (with tolerant mutual avoidance) a set of quite opposite conceptions, called the 'complexity' theories. The editors of this volume asked two representatives of this rather opposed school of thought, Berlyne and Maddi, to discuss the consistency work from their point of view in Chapters 15 and 16, and I myself return to this issue in Chapter 17. But I should point out here that any congruence formulation will fall short of an adequate depiction of human thought processes to the extent that these exhibit an attraction towards the incongruent, the novel, the unpredictable. And I do believe that there is such a component in the human personality. It perhaps appears more saliently in the leisure hours than during the workday, being more clearly manifested in art, humor, and recreation. But I suspect that it pervades every aspect of thought at least to some extent. It perhaps is the random element that has been introduced into the system because of its survival value in providing an opportunity for innovation and improved solutions to old problems.

Formal Logic as a Process Simulation of Human Thought

The 1953 formulation was developed also with a very clear realization that formal logic was not adequate as a product simulation of human thought. It was recognized that there were many other factors involving nonrational needs and limited intellectual capacities in the human which made the belief system at which he arrived somewhat different from that at which he would have arrived strictly from the considerations of formal logic. Nevertheless, I did feel that these thought processes were at least partly informed by the considerations handled by formal logic. Hence, I adopted the strategy in the model of assuming that human thought processes could be depicted in the form of a model that started with the rules of formal logic and added to them certain qualifications, limitations, and elaborations in order to approximate more closely what actually went on in human thinking.

It now seems somewhat less certain that formal logic does provide a useful core for a process simulation of human thinking, such that it, with the addition of these additional heuristic rules just cited, could provide a valid protocol of actual human thinking. This 'logic with corrections' strategy has not quite been abandoned as regards depiction of actual thought processes. However, it is much less certain that it will prove an accurate depiction than it seemed in 1953. The reason for this decline of confidence is that I now realize that so many 'corrections' must be applied to the formal logic rules in order to approximate human thinking that I have begun to fear that this 'logic with corrections' wiring might be too circuitous and inefficient an apparatus for arriving at beliefs and intellectual conclusions to have plausibly evolved. Granted that in a strictly rational world formal logic is a most efficient and powerful machine for inference, in the real 'world we never made,' with all its complexities and inadequacies, this strictly logical model seems so inadequate and in need of correction that I now wonder if nature may not have solved the inference problem in a radically different way from the logic plus corrections program.

Perhaps those of us who are interested in the process simulation of human thought should pay more attention to the possibility that primitive thinking is not confined to the child's cognitive processes or those of the adult in mental institutions or in preliterate societies. Developmental psychologists, students of psychoses, and cultural anthropologists have all made some progress of late in describing, often in fairly formal terms, the rules that they feel characterize this primitive thinking. I have in mind the work of the students of early cognitive development who stem mostly from the tradition of Piaget; or the studies by Ariete and others who have tried to formalize schizophrenic thinking; or the analyses of Lévi-Strauss and other cultural anthropologists who have tried to formalize and describe the laws of thought purportedly followed by preliterate peoples. These theorists themselves, particularly the latter, have often suggested that the sophisticated thought modes followed by educated adults in our own Great Society are not as far removed from primitive thinking as is usually supposed. It might be that the more efficient and valid way of arriving at an adequate process simulation of human thinking would be to adopt a 'primitive thinking plus corrections' strategy for the model. One might, for example, take the thought modes which Lévi-Strauss intuits as operating in the savage mind on the basis of studies of their nomenclature and mythology, as the core of all human thinking. The primitive modes would thus play in a new formulation the central role which formal logic played in my 1953 formulation, with formal logic now relegated to the role of one of the correctives.

II

Intersections of Consistency Theories with other Psychological Theories

INTRODUCTION

Since this volume is focused on the topic of consistency theory, it is only appropriate that the first section contained an exposition of six variants of this approach. It is equally appropriate that Sections III and IV be devoted to the antecedents and consequences, respectively, of cognitive inconsistency. At first glance, the appropriateness of Section II might be less obvious since it consists of chapters by authors presenting theoretical positions quite different from those of the consistency researchers. However understandable such a first reaction might be, the editors think that it becomes clear on reflection that an adequate consideration of consistency theory requires its being put in the context of other theoretical viewpoints that bear on the same phenomena with which its predictions deal. Hence we felt it appropriate and even necessary to invite expositions of no fewer than ten other theoretical positions that stand in some special relationship to consistency theory.

There are four different special relationships demanding exploration in the form of chapters by researchers whose work has been guided by other theoretical orientations. First, there are some theoretical positions that relate to consistency theory mainly by providing a general theoretical housing under which it can be subsumed. Secondly, some theories stand in a supplementary relationship to the consistency position, so as to intersect with it in certain empirical areas and thus provide an opportunity for cross-fertilization. The third relationship is constituted by theories that purport to supplant consistency theory to some extent by providing alternative explanations for its confirmed predictions. In a fourth relationship are those theories more explicitly opposed to the consistency formulation, which postulate psychological needs that seem directly contrary to cognitive consistency tendencies. These four relationships are listed in order of increasing opposition to the consistency formulation and might be called respectively: consistency subsumed, consistency supplemented, consistency supplanted, and consistency opposed. At the risk of emphasizing controversy, the ten theories expounded in this Section II have been grouped under these four headings in order of increasing opposition to consistency theory.

In the consistency subsumed' category, the editors felt it appropriate to invite three theorists to comment on the consistency position from the point of departure provided by theoretical formulations which they have developed and often used in their research. We felt that each of these three alternative theories would most likely be considered to subsume the consistency formulation as a special case, and a case which could be bolstered by an exposition of the broader theoretical housing provided by these encompassing formulations. It seems appropriate to present first in order of relevance to the consistency formulation, an exposition by Nehemiah Jordan of the Gestalt position associated with Heider and himself, since this Heiderian formulation was quite clearly the historical origin of a number of the consistency theories. We asked Daniel Katz to consider consistency theory in the light of the functional approach which he has been developing and working with in recent years. Much of the consistency work deals with attitudes and behavior, and we think that the functional approach is one of the most inclusive and ambitious formulations currently available for handling attitudinal phenomena. To complete this section on broader theoretical housings that might subsume consistency theory, we asked Irving Sarnoff to discuss consistency theory in the light of the psychoanalytic approach which he has in the past applied to the attitudinal area. It seems to us that psychoanalytic theory is the most extensively applicable and intensively developed of all psychological theories and moreover has a special relationship to the consistency formulation because of its preoccupation with the problems of rationality and modes of resolution.

The second, 'consistency supplemented,' category includes approaches that provide an elucidation of consistency theory by confronting it with complementary theories that developed from different problems and proceeded in different directions, but which in the course of their development intersect with consistency formulations in ways that might promise fertile interactions. The editors invited two exponents of such positions to comment on the consistency research from their point of vantage. Vernon Allen discusses the consistency work in the light of the role theory formulation with which he has so often dealt. This role theoretical approach constitutes a well worked-out conceptualization of social processes that seems to have run parallel to the cognitive consistency work with few points of explicitly discussed contact. It seemed to us that there were analogous aspects of the two formulations that might make some bridge building here mutually profitable. Harry Upshaw was asked to examine the consistency work in the light of the work in the psychology of judgment area with which he has been concerned during recent years. We felt that researchers from the judgmental and the consistency groups have found themselves on a number of occasions rather suddenly and unexpectedly in confrontation. In view of these several points of contact and the fact that the two groups seem to elaborate different aspects of the problem areas, we felt again that an explicit comparison here might be mutually stimulating.

In the two preceding classes of relationships in which other theories stand to consistency theory, a large number of alternative formulations might have been invited, but we felt constrained to limit the invitation to particularly appropriate sets of alternatives. The same embarrassment of riches obtained with regard to the third type of relationship constituted by 'supplanting theories,' which provide alternative explanations for the predictions that are particularly associated with the consistency theory approaches. The editors chose to confine the discussion in this category to three widely varied alternative formulations which seem to have a particularly close relevance to the domains of behavior to which the consistency theories have been applied. Hence, we asked Helen Peak to discuss the consistency work from the vantage point of her activation theory, which grew out of her early concerns which also gave rise to some of the consistency formulations, and yet differs quite dramatically in conceptual flavor from those formulations. Secondly, we asked Barry Collins to comment on consistency theory from the vantage point of reinforcement-behavioristic theory, since this formulation has been widely influential in psychology in general and more specifically because its proponents have often either made alternative predictions to those derived from consistency theory or offered alternative explanations for the same predicted relationships. As a third example of a 'replacement' theory, we asked Daryl Bem to discuss consistency theory from the Skinnerian (or perhaps Jamesian) form of 'radical behaviorism' that he has recently been developing and applying quite specifically to provide an alternative explanation to some of the more dramatic consistency theory findings.

The fourth class of alternative theories confronted us with a lesser embarrassment of riches, since there are fewer theories that posit processes diametrically opposed to those postulated by the consistency theorists. What we call 'complexity theories' come closest to being in direct opposition, since they postulate that the organism seeks out novelty and surprise rather than confirmation of his expectancy. Two rather divergent exponents of this complexity-need approach were asked to discuss consistency theory in the light of their viewpoints. Daniel Berlyne, who is one of the earliest developers of the curiosity drive notion, evaluates the consistency theory approach from his complex but moderate complexity viewpoint, and Salvatore Maddi discusses it from his more radical complexity approach.

Hence while all ten of the theoretical chapters that follow deal with alternative theoretical formulations relevant to the consistency approach, they have been selected and arranged to cover the whole spectrum from worried progenitor to radical oppositionist. Despite their faithfully playing the role of opposition theorist, the authors of these ten chapters, with remarkable unanimity, take a positive approach and have been constructive in their criticism of the consistency formulation. In general, they attempt to suggest the elaboration, modification, and improvement of consistency theory rather than its abandonment. Understandably in view of their very different origins, conceptual mechanisms, and purposes, these ten theorists choose to throw light on different areas of consistency research. Some central themes tend to recur, however, with remarkable frequency. Dissatisfactions with the motivational status of consistency theory seem to be felt by almost every one of these alternative theorists. (Quite independently, this communal brooding arises again in Section III A.) A feeling that the consistency researchers have neglected the topics of individual differences and of alternative modes of resolution seem almost as unanimous. Other complaints tend to reappear in subsets of the chapters. Where the complaints are voiced, the theorists are rather positive in going on to suggest how the consistency formulation should be appropriately elaborated, in the light of the alternative theory being discussed. After all ten of these theorists have (in Chapters 7 through 16) presented their viewpoints, Chapter 17 will be devoted to a reconsideration from the consistency theory approach of the points raised by these alternative theorists.

CHAPTER 7

Cognitive Balance as an Aspect of Heider's Cognitive Psychology

Nehemiah Jordan

International and Social Studies Division
Institute for Defense Analyses

A 'new field' has developed in social psychology during the last decade. It goes under many names: dissonance (Festinger, 1957), congruence (Osgood, Suci, & Tannenbaum, 1957), symbolic psycho-logic (Abelson & Rosenberg, 1958), the strain towards symmetry (Newcomb, 1953), and structural balance (Cartwright & Harary, 1956). Adopting a term seemingly first to appear in print in 1960 (Katz, 1960; McGuire, 1960a), these various names are now subsumed under "cognitive consistency."

All these approaches have at least one feature in common. They all assert that the perception or cognition of inconsistency or contradiction, of whatever form, generates tension within the perceiver which, in turn, leads to some action on his part. By and large the action the several investigators were interested in was either attitude change, cognitive distortion, or behavioral change. They usually treat cognitive inconsistency as motivating behavior or selective perception outside the context of any more inclusive theoretical approach or model. Most also explicitly treat it as a constant factor and some, notably Festinger, stress that it is a very important factor in daily behavior (Festinger, 1957, pp. 275 ff.).

These approaches have another feature in common. They all cite Heider's principle of cognitive balance as an approach either similar or parallel to their approach and admit to its historical priority. (Heider explicitly discussed cognitive balance in a paper published in 1946 and it was adumbrated even earlier, in a paper published in 1944.) Some, particularly Cartwright and Harary, and Abelson and Rosenberg, also admit their intellectual debt to Heider as having influenced them directly.

Cognitive balance is an integral part of a larger, coherent theoretical approach aimed at attempting to understand how a person cognizes the social world, i.e., it is an important but only a partial aspect of Heider's cognitive psychology. To use it as Heider uses it, or even to mention Heider's principle of cognitive balance adequately, demands that Heider's total cognitive psychology be taken into account since so much of its meaning and implication stems from its embeddedness in Heider's system. Not that there is anything intrinsically improper about taking an idea or concept from a system and then developing it independently of that system; scientists have the right to take their ideas from whatever source they wish and develop them in whatever way they feel is valuable—but they should be clear about what they are doing.

HEIDER'S SYSTEMATIC COGNITIVE THEORY

Heider has been remarkably consistent in his scientific interests throughout his entire career; he is a student of perception. Most of his work, since the early 1940's at the very least, has been devoted to an attempt at understanding social perception or, a term he uses more frequently, person perception, e.g., the perception of social objects.[1] The earliest publication where this interest predominates is a paper written jointly with M. Simmel (Heider & Simmel, 1944), although it is already implied in two earlier papers which treat perception from a more general standpoint (Heider, 1927, 1930).[2]

The 1944 paper reports the results of an experiment in which 114 subjects viewed an animated movie showing three objects, two triangles of different sizes and one disc, moving about in a simply structured field. Thirty-four of these subjects were merely asked to describe what they saw; the other 80 subjects were instructed to interpret the movement of the objects as actions of persons and then to describe what they saw. All but 1 subject of the first group of 34 subjects described the movements in terms of animated beings, chiefly of persons. Almost all the descriptions were in terms of unit actions with well defined beginnings and ends. In other words, the subjects 'broke up' the continuous movement presented on the screen into organized, discriminated events, each different and isolated from the other. This organization of a manifold of discrete movements into unitary events is not, in principle, different from the organization of a manifold of discrete point stimulations on the retina into a perceptual figure with a well-defined boundary segregating it from the ground. It follows therefore that the perception of social events or social action is not in principle different from the perception of physical objects; both entail an organization of discrete elements to create a unitary whole. A social event is consequently as much a perceptual object as is a physical thing.

The experiment disclosed more; it disclosed the principle underlying the organization of the movements into social objects. Every perceived action was organized about the motives perceived to hold for the actors involved; by what they *wished to cause*. As soon as these perceived motives changed an 'old' event terminated and a 'new' event began. One is necessarily reminded here of the classical Gestalt laws of perceptual organization. Given a manifold of elements then, all other things being equal, elements in proximity to each other will be grouped (organized) to constitute a unit, elements similar to each other will be grouped to constitute a unit, elements sharing a common fate or a good continuation will be grouped to constitute a unit. Motivation plays a similar organizing role in this experiment on social perception; the question arises whether the general Gestalt laws of perceptual organization can be applied to the perception of social objects.

---

[1] 'Social objects' is an unfamiliar term. In common parlance it should be replaced by terms like 'social events' or 'social actions.' Why it was chosen will be explained as the exposition progresses.
[2] These two early papers have been reprinted in an issue of *Psychological Issues* (Heider, 1959) devoted to his selected papers.

This question is explicitly asked in another paper published in the same year (Heider, 1944) and the answer is an unequivocal affirmative. In this paper, Heider explores many of the ways by which man organizes the field of social movement into social objects based on the principle of the motivations of the actors involved, or, in more general terms, the effect of phenomenal causality upon social perception. The paper explicitly parallels the Gestalt treatment of the perception of physical objects.

Although phenomenal causality is an important factor underlying the organization of social objects, there are other factors too. The sentiments a person has for other people or objects also lead to social-perceptual unit formation. Somehow we experience (perceive) some bond to exist between a person and the things we know he likes, a bond which acts as a *force* towards unit formation. Mere similarity, in the Gestalt thing-perceptual meaning of the term, also affects social perception. People who are similar are grouped together and are perceived as a unitary object. The same holds for proximity; parades are not perceived as collections of peoples but as organized units. And there are others. Heider's book, *The Psychology of Interpersonal Relations* (Heider, 1958), contains many examples of factors acting towards social-perceptual unit formation. When we write, using Heider's notation, that pUx, we mean that at least one of these factors exists and that p and x are perceived to constitute a social-perceptual unit in at least one respect.

In summary, Heider's main effort has been in trying to clarify social perception in a manner consistent with the general Gestalt theoretical approach to thing perception. He has succeeded in identifying factors underlying the organization of social percepts which 'parallel' the factors of thing percept organization which were first identified by Wertheimer.[3]

COGNITIVE BALANCE

Balance was 'discovered' during Heider's exploration of the social-perceptual unit-forming properties and powers of phenomenal causality; to be more precise, it was imbalance that was 'discovered'—balance poses no problems and hence does not attract attention, imbalance is problematical and does.[4] We have seen that if p is perceived to have caused x, a unit is formed in some way between p and x and they are perceived as constituting a social perceptual object (this can be represented symbolically as pUx). If, however, it is also perceived that p dislikes x ($p-Lx$) one immediately feels some sort of contradiction; dislike of an object psychologically implies a desire to disassociate oneself from the object and this desire acts in a direction opposing unit formation. If p likes x (pLx), on the other hand, no such opposition to unit formation is experienced (perceived). To paraphrase the opening sentence to Heider's first paper on balance: sentiments and causal unit formations influence each other.

At this elementary level of causal unit formation imbalance acts in op-

---

[3] A more detailed treatment of Heider's cognitive psychology can be found in my paper "The Cognitive Psychology of Fritz Heider" (Jordan, 1966).

[4] 'Discover' is enquoted because it oversimplifies the matter. It is true that judging exclusively from Heider's published works the above sentence seems to be correct. Yet Heider maintains that he developed the concepts of balance and imbalance from careful study of Spinoza's ethics. Without being able to go into the matter further, I can only say that I do not feel that there is a real contradiction here.

position to the unit forming forces whereas balance does not; even more, balance acts actually as a force towards unit formation, it supports it and enhances it; it is meet that a person should like that which he causes. Balance and imbalance have the same effect when the social perceptual situation becomes more complex. If p perceives that o has caused x and he (p) dislikes this x caused by o, balance and imbalance are determined by the relation between p and o. If p 'caused' o (let us say that p is o's parent or that p recommended o for the job, etc.) then, by virtue of causal unit formation, there will be forces acting on p to perceive himself in a unit with the x he dislikes. This effect of sentiments is carried over to the perception of o's sentiments as well. If p causes x and p likes o, then o's dislike of x is an instance of imbalance $(pUx; pLo; o-Lx)$. If, on the other hand, p dislikes o, there is no imbalance, rather balance; the forces in the situation act to segregate o from the unit, the social-perceptual object constituted by p and x.

Having discovered this influence that sentiments and causal unit formation have on each other, Heider proceeds to generalize (Heider, 1946). This he does in two ways. He first asks the question whether this influence is restricted only to causal unit formation of social objects and answers in the negative. The effect of sentiments upon any factor active in social unit formation is similar to its effect upon causal unit formation. In other words, the considerations discussed in the preceding paragraph which were restricted to, generally, the condition where p caused x, 'causing' being a proper value for the 'variable' U, are now generalized to all other factors affecting social unit organization, to all other proper values for the 'variable' U.

Secondly, he conceives of balance itself as a factor for unit organization in that the perceiver tries to organize the social object in as balanced a way as possible, i.e., there is a force towards balanced configurations of social objects. But balance is a radically different factor in unit organization than the other factors mentioned above; it can be called a dynamic factor, with respect to the perceiver, whereas the other factors are merely 'static.' By this the involvement of the perceiver in balance as such is meant, in contradistinction to the indifference of the perceiver to the other factors. In and of itself, there is no reason why p should wish to see that o caused x, or that o is similar to another person, q, or that o likes x, etc.; he is indifferent to what the case may be. However, if he happens to perceive that o caused x, or that o is similar to q, or that o likes x, etc., then these factors account for his social perceptual organization of the situation. But he is not indifferent to balance; he tries to organize the situation in as balanced a way as possible.

Something similar is to be found in Wertheimer's laws of thing perceptual organization. Four laws were mentioned in the preceding section: proximity, similarity, good continuity, and common fate. They too are static; the perceiver is indifferent as to whether two elements are in proximity, are similar, etc., but when he perceives them to be so they are organized to constitute a thing perceptual unit. Wertheimer, however, has enunciated a fifth law which has yet to be mentioned: the law of Prägnanz. Prägnanz is anything but a static law; the perceiver tries to organize the percept in as prägnant a way as possible. In determining the organization of social perceptual objects all the factors which have been considered as values for the 'variable' U play a role equivalent to the first four Wertheimer laws of thing perceptual organization, whereas balance plays a role equivalent to the law of Prägnanz.

BALANCE AND HARMONY

Up to this point the sailing has been relatively smooth. Some difficulties are now encountered. Balance and its counterpart imbalance are intrinsically ambiguous concepts and although Heider is aware of this ambiguity, he never really clarifies it. On the one hand balance is a down to earth simple factor playing its role, with other factors, in determining the organization of social-perceptual objects; on the other hand, however, it is a general principle, with Kantian a priori characteristics, which enables an ordering and grasping of what would otherwise be an inchoate collection of disparate facts.

This aspect of balance comes to the fore in his book (Heider, 1958, pp. 212–217). There balance is discussed in connection with Spinoza's theory of sentiments, general systems theory, Goldstein's concept of self-actualization, and Angyal's concept of autonomy. Here the relatively limited and well-defined problem area of studying specific problems in perception is left, and attention is turned to the general order that underlies the phenomenon of life proper. Concepts at that level of organization are not simply amenable to experimental or empirical verification. They are accepted, thrive, and prosper only to the extent that they introduce a coherent order to the knowledge gained through careful studies and experience at a more concrete level of organization. That Heider is aware of this difference seems evident from the fact that he actually introduces new terms for balance and imbalance within this extended context: harmony and disharmony.

Heider had started out primarily interested in the more limited role which balance and imbalance play in social-perceptual organization; in his 1946 paper 'harmony' is not mentioned. But as he studied the matter more closely the wider ramifications of balance and imbalance began to rise in importance. By 1950, at graduate seminars discussing the issue, Heider used 'harmony' interchangeably with and as frequently as 'balance.' By 1956, if not earlier, he expressly said that he was sorry to see 'balance' established in the literature since he feels that 'harmony' is a far more fitting word to use. But he has not made this shift in interest and change in meaning explicit. This can be attributed to the fact that Heider has explicitly eschewed attempting to formulate a rigorous system, about which more will be said in the section to follow. The fact that in his book all discussions of balance are basically in the context of harmony, whereas in the literature the latter context is not even recognized, is bound to lead to misunderstanding.

That balance and imbalance are intimately related to the most central issues of man's perception of the world seems obvious. Two examples, one for balance and the other for imbalance, sufficiently demonstrate this relatedness.

There is no denying that religion, in all its manifestations, is man's most common and, in many ways, his most serious and profound attempt to answer the fundamental question as to the meaning of his being in the world. The ultimate state which the religions offer to man become the solution they offer to his problem. The three major world religions that stem from the Old Testament, as well as others which do not, offer an identical solution, which incidentally is not found in the Old Testament: Heaven and Hell. In this ultimate state all that is evil is segregated from all that is good. To use the language of balance, all that is good is organized in one unit and all that is bad is organized in another unit and no connections, no unit-forming forces whatsoever exist between the two. This is ideal balance or harmony. It was actually rigorously deduced by Cartwright and Harary in their *structure theorem* (Cartwright & Harary, 1956, p. 286) and was intuitively deduced by other students of balance even earlier.

Another area of human endeavor which is of central importance is art. Great art is priceless, above all value. The most lasting and influential form of literary art is the tragedy, as can be seen if one compares the differential impact of Greek tragedies and Greek comedies upon modern man, or the Shakespearian tragedies and comedies for that matter. But the essence of tragedy is imbalance—just ponder Oedipus' fate. Actually the fate of Moses and that of Achilles also indicate imbalance. And what does lyrical poetry sing more of, requited or unrequited love? Balanced configurations are to be found almost exclusively in the happy-ending novel, but that generally does not serve as an example for literary quality. Formal imbalance is inextricably involved in great art, at least in art using words as its medium.

Here too balance shares a property common to Prägnanz; Prägnanz too has implications far beyond the mere perception of things. Not only do men try to perceive as Prägnant an object as possible, but they also behave in as Prägnant a way as possible, and with this Prägnanz becomes indistinguishable from self-actualization. It is obvious that Prägnanz is also inextricably involved in art. It should not be surprising to find that the study of simple perception leads to considerations involved in the most significant and profound problems confronting man; Cassirer demonstrates a similar convergence with respect to the perceptual constancies (Cassirer, 1944). The significance of perception cannot be sold short.

L AND U (LIKING AND UNIT FORMATION)

Current research on cognitive balance has concentrated on L relations; U relations have been given short shrift. The import of U is generally misunderstood. Since, as has already been indicated, balance has been considered independently of Heider's total theory, this is not surprising. As shown above, U is probably the single most important and central concept in Heider's thinking and unless it is understood, much of the power of that thinking is lost; it lacks, however, a clear independent meaning outside the system and persons not acquainted with Heider's system necessarily do not know what to do with it and feel ill at ease with it. Such is certainly not the case with liking and disliking (L and − L); these have entered the realm of psychological speculation with Plato; every psychologist feels at home with them and they do fit into whatever model of human behavior he may accept.

But Heider himself is also to blame for the current misunderstanding. It was mentioned above that Heider was not interested in formulating a rigorous system; he makes this clear in almost all of his published papers and particularly in his book (Heider, 1958, pp. 3–4 and 296). Nevertheless, it can be demonstrated that despite this disavowal, he has been remarkably consistent in his approach over his 40-odd years of professional work and that underlying it there is an implicit rigorous system free from contradictions (Jordan, 1966). There seem to be, however, a few lapses, and one of these lapses has to do with the usage of U in connection with balance. The symbol U is actually used in a self-contradictory manner and, considering all the other difficulties the relatively uninitiated reader will have with it, its usage will also confuse him—even though he may not be explicitly aware that this is the case; it can be asserted that men can feel contradictions before they see them and react to them in confusion without becoming aware of the source of confusion.

It was shown above that imbalance was 'discovered' while exploring the intricacies of causal unit formation. Heider writes: "Attitudes towards persons and causal unit formation influence each other" (Heider, 1946, p. 107); in other words, he differentiates between causal unit formation and sentiments. He then goes on to ask whether the same influence will exist for any factor that induces unit formation. He writes: "It is tempting to generalize ... and to omit the restriction to causal unit formation. Do units in general interact with attitudes in a similar way?" (ibid., p. 107). The symbol U therefore should systematically subsume all factors which, in whatever way, induce unit formation; e.g., p causes x leads to the perception of pUx; p is similar to o leads to the perception of pUo, p owns x leads to the perception of pUx, etc. As already indicated, U plays a role in social perception analagous to the role played by Wertheimer's first four laws of perceptual organization.

But if p causes x induces the perception pUx, then, a fortiori, p likes x should also induce the perception pUx. But then, in order to use U systematically, we must look at pLx as a special case of pUx, seeing L as a member of the set of specific factors determining social unit formation. If one seems to exclude L from that set, as when it is discussed as a factor or variable independently from and in conjunction with U, then U ceases to be a systematic symbol and becomes a mere notational shortcut sign for a relatively arbitrary collection of unit formation factors. In order to be systematic the notation pLx, oUx should therefore represent a social perceptual situation where *the factor of positive sentiment* acts for the inducement of a unit between p and x while some other factor or factors (which may also include a positive sentiment) acts for the inducement of a unit between o and x. The symbol U stands for a dynamic variable and is not a mere name for a relatively static state: that two discriminable entities merely form parts of some more inclusive social perceptual unit.

Imbalance was 'discovered' when it was seen that when p causes x (pCx) and p dislikes x, unit formation becomes problematical: just as pCx acts as a force for unit formation, $p-Lx$ acts as a force against unit formation. In other words, looking at U as a dynamic variable, $p-Lx$ is a special case of $p-Ux$. It can therefore be easily seen that pCx and $p-Lx$ is representable by pUx and $p-Ux$ and imbalance becomes an instance of opposing psychological forces. In fact, considering that U is obviously a symmetrical and transitive relation, e.g., if pUo and oUx, then there is a force towards the organization of a social perceptual unit between p and x, it can be asserted that pUo and $p-Uo$ is the canonic form for any form of imbalance, no matter how many entities are involved.

Let us demonstrate this for the p-o-x unit but, in order to indicate that this holds for the configuration of relations independent of the entities for which the relations hold, we will speak of a 'neutral' abc unit instead. Take the imbalanced situation: a likes b, b dislikes c, a likes c. The state of a liking b and a liking c induces a force towards the organization of a social perceptual unit containing a, b, and c; but the perception of b disliking c induces a force opposed to the organization of such a unit. In terms of transitivity this can be represented by: aUb and aUc induces a force towards bUc whereas $b-Lc$ induces a force towards $b-Uc$—hence the imbalance. No such 'contradiction' can be derived from a balanced situation. Take for example: a likes b, $b-Uc$ and a dislikes c. There is a force towards unit formation between a and b and a force against unit formation between a and b (as a unit) and c. This obviously holds for any other factor inducing a force against unit formation.

It is interesting to note that a very similar conclusion has been reached independently by Julius Marek (1966, p. 16). After reviewing the literature and analyzing his experimental results Marek concludes (using the symbol R which includes U and L as special values) that formal balance applies directly only to the R signs and not simply to the signs of L and U. Marek's use of R is harmonious with the present use of U.

A seemingly new difficulty arises with the interpretation of U as a dynamic variable. There is no problem with respect to the L relation: pLo induces pUo and $p-Lo$ induces $p-Uo$; but when we turn to causality a problem does arise. Whereas p *cause* x induces pUx, p *not cause* x does not seem to induce a force against unit formation; it just does not make sense to assume that p wishes to disassociate himself from all those things not caused by him. It must be concluded, therefore, that $p-Cx$ is neutral with respect to social perceptual unit formation, i.e., $p-Cx$ does not induce $p-Ux$. The same seems to hold for the other factors inducing unit formation. If a person owns a thing, pUx is induced; if a person is similar to another person, pUo is induced, etc.; but, on the other hand, it does not make sense to say that a person rejects all the things he does not own or all the others he is dissimilar to, etc. Offhand, it is tempting to assert that with the exception of $-L$, all other negations of unit forming factors do not induce forces against unit formation, i.e., they cannot be represented by $-U$. This is a factual finding which, however displeasing it may be to an investigator, does no violence to the system which merely speaks about forces supporting unit formation and forces opposing it. Nowhere in the system are we told that the negation of an objective state which in itself induces unit formation must necessarily induce forces against unit formation.

This assertion is satisfying in that it 'explains' Heider's tentative acceptance of Cartwright and Harary's 'rejection' of $-U$ and their argument that p-o-x units containing $-U$ are vacuously balanced (Heider, 1958, p. 202; Cartwright & Harary, 1956, p. 291). If $-U$ is interpreted as representing all the negations of unit forming factors with the exclusion of $-L$ then it does not act in opposition to unit formation, i.e., it is not imbalanced, it is vacuously balanced. And it will be assumed that Heider had exactly this in mind when he asserted agreement with the possibility expressed by Cartwright and Harary. Unfortunately, the matter is not that simple. Instances can be shown where lack of unit formation other than disliking does evoke a kind of balancing behavior that leads finally to unit formation. Think of the many times and the many different ways in which people tell other people that they ought to do something or see something or experience something even though the lack of doing, seeing, or experiencing does not lead the others to suffer any kind of deprivation. Here a force from $-U$ to U which does not involve sentiments and which leads to balance is illustrated.

THING PERCEPTUAL IMBALANCE

Part of the power, beauty, and elegance of Heider's approach to social perception is its close analogy to thing perception as worked out by classic Gestalt psychology. The comparison of balance to Prägnanz is particularly useful. With respect to imbalance, however, the analogy breaks down; the psychology of thing perception has nothing remotely resembling imbalance, it contains no antonym to Prägnanz.

So things were until several years ago. Man seemed neither able to conceptualize nor to conceive tangibly of a perceptually 'imbalanced' thing. Several years ago, however, a line drawing perpetrated by some ingenious designer began to circulate in the engineering literature.[5] It is a strange design and is often captioned: Blivet, Mark IV.

It will be recalled that in organizing a thing-figure from a line drawing the contour of the line plays a significant role in determining the organization of the figure; it marks the boundary between the figure and the ground. Since every line in a line drawing has a noticeable width, i.e., every line has two sides, then only one side, the one perceived as being external to the figure, can play the role of contour. The other side of the line blends into the figure so that it disappears as an entity as such; let the other side of the line be called the anticontour. Because the contour serves to segregate the figure from the ground in order to isolate the figure it is a unit-forming factor. The anticontour, on the other hand, fuses the line with the figure, makes it indistinguishable from the figure, hence it is a factor acting against unit formation. In ambiguous figures, obviously, any side of the line can serve as a contour or anticontour, respectively, and when,

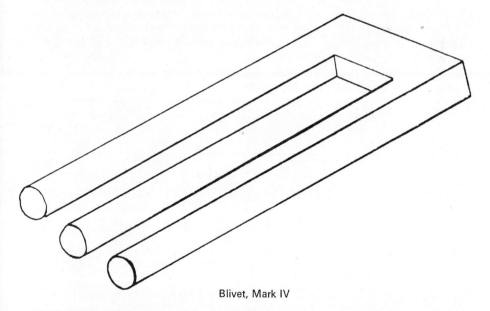

Blivet, Mark IV

---

[5] A historian of ideas might find it of some interest to trace the origins of such drawings. Gardner (1966) has an interesting article on the work of the Dutch artist Escher which incorporates representations of 'impossible objects.' At least one treatment of such 'objects' has appeared in a psychological journal (Penrose & Penrose, 1958).—Ed.

for whatever reason, the role of a side of the line changes, the figure changes. But the Blivet Mark IV is unique; if any side of any of the lines constituting the Blivet is taken as a contour, the same side will soon, without a break, begin to play the role of an anticontour. Denoting the side chosen to play the role of the contour as *side a* we find that *side a* simultaneously plays the roles of both contour and anticontour. Symbolically this can be represented by:

(*Side a*)U(Blivet Mark IV) and (*Side a*)—U(Blivet Mark IV).

This representation is imbalanced, by definition.

The figure generates all the discomfort and 'tension' to be expected from Heiderian imbalance, as the reader can see for himself.

CHAPTER 8

Consistency for What?
The Functional Approach

Daniel Katz

The University of Michigan

In a time of conflicting ideas and contradictory information from high places, of partisan pleading based upon distorted facts and illogical argument, of confused thinking and of glaring discrepancies between public profession and private practice, it is refreshing to see a revival of consistency doctrines in psychology. The hypotheses and predictions from such theories are not those which one would make from everyday observation. More encouraging still is the fact that the research inspired by these doctrines has more often than not yielded positive outcomes. Even when the predictions have not been clearly borne out, the findings have forced a critical reexamination of existing concepts and theories that has yielded novel and valuable information. The ingenuity of the research, moreover, has been a powerful force in the development of experimental social psychology.

Excellent evaluations of the research on cognitive consistency are available in the writings of Brown (1965), Weick (1965), Zajonc (1960a), and Feldman (1966c), in which the advantages of a single organizing principle as well as theoretical limitations are judiciously assessed. Though in general agreement with the balance demonstrated by these authors and with their positive appraisal, I will be more concerned with the relationship of consistency doctrines to a functional approach to attitude formation and change. A functional approach attempts to go beyond the cognitive field and deal with the motivational bases of attitudes. Though consistency and functional theories address themselves to different issues, they are both concerned with changes in beliefs and attitudes. The nature and strength of the cognitive discrepancy and the modes of its reduction can conceivably be more adequately assessed by looking at the functions which beliefs serve for the individual.

THE FUNCTIONAL APPROACH TO COGNITION AND BEHAVIOR

A functional approach would ideally require some definitive typology of human needs and their characteristic properties. Attempts at such typologies, however, have produced little agreement and it is not difficult to understand why. Even the simplest biological drives become so intertwined with social motives that they are difficult if not impossible to unscramble. People seek gratification of hunger, sex, and shelter in ways which accord with their self-esteem. Moreover, the nature of ego needs and the direction they assume is so complex as to defy classificatory analysis. The difficulties with motivational analysis in fact constitute one of the reasons for the increasing interest in cognitive theory. There is, however, one way of dealing with the problem which does not bog down in seeking to pinpoint needs according to their origin and that is to work with broad motivational patterns of differing characteristics. This is the approach of Kelman (1961) in his distinction among the influence processes of compliance, identification, and internalization. Specific needs are not described but it is assumed that the change processes will be differentially related to the power of the influencing agent, his attractiveness and his credibility. The sources of power as described by French and Raven (1959) represent another attempt to deal with motivational factors at the general level of the bases for the exertion of influence. In a more direct functional attack Smith, Bruner, and White (1956) analyzed the functions of attitudes as they were directed toward object appraisal, social adjustment or externalization. Katz and his colleagues (Katz, 1960; Sarnoff & Katz, 1954; Katz & Stotland, 1959) have been concerned with a similar analysis and have maintained that we can understand attitude change more adequately if we distinguish among four functions which attitudes serve for the individual. (a) They can be utilitarian or adjustive, i.e., can be instrumental to the individual in maximizing gains and minimizing losses with respect to the external world. (b) They can be ego-defensive in allaying anxieties generated by internal conflict. (c) They can be value expressive in giving expression to the positive values the individual holds about his social world and his relations to it. (d) They can meet his needs for cognitive structure and understanding. Utilitarian attitudes are a means to an end and can be changed if there are alternative and better ways of achieving the objective. Value expressive attitudes are ends in themselves and their content is internalized by the person. A change in them requires genuine restructuring of the individual's belief systems or a change in his available modes of expression. Ego defensive attitudes are also internalized, but more as symptoms than as causes. They are highly resistant to change and require some modification of the personality before they are extinguished. They can show change of a superficial character, as where an authoritarian individual is ordered by a person in authority to show less discrimination toward a scapegoat group. The specific order may be obeyed but the prejudice may be revealed in other ways. Attitudes serving the knowledge function are modifiable where existing organizations of beliefs are inadequate to give cognitive structure to a changing world furnishing new informational and experiential inputs, provided that the person has available some new belief that will more adequately subsume the body of information and experiences.

In essence, then, we are dealing not with a set of original and basic needs but with developed motivational patterns of varying characteristics. These characteristics enable us to predict something about the ease of change, the conditions productive of change, the direction it will take, and the stability of the change. The objectives here are not the same as those of the dissonance theorist. Nevertheless, the two approaches are related in that the conditions under which dissonance arises, the strength of the dissonance, the mode of its reduction and the stability of the new balance are affected by these underlying functions. To the extent that these forces can be fully assessed at the cognitive level there is no need to modify dissonance theory. To the extent they cannot, a more comprehensive theory is necessary to deal with both cognitive representations and patterns of motivation.

In general in the following discussion more reference will be made to dissonance theory than to balance and other consistency formulations. Though less precise theoretically, dissonance theory has led to more interesting experimentation, more novel findings, and more challenge to conventional formulation than have the other models. Perhaps because of their more specific and vulnerable formulation, balance theory, congruity theory, etc., have had less experimental support than the dissonance doctrine. For example, though people prefer balanced to unbalanced structures, and learn symmetrical patterns more readily than asymmetrical patterns, the differences are not as great nor as compelling as the theory would predict. Moreover, some experimental findings cannot be handled by the model. Zajonc and Burnstein (1965a), for example, have shown that not all structures of equal balance are learned with the same facility. Negative structures fully balanced are not learned as readily as balanced positive structures.

Even when the dissonance doctrine encounters ambiguity in its experimental results, it raises issues of consequence for further research. This is true, for example, of the search for information following a decision where not all experimenters find that consonant information is preferentially sought (see Section IV E). Similar interesting outcomes can be found in the problem of the degree of change produced by an unattractive communicator or in the matter of the amount of change occurring in the extreme proponents of an issue. It is also true with respect to the effects of size of reward for following a dissonant course of action. Festinger and Carlsmith (1959), following up an experiment of Kelman (1953), found that a small monetary incentive produced more attitude change than a large one when the task was one of publicly advocating a counterattitudinal position. These findings were confirmed by Cohen (Brehm & Cohen, 1962), and by Nuttin (1966), but not by Rosenberg (1965d) nor by Janis and Gilmore (1965). The experiment by Carlsmith, Collins, and Helmrich (1966) gives additional information on the problem by replicating the earlier findings for conditions of role playing but not for essay writing. This whole line of experimentation has called attention to the need for clearer specification by those favoring a reinforcement theory of the psychological effects of incentives and by those favoring dissonance theory of a more precise formulation of the types and amount of dissonance created by various conditions. It is such experimental confrontation, discussed more fully in Section IV F, that makes for scientific progress.

NEGLECT OF MOTIVATIONAL LEVEL IN CONSISTENCY THEORIZING

The strength of the cognitive consistency models is also their weakness. By narrowing their focus to cognitive conflict, these theories facilitate experimentation and research. Moreover, their attempts to handle a bewildering complexity of the determinants of human behavior with a single general principle follows acceptable scientific logic and strategy. The main motivational principle they invoke is that of inconsistency reduction, though other motivational aspects are discussed (see Section III A). Motivational forces, value systems, and personality dispositions are only beginning to receive adequate attention by the consistency theorists (as discussed in Sections IV B and C). Nor is there adequate theoretical recognition of qualitatively different types of inputs. Cognitive conflict is sometimes reduced to the number and importance of the incongruent cognitive elements and their degree of disparity, thus capturing only one aspect of field theory, namely the discovery of a basic field condition such as cognitive dissonance and its properties. The exploration of the types of historical forces responsible for the conflict is only beginning with the work on volition, commitment, etc. (see Sections III B and D). More attention must also be paid to the objective environment and the types of stimulus inputs it generates. How serious these inadequacies are cannot be fully assessed until the experimentation stimulated by the model has run its course. One would predict, however, that consistency models, by neglecting motivational factors and environmental pressures, will not be able to take into account a great deal of the variance in attitude change and cognitive restructuring.

Cognitive consistency models give insufficient attention to three levels of conflict. One is the objective logical level and is in evidence in Festinger's (1957) definition of dissonance as the presence of two cognitions, one of which is the obverse by which Festinger presumably meant 'contradictory' of the other. The second is the level of what Abelson and Rosenberg (1960) term "psycho-logic." Here the utilities of various functions are weighted by the individual himself in relation to his own limited experiences, his position in social space, his cognitive near-sightedness and astigmatism, his values. Actually Festinger, despite his use (or misuse) of the technical term "obverse," did develop his theory explicitly on the level of psychological, rather than logical, inference. The third level is the logic of the unconscious. Freud and his followers have directed their efforts to show how seemingly irrational behavior can be understood by imputing rationality to the play of unconscious forces. Different assumptions and different predictions are implied by these three levels but there is little specification in cognitive consistency models for handling such complexity.

One of the few direct attacks upon the nature of cognitive inconsistency is to be found in the work of McGuire (1960a). He studied the Socratic effect produced by making salient to the individual the relationships between the premises and conclusion of a given proposition. People did in fact move from wishful thinking to more logically interrelated beliefs under conditions of salience. McGuire found, moreover, that persuasive communications changed belief, not only on the explicit issue, but also on its logical derivatives. In a related experiment, Tannenbaum (1966b) first linked a single source to two attitudinal objects with four variations in his experimental groups: (a) the source being favorable toward both objects, (b) favorable toward the first but against the second, (c) against the first but for the second, and (d) against both. Then, the basic experimental manipulation consisted of both positive and negative treatments of the first attitudinal object without reference to the original source. Not only were there changes in the manipulated attitude but in the evaluation of sources and in the attitude toward the second object. Moreover, these changes were positive or negative depending upon the congruity requirements of the patterning of the source concept linkages (see Chapter 3). Logical consistency was operative as in the Mc-Guire study. In a follow-up of the McGuire experiment Dillehay, Insko, and Smith (1966) also found that changes in a belief carried through to its logical derivatives. They did not replicate the finding concerning the shift from wishful thinking. These authors suggest that the underlying mechanism even in moving toward more logically consistent positions may not be so much a matter of formal logic as of psychological association. "If persuasion produces a change in acceptance of Fact A about Object X, this change may influence the acceptance of other facts about the object, especially facts that have an experiential relationship to Fact A or are 'reasonably' related to A" (p. 654). Whatever the explanation, these experiments illustrate an approach which could be profitably pursued to examine more fully the roles of logical consistency and wishful thinking in the formation and change of beliefs and attitudes (see Chapter 6).

Dissonance theory would consider only the quantitative aspects of the dissonance created and would not be specifically concerned with the logic of the unconscious. A functional approach would start by assuming that these three levels of inconsistency should not be equally weighted. Logical inconsistencies would be regarded as weak in their tension properties unless they had to do with conflicts in motivational patterns. Logical inconsistency would have little force in its own right, and then more within a single set of beliefs rather than across cognitive patterns. It would be tolerated if it were a matter of contradictory means for achieving the same end. It would also be tolerated if it were a contradiction between a method for achieving a goal and the goal itself, provided that the method had some prospect of success. There are many, many believers in peace as a goal but few adherents of nonviolence as a means to achieve peaceful outcomes.

Logical inconsistency according to functional theory could be readily converted to psychological consistency in that the individual could make sense out of discrepant elements under appropriate motivational conditions. The more attractive the goal, and the more difficult alternative routes to it, the more likely the individual is to accept an available path which may be logically inconsistent with it.

Inconsistencies at the *psychological* level would pose more difficulty for the individual, according to a functional approach, because they upset previous arrangements for handling conflict. The sensible pattern he has achieved for himself in accepting an undesirable means for a desirable objective was based upon the heavy rewards of attaining that goal. Now if he is thwarted he does not even have the pragmatic justification that his unethical behavior worked. The dissonance aroused is sufficiently great as to polarize his reactions either toward renunciation of such unethical tactics or a complete acceptance of immoral means to an attractive goal.

Inconsistencies at the unconscious level where the individual suffers from internal conflict affect cognitions in an indirect and symbolic way. Here the conflict is so severe that it is not directly represented in the cognitive field. The cognitive discrepancies which do appear are so muted and so remote from their origins in content that they apparently produce little dissonance. Yet the underlying conflict which is concealed can be triggered into action by making the discrepancy salient. This does not mean that the anxiety aroused will lead to a solution of the conflict. Rather the individual will only work harder to build his defenses. In this case the cognitive discomfort is only temporarily reduced and is reinstated, perhaps in greater magnitude, another time.

A general question to be raised has to do with the adequacy and validity of the cognitive representation of motivational forces which arouse conflict in the individual and affect its resolution and the manner of the resolution or compromise. The strength of a motivational determinant may be poorly reflected by the individual's report of how important a given belief is to him. Nor is the individual necessarily knowledgeable about the complex of motivational factors affecting him. His inner conflicts are represented in the cognitive field very sketchily, often symbolically, and often in distorted fashion. The cognitive elements which result from reaction formation cannot be treated for predictive purposes in the same fashion as cognitive elements which serve some clearly recognized objective of the individual. The failure to take account of the different qualitative inputs into cognitive conflict is a major limitation of consistency theories. The same lack of qualitative analysis makes difficult the prediction of various outcomes of imbalance or dissonance.

The critical issue concerns the strength and persistence of cognitive dissonance and whether this can be determined fully and understood adequately without going beyond the dissonance doctrine. We have had many demonstrations of dissonance and its effects, but little study of the strength of cognitive discomfort and its parameters. The only specification is the number, importance, and disparity of cognitive elements. Since the theory does not go beyond the cognitive level of representation we encounter problems when the cognitions poorly reflect or even misrepresent the basic motivational forces. As already noted the belief assessed by an individual as important may be unimportant, or in other cases the belief may really mean the opposite of what it states. Nor is there any specification about how far to go in sampling from the large number of possible cognitive elements.

Take the case of two individuals who both have the same cognitions about the immorality of antisocial behavior, specifically the use of physical brutality against helpless victims but for whom these beliefs serve different functions. Both individuals are now placed in a situation in which brutality receives some social sanction and in which they are called upon to approve the brutality. In the one case there may be severe cognitive dissonance; in the second case scarcely any. In the first instance the relevant value pattern of the person represents an end in itself. In the second case it is based upon repression of aggressive impulses in which the inhibiting forces have been social, i.e., other people. Now in a situation in which the social environment serves as a facilitating rather than an inhibiting force, this individual can readily approve of the brutal action. The cognitive conflict between old beliefs and the new information is transformed into a consonant pattern by a redefinition of the situation. Yet the cognitive representation of the repressed hostility and of the nature of the inhibiting force would be difficult to ascertain if one did not take account of the psychodynamics involved. It is true that this could be picked up in part by examining rationalizations after the fact, but dissonance theory is not very helpful in telling us where to look in assessing the strength of dissonance in cases of this sort.

How much is to be gained by ignoring the questions of where cognitions come from and what functions they serve? Dissonance theory is content to deal with beliefs such as might appear straightforwardly in the cognitive field and to predict outcomes when they are discrepant. But sooner or later do we not need to extend the theory to make qualitative distinctions about types of beliefs? Cognitions are not just the random residue of information and experience. Sometimes they are the clear statement of an integrated value system, sometimes they are the rationalizations of only partially recognized objectives, sometimes they are instrumental for achieving a practical end, at other times they are the denial of deep wishes, sometimes they are entertained for purposes of the deception of others and sometimes for self-deception, and sometimes as a means for understanding one's world. Even if one is solely interested in the magnitude of cognitive dissonance or in the modes of dissonance reduction it would seem necessary to understand more of the processes by which types of motives achieve cognitive representation. Certainly there is no one to one correspondence between motive patterns and their cognitive representation.

If we are restricted to dealing with a problem at the attenuated level of cognitive representations, we may be working with pale and malformed indicators which are phenotypic and unreliable. With all its limitations, Freudian theory has shown the difficulty of relating cognitive elements to one another in terms of meaningful patterns and in assessing the significance of certain elements. The representational field of the individual reflects both basic motivational conflicts and indirect and devious ways of handling them. It has a structure and properties of its own and new inputs need to be understood in relation to this field of forces. In its present form dissonance theory is too general and vague to provide the tools for ascertaining the strength and persistence of cognitive conflict and modes of resolution.

SOME FAILURES OF CONSISTENCY THEORY DUE TO NEGLECT OF MOTIVATIONAL LEVEL

Dissonance workers have been able to get very good mileage out of their general doctrine because of their insightful use of discrepancies which permit the operation of own forces. Their studies show that the mobilization of the individual's own efforts is a strong force in changing beliefs and attitudes. In fact, the greatest change seems to come from the exertion of minimal external force to induce the individual to stay with the situation so that he can maximize own forces. This is a valuable contribution and helps to tie dissonance theory to older concepts and to furnish additional specification for the older theory. There has not been, however, similar success in relating inconsistency to other motivational issues.

More specifically the following weaknesses of consistency models need to be examined: (a) What are the conditions under which conflict arousal takes place? (b) What is the nature of the inconsistency under study? Consistency for what? (c) How are conflicts resolved? (d) How stable or permanent is the new balance?

Conditions Productive of Conflict Arousal

To the extent that subjects have been moved toward cognitive congruity by fleeting exposures to manipulations in contrived laboratory situations, we might expect that everyday experiences in a continuing environment of stresses and strains would result either in well organized sets of beliefs or in psychotic breakdown. The facts are that neither outcome is typical. People notoriously lack ideological structures about their own world (Campbell *et al.*, 1960) and are full of inconsistent cognitions. It takes special conditions to make incongruity of beliefs salient to the individual. Consistency models vary in their recognition of this problem and in their inclusion of conditions of conflict arousal as a formal part of the theory. In general, balance formulations do utilize the notion of relevance. The congruity theory of Osgood and Tannenbaum (1955) does include the concept of cognitive interaction according to which conflicting elements have to interact to produce resolution. But there is no formal specification of the conditions under which cognitive interaction will occur. Brehm and Cohen (1962) have added the concept of commitment to the Festinger dissonance theory so that the individual experiences dissonance after he has committed himself to some activity inconsistent with his beliefs. This limits the Brehm-Cohen formulation to problems of resolving postdecisional conflict. Though specification of commitment is a straightforward handling of the problem, it should be recognized that it reduces the comprehensiveness of the theory. The major part of the battle in producing attitude and behavioral change is one of securing commitment.

We need, then, more study of the relationship between the constraints of the laboratory experiment in which cognitive conflict becomes salient and the conditions in social settings which are functionally equivalent. It is of interest that science is the area par excellence in which consistency and logical organization of knowledge exists. To insure such an outcome we have developed science as a separate subsystem of society with its own norms and values and with many built-in pressures and constraints. We demand that scientific theories be internally consistent. We require a fit between the theory and experimental findings. We develop elaborate experimental and statistical procedures to insure such congruence. Science, then, is the subsystem in which the role requirements exact consistency. To be a successful member of such a structure and to share in its rewards means that the individual accepts its values as his own in carrying out his work as a scientist. But this system of science is at marked variance with the other social systems. Moreover, when scientists step outside the laboratory and speak on issues foreign to their research, they are not impervious to logical contradictions in the expression of their opinions.

The Nature of Consistency and Inconsistency

What constitutes serious cognitive discrepancy for the individual? The balance, congruity, and dissonance models define imbalance as the psychological inconsistency of two or more cognitive elements. But the individual can tolerate a great deal of inconsistency if by so doing he can satisfy some basic motive pattern. The basic goal of attaining political objectives can accommodate many discrepant behaviors and beliefs. Politics makes strange bedfellows. It is of course true that the incongruity is between the various means to achieve a goal and not between the means and the goal. Thus from the larger frame of reference of the individual's personality there is no inconsistency. But then why dispense with concepts of motivation, of value systems, and of personality predispositions as is done in balance theory if we want to understand the nature of self-consistency? These

concepts give us the leverage to attack the significant problems of social behavior and provide a more adequate framework for evaluating consistency.
A motivational theory would start with the goals of the individual and
would attempt to see what beliefs and behaviors are consistent with the
attainment of the individual's motive patterns. Much persuasion consists
of the use of an armamentarium of verbal weapons often of an inconsistent
character designed to break down the resistance of an audience. The
caricature is the case of the defense lawyer who told the jury that he
would prove conclusively that his client could not have committed the
murder because of a well-established alibi, but that if this failed to convince
them he would then prove that his client was temporarily deranged when
he committed the crime. Inconsistent arguments like the statements of the
Johnson administration about its foreign policy in Asia are readily understood once we recognize what their proposers are trying to do. Why
neglect such obvious determinants of cognition and behavior in the construction of psychological theory?

Rosenberg and Abelson (1960) dealt with this problem explicitly and
experimentally demonstrated that subjects did not follow a balance prediction of achieving consistency between various relevant beliefs when the
total outcome of such a balance was unpleasant. Hence they formulated the
following general proposition (p. 145):

> In resolving cognitive discrepancies of the sort represented by our
> materials, subjects seek not only the attainment of cognitive balance
> and consistency but they seek also to alter their beliefs and evaluations
> in ways that will maximize expected gain and minimize expected loss;
> when both forces converge so that they may be gratified through the
> same change or changes a formally "balanced" outcome will be
> achieved; when these forces diverge the typical outcome will not meet
> the requirements of a simple formal definition of cognitive balance.

This general proposition modifies the usual statement of balance theory
in the direction of greater adequacy as advocated in the present argument.
But again the question arises, if we are to take account of maximizing expected gains and minimizing expected losses, would it not be more logical
to give attention directly to the motivational forces that tell us something
about such gains and losses? Why approach psychological hedonics through
a side door if it is necessary for an understanding of social behavior? Moreover, there is still the problem that not all motivational forces are clearly
represented cognitively through *expected gains* and *expected losses*. And,
motivational discomfort may be more upsetting than cognitive discomfort.

A related issue in asking *consistency for what?* is the neglect of existing
value systems and cognitive structure in balance theory. People organize
their cognitions and attitudes around objects and symbols in their world
and group their beliefs according to their appropriateness and relevance for
various types of situations. The exploration of such cognitive structuring
has been carried on under such rubrics as public and private attitudes, legitimacy, reference groups, role-related attitudes, relative deprivation, potency
of involvement in social systems, personal values and goals, linkage of attitudes to value systems, cognitive complexity, cognitive differentiation, etc.
From this work it is clear that people have some existing organization of
belief systems which not only give weighting to cognitive incongruities but

also enable them to accommodate apparent inconsistencies. For example, political scientists as well as politicians themselves are concerned with the Osgood paradigm of how much of the favorable evaluation of a highly esteemed public figure rubs off on other candidates on the ticket. In some instances there is such an effect, in other cases the endorsement of candidates by a revered public figure is ineffective. The high esteem may be based upon an organization of beliefs which is not political in nature, as in the case of a presidential candidate who is highly regarded because he is a national leader standing above political strife. A simplistic model which neglects such existing knowledge would have to be modified with all sorts of patchwork to make it fully operational. Hence, the thorough discussion of the motivational status of consistency, the role of self-involvement, and other issues taken up in Section III of this volume is of critical importance.

Modes of Resolution of Inconsistency

Another weakness of balance models is the lack of specific prediction about outcomes of incongruity. The general statement is that something will happen to restore balance but neither the Heider type theories nor the concept of cognitive dissonance specify how the conflict will be resolved. Thus Newcomb's (1961) study of Project House found that after four months the discrepancies between own attitudes and attractions toward others were resolved not through attitude change but through shifts in friendship patterns and perceptions of others (sometimes distorted). But his model provided no way of predicting whether a more harmonious adjustment would be achieved through finding congenial partners or through restructuring one's own beliefs or through misperceiving the attitudes of others. It is important, however, to be able to tell whether new situations change people's beliefs or their patterns of association or increase their autistic perceptions. [Fortunately, Sections IV B and C of this volume deal extensively with this problem—Ed.]

The mode of dissonance resolution is determined more by the total forces affecting the individual than by the fragments of experience traditionally manipulated by the experimenter. The mode of dissonance reduction can be controlled by the experimenter in that he can permit only one way of reacting to the psychological discomfort. But where various ways of reducing dissonance are possible, the individual will take that path congruent with his personality and existing social forces. And again consistency models provide no specification for such determinants. What is needed here is some variant of Maslow's (1943) hierarchy of needs in which are assessed, if not for individuals then for known groups in the population, the priority of motivational patterns. We already know that ego defensive people are resistant to informational input that challenges beliefs bolstering their defenses. Under conditions of constraint they may apparently accept new inputs but their methods of reducing dissonance will follow patterns of denial, compartmentalization, or rationalization.

There is an inconsistency in consistency theories with respect to the mode of reducing cognitive conflict and the resulting outcome. If one addresses himself to the proposition that inconsistency leads people to change beliefs and/or behavior, then why not examine the consistency of the apparent solution which is achieved? Some types of solution will be genuine resolutions of the cognitive conflict, others will be temporary expedients which postpone or alleviate the conflict. The older writers concerned with conflict such as Holt (1915) and Follett (1924) distinguished between three types of handling conflict: avoidance, compromise, and integration. But present-day consistency models tend to neglect the issue of consistent or logical resolutions of conflict which occur in integration as against the compromise outcomes or avoidance mechanisms. If one is concerned about the tensions created by inconsistency, he should continue to examine the consistent or inconsistent nature of the ways in which individuals handle the problem. Why stop when the issue of consistency really becomes interesting? Different modes of conflict reduction can be further elaborated in functional theory terms. [Just such an attempt is made in Chapter 66—Ed.]

1. One mode has been clearly presented by Freud in his description of various means of avoiding conflict through denial, compartmentalization and perceptual and cognitive distortion. These mechanisms, though effective in immediate reduction of conflict tension, are not logically consistent solutions, for the problem remains and the same tensions are readily recreated. A functional approach would emphasize the importance of determining the ego defensiveness underlying given attitudes and would anticipate the probability that the usual influence attempts would merely invoke defense mechanisms for the threatened individuals.

2. A common mode of reducing cognitive inconsistency is through compromise rather than through a genuinely logical solution. A compromise outcome is what the term literally means; namely there is some compromising of both alternatives. In general, according to a functional theory compromise is most readily achieved for utilitarian attitudes. The individual is concerned here with obtaining some return from his environment and can easily trade off one outcome for another. When value systems are involved, however, such trade-offs are difficult because the internalized values represent important principles for the individual in and of themselves. Moral beliefs are examples of such principles.

Hence, in cases of value conflict, compromise may prove a very unstable solution. The essential conflict between the two alternatives is not truly resolved. Compromise outcomes can assume a number of forms. After one alternative has been favored its conflicting counterpart is then given additional support. A business operator may indulge in some antisocial activity in his commercial operations and then increase his donations to charity. Or some middle ground is found between two contradictory positions which still reflects the same basic conflict. The person who finds his position on democratic values inconsistent with his support of segregated schooling may compromise by favoring the introduction of integrated schooling with all deliberate delay, such as supporting a program whereby integration will start at the kindergarten level and proceed a year at a time to affect higher grades. Or a business firm will accept Negroes for white-collar positions provided that they are unusually attractive, personable, and well-groomed.

3. The third basic method of handling cognitive inconsistency is through an integration in which a genuine resolution of conflict is achieved. Integration calls for a more drastic reorganization of cognitive and attitudinal structure. It deals with causes rather than symptoms. The individual who is inconsistent in holding both democratic ideas and discriminatory beliefs

about Negroes can meet the conflict not through compromise but through a new frame of reference in which he thinks through the full implications of democratic and egalitarian values in the social, economic, and individual sectors of life. A full realization of their meaning and application will lead to greater consistency than the compromise solution of an occasional concession to the deprived group.

Integration, though the most logical way of reducing inconsistency, is often the least preferred. It is psychologically more expensive than avoidance or compromise from a short run point of view, though less expensive in the long run. Immediate costs outweigh distant costs, especially for those whose psychological time perspective does not extend very far into the future. Moreover, there are circumstances in which the more remote consequences are difficult to assess in a dynamic world. To come up with an answer of what to do next is less difficult than to formulate wise policy for the future. Then, too, the individual often finds that his compromises have worked for him with some degree of success in the past. March and Simon (1958) point out that even decision makers in organizations do not follow a rational utility model in exploring all possible utility functions. These authors emphasize a *satisficing criterion* according to which a solution is reached which will apparently meet the immediate demands. Only in exceptional cases, they contend, is decisionmaking concerned with the discovery and selection of an optimal alternative.

Another consideration in the resolution of inconsistency is the salience of the moral nature of the incongruity. Moral dilemmas by definition cannot be compromised if genuine solution is to be achieved. The individual, however, can frequently redefine the problem to cast it into pragmatic rather than moral terms, e.g., to consider the means rather than the ends. By so doing he can meet the problem by compromise rather than by attempting integration.

The use of compromise thus is facilitated under conditions (a) in which the people involved have short time perspectives, (b) where long-term outcomes are ambiguous and difficult of assessment, and (c) where moral issues are not salient.

STABILITY OF THE COGNITIVE BALANCE ACHIEVED

The modes of inconsistency reduction are significant with respect to the stability of the solution achieved. If the mode is one of defensive behavior there is little if any change in reducing basic conflict. The defense mechanisms are merely ways of sidetracking anxiety-producing inconsistencies either through primitive forms of leaving the field or more subtle forms of rationalization. The experimental situation which takes no account of the temporal dimension gives too little weight to the role of rationalization. People over time can develop their own rationalizations to handle the problem or can search for them until they find them.

Research indicates that people with boring and disagreeable jobs are much more likely to dislike their work than to overvalue it. Adams (1963) has proposed an interesting theory of wage inequity as a special case of dissonance. Adams and Rosenbaum (1962) found that overpaid interviewers were more productive than their more poorly paid colleagues. The question remains, however, if such effects persist over time. Though people may temporarily put forth more effort to justify a wage inequity they can easily find some way of rationalizing their good fortune. Higher wage scales of a differential character do not necessarily lead to greater continued productivity for the favored group.

If the mode is one of compromise, the solution is still essentially unstable. There is no genuine reconciliation of inconsistent elements and so people will move toward one or the other of the opposed sets of beliefs as situational forces change. Compromise solutions work only until the next round of competing pressures.

Integrative solutions, however, are more permanent in that the discrepant elements or antitheses are truly resolved in some creative new synthesis. In general, such integrative solutions are much less frequent than either defensive reactions or compromises. It would seem as if most people move from compromise to compromise and emerge with a well integrated set of cognitive structures of a unifying type only under circumstances of recurring confrontations in clearly structured situations.

In conclusion, the argument is that dissonance theorists have made their greatest contribution in revitalizing experimental social psychology and in their interesting findings which challenge traditional concepts. The lack of precision in their own theory has been conpensated by the careful and extensive experimental manipulations which clarify the issues they attack. No recent movement has done as much to bring problems within the laboratory for systematic investigation. Dissonance theorists, however, have somewhat neglected what comes before and to some extent what happens after immediate dissonance reduction though some temporal aspects are explored in Section IV A. Moreover, by limiting themselves to certain aspects of the cognitive field these researchers have omitted significant relevant information in dealing with attitude change and cognitive restructuring. Existing value systems, personal goals, ego defenses, and methods for tolerating incompatible objectives are critical for an understanding of attitude change. The cognitive level can distort and fail to represent conflict. The question remains as to whether dissonance theory in not concerning itself with motivational problems can adequately deal with the outcomes of cognitive inconsistency. It should be remembered that classical conditioning in time was supplemented, if not replaced, by instrumental learning. A similar functional corrective may be necessary for dissonance theory.

CHAPTER 9

Psychoanalytic Theory and Cognitive Dissonance

Irving Sarnoff
New York University

In the past decade, a rising volume of research has been inspired by various theories of cognitive consistency, which, despite their differences, share the same fundamental assumption. "Generally, these models contend that the introduction of any inconsistency in a set of cognitive relationships sets up mechanisms which operate, directly or indirectly, to restore consistency" (Tannenbaum & Gengel, 1966, p. 303). Thus, as their prototypical problem, these theories address the situation in which an individual is motivated to reduce tension generated by cognitive inconsistency.

Theorists who have attempted to provide a fuller account of human behavior and experience would regard these consistency formulations as neglecting other sources of motivation that may profoundly affect the ways in which an individual deals with discrepancies between his cognitions. They have also tended to neglect individual differences in personality that may habitually mediate the individual's reduction of his motivational tensions, including those emanating from cognitive inconsistencies [though Sections IV B and C attempt to rectify this neglect]. Hence, although the theories of cognitive consistency are implicitly motivational ones, they have not been sufficiently brought into relationship with other theories of motivation. Certainly, it is difficult to dispute the view on this matter recently expressed by Price, Harburg, and Newcomb (1966): "Our basic point is simply that theories of balance and consistency, like any others, need to be, as nearly as possible, whole theories. This requires that we bring to bear all possible psychological sophistication concerning such fundamental matters as the processing of information, interpersonal needs, and cognitive structuring" (p. 270).

This paper is an attempt to contribute toward putting consistency theory in a broader theoretical context. Specifically, I shall briefly comment on some relationships between Festinger's (1957) theory of cognitive dissonance and psychology's most comprehensive account of human motivation, psychoanalytic theory. And, in the ensuing discussion, it is assumed that the theory of cognitive dissonance can serve as an appropriate vehicle for illustrating potential lines of rapprochement between psychoanalytic concepts and those found in the theories of cognitive consistency.

I. *The Comparative Scope of Psychoanalytic Theory and the Theory of Cognitive Dissonance*

Psychoanalytic theory is as encompassing and presumptuous as the theory of cognitive dissonance is narrow and modest. For Freud roamed over a vast terrain of human motivation, innate and learned, having the temerity, moreover, to postulate conscious as well as unconscious motives. At the same time, he invented a profusion of mediational concepts, such as the mechanisms of ego defense, which permit one to predict how different people are likely to respond to identical situations. Indeed, it may be fair to say that psychoanalytic theory is actually a collection of theories, loosely stitched together by the silken thread of Freud's literary style. And it may not be unduly rash to add that the components of this theoretical federation may ultimately show varying degrees of success in weathering the crucible of scientific evaluation (Sarnoff, 1965).

By contrast, Festinger's theory confines itself to but a single dimension of motivation, cognitive dissonance, whose very origin, by definition, depends upon the individual's awareness of discrepancies among his cognitions. Moreover, although Festinger (1957) and Brehm and Cohen (1962) have taken note of the probable importance of individual differences in personality in mediating the reduction of dissonance, the theory of cognitive dissonance per se does not contain a specification of such personality variables.

Given this enormous difference in scope, psychoanalytic theory cannot be meaningfully compared—concept by concept—with the theory of cognitive dissonance. Consequently, this discussion shall be restricted to a general consideration of the following three questions: Does psychoanalytic theory contain concepts sufficient to account for the phenomena predicted and explained by dissonance theory? How can psychoanalytic theory contribute to an understanding of the determinants of phenomena which are relevant to dissonance theory but which that theory neither predicts nor explains? How can dissonance theory contribute to an understanding of the determinants of phenomena which are relevant to psychoanalytic theory but which that theory neither predicts nor explains?

II. *Does Psychoanalytic Theory Contain Concepts Sufficient to Account for the Phenomena Predicted and Explained by Dissonance Theory?*

Like other theories of cognitive consistency, the cardinal motivational assumption of dissonance theory holds that human beings are impelled to reduce the inner tensions they experience. This homeostatic principle is, of course, also central to psychoanalytic theory and constitutes the one unequivocally common bond between psychoanalytic theory and the theory of cognitive dissonance. The relevant points of contention between dissonance theory and psychoanalytic theory revolve about the following issues:

A. The properties of the particular tension the individual feels obliged to reduce; that is, the specific motives determining his tension-reducing behavior.

B. The mediating processes by which his specific motives are translated into specific behaviors.

For Festinger, the handling of these issues is quite a simple and general matter. When an individual decides, for example, to do something at odds with his beliefs, he is assumed by Festinger to experience dissonance. But the precise psychological properties of the motivational state labelled 'dissonance' are not articulated by the theory of cognitive dissonance. Nor does that theory indicate how the motive of dissonance may be conceptually or operationally distinguished from any other motive in the human repertoire, despite Festinger's (1957) assertion that it is "a very different motivation from what psychologists are used to dealing with" (p. 3). Festinger's theory merely states that, under the conditions it describes, individuals will experience dissonance and be driven to reduce it. "The existence of dissonance, being psychologically uncomfortable, will motivate the person to try to reduce the dissonance and achieve consonance" (Festinger, 1957, p. 3). The theory further holds that the individual may reduce dissonance in a number of different ways. But these ways are not systematically conceptualized in terms of individual differences in variables of personality that habitually mediate the reduction of dissonance. While duly recognizing the potential role of these individual differences, Festinger (1957) concludes: "But I have little to say on this point beyond the acknowledgement that such differences among people certainly exist" (p. 271).

For the psychoanalytic theorist, however, the foregoing issues of motivational specificity and individual differences in mediational processes are much more contingent upon knowledge, on the one hand, of the concrete activities and incentives involved in a person's choice to engage in a particular task. The psychoanalytic theorist needs such information to infer what kinds of motives may be evoked by the conditions under study. On the other hand, the predictions of the psychoanalytic theorist are contingent upon knowledge of the habitual ways in which individuals tend to reduce the tensions of the specific motives aroused by those conditions. Thus, totally lacking the motivational concept of dissonance, the psychoanalytic theorist is required to conceptualize the individual's motivational state in psychoanalytic terms before he can apply the explanatory and deductive principles with which he is familiar.

Before proceeding with an example, however, the reader should be cautioned to keep in mind that no monolithic consensus exists among psychoanalytic theorists concerning the proper application of psychoanalytic concepts to 'dissonance' phenomena. Accordingly, the illustration given below represents solely the viewpoint of the present author and is developed more fully in his book *Personality Dynamics and Development* (Sarnoff, 1962, pp. 458–459).

If one considers the subjects' behavior in such an archetypical dissonance experiment as Festinger and Carlsmith's (1959), it becomes obvious that there must be complex motivational forces acting on the subject which the dissonance theorists have left completely unexamined. In the Low Incentive condition, the $1 reward would hardly seem adequate to motivate by itself the subjects' overt compliance and yet, despite their being given opportunity to drop out of the experiment at that point, almost all subjects chose to comply. Possibly the desire to contribute to scientific research added some motivation. Even more important a motivating factor, I suspect, was the subjects' need for the approval of the experimenter and their reluctance to endure the disapproval he might show if they refused to 'go along' with the request of this authority figure. Still, acquiescence under such conditions would tend to leave some residue of unpleasantness and shame to be experienced by the subject which, in turn, would motivate his rationalization that perhaps the task was not quite so uninteresting after all.

It will have been seen that the above explanation nowhere invokes the motive of cognitive dissonance. Instead, it posits the arousal of two conflicting motives—the need for approval and shame—one of which (shame) is presumably pushed out of consciousness by the ego defense of rationalization, which is assumed to manifest itself in the form of attitude change. Obviously, to demonstrate the cogency of such an explanation, one would have to obtain independent measures of the motives postulated; and one would also be obligated to show that consciously experienced shame was reduced as a concomitant of attitude change and that, moreover, subjects who were most inclined toward the use of rationalization in coping with consciously unacceptable shame showed the greatest change in their attitude toward the task. One might, in addition, undertake to demonstrate empirically that shame was less consciously acceptable a motive than the need for approval, thus leading the individual to resolve his motivational conflict in such a way as to minimize the awareness of his shame. Finally, since psychoanalytic theory differentiates between the repression of motives from consciousness and the reduction of their tension, one would wish to seek ways of detecting the ongoing, albeit unconscious, tension of the shame motive.

To be sure, dissonance theory offers a much more parsimonious account of the effects under consideration. But, however convoluted its application may appear to be in this instance, psychoanalytic theory *can* be employed to offer an alternative explanation of the phenomena—and one that makes no use of the concept of cognitive dissonance. So, in this sense, it appears plausible to conclude that psychoanalytic theory could adequately, if not parsimoniously, embrace the phenomena predicted by dissonance theory.

But it should be immediately said, in all fairness, that the kinds of predictions made and substantiated by Festinger and others—the recent criticisms (Chapanis & Chapanis, 1964; Janis & Gilmore, 1965; Rosenberg, 1965d) of their research notwithstanding—would probably never have been put forward by any psychoanalytic theorist. And it cannot be too ardently stressed that one of the best justifications of any theory lies in its ability to generate hypotheses that other theories are unlikely to make, however archly they may undertake to explain them after the fact. Moreover, the fact that dissonance theory yields predictions contrary to "common sense" (Festinger & Bramel, 1962, p. 256) is all the more to its credit, especially from the standpoint of the esthetic needs of the experimenters who work with it.

Nevertheless, because of its very paucity of guiding assumptions about the determinants of behavior, dissonance theory cannot possibly generate predictions concerning individual differences in the behavior of people placed in identical dissonance-arousing conditions. Dissonance researchers have shown very little interest in such individual differences, which might conceivably account for a good deal of the unaccounted variance in the behavior of subjects in their experiments. This neglect is very puzzling when one considers that almost any social psychologist would be willing to subscribe to Kurt Lewin's (1954) formula about behavior being a function of the individual interacting with his environment. [Sections IV B and C of this volume do give commendable attention to individual differences.]

Besides, dissonance theory focuses so heavily upon the individual's internal state that one would have expected its adherents to pay fuller attention to the problem of assessing the vicissitudes of that state. The consideration thus far given to this problem [cf. Section III C] is only a beginning. In this task the consistency theorists need whatever help they might obtain from theoretical approaches, such as Freudian theory, which have devoted themselves strenuously to the conceptualization of man's private world. At any rate, it seems eminently reasonable to utilize research designs which, following Cronbach's (1957) advice, seek to study the interactions between situational and organismic variables. Hopefully, through the application of such interactive designs, all of us may "come to realize that organism and treatment are an inseparable pair and that no psychologist can dismiss one or the other as error variance" (Cronbach, 1957, p. 19).

III *How Can Psychoanalytic Theory Contribute to an Understanding of the Determinants of Phenomena which Are Relevant to Dissonance Theory but which that Theory Neither Predicts nor Explains?*

It has already been suggested how various concepts from psychoanalytic theory may be able to account, *on a post hoc basis*, for the results of a dissonance experiment. It now remains to be illustrated how concepts from psychoanalytic theory can be applied to and integrated with a dissonance experiment *on an a priori basis*, yielding predictions, *before the fact*, which could not have been derived from dissonance theory because that theory simply lacks the necessary conceptual ingredients for such derivations.

In the example given below, cognitive dissonance is explicitly assumed as a separate motivational force, operating simultaneously with a motive whose predicted effects are derived from a psychoanalytic concept of individual differences in a dimension of personality structure.

A. *Psychosexual Fixation and Dissonance: An experiment on the anal character.* Conducting a modified replication of the Festinger and Carlsmith (1959) experiment, Frances Bishop (1967) argued that the relationship between incentive and attitude change found by those experimenters would not necessarily hold up for all possible individuals. Utilizing the psychoanalytic concept of the anal character (Freud, 1949a), she reasoned that subjects who differed in anality would differ in their response to monetary privation. Thus, she predicted an interaction between anality and privation in determining the attitude of subjects toward a boring task which, as in the Festinger and Carlsmith experiment, they had volunteered to describe as interesting to other purported subjects. Specifically, Bishop anticipated that, when privation was low, the high anals would find the task *less* boring than would the low anals. However, under conditions of High Privation, she predicted that the high anals would rate the task as *more* boring than would the low anals. She varied the degree of privation by inducing subjects to expect a $20 reward for participating in the experiment—and later having a 'drawing,' from a punch board which deprived the High Privation group of $19 and the low privation group of $1.

Bishop's results gave clear support to the interaction she had predicted, thus illustrating the potential scientific benefit to be gained by including theoretically cogent personality variables in experimental studies of cognitive dissonance. In particular, her study highlights the significance of Freud's concepts of psychosexual development, suggesting how other experimenters may be able to postulate, in advance, the unconscious or symbolic relationship between a given incentive or deprivation and a given stage of psychosexual development.

B. *The Concept of a Motivational Hierarchy and Dissonance.* Bishop's study also lends some empirical credence to the usefulness of attempting to conceive a hierarchy among simultaneously operative motives (Sarnoff, 1960a). Assuming the high anals in the High Privation condition were motivated by both a high degree of cognitive dissonance and a high degree of resentment, she was able to predict that those subjects would be more inclined to express their resentment to privation than to reduce their dissonance—the former occupying a more dominant place in the individual's motivational hierarchy because it is developmentally more closely linked to the functioning of vital bodily processes and, ultimately, to survival itself. For the low anals in the same condition of High Privation, however, she expected little arousal of resentment, thus permitting cognitive dissonance to occupy a relatively more important position in their activated motivational hierarchy.

C. *Ego Defense and Dissonance.* Because psychoanalytic theory is replete with concepts of mechanisms that individuals use to obscure or preclude the awareness of consciously unacceptable motives, it can serve as a source of ideas about variables which might determine:

    a.   The relative susceptibility of individuals to the experience of dissonance;

    b.   Individual differences in preferences for modes of dissonance reduction; and

    c.   Individual differences in readiness to reduce dissonance by means of altering initial cognitions of the dissonance-arousing activity.

From the vantage point of psychoanalytic theory, it seems plausible to assume that a number of the mechanisms of ego defense may play a role in regard to each of the spheres of individual differences mentioned above. But it should be reiterated that these mechanisms are thought to function as defenses against motives whose conscious awareness cannot be tolerated by the individual. Thus, the following suggestions are pertinent only insofar as it may be theoretically reasonable to regard cognitive dissonance as: (a) a separate motive in its own right, having special, if as yet unspecified, psychological properties that distinguish it from all other motives; and (b) a motive against whose painful awareness individuals have learned to defend themselves in the same way as they defend against other motives they have found to be consciously intolerable. And since both of these assumptions have, in fact, been made by Festinger, the discussion below shall adhere to them.

1. *Denial and dissonance.* The mechanism of denial may operate to prevent or limit the input of information pertaining to the fact that the individual is, indeed, participating in an activity which is repugnant to him. As in the case of an obese person who continually avows a desire to lose weight, the individual may simply tend to deny the extent to which he actually eats. That is, he may not 'notice' the number of candies, for instance, that he happens to slip into his mouth while reading a book. Such

a mechanism of denial may also have functioned to obscure the input of painful electrical stimulation in an experiment reported by Zimbardo *et al.* (1966). Thus, at least some of the high dissonance subjects—voluntarily committed with minimum justification to the receipt of painful shocks after having already experienced them—may have used denial to reduce their perception of the electrical input per se. Hence, their subjective reports of low painfulness may result from a perceptual obscuring of the input rather than from a process of dissonance reduction following the full, conscious registration of the electrical charge.

2. *Compartmentalization and dissonance.* Similarly, the mechanism of compartmentalization may permit an individual to place each of his discrepant cognitions into separate and impermeable mental niches while participating in an experiment on cognitive dissonance. Hence, he may experience no urgent psychological pressures to resolve those discrepancies. For his defense may allow him to contain incongruities without bringing their conflicting elements into either simultaneous or emotionally perturbing juxtaposition. Thus, a high compartmentalizer who is given little justification for engaging in a distasteful task may go through the experiment without letting himself become disquieted by the incongruity between his choice and the task chosen. His defense may make it possible for him to go cheerfully through the task, entirely focused, *for that time,* on the cognition of his choice. Only afterward, perhaps, may his thoughts shift to the cognition in his other compartment, at which time he may be beset by distaste for the task, his cognition of his choice safely tucked back into its compartment. [The temporal effects considered in Section IV A might well be analyzed in terms of such a psychoanalytic mechanism—Ed.]

3. *Reaction formation and dissonance.* Concerning preferences for various modes of reducing cognitive dissonance, the individual who uses reaction formation as a way of dealing with consciously repugnant motives may, insofar as those motives are experimentally aroused to the point of conscious awareness, tend to reduce his dissonance in quite a different manner from individuals who have learned to use the previously described ways of obscuring their awareness of the same motive. Thus, for example, if made aware, by means of experimental manipulation, of the possession of habitually repressed affection, the individual who prefers reaction formation may seek to blot out that awareness by generating cynical cognitions, which grant no altruism to others (Sarnoff, 1960b).

4. *Projection and dissonance.* By contrast, the person who uses projection as means dealing with his own hostility may, following the experimental arousal of his hostility, develop cognitions that stress the inherent aggression of others. Regarding the employment of projection as a mechanism for reducing dissonance, Bramel (1962) conducted an experiment in which he induced subjects to reduce their dissonance by attributing a purported and unwanted motive, homosexuality, to others. However, although that experiment may be regarded as an intriguing analogue of the defensive projection of homosexuality, neither Bramel nor anyone else has yet designed or conducted an experiment in which individual differences in habitual tendency to use projection as a mechanism of defense against the awareness of homosexuality are *premeasured*—after which those habitual individual differences are studied in interaction with the experimental arousal or attribution of the motive relevant to their defense.

IV. *How Can Dissonance Theory Contribute to an Understanding of the Determinants of Phenomena which Are Relevant to Psychoanalytic Theory but which that Theory Neither Predicts nor Explains?*

For all its coverage of behavioral phenomena, psychoanalytic theory has virtually nothing to say on the vitally important subject of human volition. Indeed, Freud tended to see human psychological development largely in terms of the vicissitudes of implacable instinctive drives; and he was inclined to regard consciousness as a mere epiphenomenon, a rather captive shadow-graph for images that reflect the play of unconscious forces seething in the wellsprings of human behavior.

But in his role as psychotherapist, Freud invoked the desirability of willful effort for therapeutic progress. Determinist par excellence as a theoretician, Freud found it sensible to speak of the felicity of deliberate, conscious, and freely bestowed commitments in attempting to apply his theory to actual work with human beings. "The patients who are most welcome to the psychoanalyst will be those who desire complete health so far as they are capable of it and who will place as much time at his disposal as the process requires" (Freud, 1949b, p. 351).

Yet, Freud never attempted a systematic theoretical reconciliation between the phenomena of volition and his concepts of the unconscious determinants of behavior. Therefore, concepts leading to predictions about specific psychological consequences of voluntary choice and commitment lie outside the realm of psychoanalytic theory. And it is precisely in regard to such consequences that the theory of cognitive dissonance has the most to offer the psychoanalytic theorist. For dissonance theorists have typically taken, as their theoretical and empirical points of departure, the very acts and effects that psychoanalytic theory has neglected: the act of choice and its psychological effects upon the individual who has made it.

Up to the moment of choice or commitment, the psychoanalytic theorist is in a better position than the dissonance theorist to predict which individuals are likely to opt for which alternatives; to predict, for example, which individuals are likely to choose to be alone rather than with others after an upsetting experience (Rapaport, 1963), and to predict, moreover, how confident different individuals will be in the choices they make (Gordon, 1966). Nevertheless, it is the dissonance theorists who have had the verve and imagination to seize upon that critical moment of decision—so easily disregarded, even by a genius of Freud's stature—and to begin to map its psychological aftermath. And, in the last few years, investigators of dissonance have demonstrated that the immediate effects of choice inconsistent with one's cognitions about the chosen behavior may show up not only in altered attitudes, but also in changes in patterns of learning and in both subjective and physiological responses to pain (Zimbardo *et al.*, 1966). Further, a recent experiment by Bonchek (1966), drawing upon the earlier studies of Bergin (1960) and Zimbardo (1960), indicates how voluntarily expended effort may increase the readiness of individuals to accept unpleasant clinical interpretations of their personality—even when the interpreter is a person whose credibility is low. And, in the same vein, Levy (1963) has sought to spell out various implications of cognitive dissonance for the process of psychotherapeutic interpretation.

Certainly, the experimental evidence already accumulated underscores the power of dissonance theory to predict diverse consequences of consciously formulated decisions, irrespective of individual differences in personality that may be germane to those decisions. This work is thus pointing the way toward the situational parameters of decision making that can provide guidelines for all research on human behavior. For is not the very participation of all subjects in all laboratory experiments the result of a conscious decision? And do not every subject's ratings of every questionnaire represent choices among alternatives? And even if a subject is wired up for physiological measurements exclusively, has he not made a decision to remain in the apparatus rather than to shed it?

These rhetorical questions merely accentuate the fact that decision-making is an integral part of every facet of every conceivable psychological experiment. And just as the implications of the Heisenberg principle have found their way into scientific psychology (Orne, 1962; Rosenthal, 1964), so may the ubiquitousness of volitional behavior in psychological investigations, whatever their theoretical orientation, be enduringly highlighted by the systematic experiments stimulated by dissonance theory.

Clearly, the psychoanalytic theorist can no longer feel smug about ignoring the psychology of volition. What most laymen believe and what Freud himself felt obliged to invoke, research on dissonance has dramatically demonstrated: conscious decisions, made on the basis of consciously perceived alternatives and highly aware cognitions, can profoundly affect behavior. But to focus entirely on the conscious determinants of behavior is to seek to correct the errors of psychoanalytic theory by committing equally blatant ones. It seems most reasonable, instead, to assume that man's behavior is wholly determined by neither voluntary nor involuntary factors; that the picture of man driven totally and uncontrollably by unconscious urges is just as grotesque a distortion of human complexity as is the image of man functioning entirely on the basis of consciously formulated decisions. Thus, genuine hope for a portrait of man that resembles the actuality of his behavior would appear to reside in a strategy of research, such as is exemplified in the previously mentioned experiment of Bishop (1967), whose objective is to bring together both conscious and unconscious determinants of behavior. By studying the interactions between these determinants, we may begin to sort out how much each contributes to a particular behavioral phenomenon. And such studies may gradually induce psychologists to think in fresh theoretical terms, breaking down the invisible conceptual walls that now separate 'depth' psychology from the psychology of cognition.

CHAPTER 10

Role Theory and Consistency Theory

Vernon L. Allen
University of Wisconsin

Role theory and consistency theory may seem on first reflection to have little if anything in common; if so, only slight mutual gain would be expected from an exchange of ideas between the two approaches. Further consideration, however, will disclose several areas of contact between the theories, suggesting that mutual contributions may be possible. Moreover, even if they are irreconcilable on some points, such differences between the theories may help to increase our understanding of social behavior.

A plentitude of reinterpretations of specific experimental results seems assured in this volume; some of the consistency studies may soon have the distinction of being the most reinterpreted and overinterpreted experiments in psychology. Since both role and cognitive consistency approaches to social behavior aspire to the lofty status of theory, perhaps the most useful point of departure in this paper is to discuss them at a general level befitting the dignity of approaches called "consistency theory" and "role theory." Therefore, rather than discussing in great detail the results of a large number of specific experiments, the main goal of this paper will be to examine basic assumptions that appear to underlie the two theories and to compare them with a view toward their adequacy as general approaches to the understanding of certain kinds of social behavior.

Following a brief description of role theory, the two approaches will be compared in terms of their theoretical structure. Finally, contributions of consistency theory to role theory, and vice versa, will be presented.

ROLE THEORY

The term 'role theory' in the singular is perhaps misleading; there are in fact several versions of role theory and differences among them are important enough to warrant the specification of which particular version one is using. Role theory as presented by T. R. Sarbin will be the orientation used in this paper (Sarbin, 1954, 1964; Sarbin & Allen, 1968); in this approach there are many concepts and basic assumptions in common with approaches of other contemporary role theorists such as Newcomb (1951), Merton (1957), Goffman (1959), and Sargent (1951). The role theory approach is a very broad framework for the analysis, prediction, and control of social behavior. Role theory represents the convergence of two intellectual traditions, one deriving from theoretical investigations of the growth of self and social awareness (Cooley, 1902; Mead, 1934) which emphasizes cognitive processes in social interaction, the other coming from the sociological and anthropological tradition (Durkheim, 1933; Linton, 1936, 1945) which focuses on implications of status differentiation and division of labor within society.

A role is a part assigned to a person, whether the part is in the drama of the stage or in the drama of everyday life. To a part accrue certain requirements: requirements for a particular set of overt behaviors and actions, and also for the possession of particular dispositions, such as attitudes and values. In other words, the part or role specifies what one should do, how one should do it, and what sort of person one who enacts the role should be. A role has its complementary role, e.g., father and child; each has rights and obligations vis-à-vis the other. Society is composed of differentiated social positions, both formal and informal, which are often identifiable by a label or name. Integral to each position is a set of norms specifying the appropriate and expected social behavior for a person occupying such a position. Behavior of a person in accordance with the expectations of the position is role enactment. Another basic concept in role theory is the cognitive organization of qualities called the self or self-conception, which refers to phenomenal experience.

Role enactment can be viewed as a dependent variable which is affected by the following variables taken from role theory: role expectations, location of a role in the social system, role-taking skill, role demands, reinforcement from the social ecology, and self-role congruence. For a discussion of these and other concepts in role theory see recent articles by Sarbin (1964) and Sarbin and Allen (1968). The concepts above, along with more complicated phenomena such as multiple roles, role conflict, and role-set, form a complex and subtle theory of ongoing social behavior. A good example is found in Goffman's (1959, 1961) fascinating work.

It has often been observed that role theory is unique is providing a theoretical integration of individual and society. Social behavior or role enactment is a function both of the individual in terms of his unique conception of self, and of the social system in terms of the social position occupied by the person.

COMPARISON OF ROLE THEORY AND CONSISTENCY THEORY

Let us now compare the approach to social behavior taken by role theory to that taken by consistency theory as represented by Heider (1958), Festinger (1957), Osgood and Tannenbaum (1955), Newcomb (1953), and others. The basic assumption underlying the role theory approach to social behavior is that, in Peters' (1958) words, "Man is a rule-following animal." This is to say that all societies conventionalize behavior; even in the case of biologically based behavior such as food-seeking and sexual activity, expression is governed by an elaborate set of rules which differs across cultures. Rules also govern the behavior of persons having specific statuses in society —such as husband or wife, teacher or student, host or guest. Rules for a particular social position are role-expectations which define how the occupant of the position ought to behave. Such role-expectations exist for each social position within a society and define the appropriate behavior for an occupant of the position. We can say, then, with Peters, that man is indeed a rule-following animal, and further that roles constitute the rules for behaving appropriately in accord with one's social position. Why is man a rule-following animal? Why do we conform to role-expectations? The reasons are complex, but can be found in the nature of the life-long processes of socialization from which we attain self-identity, gain the ability to predict and control the social environment, and obtain approval or disapproval from our fellows. We behave according to role-expectations of father, for instance, because such role enactment validates our occupancy of the position, maintains our self-system, elicits predictable behavior from reciprocal roles, and produces positive reinforcement from other persons.

Much of an individual's behavior consists of role enactment, be it the enactment of a formal social role such as teacher or of an informal social role. Location of a person's position in the formal and informal social systems enables us to understand and predict his behavior because individuals are rule-followers and hence adhere to role-expectations. The primary task of predicting social behavior according to role theory is to locate the other's role in the social ecology.

The basic assumption of consistency theory is that the cognitive system tends toward a state of simplicity and harmony, creating balance or consistency among cognitive elements. Cognitive inconsistency presumably motivates a change among inconsistent cognitions in such a way that equilibrium or consistency results.

In essence, consistency theory is a tension-reduction model of cognitive structure. A change in behavior can be produced, according to the theory, by inducing a state of cognitive inconsistency which will act as a motivational force. Role theory is not a motivational model in this sense. According to role theory, a change in behavior requires a change in role or in one of the variables affecting role enactment. One adheres to role-expectations for reasons mentioned above; conformity to role-expectations need not be due to motivational factors such as cognitive tension or psychological discomfort.

Several other points of contrast between role theory and consistency are immediately apparent. First, the level of abstraction employed by the two theories differs greatly. Role theory is a very broad and abstract theory which explains social behavior in terms of the interrelation among variables at the conceptual levels of individual (the self), social system (position), and culture (role). As mentioned earlier, the theory attempts to integrate individual and society. Consistency theory, on the other hand, does not attempt to treat social behavior at such a broad, abstract, and inclusive level. Although the scope of some consistency theories is relatively broad, most are more restricted. Still, even the broadest consistency theory does not attempt to explain all social behavior.

A comparison of the unit of analysis used by role theory and consistency theory will shed some light on their differences as theories. For consistency theory the unit of analysis is intraindividual; primary concern is directed at the relation existing between cognitive elements. The explanatory mechanism is the state of consistency or inconsistency that exists between cognitions inside the head of a person. These inside-the-head cognitions may, of course, represent social events outside the head. As a theory of cognitive functioning, however, consistency theory has relevance to social behavior only when the cognitive elements represent social objects and situations, or have consequences for behavior that is incidentally social in nature [see Section III G]. In Brunswik's (1952) terminology, "encapsulated centralism" would describe consistency theory. Role, as a unit of analysis, is explicitly interindividual in nature. A role is meaningful only in relation to its complementary role—e.g., husband-wife or teacher-student —and therefore role enactment is always social interaction. Thus, role as an explanatory mechanism for social behavior constitutes an interpersonal rather than an intrapersonal unit of analysis. It is the social act, in Mead's (1934) terms, that forms the basic unit of role theory.

CONTRIBUTION OF CONSISTENCY THEORY TO ROLE THEORY

Several behavioral phenomena that are traditionally discussed in role theory acquire greater clarity when interpreted in terms of consistency theory. One aspect of consistency theory's contribution is obvious: the effect of role enactment on cognition (attitudes, beliefs, values, self). Long ago role theorists pointed out that prolonged enactment of a role produces changes in the self-system ('personality') congruent with role-expectations. Merton's (1940) analysis of the rigid personality of the bureaucrat and Waller's (1932) analysis of the effect of teaching on the teacher are early examples.

Precisely how—by what psychological processes—role enactment produces a change in cognitive structure was not specified in role theory; nor did role theory stimulate much research on this problem. Interpretation of a change in the self-system accompanying long-term enactment of an occupational role of teacher or bureaucrat is hazardous methodologically. Since personality characteristics influence occupational choice, self-selection might account for the observed congruence between self-characteristics and role-expectations of particular occupations. Less equivocal data are available, fortunately, from a longitudinal field study conducted by Lieberman (1956). Attitudes toward union and management were obtained from a large group of factory workers. During the ensuing year many workers changed roles, some becoming foremen and some union stewards. New foremen became more favorable toward management, and new union stewards became more favorable toward the union. Moreover, persons who subsequently resumed their former role of worker reverted to their earlier attitudes. This study shows convincingly the direction of causation; a change in attitude follows role enactment.

A clearer understanding of the psychological mechanisms in cognitive change resulting from role enactment came in the wake of an analysis of the forced compliance situation by cognitive dissonance theorists. Stimulated by predictions of dissonance theory, many investigators have recently studied the effect of role enactment on attitude change. Many studies support the conclusion that attitude change following enactment of attitude-discrepant behavior can be accounted for, under certain conditions, by reduction of cognitive inconsistency. Incongruence between behavior and private attitude is reduced by changing the private attitude. Other factors in addition to dissonance reduction, such as reinforcement and self-persuasion (Scott, 1959; Janis & Gilmore, 1965), probably also contribute to opinion change in real-life situations of role enactment. But by focusing on dissonance reduction as an explanation of opinion change produced by opinion-discrepant behavior, consistency theorists have provided one theoretical explanation for role theorists' observations that changes in personality, opinions, and values frequently accompany role enactment.

Research conducted within the dissonance theory framework enables us to specify the conditions under which greater cognitive dissonance, and thereby greater attitude change, would occur. This knowledge can be applied to role theory. As a single example, dissonance research has shown that greater dissonance is produced when one's performance of discrepant behavior is perceived to have been voluntary (Cohen, 1960; Zimbardo, Chapter 36). An individual's degree of choice in occupying a social position is one widely discussed dimension of roles. Linton (1945) called this the ascribed-achieved dimension. Ascribed roles are those that a person has little choice in occupying by virtue of biological, kinship, or other reasons. In other words, ascribed roles are those that are granted to a person through no effort or choice on his part. Achieved roles are those that the individual occupies voluntarily through his own free choice, or that he strives for. This distinction between ascribed and achieved roles is not a dichotomy, needless to say, but rather a continuum of one's degree of control in attaining a social position. Adding to our understanding of this aspect of role theory, dissonance theory would predict greater personality change as a result of enacting roles which are located toward the achieved end of the ascribed-achieved dimension. Many such findings from dissonance theory that may be relevant to the effect of role enactment on cognitive change have not yet been tested in real-life situations with persons enacting social roles over a long period of time.

A second selected contribution of consistency theory to role theory is in the area of self-role congruity, which is used in role theory as a variable affecting role enactment (Sarbin, 1954). According to role theory, when characteristics of the self are incongruent with requirements of the role (role-expectations), role enactment will be poor in terms of appropriateness, effectiveness, and convincingness. A considerable amount of evidence supports this hypothesis (Bunker, 1965; Milton, 1957; Smelser, 1961). If a person believes himself an honest and upright individual, his performance of the role of price-fixer in industry would be less effective (we hope) than if his self-characteristics and role-expectations were congruent. This concept of self-role incongruity can be viewed in terms of consistency theory as a simple instance of inconsistency between two sets of cognitions. The less effective role performance in the incongruent self-role condition can be seen as a case of a person's dealing with disturbing inconsistencies between cognitions. Poorer performance may be the result of attempts by the person to reduce inconsistency through a change in behavior, since self-characteristics are likely to be more difficult to change initially.

Finally, consistency theory can make a contribution to another important topic in role theory that has been the subject of a great deal of investigation—role conflict. In spite of a considerable amount of research on role conflict, conceptualization of the problem has proceeded at a very low order of theorizing, often taking the form of specifying in detail the concrete content of conflict among roles and the way the conflict is resolved. Instances of role conflict such as role conflict in the funeral director

(Fulton, 1961), role conflict in the chaplain (Burchard, 1954), and role conflict in the school superintendent (Gross *et al.*, 1958), probably differ considerably at the concrete level but little at the theoretical level. Role conflict can be viewed as inconsistency between cognitions, and specific content can probably be ignored as irrelevant to our theoretical understanding of the problem. We would expect from consistency theory that attempts would be made to resolve the inconsistency, as indeed occurs in studies of role conflict. There are advantages to conceptualizing role conflict at the more general level of consistency theory rather than at the level of content. One benefit is in providing a language for describing role conflict in terms of cognitive elements, the number and importance of consistent and inconsistent elements, and so on. Translating role conflict into a general cognitive consistency model would also enable us to make predictions about role conflict resolution at a more general level. An even more useful contribution could be made to the analysis of role conflict resolution by the application of models of resolution of cognitive inconsistency developed within the consistency theory framework. Perhaps the fullest discussion by consistency theorists of the problem of modes of resolution of inconsistency and the hierarchy of modes of resolution is found in Sections IV B and C of this volume. Abelson's (1959) interesting theoretical paper offers one possibility for application to role conflict resolution. In fact, Abelson's theorizing bears some similarity to treatments of role conflict resolution by investigators working within role theory.

CONTRIBUTION OF ROLE THEORY TO CONSISTENCY THEORY

As a first point, consider the basic assumption of consistency theory: persons tend to minimize inconsistency among cognitions due to the dynamics of the cognitive system. Let us look at the well-documented fact that persons tend to reduce cognitive inconsistency. How would this be viewed from the vantage point of role theory?

First of all, remember that a basic component of role theory is the self. Many years ago, in a little book called *Self-consistency*, Lecky (1945) advanced the thesis that persons strive to maintain consistency in their conception of self. Since most persons have a positive conception of self, a very pervasive tendency in social interaction is to maintain a presentation of self consistent with the favorable conception. Many instances of reduction of cognitive inconsistency could be interpreted as an attempt to maintain one's positive self-conception during the course of social interaction, rather than to minimize inconsistency between cognitions.

Next, it should be remembered that in any social interaction a person is attempting to validate his occupancy of several important social positions. Consider, for example, a male subject in a cognitive consistency experiment. One important role, the one most salient at the moment, perhaps, is the role of subject in a psychology experiment. As Orne (1962) and others have shown, this social role carries role-expectations that may influence the outcome of psychological experiments. Other important roles, in addition to the role of experimental subject, are age and sex roles. Other latent formal and informal social roles may become active when appropriate cues are present. Furthermore, influence of the complementary roles in a social situation should not be overlooked. In the psychological experiment, the experimenter and other subjects may be present. Role expectations of all these roles probably serve to emphasize the importance of rationality and consistency in behavior.

In other words, it is suggested that inconsistency reduction may not be solely a cognitive process. Rather it may be in part a social process dependent on, first, maintaining a positive self-conception, and secondly, validating one's occupancy of formal and informal social positions by appropriate role-enactment.

Several experimental findings point up the importance of the social interaction context in consistency research. In one study, postdecision dissonance reduction occurred only when the decision was relevant to valued aspects of the self, such as leadership potential (Deutsch, Krauss, & Rosenau, 1962). Carlsmith *et al.* (1965) did not obtain dissonance reduction in a forced compliance situation when subjects' opinion-discrepant behavior was anonymous rather than face-to-face with the stooge. In the Davis and Jones (1960) study, when subjects anticipated meeting the person they had deevaluated, there was less dissonance reduction (private derogation) than when such meeting was not possible. The reciprocal role of the experimenter is an important part of social interaction in the experiment. Studies by Rosenberg (1965a), and by Elms and Janis (1965) underscore the influence of the experimenter. All these studies, and many others, highlight the important effect of the social context on a person's reaction to cognitive inconsistency.

The role theory view would also suggest that the tendency to reduce inconsistency may be a product of cultural values. It seems likely that striving toward consistency would be characteristic of western societies in which science, rationality, and order are valued. Consistency among cognitions, and between behavior and belief is role-appropriate behavior for a socialized person in western society. Interestingly, in this regard Leonard Doob has informally remarked that the primitive peoples of Africa do not seem to attempt to resolve inconsistency. Apparently, cognitive inconsistency is not disturbing to them. [Section III G of this volume discusses the historical and cultural forces that give rise to a need and tendency toward cognitive consistency.]

Hovland (1960) and others (including Berlyne, Maddi, and Sears in this volume) have pointed out that under some conditions inconsistency is tolerated or even sought out, rather than avoided. A role theory approach to the problem would point out that inconsistency reduction is partially a function of the social situation, particularly when inconsistency has important implications for the self or for salient roles. However, inconsistency will be tolerated when it has no implication for self and role. For example, we should expect little postdecision dissonance reduction for males if making correct decisions were a strong role-expectation of the female role but not of the male role. [Steiner, in Chapter 62, deals with some sex differences of this type.] Or suppose the most important requirement of one's role is financial success. When this—or any other important role-expectation—runs counter to inconsistency reduction, inconsistency will readily be tolerated. Noteworthy in regard to the last example is Rosenberg and Abelson's (1960) study. Imbalanced states were preferred when a balanced state would have precluded adhering to an important expectation of the subjects' role (maintaining high sales). [This issue of the centrality of the self concept in consistency theorizing is discussed at length in Section III B.]

There are other instances in which inconsistency will not be resolved. Some consistency theorists predict that inconsistency must be brought to the attention of the individual for inconsistency resolution to occur. By the use of social techniques such as spatial and temporal segregation of roles which contain inconsistent elements, the inconsistency need not be thought about and therefore not resolved. [An example of this sort occurs in Chapter 66. The general 'awareness' issue is dealt with in several chapters in Section III, below (e.g., Brock's Chapter 32).]

To consider another point, can role theory make a contribution to the problem of modes of resolution of inconsistency? Abelson (1959) hypothesized that modes of inconsistency resolution will be attempted sequentially, starting with the easiest technique. All the techniques suggested by Abelson involve cognitive reorganization. Role theory would suggest that criteria other than cognitive difficulty be used for predicting the order in which various modes of resolution will be tried. Theoretical work in the structure of role relationships in society offers suggestive leads (Goode, 1960; Toby, 1952). Norms exist within society concerning the hierarchy of role obligations for resolving role conflicts or inconsistency. For example, attending the funeral of one's mother would take priority over attending a seminar meeting. The criterion used in role conflict resolution is entirely different from Abelson's criterion of cognitive difficulty; the hierarchy of role obligations represents the socially approved priority among techniques for resolving role conflicts. Furthermore, many techniques used to resolve role conflicts do not involve cognitive reorganization at all, but are based on provisions available within the social system for dealing with role conflicts. One socially accepted way of dealing with conflict, for instance, is to segregate roles spatially or temporally.

Consistency theory might profit from literature on role conflict in two ways. First, role theory calls attention to many modes of inconsistency resolution that exist in everyday social behavior. In practice consistency theory research places excessive emphasis on cognitive reorganization by restricting the possible modes of inconsistency resolution. Secondly, role theory suggests the possibility of using normative criteria, such as institutionalized obligations, as a basis for a theory of modes of inconsistency resolution.

CONCLUSIONS

As suggested in the introduction, role theory and consistency theory do have points of contact in terms of common concern with certain areas of social behavior; in such cases consistency theory does make contributions to role theory. The nature of the contribution seems to be primarily in a further specification of the cognitive factors responsible for particular behavior. In a sense, consistency theory supplies a more molecular (intrapersonal) explanation for areas of social behavior discussed at a more molar (interpersonal) level in role theory. Consistency theorists concern themselves with internal cognitive dynamics; perhaps, though, they have been too occupied with inside-the-head happenings to see what is happening outside the head and between heads. Role theory can add perspective to consistency theory by emphasizing broader aspects of social interaction such as roles and social positions. The socialized head exists in a culture, occupies social positions within a social system, and engages in role enactment; all these factors are important determinants of behavior—even in a psychology experiment. This is not to gainsay the importance of cognitive dynamics in social behavior; on the contrary, consistency theory and role theory should be viewed as complementary approaches to the understanding of social behavior.

CHAPTER 11

Cognitive Consistency and the Psychology of Judgment

Harry S. Upshaw
University of Illinois at Chicago Circle

The various cognitive consistency theories have often been applied to data consisting of subjects' appraisals of stimuli in terms of some variable properties. In such applications the theories seek to account for phenomena such as the change in a person's judged desirability of an object consequent upon his gaining ownership of it, his change in evaluation of a source resulting from information linking that source to high- or low-valued concepts, etc. Hence, the field of research in psychology, ambitiously called "the psychology of judgment," is obviously relevant to consistency theories but the two research areas have developed in recent years with virtually no point of contact. The purpose of the present paper is to explore the possibility of bringing these two areas of research together. In the course of the discussion, I shall suggest some research problems in terms of cognitive consistency theories that follow from the judgmental orientation. Likewise, I shall suggest some research issues in the more conventional judgmental areas that follow from consideration of cognitive consistency.

SOME PRINCIPLES OF JUDGMENT

The traditional concern of the psychology of judgment is with problems derived from psychophysics dealing with the efficiency and accuracy of the human being as an observer of environmental change. In the typical psychophysical experiment a subject is presented a series of stimuli which differ in terms of a specified attribute. He is instructed to 'judge' each stimulus, which, in this context, may correspond to one of three tasks. It may entail deciding which of a pair of stimuli has more of a particular property. On the other hand, it may consist of the subject's sorting stimuli into prescribed categories according to his perception of the magnitude of each stimulus in terms of the property. Finally, it may consist of the assignment of the subject's own numbers to the stimuli to indicate perceived

The preparation of this manuscript was aided by support of a grant from the National Science Foundation. Some of the ideas expressed were developed through discussions with colleagues and students. Grateful acknowledgment is made to them, particularly to John Schopler.

210

magnitude. Whatever the specific experimental task, typically the judgments collected as data in a psychophysical study are compared with measures of the same stimuli on a physical scale. The investigator's particular interest is likely to be in one of two types of discrepancies between judgmental and physical values. One type of discrepancy is generally attributed to the sensory apparatus of the organism. 'Errors' of this type systematically pervade all judgments involving a particular sensory modality. The second type of discrepancy in which psychophysicists are sometimes interested is attributable to stimulus context, personality characteristics, and past experiences of judges, etc. Discrepancies of the second type tend to be less general in their manifestations than those of the first type. Psychologists who seek to discover 'the psychophysical law' are particularly interested in discrepancies of the first type, and tend to consider those of the second type to be 'noise.' At the same time, however, other investigators devote their primary attention to data of the second type, treating them as manifestations of orderly judgmental processes. These are the processes that are to be integrated with consistency phenomena.

Many of the phenomena of judgment which classically refer to discrepancies of the second type have been found not to depend upon the comparison of judgments with physical values. They have been observed, for example, with social stimuli for which 'true' values are not only unknown, but are theoretically unknowable. It is probably true that most examples of phenomena to which cognitive consistency theories apply likewise do not permit a comparison of judgments with physical values. This seems to be true despite the fact that theorists often speak of overvaluation and undervaluation of stimuli as though there were a known point of reference by which to assess judgmental displacement. In the present discussion any implication of a comparison of a subject's judgments with 'real' stimulus values will be avoided. Therefore, judgmental phenomena will be conceived in terms of the comparison of two sets of judgments, those of one subject on two occasions, or those of two subjects on a single occasion.

As an aid in the discussion, the concept of *reference scale* is needed. Mathematically a scale is defined as a set of elements each of which has three components: a stimulus, a number,[1] and a set of rules linking the stimulus and the number in order to represent the value of the stimulus in terms of a variable property (Suppes and Zinnes, 1963; Upshaw, 1968). The term reference scale refers to a hypothetical scale which is assumed to intervene between the instigation to the act of judgment and the act itself. Thus, if a subject is asked to indicate his perception of a set of stimuli in terms of some variable property, he presumably complies by referring the stimuli to his preexisting rules, thus incorporating the experimental stimuli into his reference scale. Each judgment that he makes may be assumed to reflect the location of the appropriate stimulus on his reference scale.

All of the numerical values associated with the stimuli of an individual's reference scale correspond to the judged status of stimuli in terms of what is for him a single variable property. The numbers imply unidimensional

---

[1] For simplicity it is assumed here that the scale values of objects are expressed in numbers. Actually any magnitudes may serve in place of numbers, although it is likely that any such non-numerical magnitudes would ultimately be expressed as numbers in order to perform arithmetical operations on data.

comparisons among the stimuli. It is conventional to represent a scale of any sort as a straight line in which stimuli are located by points according to their values in terms of a variable property. It should be noted, however, that this straight-line representation presupposes a single scale property by which all of the stimuli can be evaluated.

The concept of a scale generally implies the notion of *origin* and *unit*. The origin of a scale is a parameter referring to elevation, and the unit is a parameter referring to dispersion. In comparing two judges who differ only in reference scale origin, the one with the lower origin is the one who generally assigns higher values to stimuli in the scale. In comparing two judges whose scales differ only in unit, the one with the greater dispersion of stimulus scale values is the one with the smaller reference scale unit. As parameters of a straight line, a judge's origin, corresponding inversely to intercept, and unit, corresponding inversely to slope, determine his reference scale. The phrase 'standards of judgment' refers, in the unidimensional case, to the origin and unit of a reference scale.

Both in social psychology and in psychophysics considerable research has been devoted to the determinants and to the consequences of changes in standards of judgment. Most of this work has been focused on the change of reference scale origin as a function of various experimental and real-life factors. Theoretical conceptions referring to these effects are represented by the familiar concepts of 'adaptation level' (Helson, 1964), 'comparison level' (Thibaut & Kelley, 1959), and 'relative deprivation' (Merton & Kitt, 1950). Much less work has been devoted to the reference scale unit than to origin. White and Harvey (1965) and Murdoch (1965) have related unit phenomena to personality correlates, Tajfel (1957) has related them to value as a variable, and Upshaw (1964, 1965) and Ostrom (1965) have related them to the effective stimulus range, or *perspective*.

The typical result in studies concerned with reference origin, whether in psychophysics or in the judgment of social stimuli, is that the increased salience of any stimulus tends to shift the reference scale origin toward that stimulus, with the consequence that judgments of a given set of stimuli all shift in the opposite direction. This effect is often called *judgmental contrast*. Examples of apparent judgmental contrast are many and varied, ranging from shifts in the ratings of lifted weights through the expressions of satisfaction with military life by Negro troops.

The most common consequence of increasing the salience of a particular level of stimulation is a shift in reference scale origin toward that level. Some investigators, however, have reported a shift in stimulus judgments toward the more salient stimuli, implying a shift in origin away from these stimuli. This phenomenon is *judgmental assimilation* (Hovland, Harvey, & Sherif, 1957; Campbell, Hunt, & Lewis, 1957; Berkowitz, 1960). Several 'explanations' of assimilation phenomena have been offered. Parducci and Marshall (1962) have accounted for at least one demonstration of the effect as an artifact involving restrictions in the subject's use of numbers as a judgmental language. Ostrom (1965) and I (Upshaw, 1964, 1965) have interpreted manifestations of the phenomenon as effects due to reference scale unit. Sherif, Taub, and Hovland (1958), Hovland, Harvey, and Sherif (1957), and Sherif, Sherif, and Nebergall (1965) interpret the phenomenon as a bilateral displacement of some stimuli toward the level of increased salience and of other stimuli away from it. In the language of the reference scale, the Parducci and Marshall interpretation of assimilation is that of an artifactual manifestation of a change in reference scale origin. The Upshaw and Ostrom interpretation is that of a change in unit. The interpretation offered by Sherif and his colleagues is multidimensional in that the changes ascribed to the increased salience of certain stimuli cannot be represented in terms of a linear model.

A REFERENCE SCALE REPRESENTATION OF COGNITIVE CONSISTENCY PHENOMENA

Most explanations of judgmental contrast and assimilation are based, in one way or another, on the concept of adaptation. This concept refers to processes within the organism which are normal, continuing, and affectively neutral. Most explanations of cognitive consistency phenomena, on the other hand, are based on the notion that people seek to eliminate the noxious stimulation resulting from inconsistency. This notion implies special processes that are triggered by a sufficient stimulus, and which are recurring, rather than continuing. Furthermore these consistency-restoring processes are presumably gratifying. The search for common ground between cognitive consistency theories and judgment theories involves bringing the rationale of each to bear on phenomena associated with the other.

Consistent with the concept of the reference scale, the fundamental phenomena of judgment tend to be effects that pervade all of the judgments that a subject makes for a series of stimuli. Cognitive consistency phenomena, on the other hand, tend to be stimulus-specific, according to prevailing research traditions, if not according to theory. It may be instructive for present purposes to examine how cognitive consistency phenomena *might* be related to reference scale phenomena. For this discussion it is desirable to consider a concrete example, even at the risk of being distracted from the more general issues by specific aspects of the experiment. Let us, therefore, consider a study by Brehm (1960b) in this light. In that study junior high school students rated the palatability of a disliked vegetable before and after an experimental treatment evoking a commitment by the subject to eat a lot, a little, or none of the vegetable. A second experimental manipulation was also part of the design. It consisted of the presentation to the subject of a communication from a highly authoritative source which was either supportive or nonsupportive of eating large quantities of the vegetable by arguing that it had high or low vitamin content. As expected on the basis of the cognitive consistency principle, and more specifically by the theory of cognitive dissonance, an interaction effect on liking the vegetable was found between the commitment variable and the support vs. nonsupport variable. This effect was such that the change toward liking the vegetable was nonsignificantly greater for those subjects committed to eating large quantities when the intervening communication was derogatory, and significantly greater for those subjects committed to eating small quantities or none at all when the communication was complimentary to the vegetable.

In the tradition of the psychology of judgment it may be imagined that the students in Brehm's experiment responded to the task of making palatability ratings by invoking a reference scale. Each stimulus that was judged was presumably evaluated against the subject's standards of palatability, standards which define a point of indifference (the origin) and a characteristic amount of palatability corresponding to the difference between two consecutive numerical values (the unit). With this orientation to Brehm's experiment it is interesting to speculate concerning the possibility that the increased palatability of the disliked vegetable, which was observed to follow experimentally induced cognitive consistency, is a manifestation of a shift in reference scale origin in the direction of the critical stimulus. As was noted earlier, the reference scale origin generally tends to shift in the direction of stimuli that become more salient. A necessary consequence of an origin-interpretation of these experimental results is that every item in the reference scale, including that stimulus the increased salience of which produced the shift in origin, would be expected to show increased palatability. Furthermore, if data were collected that permitted generalization to the entire reference scale, it seems likely (although not logically necessary) that effects would be found reflecting a change in reference scale unit as well as origin.

This analysis of the Brehm data as mediated by a shift in reference scale parameters has assumed that the shift was caused by the increased salience of the particular vegetable to which the subject was committed. This assumption is consistent with the adaptation concept underlying current theoretical orientations in the judgment area. As an explanatory principle, adaptation is in competition with the principle of consistency-motivated judgmental effects. However, the analysis of cognitive consistency phenomena in reference scale terms does not require the surrender of consistency theory to judgment theory, or the reverse. The demonstration that an experimental result affects an entire reference scale would not, in itself, constitute evidence in support of any particular theory. It would indicate merely that an appropriate theory should be directed toward the explanation of scale-wide effects rather than those that are stimulus-specific.

Let us imagine that Brehm had demonstrated changes in palatability that involved an entire reference scale. The question then arises as to whether there is an alternative to the adaptation concept as an explanation of these effects. There are at least four possibilities that will be explored here because of their clear judgmental implications.

1. *Protective anchoring.* It is conceivable that a noxious state associated with cognitive inconsistency provides the motivation for a subject to augment his reference scale with stimuli not previously included. Thus, the commitment to eat a large quantity of, let us say, spinach, might remind the subject that some people eat insects, weeds, and other unappealing items. Thus his reference scale is extended in the unpalatable direction, causing a shift of origin in that direction, and a perception of increased palatability for spinach and all other items in the reference scale. This hypothetical process by which the parameters of a reference scale are altered to produce the phenomenon of particular interest to cognitive consistency theories might be called *protective anchoring*. The process is essentially that described by Abelson (1959) as the "mote" resolution or by Brown (1962) as the process underlying the "greater peril" explanation of why heavy smokers have disproportionate interest in information relating to the highway death toll.

2. *Alteration in the perception of personal power.* A mechanism somewhat similar to that of protective anchoring is suggested by the work of

Thibaut and Kelley (1959). These investigators argue that the stimulus range that is taken into account by a judge when he evaluates outcomes is a function of the personal power which he attributes to himself. If we imagine that the knowledge that one is committed to the performance of an undesirable act serves to lessen his perceived power, then Thibaut and Kelley might expect that the reference scale is thereby constricted, with the better (more palatable) stimuli dropped from consideration. With scale constriction, the origin (which they call 'comparison level') is expected to be displaced toward the unpalatable end of the scale, resulting in increased satisfaction with every item in the scale. The hypothesis relating the change of reference scale origin to the perception of personal power does not, of course, presuppose discomfort due to inconsistent cognitions. As a matter of fact, any agony suffered during the hypothesized process would most likely be attributed to the frustration involved in acknowledging reduced personal power.

3. *Reinterpretation of the experimental task*. Both the protective anchoring hypothesis and the personal power hypothesis are directed toward the parameters of the subject's reference scale. These two hypotheses, therefore, may account for quantitative, but not qualitative changes in judgment following the usual experimental manipulations of cognitive inconsistency. There are at least two avenues through which cognitive inconsistency might produce qualitative changes in a subject's judgments. One of these involves a redefinition of task demands, and the other involves the redefinition of the property in terms of which judgments are made. The first possibility is not particularly provocative in the case of the Brehm example, although it may have greater potential in the more general case. The mechanism that is suggested here is similar to one described by Sherif *et al.* (1965). Their hypothesis is that subjects who are motivationally aroused during a judgmental task tend to evaluate stimuli according to how much they like them rather than in terms of attributes of the stimuli. To generalize, we may perhaps describe this mechanism as one of selective task-setting. Surely, the instructions for most experiments in social psychology are sufficiently inexplicit that a subject, when goaded by experimentally aroused motives to do so, can produce an accommodating reinterpretation in the postinduction session of what the experimental task really was. Accordingly, subjects might shift from reference scales relating to private views to those relating to public views, from those relating to acceptability of means to those relating to the acceptability of ends, from those referring to short-term time perspectives to those referring to long-term time perspectives, etc. If the unpleasantness of cognitive inconsistency drove one to seek relief through this mechanism, the results would be effects pervading the judgments of all stimuli in the series. As a matter of fact, the mechanism may be viewed as the motivated substitution of one reference scale for another. Most likely, therefore, the comparison of a subject's judgments before and after the experimental induction of cognitive inconsistency would reveal a nonlinear relationship under the present hypothesis, whereas the first two hypotheses would always result in linear relationships.

4. *A redefinition of the scale property*. Most variable properties that underlie reference scales are compounded from simpler properties. Consider the familiar example of the evaluation of automobiles according to their desirability. A subject's preference ratings are likely to reflect an idiosyn-

cratic composite of attributes such as estimated safety, economy, prestige, and comfort. Any one of these components could, itself, be analyzed into components. The selection and weighting of components in defining the scale property provides another potential avenue for the restoration of cognitive consistency (Asch, 1940). Penner, Fitch, and Weick (1966) recently presented experimental evidence of the operation of this mechanism. Applied to the Brehm data this approach to dissonance reduction entails a qualitative change in what it means to like a vegetable. As in the case of the change of experimental task, redefining the scale property is likely to result in non-linear relationships among the pre- and postinduction judgments.

Knowledge Gaps in the Psychology of Judgment

By viewing cognitive consistency phenomena in reference scale terms, an investigator is led to look for more widespread judgmental effects than those conventionally discussed in the cognitive consistency literature. Furthermore, he is led to entertain a wider range of theoretical approaches than usual to account for consistency phenomena. The search for common ground between judgmental and cognitive consistency approaches has implications for both fields of research. Of particular importance to the psychology of judgment is the imprecision of the judgmental framework which is revealed when one seriously attempts to apply principles of judgment to cognitive consistency phenomena.

To document the inadequacy of judgmental approaches as presently formulated, consider a judgmental representation of Heider's (1944) observation that the same joke that one would consider funny when told by a person known to be witty would appear to be silly when told by a silly person. This observation conforms to the expectations of any number of cognitive consistency theories, notably those due to Heider (1946) and to Osgood and Tannenbaum (1955). However, in order to transform the observation into a hypothesis concerning a reference scale, assumptions must be made which can lead to the prediction of assimilation, as expected by Heider, or of its opposite, contrast. The difficulty that produces this ambiguity in the application of the reference scale concept resides in the fact that, outside of the laboratory, the investigator has little control of, and minimal access to, the stimuli that comprise a subject's reference scale. Since we can only guess the class of stimuli with which the joke is compared by any given subject, we cannot specify on the basis of the adaptation concept what the effect of authorship on its humor-value should be.

Suppose, for example, that the subject holds two reference scales, consisting of jokes previously associated with silly-source A, on the one hand, and witty-source B, on the other. In assuming the two scales to be separate, we assume that each is characterized by its own origin (and unit, as well, though the present argument concerns only the scale origins). The wittiness of any single joke is presumably a function of its scale distance above or below the origin. A's origin compared to B's corresponds to objectively sillier jokes. Any single joke would be expected, therefore, to be rated as funnier when attributed to A than when attributed to B. This prediction is contrary to that of Heider.

Instead of two reference scales, each referring to a particular joke-teller, let us imagine that the subject holds one scale consisting of comedians ordered according to their perceived merit. In terms of this scale the origin corresponds to a person whose anticipated level of performance in telling jokes is neither witty nor silly (to use Heider's designation of the scale property). Source A, having been previously judged to be silly, has a scale location on one side of the origin, and B, having been judged to be witty, has a location on the other side of the origin. A and B presumably earned their scale locations by authoring a series of jokes sometime in the past. Some weighted average of the humor-values of the jokes of each source apparently accounts for the subject's estimate of how funny the source is likely to be in the future (which is another way of viewing the nature of the property underlying the hypothetical scale). According to this conception of Heider's situation, a subject who hears the new joke, but attributes it to a new source, will judge the source to be at position C on the scale. When attributed either to A or B, the new joke causes A's or B's position to move toward C. Thus the addition of the new joke to A's repertoire may make him appear less silly, just as it may cause B to appear less witty. However, the new location of A, i.e., $(A + C)$, is still sillier than the new location of B, i.e., $(B + C)$. It is possible that Heider's observation refers to this type of judgment of the sources based on the new joke, rather than of the joke per se. If it does, by the analysis we have made, the result is the apparent assimilation effect which Heider assumed.

Finally, it should be recognized that a subject might hold a single reference scale for jokes, in terms of which he evaluates any joke, without regard to author. In this case, of course, the source is expected to have no effect on the subject's judgment of the joke.

Most of the research in the psychology of judgment has been directed to a particular experimental setting in which the subject is provided with a series of stimuli, and he is told when to judge and in terms of what property. When removed from the laboratory, judgmental approaches lose much of their apparent rigor. The search for common ground between cognitive consistency and judgmental concepts points to the need to expand the scope of both research areas. Specifically, the analysis in this paper suggests the desirability of studying the effects of resolving cognitive inconsistency on an entire class of stimuli, the reference scale, rather than on particular stimuli removed from their perceptual context. The analysis also suggests the need to consider alternatives to the adaptation process as an explanation for judgmental phenomena. Some of these alternatives derive from considerations of cognitive consistency. These suggestions imply an end to apathetic quiescence in the coexistence between the psychology of judgment and the psychology of cognitive consistency.

CHAPTER 12

Activation Theory

Helen Peak

The University of Michigan

The theory to be sketched had its beginning in an exploration of the properties of attitude structure and of the relation between attitude and motivation (Peak, 1955), topics which proved to harbor most of the basic issues of behavior theory. Since then, the elements of a more general theory of action have been proposed (Peak, 1958a, b), and these earlier versions provide a background for the present discussion, which will inquire whether a theory stating the conditions of transmitting change from point to point in structures of various kinds, has any utility in the interpretation of inconsistency phenomena. The theory will be described briefly and applied to the prediction of behavior outcomes in a dissonant situation.

From time to time investigators of inconsistency have supplemented their stated principles by less clearly formulated assumptions about familiar issues, such as the role of ego involvement (volition and commitment) in motivation and the effects of punishment and resulting negative affect on restructuring and performance, to mention but two examples. Although the use of such variables in setting up predictions may have been an important factor in the relatively greater predictive success of the dissonance version of inconsistency theories, the increasing eclecticism and complexity of that version and of the experiments generated by it have tempted us to examine the possibility of subsuming some of these observations under more general principles. Though activation theory was not designed to deal specifically with the inconsistency data of the last ten years, it will be of interest to consider how the theory might be adapted for this purpose.

THE INITIAL HYPOTHESIS

Our early concern with motivation led inevitably to questions about the function of goals, for as everyone knows, goals are somehow related to action. A child sees a toy and sets out to get it. When it is in his hand, he stops his pursuit ending that behavior episode, and we say that he has reached his goal. What is the important difference in the conditions prevailing during his pursuit and after the toy is possessed, which magically removes its goal properties for a time?

The initial article (Peak, 1955) suggested first of all that an essential condition of "goal-directed" action was to be found not simply in the presence of some object, nor in the activation of the concept of such an object endowed somehow with powers of attraction, but rather in the activation of two or more disparate psychological events, such as the child's perception of where the toy is and his concept of where he would like it to be, his pursuit tending to last as long as the disparity exists. In a similar manner goal-directed action of some kind would be initiated by Mr. Big's concept of his high status and a related perception that he has just been blackballed by the Town Club.

Having formulated this statement, a second and equally important condition of persisting action became apparent as disparities of various kinds were considered. If I look out of the window at the skaters in the park, my perception of that scene will be different from my concept or percept of the house next door, but this difference as such would hardly be expected to generate or maintain activity. The activated events must be not only different but related as well. They may, for example, possess different properties as well as similar ones; they may be different and associated, or different parts of the same whole. Thus the child's percept of the present position of the toy and his concept of possessing it have the toy as a common feature at the same time that they represent different distances between child and toy.

It was suggested that the activation of a pattern such as this, composed of psychological events which are different but related, is a *goal state* or an aroused motive, and the cluster of behaviors associated with such a process and coterminous with it, is a *behavior episode*. Assuming this dependence of the episode on a goal state, it follows that when activation of the goal state ceases for any reason, the episode will end. Among the reasons for the disappearance of a goal state is a change in the environmental situation, such that the reactor's perception of the state of affairs matches his goal concept; e.g., the child perceives the toy to be in his hand (or mouth). The goal state will also be likely to end if a change in the situation results in a percept whose properties are drastically different from those of the goal concept. In short, either a great decrease in disparity or in relatedness will increase the probability of the disappearance of a goal state. (The terminology of the 1955 discussion has been altered to correspond with our current somewhat modified usage.)

Although a goal state may be either maintained or ended by perceptual feedback, the properties of the psychological structure underlying such a state also influence the duration of activation within the structure, and the disparate but interrelated parts of a goal state were thought of as constituting a feedback structure with some potentiality for self-maintained activity. In summary, the initial hypothesis was this:

A goal or motive state exists as long as disparate psychological events, related in such a way that they constitute a feedback circuit, are activated. The probability of the duration of this state is influenced by changes in the disparity and/or degree of relatedness of the events activated. The cluster of overt behaviors associated with a goal state is a behavior episode. It is coterminous with a goal state and is terminated by its disappearance.

From this point of view, goal states of varying duration are involved not only in conventional goal-seeking situations, task sets and intentions, but in innumerable others. Startle, surprise, humor, and fear behaviors appear as a result of difference in the familiar and the novel or the expected and the actual (McDougall, 1908; Hebb, 1949; Berlyne, 1960), and vanish when the novel becomes familiar or when the once unexpected outcome is predictable (e.g., the punch line of a joke). Perception of an object is 'achieved,' according to Brunswik (1939), when the properties of a distal object match a category, and a mismatch often produces continued activity and search (Bruner, 1957). Reactions to inconsistency also belong here, for disparity between related events is characteristic of inconsistency. Different conclusions drawn from the same premises, or different evaluations of a person by the same observer or by different observers somehow related to each other, are called inconsistent, imbalanced, incongruous, dissonant. And again, consistency is restored if the difference is reduced by deciding that the conclusions are actually the same, or if relatedness of the premises leading to the conclusions is reduced by discovering that the premises are different.

Although this working hypothesis was plausible, predictions were impossible without more precise statements of the meaning of structural concepts, such as disparity, similarity, association, and interdependence, and of the manner in which such structural properties determine behavior. The principal features of a concept of psychological structure will be outlined briefly, and postulates will be stated regarding the effects of specific input to particular structures on the course of change from point to point in the structure, leading to behavior.

A SUMMARY OF THE BASIC CONSTRUCTS OF THE THEORY

Behavior depends on the transmission of change within the psychological structure of a reactor. The course of change is a function of the properties of that structure and of the pattern of input to it on a given occasion. The full elaboration of the theory requires, therefore, a description not only of psychological structure and its relation to behavior but also of environmental structures, some of which are the sources of proximal stimuli (Brunswik, 1939), while others are what Tolman has called behavior supports (1932), such as the tools we use, the food we eat, the persons who help or interfere with our acts—in short, all kinds of resources, physical, biological, and social. The importance of such factors can be recognized at this time only by emphasizing that there is no such thing as behavior which is determined exclusively by psychological structure or exclusively by input from the environment.

Psychological Structure

Any structure consists of a set of parts that have some relation to each other. The related parts of psychological structure lie within the person, and determine (a) the probability of the transmission of change along various pathways following input at particular points, and (b) the probability of particular patterns of overt behavior. The boundaries of psychological structure are not precise but it will be convenient to include sense receptors involved in reactions to proximal stimuli, and effectors that produce proximal and relatively molecular reactions (Brunswik, 1939), as well as the more central structures that intervene.

Because psychological structures must usually be inferred from behavior-in-situations by convergence procedures (Garner, Hake, & Eriksen, 1956), they are hypothetical constructs to which neither uniquely anatomical nor uniquely 'mental' properties are attributed for present purposes. It is intended, nevertheless, that any properties assigned to these inferred structures should be compatible with known behavioral or neurological facts.

The term *event* will refer to any distinguished happening, whatever its properties. It may be inside or outside the reactor, complex or simple, static or changing, of any duration. A cloud, an atom, an attitude, a concept, a stimulus, an activation pattern, a response—all are events. A *part* is an event distinguished from some other event and included in a structure. A part may be homogeneous or internally differentiated. If homogeneous, or treated as such, it is called a *point*. If internally differentiated, a part is composed of *subparts*. Thus a concept is a part of psychological structure which is differentiated into its subparts or defining properties.

A *relation* is a property that can be predicated only of two or more events taken together. Although scores of different relations have been of interest to psychology, *similarity-difference* on the one hand, and *association* on the other, are the basic relations in psychological structure in the sense that (a) many, if not all, complex relations can be described in terms of similarity-difference or association or both, and (b) neither similarity-difference nor association is reducible to the other. Two parts are similar if they share one or more subparts. They are different if one or both possess parts not shared with the other. For example, the concepts of woman and of girl have femaleness in common, while they differ in the unshared properties of maturity and youth; they overlap in some degree. Nonoverlapping parts may be associated. Structurally speaking, association between parts implies continuity between them which mediates the transmission of change. Operationally, the presence of such a structure is inferred if there is some probability of the activation of B when A is activated, even though A and B do not overlap and B receives input only from A. It may be assumed, for example, that a reply to a stimulus phrase, such as "What is your name?" is mediated by associative structures.

Both similarity-difference and association imply degrees of closeness, proximity, or distance (Shepard, 1962), and it is this property of relations which is assumed to be correlated with the probability of transmitted change in Postulate II below. Such distances may or may not be metric.

Given the concepts of part and of relations of the kinds indicated, it will be evident that the *position* of any part in a structure may be described in terms of its overlap and/or association with other parts. In view of the fact that *the* important characteristic of a part is its position in a structure (i.e., what it is related to and how), a part will often be referred to simply as a *position*. The importance of position derives from the following considerations. When one speaks of positions as 'representing' a stimulus property or object or referent, this means (a) that the representing positions have a high probability of activation when the stimulus object is present because of associative connections, (b) that similarly, the representing positions mediate more or less consistent identification of the referent, and (c) that even in the absence of the referent event, the representing positions, activated perhaps by verbal stimuli, may yield outcomes similar to those produced when the referent itself is present, as when the remembered characteristics of a hurricane lead the victims to leave their homes promptly at the first warning of the next hurricane. In other words, each of the parts in such a network has a postion vis-à-vis the other parts. Events which have no position do not belong to a structure and do not mediate change.

Activation, Input, and Behavior

A few nonstructural terms must be defined.

When change occurring at a receptor or at any other point in psychological structure, produces change elsewhere, *activation* is said to have occurred. Activation is, therefore, simply change at one point depending on change at another. Although no part of a living organism is ever totally quiescent, change introduced at points in psychological structure will alter the activation pattern.

A *stimulus* is a change *at a sense receptor* which produces change at some other point or points in psychological structure; that is to say, there is no stimulus unless it has effects.

Input is change anywhere in a structure which may or may not produce change at other points.

Behavior includes what Brunswik has called proximal and molecular response, as well as the more distal and molar effects of these reactions, 'behavior achievements' (1939).

Postulates

Six Postulates will make it possible to use information about structures and the input to them in predicting behavior.

I. Learning and Restructuring through Activation.

A contiguity principle, similar to Hebb's (1949), assumes that learning is dependent on contiguous activation of parts of psychological structure, whether the input to these positions comes from external stimuli or from central sources. The Postulate differs from Hebb principally in its non-neurological formulation:

The probability of change in the closeness of the association between any two parts of a psychological structure is a monotonic function of the frequency of their paired activation, of the time interval between their activation, and of the relations already existing in the structure.

It follows from this Postulate that anything which increases the probability and frequency of paired activation of particular positions will influence the probability of their becoming associated. For example, Bruner and Olver observe that the associative grouping of objects, words, and other events by a person depends on 'what he is up to' (1963, p. 126). That this should be so follows from Postulate I as well as III below. The prevailing goal state ('what the person is up to') provides input to positions representing goal objects and associated with the goal state. As a result, these positions will have an increased probability of activation and hence a higher probability of being activated together, which produces the 'associative grouping.'

Effects of 'reinforcement' are assumed to depend on the fact that any position A, which becomes associated with situation cues and with the affective arousal resulting from reward or punishment will on reinstatement of the situation, receive input not only from the stimulus cues but also from the associated affective sources. As a consequence, the probability of A will tend to exceed that of positions not associated with reward or punishment (Postulate III). This notion bears some resemblance to Tolman's concept of emphasis (Tolman, Hall, & Bretnall, 1932). It is assumed further that differential influences of positive and negative affect result from the generally greater intensity and diffuseness of the activation pattern of the latter, with consequent increase in the number of interfering responses activated.

II. Transmitted Change as a Function of Distance.

The probability that change at any point A *will be transmitted to point* X *along some specified pathway is an inverse monotonic function of the distance between* A *and* X *along that pathway.*

In other words, the closer the relation of A and X, the more likely it is that change will be transmitted from one position to the other. If A is the only source of input to B, and B the only source of input to C,

$$p(C/A) = p(B/A) \cdot p(C/B).$$

(To be read, "The probability of the activation of C, given the activation of A, equals the probability of B given A, times the probability of C given B.")

A *pathway* in a psychological structure consists of that series of positions activated successively in the process of transmitting change from any point A to point X. It is assumed that change is transmitted from A to X and from X to A over different pathways, and that $p(A/X)$ and $p(X/A)$ may or may not be identical.

A theorem may be derived from Postulates I and II:

As distance between A *and* X *decreases, the probability increases that any part of a psychological structure which becomes associated with* A *will also be associated with* X.

This follows from the fact that when the relation of A and X is close, the probability is high that whenever A is activated X will also be activated in close temporal relation (Postulate II). Moreover, if A is activated contiguously with R, the probability is high that X and R will also be activated in close temporal relation, resulting in an increase in the association not only between A and R but between X and R as well (Postulate I).

III. Activation of a Position by Multiple Input.

The great flexibility of behavior argues against too much emphasis on the distance between any single source of input A and some outcome X as the principal determinant of the probability of X. It appears more reasonable to suppose that the probability of the activation of X given only A, is relatively low as a general rule, unless the two positions overlap. When, however, there is convergence of input on X from additional sources, then the probability of its activation will increase. These sources include all kinds of stimulus patterns, contextual as well as focal, and the recurrent input from central sources such as persisting goal states with which X is associated. Therefore, Postulate III is added to Postulates I and II in order to account for both the flexibility and the predictability of behavior:

The probability that any position X will be activated is some positive monotonic function of the combined probabilities that change will be transmitted to X from all activated parts of psychological structure within some specified time interval.

This Postulate is not intended as a threshold principle but is simply a recognition of the effect of combining probabilities of activation at a point. Suppose X receives input from independent sources, *A* and *B*, and that $p(X/A) = .5$ and $p(X/B) = .4$. In this case, X will be activated 50 per cent of the time when input comes from *A* alone and 40 per cent of the time by *B* alone. If *A* and *B* are both present, the probability that *X* will be activated by *neither A* nor *B* is expressed in the following equation:

$$p(\overline{X}/A,B) = [1 - p(X/A)] \cdot [1 - p(X/B)] = .30.$$

Consequently, $p(X/A,B) = 1 - [p(\overline{X}/A,B)] = 1 - .30 = .70.$

IV. Activity Decrement.

Activation of a position in psychological structure results in reduced probability of its reactivation under specified conditions of input. The probability of activation of the position given the same probability of input increases as a positive monotonic function of the time since its activation.

This Postulate is important in accounting for the termination of behavior episodes. It also avoids the deduction that all parts of any highly integrated structure will remain in a state of maximal activation at all times.

V. Forgetting.

Following the period of recovery from activity decrement, the probability of the activation of X, given the activation of some point A, is a monotonically decreasing function of the time elapsed since the paired activation of A and X (without implying that time as such has a causal function).

VI. Time for the Transmission of Change as a Function of Distance.

The time required for the transmission of change from one position to another in a psychological structure is a monotonically increasing function of the distance between the positions.

Activation in a Conceptual Network

The earlier statement of our 1955 hypothesis regarding the structures underlying motive and goal states and their related functions referred to percepts and concepts as basic components of these processes. Therefore, it will be instructive to consider what kind of arrangements would mediate some of the functions of the conceptual network. (The closely related attitude construct has not been discussed but is simply a concept which includes evaluative or affective properties.)

Defining a concept as "a network of inferences that are or may be set into play by an act of categorization," Bruner, Goodnow, and Austin (1956, p. 244) go on to assign the following functions, among others, to such a network. (a) It makes possible the identification of a stimulus object as a member of a class; i.e., the object is categorized on the basis of the properties that define the concept or category. (b) On any particular occasion some of the defining properties may be missing. Nevertheless, there is some probability that the object will be identified correctly, for the perceiver 'goes beyond the information given.' For example, the sound of a friend's voice over the telephone usually leads to his immediate identification. And (c) once the identification is made, one goes on to react appropriately to the friend and his characteristics even though the stimulus cues that would reveal these properties are not visible. This is to say, the missing properties are inferred.

The first problem encountered in tailoring a structure appropriate for these functions is how to conceptualize the relation of the concept as-a-whole to the parts or positions which define it. One usually thinks of a whole as including its parts as a plant includes its cells. This manner of conceiving the relation between defining parts and the concept whole would entail simply listing the components as set theory lists or counts the elements of a set. It is to be noted, however, that if the component elements are regarded as independent (as is the case in set theory), there is no structural property that identifies them as belonging to a whole.

An unusual notion of a part-whole structure has been suggested by

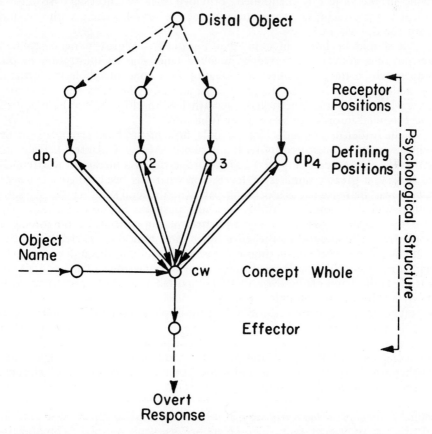

FIGURE 1.   A conceptual network. Lines joining positions indicate the probability is greater than zero that change will be transmitted between the positions. Dotted lines represent relations external to persons; solid lines are within this psychological structure. Arrows indicate direction of transmitted change.

Hebb in his discussion of what amounts to a conceptual network (1949, pp. 95ff.). After considering the organization of the parts involved in the perception of a triangle, the three corners and three lines, he goes on to observe that in addition to these parts, it is necessary to think of a 'new structure' that mediates the perception of the triangle as a 'distinctive whole.' This whole is associated with the cell assemblies activated when the corners of the triangle are fixated, but it is "something other" than those assemblies. In our terms, it is a separate position in the structure of a concept, associated with those parts or positions that define the concept.

Figure 1 presents such an arrangement, in which a position, a distinctive concept whole (cw), is related to each of the defining parts (dp's) and so has some probability of activation when one or more of those parts are activated. Moreover, in such a structure, activation of the concept whole will have some probability of leading to the activation of dp_4 which is represented in Figure 1 as receiving no input from the stimulus object itself. In short, the whole (cw) may be 'inferred from' the defining parts which happen to be activated, and the defining parts (e.g., dp_4) are inferred from the whole (cw). The whole and the parts may also be activated when the name of the object is mentioned, provided that the necessary structural relations are present; i.e., the association of the stimulus name with cw, and with the dps via cw.

It should be borne in mind that Figure 1 is a greatly oversimplified version of a conceptual network, intended chiefly as an illustration of the way in which the probability of activation of a concept whole is increased by multiple input from its defining parts, and how the parts may be recovered when the whole is activated. Nevertheless, the Figure may be modified and extended in order to serve other functions.

The reader may wonder, for example, how hierarchical arrangements or schema can be represented by such a network (Miller, Galanter, & Pribram, 1960, Ch. 11). Actually Figure 1 has the properties of a hierarchy if extended to include a greater number of levels, for what has been called a *concept whole* may be regarded as a defining part when several such wholes are subsumed under a more superordinate whole position. Suppose, for example, that the cw in Figure 1 is taken to represent the concept of borrowing a book from a colleague in the next office, and that the dps represent the defining parts of that act: getting up from desk, walking through door, turning to right into hall, walking through door of colleague's office, and asking for the book. Each of these dps may be regarded as a whole, associated with its own subordinate defining parts.

The structure of Figure 1 may be prototypic in still another sense. Any and all events inside or outside the reactor—an object or movement of an object, the acts of a person and their consequences, relations of all kinds and complex systems of plans and rules about grammar, counting, logical and mathematical operations—these and many other events may be the referents of such a conceptual structure.

Finally, it will be apparent that this hierarchical arrangement, though called a *conceptual network*, may also be considered to represent a portion of a hierarchy of goal states—incomplete because some necessary components of feedback systems are missing in Figure 1. Returning to the earlier example, if the cw position representing a concept of the act of borrowing a book is to become part of a goal state, it must be related to other positions in such a way that the component positions when activated will have some capacity for maintaining activation. The concept of borrowing-a-book might, for example, be related in the requisite manner to a concept (or percept) of not-having-the-book.

Behavior Outcomes, Blocking, and Reactivation

When a structure receives input A and at the same time somewhat different input B, the behavior resulting will be related in various ways to the outcomes produced by A or B alone. Sometimes the resulting pattern will be recognizable as a compound of responses to A and to B. Thus the words of a poem may be read and a tune may be hummed, or words and tune may be coordinated into a song. In the case of those combinations variously referred to as assimilation, averaging, pooling (Hovland, Harvey, & Sherif, 1957; Peak, 1958a; Helson, 1964), the outcome is a compromise between the responses to the separate stimuli. Compromise responses tend to occur when stimulus inputs activate points lying relatively close together. At greater distances, the difference in response patterns will be increased and contrast may result.

In still other conditions, combined inputs yield patterns which bear no recognizable relation to those produced by either input alone. Gestalt psychologists, among others, have provided many examples of 'emergents,' such as the *phi* phenomenon in which two spots of stationary light presented in certain spatial and temporal relations, produce the perception of a single light moving from one position to the other and back again.

These and other outcomes are presumably predictable given the postulates of activation theory, knowledge about the particular structures, and the loci of input, but there is one resultant that requires special comment at this time. Some responses and movements, which may occur alone, cannot be produced at the same time, so that simultaneous input to the effectors controlling these responses results in blocking, or response reduction and delay. It is physically impossible to walk forward and backward at the same time and the effort to do so is likely to result in no movement. Neither can the lips be parted to pronounce "t" and pressed together to say "p." These acts can only be performed successively.

This raises the question whether an additional postulate is needed to handle this and other instances of reduced reaction or response failure. Although the occurrence of central inhibition, one possible source of response reduction, has been demonstrated, the concept has not been made part of our postulate set, first because the conditions under which activity in one central area is inhibited by activity in another are not sufficiently identifiable for incorporation into a postulate about the behavior of intact organisms. A second justification for omitting such a postulate is that the principles already stated (e.g., Postulates IV and V) predict response reduction in a number of situations which should be explored more fully before other complications are introduced. It has been assumed, therefore, that blocking does occur at the response level but that central positions may, as a rule, be activated at the same time, if they receive input, and if they are not in a state of activity decrement from previous activation when the input arrives (Postulate IV).

What happens, then, when effectors controlling incompatible movements receive input at the same time so that overt response is blocked? If a person is operating under a task set to respond, failure to do so for any reason will tend to lead to the perception that no response has occurred and to reactivation of the structure involved in producing the responses associated with the task set, until the perceived outcome matches the goal concept which is part of the goal state. In the absence of a goal state, blocking of incompatible movements will produce no action unless new input is supplied. The operation of the reactivation process will be explored further in a later section.

THE ANALYSIS OF A DISSONANCE STUDY

The characteristics of activation theory, its strengths and weaknesses, will become clearer when it is put to the test of describing a specific action situation and predicting observed behavior outcomes, as well as the results to be expected when the conditions are modified.

In selecting an inconsistency study for this purpose it was important that the procedures be sufficiently simple and clear to permit reasonable inferences about the principal mediating events involved. Marlowe, Frager, and Nuttall (1965) have reported an investigation which is reasonably satisfactory in this respect. The structures required to mediate the outcomes are considerably simpler than is usually the case in dissonance studies, and problems of interpreting attitude-change measures are avoided because the principal dependent variable is agreement or refusal to volunteer to guide visiting Negro students on a campus tour. It was predicted that students who had been made to 'suffer' for their attitudes toward Negroes would be most likely to volunteer because of the dissonance created by this procedure and the pressure to reduce it.

The analysis of this study will consider the following matters:

1. The procedures of the experiment.

2. The inference of hypothetical structures established by the procedures and involved, along with the input at the time of the request to volunteer, in determining the student's choice between saying "yes" and "no" to this request.

3. A method of predicting from activation theory the probability of volunteering under high and low dissonance conditions.

4. The conditions under which dissonance produces higher probabilities of volunteering.

5. Volunteering as an equivocal indicant of dissonance.

6. Restructuring as an index of dissonance.

The Experiment

We are concerned here with Experiment I in the Marlowe *et al.* article (1965), which involved two groups of Ss, all of whom were first asked to indicate their attitudes toward Negroes by filling out a questionnaire. E then announced that if the questionnaire showed the "right attitudes," S could stay after the experiment and fill out more questionnaires for which he would be paid $1.50 (Group I), or $20 (Group 2). After E examined the answers, he said to S, "I am sorry but you don't have the right attitudes. You won't be able to fill out the other questionnaires for $20 ($1.50). I'm looking for people a little less open-minded."

The E then explained that another person in the building wanted to see *S* for a few minutes, disclaiming any knowledge of "what it was all about." When *S* arrived in the second room, E_2 described a Visiting Student and Exchange Program for which he was organizing a volunteer guide service. A group of Negro students was to come to the campus in ten days, he said, and asked if *S* would be willing to volunteer.

The number of *S*s volunteering to guide the Negro students was significantly greater for persons who believed they had 'lost' $20 than for those 'losing' only $1.50.

The authors interpret these results as support for dissonance theory, noting that the state of dissonance might be thought of by *S* in this way: "I believe something which is true and good and it has cost me $20." As is often the case, it is difficult to judge the extent to which the outcome of the experiment should be regarded as support for dissonance theory, since the predictions evidently depend on a good many assumptions which are not made explicit. We return to the problem later.

Hypothetical Structures

The first task in this analysis is to infer the structures that might reasonably have been established by the experimental procedures prior to the time when *S* was asked to volunteer. Whatever the difficulty of making these inferences, the attempt forces a decision about the locus of the difference between high and low dissonance structures. Hypothetical structures are presented in Figures 2 and 3, representing, respectively, the structures for *S*s undergoing the 'loss' of $20 and for those 'losing' $1.50. The validity of such inferences can be determined only by the familiar methods of construct validation (Peak, 1953) and by convergence operations (Garner, Hake, & Eriksen, 1956).

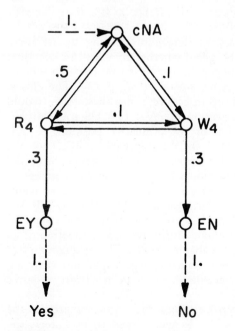

FIGURE 2.   High Dissonance ($20).

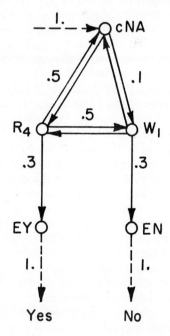

FIGURE 3.   Low dissonance ($1.50).

Each figure has these features: (a) a source of input; (b) a three-termed loop composed of positions, cNA, R, and W; and (c) effectors (EY and EN) involved in producing overt responses.

A three-termed loop. cNA is a concept whole which integrates the defining parts of S's concept of his *attitude toward Negroes*. Only two of these dps are present in Figures 2 and 3. One is R_4, which represents S's evaluation of his attitude as Right or Correct. Since Ss in general judged this attitude to be highly important, it is reasonable to suppose that it was evaluated as Very Right (R_4). The other defining part of cNA represented in the Figures is what S judges to be the experimenter's evaluation of cNA. In Figure 2 this is W_4, the evaluation Very Wrong, while in Figure 3 the evaluation is taken to be Slightly Wrong or W_1. The assumption is that a more negative evaluation of cNA is implied when E deprives S of \$20 (Figure 2) than when he withholds \$1.50 (Figure 3).

The association between positions cNA and R_4 is assumed to be closer $[p(R_4/cNA) = .5]$ than that between cNA and W $[p(W/cNA) = .1]$. This is intended to reflect the assumption that S's own evaluation of cNA should be more closely associated with that important attitude than is his concept of E's evaluation of the attitude, since the latter association is formed by only one comment and one act of E (Postulate I). The same values are assigned to the relation of cNA and W_4 in Figure 2 and to the relation of cNA and W_1 in Figure 3, because of the foregoing assumption that the association between cNA and the evaluation—Wrong—was established in both cases by E's single comment and act.

R_4, W_1, and W_4, as well as other values of R and W, are assumed to constitute an ordered dimension. The R and W ends, separated by a zero position, may be thought of as two subcategories of the larger evaluative dimension. It will be apparent that R_4 is closer to W_1 on this dimension than it is to W_4, and that as a consequence, $p(W_4/R_4) < p(W_1/R_4)$; likewise, $p(R_4/W_4) < p(R_4/W_1)$ (Postulate II).

Does Figure 2 represent dissonance? Before proceeding to use these structures for predictions, it should be asked whether they will be accepted as representing high and low dissonance. According to Festinger, elements X and Y are dissonant if Y is followed by *not-X* (1957, p. 13). The closest approach to a translation of the relations in Figure 2 into these terms would be something like the following. Activation of cNA (Y) has some probability of being followed by activation of the evaluative position, $R_4(X)$. There is also some probability that cNA will be followed by W_4 (*not-X*). So perhaps Figure 2 will be accepted as representing the structure of the average S in the High Dissonance condition when he comes to volunteer.

The Low Dissonance situation where S regards his attitude as Right (R_4) while E is judged to evaluate that attitude as Mildly Wrong (W_1) is referred to as "neutral" by Marlowe *et al.*, so that dissonance, unlike incongruity, does not depend on just any amount of difference in evaluation of an object or event (Osgood, Suci, & Tannenbaum, 1960). The evaluative positions must be in different and opposite categories (e.g., Right and Wrong), and for Marlowe *et al.* the negative evaluation must be markedly negative in order to be dissonant.

Input sources and effector structures. Since the Figures represent the experimental situation at the point when Ss were asked to volunteer, the focus of stimulus input is shown to be position cNA, activated when E remarks that he is organizing a guide service for Negro students. The request that S volunteer for this service must have also activated a task set or goal state (not shown in the Figures), consisting in part of the activated concept of responding with an agreement or refusal to volunteer and the related perception of not having done so. In the conditions of the study S's concept of a positive attitude toward Negroes will share parts with the concept of volunteering and so both will become associated with Right (R_4) and with the response *Yes* (Theorem above). If, however, S's own attitude toward Negroes is negative, it will share positions with the concept of refusing to volunteer and with response *No*.

The assumed values of the probability of response *Yes* given activation of R, and of *No* given W, are made equal in both Figures 2 and 3, in order to observe the less obvious effects of different relations within the cNA-R-W structure.

The Probability of Volunteering under High and Low Dissonance Conditions

What outcomes are to be expected from these structures according to activation theory?

The method of deriving predictions will now be described in detail for the dissonant situation in Figure 2. This involves calculation of the probability of activation of positions at successive steps following input at cNA, using the probabilities of transmitted change between positions specified in Figure 2. The combination of these probabilities, when they occur in series, or when they constitute input to the same position, is made according to Postulates II and III, respectively. The predictions presented at this time do not take account of the fact that input to the effectors governing *Yes* and *No* responses is not wholly independent; both receive some input from positions R and W. Since the method which assumes independence of these input sources is the simpler, can be described more briefly, and does not alter the conclusions to be drawn at this time, it is employed, despite the fact that some differences in the level of predicted probability of response patterns result from the two methods.

It is suggested that the reader refer to Figure 2 as the following steps are described:

Step 1. Activation of cNA is assumed to have a probability equal to unity, when S is asked to volunteer.

Step 2. Change at cNA may be transmitted to R and/or to W. $p(R_a/cNA) = 1 \times .5 = .5$; at the same time $p(W_a/cNA) = 1 \times .1 = .1$. The symbols, $p(R_a)$ and $p(W_a)$, refer to the probability of activation of positions, R and W on the first occasion of input to these positions. $p(R_b)$ and $p(W_b)$ below refer to the second occasion of input to the specified positions, arriving by a different route from the first.

Step 3. At this juncture, there is some probability that changes occurring at Step 2 will be transmitted from R to EY, the effectors controlling response *Yes*, and also from R to W. At the same time, change at W may be transmitted to EN, the effectors controlling *No*, and to R. Consequently, $p(EY_a/R_a) = .5 \times .3 = .15$; $p(W_b/R_a) = .5 \times .1 = .05$; $p(EN_a/W_a) = .1 \times .3 = .03$; and $p(R_b/W_a) = .1 \times .1 = .01$.

Step 4. The changes at R_b and W_b in Step 3 now provide input to EY and EN, respectively. And $p(EY_b/R_b) = .01 \times .3 = .003$; $p(EN_b/W_b) = .05 \times .3 = .015$.

Step 5. If it be assumed that the successive inputs (a) and (b) to EY or to EN arrive within a time interval short enough so that they combine (Postulate III), $p(EY) = 1 - [(1 - pEY_a)(1 - pEY_b)] = .153$; and $p(EN) = .045$.

Step 6. The responses, *Yes* and *No*, cannot be made simultaneously since they are mutually exclusive. In order to predict their probability under these circumstances, we must first determine the probability of each of the possible patterns of input to EY and EN when the total probability of $EY = .153$, and of $EN = .045$ as in Step 5. The four possible patterns and their probabilities are found in Table 1.

TABLE 1

Probability of Input Patterns to Effectors
(High Dissonance Structure—Figure 2)

Both *EY* and *EN* receive input	$p = .0069$
Neither receives input	$p = .8089$
Only *EY* receives input	$p = .1461$
Only *EN* receives input	$p = .0381$

Since the effector pattern, involving simultaneous input to both EY and EN, leads to response blocking, while the pattern of no input to either EY or EN also produces no response, both represent response failure and occur 81.5 per cent of the time in Table 1. But this is not what seems to happen in such experiments. In the Marlowe *et al.* study everyone replied to E's request to volunteer. How did this come about? It was suggested earlier that if S is operating under a task set to respond in some fashion, response failure will be followed by reactivation of the network until a response is produced or until the set is disrupted.

It is safe to assume that when E is standing by waiting for S's answer, the set to respond will be reactivated even if it has disappeared, and that this will provide input to the structure involved in the production of a reply to E. When such reactivation has caused everybody either to volunteer or refuse, the proportion of *Yes*es and *No*s should approximate $\frac{.146}{.184} = .79$, and $\frac{.038}{.184} = .21$, respectively. That is, 79 per cent of the persons in the High Dissonance group should say *Yes* and 21 per cent, *No*, assuming in both cases that relations within the structures have the stated values.

The corresponding values for the Low Dissonance condition depicted by Figure 3 would approximate 63 per cent and 37 per cent. In other words, activation theory would anticipate that the probability of volunteering will be greater in the High than in the Low Dissonance group, which is the result predicted and observed by Marlowe *et al.*

This difference between the probability level of the competing responses (p *Yes* = .79 and p *No* = .21) and of the input to the efforts determining those responses (p EY = .146 and p EN = .038) is an important fact which has often been neglected.

The Essential Conditions of the Predicted Relation of Dissonance and Volunteering

At this point the reader may well ask whether any generality can be attributed to these predictions based as they are on arbitrarily selected values of the variables. This question can best be answered by examining the results produced when probability of volunteering is predicted from a full range of values of the critical variables. This will reveal the limits within which higher dissonance is associated with higher probability of volunteering. It will also demonstrate that predictions from activation theory can be useful even when measurement techniques do not provide absolute values of variables, such as distances between evaluative positions or the corresponding $p(R/W)$s. In many cases, the inference of relative values expected under different conditions is sufficient for making predictions.

What, then, are the particular properties of Figures 2 and 3 responsible for the predicted increase in volunteering with increase in dissonance? Within what limits does this relationship hold and what happens when these limits are overstepped? Three variables will be examined: (a) the distance between cNA and the position on the R-W dimension of S's evaluation of cNA, and the distance between cNA and the position of E's evaluation, which determine $p(R)$ and $p(W)$, respectively; (b) the distance on the R-W dimension between the positions representing S's and E's evaluations of cNA; and (c) the sign of S's attitude toward Negroes and its relation to the sign implied by the act of volunteering or refusing to volunteer.

The limits within which volunteering increases with increase in dissonance are set by the following statements:

1. S's *evaluation of* cNA *as Right must have a higher probability of activation than* S's *concept of* E's *evaluation of his attitude as Wrong; i.e.,* p(R) *must be greater than* p(W). Table 2 presents the predicted probabilities of volunteering for a range of $p(R)$ and $p(W)$ values under conditions which in other respects are those of Figures 2 and 3. When $p(R) > p(W)$, the probability of volunteering is greater than that of refusing, at all values of $p(R)$ and $p(W)$. Moreover, the probability is higher in the High Dissonance than in the Low Dissonance structures in all cases where $p(R) > p(W)$.

TABLE 2

Probability of Volunteering as a
Function of Relations in cNA-R-W Structures

$p(W/cNA)$	.9		.7		.5		.3		.1	
$p(W/R)$ $p(R/W)$	.1ᵃ	.5ᵇ	.1ᵃ	.5ᵇ	.1ᵃ	.5ᵇ	.1ᵃ	.5ᵇ	.1ᵃ	.5ᵇ
$p(R/cNA)$										
.9	(.50	.50)	.58	.51	.66	.57	.76	.62	.85	.67
.7	.42	.47	(.50	.50)	.58	.54	.70	.59	.83	.65
.5	.34	.43	.42	.46	(.50	.50)	.63	.55	.81	.63
.3	.24	.38	.30	.41	.37	.45	(.50	.50)	.70	.60
.1	.15	.33	.16	.35	.19	.37	.30	.40	(.50	.50)

ᵃ High Dissonance
ᵇ Low Dissonance

In Figures 2 and 3, the higher probability of R is obviously due to its closer relation to cNA, but this need not be the only determinant of the relative values of $p(R)$ and $p(W)$, for either may be increased by input from sources not represented in these overly simple structures. One possible source of added input to R is of particular importance, namely, the activation of a self concept structure which is related to structures such as Figures 2 or 3. Brehm and Cohen (1962) and others have emphasized the role of personal responsibility and commitment in the creation of dissonance effects.

2. Although clearly necessary, the higher probability of positive than of negative evaluation is not sufficient to produce more volunteers from High than from Low Dissonance groups. Indeed, the values of $p(R)$ and $p(W)$ are assumed to be the same in Figures 2 and 3. A second condition must also be present: *the difference between the two evaluations of* cNA *must be greater in High than in Low Dissonance conditions, and in both cases one evaluation must be positive and the other negative.* Thus R_4 is farther from W_4 in Figure 2 than R_1 is from W_1 in Figure 3. As a consequence, the probability of transmitted change from R_4 to W_4 (and W_4 to R_4) is less than from R_4 to W_1 (and W_1 to R_4). In general, the greater the probability of transmitted change between the evaluative positions, the greater will be the tendency toward equalizing any initial difference in $p(R)$ and $p(W)$ and hence in $p(Yes)$ and $p(No)$. This follows from the fact that a relatively high probability of transmitting the more frequent change at R to W, and of transmitting the less frequent change at W to R produces a greater increase in the initially smaller $p(W)$ than in the initially larger $p(R)$. As distance between evaluations increases, less equalization of $p(R)$ and $p(W)$ occurs. Support for this conclusion will be found in Table 2 where volunteering is consistently more probable when $p(R/W) = .1$ (High Dissonance) than when $p(R/W) = .5$ (Low Dissonance), provided that $p(R) > p(W)$. When $p(R) < p(W)$, this is no longer true.

3. The third necessary condition of the higher probability of volunteering in the High Dissonance structure is that S's *attitude toward Negroes be positive.* As already explained, overlap in the defining positions of S's concept of his positive attitude toward Negroes and the defining positions of his concept of volunteering is responsible for the association of both these concepts with the same evaluation, Right, and with the act of volunteering. If, on the other hand, S's attitude is negative, cNA will share positions with the concept of refusing to volunteer and both will be seen as Right. In this case, the more dissonant structures will be associated with a higher probability of refusal.

The foregoing analysis indicates that the predicted higher probability of volunteering in High Dissonance Figure 2 than in Low Dissonance Figure 3 is not restricted to the particular values assigned to the principal variables in those Figures but has the generality indicated in the above statements. It remains to note some of the results predicted when the values of the variables go beyond the stated ranges.

Volunteering as an Equivocal Indicant of Dissonance

The results expected under the following conditions in Marlowe-type situations suggest that volunteering cannot be regarded as a consistent indicant of the presence of dissonance.

1. $p(R) < p(W)$. It is evident in Table 2 that although High Dissonance structures should produce higher rates of volunteering than Low if $p(R) > p(W)$, the former will actually result in the lower probabilities when $p(R) < p(W)$. These results are to be found in that portion of Table 2 under the diagonal.

2. $p(R) = p(W)$. Under these circumstances the probability of volunteering is at the chance level ($p = .5$) for all values of $p(R)$ and $p(W)$, and for both Low and High Dissonance conditions. This case is of particular interest because it calls attention to High Dissonance structures with equal probabilities of volunteering and refusal. Let us assume a structure (X) having the same characteristics as Figure 2, except that $p(W_4/cNA) = .5$, instead of .1 as in Figure 2. At the same time, $p(R_4/cNA) = .5$, just as it does in Figure 2. Such a structure is not only highly dissonant by definition, because the two evaluations of cNA are opposite and far apart, but it appears to be even more dissonant than Figure 2, according to one common index. It is often held that dissonance creates pressures to change the structure, and that this pressure increases as dissonance increases. In the next Section it will be argued that structure X should afford more opportunity for restructuring than Figure 2, because of the higher and equal probabilities of R and W and the consequently higher expected frequency of their paired activation, an important condition for restructuring (Postulate I). The point is this. Less potentiality for restructuring is inferred to exist in the structure of Figure 2 than in structure X, but the latter is predicted to yield the lower probability of volunteering. Therefore, it will be asked later which of these contradictory criteria of the presence of dissonance is to be accepted, the probability of restructuring or of volunteering.

3. *Changing the distance between evaluations* of cNA. In Figures 2 and 3, one evaluation is positive and the other, negative. In Figure 2 the evaluations are extremely positive and extremely negative, while in Figure 3, one is extremely positive and the other mildly negative. As the distance between these evaluations approaches zero by making S's evaluation of cNA less positive or E's less negative, the probability of volunteering approaches .5, provided the two evaluations remain in different categories. If, however, both are in the same category, the function changes. Suppose, for example, that S evaluates cNA as Right and E rewards the attitude instead of punishing it ($+ +$ input pattern). Both of these positive evaluations will be associated with volunteering which should be enhanced in probability by the double input from the two activated R positions to the effector (EY), which produces a *Yes* response (Postulate III). At the same time, the probability of the competing response, *No*, will be low relative to *Yes*, because the effectors governing it will receive only indirect input transmitted along the R-W dimension from the activated R position at the opposite end. In the same way, if S believes his attitude to be Wrong and E makes the same evaluation of it ($--$ input pattern), the probability of volunteering will decrease as distance between these two negative evaluations decreases.

In other words, two features of the relation between points receiving input on the R-W dimension are important: whether the positions are in the same or different categories of the dimension and hence associated with the same or different responses, and how far apart they are on that dimension. When inputs from cNA are to positions in the same category (Right *or* Wrong), the directly associated response (volunteer or refuse) is increased in probability by the multiple input, but when inputs are to different categories, competing responses will be activated directly, tending to equalize probabilities of the two types of response. Consequently, it is to be expected that in the Marlowe-type situation probability of volunteering will tend to decrease as conditions change from rewarding a positively valued attitude (+ + input pattern) to punishing a positively valued attitude (+ − pattern) to punishing a negatively valued attitude(− − pattern).

Restructuring as an Index of Dissonance

The most widely accepted generalization of inconsistency theory is that inconsistency generates forces to restore consistency and that this may be accomplished by a change in structure. Although the Marlowe *et al.* experiment provides no evidence that dissonance was reduced by restructuring, it is of interest to ask how activation theory would proceed to predict potentialities for restructuring in different structures.

It will be recalled that Postulate I assumes that increase in the association between two central positions depends on the frequency of paired activation of those positions, the time interval between the activations (the shorter the interval, the greater the probability of change), and on the relations already existing between the positions. Since activation in psychological structures is the *sine qua non* of restructuring, the following questions are of first importance: (a) What is the probability of activation of specified positions in a particular structure under stated input conditions? (b) What is the probability of paired activation of those positions, given the probability of each? (c) How frequently will input to the structure occur?

The first two questions may be answered in a straightforward manner if the properties of a structure and of stimulus input to it are known or assumed. The third question requires additional considerations. Simultaneous activation of positions in a psychological structure may result, of course, when there is input to those positions from external stimulus events in close temporal relation. But in the absence of this source of input, the frequency of paired activation will be dependent on the properties of the structure itself, such as feedback arrangements capable of sustaining activation for a time, or a tendency to produce competing responses and response failure and reactivation (see page 227).

Since in the presence of input there is some probability of the activation of each of the positions in a structure, and hence of their paired activation, the number of pairings will increase as the number of such input occasions increases (Hays, 1963, p. 58: the Bernoulli theorem). Therefore, a rough index of the expected frequency of paired activation may be constructed by multiplying the probability of activation of any pair of positions on each input occasion by the expected frequency of the occasions. The probability of response failure and reactivation in a given structure is used to estimate the frequency of input. Such an index takes the following more specific form for the family of structures and input conditions discussed in this Chapter. If the *S* is operating under a goal set, *FPA* equals the probability of paired activation on each input occasion, of two or more positions such as *R* and *W*, times the probability of response failure assumed to determine the frequency of reactivation. The resulting value is multiplied by 100 as a matter of convenience. The probability of paired activation of R and W is, of course, equal to the product of their probabilities, and the method used to determine the probability of failing to respond with either volunteering or refusal is that described on page 232.

$FPAs$ have been calculated for a set of High Dissonance structures, like Figure 2 in all respects except that $p(W)$ and $p(R)$ values vary over the whole range of probabilities; and for another set consisting of Low Dissonance structures, like Figure 3 except that again $p(R)$ and $p(W)$ cover the range. This analysis reveals that High Dissonance structures, defined as such by the greater distance between the Right and Wrong evaluations of S's attitude, prove to have consistently higher FPA indices than do the corresponding Low Dissonance structures.

The suggestion was made earlier that a structure X, producing high and equal evaluations of an attitude, and hence high probabilities of response failure, would be expected to result in more restructuring than the High Dissonance structure of Figure 2, provided the S is responding under a goal set of some kind. This notion is compatible with the FPA values of these two structures, which are 18.25 and 3.75, respectively. But this brings us back to the fact that although the former is expected to produce more restructuring than the latter, the probability of volunteering should be greater for Figure 2, according to activation theory. Which of these two indices of dissonance is the more justifiable?

Only these conclusions can be made at this time: (a) Activation theory leads us to expect that restructuring should be more consistently related to dissonance than is volunteering, *over the range of conditions considered here.* (b) It is evident, however, that dissonance as defined, is not invariably or exclusively correlated with restructuring. The conditions of restructuring may be established by means other than the creation of dissonance. Furthermore, Postulate I includes other parameters of restructuring than paired activation. Of particular importance is the nature of the existing structure which helps determine both the amount and locus of restructuring. In short, the utility of restructuring, like that of any index of any hypothetical construct, is subject to limitations which are implicit in the postulates.

ACTIVATION THEORY, DISSONANCE THEORY, AND CHOICE

So far, the postulates of activation theory have been used to predict the effects on response choice (to volunteer or to refuse) of the following features of psychological structures and input to them: (a) degrees of dissonance (defined as distance between two opposite evaluations of an attitude); (b) different degrees of relatedness (i) between S's attitude toward Negroes and his evaluation of that attitude, and (ii) between S's attitude and E's evaluation of the attitude; (c) the sign of S's attitude in relation to his concept of volunteering or refusing to do so (overlap in positions defining the two concepts); (d) rewarding S's attitude vs. punishing it; and (e) other sources of input to the Right or Wrong evaluative positions. In any action situation, the properties of psychological structures activated by given input must be inferred and predictions of the direction of choice made therefrom in accordance with the postulates, as was done in this case.

The statements of dissonance theory about the factors governing choice are not always clear. At the most general level, a principle states that dissonance will be followed by events which reduce dissonance. In specific situations, the experimenters must presumably decide whether a given outcome will reduce dissonance, and hence be chosen, on the basis of principles that are often esoteric. Marlowe *et al.* indicate that their "prediction follows from the assumption that by taking action the person can overtly demonstrate to himself how important the beliefs are, thereby minimizing further the discomfort of having suffered for them" (1965, p. 865). While a case may be made on various grounds for expecting an increase in volunteering as a function of the importance of beliefs in this situation, it is not explained why further increase in the importance of a belief should reduce a dissonance assumed to be generated in the first place by punishing an important belief. Further doubts are raised about this rationale by the fact that the predicted increase in judged importance of ethnic attitudes in the dissonance group did not actually occur. If volunteering was chosen because it would reduce dissonance by making S see his punished attitude as more important, what interpretation is to be made of the fact that Ss chose to volunteer even though doing so had no effect on the importance of their attitudes? Because of these ambiguities it is difficult to be certain just what aspects of dissonance theory are supported by this experiment. Similar ambiguities are very prone to exist in other dissonance experiments.

SUMMARY

1. It is proposed that the behavioral outcomes of inconsistency and other goal states are predictable from the principles of an activation theory which are sketched.

2. Psychological structures are described in terms of parts and relations between them, the basic relations being similarity-difference and association between parts, both of which imply degrees of relatedness. These structures have their locus in the person but are not assigned properties uniquely anatomical or 'mental.' They are assumed to mediate processes which determine behavior, such as stimulation, perceiving and categorizing, goal states (e.g., task sets, inconsistency states, motives), and learning.

3. A set of postulates is stated concerning (I) learning and restructuring, (II) the relation of distance between positions and the probability of the transmission of change between them, (III) the combination of multiple inputs at a point, (IV) activity decrement, (V) forgetting, and (VI) time for the transmission of change as a function of distance. It is recognized that overt responses may block each other if mechanically opposed but the outcome of blocking depends on the presence or absence of a goal set. If none is present, blocking prevents action. If a goal state is operating, failure of response or of some specified outcome may be followed by perceptual feedback and reactivation, until S perceives that he has produced an act or outcome matching his goal concept.

4. A study, intended by the experimenters to test predictions from dissonance theory (Marlowe, Frager, & Nuttall, 1965), is interpreted in terms of activation theory. High Dissonance was assumed to be created by depriving S of $20 because his attitude toward Negroes "was not right"; that is, E punished S's attitude. In a Low Dissonance condition, S was deprived of $1.50 under conditions otherwise the same. The prediction that a

greater proportion of the High Dissonance group would volunteer to guide Negro students on a campus tour was supported by the results.

a. Hypothetical structures are inferred from these experimental conditions and described in terms of their parts and the relations between them. The chief difference in the High and Low Dissonance structures generated by the conditions is judged to be the greater distance in the former between S's and E's opposite evaluations of S's attitude. The behavior predicted by activation theory to result from the request to volunteer is essentially the same as that predicted and observed in the Marlowe, Frager, and Nuttall study; that is, a higher probability of volunteering in those subjects operating under higher dissonance.

b. Further predictions suggest that this relation between volunteering and dissonance holds only within certain limits: (i) In both High and Low Dissonance conditions, S's positive evaluation (R) of his attitude toward Negroes must be more closely associated with that attitude than is his concept of E's negative evaluation (W) of the attitude, with the result that $p(R) > p(W)$. (ii) The difference between these two evaluations must be greater in the High than in the Low Dissonance structure, one evaluation being positive in both structures and the other extremely negative in the High and mildly negative in the Low Dissonance case. The closer relation between the two evaluations in the latter has the effect of equalizing the probability of volunteering and refusing to do so. On the other hand, the greater distance between these evaluations in the high dissonance structure results in conserving any existing difference between $p(R)$ and $p(W)$. Therefore, when $p(R) > p(W)$, more frequent volunteering will result if dissonance is high. (iii) The S's attitude toward Negroes must be positive.

c. In conditions such as the following, the generalization fails: (1) When $p(R) < p(W)$, the probability of volunteering will decrease with increasing dissonance. (2) When $p(R) = p(W)$, the degree of dissonance makes no difference, and the probability of volunteering and of refusal are at the chance level.

These and other predictions indicate that volunteering is a somewhat equivocal index of dissonance. They also emphasize the importance of determining the limits within which any relation is expected to hold.

d. An estimate of the potentialities for restructuring afforded by various structures under particular input conditions is based on a combination of the probability of temporally contiguous activation of each pair of positions in a structure and the frequency of input. According to activation theory, this Index will not be highly correlated with the probability of volunteering, even though the two dependent variables may be mediated by some of the same structures. It can be shown that the probability of restructuring should increase as the probabilities of activation of positions R and W become more nearly equal and high, conditions which reduce the probability of volunteering. Activation theory suggests a basis for predicting the conditions under which such dependent variables will be influenced in the same or different ways by changes in the intervening variables without reference to a construct of dissonance as such.

CHAPTER 13

Behavior Theory

Barry E. Collins

University of California, Los Angeles

Typically, a writer assigned one of the 'outgroup' theories in a volume such as this one is expected to focus on the *differences* between behavior theory and cognitive consistency theories. I will argue, however, that the important interfaces between behavior theory and cognitive consistency theory are found when the two distinct theoretical orientations converge to make the same empirical predictions. Although cognitive and behavioral theories can be interpreted so as to make different predictions, important differences between the two orientations are also found in their contrasting initial assumptions, in their ideas about what aspects of human behavior are most important and interesting, in their contrasting research strategies, and in subtle connotative differences in the words they use.

A quick review of four metatheoretical characteristics of behavior theory illustrates some of the philosophical differences between behavioristic and cognitive consistency traditions. These characteristics indicate the different perspective that the behavior theorist brings to bear on the data generated by consistency theories. Hopefully, they also provide a context in which it is possible to separate genuine empirical controversy from mere difficulties in communication from one inbred culture to another.

1. *Emphasis on the adaptive aspects of human behavior.* Learning theorists have followed closely in the footsteps of the "Chicago Functional" school of psychology. As Keller (1937) has indicated, the functionalists were interested in the "stimulating concepts of Darwinian biology. Impressed by the ideas of mental evolution and 'survival of the fittest,' they sought to determine the place occupied by mind in helping human or animal organism to hold its own in the struggle for existence" (p. 42). In general, behavior theorists have found joy in discovering the techniques by which an organism—animal or human—goes about the processes of survival.

This emphasis contrasts sharply with the phenomenological approaches of the field-theoretic school—the intellectual predecessor to most cognitive consistency theories. Lewin's term for the objective environment—"foreign hull"—captures connotatively the importance he attached to the impact of the objectively defined environment.

2. *Historical explanation.* Considering this stress on the adaptive aspects of human experience, it is not surprising that behavior theory should look to an individual's past interaction with his environment in order to explain or understand current attitudes. Leonard Doob (1947), in a frequently cited behavioral discussion of attitudes, argues that "There are no psychic rays which enable the investigator, even though he be equipped with a poll or a scale, to determine the 'strength' of an attitude, the overt responses with which it has become associated, or its present functioning within the personality. Such knowledge can be obtained only from knowing approximately under what conditions the attitude was acquired in the first place and the extent to which it secures present and future reinforcement" (p. 138).

3. *Strict operationalism—the psychology of the other person.* Behavior theorists set about to discover lawful relationships between objectively measured stimulus variables and overt responses—thus the shibboleth "S-R psychology." The behavior theorist's interest in the measuring units of physics as a basis for the laws of psychology is partly methodological. By building 'a psychology of the other person' the psychologist is able to stand apart from his subject matter as do the other natural scientists. The preference for stimulus-response variables, although initially a purely methodological one, has led inevitably to a substantive preference. Cognitive consistency theorists would probably disagree with both the methodological and substantive preferences.

4. *Foundation on data from animal experiments.* Behavioral theories of attitude change typically begin their work on the foundation of several well-established principles of animal learning. This has led to the infusion of a number of terms and jargon into theories of attitude change (organism for individual, habit for cognition, etc.) which sometimes make the theories seem technical and far removed from day-to-day life. While these concepts are almost inevitably 'liberalized' to some extent in their metamorphosis from their foundation in the explanation of animal behavior to explanations of human behavior, their simplicity has sometimes offended humanistically oriented organisms.

Two Behavioristic Conceptions of Attitudes

Leonard Doob defines an attitude as "An implicit response with drive strength which occurs within the individual as a reaction to stimulus patterns and which affects subsequent overt responses" (1947, p. 136). Doob argues that an attitude is an implicit response to an objective stimulus pattern. This implicit response, in turn, serves as stimulus and drive for overt, observable behavior. While Doob discusses several implications of this definition, the point of emphasis here is that the attitude is intimately bound up with overt behavior—the attitude is an immediate cause, both as stimulus and drive, for overt responses.

Donald Campbell (1963) argues that attitudes—as typically measured— are manifestations of behavioral dispositions. He argues that an attitude is a manifestation or symptom of the more generic "acquired behavioral disposition." He notes that "Behavior is modified as a result of experience, that somehow a person retains residues of experience of such a nature as to guide, bias, or otherwise influence later behavior" (p. 97). Once the residue of experience or acquired behavioral disposition exists, Campbell argues, then it can be diagnosed through any number of techniques—which range from observation of behavior to standard interview and questionnaire techniques. Although he is careful to exclude the causal role for attitudes assigned to them by Doob, Campbell does stress the close relationship between an attitude and overt response: both are alternate means of expressing or diagnosing the same acquired behavioral disposition.

In summary, these conceptions of attitude have two characteristics important for a contrast with cognitive consistency theories: (a) The assumption that an attitude has been forged out of the individual's past experience with his environment, and (b) the statement that the attitude is intimately bound up with behavior systems. With respect to the second point, Doob argues that the attitude plays a causal role in the stimulus-response sequence, and Campbell argues that pencil and paper attitude tests are simply another diagnostic method for acquired behavioral dispositions.

Illustrative Applications of a Behavioral Orientation to Problems of Cognitive Consistency

Balance. Two direct applications to cognitive consistency issues will be sketched briefly. First, consider a classical unbalanced Heiderian triad. Hugo likes Hortense, I like Hugo, and I dislike Hortense. If we assume that liking attitudes are bound up in approach responses to the liked object and disliking attitudes are bound up in avoidance responses, then the state of affairs described in the above triad creates a behavioral dilemma. If, for instance, we see 'Hugo' as a complex stimulus, the statement "I like Hugo" can be translated to mean that I have approach responses conditioned to most, if not all, elements of the Hugo stimulus, and the statement "I dislike Hortense" can be translated to mean that I have avoidance responses conditioned to most, if not all, elements of the Hortense stimulus.

So long as Hugo and Hortense remain separated, I can go right along approaching and avoiding to my heart's content. But the statement "Hugo likes Hortense" (or the Heiderian equivalent "Hugo and Hortense are married") can create problems in several ways. Considering just the Hugo stimulus, it might mean that I approach most of the stimulus elements of Hugo, but I avoid that element which likes Hortense. Or since both liking and unit relationships imply propinquity, it might mean that I tend to approach the Hugo element and avoid the Hortense element of the Hugo-Hortense stimulus complex. In short, 'unbalanced' triads may be unpleasant, not because of any formal cognitive rules, but because the situation will eventually lead to a *behavioral* dilemma.

Such an approach would resolve the dilemma posed by the triad, I like chickens, chickens like chicken feed, and I dislike chicken feed. While formally unbalanced, the triad does not seem subjectively unpleasant. All is resolved if we can establish that the cognition "I dislike chicken feed" does not imply any behavior incompatible with the behavior implied by "I like chickens."

To the extent that different triads imply different degrees of potential behavioral conflict, the triads should be rated as differentially unpleasant and should result in differential attitude change. Thus if we substitute Hugo has dated Hortense for Hugo is married to Hortense or if we substitute Hugo likes Hortense's money for Hugo likes Hortense, and *if we find that the behavioral dilemma is less severe*, then the new triads should be rated as more pleasant and should produce less cognitive reorganization.

Cognitive dissonance. When Lawrence and Festinger (1962) argued that dissonance concepts could subsume the operations previously called conflict and frustration in the rat laboratory, they made it even easier for behaviorists to argue that conflict and/or frustration could subsume the operations previously called dissonance in the human laboratory. Festinger (1957) states that a cognition is "any knowledge, opinion, or belief about the environment, about oneself, or about one's behavior" (p. 3). If we make the standard behavior theory assumption—that 'knowledges, opinions, or beliefs' have behavioral implications—then cognitions may be 'dissonant' or 'nonfitting' because the behavioral implications are incompatible. The lack of fit, then, would not be between the cognitions themselves but between the behavioral implications of the cognitions.

Festinger (1964) has made a strong attack on a conflict interpretation of the dissonance data. His entire argument, however, is based on *his* definitional distinction which limits conflict to predecision processes. He argues that an individual is in conflict during the predecision period, but "once the decision is made ... dissonance-reduction processes begin" (Festinger, 1964, p. 8). The data (Festinger, 1964; cf. also Section IV A) do indicate that much of what has been called dissonance reduction, particularly in the choice paradigm, occurs after the decision has been made. But these data do not argue against a conflict interpretation unless we limit conflict processes to 'predecision' or 'preresponse' processes—and such a limitation is arbitrary and idiosyncratic to some dissonance theorists.

In the first place, investigators (Murray & Berkun, 1955; Berkun, 1957) working within Neal Miller's conflict orientation studied the postresponse implications of conflict prior to the original presentation of dissonance theory. An approach-avoidance conflict was established in a black alley and then the subject was placed in a white alley where he resolved the conflict by approaching the goal. When the subject was placed back in the original black alley after making a response (decision) in the white alley, the investigator was clearly examining the dynamics of behavior after the white alley response—i.e., postdecisional behavior.

Even if this prior claim to postdecision processes is not allowed to conflict theory, the fact that cognitive consistency researchers first investigated the phenomena would not entitle them to christen the phenomena dissonance and then, by definitional fiat, fence out other theoretical interpretations. The process of psychological exploration, unlike the exploration of new world geography, does not allow the first arrival to lay claim to the new territory in perpetuity. In fact, even the most ethnocentric of the behavior theorists have a long history of land grabbing in which they frequently extend their theories to accommodate new phenomena first discovered by Tolman or other cognitive theorists.

At the risk of redundancy, let me make the argument for a behavioral definition of dissonance in another way. Festinger's original definition of dissonance stated "... two elements are in a dissonant relation if, considering these two alone, the obverse [sic] of one element would follow from the other" (1957, p. 13). From this definition it would appear that dissonance can be analytically defined within some set of formal rules of cognitive logic —thus Festinger and Carlsmith (1959) speak of "X" and "not-X." In fact, however, the 'dissonant' cognitions studied are never simple opposites such as "I do like the task" vs. "I do *not* like the task." Probably for this reason, Lawrence and Festinger (1962) abandon a strictly formal basis for the definition of dissonance or nonfittingness of cognitions:

> Two items are in a dissonant relationship if ... the obverse of one follows *psycho*logically [emphasis mine] from the other. ... Psychological implication ... is to be interpreted as follows: if the acceptance of one item of information as true sets up an expectation that some other item of information is also true, then the first item psychologically follows from the other (pp. 36–37).

But why is it that the cognition "I know the task is dull" should set up the expectation that "I *said* the task was dull?" Possibly it is because the cognition "I know the task is dull" is tied up in a behavioral system which includes the response "I said the task is dull." (Bem's Chapter 14 presents suggestive evidence in this regard.)

In short, the behavioral interpretation of dissonance makes possible a straightforward empirical definition of dissonant or nonfitting relations. First, the experimenter determines what behavior is emitted by subjects who hold (or who have been taught to hold) cognition A. In the Festinger and Carlsmith experiment, for example, the subject could be asked to describe the task to the next subject without any pressure from the experimenter. Then, if the subject is tricked or induced into making any response inconsistent with that behavior which would have been freely emitted, the awareness, cognition, or knowledge of the induced behavior will be dissonant or nonfitting with cognition A.

Having argued that the essence of dissonance arousal is that the two cognitions imply different behaviors, it remains to ask why the organism should be bothered by such a state of affairs. It is possible to argue for a drive associated with conflict (Spence, 1951; Berlyne, 1957; Miller, 1959, p. 236; Kimble, 1961, p. 459) and frustration (Brown & Farber, 1951; Amsel & Roussel, 1952). Imbued with drive which continues after the decision is made, the argument for 'conflict-drive reduction' would parallel the argument for 'dissonance reduction,' and both would be diametrically opposed to the kind of 'variety' drive postulated by Maddi in Chapter 16.

The main argument here is that the definition of dissonance is closely parallel to the definition of conflict; that the magnitude of predecisional conflict is highly correlated with the magnitude of the postdecisional conflict-dissonance; that those manipulations which increase or decrease the magnitude of predecisional conflict also increase or decrease the magnitude of postdecisional conflict-dissonance. No position is taken on whether or not the specific dynamics of postdecision conflict-dissonance reduction are similar to the specific dynamics of predecisional conflict resolution. In other words, I have tried to suggest a behavior theory mechanism for the arousal of dissonance, but, at present, no behavior theory mechanism for dissonance reduction has been presented.

Furthermore, it is not necessary to argue that the state of conflict, *per se*, exists after the decision or response is made. It is only assumed that the individual somehow stores information about the conflict and that the causal impact of conflict continues even after a decision or response has been made.

Although I shall avoid the temptation to spin out a Hull-Spence mechanism which would explain how conflict could extend its causal impact after the response has been made, I shall provide a more literary illustration of the postresponse impact of conflict.

If one were to take Neal Miller's conflict model literally, it would be necessary to predict that the caveman—in conflict about whether to run or fight the local dragon—would fight only with the enthusiasm remaining after the tendencies to run had been subtracted (or run with the vigor remaining after the inclination to fight had been substracted). If an ancestor who was almost as inclined to fight as to run merely walked away (as would be predicted when the strong approach response tendency was subtracted from the slightly stronger avoidance tendency) he probably would not live to be an ancestor. It seems reasonable that an individual, *after* resolving a conflict between environmental pressure and personal inclination, can find some way to commit himself wholeheartedly to the alternative chosen—both at present and on future occasions when the two response tendencies are again simultaneously evoked. The position of the dominant response could be consolidated by weakening the lesser of the two response tendencies; any attitudes and cognitions associated with the weakened response tendency would, of course, also be changed.

SUMMARY

If the connotative differences between cognitive and behavior theories are ignored and the causal impact of conflict is not arbitrarily stopped at point of decision, behavior theory can make a contribution to the troublesome problems of defining dissonance and imbalance. Two cognitions or attitudes are dissonant if each is associated with a different, and incompatible, overt response. Thus a series of statements are dissonant or imbalanced if they describe a situation which would evoke incompatible responses.

The magnitude of predecisional conflict is highly correlated with the magnitude of postdecisional conflict-dissonance; those manipulations which magnify predecisional conflict magnify postdecisional conflict-dissonance. This is not to say that the mechanisms of conflict *resolution* are identical with the mechanisms of dissonance *reduction*. But it *is* to say that the independent manipulations which create conflict also create dissonance. Given this similarity, cognitive theorists can probably benefit from the relative ease with which behavior theorists have been able to define conflict and specify the conditions of its arousal.

The argument that dissonance and imbalance concepts are related to conflict is not new; but such an integration of behavioristic and cognitive theories has been rejected by the cognitive theorists (e.g., Festinger, 1964). It is true that the cognitive theories 'got there first' with specific predictions for conflict-dissonance-imbalance reduction. But the (disputed) claim to historical precedence is irrelevant to the assertion that the phenomena explored under the name 'conflict' by behavior theorists are similar to the phenomena explored under the name 'dissonance' by cognitive theorists.

CHAPTER 14

Dissonance Reduction in the Behaviorist

Daryl J. Bem
Carnegie-Mellon University

If a behaviorist holds cognition A, a firm belief in the empirical Law of Effect, and he is confronted with the apparently inconsistent cognition B, the fact that a \$1 reinforcement given to a subject for role-playing produces more attitude change than a \$20 reinforcement (Festinger & Carlsmith, 1959), he is likely to experience cognitive dissonance, an aversive state which he will seek to remove. But how will he do so? Clearly relinquishing cognition A would be too shattering, and denying cognition B would be a gambit which runs counter to the mores of the scientific community. It would appear that reinterpreting cognition B is the only socially sanctioned mode of dissonance reduction remaining open to him. Accordingly, it is in this way that the behavioral analysis presented here attempts to assimilate the 'dissonant' datum and thus restore cognitive quiescence once again. I seek, in short, to demonstrate the plausibility of an alternative interpretation of data drawn from one of the current consistency theories, the theory of cognitive dissonance (Festinger, 1957).

Like the other consistency theories, the theory of cognitive dissonance attempts to account for observed functional relations between current stimuli and responses by postulating some hypothetical structure or process within the organism, in this case, an inferred motivational process of dissonance arousal and reduction. Also like most of the other consistency theories, dissonance theory is further characterized by an emphasis on the individual's current phenomenology; the explanatory account in the theory itself is ahistorical.

In contrast, the alternative formulation to be presented here eschews any reference to hypothetical internal processes and seeks, rather, to account for observed functional relations between current stimuli and observable

Preparation of this article was supported by National Science Foundation Grant GS 1452 for the study of 'Self-Awareness and Self-Control.' The article is based on the extended discussion of dissonance theory in Bem (1967). Permission to reproduce materials from that discussion was granted by the American Psychological Association and is gratefully acknowledged. The author is also grateful to George R. Madaras and Kenneth M. Peterson for aid in conducting the research and to Sandra L. Bem for critical comments on the manuscript.

responses in terms of the individual's past training history. This approach has been called 'radical' behaviorism (see Scriven, 1956, for example), a position most often associated with the name of B. F. Skinner. In analyzing a complex behavioral phenomenon, the radical behaviorist attempts to establish it as a special case of some previously substantiated functional relation discovered in the experimental analysis of simpler behaviors. His functional analysis is thus based on empirical generalization and, accordingly, is frankly inductive not only in its experimental execution, but in its formal presentation.

A functional analysis characteristically begins by inquiring into the ontogenetic origins of the observed dependent variable and attempts to ascertain the controlling or independent variables of which that behavior is a function. The present analysis proceeds in the same way by noting first that the dependent variable in cognitive dissonance studies is, with very few exceptions, a subject's self-descriptive statement of an attitude or belief. Indeed, this is the dependent variable in most of the other consistency theory experiments and in nearly all of contemporary social psychology as well. But how are such self-descriptive behaviors acquired? What are their controlling variables? It is to these questions that the analysis turns first.

Self-Perception: A Special Case of Interpersonal Perception

Self-perception, an individual's ability to respond differentially to his own behavior and its controlling variables, is a product of social interaction (Mead, 1934; Ryle, 1949; Skinner, 1957). Verbal statements that are self-descriptive are among the most common responses comprising self-perception, and the techniques employed by the community to teach its members to make such statements would not seem to differ fundamentally from the methods used to teach interpersonal perception in general. The community, however, does face severe limitations in training the individual to make statements describing internal events to which only he has direct access. Skinner (1953, 1957) has analyzed the limited resources available to the community for training its members thus to 'know themselves,' and he has described the inescapable inadequacies of the resulting knowledge.

Skinner suggests that some self-descriptions of internal stimuli can be learned through metaphor or stimulus generalization. The child, for example, can easily learn to describe 'butterflies in the stomach' without explicit discrimination training. More often, however, a socializing community must teach the descriptive responses more directly. In training a child to describe pain, for example, the community, at some point, must teach him the correct response at the critical time when the appropriate private stimuli are impinging upon him. But, the community itself must necessarily identify the 'critical time' on the basis of observable stimuli or responses and implicitly assume that the private stimuli are, in fact, accompanying these public events.

This analysis suggests that many of the self-descriptive statements that appear to be exclusively under the discriminative control of private stimuli may, in fact, still be partially controlled by the same accompanying public events used by the socializing community to infer the individual's inner states. Private stimuli may play a smaller role than the individual himself suspects. For example, by manipulating the external cues of the situation, Schachter and Singer (1962) were able to evoke self-descriptions of emo-

tional states as disparate as euphoria and anger from subjects in whom operationally identical states of physiological arousal had been induced. It appears
that these subjects utilized internal stimuli only to make the gross discrimination that they were emotional, but that the more subtle discrimination of
which emotion they were experiencing was under the control of external
cues.

A similar division of control between internal and external stimuli appears to operate in the domain of attitude statements. Osgood, Suci, and
Tannenbaum (1957) theorize that a pattern of internal responses elicited
by a word or an object comprises the connotative or 'emotional' meaning of
the stimulus for an individual, including his attitude toward it. Using the
Semantic Differential technique, these investigators report that an individual's verbal descriptions of these hypothesized internal responses can be factor analyzed into a very small number of factors, factors which appear to
have extensive cross-cultural generality as well (Osgood *et al.*, 1957). These
findings, too, are consistent with the view that an individual is unable to
make more than a small number of independent discriminations among
stimuli that have never been publicly available to a socializing community.
It is suggested that the many subtle discriminations which individuals do
make when describing their attitudes are based, rather, on the kinds of cues
that are potentially available to an outside observer. In particular, it is suggested that self-descriptive attitude statements can be based on the individual's observations of his own overt behavior and the external stimulus conditions under which it occurs. A number of recent experimental studies
provide support for this proposition.

Several studies have shown that an individual's belief and attitude statements can be manipulated by inducing him to role-play, deliver a persuasive communication, or engage in any behavior that would characteristically
imply his endorsement of a particular set of beliefs (Brehm & Cohen, 1962;
King & Janis, 1956; Scott, 1957; 1959). A recent experimental analysis
of these phenomena of 'self-persuasion' demonstrates that an individual bases
his subsequent beliefs and attitudes on such self-observed behaviors to the
extent that these behaviors occur under circumstances that have in the past
set the occasion for telling the truth (Bem, 1965; 1966). For example,
in one of three studies reported in Bem (1965), subjects were first trained
to tell the truth in the presence of one colored light and to tell lies in
the presence of another. Later in the experimental session, subjects were
required to state attitudes with which they disagreed; one of the two colored
lights was illuminated as each attitude statement was made. It was found that
subjects subsequently endorsed the attitude statements they had uttered in
the presence of the 'truth light' significantly more than attitude statements
they had made in the presence of the 'lie light'; the lights, in short, deter-
minded the degree to which the subjects believed what they had heard themselves say. Furthermore, no subject could report any awareness of the control
exerted by his statements or the lights over his subsequent attitudes.

In another study, the same technique was employed to demonstrate that
an individual can be induced to believe in 'false confessions' he has made,
but only if they are uttered in the presence of the 'truth light' (Bem, 1966).
These several studies also illustrate that the control over an individual's beliefs and attitudes exerted by his overt behavior is vitiated to the extent that
situational cues imply that the behavior is deceitful or, more generally, is

being emitted for immediate specific reinforcement. For example, just as a communicator is more persuasive to others if he is known to be receiving no payment for his communication, so too, it is found that he is more likely to believe himself under such circumstances (Bem, 1965). The effectiveness of self-persuasion can thus be altered by many of the techniques typically used to manipulate the credibility of any persuasive communicator.

The major implication of these findings is that, to the extent that internal stimuli are not controlling, an individual's attitude statements may be viewed as inferences from observations of his own overt behavior and its accompanying stimulus variables. As such, his statements are functionally similar to those that any outside observer could make about him. When the answer to the question, "Do you like brown bread?" is "I guess I do, I'm always eating it," it seems unnecessary to invoke a fount of privileged self-knowledge to account for the reply. In such a case the reply is functionally equivalent to one his wife might give for him: "I guess he does, he is always eating it." Only to the extent that 'brown bread' elicits strongly conditioned internal responses might he have additional evidence, not currently available to his wife, on which to base his self-descriptive attitude statement.

The present analysis of dissonance phenomena, then, will rest upon the single empirical generalization that an individual's belief and attitude statements and the beliefs and attitudes that an outside observer would attribute to him are often functionally similar in that both are partial 'inferences' from the same evidence: the public behaviors and accompanying stimulus cues upon which the socializing community has relied in training him to make such self-descriptive statements in the first place.

THE FORCED-COMPLIANCE STUDIES

The most frequently cited evidence for dissonance theory comes from an experimental procedure known as the forced-compliance paradigm. In these experiments, an individual is induced to engage in some behavior that would imply his endorsement of a particular set of beliefs or attitudes. Following his behavior, his 'actual' attitude or belief is assessed to see if it is a function of the behavior in which he has engaged and of the manipulated stimulus conditions under which it was evoked. The best known and most widely quoted study of this type was conducted by Festinger and Carlsmith (1959). In their experiment, 60 undergraduates were randomly assigned to one of three experimental conditions. In the $1 condition, the subject was first required to perform long repetitive laboratory tasks in an individual experimental session. He was then hired by the experimenter as an 'assistant' and paid $1 to tell a waiting fellow student (a stooge) that the tasks were enjoyable and interesting. In the $20 condition, each subject was hired for $20 to do the same thing. Control subjects simply engaged in the repetitive tasks. After the experiment, each subject indicated how much he had enjoyed the tasks. The results show that the subjects paid $1 evaluated the tasks as significantly more enjoyable than did subjects who had been paid $20. The $20 subjects did not express attitudes significantly different from those expressed by the control subjects.

Dissonance theory interprets these findings by noting that all subjects initially hold the cognition that the tasks are dull and boring. In addition, however, the experimental subjects have the cognition that they have expressed favorable attitudes toward the tasks to a fellow student. These two cognitions are dissonant for subjects in the $1 condition because their overt behavior does not 'follow from' their cognition about the task, nor does it follow from the small compensation they are receiving. To reduce the resulting dissonance, they change their cognition about the task so that it is consistent with their overt behavior: They become more favorable toward the tasks. Subjects in the $20 condition, however, experience little or no dissonance because engaging in such behavior 'follows from' the large compensation they are receiving. Hence, their final attitudes do not differ from those of the control group.

In contrast with this explanation, the present analysis views these results as a case of self-perception. Consider the viewpoint of an outside observer who hears the individual making favorable statements about the tasks to a fellow student, and who further knows that the individual was paid $1 ($20) to do so. This hypothetical observer is then asked to state the actual attitude of the individual he has heard. An outside observer would almost certainly judge a $20 communicator to be 'manding' reinforcement (Skinner, 1957); that is, his behavior appears to be under the control of the reinforcement contingencies of the money and not at all under the discriminative control of the tasks he appears to be describing. In other words, the $20 communicator is not credible in that his statements cannot be used as a guide for inferring his actual attitudes. Hence, the observer could conclude that the individual found such repetitive tasks dull and boring in spite of what he had said. Although the behavior of a $1 communicator also has some mand properties, an outside observer would be more likely to judge him to be expressing his actual attitudes and hence would infer the communicator's attitude from the content of the communication itself. He would thus judge this individual to be favorable toward the tasks. If one now places the hypothetical observer and the communicator into the same skin, the findings obtained by Festinger and Carlsmith are the result. There is no aversive motivational pressure postulated; the dependent variable is viewed simply as a self-judgment based on the available evidence, evidence that includes the apparent controlling variables of the observed behavior.

If this analysis of the findings is correct, then it should be possible to replicate the inverse functional relation between amount of compensation and the final attitude statement by actually letting an outside observer try to infer the attitude of a subject in the original study. Conceptually, this replicates the Festinger-Carlsmith experiment with the single exception that the observer and the observed are no longer the same individual. More precisely, this provides a *simulation* of the Festinger-Carlsmith experiment, a test of the hypothesis that self-judgments and interpersonal judgments are 'outputs' of the same 'program.' Like a computer simulation, then, a successful simulation provides a sufficiency test of the model of the process that we propose lies behind the dissonance phenomenon.

AN INTERPERSONAL SIMULATION OF THE FESTINGER-CARLSMITH EXPERIMENT

Seventy-five college undergraduates participated in an experiment designed to "determine how accurately people can judge another person." Twenty-five subjects each served in a $1, a $20, or a Control condition. All subjects listened to a tape recording which described a college sophomore named Bob Downing, who had participated in an experiment involving two motor tasks. The tasks were described in detail, but nonevaluatively; the alleged purpose of the experiment was also described. At this point, the control subjects were asked to evaluate Bob's attitudes toward the tasks. The experimental subjects were further told that Bob had accepted an offer of $1 [$20] to go into the waiting room, tell the next subject that the tasks were fun, and to be prepared to do this again in the future if they needed him. The subjects then listened to a brief conversation which they were told was an actual recording of Bob and the girl subject who was in the waiting room. Bob was heard to argue rather imaginatively that the tasks were fun and enjoyable, while the girl responded very little except for the comments that Festinger and Carlsmith's stooge was instructed to make. The recorded conversation was identical for both experimental conditions in order to remain true to the original study in which no differences in persuasiveness were found between the $1 and the $20 communications. In sum, the situation attempted to duplicate on tape the situation actually experienced by Festinger and Carlsmith's subjects.

All subjects estimated Bob's responses to the same set of questions employed in the original study. The key question required subjects to rate Bob's attitude toward the tasks on a scale from -5 to $+5$, where -5 means that the tasks were extremely dull and boring, $+5$ means they were extremely interesting and enjoyable, and 0 means they were neutral, neither interesting nor uninteresting.

Results

Table 1 shows the mean ratings for the key question given by the subjects in all three conditions of both the original Festinger and Carlsmith experiment and the present simulation.

TABLE 1

Attitude Ratings and Interpersonal Estimates of
Attitude Ratings toward the Tasks for Each Condition

		Experimental Condition	
Study	Control	$1 Compensation	$20 Compensation
Festinger-Carlsmith (*N* = 20 in each condition)	−0.45	+1.35	−0.05
Interpersonal Simulation (*N* = 25 in each condition)	−1.56	+0.52	−1.96

The results show that in both studies the $1 and Control conditions are on different sides of the neutral point and are significantly different from one another at the .02 level of significance ($t = 2.48$ in the original and $t = 2.60$ in our study).[1] In both studies, the $1 condition produced signifi-

---

[1] All significance levels reported are based on 2-tailed tests.

cantly more favorable ratings toward the tasks than did the $20 condition ($t = 2.22$, $p < .03$, and $t = 3.52$, $p < .001$ in the original and present studies, respectively.) In neither study is the $20 condition significantly different from the Control condition; and, finally, in neither study were there any significant differences between conditions on the other questions asked of the subjects about the experiment. Thus, the inverse relation between amount of compensation and the final attitude rating is clearly replicated; and, even though our conceptual model does not require the interpersonal judgments actually to duplicate those of the original subjects, it is seen that the two sets of ratings are quite comparable on the 10-point scales.

Since the above interpersonal study was conducted, Jones (1966) obtained subjects' attitudes and observers' judgments in the same experiment. Again, the observers' judgments not only replicated the inverse functional relation displayed by the attitude statements of the subjects themselves, but the actual scale positions of observers and subjects were again similar.

These successful replications of the functional relation reported by Festinger and Carlsmith provide support for the self-perception analysis. The original subjects may be viewed as simply making self-judgments based on the same kinds of public evidence that the community originally employed in training them to infer the attitudes of any communicator, themselves included. It is not necessary to postulate an aversive motivational drive to avoid inconsistency.

The merits of alternative formulations to an established theory are often sought in their ability to explicate functional relations about which the original theory must remain mute. Accordingly, the analysis now turns to a pattern of related findings which have not been adequately accommodated by dissonance theory: the observed relationships between the *amount* of behavior evoked from the subject in a forced-compliance setting and his final attitude statements.

A number of forced-compliance experiments have demonstrated that the differential effects of the stimulus manipulations on attitude statements can be obtained even before the individual engages in the behavior to which he has committed himself (Brehm & Cohen, 1962, pp. 115–116). That is, the behavior of volunteering to engage in the behavior is sufficient to control the individual's subsequent self-judgment of attitude. (The self-perception interpretation of this effect has also been confirmed by an interpersonal simulation [Bem, 1965].) In fact, in an experiment in which subjects volunteered to write essays against their initial opinions, Rabbie, Brehm, and Cohen (1959) report that the mean of attitude ratings obtained before the essays were actually written was not significantly different from the mean of attitude ratings obtained after the essays were written. But the variance across subjects was much greater in the latter case. That is, actually writing the essays increases *and* decreases the initial effect of volunteering. In addition, there was a negative relationship between the number of arguments the subject wrote and the degree to which his final attitude statement agreed with the position advocated in the essay. On the other hand, Cohen, Brehm, and Fleming (1958) report a positive relationship between "original arguments" and amount of attitude change, but this relationship appeared in only one of the experimental conditions. Unpublished data from the Festinger-Carlsmith experiment show a negative correlation in one condition between attitude ratings and "number and variety" of arguments and a positive correlation in the other (reported by Brehm & Cohen, 1962, p. 119). Finally, when subjects themselves rate the quality of their persuasive communications, the confusion is further compounded. Brehm and Cohen conclude that "the role of discrepant verbal behavior in the arousal and reduction of dissonance remains unclear" (p. 121). Additional complexities in the relationships are presented in Section IV F of this volume. How might the self-perception analysis treat these effects?

If an outside observer begins with the discrimination that a communicator is credible, then the more arguments put forth, the more persuasive the speaker might well become, *if* nothing intervenes to change the observer's judgment of the communicator's credibility. If, however, the observer discriminates the communicator as manding reinforcement, then it may be that the more insistent the speaker becomes in pushing his point of view, the more it appears to the observer that he 'doth protest too much,' and the less likely it is that the speaker's statements will be taken to express his 'actual' attitudes.

Now consider the self-observer. If subjects in the dissonance experiments begin with the discrimination that they are not manding (subjects in the Low Compensation conditions, for example), then the more arguments they put forth, the more self-persuasive they might become. For any given subject, however, presenting a communication counter to his initial position might itself provide him with the cues that he is manding and hence destroy the initial effect of volunteering under nonmand conditions; he will become less self-persuasive as he continues. This analysis, then, leads one to expect the increased variability in postessay as compared to pre-essay measures of attitude. It is clear, however, that to confirm this analysis, the hypothesized discrimination of credibility must be brought under experimental control rather than being left under the control of the unique past histories of individual subjects. To do this, the Festinger-Carlsmith experiment is again used as an illustrative example.

AN EXTENDED INTERPERSONAL SIMULATION OF THE FESTINGER–CARLSMITH EXPERIMENT

Festinger and Carlsmith found that within the $1 condition, the greater the number and variety of arguments stated by the subject about the tasks, the more favorable his final evaluation was of them. Within the $20 condition, however, the greater the number and variety of arguments, the less favorable his final rating. The following study thus seeks to replicate this pattern of results with interpersonal observers.

Method

In the earlier simulation, the persuasive communication heard by the subjects was identical for both conditions. All subjects heard the speaker present a fairly imaginative and lengthy set of reasons as to why he had enjoyed the tasks. For the present extension, a second communication was designed, which was somewhat shorter and contained comparatively unimaginative arguments. The simulation was then re-run on an additional 50 subjects assigned either to a $1 or a $20 condition. Subjects were again asked to estimate the actual attitude of the speaker. Thus, except for the length and variety of arguments in the communication, this simulation is identical with the earlier one. The total design, then, contains four experimental groups: $1-long communication, $1-short communication, $20-long communication, and $20-short communication.

If the present analysis is correct, then within the $1 condition, where the communicator is more likely to be perceived as credible, the long communication should lead interpersonal observers to infer that the communicator enjoyed the tasks more than the short communication would. Within the $20 condition, however, the long communication should be *less* persuasive than the short one; the longer the speaker carries on, the harder he appears to be trying to earn his $20. He "doth protest too much." Thus, an interaction effect is predicted between the two variables of communication length and amount of compensation. It will be noted that this is equivalent to saying that the 'dissonance' effect, the inverse functional relation between compensation and attitude change, is itself a function of communication length. The shorter the communication, the smaller the inverse relationship should become, perhaps even reversing itself at very short communication lengths.

Results

Table 2 displays the results. It will be recalled that scores can range from −5 to +5, the higher the score, the more favorable the communicator is judged to be toward the tasks.

TABLE 2

Interpersonal Estimates of
Attitude Ratings Toward the Tasks
($N = 25$ in each cell)

Experimental Condition	Long Communication	Short Communication
$1 Compensation	+0.52	−1.04
$20 Compensation	−1.96	−0.64

An analysis of the results in Table 2 indicates that the interpersonal model of self-perception is supported. By employing attitude estimates of outside observers, the study replicates Festinger and Carlsmith's positive correlation between number of arguments and attitude change within the $1 condition and the negative correlation between these two variables within the $20 condition. The interaction effect is significant at the .01 level ($F = 7.80$, $df = 1, 96$). The primary 'dissonance' effect, reported earlier, is revealed by a significant main effect of the compensation variable ($F = 4.07$, $p < .05$). As also noted earlier, however, the 'dissonance' effect is itself a function of communication length, and the main effect is due entirely to the inverse relation appearing in the conditions employing the longer communication, the communication designed to duplicate those found in the original Festinger-Carlsmith experiment. A nonsignificant reversal actually appears when the very short communication is employed. It may be that communication length is thus one of the confounding parameters responsible for the conflicting findings, including reversals, reported in forced-compliance experiments, a point discussed by Aronson (1967). If this is so, then the present conceptualization might provide a reconciliation of the conflicting results (cf. Bem, 1965; McGuire, 1966a, pp. 494–496).

The interpersonal simulations presented here are illustrative of others which have been reported elsewhere (Bem, 1965; 1967). It has been shown that the present analysis applies as well to forced-compliance experiments which utilize compensations much smaller than $20, to studies which manipulate variables other than the amount of compensation, and to studies which evoke different behaviors from the subject. Alternative dependent variables, including nonverbal measures, have also been discussed; and, finally, experiments that employ paradigms other than the forced-compliance procedures have been successfully analyzed and simulated within the present theoretical framework (Bem, 1967). In sum, it is suggested that the interpersonal model of self-perception provides a viable alternative to the theory of cognitive dissonance in accounting for its major phenomena.

SOME METATHEORETICAL CONSIDERATIONS

At the beginning of this chapter, some contrasts were noted between the conceptual approach typified by dissonance theory and the behavioral approach respresented here by the functional analysis of self-perception. It was pointed out that the behaviorist's goal is to account for observed relations between current stimuli and responses in terms of an individual's past training history and functional relations discovered in the experimental analysis of simpler behaviors. The behaviorist's functional analysis of complex behaviors like dissonance phenomena was thus seen to be based on empirical generalization, a feature which infuses it with an inductive flavor and spirit.

In contrast, the dissonance theorists clearly prefer the 'deductive' nature of their theory and explicitly derogate the "weakness of an empirical generalization as compared with a true theoretical explanation" (Lawrence & Festinger, 1962, p. 17). This criticism of the behaviorist's functional analysis, namely, that it has no deductive fertility or predictive power, is often expressed. The radical behaviorist, so the criticism goes, will not venture a specific prediction without knowing the complete reinforcement history of the organism. He cannot provide a 'true theoretical explanation.'

It is suggested here that a functional analysis appears to have limited predictive power only because it makes explicit the kinds of knowledge about the past and present controlling variables that any theorist must have if he is to predict behavior accurately. How, for example, do the dissonance theorists conclude that dissonance is present in a particular case? That is, how do they decide when one cognition does not 'follow from' another? According to Festinger, "the vagueness in the conceptual definition of dissonance—namely, two elements are dissonant if, considered alone, the [contradictory] of one follows from the other—lies in the words 'follows from' .... One element may follow from another because of logic, because of cultural mores, because of things one has experienced and learned, and perhaps in other senses too" (1957, p. 278). Five years later, Brehm and Cohen note that "the 'follows from' relationship can sometimes be determined empirically but is limited by our abilities to specify and measure cognitions and the relationships among them ... the 'follows from' relationship is not always clear and specifiable" (1962, pp. 11–12).

In actual practice, however, the dissonance theorists do not experience difficulty in inferring the existence of dissonance from their stimulus operations. But this is so precisely because in that inference the dissonance theorists sneak through the back door the very knowledge they claim to do without. It is in that inference that they implicitly make use of the fact that they have been raised by the same socializing community as their subjects. The dissonance theorists can thus infer that a $1 compensation will produce more dissonance than a $20 compensation, just as it has been *our* common history with these same subjects that permits *us* to speculate that the difference in compensation represents a difference in the mand properties of the induced behavior. Interpersonal observers are successful in replicating dissonance phenomena for the same reason. Dissonance theorists and radical behaviorists need the same kinds of knowledge. Only the behaviorists, however, take as their explicit obligation the necessity of accounting for both their subjects' *and their own* responses to such variables.

In sum, it is concluded that the greater 'deductive fertility' of dissonance theory is largely illusory. In the process of adequately explicating the phrase 'follows from' in their fundamental statement, the dissonance theorists will necessarily have to perform the explicit functional analysis they had hoped to finesse. It remains our conviction that the appeal to hypothetical internal states of the organism for explanations of behavior can become heuristically undesirable. Such diversion often appears to retard and deflect the thrust of the analysis that is ultimately required.

CHAPTER 15

The Motivational Significance of Collative Variables and Conflict

D. E. Berlyne
University of Toronto

Since about 1950, it has become clear that the events that motivate behavior and the events that reinforce learned responses do not belong to special classes with limited membership. Stimuli associated with activities like feeding and mating, and with pain or protection against pain have unusual motivational potency and reinforcement value. They have obvious and exceptional biological significance, and they are known to activate special centers in the limbic system and hypothalamus. But they are not by any means the only sources of motivation or reinforcement. On the contrary, it is now evident that virtually any kind of stimulus, external or internal, can be motivating or reinforcing in suitable circumstances.

This lesson has been brought home to us by quite a variety of experimental findings. As studies of exploratory, aesthetic, and playful behavior have demonstrated, higher animals and human beings will put a great deal of effort into exposing themselves to stimuli with no biologically important impact on tissues outside the sense organs and nervous system (Berlyne, 1960, 1967). Rats and human infants, among other species, can be quite powerfully rewarded by such arbitrary external occurrences as a light coming on or getting brighter, a buzzer or tone sounding, or even a mild electric shock (Berlyne, 1960; Stevenson & Odom, 1964; Berlyne, Salapatek, Gelman, & Zener, 1964; Harrington & Linder, 1964). One particularly significant fact is that the relation between the reinforcer and the reinforced can be reversible. Interestingly enough, this has been demonstrated both for instrumental conditioning in the United States and for classical conditioning in the USSR. Premack (1965) has shown that, if an opportunity to indulge in activity A reinforces activity B, an opportunity for B can reinforce A if the situation is somewhat different. For example, the rat may learn to run more vigorously if he can drink afterwards, or he may learn to drink more vigorously if he is able to run afterwards. Asratian's (1965) experiments have indicated that the usual classical-conditioning experiment, in which an indifferent

The preparation of this paper and research mentioned in it were supported by grants MH-06324 and MH-12528 from the U.S. National Institute of Mental Health, APT-73 and APB-73 from the National Research Council of Canada, and No. 70 from the Ontario Mental Health Foundation.

stimulus is paired with a powerful stimulus of biological importance, can be misleading and suggest an asymmetry that is not necessarily there. If two indifferent stimuli (e.g., a passive flexion of a limb and a tone) or two biologically important stimuli (e.g., a puff of air to the eye and a shock to a limb) are paired, symmetrical two-way associations can be established. So whether something reinforces or is reinforced depends on the situation. Various factors can incline it more toward the one role or the other or give rise to bidirectional learning in which both roles are more or less equally evident.

It seems, therefore, that many kinds of stimuli can be motivating or reinforcing. But not all stimuli are, and so we have to identify the conditions in which stimuli without special biological significance (so-called indifferent stimuli) take on motivational properties. One answer, implicit in the Freudian theories of the wish and of cathexis and in neobehaviorist theories of secondary (acquired) drive and secondary (conditioned) reinforcement, is that this occurs when indifferent stimuli become associated, through contiguity or through similarity, with primary distress or gratifications. An additional answer, to be found in the version of Hullian theory propagated by Miller and Dollard (1941) but also adumbrated by Freud (1915), is that all stimuli are motivating or drive-inducing in proportion to their intensity and that any event that reduces the overall intensity of stimulation or excitation will be rewarding.

These two hypotheses have certainly broadened the scope of motivation theory focused on the concept of 'drive' and can account for many cases. But they certainly do not tell the whole story. By now, many different lines of evidence (Berlyne, 1960, 1963, 1966a) have shown that disturbing and rewarding potentialities of stimulus patterns can depend on how novel they are, how far they tally with, or deviate from, what was expected, how complex they are, how strongly they contrast with their backgrounds, their rate of change, how strange or puzzling or inexplicable they are, and how much uncertainty they induce about their sequelae or accompaniments. These are the properties for which I have proposed the term 'collative,' since they all involve collation or comparison of stimulus elements. Sometimes it is a matter of comparing elements that appear simultaneously in different sectors of one stimulus field. At other times, it is a matter of comparing what is perceived now with what has been perceived in the past.

Although for convenience we often speak of novelty, complexity, and the like as attributes of external stimulus patterns, they are actually relations between physicochemical and statistical attributes of external events and attributes of the subject. They depend on interactions between what is outside and what is inside, the most important internal factors in this regard being traces left by prior encounters with relevant events in the past. Something may be highly novel, surprising, or complex for an individual on one occasion, but a physically identical pattern will be far from novel, surprising, or complex for the same individual on another occasion. It all depends on the kinds of learning or short-term retention that permit us to recognize a stimulus pattern as familiar or not, to form expectations and to see whether they are fulfilled or violated, to organize intricate combinations of elements into coherent subwholes, to note repetitions or discrepancies among components.

COLLATIVE VARIABLES AND INFORMATION THEORY

Since indications are steadily accumulating (Berlyne, 1960, 1967) that the collative variables have similar motivational effects and are interchangeable in many respects, we have to ask what they might all have in common to give them these effects. Little has been done to attack this problem directly and comprehensively, but the makings of several possible solutions are to be found in the literature.

Some hints regarding the common essence of the collative variables may come from their affinities with the concepts of information theory. Novel, surprising, or highly complex patterns tend to occur with relatively low probability, which implies that they have relatively high information content. We can argue that more complex or irregular patterns bear more information on the grounds that they are selected from larger populations (Garner, 1962). They can be said to involve greater uncertainty in the sense that, when one portion has been examined, it is relatively hard to predict what other portions will be like (Attneave, 1954). The more novel or surprising a stimulus, the more uncertainty there is apt to be about its antecedents or about what will follow it. In general, there are close associations between uncertainty and entropy or disorder and between redundancy or information transmission and recurrent sequences or highly organized structures.

Nevertheless, these information-theoretic analyses have their limitations. First of all, information-theoretic (i.e., objective) amount of information and uncertainty depend on objective probability distributions, and there is good reason to believe that the motivational phenomena in which we are interested depend more closely on subjective information content and on subjective uncertainty, which can be conceived as analogous functions of subjective probabilities. Subjective probabilities and uncertainties tend to increase with their objective counterparts (e.g., Berlyne, 1962; Driscoll, Tognoli, & Lanzetta, 1966), but they do not mirror them faithfully. Furthermore, informational measures, whether objective or subjective, depend solely on probabilities, which means on relative strengths of responses corresponding to stimulus events. They are incapable of reflecting absolute strengths, and yet there is good reason to suppose that motivational effects can vary with absolute strengths when relative strengths remain constant (Berlyne, 1957, 1960).

THE CONFLICT HYPOTHESIS

Three other kinds of approach have acquired some following and thus warrant consideration. First, there are those who hold the critical condition for exploratory behavior or affective reaction to be some kind of *disparity* or discriminable difference between the kind of stimulus that an organism receives and the kind of stimulus that it was prepared to receive (e.g., Mc-Clelland *et al.*, 1953; Anokhin, 1958; Voronin & Sokolov, 1960). Secondly, some place the emphasis on *inconsistency* or lack of agreement between information contents of different stimulus inputs, whether received simultaneously or received at different times. This inconsistency depends on similarity or dissimilarity of implications rather than of physical attributes, which is what distinguishes this view from the disparity view. One of its principal exponents has been Hunt (1963, 1965), but many theories using notions of 'cognitive inconsistency' can presumably be placed in this category. Finally, there is the conceptualization offered by Dember and Earl (1957), who focus on the degree of *stimulus change* experienced as simultaneously present or successive stimulus elements are scanned in turn, and the somewhat similar conceptualization offered by Andrew (1963), who discusses the special biological roles of stimuli that contrast strongly with their contexts.

The chief shortcoming of all three of these approaches is that each of them fits one particular group of cases admirably but is difficult to apply to other situations in which collative variables have motivational effects. Thus none of them can satisfy our quest for a crucial ingredient that might account for effects common to such an apparent diversity of factors.

The hypothesis that I myself have been pursuing is that collative variables all work through *conflict*. Rather similar suggestions have been offered by Polezhaev (1958) and by Grastyan's group (Karmos *et al.*, 1965) with special reference to the determinants of the orientation reaction in animals. By 'conflict' is meant a state of affairs containing stimulus conditions that are associated with incompatible responses, i.e., responses whose simultaneous performance is excluded. This notion of conflict is of course most clearly applicable to situations in which mutually exclusive motor responses are instigated. It can, however, be extended to situations in which central neural events seem alone to be involved and there is no immediately manifest motor output. It is assumed that, in the cases in question, neural processes are initiated, each of which would complete itself with a motor output if it were acting alone. When, however, several are initiated together, reciprocal interference causes all of them to be curtailed or attenuated, so that the corresponding bodily movements do not ensue.

Conceived in this way, conflict is a matter of degree. When one considers how many stimulus events are bombarding sensory surfaces during every movement of waking life and how every perceived object and event must be associated with some motor response, if it is only a descriptive verbal response or a locomotor approach response, we can see how conflict must always be present to some extent. But most of the time there are evidently mechanisms at work to keep its disturbing effects within bounds (Berlyne, 1965, Ch. 2). Degree of conflict will, however, fluctuate continually, reaching uncomfortable levels from time to time.

We therefore need at least some rudimentary conception of a degree-of-conflict function. In considering the properties such a function should have, one arrives at what seem to be three reasonable principles, namely that degree of conflict should increase with (a) the number of competing response tendencies, (b) the extent to which their strengths approach equality, and (c) their total absolute strength. In order to extend the conception to cases of partial compatibility (which might be of importance in the domain of intellectual processes), one can add (d) degree of incompatibility. These principles (Berlyne, 1957; 1960, Ch. 2) extend some suggestions of Brown and Farber (1951). It is noteworthy that the first two of them resemble, in a way that surely excludes coincidence, the two salient characteristics of the uncertainty function in information theory. The similarity to the principles determining degree of 'dissonance' in Festinger's (1957) theory is also interesting.

The drawbacks of the conflict hypothesis are obvious. It lacks precision, particularly when applied to some situations in which collative variables are at work. Nevertheless, as pointed out elsewhere (Berlyne, 1964; 1965, Ch. 1), imprecision must not be confused with vagueness and is part of the price that must be paid for attempts at integration.

The conflict hypothesis has, however, certain virtues to be claimed for it. First, it arises out of an attempt to find a conceptualization that can be applied to all the situations in which collative stimulus properties play important motivational roles. Secondly, it enables us to speculate about the manner in which motivational consequences of collative properties are produced in the central nervous system. It is agreed implicitly by the adherents of all the approaches we have just reviewed that, in the situations in question, a number of neural processes, whether they be set in motion by external stimuli or deposited by previous learning and revived by central events, interact in an inharmonious manner. Mutually interfering constellations of activity can presumably occur at widely separated points of the cerebral cortex, and yet common motivational effects must result from excitation in some one controlling area, presumably in the brain stem. One conjecture that does not seem incompatible with neurophysiological knowledge (see Berlyne, 1960) is that the reticular formation, having been activated by incoming stimulation, remains activated until it receives an inhibitory signal from some higher, cortical center. Such a signal may be given when the stimulation has been recognized or organized or evaluated. If, on the other hand, mutually discrepant neural processes meet one another somewhere in the cortex, the reticular formation may fail to receive quieting impulses from above, so that arousal remains high (see also Back's comments on the reticular formation, Chapter 19). Thirdly, the conflict hypothesis permits us to venture a speculative answer to the question of why subjection to inconsistent items of information or to something unprecedented and unaccountable or to something that does not fit expectations can be so disturbing. If we recall that the whole brain can be regarded originally and ultimately as an instrument for selecting motor responses (see Sperry, 1952), we can understand that failure to resolve conflict may threaten adaptation by preventing any motor activity from achieving prepotency and completing itself while competitors are held in check. The vigor of reactions to conflict or to harbingers of conflict is thus explicable.

COLLATIVE VARIABLES AND AROUSAL

One clue that we can hardly afford to ignore is the ability of the collative variables to raise arousal. If, as several writers have suggested (Berlyne, 1960, 1963), arousal is identifiable with drive, in at least some of its aspects, the implication is that collative properties can give external or internal stimulus patterns the power to induce drive. There are actually three main kinds of evidence linking the motivational role of collative variables with changes in arousal level. First, work on the orientation reaction (Sokolov, 1958) shows that exploratory behavior, whose strength and direction depend so heavily on collative variables, is accompanied by most of the recognized indices of heightened arousal. Secondly, some of our own experiments (Berlyne, 1961; Berlyne, Craw, Salapatek, & Lewis, 1963; Berlyne & McDonnell, 1965), in which human subjects were exposed to visual patterns while galvanic skin response or duration of electroencephalic desynchronization was recorded, have shown the principal collative properties—novelty, surprisingness, incongruity, complexity—to affect the magnitude of the orientation reaction. Lastly, there is evidence that the reward value of 'indifferent stimuli' depends on collative properties interacting with arousal level, which seems to imply at least some convergence between the neural processes through which these properties exert their motivational effects and those controlling arousal level (Berlyne, Koenig, & Hirota, 1966; Berlyne, in press).

Since we have been pursuing the hypothesis that the motivational effect of the collative variables depends on conflict, the prediction that indices of arousal will be affected by degrees of conflict is a particularly crucial one. In an experiment (Berlyne, 1961), in which care was taken to separate degree of conflict from other variables with which it is often confounded, a tendency of GSR amplitude to be greater with high conflict than with low conflict was demonstrated. The effects of subjective uncertainty on arousal measures are also of interest, in view of the assumption that subjective uncertainty is a form of conflict; the competing responses will in this case be internal representations of alternative events that are inaccessible to the sense organs, whether because they belong to the future or for some other reason. In our laboratory, Nicki (1968) has used pictures of varying degrees of blurredness and measured subjective uncertainty by asking subjects to make guesses regarding the object that might be represented. Subjective uncertainty, judged by the number of guesses offered and the subjects' estimates of confidence in them, varied curvilinearly with blurredness, reaching a maximum at an intermediate degree. Berlyne and Borsa (1968) exposed pictures with approximately this same degree of blurredness for 4 seconds each in an EEG experiment and found them to evoke longer-lasting desynchronization than clear versions of the same pictures. That this effect was due to subjective uncertainty was confirmed in a second experiment. The effect did not appear when each blurred picture was immediately preceded by the corresponding clear picture, so that uncertainty with regard to the content was eliminated, but it was still in evidence when each blurred picture was immediately followed by its clear counterpart.

Another electrocortical measure has likewise been found to indicate greater arousal in situations where greater subjective uncertainty could be expected. Slower d.c. baseline shifts appear when a subject is expecting a faint tone that he is told will be difficult to detect than when he is expecting a louder tone (Rebert et al., 1967). Averaged evoked-potential amplitude increases with the information content of a stimulus, i.e., with the degree of uncertainty that its occurrence resolves (Sutton et al., 1965, 1967).

UNCERTAINTY REDUCTION AND REWARD

Nicki (1968) has obtained evidence that subjective uncertainty is an aversive condition, i.e., a condition whose termination is rewarding. Such a condition may be identified with what has in previous writings (Berlyne, 1957, 1960) been termed 'perceptual curiosity.' He studied human subjects in a situation analogous to the familiar T maze that has so often been used with rats. In one experiment, the subject on each trial pressed either of two telegraph keys, which resulted in the replacement of a blurred picture by a clear picture on a screen. For half of the subjects, the blurred picture to which they were exposed before making the response was a blurred version of the clear picture produced by the left-hand key. For the remainder, it was a blurred version of the clear picture produced by the right-hand key. Subjects learned within a few trials to press predominantly the key that cleared up the blurred slide, the asymptote being around 80 per cent. When three different degrees of blurredness were used in a later experiment, the effect was found only with the intermediate degree of blurredness, which was the one that had been shown previously to generate the most subjective uncertainty. The effect disappeared when projection of the blurred picture was preceded by the corresponding clear picture, so that, when the clear picture appeared for a second time as a consequence of key pressing, it no longer reduced any uncertainty. These experiments seem to indicate that termination of subjective uncertainty can reinforce an instrumental response. In other words, the reward value of seeing a picture is increased by prior induction of subjective uncertainty regarding its properties.

AVERSIVE AND REWARDING EFFECTS OF AROUSAL INCREMENT

So far, this discussion has concentrated on the aversive or disturbing effects of collative stimulus properties. It has been hypothesized that these effects occur because novelty, surprisingness, complexity, and ambiguity induce subjective uncertainty and other forms of conflict, through which arousal is driven up to uncomfortably high levels. When an aversive condition is generated in this way, it can be relieved by withdrawal from the stimulus responsible for it or alternatively by continued exposure to this stimulus. Continued exposure to stimuli high in collative properties may alleviate the disturbance (and consequently be sought) either through habituation or by affording access to additional information that reduces uncertainty.

A certain amount of arousal potential (to use a term meant to cover the various collative and other stimulus properties that tend to drive up arousal) may be welcomed as a means of relieving boredom, an aversive condition induced by environments that are inordinately monotonous, familiar, or devoid of stimulation. Various considerations favor the supposition that boredom involves intolerably high arousal, due to release of brain-stem centers from inhibitory influences that they normally receive from an active cerebral cortex (Berlyne, 1960, 1963). According to available psychophysiological evidence, autonomic and somatic indices manifest high arousal during sensory restriction, although EEG waves are generally slow and thus indicative of a relatively inactivated cortex (Schultz, 1965).

Some forms of animal and human behavior, however, apparently represent searches for arousal-raising stimulation that do not fit any of these cases. The reward value of the stimulation resulting from them does not seem to come from alleviation of any prior aversive condition. This applies to "diversive exploratory behavior" (Berlyne, 1960), which does not seek out stimulation from specific sources and has nothing to do with 'perceptual curiosity.' A large part, but not all, of the behavior covered by terms such as 'play,' 'entertainment,' 'art,' and 'humor' (Berlyne, 1960, 1968) fits this category.

The fact that stimulus patterns high in collative properties are sometimes avoided, sometimes sought because they relieve some aversive condition, and sometimes sought for reasons that have little to do with relief of an aversive condition is what we should expect if collative variables exert their motivational effects through changes in arousal. The evidence on relations between arousal and reinforcement has been reviewed elsewhere (Berlyne, 1967). Data from a great variety of lines of research, including neurophysiology, animal learning, verbal learning, psychopharmacology, and experimental aesthetics suggest that, whereas extreme increases in arousal are aversive and their alleviation is rewarding, moderate arousal increments are rewarding regardless of whether they are soon reversed or not. It seems likely that two antagonistic systems in the brain can be activated by the factors (including the collative stimulus properties) that increase arousal. One is a reward system, and the other, requiring a higher input of arousal potential for it to be activated, is an aversion system which inhibits the reward system.

CONCEPTUAL CONFLICT

With some additional superstructure, the conflict hypothesis can be expanded to cover motivational aspects of epistemic behavior, by which is meant behavior aimed at the acquisition of knowledge, i.e., of information to be stored in the form of symbolic structures. The kind of motivational condition (epistemic curiosity) that motivates intellectual inquiry (directed thinking, consultation of textual or oral authorities, observation, and experimentation) can be induced by strange or puzzling external situations, but here the ideational or symbolic responses associated with external stimuli are critical. The kind of conflict that is pertinent here is 'conceptual conflict.' The mutually interfering responses are implicit symbolic responses—beliefs, attitudes, evaluations (Berlyne, 1954a; 1960, Chs. 10, 11; 1965, Chs. 9, 10). To apply to intellectual functions a terminology that originated in very different fields of study and, above all, to speak of intellectual processes as 'implicit responses' are practices that have both their pros and their cons. If pursued with all due caution, however, they can be defended as aids to arriving at an integrative view of a variety of psychological phenomena (Berlyne, 1965, Ch. 1). When we are worried about intellectual problems that seem to have no immediate bearing on practical issues, the presence of conflict may plausibly be inferred, since sooner or later we may be called upon to select a course of action in accordance with our beliefs, attitudes, or evaluations, and this selection will be gravely hampered if inconsistencies have not been resolved.

The convergence between the line of thought outlined here and those that have led to concepts of cognitive inconsistency from other starting points is evident. There are, however, two important differences.

First, I myself have avoided both the word and the concept of 'cognition' because I can see no satisfactory way of defining the 'cognitive' that does not either encompass everything in psychology or commit one prematurely to a particular position on issues that must still be regarded as controversial (Berlyne, 1967). On the other hand, the distinction between symbolic and nonsymbolic responses seems to be one that can be drawn with at least a provisionally tolerable degree of clarity and corresponds to a nonarbitrary boundary line (Berlyne, 1965).

Secondly, the notion of conceptual conflict does not segregate the motivational consequence of discrepant thought processes as if they were unique and without cognates at nonsymbolic levels of behavior. It permits us to view them in proper perspective as variants of a broad class of motivational phenomena with ramifications throughout psychology.

In my own work, the notion of conceptual conflict first arose out of the study of epistemic behavior and epistemic curiosity (Berlyne, 1954a, b). This area of investigation deals with situations in which unbiased search for information (whether from the external environment or from internal storage) is likely to be helpful and consequently likely to occur. To be more exact, the search is likely to be biased toward sources that can be expected to supply the greatest amount of relevant information, i.e., the greatest reduction of epistemic curiosity, subjective uncertainty, conceptual conflict.

One of Nicki's (1968) experiments demonstrated the reward-value of relief of epistemic curiosity—an aversive condition induced and removed by informative material in symbolic (e.g., verbal) form—by a technique analogous to the one he used in studying perceptual curiosity. A typed question was projected on the screen, and, if one of the two keys were pressed, it would be replaced by a sentence recognizable as an answer to the question. If the other key were pressed, a sentence bearing no relation to that question appeared instead. Again, the subjects learned quite rapidly to press the key providing the answers to the questions, the asymptote being around 90 per cent. An earlier experiment by Mittman and Terrell (1964) had yielded findings consistent with their prediction that reduction of epistemic curiosity would reinforce discrimination learning in grade-1 and grade-2 children. Errors were fewer when, after each correct response, an additional line was added to an incomplete dot drawing.

Information often relieves conceptual conflict by strengthening one of the competing beliefs or lines of thought and weakening the alternatives. If this is how it works, it will invariably mitigate conflict when the conflicting response-tendencies are of equal strength. If they are unequal, incoming information may make matters worse by strengthening weaker elements and thus aggravating the conflict by making it more even. It may heighten conflict even when competing response-tendencies are initially comparable in strength, by adding new possibilities that had not previously been entertained. Recourse to epistemic behavior may occur, however, despite the dangers of exacerbation, if the temporary worsening does not exceed the bounds of the endurable and if it can be recognized as a prelude to lasting relief. It all depends, presumably, on personality traits (intolerance of ambiguity and the like), amount of arousal due to other factors, and previous successes or frustrations from attacking problems head on.

At other times, an unbiased search for information is virtually bound to heighten conflict. The situations on which Festinger and other exponents of dissonance theory (Festinger, 1957; Brehm & Cohen, 1962) have concentrated are cases in point. Once a decision has been made, the tendency to believe that it is a good decision receives strength from many obvious sources. Whatever factors made the subject favor the alternative that he chose rather than its competitors are likely still to be operative, and he will be pained by anything suggesting that he has made a mistake. Consequently, we should expect a subject who has committed himself, in contrast to a subject who has not yet made up his mind, to seek information selectively, favoring stimuli that will support his belief in the rightness of his decision and shunning stimuli that might cast doubt on it [but see Section IV E].

In other cases, behavior depends on subjective interpretations and evaluations, such as are unlikely to be unequivocally upheld or refuted by information inherent in external stimulation. Unbiased inquiry will once again be unavailing and thus not a likely reaction. Relevant external information may very well make conflict more severe, making the issue seem more complicated and unclear than it seemed before and thus strengthening several competing response tendencies simultaneously. When such is the case, the subject may be forced into rearrangement of symbolic structures and endogenous attitude change. Some, at least, of the situations to which Abelson and Rosenberg's "cognitive imbalance" theory (1958) and Osgood and Tannenbaum's "incongruity" theory (1955) have been applied are presumably of this sort.

So, the mechanisms to which a subject may resort when beset by conflict are numerous and diverse. Which will come to the fore will depend on the nature of the response-tendencies in conflict, the stimulus context, and constitutional or learned proclivities within the subject. Nevertheless, there are plenty of reasons for believing that all situations of which conflict is a major component have characteristics and governing principles in common. There can be little justification for marking out proprietary enclaves within this vast field of interrelated psychological phenomena and shutting them off from one another by unnecessarily divisive terminological barriers.

CHAPTER 16

The Pursuit of Consistency and Variety

Salvatore R. Maddi
University of Chicago

I take it that the essential message of consistency theories is that people want to avoid incompatibilities in their experience. If they believe one thing, they do not want to find evidence supporting something else. Nor do they want to perceive themselves acting in a manner that belies their opinions and principles. Expecting a particular thing to happen, they do not want to be confronted with some disconfirming event. They do not even want to entertain two opposing opinions or beliefs at the same time. If they are threatened with the experience of inconsistency, they will bend every effort, even to the point of distortion and defense, to ensure that the threat does not materialize. If they should be unfortunate enough actually to experience inconsistency, they will feel discomfort and anxiety, and learn through these feelings to be more careful to avoid inconsistency in the future.

The consistency position is best known in the study of attitude change. But it has also found expression in such more comprehensive frames of reference as personality theories. Lecky (1945) furnishes one early example and even better known is Kelly's (1955) psychology of personal constructs, the major thrust of which is that people lead their lives much like scientists. People formulate cognitive constructs which permit them to have hypotheses about what the world is like, and what will happen. If a hypothesis does not match experience, the person feels the inconsistency as anxiety, and takes steps to avoid the feeling in the future, either by changing the hypothesis and its underlying constructs, or by avoiding the domain of experience leading to the inconsistency. It is true that Kelly sees the pursuit of consistency more in rational terms than do many of the attitude-change theorists, who tend to exploit the dramatic instance in which people avoid inconsistency by distorting and defending, but this difference is not crucial.

On the face of it, the consistency position is unassailably valid. To perceive something different than what one thought or expected is to have been wrong, and who can rest easy with that? To think one way and perceive yourself acting another way is to be dishonest or cowardly or inept, none of which would be very acceptable. To harbor two discrepant thoughts or beliefs at the same time is to be confused, and who wants that? Inconsistency seems an unpleasant thing, whether it be large or small, important or unimportant. It certainly is not surprising that consistency theories arouse so much enthusiasm, and are so popular in contemporary psychology. Actually, what is surprising and intriguing is to find that the essentially opposite point of view also has ardent adherents these days. Let us call this opposing view the 'variety' position. Its essence is that novelty, unexpectedness, change, and complexity are pursued because they are inherently satisfying. The definition of novelty and unexpectedness must stress the difference between existing cognitive content and current or future perceptions, and hence, the experience of variety is very likely to also be the experience of inconsistency. If the consistency position is so sensible, how can there be so many reasonably reputable psychologists, such as Hebb (1955), Harlow (1953), Dember and Earl (1957), White (1959), Montgomery (1954), Duffy (1963), and Fiske and Maddi (1961), in the variety camp?

The truth is that the variety position sounds sensible too. Faced with the obvious way in which inconsistency is a sign of such unpleasant things as dishonesty, ineptitude, and confusion, variety theorists suggest that life is much too complex to be properly lived and understood through a reliance on easy consistencies. They would use as a rallying cry the crackling assertion from Ralph Waldo Emerson's Essay on Self-Reliance that "consistency is the hobgoblin of little minds." To insist on consistency is to take an unnecessary risk of trivializing life. To theorize that the pursuit of consistency is the major directionality in life is to underestimate man. This general theme is older than Emerson, and as contemporary not only as variety theory, but also as Rogers' (1959) emphasis on the actualizing tendency and the self as process, and Susan Sontag's (1966) outcry against the reduction of experience to overly intellectual versions of what is familiar and orthodox. Variety theorists would also dispute that consistency is so satisfying as it sounds at first. According to them, the consistency position is incapable of giving due significance to the unpleasant experience of boredom. The consistent life is the humdrum life, by the most straightforward definition of consistency. Variety theorists would turn for support in this to artists and poets, like Lord Byron, who considered boredom the signal form of torture, and Gerard Manley Hopkins, who thanked the Lord for "dappled things."

LIKE SHIPS THAT PASS IN THE NIGHT

The variety and consistency positions both seem reasonable in that they are believed by serious men and can be argued sensibly. Can any further light be thrown on the question of which of the positions is more accurate by considering the results of systematic research? I think not, because the research has expressed exclusive interest in one or the other position, and hence, the issue of their relative merit is not addressed. There is empirical support for both positions, a common enough situation when research proceeds single-mindedly and theories pass each other like ships in the night.

We need not review here the research supporting the consistency position. Other chapters discuss in detail the ingenious experiments testing the hypotheses that counterattitudinal advocacy, in the absence of grounds whereby the person can accept what he has done, leads to attitude change in the direction of the position advocated (see Section IV F) and that people may tend to show selective perception in a direction supporting a decision they have already made (see Section IV E). These kinds of experiments have generally dealt with important, realistic social events, and have been designed so as to test predictions from consistency theory that would not have been expected on the basis of simple reinforcement theory. While it is certainly true that the designs involved have tended to confound a number of variables in an unfortunate way, and that the treatment of data has sometimes been overzealous (Chapanis & Chapanis, 1964; Rosenberg, 1965d), it must be said that dissonance-reduction research has had quite an impact on psychology. Many psychologists are convinced of the empirical soundness of the consistency position.

But so too can variety theorists point to formidable empirical support for their view. The relevant studies are hardly without drama and importance, and have led to much less controversy and criticism than those performed in the name of consistency. The first conclusion that seems justified is that organisms orient toward and seek out variety for its own sake. This statement is supported by the mass of the research on exploratory and alternation behavior (e.g., Welker, 1961; Dember, 1961; Maddi, 1961b; Berlyne, 1950, 1955). The studies of exploratory behavior show that when a new element is introduced into the environment, animal and man alike will approach, contact, and perhaps even play with it. The studies of alternation behavior show that when an organism's initial response has exposed it to only a part of a larger environment, the next response will be made such that the unexperienced parts of the environment can be experienced. It has been definitely shown in ingenious experiments (Dember, 1956; Fowler, 1958) that alternation behavior cannot be explained by such concepts as reactive inhibition and stimulus satiation. This behavior emerges clearly as expressive of the pursuit of variety. The second conclusion supported by variety research is that variety seems to produce a positive affective response in people. Studies utilizing direct and indirect report of human subjects show that at least small degrees of novelty and unexpectedness are pleasurable, whereas completely predictable events quickly become boring (e.g., Maddi, 1961c; Platt, 1961). The third conclusion coming out of variety research is that variety is not only pursued and enjoyed, but that it seems necessary to normal functioning and development. The relevant research (e.g., Reisen, 1961; Thompson & Schaeffer, 1961; Fiske, 1961; Brownfield, 1965) concerns the marked reduction of stimulus variety and intensity as a long-term rearing condition of young organisms and as a temporary condition imposed upon adult organisms. The rearing condition leads to debilitating, and rather irreversible sensory, motor, and cognitive defects. The temporary condition produces similar, though less marked and persistent defects in adults.

The variety position has also been a stimulus to personality research. Elaborating upon the views of Fiske and Maddi (1961), Maddi and his associates (Maddi & Propst, 1963; Maddi & Berne, 1964; Maddi, Propst, & Feldinger, 1965; Maddi & Andrews, 1966; Maddi, 1968a) have offered theory and research to the effect that the need for variety is an underlying characteristic of personality expressed in different degrees and forms in different people. Through a series of multivariate studies, they have shown that there is an active and a passive form of the need for variety. The person possessing the active form in strong degree will (a) produce his own variety through responding in a complex, novel, and changing manner in unstructured tasks, (b) express a preference, in describing himself, for change and divergent thinking, as well as an aversion to order and rigidity, and (c) rely upon internal rather than external sources of stimulation in seeking variety. The person possessing the passive form of the need for variety in strong degree will (a) express dissatisfaction with the status quo because of its boring nature, (b) express the wish that something new and interesting would happen, and (c) describe himself as sufficiently without energy, reflectiveness, impulsivity, and sentience, that his continued frustration would be understandable.

A HOMEGROWN INCONSISTENCY

The importance of the preceding discussion is that in the consistency and variety positions we have two essentially opposing, but rather plausible views of the basic tendencies in man. One view is that man seeks, enjoys, and needs consistency, and the other is that man seeks, enjoys, and needs variety. Lo and behold, ours is no longer a dispassionate analysis! We are no longer merely talking about what the experience of inconsistency is like, we actually have our own homegrown inconsistency. We might as well make the best of the situation, and see whether our reactions to the inconsistency can enlighten us further on the relative value of the consistency and variety positions.

Do we respond to the incompatibility between viewing man as the pursuer of both consistency and variety in the manner prescribed by consistency theory or variety theory? The answer for me is both, and I find that very instructive. One part of my reaction is that it is a marvelous and mysterious organism that includes two such opposing tendencies. The excitement and wonder aroused by paradoxes such as this is very close to the kind of thing variety theorists see as the positive affective value of novelty. We often fail to recognize this reaction because it is easily covered over by more serious concerns. But the other part of my reaction is that the incompatibility is disconcerting, and this is the kind of thing stressed by consistency theorists. How can any rational organism seek two opposing things? Caught in the grip of dissonance, we must search for a basis whereby the incompatibility is reduced. There are a limited number of ways of doing this, ways described by consistency theorists in Section IV C. Having experienced two things as incompatible, one can attempt to reduce the incompatibility essentially by either reconstruing the presumed relationship between them, or reconstruing the presumed nature of one or both of the things. (More elaborate techniques need not be considered here.) Both basic techniques have been tried concerning the incompatibility between the pursuit of consistency and variety. I shall spend the rest of this paper discussing the relative merits of these techniques and some specific applications of them.

RESOLUTION BY DENYING THE TENDENCY TOWARD VARIETY

Consider first the technique of reconstruing the presumed nature of one or both of the things seen as incompatible. To my knowledge, this technique has been used only by theorists who fall in the consistency camp, and the position developed has been that only the tendency to pursue consistency is genuine, with the tendency to pursue variety being more apparent than real. Berlyne's (1957, 1963) theory (see Chapter 15) is a good example. Agreeing with other general behavior theorists, he would say that tension reduction is the basic principle of motivation, and that stimulation has the function of increasing tension. Novelty, unexpectedness, and complexity— in short, variety—are seen by him to arouse conflict, which is clearly an increase in tension. That Berlyne is really a consistency theorist is suggested by his defining conflict as the simultaneous arousal of incompatible response tendencies, as does Collins in Chapter 13. In essence, conflict and dissonance are not very different, even though Berlyne's general behavior theory ancestry is apparent in his action-oriented definition of incompatibility of experiences.

In his theorizing Berlyne depicts variety experience as having negative rather than positive affective value. Variety is conflictful and tension-provoking, it is not at all rewarding or pleasing. Of course, Berlyne recognizes the existence of exploratory and alternation behaviors, but does not by any means consider them to indicate pursuit of variety. After all, why should something unrewarding be pursued? Actually, he asserts that exploratory and alternation behaviors have the aim of destroying variety. Variety arouses conflict, and the ensuing exploration is a way of gaining enough information about the unfamiliar stimuli so that they become familiar. When the stimuli are familiar, they no longer arouse conflict, and hence, need no longer be the subject of attention. Berlyne postulates that variety is painful rather than needed, avoided rather than pursued, and threatening rather than appealing. This formulation clearly assumes the overwhelming centrality of the consistency tendency.

The major drawback of this procedure for resolving incompatibility by assuming only one of two apparently opposing tendencies to be fundamental is that when both tendencies seem reasonably plausible, the assumption seems to explain away, rather than resolve, the incompatibility. Berlyne's position does not explain self-report data to the effect that at least moderately unexpected and unusual stimuli are more affectively positive than are common stimuli (Maddi, 1961a; Platt, 1961), and the evidence (Maddi & Andrews, 1966) that people who are most productive of variety also say that they enjoy it. One could refuse to admit these findings because they are based on self-report data, but while this stance was popular among the rigid Behaviorists of 40 years ago, it is just too unnatural and arbitrary to be justified these days. Alternatively, one could recognize the self-report data, but argue that the underlying effect of variety is conflict nonetheless, with the report of pleasure reflecting a social desirability response bias because everyone knows that variety is supposed to be enjoyable. But in the absence of concrete evidence that a set to respond in this fashion produced reports that were opposite to the actual experience, such a rejoinder does not loom very formidable.

My second worry about Berlyne's position is that it tends to collapse the distinction between approach and avoidance behavior. If variety arouses conflict, and conflict is uncomfortable, then one could with equal theoretical sense predict that the stimuli comprising the variety would be avoided or approached. To run from the stimulus would reduce the conflict as much as would exploring it, and yet running and exploring are so clearly opposite in nature. The disadvantage in collapsing these two categories of behavior is illustrated in Welker's (1959) studies of exploratory behavior, where the rat is placed in a rectangular, well-illuminated box with a small, dark box opening off of it. Many rats scurry around the illuminated box, and, when they find the small, dark box, dart into it, remaining thus protected for a while. Then after a time some gradually poke their heads into the larger box and finally enter it again with more deliberate behavior. It is not hard to see that the behavior preceding entry into the small box is avoidance, whereas the subsequent behavior is approach. While the early form of exploration seems properly understood as the result of conflict, extending that explanation to the latter form of exploration smacks of explaining away, rather than understanding, the pursuit of variety.

Whether an explanation is convincing will always rest, in the final analysis, on its coverage of observational facts. But covering the facts is not the same as sweeping them under the rug, and it is the latter, most unconvincing to the test of reason, that is usually achieved when the attempt to resolve two contradictory phenomena takes the form of considering only one of them to be fundamental. To justify this technique on the grounds of parsimony is a misuse of the concept. Parsimony only applies to assumptions, not to the obvious phenomena that comprise data. To collapse an observational distinction, like that between running away and contacting a stimulus, and to overlook data, like the self-report that variety is enjoyable, is overzealousness rather than parsimony.

RESOLUTIONS THAT ADMIT BOTH TENDENCIES

There are at least three concrete ways of resolving the incompatibility between the pursuit of consistency and of variety by harmonizing the relationship between the two. Since all three of these ways accept the genuineness of both tendencies, they are more likely to be convincing than the technique just discussed. I will present the three ways separately, though they bear many similarities, and might well be used in combination.

The first position assumes that everyone has tendencies toward both consistency and variety, but presents the specific conditions, in the personality and in the situation, that determine when one tendency as opposed to the other will be apparent. Even with such simple theorizing, one can retain the belief in both tendencies without endorsing a view of man as irrational. This position is exemplified most completely in the work of Fiske and Maddi (1961), who built on the thoughts of other variety theorists. To the best of my knowledge, consistency theorists have not utilized this particular incompatibility-resolving technique.

In specifying the personality conditions determining which of the two tendencies will be shown, Fiske and Maddi assume that there is a level of activation at which the person feels most comfortable, and is most effective. Whenever the level of activation actually being experienced is lower than this optimal level, the person will engage in behavior designed to increase activation. A notable form of such behavior is the pursuit of variety. And conversely, whenever his actual level of activation exceeds that which is comfortable for him, he will engage in activation-decreasing behaviors, notable among which is the pursuit of consistency. As Fiske and Maddi believe that there are individual differences in the height of the comfortable

level of activation, [as does Pilisuk in Chapter 68] it follows that the proportion of time spent pursuing variety and consistency would vary predictably from person to person (Maddi, 1968b).

But personality is only one determinant of behavior. Concerning situational determinants, Fiske and Maddi suggest that the tasks confronting a
person can be roughly ordered as to the level of activation they require
for optimal performance. If the person's actual level of activation is below
that necessary for optimal performance of the task he has undertaken, he
will engage in activation-increasing behaviors, such as variety-seeking. And
conversely, if his actual level of activation is above that necessary for optimal
performance of a task, he will engage in activation-decreasing behaviors,
such as consistency-seeking. Take as an example of the use of this theory
a prediction concerning attitude change: regardless of the content of attitudes
and of influence attempts, attitude change will be easier or harder when the
person's actual level of activation is, respectively, lower or higher than that
which is characteristic for him.

A second way of resolving the incompatibility between pursuing consistency and variety by elaborating the nature of the relationship between
them rather than denying either tendency, considers these phenomena to
be dependent upon the overall expectancies of the person. Although I do
not know of any concrete statement of this position, it could be put as
follows: If variety is considered to be natural and likely, then the experience
of variety will be pursued and enjoyed, just as the experience of consistency
will be pursued and enjoyed if consistency is considered natural and likely.
[See Aronson's 'magician' examples, Chapter 1, pp. 25-26—Ed.] Since each
case involves the confirmation of an expectancy, this position makes consistency the basic tendency in man, but does not explain away the pursuit
and enjoyment of variety, as does a position like that of Berlyne. Of course,
it remains to be seen whether people enjoying and pursuing variety do indeed believe in its pervasiveness. Stated as simply as I have done, this position
has the probable disadvantage of viewing people as either variety-seekers
or consistency-seekers, rather than some combination of both. But this disadvantage could be easily overcome by classifying expectations according
to domains of experience, and theorizing that in one domain, variety might
be expected, whereas in another, consistency might be expected. Hence, one
could understand when and why variety and consistency would be pursued
and enjoyed by the same person.

It is my impression that Kelly (1955) was aiming at this kind of position,
though his statements are too vague for me to be sure. Kelly has indicated
that in the person's attempt to achieve consistency between his hypotheses
and the perceived world of events, he will act either conservatively so as to
restrict himself to the already well-known routines of living, or adventurously so as to expand his experience. Whether the choice is made conservatively or adventurously will depend upon which of the two courses of
action seems likely to lead to greater overall definition of the construct system upon which hypotheses are made. Perhaps Kelly meant that if the construct system predicts variety in one domain of experience, the adventurous
choice will be made, whereas if the construct system predicts consistency,
the conservative choice will be made.

There is one more manner in which the apparent incompatibility between the pursuits of variety and consistency can be resolved through

elaborating the relationship between them. This position accepts that both variety and consistency are sought after and satisfying, but attempts to relate them to each other in such a way that their positive properties are partially dependent upon each other. Variety and consistency, in the absence of each other, are considered to have positive but rather trivial effects. To experience variety alone may be entertaining, and to experience consistency alone may be reassuring, but the most profound psychological effects are reserved for a particular combination of the two. In considering the nature of aesthetic satisfaction, Platt (1961) exemplifies this position by giving the highest place to a combination of variety and consistency, though recognizing the separate value of each as well. According to him, we find a work of art, say a piece of music, aesthetically worthwhile in a formal sense when, whether we realize it precisely or not, it first surprises us by disconfirming expectations it built up or we had anyway, and then provides the basis for a new, more comprehensive expectation that incorporates the events that were surprising. It is variety that produces the experience of surprise, and a new consistency that produces the subsequent experience of insight and deeper meaning. The total experience is a little like being stretched to a new height. It is the experience of growth. And the experience of growth—clearly satisfying—requires this particular combination of variety and consistency.

It seems to me that Platt's view has much broader application than aesthetic appreciation alone. The growth experience is very likely that of the creator as well as of his audience, and it may determine the creator's course of action in the sense that it is this very experience that he uses as a criterion of the excellence of his work. In a more everyday sense, this experience of growth must be so striking when it occurs in our lives that we come to pursue as well as enjoy it, even if we personally do not achieve creative heights.

In conclusion, I would suggest that single-minded emphasis on either the consistency or the variety positions—simple and sovereign theorizing, in Allport's (1954) terms—is short-sighted. Both consistency and variety are pursued and enjoyed, and it is incumbent upon us to recognize this in some harmonious and creative fashion in our theorizing.

CHAPTER 17

Résumé and Response from the Consistency Theory Viewpoint

William J. McGuire

University of California, San Diego

The introduction to this Section II (pages 165-167) outlined the bases for selecting the ten theoretical viewpoints from which consistency theory was to be assessed in the subsequent chapters, 7 through 16. The first three were selected as representative of broad theoretical housings that subsume the consistency tendencies and thus illustrate their functioning in the broader psychological economy. To this end, Jordan uses a Heider derivative of Gestalt theory; Katz, a functional approach; and Sarnoff, a psychoanalytic position, as broader contexts in which consistency theory might be subsumed and elaborated. The two chapters following, by Allen on role theory and by Upshaw on the psychology of judgment, were selected as supplementary positions that examine consistency theory in the light of formulations deriving from quite different considerations but which often focus on similar empirical areas. It was our hope that consistency theory might be enriched by a discussion in terms of quite different theories with which it intersects in the enterprise of totally predicting behavior. The third set of chapters— Peak's on activation theory, Collins' on an incentive-reinforcement theory, and Bem's on a radical behaviorism—were selected to illustrate formulations that might 'supplant' consistency theory by providing alternative explanations for its predictions. The final two chapters, Berlyne's on his collative approach and Maddi's on his need-variety position, were selected to stimulate consistency theory by a confrontation with formulations that postulate diametrically opposed processes.

Although the authors of these ten chapters were not explicitly cast in the presumptive roles I have outlined here and were, of course, left completely free to develop as they pleased the interfaces they saw between consistency theory and the theoretical formulations with which they resonated, their comments fall sufficiently within the presumed framework to allow discussing them in this context. Each of the ten 'opposition' theorists was properly critical and explicit about the shortcomings of consistency theory, pointing out its theoretical and (less fully) its empirical shortcomings, its narrowness, incompleteness, and ambiguities. They were uniformly constructive in this criticism, exceeding even our high expectations in this regard. Rather than simply pointing out the imperfections of consistency theory and suggesting its abandonment, these expounders of alternative theoretical positions preferred, as the editors hoped they would, to suggest remedies for the consistency theory shortcomings in terms of their own theoretical orientation.

In one sense it might be proper to let these alternative theorists have the last say, since they were invited to contribute to this volume in the status of guests, since their task was such that it would more likely contribute to consistency theory than to their own position, and since they were so uniformly gracious in their treatment of consistency theory. But while propriety might suggest that our invitees be allowed the last word, I am in this chapter stretching my editorial prerogative in the interest of extending the dialogue, to allow a consistency theorist to comment in reply to the criticisms and suggestions made by the alternative theorists. My main embarrassment is not that I thus continue the exchange, but that it cannot (for practical reasons) be allowed to continue still further in the form of a reply by the alternative theorists to the comments in this chapter. In my comments here I shall consider in turn each of the four classes of theories as designated above.

FORMULATIONS THAT SUBSUME CONSISTENCY THEORY

Even the most imperialistic advocates of consistency theory would probably grant that it has explanatory value only for a narrow band of the total range of human experience and behavior with which psychology deals. It must be further admitted that even in those areas with which it most specifically deals, consistency theory can yield testable predictions only when we take into consideration a wide variety of other factors and make numerous assumptions about the parameters of the situation. Hence the consistency theorists who use the formulation creatively and productively are usually operating, implicitly or explicitly, in some larger theoretical context. Jordan, Katz, and Sarnoff have each analyzed consistency theory in terms of a different broader theoretical formulation by which it could be enriched. Each has pointed out numerous shortcomings in consistency theory due to its narrowness and have suggested possible remedies by elaborating the consistency position in the broader theoretical framework being discussed in each of their chapters. I shall consider each chapter in turn, commenting on the criticisms and suggestions made by each author. In the interest of productive dialogue, points of disagreement will be stressed more than points on which I fully concur with these alternative theorists. The reader will, I hope, appreciate that these comments will stress what is most debatable in the preceding chapters, rather than what is most valid. As regards the latter points, while I attempt here to recapitulate some of the salient contributions of each chapter with which I agree, I am for the most part content to let the authors of the separate chapters speak for themselves.

Jordan's Heiderian-Gestalt Analysis

Like many of our alternative theorists, Jordan feels that as now developed consistency theory has too much of an ad hoc quality. Along with Katz, Sarnoff, and others, he believes that consistency theory would be enriched if placed in the context of a broader theoretical superstructure that would make more explicit its hidden restrictive assumptions and would even allow the theory to be extended beyond those limitations, increasing its predictive adequacy and extensivity. Since Jordan has chosen to build upon Heider's approach, he naturally proposes a Gestalt theory housing. Jordan brings out the fuller meaning of Heider's own balance theory by putting it in this theoretical context. Thus balance becomes for the cognitive arena what Prägnanz is for the perceptual realm, and both are subsumed under the more general notion of harmony.

From this broader perspective it must be admitted, as Jordan points out, that the L-type relationship posited by Heider has been overstressed by the later consistency theorists at the expense of the type-U relationships. Newcomb, Cartwright and Harary, Osgood and Tannenbaum, Abelson and Rosenberg, and McGuire all focus rather exclusively on the liking relationships as opposed to other forms of belonging relationships. The later-mentioned theorists in this list do also deal with a kind of 'going with' relationship among their concepts, but the ego's relationship to these concepts is almost exclusively in terms of liking. Festinger and the other dissonance theorists seem less deserving of this charge of overconcentration on liking relationships, since the dissonance theorists often deal with other unit-forming ties as varied as choosing, eating, causing, etc.

In Jordan's opinion, consistency theorists have been misled, or at least made somewhat myopic, by their overconcentration on liking relationships which are but one type of unit forming bonds which in turn constitute only one aspect of the harmony characteristic which the richer Heiderian formulation develops. This narrowness is worrisome only to the extent that the liking relationship is an atypical manifestation of the broader constructs. If all the unit-forming components behave rather similarly, there is little need for the consistency theorists to be embarrassed at having availed themselves of the experimental convenience of concentrating on the liking bond. It seems to me that Jordan is somewhat ambivalent on this point of the peculiarity of the liking relationship. He astutely and frankly points out that Heider himself was perhaps misleading by singling out L relationships as something different from U relationships. Jordan points out that this opposition between L and U is rather arbitrary and unesthetic, and that L should be considered a special case of U. On the other hand, Jordan does admit that there is something peculiar about the liking relationship in that its negation leads symmetrically to a force against unit formation, whereas the negation of such other relationships as causality does not necessarily impede unit formation.

I feel that Jordan has overstressed the peculiarity of the L relationship. This contention revolves around the complex question as to when the contradictory and when the contrary of a proposition constitutes psychological negation. Let us consider the question in terms of the other relationships that Jordan uses to illustrate the problem: liking, causing, and similarity. It seems generally agreed that the positive poles of these three relationships give rise to unit-forming forces. The psychological implication of their negation is more debatable. Jordan argues that disliking gives rise to forces against unit formation, while not causing and not being similar tend only to induce no force toward or against unit formation. I feel that the distinction is to some extent based on the play of words, namely, whether the negation of the concept is done with the preface dis- or non-. If some contradictory-forming preface like 'non' is used and understood by the subject, we feel that p's not liking o (which is taken to include being utterly unfamiliar with him) does not necessarily induce forces against unit formation any more than does the relationship of p not causing o in this contradictory-forming sense. The stronger negations yielding mutually exclusive or contrary states of affairs, such as p's disliking o or p's causing *non-o*, do induce forces against unit formation. The similarity relationship behaves even more like the liking relationship than does the causality: 'dissimilarity' induces forces against unit formation while 'not (necessarily) similar' gives rise to forces neither toward nor away from unit formation.

I would suggest in conclusion that psychological negation is actually more complex than either Heider, Jordan, or I have indicated here. For example, the strong negation which gives rise to forces against unit formation for the liking dimension is "p dislikes o;" while for the causality dimension it is not "p does not cause o" but rather the logically very different "p causes *not-o*." Hence, while quibbling about Jordan's example, I find myself agreeing with Jordan's basic contention that the world of cognitive organization is more complex than we liking-preoccupied consistency theorists dream of. Returning to the theme which was developed more fully in Chapter 6, I would argue once again that the cognitive consistency approach offers rich dividends when used for a tool to study cognitive organization, both its structure and its functioning. But as Jordan argues, to realize this dividend fully we must mount the consistency notion in some broader theoretical framework.

Katz's Functional Approach

As a second possible theoretical housing for the consistency notion, Katz points out the usefulness of the functional theory with which he has been identified for the past 10 or 15 years. According to this view, cognitive consistency theory is too exclusively cognitive and neglects the motivational aspects of behavior. It is the essence of the functional theory approach to explain attitudinal behavior in terms of the person's goals and values and his perceptions of the instrumentality of given behaviors or cognitions for attaining these goals. According to Katz's functional analysis, inconsistency becomes psychologically uncomfortable (and theoretically interesting) only when it is perceived by the person as standing in the way of his goal attainment.

Because of their neglect of a broader motivational context, Katz suggests that the consistency approaches are inadequately developed on both antecedent and consequent sides. They have given too little attention to the psychologically important differences among the types of inconsistencies resulting from different antecedent situations. Likewise, they have neglected the motivational factors which give rise to different modes of resolving the inconsistencies that do occur. I think that Katz somewhat exaggerates the extent of this neglect and, more important, I feel neglect would be less serious than he does.

I feel that almost from the outset of consistency theory research, considerable theoretical and empirical grappling occurred as regards its motivational status. Motivational issues are confronted frequently in the dissonance theory work as reviewed by Brehm and Cohen (1962) and they constitute a dominant theme in the volume of collected papers on consistency theory recently edited by Feldman (1966). When the present volume was designed, the motivational issue was sufficiently salient so that Section III A was devoted explicitly to it and constitutes one of the longest sections in the volume. As Katz points out, concern with motivational factors gives rise to interest on the consequent side in preferred modes of resolving inconsistencies and in how situational and individual difference variables interact in affecting the choice among these modes. Hence the extensive Sections IV B and C exploring the current theoretical and empirical state of these questions were included in the present volume. Debates about whether a certain area has been neglected in a science tend to deteriorate into a quibble about words and priorities. Inevitably, the scarcity of time, funds, and especially talent, causes all areas to be neglected. Had more thought been given to the motivational surround for consistency theory we would now be further advanced as regards our theoretical mastery of both the antecedents and consequences of cognitive inconsistency. But the more realistic question is whether this area should have been more vigorously pursued at the cost of other important areas.

I would disagree somewhat with Katz on a more important point by arguing that consistency theories *should* be developed vigorously on the strictly cognitive level even at the cost of neglecting the motivational aspects of the total person. As a functional theorist, Katz stresses the importance of motivational aspects, and postulates that inconsistencies are not bothersome per se, but only if they interfere with some goal attainment. I am more inclined to believe that, aside from the frustration of any other goal tendency, the introduction of a new or inconsistent cognition into the person's belief system causes some peculiar and predictable perturbation in his constantly churning information-processing apparatus. Phylogenetic and ontogenetic states of affairs that could have produced an ipso facto need for consistency seem as plausibly imagined as those that would give rise to many of the other, commonly accepted need states. If we can imagine, say, a need for abasement having survival value, it takes even less imagination to imagine a need for consistency offering similar value.

I contend that the most useful potential contribution of cognitive consistency work is in furnishing us with a probe to explore cognitive processing, a point which is developed more fully in Chapter 6 of this volume. I would accept as a working postulate that there is some fairly pervasive need to maintain cognitive consistency such that the introduction of an inconsistent cognition into the person's ideological system has traceable cognitive ramifications that provide a probe for studying how the cognitive system is structured and how it functions. I feel that the concept of the organism as an information-processing machine is an idea whose hour has come. It would follow that our efforts would more usefully be put into using the cognitive consistency notions to trace human information processing than to further the mapping of the total motivational panorama. I must admit however, as Katz points out, that there is an apparent and appalling lack of consistency in peoples' cognitive systems when they are studied in the natural environment, and this calls into serious question how pervasive is the need for cognitive consistency which I have here posited. Section III F of this volume calls further into question my 'maximalist' assumption.

I take similar ambivalent exception to two other shortcomings which Katz sees in the neglect of the dynamic aspects of the person by the consistency theorists. I feel that Katz overstresses the logicality of the consistency posited by these theorists. Even Festinger, whom Katz particularly classifies with the logical theorists, has emphasized that the inconsistency about which he is speaking is psychological rather than formal. Admittedly, the consistency theorists have been quite unexplicit and wavering in their handling of unconscious motivation and the whole question of awareness. This issue is faced at various places in the present volume. Katz also points out as somewhat embarrassing to the consistency theorists the results which indicate that not all kinds of balance are equally satisfying, for example, that positive balance seems preferable to negative balance. But, of course, consistency theory is not intended as a total solution of the psychological economy. I know of no consistency theorist so imperialistic as to deny that other forces are also acting on the organism, so that he might prefer positive structures as well as balanced ones. Consistency theorists do not really make the mistake of the man who believed so strongly in Boyle's law that he could never accept Charles' law.

Sarnoff's Application of the Psychoanalytic Approach

Any serious attempt to place a particular conceptual position within broader theoretical contexts must inevitably utilize psychoanalytic theory as one of the encompassing formulations. With stimulating and irrepressible verve, the psychoanalyst takes the whole human condition as his rightful domain. Sarnoff in his chapter responds to the challenge of subsuming the consistency formulations (and particularly dissonance theory) under the broad mantle of psychoanalytic theory. In the course of his exposition, he points out how psychoanalytic theory can subsume some of the dissonance findings, give alternative explanations for others and enrich it by adding additional dimensions for its consideration. While he appropriately notes the subordinate nature of dissonance theory within the broader explanatory task that psychoanalytic theory has set for itself, Sarnoff also graciously points out that consistency theory can, in turn, offer some enrichment for the psychoanalytic formulations, in that the latter, while it appropriately encompasses the whole man, has traditionally stressed the unconscious to the neglect of conscious processes. Sarnoff sees a more adequate depiction of man deriving from the wedding of the depth psychology and the psychology of cognition developed by the two approaches.

Despite Sarnoff's *noblesse oblige* in suggesting that there is stimulating intellectual traffic potential in both directions between the consistency and psychoanalytic positions, it behooves us as consistency theorists to give special consideration to the possible gains that this theory might obtain from a psychoanalytic housing. Sarnoff sees consistency theories as underdeveloped in at least three regards where a confrontation with psychoanalytic theory could result in a needed elaboration. These include a fuller consideration of the various modes of coping in both their conscious and unconscious aspects, individual differences in preferred modes of tension reduction, and a better understanding of the intervening tension processes themselves. One might quibble regarding the extent to which the consistency theories have indeed neglected these three areas, feeling that Sarnoff somewhat exaggerates the lack of interest in these topics. The present volume contains several extensive sections in which consistency theorists review their theoretical and empirical work on these very topics (for example, Section IV C on modes of resolution; Section IV B on individual differences; Section III C on mediational processes, etc.). However, it is more useful to admit that the psychoanalytic theorists have been particularly fertile in their elaboration of these areas, for example, of modes of coping in terms of myriad defense mechanisms or adjustment dynamisms. Sarnoff is particularly provocative when he outlines the range of responses that the person might make to inconsistency tensions.

As in the case of so many of the chapters in this volume by authors who are asked to examine the consistency research from the vantage point of other theoretical approaches, Sarnoff is rather dismayed by the parochialism of the consistency theorists as regards human motivation. He also finds it necessary to point out that in many of the situations in which the person's behavior is discussed solely in terms of the need for consistency, the individual is actually responding to a wide variety of other motivational needs as well. This leads Sarnoff to raise additional complexities on the topic of modes of coping with inconsistency, threatening to complicate still further an already difficult problem. Such consistency theory thinking as has occurred as regards the use of various modes of coping starts from the assumption that these modes are being utilized in order to deal specifically with need of consistency restoration. Even in this narrow formulation, prediction regarding which modes will be tried and in which sequence is quite difficult. Sarnoff points out that the fuller motivational analysis allowed by psychoanalytic theory suggests that the individual is actually responding on the basis of a variety of motives, conscious and unconscious. Hence the sequence question must consider, not only the order in which various modes will be utilized to reduce a given motive, but also the question of the sequence in which the person will attempt to reduce the several motives themselves. We can only hope that the recognition by consistency theorists of the full complexity of this problem will result in renewed effort rather than complete demoralization.

In Sarnoff's attempt to deal with the results of the Festinger and Carlsmith incentive experiment, I feel he is, like several of the other alternative theorists, providing an explanation that avoids confrontation with some of the more challenging predictions of the dissonance theorists. Sarnoff points out that the subjects' internalization behavior in the low incentive condition could be regarded as an attempt to deal with the shame aroused by his approval-seeking compliance and an attempt to maintain self-esteem. But we think that the more provocative dissonance predictions are those in which the subject seems to be behaving in a way which will confirm his low self-regard or will confirm his expectation of a painful experience, such as discussed in Section III E. It would be much more challenging for psychoanalytic theory to try to handle these consistency predictions that the person will behave so as to confirm his expectation even when it means loss of self-esteem and unpleasantness. I do not mean to suggest that psychoanalytic theory cannot account for such phenomena (if indeed they do occur). But I do feel that psychoanalytic theory will have to draw upon its own more controversial aspects to handle these flamboyant dissonance predictions. Aronson himself, in his early formulation of the disconfirmation-of-expected-failure prediction, actually derived the paradoxical prediction from a psychoanalytic-type position that constant failure would have caused the person to elaborate a delusional system that would justify or even demand his poor performance. The surprising experience of success would tend to embarrass such a person, since his rationalizations would have made this success seem undesirable. It might be that the psychoanalytic theorists would have to call upon the death wish, aggression turned inward, and need for abasement in order to handle some of these paradoxical predictions. Indeed, Freud was something of a consistency theorist himself when, in *Beyond the Pleasure Principle*, he developed the repetition compulsion mechanism, which I feel gives rise to some of the profoundest aspects of psychoanalytic theory.

FORMULATIONS THAT SUPPLEMENT CONSISTENCY THEORY

The first three theorists contributing chapters to this section (Jordan, Katz, and Sarnoff) were selected as having broad approaches that might subsume the consistency position as a special case, enriching it through placement in the broader context they provided. The fourth and fifth theories to which chapters in this section are devoted were selected to illustrate a different relationship to consistency theory. These chapters by Allen and by Upshaw consider the consistency notion from the viewpoint of supplementary positions, not necessarily broader in scope than the consistency notion itself. These positions have assumptions, concepts, and aspirations quite different from those of consistency theory but tend nonetheless to bear on some of the same empirical problem areas. The very contrast in the orientations of these other theories enhances the opportunities for that mutual enrichment when they intersect with consistency theory in making predictions about the same behavioral domain. Hence, it seemed that attempts in this section to build bridges between consistency theory and these supplementing approaches might prove mutually provocative.

To provide diverse illustrations of confrontation by supplementary approaches with which consistency theory seems to intersect in several empirical areas, the editors asked Vernon Allen to discuss consistency work from the role theory point of view and Harry Upshaw to discuss it from the perspective offered by the psychology of judgment. Role theory appears to run alongside the consistency position, often dealing with behavior in the same situation but from a consideration of the social factors involved, while the consistency workers focused on the intrapersonal factors. The psychology of judgment theorizing was selected for discussion as standing more in an orthogonal relation to consistency theory, frequently coming in contact with it, somewhat to the surprise of both parties, by making predictions about the same perceptual behavior. In these confrontations, the two have used supplementary strategies, with psychology of judgment work focusing on the stimulus characteristics and the consistency work, on the characteristics of the judges. Again, this supplementary relationship offers an opportunity for cross-fertilization.

Allen's Role Theory Analysis

According to Allen's analysis, there is a sufficient parallelism between role and consistency theories so that building bridges between them would permit intellectual traffic that would be mutually enriching. Both are designed to describe the behavior of the person in social situations, with role theory stressing the social variables and consistency theory, the personal variables. Allen points out how the social analyses supplied by role theorists could facilitate the work of the consistency workers, while the analyses of individual modes of coping developed by the consistency theorists would be of use in the application of role theory. I feel that Allen exaggerates the dichotomy between the two approaches. His own discussion suggests that they overlap more than run parallel. I suspect that Allen modestly underestimates the extent to which role theorists like himself have already grappled with intracognitive functioning, even in the absence of any provocation from the consistency theorists. Turning to more familiar ground, I argue more confidently that consistency theory is not so exclusively intracognitive as it is depicted by Allen, but rather has always dealt to a considerable extent with interpersonal processes.

I would agree with Allen that an exclusive focus on consistency within one skull is found in some consistency theorists, including Tannenbaum, Rosenberg, Abelson, and McGuire, all of whom present their views elsewhere in this volume (Chapters 3–6). However, there is a considerable line of theorizing which develops consistency theory as appropriate for handling interpersonal social behavior as well as intrapersonal cognitive behavior. The germ of both of these applications lay in the original formulations of Heider, which are discussed more fully in Jordan's chapter of this volume. Heider dealt essentially with mixed systems of intra- and interpersonal constructs. Admittedly, as Allen argues, much of the interpersonal formulations are actually the intracognitive representation of some external social world. However, in the formulations by Newcomb (1953) and by Cartwright and Harary (1956), the consistency approach is developed to handle interpersonal situations per se. The predicted resolution of inconsistency might involve not only intracognitive belief changes, but also changes in the social system such as the breaking of friendship bonds or division into segregated subgroups. Newcomb's views are set forth in Chapter 2, and in Chapter 53 he again returns to this issue of analogues between the social and individual applications of consistency theory. It is interesting to note that while many of the alternative theorists who have contributed to Section II feel that consistency theory neglects motivational factors, its preoccupation with intrapersonal applications makes Allen regard its analyses of motivational considerations as one source of the contribution it can make to role theory. Consistency theory can be seen to veer in either direction as regards attention paid to motivational factors, depending on one's own theoretical point of departure; if one accepts an Aristotelian golden mean notion that the truth lies somewhere in-between, then the consistency theorists must be doing something right.

A number of the role theory constructs pointed out by Allen do seem to have considerable potential for the intellectual stimulation of the consistency theorists, including Linton's distinction between ascribed and achieved status, and the notions of role conflict, role expectancy, and role-discrepant behavior. Since these concepts have been worked out more fully by the role theorists and yet bear upon the problems of the consistency theorists, their study and utilization by the latter gives promise of useful cross-fertilization. One other aspect of role theory suggested by Allen seems to us less useful for the consistency theorist, namely, his role theory reformulation of some of the kinds of behavior handled by consistency theorists as being rather an attempt to maintain self-esteem or status, than an attempt to behave in a cognitively consistent way. I would argue that the diametrically opposed tendency is one of the most provocative (though not necessarily valid) predictions of consistency theory, particularly in its dissonance version. It seems to me that dissonance theorists would gain little self-esteem from predicting that people seek resolutions which will confirm their high opinions of themselves, since almost any other theoretical formulation would predict the same (see Section III B). The consistency prediction that the dissonance theorists particularly relish is that people also seek outcomes which confirm any low opinions of themselves which they may have. The Aronson-Carlsmith experiment, which suggested that subjects who have been led to expect that they will fail at a task try to confirm this expectation by changing their answers when they are surprised by success, is probably the second most salient of the dissonance theory experiments in terms of the number of attempts at replication (with the Festinger and Carlsmith experiment, which purportedly demonstrated a negative effect of incentive, being the most notorious). Such a tendency would be directly opposed to the alternative explanation being suggested by Allen.

In the terribly complicated area of preferred modes of discrepancy resolution, I do agree with Allen that each theory, role and consistency, has insights which proponents of the other position would find provocative. As regards the hierarchy of choice of modes, I would agree that the consistency theorists have overstressed relative costs. For example, Abelson (1959) conjectured that people tend to employ the modes in sequence of ease of usage, and the same notion reappears in the present volume (e.g., in Chapter 67). I feel people work on a more complicated cost-utility economy, such that the modes are utilized in order of the excess of their perceived probability of success over their perceived cost. Allen, in his discussion of role theory, like Katz in his discussion of functional theory, makes provocative conjectures regarding the relative efficacy of the different modes.

Upshaw's Application of the Psychology of Judgment

Both role theory as discussed by Allen and the psychology of judgment in Upshaw's depiction stand in a supplementary relationship to consistency theory, approaching the same problem areas as the latter, but from different directions than it does. But while the role theory approach is seen as an interpersonal parallel to the intrapersonal approach of consistency theory, the psychology of judgment is represented as more orthogonal than parallel to consistency theory in approach. Where the judgmental and consistency theorists do find themselves in confrontation, it has typically seemed to happen by accident, with the two groups having approached the area from unrelated directions, for different purposes and with different concepts. These very differences suggest to Upshaw that each group could be enriched by contact with the other. By considering the analyses used in the psychology of judgment, consistency theorists could gain a more exact formulation of their problems and could derive predictions bearing on the parameters of the psychological scales which they use with little regard for the level of quantitative sophistication now possible. As is appropriate for one who has long labored in the judgmental vineyard and is writing for an audience of consistency theorists, Upshaw stresses the potential contribution of the former field to the latter. However, he does graciously point out towards the end of his chapter that there would be gains also in the reverse direction from bringing these two streams of research into confrontation. For example, consistency theory work has revealed complexities in the person's response, when he is confronted by a discrepancy between subjective scales and objective stimuli, that would make explicit the restrictive assumptions underlying much of the psychology of judgment work and reveal to these workers the diabolical ingenuity of the subject in eluding the supposed conditions of a given experiment. I must focus my comments here, however, on Upshaw's views of possible contributions in the opposite direction, from the judgmental to the consistency area.

I feel that Upshaw exaggerates the extent to which these two approaches, with their attractive prospect for productive cross-fertilization, remain beautiful strangers. It seems to me that there has been an open liaison between the two for over a quarter-century. The work of Sherif since the 1930's and of Asch since the 1940's has stressed that there is a 'conservation of parity' as regards cognitive consistency, which takes into account both social attitudes and perceptual judgment. Perceptual change and distortion has long been recognized in consistency theory work as one response to discrepant, novel or unexpected information. It ranks with changes in one's own attitude as a facile response to discrepancy. Indeed, Upshaw himself in his chapter documents the fairly well-worn path between the two approaches. Confronted by a discrepancy, the person may well respond by changing his perception of the position of the stimulus, as dealt with in the psychology of judgment; alternatively, he may change his own opinion, reevaluate the importance of the dimension, alter its meaning, or devaluate the source of the stimulus. One wonders whether the psychology of judgment can provide an adequate model for any wide range of stimuli unless these researchers find some way of handling alternative modes of response, either by experimental procedures or by quantitative detection and adjustment.

But if consistency theory has been in the vanguard in recognizing the problem, the considerable value of Upshaw's comments becomes apparent when the consistency theorist reads his chapter as the receiver rather than the giver of gifts and as seeking the answer, rather than the question. Particularly interesting is Upshaw's creatively aggressive derivation of judgmental predictions to serve as indices for evaluating which of the alternative underlying processes is actually being used as the mode of resolving cognitive discrepancies. For example, the use of the 'mote' or the bolstering mode is defined as preserving the rectilinearity between the pre- and the postinduction judgments, while use of redefinition as the mode would tend to destroy the rectilinearity. The use of such elegant indices and dependent variables might help the consistency researcher circumvent some of the methodological difficulties arising from the multiple modes of resolution problem. Such sophisticated indices might, in skilled hands, be made to yield a statistical adjustment procedure that would be more methodologically acceptable than such current illegal necessities as eliminating subjects on a post factum basis or use of overelaborate, hard-to-replicate experimental inductions to close off alternative modes.

Consistency theorists show an annoying (but highly predictable) tendency to evade the implications of the failure of their data to confirm the kind of rigorous predictions that Upshaw makes. But the example which Upshaw uses, Brehm's experiment on the attitudinal effects of commitment to eat different amounts of food in conjunction with information about vitamin content of the food, illustrates some of the complexities involved.

Upshaw points out that the commitment might affect salience in a way that would make judgment theory relevant, since increased salience is predicted to cause a shift of the indifference level towards the salient stimuli. In the consistency theorists' vocabulary, terms such as salience, importance, and involvement are closely related, and thus the question arises of whether the issue- or the response-salience is affected (if I may use Zimbardo's terminology). But granting that the salience is proportional to the commitment and that the indifference point shifts toward the salient stimuli, then it is strange that Upshaw's predicted lessened impalatability of the disliked vegetables as a function of the amount of commitment does not appear in the data shown in Brehm's (1960a) Table 21. The changes in judged liking rather occur in terms of the interaction between commitment and type of justifying information. Moreover, it appears to me that had the commitment involved liked, rather than disliked, foods, the judgmental approach would have to make opposite predictions which are hardly borne out in Brehm's (1956) earlier work. That earlier work showed that, quite contrary to Upshaw's prediction of a unidirectional change across the whole spectrum of stimuli, the chosen alternative increased and the rejected alternative decreased in subjective value. It seems to me that the theoretical content of judgment work is likely to be of less use to the consistency theorists than is their sophisticated suggestion regarding rigorous and quantitative derivations in terms of well-scaled dependent variables.

FORMULATIONS THAT SUPPLANT CONSISTENCY THEORY

While Allen's role theory and Upshaw's psychology of judgment tend to supplement the consistency theories by approaching the same problems from different directions, thus revealing other relevant variables, the next three chapters were invited to exhibit theories in a more intimate and menacing relationship to the consistency position. These three chapters (by Peak, Collins, and Bem) examine the consistency work from the perspective offered by theories we regarded as aspiring to replace, rather than subsume or supplement consistency theory. We are considering here theories that make many of the same predictions as consistency theories, but on the basis of quite different assumptions, and then to go on and make further predictions that go beyond, or conflict with, those derivable from the consistency position. It is true, of course, that where one deals with so complex a topic as interrelations among theories, the line between subsuming, supplementing, and supplanting is not a sharp one, and also that none of the alternative theories that are discussed in this section was historically formulated in order to contend with consistency theory on the grounds we have outlined here. Still, we feel it is enlightening to discuss these three theories as typically standing in the replacement relationship to consistency theory, challenging it by their alternative explanations to generate new valid predictions which they cannot handle.

The three theorists whose views were invited as standing somewhat in this replacement relationship were selected as being quite varied in the mode of alternative explanation which they supplied, with each being provocative and widely relevant to consistency theory predictions. On the basis of these criteria, it seemed particularly appropriate to ask Helen Peak to discuss the consistency work from the perspective of her activation theory, since this approach developed out of the same need-instrumentality work as gave rise to some consistency formulations, and yet it uses quite different modes of analyses. That Collins should comment on the consistency work from a stimulus-response incentive or reinforcement viewpoint seemed demanded by the fact that these two positions have so often come into empirical confrontation in the past, giving different reasons for the same prediction in some cases and making different predictions in others. Bem's radical behaviorist views regarding the consistency work were solicited as representing an ingenious attempt to reinterpret and extend consistency theory findings in the light of a "demand character" type of explanation (which currently seems to be offering alternative explanations of just about every theory's findings) with the added attraction of bringing to bear on consistency findings a form of the radical behaviorism associated with Skinner.

Peak's Activation Theory Approach

Although Helen Peak's chapter has been placed among the theories which tend to replace consistency theory by giving its predictions an alternative explanation, it could with almost equal justice have been classified with the first set of alternative theories, those providing a broader theoretical housing for the consistency position. Basic to human motivation (and the behavioral episodes to which it gives rise) in Peak's theory is a psychological disparity, and this has an obvious kinship with the imbalance, incongruity, dissonance, etc., constructs of the consistency theorists. While the space available did not allow Peak to give a full exposition of her activation theory, she did expound it somewhat more explicitly and apply it more concretely to consistency theory experimentation than did the other theorists in Section II. One of the dividends of this fuller treatment is that her exposition serves to put not only consistency theory, but a number of the other alternative formulations presented here, into context with one another. The activation approach postulates that the disparity is bothersome when it leads to mutually incompatible response tendencies, a restriction similar to that suggested by Collins and Berlyne in their chapters of this section. Furthermore, even when such conflict occurs, whether there are consequences depends also on the accompanying goal set, which raises issues similar to those with which Katz deals in his functional approach. Hence as regards putting consistency theory into a dynamic motivational context, Peak's activation theory weaves together several of the strands spun by the other theorists.

A more unique and perhaps more valuable contribution of the Peak approach is that it conceptualizes the structure of the cognitive system in much more detail than any of the other approaches, including consistency formulations. Many of the alternative theorists who have contributed to this section, as well as the consistency theorists themselves, have pointed out regretfully that the crucial notion of 'psychological implication' has been left extremely vague in the cognitive consistency approaches (although brave attempts have been made in some of the chapters of Section I). Most of the consistency research has circumvented the problem by such tactics as determining the structure among given cognitive elements on an ad hoc basis for their experimental purposes or selecting so flagrant a case of inconsistency as to discourage any felt need for defining just what is psychologically inconsistent. I feel this lack particularly, since I regard the elucidation of cognitive structure as the most valuable potential dividend of the consistency approach, rather than as a problem to be ignored or sidestepped, and so particularly welcome Peak's focusing on this area.

Her theory contains several aspects which deal with this crucial question of psychological implications. First, the theory's structural elements of event, part, and (particularly) relation provide one possible depiction of the components of the cognitive structure. The 'relation' construct plays something of the same part in Peak's theory as does the unit-formation construct in Jordan's depiction of the Heiderian approach. Secondly, she uses the term 'activation' in a way similar to the consistency theorists' use of such terms as psychological implication, belonging, follows from, congruent with, etc. Hence Peak's postulates regarding the flow of activation among the points of the system can be taken as one possible account of the principles of psychological implication. It seems to me that Peak's system provides a fuller depiction of the cognitive system and the flow of psychological implication than does any other formulation currently available. Since the full exposition of this theory is rather recent, its empirical validity and heuristic provocativeness remain uncertain. At this point one can simply say that it has an a priori plausibility and in Peak's hands can be made to subsume a wide variety of empirical relationships. She utilizes it to derive the results of the experiment by Marlowe and his associates which might at first glance seem to present a problem for a tension reduction, incentive theory such as this. Even more interesting is the fact that she utilizes the theory to make still further predictions about the limiting conditions for that outcome and regarding other parametric conditions under which it might even be reversed.

There remains, however, the inhibiting consideration of the theory's complexity. The variety of factors which it takes into consideration and the quantitative precision to which it aspires is a source of strength as regards thoroughness; but on the other hand is rather discouraging as regards actual utilization. Peak's analysis of the results of the dissonance experimentation is interesting in that it shows that this activation theory can handle a wide variety of results, including some which might seem rather paradoxical, provided the parameters of the experimental situation are set at the proper level. These considerations also cause us to worry that perhaps the theory is too powerful and can handle any results by making suitable assumptions regarding the parametric values in the situation. In defense of this kind of theory construction which provides a highly adaptable system, it could be argued that while it might seem untestable in terms of first order predictions, it could be empirically embarrassed by some second order outcomes involving interactions. Thus, it might be admitted that this activation theory could have predicted the dissonance outcome which was obtained in the experiment considered or the reverse of this outcome with equal facility provided one could set the parameters where one wished; but still, there are enough constraints in the theory so that it could be tested in terms of a prediction that the relationship should have been greater in a given direction under some specifiable conditions than others. It may turn out, then, that the complexities and richness of this activation theory are not too much of a good thing. We can only hope that some consistency theorists will master its intricacies sufficiently to use it creatively.

Collins' Behavioral Theory Analysis

Collins is a supplanting theorist in that, when he views the consistency work from the stance of the behavioral approach, he concludes that consistency theorists frequently make the right prediction for a wrong or superfluous reason. That such a prediction is 'right' means, of course, that it agrees with the behavioral theory prediction; and that the consistency theorist makes it for a 'wrong' reason means that the behavioral theory postulates would suffice for the derivation. Collins accounts for the joint predictions in terms of some cognitive circumstances leading to incompatible behavioral tendencies. Indeed, he would even save the balance and dissonance theorists from some of their embarrassments by arguing that only such inconsistencies are psychologically bothersome. We shall return shortly to this consideration.

Collins is too tolerant to depict a line of research that has occupied as many psychologists as the consistency work as being simply redundant with the already available behavioristic formulation. Rather, in the early part of his chapter he is at some pains to argue that, while consistency and behavioral theory often lead to the same predictions, there are metatheoretical differences of some interest between the two approaches. Presumably, he would argue that these differences in flavor have heuristic value, so that each approach suggests a somewhat different set of predictions, though once made any of the predictions can be accounted for in terms of either approach. It seems to me, however, that the metatheoretical differences which Collins points out do not really distinguish the two approaches. He cites as the first distinction that behavioral theory stresses the adaptive nature of the organism's economy; however, Lewin and the other field theorists (with whom Collins seems to classify the consistency theorists) are no less emphatic about the functional nature of the person's behavior in his environment. As a second distinction, Collins cites Doob's dictum, in his adamantly behavioristic analysis, that all attitudes derive from past experience; however, it can be pointed out that Chein, in his cognitivistic response to Doob's behavioral manifesto, was in full agreement with Doob on this point of the origin of attitudes in past experience. Nor can it be agreed that the consistency theories are less operational than are the behavioral theories. One would as soon call them 'un-American' as that. Nor do I find very compelling the fourth distinction that behavioral theories, because of their supposed origin in animal learning, have a more forbidding and technical terminology than do the consistency theories; anyone who reflects upon the theorizing of Lewin, Heider, Cartwright and Harary, etc., or the other cognitive consistency theorists (as revealed to anyone who persists through the reading of this book) will have to grant that the consistency theorists need hardly to apologize for their lack of a ponderous and technical vocabulary. I have more sympathy with a fifth distinction made by Collins, namely, the distinction based on the purported relationship between attitudes and behavior. Collins seems to regard the behavioral theorists as positing a somewhat closer relationship between these two than do the consistency theorists. I feel that there is a difference, but it lies not so much in the posited closeness as in the posited direction. It seems to me that the behavioral theorists have tended to postulate that behavior follows from attitudes, whereas the consistency theorists (particularly the dissonance theorists) have more stressed the reverse direction, with attitudes developing as a justifying consequent of behavior.

Not only is behavioral theory represented as putting its official imprimatur on the consistency theory predictions, but it is even held to save these theorists from some of their excesses by restricting the domain of significant inconsistencies to those which give rise to incompatible behavioral tendencies. Berlyne in his chapter makes a similar proposal. In this way, balance and dissonance theories are saved from some intuitive or empirical embarrassment. I feel that there are some consistency theorists (admittedly, a dwindling minority) who do not wish to be saved from such embarrassments. We touch here upon a very fundamental issue as regards cognitive organization, or the psychology of inference. Do all inconsistencies tend to be bothersome and set off agitated information processing, or is it only inconsistencies of some special kind, for example, those involving the self concept (see Section III B, especially Chapter 26) or those leading to conflicting behavioral tendencies or interfering with goal attainment, as Katz or Peak suggest in their chapters? This matter is further discussed in Chapters 6 and 48. The dwindling minority of us who are what Abelson calls 'maximalists' hold that the human is a constantly churning information processing machine, and that any new, and especially any discrepant, piece of information evokes considerable cognitive agitation until the new information is subsumed as fully as possible within the total delusional system of the individual. Almost surely the actuality in this regard lies somewhere between the extreme positions and will be defined only by considerable empirical work.

Collins concludes his discussion by ingeniously deriving the dissonance theorists' postdecisional reevaluation predictions from a phylogenetic behavioral reinforcement theory. I think the bases for an innate, phylogenetically acquired need for consistency could have been displayed as plausibly. In the course of his showing the essential equivalence between the two approaches, I wish Collins had analyzed the theoretical and empirical question which still constitutes an important open issue after considerable research by both conflict and dissonance theorists. That is, to what extent is the postdecisional phenomenon (like felt tension and reevaluation of the alternatives) a function of the ratio of the two conflicting forces, their difference, or the strength of the suppressed tendency? This is a beautifully researchable area both for the model builders and the empiricists, the outcome of which could cause basic embarrassment to neither behavioral nor consistency theory, but would enrich both.

Bem's Radical Behaviorism

Daryl Bem proposes still another alternative explanation for dissonance theory predictions that would make the dissonance explanation superfluous. A radical behaviorism can account for dissonance theory's 'classical' inverse incentive effect, according to Bem, on the assumption that we judge the subjective feelings, not only of others, but also of ourselves on the basis of their (or our) external behavior. If a person, including oneself, complies overtly when faced with trivial inducements or sanctions, we infer that he must have been feeling more in accord with what he was doing than if he complies under conditions involving massive 'manding.' Bem is able to replicate the inverse incentive effect even when the subject is reporting the feelings of another person (in which case dissonance theory has little applicability), and suggests in the interest of parsimony that a similar psychologically positivistic explanation would also account for the self reports with which the dissonance experiments have dealt. Furthermore, in the best tradition of the alternative explanation approach, Bem demonstrates that this psychological behavioristic explanation will also account for additional relationships (namely, between length or quality of the arguments and the inferred subjective attitude) for which the dissonance theorists have found no comfortable basis for predicting, though Section IV F does contain several chapters which grapple with the relationship.

Those who have followed the lively controversy regarding the paradoxical incentive effect reported by dissonance theory should note that Bem's radical behavioristic account is unrelated to the incentive-reinforcement behavioristic explanation which previously has been furnishing the opposition to consistency theory on this issue. Bem's explanation differs from the previous reinforcement theory account as regards assumptions, predictions, and experimental situations. In fact, Bem's experimental procedures rule out the operation of the factors which the reinforcement explanation regards as crucial. Therefore Bem's explanation, while providing an alternative interpretation of the dissonance effect, does not bear crucially on the factors proposed by reinforcement theory. The reinforcement theory prediction of a positive relationship between incentive for compliance and resulting internal opinion change is based on the assumption that the greater incentive operates by producing a more skillful and forceful overt compliance, which in turn results in more self-indoctrination. By bringing the quality of overt compliance under the experimenter's control (an appropriate methodological tactic considering his hypothesis), Bem rules out the operation of the mediating variable stressed by the reinforcement theorists who have previously been in contention with the dissonance theorists, leaving them in the role of interested bystanders, leisurely observing whether the dissonance formulation or Bem's radical behaviorism better accounts for relationships with which their theory does not deal.

Both the dissonance theorists and Bem are postulating an epistemic motivation quite foreign to the flavor of classical reinforcement behaviorism (even in its 'liberated' guise of dealing with subjective states after the manner of Collins in his chapter in this volume), which tends to deal with motives quite extraneous to the behavior being explained. Both the dissonance theorists and Bem implicitly assume that the individual operates with a high need to make sense out of his personal actions, to give them meaning and coherence. Until recently, in the broad dualistic tradition it has been assumed that overt behavior follows from internal states, but here both dissonance theory and Bem's radical behaviorism assume rather that the internal states follow from overt behavior. There is a slight difference in nuance between the motives that the two positions use to account for this reversal. Dissonance theorists propose that the person generates his internal feelings to justify his overt behavior; while Bem's radical behaviorism postulates that the person produces these internal attitudes to explain the behavior at all. One posits a need for self-justification; the other, a need for meaning. While Bem has invoked the fatherhood of Skinner for his formulation, it seems to us that there is more than a little suspicion that William James was involved in the paternity of this idea. James' man of feeling is unsure of the emotion he is feeling until he consults his physiological response. Bem's reactor really has no stand on the issue until he is asked to state his opinion, and then gropes for an answer by reviewing how he has behaved regarding the object of judgment, coming to a conclusion of how he must feel about it from how he has been behaving toward it. The embarrassment he is trying to avoid is that of appearing to have no opinion, no meaning. To the dissonance theorist, on the other hand, the person reports (to others and perhaps to himself as well) an opinion in accord with his action in order to avoid the embarrassment of admitting that he behaved in a way discrepant with his prior beliefs.

Bem pushes his "looking glass other" formulation to make predictions about the quality of the overt compliance and the inferred subjective states, in interaction with incentive size. Two problems regarding his derivation worry me. In the first place, his strong reversal formulation of this interaction effect requires some luck in setting the parameters (of incentive in this case) so that they fall well on either side of the underlying inflection point. One can only hope that in experimentation such good luck comes to those who deserve it. Secondly, I think Bem's "protesting too much" explanation would make an interesting prediction about, say, a dependent variable such as liking for the observed participant; but I think it is more forced to use it to make a prediction about his inferred subjective state. Still, it must be admitted that nothing succeeds like success and Bem's experiment did work as he predicted it would regarding the interaction between incentive size and quality of participation as it affected inferred feelings. Despite the fine and varied explanations for this relationship given by Bem and in the chapters of Section IV F of this volume, I retain a stubborn feeling that this relationship needs more theoretical and empirical exploration. In particular, it would seem that the incentive type of analysis (cf. Chapters 82 and 84) requires exactly the contrary relationship to that of Bem's Table 2: namely, that while short, inarticulate counterattitudinal communications might yield the dissonance effect with varied rewards, long, well-elaborated communications should yield the incentive effect (because of greater scanning of arguments and other effects of self-exposure to content).

FORMULATIONS WHICH OPPOSE CONSISTENCY THEORY

The eight alternative theories in this section which I have so far discussed stand in a less diametrically opposed relationship to consistency theory than do the final two. The approaches considered in the first eight chapters accepted the bulk of the consistency predictions, but sought to subsume, supplement, or supplant the consistency theory explanations of them. A fourth possible relationship between theories is outright opposition, and so the editors sought some representation from theories which seemed to make predictions opposite to those of consistency theories. As I have pointed out elsewhere (McGuire, 1966b), there is one such group of opposition positions which I denote under the rather unsatisfactory generic name of 'complexity theories.' It includes formulations that give an important place to such constructs as curiosity drive, need exploration, alternating behavior, stimulus hunger, need for variety or stimulation or novelty, stimulus satiation, reactive inhibition, etc. All of these notions make an assumption, opposite in flavor if not in logic to consistency theory, that the organism is oriented toward the new and unexpected. Theirs is a romantic, Dionysian view of the organism, so to speak, as opposed to consistency theory's classic, Apollonian view, which regards the organism as oriented toward the familiar and confirmation of the expected.

The complexity conceptions, like the consistency, embrace a wide spectrum of variant formulations. As an attempt to represent the range of diversity and to avoid redundancy, we asked two workers who hold what we regarded as moderate and extreme complexity positions to comment on consistency theory from their perspectives. One of these was Daniel Berlyne, who was one of the earliest theorists to make the complexity viewpoint respectable and popular through his Hullian analysis of curiosity behavior and who has continued since to develop a theoretical model that makes room for complexity-seeking behavior, while still adhering to a drive reductionist theory that has a basic kinship with the consistency position. The second theorist, Salvatore Maddi, holds a position of more extreme opposition in rejecting Berlyne's view (as suggesting that complexity behavior serves a more basic need for consistency) and positing rather that the need for variety is equally as basic a drive as the need for stability and confirmation emphasized by consistency theory. The confrontation of consistency theory with these rather diametrically opposed views was deemed particularly essential in a volume of this sort, even granting that our inviting such opposition views seems to refute a basic tenet of consistency theory. While such direct confrontations often generate heat as well as light, still they appeal to the zest for combat in many researchers and, science being a human enterprise, supply some useful motivation to experimental work.

Berlyne's Collative Approach

It is, we think, not too extreme an analogy to say that Daniel Berlyne stands in the progenitor relationship relative to the complexity theories that Heider occupies relative to the consistency theories, though this seems to put Berlyne somewhat prematurely in the role of elder statesman. As such, Berlyne should be arguing a point diametrically opposed to the consistency theory position, arguing that the organism has a need for the novel and unexpected rather than for the balance-buttressing familiar. Yet Berlyne chooses not to cast himself in this opposition role. One suspects that historic ties and his creative skill in using this formulation incline him instead to maintain a basic drive reductionist position, which some (such as Maddi) would feel makes him a consistency theorist at heart. But he accepts the challenging task of admitting that the organism does indeed seem to orient toward and be attracted by the novel and unexpected, and develops a tension reduction formulation that places these curiosity tendencies in the service of a more basic need to convert the unknown into the familiar.

It might be argued, then, that Berlyne is basically a consistency theorist, though one whose formulation is extremely complex. Unlike the explicit consistency theorists who tend to deny or ignore that the organism does behave on more than a few occasions as if motivated by a curiosity rather than a confirmation drive, Berlyne makes these neglected phenomena his focus of experimental interest. As a result, Berlyne's research, while it might seem superficially worrisome, is actually fundamentally reassuring for the consistency theorist. Berlyne very ingeniously explains how the organism can be basically tending toward a harmonious, stable, and balanced confirmation in its information consumption behavior and yet show such phenomena as have been referred to as exploratory drive, alternation behavior, stimulus satiation, novelty seeking, etc. Berlyne variously accounts for these interesting phenomena (in terms of secondary reinforcement value, quick reduction of temporarily aroused tensions, short-term detours on the path to the organism's long-term goal, etc.) without ever deserting the basic drive reductionist position. Not only does Berlyne provide a rich conceptual system to handle these phenomena, seemingly paradoxical in the light of his basic position, but he even suggests possible neural mechanisms that add physiological plausibility to the psychological theory. No explicit consistency theorist has made even a gesture toward providing such a physiological substratum. Such physiological work as has come from the consistency position has been confined to physiological indices or dependent variables of the induced inconsistency tension. Inevitably, this tour de force by Berlyne has resulted in a quite complicated theory, as he himself will readily grant, while pointing out that a complicated theory is not necessarily a confused one. If one wants to make a good omelet, one has to throw in some elaborate ingredients. Or, as Sarnoff has said in another connection, to describe a pretzel-shaped Universe, one might need pretzel-shaped hypotheses.

As elaborate as Berlyne's theory is (and his chapter in this volume really does not suffice to exhibit its full complexity and explanatory power), I would suggest that it is insufficiently complex as regards the psychological epistemology processes which bring it into confrontation with consistency theory. I feel that there is a residue in Berlyne of the classical epistemology that would make knowing a reducing rather than enriching occurrence. It views the act of knowledge as a reduction into his own terms by the knower of the object known; it gives less consideration to the act of knowing as an enrichment of the knower into the form of the thing known. As in much of the information-theory work, the organism's knowledge system seems to be viewed a little too much as a predetermined and stable set of categories, into which signals are fitted as they occur. Somewhat less thought is given to the changes in the cognitive categories themselves that result from the reception of new stimuli or to the possibility that the categories might not suffice for an extended period of time to allow processing of a given stimulus. Granting that the acquisition of knowledge involves putting signals into categories, the assumption of the information theory approach that there are preexisting categories and that the signal is inevitably fitted into one of them allows the definition that the information value of a stimulus is directly proportional to its unexpectedness. However, if we add the assumption that the probability that any category will suffice to subsume the signal goes down as its unexpectedness increases, then we are led to a more complicated, nonmonotonic definition of the relationship between the knowledge value and the unexpectedness or strangeness of the stimulus. The utility of a signal would thus depend on both its categorizability and the predictability of a signal's occurring in that category. It would follow that the person is neither a compulsive confirmation seeker nor a radical seeker after novelty; rather, he is a seeker after the mildly novel, slightly unusual, not completely expected. Hence, this consistency theorist finds himself more of a complexity theorist than Berlyne, the father of complexity theory, though less of a complexity theorist than is Maddi, who supplies the last of our 'alternative theories' chapters and the one most radically in opposition to the notions of consistency theory.

Maddi's Need for Variety Formulation

In opposition to the consistency theory assumption that the organism has a basic tendency toward balance, harmony, confirmation of the expected, etc., Maddi stresses a contrary component in the organism's motivational system. Like Berlyne, Maddi argues that behavior also manifests a tendency which makes it appear that the organism seeks novelty, surprise, and the unexpected. But while Berlyne sees these exploratory curiosity behaviors as complex modes in the service of a basic tendency toward tension reduction, Maddi takes the more radical position that both tendencies are equally basic aspects of human motivation. The two complexity theorists agree that behavior exhibits both of these seemingly opposed tendencies, and that the apparent opposition is serious enough to demand some theoretical confrontation. But Berlyne's tentative suggestion that the variety need is subservient to the tension reduction need seems to provoke more response in Maddi than does the more radical consistency theory position which ignores altogether the need for variety.

Maddi suggests several possible theoretical housings which would permit both tendencies to coexist in the organism. One possibility is that the two opposing forces are simultaneously present in the organism, and that his behavior on a given occasion veers toward one or the other, depending on personality and situational factors. This contention might seem no more demanding than my often-repeated contention that a true believer in the validity of Boyle's law need not deny the possibility of Charles' law. However, Maddi's point is perhaps more radical in that it posits a second force affecting the same behavior which is not only quite different from and additional to the first, but it is almost the exact opposite of it. Yet I feel no more embarrassed than does Maddi at accepting such a possibility. Elsewhere I have argued in this and other contexts that a dynamic equilibrium of such opposed forces is not only conceivable but is frequently indicated by the data and can be seen to have evolutionary survival value, though it does seem likely to be attended by a considerable level of psychological tension. I have argued elsewhere that the inevitable sign of such a dynamic equilibrium is the finding of nonmonotonic functions between our variables, with the optimal level lying at an intermediate point. In this case I would readily agree with Maddi that the organism probably likes a little bit, but not too much, novelty and surprise, with this optimal point shifting predictably with personal and situational characteristics.

Maddi's second and third models for handling the apparent dilemma go to second-order considerations, and are less delicately balanced in giving each tendency equal prominence. The second model stresses the consistency tendency somewhat more, in postulating that the organism does tend towards confirmation of his expectancies, but posits that these expectancies might sometimes be for the unexpected or the novel. With a fine sense of justice, his third model gives somewhat more prominence to the need for variety, postulating in effect that each of the two tendencies has a satisfaction value by heightening the contrast of the other. All three of the models seems plausible, provocative, and reassuring to all parties, since they grant that all of the researchers are working on quite basic aspects of human motivation.

The coexistence of two opposing forces in human personality, including the need for confirmation and the need for surprise, would have several important implications for empirical research. In the first place, it predicts a nonmonotonic relationship between unexpectedness and tension-induced behavior. Without adequate knowledge of the parameters, two researchers might be working on opposite sides of the inflection point so that seemingly contradictory results would be quite common in this area. To avoid such confusion, a very wide range of parametric values along the unexpectedness dimension should be investigated in any research program. The more heuristically valuable aspect of such a conceptualization is that it suggests that the inflection point (and other aspects of the overall function) will vary with personal and situational factors. Hence the model can be tested in terms of interaction effects between unexpectedness and these other characteristics.

As regards the domain in which the two forces are most operative, I think it is suggestive that the two groups of researchers, those using consistency and those using complexity theory, tend to use rather contrasting types of situations to illustrate and test their predictions. The consistency theorists tend to depict man in situations of rather deadly seriousness. They employ illustrations and experimental settings which confront the individual with considerations involving his economic well-being, his self-integrity, or his relations with significant others. The complexity theorists, on the other hand, are inclined to illustrate and test their theory by man in his 'after-hours' activities. Man is depicted at play, at his recreations or hobbies, in humorous interchanges, and in his aesthetic relaxations. It might seem at first glance that in pointing this out I am arguing that the variety needs are less basic than the consistency needs. However, it seems equally valid to draw a quite different conclusion, namely, that both needs are equally basic and that the indulgence of homo ludens is no less vital than that of rational man for the flourishing of the total human personality.

CONCLUSIONS

In inviting and displaying the panorama of alternative theories which appears in this section, the editors sought to obtain heuristic suggestions rather than definitive conclusions regarding consistency theory. I feel that the categories of 'right' and 'wrong' are inappropriate for formulations as broad as those discussed in this section. All represent broad formulations by men of good will and intellect as fitting their intuitions and the hopefully reliable data to which they have access. As such, it is rather unlikely that any will prove utterly wrong. On the other hand, each of the formulations is clearly incomplete (the abstract nature of a scientific theory requiring a degree of hopefully wise elected ignorance to certain aspects of the empirical situation), and may even involve a worried temporary disregard of data which seem to conflict with the working postulates of the theory. Hence, each of the formulations is probably inadequate and wrong, its last best service being to yield numerous hypotheses which fail of empirical confirmation; for it to be otherwise would suggest that the formulation is either tautological or trivially obvious. I suspect that the pragmatic element is sufficiently pervasive in today's scientific paradigm so that I need not belabor the point that for better or worse, theories are judged in terms of utility in provoking new research rather than in terms of their parsimony or ultimate validity.

Hence, the editors' aspiration in Section II in having consistency theory confronted by ten alternative theorists was less to have it judged than to have it provoked. Out of such a confrontation should come a clearer notion of the shortcomings and inadequacies of consistency theory and perhaps even some suggestions for dealing with these inadequacies. We think that the ten alternative theorists who contributed chapters to this section have suitably met these aspirations. Each author cited numerous omissions, ambiguities, and errors in the consistency formulations and each made suggestions regarding how consistency theorists might deal with these shortcomings. Since, as intended, the ten authors looked at consistency theory from widely different perspectives, a good number of the suggestions were idiosyncratic to a given author; however, certain complaints recurred in more than a few chapters. Among these were the feelings that consistency predictions were quite often imprecise and ambiguous and that they were based on unstated assumptions. Repeatedly, the alternative theorists pointed out that the consistency theory work failed to specify in advance which mode of resolution the subjects would use. Without such specification, it was pointed out, the theory could account for almost any outcome without being able to predict any exclusively. With almost equal frequency the alternative theorists regretted the avoidance of individual differences considerations by consistency theorists. Since this question involves not only individual differences in overall inconsistency tolerance but also in preferred modes of resolution, this point is related to the preceding one. Our awareness of the previous neglect of these topics by consistency theory had fortunately prompted us to devote two extensive subsections of this volume, Sections IV B and C, to these two topics. The most pervasive complaint regarding consistency theory, arising in almost every one of the ten chapters, is the inadequacy of its handling of the motivation problem. I have commented on this point at numerous places above, and appropriately, the next section of this volume is devoted to an extended discussion of the status of consistency as a motivational construct.

The one aspect of consistency theory's shortcomings which I feel was neglected in the preceding ten chapters is the lack of specification in this work of the structure and functioning of the cognitive system. There was an occasional suggestion in this regard in the preceding ten chapters by the alternative theorists, but I felt that the frequency of mention was not commensurate with the importance of the question. As I pointed out in Chapter 6, my own enthusiasm for consistency theory derives mainly from the hope that it can be made to throw light on the neglected problem of psychological implication, that is, how the cognitive system is structured and functions so that one cognition leads to another. This interest makes me wish the alternative theorists had pointed out more explicitly our own failure to study cognitive structure sufficiently.

III
The State of Inconsistency:
Preconditions and Properties

A. INCONSISTENCY AS A MOTIVATIONAL CONSTRUCT

As initially presented, the various consistency theory formulations included the implicit assumption of a basic tendency of the human organism to maintain a state of consistency or equilibrium within his cognitive system. While few of the theories have addressed themselves to this issue in sufficient detail, such a tendency became classified among other basic drive states regulating human behavior. This gained increasing credence as experimental results of successful applications of the theoretical premises were reported for a wide range of behavioral phenomena including some apparently non-obvious cases. As with other such seemingly pervasive demonstrations in the history of psychology, it was not unexpected that "the consistency motive" came to achieve a central status in the field (McGuire, 1966b).

In recent years, however, the pendulum has begun to swing in the reverse direction, with a healthy skepticism developing regarding the notion of consistency as a unitary motivational state—no doubt, part of the not uncommon "yin and yang" of general theory development in psychology (McGuire, 1966b). Each contributor to this section voices and documents some misgivings about a fundamental consistency motive, and each offers some modification to the basic formulation.

Leonard Berkowitz argues for less phenomenological theorizing, and suggests that we look more closely at the role of eliciting stimuli, rather than some internal single drive state, to account for changes in cognition. Similarly, Kurt Back finds it instructive to distinguish between cognitive motivation and other, more conventional psychological drive-reduction states, but still regards a tendency toward cognitive balance as a fundamental adaptive process providing the individual with an economical means of coping with environmental complexity. While also somewhat sympathetic to the notion of a consistency motive, Al Pepitone offers a corresponding and perhaps more fundamental need of the individual to continually validate his existing cognitive structures in terms of incoming information available in a given situation, with certain discrepancies between the two giving rise to different degrees and types of tension. Keith Davis introduces us to the fine distinction to be made between *needs* and *wants*. He argues that the existence of a need for a limited degree of consistency does not necessarily always imply a concomitant desire for consistency by the person.

An interesting variation of the consistency theme is offered by Herb Kelman and Reuben Baron. For them, it is not that inconsistency is a drive state in itself, but that it provides a signal to the individual that all is not well with his judgmental processes and hence with his adaptive and coping mechanisms. In this sense, the main motivational locus of an inconsistent situation is that it elicits specific searching behavior designed to assess the implications of the inconsistency for the individual's well-being. Jerome Singer also finds it necessary to add a further type of consistency mechanism to that concerned with the resolution of inconsistency. He reasons that the individual, beset by an overwhelming amount of incoming information, must process it in terms of some consistent "learning and screening" mechanism by utilizing preestablished perceptual schemata.

All this does not add up to a major controversy, but it does make for a stimulating interchange on an issue of central importance.

CHAPTER 18

The Motivational Status of
Cognitive Consistency Theorizing

Leonard Berkowitz

University of Wisconsin

The quest for simplification and parsimony in psychology has often centered around motivational constructs. Single or unitary drive states have been invoked as the explanation for a great variety of behaviors. Thus, for example, there is the psychoanalytic libido, the ethological energy reservoir (e.g., Tinbergen, 1951), Hull's general drive, and even the notion of a general activation or arousal (Duffy, 1962; Lindsley, 1951; Malmo, 1959). With the possible exception of the activation theorizing, these general drive models characteristically maintain that internal undifferentiated excitation goads the organism into action and impels many greatly different behaviors. If the conjectured inconsistency drive is not quite as sweeping as these formulations, it is at least as far-ranging as the anxiety drive postulated by some psychologists (e.g., Mowrer, 1950; Brown, 1961), and can certainly be regarded as a general drive conceptualization.

The number of these general drive models testifies to the potential utility of such unitary motivational conceptions. But they can also be dangerous. They may lead to an oversimplified, and therefore somewhat erroneous, understanding of the processes involved in a given response. Many writers now insist that traditional drive theorizing often exaggerates the uniformity among the various instigations to behavior and also does not give sufficient consideration to stimulus determinants. After briefly reviewing some of these arguments advanced by researchers from other, nonsocial-psychological disciplines, I will contend that the same points can be made in regard to many cognitive consistency investigations. Although I do believe that cognitive inconsistency *per se* can heighten the likelihood of particular responses, my major thesis here will be that the unitary drive model embodied in much of the consistency theorizing has also resulted in an oversimplified neglect of important behavioral determinants and possible distinctions among the various forms of cognitive inconsistency.

THE GENERAL DRIVE CONCEPT

Hinde (1960) has discussed some of the difficulties facing the unitary drive notion in his criticism of energy conceptions of motivation. Searching for a simplifying principle, psychological theorists (Hinde observes) all too often have reasoned by analogy with physical energies. Properties of the physical model have been attributed in an unwarranted fashion to the conjectured psychic energies. Without any supporting evidence, and requiring "the existence of decidedly improbable [physiological] entities and processes" (p. 207), libidinal energy has been described as flowing from one channel to another, as being supposedly dammed up at times, and as capable of being converted into other energy forms. The psychological energy model in the hands of many theorists is more than a permissible "as if" statement; it is treated as a portrayal of actual processes. One serious consequence, Hinde notes, has been an impeding of research. This can be seen in the case of the ethological concept, "displacement activities." An animal having conflicting action tendencies occasionally exhibits seemingly irrelevant responses, presumably because blocked energy "sparked over" into the displacement activity. Hinde believes the widespread acceptance of this idea has "hindered an analytical study of the causal factors underlying displacement behavior" (p. 207). Many investigators, until recently at least, did not adequately consider the role of external stimuli in producing the supposedly irrelevant acts (also cf. Ziegler, 1964, in support of Hinde's contention).

But whether or not the particular drive model rests on a close analogy with physical energies, or takes an 'economic' point of view as psychoanalytic theory continues to do (Gill, 1959), general drive concepts characteristically envision a unitary process (or force or energy) with far-ranging consequences. An instigating condition is said to produce an increase in *the* drive, which automatically impels many different forms of behavior until some goal is reached and the drive decreases. Contrary to this unitary conception, however, an increasing body of research demonstrates that different kinds of activities are often governed by specific and quite different mechanisms (Hinde, 1959; Cofer & Appley, 1964). This type of evidence is particularly troublesome for the idea of a single activation continuum (Malmo, 1959). The notion of a unitary arousal or activation state demands that increased excitation in one part of the body is associated with other signs of physiological arousal in other bodily systems. While there is a great deal of evidence consistent with this thesis, even its adherents admit to the existence of disturbing exceptions (Bindra, 1959, p. 213). Lacey (1965) has recently concluded that there are many experimental results sharply contradicting activation theory, showing that "electroencephalographic, autonomic, motor, and other behavioral systems are imperfectly coupled, complexly interacting systems." There can be great behavioral responsivity even though the brain shows signs of low arousal, or indications of an alerted cortex along with behavioral drowsiness. In general, somatic and behavioral arousal may be dissociated, and much more has to be known before we can specify the conditions under which the different systems are aroused together.

Hinde (1959), in discussing unitary drive concepts, has suggested that behavior is governed by specific factors as well as by a nonspecific physiological arousal. These specific determinants appear to differ greatly from one behavioral system to another. Together with Beach (cf. Cofer & Appley, 1964, pp. 175–176), Hinde maintains that hunger and thirst are greatly different from sexual motivation in important respects. No one supposed drive state can serve as an entirely satisfactory model for other drives. Social psychologists could do well to keep this in mind. Much of their motivational theorizing (e.g., Newcomb, Turner, & Converse, 1965, p. 23) assumes rather blithely that hunger and thirst provide an analogy for all motivated actions. The analogy, in actuality, is at best a very crude one and neglects a host of differentiating factors.

Specific determinants are also important within a single 'drive' condition. The various possible reactions to the same presumed drive do not necessarily operate together as manifestations of a unitary state. Thus, an animal's degree of hunger can be assessed by such measures as the amount of food eaten, the speed of running to a food goal, the latency of the response, the intensity of a noxious stimulus that the animal will withstand in order to reach the food, and so on. Contrary to the idea of a simple unitary process, the correlations among these various measures are often quite low (Miller, 1957). Each reaction is at least partly governed by a different set of determinants. The notion of a unitary and quite general hunger drive arising from food deprivation has resulted in an oversimplified neglect of relatively unique motivational factors.

These unfortunate consequences have also arisen in consistency theorizing. The pursuit of a general theoretical model based on the traditional unitary drive idea has led to an unwarranted neglect of important problems. Just as hunger and sex are governed in somewhat different ways by different determinants, it may be a mistake to assume a motivational equivalence among the several consistency approaches and the phenomena confronted by each approach. Is it necessary to make this assumption? Must the various forms of cognitive inconsistency be regarded as all producing the same general, unitary drive state? Further, is there any good empirical reason for thinking that the different reactions to any one inconsistent situation are functionally equivalent, i.e., can substitute for each other in reducing the same internal "drive"?

ARE THE VARIOUS INCONSISTENCY REACTIONS FUNCTIONALLY EQUIVALENT?

I believe it is unfair to attack cognitive consistency research on the grounds that the studies have failed to dispose of every alternative explanation (cf. Chapanis & Chapanis, 1964); surely every psychological investigation is open to this accusation. It is appropriate, nevertheless, to ask whether the research findings can be accounted for by a coherent alternative theoretical formulation of at least moderate generality. Is there a general body of ideas that can serve as a plausible alternative explanation for at least some of the consistency results? From my vantage point, not only are there such plausible coherent alternatives in many cases, but these alternative schemes also seriously question the sweep of the consistency models. There may well be quite different explanations for different phenomena typically gathered together under the consistency tent.

The frequently observed relationship between attitudinal similarity and attraction is often interpreted in consistency—more specifically, in balance—theory terms (e.g., Newcomb, Turner, & Converse, 1965, p. 130; Zajonc, 1960a). Nevertheless, opinion disagreements may provoke an emotional reaction (Burdick & Burnes, 1958) because of anticipations of disapproval rather than because of cognitive imbalance *per se*, while people holding similar beliefs could become attractive (Byrne, 1961a; Newcomb, 1961) because they satisfy a desire for social approval rather than a need for consistency. As only one of several demonstrations of this possibility, Walster and Walster (1963) showed that college students exhibited the greatest preference for people similar to themselves when they were made to be concerned about being liked by these others, and preferred to be with dissimilar others when they were assured they would be liked. The individual who seeks out or is drawn to people having similar beliefs is not necessarily governed by a balancing tendency or strain toward symmetry of orientations. If he is concerned with gaining social approval, he may be attracted to those persons he thinks are most likely to provide him with the social rewards he wants: the people possessing attitudes similar to his own. On many other occasions, perhaps when he is feeling secure, he may actually prefer variation in his social groups and may be particularly drawn to those groups whose members are greatly different from each other (Levy, 1964).

Byrne and Newcomb have also suggested that opinion similarity is desired at times because the individual wants support for a shaky opinion. By the same token, disagreements within an attractive group may be tension-producing because of the conceptual uncertainty they create. Balance theory can serve as a useful general description of the relationships among cognitive elements, but the 'theory' is quite imprecise and omits many important considerations. There are many reasons why a person may develop positive attitudes toward those people whose views are close to his own, or come to dislike the persons holding widely divergent beliefs. Whatever their exact nature, the motives are not constantly operative, however, and it could well be a mistake to think of a general, ever-active strain toward cognitive balance. The frequent failures to confirm balance-theory predictions when there are negative-negative relationships among the cognitive elements (e.g., Jordan, 1953; Harburg & Newcomb, 1966) are only some illustrations of the difficulties confronting the model (see Chapter 2).

Similarly, several supposed instances of dissonance reduction might be the outcome of still other processes. Consider the consequences of decision making. Where dissonance theorists have contended that a person will enhance the value of his choice and lessen the attractiveness of his rejected alternative in order to reduce the dissonance produced by his decision, some evidence suggests that these reactions may be pride-engendered attempts to maintain a favorable self concept (Deutsch, Krauss, & Rosenau, 1962). Thus, Malewski (1962) and Gerard, Blevans, and Malcolm (1964) found that the chosen alternative becomes more attractive primarily when the individual has a generally positive self concept, or at least thinks he is good at making this type of decision. In accord with this possibility, Glass (1964) reports that subjects who had previously indicated they were opposed to the use of electric shocks tended to derogate the person they later had shocked 'voluntarily,' but only when the subjects had been induced to have high self-esteem. The derogation evidently justified the attack on the victim and served to maintain the favorable self concept. If this type of explanation is correct, it may be more profitable to explain certain phenomena in terms of pride maintenance rather than a general striving for cognitive consistency. (See Section III B, and Chapter 68.) Moreover, should threat to a favorable self concept prove to be a major operative factor in reactions to decision making, the same maintenance of pride also might govern the individual's reactions to the imbalance produced by hearing two respected persons express widely divergent opinions on an important issue.

There are better and more direct ways to test the functional equivalence of the various inconsistency reactions than to search for alternative explanations, however, and important observations are provided by Steiner and his associates. In one experiment, Steiner and Rogers (1963) led their subjects to believe a respected associate disagreed with them on a number of issues, and then examined the intercorrelations among four different reactions to the disagreement. The subject could conform to his associate's opinions, reject the associate as being relatively incompetent, lessen the importance of the issues about which the disagreements occurred, and/or forget some of the disagreements. Although the researchers generally concluded that the different reactions substituted for each other, and hence were functionally equivalent, the evidence for this conclusion is tenuous indeed. Thus, while the intercorrelations tended to be negative, they were all very low, and none of the relationships among the four reactions were statistically significant for the male subjects.

This failure to obtain clear-cut support for the equivalence thesis has been argued away by other writers. McGuire (1966b) suggests that the strength of the dissonance has not been held constant in this research; those people having strong dissonance might employ several modes of dissonance reduction while persons with weaker dissonance could exhibit one, but not other, dissonance-reducing reactions. For some people, then, there might be positive correlations among the various dissonance reactions, but there would be negative correlations for other persons. But whatever the actual explanation for the low intercorrelations in the Steiner experiments, they certainly do not show unequivocally that the different inconsistency reactions are governed by the same processes and lead to the same consequences. In particular, I would contend that rather than the rejection of the disagreeing associate being a purposive attempt at dissonance reduction, at least for some subjects it could well be an aggressive response to the frustration established by the disagreements. Again, however, whether this latter possibility is correct or not, the unitary drive conception of consistency theory has resulted in a failure to investigate the specific situational determinants of the different inconsistency-engendered reactions.

HOW DOES "DRIVE ENERGY" OPERATE AND BECOME REDUCED?

In their basic assumptions about the nature of motivation, social psychologists typically have been slow to adopt the revised motivational models advocated by many experimental psychologists. As just one example, a number of experimentalists have insisted that food and water deprivations do *not* produce an internal energy which inevitably goads the organism into activity (cf. Cofer & Appley, 1964). Thus, where such social psychologists as Newcomb, Turner, and Converse (1965, pp. 22–24) think of the deprivation as leading automatically to an inner "push," animal investigations have suggested that the deprivation may create only an increased responsivity to external stimulation (e.g., Sheffield & Campbell, 1954). According to this view, appropriate stimuli must be present in the situation if the "drive-impelled" responses are actually to occur. These stimuli elicit the actions the animal is ready to take. Going further, some have argued that it is not necessary to characterize the internal "drive" or "arousal" condition as an energizing state (cf. Hinde, 1960). Zajonc and Dorfman (1964) proposed, in this vein, that the apparent energizing effect of a drive state could be due to the interaction of the perceived stimulus with other, internal (supposedly drive-produced) stimuli. These two sets of stimuli operating together could lead to the more intense responses.

Other consequences of the arousal or instigating condition could conceivably also affect the intensity and nature of the responses made in the situation. Consistent with Hullian learning theory, Easterbrook (1959) hypothesized that arousing conditions result in a decreased range of cue utilization; there is an increased responsivity to the central cues in the situation and a decreased likelihood of reacting to peripheral cues. Supporting observations can be found in the work of personality and social psychologists. For example, Epstein and Levitt (1962). in studying the influence of hunger on the learning of food-related words, concluded that the hunger produced a selective responsivity to food-related stimuli and an inattention to other stimuli. Similarly, Berkowitz and Buck (1967) recently created an adrenalin-induced arousal in some of their subjects and found that men who had to make an aggressive response to a certain signal showed a decreased aggressive responsivity to other, peripheral cues when under the influence of the drug; they responded selectively to the central cues to the extent that they had learned to do so previously, and were less apt to respond to the other, less relevant stimuli. (See also Bandura & Walters, 1963; Walters & Parke, 1964.) This stimulus conception could account for many of the findings used to buttress the notion of a unitary, general drive state (cf. Estes, 1958; Miller, 1959). The generality could perhaps be due to a stimulus generalization and also, as Easterbrook suggested, a decreased responsivity to the peripheral cues which could have elicited other kinds of reactions.

Whatever the exact nature of the relationship between instigating condition and external stimulus, the point is that cognitive consistency theorizing has slighted the role of eliciting stimuli. If cognitive inconsistency is stressful, as would seem to be the case in many instances, could not at least some of the reactions be evoked by the stimuli in the situation, with these responses being only facilitated by the internal arousal? I have contended that many cases of aggressive behavior are stimulus elicited (Berkowitz, 1965a). Similarly, rejection or derogation of a communicator presenting belief-discrepant information could also be a stimulus-evoked aggressive reaction rather than a purposive attempt to reduce dissonance. Other kinds of responses could also be evoked by other kinds of situational stimuli.

There are many reasons why social psychologists have failed to give more attention to the part played by such situational stimuli. One major reason undoubtedly involves social psychology's almost exclusive reliance on phenomenological theorizing. We generally assume as a matter of course that the human being acts as he does because of wants arising from his understanding of his environment. In some cases, however, this understanding may develop *after* stimuli have evoked the action so that the understanding justifies but has not caused the behavior. One of the field's most erudite scholars, Bill McGuire, has given us a quotation from Spinoza that is relevant here: "A thrown stone given consciousness in flight would think itself moving of its own volition." Much the same thing could be said about many human actions. We become aware of a given response (which actually may be elicited by some particular stimulus) and attribute the behavior to some internal motivating state; we tell ourselves we wanted to do this thing in order to achieve a certain end-state.

All of this is not to deny the frequent utility of cognitive and purposive constructs in psychology. Behavior obviously is often controlled by cognitive intervention—few would doubt this (cf. Miller, 1959, 1961; Koch, 1959) —and frequently is goal-directed. But it seems to me equally obvious that some actions are "impulsive," i.e., stimulus elicited, without being governed by anticipations of some desired end-state, whether this is a favorable ratio of rewards to costs, an equitable balance of rewards to investments, pride maintenance, or dissonance reduction.

However the action comes about, the conventional motivational theorizing employed by most social psychologists seems to suggest that the performance of a drive-impelled response "lets off steam" and produces a reduction in the central drive. This hydraulic model has been frequently applied to aggressive behavior, and is at least implicit in many discussions of inconsistency reactions. But just as available evidence fails to provide clear support for the catharsis theory of aggression (Berkowitz, 1962, 1965a), there is no really good proof that any inconsistency-engendered response will in itself reduce the inconsistency drive. In an experiment by Steiner (1964), subjects were individually confronted by the experimenter's accomplice who disagreed with them on a number of issues. Continuous galvanic skin response (GSR) readings were obtained throughout the sequence of agreements and disagreements, and changes in these readings were related to different modes of reaction to the situation. Taking these readings as indications of internal arousal, Steiner reported that the people who exhibited several of the possible modes of dissonance reduction (conformity, rejection of the accomplice, devaluation of the task, etc.) to a relatively great degree had *less* reduction in physiological arousal than the subjects displaying only one reaction pattern to a high degree. It would seem that dissonance theory would have predicted the opposite—people employing several modes of dissonance reduction at once should experience a greater tension reduction than people taking only one way out. At any rate, the findings are at best equivocal, and certainly do not constitute easy support for the dissonance theory expectation.

There is another line of investigation that merits consideration, however. Several experiments conducted by Brehm and Cohen and their colleagues (Brehm & Cohen, 1962, Ch. 8) suggest that dissonance effects can be so powerful that they apparently counter the physiological and behavioral signs of other motivational states such as hunger. A recent study by Zimbardo *et al.* (1966) is illustrative. In comparison to the subjects who volunteered to receive painful electric shocks with relatively good justification (i.e., who theoretically had low dissonance), the men volunteering for these shocks with little justification (having high dissonance) subsequently reported feeling less pain and also had a much greater reduction in GSR relative to the prevolunteering shock period. Learning, verbal report, and even physiological measures all indicate that the high dissonance somehow lessened the effects of the electric shock. How did this happen? Although the dissonance theorists do not take this view, I think we can readily rule out the possibility that the dissonance excitation (or energy) completely suppresses the pain excitation. My own preference is for a slightly modified version of the position actually taken by Brehm and Cohen (1962, p. 152). With them, I would suggest that there is a change in the individual's cognition as a result of the dissonance arousal. Among the most important aspects of this change, it seems to me, is an alteration in the perception of the instigating stimulus condition. (Many writers are now agreed, at least implicitly [cf. Koch, 1959], that a psychological stimulus can profitably be regarded as a construction established by the individual.) There may thus be an alteration in the perceived magnitude of the electric shock (which is what Zimbardo and his colleagues report) as the individual seeks to justify his volunteering to himself. An analogous phenomenon has been demonstrated in the research conducted by Lazarus and his coworkers (Lazarus et al., 1964; Speisman et al., 1964), who showed that the introduction to a filmed depiction of a primitive circumcision rite can drastically alter the observers' physiological reactions to the witnessed event. There is a much smaller reaction when the scene is introduced as a happy occasion (the boy is about to enter manhood, etc.) than when the threatening aspects and dangers are pointed up. The introduction altered the observers' cognitions, lessening the extent to which the witnessed situation served as a threat stimulus.

A similar process may govern other reactions to dissonance arousal. The desire for self-justification, pride maintenance, or whatever the dissonance entails, can produce a change in the nature and/or magnitude of the perceived situational stimuli. Thus, a previously neutral person may come to be viewed in an unfavorable manner (altering his stimulus qualities), which in turn heightens the extent to which he can evoke an aggressive reaction from the emotionally aroused subject. The expressed aggression could be an automatic, stimulus-elicited response, and in itself does not necessarily reduce whatever internal arousal may have been created by the cognitive inconsistency. Under other conditions, the person with whom the subject is in disagreement could come to be regarded as a knowledgeable expert. This altered cognition could facilitate acceptance of that person's opinions, but the overt conformity to his stated beliefs may not in itself reduce the conjectured dissonance-created drive state. There is a change in the stimulus condition, leading to a behavior change, but the behavior does not produce a reduction of the inconsistency-caused arousal. Much more has to be known before we can specify the factors governing the probability that further responses will or will not be made. It is doubtful that the present simple, unitary drive models can provide this specification.

CHAPTER 19

Equilibrium as Motivation: Between Pleasure and Enjoyment

Kurt W. Back
Duke University

The ideal simplified world of balance theory would be one divided into groups of good people and bad people, each of which stands together. The good guys wear white hats and are for law and order, fight fairly and only under duress, and always are for good causes. The bad men wear black hats, are unshaven, drink too much, and are constantly involved in crooked deals. This is the kind of atmosphere where cognitive consistency would be best realized. By testing ourselves and asking what is right and what is wrong with this picture, we may gain insight into the mechanisms and the deficiencies of the consistency theories and especially their place within the general framework of human action.

The reader's reaction to the above situation might have included any or all of the following statements: the situation is trite; it is ridiculous; it is unrealistic; it looks at the world quite childishly; or it is a caricature of the lowest values in mass entertainment. But on the other hand, we must admit that to some degree we are likely to interpret the world in this way. There are several kinds of feelings running through all these statements. First, there is some degree of truth in arrangements of this kind. Secondly, the truth is overstated; and finally, it neglects some important values.

We find here a clue to the position of consistency theories and their mechanisms. They are inherently plausible, almost trivial. But the workings of the equilibration process cannot be demonstrated as easily as the inherent plausibility of the theories would lead one to believe. And finally, even in those studies which do demonstrate the correctness of the theories, one feels that they do not tell the whole story, that there must be some opposing tendency calling for more than mere equilibration. Consistency theories are thus in a somewhat ambiguous position. This ambiguity is reinforced by the fact that in this model we take cognition as the motivating source. I propose here that ambiguity derives from the intermediate position of cognitive motives between two other types of motives, and from some basic differences between the motives.

In essence, what consistency theories say is that given the particular consistency principle invoked (for instance, dissonance, balance, or semantic equilibrium) the organism needs only this principle and a minimum number of independent data to understand the world around him and he will have a preference for a minimum of independent cognitions. This model implies that in using consistency, one cognition is derivable from the other cognition. Thus, this is a way in which reason enters psychological theory—a formulation that has its difficulties.

COGNITION: THE REDISCOVERY OF REASON

The place of reason in the model of man has almost come full circle since the Eighteenth Century. At that time, the first fruits for the development of science and the concurrent philosophy of enlightenment had given reason the supreme place in the scheme of things, among other things giving the century the name of The Age of Reason. However, it soon became apparent that this was not an acceptably complete picture of man. It also failed to be a guide for action, especially in the light of the French Revolution and subsequent violence. We may note that the insufficiency was two-fold. Enlightenment neglected the importance of emotion or instinctual drives in the make-up of the individual, and secondly, it misunderstood the nature of reason itself, taking it to be a logical arrangement of the world through sensation. Reactions to the Age of Reason—for instance, romanticism—took mainly into account the first deficiency, raising sentiment to the central place of man's structure. Romanticism stressed the importance of man's feelings, drives, and so on, and in this way argued successfully against the rationalist's point of view. This revolt against reason was so thorough that it did not need to concern itself with the second deficiency of rational theory; namely, the neglect of the properties of the cognitive process itself.

The development of scientific psychology occurred in the same period and bears the mark of the same ideas. It started out mainly as the study of sensations which were integrated into perceptions and thoughts. However, little actually was done on the process of thinking itself. Again, attention was directed more to the motivating forces of drives, later theorized as the unconscious. Understanding of human behavior as contrasted to this situation in the laboratory has come to be based on affect and emotion and needs. A further sign of the counterattack on rationalism within psychology has come out of the attention directed to the intrinsic features of cognition. We can trace this interest to the early work of Gestalt psychology, which investigated the nature of perception as different from that of physical stimulus and independent of the emotional needs of the person. It is no accident that many of today's equilibrium theories derived from the Gestalt tradition. The point of view that the human sense organs do not necessarily reproduce physical conditions but are organs through which the individual is trying to make a consistent picture of the world is no longer the property of any single school of psychology, but permeates all of it. Thus, under the guise of understanding distortions which the individual makes of physical reality, the psychologist has again introduced the importance of cognition, that is, reason. Equilibrium theory uses this more realistic view of reason to show how cognition could have a motivating base. The crucial difference from the earlier theories is that reason is not considered to be a measure of truth, but an organizing principle for behavior.

It is no wonder, therefore, that equilibrium theories sound so convincing, almost self-evident when they are enunciated, but are surprisingly elusive to demonstrate in experimental work. The difficulty comes out most clearly through studies which investigate equilibrium in cognition and the achievement of status. These studies generally find that the most important motivational factor is the desire to achieve positive affects. Thus, in studies of balance it is found that liking, by itself, is a preferred condition, and instead of status-equilibrium, one finds that people in general prefer higher status. Only if this condition is satisfied or controlled can we explore the influence of equilibrium. For instance, individuals would rather have higher status than lower status, but given the same status they prefer conditions where equilibrium will be achieved (Kimberly, 1966). Also, most people would rather be liked than hated, but if they are liked, they prefer to be liked by people who have the same values which they have (Jordan, 1953). Thus, we find first a powerful motive toward conditions favorable to the individual (liking among one's fellow men, high status) which takes precedence over any motives to organize and understand the world. On the other hand, the emphasizing of a world view completely dependent on equilibrium points toward the existence of other drives which may have the same relation to equilibrium as the latter has to need-reduction motives. These motives are the ones which lead to creativity, play or artistic endeavors such as Angyal's (1941) self-realization or Maslow's (1962) growth motivation (in contrast to deficiency motivation). Cognitive motives have thus an intermediate position between these two kinds of motives. We can investigate now in detail the meaning of this position of cognitive motives.

TENSION REDUCTION AND EQUILIBRIUM OF GOALS

First, we shall distinguish between need reduction and cognition as motives, since there are some fundamental distinctions between the two.

Physiologically and psychologically, need-reduction motives have some common characteristics. Physiologically they derive from some basic deficiency of the body (primary needs), and later as a means to satisfaction of those primary needs (secondary needs). Psychologically a need is represented by some stress on the individual or by some kind of deficiency requiring satisfaction. The consummatory response then consists of the reduction of this need and typically elicits feelings of pleasure. Correspondingly, the time to the consummatory response can be long and the response itself may be quite drawn out. During this period, progress to satisfaction can be interrupted and can lead to the typical frustration reaction, such as negative feelings and attempts to overcome the barrier, and retrogression to earlier stages or regression to a more primitive organization. Thus, the need is characterized by a sequence of distress reaction (either primary or learned) to instrumental action toward overcoming frustrating conditions, and finally to a consummatory response.

The situation is very different in cognitive drives or needs. They cannot be tied directly to any bodily deficiency; on the other hand, there is no evidence that they are derived from other drives. They occur too early in individual and phylogenetic development and are too universal for this to be very likely. The difference is shown even more strongly in the psychological description. Cognitive equilibrium is reached practically immediately, while there is no felt need to do so. Descriptions of equilibrium theories conform to this view. They generally say that equilibrium will be achieved, a balance will be reached, dissonance reduced, etc. They do not say that there are tendencies to do so which, for instance, would be interrupted. Because of this immediacy there does not seem to be any way to frustrate the need or to interrupt its consummation.

In short, we can talk about these two kinds of motivations in different ways. In drive-reduction motivation, one may talk about the kind of action which the organism may set up to satisfy the need which it feels. In cognitive drives, we talk about the results which occurred because the organism is built to achieve cognitive organization, in particular, some sort of equilibrium. We shall return later to the possible mechanisms which may be responsible for this effect.

In terms of our previous discussion, we may state the following: If we do not fall into the trap of making reason the supreme motivating force, we can recognize the distinction between tension-reduction motivation and cognitive motivation. This helps us to recognize the great importance of the first type and places cognition in the proper perspective. Recognizing the nature of cognitive needs and the manner by which they achieve equilibrium shows that cognition follows its own definite laws, and is not a supreme arbiter standing almost outside of nature. Keeping cognition distinct from need reduction will make research in equilibrium theory clearer and avoid some of the criticism to which it has been subject. Drive reduction is basically the study of a process occurring through time and is interested in people's acts. Studies of cognition are really studies of structures and organisms and make inferences about the characteristics of the structures.

The typical experiment of balance theory is to present to a subject items known by the experimenter to be unbalanced. These studies attempt to show how the subject would put these items into some kind of balance. They tend mainly to demonstrate different situations in which the balancing process occurs in order to demonstrate the consequences of this process. It is quite fitting for this approach to discount any subject for whom this process did not occur and to omit many features which could be subject to alternative explanation. The interest here is not in how people behave but in the existence of a process, its preconditions and its consequences. Thus, instead of complaining that equilibrium theorists have not followed standard experiments which could be derived from a drive-reduction theory (Chapanis & Chapanis, 1964), we can say that these theorists have modeled too much after them, not having distinguished cognition enough as a separate process. Progress in experimentation and theory will not come from a more detailed look at the temporal process of cognition. On the contrary, we may profit more from working with the place of cognition in the larger framework of human action in general and apply this to a specific problem where cognition occurs and examine the mechanisms which promote it.

PLAY: BEYOND EQUILIBRIUM

Distinguishing cognition from tension-reduction drives establishes the boundary only on one side. There is another side which is indicated by the feelings of boredom and triteness in the example at the beginning of this Chapter. The organism seldom, if ever, achieves complete and total balance. The organizing function (cataloguing, making things consistent, i.e., the preserving phase of cognition) allows characterization of equilibrium as the almost automatic reaction which lacks the feeling tone accompanying the progress and interruption of tension reduction. In balance theory we talk of the end result—that is, of the ways in which balance is achieved, and what the patterns in this achievement are, really doubting that it will in fact be achieved.

Can it ever happen that balance is not achieved? In considering this possibility, we reach the outer limit of balance processes. We have touched at this limit in our example when we talked about the triviality of the world presented in a perfect balance. Conversely, there is a point where the individual's activity tries to maintain a condition of imbalance. One of the extreme conditions under which this is noticed is the kind of behavior which we call creative. It has been shown repeatedly that one of the bases of creativity is the ability of keeping seemingly contradictory cognitions in mind for a long time and preventing premature closure or balance. We can also observe that the superior scientist sees discrepancies in the world which other people do not realize and he is able to keep them going for a long time without explaining them away (McKinnon, 1962). This ability to play one idea against the other has also been described in terms of enjoyment—an obstruction of balance leading not to frustration, but, on the contrary, to positive affect. We can contrast this "enjoyment" to "pleasure" which is the feeling accompanying tension reduction.

The same aspect of creativity can be found even more strongly in the field of art. Artists may be said not to resolve imbalances but to create new ones. The perfect balance of a geometrical design (as well as attribution of balance to human relations) is usually considered bad art or not art at all. Artistic creativity can go even further in creating imbalances than scientific creativity and is not required to eventually lead to some resolution.

The obvious creation of imbalance in the creative effort of art and science represents only the extreme manifestation of a general type of activity which can be subsumed under play (Foote & Cottrell, 1955, pp. 90–94; Russell, 1935; Koestler, 1964). Consistency makes it possible for the organism to structure the world in an economical way in order to react to facts which are connected in a consistent way. Given certain conditions, and the consistency principle, an organism usually needs only one independent event to be able to react to a whole set or network of events. From the point of view of the effectiveness of the organism, this is a necessity for survival, for otherwise, he may not be able to deal with the wealth of experiences to which he is exposed. Thus, he tries to select relevant information from the environment and react to it in a consistent way, as a form of adaptive specialization. On the other hand, this economy may go too far. The individual may organize his world so consistently that he is not able to adapt to change in the environment.

Living systems are able to simplify the organized information and to have a consistent outlook, but also to be flexible enough to adapt to new conditions. Both aspects are important on all levels of organization. In the evolution of these systems, an organism closely adapted to a static environment can become successful by adapting to the complete control of the system, becoming extremely specialized. However, if there is a change in the environment, organisms which are never as well adapted and still process contradictory information, are better able to process new information and become superior under novel conditions. This is just as true for social groups as it is for individuals. Karl Deutsch (1953) has analyzed a function of communication in creating social identity in just these terms, and Toynbee (1947–57) has pointed out the ability of border regions of a culture, which were not perfectly adapted and profiting from the richer original culture, to adapt better to social changes. In the present discussion, however, our concern is more with the effects within the individual. Here, the system which is responsible for the needs of organization, and possibly new information, is the nervous system, especially the central nervous system.

POSSIBLE PHYSIOLOGICAL MECHANISMS

The neural mechanisms through which the organism decides how to integrate experiences and how fast to react to new ones are not completely understood. They, as well as other mechanisms corresponding to the higher cognitive functions—reasoning, understanding, and creativity—are difficult to place on a physiological basis. We can speculate, however, on the nature of possible physiological correlates of balance and its limits. We are helped here by the work of two scholars in different fields, one a general humanist and the other a clinical psychologist, both of whom have dealt with the problem of the function of central control and consistency, on the one hand, and the need for creativity and imbalance on the other.

Peckham (1965) has suggested a social function of art as a producer of chaos for men and society so that the system is kept in a sufficiently alert state to be able to deal with changing conditions. He has dealt with the fact that society defines for itself some objects as art, but that once it is defined as such, there is a rapid drift in all such art productions. This drift is the patterned entry of planned disturbance into society, and is one area where the individual is not directed to solving a problem but toward creating one. Biologically, it is as necessary for the individual to be able to create problems, in order to see changes and new conditions, as it is to be able to solve the problems which have occurred. The latter is the ability of cognitive control or central nervous system control. Koestler (1964) employs a similar argument for his concept of bisociation (association from two different cognitive systems) which he takes to be the base of humor, art, and science, i.e., creativity.

Peckham himself has pointed out the possible physiological base of this theory, which may be found in Rimland's work on autistic children (1964). Rimland considers autism as a cognitive disturbance, not an emotional one as has been frequently considered. For him, the autistic child is one who has no ability at all to integrate experiences, i.e., a child for whom the balancing and equilibrium mechanism is absent or very much impaired. On the other extreme of this dimension, he would put the schizophrenic who has the ability to organize and balance his world completely, but at the cost of losing touch with a reality which is not all balanced. The range of much of the population will fall somewhere in between, with the artistic creator closer to the autistic side, and the systematizer more toward the schizophrenic. From a considerable amount of clinical evidence, Rimland is also able to show that the reticular network of the central nervous system may be the basis of this ability to integrate which is impaired in the autistic child. If we accept the theory, we can say that it is the state of this network in a particular person which will determine his need for cognitive balance. The development of the reticular system makes him see the world in a particularly balanced way and we might find it to be the basis for his cognitive equilibrium. In this sense, equilibrium is a fundamental part of a basic system of the organism. It is, in fact, the manner in which the organism can react to the world and organize it.

COSTS AND REWARDS

A basic neural mechanism may also explain why a certain amount of equilibrium and imbalance-reduction is satisfactory for an individual, but that more or less reduction may cause definite strain. The optimum level depends on an individual's particular structure of the central nervous system. Here we can return to the problems of research on cognitive balance. We have previously discussed the difficulty of the experiments on equilibrium, as they deal essentially with phenomena which are of secondary importance to the individual. Equilibrium is usually less important to the organism than tension reduction. Thus, a laboratory experiment must create the need for equilibrium by presenting unusual equilibration conditions with which the organism must cope in some way. We may suspect, however, that in these experiments it is necessary for the individual to exert more effort in achieving equilibrium than the structure normally allows. The experiment, therefore, usually measures effects in a short duration, and it is highly doubtful how long these effects will last. It is possible that at some point the organism will not be able to integrate these diverse conditions; he will recognize that they are in contrast to each other, and will allow them to remain this way.

In an experiment concerned with both the physiological reactions of dissonance reduction and its effects over a longer time period, such effects were actually detected (Brehm, Back, & Bogdonoff, 1964). Subjects who had fasted for a long period were asked, under conditions of high or low dissonance, to continue fasting. As predicted, High Dissonance subjects reported less hunger after commitment to continue. However, continuing the fast for six more hours had the effect that High Dissonance subjects were actually *more* hungry at the end of the period than the Low Dissonance subjects. That is, when inconsistency becomes stronger, these subjects were no longer able to maintain an equilibrium, and reaction to the cost of equilibrium-effort set in. Incidentally, we also see here that the achievement of equilibrium does not yield any particular pleasure but can be very difficult and effort-consuming for the individual.

The importance of time perspective in the acceptance of inconsistency can also be seen in the study of political attitudes. Individuals who engage in gambling (which implies a longer time perspective and acceptance of change of outcomes) are also less likely to present consistent political views, e.g., to accept the whole legislative program of a president they voted for (Back & Gergen, 1963).

From this perspective, then, equilibrium has both physiological and psychological manifestations for the organism. The maintenance of some cognitive equilibrium is necessary for the individual to function economically in his environment. In its normal range this is simply a function of how the organism is built, especially with regard to the central nervous system. There is some indication that the reticular network has a particular function of integrating cognitions and that it largely determines the normal level of integration for the individual. Equilibration is almost an immediate act and has no particular affect connected with it, except when the equilibrium is somewhat beyond the individual's usual capacity and may require a discomforting expenditure of effort. On the other hand, a certain amount of disequilibrium may be pleasurable. The pervasive presence of art and playful actions indicates the enjoyable affect of disequilibrium in all persons except the most pathological. Positive affect stands at both sides of equilibrium production. Preequilibrium, the reduction of tension, leads to pleasure. The maintenance of disequilibrium in play, creativity, and art leads to enjoyment or positive enhancement. Equilibrium is the cognitive effort, the base on which both positive affects rest.

CHAPTER 20

The Problem of Motivation in Consistency Models

Albert Pepitone

University of Pennsylvania

A primitive assumption of consistency models is that cognitive inconsistency is an aversive state which the individual tries to remove or reduce through bringing about consistency among the disturbing cognitions. The behavior observed, whether it be attitude change, self-evaluation, level of performance on a task, etc., is supposed theoretically to reflect the attempt of the individual to transform the aversive into a more 'satisfying' state of affairs. At bottom, in other words, consistency models are motivational models.

Of the almost limitless psychological conditions that could be motivating, putting the finger on cognitive consistency was surely a theoretical advance for psychology, and what I have to say in the ensuing paragraphs should not be construed as a detraction from this estimate. But the discovery of the interesting properties of cognitive inconsistency has opened a Pandora's box of theoretical and empirical questions. Indeed, a number of questions need to be answered in order to make further advances: (a) What is inconsistency conceptually? (b) Can the various operational versions of imbalance, dissonance, and incongruity be conceptualized as a unitary motivational construct? (c) Is inconsistency a motive in itself or are other, more basic motives mediated by inconsistency operations? In this brief paper we shall try to deal in a preliminary way with some of the questions which bear on inconsistency as a motivation; a fuller analysis has been published elsewhere (Pepitone, 1966). To put the problem into its proper perspective, it will be useful to review the motivational status of the three most well-known models.

Balance

In concluding his exposition of the balance model in interpersonal relations, Heider (1958, pp. 212–217) states that it may be integrated within a more general organismic frame of reference. By this is meant that the strain toward balanced sentiments can be taken as a special case of the tendency of man toward a state of greater 'perfection.' The idea of perfection in the organization of personality can be seen in the work of Spinoza, especially in his analysis of love and hate. In modern psychology, balance between sentiments and unit relations is seen by Heider as part of the more holistic personality theories of Goldstein (1947) and Lecky (1945). The question of why an imbalanced triad motivates the individual to change sentiments of structures so that the triad becomes balanced seems to be answered by reference to a higher order principle of organismic functioning. One detects an analogy between the basis of balance and the organization of the perceptual field according to the laws of prägnanz (see Chapter 7).

There are difficulties with this view of the motivational basis of balance. If the cognitive balancing process is an organismic phenomenon that is part of the nature of man, then it should be observed in all men, in all cultures, but evidence of such a generalization is lacking. Then too, the absence of reliable and valid criteria of perfectionism is a problem that stands formidably in the way of confirmation. Further, to propose that balance-seeking is a special case of perfection-seeking would appear to shift the question of basic motivation to a more general level which is even more refractory to theoretical analysis and experiment.

Congruity

In the original congruity paper (Osgood & Tannenbaum, 1955), there is a suggestion as to what underlies the tendency toward congruity: "Since extreme, all or nothing judgments are simpler than finely discriminated judgments of degree, this implies a continuing pressure toward polarization along the evaluative dimension ...." In effect, congruity pressures have their source in a tendency of human thinking to simplify the cognitive structure in judgmental situations. In the same vein, the congruity theorists assume that to maintain distinctions in judgments requires more energy than to create identities.

It is clear enough that attitudinal incongruities are puzzling; the individual who experiences them probably spends extra time trying to dope them out. Undoubtedly it is sometimes a bother to keep them in mind, especially when one or the other of the attitudes has action implications. But granting all this, it does not necessarily follow that difficulty is the cause, and cognitive simplification the end, of congruity-seeking.

It is relevant to note that such simplification has been cited as one basis for stereotyping (Lippmann, 1922). Thus, when we think of Uplanians as gnome-like hotbloods with a keen skill at bargaining and inclined toward technological subjects, it is because we prefer the economy of such an image and shy away from a more complex characterization that would be necessary to give a complete picture. But stereotyping may not be an avoidance of difficulty or complexity at all. Rather, the characterization of whole groups in such personalized ways may be due to an attempt to speak the 'truth' about the group—to get at the genotypic factors as they are perceived by the individual. Also, the individual who has hostile feelings toward the group tends to pick out obnoxious characteristics and generalize them to all members of the group. The generalization, however, is not necessarily for simplicity's sake but to justify his prejudice, i.e., to prove his 'theory.'

A curious problem with the cognitive simplification formulation is that the congruity between attitudes toward the object and toward the communicator is often difficult to bring about. It sometimes happens that an admired figure does disagree with one's cherished opinion, and in such a case, it not only is difficult to change one's opinions but rationalizations and differentiations are hard to make. Because of a halo effect, hero worship cannot be easily differentiated. Secondly, congruent attitudes toward object and communicator often create problems precisely because they are over-simplified resolutions of conflict. To like someone more because you discover he shares the same position on a political attitude scale can prove not only to be disenchanting but troublesome. We learn the hard way to avoid this kind of naiveté.

Dissonance

In the original statement of the dissonance model, Festinger (1957) de-scribed dissonance as a motivating factor in its own right, analogous to the hunger drive. Although Festinger discusses different ways by which pairs of cognitions can come into a dissonant relationship, once the dissonance exists such a state is sufficient to motivate the individual to try to reduce it.

In their comprehensive review of dissonance theory and experiments, Brehm and Cohen (1962) pointed out that, in contrast to balance tendencies which are based on unlearned "autochtonous" forces of the stimulus field, the dissonance motive is learned. In the developmental history of the in-dividual, states of consistency among cognitive, affective, and behavioral responses have been selectively rewarded. Add to this natural schedule the deliberate training in consistency given by child rearers and educators, and a case can readily be made for the gradual emergence of a learned motive. Brehm and Cohen enter an objection to this characterization of a general motive of dissonance primarily on the grounds that it is not too useful to add to a list of basic needs. It can also be argued that the learning formula-tion tends to confuse the issue. In examining the motivational basis of con-sistency models the Lewinian distinction should be noted between historical origin and systematic causation. The attempt to answer the question of what motivates the consistency effect at the time it is observed, i.e., the systematic question, by referring to an historical process bearing on the origin of the motive, is a displacement of the question rather than an answer to it. And even if the focus is on the question of historical origin as such, the mere positing that a reinforcement schedule must have been such and so is hardly an empirically-grounded theory. Furthermore, if the results of some of the dissonance experiments prove to be valid, e.g., the smaller the reward, the greater the attitude change in the so-called forced compliance paradigm; liking the group more when membership was contingent on a painful, em-barrassing initiation, etc., it seems very unlikely that a simple reinforcement basis for dissonance reduction could be demonstrated. On the face of it, such results are counter to the predicted effects of reward, and have been so interpreted. Finally, and this would appear to be a deficiency of all social learning theories, the argument that consistency among cognitions has been rewarded in the past does not include information as to why this was so. For example, why is cognitive consistency a value which child rearers try to get their charges to internalize?

As an alternative to the view that dissonance is a learned need or drive in its own right is the idea that dissonance frustrates other motives. More specifically, according to Brehm and Cohen, dissonance motivation is based on the frustration of motives implied in the cognitions involved in the dissonant relationship. For example, consider the dissonant cognitions: "I am smoking" and "Smoking is bad for my health." 'Implied' in these cogni-tions are the motives of seeking pleasure and the avoidance of physical harm,

respectively. Although they are not explicit as to what is meant formally by
"*motives being implied* by cognitions," the authors seem to suggest that these
motives are aroused when the individual is experiencing the inconsistent
cognitions.[1] The point is that dissonance involves conflicting motives or,
rather, conflicting response tendencies to which the motives give rise. Thus,
when response tendencies of the organism are incompatible, the motives behind these responses cannot be satisfied, and it is this underlying frustration
of motives which provides the impetus for the reduction of dissonance.
(For a more detailed discussion of the motivating properties of conflict, see
Brown and Farber, 1951; Pepitone and Feshbach, 1962.)

The systematic formulation concerning the motivational basis of dissonance overcomes the objections to the concept of a general dissonance
drive and to the historical origin of it in terms of a vague learning theory. It
is not entirely satisfying, however. One of the problems can be put in the
form of a question: Is it the cognitive inconsistency which frustrates the
motives implied in the cognitions, or are the incompatible response tendencies
reflected in the cognitive inconsistency? Concerning the first alternative, it
is difficult to see how cognitions which have motive implications necessarily
frustrate these motives by entering into a dissonant relationship. One would
have to argue that the cognition of the motive, e.g., "I get joy out of smoking," in some way determines the satisfaction of the motive. Clearly, this
would not be true in the case of biologically based motives, and it is doubtful if cognitive control over social motives is complete, especially when unconscious components are involved. On the other hand, if the second alternative is correct, then the effects of cognitive inconsistencies are mere
epiphenomena. The reduction of dissonance is but a shadow of what the
individual is trying to do in his behavioral field.

There are other problems with the "frustration-of-other-motives"
theory. For one thing, not all cognitions that are eligible for dissonant relations appear to contain motive implications. Inconsistencies among these
cognitions cannot therefore involve the frustration of response tendencies.
Using the rule that the opposite of one cognition follows from another, it
should be possible to generate dissonances which are based on contradictory
sensory information—e.g., when a subject hears a noise but does not see anything that might be the source of it. The cognition of seeing nothing does
not "fit" with the cognition of hearing something. Here the individual is a
passive victim of inconsistency. It was thrust upon him adventitiously and
he holds no motives with respect to what he hears and what he sees. Yet,
the hapless individual can be observed to explore the environment, to pull
at his ears in order to check their functioning, etc.

There are more familiar examples of 'intellectual' dissonances which do
not seem to have any simultaneous response tendencies that could be frustrated. Some of the arguments of the Middle Age Scholastics and the pure
belief crisis that must have been experienced by the disciples (If He's the
Savior and son of God, how come He died a mortal death just like I shall?)
are illustrations. It is possible to argue that, insofar as is apparent—and in
the interests of parsimony—belief-inconsistencies tend to be resolved because

---

[1] Brehm and Cohen (p. 231) say: "... discrepancies or inconsistencies ... produce a
drive toward their resolution because of *motive states insofar as a discrepancy has some
instrumental relationship to their satisfaction or frustration*" (their italics).

they disturb the integrity of the belief system. Similarly, logical inconsistencies appear to motivate the individual to seek consistency in order to obey the rules of logic rather than to reduce the frustration of action tendencies that are somehow related to the logical elements involved in the inconsistency.

Despite their intuitive plausibility, however, these arguments are not supported by the research literature. The plain fact is that in dissonance (and balance) experiments other motives have obviously been aroused by the inconsistency operation and these additional motives may well be accounting for the observed behavior. This does not affect the theoretical argument in favor of a pure cognitive motivation, and it is to this question we now turn.

Cognitive Validity Maintenance

An intuitively obvious but fundamental property of any but the most transient cognitive structures is their subjective validity—the implicit assumption by the individual that the structures correspond to some conception of social or physical 'reality' and are, therefore, right, just, and true. Indeed, the truth of his cognitive structures is so taken for granted by the individual that when queried about it he is likely to respond with: "Why would I believe that if I didn't think it were true?" Apart from its self-evident character we would propose that the tendency to seek and maintain valid cognitive structures is one of the dynamics responsible for the various effects attributed to inconsistency. This postulate is certainly not new in social psychology. Presumably, the tendency to develop a frame of reference to stabilize the autokinetic effect (Sherif, 1936), the "social comparison" ideas of Festinger (1950, 1954) are conceptually similar notions. More recently, the assumption of a need to evaluate emotions (Schachter, 1959) and a tendency to validate interpersonal and self-evaluations (Pepitone, 1964) are statements concerning a cognitive validity need.

For analytic purposes, a distinction should be made between cognitive structures which exist for the individual and the body of information he receives in the situation. In processing this situational information for entry into the cognitive field, two not necessarily independent properties are evaluated: the reliability of the information, and its consistency with existing cognitive structures to which it is relevant.

There are four possible outcomes of the evaluation process: the information may be consistent and reliable, inconsistent and unreliable, consistent and unreliable, and inconsistent and reliable. When the information is consistent, there is little trouble preserving the truth of the structure; indeed when the consistent information is reliable, validity may even be increased. Inconsistent and unreliable information can similarly be easily dismissed. Presumably, it is most difficult to maintain the validity of a relevant cognitive structure when the information is reliable and inconsistent.

The most general statement of the cognitive validity postulate then is that reliable information, obtained from the stimulus situation including feedback from the person's own behavior, which is inconsistent with an existing cognitive structure threatens the validity of this structure. Reactions to such a threat include cognitive processes and behaviors with respect to the threatening situational information designed to maintain or reinforce the validity of the existing cognitive structure, and, less frequently, changes in the structure. It should be emphasized that while such a characterization of a cognitive motivation responsible for the observed effects of inconsistency represents a conceptual differentiation, it is still too abstract for productive use. Overabstractness in the definition of consistency models has probably inhibited their capacity to generate empirical predictions. Thus, the formal definition of dissonance—when the obverse of one of two cognitions follows from the other—is of little use without knowing the rules of correspondence concerning "obverse" and "follows from" (especially when one must assume that 'opposite' was the intended term rather than 'obverse'). The formal definition of dissonance also seems to imply a universal cognitive mechanism more or less invariant across cultures, and that, within a culture, the mechanism operates regardless of the content of the mutually relevant cognitions involved in the dissonant relationship. In our view, this degree of generality is premature and could well be altogether wrong.

Theories of the cognitive processes which underlie inconsistency effects must be much less abstractly formulated and based more closely on the actual contents of cognitive fields. Rather than deal with abstract and atomic cognitive entities such as cognitions, bits of information, elements, positive and negative sentiments, etc., larger, phenomenologically present structures including concepts, values, normative prescriptions, and their derivative expectancies will be more useful for developing and testing cognitive validation and other inconsistency-linked motivations. We propose four cognitive structures which generate hypotheses concerning the cognitive validation process.

The Work-Reward Relation

Many individuals believe that there is (or should be) a correlation between the amount of work done and the amount of reward received by the worker. In most societies where labor is purchased by employers and sold by workers this work-reward concept is present in both parties. In addition, the correlation exists for believers in the Protestant Ethic who view work as a means of cleansing the spirit and perfecting the relationship with God. Finally, it is likely that such a correlation has been demonstrated in the experience of most people, including young experimental subjects who subscribe neither to capitalist nor Protestant ideology. Of course, the sheer quantity of labor is not the only determinant of expected reward-magnitude. The worker's training, ability, sacrifice, risk, education, and other qualifications are also relevant "inputs." (Adams, 1967, for example, has shown that a concept of equity determines the effects of pay incentive on worker productivity.) Depending on the strength of such normative prescriptions, and their particular terms, cognitive validity tension will be specifically aroused when (a) undeniably effortful (sacrificing, risky, etc.) work results in undeniably less than expected commensurate rewards and when (b) easy and small amounts of work result in large rewards. The effects of such validity threats need not be symmetrical. The second violation of the work-reward rule may not be much of a threat, or if it is, it may be more easily handled. Then there are additional motivations to consider.

The Punishment-Transgression Relation

People tend to believe that the amount of punishment received is (or should be) correlated with the severity of the violation committed, i.e., that punishment tends to fit the crime. Although this rule obviously varies with the nature of the violation, the person or agency who metes out the punishment, and a host of other factors, its essential form is widely and strongly believed. Given such a structure, then, cognitive validity tension can be aroused (a) when, following a serious violation, the individual is punished lightly, and (b) when, following a minor violation, the individual is punished harshly. It is interesting to note that the cognitive structure involves expectancies as to how others who commit violations should be treated. The individual himself need not be punished incommensurately for cognitive validity tension to be aroused.

The Social Reciprocity Rule

There is a law of reciprocation in social relations which has been demonstrated time and again in the experience of most people. In general, when one provides rewards for another it is expected (and sometimes demanded) that the rewards be reciprocated. The same holds true for punishment. Given this valid concept in a person's cognitive field, cognitive validity tension is aroused when (a) having rewarded someone, the person receives punishment from him; and when (b) having punished someone, the person is rewarded. There are many concrete applications of this rule in the form of social obligations. When one invites others to a party the obligation to be invited by the others is set up. When one presents a gift to someone it is expected to be appreciated in some psychologically commensurate way. There are certain ethical norms which at times run counter to the reciprocity rule, e.g., when attacked one should turn the other cheek. There are also conditions under which reciprocity does not operate. Thus, if a gift is an attempt to force an obligation, no gift in return can be expected. The presence of the reciprocity rule, its realm of application, and limiting conditions as well as the presence and strength of competing tendencies must obviously be assessed before predictions can be made in the individual case.

The Virtue-Is-Rewarding Rule

There are conceptions about virtue and its effects which are deeply imbedded in many people. To be virtuous is not only rewarding in itself but is instrumental to various rewards. Given expectations about virtuous behavior, cognitive validity tension can be aroused when (a) the behavior prescribed by the virtue is punishing and (b) the behavior proscribed by it is rewarding. Similarly for the individual who believes he lacks virtue, engaging in virtuous behavior which is then rewarding would also arouse cognitive validity tension.

Other Factors

Experimental tests of the cognitive validity hypothesis must contend with a troublesome reality. Inconsistencies expressed in attitudes and behavior, in thinking and emotional expression, are often socially undesirable. Depending upon the nature of the inconsistency, of course, it is frequently the case that individuals avoid inconsistencies or quickly try to resolve unavoidable ones because they expect to be devalued or punished by the social environment in some way. Thus, for example, the law student who is inconsistent in his arguments fears that he will be thought stupid, and the subject who works hard for a small reward or who does not reciprocate the social invitation may fear that he will be regarded as a fool or snob. In these instances, it is obviously not cognitive validity tension which is motivating him to resolve the inconsistency but his fear of losing status, being rejected, humiliated, etc. Thus, to confirm a cognitive validity hypothesis such social motivations have to be controlled or ruled out. When they are and consistency-seeking processes are not observed, one supposes that cognitive validity maintenance plays no role in the particular processes under consideration. When consistency-seeking is observed with such controls in effect, cognitive validity tensions are suspected.

We may conclude this short analysis with two summary points: (a) According to the cognitive validity approach, it is not inconsistency as such which motivates consistency-seeking; rather it is a need for subjectively valid cognitive structures which are threatened by inconsistency. (b) Inconsistency arouses other motives as well as cognitive validity tensions, and the research problem in the consistency model field is to isolate and deal with the interrelations of these motives.

CHAPTER 21

Needs, Wants, and Consistency

Keith E. Davis

University of Colorado

Two questions will be addressed in this paper: (a) Is there a need for consistency? (b) Is a state of inconsistency necessarily a motivational state? In each case the primary concern will be with the conceptual issues, not the empirical ones. Our style of analysis may be unfamiliar to many psychologists, and for background on our general approach, the reader is referred to Ossorio (1966) and to Ossorio and Davis (1968), where the concept of a person and the notion of intentional action are presented as the basic conceptual ingredients of psychological subject matter.

THE CONCEPT OF NEED AND THE NEED FOR CONSISTENCY

Needs. The word 'need' and related verbal expressions contain at least two distinct concepts. The more recent, technical sense is that which we recognize in, for example, the discussion of a 'need for achievement,' where this refers to the person desiring to excel or to accomplish some task that has standards of excellence. Need in such a use is a motivational concept. The other notion of need, and the one central to our concern here, is the conception of a condition, which if not met or satisfied, either leads to or constitutes a pathological state. Much of the nontechnical use of the word 'need' embodies this latter concept, and from this point on, I shall use 'need' only in this second sense.

It is central to a grasp of the concept of need that needs have no motivational implications whatsoever. There are no direct logical connections between being in a need state and wanting whatever will satisfy the need. Rather, the connection between the needs and wants is a matter of brute fact. In a sense, we are fortunate that we want enough of those things that we need to survive as a species.

Needs have their motivational impact through two routes. If one be-

This paper was written as part of the author's participation in the Program on Cognitive Processes, Institute of Behavioral Science, University of Colorado and is a portion of Publication No. 100 of the Institute. Preparation of the paper was facilitated by a grant from the National Science Foundation (GS-945). I am indebted to Jack W. Brehm, Willard Day, Thomas Mitchell, and Peter G. Ossorio for their detailed critiques of an earlier version of this paper. The present version of this paper is part of a longer paper, entitled "Dissonance and Consistency Theories as Viewed from the Concept of a Person," which may be obtained from the author.

comes *aware* that one needs X, then one has a reason to try to get X—not that awareness of a need is always a sufficient reason for action, but it is a reason. The second, more indirect route, is through the alteration of bodily states so that whatever is needed becomes more palatable, tasty, or attractive to the person. In this state, whenever P, say, needs X and happens to taste it, then P will find X more desirable than usual and thus have a reason to get X or more of it. Here the connection between need and motivation is indirect, for P may not be aware of his need for X. His trying to get X would not be explained by his need for it, but by his *desire* for it.

To say that P needs X is neither to imply that he wants, desires, or has a reason to get X; nor does it imply that he will strive for X. Neither is there any implication that P is aware of what he needs or of being in a need state. Nor does the removal of a need deficit imply that P is pleased, happy, or satisfied in the way that P must be when he gets what he wants and finds that what he got is what he wanted.

The Need for Consistency. Is there a 'need for consistency'? Yes. To see this, one need only consider the full-blown case of complete inconsistency between items of information or that between cognitions and behaviors. Suppose that P 'knows' that an object before him is both red all over and green all over at the same time. What does he know? Nothing intelligible about the object. Or suppose that he tries to move his leg forward, and one time it goes backward, the next time sideways, and next time remains still, and so on with no rhyme or reason. What would P be able to do then? Nothing at all that required moving his leg in a certain direction. It follows logically from the concept of intentional action that some level of consistency in the world and in what P can do are required for intentional action. And if a person literally cannot do a significant number of things that he wants to do, he is in a pathological state. The failure to achieve a condition of minimal consistency is, therefore, to be deprived of something one needs and to be arbitrarily cut off from participation in the relevant parts of human society.

When P is aware of something's being inconsistent, it is appropriate to describe him as perplexed, bothered, or puzzled. P's being confused, however, does not imply that he is aware of his state (although he may be). When what P says and what he does are inconsistent often enough, we may see him as a confused person, and if he is confused enough, we may have him committed as schizophrenic or brain damaged. States of confusion are pathological states, and they imply that P has failed to develop the degree of cognitive consistency that is essential for participation in the society. Thus when P's need for consistency is sufficiently not satisfied, he will be in a pathological state, and he may be either aware or unaware of his condition. The influence on behavior of the failure to satisfy the need is therefore indirect. For pathology implies that P is in some way arbitrarily limited in his capacity for intentional action (i.e., in what he can do); but the need condition does not imply any kind of intentional action that is done in order to remove the need deficit. Only when P believes or knows that he needs something and is able to attempt a remedy of his condition does his condition of need provide a reason for action.

That consistency in knowledge and ability is a necessary condition for intentional action is a logical point. Precisely how much inconsistency of what sorts produce what sorts of pathology is an empirical matter, as is the question of what procedures or techniques might eliminate or alleviate the need state. (It is here that one can see the relevance of Ray Miles' work on "random" environments for cats and some of the work on various ways of distorting or disturbing the relationship between perception and the world.)

MOTIVATIONAL CONCEPTS AND THE DESIRE TO REDUCE INCONSISTENCY

If the concept of a Person were analogous to the concept of a Physical Object or of a Plant, then there would be no need for the concept of motivation. It would have no application. Motivation becomes an issue because we recognize that the 'behavior' of persons is not like the 'behavior' of other physical objects. The contrast is embodied in the distinction between intentional action and bodily· motion. When we say what it is that is recognized as different between these two kinds of behaviors, we have recourse to notions such as *awareness, motivation,* and *ability*—to particulars of the intentional action paradigm (Ossorio, 1966; Ossorio & Davis, 1968).

The role of motivational concepts, as has been shown by Hart and Honoré (1959) and Peters (1958), is both distinctive and considerably more complex than that of mechanical cause in physical systems. First, the connection between reasons or motives and action is not contingent but necessary. A reason, a desire (or some other particular from the Want type), must be part of the action for there to be an action.

Secondly, any adequate, conceptually complete account of motivation must have recourse to a discussion of the full paradigm of intentional action. (It is of interest to note that the better recent treatments of the topic, such as Atkinson's [1964], exhibit just such a tendency.) For talk of motivation presupposes the concepts of knowing or being aware and those of knowing how or being able to. Furthermore, in any behavior theory currently in use, the relationship between the content of the motivational state and the overt attempt is that of means to ends. None of what has been said above holds for mechanical causes.

Wants and Awareness. The state of affairs which P wants must be a state that P either believes to exist or believes it possible to bring about—it is absurd to talk of wanting a 'nurg' if one literally has no concept of 'nurg' and no idea at all what it would be. There are, however, some important complications concerning the necessity of awareness. First, while the paradigm case of being aware of something is the case where one can say what one is aware of, there is a derivative case in which P only behaves appropriately to the state of affairs but cannot say that is what he is doing. There are numerous everyday examples of such derivative cases—e.g., driving from one's office to home without being able to say what one did at point X or what happened at point Y, when what happened at points X and Y must have been taken into account in order for P to have navigated home successfully. The point is that we have no other way of identifying such awareness than by saying that his behavior is the kind he would have done if he were aware of X and able to say so. This derivative case is directly relevant to such puzzling psychological phenomena as perceptual defense and unconscious motivation, and the Person concept, far from ruling out such phenomena arbitrarily, makes their existence intelligible as special cases of intentional action (see Ossorio, 1966). The derivative case is also essential for the legitimate extension of the concept of awareness to infants and animals.

The Desire to Reduce Inconsistency. As was argued in the discussion of needs, a minimal level of consistency among cognitions or among things that one is able to do is a requisite for intentional action. A state of greater order among cognitions or of regularity in accomplishments is something that P could try to achieve only if he already had some degree of consistency. The need for consistency is, therefore, more basic than the desire to achieve consistency.

Is the state of inconsistency among cognitions a motivational state? Not necessarily, though often enough it is. To begin with, it is possible to hold inconsistent or contradictory beliefs without being aware that they are inconsistent. Only if P is aware that his beliefs (or his actions and his beliefs) are inconsistent can the inconsistency constitute a reason for action or a basis for altering either belief or behavior. (Again, the formulation does not exclude cases of unconscious motivation, as in instances where the belief that one is a moral person is inconsistent with the belief that one has committed several very immoral deeds. One could then see either expiation, retribution, or self-punishment, among others, as ways of dealing with these inconsistent cognitions.)

To find that a set of beliefs is inconsistent in some way or that an action that one has taken is inconsistent in some respect with one's beliefs or desires is to have a reason for bringing about greater order. And it is often a compelling reason. But this is a logical and not an empirical statement, and, therefore, one does not need to assume that people want to reduce inconsistencies and then check that assumption. There could be an empirical question (and therefore an assumption) about whether a specific inconsistency were reason enough for a specific person to deal with it. Or one could be mistaken about whether a specific state of affairs was one of inconsistency or whether a specific person was aware of it. But the concept of an inconsistency would not have the meaning it has if its existence did not constitute a reason for one to try to remove or reduce the inconsistency.

A complication in the story is introduced by a nonempirical maxim that is at the heart of all behavior theories. "If a person has a reason to do something at a given time, he will do it, unless he has a stronger reason for doing something else" (Ossorio, 1966, p. 72). Even though felt inconsistency is a compelling reason, it may not be the most compelling reason for action at any specific time. Nor would the failure of the person to try to deal with the inconsistency amount to a disproof of an assumption. For no assumption need be made about reasons, and we can still go about the empirical business of finding out what kinds of inconsistencies among cognitions, in what contexts, are typically reasons enough for what persons to try to reduce them.

A fundamental contribution of the research to date has been the creation of situations in which the inconsistencies were made both salient and strong enough so that subjects typically dealt with them. There is, then, no doubt that awareness of inconsistency among cognitions can be a motivational state (i.e., that it is a state of affairs that could give P reason enough to reduce it). Rather, what could be doubted and determined empirically is whether a specific inconsistency was in fact the person's reason for performing a certain act.

CHAPTER 22

Inconsistency as a Psychological Signal

Herbert C. Kelman

The University of Michigan

and

Reuben M. Baron

Wayne State University

The major thesis of the present analysis is that cognitive inconsistency serves primarily as a *signal* to the individual that his coping mechanisms may not be functioning at a sufficiently high level of effectiveness. Through considerable prior learning, knowledge of inconsistency has become an internal discriminative stimulus for the possible existence of a threat to the individual's ability to achieve certain of his goals, or of an occasion to enhance his ability to achieve such goals. Thus, for example, if a person is confronted with a sharp discrepancy between actual events and his expectations of these events, he may (on the basis of prior experience) become concerned about the efficacy of his reality-testing, or he may sense an opportunity to achieve new insights into the nature of his environment. If a person is confronted with a discrepancy between his own opinions and those of significant others, he may become concerned about his status and acceptance within his social groups, or he may be struck with the possibility of achieving a higher level of social integration through revising his opinions or changing his group memberships. If a person is confronted with a discrepancy between his attitudes and his own actions, he may see this as a serious threat to his sense of personal integrity, or perhaps as an indication that his attitudes have not kept pace with changes in his life situation.

Thus, we would expect that confrontation with a discrepancy or inconsistency typically sets into motion active (though not necessarily conscious) searching behavior, designed to assess the functional implications of the inconsistency. That is, the individual surveys those regions of his life space that are marked by the inconsistency in order to determine whether indeed it indicates a threat to the achievement of some of his goals or a possibility of a more effective utilization of his resources for the achievement of these goals. The discovery of such implications provides a challenge to the individual to reexamine his attitudes, his actions, and his social rela-

This chapter is a product of a research program on social influence and behavior change supported by Public Health Service Research Grant MH-07280-06 from the National Institute of Mental Health.

tionships, with an eye to improving his ability to cope with his environment.[1]

The present view of inconsistency as a signal contrasts with the view of inconsistency as a drive state in its own right. We would agree that inconsistency per se has motivational character: it is inherently uncomfortable, since it threatens basic needs for a stable self concept and a coherent and predictable environment. Thus, other things being equal, human beings will tend to minimize inconsistency and to maximize consistency. In our view, however, this preference for consistency is only one of many competing motivations that determine behavior, rather than a 'master motive' under which all reactions to situations of cognitive inconsistency can be subsumed. What we would regard as the *general* characteristic of inconsistency is that it serves as a signal for possible shortcomings in the person's coping processes. Knowledge of inconsistency may or may not lead to attempts to reduce the inconsistency, since reduction of inconsistency is not an important end in itself. The nature of the person's reaction—whether or not he will move to reduce the inconsistency; if so, by what means; and if not, what alternative course he will follow—can be predicted only from an analysis of the *specific* functional implications of a given case of inconsistency.

ATTITUDE–DISCREPANT ACTIONS: AN ILLUSTRATION

To illustrate what we mean by an analysis of the functional implications of inconsistency, let us take the situation in which a person engages in actions that do not follow from his attitudes. The studies in this area that have been carried out in the dissonance theory tradition seem to involve at least two different kinds of adjustive problems. In the first class of situations, a person is somehow induced to perform an action that violates a moral precept or value. In one study, for example, students who disliked Catholicism were asked to write an essay on why they wanted to become Catholic (Brock, 1962). In other studies, subjects were induced to cheat (Mills, 1958), to lie (Festinger & Carlsmith, 1959), or to shock a helpless female (Brock & Buss, 1962). In the second kind of situation, a person is induced to perform a task that is intrinsically of little value, such as copying tables of random numbers or putting spools of thread into a box. These tasks also tend to be boring, unpleasant, effortful, or nonsensical.

Situations of the second type can be said to arouse 'hedonic dissonance,' in contrast to the 'moral dissonance' produced by the first type. Dissonance theorists treat these different situations as formally equivalent and equally likely to generate attitude change or other modes of reducing inconsistency, depending only on the strength of the dissonance aroused. In the present view, the inconsistent behavior has very different motivational implications for the individual in these two types of situations, and confrontation with it is likely to produce rather different consequences.

---

[1] The present view can be brought into line with Schachter's (1964) analysis of emotional states if we assume that inconsistency triggers an increase in the general level of physiological arousal, which in turn motivates a search aimed at providing a specific emotional label for this 'stirred up' state. To aid himself in labeling the state of arousal produced by inconsistency, the person scans both his memory storage system and the immediate situation for relevant cues. Once an appropriate label has been found, it serves as a cognitive guide for the direction of future coping behavior.

The violation of an important moral precept or the negation of an important value carries direct implications for central aspects of the person's self-image. Such an inconsistency affects both a person's basic sense of worth and his beliefs as to his defining attributes. In this kind of situation we expect that the inconsistency will create a great deal of tension and evoke an emotional label that may be described phenomenally as 'guilt.' This guilt reaction manifests itself in a concern over the goodness or badness, the rightness or wrongness, of his behavior. Such concerns may be sharply contrasted with a concern over the 'profitableness' of one's action, which constitutes the major adjustive problem in the case of hedonic dissonance.

When the person labels his affective state as guilt, then he is likely to engage in efforts at undoing his 'reprehensible' action or making reparations for it. If opportunities for such resolutions are unavailable, and if his attitude toward himself is basically positive, then he is likely to reassess the worth of the distal attitude object in a way that would justify his action. For example, having written an essay in favor of Catholicism, he may decide that Catholicism has some good points after all. Or, having cheated or harmed another person, he may decide that the other deserved such treatment. If his self-image is negative, then he may reassess his own worth rather than the worth of the attitude object; that is, he may lower his self-evaluation still further.

We would also hypothesize that, where evidence concerning the evaluative character of the distal attitude object is incontrovertible and a person has high self-esteem, a 'boomerang' effect may be expected. For example, instead of becoming more favorably disposed to Catholicism, the person may derogate it even more; instead of devaluing the one he has cheated or harmed, the person may place him on a pedestal. Such reactions would seem to increase rather than reduce inconsistency, at least in the short run; in the long run, however, they may be part of a strategy of expiation. Whatever cognitive changes emerge out of an experience of moral dissonance, we would expect them to be relatively persistent and to be accompanied by an active search for information in support of the new position the individual has taken. Such information would help to stabilize and protect the new evaluations and prepare the person for future encounters with the attitude object.

In contrast to the situations that we have just described, hedonic dissonance conditions create more transitory and peripheral discomforts. Insofar as they do touch on questions of value and self-esteem, these concern the issue of not letting oneself be 'played for a sucker' or doing something for nothing, and involve considerations of equity (Adams, 1965), of reciprocity (Gouldner, 1963), or of distributive justice (Homans, 1963). The person's discomfort in this kind of situation derives from a 'balance sheet' operation, which leads him to conclude that he has been insufficiently rewarded for meaningless, painful, or effortful activities. The basic conditions for discomfort here are high effort and low reward; the person's major focus is on justifying his 'useless' actions. Unless there are other superordinate values or goals that may be achieved by maintaining this inconsistency (see Chapter 66), the person is likely to reduce dissonance by retrospectively distorting the experience, selectively recalling pleasant and meaningful features, or convincing himself that his efforts were minimal. We assume that what is involved here is a memorial adjustment rather than attitude change, and we would predict, therefore, that effects are likely to be transitory and to produce no generalized reassessment of the attitude object.

It may be noted that such a functional analysis places a very different interpretation on the effects of reward and effort when moral as opposed to hedonic dissonance is aroused. Thus, it can be argued, in contradistinction to traditional dissonance theory assumptions, that in moral dissonance situations the greater the reward the *greater* the psychological discomfort. That is, the knowledge of having allowed oneself to be 'bought,' of having violated one's values for a price, may actually increase one's feelings of guilt. By the same token, the greater the effort (physical or psychological), the *less* the discomfort—that is, the knowledge of having suffered while carrying out the morally questionable deed may serve to mitigate one's feeling of guilt. In the case of hedonic dissonance, on the other hand, we would expect the effects of reward and effort to fit the standard dissonance model. That is, *less* discomfort will be created when there is high reward and low effort. The contradictory findings regarding the relationship between reward, discomfort, and attitude change in a number of recent studies may conceivably be attributable to the fact that different experimental settings, different issues, and different subjects have produced differing amounts of moral and hedonic dissonance.

Other parameters too may have a differential effect in moral as compared to hedonic dissonance situations. For example, choice and commitment (see Section III D) may be of central significance to the arousal of moral dissonance, but they are essentially irrelevant to hedonic dissonance. In short, then, the differences in the functional implications of the two types of situations allow us to predict differences in the way the person will react to the inconsistency and in the type of effect that different variables will have on his reaction.

IMPLICATIONS OF A FUNCTIONAL ANALYSIS

One of the weaknesses of those models that view inconsistency primarily as a drive state—or that are based on the proposition that the greater the inconsistency, the greater will be the effort to reduce it—is that they provide no systematic basis for predicting the mode of resolution of an inconsistency dilemma that an individual is likely to employ. From a social-psychological point of view, it is not particularly interesting to know that an individual will use one of a number of possible modes of resolving inconsistency. What is of more basic concern is the specific nature of his reaction. What are the conditions under which the person will change his attitude rather than distort reality, or the conditions under which he will change group membership rather than attempt to influence his fellow-members? It is answers to these questions that are likely to illuminate social-psychological phenomena. The present view of inconsistency does provide a basis for dealing with such questions in a more systematic way. It has three major implications for the delineation of modes of resolving inconsistency:

1. According to the present view, the primary motivational impact of inconsistency is that it activates searching behavior, rather than—at least in the first instance—efforts to resolve the inconsistency. If the search reveals that the inconsistency has no significant functional implications—i.e., that

it does not present any threats to or reflect any inadequacies in the person's coping mechanisms—then he will do nothing further about it. For example, a person may be confronted with a gross discrepancy between his own aesthetic judgments and those of fellow-members of an important group; in reviewing the implications of this discrepancy, he may discover that it does not result from a poor coding of reality on his part, that it is not likely to affect his status in the group, and that it is not an impediment to the achievement of those goals that are mediated by the group. Or, to take another example, a very serious, task-oriented individual may (quite contrary to his own self-image) turn into 'the life of the party' during week-end gatherings; on reflection he may find that this inconsistency in no way interferes with the effectiveness of his work and is regarded as rather charming by his associates. In these cases, we would not expect the person to make any efforts to resolve the inconsistency, since it turns out to be irrelevant to the achievement of his goals. In general, in order to predict whether, after engaging in his search process, a person is likely to resolve or to ignore the inconsistency with which he has been confronted, we would have to examine the specific nature of the motivational system to which the potentially challenged element (e.g., the person's relationship to his group in the first example, or his self-image in the second example) is linked. Only if the inconsistent element is relevant to that motivational system will any effort at resolution be set into motion. Thus, by viewing inconsistency as a signal for potential shortcomings in coping processes, one can account for those cases in which inconsistencies between important elements are ignored.[2]

2. If the individual perceives the inconsistency as relevant to a motivational system—as having implications for the adequacy of his coping mechanisms—then he is likely to react with some active attempt to improve their adequacy. According to the present view, this reaction does not necessarily take the form of reducing or eliminating the inconsistency, since the source of motivation is not the inconsistency itself but the shortcoming in coping processes signaled by the inconsistency. An inconsistency that is perceived to have functional significance will create a state of tension and activate an adjustment designed to reduce the tension. Tension reduction, however, does not necessarily mean inconsistency reduction. Thus, depending on the specific nature of the functional implications of the inconsistency, the person may bring into play mechanisms that allow him to correct for the shortcomings signaled by the inconsistency while maintaining the inconsistency itself. In other words, the present approach calls attention to mechanisms that allow the person to live with inconsistency, to tolerate it. We shall elaborate on these mechanisms in Chapter 66. For the moment, we merely wish to stress the importance of analyzing such mechanisms, since there is a great deal of phenomenological evidence to suggest that human

---

[2] Consistency models generally assume that there will be no efforts to reduce inconsistency unless the two elements are perceived as relevant to one another. They do not, however, provide any systematic basis for determining relevance, except in the logical sense. According to the present view, two elements may be logically relevant to one another, and may be perceived to be so, and yet inconsistency between them may be ignored because it is seen as irrelevant to the achievement of the person's goals. Thus, we have at least the beginnings of a systematic basis for dealing with the question of relevance.

beings do tolerate troublesome inconsistency, and there are theoretical reasons to assume that the acceptance of such inconsistencies is often functionally significant. It is an arbitrary matter whether one includes these inconsistency-maintenance mechanisms among the modes of *resolving* inconsistency; it may be less ambiguous to describe them as modes of *handling* inconsistency. The main point is that, even when we are dealing with functionally significant inconsistencies, *reduction* of the inconsistency is not the only possible type of reaction. Whether inconsistency-reduction or inconsistency-maintenance mechanisms are brought into play depends on the nature of the challenge with which the individual must come to grips.

3. Let us assume the situation is such that inconsistency-reduction is indicated. It follows, from the present view, that the different modes of reducing inconsistency are not completely interchangeable. Since inconsistency as such is not the primary motivating force, the removal or reduction of inconsistency in and of itself does not resolve the problem confronting the individual. His problem is not to reduce the inconsistency, but to respond to the inadequacy in his coping processes revealed by the inconsistency. Not every mode of reducing inconsistency is equally relevant to the particular functional problem that the individual faces. For example, if a discrepancy between a person's actions and his attitudes confronts him, above all, with the realization that his attitudes have not kept pace with important changes in his social environment, and in his own roles within that environment, then he is more likely to reduce the inconsistency by changing his attitudes than by discounting the action. Hypotheses linking the nature of a person's reaction to inconsistency with the specific functional implications of that inconsistency should provide us a systematic basis for predicting the mode or modes of inconsistency-reduction that are likely to be utilized in a given situation. The same reasoning applies, of course, to the selection among the different modes of handling inconsistency in those situations in which inconsistency-maintenance is indicated.

The implications of a functional analysis of inconsistency extend beyond those we have been able to indicate here. We have tried to convey enough of the sense in which we depart from a 'traditional' view of consistency as an end in itself, so that the reader may carry this type of analysis further. In Chapter 66, we return specifically to the question of modes of handling inconsistency.

CHAPTER 23

Consistency as a Stimulus Processing Mechanism

Jerome E. Singer

State University of New York at Stony Brook

The term *cognitive consistency* can be used in reference to three different concepts. It can be used descriptively as a name for a state of an individual's cognitive system; it can be applied to the entire process or processes which aim to bring about consistency through cognitive reorganization; or it can be applied to a consistency stimulus processing or consistency learning mechanism. In the past, both the theoretical and the empirical work on this topic have been devoted to the process of changing from inconsistency to consistency, and have started with the conception that, at times, people do have inconsistent relations within their cognitive systems. The descriptive use of consistency is widely acknowledged as valid, but it is not a very interesting case and its neglect is understandable. The conception of consistency as a mechanism of cognitive realignment has been adopted as the means by which this descriptive state is achieved.

Yet, if the motivational bases that various theorists ascribe to the forces producing resolution of inconsistency are considered, it becomes apparent that these same motivations and/or forces could equally as well suggest that people strive not only to reconcile existing cognitive inconsistency but also to screen out or avoid potential inconsistency. Such a notion was often included in consistency formulations. In dissonance theory, for example, this was the rationale for the prediction of selective attention or exposure (Festinger, 1957; Freedman & Sears, 1965a). However, considerations of consistency-screening processes based on a resolution notion link such processes with the problems of motivation implicit in the theories of which they are a part (cf. Singer, 1966). Consistency can be thought of as a screening mechanism, then, which is independent of a reorganization mechanism and which relates consistency to broader areas of psychology such as perception and psychophysics.

There is a large body of literature documenting and describing the ways in which people differ in various perceptual, conceptual, and cognitive skills. Under the general rubric of "cognitive style," reliable measures along

This chapter was written while the author was a N.I.M.H. Visiting Scholar at Educational Testing Service. The author is grateful to ETS for their generous support and use of facilities. The paper was supported in part by National Institutes of Mental Health Grant MH-07515.

dimensions such as "scanning vs. focussing" (Gardner *et al.*, 1959), field dependence vs. independence (Witkin *et al.*, 1954), or broad vs. narrow conceptualization (Pettigrew, 1958) have all been developed and utilized. It might be useful to consider the possibility that there is a tendency for people to screen incoming information so as to absorb it in consistent fashion. There are, of course, individual differences: some people exercise an extensive amount of screening, others very little. But, across a wide range of people, the tendency to process information may be considered as a general characteristic, and it is possible to work with such a characteristic from a perspective different from that usually employed in cognitive consistency. A consistency-screening process may be derived from more general considerations of stimulus processing properties.

STIMULUS PROCESSING

One of the startling facts of human life is the amount of overall stimulation impinging upon an individual. If all sensations impinging upon the retina were perceived, pattern or form perception would probably be impossible. If an ordinary conversation is tape recorded and then replayed, it becomes apparent how large an amount of background sound has been screened out or suppressed by the selective human ear in contrast with the monaural microphone. The striking study of Hernandez-Peon (1964), in which electrodes implanted in cats' auditory tracts pick up impulses in response to a clicking stimulus yet fail to register from that same stimulus when a mouse is placed in the cat's visual field, can be interpreted as a demonstration of stimulus selectivity.

Under very 'pure' and precise conditions, there is evidence that human sensory imput is limited (Miller, 1956). Under less ideal circumstances information which cuts across dimensions or which is 'chunked' is more readily absorbed; nevertheless, the amount of material cognized is finite. Consider, for example, impression formation, where one individual observes another for a short amount of time, and is then asked to record his impression of the target person. This impression is invariably selective—the observer will not record certain features of the target. Some physical characteristics or particular behaviors may have escaped his notice. In point of fact, an observer could not, under most circumstances, process all stimuli emanating from another person.

Many psychologists have dealt with the problem of the selection and coding of stimuli. For instance, this is one of the foci of Hebb's classic work (1949) and a major concern of the TOTE system of Miller, Galanter, and Pribram (1960). One widely held general conception is that people have schemata or categories. Stimuli which fit these schemata are easily processed or coded compared with stimuli which do not fit these schemata. The development of schemata, whether they are innate or learned, and similar issues will not be discussed here. Instead, the focus of the rest of this chapter will be on the use of schemata for stimuli about social relationships.

THE LEARNING OF STRUCTURE

The hypothesis that schemata, that is, preexisting assumptions about the way the world is organized, can aid in the processing of stimuli is supported by a variety of sources. Zajonc (1960b) induced such schemata by making subjects either "senders" or "receivers" in an information transmission task. The subjects organized the stimuli differently depending on their set. De Soto (1960; De Soto & Keuthe, 1959) took simple social structures consisting of groups of people and a single relationship such as "liking" or "influencing." De Soto represented each system as a series of discrete units—an ordered pair of people who were or were not connected by the relationship. He found that for each relationship certain structures were more easily learned than others. When the relationship was "likes," a symmetric structure was easier to learn than a transitive one; for an "influences" relationship, the transitive structure was easier to learn than the symmetric. One interpretation of De Soto's results is that people, when confronted with a new array of stimuli to process, make an assumption—a hypothesis or a heuristic—about the structure of that stimulus array. If the heuristic is accurate, stimulus processing (or the learning dependent upon that processing) is facilitated (see Chapter 45.).

There are many possible 'guesses' about underlying structure which people can adopt. Some, as suggested by De Soto, involve assumptions about topological properties such as symmetry, reflexivity, or transitivity. Others may be assumptions about dispositional properties; for example, in the "liking" relationship, if the stimuli are people, the assumption may be they all like each other. (Alternatively, misanthropes and cynics might adopt the heuristic that people dislike each other.) Similarly, people confronted with a host of new relationships to process or learn may assume that these relationships exist in a *consistent* structure. If a person must learn all of the sentiment relations pertaining in a particular group, he can reduce his intellectual labor by assuming consistency prevails. Two friends of a given person, for example, will be assumed to be friends of each other; if two people dislike each other, they will be assumed to be dissimilar in their likes. A heuristic of this sort may work selectively to produce consistency in several ways. It may induce a person to assume consistency where no information exists; it may lead to selective attention to cues implying consistency so that consistency is mistakenly inferred; or it may make relations which are consistent (i.e., the rule) easier to learn than those which are not consistent (the exceptions).

Evidence for some of these possibilities is provided by Zajonc and Burnstein (1965), who utilized De Soto's technique to study balance. They presented each of their subjects with a cognitive structure, a series of related attitudes and beliefs. Some of their subjects were exposed to a series of ordered pair relationships which described balanced structures. Other subjects were shown a series of ordered pair relationships which described unbalanced structures. They found that the balanced structures were more easily learned than unbalanced ones. Rosenberg and Abelson (1960) also provide data which can be applied to this point. Their experiment consisted of having subjects learn an unbalanced situation, and then studying the alternative ways in which these subjects achieved balance. They had to discard some subjects whom they described as exercising "premature balancing." These subjects, although presented with an unbalanced situation, immediately afterward reproduced this situation in a nonveridical but balanced fashion. The designation "premature balancers" implies that these people learned the unbalanced structure and then almost instantaneously modified their beliefs to bring about balance. It is equally plausible to suggest that these subjects had a set for balance (that is, used the assumption of balance as a heuristic principle) and consequently learned, albeit incorrectly, the structure as balanced. Similarly, when Kogan and Tagiuri (1958) asked a group of navy personnel to choose partners for a shore leave and also to predict the pattern of choices, the predicted pattern displayed a greater degree of balance than the actual choices. This excess of predicted over actual balance can be interpreted, in part, as the operation of a consistency stimulus-processing mechanism as well as the operation of a consistency-resolution mechanism. The balanced structure resulting from shore leave choices may be the operation of only the resolution mechanism.

THE RELATION OF PROCESSING TO RESOLUTION

In brief, the point made up to now is that there may exist two similar but independent consistency mechanisms at work. One is a mechanism in a cognitive system which responds to tension produced by inconsistency and seeks to modify the system to be consistent. The other is a mechanism which structures the perceptions and learning of a person so that his cognitive system is kept consistent by all the processes of differentially rapid learning of objectively consistent material and, perhaps, by some distortion of objectively inconsistent material. (This second possibility is not selective exposure; people expose themselves to inconsistency—often they have no way of knowing that it may be inconsistent until they encounter it—and then 'incorrectly' process it as consistent.)

Let us now consider relations of these mechanisms to each other and some useful functions to be served by considering a stimulus-processing mechanism. Logically the two mechanisms are independent of each other. There is no a priori reason to believe that those people who are the most effective consistency screeners are the ones who are most bothered by the presence of inconsistency in their belief structure. Either or both of these mechanisms may result in a consistent cognitive structure. If a survey of a belief system indicates that it is balanced, there is usually no way of determining, in retrospect, whether this balance was the result of a revision of an unbalanced system or the residual of a selective 'gating' process. However, Newcomb's (1961) longitudinal study of friendship formation provides an illustration of both processes at work. In Newcomb's design 17 college transfer students, originally strangers, lived together for a semester in a rooming house. A study of the relationships between value systems and friendship formation showed that after 15 weeks people were friendly with those of similar value orientation—a balanced and symmetric result. There were significant individual differences in the way in which this result ensued. The subjects in the study were bipolar on the California F scale. High F scorers misperceived the value orientations of the early friendship choices, so that although their friendship-belief structure was subjectively balanced, it was objectively unbalanced. Low F scorers accurately perceived others' value systems, tolerating some early discrepancy between initial attraction and coorientation of belief. The High F subjects were using consistency screening as their primary process; eventually these people have reality forced upon them, have inconsistency, and resolve it as much as the Low F scorers do. But the paths of these two groups in arriving at consistency are markedly different.

CONSISTENCY MOTIVATION

The distinction between consistency as a learning and screening mechanism and consistency as a resolving process can help in the examination of some conceptual and interpretative problems. One topic is the nature of consistency motivation. Most of the consistency theories (e.g., Festinger, 1957; Heider, 1958) deal for the most part with the resolution of existing inconsistency. They posit that inconsistency produces a tension or drive within the individual to resolve the inconsistency. The nature of such a tension-building and tension-reduction system is complex and poses many problems (cf. Singer, 1966). Some of these difficulties which involve seemingly unmotivated arrivals at consistency can be circumvented if these recalcitrant examples are alternatively viewed as consistent stimulus processing rather than as consistency resolution. The argument that people have a heuristic or hypothesis for incorporating new information into their belief system requires neither the concept of a drive mechanism nor the classification of structures into good and bad gestalten. It rests on the assumption that when people are confronted with more stimuli than their perceptual and cognitive apparatus can handle, they utilize schemata which selectively give precedence to certain categories.

ROLE PLAYING

Some of the studies that test theories of consistency have been criticized on the ground that they involve role playing (e.g., Di Vesta, Meyer, & Mills, 1964; Morrissette, 1958; Rosenberg & Abelson, 1960). In each of these experimental arrangements, subjects were asked to imagine that they were in a particular situation and state what response they would make. The focus of the criticism, of course, is the lack of correspondence between peoples' statements of what they would do in an imagined situation and their actual behavior in a real one. If the theory being tested is concerned with the resolution of ongoing inconsistency, the criticism is valid—subjects are playing at their behavior. But if these studies are viewed as testing the notion that people presume consistency unless shown otherwise, the subjects are not role playing—they are processing stimuli. The data indicate the forms into which subjects are classifying them.

Morrissette's (1958) experiment provides a convenient example. Subjects were asked to imagine that they were moving into an apartment with three other students. They were provided with some of the sentiment relations in the group and were asked to give their prediction of what remaining relationships would be apportioned with "liking" and "disliking." It is clear that the data do not necessarily indicate what would happen if the subjects were actually placed in such an apartment. They are addressed directly to the question of how these subjects envision the complete sentiment structure of the apartment; i.e., what is their hypothesis about the sentiment system? Subjects are not role playing at forming such an hypothesis; they are actually making one. And Morrissette's data provide reasonably clear evidence that people assume that an incomplete sentiment structure is as balanced as possible.

In a recent unpublished replication of Morrissette's experiment, Singer independently varied two factors: the amount of information to be processed, and the degree of the subject's involvement in the situation. The first variable relates most directly to the stimulus-processing mechanism; the second variable relates most directly to a role-playing test of inconsistency resolution. If the consistency-screening mechanism is similar to the more general stimulus-processing mechanism, then it should be sensitive to the number of stimuli handled at one time. If a large number are presented simultaneously, then the efficiency in processing consistently should be impaired. On the other hand, for a given number of stimuli, the extent to which a subject is involved in a situation should affect the validity of his role playing. The more involved the subject is, the closer the role playing should be to his actual behavior. The first variable was associated with a much larger proportion of the variance than was the second: the structure completion technique was more sensitive to processing influences than to role-playing form.

INDIVIDUAL DIFFERENCES

Difficulties in the area of individual differences may also be lessened if the consistency tendency is cast in stimulus processing terms. If consistency is considered only as a resolving process such as dissonance reduction, then the postulated internal mechanisms make it difficult to isolate the dimensions on which people differ. It is a well-documented phenomenon (Festinger, 1964) that after a subject chooses between several relatively attractive alternatives, he will probably display a reevaluation of the alternatives, the chosen one becoming more attractive and the unchosen ones less attractive. Individuals will differ in the extent to which they show this reevaluation, and questions can be raised as to why they differ. For example, those who show little reevaluation may be resistant to inconsistency; hence, they feel no pressure to change ratings of alternatives. Or they may develop as much dissonance as others but be more able to tolerate it. Or they may experience dissonance and be very efficient in reducing it so that just a little reevaluation provides a great deal of relief. Since there is no way of measuring either engendered or residual dissonance, it is impossible to distinguish among the several possible dimensions of variability.

Of course, it is possible to give subjects a battery of personality tests and find the correlates, if any, of the measured hypothesized dissonance reduction. But this technique will have bearing on the original question of the nature of the individual differences only if some of the personality traits can be independently linked to dissonance arousal and others to dissonance reduction. When people differ in the extent to which they process stimuli consistently (measured by either the Morrissette or the Zajonc and Burnstein technique), it may be possible to isolate the nature of these differences. Tolerance for ambiguity, speed of perceptual closure, extent of focusing, and field dependency, to name but a few, are all perceptual dimensions which can independently help to isolate the precise components of the variability in stimulus-processing consistency.

To recapitulate: cognitive consistency may be due in part to the ways in which people order and learn a stimulus-rich world. This conception may help to explain phenomena such as learning of structure, unmotivated consistency, consistency in role-playing, and aspects of individual differences which are difficult to explain if consistency is regarded only as a process of resolution of an inconsistent system. The conception of consistency as a stimulus-processing mechanism may also relate consistency to a wider body of psychological theory.

CHAPTER 24

Summary: Is Anything Special about Consistency?

Percy H. Tannenbaum

Undoubtedly, a major appeal of the consistency/inconsistency formulation for many psychologists stems from its underlying motivational properties. The promise of a new basic and comprehensive principle that would account for a wide variety of judgmental and behavioral phenomena is an understandable lure, and it is not difficult to see how the notion of a consistency motive and/or an inconsistency-reducing drive had such seductive appeal. But motivational issues in psychology have proven to be rather hard to pin down—at least in the sense of obtaining clear-cut evidence of proof or disproof—and the consistency theories are certainly no exception. McGuire (1966b) has recently documented the give-and-take that has characterized this area, and our present contributors—in other parts of this volume as well as within this particular section—add to the debate. While there is considerable diversity in their viewpoints, some issues of substantive agreement are also apparent. And while much of the discussion is almost of necessity speculative, it does hold out the promise of conceptual refinement if not theoretical closure.

The most salient point of agreement is the unanimous rejection of a unitary, drive-reduction nature of inconsistency—essentially, that inconsistency is an aversive state, and generates activity for its own resolution. In general, this is regarded as being too gross and unrefined a basis upon which to build an adequate theory. Berkowitz, for one, strongly argues that such an explanation may well be inappropriate to accommodate such conventional physiological drive states as thirst and hunger, and to extend this conceptual scheme to cognitive processes only compounds the original error. Though the others may not share this sentiment completely—for example, Back may accept both need-reducing drives and cognitive motivation, but insists that they are functionally independent and different—they each voice objections to the single, undifferentiated drive state model for cognitive inconsistencies.

But rejection of an inconsistency drive does not mean the rejection of a consistency position. Each of our contributors' offerings of dissent is accompanied by the qualification that it is indeed reasonable and necessary to assume a fundamental need for consistency (although after Davis' detailed discussion, one hesitates to use the term). For the most part, the reasoning behind such an assumption relates to the organism's presumed need to apprehend and comprehend things and events about him. In monitoring, processing, and interpreting information from the environment, some degree of consistency and equilibrium is seen as essential for reasons of parsimony and economy of effort, as well as to allow for the predictability of, and hence adaptability to, subsequent encounters. The arguments for such a position are well reasoned in our various contributions and need not be repeated here. Suffice it to say that most assume a universal survival value for the organism in his having a stable predictive view of his environment. This is not to imply that individuals will not vary from one another in their expectations as a result of different previous experience. Indeed, one can readily imagine an individual trained, as it were, to expect inconsistencies, although it is difficult to conceive of a totally random environment. Presumably, such a person would develop expectations that would seem misguided to others but which would still be functional for him.

Given the acceptance of such a fundamental need for consistency, the important question is what happens when inconsistencies are introduced, when the stability is disturbed. Clearly, the tenet that consistency is adaptive implies that inconsistency is maladaptive. Thus, while not all our contributors address themselves to this issue directly, strong violations of established patterns of relationship and expectation are to be taken as being intrinsically disturbing and psychologically dysfunctional. A prevailing viewpoint, then, is that there is indeed something special and distinctive about consistency—if nothing else, that there is a limit to any given individual's tolerance for inconsistency. To complete the loop initiated earlier, inconsistency is regarded as an aversive state to be avoided, but not necessarily one that generates the motive power for its own resolution—at least not in terms of a unitary drive-reduction model.

What, then, does inconsistency lead to? It is on this issue that our contributors go their separate ways, or so it would seem. Back, once he has made his separation between need reduction and cognitive motivations, sees the latter in terms of a built-in mechanism to achieve and maintain equilibrium. Although Back also reasons that such a tendency toward consistency must also have sufficient flexibility to allow for equally pleasurable, creative nonbalances, his formulation comes closest to the earlier positions implicitly advocating a cognitive analogue to physiological homeostasis. Indeed, by treating equilibrium as a feature of the reticular formation system, Back takes a stab at giving the concept a more specific and fundamental locus than hitherto offered.

Feelings of revisionism run deeper among some of the other contributors. Kelman and Baron, for example, argue that the "reduction of inconsistency is not an important end in itself." Instead, they claim, the individual, sensing an apparent malfunction of his scanning and coping system as a result of the awareness of an inconsistency, is thus stimulated to explore the basis of that inconsistency and its consequences for him. The end result may or may not include an attempt to resolve the inconsistency itself. In either case, it is not as immediate and direct a reaction as the notion of a built-in mechanism would suggest, and the essential impact of the inconsistency is its signalling rather than reductive capacity.

It is of more than passing interest to note that several of the other proposed mechanisms have much in common with this concept of a signal-

and-search process, which is itself close to Schachter's (1964) more general theory of emotional arousal. Pepitone's cognitive validity model shares some similar features in pointing to the interplay between the incoming situational information and the existing cognitive structure, as does Singer's notion of the screening of incoming information in terms of existing cognitive schemata in the interests of economy and harmony. Pepitone's enumeration of a few schemata in detail is of considerable heuristic value.

Such models have an obvious intuitive appeal, and have the added feature of fitting into a current trend in psychology to view man as essentially an information-processing animal. In engaging in such activity, the individual may be faced with an assortment of inexplicable and inconsistent—the two are not necessarily the same—phenomena, and the awareness of an apparent discrepancy, either between different inputs or in relation to already existing perceptions, should elicit the kind of searching and support-seeking behavior postulated. It is likely that many such inconsistencies are readily accommodated by the individual having some kind of legitimate explanation available, even if it is somewhat incomplete. For example, a magician's trick may be perplexing but it hardly generates much discomfort or searching behavior if the person is aware that some sleight-of-hand is involved even if he does not know the particular ruse employed. In conditions where no ready explanation presents itself, the dilemma becomes more pressing and the individual is forced to question himself. The companion issues of awareness (Section III C) and the self concept (Section III B) thus enter the picture in such instances and become intimate ingredients in the final resolution.

Is such a model totally incompatible with that suggested by the homeostatic mechanism? I submit that both models may be operative under different circumstances, neither being an all-or-none explanation. The information-processing paradigm seems most suited to situations where the input is of a factual or perceptual nature, or where cognitive 'implications' are involved, as in dissonance theory. When the inconsistencies involve purely affective relations, such as in the typical balance or congruity type of study, the mechanism may be more along semi-automatic homeostatic lines. As I have suggested elsewhere (pages 63-69), attitudes are assumed to exist in some established relationship to one another, and change in one immediately sets off modifications to reestablish attitudinal equilibrium without specific searching or reasoning activity. In such cases, awareness need not occur, and threats to the self concept, as such, need not be involved.

Such explanation by differentiation is certainly not very elegant or persuasive in and of itself. It is offered here merely as a possibility for consideration, to be included along with the other types of differentiation that characterize some of the current theorizing. In their own aversion for the single aversive state model, several of our contributors have noted that different kinds of inconsistency may exist and that these may lead to different kinds of subsequent behavior, including a variety of modes of resolution (Section IV C). A particular case in point in the foregoing section is Kelman and Baron's proposal of a significant distinction between hedonic and moral dissonance, which they have applied to account for different, seemingly contradictory results. In a somewhat related vein, Berkowitz has argued for alternative explanations in terms of "increased responsivity to external stimulation," a critical distinction here being that under conditions of arousal the individual becomes more sensitive to central cues of the stimulus situation and disregards the more peripheral ones entirely. Similarly, Pepitone's formulation of different types and degrees of match and mismatch between existing and situational information would appear to have a parallel potential.

It is of some significance that such differentiation models may possibly account for past and present findings. But even more important, by suggesting the kinds of distinctions that may be critical, and by linking specific different consequences to those distinctions, they point to experiments based on a priori predictions rather than the kind of hindsight thinking that has marked most of the activity in this area. Assuming that the various differentiations can be appropriately operationalized, these may lead to the kinds of refinements that will avoid the pitfalls of going overboard along one exclusive line of theorizing or another. There is a need for some degree of empirical closure in this area, and hopefully some of the Monday morning quarterbacking will be translated into some specific pregame strategy.

The motivational question is generic to the entire range of problems and issues that are involved in the central consistency formulation—e.g., the issues of botherment, the self concept, commitment, etc.—and it is hazardous to treat it apart from such considerations. The contributors to this section have raised some penetrating challenges, and several offered suggestions for further refinement and clarification. One could take issue, if not actually find fault, with each of these models, but progress is apt to be advanced more if these suggestions are seriously considered and accommodated within the treatment of each of the individual problem areas involved. By the same token, the drafting of a more general motivational model undoubtedly must take into account developments in the various subordinate areas. It is there, more than in the general arena, that the relevant and critical empirical findings will accrue, and from which the theoretical generalizations can be drawn.

B. SELF AND THE CONSISTENCY PROCESS

The general task of this section is to make some further theoretical sense of consistency processes by relating them to self, and of self-processes by relating them to consistency.

Paul Secord, drawing upon his own and others' experimental work, points to one important case in which a basic balance proposition is complicated by "self" variables. This proposition, stated in its Heiderian form, is: *P dislikes X* and *O dislikes X* induces *P likes O.* Where this seems to fail is in the situation in which *X* is an attribute of person *P*.

Along related lines Thomas Ostrom and Timothy Brock report in Chapter 28 a study from which it might be concluded (though this is not the precise meaning that they impose upon their data) that the basic consistency proposition does not fully comprehend the case of an attitude bolstered by values central to the attitudinalizer's self. The receipt of information inconsistent with the attitude's cognitive content will move the attitude and its holder less than in the case where only peripheral nonself values support the attitude.

These authors, then, reveal an awareness of the limits that the cognitive defense of self imposes upon the consistency restoration process. A particular persisting theme throughout the section concerns the way in which self-processes may influence the testing of dissonance hypotheses. Dana Bramel carries this theme to its full development. Through a stringent re-examination of propositions and experiments in the dissonance realm he comes to this rather dramatic conclusion: ". . . Dissonance is a feeling of personal unworthiness . . . traceable to rejection of oneself by other people in the present or the past" (and thus leading to anticipatory rejection by oneself).

In these contributions, analysis of the concept of self is used to illuminate problems in consistency theories. Can the consistency approach return the favor? Does it highlight problems in the conventional understanding of how the person develops and maintains a viable self concept?

M. Brewster Smith's contribution partially emphasizes this direction. In a useful convergence with some of Secord's speculations, Smith elaborates a distinction between two types of processes involved in the development and maintenance of a cognitive orientation toward the self. One of these is the familiar trend "toward internal consistency with as simple a structure as possible . . . ." The second is ". . . an essentially unrelated trend, a bias toward thinking as well of oneself as one can get away with." Though these trends are *essentially* unrelated they do often appear to intersect one another. The interaction traceable to that intersection has some significant consequences for our ways of conceptualizing the self in action.

Some of the interesting issues raised by the authors, along with some further ones posed by the editor, are interwoven in the final chapter of this section.

CHAPTER 25

Consistency Theory and Self-Referent Behavior

Paul F. Secord

University of Nevada

The present paper is restricted to the following aims: (a) to treat the self concept from a behavioristic point of view while at the same time emphasizing its social psychological nature, and (b) to answer the question of whether, in applying consistency theory to behavior, a cognitive element that is part of the self concept must be treated differently from one that is not.

Much early work on the self dealt with the concept as a coherent, organized set of cognitions and feelings about one's person and behavior as an object. Frequently it has been viewed as a relatively stable entity comprising the core of personality, and, even further, as a kind of independent variable determining behavior. The very term *self concept* in part implies these connotations. Yet, this customary approach has always been vague in that the organization of these cognitions has seldom been specified and has rarely been studied empirically. Moreover, little research has been carried out to test the stability of the self concept over time; what findings there are do not increase our confidence in its stability (Engel, 1959; Haas & Maehr, 1965; Tippett & Silber, 1965).

Recent work in social psychology suggests that a view of self as process rather than as a mental construct would fit empirical findings more adequately and would increase our understanding of behavior. Instead of focusing upon some inferred entity, it appears wiser to examine closely the behavior of the individual from which the investigator generally draws his inferences, as well as the context in which such behavior occurs. For an approach of this kind, the term *self-referent behavior* appears more suitable than *self concept*.

In the present discussion, self refers to verbal and affective behaviors an individual displays with respect to himself as an object. Self does not exist apart from these behaviors enacted by the behaving person. Thus, *it is not an entity, and these behaviors take different forms under different conditions and in interaction with different persons.*

For the social psychologist, personality theorist, and clinician, the most important of these self-referent actions is self-evaluative behavior. By such behavior is meant any action by an individual, verbal or otherwise, which expresses a value judgment about himself as a person, about some act of his, or about some other aspect of self.

Evaluation should be thought of in a broad sense. Included here would be not only such direct evaluative statements as: "That was stupid of me," or "I made a mistake," but also expressions that might indirectly carry an evaluative connotation. For example, in some contexts, a statement or thought about one's status or role category might have evaluative implications. A patient might feel inferior in the presence of a psychiatrist, a private in the presence of a general, an entering freshman in the office of a dean.

Another important form of self-referent behavior has been termed *self-presentation* (Goffman, 1959). This refers to behavior conveying a clear impression to another person of one or more definite traits or characteristics and ordinarily eliciting some reaction from the other person. Presentation of self in this manner may be carried out deliberately and for the purpose of manipulating the other individual, but alternatively, it may be performed with little awareness. For example, an individual may intentionally ingratiate himself to gain another person's approval: he presents himself in a manner that will be agreeable to the other person even though his presentation is at variance with his own preferences (Jones, 1964). Or, a person may present himself as incompetent in some respect without realizing that he does this to elicit reassurance from the other person. Self-presentation may or may not involve evaluation of self, as in the last example.

The assessment situation, where a psychologist or other individual asks for a self-assessment according to a questionnaire or other device is a special case of self-presentation. In a sense, an assessment situation requires an individual to make evaluations publicly which might under normal circumstances never be revealed in any direct way to other persons. In fact, the assessment process may produce evaluations that are unique to it and occur only as a consequence of it. It follows that the demand characteristics of the assessment situation must always be kept in mind when interpreting its results. Indeed, there would be merit in assessing self through a series of observations of the behavior of the individual in situations calculated to evoke display of self-evaluative behavior, rather than through the usual questionnaire.

Other forms of self-referent behavior that are neutral rather than evaluative, or that are not intended to influence the behavior of another person, have less social significance. Statements referring to bodily processes, for example, may often have little social significance. An individual may say, "I feel cold," or "I feel tired," or even "I have a headache," without implying anything of enduring importance. At other times references to bodily processes may have great social significance. Sexual impotence, for example, would have considerable evaluative connotations because of the implication that the individual is not capable of fulfilling his role in a normal fashion.

Certain social contexts are more apt than others to evoke self-evaluation. These are of great importance for understanding self-referent behavior. *One context evoking self-evaluation is that in which an individual deviates from some self-standard.* He may perform some uncharacteristic action (such as a violent outburst or an unusually clumsy act) which in turn leads him to make some evaluative response to his own behavior.

A second context is comprised of competitive situations. Here, too, a self-standard may be involved, but the nature of the situation also focuses public attention on performance, and there may be some standard of performance expected by opponents or bystanders. *A third context is also closely related: it involves public performances of an individual nature,* such as giving a concert or a lecture. Once again it is deviation from a standard held by him and by his audience that heightens self-evaluation: either exceeding or failing to meet the standard provokes evaluative judgments on his part.

A fourth context that is apt to evoke self-evaluation takes a more general form. *In much social interaction, the individual has a particular identity that he presents. As Gross and Stone (1964) have noted, he may inadvertently present himself in a manner that violates this accepted identity; often this gives rise to an acute self-feeling, most particularly, embarrassment.* For example, if a man accidentally enters a public ladies' room, he has momentarily presented himself in the wrong identity and is apt to feel quite sheepish about his mistake. Or, if, while playing the genial host, an individual insults his guest through some faux pas, his presented self is contradicted, and he is discomfited.

Finally, in many social contexts direct or implicit evaluations of an individual are made by other persons; these lead him to evaluate himself. Others may say, "You made a good speech," "I think you are wrong about that," or, "You are a poor tennis player." Of course, they may also evaluate without saying anything; a conspicuous silence in some situations, a certain facial expression, or other nonverbal actions may clearly convey an evaluation leading to some self-reaction in the target individual. In these situations where another person engages in evaluative behavior, what we call self is expressed by the manner in which the individual receives the other's evaluation: he may accept it, reject it, ignore it, or distort it in some fashion.

Self-evaluations and presentations are not always restricted to the person of the individual. He may display similar behavior with respect to individuals close to him—his best friend, sweetheart, wife, children, or, for that matter, even his property. Criticisms of these objects are responded to as if they were extensions of self; similarly, praise or admiration of them is apt to raise one's self-esteem. The familiar expression "Love me, love my dog" illustrates a similar investment in one's pet.

Prelinger (1959) has shown that individuals vary markedly in the extent to which they invest other objects with selfhood. He administered a set of 160 items, 20 in each of eight categories developed from the ideas of James (1890) and Allport (1937). Sixty soldiers were asked to perform a double sort of the item cards, first into self and nonself, and then each of these into piles of items about which judgments were more certain and less certain. This provided weights ranging from 0 to 3 on a continuum from nonself to self.

Random subsamples of the total sample agreed perfectly in the way averages of the item weights ordered the eight categories on a continuum from self to nonself. Body parts were considered self with greatest frequency and certainty. Next were intraorganismic processes, personal identifying characteristics, and possessions and productions. These four categories were more often self than nonself; categories in the nonself region in descending order were bodies of knowledge, other people, close physical environment, and distant physical environment. The fewest number of items regarded as self by an individual was 25, the greatest number, 153. Total scores based on item weights ranged from 82 to 387. In other words, at one extreme, some individuals excluded the great majority of items from self and, at the other, some included almost all of them.

Thus, the limits of self cannot be universally defined in terms of content; for any one individual almost anything may be included or excluded. There is a further complicating factor: self and nonself may not have the same content in different social contexts. For example, members of one's family are more apt to be regarded as part of self when some crisis confronts the group—this is consistent with the well-known increase in group cohesiveness in a situation involving common fate and an external threat (Sherif, Harvey, White, Hood, & Sherif, 1961). Prelinger's situation is almost neutral, or at most mildly evaluative. In a situation evoking strong self-judgments, some individuals may contract self and others expand it.

Consistency theory and self theory. Now that a position on self-referent behavior has been outlined, *we may turn to consistency theory, and give particular attention to the question of whether a cognitive element that is part of the self concept must be treated differently from one that is not.* There are two basic ideas underlying all consistency theories. The first of these is that certain cognitive elements have a logical relation to each other, and others do not. The second is that a logical inconsistency between two related elements is apt to be disturbing and to lead to attempts to resolve it. These ideas we will take for granted without further discussion.

The major argument presented here is that elements that involve self-referent behavior must be treated differently from elements that do not, because of the many variables influencing self-referent actions. The following discussion outlines some of the reasons for this position.

One factor making self-elements distinctive is that they are often related to one another in some organized fashion. While it is true that nonself-elements may also be related, the organizing factors operating in the case of self-elements are often powerful and overriding, in a manner confounding predictions from consistency theory. Unfortunately, the structural properties of self-elements are little understood, primarily because of the lack of systematic research on the topic. Generally the structure of the self has been treated only in theoretical terms without benefit of a systematic research program. If we restrict ourselves to self-referent behavior, however, some ideas concerning its organization can readily be derived from social psychological principles.

It is reasonable to suppose that there is some linkage between the specific elements making up a general ability which is called upon repeatedly in certain situations. Because the situations require a particular level of performance based upon a complex of specific skills, the skills are not only apt to be learned together, but the individual is likely to develop the same evaluation of each of the skills in the complex. For example, grade-school teachers are apt to expect students who are competent in oral reading to be competent also in writing, in spelling, and perhaps even in arithmetic. Similarly, a boy who excels in one or two athletic skills is expected by other boys to do well in most athletic skills. This expectation of status congruence (Homans, 1961) is apt to shape behavior in a manner appropriate to the expectations and also to produce a common attitude toward the different components of self.

Some empirical evidence suggests that such components do indeed act as a functional unit. Where a person makes a negative evaluation of some specific aspect of an individual, the individual reacts to the evaluation as if it also applied to components other than the target aspect. For example, in one experiment individuals were criticized by an expert on their performance of a few specialized motor tasks; as a result they lowered their self-evaluation of their general athletic ability (Maehr, Mensing, & Nafzger, 1962). In an unpublished experiment, this investigator found that individuals evaluated by an assistant as poor in a rather narrow specific ability defined as 'abstract thinking' responded by also evaluating themselves as lower in general intelligence than those who were led to think they were good at abstract thinking. Moreover, those who thought of themselves as high in general intelligence resisted more strongly the suggestion that they were poor at abstract thinking, supporting the idea that this specific component was linked to the more general one.

A second social phenomenon apt to produce linkage between elements of self consists of the major roles that a person assumes in life. Both age-sex and occupational roles are likely to produce ties between certain self-traits. If so, a strong negative or positive evaluation of an attribute central to the role would be expected to spread to other attributes of the role as well.

The point of these examples is that what looks like a simple consistency experiment is in fact made more complex because it involves self-referent behavior. According to interpersonal congruency theory, an individual should like another person who evaluates him in the same way he evaluates himself. Through suitable manipulations, an experimenter successfully leads an individual to believe that he is either good or poor at abstract thinking. A straightforward prediction would be that another person who evaluates him in the same way should be liked. But this ignores the relatedness of self-elements.

If the evaluation is positive and congruent, liking increases, and the prediction is apparently confirmed. But if the evaluation is negative and congruent, the prediction is not confirmed. What apparently happens is that negative evaluations have the property of spreading to other related aspects of self which have a positive valence. Thus, the negative evaluation is congruent with the target attribute but not with related attributes, and the conceptualization in terms of consistency theory has had to be modified because self-referent behavior is involved.

A further complication is that linkages among components of self may vary in interaction with different persons. A common case is the sensitivity of an individual to criticisms offered by a person he loves. In this instance, a negative evaluation of some aspect of self is apt to be applied to the whole self. A proverbial example is that of the wife who, told by her husband that her new hat looks funny, bursts into tears and says, "You don't love me!" Yet she may well have totally ignored a suggestion by the salesgirl that the hat was not becoming to her. This suggests that the role category of the evaluator must be taken into account, a point consistent with Harvey's finding (1962) that reactions to evaluations by friends and strangers differ. Of course the ultimate demonstration would be one showing no difference between friends and strangers for nonself-elements vs. a difference for self-elements.

Another way in which the structure of the experiment may arouse self-evaluations that confound the results is illustrated by Rosenberg (1965). He suggests that the familiar Festinger and Carlsmith (1959) study, in which small rewards for performing attitude-discrepant behavior brought about more change than large rewards, can be readily explained by interpreting the situation as one in which the subject is anxious about being evaluated by the experimenter, and that the dissonance interpretation is gratuitous. His replication, which was structured to deemphasize self-evaluation, demonstrated a direct relation between attitude change and reward, in contrast to the previously obtained inverse relation. A subsequent investigation has obtained similar results for anonymous essay-writing, but with face-to-face role-playing, findings are consistent with the earlier Festinger and Carlsmith study (Carlsmith, Collins, & Helmreich, 1966; see also Section IV F of this volume).

Other contrasts between self and nonself-elements arise because the individual may have strong motives for presenting self in an inconsistent manner. For example, he may occasionally behave contrary to expectation just to confound another person; being too predictable may well weaken his power over the other. Or he may present self in an inconsistent manner to annoy the other person or to provoke from him a response against which he can retaliate. Presentation of self may frequently be inconsistent with private views of self. A bold manner may in fact be a front for a lack of confidence in one's ability to succeed. Certain role positions require behavior at odds with self; nevertheless the role incumbent must play the part. Self-mechanisms probably operate here to counter the inconsistency; such mechanisms are unlikely to be found in studies of nonself-elements. An example is Goffman's (1961) concept of role distance: the individual adopts some mannerism or sign indicating a separation between role and self. This is illustrated by the hospital psychiatrist who is sympathetic to patients and who maintains distance from his administrative role by wearing his shirt without a tie and open at the collar.

One of the most perplexing problems is that many elements will vary markedly among individuals in the extent to which they are invested with self. Because of this, considerable thought must be given to the choice of elements and to the structure of the experiment on consistency theory. Preferably, important aspects of the experiment should be either clearly relevant or clearly not relevant to self for the great majority of subjects in the investigation. When they are relevant to self, special consideration must be given to the effect of this relevance upon the outcome of the experiment.

CHAPTER 26

Dissonance, Expectation, and the Self

Dana Bramel

State University of New York at Stony Brook

A close look at the writings of the people who claim to speak within the dissonance theory stream reveals that there is more than one theory of 'cognitive dissonance,' and it is not always clear which of these is being advocated by any given writer at any given time. Most of these differences are traceable to the ambiguity of Festinger's definition of dissonance; some must be faced before we can say with any confidence what the role of the self is in 'the' theory.

In the first detailed exposition of his theory, Festinger (1957) stated in effect that two cognitions are in a dissonant relation if the opposite of one follows from the other in the subjective world of the person holding both cognitions. The meaning of the words 'follows from' has never been made completely unambiguous in any published account. [However, see Chapter 1, pp. 9 and 23, and Chapter 5, pp. 128–132—Ed.] A careful reading of Festinger's theoretical writings seems to lead to the conclusion that, in his theory, dissonance is aroused whenever an expectation about what will be observed is disconfirmed. Thus, X follows from Y if, believing Y, the organism therefore expects X. But even the term 'expectation' is vulnerable to misinterpretation. When the invitation reads, 'Guests will be expected in formal attire,' something more than a mere prediction of how the guests will in fact dress is implied. Festinger has rarely been completely explicit about distinguishing the disconfirmation of an expectation (in the Tolman and Brunswik, 1935, sense) from the unfulfillment (or frustration) of a desire. The most documentable conclusion would be that he intends to say that dissonance occurs if, and only if, an organism attends to some information which is contrary to what it expected. The non-occurrence of an event which is desired but not expected apparently does not arouse dissonance according to Festinger's version of the theory (cf. 1957, pp. 277–278). A similar line of reasoning is presented in a later article (Festinger & Bramel, 1962) and in *Deterrents and reinforcement* (Lawrence & Festinger, 1962). Others who have interpreted the theory in this way are Aronson and Carlsmith (1962, 1963), Malewski (1964), Gerard, Blevans, and Malcolm (1964), Deutsch, Krauss, and Rosenau (1962), and Brown (1965).

If dissonance theory is interpreted to bear only upon the confirmation and disconfirmation of expectations, then it is clear that most of the experiments claimed as tests of the theory are seriously confounded with frustrations and anxieties aroused by the same manipulations intended to arouse dissonance. The unfortunate subject in the High Dissonance condition typically finds himself behaving in a way that is not only unexpected but which also arouses additional uncomplimentary implications about himself. With a few exceptions (mostly reflecting Aronson's influence), dissonance theorists have not bothered to distinguish in their research among the various sources of affect and unpleasantness aroused by so-called dissonance manipulations. Nearly everyone seems to have been content to refer to this mixed bag of stimuli as 'dissonance arousing.' I think it is important now to take a closer look at the nature of dissonance and the conditions that arouse it.

Let us begin by examining one of the basic dissonance-arousing situations—the one in which a person chooses from among alternative actions which are comparable in attractiveness. There are at least two sources of unpleasantness which are peculiar to the case where the person feels responsible for the choice he has made. Dissonance theorists agree that one or both of these sources arouse dissonance. The first source is the encountering of information which disconfirms an expectation (often about oneself). This can occur also in situations not involving an explicit choice among alternatives. The second source is the discovery that one has chosen incompetently or immorally, regardless of whether one had expected to do so. I shall deal with each source in turn.

DISCONFIRMATION OF EXPECTATION

The chooser ordinarily expects himself to choose one of the best of the available alternatives, at least given the information at his disposal at the time of the decision. Hence, after the decision has been made, any piece of information (especially if available at the time of the decision) which implies the decision was a bad (irrational) one violates his expectation that he behaves rationally. It questions his ability to predict his own behavior. This argument can be applied equally to the case of the person who expects himself to behave irrationally. Such a person (if he exists) will have his expectations about himself disconfirmed by information implying that the decision was a rational one. The theory states that an unpleasant emotional state is aroused by attention to contraexpected information, regardless of whether that information has other implications of a predominantly desirable or undesirable nature.

Several studies have produced results consistent with this version of dissonance theory. Malewski (1962) reports correlational data indicating that subjects with (unmanipulated) low self-esteem show less of the typical dissonance reduction effects after a decision than do subjects with high self-esteem. The same finding is reported by Gerard, Blevans, and Malcolm (1964), who manipulated their subjects' evaluation of their own artistic ability. Those with higher expectations about their ability to choose among paintings were the ones most likely to push the choice alternatives farther apart after their decision among paintings had been made.

In my own devilish experiment relevant to this issue (Bramel, 1962) I manipulated the global self-esteem of male subjects with an array of faked personality test analyses. Half were led to believe that they were very exemplary specimens of humankind, while the others were told that their adaptation to life was shaky indeed. The intended effect of this manipulation was to set up differential expectations in these two groups concerning the nature of future information to be 'revealed' about themselves. All subjects were shortly thereafter made to believe that they had clearly detectable (but not extreme) homosexual tendencies. The design attempted to vary the amount of expectation-disconfirmation introduced by this information while holding constant the extent to which subjects would find the information otherwise undesirable. Presumably, subjects in both self-esteem conditions found it very unpleasant to 'discover' that they had homosexual motivation. For both groups this unpleasantness included a dose of frustration of their desire to be masculine; it also included a specific disconfirmation of their belief that they were not at all homosexual. The main difference between the groups theoretically was that the information would be less expected by those with high self-esteem, since it contrasted so strongly with all the information they had received in the personality report. It was hypothesized that dissonance could be reduced by projecting the trait onto others; the data showed that subjects in the High Self-Esteem group attributed more homosexuality to another person that did those with low self-esteem. In a related experiment, Glass (1964) showed that subjects with manipulated high self-esteem are more likely to rationalize their aggressive behavior.

Although the belief that one is homosexually motivated or aggressive is more unexpected for the person with high self-esteem, one could reason that it is more frustrating in other ways for the person with low self-esteem; perhaps he is more motivated to *raise* his self-esteem than the person with high self-esteem is motivated to *maintain* his high level. Assuming that a person can raise his self-esteem by attributing undesirable traits to others, one could reasonably make a prediction opposite to that made from the 'expectation' version of dissonance theory. A full experimental design therefore requires variation not only in the unexpectedness of the information, but also in its 'intrinsic' desirability. Subjects with high and low expectations about themselves must be exposed to information which, aside from its unexpectedness, is otherwise desirable or undesirable (i.e., signals positive or negative reinforcement of some kind).[1]

One of the first experiments employing the four-cell design was done by Deutsch and Solomon (1959). They manipulated their subjects' evaluations of their own performances on a task; then each subject received a note (purportedly from another subject) either praising or derogating her performance. The dependent variable was the final level of liking for the note-sender. The data showed the predicted effects both of the favorability of the note and of the confirmation or disconfirmation of the subjects' expectations. Those most displeased by the note were the ones who were both derogated and expected praise. Those most pleased were the ones who

---

[1] Pepitone (1964) performed such an experiment on projection, in which subjects with manipulated high and low self-esteem were then presented with either favorable or unfavorable information about themselves. The overall interaction predicted by dissonance theory failed to reach significance, but the data on projection of the favorable information were consistent with the theory. Subjects with low self-esteem attributed the favorable trait to others more than did the High Self-Esteem subjects, for whom the information was not unexpected.

were both praised and expected praise. A similar experiment was done by Wilson (1965) and gave confirmatory results. Subjects who were induced to make a public commitment to a low self-evaluation actually disliked the confederate who praised his performance more than the one who called it poor. By contrast, when the subject was not firmly anchored in his low self-evaluation, he preferred the praiser to the derogater.

A related series of studies was initiated by Aronson and Carlsmith (1962). Subjects were led to expect themselves to perform either at a high or a low level on a task. Then, after a number of consistent trials, a critical trial was presented, and the subject was told either that he had performed well or poorly. For some subjects, this critical trial performance was consistent with their expectation; for others it constituted a sharp change in performance level. The dependent variable was the tendency of the subject to revise his performance on the critical trial when given a chance to take that trial over again. The assumption was that the more unpleasant the feedback, the more likely that the subject would attempt to change his performance on the retest.

First, let us be clear about the prediction from the theory. Naturally, since other forces than expectation disconfirmation exist in the world, they must be taken into account in the forecast. There are four conditions. Subjects who have been performing well and then find they have performed well once again are presumably content. They have neither dissonance nor frustration of the desire to perform well. Those who have been performing well and suddenly perform badly should have strong motivation to revise their performance. Their expectation has been disconfirmed, and they may, in addition, feel ashamed or guilty after such a poor performance. Among the subjects who have originally performed poorly, the latest performance should not produce such differential reactions. Those who suddenly find themselves doing well have their expectation disconfirmed but the rest of their desires fulfilled; those who find themselves still doing poorly have their expectations confirmed but their other hopes dashed. Both of these Low Expectation groups have conflicting reactions, since the expectation and desire forces operate in opposite directions within each group. One would thus expect less difference between these groups in the tendency to revise performance when given a chance. The overall prediction, then, is that the tendency to change performance will be greatest for the High Expectation-Low Performance group and least for the High Expectation-High Performance group. The Low Expectation groups would fall in between the other two. Although it would be foolhardy to predict the direction of difference between the two Low Expectation groups, one can clearly predict an overall interaction between the Expectancy and 'Subsequent Performance' manipulations.[2]

---

[2] Aronson and Carlsmith (1962) were relatively clear on this point in their theoretical introduction but then tended to overstress the theoretical importance of an obtained difference between the two Low Expectancy groups. In an excellent review and report of further studies Brock, Edelman, Edwards, and Schuck (1965) incorrectly imply that dissonance theory requires more changes in the Low Expectancy-High Performance than in the Low Expectancy-Low Performance group. It is indeed true that dissonance should be greater for the High Performance subjects, but frustration of the desire to do well (not part of this dissonance analysis) would be greater in the Low Performance subjects. The resultant tendencies to change the performance cannot be predicted without some way of assessing the relative strengths of these two opposed processes.

I have seen the data of nine experiments which seem, on the face of it, to satisfy the requisite conditions for a test of the foregoing dissonance hypothesis. They are reported by Aronson and Carlsmith (1962), Cottrell (1965), Lowin and Epstein (1965), and Brock et al. (1965, experiments Nos. 1, 2, 3, 4, 6, and 7).[3] Of the nine experiments, eight produced interaction effects in the predicted direction; the only exception (Brock et al., experiment No. 6) had a nonsignificant interaction in the opposite direction. Of the eight instances in the predicted direction, three were reported to reach conventional significance levels.[4] Certainly this array of data on performance expectancy does not constitute impressive support for the hypothesis that disconfirmation of expectation is aversive. However, there is reason to believe that the particular dependent variable used in these experiments is of low validity (cf. the discussions in Brock et al., 1965; Lowin & Epstein, 1965; Waterman & Ford, 1965).

A number of other strategies for testing the role of expectations have been initiated by Aronson, Carlsmith, and others (e.g., Aronson, Carlsmith, & Darley, 1963; Carlsmith & Aronson, 1963; Goldberg, 1965; Sampson & Sibley, 1965; Lamb & Singer, 1966). As with the above-discussed performance expectancy research, the results in these other areas have also been mixed in their support for this version of dissonance theory. There is some evidence that the dissonance effect is reliable only when the disconfirmed expectation had been firmly held. Only then, perhaps, is the affective arousal sufficiently great to be aversive. [The topic of disconfirmed expectancies is further treated in Section III E.]

BEHAVIOR IMPLYING INCOMPETENCE OR IMMORALITY

The second source of discomfort said to be peculiar to the person who feels responsible for the outcomes he has received is as follows: Any information about the chosen or rejected alternatives which implies the decision was a bad one (irrational, signaling punishment) implies that the chooser is incompetent and/or immoral—not capable of choosing intelligently or ethically. It is very easy to confuse this source of discomfort with the case discussed above, in which the person was allegedly disturbed because he could not understand his own behavior (it violated his expectation about himself). In the present focus, the person is, theoretically, disturbed *whether or not* he expected himself to behave rationally.

The distinction is clearest if we examine the case of the person who expects himself to behave irrationally, or who at least has a low opinion of his general ability to make decisions of the sort he is currently induced to make. Presumably, such a person does not firmly expect to find, after the decision is made, that the decision was a good one. His confidence in himself being low, he is prepared to discover that he made a mistake. What happens

---

[3] Several experiments are not precisely relevant to this issue for various reasons. Ward and Sandvold (1963) did not establish strong expectations about performance. Waterman and Ford (1965) did not report data on tendency to change performance after disconfirmation of expectation. Silverman and Marcantonio (1965) did not include the essential high-expectation conditions. Brock et al. (1965, experiment No. 5) probably allowed the subjects to revise their expectations before the dependent measure was taken.

[4] The published report of a fourth experiment (Brock et al., experiment No. 2) mistakenly attributed statistical significance to a weak interaction F.

when such a person attends to information implying that the decision really was a bad one? It comes as no surprise; it disconfirms no strong expectation, and may even confirm his expectation about himself. Does this mean that he is not disturbed about the irrationality of his decision? No.[5] Even though he has not mispredicted his own behavior, he has nevertheless made an incompetent or immoral decision. He has brought undesirable consequences upon himself and perhaps other people as well. This probably rearouses anxiety associated with past situations in which he has been punished for incompetent or immoral decisions.

To make the analytical separation between the two sources of unpleasantness even clearer, imagine how this person with low self-confidence feels when he attends to information implying that his decision was really a very good one. This is inconsistent with his expectation that he will bungle the decision. Hence it questions his understanding of his own ability. But this information certainly is pleasant in other respects. It allows him actually to raise his self-esteem and pat himself on the back. In such a situation this person theoretically has dissonance aroused by his failure to confirm his expectations about himself, but at the same time he is free from the anxiety which would have been aroused if he believed he had made an incompetent decision.

The confusion between these two sources of affect is easily made, simply because the typical person probably expects himself to behave in his own best interests (i.e., rationally). Hence, information implying that a decision was a bad one both disconfirms his expectation about himself and makes him feel incompetent as a decision-maker. The entire situation is bleak for such a person. The distinction only becomes clear theoretically when the two determinants work in different directions, as with the person with very low self-esteem, for whom, theoretically, some dissonance is aroused by the discovery that what he has done is very competent or morally praiseworthy.

These same two sources of discomfort can be traced through a number of areas of traditional dissonance research. It is clear that whenever a person chooses from among alternatives, information implying that the choice was a poor one is relevant both to his expectations about his own behavior and to his feelings of competence and moral goodness as a decision-maker. A person who decides to tell a lie may or may not be surprised to see himself behaving in this way, and, in addition, he will probably experience the guilt feelings associated with past punishment for such immoral behavior. A person who performs a task may or may not be surprised by the level of his performance, but if his performance is poor he will probably experience the feeling of shame often associated with past ridicule. A child who obeys an injunction against playing with an attractive toy may or may not be surprised to observe his own docility, but may be ashamed of it nevertheless. The person who agrees to go several more hours without food or who agrees to undergo electric shocks is a precisely parallel case.

---

[5] It is difficult to speculate about the person who is certain that he will choose the wrong alternative. He would be better off flipping a coin or choosing the opposite of what his reasoning has generated. Further, such a person may have become emotionally adapted to dissonance so that it has ceased to disturb him. For purposes of exposition, it is sufficient to assume a person who believes that his decisions are scarcely better than could be achieved by flipping a coin. Such a person has no strong expectation about the rationality of his decision, hence expectation disconfirmation adds relatively little to his discomfort.

All of the experiments in which a subject is induced with minimum justification to choose a course of action which leads to foreseeable negative consequences potentially include both sources of unpleasantness. The typical subject is probably baffled to see himself acting in a self-punishing manner, because he does not expect himself to behave in this way. Further, even if he expects himself to get the short end of the stick, it is still a humiliating experience, for very few people enjoy believing either that they have acted foolishly or that an audience may take them for a sucker.

I have already discussed some of the experiments which have tested for the effect of expectation disconfirmation independent of the 'intrinsic' desirability of the information. Have there been any tests of the effect of information implying incompetence or immorality in situations where this information is not unexpected? Such a design would require ideally that subjects be led to expect to behave incompetently or immorally and then be exposed to information consistent with this expectation vs. no information (as a control). Experiments employing subjects with high expectations are irrelevant for obvious reasons. I know of no data testing this specific issue. There are some difficult problems in designing such an experiment. If the undesirable consequences of a decision are known to the subject in advance of his decision, then it is difficult to keep the control subjects (no attention to undesirable consequences) from thinking about them. An alternative is to use the fait accompli technique, whereby new undesirable information is fed to one group of subjects after the decision has irrevocably been made. This technique encounters several objections. The magnitude of dissonance thus introduced may turn out to be slight since the person may not feel responsible for consequences he could not have anticipated. Secondly, the fait accompli information is unexpected (by definition) and therefore might arouse 'disconfirmation' dissonance in this group of subjects, thus reintroducing the confounding factor the design was intended to exclude. Another way to test this version of the theory would be to allow the disconfirmation-of-expectation variable to be present but theoretically operating in a direction opposite to the 'intrinsic-undesirability' variable. Positive results would then imply that the effect is a strong one.

A CONFRONTATION AND A PROPOSED RESOLUTION

Is the subjective state aroused by both of these distinct antecedents to be called cognitive dissonance? If dissonance is aroused only by the disconfirmation of an expectation, then the person who expects himself to make a bad or mediocre choice has very little dissonance when he discovers that indeed the choice was precisely that. If Festinger held strictly to this view, then he would have to conclude that most 'dissonance' experiments were badly confounded with conditions arousing guilt and shame, as in the above examples. In practice, however, many of these 'confounded' experiments were designed by Festinger himself, or under his supervision.

The confusion potentially arising from the confounding of these factors is strikingly illustrated in the book by Brehm and Cohen, *Explorations in cognitive dissonance* (1962). They conclude their painstaking review of the area by calling 'dissonance arousing' only those factors which have been confounded with the disconfirmation of expectations in most relevant research. They argue that dissonance is aroused, not because expectations have been contradicted, but rather because the person has caused unpleasant (unwanted, frustrating) consequences for himself. Consider the following quotation:

> In any one of the experiments mentioned, the simple existence of inconsistency has not been shown to be enough to motivate behavior; in each case the person has arrived at a state of dissonance as a consequence of some prior commitment that has consequences for satisfaction of important needs (p. 230).

By this statement they seem to mean that the disconfirmation of an expectation ("inconsistency," in their terms) is at best a very minor source of dissonance. Brehm and Cohen's position, that no dissonance exists unless important motives are being frustrated, would clearly rule out those instances in which an event more desirable than expected is perceived to occur. Although they are unquestionably correct in attributing part of the power of 'dissonance' manipulations to the fact that almost all of them have indeed produced strong frustrations or anxieties in addition to the affect aroused by disconfirmation of expectations, it is curious that their use of the term dissonance practically excludes Festinger's original notion from the domain of the concept!

How can one make sense of this disorder? What do disconfirmation of expectations and feeling responsible for getting oneself into punishing situations have in common, if anything? If, hopefully, they both produce essentially the same kind of emotional state in the person, one could call that state dissonance and even go on to find out whether there are yet other circumstances that also funnel into the same organismic response. This is of course difficult at present because we do not have very adequate measures of emotional states—either subjectively or objectively defined.

I offer the following tentative speculation: Consider first the case of the person who finds that he has voluntarily chosen a course of action which has punishing consequences for him. How does he feel? He feels stupid, foolish, irrational, perhaps guilty. But what does that mean? What is the source of these feelings? Perhaps in the past he has been punished in various ways for making bad choices. People have probably laughed at him, scolded him, excluded him from their group, etc. (Perhaps he has occasionally received sympathy, but that is not the dominant audience response, for, if the socializing community rewarded incompetence, the group would not last very long.) What is rearoused in the present instance of incompetent or immoral behavior may be the conditioned emotional component of those earlier punishment situations.

How does this compare with what happens when an expectation is disconfirmed? If the person has acted on the basis of his expectation about something, and the expectation turns out to have been incorrect, chances are that the action will be punished. Action based upon a misreading of a situation is less likely to be rewarded than that based upon a correct interpretation. The person who acts on the basis of incorrect assumptions incurs also the same kinds of social rejection listed above. That is, from the point of view of the social environment, the action was incompetent. The emotional state induced by the punishment is likely then to become conditioned to the cognitions that occurred prior to the punishment, including the discovery that one's expectation about events had been wrong. The experience

of a disconfirmed expectation becomes associated with the aversive consequences of the punishment that was in part caused by the cognitive error.
This aspect of the conditioned emotional reaction to a disconfirmed expectation may thus turn out to be identical to the conditioned reaction to incompetent behavior. The socializing community punishes incompetent behavior, and in so doing in effect punishes disconfirmed expectations at the
same time.

However, there are also many times when an expectation does not
serve as a clear basis for action, so that when it is disconfirmed the social
community is not aware that the person has made an error. The greater
the proportion of such instances among the total set of occasions when
expectations are disconfirmed, the more 'diluted' would be the conditioned
emotional reaction based upon punishment from outside the person. It seems
plausible to argue, then, that the effects of past punishment for incompetence are aroused more weakly in the case of disconfirmed expectations than
in the case of overtly incompetent acts. Nevertheless, even in the absence
of public knowledge of the disconfirmation, the person can draw his own
implications about his incompetence. The stronger these implications, the
greater the dissonance (cf. Deutsch, Krauss, & Rosenau, 1962; Zimbardo,
1960).

There may be an additional emotional reaction to the disconfirmation
of an expectation which is not present when a person has merely *acted* irrationally. Hebb (1949), for example, contends that incongruity in the midst
of a familiar surround is innately disturbing to organisms. He cites the reactions of chimpanzees to peculiarities in the looks or actions of otherwise
familiar keepers or cagemates. If he is correct that this is an inherent property of the nervous system, then this source of arousal when an expectation
is disconfirmed is not traceable to punishments in the ontogeny of the
individual organism.

If Hebb is correct, and if the arousal to which he refers has consequences which are different from those following the arousal of a conditioned emotional response deriving from past punishment, then there is not
a perfect correspondence between reactions to disconfirmed expectations
and to overt incompetent or immoral acts. This is an issue which is perhaps
too far removed from empirical anchors to be discussed here. Nor is this
the place to attempt to deal with the possibility that relatively small disconfirmations of expectations may be reinforcing under some circumstances,
as is argued by McClelland, Atkinson, Clark, and Lowell (1953), Berlyne
(1960; Chapter 15), Maddi (1961; Chapter 16), and others. Possibly the
same is true of low levels of guilt and shame following overt actions.

It appears that there may be considerable correspondence between the
emotional reactions to disconfirmed expectations and to incompetent acts.
If this speculation is sound, there is nothing to prevent anyone from saying
that both antecedents produce dissonance, even though the antecedents are
analytically distinguishable. They appear to be sufficiently correlated in
the history of the organism to result in their arousing the same kind of
conditioned emotional reaction.

What do the punishments for incompetent cognition and incompetent
and immoral behavior have in common which distinguish them from other
kinds of punishment? After all, if they are in no important way distinctive,
there seems little point in giving them a special name. Does the arousal of

any conditioned emotional response based upon punishment qualify as cognitive dissonance? It seems to me that the factor common to the conditions claimed to produce dissonance is that they arouse feelings associated with social rejection. It is the deprivation of positive, affectionate response—originally from other people, but perhaps later from oneself also. An analysis of the past punishments for incompetence and immorality suggests that, for humans, the most potent and predictable consequence of these is social rejection. This is because incompetence and immorality are so often relative. The person does not usually know whether his behavior is competent (or moral) or not until someone points it out to him or until he is able to compare his performance with that of other people. Although the inability to jump far enough to cross the stream brings its own appropriate punishment, the more typical case requires a social definition of adequate behavior (Festinger, 1954). The reinforcing and punishing responses of the socializing community, initially originating outside of the person himself, are eventually 'internalized' so that the person punishes or rewards himself even in the absence of an observing audience.

Following this line of reasoning to its conclusion, it seems reasonable to attach the label 'dissonance' to the arousal of feelings of social rejection. Any set of circumstances producing such an emotional state is likely to be followed by responses which have successfully reduced such feelings in the past. Those situations which do not arouse feelings associated with social rejection do not arouse dissonance, although they may arouse other unpleasant emotional states. And, it must be added, situations involving social rejection often include other emotionally arousing stimuli whose effects must be separated from dissonance.

How far away have we gotten from Festinger's original statement? Very far indeed! The reason is that we have explored a different stategy in setting up the concept. Festinger started with a set of determining conditions, saying that whenever two cognitions contradicted each other, an unpleasant emotional state was produced. If one then goes on to ask about the life-historical variables which contribute to this emotional state, one finds that various other kinds of situational conditions would also be expected to arouse this kind of emotional state. We must deal eventually with all of the conditions which produce it. In so doing, we may very well find that contradictory cognitions constitute only one of a variety of antecedents capable of arousing essentially the same emotional state. Dissonance could be aroused by the unconditioned stimulus itself (social rejection) or by any stimulus which has been appropriately temporally associated with such rejection.

It should be clear that these speculations imply a considerable broadening of the scope of the theory beyond Festinger's original statement. Although he seemed to be restricting his theory to the effects of disconfirming expectations, much of his own research clearly has contained confounding variables. Brehm and Cohen (1962) reformulated the theory in such a way that the confounding variables became the prime determinants of dissonance and the role of expectations was reduced to virtually nothing. I have attempted here to discover what these variables have in common insofar as their impact upon the person's emotional state is concerned. There does appear to be some overlap, owing to the likelihood that wrong expectations and incompetent or immoral overt behavior are correlated in the experience of the organism and therefore tend to become conditioned to the same punishing consequences from the social environment.

How is dissonance different from other varieties of anxiety? It has not been demonstrated that the drive or emotional component of dissonance is subjectively or physiologically different from anxiety aroused by other stimuli. Nor has it been shown convincingly that dissonance is reduced in ways other than those employed by organisms to reduce anxiety aroused by other stimuli. This is not to deny that important differences—both in the emotional state itself and in the ways organisms respond to it—will eventually be demonstrated. However, I think it is important to note that the characteristics distinguishing dissonance from other kinds of anxiety have not received much attention either theoretically or empirically.

My own hunch is that it is worthwhile to subdivide the concept anxiety, reserving the name 'dissonance' for anxiety associated with social rejection. The feeling of unworthiness, incompetence, unlovableness is probably aroused both by the failure to predict accurately and the failure to behave competently or ethically. The consequences of anxiety about one's worth are likely to be such things as self-justification and the search for information that will reflect favorably upon the self. These responses seem much less probable following the arousal of other kinds of anxiety, such as fear of physical pain. Thus, I think a plausible armchair case can be made for distinguishing a type of anxiety called 'dissonance' from other anxieties, both in its subjective aspect and in its response consequences.

The theoretical relevance of the self in this view of dissonance theory now becomes clearer. I am arguing that dissonance is a feeling of personal unworthiness (a type of anxiety) traceable to rejection of oneself by other people either in the present or in the past. Any information which implies that one is incompetent or immoral arouses dissonance. The reason dissonance is greatest when the person feels personally responsible for his behavior is that rejection by other people is usually greatest when they believe the person voluntarily acted in an inappropriate way. Further, a person's expectations about his own behavior should be aroused most clearly when he perceives his behavior as emanating primarily from himself rather than from environmental pressure. Most dissonance experiments have induced the subjects to behave in ways that lead both to disconfirmation of expectation about oneself and to the arousal of implications that one's behavior has been incompetent or immoral. Experiments attempting to test for the effect of expectation disconfirmation by itself present a confusing array of support and nonsupport for dissonance theory, while no experiments have been reported testing the effect of immorality or incompetence in the absence of disconfirmation of expectation. It is not possible at this point to say whether either one or a combination of these factors is the necessary condition for the arousal of dissonance; but we do know that the strongest and most consistently self-justifying (dissonance-reducing) behavior seems to occur in conditions which confound large amounts of both variables.

CHAPTER 27

The Self and Cognitive Consistency

M. Brewster Smith

University of California, Berkeley

The seemingly straightforward notion of a psychological trend toward consistency comprises a host of problems that require explication, as this volume as a whole makes amply clear. If we ask, as this section does, how such trends are conditioned by relations to the self or *self concept* as a cognitive structure, we immediately face similar complications. In spite of the apparent solidity of the term self concept, even a mildly critical look at the literature of research and theory bearing on the topic should suffice to indicate that the solidity is illusory. Concerning neither conceptualization nor measurement is there satisfactory agreement, and what traditions of measurement have emerged—particularly the self-report methods—are not very well grounded in theory. Wylie's (1961) review volume displays this unsatisfactory situation, which remains essentially unchanged since 1961, without doing much to improve it.

Given this state of affairs, a necessary preliminary to the present chapter is to sketch in the bare bones of a working conception of the self. Here I will be brief and dogmatic, so as to get on with the main task, even though the state of self theory would call for tentativeness, qualification, and prolixity. The minimal distinctions that I introduce are conceived within a general frame of reference I outlined some years ago (Smith, 1950).

Phenomenological inspection yields references to the self as actor in relation to other actors, as ground against which experience of an external world is figural, as maintaining identity in time, as reflexive object. Some tender-minded theorists, playing by rules that I do not accept, try to put such a phenomenal self to immediate theoretical work. However, I have always thought that proper scientific discourse requires us to use what insights we can glean from what is given phenomenally so as to frame subjective constructs—ones conceptualized from the actor's point of view—that are as firmly grounded in the observer's frame of reference as we can make them. We cannot expect to find good theoretical concepts given directly in experience. The question is, rather, what inferential conceptual distinctions do we need in the domain vaguely identified by phenomenal experiences of self?

One distinction seems to me clearly useful in the present context; a couple of others will be noted as likely to be useful, though I am less clear about how. The one I would stress is between the person's more or less stable *self concept*, and the transitory *self percepts* that are evoked in the course of his transactions with the environment. Self percepts will depend not only upon the individual's persisting beliefs about himself (self concept), but also upon his ongoing behavior and the informational feedback that it brings, as well as upon the treatment he is accorded by others as it varies from one situation to another. The responses evoked by self-report procedures are highly fallible means for developing inferences about either level of construct, and the sloppy habit of *identifying* self-reports with constructs is sure to lead to confusion.

Within the sphere of the self concept, a further minimal distinction will probably turn out to be necessary, though I will not put it to use here. One can probably distinguish a *core of identity beliefs* that have persisting transsituational relevance for a person's view of himself (these varying in centrality or importance and saliency—thus sex vs. eye color) from the set of subidentities that correspond to William James' notion (1890, pp. 293–296) of the person's multiple social selves, systems of beliefs that are bound to the major distinguishable contexts of role relations in which the person participates. One may expect pronounced individual and societal variation in the extent to which such subidentities are differentiated from one another and from core identity.[1]

The psychoanalytic tradition suggests the relevance of additional distinctions, which are introduced here not because I intend to use them directly, but to suggest the absurdity of treating *the* self concept as a concrete entity. We may infer that a person entertains views of himself that he fears or disavows, 'negative identities' that may not be accessible to self-report; he also has conceptions of himself as he would like to be (research has picked up the latter theme for emphasis). In the sphere of percepts, he may reject self-regarding experiences as 'ego'-alien, as not pertaining to the acknowledged self.

With this sketchy foundation, we can return to the task at hand. In order to consider what the self has to do with trends toward consistency, we can begin by noting, with Lecky (1945), the importance of such trends in the very constitution of the self. As consistency theories become more mature, we can expect that one important direction in which social psychology may seek integration with personality theory is in further specifying the role of consistency-directed processes in the formation and development of the self. Pending such an elaboration and application of formal theory, several things can be said.

First of all, the formation of a person's core identity, the differentiation of his subidentities, and the extrusion of his negative identities would seem to be heavily influenced by trends toward consistency of two kinds: toward internal consistency with as simple a structure as possible, and toward external consistency, such that surprise and disconfirmation by new percepts are kept within tolerable bounds. Heider (1958) emphasized how differentiation can be one outcome of strains toward cognitive balance; the theories derivative from Heider would seem to hold more promise than dissonance

---

[1] See Miller (1963) and French and Sherwood (1965) for more formal treatments of self theory that are generally congruent with the approach taken here.

theory as aids toward the understanding of differentiated structure in the self.

But secondly, consistency-seeking processes operate in conjunction with an essentially unrelated trend, a bias toward thinking as well of oneself as one can get away with. Just as Festinger's version of consistency theory weights the discrepancy between cognitions by their importance, so the self-esteem-maximizing trend would seem also to involve a weighting by importance or centrality to one's self concept (see French & Sherwood, 1965). Among social psychological consistency theories, McGuire's (1960c) formulation, which pits logical consistency against wishful thinking, runs somewhat parallel here.

The joint operation of these trends over the course of a life in progress, moreover, will likely give rise to affectively charged cognitive structures that have great stability, exceeding that of all but a very few "primitive beliefs" (Rokeach, 1960) about the external world that also operate like Kantian categories as ground for the whole succession of perceptual experience. The self concept as comprised of such structures is not likely to be much disturbed by single bits of incoming information, or by brief communications. We know how resistant it is to change in psychotherapy, and we know the heroic (or diabolical) efforts that seem to be required for 'brainwashing' to have substantial impact. When experimental manipulations and communications purport to produce measurable changes in the self concept, we may rightly be suspicious and look rather for momentary changes in self percepts—or for temporary yielding to the demand characteristics of the experimental situation (see Orne, 1962).

Finally, if the inferred self concept of a normal person is bound to be a strong and stable structure, the same cannot be said about momentary self-perceptions. These are also subject to pressures toward internal and external consistency and toward high self-evaluation. They should be under particularly strong pressure toward consistency with the person's enduring self concept, given the greater stability and importance of the latter. Their relation to the self concept should be asymmetrical: in the single encounter, the percept should give way, not the self concept. If there is not enough stimulus ambiguity for the self-perception to be brought into line, other maneuvers of isolation, rationalization, and so on, will be drawn upon, including the ones explored in dissonance theory.

So much (and little it is) for consistency phenomena in the self. What of the bearing of self on consistency phenomena as currently under view in social psychological research and theory? Let us first sample some of the ways in which the recent literature reflects explicit or implicit reference to the self.

Perhaps the most interesting of these involves implicit reference. As I read the focused reformulation of dissonance theory in Brehm and Cohen (1962) and in Festinger (1964b), the claims for dissonance theory are now restricted to a sphere in which one of the terms in the cognitive relationship involves a self-perception. Although Festinger's original (1957) formulation was extremely general, purporting to deal with the relations between any two cognitions, research as it developed was preponderantly concerned with the important but very special class of situations in which one of the cognitive elements is the subject's knowledge of how he has in fact behaved. Brehm and Cohen's contribution, in their own research and in their thorough review of the work of others, was to stress the role of commitment and voluntary choice as requisite for the generation of dissonance. But knowledge of how one has behaved is an instance of self-perception, and the requirement of choice and commitment insures that the percept will be in relatively close communication with the self concept. Festinger's own recent (1964) reaffirmation of dissonance theory as a theory of postdecisional processes is congruent: the act of decision binds the self to a particular alternative or course of behavior.

The suggestion that the phenomena of dissonance depend upon involvement of the self has been made by others outside the directly Festingerian research tradition (see Deutsch, Krauss, & Rosenau, 1962). Intuitively, it makes good sense that the trend toward consistency should be particularly noticeable in matters that touch on the self. But are consistency effects limited to such matters? Evidently not: witness the success of Osgood and Tannenbaum's (1955) congruity model in its even more restricted sphere that in effect excludes the self; witness also the success of Rosenberg and Abelson's (1960) potentially very general balance model and of McGuire's (1960c) narrow syllogistic one, neither of which involves self-reference. For each of these cases the research data are limited, but there is no reason to doubt the existence of consistency effects that fall outside the sphere of self. Is the restriction of dissonance theory to self-related cognitions a matter of historical accident? Or can reasons be found for this restriction?

Three considerations occur to me as pertinent. For one, there is the formal defect of dissonance theory that, unlike balance and congruity theories, it does not deal explicitly with the unit relation. To limit its scope to relations that involve self percepts resting on voluntary commitment may, as Brehm and Cohen imply, make it more likely that the cognitions in question will be taken as relevant to one another.[2]

Perhaps also germane is the iceberg-like quality of dissonance theory as it is revealed in practice, in which experimental ingenuity tends to substitute for theoretical explicitness. Buried in experimental manipulations that are arrived at intuitively and refined through pilot work is a lot of implicit theory about how to 'con' subjects into voluntarily engaging in dissonance-producing behavior, as well as additional implicit theory about how alternative channels of dissonance reduction may be blocked. The high valuation that Festingerians set on experimental ingeniousness may have helped to disguise the extent to which the generality of the theory had in effect become limited until Brehm and Cohen did their stock-taking.

Finally, there is the effect of the competition between dissonance theory and conflict theory cast in terms of incentives and reinforcement (Janis, 1959; Chapter 82). The pressure to make dissonance theory distinctive pushed it to make its special claim for postdecisional processes, leaving predecisional ones to conventional conflict formulations. But, as we have seen, postdecisional phenomena are intrinsically self-referential. To get outside the bounds of self, dissonance theory would have to leave the postdecisional domain where its claim for exclusiveness rests.

So far, we have been considering ways in which dissonance theory has been implicitly concerned with the self. In regard to *explicit* self-reference,

---

[2] McGuire's special case may assure the mutual relevance of cognitions through its restriction to highly artificial materials drawn from the formally defined domain of propositional fragments of syllogisms.

at least two lines of research may be noted. One suggests that high momentary self-esteem (presumably a composite dimension of self-perceptions rather than of the enduring self concept, since it is manipulated experimentally) may be an essential condition for the generation of dissonance under certain circumstances. Thus, Bramel (1962) predicted and found that subjects in whom high self-esteem had been induced engaged in more dissonance-reducing behavior than subjects whose self-esteem had been lowered, when all subjects were given credible information implying that they had strong homosexual tendencies. Similarly, in an experiment in which subjects who were opposed to the research use of electric shock on human beings were induced to administer apparently painful shocks to a seeming fellow student, Buss (1961) found that only the subgroup among whom high momentary self-esteem had been experimentally induced showed the predicted indications of dissonance-reducing behavior (increased unfriendliness toward the target of their aggressions). In both these cases, it is implied that negatively valued information about the self should produce more dissonance for subjects whose self-esteem is momentarily high than for subjects who for the nonce have been made to think less well of themselves. The employment here of concepts relating to the self seems to be well within the bounds of conventional dissonance interpretations.

The other line of research, exemplified by Aronson and Carlsmith (1962), pits the predictions of dissonance or consistency theory against those that would follow from people's general tendencies to maximize their self-esteem. They found that subjects in whom an expectation of failure on an experimental task had previously been established and who were then led to experience strong success used an opportunity with which they were provided to revise their performance in a downward direction, just as those in whom an expectation of success had been established and who then were made to fail used the opportunity to improve their performance. Put in general terms, subjects who were given information about their performance that was inconsistent with their expectancies changed a significantly greater number of their responses than those who were given consistent information. The results are startling, because common sense, which knows about self-esteem and the desire for success, has not yet been educated in dissonance theory. Theoretically, these results only begin to open the problem of what conditions govern the relative weight of consistency-producing and esteem-enhancing processes when these compete with each other. Certainly the existence of neither sort of process is in doubt.

As for the versions of cognitive consistency doctrine other than dissonance theory, we have already noted that neither Osgood and Tannenbaum (1955), McGuire (1960c), nor Rosenberg and Abelson's (1960) version of balance theory has anything distinctive to say about the self. But Heider's own formulation of balance theory in his chosen domain of cognized interpersonal relations requires reference to sentiments toward the self. Thus, Heider (1958, p. 180) introduces his discussion of balance and imbalance with the following intuitive examples of imbalance:

p hates o because he is similar to o.
He always imitates people he dislikes.
He avoids people he likes.

For these examples to represent imbalance, according both to common sense and to Heider's noncommonsense version of commonsense psychology, one must assume—as will usually be the case but not always, that p likes p; in other words that p has relatively high self-esteem. For a person whose self-esteem is pathologically low, it is plausible enough to regard the examples as balanced.

Evidence that self-esteem can indeed be a predictive variable in a version of Heider's theory that is modified to treat relations between elements as continua rather than as dichotomies is provided by Wiest (1965), who finds with sociometric data from schoolchildren that the extent to which a person believes that his evaluations of others are reciprocated by them is a positive function of his self-esteem.

Involvement of the self presumably also bears upon stability and change in attitudes in ways other than those mediated by consistency-seeking processes. (For the conventional term ego-involvement read self-involvement in the present context.) For example, consider the so-called discrepancy-involvement controversy as recently summarized by McGuire (1966a, pp. 485–487). Sherif and Hovland (1961) and, most recently, Sherif, Sherif, and Nebergall (1965) have claimed in the context of assimilation-contrast-judgmental theory that with stronger involvement, larger discrepancies between a person's own prior attitudinal position and the position advocated by a persuasive communication should result in decreased attitude change, because of the narrower latitude of acceptance that accompanies high involvement. Zimbardo (1960) arrived at contrary predictions from dissonance theory, and found evidence to support them. The confusing array of results from the series of studies that have ensued suggests the importance of differentiating types of 'involvement,' and the relevance of other features of the experimental situation. [See Chapter 28 for one attempt at resolving this issue—Ed.] The bearing of this entire controversy on consistency theory is ambiguous, however, in that dissonance theory must be stretched a good deal beyond what its formal properties can strictly support if it is to deal with quantitative phenomena such as degree of discrepancy. Dissonance-consonance, after all, is presented as a dichotomous relationship, with quantification entering only through the manipulation (not rating) of importance and the fictive counting of consonant vs. dissonant elements.

Outside the laboratory, the work on 'brainwashing' (Lifton, 1961; Schein, 1961; Biderman, 1963) contains suggestions that processes involving the self may set some limits to predictions that follow from consistency principles in other settings. Thus, dissonance theory predicts that the more coercive the sanctions that are applied to a person to secure his compliance, the less he will change his private opinions in the direction advocated. On the whole, this prediction seems to have been well enough sustained in the experience of Korean POW's (see Biderman, 1963), among whom conversions were few in spite of some token compliance. The more intensive and efficient procedures that the Chinese Communists applied to American and other civilian prisoners seem to have led to a somewhat different outcome, if we are to believe Schein (1961) and Lifton (1961) who report instances of pronounced attitude change. Here the crux of the matter would seem to have been a prolonged and efficiently contrived assault upon the self, in which coercion was an essential ingredient. The central use of self-produced confessions, of course, can be interpreted in terms of dissonance theory as a technique that undermines the prisoner's previous self-structure and helps to reformulate it along desired lines. Attitudes deeply anchored in the self could thus be susceptible to coercive persuasion by this painful indirect route.

This sampling of ways in which conceptualizations of the self have come in contact with consistency theories can be summed up in a few declarative sentences to which the reader can add his own qualifications:

1. The formation, structure, and dynamics of self concepts and percepts is a field of personality study to which the present crop of consistency theories and their successors can profitably be applied.

2. Those consistency theories to which the topic is directly relevant seem to have no difficulty in bringing the self into their formulations. As a class of cognitive structures, the self concept has properties of stability, differentiation, and importance that should weight it heavily when it is out of balance with other types of cognitions. These features do not seem to require the special modification of consistency theories, however.

3. The tendency to think well of oneself may complicate predictions from consistency theories, since it appears to be independent of trends toward consistency.

4. The variable(s) of self-involvement should be played against less ambiguous questions of consistency theory than the issue concerning the effects of communication discrepancy.

5. Dissonance theory seems to have limited itself in practice to cases in which one of the terms in the cognitive relationship involves a self-perception. Whether this is a necessary restriction warrants closer examination.

6. To be useful in the development of consistency theory, more precise and better specified conceptions in the sphere of self are obviously called for.

CHAPTER 28

A Cognitive Model of Attitudinal Involvement

Thomas M. Ostrom and Timothy C. Brock
The Ohio State University

One striking, and at times bothersome, feature of attitudes is the wide range of individual differences found in response to a standard persuasive communication. Differences are observed both over individuals for a given topic, and over topics for a given individual. Responses vary from changing one's attitudes away from the position advocated to adopting a position more extreme than was advocated. The concept of ego involvement has been offered as one possible determinant of these individual differences. A person highly involved in his attitude is viewed as being very resistant to change. This chapter considers existing formulations of ego involvement, proposes an alternative model, examines past research, and presents the results of an experiment conducted to test the proposed model. Although we confine attention here to attitude change phenomena, much of what we say can be extrapolated to the relationships between ego involvement and responses to inconsistency other than attitude change.

DEFINITIONS OF INVOLVEMENT

The classic and most exhaustive analysis of ego involvements was made by Sherif and Cantril (1947). They describe ego-involved attitudes as "attitudes that have been learned, largely as social values; that the individual identifies himself with, and makes a part of himself; and that have affective properties of varying degrees of intensity" (pp. 126–127), and "All attitudes that define a person's status or that give him some relative role with respect to other individuals, groups, or institutions" (p. 96). Thus, attitudes characterized by high involvement are defined by Sherif and Cantril to be those which are incorporated into the individual's ego, into his definition of himself. Their view of the ego is summarized in the following passage.

> We have said that what an individual comes to regard as himself is a genetic development, a product of learning. In the normal course of affairs, the components of the ego include the individual's body and

This paper was partially supported by grants to Brock from the National Science Foundation, GS-606, and the Advanced Research Projects Agency, monitored as AF-AFOSR-1159-66. The authors gratefully acknowledge the assistance of Franz Epting in data collection and analysis.

physical characteristics; the things he learns belong to *him,* such as *his* clothes, *his* toys, *his* keepsakes, *his* room, *his* hut, *his* house, *his* mother, *his* sweetheart, *his* children; together with a whole host of social values he also learns and with which he identifies himself—*his* country, *his* politics, *his* language, *his* manner of dressing, the characteristics of *his* particular society.

In spite of the relative similarity of the norms to which an individual in a given society or a group may be exposed, the content of any single individual's ego, what he regards as himself, is a rather distinct constellation of social and personal values that vary not only in their number and nature but also in the intensity with which they are held (p. 117).

One of the major consequences of being involved in an attitude is that:

This degree of ego-involvement, this intensity of attitudes, will determine in large part which attitudes he will cling to, how annoyed or frustrated he will feel when his attitudes are opposed, what action (within the range of his individual temperament and ability) he will take to further his point of view (p. 131).

The feature most frequently studied in the current attitude literature has been the determination with which an individual 'clings to' his initial attitudes. This shall be the focus of the present paper.

This view of ego involvement has been retained by Sherif in his recent work in the area (Sherif & Hovland, 1961; Sherif, Sherif, & Nebergall, 1965). However, other investigators appear to define involvement in terms of its consequences rather than its structural and dynamic properties. Freedman (1964) defined it as "interest in, concern about, or commitment to a particular position on an issue" (p. 290). Greenwald (1965) applied the label "position involvement" and defined it as "adherence to a prior behavior" (p. 3). By behavior, he meant a judgment, decision, or attitude position. Nowhere did Freedman or Greenwald discuss the relationship between ego-involved attitudes and the individual's network of social and personal values.

Other forms of involvement have also been discussed by these authors. Freedman (1964) identified "general level of interest in or concern about an issue without reference to a specific position" (p. 290) as another type of involvement. Greenwald (1965) proposed the term "solution involvement" to denote "commitment to the seeking of a 'good' solution to a problem" (p. 4). These forms of involvement were viewed by their contributors as independent of ego involvement.

Finally, a further definitional viewpoint was offered by Miller (1965). He identified four components of attitudinal ego involvement: social support, salience or importance of the issue, commitment to a position, and frequent rehearsal of arguments supporting one's prior position. High involvement is implied when an individual's attitude possesses all these features. It was not completely clear from Miller's discussion which of these components are to be regarded as antecedents or determinants of ego involvement and which are produced by high involvement.

THE MODEL

In formulating the following model, an attempt was made to retain the fundamental character of attitudinal ego involvement as described by Sherif and Cantril (1947). However, it was felt that the process of involvement could be better understood in the context of cognitive structure. Stating ego involvement in these terms permitted a broader integration of involvement phenomena with other cognitive models of attitude formation and change.

The basic feature of an ego-involved attitude is its relation to the manner in which the individual defines himself. The individual defines himself primarily in terms of that 'distinct constellation of social and personal values' he has acquired. The closer the relation between his attitude and these values and the more central these related values are, the higher the degree of attitudinal involvement. The major consequence of heightened involvement is increased resistance to persuasion. This brief description represents our summary of the critical properties of attitudinal ego involvement as described by Sherif and Cantril (1947).

Scott's (1963) discussion of the conceptualization and measurement of cognitive structure influenced the formation of the model. The model is intended to work within the limitations and ambiguities of contemporary cognitive theory, as noted by Scott (1963), rather than to offer refinements to general cognitive theory.

The *elements* of the present cognitive model are the social and personal values of the individual and the particular attitudes held by the individual. Three structural properties of cognition are employed in the model. *Centrality* of a value is defined as the extent to which the value is integral to the individual's self-definition. The degree of *relatedness* between an attitude position and a value refers to the amount of similarity, relevance, association, dependency, or distance existing between the pairs of elements. The most directly pertinent synonyms are "dependency" as defined by Zajonc (1960b) or "bond," in Brock's (1962) terms. One element is dependent on another to the extent that a change in one produces a change in the other. The third structural property is the *number* of value elements which are engaged by the focal attitude.

The proposed model postulates three primary determinants of the magnitude of ego involvement.

1. Involvement is greater where the attitude is related to more *central* or important values. An attitude related to values integral to the individual's self-definition will be more ego involving than if the values are tangential to the content of his ego.

2. Involvement is greater under high *relatedness*. As the attitude is personally more relevant to the individual's values, the more involved he is in that attitude.

3. Involvement is greater when a larger *number* of values are engaged. The wider the array of social and personal values bonded to the attitude, the higher the resulting involvement of the individual in his attitude position.

The first two factors combine in a multiplicative fashion in determining ego involvement. A value having zero relatedness (no relevance) to an attitude would not contribute to involvement. A value of zero centrality (no importance) which may be related to the attitude would not increase involvement. Combining all three factors, the magnitude of attitudinal ego involvement is defined as the sum over values of the products of the value centrality and the value-attitude relatedness.

It is clear from the above discussion that a highly ego-involved attitude is one characterized by being well imbedded in the cognitive structure, linked firmly and often with highly central elements. Since changing this attitude would cause extensive cognitive restructuring, and since the organism is presumed to prefer stability and consistency in his cognitive world, the major prediction of this model is that the highly ego-involved attitude is more resistant to change than an attitude in which the individual is not so deeply involved. This should hold true both when comparing individuals for a single attitude topic and when comparing different attitude topics within a single person.

Certain basic similarities exist between the present formulation and that proposed by Rosenberg (1956). Rosenberg was concerned with the relationship between the magnitude of attitudinal affect and cognitive structure. He proposed the following formulation:

> The degree and sign of affect aroused in an individual by an object (as reflected by the position he chooses on an attitude scale) vary as a function of the algebraic sum of the products obtained by multiplying the rated importance of each value associated with that object by the rated potency of the object for achieving or blocking the realization of that value (p. 367).

Rosenberg identified the same three cognitive factors of centrality, relatedness, and number as being determinants of magnitude and signs of attitudinal affect. However, attitudinal affect and ego involvement are conceptually independent although they have been found to be frequently associated with each other (e.g., Sherif *et al.*, 1965).

The difference between the two models lies entirely in the definition of the attitudinal element which is being linked into a cognitive structure. Rosenberg was utilizing the attitude object and the present model uses the individual's particular stand or position regarding the attitude object. An individual who is highly involved in his neutral attitude sees his neutrality as highly related to important values. A man who holds the view that 'war should be used on some occasions and not on others as an instrument of foreign policy' holds a neutral position, but may be very involved in it and highly resistant to change. For this man, the concept 'war' stands in one relationship to his value system, while his particular attitude position occupies a different location in his cognitive structure. Thus the two formulations may compatibly coexist, with Rosenberg's model predicting the level of attitudinal affect to an object and the present model predicting resistance to changing the particular belief or stand. (See Chapter 4 for a full treatment of the Rosenberg model.)

EXAMINATION OF PAST EXPERIMENTS

Several studies have been reported in which the magnitude of ego involvement was experimentally manipulated. The procedures employed in these studies can be examined to determine the correspondence between the present theory and the operations used by others to vary involvement.

In each of the following experiments subjects were asked to respond twice to a task. The tasks were diverse; they varied from estimating the number of dots on a card to concept formation. The responses were making a judgment or taking a stand on an issue. The second response was requested after a discrepant communication was administered; it served as the postmeasure. The difference between the two responses was the measure of attitude change. The cognitive model of ego involvement predicts greater resistance to change in a high-involvement condition than in a low-involvement condition.

Zimbardo (1960) induced high involvement by telling subjects that their response to a task would be a "good indicator of their basic social values, their personalities, and their outlook on important life problems." Subjects in the Low Involvement group were told that their response would not reveal their values or personality; it was implied that their response was unimportant and would contribute nothing to the experiment. The task was to identify the locus of blame for a crime committed by a juvenile delinquent. These operations must be examined to determine whether they constituted a proper manipulation of ego involvement as defined by the present model. The choosing of an attitude position in both conditions was presumably determined on the basis of which alternative had the highest congruence with the subject's value system. It could be argued that those in the High Involvement condition induced by Zimbardo saw greater relevance between their chosen first response and the valued state of a healthy personality and life outlook. However, at the time of their second response, they were told that their first response was not the important one in that it was necessarily made in haste. This would have the effect of removing the perceived bonds between their first response and their values in both his experimental conditions. His instructions to the High Involvement group likely aroused "evaluation apprehension" (Rosenberg, 1965d) and consequent monitoring of the environment for clues as to the 'correct' response to the task. Zimbardo's manipulation had a significant effect on resistance to attitude change; his High groups changed more than his Low groups. However, it must be concluded that his manipulation, and consequently his findings, cannot be considered relevant to the model presently being proposed. No differential value bonding existed *at the time* his subjects were asked to reassess their attitudes.

Freedman (1964) studied the effects of an involvement manipulation on the readiness to relinquish a concept definition in a concept formation task. All subjects were told that their performance on the task was indicative of their intelligence and perceptiveness. The correctness of their response, then, was directly linked to the values of being intelligent and perceptive. Freedman's High vs. Low Involvement manipulation differed only in terms of which response was asserted to be related to these values. His High Involvement groups were told that their first response was the important one; his Low Involvement groups were told that their second response was the critical one. The theoretically postulated differences in ego involvement would clearly correspond to the manipulated categories in this study. The initial response would be characterized by high relatedness in Freedman's High Involvement condition, and characterized by low relatedness in his Low Involvement condition. As would be predicted, greater change was found under low involvement than high in this study.

Greenwald (1965) employed a dual manipulation of involvement. His experimental task required subjects to estimate the number of dots on a card as a test of perceptual acuity. In his High Importance (High Solution Involvement) treatment, he told the subjects that their second response would reveal important personality characteristics and indicate possible mental disturbance. Those in the Low Importance (Low Solution Involvement) treatment were told that the test was dull, routine, and generally unsuccessful. Clearly, more central values were linked to the response under the High condition than the Low condition, but it was the subject's second response which related to these values rather than his first. The cognitive model of ego involvement can therefore make no prediction regarding the effect of this solution involvement manipulation on attitude change. This manipulation was very similar to Zimbardo's (1960) and had much the same effect. Greenwald observed, under high levels of discrepancy, greater shift in judgment for his High Importance subjects than for his Low Importance subjects.

In the same study, Greenwald comanipulated a factor which he termed "position involvement." All subjects were told that a critical discussion of their responses would follow the acuity task. The discussion would include all four subjects in that experimental session. In his public (High Position Involvement) condition, the discussion was to examine both the first and second response of each participant. This can be interpreted as arousing the values of personal consistency and inner directedness, and relating them to the subject's *first* response. The private (Low Position Involvement) condition subjects were told their first responses were only for practice and would remain anonymous. Only their second response would be considered in the discussion session. In this private condition, no values were experimentally linked to the subject's first response. In terms of the cognitive model of ego involvement, this private-public manipulation would constitute a proper and interpretable variation. As the model would predict, Greenwald found more resistance to change in the public than in the private treatment.

Miller (1965) used attitude toward fluoridation in studying the effects of involvement. He induced high involvement by telling the subjects that the Department of Health, Education, and Welfare was sponsoring his survey. They were further told that this sponsor considered fluoridation an important national problem, believed the subjects' opinions were particularly important, agreed with the views the subjects had expressed on fluoridation (their first responses to the task), and felt that there was striking evidence to support this position. The subjects were next requested to list the arguments which supported their positions. The final step in the manipulation was to have the subjects sign a pledge agreeing to distribute supportive materials to family and friends. In low involvement, none of these activities were related to fluoridation but to a secondary, irrelevant topic. Being convinced that one's attitude is considered important and is supported by an authority would have the effect of linking the attitude to such values as respect for authorities; commitment to promulgate one's beliefs would link those beliefs to the values of being consistent and honoring one's obligations. The implication of listing supporting arguments is to increase the salience and perceived relatedness between the attitude position and value system. Miller's manipulation did constitute a proper variation in the terms of the cognitive model of ego involvement. The observed effect of Miller's manipulation was to increase resistance to change in his High Involvement condition.

This examination of selected involvement experiments has illustrated several important points. It is clear that involvement can be manipulated in an experimental setting, but that not all such manipulations of 'involvement' can be considered pertinent to the proposed cognitive model. A proper manipulation requires that values be related to the attitude position the individual personally endorses. This induction must precede any introduction of a discrepant communication. Also, other experimental variations should not be confounded with the involvement manipulation.

Of the several experiments which included an interpretable variation of ego involvement, none could be described as systematically varying any of the three major factors in the present model. A more critical test of this cognitive model demands a series of experiments in which each factor is independently varied. Experiments need to be conducted which link an attitude to central vs. peripheral values, vary the perceived relatedness to the value system, and/or vary the absolute number of values involved. One such study (Ostrom & Brock, 1968) is partially reviewed below.

A TEST OF THE MODEL

In the above instances of manipulation of ego involvement satisfying our definition, it was found that heightened involvement increases resistance to change under conditions of large communication discrepancy. This is in accord with the expectations of the present model. Resistance to change is a direct function of the magnitude of ego involvement. An individual with low involvement would alter his attitude a large proportion of the distance advocated; a highly involved individual would shift only a small part of the distance between his initial attitude and the position advocated. This leads to the prediction of a significant interaction between involvement and discrepancy when the dependent measure is the absolute number of attitude units changed.

An experiment conducted as a first step in testing the proposed cognitive model examined the relationship between ego involvement, communication discrepancy, and attitude change. Two of the three components of ego involvement were independently manipulated in a 'value-bonding task' which permitted values to be experimentally related to an attitude position. The component of major concern here is the centrality of the related values. (Many details of the experiment are omitted from the description which follows.)

In the experimental booklet given to all subjects, the following occurred in fixed sequence: explanation of attitude topic, attitude-inducing communication, value-bonding task, and discrepant communication. A separate section contained the dependent measures. An attitude issue was devised which would be free of prior individual background differences. Greenland was said to be applying for membership in the Pan-American Bank and a Consortium on Membership had been formed to review the case.

The next section contained excerpts from an authoritative speech which advocated that Greenland should not be extended membership in the bank. The major arguments were that its membership would be a financial loss to the bank, that Greenland had only one prominent industry in the mining of cryolite, that it is the world leader in the production of icebergs (apparent sarcasm), that because of its ties with Denmark, European financial interference may result, etc. It was expected that most subjects would adopt the advocated position that Greenland should not be permitted to participate in the bank.

The value-bonding task, administered next, was described as a new approach in speech interpretation. Statements from the speech the subjects just read were to be related to general ideas. On each of nine following pages, a one-sentence excerpt from the speech would be found paired with a general idea which was supposedly relevant to the excerpt in some way. The subject was first to indicate on a rating scale the level of appropriateness between the excerpt and the general idea. The second step was to circle one key word in the excerpt and one key word in the general idea and then to draw a link between them. They were instructed to choose the link which 'seems best.' An example of the format used in the value-bonding task is provided in the Figure. Note the check and 'dumbbell' as drawn by a hypothetical subject. The purpose of this dual task was to present values in a context which would facilitate relating them to the subjects' new (anti-

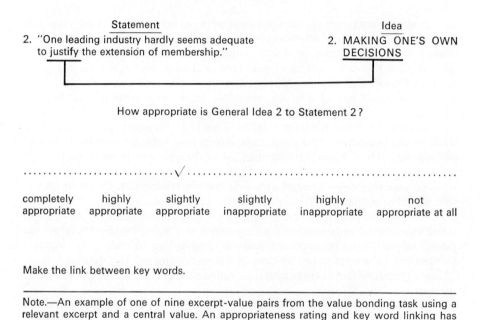

Statement

2. "One leading industry hardly seems adequate to justify the extension of membership."

Idea

2. MAKING ONE'S OWN DECISIONS

How appropriate is General Idea 2 to Statement 2?

| completely appropriate | highly appropriate | slightly appropriate | slightly inappropriate | highly inappropriate | not appropriate at all |

Make the link between key words.

Note.—An example of one of nine excerpt-value pairs from the value bonding task using a relevant excerpt and a central value. An appropriateness rating and key word linking has been added to illustrate the response of a hypothetical subject.

FIGURE.   An Item from the Instrument Used to Induce Value-Attitude Bonding (Hypothetical Response)

Greenland) attitude position. No specific relations were suggested at any time; the relations the subjects perceived were self-generated. It was within this phase of the booklet that the factor of centrality was manipulated.

Centrality was manipulated through differential selection of the general ideas or values which were used in the value-bonding task. The selection of values was based on the results of a previous scaling study conducted for this purpose. A set of 64 value statements was assembled, including those listed by Rosenberg (1956) and Carlson (1956). This basic set was augmented by the present investigators to provide greater representation of distinctly peripheral values. This entire set of values was presented to a group of 49 judges who were instructed to rate each item in terms of its "personal importance." Nine of the most important items (e.g., "keeping promises to others" and "having a steady income") were used in the central variation of the value-bonding task, and the nine least important items (e.g., "people honoring their ancestors" and "people paying inheritance taxes") were used in the peripheral level of the centrality manipulation. All the values were positive, 'good things' to do or have. The same nine speech excerpts were used in both conditions. The pairing of values with excerpts was done on a random basis.

The discrepant communication was described as containing excerpts from a second expert's speech given at the same meeting as the previous speech. Two levels of communication discrepancy were used. Both advocated that Greenland be admitted to the bank. In the Slight Discrepancy condition, 50 per cent participation was advocated. This was supported by a 450-word speech which argued that while Greenland had shown some economic development, future advance would be slow. The Large Discrepancy communication urged that a full 100 per cent participation be permitted for Greenland in the bank. This position was contained in a 450-word speech which argued that Greenland possessed an ideal combination of natural resources and stable economy, and that with the support of the bank she would be able to sever her economic ties with Denmark.

The dependent variable was the self-rating of attitude toward Greenland's participation in the Pan-American Bank. It was presented in the form of a rating scale on which the subject indicated the extent of participation he believed appropriate. The scale was labeled 100 per cent participation at one end and 0 per cent participation at the other. Identification labels of 10 per cent, 20 per cent, etc., were provided at equally spaced intermediate intervals.

The cognitive model of ego involvement predicted greater resistance to influence under conditions of higher ego involvement, manifested in an interaction between centrality and discrepancy. The Peripheral Value condition subjects should be less committed to their initial attitude and therefore shift readily when presented with a discrepant communication. Those in the Central Value condition should be relatively uninfluenced regardless of the magnitude of discrepancy encountered.

The means for the significant discrepancy main effect $(F = 6.32; d.f. = 1/128; p < .05)$ and its interaction with centrality $(F = 14.78; d.f. = 1/128; p < .01)$ are in the Table. The interaction resulted because those in the Peripheral condition changed their attitude in accordance with the magnitude of discrepancy encountered, whereas those in the Central condition were unaffected by the differences in discrepancy. Control group data (Ostrom & Brock, 1968) indicated the prediscrepancy percentage participation rating averaged 35.9. Positive attitude change was obtained for all conditions in the Table.

Mean Per Cent Participation Ratings as a Function of
Discrepancy and Centrality

Value Centrality	Communication Discrepancy	
	Small	Large
Peripheral	39.9	68.5
Central	51.5	45.5

A Newman-Keuls test was computed to determine which differences between the four means in the Table were significant. It was found that the
mean for the Peripheral Value, Large Discrepancy group was significantly
higher ($p < .01$) than the other three means and that all the other differences were insignificant. The form of this interaction supports the predictions of the ego-involvement model.

DISCUSSION

The power of any theoretical orientation is determined in part by the
diversity of phenomena it can integrate and explain. This chapter extends
the widely applied cognitive orientation to yet another domain of psychological phenomena, that of attitudinal ego involvement. It was proposed
that ego involvement results from a value-bonding process which includes
the three variables of value centrality, magnitude of relatedness, and number
of values incorporated in the structure. Centrality and relatedness were proposed to combine multiplicatively, the magnitude of ego involvement being
a function of the sum of these products.

Since Sherif and Cantril's original 1947 contribution, there has been
insufficient concern in the attitude and ego involvement literature regarding
the nature of the intervening process. Empirical pursuit progressed to the
laboratory before a specific theoretical statement of the causal antecedents
was available. As an example, several investigators (Freedman, 1964; Greenwald, 1965; Miller, 1965) have attempted to induce greater public commitment to initial attitudes as a technique to produce higher ego involvement
in those subjects. This was justified on the grounds that the ego-involved
individual is concerned about and committed to his position on the issue.
While it is clear in terms of the construct as presented by Sherif and
Cantril (1947) and by the present authors that heightened involvement
should always produce heightened commitment, it is not clear that heightened commitment will necessarily produce heightened involvement.[1] A commitment variation can be defended only as affecting level of involvement
if differential value bonding can be shown to result. Indeed, this was the
principal focus of the logical analysis we performed on selected experiments.
Our three proposed determinants of involvement are sufficiently explicit so
that any investigator can assess whether his manipulations are in accord
with the theoretical structure of the present model. The major procedural
requirement of the present model is that any bonding of attitude and values
must focus on attitudes held prior to the introduction of persuasive messages.

The present model, by defining ego involvement as the product of a
value-bonding process, suggests rather unique manipulative techniques. The
task employed in the experiment reported here was perceived as novel by
the participating subjects. Although some were perplexed, the task proved
effective in altering resistance to attitude change. Any technique which has
the effect of increasing the centrality, relatedness, or number of values linked
to an attitude position should have the consequence of heightening the magnitude of ego involvement and consequent resistance to attitude change.

---

[1] True, but heightened commitment might itself produce resistance to attitude change
without the mediation of heightened involvement. Commitment is treated at length in
Section III D—Ed.

The predicted interaction between magnitude of ego involvement and communication discrepancy on attitude change, which had been supported in our analysis of other experiments, also emerged significantly in our experiment. The High Involvement subjects were not differentially affected by the size of discrepancy; the Low Involvement subjects changed significantly more under high than under low discrepancy.

Incidentally, it was found in another condition of the experiment (Ostrom & Brock, 1968) that the predicted interaction also emerged when the bonding task utilized irrelevant excerpts rather than excerpts from the attitude-inducing speech. One possible interpretation is that since the attitude-inducing speech was fresh in their minds, the subjects were still actively rehearsing the arguments and comparing them to the provided values during the value-bonding task.

The involvement model presented here has a quality of specificity and rigor which could potentially mislead one into interpreting it as a finished product. The model is not offered as a polished, final definitive statement, but rather as a tentative beginning which appears to have promise. The specificity was deliberately sought, even at this primitive stage, to facilitate hypothesis-testing and theory modification. The three determinants of ego involvement and their hypothesized combinatorial rule are stated so as to be refutable. Other determinants may well exist which are not presently incorporated into this model; no claim is made that these three are exhaustive.

The theory asserts that attitudinal ego involvement can be explained in terms of cognitive structure. However, no indices of cognitive structure change were incorporated in the present study or in any of the studies reviewed. This hypothesized intervening process should be directly examined (e.g., Brock, 1962) in future studies on involvement through assessing the bonds between the subject's own attitude and his value system. Greater linkage should be found for the more involved subjects. Other measures of involvement, such as the width of the region of rejection (Sherif *et al.*, 1965), need to be studied in relation to cognitive structure. These measures should be predictably affected by the value-bonding procedures employed in the present experiment. Work should be done to assess the phenomenal experience of ego involvement. Does the involved individual report that the issue is important, that his particular beliefs are important, and/or that he feels committed to his beliefs? These kinds of self-reports may or may not be affected by value-bonding treatments.

The past attitude literature has been somewhat restricted in its focus upon resistance to attitude change as the sole consequence of ego involvement. Sherif and Cantril (1947, p. 131) suggest there are other consequences, such as the annoyance felt when one's attitudes are attacked and the kinds of actions taken to further one's own point of view. The range of variables which attitudinal ego involvement, as an intervening process, influences should be theoretically and empirically expanded, especially to the responses treated elsewhere in this volume as various forms of dissonance reduction. (cf. Chapters 67 and 68).

The proposed cognitive model of attitudinal ego involvement, supported by an analysis of past research and present data, gives new coherence to previous studies, integrates them with research on cognitive structure, and opens up new research problems.

CHAPTER 29

Discussion: The Concept of Self

Milton J. Rosenberg

As the authors of this section have perused the concept of self and the processes that are commonly employed in the defense and enhancement of self, they have seemed in their separate ways to be working toward a major revision of the consistency approach, one in which self-related processes will play a far more central role than they have hitherto done.

Precisely what failings in the consistency approach have forced this revisionist mood? The most important seems to be the experimental affirmation of this hard, intractable fact: The need for (or trend toward) the maintenance of internally consistent affective-cognitive structures is often subordinated to man's penchant for trying to think well of himself and optimistically of his prospects. Experimental evidence to this effect was already apparent, though not yet rigorously examined, over a decade ago. One early example is Jordan's (1953) study of reactions to abstractly stated balanced and unbalanced triads. Somewhat indirectly the data revealed that unbalanced triads are less displeasing when their content is ego-enhancing than when this is not the case. Similarly, studies by Morgan and Morton (1944) and by McGuire (1960c) made clear that syllogistic reasoning (logic to be sure is not "psycho-logic," but they are related) is often subordinated to "wish fulfilment."

Further evidence in the same direction was apparent in the "Fenwick" studies that Abelson and I conducted (Rosenberg & Abelson, 1960). In summary of some of our findings we offered the general proposition that "In resolving cognitive discrepancies ... subjects seek not only the attainment of cognitive balance ... but also to alter their beliefs and evaluations in ways that will maximize expected gain and minimize expected loss; when both forces converge ... a formally 'balanced' outcome will be achieved; when these forces diverge the typical outcome will not meet the requirements of a simple formal definition of cognitive balance" (p. 145).

Where we spoke of the tendency to "maximize expected gain and minimize expected loss" we had in mind the kinds of cognitions which forecast or summarize actual need-reduction or frustration in one's dealings with persons, agencies, and events beyond the self. The papers in this section are, I think, quite persuasive in suggesting that the maximization of gain in self-esteem and the minimization of loss in the same realm are desiderata which also intrude into the cognitive processes of the individual, and which thus also turn him away from the simple pursuit of consistency in his ordering of cognitions referring to some common object or set of related objects.

While Secord offers a few particular exemplifications of this sort of self-oriented contamination of consistency processes, and while Smith conveys a general conviction that the former can often overwhelm the latter, they tend more to demark an important problem area than to fill it with testable, variable-specifying propositions. This is clearly the next required phase if consistency theory is to be expanded in a way that will make it more veridical and more broadly applicable to the wide range of cognitive dilemmas that humans encounter in real, as contrasted to laboratory, life.

In the light of the present contributions and some related recent work (cf. Pepitone, 1966) we can probably specify some of the important variables and processes that will have to be encompassed in the required expansion of the consistency approach. One of these is, certainly, the individual's generalized level of self-esteem. Quite possibly we shall find that where self-esteem is truly high and stable, the person is more prone to process incoming information in ways that are keyed to consistency restoration even when that can only be achieved at the cost of internalizing some negative judgments about the self.

The variable of ego-centrality is also likely to be confirmed as having great importance. For example, common insight suggests that when negative judgments or information about the self intrude into an otherwise favorable self-cognition system, the extent to which this will be tolerated, despite the inconsistency it arouses, may vary as an inverse function of the importance within the self concept of the particular positive attribute that is being called into question. Most readers of this volume would certainly have lower thresholds of response to inconsistent (that is, evaluatively negative) information about their competence as psychologists than about the forthrightness of their handshakes.

Or would they? The secret side of the self concept may contain many surprises. Probably as one goes from person to person within the same role category one would find highly idiosyncratic patterns of cherished attributes. Thus, apparently similar individuals might differ considerably in the degree of ego injury associated with accepting some particular kind of negative information about the self and then having to reorganize the self concept into consistency with that information.

These last comments may, in turn, suggest some of the quite complex problems that are likely to be encountered as we attempt to develop a more precise theoretical and research approach to the interaction of consistency and self-enhancement. Better techniques than we now possess will probably be needed to obtain valid maps of the elements of any particular self concept and of the patterns of interconnection between those elements. Indeed, we must remember that the self as represented to another (as in psychological testing or research inquiry) may be more favorably toned or more internally consistent than would be the case in the person's unrevealed perception of himself.

Further theorizing and research in this realm will probably also have to confront one phenomenologically available fact that the present investigators seem to have slighted: namely, that some individuals most of the time, and most individuals some of the time, find psychological gain in maintaining an image of a 'bad' or unattractive self along with the usually dominant 'good' or attractive self. Is it an attribute of the 'normal' person that he achieves some integration between these and that he has developed cognitive processing skills enabling him to do this?

Similarly, we must ask whether a negative portion of the self concept persists (in the face of the need, as Smith puts it, for "thinking as well of oneself as one can get away with") because we are able to link to it our inadequate and culpable actions? The paradoxical suggestion I would offer is that a positive self concept can best be defended from the inconsistency generated by 'bad' behavior if one also maintains an alternative or coexisting negative self concept. (Incidentally, do these last speculations suggest that Bramel may be overstating the case when he attributes to the person a pervasive, unopposed need to have others, and himself, judge him in approving terms?)

In the foregoing comments, by focusing upon the problems that are posed for consistency theory by the trend toward cognitive enhancement of the self, I have been responding to the major theme that ties together the contributions of Smith, Secord, and Bramel. Without attempting any overall integration I should now like to submit various other of their suggestions to brief discussion. Some consideration of the rather different issues broached by Ostrom and Brock is given in Chapter 4.

An extremely important problem is raised, and a compellingly elegant answer is offered, in Bramel's paper. His suggestion, it will be recalled, is that the intolerance for dissonance derives from a learning sequence that is frequently and universally experienced. Discrepancy between overt behavior or socially visible choice on the one hand and, on the other, private conviction, competence, or interest, will often lead to receipt of social disapproval. Since social disapproval is a potent negative reinforcer the ultimate effect of the frequent repetition of this sequence is that the person acquires a conditioned avoidance orientation toward situations in which such discrepancies or 'dissonances' are encountered. Thus his efforts to reduce such discrepancies, whether by altering his private convictions or his estimates of his own competence and rationality, are ultimately derived from his need for social approval.

This argument need not be restricted to account only for the rather special types of cognitive-behavioral discrepancy highlighted in dissonance theory. Much the same point might be made regarding the kind of intercognitive and affective-cognitive imbalances of focal prominence in the other major consistency theories.

However, one important further consideration seems to me to be required. Even if the reinforcing community were totally benign toward visibly inconsistent cognitive substructures (whether in the form of Heiderian imbalance or Festingerian dissonance) the person entertaining such substructures would experience them as leading to negative consequences more often than to positive consequences. This would be because cognitive inconsistency generates ambivalent evaluation of the objects involved in the inconsistently structured subsystem, and ambivalence impedes effective approach and avoidance toward consummatory and frustrating states, respectively. Confusion and delay in decision and action, uncertainty over the likely outcome of action—these, in themselves, are likely to be negatively reinforcing. Thus the person would be likely, rather early in life, to acquire a conditioned negativism toward inconsistency as such—and a comparably positive orientation toward those gradually acquired cognitive skills that can be employed to reduce inconsistency and thus to facilitate effective approach and avoidance. (This point of view is further elaborated in Chapter 13.)

This perspective is not in conflict with Bramel's argument—but it may add to it in a way that brings us a bit closer to a comprehensive theoretical account of the acquisition of that 'intolerance for inconsistency' assumed by all of the available variants of consistency theory. Though obvious, it is also worth noting here the compelling need for studying such matters through the techniques available in developmental psychology. We do not yet have any close, longitudinal studies of the emergence of the need for consistency maintenance or of the "cognitive micro-process" techniques (Rosenberg & Abelson, 1960) which are available to adults, and even to school-age children, as they attempt to reduce cognitive inconsistency.

The last matter I should like to comment upon is Smith's distinction between "the person's more or less stable *self concept*, and the transitory *self percepts* that are evoked in the course of his transactions with the environment." The former, as Smith suggests, is marked by considerable internal consistency between its positive (esteem maximizing) cognitive elements. But both its inner consistency and its positive evaluative orientation are often challenged by the actual content of the experience-generated self percepts that reach the individual's awareness.

This useful conceptualization brings to mind at least two further questions. The first concerns mediational mechanics: Just how are the inner consistency and positive orientation of the self concept maintained against the discrepant inputs that are directed at it in the form of transitory self percepts?

In formulating this general problem, let us consider the self concept metaphorically as an armored tank rolling across dangerous terrain and assaulted by occasional bursts of machine gun fire. The bullets that reach the tank and bounce off its armor represent negative self percepts potentially capable of arousing inconsistency within the self concept. What we do not presently understand is the nature of the armor, or—to set aside the metaphor—we do not understand in any but the most general terms the kinds of routine, day-by-day cognitive processing through which negative or inconsistent information relevant to the self is rendered noncredible or, when this is not possible, is transformed so that it can be incorporated into the self concept without doing it any significant injury.

A proper approach to this sort of problem could begin, I think, with descriptive studies (based, necessarily, upon introspective reports) of the kinds of cognitive processes which provide the self concept with its armor plating. Since these are highly practiced 'subroutines' they need somehow to be slowed down if they are to be scrutinized. Also one needs to adopt some set of concepts concerning ultimate elements and unit events. I should think that one way to begin would be to recognize that any self percept (e.g., 'The Professor thinks my dissertation proposal is uninspired') is comprised of objects and relations each of which is in turn comprised of subparts organized in some discernible structure. Some of these subparts could be easily elicited. (E.g., The concept of 'The Professor' may contain 'distant authority,' 'barks rather than bites,' 'hard task master,' 'not up-to-date on my problem area,' as well as other, less relevant elements.) The reshuffling of the component parts of the separate concepts and of the relations between those concepts may be the key to balance restoration or to the isolation of an inconsistency generating percept that cannot be balanced out.

A particularly promising exemplification of how such an approach can be used to develop a conjectural analysis of cognitive microprocessing has been provided by Abelson (1959, 1963). Similar concepts and analytic procedures might be put to work in the planning of observational research on just how the negative self percept bullets get bounced off the self concept tank.

Before I abandon this metaphor I might note that at times a more overwhelmingly disruptive self percept gets into the self concept tank. (Shall we say it is a heavier bullet that penetrates the armor or shall we conceive it as an enemy soldier who drops in through the top hatch, pistol blazing?) This represents the true "crisis of identity," and it is quite likely that cognitive events of a very different order are involved in handling this sort of problem. Thus we must ask: What, if anything, can the consistency theory perspective add to our understanding of identity disruption and collapse, of conversion or, for that matter, of a truly effective psychotherapeutic process?

I noted above that Smith's distinction between self concept and self percept brought two large questions to mind. The second is a sort of reversal of the first: Can inconsistency *arousal*, rather than reduction, facilitate the maintenance of a coherent, subjectively attractive self concept? Obviously I raise the question because I believe that an affirmative answer is required. I have in mind, first of all, the widely credited observation that an ego-enhancing sense of competence can be maintained by seeking out, or stirring up, cognitive inconsistencies and then proceeding to resolve them. From either the instrumental or operant conditioning points of view this observation has larger significance; for it suggests that the individual who has frequently tested his competence in this way would come to welcome cognitive inconsistencies as directly gratifying, particularly if they were of low magnitude and were not located in ego-central areas.

Perhaps the frequently assumed 'need for variety' or the 'curiosity' drive, at least as these operate at the human level, are outcomes of the sort of learning sequence that I have referred to here. Or if they are assumed to have a different, more intrinsic, origin, it must nevertheless be noted that such needs are likely to converge with the acquired preference for manageable cognitive inconsistencies.

However, these considerations do not fully encompass some of the additional problems encountered when one tests the limits of the 'intolerance for inconsistency' proposition. Daily life at least as lived in the academic world (which, to be sure, may be a subculture that has elevated the search and tolerance for inconsistency to a positive normative standard) affords some examples in which the involvement in unresolved inconsistency seems to have ego-enhancing value. One common form that this takes is the courting of P-O-X paradoxes. Who does not have in the circle of his acquaintances at least one person who seems to specialize in seeking out the sentiments of relevant others (O) toward common objects (X) so that he (P)

may then strongly state opposite sentiment toward X? Possibly this is often little more than a practiced "lifemanship" gambit—but I would hazard the observation that, for some persons at least, there is positive ego investment in the development and employment of skillful and authentic attitudinal deviance. Nor could we wish it to be otherwise, living as we do in a social epoch in which professional and associational life are characterized by so much orthodoxy in the internalization of 'received,' consensually structured political and social attitudes.

There are many other unsystematic observations suggesting that inconsistency arousal (and perhaps even the maintenance of inconsistency) sometimes serves to bolster the positive core of the self concept. For example: What of the person who celebrates the continuing discrepancy between his aspirations and his achievements and uses this to justify his estrangement from 'a world I never made'? What of the person who insists upon the necessary opposition between the real ('how I live') and the ideal ('how one ought to live')? It would appear that life, or at least the contemporary social system, imposes existential inconsistencies upon some of its participants and that ego defense and enhancement require such persons to make a virtue of the necessity of inconsistency. Whether or not this is an adequate explanation is a question I would commend to those who are attempting to improve the consistency theory approach.

More generally I would suggest that if we are going to construct a viable integration of what we know about cognitive consistency processes and about the development and stabilization of the self concept, this much is required: that we focus as closely upon the ego-enhancing uses of inconsistency as upon the more directly visible ways in which the self is served by skills in inconsistency reduction.

C. INCONSISTENCY AND PSYCHOLOGICAL STRESS

A common feature of the various consistency theory formulations is the belief that a state of 'psychological stress' is associated with the condition of inconsistency. Thus, Zajonc (1960a) speaks of the assumption that "inconsistency (is) a painful or at least psychologically uncomfortable state" (p. 282), while Hovland and Rosenberg (1960) refer to "the special tension caused by being in (cognitive) conflict" (p. 224). This notion was perhaps most explicit in Festinger's (1957) original presentation of dissonance theory with numerous references to, for example, "psychological discomfort ... in the presence of inconsistency" (p. 2). Heider, too, speaks of situations of imbalance "leaving us with a feeling of disturbance" (1958, p. 160). The stress component is perhaps least apparent in the congruity principle formulation. Osgood and Tannenbaum (1955) speak only of a "pressure toward attitude change" generated by an evaluative incongruity (although at a later date, Osgood [1960] does comment on "the psychological stress produced by cognitive inconsistencies" [p. 345]).

But while references to an association between inconsistency and a state of bothersomeness are common enough in the various consistency theory statements, the specific locus and role of the stress component remains a conceptually unclear issue. While it is mostly referred to as a condition mediating the inconsistency and its resolution, it has received surprisingly little direct attention in research to date. With few exceptions, its existence has been assumed or inferred rather than demonstrated or assessed.

The contributors to this section take note of this situation, and in the process of giving it its due consideration, raise a number of pertinent theoretical and methodological considerations. Jerome Singer gets directly to the point by noting the not always obvious distinction between the state of dissonance or inconsistency itself and the often accompanying feelings of discomfort. He then addresses himself to a number of possible factors limiting or enhancing—and often contaminating—the appearance of the psychological stress. Approaching the problem from a somewhat different standpoint, Leonard Berkowitz questions the need to invoke the intervention of a discomfort state into the consistency paradigm. Rather than the ʾore 'traditional' aversion-avoidance mechanism, he tends to opt for a positive pleasure-seeking explanation of the type suggested by Berlyne (see Chapter 15).

Also relevant to consideration of discomfort or other intervening conditions is the important issue of awareness. Timothy Brock addresses the problem within the dissonance theory framework where it is most salient, particularly in the Brehm and Cohen version, with its relation to their key concept of commitment. He cites a number of studies which raise doubts about awareness as a necessary component of the inconsistency induction-reduction process.

Undoubtedly, a main reason why the assumed psychological stresses have so rarely been studied is the lack of acceptable measures of such affective states. Among the measures that have been employed are verbal indices. Eleanor Norris comments on these generally, singling out the Nowlis mood scale for particular attention. She surveys a number of studies utilizing such self-report techniques, and raises a number of problems inherent in their use. Possibly of more promise is the application of a variety of physiological stress indicators. Harold Gerard traces some of his own work using such measures as skin resistance, blood flow, and pupil size with encouraging results. Of particular interest is the fact that in one instance the physiological indicators led to a different and less apparent interpretation of the cognitive results.

CHAPTER 30

The Bothersomeness of Inconsistency

Jerome E. Singer

State University of New York at Stony Brook

Imagine a bright high school student who, in his senior year, has to choose between several very desirable colleges to attend. The colleges differ in several ways and all the alternatives open to him are attractive. His deadline draws near and he finally makes his choice. The night after he makes his choice, he has trouble sleeping. He sweats, he is uncomfortable, he keeps tossing back and forth. The characteristics of the college he has chosen and of those which he has rejected pervade his thoughts. He is bothered, disturbed, and upset after having made his decision. This young man, however, is of an intellectual bent and is self-analytical and perceptive. Curiously, he finds himself puzzled by the dilemma. On the one hand, he had nothing but desirable alternatives to select from; any one of them would be a fine school to attend; yet, on the other hand, having made his choice between the schools he finds himself totally bothered by his choice.

Not being a dissonance theorist, his curiosity is piqued at the seeming inconsistency of feeling distress and anguish where logically it seems he should be experiencing nothing but pleasure and joy. The young man is caught in two inconsistency-producing situations. The first, post decision dissonance, he finds bothersome and pervaded with negative affect. The second one, inconsistency between his good fortune and the inappropriate bothersomeness it has engendered, is an intellectual sort of inconsistency which he does not find particularly troubling, but merely curious and interesting. This, then, is the general proposition—that there are different kinds of cognitive inconsistency. Some of these have a noncognitive component; they are disturbing, bothersome, and accompanied by negative affect. Others are strictly cognitive with no corollary bothersomeness or negative affect.

The particular problem poses several questions: How is it possible to demonstrate rigorously that there is some sort of bothersomeness connected with inconsistency? Secondly, is it possible to show that some kinds of inconsistency are bothersome whereas others are not? Finally, what are the

This chapter was written while the author was a N.I.M.H. Visiting Scholar at Educational Testing Service. The author is grateful to ETS for their generous support and use of facilities. The paper was supported in part by National Institute of Mental Health Grant MH-07515.

general rules or under what circumstances is a cognitive inconsistency bothersome?

It is not possible to deduce that inconsistency will be accompanied by negative affect or bother from an analysis of the theoretical bases of inconsistency theories themselves. Most of them have some motivational base. Usually it is tied to a drive-like tension system (dissonance theory, Festinger, 1957) or a Gestalt-like tension system (balance theory, Heider, 1958), although it may be related to the presence of tendencies to make two incompatible mediations (congruity theory, Osgood & Tannenbaum, 1955). None of these motivational or impelling systems necessarily implies that there will be unpleasantness connected with the inconsistency, just as it may be possible to have a Zeigarnik effect with no accompanying negative affect. It would also be difficult to state a set of procedures which would enable one to find out experimentally whether or not a given kind of inconsistency were bothersome. Clearly, any physiological measure would confound bothersomeness or affect with excitement, interest, attention, and cognition. There is no present reason to believe that there will be physiological measures sensitive and subtle enough to pick up the difference between bothersomeness and pleasure. Experimental attempts to isolate the bothersomeness must rely, at present, either on behavioral indices or on self-rating or self-report scales.

Any case for bothersomeness of inconsistency must be made at first on an anecdotal level, which is to say that the instances given must be so compelling that although their documentation is nonexperimental, they will elicit a wide range of agreement. There are other instances where such forceful anecdotes can be found. For instance, it is equally difficult to document the existence of something called castration anxiety. Yet it is not easy to listen to the Tom Lehrer song which contains the line "sliding down the razor blade of life" without experiencing a resonant twinge which serves as testimony to the intuitive validity of the castration anxiety concept. Although it is not possible to choose as immediately compelling an anecdote for bothersomeness of inconsistency, anybody who has purchased a car or a house or gotten married will immediately have some intuitive feeling for the notion of postdecision dissonance. The bothersome aggravation that occurs after the decision has been made seems to have almost universal applicability. Indeed, one of the problems of teaching dissonance theory to an undergraduate course in social psychology is not arousing this intuitive understanding, but rather keeping it restricted to dissonance problems. Intuitive agreement is so great that students tend to view everything and anything in dissonance terms.

A more difficult question is that which asks whether or not the bothersomeness produced by different sorts of inconsistency is similar. The whole question of comparative aspects of phenomenology is one which has been strenuously debated in other areas of psychology. Suffice it to say there is no immediately recognizable or easy way to tell whether or not the bothersomeness engendered by being attracted to an object we cognitively dislike is the same as the bothersomeness engendered by having to choose or having chosen between several relatively attractive alternatives. Clearly recognizing that later research may demonstrate that different sorts of affect accompany different types of inconsistency, we will nevertheless assume that the bothersomeness which accompanies inconsistency of different types is essentially the same.

Factors Influencing Bothersomeness

We can now turn to the broad question: Are there any general circumstances under which inconsistency will be bothersome as opposed to ones where the pressures to achieve cognitive reorganization are not accompanied by negative affect? In examining this question, it will be helpful to look at five variables which, accompanied by inconsistency, may be responsible for producing bothersomeness—pervasiveness, intensity, salience, ego involvement, and response incompatibility.

Pervasiveness. In recent years the study of the topic of attitudes has shifted from the consideration of attitudes as independent conceptual entities, each of which could be individually manipulated or changed, to the conception of attitudes as structures or organizations of cognitions and beliefs. This reformulation incorporated the recognition that changes in particular beliefs, attitudes, or opinions often may reflect not so much a reevaluation of a position on one particular topic, but rather a restructuring of the system into which that topic was interwoven. Alternatively, as consistency theories developed, the traditional attitude-change mechanisms came to be seen as handmaidens of a general process by which consistency resolution is obtained and maintained.

It is possible to conceptualize an inconsistency which arises between cognitions as being more or less pervasive—that is, it affects a relatively large part of the structure or a small part of it. Bothersomeness may covary with pervasiveness such that, other things being equal, the more pervasive an inconsistency is, the greater will be the amount of cognitive effort or cognitive change or restructuring necessary to restore consistency, and the greater the pressures to attempt to restore consistency. The work of Rosenberg and Abelson (1960) demonstrates that a principle of least effort applies in cognitive restructuring. People prefer to do less work to restructure than to do more work. To the extent that a pervasive stimulus requires more work, it can be thought of as producing more negative affect and more bothersomeness than a stimulus which is less pervasive and which requires less overall work to change the structure.

McGuire's (1960c; Chapter 6) experiments on consistency in logical syllogisms also supply some inferential support for this notion. He found, for example, that people were not able to keep the belief in the conclusions of syllogisms logically consistent with belief in their premises and at the same time consistent with the desirabilities of the conclusions. Conclusions which were thought desirable were believed to a greater extent than warranted by belief in the premises on which they were based. Changes in either the desirability of or the belief in a premise required adjustments in the desirability and belief of its derivative conclusions in order to maintain a new optimal level of consistency. To the extent that a particular belief is pervasive—i.e., that it is a premise in a large number of syllogisms—it will require more effort to get a new balance of consistency in all of its derivative conclusions, and the more effort required, the more bothersome the results. The choice of college may be more pervasive an inconsistency for our apocryphal high school boy than speculation about human nature.

Intensity. So far, the use of the word importance has been avoided in this discussion of inconsistency, for importance appears to be a multi-dimensional quality. One characteristic of importance is pervasiveness, as discussed above. Another is intensity. A person's belief system may contain two cognitions which are equal in their pervasiveness but differ in their intensity. If a person could order his beliefs in the extent to which their truth mattered to him, or the extent to which their desirability varied, then the more desirable the truth of a particular belief or the more concern that he would have were that belief not true, the more intense that belief.[1] Bothersomeness may thus be a function of the inconsistency of intense beliefs. That is, beliefs which, although pervasive, are not deemed very important to a person may not produce bothersomeness when involved in inconsistency; but beliefs whose truth is greatly desirable may produce a great deal of bothersomeness if involved in inconsistency or if threatened. There may be equal reasons or equal pressures upon a person to reorganize his cognitive system to relieve the inconsistency of the threat to any of several beliefs, but the more intense ones may be accompanied by negative affect while the less intense ones are not. In other words, there must be an intensity level which serves as a threshold for bothersomeness. Intensity seems to be the sense in which Festinger (1957) uses "importance" when he states that more dissonance arises from an important inconsistency than from an unimportant one. For our high school senior, choice of a college is a more intense set of cognitions than his paradoxical intellectual bother.

Salience. A third factor which may relate to the production of bothersomeness accompanying inconsistency is the salience of the belief, that is, the extent to which it predominates the subject's cognitive system at any given time. Imagine a person who reads a bit of doggerel poetry with a particularly captivating rhythm: Mark Twain's story about the ditty "Punch brothers, punch brothers, punch with care"[2] is such an example. After hearing or reading this ditty a person finds that, try as he will, he cannot avoid reciting it mentally, rehearsing it, practicing it; in short, he cannot get rid of it. It is with him day and night, preventing him from thinking about other things, it distracts him from his immediate work, and it begins to irritate him solely because of its continued presence. Possibly some of the irritation engendered by the continued salience of a relatively trivial topic is due to the general inconsistency between the cognitions that other business needs to be transacted and that only the trivial subject is immediately available. In addition, it could be that a salient inconsistency interacts with temporal phenomena so that what was previously a neutral inconsistency becomes bothersome. Just as Schachter (1951) and Festinger (1950) postulated that a perceived discrepancy of agreement or opinion in a group increased through time as actual discrepancy remained constant, so it very well may be that perceived inconsistency increases over time as actual inconsistency remains constant. An unintense and relatively unmeaningful inconsistency may become more and more intense in time, and the desirability of, or pressures for,

---

[1] Singer's concept of intensity is very similar to Colby's concept in Chapter 47 of "charge" on a belief—Ed.

[2] In the story "Punch, Brothers, Punch," Mark Twain documents his personal agony in trying to make a rhythmic ditty unsalient. He finally succeeds by infecting a friend with the rhyme and saves his friend from "an asylum" by taking him to a university and having him "discharge the burden of his persecuting rhymes into the eager ears of the poor, unthinking students."

getting it resolved may increase as it remains unresolved over extended periods. The high school student may resolve his choice dissonance and be still thoughtful about his incongruous negative affect. If these thoughts remain salient for a long enough time, they may become bothersome in themselves.

Ego involvement.[3] One of the main distinctions to be made between bothersome and nonbothersome inconsistencies is the extent to which the inconsistency is ego involving—i.e., the extent to which it poses a threat to a person's self-image. Inconsistencies which involve logical disturbances and discrepancies but do not particularly reflect back upon or imply any unfavorable self-connotations might not produce negative affect. On the other hand, those which either in their statement or in their resolution would involve some threat to the ego would be bothersome. Thus, in Bramel's (1962) study of defensive projection as a dissonance-reduction mechanism in which subjects were given the cognition that they had homosexual tendencies, the threat to the ego is clear and distinct, the dissonance is precisely between self-image and the possession of an unfavorable and unwanted characteristic. Under such circumstances the inconsistency produced would be quite bothersome and irritating. It would be instructive to find a case which could be matched in general for other characteristics previously mentioned and yet would not be ego involving. Perhaps Brehm's (1962) study of cognitive control of thirst and hunger provides such a parallel. His subjects have inconsistencies between the fact they are hungry or thirsty and the fact that they have voluntarily agreed to go without food and water. While such cognitions may be physically unpleasant (although the point of Brehm's work is that dissonance mechanisms will prevent them from being so), they are not necessarily ego threatening, and to that extent the inconsistency in the Brehm study should not be as bothersome as the inconsistency in the Bramel study.

The same point could be demonstrated in another fashion if two groups of people could have similar inconsistencies where it would be ego threatening for one group and non-ego threatening for the other. At a trivial level, the example of an inconsistency in a mathematical proof might be bothersome for the mathematician but not for the layman. This, of course, could be attributed to the intensity and the pervasiveness of the inconsistency as well as to the ego involvement, but in part it could be that an inconsistent formulation in mathematics may be more ego threatening for the mathematician than for the layman. Similarly, Carlsmith and Aronson (1965) have reported that violation of an expectancy produces unpleasantness, and Lamb and Singer (1966) report that this effect is more likely to occur in ego-involving situations than in non-ego-involving ones. The choice of college may be ego involving for the high school boy, while speculations on human nature may not carry any self-derogatory implications.

Incompatible response tendencies. It may be that bothersomeness will not occur when the inconsistency is between two purely cognitive elements, but only as between cognitive elements which are related to incompatible response tendencies. These may be between two behaviors which are inherently incompatible, or between two behaviors which, although not

---

[3] See Section III B for a more detailed and thorough consideration of this variable in the consistency theories.

necessarily incompatible, are to be performed simultaneously and hence are temporally impossible. (See Collins' discussion in Chapter 13, pp. 243-244). To the extent that incompatible responses or behaviors are involved in the inconsistency, this may produce bothersomeness, while, on the other hand, if the inconsistency is purely cognitive in nature it may not be particularly bothersome.

The notion of inconsistency stemming from incompatible behaviors is implicit in the Osgood and Tannenbaum (1955) formulation of congruity theory, for indeed it would appear that the reason that incongruity motivates people to resolve their attitude structure is precisely to avoid having to make incompatible responses to two objects of judgment. Although seemingly dissimilar, Rosenberg's (1960a) notion of the consistency between affect and cognition may also be interpreted on an incompatible behavior basis. That is, if someone has a positive valence for an object, a belief, or a behavior which produces negative affect, this can be thought of as producing a kind of ambivalence of incompatible responses which is bothersome. Logically, of course, there would be an inconsistency if somebody were cognitively repelled by an object which gave him positive affect, and this should also produce bothersomeness of cognition: somebody would have both approach and avoidance tendencies to the same object or belief. The study by Yaryan and Festinger (1961) in the format of the recent replication by Arrowood and Ross (1966) provides a case of an inconsistency which is not behaviorally oriented. Subjects are told they are to take one of two kinds of tests. One of the tests will necessitate a great deal of difficult preparatory work, the other will not require much difficult work. Subjects increase the subjective probability of their being given the difficult test although they realize the objective probabilities are even. Although this prediction derives directly from dissonance theory, no incompatible behavior is involved, and hence it would be predicted that in contrast to a study which involved two different actions, such as choosing one of two objects in a decision task, there should be less bothersomeness for the Arrowood and Ross situation. Choosing two different colleges is impossible for our high school student; reflecting on puzzling observations does not result in response conflict.

Testing Bothersomeness

Although it is possible to speculate on additional factors or sources of bothersomeness, several comments remain pertinent. The existence of the bothersomeness accompanying inconsistency is one which rests on a consensual basis rather than on any rigorous proof. The belief that only certain inconsistencies are accompanied by bothersomeness rests on a similar basis. It is difficult to test or to ascertain which factors are involved in inconsistency and bothersomeness, and to what extent they are so involved without having a good measure of bothersomeness. Unfortunately, it appears that neither the physiological nor the verbal methods currently used provide clearcut possibilities and experimental tests of these notions. But there are some procedures which would enable experimental tests of the conjectures on which factors produce bothersomeness, although these procedures require especially modified instruments.

There are joint difficulties in getting scales phrased subtly enough to separate the bothersomeness of some kinds of inconsistency from the general, curious prodding of almost all inconsistency, and the incorporation of such measures into experiments so that they would not be inappropriate or im-plausible. These difficulties may be solved, for instance, by presenting sub-jects with a Nowlis (1953) mood adjective check list after each dissonance-arousing manipulation (see Norris, Chapter 33) or as in the Rosenberg and Abelson (1960) study in a general postcommunication questionnaire, but this still would leave the problem of dissemblance. The dissonance-producing experience may lead subjects to report on the mood adjective sheet in a self-protective or ego-enhancing way. What would be picked up is not only bothersomeness, but might include chagrin, pride, social desirability, or a host of other extraneous feelings also produced by the dissonance situation but not necessarily one of the concomitants of bothersomeness. One solution to the problems of assessing bothersomeness produced by inconsistency might lie in the development of a standard measuring device. For various reasons, most of the consistency experiments employ idio-syncratic or ad hoc measures[4] for the assessment of attitude, belief, or cog-nition. If a scale of bothersomeness were constructed, accommodating the usual caveats (cf. Vernon, 1964), it could then be used in a wide variety of studies to isolate and refine both the necessary conditions and the thresh-old values required for inconsistency to result in bothersomeness.

In summary, there are two major problems concerned with bother-someness of inconsistency: the specification of factors and the nature of its measurement. Both problems are amenable to experimental solution; but, at present, an actual body of pertinent data does not exist.

---

[4] The words *ad hoc* and *idiosyncratic* are used advisedly. Osgood and Tannenbaum, for instance, use the semantic differential which is hardly ad hoc, but in a real sense it is idiosyncratic in consistency research. The terms refer to the use of measures in such re-search even though the instruments may be well known and documented for other purposes.

CHAPTER 31

On the Discomfort of Cognitive Inconsistency

Leonard Berkowitz

University of Wisconsin

I must admit to being conceptually uncertain, cognitively inconsistent, and generally bothered by this 'discomfort' problem. The research evidence is seriously incomplete, and considerations of parsimony and common sense appear to be in conflict. Given this state of affairs, the easiest and most discreet path is to be eclectic and to note that most of the contentions regarding the role of 'botherment' in cognitive inconsistency probably have some degree of validity. My theme here will be that there are many different kinds of behavioral determinants, and the processes governing behavior vary from one type of situation to another. Under some conditions the responses to cognitive inconsistency may well be attempts to lessen discomfort, but other determinants may become dominant in other situations.

When the several cognitive consistency models were first introduced, it was typically assumed that cognitive inconsistency was unpleasant. Festinger (1957, p. 3) was quite explicit in making this point, and he had company in the proponents of the other consistency approaches (e.g., Jordan, 1953). In the succeeding years, however, dissonance theorists at least seem to have developed some doubts about the necessity of invoking experienced discomfort as the spur to dissonance-engendered responses. Thus, Brehm and Cohen (1962) did not mention felt unpleasantness as a mediating condition in dissonance reactions, and, with Lawrence and Festinger (1962), chose to define dissonance only as a state of tension.

It is possible that Festinger was being overly *phenomenological* in his original linkage of dissonance with subjective discomfort. Contemporary social psychology has a great tendency to anchor its explanatory concepts in experience—even when, following the logic of theory construction, it is not necessary to do so. Reflecting this tendency, and perhaps also showing the influence of folklore, consistency theorists readily think of inconsistency as generating an experienced discomfort. It may not always be necessary, however, to assume that discomfort arises from cognitive inconsistency. Cognitive inconsistency might affect subsequent behavior without the intervention of any experienced unpleasantness. This possibility is also relevant in some ways to other motivational formulations. Most motivational discussions, at least until the onrush of studies of stimulus-seeking in the 1950s, assumed as a matter of course that all instigations to behavior were essentially aversive in nature. The organism supposedly acted primarily in order to reduce a disturbing internal excitation. Consistency theorizing is still dominated by this aversive-state conception of motivation.

Dissonance and Information-Seeking

Investigations of reactions to belief-discrepant information provide some important observations. In particular, consider the matter of selective exposure. Social scientists have long maintained that people will accept and even seek out information supporting their beliefs but will tend to avoid incompatible information, and the phenomenon has been given renewed emphasis by dissonance theory. Freedman and Sears (1965a) have shown, however, that there is very little clear-cut experimental evidence in favor of the selective exposure proposition, and dissonance theory is not upheld unequivocally in this regard (see Section IV E). These doubts exist, furthermore, even when there is a narrowing of the conditions said to produce cognitive dissonance. In accord with Brehm and Cohen (1962), Festinger (1964b) has recently suggested that commitment is necessary for the occurrence of dissonance after a decision has been made. A person presumably will not demonstrate selective exposure prior to reaching a decision, and will demonstrate selectivity following a decision only if he has committed himself to a course of action that would unequivocally affect his subsequent behavior.

This type of commitment was probably established in the experiments by Mills, Aronson, and Robinson (1959) and Rosen (1961). College students were given a choice as to the nature of the examination they would have in a course; by Festinger's definition, their decisions would influence their subsequent actions. But contrary to the original dissonance-theory prediction, the students tended to prefer material having the greatest relevance to their choice—whether or not the article supported the choice to which they had committed themselves. Similarly, many cigarette smokers probably feel somewhat committed to their smoking behavior, yet smokers have been found to have a greater interest than nonsmokers in articles pertaining to smoking, and again whether or not the information is consistent with the continuance of smoking (Feather, 1963). Smokers do not generally avoid information that smoking can lead to lung cancer even when they have committed themselves to reading this material right away (Brock, 1965).

Several attempts have been made to preserve the dissonance theory-dictated notion of selective exposure, and a number of these arguments seem quite reasonable. Festinger has pointed out (1964b, p. 82), as an illustration, that merely telling the individual of the existence of information going counter to his beliefs can actually generate dissonance, causing him to mobilize his dissonance-lessening defenses. It has also been suggested that the person's self-confidence can be an important contingency condition; the higher his self-confidence, the less likely he is to display selective exposure (Canon, cited in Festinger, 1964b, pp. 83–96). This last-mentioned possibility has been brought into question, however, by the negative results in a more recent experiment (Freedman, 1965a). There is better evidence supporting yet another hypothesis regarding factors governing selective exposure. Several writers (e.g., Mills et al., 1959; Rosen, 1961; Festinger, 1964b, p. 84) have suggested that people will tolerate increased dissonance if they believe it is to their benefit to do so; information will be sought out, even if it is inconsistent with established cognitions, to the extent that the information is thought to be useful for the attainment of other rewards. Two direct tests (Canon, cited in Festinger, 1964b; Freedman, 1965a) have confirmed this contention.

It is apparent that selective exposure is not an all-or-nothing proposition, and even the most sympathetic adherents of dissonance theory (Brehm & Cohen, 1962, pp. 68-69; Festinger, 1964a, Ch. 4) now appear to recognize that people generally are not as quick to stick their heads, ostrich-like, in the sand, as their formulation had initially maintained. Other factors may determine whether or not the selective avoidance will occur, but whatever these factors may be, the selective avoidance tendency does not seem to be very strong.

Such a conclusion is pertinent to the description of dissonance as a state of discomfort. Assuming the belief-discrepant information is dissonance producing, the failure to avoid this kind of information implies (a) that increased dissonance is not necessarily very unpleasant, and/or (b) that behavior can be governed by determinants that, at times at least, are stronger than the striving to lessen discomfort. I would suggest that both implications are correct.

Nondissonance Interpretations of Information Seeking

Studies of exploration and curiosity can provide an alternative explanation of a number of observations obtained from dissonance-theory investigations of information seeking. In recent years several writers (e.g., Berlyne, 1960; Hunt, 1963) have maintained that the detection of incongruity can instigate behavior. This incongruity encompasses dissonant states, as defined by Festinger and his colleagues, but is apparently much more extensive; to my knowledge, none of these alternative formulations have confined perceived incongruity to situations in which the individual has committed himself to a particular cognition. Incongruity in this sense appears to be more of a perceptual and less of a self-defensive matter than dissonance (see Hunt, 1963, for one taxonomy of such incongruities).

Berlyne's analysis of stimulus seeking (1960, 1962, 1963; Berlyne & Lewis, 1963) is particularly suggestive. Since Berlyne has his own contribution to this volume (see Chapter 15), his general position as outlined in his 1960 book will be but briefly summarized here. A major feature of this conception is the postulated connection between the individual's internal arousal level and the nature of the external stimuli he will attempt to encounter.[1] The organism presumably desires to maintain an optimal "arousal tonus." Substantive departures from this optimal level are aversive, while a return to the tonus level is rewarding (p. 194). Increases in arousal level are not invariably avoided, however. According to Berlyne, momentary jumps in arousal are pleasurable "as a consequence of the drop in arousal" terminating these jumps; these "arousal jags," or brief increases and decreases in arousal level, are pleasant (pp. 198–200). Certain conditions possess

---

[1] In this discussion we shall, for simplicity, consider arousal as a unitary condition. There is some generality of arousal effects, as activation theorizing contends, but the extent of this generality can easily be exaggerated. Nevertheless, these complex differentiations will be ignored here.

"arousal potential" in that they are capable of either increasing or lessening the arousal level, and the organism generally will seek an intermediate arousal potential (p. 200). These arousal-modifying conditions are termed "collative variables" and include such things as change, complexity, novelty, and uncertainty. The organism may then seek out a novel, complex, or possibly even dissonance-producing stimulus because of the pleasant change in arousal level that will result.

Taking a very general drive position, Berlyne also suggested that various forms of arousal potential have equivalent effects: "an individual whose arousal has already been raised by one kind of arousal potential can be aroused far beyond the tonus level by ... arousal potential from a different source" (p. 209). Thus, making an observation to which we will return later, Berlyne contended that anxious people "will be distressed by an amount of novelty, change or complexity that others would take in their stride" (p. 209). For example, subjects who have just been frustrated tend to make relatively quick guesses as to the nature of an ambiguous stimulus that is shown to them (Smock, 1955). By classifying the unknown stimulus, the guess reduces its uncertainty and thereby lessens the arousal potential of the stimulus to a level that can better be tolerated by the emotional subjects.

Especially relevant to the present discussion is Berlyne's concept of "epistemic curiosity" (1960, Chapter 11). Explicitly likened to the cognitive inconsistency with which we are here concerned, epistemic curiosity is said to be a motivational state arising from conceptual conflict (conflict between opposing symbolic-response tendencies) that "actuates quests for knowledge and is relieved by acquisition of knowledge." The greater the number of competing response tendencies, the greater their mutual incompatibility and their absolute strength, and the more equally matched their response strengths, the greater is the conceptual conflict and the resulting knowledge-seeking. To demonstrate this, Berlyne (1962) conducted an experiment in which high school and college students were given a number of quotations, each coupled with the names of possible authors and also some fictitious experts' guesses as to the true authors. In accord with his formulation, he found that reported curiosity as to the authorship of the quotation increased with two determinants of conceptual conflict (regardless of whether or not the subjects had correctly guessed the name of the author)—the number of possible alternatives and the evenness of their probability of being correct.

I do not claim that the Berlyne analysis of information seeking is necessarily superior to other interpretations. It does have some appeal, nevertheless, in being quite general in its coverage and also relatively parsimonious. The quest for information does not have to be attributed to some conjectured drive for "mastery" (Fenichel, cited in Berlyne, 1960, p. 199) or "competence" (White, 1959) in a strained attempt to preserve the structure of traditional personality theorizing. Moreover, where dissonance-theory analyses of communication behavior generally interpret information-seeking as being essentially a search for support, the Berlyne view holds that information may be sought for the intrinsic pleasure it will bring.

Social psychologists might be well advised to consider this type of conception in their research on information seeking and interpersonal communication. While it is undoubtedly true, as we have already seen, that the perceived utility of a given information set is an important determinant of the individual's preference for this material, available evidence also indicates the search for information can be heightened by the sheer novelty of the available information and by conceptual conflict independently of utility or defensive considerations.

Freedman and Sears (1965a) have reported a number of studies demonstrating the preference for relatively unfamiliar information. In several experiments by Sears, for example, subjects placed in a simulated jury situation expressed the strongest desire to read arguments they had not encountered before. The writers concluded (p. 86), "If in some controversy ... [the individual is] exposed to one side's arguments but not the other's he seems to prefer the side with which he is unfamiliar, even if it means being exposed to nonsupportive information" (i.e., material opposed to his initial beliefs).

Brief mention can also be made of several findings consistent with the Berlyne emphasis on conceptual conflict. Thus, Spitzer (1964) gave his college-student subjects fictitious information as to both what a 'foreign student' thought about the role of the American college student, and what their peers' opinions were on this issue. There was the greatest expressed interest in meeting the foreigner in the condition in which conceptual conflict was greatest—i.e., when the foreigner disagreed with the peer group opinion and there was a high degree of opinion consensus within this peer group—in other words, when there were opposing strong symbolic-response tendencies. Similarly, Berkowitz (1965b) used the number of words written by subjects to their fellow group members as an index of the subjects' motivation to communicate. He found that this motivation was strongest in the subjects presumably possessing strong opposing cognitions. These were men who had heard an expert give a talk opposed to their beliefs but who remained confident that their original views were correct. The motivation to communicate was lower in the people supposedly under less conflict, either because the expert's speech had supported their position or because their confidence in the correctness of their opinion (opposed to the expert's statement) had declined.

This is not to say, of course, that conceptual conflict is the only or even major process affecting communication behavior. Information-seeking and communication behavior generally can be influenced by a variety of determinants. Berlyne (1960, pp. 274–280) acknowledged the role of extrinsic motivation; information-seeking can be in the service of practical problems, and can be an outgrowth of habits developed from the past history of extrinsic rewards. But other motivational factors also play some part. It is important for psychological theory to specify the conditions governing which processes become operative on a given occasion.

One of the conditions influencing the quest for information, it has been suggested, is the level of arousal within the individual. A number of studies point to this relationship. In one of these, Berlyne and Lewis (1963) demonstrated that there is some generality in the effects produced by different arousal sources. Subjects received either (a) white noise, (b) information that they would soon get electric shocks, or (c) information that they would take a memory test, or (d) were placed in a nonaroused control group, and then were given two tasks involving different forms of exploratory behavior. One task supposedly dealt with 'specific exploration' (instigated primarily by incomplete information) and required the subjects to look at designs presented one at a time on a screen. In this situation the three aroused groups spent significantly more time looking at the designs than did the control group. On the other task, however, presumably having more to do with 'diversive exploration,' two patterns at a time were first shown briefly to the subjects who were given a choice as to which pattern they could look at again. Here the three aroused groups chose to look at the more complex or incongruous pattern significantly *less* often than did the nonaroused subjects. As a result of their already heightened internal arousal, the experimental subjects preferred not to encounter those complex and incongruous patterns which would produce even greater arousal—when they had a choice and could easily avoid the arousing stimuli. Haywood (1962) obtained similar results in a study in which the heightened arousal (manifested in increased palmar sweating) was brought about by requiring subjects to listen to a tape-recorded incomprehensible message. When they were next asked to choose between novel or familiar cards, the aroused subjects expressed less of a preference for the novel cards than they had displayed earlier, while a nonaroused control group actually had an increased preference for these novel cards.

A variety of social psychological observations can also be understood as a decreased preference for novel, incongruous, or complex stimuli under arousing conditions. In particular, consider the gambling experiment, first reported by Festinger (1957) and then replicated by Cohen, Brehm, and Latané (1959), which is frequently cited in support of the selective exposure thesis. College students played 12 hands of a card game against the experimenter for money and then, before going on with the game, were shown a complicated graph from which the true probability of winning supposedly could be computed. Reasoning that the amount of money lost by the subjects could be coordinated to the dissonance within them (since the subjects were somewhat committed to their initial strategy), the investigators maintained that the time the subjects spent looking at the graph was governed by the intensity of their dissonance. The subjects who had lost only slightly up to that point, and who presumably had relatively weak dissonance, looked at the graph for the longest period of time. They supposedly expected the graph information would support their strategy and thus reduce their dissonance. The people experiencing stronger dissonance, however, gave little attention to the graph, theoretically because they expected the information would be opposed to the strategy to which they were committed; they therefore avoided the information that probably would increase their dissonance still more.

Without insisting on the superiority of any particular interpretive scheme, it would seem that a Berlyne type of analysis might well apply to these findings; at least, it poses an alternative explanation that should be tested. Some of the increased time spent looking at the graph by the Weak Dissonance group might be due to conceptual conflict rather than the hypothesized search for support. And similarly, some of the decrease in time given to the graph by the High Dissonance group might be due to a lessened tolerance for complex stimuli stemming from the loss-engendered strong arousal in this group. (If this latter notion seems contrary to the first set of results obtained in the previously cited study by Berlyne and Lewis, let me suggest that even the Berlyne-Lewis subjects might have shown a decreased desire to look at the complicated patterns—i.e., a lessened specific exploration—if their arousal level had been much stronger. First, the choice of what pattern to look at is affected by arousal level, and then, as arousal mounts, there is also an avoidance of very complex, novel, and/or incongruous stimuli when no choice is given.) At any rate, in order to rule out the effect of strong arousal on the avoidance of all complex information, the gambling experiments require a control condition in which the chart presented to the subject is equally complex but the information is irrelevant to the card game strategy.

There is another line of research to which this postulated connection between arousal level and stimulation preference is also pertinent: the series of studies on affiliation behavior conducted by Schachter (1959). As is well known, Schachter demonstrated that anxious people generally want the company of other persons, and particularly prefer to be with people undergoing the same unpleasant experience. Rabbie (1963) extended this observation by showing that anxious women tended to prefer being with those other women who supposedly were just as aroused as they were. To modify Schachter's apt summary, "misery loves miserable company," as long as it is just as miserable but not too miserable. Schachter and his colleagues view these results as stemming from a drive for social comparisons: the anxious person presumably wants to evaluate his emotional state and seeks out people who are just as aroused as he is so that he can compare himself with them. The present reasoning suggests a somewhat simpler process might be at work. Instead of wanting to understand his feelings, the anxious individual (a) wants social companionship because he expects the presence of other people to be anxiety reducing, and (b) wants the kind of companionship that would provide the least amount of novelty, incongruity, and complexity: other people who are similar to himself in the experiences they are undergoing, the magnitude of their emotional arousal, and even in their attitudes and values.

Discomfort and reactions to external stimuli

The apparent decreased preference for novelty-complexity-incongruity under high arousal could undoubtedly be viewed in discomfort-avoidance terms. The findings could also be interpreted, however, without invoking *experienced* (i.e., verbally discriminated) discomfort; with the latter-day dissonance theorists and Berlyne, we can speak of the avoidance of potentially arousing stimuli as being produced by some internal excitation or tension. Berlyne postulated an "anticipatory arousal" (1960, p. 185) in a manner somewhat analogous to Freud's concept of anxiety. This anticipatory reaction, stemming from the detection of a certain class of stimuli, could conceivably lead to the avoidance of further contact with such stimuli without the intervention of a recognizable discomfort state.

The quest for external stimuli certainly does not always have to be explained as an attempt to reduce discomfort. These stimuli may be sought out, even though they are incongruous or a source of conceptual conflict, because encounters with them are pleasurable; indeed, it is their novelty, complexity, and/or incongruity that provides the pleasure. Here, then, is the answer to the apparent paradox mentioned by Zajonc (1960a, p. 295). "Almost everybody enjoys a magician," he pointed out, "and the magician only creates dissonance ...." The slight-to-moderate incongruities (or deviations from expectation, or opposing cognitions) established by the magician produce the enjoyment. Having stable, confirmed expectations may be a source of comfort, as is often maintained, so that drastic departures from expectation are unpleasant (cf. Carlsmith & Aronson, 1963). Nevertheless, *moderate* deviations from expectation, or moderate incongruities generally, can be pleasurable. Maddi has reported, for example, that "greatly unexpected and completely expected situations arouse negative affect, while moderately unexpected situations arouse positive affect" (1961, p. 345). His point of view is explicated in Chapter 16.

In the present chapter the Berlyne (1960) analysis has been employed as the framework around which I discussed stimulus seeking. It should be clear, however, that this type of behavior might not be motivated by increases and decreases in tension or arousal as Berlyne had suggested. As some writers (e.g., Pfaffman, 1960; Young, 1961) have demonstrated, certain stimuli are inherently pleasurable for many organisms; these stimuli are evidently sought out for the pleasant affect they produce independently of any tension, arousal, or discomfort. Similarly, Hebb (1949, 1955) and McClelland and his colleagues (1953) have argued that moderate discrepancies from expectation are pleasant without invoking any conjectured arousal changes. For Hebb (1949), the pleasure comes from the process of developing an organized neural structure within the central nervous system, while McClelland *et al.* attribute the affect to the given stimulus pattern's degree of discrepancy from the organism's adaptation level. Whatever the exact processes that are involved here, it is clear that there are more things involved than are included in the traditional aversive-state motivational scheme customarily followed by cognitive consistency theorizing.

CHAPTER 32

Dissonance Without Awareness

Timothy C. Brock
The Ohio State University

Several months before the publication of *Explorations in cognitive dissonance* one of its co-authors, Cohen, wrote to me,[1] "if you are right that unconscious cognitions can produce dissonance, why then Jack [Brehm] and I have been too narrow in basing our notions on commitment-producing decisions." Perhaps more is at stake than a possible "narrowness" in the Brehm-Cohen (1962) reformulation of dissonance theory (Festinger, 1957). Dissonance without awareness may require sweeping reappraisal of the necessary and sufficient conditions for dissonance arousal; it may increase the intellectually exciting prospect of applying dissonance theory and psychoanalytic theory to the same empirical domain. The present essay considers earlier comment on the awareness issue and inspects several pertinent experiments (McGuire, 1960a; Brock, 1963; Brock & Grant, 1963; Cohen, Greenbaum, & Mansson, 1963). The recommended conclusion, that awareness is unnecessary for dissonance arousal and reduction, has several interesting implications.

In his initial presentation of dissonance theory, Festinger (1957) did not directly face the awareness issue. His first basic hypothesis (Festinger, 1957, p. 3) asserted that dissonance involved psychological discomfort, and his analysis in terms of cognitive elements and the mapping of reality by "knowledges" suggested that the subject must know x and y and know further that there is some sort of relationship between x and y. When Festinger spoke about reality impinging on persons, he seemed to have in mind opinions, behavior, and aspects of the person's ecology that could be labeled. His discussion of "selective forgetting of cognitive elements" (p. 271) undoubtedly depended upon assuming the prior existence of elements in some state of ready availability to thought and verbalization. Thus, while Festinger did not take an explicit stand on the problem, his notions of "felt discomfort" and "knowledges" implied that awareness of the involved cognitive elements and/or of their inconsistency was necessary for dissonance arousal.

Supported by a grant, GS-606, from the National Science Foundation. I thank T. M. Ostrom and H. L. Fromkin for their comments.
[1] Personal communication from A. R. Cohen, March, 1962.

Brehm and Cohen (1962) were more explicit about the role of consciousness in dissonance arousal:

> Unequivocal dissonance arousal may be based on the choice to commit oneself to a discrepant situation. For choice to be present, it may be necessary that there be some perception of uncertainty, conflict, or potentiality of alternative responses in the situation of discrepant commitment. There seems to be some basis for assuming that some awareness of the individual's own responsibility for his discrepant commitment is a necessary condition for the unequivocal identification of dissonance arousal. However, because of the lack of any direct evidence, the entire question of whether responses to inconsistency require awareness must remain an unresolved one at this time. We can only speculate, although with some degree of confidence, about whether the dissonance formulation demands a specification of the consciousness issue in terms of choice, responsibility, and commitment (p. 168).

Their scholarly tentativeness about the role of awareness notwithstanding, it is quite clear that Brehm and Cohen preferred to assume that awareness was necessary to dissonance arousal. For example, in their important extension of dissonance theory to the psychology of motivation, Brehm and Cohen found it most rewarding "to consider the possibility that it is *only* the cognitive component of motivation that affects consummatory behavior and other psychological processes. That is, it may be that physiological states can affect consummatory and other processes only insofar as they have cognitive representation, or even that a state of deprivation, short of debilitating the organism entirely, would have to have cognitive representation in order to have any kind of psychological effect at all" (Brehm & Cohen, 1962, pp. 152–153).

Since a major theme of the Brehm-Cohen revision is the choice-commitment-discrepancy requirement, it is quite evident that full acceptance of dissonance without awareness would pose formidable conceptual difficulties. Can a person choose, be responsible, feel commitment, and experience discrepancy, without awareness? Another important theme is explicitness about the motivational character of dissonance.

> *Cognitive dissonance is a general "motivational state" that always occurs when there is some prior motive associated with the cognitions that are dissonant* .... The strong effects of the dissonance manipulations are in fact due to *the commitment on the part of a person to a behavior that has implications for the frustration of important motives.* Every experiment evokes another motive whose instrumental connection to inconsistency produces drives toward the resolution of the inconsistency. Basic to the arousal of dissonance appears to be the incompatibility introduced by the individual's commitment to behave in some way ... which frustrates another strong motive (Brehm & Cohen, 1962, pp. 228–230, italics theirs).

That dissonance arousal trades on the arousal of other motives was considered a valuable theoretical distinction between dissonance theory and competing inconsistency theories. The distinction is valuable but, at the same time, the unresolved issue of awareness is again brought into play. Hovland and Rosenberg (1960) were sensitive to the implications.

> The question of "consciousness" is implicit in any theorizing about motives .... The whole problem of whether responsiveness to inconsistency requires awareness seems to be an open one. It is often convenient to speak in these terms since in attitude studies we are primarily concerned with processes which are conscious and capable of verbalization and articulation. But at the same time we must recognize that other writers find it important to stress the extent to which attitudes are derivative from, and indirectly reductive of, unconscious conflicts and motivation (e.g., Smith, Bruner, & White, 1956; Sarnoff, Katz, & McClintock, 1954). Similarly, psychoanalytically oriented personality theories clearly assume that patterns of response inconsistency of which the person is quite unaware (i.e., repressed, unconscious conflicts) are motivating: they generate behavioral attempts at inconsistency reduction (pp. 222–223).

In their brief analysis of dissonance theory and psychoanalytic theory, Brehm and Cohen (1962, pp. 168–171) skirted the awareness issue: for them, psychoanalytic theory posed unconscious forces and dissonance theory specified conscious ones. The missing link appeared to be a viable operational notion of unconscious commitment.

Empirical Evidence on Consistency Restoration Without Awareness

Awareness has many meanings and levels;[2] as applied to psychological inconsistency, several might be crudely delineated.[3] In the lowest, the individual experiences psychological malaise or puzzlement while being unable to articulate an appropriate referent. An onlooking experimenter, who had previously introduced to the subject what appeared, on a priori grounds, to be inconsistent cognitions, might regard the observed botherment and perplexity as indicative of awareness. The naive observer, of course, would be unable confidently to interpret the subject's behavior. At a less inchoate level, the individual is able to verbalize cognitive elements x and y but not their relationship. Nevertheless, the individual's observed behavior may seem to the experimenter to be best interpreted as an attempt to reduce subjective inconsistency between x and y. At a higher level, the individual has cognitive representation of both the elements and their relationship. And, finally, it is possible to imagine an individual who can say that his ongoing behavior is aimed at reducing a verbalizable inconsistency. (The proposed hierarchy excludes at least two cases: an individual aware of a relationship but not of the terms; an individual aware of his attempt at inconsistency reduction but unable to verbalize the troublesome inconsistent relationship.) Evidence of dissonance reduction at or below the lowest levels of the awareness

---

[2] A technology of awareness measurement has arisen in the burgeoning verbal conditioning literature (Krasner, 1958). More than 100 experiments have failed to produce agreement concerning the role of awareness of the response-reinforcement contingency. To illustrate, experiments by Spielberger (Spielberger, Bernstein, & Ratliff, 1966; Spielberger, Southard, & Hodges, 1966) typically find that unaware subjects do not exhibit conditioning. At the same time, other investigators, using Spielberger's (1962) procedure for detecting awareness of reinforcement contingencies, do find conditioning in unaware subjects (e.g., Bryan & Lichtenstein, 1966). Such conflicting results have not moved the controversy nearer to solution in recent years. Nevertheless, students of awareness and inconsistency can profit from the methodological sophistication developed in the conditioning domain (Eriksen, 1962).

[3] Hilgard's (1962) more sophisticated taxonomy did not seem clearly applicable to the present problem.

hierarchy would argue for the possibility of inconsistency reduction behavior without awareness of inconsistency.

A study by McGuire (1960a) seems to invoke the next to lowest level of awareness. That is, his subjects were able to verbalize the elements of an inconsistency but not the inconsistent relationship among the elements. McGuire's subjects were teenagers whose modal high school grade average was below the statewide 30th percentile; none had taken a course in logic or probability. In the first session, opinions regarding the likelihood and desirability of syllogistically related propositions were obtained. In the second session, persuasive messages, supporting a premise for each syllogism, were communicated and immediate opinions were obtained about the propositions. Each subject received communications about half the issues and served in a Control, No-communication condition, for the other half. McGuire found that "simply eliciting opinions on logically related issues does tend to move those opinions toward greater mutual consistency when subsequent elicitation occurs one week later" (1960a, p. 348). He also found a "consistency tendency sufficiently strong to cause a persuasive message to have an impact on logically related issues not explicitly mentioned in the communication" (p. 350). McGuire appeared to favor a model in which consistency restoration occurs as quietly as metabolism:

> In the present study several procedures were employed in an attempt to minimize the degree of conscious awareness. (For example, no mention was made to the Ss that their consistency was being assessed; the related propositions were widely separated from one another in the questionnaire; a quantitative expression of opinion was required and the assessment of inconsistency involved a mathematical model unfamiliar to the Ss.) Hence, the present findings indicate that the effects occur even under conditions that attempt to avoid any suggestion of inconsistency (p. 352).

But suppose McGuire had told his subjects that he was testing their ability to be consistent. Suppose further that they were given some instruction in elementary logic. Would such heightened awareness have augmented the results described above? Perhaps, but an opposite outcome seemed just as likely to McGuire. "Such a procedure could well have the opposite effect by provoking the person's hostility or defensiveness, and so result, not in a greater change towards consistency, but in some other reaction such as rejection of consistency, with Carlyle, as the hobgoblin of little minds; or in the repression of some of the conflicting issues" (McGuire, 1960a, p. 352). I know of no consistency experiment in which level of awareness has appeared as a systematically manipulated independent variable. The hierarchy of awareness proposed above could provide a conceptual starting point for such controlled variation.

A developmental approach provides another point of view for considering the question of whether responsiveness to inconsistency requires awareness. Presumably young children are less able to conceptualize violation of psychological implication than older children. The proportion of older to younger children should increase as one ascends the proposed awareness hierarchy. If awareness is needed for dissonance arousal and/or reduction, inducing dissonance in children of different ages should produce a function in which measurable dissonance reduction is positively related to age. A flat function would suggest that verbalization of dissonance is unnecessary or, what seems less likely, that other motives compete more with consistency-reduction as age increases.

There is an experiment by Brock (1963) in which children at four age levels (3–4, 5–6, 7–9, and 10–12) were exposed to postdecisional dissonance after they were given an opportunity to be dishonest. The decision involved choosing among small toys and bags of crackers. It may be assumed that all the cognitive capabilities which could contribute to heightened awareness were more fully developed in the 10–12-year-old group than in the younger groups, particularly the preschoolers. Consequently, the older group should be more sensitive to the loss of the relinquished alternative and more capable of reducing dissonance by the familiar (Brehm, 1956; Festinger, 1964b) evaluative spreading of alternatives after the decision. If awareness contributes little to postdecision dissonance reduction, then no relationship between age and magnitude of dissonance reduction would be observed. In a three-way analysis of variance the independent factors were dishonesty (peeked or did not peek), dissonance (choice from among dissimilar vs. similar alternatives), and age, as already described.

Both dishonesty and dissonance produced very reliable main effects on postdecision dissonance reduction, while the age factor yielded an F less than unity and age did not contribute to any substantial interactions. This result suggests that, to the extent awareness is correlated with age, awareness does not affect dissonance arousal and/or reduction.

There seems to be only one experiment in the literature which was principally addressed to the problem of dissonance arousal with limited awareness. Brock and Grant (1963) hypnotized intellectually superior high school students to a depth adequate for assuring amnesia for all suggestions and, before awakening the subjects, provided a signal for subsequent hypnosis. Under the guise of product testing research, half the subjects were given crackers with sauce that was very hot and thirst-arousing and half, crackers with sauce that was not hot, that aroused little thirst. Placed under hypnosis again, subjects in the experimental group were told that, on awakening, they would feel water bloated while the control subjects were told that they would feel fatigued. Subjects were awakened, offered water, and told to fill out a questionnaire relevant to the experiment. There was an additional control group, in which subjects received brief training in role-playing and, after eating the cracker-sauce combination, were asked to role-play a feeling of water bloatedness. The dependent variable was water consumption measured in cubic centimeters. It was hypothesized that bloatedness juxtaposed to high thirst would create more dissonance than bloatedness juxtaposed to low thirst. The subject could reduce dissonance by lowering his thirst drive and that lowering could be reflected in less actual water consumption. If the hypothesis was correct, high thirst should lead to greater water consumption than low thirst in the Control condition (where subjects were given a suggestion of fatigue) but that difference should be minimized or perhaps reversed in the Experimental (bloated) condition. A very reliable interaction was obtained for the High Thirst vs. Low Thirst and the Experimental (bloated) vs. Control (tired) factors. High thirst, as compared to low thirst, led to less water consumption when bloatedness was juxtaposed and to more water consumption when fatigue was juxtaposed.

Of major interest to any discussion of awareness and inconsistency reduction is the fact that the bloatedness suggestion was not available to verbalization. Brock and Grant (1963) reported that:

Although waking amnesia for "bloat" or "tired" was not specifically suggested, the general ban on recalling any part of the hypnosis was apparently potent: none of the hypnotic subjects verbalized the induced feeling either spontaneously or after the experimenter's probing . . . . The subjects were able to write or say little more than that the hypnosis had been a pleasant, relaxing and enjoyable experience . . . . The experimenter, and the questionnaire, asked the present subjects to report what they were told, what happened, and how they felt during hypnosis, and both the experimenter and the operator inquired about the subjects' current feelings. If more intensive questioning were necessary to elicit reports of "bloated" or "tired" this would be congenial with assuming that the critical sensations were not readily verbalizable (p. 56 and p. 59).

Thus, the Brock-Grant experiment seemed to offer an instance of dissonance reduction with awareness at or below the lowest levels of the proposed hierarchy. There was no observed indication of botherment and one of the terms in the dissonant relationship was not verbalizable. The Brock-Grant results are comparable to work by Blum (1961) in which the subject is introduced to inconsistent affects (e.g., anxiety and contentment) attached hypnotically to letters of the alphabet. Blum likewise assumed that inconsistency arousal occurs and resolution proceeds without awareness (Blum, 1961, p. 70). The Brock-Grant study may also be compared with an investigation by Rosenberg (1960b) in which some experimental subjects were so completely unaware of their attempts to restore the inconsistency set up by a hypnotic affect reversal that they did not feel they had changed their original beliefs.[4]

In a verbal conditioning experiment by Cohen, Greenbaum, and Mansson (1963) the dependent variables were scores reflecting the difference between operant level and mean response during 100 reinforcement trials and the difference between operant level and mean response during 80 extinction trials. First it was demonstrated that socially deprived subjects would be more affected by social approval on subsequent verbal conditioning trials than subjects who were not socially deprived. Then the dissonance hypothesis was tested: the augmentative effect of social deprivation on responsivity to social approval will be countervailed by dissonance-reduction processes to the extent the subjects commit themselves to social deprivation for inadequate justifications. In other words, the social approval motive would be lowered as a function of the magnitude of dissonance aroused by commitment to social deprivation. In support of the hypothesis, the second phase of the Cohen et al. experiment demonstrated that responsivity to

---

[4] Many individuals are apparently troubled by hypnotic interventions in research—possibly because hypnosis is so imperfectly understood—and might be more convinced of the evidence here if the procedures themselves were not controversial. It is not easy to give a satisfactory reply to this misgiving, but two arguments may be mentioned. First, hypnosis can be used to achieve certain effects without fully understanding the pertinent mechanisms. Medicine has effectively employed certain potions and herbs for centuries without correct understanding of the phenomena. In the Brock-Grant (1963) investigation there was a job to be done—namely, to induce a powerful yet unverbalizable feeling—and hypnosis seemed to do that job perfectly well. Second, it is of more than historical interest that Freud's conceptual development of System Unconscious was considerably abetted by his experience with hypnosis (Rapaport, 1959, pp. 61, 64, 112). Freud would not have been hesitant to regard the effects of hypnotic suggestion as attributable to an unconscious force.

social approval during verbal conditioning was less under the High Dissonance (low incentive) than under the Low Dissonance (high incentive) and Control conditions. The effect was statistically reliable for both the reinforcement and extinction measures. It was concluded that the High Dissonance subjects reduced their motivation to respond to social reinforcement after having committed themselves to forgo such reinforcement in a future situation. That the main finding was best interpreted in terms of dissonance arousal and reduction was borne out by internal analyses of alternative avenues of dissonance reduction such as choice, obligation, and perceived pleasantness (cf. Cohen, Greenbaum, & Mansson, 1963).

Cohen and his associates measured awareness of the response-reinforcement contingency by means of questions "modeled after those developed by Dulany (1961)" and presumably scored in Dulany's manner. In the Control condition greater evidence for conditioning was obtained by aware than by unaware subjects, a finding in accord with the majority viewpoint in the verbal conditioning literature (see footnote 2). In the Low Dissonance condition, the aware-unaware difference was no longer reliable and, in the High Dissonance condition, there was a reversal with aware subjects conditioning *less than* unaware subjects. (The High Dissonance reversal was unreliable, however.) Cohen *et al.* suggested that awareness enabled the subject to inhibit social responsivity "where the push is in the direction of reduced motivation for social reinforcement" (p. 418), that is, where dissonance increases. Unfortunately, the differences in the data did not approach statistical significance and the analysis dealt only with the reinforcement measures, the results from the extinction score being omitted because they were unclear. Hence, viewed conservatively, the data actually indicated no interaction between awareness and dissonance. As already noted, the High Dissonance subjects conditioned less than the Low Dissonance subjects and this statistically reliable effect was approximately the same for both aware and unaware subjects. This experiment has provided a new and worthwhile approach to the dissonance and awareness issue. A demonstrably sensitive measure of awareness was employed but neither dependent measure of verbal conditioning revealed clearcut relationships between awareness and dissonance reduction.

SELECTED IMPLICATIONS

Dissonance Theory

Dissonance without awareness poses a conceptual difficulty for dissonance theory, at least as reformulated by Brehm and Cohen (1962). At first glance, perception of discrepancy, feeling of volition and commitment, and sense of personal responsibility are psychological events which, by definition, demand awareness. An inelegant solution is to posit more than one kind of dissonance: perhaps different principles govern arousal and reduction of dissonance depending on the subject's degree of awareness. An interaction between level of awareness and other determinants of magnitude of dissonance would support this possibility.

A preferred solution would integrate level of awareness with other previous theoretical advances. Although "commitment," "obligation," and "choice" are themselves still problematic (Brock & Becker, 1967) these concepts can not be easily jettisoned. The concepts distinguish dissonance

theory from other inconsistency theories, explain why some alleged dissonance experiments fail to provide corroborative results, and, more importantly, allow unequivocal derivations from the theory. Perhaps only a
slight modification of the Brehm-Cohen statement is needed to conserve the
choice-commitment-discrepancy rule while providing a place for dissonance
without awareness.

A proposed accommodation is suggested by data from the Brock-Grant
(1963) experiment, not previously considered here. Recall that there was an
additional Control condition in which subjects were given motivating instructions to role-play a feeling of bloatedness. The results in the Role Play
condition were about the same as those obtained in the Hypnotic Control
(fatigue) condition. In other words, role-played bloatedness did not have
dissonant effects on the water consumption of differentially thirsty subjects.
Brock and Grant (1963, p. 58) explained that the "critical factor was
acceptance of a feeling of bloatedness as 'literally true' (Barber, 1958)."
Studies exist by Barber (e.g., Glass & Barber, 1961) in which such *complete
acceptance* does not characterize the Role Playing subjects. The difference
between the Brock-Grant Role Playing subjects and the Hypnotic Experimental subjects may be understood in theoretical terms as a difference
in degree of *commitment* to bloatedness. Hence, unawareness may strengthen
commitment. An individual's commitment (as measured by, say, resistance
to change) to a feeling, motive, value, etc., increases to the extent the object
of commitment becomes less available to verbalization. This notion, which is
familiar enough in the psychoanalytic tradition, fits the data of the Brock-
Grant experiment and suggests that hypnosis and kindred procedures may
provide a means of supplying the "unconscious commitment" which was
earlier inferred to be the missing link in the somewhat indecisive Brehm-
Cohen (1962, pp. 160–171) discursion on dissonance theory and psychoanalytic theory.[5] However, even if awareness is handled as a determinant of
magnitude of commitment, there still remains the problem of the relationship
between awareness and choice. It is now suggested that, while the person
must experience volition about getting himself into the situation in which a
discrepant commitment occurs, it is perhaps not necessary that he be aware
of a voluntary commitment to the specific critical violation of psychological
implication. The Brock-Grant subjects volunteered to be hypnotized, obtained their parents' written consent, and made their own arrangements for
evening transportation to the site of data collection. Once voluntarily engaged in the experimental activities, dissonance-producing discrepancy could
be introduced with or without the subject's awareness. Indeed, the discrepancy, acceptance of bloatedness while very thirsty, was more powerful
under limited awareness than under full awareness.

Learning vs. Performance

Even the most outspoken critic (Eriksen, 1962) of human learning and
human discrimination without awareness readily concedes that *performance*
proceeds without awareness. If dissonance reduction can be construed as
automatic performance, Eriksen's analysis suggests (p. 23) that it would be
worthwhile to investigate ways and techniques by which the dissonance
reduction process *can be brought back into awareness*. A person made aware

---

[5] See Sarnoff, Chapter 9, for more detailed discussion of the relevance of psychoanalytic theory to the general consistency paradigm.

of dissonance, or of his attempt at dissonance reduction, might be inhibited by that awareness from effectively restoring consistency. (Perhaps that is why the data from our keen and sensitive college sophomore subjects display effects that are often disappointingly small in absolute magnitude.) Festinger (1957, p. 268) assumed that persons have learned how unpleasant dissonance is and so presumably they have developed skill at avoiding and reducing dissonance. Are dissonance confrontation and dissonance reduction so over-learned that these behaviors proceed automatically with negligible awareness? The learning vs. performance distinction could stimulate research on incon-sistency that would shed further light upon dissonance without awareness.

SUMMARY

This essay appraised the possibility that persons can be responsive to incon-sistency without awareness. A study by McGuire (1960a) showed that simply eliciting opinions on logically related issues tended to move those opinions toward greater mutual consistency. Brock (1963) found postdecisional disso-nance reduction in children to be unaffected by age, a presumptive de-terminer of awareness. Brock and Grant (1963) found that a hypnotically induced feeling, which could not be verbalized by the subject, led to apparent attempts at dissonance reduction when the feeling was juxtaposed to a contrary need. In an experiment in which dissonance affected responsiv-ity to social approval in a verbal conditioning paradigm, Cohen, Greenbaum, and Mansson (1963) found no effect of awareness on dissonance reduction as reflected in conditioning scores. The conclusion, that responsiveness to disso-nance does not require awareness, was shown to have implications for core assumptions concerning dissonance arousal.

CHAPTER 33

Verbal Indices of Psychological Stress

Eleanor L. Norris

American Institutes for Research

This chapter takes as its point of departure the existence of some state of psychological discomfort or stress ostensibly induced by conditions of cognitive or affective inconsistency. Given that stress is a variable worthy of investigation within the consistency theory arena, how does one go about measuring it? This chapter restricts its domain to one such set of procedures—self-reports or rating scales. A number of such essentially verbal measures will be discussed, with particular attention given to the so-called mood scale developed by Nowlis (Green & Nowlis, 1957; Nowlis, 1963).

VERBAL MEASURES OF STRESS

A wide variety of measures of stress, anxiety, or nervousness have been used both in consistency theory and other research. Outside the consistency theory work, measures range from the very simple and straightforward to the more complicated. Schachter, for example, has asked Ss to indicate how irritated or angry, how happy and good (Schachter, 1964), and how uneasy or calm (Schachter, 1959) they feel. Korobow (1955) had Ss respond, on a six-point scale, to such statements as "I feel ill at ease," and "I feel aggressive," before the experimental manipulations, and to such items as "I felt like walking out of the room," "I felt angry," to describe at the conclusion of the manipulation their feelings during the experiment. Assuming that Ss' description of their physiological reactions during a testing situation would be a valid index of anxiety, Mandler and his associates had Ss respond to a questionnaire designed to assess "uneasiness, accelerated heartbeat, perspiration, emotional interference, and worry" (Mandler, Mandler, Kremen, & Sholiton, 1961; Mandler & Sarason, 1952). A Subjective Stress Scale was derived for use in a series of experiments by Berkun, Bralek, Kern, and Yogi (1962). This scale consisted of a list of 15 adjectives ranging from "wonder-

---

The research reported in this Chapter was conducted as part of Professor Percy H. Tannenbaum's research program on communication and attitude change. It was supported in its earlier stages by a grant from the Graduate Research Committee at the University of Wisconsin, and later under Grant G-23963 from the National Science Foundation.

ful" to "scared stiff," from which Ss chose the one which best described their own feelings during the experiment.

Although much of the consistency theory research has not directed attention to the variable of stress, a few studies have included this for attention, peripherally if not directly. McNulty and Walters (1962), for example, investigating the consequences of inconsistency on susceptibility to social influence, used a verbal anxiety measure similar to Schachter's (1959) to check on the success of their experimental manipulation. In a study designed to determine, among other things, whether Ss in an imbalanced condition will "feel more tense or nervous" than those in balanced conditions, Sampson and Insko (1964) asked Ss to indicate on a seven-point Semantic Differential Scale (Osgood, Suci, & Tannenbaum, 1957) whether they felt "nervous or calm" while participating in a dissonance-producing situation. Exploring the affect associated with interpersonal relationships which are balanced or imbalanced, Price, Harburg, and Newcomb (1966) asked Ss to indicate how they felt by placing a check along a line 90 mm. long and extending from "uneasy" to "pleasant," when presented with descriptions of interpersonal relationships varying in the sign linking Person P (oneself), Person O, and Person Q (see Chapter 2).

The number of verbal methods used to assess stress almost matches the multiplicity of physiological measures which have been used to measure this variable (cf. Malmo, 1958; Lazarus, 1962). Despite the variety of manifestations, all the verbal measures place heavy reliance on three premises common to all self-report measures—that the subjects know how they feel; that they are able to describe how they feel; and that they can and will report their feelings without distortion, conscious or unconscious. An assumption underlying the use of verbal measures of psychological stress has been that individuals do know how they feel in a variety of situations, and that they are able to describe, to some extent, these feelings—if not necessarily of being stressful or not, at least in terms of certain provided judgmental attributes. In everyday circumstances, it is not uncommon for individuals to describe feeling angry, upset, anxious, happy, and so on. The third question—will subjects respond with honesty and accuracy—is one which may be met by creating conditions under which obvious lying is apparent, or by giving subjects every reason to respond honestly (e.g., through anonymity, by explaining the reasons behind the study, the need for honest responses, etc.).

One stress measure which was based on the assumption of labeling ability, and which has undergone extensive validating procedures as well, is the Mood Scale developed by Green and Nowlis (Green & Nowlis, 1957; Nowlis, 1963). This scale has been widely used in consistency theory and other research and, in turn, has undergone several modifications in the course of its use in consistency theory work.

THE MOOD SCALE

The Mood Scale was developed on the assumption that individuals have learned to use certain adjectives (verbal responses) to describe their moods, defined as "perceptual and cognitive responses to presumed information or discriminable cues within the organism concerning its current function and orientation" (Green & Nowlis, 1957, p. 1). In choosing adjectives to form the scale, Green and Nowlis first developed hypotheses as to what the dimensions of mood might be, and then selected 120 adjectives to represent these dimensions.

To test the validity of their hypotheses, Green and Nowlis exposed male Ss to different situations, over a six-week period, designed to evoke different moods—aggression, a change in level of control, a change in pleasantness, and a change in motivation. Data were obtained by having each S respond, before and after each treatment, to each of the 120 adjectives. Ss indicated how well each adjective described how they felt "at the moment." In scoring responses, a 0 was given a response of "does not apply," a 1 to "don't know," a 2 to "applies slightly," and a 3 to "definitely applies."

Several adjectives were omitted from the analysis because of skewed distributions or because they were affected by order of presentation. The remaining 99 variables were subjected to factor analysis and subsequent oblique-rotation procedures. Eight common factors (including four of those originally hypothesized) were extracted. After rotation, they were represented by the following sets of adjectives:

Factor I. Aggression (hostility): rebellious, fed-up, annoyed, defiant, grouchy
II. Anxiety: clutched-up, fearful, jittery.
III. Pleasantness: elated, lighthearted, pleased.
IV. Concentration: concentrating, intent, serious, contemplative.
V. Fatigue: drowsy, tired, sluggish.
VI. Social Affection: kindly, warmhearted, affectionate.
VII. Depression: sad, regretful, sorry.
VIII. Egotism: self-centered, egotistic, boastful.

A series of studies using the Mood Scale, a questionnaire-interview, and various physiological measures has been conducted by Lazarus and his associates to investigate certain aspects of what they refer to as psychological stress, identified as a "construct intervening between antecedent conditions of thwarting and behavioral reaction of the person" (Lazarus et al., 1962, p. 2). Certainly this definition does not differentiate psychological stress from mood, and in fact it could easily be translated into consistency theory terms, although this was not the theoretical framework within which these studies were conducted. The significance of this work in our discussion of measures of stress is not only that it provides further validating evidence for the Mood Scale as a discriminator between conditions of experimentally-induced stress, but also that it includes two independent measures of psychological stress against which we may compare the Mood Scale.

As an early step in the study of psychological stress, the general purpose of the Lazarus et al. (1962) work was to "explore some of the antecedent conditions which produce psychological stress ... [and] a number of the physiological and behavioral consequences" (p. 3). Specifically, the studies were designed to determine the value of the motion picture film as a laboratory technique for inducing psychological stress, to identify appropriate response dimensions for evaluating film induced stress (i.e., verbal and physiological indices), and to examine the relationships among these response dimensions. Lazarus used as his stressor a highly anxiety-provoking film,

Subincision, vividly depicting a painful operation performed on the genitals of several adolescent boys as part of an important ceremonial of an Australian tribe. The control film, *Corn Farming in Iowa*, portrays a day in the life of a corn farmer and his family.

The physiological measures of psychological stress were skin resistance and heart rate. Adjectives representing the mood dimensions described above were selected from the Green and Nowlis work for the Mood Scale. In addition to this self-report measure, another verbal measure of stress was included, a questionnaire-interview consisting of three open-ended questions designed to get at Ss' cognitive and emotional reactions to the movie they saw. Content analysis of the interviews yielded several different indices to assess stress.

It was found that all three measures—autonomic reactivity, the Mood Scale, and the interview questionnaire measures—showed significant increases in response in the stressor condition as compared to the control film. The results also showed differential sensitivity within each of these types of measures. Thus, for the mood scale, although all factors showed greater stress in the experimental than in the control condition, by far the greatest difference occurred for the Anxiety factor (a difference of 16.3 points between experimental and control groups, compared to 9.3 for the next closest factor, Unpleasantness, and 1.1 for the factor showing the least difference, Concentration).

The applicability of these measures to the study of stress associated with cognitive inconsistency is readily apparent, and in fact it has been used in a number of studies conducted recently at the University of Wisconsin. In the course of three studies in which stress was one of the main dependent variables, the measuring instrument evolved from the multivariate measure of mood developed by Green and Nowlis to what may more specifically be called a Stress Scale, a direct modification of the Mood Scale.

Use of the Mood Scale in Consistency Studies

In all three studies, the experimental manipulation involved inducing cognitive inconsistency and, presumably, its associated psychological stress. The relative degree of stress *reduction* as a function of certain behaviors or manipulations was among the main effects then investigated. Certain operations in the three studies were similar—stress was to be induced by presenting Ss with a cognitively inconsistent message, i.e., one attacking a highly positively evaluated topic. Further stress was induced in two of the studies by telling Ss they were to encode messages about the topic just attacked. Stress was measured before and after these stress-inducing operations, and the difference taken between the two measures, to check the effectiveness of the experimental manipulation. The next step in all three studies was to create the conditions for stress reduction, either through prescribed behavior or through direct experimental manipulation. Whether stress reduction did occur, and to varying degrees in different conditions, was assessed by measuring stress level before and after these experimental conditions were imposed, and taking the difference between these two scores. At each of the testing times, Ss indicated how much each adjective described how they felt "at this moment."

In the first of these studies, Greenberg (1961) investigated the consequences of engaging in communication behavior under stress in terms of certain performance and message characteristics. Conversely, he investigated the consequences of communication behavior—presumably a rebuttal to a strong attack on a cherished belief—for stress reduction.

As his measure of stress, Greenberg used a 24-adjective Mood Scale, selecting 3 adjectives from each of the 8 factors empirically derived by Green and Nowlis. Rather than the 4-point scale previously used, the scale was expanded to allow a 5-point range of responses. As in the Green and Nowlis work, factor scores for each subject at each measuring time were computed, and the difference was taken between the appropriate scores. However, rather than examining changes for each factor separately, Greenberg summed across these factor change scores to provide a single *overall* index of stress change. Thus, for each individual, a single score indicated how much mood change had occurred and in what direction—i.e., increased or decreased stress. Using this overall score, Greenberg determined that significantly more people in the experimental condition exhibited heightened stress after the stress-inducing manipulation than did control Ss, and that more Ss reduced stress in Communication than in No-Communication groups.

The advantage of computing one overall score, rather than investigating mood scale factor scores separately, is primarily that it simplifies the investigation of the question of greatest interest in this particular consistency theory research—was stress induced and reduced to a greater extent in the experimental than in the control groups? This procedure assumes, of course, that each factor maps validly onto the basic underlying stress dimension.

Continuing this logic, Lynch (1963) bypassed the intermediate step of forming factor scores, and simply summed across the adjective scores to form a single stress index for each measuring time. He assessed the degree of stress induction by taking the difference, for each S, between the single stress score taken before and after a stress-inducing attack message was read, finding, as expected, significantly heightened stress.

Among the variables which Lynch was investigating was the relative degree of stress reduction in communication conditions in which the task was to actively encode or to passively read a message arguing either for or against the belief which had been attacked in the initial stress-inducing procedure. Taking the difference for each S between the summed stress score obtained before and after communication behavior (or before and after a no-communication waiting period for the control group), Lynch found stress was reduced significantly more in the Communication condition (combined preparing and reading, for and against groups) than in the control groups.

As these studies were done, it became more apparent that the central variable of interest was not so much the general one of 'mood,' indexed by the several factors of the Green and Nowlis work, but one more geared to the notion of discomfort, and which might better be described by such adjectives as "tense, nervous, jittery, and anxious," at one extreme, and "relaxed carefree, and pleased," at the other. The Green and Nowlis work itself showed a differential sensitivity of the eight factors to the different experimental situations they used. In fact, inspection of their change scores on each factor in each of their six situations (Green & Nowlis, 1957, Table 2) suggests that relatively more change was induced during the showing of a film depicting the Nuremberg trials, and that the most sensitive of the eight factors was the Anxiety factor, followed by the Pleasantness factor. Recall, also, that in the Lazarus *et al.* (1962) work, the Anxiety factor was the most sensitive indicator of a difference between experimental and control conditions, followed by what Lazarus termed an Unpleasantness factor, the reciprocal of Pleasantness. An implication of these findings is that the most sensitive indicator of differential levels of stress would be a scale heavily weighted with adjectives representing these two factors.

Accordingly, in a third study requiring a measure of stress (Norris, 1964), a scale was formed by selecting adjectives to represent only those factors which had been most sensitive to stress- or anxiety-inducing situations in previous work. An investigation of the motivating mechanism operating in cognitively inconsistent situations (the cognitive inconsistency, as such, or the accompanying stress) and the consequences of inconsistency (i.e., resolution of the cognitive inconsistency or the stress reduction *per se*), the study required that the inconsistency and stress variables be independently manipulated and the consequences for inconsistency resolution and stress reduction be examined.

To assess the differential stress change among the experimental conditions, adjectives were chosen from the Anxiety and Pleasantness factors, and other adjectives were included which had been sensitive to stressful situations in previous work. As a pretest of the 18 adjectives chosen in this fashion, Ss read a message attacking a favorably judged belief, and then were placed in the highly stressful situation of being assigned to give an impromptu speech[1] about a belief which had just been strongly attacked in the written communication—the stress-inducing procedure. For half the Ss, this assignment was then cancelled—the stress-reducing manipulation. Ss responded on the Stress Scale twice, once before reading the attack message and the speech assignment, and again at the conclusion of the experiment.

All 18 adjectives reflected to some degree a difference between the Speech and the Cancelled Speech conditions. Seven of the more sensitive, plus 5 more chosen *a priori* to be more descriptive of reactions in the speech situation, were chosen to form a 12-adjective scale to be used in the main study.

This final scale was heavily weighted with adjectives from the Anxiety factor (e.g., jittery, anxious, fearful, upset), but also included some from other factors which had been sensitive to differences between the Speech and No Speech groups in the pretest (e.g., carefree and relaxed, from the Pleasantness factor; concentrating and serious, from the Concentration factor).

This scale served as the measure of differential stress between experimental conditions in the main study, which employed the same procedures as those in the pretest. The dependent variable of stress was the sum of each subject's responses to all 12 adjectives, obtained before and after the experimental manipulations. Any implications of tautology aside, the success of the scale in discriminating between conditions of experimentally manipulated

---

[1] Instructors of college speech classes vouched for the inconsistent and highly stressful nature of such an assignment, and informal observation of the Ss in both the pretest and the main experiment confirms this judgment—behavior of Ss after receiving the information that they would give an impromptu talk during the same class period ranged from that which could be termed 'nervous' at the mild end of the continuum, to 'anguished' at the other end. After assigning this speech task, reasons were given for cancelling the assignment for half the Ss. Again, Ss' overt behavior (laughs, sighs of relief) indicated that the cancellation was successful in reducing stress.

stress induction and reduction supported the consistent findings of the other studies in which the Green and Nowlis scale had been used.

Considerations in the Use of Verbal Indices of Stress

A wide variety of self-report measures of stress have been used extensively, the Mood Scale receiving the greatest attention here. The consistency with which this scale has discriminated between conditions of differential stress and between different conditions of experimentally-induced stress, gives considerable validating support for its continued use.

Whatever verbal measure is chosen, however, a number of problems still remain. In addition to the usual problems faced when relying on self-report—i.e., does the subject know, can he report, and will he report honestly—difficult procedural questions also must be considered. For example, is one assessment of stress sufficient to answer the questions posed in the study? If more than a single measuring application is required, how does one combat the drawbacks of repeated testing? That is, will filling out a stress measure at one time affect the response the next time? Will filling it out intrude into the experiment with negative consequences for the study?

It is also quite possible that in many studies a continuous measure of stress, which would show at any given moment the level of stress and whether it is increasing or decreasing, is desired. Lazarus, in discussing the changes in stress in Ss viewing the anxiety-provoking film, as indicated by physiological indices, suggests that the value of such continuous measurement argues for developing appropriate verbal measures paralleling ongoing physiological measures. In order to approximate continuous self-report measurement, of course, it would be necessary to simplify the response domain down to a single global mood variable.[2]

The need for frequent measures of stress level was recognized in the Greenberg (1961), Lynch (1963), and Norris (1964) studies, in which stress induction and stress reduction had to be assessed. In the Lynch and Norris[3] studies, in fact, stress was measured four times during a 50-minute period. Certainly one must ask whether Ss responded honestly and accurately each time they were asked for their ratings. To minimize as much as possible any lying or malingering, instructions for all three studies were devised with the intent of gaining Ss' cooperation. The importance of honest answers and the necessity for measuring at various times during the experiment were emphasized. The true purposes of the studies were not revealed, since all included attitude change as a second major dependent variable, but acceptable reasons for the studies and the measures were given.

While instructions may be used to gain Ss' cooperation in filling out the forms as honestly as possible, they cannot overcome any effect of the sheer repetition of filling out the same form—repetition which may lead to the remembering and copying of previous responses. Studies using the Mood or Stress Scale have attempted to overcome this possibility by rotating the

---

[2] A step in the direction of simple continuous mood measurement was taken by Iwao (1963), who elicited the subject's 'annoyance' with each of six consecutive brief dissonance-producing statements from a peer. The rating procedure was designed so as to dramatize possible annoyance—the subject stuck a hatpin at an appropriate place along each rating scale—Ed.

[3] The above discussion of the Norris study referred to only two stress measures. Subsequent experimental operations called for two additional assessments.

adjectives so that Ss did not start with the same adjective each testing time. Adjectives could be completely reordered to achieve the same purpose, but scoring would be complicated if change scores between certain adjectives were to be examined.

Repeated testing problems also may be handled by the appropriate experimental design, adding control groups which receive experimental manipulations but not all the measures (cf. Solomon, 1949). In a simple before-after design, this would involve adding a control group which receives the same treatment as the experimental condition, but is measured only after the experiment (and the usual control measured both before and after but receiving no treatment).

When more than the before and after measures are used, the number of necessary control conditions could become rather overwhelming. Certain statistical procedures for handling the data then may be used to control for possible effects of prior testing. Among these is the repeated measures analysis of variance (cf. Winer, 1962), which treats the test repetitions as a source of variance, thus removing it from the main effects which are being investigated.

Another statistical method for dealing with repeated measures is the analysis of covariance, in which prior test scores for all groups are treated as the covariates while the main effect of the experimental manipulation is investigated (cf. Cochran, 1957; Cox, 1958). Thus Lynch (1963) analyzed the final stress score (T_4), covarying for the first three test scores (T_1, T_2, and T_3). A similar procedure was used by Norris (1964). The reasoning underlying this use of covariance is that if prior test scores (T_a, T_b) for all experimental conditions are held constant, and conditions differ only in the experimental treatments received subsequently (after T_b), any differences between conditions at T_c may be attributed to those treatments, and not to any differential effect of prior position of the subjects.

When using the Mood or Stress Scale to assess psychological stress, a further question involves the selection of adjectives to form the scale. All the studies reported above found differential sensitivity to stress for different adjectives. Should one, then, include adjectives to represent all the factors found in the Green and Nowlis work, or choose only those which will reflect the response to the particular experimental situations to be used? If adjectives are chosen on the basis of some independent criterion of stress (e.g., after a pretest in which psychological stress is experimentally manipulated), one may argue that by selecting only adjectives relevant to the experimental situation, as Norris did in her study, one is measuring only that variable of major interest, omitting irrelevant adjectives which would not be expected to assess that particular stress reaction. By the same token, however, if each selection is made on *a posteriori* grounds, an element of tautology is introduced, and thus some independent means of item selection is preferred.

The finding that adjectives are more descriptive of some stressful situations, but not of others, has several possible implications, one of which is that stress is not a unitary concept but a multidimensional one. This point is of obvious methodological and theoretical significance—a more specific definition and understanding of the psychological stress assumed to accompany conditions of cognitive inconsistency is called for if the theory itself is to be unambiguously expressed.

CHAPTER 34

Experimental Investigations of Mediational Events

Harold B. Gerard

University of California, Riverside

The basic postulate underlying certain theories of cognitive consistency is that inconsistency produces a drive state which can be reduced by the reduction of the inconsistency that gave rise to it. In experiments testing derivations from the theories, the typical procedure is to contrive situations that are presumed to give rise to different levels of inconsistency and then make inferences, from some measurable effect, about the degree and kind of cognitive work the person engaged in. A singular weakness of most of the research is that the effects that are measured are generally gross and simple whereas the inferences made are refined and complex. For example, in the typical dissonance experiments on decision making (e.g., Brehm, 1956; Brehm & Cohen, 1959), the relative attractiveness of the choice alternatives is measured before and after the choice in order to obtain what is assumed to be a measure of dissonance reduction. The so-called dissonance effect in these experiments is supposedly reflected in the amount of spreading apart in value of the choice alternatives when their values after the choice are compared to what they were before the choice, the chosen one increasing in value relative to the nonchosen one. One or another aspect of the decision situation that would be expected to affect the amount of dissonance has been manipulated in these experiments.

On the basis of data on how much the alternatives spread apart after the choice, or on how much the subject wants to expose himself to information about the chosen or nonchosen alternatives, a rather elaborate theory of decision making is said to have been supported. It is my contention that these simple measures of effect provide an inadequate data base from which to decide whether or not particular inferences are supported. A major problem in much of the research is that since the data base is so meager, it supports other theories as well as dissonance theory. Chief among the contenders is a "conflict theory" which assumes that the spreading apart in value of the choice alternatives occurs before, rather than after, the decision. The underlying assumption is that the person spreads the alternatives apart in order to facilitate making the decision. Dissonance theory, on the

The work reported in this paper was in part supported by Grant GS-392 from the National Science Foundation.

other hand, assumes that the spreading apart occurs after the decision in order that the person justify having made the decision in the first place. Attempts have been made to muster support for the dissonance theory interpretation by examining the information-seeking behavior of the subject. The chapters by Mills, Sears, Berkowitz, and others in this volume point out that to date the evidence on information seeking and avoiding provides very little support for dissonance theory. Festinger (1964b) in a valiant attempt at firming up the data base by providing additional experimental evidence on information seeking and valuational spread, falls far short of doing so. The ten experiments presented in that volume still have not sharply contrasted theoretical alternatives with either kind of data.

It is apparent that we need more information about the details of how a person makes a decision and comes to terms with it subsequently. Only with this kind of detail will we ever be effectively able to rule out competing interpretations. But what kind of data should we collect? Much of the controversy could be settled if we knew when in the decision sequence certain events occur, such as when the alternatives spread apart in value. Our power to contrast alternative interpretations would be increased if we also were able to measure moment-to-moment changes in information seeking and in the subject's stress level. This last measure should differentiate between the conflict and dissonance interpretations since the former would predict the greatest stress immediately before the decision whereas the latter would predict its occurrence immediately after the decision.

In this connection, I will first discuss some data from an early experiment on conformity (Gerard, 1961) which originally aroused my interest in decision making; then I will briefly describe a recent study on decision making itself (Gerard, 1967); and finally I will allude to some of the research which is currently going on in my laboratory that focuses extremely closely on the events taking place during the decision sequence.

SOCIAL COMPARISON: JUDGMENT AND SKIN RESISTANCE MEASURES

The early experiment on conformity was a real shocker to me. The data, which were dramatic and unpredicted, had a profound effect on my subsequent conceptions of social influence processes. That experiment grew out of some of the earlier work on social comparison processes, and tried to focus on an issue that was both confused and confounded in the earlier studies. Festinger (1954) discussed ability and opinion comparison as two distinct processes. I think the field has been misled by this original distinction since the two processes are inextricably connected, ability comparison being the more fundamental of the two. A person refers his opinion to someone else in the light of what he assumes to be the ability of the other person to form and hold an opinion on the issue in question. He first attempts to estimate the relative ability of the other person before attributing credibility to his judgments.[1] In the experiment I conducted, both relative ability and discrepancy were varied in order to study the relationship between ability and opinion referral. The prediction which derived directly and simple-mindedly from social comparison theory was that when a person is confronted by a judgmental discrepancy between himself and others he should: (a) ex-

---

[1] Another basis for opinion referral, which we shall not elaborate on here, is the degree of coorientation or commonality of value perspective between one person and the other.

perience less stress to the extent that the others differ from him in the ability underlying the judgment; (b) through cognitive work, achieve greater self-other evaluational consistency to the extent that an ability differential exists; and (c) manifest both of these effects to a greater degree the greater the discrepancy in judgment. These predictions grew out of the confused state of the theory at the time which simply stated that a person will tend to compare himself with others to the extent that these others are equal to him in ability. The basic inadequacy of the formulation was my failure to realize that *a judgmental statement is a performance*, and that a performance can reflect a person's ability and/or can be evaluated in terms of any ability information that is available about the person. In Festinger's original formulation any differential in ability can provide a 'basis in fact' for rendering the other person noncomparable. This, however, fails to take account of bases for credibility attribution.

The basic experimental setup fits the dissonance paradigm in that the subject was put in the position of disagreeing with what he assumed to be the judgments of the others in the group on 12 of 18 line adjustments. These were the same judgments used previously by Asch (1951) in which the subject had to match the length of a single line to one of three comparison lines. In actual fact, the subject, who was isolated from the three other subjects, was fed false information as to what the others' judgments were. Certainly, information as to the relative ability of the others would affect the degree to which the subject could feel justified in disagreeing with them. An attempt was made to induce differential ability attributions by providing the subject with false feedback concerning the scores he and the others had made on a preexperimental task which was supposed to be a test of visual judgment ability. In one condition the subject discovered that his performance had been superior to the others; in another treatment the false feedback indicated that he and the others had performed about equally well; and in the third treatment he found that his performance was below theirs. The straightforward prediction from social comparison theory was that the subject would make short shrift of the discrepancy confrontation in both of the unequal ability treatments. Common sense, on the other hand, would predict that the greater his ability relative to the others, the less the discrepancy confrontation would matter to the subject. I checked this out with a number of intelligent nonpsychologists and the commonsense prediction was the one they invariably made. On the critical trials in the Small Discrepancy treatment, 'the others' chose a comparison line that was only slightly discrepant from the correct line, whereas in the Large Discrepancy treatment they chose a line that was very discrepant. In order to measure the amount of difficulty experienced by the subject, a continuous measurement was taken of the subject's skin resistance.

The skin resistance data provided a strong and clear disconfirmation of both predictions. All six treatment combinations (two levels of discrepancy by three levels of ability) showed a gradual rise in skin conductance (the reciprocal of resistance), suggesting that the discrepancy confrontation was a generally stressful situation. Furthermore—and this is the important fact— the greater the subject's ability relative to the others, the larger was the rise in skin conductance. Thus, there was no support for the derivation from comparison theory, and the results were also opposite to what one might expect from a commonsense theory. Since I found it difficult to believe the data, I checked and rechecked the setup, assuming that somehow there had been a polarity reversal in the equipment. These equipment checks were all in vain. The recording was a faithful reproduction of resistance changes between the skin resistance electrodes.

When I was thoroughly convinced that the data were correct, I thought of a plausible explanation that hinged on two crucial facts. The first fact was that some other data collected during the experiment indicated that the subject in all treatments perceived the others as having relatively high ability but judged himself to have even higher, equal, or lower ability as a function of the particular ability treatment he had been exposed to. The other crucial fact was that the other subjects were perceived as making their judgments independently of one another. This is a reasonable assumption since all of the judgments were made at the same time and displayed simultaneously on each subject's response panel. This method of presenting the judgments precluded the possibility of mutual influence occurring among the other subjects, short of mental telepathic influence, of course. This attributed independence probably made the group consensus very compelling to the subject in all three ability treatments. If he believed himself to be low in ability, it would be relatively easy for him to attribute the discrepancy between his own judgments and the unanimous and independent judgments of the others to his own lack of ability and thus justify his disagreement. To the extent, however, that he was high in ability, this avenue of accounting for the discrepancy was closed to him. Under such circumstances the tension he experienced would tend to be sustained. There is some corroboration in the data for this interpretation. The subject was asked halfway through the session and then again at the end of the session to evaluate himself and the others, and to guess their evaluation of him. Measurement of the internal consistency of these ratings indicated that the less the subject's ability relative to the others, the greater was the tendency for him to achieve internal consistency of the self-other ratings halfway through the session, this trend becoming even more marked by the end of the session. This linear effect of relative ability on the achievement of internal consistency was more pronounced under the Large than under the Small Discrepancy treatment, which adds even further weight to my *post hoc* explanation since we would expect the severity of the predicament to be greater under the Large than under the Small Discrepancy treatment.

Imagine where I would have been had I not taken skin resistance measurements! I would have spent weeks staring at the consistency data which are incompatible with social comparison theory and conjured up explanation after explanation without any hope of being able to prefer one over another. The physiological data taken by themselves would have put me in a similar position. Both sets of data taken together, however, dovetailed nicely into an explanation that I found satisfying. The discrepancy confrontation produced different levels of arousal as a function of the subject's relative ability. This can also be seen in the ease with which he was able to cognitively resolve the predicament produced by the discrepancy.

DECISION PROCESS: BLOOD FLOW AND ATTENTION MEASURES

After a series of further experiments on conformity, the decision process itself became the focus of my research. In a recent experiment (Gerard,

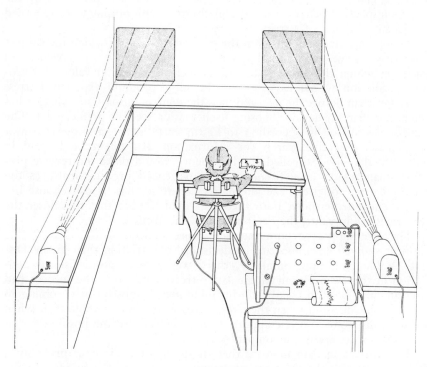

FIGURE

1967), I employed the paradigm originally developed by Brehm (1956) for studying decisions and tracked the subject's inspection behavior of two choice alternatives as well as his arousal level. The experimental setup is shown in the Figure. The two choice alternatives, which were prints of famous paintings, were projected on the two screens and the subject was instructed to indicate which one he wanted as a gift by pressing one of two buttons. Two photocells and a light source were mounted on a tripod and placed directly behind the subject's head. A shaving mirror that was attached to the back of the subject's head deflected the beam of light to trigger one of two photocells, depending upon which screen he was looking at. These photocell closures provided a record of his inspection behavior. After he made his choice, the paintings were left projected for 60 seconds and any further inspection behavior was recorded.

In addition, a photoelectric plethysmograph was attached to the forefinger of the subject's nonpreferred hand. This is a transducer that records changes in blood flow into the capillary bed of the fingertip. The probe consists of a very small light bulb which shines into the capillary bed and a small photocell adjacent to the light bulb which picks up the light reflected back from the capillary bed, the amount of light being inversely proportional to the amount of blood in the finger. The output of the photocell has a roughly sinusoidal waveform that reflects both pulse rate and the degree of constriction of the arterioles feeding the capillary bed. A stressor has the effect of constricting these arterioles which in turn reduces the amplitude of the pulse beat. The approximate physiology involved is described by Davis, Buchwald, and Frankmann (1955). The photocell closures produced by the subject's inspection behavior and the plethysmograph output were recorded on adjacent channels of a strip-chart recorder.

There were two treatments in the experiment—one in which the subject chose between two paintings that were of approximately equal value, and another in which the choice alternatives were disparate in value. A dissonance prediction would have it that the subject should experience stress after rather than before the decision; it is the confrontation with what he has done rather than the act of choosing itself that creates the predicament. The predecision situation is, according to Festinger (1964b), characterized as a dispassionate, objective search for information that might be helpful in making the decision. So-called conflict theory would make the reverse prediction—that greater arousal should be experienced predecisionally as the person attempts to spread the alternatives apart so that he can choose between them. Furthermore, both theories would predict that the closer the alternatives are in value, the greater will be the arousal.

The data supported both theories! More subjects in the Close Value treatment showed an immediate predecisional constriction than in the Disparate Value condition. Similarly, there was greater postdecisional constriction in the former than in the latter treatment. Thus, the subject had more difficulty both in making up his mind *and* in subsequently coming to terms with his decision when the alternatives were close in value than when they were disparate. No one appears to have considered the possibility that the two processes are not incompatible.

The inspection data indicate that the point of decision is probably a critical juncture in the information-seeking behavior of the subject. In the predecision period most subjects spent more time looking at the alternative they eventually did not choose, whereas postdecisionally they turned their attention to the chosen alternative. It is as though, in the predecision situation, the subject had made a tentative decision at the outset and was attempting to come to terms with what he would be giving up if he followed through on his tentative decision. Once he had decided, looking at the nonchosen alternative would confront him with its desirable features which would heighten his dissonance. There was no difference in this pattern as a function of the closeness in value of the choice alternatives.

RECENT STUDIES: GAZE AND PUPIL SIZE MEASURES

Although these continuous measures have enabled us to sketch some of the details of a theory of choice, the picture needs considerable filling in. Our hypothetical description has certain obvious implications that we might be able to test. I am now using a more refined decision situation in order to make such tests. In discussing the inspection data I have commented on the relative amount of time spent inspecting each alternative. This should not obscure the fact that nearly every subject in both treatments spent some time inspecting both alternatives both before and after the decision. Assuming that each of the paintings had both positive and negative features, and assuming that our description of the decision sequence is tenable, we would expect the subject to be paying differential attention to the positive and negative features at different points of the sequence. One of the problems in using paintings is that it is difficult to separate positive from negative features. One runs a high risk of being exposed to negative features while inspecting positive ones and vice versa.

In the research we are contemplating we will be using alternatives that consist of composites of features which are easily isolable visually. Some of the features of each of the alternatives will be positive (as premeasured) and some will be negative for the subject, and we will be able with the new setup to determine what he is looking at when. Thus, if we are correct in our characterization of the decision, in the predecision phase, when the subject looks at the alternative he eventually does not choose, we would expect him to be looking at its positive features; when he looks at the alternative he eventually chooses, we would expect him to be looking at its negative features. Perhaps initially he is attentive to the positive features of both, makes his tentative decision, and then exposes himself selectively to various features of the alternatives, in order to come to terms with the positive things he would be giving up and the negative things he would have to live with if he followed through with the tentative decision. It is also possible that the predecision situation consists of a sequence of tentative decisions, in which the subject views the alternatives first from the vantage point of the tentative choice of one of them and then from the standpoint of choosing the other, and then perhaps back and forth several times. We might expect that the more important the decision, the greater will be the number of alternations. In the postdecision situation the dissonance prediction is clear. We would expect that when the subject looks at the chosen alternative he would fix his gaze on its positive features and avoid its negative ones. This would reflect the kind of postdecisional justification or regret minimization that the dissonance theorists write about. We would also expect these differentials in gaze to diminish over time as the subject 'worked through' the problem represented by the decision. Furthermore, we would expect the initial differences in gaze to be more pronounced the closer in value were the alternatives to start with.

A further refinement of the new experimental setup will now enable us to track pupil size which, according to Hess and Polt (1960), reflects the attractiveness of the object fixated. If the technique is sensitive to what is going on during the heat of a decision, with these new measurements, we will be able to determine with some precision just when in the decision sequence, if at all, the alternatives are spread apart in value. Positive results that suggest a particular part of a sequence as the point at which spreading apart occurs would be fairly conclusive. Negative results, however, indicating that the technique reveals no particular point in the sequence as special in this respect, would leave the matter up in the air since one could argue that Hess' technique is not sensitive to these fleeting changes.

Hopefully this brief rundown of experimental results and the indication of the direction in which I am going have served to illustrate some of the possibilities for getting closer—through some ongoing physiological measures—than we have in the past to the psychology of decision making and the cognitive work which underlies it.

CHAPTER 35

Comment: Models of the Role of Stress

Percy H. Tannenbaum

A number of pertinent and interesting issues are raised in the foregoing contributions. As is often the case in such commentaries, there are perhaps more questions raised anew than old ones answered. Several of these bear additional consideration since the entire matter of a psychological stress mechanism is most fundamental, related as it is to the nature of inconsistency as a motivational drive state.

The most basic question, of course, is whether there is a need to postulate such a stress state to begin with. Of our contributors, Singer, Gerard, and Norris appear to assume its presence, while both Berkowitz and Brock express some reservations. In this connection, it is also instructive to note another present-day Doubting Thomas amongst the dissonance theorists. In December, 1965, at an informal conference foreshadowing the present volume, the editors met with a number of colleagues to discuss some of the more pressing issues underlying the consistency area. Leon Festinger was present, and when asked if he would retain the emphasis on an aversive discomfort condition, he surprised several of his listeners by indicating he would be inclined to deemphasize it, if not discard it altogether. In retrospect, he felt he had been too prone to "psychologize psychology" in this respect, and that such a postulation was not essential to the theory.

Perhaps this should not have been too much of a surprise. While the notion of psychological discomfort was inherent in many of the dissonance presentations, it was more a concept which was assumed and to which lip service was paid than an actual focus of investigation. Very few of the many studies spawned by the theory dealt with the phenomenon in any direct manner, with the concept of a mediated state being rather loosely inferred from some observable consequences which could probably be accounted for just as readily without it. Brehm and Cohen's (1962) reformulation of dissonance theory did not give strong emphasis to a stress mechanism as such, nor, for that matter, did Lawrence and Festinger (1962) or Festinger (1964b).

There is, nevertheless, evidence of some sort of stress activity being associated with various conditions of inconsistency. Gerard's data in a problem-solving situation, along with findings by Brehm, Back, and Bogdonoff (1964) under conditions of deprivation, testify to a degree of physiological stress activity. Similarly, Buckhout (1966) has demonstrated heart rate modification accompanying attitude change, while the experiments cited by Norris show similar effects using a verbal Mood Scale measure. Are such results merely artifacts of the testing situation, or do they reflect something more directly linked to the various inconsistencies created? As each of our contributors has indicated, the data at hand are insufficient in a number of ways, but in the absence of more definitive data, such findings cannot be totally ignored.

Assuming the results are not altogether irrelevant or artifactual, it is of obvious interest to determine the locus of any such stress component (S) in the scheme of relationships between the introduction of a state of inconsistency (I) and activity appropriate to its reduction or resolution (R). Several general paradigms are suggested for such a specification, each carrying its own implications.

Stress as a Mediator. The most common model, the one featured in most of the current literature and in the present contributions, assumes the stress state mediating between the instigation of an inconsistency and the subsequent behavior. The onset of the inconsistency directly evokes psychological discomfort which, being a 'naturally' aversive state, in turn elicits appropriate stress-reducing activity (i.e., $I \longrightarrow S \longrightarrow R$).

Such a formulation would tend to make inconsistency merely a special case of a more general psychological model (e.g., Lazarus, 1966) whereby the induction of stress, no matter what its origin, precipitates a general coping-response syndrome which is terminated only when the stress, as such, is accommodated. The inconsistency initiates the process, but it is not the main motivating factor. The resulting behavior is more a response to avoid or reduce the aversive stress state than to resolve the initial cognitive discrepancy.

Stress as a By-product. A second model that may be entertained suggests that it is the inconsistency itself which generates the power for its own resolution and that the accompanying stress is a side effect, part of the general fallout resulting from this process. That is, the *I-R* relationship is taken as a direct one, without the necessary intervention of a noxious mediating state. The stress component also derives from the inconsistency but responses to it are presumably independent of the responses to the inconsistency (i.e., $I \longrightarrow R$, and $I \longrightarrow S$).

Some of the points raised in Singer's contribution to this section can be adapted to such a model. Singer provides us with a detailed description of a number of possible concomitants to the induction of a state of inconsistency. Some of these can then induce feelings of botherment on their own, separate from any discomfort brought on by the inconsistency per se. The fundamental inconsistency induction-reduction relationship then remains a special and distinct process, separate from any stressful side effects which may accompany it.

Stress as a Consequence. A third general model suggests itself for accommodating the stress component. Here, the stress is not the result of the inconsistency, but of the activity elicited by the inconsistency. That is, the activity appropriate to reducing the inconsistency is seen as inducing a subsequent state characterized by psychological discomfort (i.e., $I \longrightarrow R \longrightarrow S$).

In their contribution to another Section (III A, Chapter 22), Kelman and Baron allude to such a possibility. They offer the suggestion that awareness of the inconsistency and of the need to handle it can serve as a signal to the individual that something was amiss. We found evidence of a similar effect in our recent research on the generalization of persuasion (Tannenbaum, 1967). When subjects were queried for their reasons for showing fairly substantial attitude change toward one concept as a result of reading a 300-word message on another concept, a considerable number first indicated surprise and doubt that they had changed. When their pre- and post test scores were made available and they were convinced that they had indeed changed their beliefs, they voiced considerable resentment and were clearly upset with themselves. The discomfort reported in this case appeared after the inconsistency-reducing attitude change became apparent. This finding was confirmed in a subsequent study which effectively manipulated the apparent susceptibility to different types of persuasion appeals. Subjects fed information of a higher degree of belief change showed more botherment (as indexed on the Mood Scale reported on by Norris) than those informed that they had changed little or not at all.

Between-model Comparisons. It is obvious that one of the desiderata for investigating the stress component and for deciding between these general models is a set of appropriate stress measures. Norris reports on various verbal report measures and points to several of their possible shortcomings. Gerard comments on several physiological indices, and there are other such measures available—e.g., the release of catecholamines, particularly epinephrine (cf. Schildkraut & Kety, 1967)—although Singer, for one, remains to be convinced of their applicability to the consistency situation.

Clearly, a major difference between the three models rests in the sequence of events and hence in the temporal relation between *I*, *R*, and *S*. Because reactions are apt to occur with great rapidity and because periodic interventions of the measuring instrument itself could constitute a confounding element, a continuous monitoring of the stress symptom is preferred, particularly if reliable base-line means can be assumed. Given an instrument of sufficient sensitivity and shielded from 'outside' influences, we could obtain evidence on the major paradigms for the stress locus suggested here. If the mediation model obtained, the *S* symptoms should occur after the *I* but prior to evidence of *R*. The by-product model is less explicit on this point; *I* should precede *S*, but whether *S* occurs before, simultaneous with, or following *R*, is unspecified. The consequence model, on the other hand, predicts *S* to occur after *R*, and thus provides a clear contrast with the mediation model.

Another difference between these general models stems from the respective roles they grant to the inconsistency and to the stress components as central motivational factors. What would be the consequences of treating each of these factors independently of the other? Since all three models start with the inconsistency state as the initiator of the problem, they would each predict that—directly (the mediation and by-product models) or indirectly (the consequence model)—appropriate treatment and reduction of the inconsistency would tend to reduce the stress as well. Such a resolution should be reasonably permanent unless some new situation imposes another inconsistency.

Further information may be revealed by treating the stress factor separate from the original inconsistency (e.g., by use of some tranquilizing agent, or the like). For the mediation model, this would be akin to 'treating the symptom rather than the disease.' Although its momentary effect might be quite pronounced, it should not have a relatively high degree of permanence since presumably the stress-initiating source still lingers on. Especially if it is reinstated for the subject, the unresolved inconsistency may again generate discomfort which will have to be coped with, possibly in the fashion of the Freudian mechanism of repression. In the by-product model, direct treatment of the stress should take care of it alone, without appreciably influencing the inconsistency induction-reduction process which is taken as operating independently from the stress state. Similarly, in the consequence model, since the stress supposedly results from the inconsistency-motivated activity, treatment of S should not effect the I-R relationship. The S state should persist until the inconsistency-reducing activity is accepted and integrated by the organism.

The study by Norris (1964) referred to in her chapter represented one attempt to treat the inconsistency and stress factors independently. For a variety of reasons, however, the separation was not sufficiently complete, and the study lacked the required continuous measurement to allow for adequate probing of the mechanisms involved. The proper experimental setting and the appropriate instrumentation are difficult to come by, but unless some such investigations are conducted we will probably have to continue to entertain the possibility of all three general models.

The lack of specification of the stress factor in the various consistency theories is matched by a lack of specification of the awareness factor. Does this factor imply awareness of the existence of the inconsistency itself, or awareness of any associated stress, or awareness of the inconsistency-resolving activity, or of all three? We have had little speculation and less research on such questions. Brock's contribution here marshals considerable support for the position that awareness is not a necessary condition for the dissonance theory formulation, where the awareness issue is perhaps most clearly evident.

Some of my recent work on the congruity model (cf. Tannenbaum, 1967) leads to a similar conclusion. Questioning of subjects who had exhibited appropriate (to the theory) attitude change indicated little or no awareness of the incongruity, to begin with, or of the subsequent opinion modification. Moreover, when informed that they had indeed changed their beliefs in response to certain persuasive appeals, the same subjects subsequently showed heightened resistance to persuasion by the same types of appeals—i.e., awareness seemed to decrease rather than increase susceptibility to inconsistency effects. Awareness of the susceptibility also, as we reported earlier, appeared to lead to increased stress.

Evidence of this sort and of the type reported by Brock is, however, largely circumstantial. Lacking a sensitive and uncontaminated measure of the awareness factor, as such, it is difficult if not impossible to examine it and its effects directly. Self-report, particularly in the presence of possibly associated discomfort, is not the most reliable procedure, and fully reliable and applicable physiological measures are still lacking. Again, the absence of an appropriate technology continues to inhibit the resolution of a perplexing theoretical issue.

D. COMMITMENT AS A MEDIATING VARIABLE

One of the most important and ubiquitous variables in the dissonance literature is that of commitment. Even though it is not always explicitly identified, commitment can be found at the core of virtually all of the major empirical breakthroughs generated by dissonance theory. For example, experiments on postdecision dissonance involve commitment in the form of the individual's irrevocably linking himself to participation in some future event or acquisition of some object. The experiments on effort and initiation implicitly involve commitment—commitment to the proposition that the pot of gold at the end of this endeavor is worth the price paid in effort. The experiments on insufficient justification are concerned with commitment in the sense that the individual performs an undesirable or counterattitudinal activity in a manner and under circumstances which make the consequences of the action impossible to undo or set right. The experiments on the self concept involve commitment through self-involvement.

In the following essays the role and importance of commitment are explored by three of the people currently and deeply involved with (committed to?) the concept. Philip Zimbardo explores the proposition that the reduction of cognitive dissonance (following commitment) can influence biological drives as well as social motives. He begins with a whimsical account of insufficient justification as an antecedent of thirst tolerance in the camel, but quickly removes his tongue from his cheek and proceeds to describe and analyze a series of fascinating experiments, both from his own laboratory and elsewhere. In his essay, Charles Kiesler discusses his recent work on commitment to *consonant* behavior and commitment to future interaction. From the results of these experiments he draws two interesting and rather controversial conclusions: (a) that commitment can vary independently of dissonance and (b) that commitment, in and of itself, has no motivating properties. We do not need to wait very long for the controversy to develop as Harold Gerard, in his essay, disagrees with Kiesler's position, asserting that commitment is a necessary antecedent of dissonance. He supports his view by presenting evidence that choosing one alternative (i.e., committing oneself to give up the other alternative) arouses more dissonance than a mere statement of preference involving little or no commitment.

CHAPTER 36

Cognitive Dissonance and the Control of Human Motivation

Philip G. Zimbardo
New York University

Can the resolution of cognitive inconsistency influence social motives and biological drives? Since the publication of Jack Brehm's provocative analysis and research on this problem (1962), I have attempted to test the generality of his affirmative answer to this question across a wide range of drives, and across a spectrum of response dimensions. This paper will describe the general research strategy employed and the kind of results which emerged, and then focus upon the question of whether the obtained effects reflect a simple functional reduction in level of motivation, or a more complex process of active, defensive coping with the cognitive dissonance which eventuates in motive reduction.

TRAINING COGNITIVE CAMELS

Since the studies done in our laboratories at New York University (about a dozen experiments) all employ similar research designs and comparable independent variables and experimental procedures, perhaps their exposition would be facilitated by presenting an analog which contains all of the essential aspects of these laboratory studies. Such a presentation may also have the incidental value of revealing to students of psychology how a research idea is born.

While listening to an Elaine May, Mike Nichols parody of the movie "Brief Encounter," I became intrigued with the question of how Saudi Arabian camels could cross those long hot deserts without becoming thirsty. Rejecting as too simple a physiological answer, I naturally searched for a cognitive or experiential one. Was there something special in the techniques used by Saudi Arabian camel trainers which could account for this phenomenon? A field-observation study was performed to uncover the nature of the verbal and nonverbal interaction between the camel trainer (CT) and his camel subject (CS).

What we observed can be summarized as follows:
1. From a large pool of naive camels, a sample was selected without reference to their size, color, or hump formation.
2. They were made slightly thirsty by having them eat spicy pomegranates, or foregoing liquids for a day or so.

3. Then they were given a simple task to perform like walking a short distance in the noonday desert sun.

4. At the end of this distance they were led to believe they would not have to go further and would receive water.

5. Just when they were about to partake of the water, the camel trainer would say, "Dear ship of the desert, I have a favor to ask you, would you walk another mile without partaking of water now? To be sure, O symbol of Arab Unity, the decision is up to you, it is purely a voluntary commitment."

6. Surprisingly, most of the camels silently acquiesced and, after having walked that extra mile for that CT, drank *less* water than camels who were not given the request, than camels who refused it, or than camels who were given no choice in whether to cross further into the desert!

7. On other behavioral measures these camels, who were acting in a manner inconsistent with (i.e., not predictable from) their level of thirst motivation, were also different. They traversed the distance faster, with a more sprightly step, and could even carry a heavier load than the other camels.

8. The Chief CT was not pleased however, because there were some deviant camels who did not respond to this choice situation in the manner described above. They drank as much or more than the other camel groups and tended to project water imagery on all things regardless of their natural nonliquid essence.

9. An internal analysis of this subset of camels revealed that they were all under the influence of a single trainer, el-Jannes, who, after the choice manipulation described above, would add: "If you do this favor for me, your efforts will be rewarded a hundred fold by Allah. Perhaps there will be an oasis at the end of our journey, with honey, dates, and cool spring water, maidens to sooth your brow, and a contract from M-G-M pictures."

10. All of these camels complied with his request, but the extent of the *extrinsic* justification he provided for them negated the effects of the freely made decision to comply with a request which did not follow from a consideration of the CS's relevant salient motive (i.e., thirst).

11. In order to be certain that anyone who was interested in the understanding and control of the camel's motivation could have the truth available, Noel, the Chief of All Trainers, formalized his observations and conjectures (even the nonobvious ones) into what has become a wise and trusted theory—at least among Saudi Arabians. And even today, many years later, camels can be seen in endless caravans enduring the heat of the desert and the thirst within, not with weary resignation, but with contentment borne of living a life according to the derivations of the Theory of Cognitive Dis-o-nance.

BIOLOGICAL DRIVES AND SOCIAL MOTIVES SHOWN TO BE INFLUENCED BY DISSONANCE REDUCTION

These (perhaps biased) observations and the theory were then put to a more serious test in a series of well-controlled laboratory studies. The experimental results to be described come from these experiments which: (a) have employed college students as subjects, (b) have attempted to arouse a motivational state via deprivation or aversive stimuli, (c) have given some subjects a choice to postpone motive satisfaction (to endure more of the drive state) and others no choice, (d) have manipulated justification for this decision and, occasionally, severity of the anticipated experience, and finally (e) have employed a variety of response indicators such as verbal self-reports, learning, perceptual, consummatory, and physiological measures.

Brehm's finding (1962), that subjects who commit themselves to further thirst for minimal justification (High Dissonance) experience less thirst, and drink less water than the Low Dissonance subjects, has been replicated and extended by Brock and Grant (1963) and by Mansson (1965). Mansson showed that under experimental conditions which should produce a high level of dissonance, thirsty subjects said they were less thirsty and drank less, and their scores on learning, perceptual, and fantasy measures were more comparable to controls who were not at all thirsty than to those whose thirst experience was physically similar. In fact, he obtained a linear relation between three levels of dissonance and performance on these measures (all of which were chosen as reflecting the extent of thirst motivation). Low Dissonance subjects behaved like thirsty controls while Moderate Dissonance subjects (high justification, long anticipated deprivation or low justification and short anticipated deprivation) were always in between the Highs and Lows on all five measures.

Brock and Grant demonstrated that when dissonance arousal can be assumed by coupling the experience of a hot, dry mouth (a sensation often correlated with thirst) with a hypnotic suggestion of feeling one's stomach is bloated with water, subjects drank almost no water at all, and the effect did not require conscious awareness of the cognitive elements which were in an inconsistent relationship.

That hunger is affected in the same way was also demonstrated by Brehm (1962), using self-report measures. Some of his findings were replicated by M. L. Brehm, Back, and Bogdonoff (1964), using a physiological measure. Their index of hunger was free fatty acid (FFA) level in the blood, which has been shown to increase as a function of hours of food deprivation. Typical of their findings is the one showing that subjects who report feeling most hungry after about 16 hours of food deprivation exhibit the least increment in FFA levels of any group when they commit themselves to further food deprivation for minimal justification.

The pain experienced by intense electric shocks to the fingers can be modified rather extensively by dissonance manipulations. We have been able to show that subjects who agree for minimal justification to endure a second series of painful shocks behave as if the second shocks (of physical stimulus value identical to the first series of shocks) were less aversive (Zimbardo, Cohen, Weisenberg, Dworkin, & Firestone, 1966). They say the shock hurts less, they learn faster on a task where learning is more disrupted the higher the shock, and their galvanic skin response is significantly reduced.

Grinker (1967) employed a different learning paradigm in which learning is facilitated by increases in motivation level, and then demonstrated that dissonance reduction could weaken the learning through its presumed effect on the intervening motivation. Using the Spence and Goldstein (1961) paradigm for classical conditioning, she had subjects commit themselves to an increase in intensity of the unconditioned stimulus (US), an air puff to the eye, in the second part of an eyelid-conditioning study. Under the no-choice conditions typically employed by experimental psychologists, she replicated the previous results that threat significantly increased the percentage of conditioned responses (CRs). However, under conditions of cognitive dissonance (free choice to be exposed to the US and minimal justification), the relative aversiveness of the stimulus event should be lessened. Indeed, she found only a nonsignificant increase in percentage of CRs to the US for the High Dissonance group but a significant increase for both the Low Dissonance group and the Controls. (In fact, these groups showed an increase that was four to five times as great as that of the High Dissonance group.)

Obviously, this cognitive control of behavior (though the presumed modification of intervening motivational states) is applicable to social motives as well as to drives based upon physical stimuli and biological states of the organism.

Cohen and Zimbardo (1962) showed that motivation to avoid failure could be changed by a dissonance manipulation to such an extent that subjects would actually behave so as to guarantee the likelihood of their failure. After having experienced a very difficult, novel task for which there was no prior standard for assessing success, subjects were led to believe that for minimal justification they would have to (if they so chose) be exposed to a much longer session on the same task. While half the subjects were told they would probably perform about average on this next session, higher dissonance was presumably aroused in the other subjects by telling them that it was quite probable they would perform very poorly, far below average. The task was reciting and interpreting modern poetry under conditions of delayed auditory feedback. When given the opportunity to choose the interval of delay to be used for the initial phase of the alleged next session, those in the Low Dissonance condition all chose to keep it at the moderately disturbing level used in the first session, or to make it less disturbing. In sharp contrast, most of the High Dissonance subjects set the interval selector at a point which would make the task more difficult, more disturbing, and more likely to produce failure.

Several methodological weaknesses in this exploratory study were remedied in a fine thesis by Peter Schlachet (1965) which enabled him to demonstrate a similar phenomenon more convincingly. Using appropriate controls and a conceptually clearer manipulation of dissonance, he was able to demonstrate a reversal of the usual finding relating poorer recall to stimuli previously associated with failure. When a subject who wants to achieve success on a given task commits himself to an experience which promises failure—under the appropriate dissonance conditions—we predict that his achievement motivation will be reduced (or that his failure motivation will be increased). This was indeed reflected in the significant superiority in recall of specific stimuli associated with *failure* for the High Dissonance subjects.

Interpersonal social motivation is also subject to modification by providing people with a choice of whether or not to expose themselves to a situation of anticipated motive arousal. In one study verbal conditioning, shown to be affected by social deprivation, was changed by the intervention of dissonance arousal and reduction, while in another commitment to frustration was shown to lead not to aggression but to increased liking and nonaggression.

Cohen, Greenbaum, and Mansson (1963) first demonstrated that re-inforcing the emission of personal pronouns with social approval led to a higher level of verbal conditioning for subjects who had experienced more prior deprivation of approval from the experimenter. When, however, other subjects voluntarily committed themselves to an additional postexperimental social deprivation experience for low monetary reward, they behaved as if their social motivation was low rather than high. These High Dissonance subjects showed none of the effects of initial social deprivation on verbal conditioning; in fact, for over 100 conditioning trials they exhibited virtually no acquisition of the socially reinforced response.

In studies by Brock and Buss (1962) and others, one observes a Nazi-like reaction: after aggressing against a helpless victim their dissonance-aroused subjects felt an obligation to have done so; they minimized the pain felt by the victim, and then derogated the victim. In contrast, Ira Firestone's thesis (1966) raised the question of whether dissonance theory could help to explain the turn-the-other-cheek reaction to social aggression. What happens when a 'victim' has been frustrated and verbally insulted by another person, and after interacting with him is provoked and physi-cally insulted? Will *he* retaliate if given the opportunity in a situation where he could clearly do so?

Subjects tested singly in an alleged impression formation study were frustrated in their desire to make a favorable impression upon their psychol-ogy professor by a public statement about them from a (tape-recorded, programmed) partner. This partner, supposedly a student from another col-lege, reacted to a series of benign getting-to-know-you information ex-changes with a scathing public attack, denouncing the subject as simple-minded, banal, etc. Obviously, the attacked subjects gave a more negative evaluation of their partner than other subjects who did not receive this insult treatment.

Each subject was then either required, or given a choice, to interact again with this same partner on a subsequent task in which cooperation and contact were made salient.

The dissonance produced solely by voluntarily agreeing to interact with someone who had been hostile was reduced by two-thirds of the High Dissonance subjects, who immediately increased their positive evalua-tion of the partner. The Insulted-No Choice subjects disliked the partner more, while the other groups did not change their liking for the partner.

To demonstrate that this attitudinal effect of dissonance was not tran-sitory and that it had motivational significance, the second part of the study included a manipulation of an additional source of cognitive disso-nance. Half of all the subjects were given a high degree of provocation by their partner, while the rest of the subjects received minimal provocation. This was accomplished by leading the subjects to believe that Firestone was studying the effects of various types of distraction on learning performance. The alleged partner was supposed to deliver blasts of white noise into S's earphones while S was trying to solve a problem. The experimenter sug-gested a possible range of the number of blasts which could be administered, leaving the final determination up to the partner. In the Low Provocation treatment, the minimal number E had suggested were delivered, while in the High Provocation treatment more than the upper suggested limits of white noise were given to the subject.

Then it was the subject's opportunity to retaliate! The subject's task was to administer distractions to the partner while he now tried to solve a problem. However, his distractions were allegedly in the form of electric shocks. Moreover, the subject knew that this was the final round of the study and that he could have the last laugh (since he would not see the partner, who was supposed to be returning immediately to his college).

The retaliative aggression of only one group was significantly different from the other groups. Subjects who were insulted, given a choice to interact further with the agent of their frustration, and then given maximal provocation were *least* aggressive! The High Dissonance subjects administered fewest shocks and maintained them for the shortest duration. While all other groups shocked their partner more the more provoking he was, for the High Dissonance group the high provocateur was treated just like the more gentle provocateur.

Clearly, then, the intervention of cognitive dissonance led subjects not to behave according to the expectations of a frustration-aggression model, but according to a turn-the-other-cheek model of social motivation.

These studies (and others not reported here due to space limitations) lead to the following conclusions: Providing human subjects with freedom to choose to enter a state of deprivation, or to expose themselves to aversive stimulation does not produce the dramatic effects on behavior that we have been led to believe ought to occur from our traditional models of motivation. Indeed, it is precisely the important role of choice and volition which separates human from nonhuman subject populations and experiments in which humans are treated like rational people instead of like rats. Our control subjects given no choice behave like other subjects in previous 'classic' experiments on learning and motivation regardless of species.

When subjects perceive that they must make an important decision and that they have a choice in committing themselves to one of the possible alternatives, they must then assume responsibility for that decision. This process is one of the few behavioral events which makes them (and us) uniquely human (cf. J. Milton, *Paradise Lost*).

As the justifications (be they hedonistic, mystical, or rational) for making a given decision increase, the decision becomes more 'externalized;' the individual can point to circumstances which compel a given course of action, limit his choice, and reduce the risks attendant upon personal responsibility. In short, extrinsic justification minimizes the necessity for intrinsic justification—for psychological reevaluation of the alternatives, for changing one's values, attitudes, or motives.

But let me not paint too bright a picture of a distinctly human subject. It appears, from observations of our subjects' behavior in these experiments and also from less controlled observations, that most people try to avoid making decisions or accepting responsibility and situations of free choice. Moreover, one might assert that the theory of cognitive dissonance is basically little more than a theory of face-saving. It describes the conditions under which people will distort social and physical reality rather than admit that their decision was wrong.[1] Dissonance theory ought to work best for those

---

[1] This statement converges well with Bramel's view (Chapter 26) that dissonance reduction involves responses to "feelings of social rejection"—Ed.

whose ego structure is such that they cannot accept the risk of being wrong, or who when they might be wrong never want to admit it. On the other hand, one could imagine a reinforcement schedule which would lead subjects not to prize consistency for its own sake, but to find virtue in veridical perception regardless of its implications.

Given these general considerations, the results of my research and that of my students and colleagues have been consistent and strong enough for us to believe in the tremendous potency of the cognitive control of a wide range of motives and behaviors generated by these motives. In some studies we have been able to bring behavior under as complete control with verbal-cognitive manipulations as with manipulations of the physical parameters of drive-arousing stimuli. The extent of this control and the precise determination of the central mediating mechanisms which will account for it await further research.

The last point to be discussed in somewhat more detail than those above is the theoretical status of the interaction between cognitive dissonance motivation and the specific social or biological motive aroused in a given experiment. It has been assumed that there is a cognitive component associated with any motivational state which provides information to the individual about its unpleasantness. When in our own experiments a commitment was made to experience more of this unpleasant state then we assumed that the individual emphasized the cognition that he had no choice to do otherwise (No-choice Control groups), or had to face the unpleasant experience because of money he would receive or because of nonmaterial incentives supplied him (Low Dissonance). But what alternatives were available to a High Dissonance subject? For example, he received a series of painful electric shocks, which made him want to leave the situation as soon as possible. But then he was 'made to agree voluntarily' to take still more shock with only minimal justifications for doing so (i.e., not strong enough for him to convince his grandmother why he did such a foolish thing). He could generate justifications for himself to increase the importance of the research or his pioneering or his martyr role in it. However, the manipulation was designed to make this an unlikely possibility by specifically denying that anything more could be discovered than was already discovered in the first (part of the) experiment. An alternative dissonance-reducing cognition would then be, "The shocks won't hurt so much," or some similar verbal statement. "I'm really not very hungry," or "That partner of mine may not be a bad guy once I get to know him," might be other cognitions which would be appropriate for some of the other motives aroused in the hunger or frustration studies. If indeed the shocks are perceived as not painful, then agreeing to endure more of them would not be dissonant.

This explanatory mechanism was put to a direct test by inducing this self-persuasive anesthesia cognition via hypnotic manipulation. In a study by Zimbardo, Rapaport, and Baron (1965) subjects were trained to be excellent hypnotic subjects (after 9 hours' training all could reach a somnambulistic level). An exact replication of the commitment to shock study was then run in which the dissonance manipulation was replaced by telling one-third of the subjects under hypnosis that the shocks would not hurt as much as they did before. A second group of hypnotic subjects was given an achievement induction which did not mention the shock, only that they should concentrate and try hard during the learning task and they would learn faster. An unhypnotized control group was led to role-play the anesthesia condition.

The results demonstrated an equivalence only between the High Dissonance subjects and hypnotized subjects for whom the suggestion was implanted that the shocks would not hurt. It appears that the High Dissonance subjects engaged in a process of self-persuasion which had an effect on behavior (subjective, learning, and physiological) which was similar (though weaker) to the internalized persuasion initiated by the hypnotist.

Although our confidence in the explanatory mechanism was strengthened by these findings, there nevertheless remains a disturbing thread running throughout most of the studies reported previously. In one sense, the results are too good! Most of these studies include two control groups in which the relevant drive is aroused at a high or low level, in which there is no choice or justification, and in which all the same tasks are performed as in the dissonance groups. Obviously, their function is to demonstrate the differential effect of drive on these tasks and response systems, and to provide the extreme baselines within which the dissonance groups can be expected to array themselves. While the Low Dissonance group should approximate the High Arousal controls, the High Dissonance group should be comparable to the Low Arousal controls. Generally this is what was found. However, there are a number of instances when the High Dissonance subjects behaved as if they were even less motivated than the low motivation control subjects! Let me illustrate this in outline form.

In the shock-dissonance study (Zimbardo et al., 1966), the High Dissonance subjects were either no different from or showed less effect of the electric shock on some of their behavior than a control group for whom the shock had been physically lowered by over 20 volts. This was even true of decrement in Galvanic Skin response (GSR) to the shocks.

In the Cohen et al. (1963) social deprivation study, the High Dissonance group showed less conditioning following deprivation than even the control group without any deprivation.

In Mansson's (1965) thirst study, the High Dissonance group was even more extreme than the No Thirst group in both a learning task and a perceptual task. Moreover, when asked to construct stories to TAT-like pictures, all groups but one had a higher frequency of water responses to a picture which was drive-related (water in it) than to a nondrive-related picture (no water or liquid). Only the High Dissonance group saw *less* water where it was than where it was not. When responses to this ambiguous stimulus were rated for the degree to which they exhibited 'trouble' (undifferentiated concern, uneasiness, conflict, etc.), the High Dissonance subjects exhibited more trouble themas than any other group.

In Grinker's (1967) eyelid conditioning study the High Dissonance group showed virtually no increase in conditioning after being given the threat of an increased US (less than 2 per cent for male Ss).

In the study by Brock and Grant (1963), the Hypnotic Dissonance group drank even less water than subjects who were not thirsty.

Finally, in Firestone's (1966) frustration study, the High Dissonance subjects who had been frustrated and insulted were less aggressive under conditions of high provocation (they delivered fewer shocks and for a shorter duration) than the subjects who had not even been insulted.

Thus the theory of cognitive dissonance has directed our attention toward a set of new variables which influence human motivation. The group differences predicted by the theory have been validated in many independent studies across many response dimensions. However, the simple conception we entertained initially of dissonance reduction leading to a direct functional resolution of the motive being studied does not seem to be substantiated. Rather, what we seem to be tapping is a dynamic process taking place, in which the individual is attempting to cope with the physical reality of repeated shocks of high voltage, stomach contractions, the sensation of thirst, etc., while trying to convince himself that he did not make a mistake in agreeing to endure these things. Some of the data reflect a denial of any motivation at all, rather than a reduction in the intensity of the motive. Of course, it is important to remember that most of these experiments are 50-minute studies (the duration of one college class period). Perhaps during this short time interval the confrontation between the competing levels of reality is most severe and requires the most dramatic suppression of cognitions relevant to the internal drive state. It may well be that the subject would not protest as much that he is not motivated if the drive stimulus were maintained or repeatedly presented over a longer period of time—requiring a more veridical adaptation to the demands of the stimulus.

What is clearly needed, then, is systematic research to uncover the cognitive-physiological mechanisms responsible for the control of human motivation. Festinger's theory of cognitive dissonance appears to offer us at least one existing point of departure. Perhaps it is also time to stop trying to demonstrate phenomena to skeptics, and to become concerned with understanding some of the more subtle processes involved—processes which link this theory with the mainstream of psychological inquiry on human behavior.

CHAPTER 37

Commitment

Charles A. Kiesler
Yale University

The purpose of this chapter is a modest one. I will very briefly review some of the current uses of the term commitment, present some of my own data bearing on theoretical issues, and end with some speculative notions for future research.

The most frequent use of the concept of commitment pertains to research on dissonance theory, especially in decision making and forced compliance settings. Festinger (1964b) says that "... a decision carries commitment with it if the decision unequivocally affects subsequent behavior ... that the decision has clear implications for the subsequent unrolling of events as long as the person stays with that decision" (p. 156). In a similar vein, Gerard (1965) reasons that "In general, then, any constraints that operate against changing behavior serve to commit the person to that behavior" (p. 264). Kiesler and Sakumura (1966) define commitment as a "pledging or binding of the individual to behavioral acts" (p. 349).

These three notions tend to restrict commitment to refer to the difficulty in changing one's behavior, but with special emphasis on the implications of present behavior for future behavior. This emphasis on behavior is seconded by Brehm and Cohen (1962), who say:

> ... We assume that a person is committed when he has decided to do or not to do a certain thing, when he has chosen one (or more) alternatives, and thereby rejected one (or more) alternatives, when he actively engages in a given behavior or has engaged in a given behavior. Any one or a combination of these behaviors can be considered a commitment .... A major point about commitment is that it generally provides a clear specification of psychological implication (p. 7).

But then Brehm and Cohen also bring in the matter of cognition and cognitive elements: "In addition ..., commitment increases the resistance to change of an element (or set of elements) and thereby affects the kinds of attempts to reduce dissonance that may occur" (1962, p. 8). This dual emphasis on the difficulty of changing behavior (with the concomitant

448

aspect of implications for future behavior) and the resistance to change of a cognitive element does not necessarily produce dissonance for the theorist himself. It does, however, demand an isomorphism between the difficulty in changing behavior and the resistance to change of the cognitive element corresponding to that behavior. This is not an unreasonable assumption and is one that Brehm and Cohen implicitly make. Their notion that commitment allows a "clear specification of psychological implication" really refers to cognitive elements' resistance to change. The relative resistance of cognitive elements to change is the sine qua non of dissonance theory predictions.

According to popular usage, then, commitment may refer either to the difficulty in changing (or psychologically undoing) some overt behavior or act, or to the resistance of some cognitive element to change. The cognitive element or elements ordinarily would represent some behavior, but they need not. The crucial thread in both usages lies in the implications of such behavior or cognitions for future behavior or cognitive work—"the subsequent unrolling of events," as Festinger has referred to it. This appears to be the essence of the current uses of commitment in the psychological literature. At a later point in this paper I will return to the problem of definition.

Let us now turn to some empirical work carried out by my students and myself. I will emphasize two topics here: commitment to consonant behavior; and commitment to future interaction with a group, or another person in a dyad. After discussion of these data, I will sum up and speculate about possible directions for future research.

COMMITMENT TO CONSONANT BEHAVIOR

Generally, research on commitment has focused on dissonant behavior: behavior that is discrepant with S's beliefs or attitudes. The experiments I will discuss here (Kiesler & Sakumura, 1966) differ in that commitment to consonant behavior was experimentally varied.

Briefly the procedure was as follows. The Ss were led to believe they would be participating in two separate experiments during the experimental hour, for two different faculty members, Drs. E. and M. The S filled out some attitude items, and then read a communication into a tape recorder, identifying himself by name. We told the Ss we would use their tape for the future study of regional accents.

Two things are important about this communication: (a) the attitudinal position the communication advocated was consistent with S's own attitudinal position, as determined by the previously administered attitude scales; (b) Ss were differentially paid for their effort; half were paid $1.00 and the other half $5.00.

Later, in what presumably was the second experiment, experimental Ss received a countercommunication on the same topic. In sum, all Ss performed some consistent behavior for which they were differentially paid. All experimental Ss also subsequently read a communication advocating the contrary position. They then completed a disguised posttest on the same issue. The dependent variable was the resistance of this attitude to attack as a function of the prior differential payment for the consonant behavior.

The theoretical model proposed by Kiesler and Sakumura asserts that the less the inducement to perform some consonant behavior, the greater the commitment to that behavior.[1] The greater the commitment to the behavior, the greater the resistance to change of the cognitions consistent with that behavior (e.g., "I believe X"). Consequently, we predicted that the *less* the payment for the consonant behavior, the *greater* the resistance to subsequent attitudinal attack. The results supported this prediction. The Ss who were paid $1.00 for performing the consonant behavior showed less attitude change toward the position advocated in the countercommunication than did Ss who were paid $5.00.

The theoretical notions proposed in the Kiesler and Sakumura article concerning the effects of commitment to consonant behavior are consistent with other research as well (e.g., Hovland, Campbell, & Brock, 1957; Freedman & Steinbruner, 1964). Taken together, these results suggest a more general paradigm for forced compliance studies than previously conceptualized: the less one is pressured to perform an act, either consistent or inconsistent with one's beliefs, the more one is committed to that behavior. The greater the commitment, the greater the resistance to change of the cognitions representing that behavior. Assuming one attempts to resolve inconsistencies between act and attitude, the following two propositions should hold: (a) If an act is inconsistent with one's attitudes, then the greater the commitment to the act, the greater the attitude change towards consistency with the act; (b) If an act is consistent with one's former attitudes, then the greater the commitment to the act, the greater the resistance to subsequent attack.

Thus, in this sense, commitment affects mainly the resistance of a cognition to change. I wish to add one important point here: there is no reason to believe that commitment, in and of itself, has any motivational component. This is an important theoretical point and there are several pieces of evidence related to it. First of all, in the Kiesler and Sakumura study there were no differences between control conditions (i.e., Ss who were paid $1.00 or $5.00 for the consonant behavior, but did not receive a countercommunication). That is, differential commitment to the consonant behavior had no systematic and differential effects on existing attitudes.[2] Secondly, Michael Pallak and I have run a series of studies in which

---

[1] This is explicitly an *assumption* of the model. Space limits detailed consideration and justification of this assumption, but one might briefly speculate about the psychological process involved. To behave consistently with one's beliefs, for whatever amount of money, need not produce much discomfort or psychological work for S. I would think that commitment thus produced would not initiate any active process for S. But the cognition "I did consistent act X" becomes part of the cluster of cognitive elements representing the attitude. It should be only later, when one receives the countercommunication, that any active process occurs. At that time, if one is to change one's opinion, then one has to live with this prior behavior (if only by denial, distortion, or reinterpretation of the act). At that time, but not before, the greater the amount of prior inducement or pressure, the easier it is to say, for example, "I only did it for the money." Since this represents a modification of the cognition "I did act X," that cognition is made less resistant to change with greater inducement for the act. It follows therefore, that greater inducement for the consonant behavior should produce less resistance to subsequent attitudinal attack.

[2] This lack of difference between Commitment Control conditions was also obtained in a study just completed (Kiesler, Pallak, & Kanouse, 1968). In that study, commitment and dissonance were manipulated independently on two logically related issues by two

Ss were differentially committed (i.e., via differential payment and degree of volition) to some consonant behavior. We found no systematic effect on previously existing attitudes. In addition, there were no systematic effects on the way Ss evaluated group discussions of Ss holding extreme but 'same-side' attitudes. Thirdly, as we shall discuss shortly, commitment to future interaction with a group has a strong effect for low-attracted Ss, but not for medium- or high-attracted Ss.

Other things equal, commitment does not appear to be motivating. However, there are aspects of the typical commitment manipulation which may have a motivational component, and, thus, a systematic effect on attitudes. For example, in the Kiesler and Sakumura study, we attempted to control for other relevant variables, such as the degree of effort expended and S's degree of satisfaction with a job he did. It is reasonable to suppose in more freely varying situations, an S who is paid more to defend his position might work harder at the task, and also be more disappointed with the lack of excellence in his performance. There are also other aspects of a presumably consistent task which may indeed be dissonant, e.g., giving a speech that is on the same side of the issue but more extreme than S's position.

Thus, I argue that proattitudinal advocacy need not have any effect on existing attitude. Adding a cognition or making it more resistant to change need not systematically affect the attitude in terms of its importance, extremity, and so forth. I do add, however, that there can be dissonant elements involved in the act of proattitudinal advocacy. That is, the performance of what appears to be a consonant act can create dissonance. As mentioned, one way to do this is to confound the commitment manipulation with differential effort expended. Under such circumstances, dissonance theory will even allow differential prediction of amount of change and direction of change. Indeed, most experiments using a commitment manipulation confound the degree of commitment with the degree of dissonance.

The studies discussed above are related to an atypical experimental situation: the effect of commitment to consonant, rather than dissonant, behavior. Space limits going into great detail about the theoretical underpinnings of this research, but the interested reader may wish to consult the Kiesler and Sakumura article for a more formal presentation. For the moment, let us turn to a quite different aspect of this theoretical topic: commitment to future interaction in groups.

COMMITMENT TO FUTURE INTERACTION WITH OTHERS

Several of the studies in this section are concerned with the effect of a group on the individual. More often than not, the group as an influencing agent is left out of discussions of attitude change or consistency theory. There is no reason for this to be done, providing that adequate control over the group interaction is experimentally achieved.

In the studies to be discussed here, the crucial variable is the commitment to (or strong anticipation of) future interaction with others. As we

---

different experimenters. The posttest was given by a third experimenter in a different building. Commitment by itself had no systematic effect on either issue. In general, the experimental results supported the findings of Kiesler and Sakumura, but further suggested that under conditions of High Commitment and High Dissonance, the subject compartmentalized the two issues.

shall see, this is an important variable whether the 'others' are a group, or merely one other S in the experimental situation. Let us quickly look at some of the data and then return to the theoretical implications of this variable.

In one series of studies (Kiesler, 1963; Kiesler & Corbin, 1965; Kiesler, Zanna, & De Salvo, 1966), we have used an experimental paradigm in which we manipulate: (a) S's acceptance by the group (and hence his attraction to the group); and (b) whether S anticipates future sessions with the same group. That is, all Ss must return for future sessions presumably, but some Ss must continue with the same group, while others expect to be switched to different groups. By manipulation, all Ss express their attitudes toward an array of attitude objects; they then find out the group disagrees with them, with the extent of disagreement constant for all Ss; and finally, they take a privately expressed posttest of attitudes toward the objects. The dependent variable is attitude change as a function of attraction to the group and commitment to continue interaction with the group.

Typically, others have found a monotonic positive relationship between attraction to the group and attitude change as a function of disagreement with the group: the less the person is attracted to the group the less the group can influence him (cf. Hare, 1962). We found this also, but only when S did not anticipate future interaction with the same group. Commitment to continue interaction produces a quite different effect, and the differential effect is concentrated in the Low Attraction condition. When the Low Attraction S is not committed to continue in the same group, little attitude change takes place as the result of disagreement with the group. However, when the Low Attraction S is committed to continue the interaction over several sessions, the group's influence upon him is considerable, indeed, almost as much as in the High Attraction condition (Kiesler & Corbin, 1965). This is not a simple compliance reaction by Ss. In a subsequent study (Kiesler, Zanna, & De Salvo, 1966), we showed that the attitude change thus produced is relatively resistant to subsequent attack.

These data indicate quite clearly that commitment to the group, in this case the anticipation of future interaction with the group, strongly and systematically affects the ability of the group to influence the individual.[3] In the above studies, however, the effect of commitment is concentrated in the Low Attraction condition. This suggests that the attitude change thus produced is not a preferred alternative for S, and is used only when other avenues of psychological escape are closed off.

There is no doubt that these group data have rather interesting implications for social psychology. However, the reader may well ask if the crucial variable here is really commitment. That is, does this descriptive term, the anticipation of future interaction, reflect the underlying psychological variable of commitment? In spite of obviously incomplete data, I would like to argue that anticipation of future interaction is most parsimoniously viewed as a form of commitment. Let us look at this issue more closely.

The S agrees to return for the future sessions with the same group. As I have argued elsewhere (Kiesler, Zanna, & De Salvo, 1966), the effect of this

---

[3] Perhaps more importantly, the data suggest that various empirical 'laws' concerning the relationship of particular variables to group influence may be limited to more fleeting interactions (Kiesler, 1967a, b).

anticipated future interaction is to make certain alternative responses (e.g., rejection or devaluation of the group) more difficult and less probable. That is, suppose S disagrees with a group. Presumably this is an uncomfortable situation for him. As one set of possible reactions, S may reject, devalue, ignore, or generally dissociate himself from the group. However, when one must continue the interaction over several occasions, this set of alternative reactions becomes less viable. The S must somehow make his peace with the group. Thus, the commitment lies in the act of agreeing to return for future sessions. Consequently, the cognitions inconsistent with rejecting or ignoring the group become more difficult to change.

Let us view another situation where commitment to future interactions forces Ss to deal with a situation they would rather ignore. I am now collaborating with Sara Kiesler and Michael Pallak on a series of experi... investigating how people react to a social faux pas of another (Kiesler, Kiesler, & Pallak, 1967). Folklore suggests we try to 'save the other's face' when he commits a faux pas; in other words, gloss things over. However, we have found a quite different reaction when Ss anticipate future interaction with the other. In that case, Ss are quite blunt and privately attempt to change the offending other's behavior. Apparently commitment to continue forces S to deal with the situation, since repetitions of the faux pas could produce increasing discomfort over time. (The reader may have noticed a similar effect between husbands and wives.)

I have been asked several times whether the notion of the effects of anticipation of future interaction is intimately tied to the model proposed by myself and Sakumura. Clearly it is not. Furthermore, it is still an open question whether the one concept, commitment, is adequate to describe both the effects of anticipated future interaction and commitment to consonant behavior. Nonetheless, I regard the possibility of such a parsimonious view being valid as intriguing. The ubiquitous plea for more data becomes especially applicable in the present case.

CONCLUSIONS

I have presented some of the data obtained in our laboratory on the effects of psychological commitment. Space limitations prohibit an exhaustive review of the relevant literature, or even other relevant data we have obtained. In spite of this, I would like to spend a little time speculating about this variable of commitment.

I think it is most productive and precise to view commitment in terms of the relative resistance to change of particular cognitions. These cognitions may or may not represent particular behaviors or behavioral acts. Elsewhere (Kiesler & Sakumura, 1966), I have discussed commitment as a "pledging or binding of the individual to behavioral acts." This is a perfectly reasonable, if somewhat limited, view to take about commitment, providing one further posits that the *effect* of this commitment is to make the cognition representing the behavioral act more resistant to change. It is this further assumption that would allow one to account for the data in the broad area of commitment (a breadth the former model was not intended to encompass).

One of the primary implications of this view is the denial of a motivational component to commitment. This question of whether commitment is motivating is a crucial one for future research, and for interpreting past research. The question is still not resolved, but both our group data and our data on consonant behavior strongly suggest that commitment, in and of itself, is not motivating.

Let us take the Kiesler-Sakumura experiment as an example. We differentially paid Ss to perform a behavior consonant with their beliefs. We found no consequent differential change in belief as a function of payment alone. However, later Ss in the $5.00 condition changed their attitudes more as a result of attack than Ss in the $1.00 condition. Why? Each S presumably has some cluster of cognitive elements consistent with the cognition "I believe X." If S changes one of these, he theoretically must change them all (excluding for the moment a process of compartmentalization). Between conditions there are presumably no systematic differences in these clusters except for the cognition "I performed consistent act Y for Z amount of money." The differential resistance to attack between the conditions is not due, theoretically, to any differential amount of dissonance produced by the attack. It is due to the differential resistance to change of the clusters of elements; specifically one of the elements in the cluster.

This is not to deny, of course, that some operations designed to produce differential degrees of commitment may also concomitantly produce differential degrees of dissonance. For example, a public-private manipulation has often been used to manipulate commitment. However, there are aspects of a public manipulation that could produce dissonance as well. Further, one would suspect the dissonant relationships involved are more salient in a public situation.

This brings up the general question of the relationship of the degree of commitment to the degree of dissonance. If commitment is to be a scientifically useful term in social psychology, then it must, by definition, be independent of dissonance. The confusion of these two terms can only lead to theoretical ruin. Viewing commitment in terms of the relative resistance of cognitions to change allows one to distinguish conceptually between dissonance and commitment. Resistance to change of a particular cognition does not theoretically affect the degree of dissonance.[4]

There have been a few attempts to specify the relationship between commitment and dissonance in the experimental literature. A casual perusal of recent experiments will reveal the following implicitly stated relationships of commitment to dissonance: (a) unless S is committed, we cannot make an unequivocal prediction from dissonance theory; (b) unless S is committed, there may be no dissonance; (c) the more S is committed, the greater the dissonance.

These are quite distinct statements and they have led to considerable confusion. However, viewing commitment in terms of the relative resistance of cognitions to change allows us to distinguish among these statements. That is, the first statement, that commitment aids one in specifying how dissonance will be reduced, is true *by definition*. Knowledge of the relative resistance of cognitions to change is a necessary condition for the specification of mode of dissonance reduction. The last two statements relating commitment to presence and degree of dissonance, are not true, at least by definition alone. They may however have some validity in a given experi-

---

[4] It may, however, affect the maximum dissonance possible for a given situation (Festinger, 1957).

ment in the following two ways: (a) commitment may increase the salience of dissonant relations for S; (b) the experimental operations used to produce a difference in dissonance may also systematically affect the degree of commitment.

Commitment must be conceptually distinguished from dissonance. The first step (and a minimal one) in such a distinction would be to indicate the conditions under which one may vary commitment without affecting dissonance. Without at least this, the term commitment has no conceptual status independent of that of dissonance. I would argue that without the independent status, the term commitment is superfluous to social-psychological theory. One of the initial steps in making the distinction is to answer the question: Is commitment in and of itself motivating? I argue that it is not. If one wants to take the opposite position, he must clearly indicate the motivational properties of commitment that are distinct from those of dissonance.

Commitment appears to be a scientifically useful term. However, a clearer distinction between commitment and dissonance is needed. Two types of experiments are needed here: experiments in which commitment is varied, but dissonance is not present; experiments in which commitment and dissonance are varied independently. Research on commitment to consonant behavior and the anticipation of future interaction represent a modest beginning.

CHAPTER 38

Basic Features of Commitment

Harold B. Gerard
University of California, Riverside

In their revision of dissonance theory, Brehm and Cohen (1962) added freedom of choice and commitment to the decision as necessary conditions for the arousal of postdecisional dissonance. The focus in this paper is on commitment, but I will first make a few remarks about voluntariness since the two conditions are interrelated.

Voluntariness turns out, on close analysis, to have no special distinction as a condition but serves rather to point out a basic relationship that has been enunciated over and over again in the dissonance literature, namely, that the greater the justification for engaging in some act, the less will be the postdecisional dissonance associated with that act. When a person's freedom of choice is restricted so that there are strong pressures on him to engage in some behavior alternative, a situation of high justification exists. We can therefore expect that high pressure to engage in a particular act, which can arise because of either a severe threat or a high incentive, will result in a lack of perceived choice. Cohen (in Brehm & Cohen, 1962) reports data that bear out this relationship. In a study which varied the monetary incentive for engaging in discrepant behavior, the higher the incentive the less was the subject's perceived freedom in choosing whether or not to engage in the behavior.

The unique contribution of the Brehm and Cohen volume is their hypothesis that commitment is a necessary condition for the arousal of dissonance. Festinger (1964b) has acknowledged this important contribution. Brehm and Cohen state that "a person is committed when he has decided to do or not to do a certain thing, when he has chosen one (or more) alternatives and thereby rejected one (or more) alternatives, when he actively engages in a given behavior or has engaged in a given behavior. Any one or a combination of these behaviors can be considered a commitment" (p. 7). They go on to say that the act of commitment serves to define psychological implication which, as other papers in this volume have pointed out, is the basis for a cognition being dissonant or consonant with some other cognition. This is an extremely important point. But Brehm and Cohen did not go far enough in specifying the nature of a commitment.

It is my thesis here that cognitive consistency attainment is a derivative

456

of the requirements of action; that the requirements of action determine which cognitive elements will be dissonant and which will be consonant with the act. It is only when a cognition (or belief) has behavioral implications for the person that the stage is set for the arousal of cognitive inconsistency. Another condition necessary for inconsistency to be experienced is that some other cognition have behavioral implications that are somehow incompatible with those of the first cognition (see Chapter 13). Furthermore, this perceived inconsistency will not produce any psychological tension, or dissonance, unless the person has decided to engage in the behavior following from one of the cognitions, and that behavior is to some degree irrevocable. Merely thinking about the ways in which various cognitions are inconsistent with one another will not, in and of itself, arouse dissonance. In making a decision the cognitive work engaged in by the person presumably consists of considering the various implications of choosing one or another alternative. It is then that the inconsistencies inherent in the situation confront the person since certain anticipated implications of choosing one alternative are incompatible with other implications of choosing that same alternative. Thus, if a person is choosing between a Ford and a Chevrolet he must, of course, realize *while he is making his choice* that an implication of choosing the Ford is that he cannot have the Chevrolet and vice versa. Unless he is willing to buy both cars he cannot own both. More specifically, desirable features of the Chevrolet and undesirable features of the Ford are inconsistent with choosing the Ford. Once he has put his cash on the barrelhead for one or the other, the inconsistency experienced during the decision-making process gives rise to postdecisional dissonance.

Why is this so? What is the basis of dissonance arousal? I contend that dissonance arises because it is simply nonadaptive for the person to imagine all of the desirable features of the Chevrolet or to be preoccupied with the Ford's negative features after he has bought and is stuck with the Ford. He must maintain an *unequivocal behavioral orientation* toward the Ford. Continuing to long for the Chevrolet or being preoccupied with the Ford's faults would take the edge off his enjoyment of the Ford and would create a situation in which he would have tendencies to approach both his Ford and the Chevrolet. In order to behave in an adaptive way he must follow through on his choice. This follow-through is necessary in order that he be able to live comfortably with what he has done. To the extent that the choice was difficult and important this follow-through will involve the now familiar cognitive work of justifying what he did, i.e., dissonance reduction. To the extent that he is unable to justify his decision, he will continue to suffer postdecisional regret, a state that is presumably difficult to live with.

There appear to be two basic conditions that define commitment. Commitment exists to the extent that the person is unable to reverse his decision, i.e., that there are high psychological costs for doing so, and to the extent that the chosen behavior has future reward-cost implications for the person. Since irrevocability implies that there are costs involved in reversing the decision, both necessary conditions reduce to cost considerations.

A recent paper by Kiesler and Sakumura (1966) points up some confusion in the use of the term commitment. They equate commitment with voluntariness. Essentially their argument is that a person will be committed to a given behavior to the extent that he exercised freedom of choice in deciding whether or not to engage in that behavior. This use of the term commitment is in striking contrast to the one I have suggested above in which commitment was defined in terms of the costs of engaging in and of undoing or changing the behavior. In my use of the concept, voluntariness tends to enter the picture to the extent that it results in cost implications for the person. If anything, commitment will be greater to the extent that the person had *no* freedom of choice since it is generally easier, although not always so, for the person to change his behavior to the extent that he had freedom of choice in originally deciding whether or not to engage in it. Furthermore, other things being equal, the more justified was the decision to start with, the greater will be the anticipated cost in changing it. The person is thus *committed* to continuing to engage in the behavior.

I believe that Kiesler and Sakumura's problem lies in a confusion between commitment and *conviction* which derives from the context in which they employ their commitment concept. The subject in their experiment was induced, either for a small or a large monetary reward, to read a statement espousing an attitude with which he agreed. Kiesler and Sakumura argue that when the subject read the statement for a small reward he was more committed than he was when he read it for a large reward. Committed to what? To the act of reading the statement or to the attitude expressed in the statement? Kiesler and Sakumura do not specify whether it is the attitude or the reading to which the person is committed. They start off by using the concept as Brehm and Cohen had defined it as referring to behavior but then slip into using it to refer to the person's commitment to an attitude for which something like 'depth of conviction' is more appropriate. Only by distinguishing between behavioral commitment and attitudinal conviction can we ever hope to understand the way in which attitudes accommodate to behavior, which is the central problem originally spelled out by Festinger (1957).

Thus, to the extent that a person voluntarily agrees to advocate an opinion, he is not necessarily committed to the advocation itself but he will tend, because of the minimal pressure, to add 'justifications' for having agreed to advocate the opinion. As a great deal of research has shown, attitudinal adjustments can provide such justification. If he was originally in disagreement with the position advocated, the person will tend to change toward the advocated position, whereas if he was originally in agreement with it, his depth of conviction in the opinion will be increased. An implicit assumption here is that even in the case of proattitudinal behavior there is some cost to engaging in the behavior, i.e., the effort required. The person's cognitions concerning cost will be discrepant with the cognition that he is engaging in the behavior. The monetary or other reward offered would provide consistent cognitions which would counterbalance the discrepant ones. Given this assumption I cannot accept Kiesler and Sakumura's verdict that dissonance theory does not apply to proattitudinal advocacy.

My purpose in belaboring the Kiesler and Sakumura use of the term commitment is to clarify what I mean by commitment and to indicate how commitment and voluntariness may be interrelated.

EXPERIMENTAL EVIDENCE

The two basic features of commitment are irrevocability and reward-cost implications. If either of these factors is missing from a decision there will be no sense of psychological commitment to it. Oddly enough there is no good evidence on the effects of irrevocability. Two years ago a student of mine started an experiment on this issue but never finished it. The subject in that experiment evaluated items of haberdashery and was then asked to make a decision as to which one of two of these items he would like to receive as a gift. In one treatment the decision was presented as tentative since he could at a later time change his mind whereas in the other treatment the decision was final and irrevocable. Following the Brehm-type format of having the subject rerate the alternatives after the decision, we found a trend, although the Ns were too small for it to be reliable, indicating that the alternatives spread apart in value (the dissonance effect) only when the decision was irrevocable. I intend to complete the experiment in the near future.

A decision may be irrevocable, but the person may not be certain that he has really rejected the nonchosen alternative. Until the person is certain of this there are no clear reward-cost implications for him. He will therefore not attempt to maintain an unequivocal behavioral orientation toward his choice and consequently, he will not accommodate cognitively to the decision. Evidence on this point comes from experiments by Jecker (1964a) and Allen (1964) in which the subjects, who were high school girls, evaluated 15 phonograph records and then made a choice between two of the records. In the Jecker experiment the subject was led to believe, before the choice, that she might possibly get both records and this would be determined by chance. Half of the subjects were told that their chances of getting both records were 1 in 20 whereas the other half were told that the chances were 19 in 20. After the subject made her choice, she drew a slip of paper from a box, the chance event, which indicated in one condition that she was to receive only the record she chose whereas in the other condition she was to receive both records. The subject was then asked to rerate all of the records including the ones involved in the choice.

The results were striking. Spreading apart in value of the choice alternatives (the dissonance effect) occurred when the subject received only the chosen record but not when she received both records. This was true regardless of whether before the choice there had been a 1 in 20 or a 19 in 20 chance of her getting the second record. Since it is impossible from the data to tell if the reevaluation in the Chosen Only treatment occurred after the choice or after the subject found out that she would get only the chosen record, both '1 in 20' and '19 in 20' treatments were run in which the subject was asked to rerate the choice alternatives after the choice but before finding out whether she was to get one or both records. In both treatments there was no postdecisional spreading apart of the alternatives. Even when there was only a five per cent chance of getting the second record, postdecisional accommodation appears to have been held in abeyance!

The subsequent experiment by Allen was designed to counterpose two possible interpretations of the Jecker findings. One interpretation assumes that the person will not accommodate to the decision unless he has definitely rejected one of the alternatives, whereas the other interpretation assumes that postdecisional accommodation will not occur as long as there is some uncertainty in the outcome regardless of whether or not one of the alternatives was rejected. These interpretations were counterposed by independently varying uncertainty of outcome and whether or not the decision involved rejection of the nonchosen alternative. Allen used the same

Jecker procedure with four treatment combinations. In the Chosen Only condition the subject was told simply that she would receive the record she chose. This is the typical decision condition used in the previous research and in one of the conditions in the Jecker experiment. Under this decision situation postdecisional accommodation is the typical finding. In the Nothing or Chosen condition the subject was told that there was a 50 per cent chance that she would receive the record she chose. Here the nonchosen alternative was definitely rejected, but there was uncertainty about whether or not she would receive the record she had chosen. The Chosen or Both condition was like two of the Jecker conditions except that the subject was told that there was a 50 per cent chance (rather than a 5 or 95 per cent chance) that she would receive the nonchosen record in addition to the chosen one. In this condition, therefore, the decision did not necessarily involve the rejection of the nonchosen alternative. In the Nothing, Chosen, or Both condition the subject had equal chances of getting nothing, of getting the record she chose, and of getting both records. Here, therefore, there was both uncertainty about the outcome as well as the possibility of getting the nonchosen record. In all four conditions the subject rated the records before the choice and then again immediately after the choice and before the subject in the three uncertain conditions knew what the outcome would be. If the uncertainty interpretation of the Jecker data is tenable, we should find spreading apart in the Chosen Only condition, where there was no uncertainty, and in none of the other conditions, whereas if the definiteness of rejection interpretation is more tenable we should find spreading apart not merely in the Chosen Only but also in the Nothing or Chosen condition since in both of these conditions the subject *knew for certain* that she would not receive the nonchosen alternative.

The data show clear support for the latter interpretation. Thus, it is only when the decision commits the person to giving something up that we find the typical postdecisional accommodation to the choice. In our terms, it is then that the person must maintain an unequivocal behavioral orientation toward the chosen alternative since it is only then that the fact of his having given up something valuable will tend to intrude on his enjoyment, or possible enjoyment of the chosen alternative. Giving up the nonchosen alternative falls into the general category of reward-cost implications of the choice. Presumably other kinds of reward-cost implications will produce similar effects.

If commitment is a necessary condition for the arousal of postdecisional dissonance, we would expect that a decision between two alternatives that involved a mere statement of preference would tend to arouse less dissonance than a decision involving a choice in which the person would actually be giving up the nonchosen alternative. A pure statement of preference would presumably arouse no dissonance at all. It is difficult, however, to realize its pure form in a laboratory situation in which the subject, at the very minimum, commits his ego to the choice vis a vis the experimenter. He may feel that somehow the decision reflects upon him.

In a recent experiment (Gerard, Blevans, & Malcolm, 1964) we contrasted a preference decision with a decision that involved giving up the nonchosen alternative. The subject, who was a high school art student, was asked to rank order 15 paintings and was then given a choice between two of them. In one treatment he was asked merely to indicate which of the

two he thought was nicer and in the other treatment he was asked to indicate which of the two he would like to receive as a gift. He reranked the
paintings again after the choice. We manipulated three other factors in the
experiment but I will consider only one of these since it is the only one that
bears directly on our argument. Since there is an implicit assumption in much
of the dissonance research that the subject has a positive self-evaluation, we
manipulated the subject's self-ability estimate through false performance
feedback on a prior art judgment task. Some subjects were told that their
ability was superior, some that it was average, some that it was below
average, and still others received no ability evaluation whatsoever. We predicted that the choice alternatives would spread apart postdecisionally only
when the subject had a positive self-ability estimate and that he would show
regret, which would be manifested by a coming-together or convergence of
the choice alternatives postdecisionally, where he had a negative self-ability
estimate. These effects would tend to occur only where there was a commitment of some sort. As in the Jecker and Allen experiments, if the choice
involved a clear case of giving something up we would expect to see accommodation effects that would be consistent with the subject's ability
evaluation.

The Effect of Ability and the Gift-Preference
Instructions on the Change in Relative
Ranking Between the Choice Alternatives. *

	Ability			
	High	Average	Low	No Information
Gift	+1.14(7)	—1.00(4)	—1.20(5)	+1.75(4)
Preference	+0.60(5)	—0.28(7)	—0.57(7)	—0.50(2)

* Adapted from Gerard, Blevans, and Malcolm (1964). A positive number indicates spreading apart, a "dissonance effect" whereas a negative number indicates convergence, a "regret effect." N's are indicated in parentheses.

The data, which are presented in the Table, confirm this prediction. In
the Table a positive number indicates spreading apart in rank whereas a
negative number indicates convergence. In the Gift condition we see a
linear effect of ability on postdecisional accommodation as measured by
the change in ranking of the choice alternatives from before to after the
decision. There is a similar linear trend in the Preference condition although
it is much less steep. Presumably a statement of painting preference by an
art student to the experimenter has some reward-cost implications which we
were not able to specify. To the extent that there were such implications we
would expect to find postdecisional accommodation. That there is spreading
apart in the No Information condition appears to indicate that an art student
will tend to have a positive self-ability estimate.

In describing the above experiment we alluded to possible reward-cost
implications for the subject in confronting the experimenter. In an earlier experiment by Deutsch and Gerard (1955) there are findings, as reported by
Gerard (1964), that bear on such effects of a public confrontation. In the
original conformity experiments by Asch (1956) the subject experienced
unanimous disagreement most of the time from a group of peers on a
sequence of unambiguous line judgments. The subject and the others, who

were confederates of the experimenter, were in full view of each other while the judgments were being made. Asch found that if a subject maintained his independence of the others at the outset by reporting the correct judgment, he tended to remain independent throughout the entire series of judgments. If, on the other hand, he tended to conform early in the series, he continued to conform. The amount of evidence in the form of the others' judgments that disconfirmed the subject's own judgments increased with successive disagreement. We would thus expect that the subject's confidence in his ability would decrease with time. Therefore, the initially independent subject would tend to give in to the group at some point. That this did not occur is puzzling.

This puzzle may be solved if we assume that when the subject is in a face-to-face confrontation with the others he is responding not only to the discrepancy in information about the stimulus but also to what he believes the others may be expecting of him. If he initially commits himself publicly to a discrepant stand he would tend to 'lose face' in his own eyes and in the eyes of his peers if he yielded on subsequent trials. This public commitment would then tend to fix his behavior in such a way that he would continue to be independent. We would expect that the confidence an independent subject has in his judgments would decrease with continued disagreement if he were not being held to his independent stand by his public commitment and we would therefore expect him, at some point in the sequence of judgments, to begin to yield to the others. Thus, if we could compare a situation in which the subject has not been publicly identified with his judgments with one in which he is so identified, we would predict that in the anonymous situation, the initially independent subject would tend at some point to begin to yield whereas he would tend to remain adamant in the public situation.

The Deutsch and Gerard experiment offered the opportunity to examine this interpretation of the puzzle in the original Asch results since some of the subjects were run in a face-to-face condition and others were run in cubicles and their identity during the experiment was not revealed.

The data clearly support the proposed interpretation of the Asch results. During the first series of 18 trials 13 subjects in the anonymous and 12 in the face-to-face treatment turned in an errorless performance. During the second 18 trials only four of these remained adamant in the anonymous treatment as compared with nine in the face-to-face treatment. This seems to indicate that confidence may in fact decrease for initially independent subjects with continued disagreement. Also, in the anonymous condition the number of yields tends to be normally distributed. There are very few subjects who are either completely independent or who yield a great deal. In the face-to-face situation, on the other hand, there are relatively large numbers of subjects in both extreme categories. This again points to the role of commitment: conformers tend to conform a great deal and independent subjects continue to be independent. Conformity and independence in the face-to-face condition appear to be determined both by the subject's confidence in his ability and by his having made a public commitment.

To reiterate, commitment is a necessary condition for the arousal of dissonance. The sufficient condition is that the decision he has made confront the subject with a cognitive discrepancy. Commitment involves two basic features: irrevocability and reward-cost implications. The latter feature can be satisfied in a number of ways that include the rejection of something desirable or the implications of the decision for one's ego. Both of these features induce in the person the requirement of maintaining an unequivocal behavioral orientation to the decision. This in turn tends to produce the cognitive work referred to as dissonance reduction.

Growing out of the Gestalt tradition, most theories of cognitive consistency such as balance theory (Heider, 1958) and dissonance theory (Festinger, 1957) assume that the tendency toward cognitive consistency is a built-in autochthonous tendency toward the good Gestalt. We have assumed, however, that the maintenance of unequivocal behavioral orientations, since they are adaptive, is the basis for supportive cognitive work since that work may help maintain the person on a course of action he has chosen. Furthermore, unless a cognition has reward-cost implications for the chosen course of action it will have no effect on the person's cognitive work and will itself be unaffected.

CHAPTER 39

Discussion: Commitments about Commitment

Elliot Aronson

The three papers in the current section present a wide variety of interesting material and an equally wide variety of interesting problems. Zimbardo's paper provides an excellent summary of some of the recent work linking dissonance-reducing behavior to biological drives and social motives. Brehm's pioneering finding that people who commit themselves to a thirst-producing situation in the absence of an abundance of justification report that they feel less thirsty and actually drink less water than people in a High Justification (Low Dissonance) condition has now been bolstered by the results of several carefully controlled experiments involving thirst, hunger, and pain. Social psychologists tend to be made a little uncomfortable by total reliance on attitude questionnaires as dependent variables. Thus, one of the truly impressive aspects of Zimbardo's report is the fact that it describes not only attitudinal responses, but behaviors as well (i.e., drinking behavior of thirsty subjects). Moreover, these experiments go still further by employing physiological indices of hunger (free fatty acids) and of pain (GSR). The movement away from complete dependence upon verbal and questionnaire responses is both a healthy sign and an important methodological advance.

Zimbardo also has the perspicacity to see an interesting methodological problem that runs through much of the research that he has reviewed—the problem of the results being too good. Superficially, this hardly seems like a problem to those who toil in the vineyard of experimental social psychology. Given the lack of standardization of our experimental variables and the lack of control over the subject population that characterize most research in this area, experimenters generally do not worry about results being too good. But Zimbardo's concern is justified. Specifically, Zimbardo observed that in many of the experiments which he has reviewed people in a high drive state who are experiencing dissonance (i.e., who have committed themselves to be in that state) not only experience the predicted lower drive than people who are in a high drive state with low dissonance (i.e., low commitment), but also seem to be *less* motivated even than individuals in a low motivation control condition. This is strange indeed. Theoretically, it has been assumed that in order to avoid feeling stupid about committing himself to an unpleasant situation, the individual makes that situation seem less unpleasant than it really is; e.g., a water-deprived person experiencing dissonance seems less thirsty than a water-deprived person without dissonance. But, within this conceptual paradigm, how can we account for the fact that he is less thirsty than someone who has not even been deprived of water? To me, this is far more interesting than most methodological problems because it suggests the possibility that we may be on the verge of a reconceptualization of the phenomenon. To his credit, Zimbardo offers no pat explanations for these data; rather, he suggests further research to help pin down exactly what is going on. This may well be one of the more exciting lines of research in contemporary social psychology.

Zimbardo takes the position that much of the research testing predictions from the theory of cognitive dissonance is based upon the variable of commitment. Indeed, he maintains that dissonance theory is little more than a theory of face-saving. In this regard, his ideas on dissonance theory are closely allied to those I expressed elsewhere in this volume (pp. 23-24). At the same time it should be clear that Zimbardo avoids *equating* dissonance theory with a theory of commitment. That is, although he suggests that dissonance theory almost always involves self-justification following commitment, he does not assert that the two are identical or isomorphic. In his essay, Harold Gerard carries this one step further and maintains that there is no dissonance without commitment. The seminal experiment for Gerard is one that he performed with Blevans and Malcolm in which it was found that subjects who truly committed themselves (i.e., irrevocably gave up the unchosen alternative) manifested far more evidence of dissonance than subjects who simply announced a preference (without giving anything up).

Gerard's position stands in contrast to the position expressed by Charles Kiesler that commitment, in and of itself, has no motivating properties and that dissonance and commitment can and should be separated from one another. In my judgment, the major aspect of the disagreement between Gerard and Kiesler does not rest as much on a major difference in the way they conceptualize commitment as on a difference in the operational definitions they employ. Conceptually, Kiesler, in his study with Sakumura, suggests that "the effect of commitment is to make an act less changeable" (1966, p. 349). This is not so terribly far from Gerard's definition in terms of irrevocability. However, Gerard takes issue with the empirical context in which the variable was employed by Kiesler and Sakumura; Gerard maintains that it was conviction rather than commitment that was varied. Clearly, Kiesler does not agree.

In the Kiesler-Sakumura experiment the subjects were induced to read a communication which was consonant with their own opinion, either for a high reward or for a low reward. They then were faced with a countercommunication. The results showed that people in the Low Reward condition were more resistant to this countercommunication. In addition, Kiesler and Sakumura found that unless this counterargument was presented, there was no difference between the attitudes of the subjects in the High Reward condition and the subjects in the Low Reward condition. It is primarily these data which lead Kiesler to conclude that mere commitment is not motivating but does affect resistance to cognitive change. According to Kiesler and Sakumura, since prior to being exposed to the countercommunication the subjects underwent commitment but no dissonance and did not change their attitudes, then commitment itself has no motivating properties. The commitment resulted only in resistance to change.

It should be emphasized, however, that these data can be viewed as being highly consistent with similar data derived from experiments on counterattitudinal advocacy. In the counterattitudinal advocacy experiments, people were paid varying amounts of money for making statements *dissonant* with their own point of view; the less the justification, the greater the tendency for them to believe what they have just said. It involves only a minor stretch for dissonance theory to suggest that if a person makes a consonant statement, although he may experience no dissonance at the time, he will experience dissonance when subsequently exposed to a counterargument. In this situation, insufficient justification should lead to greater resistance to change. Thus, although Kiesler argues for a conceptual separation between dissonance and commitment, as he well knows, he has not accomplished this in his experiment with Sakumura.

As is apparent from a reading of their essays, Gerard and Kiesler disagree on many things; all of these divergences need not be repeated here. But the crux of their disagreement involves the extent to which dissonance and commitment are and should be separated. In consonance with my present role as editor, I find my own position somewhere between Gerard's and Kiesler's. While I agree with Gerard's general position that commitment is an important aspect of dissonance theory, I do not believe that it is necessary for the arousal of dissonance. There appear to be clear predictions from dissonance theory that do not easily fit the commitment paradigm. For example, consider the experiments on communicator credibility and communication discrepancy (Zimbardo, 1960; Bergin, 1962; Aronson, Turner, & Carlsmith, 1963). Aronson *et al.* reasoned that subjects would experience maximum dissonance if presented with a communication which was highly discrepant from their own opinion if it was attributed to a source of high credibility. Consequently, with a high-credibility source (as opposed to one of low credibility) there should be a positive linear relationship between discrepancy of communication and attitude change. The results confirmed this prediction. Since the subject's initial expression of opinion was not stated publicly, these data cannot be easily attributed to commitment, nor can they be handled as adequately by any theory but dissonance theory.

At the same time, while possible, it is not altogether obvious to me that any great theoretical advance will be accomplished by separating dissonance from commitment as Kiesler advocates. Whether it is more parsimonious and *clearer* to continue to view commitment as a major variable under the rubric of dissonance theory or to separate the two remains a moot question. But, as Kiesler has stated, it is an empirical question as well. Kiesler suggests that in order to determine whether or not commitment has any importance irrespective of dissonance, one needs to vary the two orthogonally within the same experimental design. Kiesler is setting himself to this task in a workmanlike manner; specifically, he is currently completing an experiment in which he feels that the design allows him to assess the effects of dissonance and commitment independently. The results of this and future experiments on this issue should prove enlightening.

E. DISCONFIRMED EXPECTANCIES
AND BAD DECISIONS

Several years ago Elliot Aronson suggested that experimental demonstrations of dissonance reduction had been based upon the tacit assumption that people have high self concepts. He maintained that researchers had unwittingly assumed that people expect to perform well, to make reasonable decisions, and to tell the truth. Aronson reasoned that if a person had low self-esteem or knew he was a pathological liar, he would *not* experience dissonance if he failed, purchased an inferior car, or lied to a fellow student. In collaboration with Merrill Carlsmith and John Darley he performed a series of experiments which showed (a) that people who expect failure turn their backs on success and actively behave in a manner that guarantees a poor performance, (b) that a disconfirmed expectancy produced negative affect, and (c) that people who expect to perform an unpleasant task, when subsequently given their choice between performing that task and an innocuous one, tend to choose the expected albeit unpleasant task.

A number of other people have since pursued experimentation in this area, among them William Watts and Irwin Silverman. Their papers in this section provide critical examinations of a whole series of experiments related to the disconfirmation of expectancies. They discuss reasons for conflicting results and spotlight some of the methodological problems a researcher encounters when he attempts to demonstrate the existence of a phenomenon in a situation where strong opposing drives are known to exist.

A separate outgrowth of the original line of reasoning and research on expectancies concerns the consequences of bad decisions. In their essay, Carlsmith and Jonathan Freedman follow the suggestion that "nobody's perfect" to its logical conclusion, playing it back into dissonance theory and coming out with some intriguing suggestions for a modification of the theory. Interestingly enough, Watts' contribution in this section independently touches on a similar analysis and reaches a similar conclusion.

CHAPTER 40

Predictability and Pleasure: Reactions to the Disconfirmation of Expectancies

William A. Watts

University of California, Berkeley

Research on the effects of expectancy and man's desire for a predictable environment received considerable impetus from Aronson and Carlsmith's (1962) extension of Festinger's (1957) theory of cognitive dissonance. According to this theory, if an individual expects a certain event to occur and it does not, he will experience dissonance since his cognition that he expects the event to occur is inconsistent with his knowledge that the event did not occur. Because dissonance is presumably an unpleasant psychological state, disconfirmations should result in negative affect and, therefore, be avoided when possible; or, if disconfirmations do occur, should lead to a cognitive restructuring on the part of the person so as to maximize consonant elements.

Expectations about future events form the basis for most purposive behavior; hence, it is not uncommon for a person to have made a considerable commitment (both psychologically and behaviorally) to an expected event. Should the event fail to materialize, it is clear that the dissonance experienced should be greater when the person has prepared for it, both behaviorally as well as psychologically, since the cognitions of his wasted preparation add to the number of dissonant elements. Hence, the greater the cost in effort or unpleasantness of the preparation, the stronger the motivation should be to avoid disconfirmation; or, in the aftermath of disconfirmation, to reduce the resulting dissonance or justify the preparation.

For the sake of clarity, the more relevant studies have been categorized into those involving the effects of expectancy without behavioral preparation and those for which the subjects had prepared. After a brief review of these studies, many of which have been covered elsewhere (e.g., McGuire, 1966a), attention will be turned to certain troublesome methodological problems inherent in this area of research.

THE EFFECTS OF EXPECTANCY WITHOUT BEHAVIORAL PREPARATION

Altering Performance to Maintain Consistency.

One of the most controversial of these studies was that of Aronson and Carlsmith (1962). For four sections of a test of "social sensitivity" subjects were led to believe that their performance was either high or low. Then, on the fifth section of the test, half of the subjects were given performance scores inconsistent with the expectation they had developed during the previous four sections. The other half of the subjects were told that their scores were such as to be consistent. Subjects were then asked, on the pretext that the experimenter had forgotten to time that section of the test, to repeat it as if they had not taken it before. Those subjects whose performance was consistent with their expectancy changed fewer responses on the repeated version than did those whose performance was inconsistent. The interaction effect between expectation and performance was significant beyond the .001 level. More importantly, subjects in the Low Expectancy, High Performance condition changed significantly ($p < .01$) more responses than their counterparts who were low in both expectancy and performance. Since subjects whose performance was high would almost inevitably lower their performance level by changing many responses on the retake, whereas their Low Performance counterparts would stand to gain from many changes, these results are directly opposite to what would be expected from an achievement-maximization principle; namely, that Low Expectancy, Low Performance subjects would change more responses, thus raising their performance level. This paradoxical effect offers strong support for the predicted sacrifice of achievement satisfaction for the sake of consistency.

Since Aronson and Carlsmith had stressed the reliability and validity of the test, the results might be due to the subjects trying to do the experimenter a favor by responding consistently; however, the authors felt that available indirect evidence did not support this interpretation. Nevertheless, this and other "demand characteristic" (Orne, 1962) explanations of the results were soon resurrected and tested in a number of studies.

Ward and Sandvold (1963) deleted the emphasis upon validity and reliability and obtained only a strong performance effect so that subjects maximized their achievement irrespective of expectancy. However, this deletion may also have weakened the subject's expectancy, since a test of questionable validity and reliability could easily be derogated as not providing a true measure of his performance level. If so, the inconsistent feedback on the fifth trial would not constitute a violation of expected performance.

Silverman and Marcantonio (1965) emphasized reliability and validity of the test for half of the subjects and deleted it for the other half. The results supported neither a dissonance-avoidance nor a demand-characteristic explanation and were directly opposite to predictions based on the latter. One might attribute these discrepant results to the fact that Aronson and Carlsmith's subjects were paid, which should have heightened their tendency to be kind to the experimenter, whereas subjects in the latter studies were not. However, this conjecture received no support by Lowin and Epstein (1965). After failing to replicate Aronson and Carlsmith's original findings while using volunteer subjects, they tested the effects of paying subjects as well as the effects of status of the experimenter (paid subjects, high-status experimenter vs. volunteer subjects, low-status experimenter) and obtained no evidence of an expectancy effect in either condition.

Cottrell (1965) reasoned that Ward and Sandvold's instructions implied that the subject's classmates would learn his score, thus increasing his desire to perform well and overriding any expectancy effect. Therefore, he manipulated the subject's belief as to whether his score would be made public or kept confidential, but obtained no support for the hypothesis that the expectancy × performance interaction would be contingent upon the public-private variable. Instead, a significant expectancy × performance interaction was obtained, thus replicating Aronson and Carlsmith's finding. The significant interaction, however, was mainly due to the High Expectancy conditions; among subjects in the crucial Low Expectancy conditions, those receiving low performance scores changed slightly more responses than their presumably dissonant counterparts who received unexpectedly high scores.

Another type of artifact, differential recall, was suggested by Waterman and Ford (1965) as a possible explanation of the paradoxical effect obtained by Aronson and Carlsmith. They hypothesized, and found, that subjects in the Low Expectancy conditions recalled fewer of their responses. Hence, they argue that subjects in the Low Expectancy condition who suddenly received high-performance feedback would inevitably change more of their responses on the retake than their High Expectancy counterparts because they could not remember their previous responses. Similarly, even though Low Expectancy, Low Performance subjects might want to change their scores in an upward direction, they would be handicapped by being unable to recall their previous responses. This sounds very compelling on the surface and, indeed, could account for a performance × expectancy interaction such as Cottrell (1965) obtained; but, as Hendrick (1966) has already pointed out, it cannot account for Aronson and Carlsmith's finding that within the Low Expectancy conditions, inconsistent high performers changed significantly more scores than consistent low performers since the recall scores for these two groups were almost identical. Lowin and Epstein (1965) also found evidence of poorer recall among Low Expectancy subjects as did Brock, Edelman, Edwards, and Schuck (1965). But when Lowin and Epstein corrected Aronson and Carlsmith's results for differential recall, it strengthened, rather than weakened, the consistency interpretation of Aronson and Carlsmith's data.

In a different context, Conlon (1965) partitioned subjects on the basis of predispositional chronic level of self-esteem in mathematics .(high and low) and then orthogonally manipulated expectation of success or failure by feedback over trials. The subjects chronically low in self-esteem would be expected to have developed over years of experience an elaborate system of rationalizations excusing and even glorifying poor mathematics performance. Hence, for those subjects low in both chronic and acute (manipulated) self-esteem, there was a stronger basis for predicting consistency-seeking behavior since sudden success would be dissonant not only with their induced expectancy, but with their various rationalizations for failure (e.g., people good in mathematics are bores). No such results were obtained, however; rather, the data conformed to a straightforward achievement maximization and inattention interpretation. Conlon also tested differential recall introducing a no-feedback condition as well as the confirm and disconfirm conditions, but obtained no results that could account for the Aronson and Carlsmith finding.

Despite these repeated failures to replicate Aronson and Carlsmith's finding, the picture is not entirely negative. Brock *et al.* (1965) successfully replicated it once under the original conditions and once while reducing the number of blocks of trials by half. When in two other experiments information feedback was given trial-by-trial, rather than after blocks of trials, they failed to obtain the paradoxical effect. Three additional studies, two varying feedback rate (trial-by-trial vs. block-by-block) in expectancy and performance trials with the third using different stimuli (judging color brightness), offered no support for the predicted effect.

Volunteering to Perform an Unpleasant Task as a Function of Expectation.

Aronson, Carlsmith, and Darley (1963) demonstrated that expectancy alone is sufficient to increase the probability of a person's choosing the expected task even though it may be more unpleasant than the alternative. Subjects performed two tasks, one unpleasant and one neutral. Some subjects expected to repeat the unpleasant task, others the neutral. These expectancies were held for either 20 minutes (termed the Strong Expectancy condition) or for seven seconds (called the Weak Expectancy condition). All subjects were then given their choice as to which task they wished to repeat. For subjects in the Strong Expectancy condition, 41 per cent of those expecting the unpleasant task chose it, while no subject expecting the neutral task chose the unpleasant. This difference was significant at the .02 level. The 'strength' of the expectancy also contributed significantly to choosing the unpleasant task ($p = .04$).

Goldberg (1965) replicated the study and obtained no support whatsoever for the predicted effect of expectancy. On the other hand, in the presence of a confederate who gave his choice first, the combination of conformity pressures and expectation was sufficient to cause 5 out of 20 subjects to choose the unpleasant but expected task.

In a study involving preparation (unpleasant or neutral) for a painful event that failed to occur, Watts (1965) found a discernible, although insignificant, relationship between unpleasantness of the preparation and volunteering to return at a later time to go through the painful experience.

Negative Affect Resulting from Disconfirmed Expectancies.

An experiment by Carlsmith and Aronson (1963) provides evidence that the disconfirmation of even a negative expectancy is unpleasant and generalizes to other aspects of the experiment. They reasoned that if a person expects a particular event (X) and, instead, a different event (Y) occurs, he will experience dissonance; and, assuming this negative hedonic state generalizes to objects in the experiment, he will judge (Y) to be less pleasant than if he had no previous expectancy. Subjects predicted on the basis of rather obvious cues whether each solution they were to taste in a purported psychophysics experiment would be sweet or bitter. Disconfirmations consisted of the experimenter periodically giving the signal for one solution while presenting the other. In close accord with the experimental hypothesis, the differences between incorrect predictions without an expectancy and disconfirmation (incorrect with a strong expectancy) were significant at the .02 level for the sweet-tasting solution and beyond the .001 level for the bitter solution.

Sampson and Sibley (1965), using a somewhat different design, were able to replicate these results for ratings of the sweet solution but not the bitter. They suggest the difference may be due to the greater potency of disconfirmation for subjects in the Carlsmith and Aronson study where each incorrect trial cost the subject $1.00 and without which effects of disconfirmation may have failed to reach a just-noticeable difference in unpleasantness above the already foul-tasting bitter solution.

BEHAVIORAL COMMITMENT TO THE EXPECTED EVENT:
THE PSYCHOLOGY OF UNNECESSARY PREPARATION

It is clear that a stronger prediction of unpleasantness resulting from disconfirmed expectancies can be derived when the subject has undertaken some preparation in readiness for the expected event. In this case, not only is the cognition that the event will not occur dissonant with his belief that it would, but it is also dissonant with the individual's knowledge that his preparation has been in vain.

Two field studies involved the disconfirmation of an expected event for which people holding the expectancy had undergone considerable preparation. Festinger, Riecken, and Schachter (1956) studied a small group of people who predicted the end of the world on a certain date. Most of the members had made a considerable investment in preparation for this expected event. After it was unequivocally disconfirmed, the group showed a sudden interest in proselyting which had been absent prior to the disconfirmation. Mass proselyting would provide an effective means for reducing dissonance in this situation since trying to convince others might bolster the subject's own belief through the improvisation of new arguments supporting his side, etc. Furthermore, when successful, it bolsters his faith to see others come over to his side, and the converts in turn will feed back supportive information to him. A second study of a similar group by Hardyck and Braden (1962) failed to replicate this finding. Proselyting did not occur after the disconfirmation of their prediction of Armageddon. The situation would appear to fulfill the requirements for dissonance arousal and proselyting, although the authors suggest that perhaps the requirements really were not met since this group was awarded a medal by Civil Defense authorities and because nuclear holocaust (the predicted event) is a possibility feared by all. Hence, they suffered little derision compared to the former prophetic group, and, consequently, dissonance may have been of a lesser magnitude and resolved by less extreme means.

Watts (1965) manipulated unpleasantness of preparation for an expected event (painful electric shock) and choice in undergoing this preparation. From a dissonance-theory standpoint, those subjects undergoing the more unpleasant preparation should experience greater dissonance when the event failed to occur than their neutral-preparation counterparts since the cognitions concerning its unpleasantness are inconsistent with the knowledge that it has been rendered useless. Furthermore, subjects who prepared of their own volition should feel more dissonance than those having no choice in the matter as they are stuck with the knowledge that they could have avoided the unnecessary preparation.

Subjects might reduce their dissonance or justify their wasted preparation in a number of ways, including the following: minimizing the unpleasantness of the preparation, or their choice in preparing; enhancing the value of the experiment and their willingness to recruit other subjects; volunteering to return and complete the experiment at a later time; and, finally, magnifying the unpleasant characteristics of the expected event (i.e., it was so dreadful that the only rational course of action was to prepare).

The different conditions of pleasantness of preparation failed to produce the cognitive changes expected. Choice consistently affected the dependent variables in a direction opposite to that predicted so that subjects taking the preparation of their own volition thought the experiment was less valuable ($p < .05$), were less willing to recruit other subjects ($p < .01$), and perceived the preparation as somewhat more unpleasant than their counterparts for whom preparation was mandatory.

Preparatory effort was again varied (Gailon & Watts, unpublished data) in the context of getting ready for a test in a manner similar to that employed by Yaryan and Festinger (1961). Experimentally-naive high school subjects were used, half of whom spent 5 minutes preparing by looking at a list of transformations of the English alphabet into three-digit numbers while the other half spent 20 minutes memorizing this list. After preparation, half of the subjects were given a plausible pretext why they would be unable to take the test while the others were informed that they would be given the test shortly. At this point, the dependent variables were measured. No significant effects were obtained from the different degrees of effort in preparing, although a check on the effort manipulation showed it to be very successful.

It is strange that in two separate attempts we have been unable to obtain any effects caused by differences in preparation when they are so clearly predicted from the theory. It may be that, although the manipulations were successful, the differences in unpleasantness or effort involved in the preparation seemed unimportant compared to facing the event unprepared, and any effects were overshadowed by the surprise reaction to the disconfirmation.

Yaryan and Festinger (1961) did obtain differences in subjects' perceived probability that they personally would be given a test (with a stated objective probability of .5) as a function of effort expended in preparing, with subjects who had undergone a more effortful preparation increasing their belief that they would be given the test. Although Johnson and Steiner (1965) reported data suggesting that this effect is more likely due to the subject's interpretation of the experimenter's behavior, rather than to justification of the effort expended (a charge previously made by Chapanis and Chapanis, 1964), a recent study by Arrowood and Ross (1966) questions this alternate interpretation. These investigators found that the mere anticipation of expending effort was sufficient to increase the subject's belief that he personally would take the test and they marshalled compelling arguments against the 'experimenter concern' interpretation of their data.

Watts (1966) hypothesized that a logical decision to prepare for an event that is presumably certain to happen but which, due to a capricious universe, fails to occur, will not result in dissonance reduction or attempts to justify the preparation. More likely, frustration and anger would result. However, if an individual decides to prepare for an event whose occurrence is clearly problematical, one would expect him to feel self-reproach for having acted rashly and to make strong attempts to justify the previous act when the event did not occur. To test this conjecture, three independent variables were manipulated: probability of an unpleasant event (.50 vs. .95), choice vs. no choice in preparing, and outcome (whether the event prepared for did or did not occur). As predicted, when the event did not occur and the preparation proved unnecessary, subjects who had prepared under the .50, but not the .95 probability condition, manifested dissonance reduction or attempted to justify their actions. This relationship was evinced in subjects' distortion of the unpleasantness of the preparation taken as a consequence of their decisions, exaggeration of their fear of the event for which they had prepared, and in a composite measure of their usage of the various modes of dissonance reduction.

These data would suggest that if a person cannot foresee the negative outcome at the time of decision and, consequently, feels that he made an intelligent and rational decision on the basis of the information available, he will feel no need to defend his actions. If this is correct, disconfirmed expectancies should not result in cognitive restructuring in order to reduce dissonance unless other factors are present which make the disconfirmation ego-involving. To elaborate briefly, even if the event had seemed certain, disconfirmation might threaten the subject's self-esteem if he felt that he should have foreseen this possibility (if the majority of people thought that the event would not occur, or thought the belief to be absurd, etc.). For further discussion of the role of ego involvement or defensiveness see, for example, Deutsch, Krauss, and Rosenau (1962); the discussion section of Carlsmith and Aronson (1963); or McGuire and Millman's (1965) comparison of self-esteem theory with dissonance theory (in their discussion section).

Another factor that seemed important in studies of cognitive reorganization following disconfirmed expectancies was the time of measurement of the dependent variables. Festinger and Walster (in Festinger, 1964b, pp. 97-127) have hypothesized a brief period of regret prior to dissonance reduction. It would seem likely that upon receiving the information that an event for which an individual had been preparing would not occur, the first reaction would be one of surprise and regret. However, since regret or negative affect is itself unpleasant, we might expect that, over time, the average person begins to make the best of a bad situation by finding other uses for the preparation, minimizing its unpleasantness, etc. (although, no doubt, with enormous individual differences). Gailon and Watts (1967) tested this conjecture by manipulating, in the context of preparing for a test, the probability of the test (.50 or 1.00) and time of measurement after subjects learned that they would not take the test (immediate or 20-minute delay). In one of the more direct modes of dissonance reduction, minimizing the effort expended in preparing, a significant interaction was obtained with subjects in the High Probability, 20-minute Delay and the Low Probability, Immediate Measurement conditions perceiving the preparatory effort as less difficult than subjects in the other two groups. On several other measures of justification of the preparation, only a main effect of probability was obtained, with those subjects who had prepared under low probability manifesting greater signs of dissonance reduction than their counterparts in the High Probability group. Unfortunately, certain methodological problems encountered in this first study rendered its interpretation ambiguous. A replication of the study, with these deficiencies corrected, offered further support for the hypothesis although, in this case, justification of the wasted preparation took the form of the subjects magnifying the difficulty of the test and their anxiety about taking it. Such exaggerations would effectively serve to justify the wasted preparation since, for an extremely difficult test, one could not afford to take the chance of not preparing. The fact that different modes of dissonance reduction were utilized in the two studies may reflect the extent to which subtle changes in the environmental cues predispose subjects to the use of one means of justification vs. another.

OVERVIEW AND PROBLEMS IN STUDYING EXPECTANCIES

Recent studies of expectancy conducted within the framework of cognitive dissonance have tried to demonstrate three kinds of effects: avoiding disconfirmation of even a negative expectancy, generalized negative affect resulting from the disconfirmation of an unpleasant expectancy, and cognitive restructuring following disconfirmation of an expectancy in order to increase consonant cognitions.

Of the numerous attempted replications of Aronson and Carlsmith's (1962) original study showing that subjects would lower their performance to be consistent with the expected level, only two (Brock et al., 1965) have been entirely successful and one (Cottrell, 1965) partly successful. On the other hand, the 'demand characteristic' explanations have fared no better. Evidence is balanced evenly on the question of whether a subject will volunteer to undergo a more unpleasant task because of a strong expectancy. Aronson, Carlsmith, and Darley (1963) showed clearly that he would, whereas Goldberg (1965) found that he would not. Clearly, at least one more replication is needed to avoid a stalemate. Somewhat stronger evidence has been obtained for the prediction that disconfirmed expectancies result in negative affect inasmuch as the original findings were partially replicated by Sampson and Sibley (1965).

Experimental studies of the aftermath of disconfirmed expectancies for which the subjects have prepared offer no support for an immediate dissonance-reducing cognitive reorganization so as to supply consonant cognitions. However, Gailon and Watts (1967) found some evidence that such a reorganization does occur after a period of time when the probability of the event had seemed very high. In contrast, subjects who prepare for an event whose occurrence is seen as clearly problematical at the time of preparation show immediate manifestations of dissonance reduction.

While this area of research is certainly disquieting because of the numerous failures to replicate, it might be helpful to consider some of the problems inherent in studies of the disconfirmation of expectancies before making a hasty evaluation of these mottled results.

If the theory of expectancies stated in the introduction of this paper is correct, which there is yet insufficient reason to assume, it is still a tenuous basis for predictions in any particular case. These studies pit a hypothesized consistency principle against some other source of motivation such as achievement. No one contends that consistency is the prime motivating factor in human behavior; as Aronson, Carlsmith, and Darley (1963) point out, if the difference in desirability between the expected and the alternative outcomes is sufficiently great, the effects of any negative affect resulting from disconfirmation would be trivial by comparison. Hence, if the positive subjective utility of the unexpected outcome exceeds some unknown quantity, the utilitarian motivation would be expected to predominate over any consistency pressures. In the complex experimental settings utilized, any one of a variety of factors may change sufficiently, unbeknown to the experimenter, to shift that delicate balance away from consistency. This would suggest, assuming for the moment the veracity of the theory, that much work would be required in order to establish an empirical domain within which the predictions would hold.

Another source of ambiguity lies in the fact that a particular outcome seldom confirms or disconfirms just one expectation. As Harvey, Hunt, and Schroder (1961, pp. 60–62) have pointed out, multiple concepts are generally involved in confirmation and refutation. Thus, for example, in the Aronson and Carlsmith (1962) study, the disconfirmation of the subject's expectation of poor performance on the given task may have confirmed his previous expectation, based on past experience, that in general he does well on all things, as well as validating a host of other cognitions. The resultant reaction would then presumably be determined by the pooling of these consistent and inconsistent cognitions according to some unknown mathematical, or quasi-mathematical, function. Conlon (1965) tackled this problem by attempting to increase the number of expectations disconfirmed with her orthogonal manipulations of chronic and acute (induced) self-esteem in mathematics (previously discussed), but was still unable to show a consistency effect.

A troublesome problem concerns the mode of dissonance reduction a subject will utilize. Two strategies are prevalent: (a) attempting to block off all but the one measured mode of reducing dissonance, and (b) providing a number of a priori modes and measuring the resultant usage of each. Ingenious as experimenters may be, the subject may perceive the experimental situation in a much different perspective and, consequently, use some mode of dissonance reduction other than those measured. Since it has been repeatedly demonstrated (Steiner & Johnson, 1964; Steiner & Peters, 1958; Steiner & Rogers, 1963; Watts, 1966) that subjects' usages of alternative modes tend to be independent if not negatively related, it is quite possible that the subjects may be reducing dissonance according to theory but via some unmeasured mode, thereby yielding negative experimental results. This problem is not resolved by simply measuring multiple modes so as to increase the probability of tapping the preferred ones. Subjects' preferences for particular modes are likely quite idiosyncratic; hence, different subjects utilizing different modes may mask mean differences between dissonant and nondissonant conditions. Indeed, measuring one specific mode would be not unlike counting the people exiting from one door of a burning hotel building, except that each person can leave the hotel through only one exit, but nothing prevents a subject from using more than one mode of dissonance reduction despite the general independence among modes. (Of course, not even the most indoctrinated dissonance theorist would equate the motivational effects of cognitive dissonance with those of escaping a burning building.) It was because of this problem that Watts (1966) employed a composite index of the subjects' usage of all modes of dissonance reduction measured in the experiment. This technique, however, does nothing to solve the problem of subjects using unmeasured modes of dissonance reduction.

Time of measurement of the dependent variables, typically a neglected variable in psychological research, may be an important determinant of the effect obtained not only in studies of disconfirmed expectancies, but in dissonance theory studies *per se*. Walster (see Festinger, 1964, pp. 112–129) reported data concerning temporal effects in a single situation with results ranging from significant regret to significant dissonance reduction depending upon the time the measurements were taken. Similarly, Gailon and Watts (1967) found the time-of-measurement parameter to be important in subjects' reactions to a disconfirmed expectancy (previously discussed). The amount of time elapsing before dissonance reduction occurs is presumably a function of the difficulty of reducing dissonance in a particular situation (Festinger, 1964b, see Ch. 5, especially p. 112). Hence, unless the time parameter can be specified in some detail for various situations, multiple measurements would be required for a rigorous test of the theory since, otherwise, any result could be attributed to the time-of-measurement factor.

Another problem concerns the unusual amount of deception involved in the experimental studies of disconfirmed expectancies. While the demand characteristics of these complex experiments have been much discussed and investigated, the histrionic requirements have been relatively neglected. An experimenter's failure to play a convincing role would drastically alter the experimental situation and, thus, could generate an inexplicable array of results. Indeed, it might be a wise strategy to demand that future experimenters be bona fide members of the Actors' Guild.

In contrast to dissonance theory, a number of investigators (e.g., Berlyne, 1960; Hebb, 1949; McClelland, Atkinson, Clark, & Lowell, 1953) contend that small departures from the expected are pleasurable whereas large discrepancies, as well as complete predictability, result in negative affect. Since none of the studies cited has considered the magnitude of the disconfirmation, it is conceivable that this factor is responsible, in part, for the inconsistent results. However, it is probably safe to assume that the disconfirmations were potent enough to fall in the negative affect range according to such optimal discrepancy theories; and, if so, the power of this variable to reconcile the contradictory findings concerning avoidance of disconfirmation vanishes.

If any precise understanding of the parameters affecting an individual's reaction to disconfirmed expectancies is to be reached, it is clear that much work remains to be done. One might begin by doing a little introspection about how it feels to have predictions disconfirmed and here, quite conveniently, the investigator can serve as his own subject.

CHAPTER 41

Expectancy Disconfirmation and the Choice of Negative Alternatives: Dissonance Avoidance or Situational Demands?

Irwin Silverman

State University of New York at Buffalo

Nearly 40 years ago Tinklepaugh (1928) demonstrated that if a monkey is given the expectancy that he is going to eat a banana but is then given a lettuce leaf, which is generally less preferred, he will refuse to eat this otherwise acceptable food. This observation was probably not surprising to anyone who has tried to feed cereal to a pet dog with the odor of fresh meat present, but it may represent the earliest systematic demonstration of the motivational properties of expectancy disconfirmation. One theorist (Bugelski, 1960) has offered an expectancy disconfirmation interpretation of this finding in terms of the Hullian concept of fractional anticipatory goal responses (rgs), maintaining that the rgs made to the banana, such as "salivating to a certain degree, of preparing lips and teeth in appropriate positions for bananas and no other food" (p. 298), interfered with the development of rgs for eating the lettuce. The difficulty with this explanation is that any type of frustration may readily interfere with the animal's eating behavior, and this latter interpretation, in contrast to Bugelski's expectancy notion, can account for the observation that when Tinklepaugh prepared his monkeys for lettuce leaves, these rgs did not seem to interfere with their eating of bananas. For further evidence on this point, 11 of my students and I conducted a rather informal investigation where each experimenter used his own pet dog and selected two foods which the animal ate regularly but which could be ranked in terms of preference. At a time shortly before the dog's regular feeding, he was allowed to inspect closely the less preferred food for about 20 seconds, then freely choose between both foods. Of the 12 animals, 11 ignored the expected food and ate the preferred food apparently without hesitation.

This brief demonstration closely resembles some of the recent studies by Elliot Aronson and his colleagues, based on dissonance theory, on the motivational properties of expectancy disconfirmation in humans. These studies, however, have put the effects of expectancy disconfirmation to a sterner test. Rather than using pleasant alternatives of varying degrees of preference, subjects were given expectancies for an unpleasant event and

This chapter was prepared with the support of Grant No. GS-1023 from the National Science Foundation.

then a choice between experiencing this or either a neutral or pleasant event. The results of at least some of these studies indicated that, unlike our dogs, the experience of expectancy disconfirmation does frequently lead the human subject to choose the negative alternative.

These data have received a good deal of attention. We are disposed, both in our academic and intuitive psychology, to give much credence to the 'pleasure-pain' principle, and the contention that the consistency motive can supplant hedonistic tendencies in such a direct manner has basic implications about human motivation. Research on this question is in its earliest phase, however, and it is incumbent upon us to explore fully the extent to which the Aronson findings are congruent to the interpretations given them. Subsequent investigators have, in fact, postulated alternate explanations, and it will be the task of this chapter to examine these, to provide some additional ones, and to review generally the status of the question of whether, in any circumstance, the cognitive consistency motive can dispose a person to choose a less pleasant behavioral alternative.

In a study by Aronson, Carlsmith, and Darley (1963) subjects were given a series of trials in both a weight discrimination task (neutral) and a bitterness discrimination task (unpleasant), and were told that they would have to repeat either one or the other. Within these two groups, subjects were kept waiting either 20 minutes (strong expectancy) or approximately seven seconds (weak expectancy). Then the experimenter stated that ". . . a preliminary analysis of the data shows that it makes absolutely no difference in the results whether or not we randomly assign the task you have to repeat. Therefore, I think that it's only fair to give you the choice of what to repeat . . ." (p. 221). No subjects in the Weight Expectancy conditions chose the taste task, but 11 per cent of subjects in the Weak Taste Expectancy condition and 41 per cent of subjects in the Strong Taste Expectancy condition did so.

Aronson et al. predicted their findings on the basis that Taste Expectancy subjects would choose the unpleasant alternative to avoid dissonance concerned with the preparations they had made for the event. From another point of view, however, the act of agreeing to perform an unpleasant task can be considered, in itself, to be dissonance provoking, and has been used as a manipulation of dissonance in several studies (Aronson & Mills, 1959; Brehm, 1960a; Brehm & Cohen, 1959a; Mills, Aronson, & Robinson, 1959; Rosen, 1961; Cohen & Zimbardo, 1962). In one of these (Brehm, 1960a), in fact, the unpleasant task was eating a disliked food. Thus, it would appear that subjects who chose the taste task were avoiding dissonance from one source, that is, their cognitions about their preparations, at the expense of dissonance from another, that is, their cognitions that they had chosen a less pleasant alternative than they could have, and one needs to assume that the first source of dissonance has stronger motivating properties than the second. This assumption is tenable, but it requires empirical confirmation. If it is rejected, then the task remains to explain the behavior of subjects in the Aronson et al. study who chose the negative alternative.

In an attempt of this kind, Goldberg (1965) took the position that the Taste Expectancy-Taste Choice subjects were complying with the perceived demands of the experimental situation (Orne, 1962) but his data do not offer clear support for either his view or the expectancy disconfirmation view. He failed to replicate the findings of Aronson et al., using an identical procedure; all but one subject chose the weight task. In a further study, using the 20-Minute-Wait condition only, both Taste and Weight Expectancy subjects made their choices after hearing another subject, who was actually the experimenter's confederate, choose one or the other. Goldberg expected the confederates' choices to affect the subjects' choices in all conditions, but the only subjects who chose the taste task were 25 per cent of the group with taste expectancies when confederates made this choice also.

Situational demands may have determined the results of Aronson *et al.* in a somewhat different manner, however. Orne (1962) and Rosenberg (1965d) have described convincingly the strong need of subjects, in a university research setting, to favorably impress the experimenter. Orne has shown, for example, that subjects will perform tedious and obviously meaningless work for hours, with "few errors and little decrement in speed" and "relatively little sign of overt hostility." In the paradigm used by Aronson *et al.*, the experimenter assigned the subject to an unpleasant task without identifying it as such, then gave him the option of changing to a more pleasant alternative on the grounds that it did not matter who performed which task. In this situation it is plausible that 41 per cent of the subjects stayed with the unpleasant task *in order not to indicate to the experimenter their original displeasure with his assignment.* This interpretation may be tested directly by varying conditions which may be assumed to affect approval-seeking by subjects, such as the experimenter's status or manner, or indirectly by comparing subjects who go counter to their expectancies with those who do not, to see whether these groups differ in characteristics related to approval-seeking or consistency-seeking.

With this interpretation as opposed to the consistency concept, it is easier to account for Goldberg's failure to replicate. Experiments may readily differ in factors determining the degree to which subjects wish to impress the experimenter, but the consistency motive would be expected to be more resistant to extraneous variables inherent in different experimental settings. Further, Goldberg's findings with regard to the facilitating effect of the confederate supports the present view; the knowledge that another subject stayed with the unpleasant task would be expected to add pressure to the subject not to be unfavorably compared.

This explanation does not, however, account for the differences in the Aronson *et al.* study between Strong and Weak Expectancy groups, whereas the dissonance explanation does. Those authors did suggest as an alternate explanation of this finding that the longer wait period in the Strong Expectancy group may have dispelled the aversive effects of the taste task to a greater degree. They performed an analysis which suggested that the effects of such dissolution on choice would have had to occur in the last 10 minutes of the 20 minute wait period, but this is not an infeasible possibility.

For me, there are no clearcut empirical grounds at present to favor either the dissonance-avoidance or the situational demands explanations. Further research, perhaps along some of the lines described above, may be expected to show the more fruitful theoretical direction.

A second line of research on the general question of expectancy disconfirmation and the choice of negative alternatives was launched by Aronson and Carlsmith (1962). In this study subjects were given an alleged test of social sensitivity requiring them to make judgments pertaining to emotional stability from photographs and consisting of five trials of 20 judgments each. Subjects were given fictitious scores after each of the first four trials, which were either consistently high or low. The feedback for the fifth trial was either consistent or inconsistent with the first four. Then, on the pretense that the experimenter had forgotten to time the last trial, subjects were requested to take it over and "... pretend that it is a completely new set of pictures." In terms of the number of changes made on this retest, subjects tended to adjust their scores in the direction of their expectancies even when this required the seeking of a lower score.

This study was followed by numerous replications, attesting to the importance of the finding both theoretically and practically, considering the effects of failure in educational settings. These replications produced a variety of results, some of which confirmed the original findings. Others led to several alternative interpretations; however, none of these alternative interpretations have successfully stood the tests of subsequent research.

Ward and Sandvold (1963) contended that Aronson and Carlsmith's statement to their subjects stressing the reliability of the test established a demand for consistency, and reported that when the study was conducted without this statement, success-seeking rather than consistency-seeking was observed. Silverman and Marcantonio (1965), however, replicated the paradigm both with and without the reliability statement and their data indicated that its effect was to increase success-seeking, which was explained on the grounds that subjects receiving the statement were more ego-involved in their performance. The latter investigators, in attempting to account for differences in findings among the three studies, suggested that consistency-seeking may be a response to experimenter demands, though these are not contained in the reliability statement, and, with Ward and Sandvold, they speculated that the fees given subjects by Aronson and Carlsmith may have heightened responsiveness to these demands. Lowin and Epstein (1965), however, obtained success-seeking with paid subjects and Brock *et al.* (1966) obtained consistency-seeking in two replications with unpaid subjects. In three separate studies, Lowin and Epstein, Waterman and Ford (1965), and Brock *et al.* demonstrated that Low Expectancy subjects have poorer recall of their prior judgments than High Expectancy subjects. Waterman and Ford described how this can account for an expectancy × fifth trial interaction, but Hendrick (1966) has correctly pointed out that differential recall cannot account for a greater number of changes by high fifth trial subjects as compared to lows within the Low Expectancy condition, which was obtained by Aronson and Carlsmith and in two replications by Brock *et al.* When an expectancy × fifth trial interaction is observed without this difference, however, as in the study by Cottrell (1965), Waterman and Ford's explanation is a valid alternative.

In consideration of the differential recall factor, a conservative criterion for determining success-seeking vs. consistency-seeking is the direction of differences between high and low fifth trial, Low Expectancy subjects. On this basis, three studies have demonstrated consistency-seeking (Aronson & Carlsmith and two replications by Brock *et al.*) and eight studies have shown success-seeking (Ward & Sandvold, two replications by Lowin & Epstein, and five by Brock *et al.*). Cottrell's (1965) may be included as a fourth study supporting the consistency view with the reservation that the differential recall factor can account also for his data. The 'score,' however, is not of primary importance. Given that consistency-seeking was observed in four separate investigations, Aronson and Carlsmith's hypothesis is a viable one and the source of differences among the studies should be pursued to some ultimate conclusion. Some considerations about this question and some possible directions for further research are offered below.

One suggestion is that different subject populations may differ in the intensity of either motive; for example, Silverman and Marcantonio, at the time of their report, reasoned that the nurses of Ward and Sandvold's replication may have been more disposed to demonstrate social sensitivity than the general undergraduate population used by Aronson and Carlsmith. With the subsequent studies by Brock *et al.* and Lowin and Epstein, however, success-seeking has been obtained with a variety of subjects and no systematic subject factor has emerged to account for differences in results. Marcantonio (1966) has pursued this approach further and has obtained some support for the notion that subjects with less tolerance for dissonance show more of a consistency-seeking effect.

When the same paradigm yields distinctly different findings in different experimental settings, it is feasible that role-related behavior of subjects and experimenters, which may be expected to show some variation between settings, is at least a partial determinant of the results. One apparent notion is that either success-seeking or consistency-seeking or both represent the effects of experimenter bias (Rosenthal, 1963), that is, cues given the subject by the experimenter regarding his expectations. Cottrell's study was designed to account for this possibility but his data, as noted above, may reflect factors other than either motive.

In terms of the variable of the experimenter's awareness of the consistency hypothesis, the pattern of findings does not appear to support the experimenter bias hypothesis. For the three studies besides Cottrell's showing consistency effects, the experimenters were aware in one and not in the other two. For seven of the replications showing success effects (Ward and Sandvold's is excluded because they hypothesized success-seeking), the experimenters were aware in six. Experimenter bias may operate in a more indirect way, however, through "modeling effects" (Rosenthal, 1963); hence, the effect that is obtained may reflect the degree to which consistency or social sensitivity needs are reflected in the personality of the experimenter.

A parallel suggestion is that responses in the Aronson and Carlsmith paradigm may reflect role-related motives of the subject, which may account for either success-seeking or consistency-seeking. The assumption here is that subjects are suspicious of the legitimacy of the experimenter's ruse to ask them to take the fifth trial again. For subjects in the Low Expectancy, high fifth trial group, this may be interpreted as dissatisfaction on the experimenter's part with their atypical fifth trial score; hence changes in this condition will reflect responsiveness to experimenter demands rather than consistency-seeking. On the other hand, Low Expectancy subjects may perceive the experiment as a test of the effects of repeated failure on the adaptiveness of their behavior, and "evaluation apprehension" (Rosenberg, 1965d) would lead them to respond in the direction of success-seeking.

Given these possibilities, the key to the differences among studies would appear to be in the believability of the experimenter, which may vary considerably with a procedure requiring as much acting skill as Aronson and

Carlsmith's. The question of which effect, if either, is obtained by more or less believable experimenters would indicate whether success-seeking or consistency-seeking is a function of role-related subject behavior.

Considering the differences in results among replications and the possibilities for alternate interpretations of the original findings, the next logical step may be the development of other paradigms to test the consistency hypothesis. It would appear that performance expectancies could be disconfirmed and measures taken of the subjects' adjustive behaviors in a number of other ways, with less likelihood of provoking suspicion. One suggestion, using the essential design of Aronson and Carlsmith, is to test subjects twice on each trial, telling them that they may change any responses that they wish, and explaining that the experimenter is interested in which judgments they were more or less sure about. In this context, also, suspicions have probably been enhanced in previous studies by the unnecessary procedure of indicating to subjects that they scored consistently below chance. Subjects at the university level undoubtedly would assume that chance performance is failure on this type of test, but continual below chance scores would seem to represent a devious and atypical judgmental process.

What can be said at this juncture about the status of the entire question of whether subjects will choose negative alternatives to avoid expectancy disconfirmation? It appears to be just as much open as it was at the time of Tinklepaugh's experiment, though the issues raised by the Aronson studies are empirical and will, hopefully, be resolved as such. To me, the discrepancies among replications are as interesting a phenomenon as the nature of the findings themselves, and my predilections lead me to anticipate that we will learn as much about the complex interactional processes of the psychological experiment as about the mechanisms of dissonance avoidance.

CHAPTER 42

Bad Decisions and Dissonance:
Nobody's Perfect

J. Merrill Carlsmith and Jonathan L. Freedman
Stanford University

What can we expect to happen to a person when he makes a decision and it turns out badly? It has sometimes been assumed that all decisions with negative outcomes will arouse cognitive dissonance and lead to attempts at dissonance reduction (see Festinger & Aronson, 1960). The position to be taken here is that there is no theoretical reason to expect dissonance to be aroused when the outcome could not have been known in advance, and that in many such situations dissonance is probably not aroused.

The theory is very clear about the effects of cognitions which a person holds when he makes the decision. Once he has decided to eat spinach, all cognitions about how lousy spinach tastes, how he breaks out in boils whenever he eats it, how it makes him nauseous, are dissonant with the cognition that he chose to eat it. The more such negative cognitions there are, the more dissonance will be aroused by his decision, and the more pressure there will be to reduce dissonance in any way possible. This is straightforward, is clearly deducible from the theory, and is well supported by experimental research (cf. Brehm & Cohen, 1962, Ch. 3, 4). We have no complaints with this.

Consider, however, the situation in which a person makes a decision on the basis of limited information. Suppose further that at some time following that decision, new information is introduced which shows that the decision will have or does have negative consequences. This kind of situation has been labelled "fait accompli" (Brehm, 1959) or "faulty anticipation of the environment" (Festinger & Aronson, 1960), and it is entirely different from the previous situation. Here we have someone making what seems to be the best decision on the basis of current information, only to find out later that something which he knew nothing about makes it the wrong decision. The poor unsuspecting boy who agrees to eat spinach must feel some dissonance because he has negative cognitions about spinach. But if it then turns out that the spinach was actually mixed with swiss chard and tastes worse than he could possibly have imagined, or that his mother is going to be told and he will have to spend the rest of his life eating spinach three

The writing of this paper was facilitated by National Science Foundation grants GS 1115 and GS 1083 to the authors.

times a day, does this arouse more dissonance? Certainly this new cognition is exceedingly unpleasant, but we would argue that this new, unsuspected cognition does not arouse dissonance, or at least that it does only for a person with a curious cognitive system.

Let us expand on this point. Does it follow from the cognition "This spinach turned out to have swiss chard in it" that I should not have agreed to eat it? If I knew beforehand that it had swiss chard, obviously it does because the chard would be a reason for not eating it. However, if I did not know and could not have known about the swiss chard when I decided, then the fact that chard turned out to be present is essentially irrelevant to my decision and it does not follow that I should have refused to eat the stuff. In other words, dissonance should be aroused by the negative cognition only when the person knew or thinks he should have known about the negative consequences when he made the decision. It may be that many people do think that whatever happens, somehow they should have foreseen it. For these people, new negative information will always increase dissonance. It does seem, however, that most people feel less omniscient than this and that in many situations they will not feel responsible for negative consequences which they could not have foreseen.

In other words, a piece of negative information introduced after a decision should arouse dissonance only when the person feels he should have known about it before the decision. The critical factor determining whether or not dissonance is aroused in these situations is, therefore, the extent to which a person could reasonably have foreseen the negative consequences. Situations range from those in which the negative consequences were completely unforeseeable to those in which they were clear from the beginning, and the likelihood of dissonance being aroused should range from approximately zero at one extreme to 100 per cent at the other. Let us consider some relevant experiments and see how they fit this analysis.

An experiment by Freedman (1963) provides a clear example of a situation in which some subjects could not have foreseen the negative cognition which was later introduced, while other subjects had the negative information right from the beginning. Subjects were asked to generate a large quantity of random numbers and write them in the small squares on a piece of graph paper (presumably an unpleasant task). Before they began, some subjects were told that the task was extremely useful (high justification) while others were told that the experimenter already had enough numbers so that the task was useless (low justification). Another group of subjects was told nothing about the utility of the task before beginning. Instead, when they had finished writing numbers for 12 minutes, half of them were told that it was very useful (high justification) and the others were told that it was a useless task (low justification). There were thus four groups: high and low justification given before the dull task; high and low justification given after the task. The dependent measure was how much the subjects said that they enjoyed the number-writing.

This situation illustrates the two extremes of foreseeability that we described above. When the justification is given before the task, everything is clear to the subjects. They know what they are getting into. Under these circumstances, the low justification serves as a negative cognition which is inconsistent with engaging in the task, while the high justification is positive and is consistent with doing the task. Thus, there should be more dissonance in the Low Justification condition. This dissonance can be reduced by deciding that the task was enjoyable, and subjects in the Low Justification condition should therefore rate the task more enjoyable.

When the justification instructions are given after the task is performed, we have the opposite end of the continuum. No one could have possibly foreseen that the experimenter was going to throw the numbers in the wastebasket—this new, unpleasant piece of information is entirely gratuitous and unexpected. It may be very unpleasant, but it should not arouse dissonance. Thus, we would not expect a dissonance effect here.

The results of the experiment support the interpretation. Whereas there was a clear dissonance effect when the justification was presented before the decision (subjects in the Low Justification condition rated the task as more enjoyable), there was a reversal when the justification was presented after the decision (subjects who were given low justification actually rated the task as less enjoyable).

Watts' (1965) experiment is another in which no evidence of dissonance reduction was found when the supposedly dissonant cognition was introduced after a choice had been made. He had subjects choose to taste a very unpleasant solution which would act as an anesthetic to protect their tongues against a shock. After the subject had drunk the solution, it turned out that the doctor who was to deliver the shock had been called out on an emergency and that the shock would not be given. Watts argued that taking the unpleasant anesthetic was dissonant with the cognition that it was not needed. We would argue that in fact it was not dissonant. The cognition that it was not needed was introduced only after the decision had been made and could not have been foreseen. It was not inconsistent with the decision, and should not have aroused dissonance. This interpretation is supported by the fact that Watts found no dissonance effect.

These two studies illustrate very clearly the situation in which the subject is unlikely to feel that he should have foreseen the negative consequence of his decision. In both studies there is no dissonance effect. There are a great many experiments that illustrate the other end of the continuum; the data from these clearly show that when the subject is aware of the dissonant cognition before the decision, dissonance is aroused. What of the situations that fall between these two extremes?

Sometimes the subject knows that a particular negative outcome might occur. He is not certain that it will, but it is a definite possibility and should probably be taken into account beforehand. In Aronson's (1961) experiment on the effects of effort on attractiveness, he had subjects fish for containers, some of which contained money and some of which did not. Although the negative cognition (no money in this container) was introduced after the subject had engaged in the unpleasant behavior, the subjects did know that some of the containers would be empty. One could argue that in this study there is dissonance between the cognition that one is working hard and the cognition that one may not get any reward for the work. On those trials when the subject is rewarded, there is of course no more dissonance. When the reward is not present, however, the dissonance remains and may be reduced by increasing the perceived attractiveness of the empty containers. This is consistent with what Aronson found. In other words, when the possibility of a negative outcome is known ahead of time, dissonance may sometimes be aroused by a negative consequence.

In contrast, there are situations in which the person did not expect a negative outcome and may not have actively considered the possibility of one. When the negative outcome appears, however, the person feels that he should have anticipated it.

An example of this is the study by Aronson and Mills (1959). Subjects decided to go through a painful initiation in order to join a group which turned out to be very dull. It is possible that for some subjects dissonance was actually aroused. The fundamental relation of dissonance theory is 'psychologically follows,' and if a person believes that it follows from his cognition that the group is dull that he should not have decided to go through the initiation, then dissonance will be present. Note, however, that this depends upon the subject having the belief that he 'should have known' beforehand that the group would be dull. Only if he believes this will it 'psychologically follow' that he should not have gone through the initiation. Such a belief system is not entirely implausible in this situation, but on the other hand it is quite a distortion of reality. And, to repeat, we are arguing that there is no dissonance without such a distorted belief system.

The above line of reasoning explains why dissonance might be aroused by an unexpected negative consequence of a decision or action. Our own feeling is that in most of these situations dissonance is probably not aroused. Although in the Aronson and Mills experiment liking for the group changed in the direction predicted by a dissonance analysis, this is not strong evidence for the presence of dissonance. We would argue that an entirely different process could explain this result and equivalent ones in similar studies.

We imagine a person in the situation having a cognitive system which says in essence: "This is a lousy group and I went through a lot of pain to get into it. True, I couldn't have known how lousy it was going to be when I made my decision, but that doesn't make the unpleasantness of the situation any less." Faced with such a series of cognitions, the person may very well reduce the unpleasantness by convincing himself that it isn't such a bad group after all. Such rationalization or distortion of reality must occur often when someone wants to make his lot seem better than it is. This process, which in no way depends upon dissonance, does depend upon how painful the initiation was, because of course it is worse to go through severe pain for nothing than to go through mild pain (worse not in the sense of more dissonant, but worse in the sense of just plain nasty and unpleasant). There should accordingly be more reevaluation of the group in the severe initiation condition than in the mild, and this is what was found.

Brehm's study on the fait accompli may be interpreted similarly. In that study a child was induced to eat a vegetable which he did not like. While he was eating the vegetable, the experimenter mentioned that he was sending a letter to the child's parents informing them that the child was eating the vegetable. The implication was that this would increase the likelihood that the child would have to eat the vegetable at home in the future. Again, we would argue that the child finds himself in a situation which is very unpleasant, but that without a belief that he should have known that the outcome would be negative, it is incorrect to assume that dissonance will be present.

At the moment the available evidence does not allow us to choose between the dissonance interpretation of these results and the one we have proposed. The interpretation we have offered appears to be at least as plausible as the dissonance analysis, and it fits the data just as well. We feel that in many of these situations it is highly unlikely that dissonance actually is aroused, and we have presented our interpretation primarily to show that the results do not constitute unequivocal support for the assumption that dissonance was present.

We are left with the puzzling problem of accounting for the presence of change in experiments like those of Aronson and Mills and of Brehm, while at the same time explaining its absence in the studies by Freedman and by Watts. One possible explanation, of course, is that dissonance was present in the former two experiments, since it was more possible to foresee the negative outcome. This is not terribly plausible in the Brehm study, since only a pretty paranoid child would expect his parents to be told that he was eating the spinach.

We would suggest that the unpleasantness leads to strong pressure to change one's beliefs only in a situation where there are implications for future unpleasantness. In the study by Freedman, the person was no longer involved in the unpleasant behavior when the negative information came, and he was not committed to any future behavior. Similarly in the study by Watts, there was no future unpleasantness to be dealt with; the anesthetic had been drunk and the taste was gone. In contrast, Aronson's and Mills' subjects expected to continue in the dull group, and Brehm's children expected to have to eat more spinach in the future. If there are no future consequences, little is gained by changing one's evaluation of the negative stimulus. The worst is over and all that will improve is your memory of it. If, on the other hand, you are going to have to experience this negative stimulus in the future, a great deal is gained by deciding that it is not so bad—it makes the whole future appear less unpleasant. Therefore, it seems plausible that we should find the effect when there are future consequences and not find it when there are no future consequences. This is only conjecture at the moment, but it does seem to explain the contradictory results quite well.

In summary, we would assert that whether or not dissonance is aroused by negative cognitions about a decision depends upon the extent to which the subject thinks that he should have foreseen the negative cognition. When he knows the negative aspect beforehand, dissonance is definitely aroused (e.g., Festinger & Carlsmith, 1959; Brehm & Cohen, 1959a; Freedman's pre-task condition; and most postdecision studies). When he knows of the *possibility* of negative consequences, dissonance will probably be aroused much of the time (e.g., Aronson, 1961). As it becomes less and less possible to have foreseen even the possibility of the negative consequence, as bad result becomes more and more unexpected and gratuitous, it becomes less and less likely that dissonance will be aroused. In these situations the negative result will be unpleasant and may, if there are consequences for future action, produce cognitive reorganization. But dissonance will usually not be aroused. And in the extreme case where it is impossible to have foreseen the bad result or the negative aspect, no dissonance will be aroused (e.g., Freedman's postdecision groups; Watts, 1965).

Although the available evidence is generally consistent with this analysis, it does not provide unequivocal support for it. In particular, the ambiguous instances such as the Aronson and Mills (1959) study cannot be interpreted without additional data; and our explanation of the Brehm "fait accompli" study, while it seems plausible, certainly needs independent verification. Future research will presumably clarify these issues. Our main point, however, does not seem to require additional support. This is that as dissonance theory stands, it does not lead to the expectation that dissonance will be aroused by negative information introduced after a decision has been made. On the contrary, the theory states quite clearly that under those circumstances, if the person did not foresee the negative consequence, the new cognition should usually not arouse dissonance. Exactly when, if ever, new negative cognitions will arouse dissonance is an empirical question. We hope, however, that it is evident that the theory does not predict such arousal and that experiments involving such situations fall largely outside of the framework of the original theory.

CHAPTER 43

Discussion: Expectancy vs. Other Motives

Elliot Aronson

Both Silverman and Watts have done an excellent job of summarizing and interpreting the literature on the disconfirmation of expectancies. The most general conclusion we can draw from their analyses is that although a phenomenon exists, it is far from being completely understood. In short, people do seem to be motivated to confirm expectancies and do seem to experience some discomfort when their expectancies are disconfirmed—but they frequently experience competing motivations as well. Frequently these competing motivations override the negative effects of disconfirmation and lead people to behave as though disconfirmations were unimportant to them. Indeed, in certain situations, compared to the strength of some of these competing motives, the drive to confirm expectancies is frequently miniscule. Thus, in framing their hypothesis, Aronson, Carlsmith, and Darley (1963) expressed the following qualification:

> ... It seems reasonable that the negative affect resulting from discon-
> firmation will rarely be of such magnitude as to override the extreme
> negative aspects of some undesirable expected alternatives. For exam-
> ple, if a person firmly expects to die a painful death, and at the last
> moment is offered a choice between this alternative and a long and
> happy life, we have few doubts as to the nature of his choice (p. 221).

One of the most salient of these competing motives is the need to achieve; most of us obtain some intrinsic and extrinsic enjoyment from success. In the experimental situation created by the "performance ex-pectancy" experiments, the drive to achieve is placed in direct and dramatic confrontation with the drive to confirm expectancies. It seems reasonable to assume that people in many situations would almost certainly strive to succeed and would be relatively pleased by success even in the face of a disconfirmed expectancy. But as both Watts and Silverman suggest, it is not enough to recognize that the world is a complicated place and that, fre-quently, competing drives influence behavior in different directions. The intriguing methodological question remains: How do we account for the fact that even when using essentially the same procedure, some investigators have found evidence favoring an "achievement-seeking" prediction while others have found evidence favoring a "confirmation of expectancies" prediction?

It may be that the key to this problem lies in the phrase *"essentially the same"*—for if there is one thing we have learned in the past few years, it is that in social psychological experiments, experimental procedures are rarely identical. If nothing else, the experimenter himself is frequently a variable. From his analysis of the existing experiments, Silverman makes a convincing case against the possibility that the experimenter's awareness of the hypothesis could have had a systematic effect on the pattern of the results of these experiments. But the experimenter may affect the results in less obvious ways. Silverman suggests that acting ability may be important. This is clearly true, for if a subject questions the legitimacy of the information he has received, he will not behave as predicted. Another important variable in this situation might be the experimenter's personality characteristics—it is possible that these characteristics could manifest themselves in subtle ways which might have a profound effect upon the behavior of his subjects. For example, in a recent paper, I (Aronson, 1966b) suggest that if an experimenter himself has a high drive for achievement, the subject might perceive this and, consequently, might feel more uncomfortable after failure than he would if he were being run by an experimenter who manifested behavior indicating a lower need for achievement. This could result in greater achievement-seeking behavior. Such a phenomenon is quite different from the bias investigated by Rosenthal (1966), for unlike Rosenthal's situations, it does not involve an interaction between the experimenter's behavior and the subject's experimental condition. The problem here is a more difficult one to avoid because it suggests that there is an unknown and unreported piece of the experimenter's behavior which may be pushing everyone in all conditions in the same direction—toward greater concern with achievement.

But this is admittedly conjectural. How might we be certain whether or not such an event actually occurs? Happily, this question, like most of the others raised by Watts and by Silverman, is an empirical one. This suggests that, in spite of the formidable methodological problems outlined in their papers, more answers will be forthcoming through further research.

Another way to 'resolve' the above methodological problem is to avoid it entirely. Such a solution is suggested by Bramel (Chapter 26), who makes a convincing case for using a less stringent criterion than that employed in the performance expectancy experiments. According to Bramel, (a) if one is interested in demonstrating the effects of a disconfirmed expectancy, (b) if one knows that achievement needs will produce opposing tendencies, and (c) if one has no a priori way of predicting the relative strengths of these forces, then (d) a statistical interaction may be the only sane prediction. Thus, Bramel's contention is that if the conditions are such that the achievement effects predominate, these effects should be less manifest in those experimental treatments which involve disconfirmed expectancies. According to Bramel's use of this criterion, eight of the nine relevant experiments produced interactions in the expected direction; of these, three were significant (confirming the dissonance prediction), and only one experiment produced an interaction (nonsignificant) in the opposite direction (see p. 359 of this volume).

There are a myriad of theoretical implications of the notion of disconfirmed expectancies and low self concepts. One of these, suggested by

Carlsmith and Freedman in this section, is the proposition that most people do not feel that they have the Midas touch. It is part of our general expectancy that, occasionally, our decisions and actions will turn out badly for reasons that are beyond our control. Carlsmith and Freedman's important contribution is to specify clearly that such events do not involve dissonance. This has not been made clear in the past—leading to some confusion in interpreting negative findings. The extremes are very clear: In Freedman's (1963) experiment, subjects who chose to participate in the experiment, knowing in advance that the experimenter was going to throw away their data, should experience dissonance and, consequently, should seek to justify their participation. In effect, they should have known better —dissonance arose (to use Festinger and Aronson's [1960] phrase) because of "faulty anticipation of the environment." At the other extreme are the subjects in the other condition of Freedman's experiment who were not informed until *after* they had participated. Since experimenters are not expected to run subjects with the *intention* of throwing away the data, it is inconceivable that the subject could have felt silly about not having predicted such ludicrous behavior in advance. Consequently, he should have experienced no dissonance.

Carlsmith and Freedman are well aware of the fact that there is a great deal of acreage in between these extremes; middle ground always introduces some ambiguity. Furthermore, although Carlsmith and Freedman suggested that there is a continuum of dissonance between 0 (it was inconceivable) and 100 (I should have known better), it is by no means clear that in such a situation a continuum exists; on the contrary, the data seem to favor an all or none law. It may be that people tend to assume maximum responsibility for bad outcomes whenever there is some real possibility that they might have anticipated this outcome. For example, let us examine the Aronson and Mills (1959) initiation experiment. Since people know that some groups are dull, it is easily conceivable that individuals in the severe initiation condition experienced dissonance for going through so much to obtain a pig in a poke. They probably would not say "I should have known," but they might say "I might have known"—and that could be (and apparently was) enough to trigger a high degree of dissonance.

Although Carlsmith and Freedman allow that some dissonance might have been present in the Aronson-Mills experiment, they lean toward explaining the results (as well as the results of Brehm's [1959] fait accompli experiment) by suggesting that unpleasantness in and of itself "leads to strong pressure to change one's beliefs only in a situation where there are implications for future unpleasantness" (p. 489). This analysis neglects the fact that future unpleasantness was also present in the mild initiation condition—and subjects in this condition showed no tendency to believe that the group was attractive.

Carlsmith and Freedman have made an important step toward clarification, but as they are well aware, much work remains to be done in order to determine the exact conditions which allow a person to dodge the responsibility for a bad outcome.

F. ASSUMPTIONS ABOUT COGNITIVE STRUCTURE

Each cognitive consistency theory pursues its predictions in its own special defining circumstances, but none of them go into much detail on the general nature of cognitive structures or systems. Are cognitive structures typically highly elaborate? Does much cognitive organizing and reorganizing activity take place even in the absence of inconsistency? Or have cognitive psychologists tended to oversystematize desultory and isolated cognitive events, assuming a greater structural basis than in fact exists?

Jonathan Freedman argues in this section that although certain dissonance theory predictions have led to striking experiments and results, in general the assumed motivation toward cognitive consistency has been vastly overplayed because people are not very 'cognitive.' In its extreme form, this position would say that cognitive structures do not exist or do not matter.

A variety of opposed positions may be held. Clinton De Soto and Frank Albrecht argue that cognitive structures, if they are very neat and simple ("conceptual good figures") may exert powerful influences. Karl Weick speculates about the gamut of structural possibilities from the most rudimentary to the most complex, attempting to identify variables disposing toward greater complexity or 'ramification' of cognitive structures. Finally, Kenneth Colby presents a terse summary of his theory of how belief systems operate, a theory which has been programmed for a computer. Colby's position is toward that end of the spectrum where cognitive structures are assumed to be both influential and complex.

CHAPTER 44

How Important Is Cognitive Consistency?

Jonathan L. Freedman
Stanford University

Most formulations of cognitive consistency theory picture man as a somewhat misguided and perhaps slightly devious electronic brain. Their descriptions of him make him a walking, breathing, talking computer, albeit an unpredictable, irrational one with some built-in idiosyncracies and imperfections. The dominant theme of these theories is that the mind is always working, and that one of the most important things it is doing is working to produce a logical, rational, consistent view of the world. The balancing man (Heider, 1958; Abelson, 1959) accepts input about people and things and then carefully, according to a simple formula, decides how much he will like those people and things. In order to do this he displays a high degree of ingenuity and virtuosity in constructing, tearing down, and inventing complex structures which will serve the purpose of bringing balance out of chaos; but he does succeed in producing this balance. The congruous man (Osgood & Tannenbaum, 1955) has a little less to do because various problems that bother the balancing man do not upset him. The congruous man simply assesses the situation, assigns weights to various factors, and moves his position the appropriate number of units so as to maximize congruity. The dissonant man (Festinger, 1957) has a lot more to think about because potentially dissonant elements can come from any quarter, but he is nevertheless equal to the task. He assesses the potential dissonance of information and meticulously avoids the bad stuff while searching for the good; he ponders decisions he has just made and slides washing machines up and toasters down on a variety of evaluative scales so as to improve his decision; he attends to dissonant characteristics producing regret, then to consonant characteristics, reducing regret and dissonance at the same time; and so on. Throughout all of these formulations there is the implication that this process of inconsistency reduction goes on continually, is very effective, and is one of the major determinants of how a person acts and thinks.

Perhaps I have been overstating the case somewhat, but I hope I will be forgiven since it is difficult to give the flavor of these theories without going

The preparation of this paper was supported in part by Grant GS-1083 from the National Science Foundation.

into lengthy examples and direct quotations. I have been trying to dramatize the point that consistency models present us with a very cognitive man who is extremely concerned about and devotes a great deal of energy to maximizing cognitive consistency. I think all of the theories do take this position to a large extent[1] although it is not often made as explicit as in McGuire's strong statement in Chapter 6. The question is whether or not this is an accurate description of human beings.

Let me start by saying that I am very sympathetic toward cognitive consistency theories. I think that men do tend to reduce inconsistencies in their lives and among their beliefs; and I think the various theories have said this quite well. I happen to think dissonance theory is by a large margin the best and most meaningful statement of this position, but the other statements are also significant. I think the research growing out of these theories has been extremely useful and informative. In other words, I am not writing as an opponent of this general position in social psychology.

I do not agree, however, that the tendency to strive toward cognitive consistency is as important, ubiquitous, or continuous as these theories seem to be saying. I do agree, and I think that experimental evidence has amply supported this, that people strive toward cognitive consistency and that this can have significant effects on their behavior and beliefs. It also seems likely that under some circumstances these inconsistency-reducing activities are quite important and may even be a major determinant of behavior and beliefs. But in my opinion these would be very special circumstances. I think that most of the time tendencies toward cognitive consistency are of relatively minor importance, are not in fact going on continuously, and consequently have relatively minor consequences for behavior or even for attitudes and opinions.

Let us consider first cognitive factors in general in the context of other factors affecting behavior and opinion. It seems evident that to a man who has endured electric shock or tasted vile substances or been through an air raid, the pain and suffering itself is generally much more important than his knowledge that he endured this pain and suffering. A man who is terribly hungry is motivated more by his feelings of hunger than by his knowledge that he is hungry. This is not to say that cognitive factors may not be very important—only that noncognitive motivational factors are extremely important also. It seems to me that only very potent cognitive factors are as strong as typical noncognitive motivational factors.

The main point for our present purpose is that the effect of purely cognitive factors of any kind must be considered in the context of other kinds of factors which are also very powerful. This means that any one special kind of cognitive factor must perforce account for only a fairly small amount of the total variance in behavior and even attitudes. I think it is important to keep this in mind because some discussions of cognitive consistency sometimes seem to lose this perspective and to picture a world more or less entirely controlled by a few cognitive factors. No one really believes this, but it is occasionally proposed in the current fascination with Cognition. Despite all of this, it is clear that the one cognitive factor with which we are concerned, the tendency toward cognitive consistency, might

---

[1] Abelson's formulation is somewhat of an exception since he stresses that the person must be aware of imbalance for it to have any effect. Other theorists are mostly silent on this point, but they imply that awareness or salience is not a particularly crucial factor.

still be pretty important in the big picture. Let us now turn to a consideration of this specific question:

How important and continuous is the trend toward cognitive consistency? There are two separate points: (a) To what extent are people attuned to discovering inconsistencies? (b) When they are discovered, to what extent do people try to reduce them? It seems to me that the answer to both of these questions is that the extent of the phenomenon is quite limited—people are not particularly on the look-out for inconsistencies among their cognitions, they are not aware of most such inconsistencies, and they do not spend much time trying to find them. In addition, once they find them, it generally does not bother them terribly and therefore does not activate very strong processes of reducing or minimizing the inconsistencies. In other words, although most people probably prefer having their cognitions consistent with one another, under most circumstances this is not one of their major concerns and it does not have a major effect on their behavior or cognitions. It is easy to say this, but harder to defend it. Let me try to adduce some evidence for this position.

The first piece of evidence comes from work on selective exposure. If people are concerned about cognitive inconsistency, it seems very plausible that they should avoid exposure to information which is likely to produce or increase such inconsistency, and they should also seek out information which will decrease inconsistency. This prediction is one of the core propositions of the theory of cognitive dissonance, and it is certainly a reasonable deduction from any of the other theories.

In fact, however, there is very good reason to believe that people do not show either of these tendencies. There is by now a fairly extensive literature on selective exposure and the data are available for all to see. It is very clear that this evidence does not provide support for the selective exposure hypotheses. In a few experiments people do show a preference for supportive information over nonsupportive, but the opposite preference is shown in other studies. By far the modal finding is that whether or not the information is likely to increase or decrease cognitive consistency has little or no effect on subjects' exposure preferences. This holds for trivial issues (mock jury vote) as well as for very important ones (smoking and cancer). And there is no evidence that increasing the importance of the issue increases the preference for supportive information. Several more complex hypotheses dealing with people who show selective exposure have been offered, but none of these has received consistent support. The whole issue of selective exposure has been covered in detail elsewhere (Freedman & Sears, 1965a) and is discussed at length by David Sears[2] in Chapter 77. For our present purpose suffice it to say that the research does not indicate that people prefer consistent to inconsistent information.

This finding should not be considered terribly serious for dissonance theory or for the other theories of cognitive consistency. It does not mean that the theories are incorrect in general. What it does suggest quite strongly is that the strength of the drive toward cognitive consistency is relatively weak compared to other factors such as the interest, utility, or novelty of information. That is, we may still believe that people prefer cognitive consistency and that they strive to produce such consistency; but we

---

[2] A competing point of view is expressed by Judson Mills in Chapter 78—Ed.

must realize that this preference and this striving are not particularly strong factors in most situations.

Other evidence comes from work on attitude change and resistance to change. On the one hand, most of this work supports the idea that people are quite cognitive. Nice regularities appear which indicate that stronger arguments lead to more change. Within limits greater discrepancy leads to more attitude change (Hovland & Pritzker, 1957); more prestigeful communicators produce more change (Kelman & Hovland, 1953); and even the interaction between prestige and discrepancy makes good sense in terms of a rational man (Aronson, Turner, & Carlsmith, 1963). We also have evidence collected specifically to test various consistency theories. The work on congruity and balance models generally supports these models in the limited situations to which they apply; and the extensive work on dissonance theory pretty much supports the main point of that theory (with the exception of the selective exposure hypothesis). In other words, the evidence does indicate that people are sometimes quite cognitive and furthermore that to some extent the theories that stress cognitive consistency reflect what actually goes on. But, and this is the main issue here, the evidence also very strongly suggests that people are far from being totally cognitive and in particular that stresses toward cognitive consistency, even in the area of attitude change, are rather limited.

Subjects in the laboratory who are exposed to extremely strong, seemingly convincing arguments from impeccable sources are much influenced—they change their attitudes toward the new arguments. This shows that people are cognitive and that they reduce inconsistency. On the other hand, few people change their attitudes all the way to the proposed position. Far from it. In most studies they change their attitudes only slightly. Their new position is consistent with neither the information they have just heard nor their former behavior and opinion. It is a compromise of sorts, but not a logical one. The new position is inconsistent with everything—both new and old. The amount of change is much less than would be required for inconsistency reduction. It appears that subjects are momentarily influenced by the force of the current argument and move a little in its direction. This is not a logical, thoughtful move but rather a nonlogical move caused by the exigencies of the moment. My feeling is that even in this very cognitive situation (i.e., sitting and listening to a persuasive communication) most subjects react in a largely noncognitive manner. They hear the arguments, they find out what position the speaker is taking, and they then tend to move a little toward it much as a ship is pushed slightly by a large wave.

Subjects do not move to reduce cognitive inconsistency—they move because there is a lot of pressure, mostly noncognitive, on them. By moving a little, they reduce this pressure even though in fact they probably increase the amount of inconsistency in their cognitive structure.

The research on resistance to influence seems also to be in line with the above argument. For example, McGuire has shown that giving a person arguments which support his position is not as effective a way of increasing his resistance to persuasion as is giving him a refutation of arguments against his position (e.g., McGuire & Papageorgis, 1961). Although he interprets this in quite cognitive terms, I would take the opposite position. In terms of cognitive consistency, the supportive arguments should balance the counterarguments and should greatly increase resistance. This is because they provide as many arguments consistent with the person's initial position as the counterarguments provide arguments against it. With the new supportive arguments the person should be much more resistant than without them. The refutations, on the other hand, supposedly make him more resistant to new attacks by arousing the subject's defenses—a process which is essentially outside the cognitive-consistency framework. It turns out that the supportive arguments are actually less effective than are the refutations. I interpret this to mean that the force of the tendency toward cognitive consistency is relatively weak compared to the force of other factors such as the determination to resist, arousal of the drive to resist, confidence, or whatever else causes the refutation to be so successful. It seems clear to me that from the point of view of cognitive consistency the supportive arguments should be superior and the fact that they are not suggests that cognitive consistency is not the important mechanism operating in this situation.

The work on the effect of forewarning on resistance leads to a similar conclusion. Telling someone that he is going to hear an argument against his position helps him resist the argument; and telling him ten minutes ahead of time helps more than telling him only a few seconds ahead of time (Freedman & Sears, 1965b). In addition, there is evidence that the intervening time is not spent rehearsing or constructing counterarguments.[3] In any case, the effect was found when all or most of the subjects were extremely familiar with the available arguments on both sides of the issue (teen-age driving). Once again it sounds to me as if what is producing the increased resistance is some kind of emotional, gut reaction rather than some simple cognitive activity. The warned subject becomes determined to resist and does; whereas the unwarned is less determined and resists less. The evidence does not by any means provide unequivocal support for my position, but it does seem to be more consistent with it than with an explanation in terms of cognitive consistency.

Opposed to the evidence mentioned above, I freely admit (particularly since I was involved in some of this research) that the work on forced compliance has produced some impressive demonstrations of the strength of the drive toward cognitive consistency. In some studies really large effects were produced, and in a few there were actual behavioral effects that in one case were found as much as seven weeks after the experimental manipulation. These studies (e.g., Aronson & Carlsmith, 1963; Freedman, 1965b) are examples of those special circumstances which I mentioned earlier. I think the reason they produced such strong effects is that the situations were arranged so the cognitive factors would be dominant and other factors would be minimized or in fact would operate so as to maximize the importance of the cognitive factors. A young boy is left alone in a room with a marvelous toy and is told not to play with it. Presumably he wants very much to play with it, but a mild threat was just about enough to prevent this transgression in the few minutes he has to think about it. Instead he plays with a few miserable toys that are available and which probably serve only to dramatize how wonderful the other toy is. In this rarefied situation, the inconsistency between what he wants to do and what he is doing is very clear and salient— he wants to play with the toy and yet there he is, not touching it. There is nothing else to think about, not much else to do. He is a starving man in

---

[3] Freedman—unpublished data.

front of food and his whole person is attending to the desired object. Apparently under these circumstances the cognitive inconsistency is very important to him and he does something about it; this eventuates in him not playing with the toy at a later date. This is true at least for a large enough percentage of the boys to produce a significant experimental result. But this is a very special kind of situation—stripped clean of all extraneous factors, designed to force the subject to attend to the inconsistency. I feel that it shows there is an appreciable drive toward cognitive consistency which can sometimes be mobilized to produce big effects. However, the paucity of such behavioral and long-term effects in the experimental literature and the generally small absolute size of the effects that are usually obtained suggest that this drive is relatively weak compared to other determinants of behavior and that only in very unusual circumstances can it produce such effects.

There are a number of other areas in which the available evidence seems to me to suggest the same conclusion, but this is not meant to be by any means an exhaustive compilation of such data. It does seem likely that in general, research in which subjects are actually exposed to a real situation (even those as simple as hearing a persuasive message) tend to produce the kind of data I have been describing. In these relatively realistic situations, subjects do not behave in perfectly consistent ways. In contrast, in what I tend to think of as 'nonsituations,' in which the subject is asked how he *would* feel or would respond *if* he were in a real situation, occasionally the data may indicate that cognitive consistency is a dominating factor. My point here is that subjects who are, in a sense, *asked* if they behave logically, will sometimes answer "yes." For example, given a series of both positive and negative adjectives which supposedly apply to someone, they may form a conclusion which is logical and fits a nice formula; or asked to imagine a situation in which various factors are inconsistent with each other, they may occasionally produce a perfectly balanced solution. In contrast, subjects who are *actually* put in these situations would never behave in this way—they would be much less logical and would look very little like people who are terribly concerned about cognitive consistency.

Thus, it seems that people are not usually looking for inconsistencies among their cognitions, do not notice many that exist, and therefore do not act on them. This lack of concern with inconsistencies is, I believe, because it is not a very important consideration for most people in most circumstances. And when they do notice inconsistencies, people seem to endure them without being particularly troubled. Individuals behave in ways which are drastically inconsistent with their beliefs without bothering to change those beliefs; they hear extremely sound convincing arguments from a high prestige source but do not change their attitudes on the issue; and so on. The pressures caused by these inconsistencies may produce some small changes in the direction of reduced inconsistency, but other factors are more important and seem to swamp these relatively weak pressures toward consistency. In other words, I feel that there is a general, persistent tendency to reduce cognitive inconsistencies when they are apparent; but that this tendency is quite weak, and that most of the time it is not producing any sizable changes in the person's behavior or attitudes.

This brief paper is not meant to be a complete analysis of this complex problem and I have not attempted to go into the available data in detail. In fact, I feel that at the moment the evidence does not allow us to choose between the alternatives with any degree of confidence. Arguments can probably be presented on both sides. I have attempted to give my position and to give some of the concrete reasons for it. Since this is a question of degree of importance rather than disagreement on the basic notion of cognitive consistency, it is difficult to find experimental evidence that is unequivocally for either side. Hopefully, additional research will clarify the problem and allow us to reach more definitive conclusions about the importance of cognitive consistency.

CHAPTER 45

Conceptual Good Figures

Clinton De Soto

The Johns Hopkins University

and

Frank Albrecht

Hollins College

In the study of perception it has long been noted that, in Köhler's words, "the order of sensory fields ... shows a strong predilection for particular kinds of organization" (Köhler, 1947, p. 145). In vision, such kinds of organization are "single, regular wholes, also closed areas," as opposed to "irregular and open wholes." These preferred organizations are generally called good figures, and the phenomena associated with them are succinctly, if vaguely, summarized in the law of prägnanz. This principle was first introduced by Wertheimer; Koffka states it as follows (1935, p. 110): "psychological organization will always be as 'good' as prevailing conditions allow. In this definition the term 'good' is undefined. It embraces such properties as regularity, symmetry, simplicity and others ...."

These notions, perhaps the most familiar and enduring contributions of the Gestalt psychologists, have been given remarkably little elaboration and extension since their introduction. There have been some recent theoretical attempts to account for what makes perceptual good figures (Garner & Clement, 1963; Glanzer & Clark, 1962), and the various theories labelled consistency theories can be viewed as dealing with similar phenomena in that they, too, speak of the strain toward preferred configurations of entities and the relations between them. However, as Heider (1960) indicates, there is an important difference between these theories and the earlier work on good figure: the consistency theories invariably speak of attitudes, sentiments, or ego-object forces, whereas the Gestalt psychologists mainly treated neutral (usually spatial) relations. Additionally, the consistency theories are more truly cognitive than most of the work in the Gestalt tradition—consistency theories deal with thinking and conception, not just sensation and perception.

The Gestalt psychologists did not intend the law of prägnanz to be limited in application to perception, even though most of the work on it turned out to be so limited. Koffka's statement of the law was very general in nature; he wrote of "psychological organization" rather than of "perceptual organization." In fact, Koffka believed that "perceptual and thought

This work was supported in part by Grant GS-653 from the National Science Foundation.

504

configurations are most closely related ... in principle identity obtains between them (Koffka, 1935, pp. 13ff., p. 175; Petermann, 1950, p. 265). Koffka therefore asserted that the configurational laws of perception applied to cognition generally. He did, however, admit that "The task of working out the basic types of thought configurations in the same way as for the perceptual configurations is one which still remains before us ..." (Petermann, 1950, pp. 265–6). Köhler held a similar belief (Köhler, 1947, pp. 177ff.). This approach has been savagely attacked on conceptual grounds (Petermann, 1950, pp. 265ff., 301ff.), but the really decisive question is whether conceptual good figures can be discovered empirically. The search has not been seriously attempted, and as a result, the law of prägnanz has come to be treated almost exclusively as a perceptual law (see, for instance, Osgood, 1953, pp. 204, 216).

The aim of this article is to argue that there are indeed conceptual good figures besides those treated by the existing consistency theories and to suggest that their coerciveness and range of effects exceed what one might offhand expect.

BALANCE AND THE GROUPING SCHEMA

We would like to describe the results of a recent experiment (De Soto, Henley, & London, 1968), partly to show the feasibility of experimental investigation of conceptual good figures, and partly to show the distinction between what is good figure in the case of configurations involving sentiment relations and what is good figure in other cases.

In this experiment, goodness of figure was evaluated by the ease with which a structure was learned and remembered. There is some precedent for using memory tasks to measure goodness of figure, both under the Gestalt tradition (e.g., Glanzer & Clark, 1962), and under the consistency theory tradition (e.g., Zajonc & Burnstein, 1965a). However, this experiment appears to be the first one in which attention was paid to goodness of figure in both senses simultaneously.

The subjects in this experiment were required to learn a fictitious social structure made up of ten men's names and the relations among them. In some conditions, the relations were sentiment relations of the kind treated by consistency theories (friends-enemies); in other conditions, the relations were neutral or unit-forming relations (acquainted-unacquainted), which in general are not treated by consistency theories or not treated separately from sentiment relations.

One general hypothesis for the experiment, deriving from classic Gestalt findings on perception and from recent studies of social schemas (De Soto, 1960; Kuethe, 1962), was that the simple grouping is a basic conceptual good figure. In support of this hypothesis, it was found that simple groupings, with positive relations (friendship or acquaintance) within groups, and negative relations (enmity or lack of acquaintance) between groups, are learned relatively easily. Subjects had difficulty with structures in which the simple grouping was violated by incompleteness (some relations not stated) or by reversed relations (a negative relation within a group, a positive relation between groups). This finding held for both unit-forming and sentiment relations, but most clearly in the case of unit-forming relations. For in the case of sentiment relations there was an overlay of other tendencies—tendencies in accord with Heider's balance theory, as formulated by Cartwright and Harary (1956). That is to say, whereas two *or* three groups are good figure for unit-forming relations, two groups are much better figure than three groups for sentiment relations. Also, whereas incompleteness and reversals, as violations of a simple grouping, produce roughly equal difficulty for unit-forming relations, incompleteness (which does not unbalance the structure) does not produce as much difficulty as reversals (which do unbalance the structure) in the case of sentiment relations.

In short, this experiment showed that balance does make for conceptual good figure, but that balance does not work in isolation and extra-balance characteristics of a structure also determine goodness of figure.

LINEAR ORDER AS CONCEPTUAL GOOD FIGURE

We will now turn to another structure, the linear ordering, which we believe to be a preeminent conceptual good figure. By no means do we wish to imply that the simple grouping and the linear ordering are the only conceptual good figures, but we believe they hold a sway which it is hard to appreciate. Indeed, with few exceptions (e.g., Sampson, 1963), workers in the consistency theory tradition have shown even less recognition of the good figure character of the linear ordering than of the simple grouping.

There is experimental evidence to support some of our assertions (De Soto, 1960, 1961; De Soto & Bosley, 1962; De Soto, London, & Handel, 1965; Kuethe & De Soto, 1964), but we intend to rely mainly on more anecdotal evidence to point up what we consider a far-ranging and dimly perceived problem in human cognition.

Consider the following dialogue between an interviewer for *Playboy*[1] magazine and the jazz trumpeter Miles Davis (*Playboy*, 1962):

PLAYBOY: You've won all the trumpet polls. After yourself, how would you rank others?

DAVIS: *After* me! Hell, it's plenty great trumpet players don't come *after* me, or *after* nobody else! That's what I hate so about critics—how they are always *comparing* artists ... always writing that one's better than another one. Ten men can have spent all their lives learning technical expertness on their instruments, but just like in any art, one will play one style and the rest nine other ways. And if some critics just don't happen to like a man's style, they will knock the artist. That bugs the hell out of musicians. It's made some damn near mad enough to want to hang up their horns.

Trumpet players, like anybody else, are individualized by their different ideas and styles. The thing to judge in any jazz artist is does the man project, and does he have ideas. You take Dizzy—he does, all the time, every time he picks up his horn. Some more cats—Clark Terry, Ray Nance, Kenny Dorham, Roy Eldridge,

> Harold Baker, Freddie Hubbard, Lee Morgan, Bobby
> Hackett—a lot of them. Hell, that cat down in New
> Orleans, Al Hirt, he blows his ass off, too!

What Miles has to say, in short, is that these trumpet players are incomparable or incommensurable. Why doesn't he say it thus briefly? Not from a weak command of English. On the contrary, he does an unusually telling job of making English say something it is ill-equipped to say. We would like to recommend that he say simply the players have different styles and are incomparable, but we cannot. Few would understand the rarely used words, incomparable and incommensurable; he would sound pedantic to those who did; and worst and most curious, he would probably not convince them.

Compare the accomplishments of the two statements. In a few words, the interviewer proposes that trumpet players can be arranged in a certain way: that they can be ranked, or ordered, and asks for an exact ordering. In many more words Miles protests the interviewer's proposition. We repeat that Miles' words are well chosen; he is not being verbose. One reason Miles has to argue at length is that the onus of establishing his claim seems to be on him, rather than on the interviewer. The proposition that the trumpet players can be ranked seems almost self-evident; denying it is what requires proof. It is hard to fight good figure. It is no accident that the generic term for good arrangement in English is order: the prototypic example of good arrangement is order in its narrow sense of linear order.

LINEAR ORDER VS. PARTIAL ORDER

Implicit in the Gestalt writings about the law of prägnanz is the principle that structures which suffer the most strain and distortion are ones which objectively resemble some good figure. It could be argued that Miles' plight stems partly from the fact that objectively the arrangement of trumpet players does indeed resemble a linear ordering—but that it is a poor relative, the partial ordering. Let us make some definitions. Objects are in a linear ordering if there is a relation among them that has these key properties: *asymmetry*, meaning that if one object bears the relation to a second, the second does not bear it to the first; *transitivity*, meaning that if one object bears the relation to a second, and the second bears it to a third, then the first must bear it to the third; and *completeness*, meaning that for every possible pair of objects in the set under consideration, one bears the relation to the other. Objects are in a partial ordering if the relation among them is asymmetric and transitive but lacks completeness. A familiar example is the *family tree* yielded by the relation of descent. We would suggest that such a branching structure would best characterize the world of trumpet players. Although Miles, in effect, argued that they could not be put in any arrangement with clear properties, he would, if pushed, doubtless have to admit that some trumpet players are better than some others. He would have to agree to a relation that was asymmetric and transitive, but he would persist in denying completeness. Sometimes neither A nor B is better than the other, either because they are equally good or (more in keeping with his emphasis on stylistic differences) they are on different branches of a tree of attainment and therefore incomparable. But neither 'tree' nor 'branch' nor 'partial ordering' is available for this use in standard English, nor is there any other convenient way of elucidating such an expression.

LINEAR ORDER VS. NONTRANSITIVE STRUCTURES

We wish to give one more example of the inadequacy of the relational vocabulary of English, again in handling a poor relative of the simple ordering. Some years ago various zoologists and psychologists made intensive studies of dominance relations (peck rights) among birds. They learned that if bird A dominated bird B, and B dominated C, it was quite possible that C dominated A. The explanation was not too difficult—the birds established enduring dominance on the basis of the rather chancy outcomes of pair-wise encounters, a process which ensured that the resulting social structure was asymmetric and complete, but not that it was transitive. But when they tried to describe these pecking orders which were not orderings, the scientists showed dismay and difficulty. They spoke of "pecking out of order," "curious exceptions," "irregularities," "imperfect orderings," "lack of a hierarchy," "polygonal dominance," "cyclic pecking," "triangular pecking," and "complex, triangular hierarchies" (De Soto, 1960). None of these terms adequately characterizes the birds' social structure. The first five intimate that a linear ordering does not prevail but make no attempt to say what *does* prevail. The remaining four are valiant efforts to bend English to a task for which it is clearly unsuited. There seems little likelihood of a reader grasping the nature of the social structure from any of those terms alone; the only way it can be put to him in standard English is through extended explanation. English, so bountiful with words to say things are ordered, provides no words to say things are interrelated in this slightly different way. Mathematicians have given the names "dominance structure" and "tournament" to relations and structures of this type, but it goes without saying that these terms are not part of standard English.

THE SCOPE OF THE PROBLEM

Accepting that there are conceptual good figures which can be as compelling on occasion as perceptual good figures, one can inquire further as to the range of conditions under which they pose problems for thought. We can make some general suggestions, continuing to use the linear ordering as our prime example.

A general prediction is that problems will arise when people are *thinking*. Conceptual good figures are traps primarily for rationalistic, intellective behavior as opposed to nonintellective behavior such as affective and sensory reactions. As thinkers, scientists and scholars may be more, not less, vulnerable than other men to the appeal of good figure.

A few more specific predictions follow, based on the principle of prägnanz, which says that thought will tend toward good figure to the extent conditions permit it.

1. When people can't see how things are. Old-fashioned naive realism—the assumption that our perceptions are veridical even if our thoughts are not—is no longer a tenable position. Nevertheless, perceptions are likely to reflect reality more faithfully than thought, and the evidence of eyes and ears may so disprove a linear ordering as to prevent its appearance in thought.

In the absence of such evidence our thoughts drift toward good figure.

2. *When people think of more than they grasp.* People have a prodigious store of memories which they can recall, one by one, under suitable provocation. In contrast, the number of elements people can carry in their heads simultaneously—their span of apprehension—is absurdly small, on the order of six or seven. Even more limited is their capacity to interrelate these few elements in arrangements other than simple groupings or linear orderings. And when people's mental reach exceeds their mental grasp, what happens? They simplify. Inevitably, their simplification tends toward good figure.

3. *When a linear ordering has somehow been suggested.* We have mentioned that a resemblance of an actual arrangement to a good figure tends to induce the good figure. For example, the family tree may induce the better figure: the family line. Moreover, the good figure may be positively encouraged and supported by various sources.

The several conditions that foster good figure can obviously coexist. Indeed, they are likely to be found together. Consider once more the plight of Miles Davis. He was asked to intellectualize about trumpet players rather than give an affective or aesthetic reaction to them. He was asked to think about a rather large number of them. And a linear ordering of them was suggested explicitly by the *Playboy* interviewer and implicitly by the background chorus of critics. No wonder Miles had a struggle.

Compare Anna Karenina's easier triumph in the following exchange:

Oblonsky says: "You'll end up by being more fond of her than of your own daughter."

Anna replies: "You talk like a man. There's no such thing as more or less in love. I love my daughter with one kind of love and her with another."

What has happened? Anna, like Miles, has demolished a linear ordering. Perhaps it is Tolstoy's genius that enables her to do it so effectively in fewer words. Perhaps the contest is subtly different. Anna, as a woman, may be able to deny intellectualizations more effectively than a man. Perhaps the restriction of discussion to two people as elements makes it easier to insist on kinds as opposed to degrees. Perhaps the suggestion that love can be ordered has less conventional acceptance to give it strength than the suggestion that merit can. All these things may work to make the linear ordering less compelling in this example than in the earlier one.

What, then, if we examine cases where conditions are even more encouraging of good figure than those confronting Miles, cases where people are truly intellectualizing, trying to arrive at an overall organization or scheme of things, cases where the organization is far from visible, where the number of elements is exceeding, and where a linear ordering is vigorously proposed? In such cases, we believe, the linear ordering has held immense sway and given mankind some of his foremost intellectual traps. In particular, the predilection for linear orderings has afflicted man's great framing conceptions about what he is, where he is, and what he is doing.

Perhaps the most outrageous linear ordering of all time was the Great Chain of Being or Scale of Nature—the notion, traceable to Aristotle, that the entire universe is structured as a single, simple, continuous ordering. This ordering ranged from the most perfect, most worthy being (God) on top to the basest element on the bottom with no breaks, no branches, and no exceptions. We may recognize the Great Chain as a historical aberration, but it dominated Western thought for 2,000 years and had profound and diverse consequences (Lovejoy, 1936). It worked against social change because to uplift the poor and oppressed would be to leave empty their grade on the Great Scale, an unthinkable happening. It encouraged scientists to search for missing links in the Great Chain (this was the expressed original aim of the Royal Society). It facilitated the acceptance of the doctrine of evolution, which was in a sense merely a temporalization of the static Great Chain, but it saddled thought about evolution with a linear organization which plagues it to this day. In 1816 the anatomist Cuvier showed that the partial ordering or tree, not the Chain, is the appropriate structure for the animal kingdom, but 150 years later the evolutionary ladder still tends all too often to displace the evolutionary tree.

So with thought about social and cultural evolution; it too has suffered throughout its history from crippling efforts to make the linear ordering the overall organizational scheme. Even in viewing the history of their own discipline, as Kuhn (1962) has recently shown, scientists have an unfortunate tendency to see it as developing in a linear sequence to its present state, and toward an ultimate goal. (The equally dubious and equally compelling notion of the hierarchy of sciences is too familiar to require documentation.)

So too with thought about social structures, although the problem becomes curiously complicated in this case by the fact that social structures are in part *constructed* by man to suit his fancy (De Soto & Albrecht, Chapter 49).

Indeed, even in the singular case which has been mentioned in which man places himself in a well-defined structure other than a linear ordering or simple grouping—the *family tree*—he often lapses into the less valid but somehow more appealing and elegant *family line*. It is interesting to note that the majority of societies studied by anthropoligists, in which kinship typically is a topic of much more thought and reflection than in our own, view descent as unilineal rather than bilateral. The cognitive considerations we have spoken of would predict this finding, probably better than the explanations traditionally advanced by anthropologists, which have run into difficulties recently (Davenport, 1959; Wunderlich, Youniss, & De Soto, 1962). It is perhaps less well known that the majority of thoughtful students of biological heredity in western civilization believed for milennia, until the 1880's, that descent is unilineal, either patrilineal or matrilineal. Even when the sperm and egg had both been discovered, most scientists seemed incapable of conceiving of biparental inheritance: the issue was between the ovists (descent from the mother) and the animalculists (descent from the father), between family lines, not between family line and family tree (Grant, 1956).

We do not wish to prolong or detail further the list of problems that result from the predilection for linear orderings. In fact, it may be worthwhile after our diatribe to make clear that we do not consider the linear ordering to be all bad. Some things in the world are, after all, truly arranged in linear orderings; and it can often be a convenient and even necessary simplification to treat things as in linear orderings when in truth they are quite differently arranged. Coombs (1964, pp. 284–291) for example, has recently written on the need for compressing partial orderings into linear orderings when decisions are to be made, some elements chosen over others. Even if the most valid arrangement of trumpet players is a partial ordering, a night club manager who has to decide which ones to hire must somehow compress the partial ordering into a linear ordering, a simple ranking.

CONCLUSIONS

Overall, however, we suspect that in the majority of cases in which we arrange things in linear orderings there is little justification, that we are doing nothing more than falling into an intellectual trap. We think also that there is value in viewing the linear ordering as a conceptual good figure; this view reminds one that it is not an inevitable way of organizing things, that we are capable of conceiving of other arrangements, but that it is a seductive and coercive organization. It further indicates some of the conditions under which it is likely to be an intellectual trap, including the perhaps unexpected implication that it may be more of a problem for serious thought about important topics than for casual thought about trivial matters—that scientists and scholars may be more prone to this kind of simplistic thinking than less meditative people.

As an illustration of the possibilities of systematic experimentation on goodness of figure we would like to cite a recent unpublished experiment by Nancy Henley. Subjects were required to learn a five-element structure in which the relation was asymmetric and complete, but in which there were intransitivities (loops or cycles) ranging in number from 0 (a linear ordering) through 5. She obtained a correlation (rho) of .83 between number of loops and difficulty as measured by errors. Such regularities are rare in learning experiments, and suggest that the approach we have been advocating is a fruitful one.

We wish to reiterate that we do not regard the linear ordering as the only important conceptual good figure; rather, we have used it as an illustrative example. We do believe, however, that it has been overlooked as an intellectual trap in comparison with, say, the simple grouping. One does not need to look far to find warnings against the dangers of categorizing, classifying, stereotyping, dichotomizing. Warnings about linear orderings are much rarer.

Finally, we wish to remark that we hold no brief for the use of anecdotal evidence in the study of conceptual good figure. We have indeed used anecdotal evidence primarily, but the reason is partly that we wished to suggest the place of good figure in human thought and, more, that experimental evidence seems scarce. We would encourage experimentation on conceptual good figure and see no reason why it cannot be done. Much of the experimentation stimulated by the consistency theories can be regarded, as we have indicated, as being concerned with certain special classes of conceptual good figures. What is needed now is an extension of this experimental approach to the areas traditionally labelled judgments, reasoning, concept-formation, learning, and so on, where the dominant influence of associationistic, S-R psychology has led to very different experimental emphases.

CHAPTER 46

Processes of Ramification Among Cognitive Links

Karl E. Weick
University of Minnesota

The sine qua non of consistency theories is the property of cognitive linkage. Unless isolated cognitive elements are related in some manner, pressures toward accommodation are nonexistent. Even though this assumption is basic for all consistency theories, many of its implications have been ignored. Still unanswered and largely unstudied is the question, do persons, regardless of whether they are in a state of consistency or inconsistency, tend to maximize the linkages among cognitive elements, minimize them, or effect some compromise? As we will see, it is important to answer this question whether one studies balance, congruity, cognitive dissonance, symmetry, or any other theory of cognitive consistency.

To preserve some important properties of this question, we have labeled it as the issue of 'cognitive ramification.' Presumably when at least two elements are linked, forces of some magnitude will be generated to include other isolated elements for the sake of psychological economy (Lewin, 1951). A process of branching may occur in which the original linkage is extended, new elements are incorporated, and these new links induce still other links. However, once a specific linkage begins to ramify, maximum interconnection of elements is not inevitable. Different degrees of ramification have different implications for the arousal and resolution of inconsistency. If a cognitive system is maximally interconnected (high ramification) then it should be difficult for an inconsistent element to penetrate the system (it does not fit with anything which exists); if an inconsistent element is implanted, tension should be more intense because more extensive changes will be required to incorporate the element; and, resolutions should involve removing the element or minimizing its importance through greater attention to other portions of the interconnected system (e.g., the mechanism of bolstering). A system which is less interconnected (low ramification) allows more inconsistent elements to penetrate; once the inconsistent element has been implanted tension should be less intense because fewer changes are needed to incorporate the element; and resolutions should involve more attempts to retain the inconsistent element in some manner that isolates it

Preparation of this paper was facilitated by the National Science Foundation through Grant GS-1042.

from adjacent elements. Notice that both systems are functional. Highly ramified systems are relatively immune to inconsistent elements, but once they intrude, the system is vulnerable and discomfort is substantial. Systems with low ramification are less immune to inconsistency. Discomfort may be present because there is more residual inconsistency, but the system is less vulnerable and the discomfort less intense, when inconsistent elements do intrude.

The purpose of this chapter is to initiate thinking about the issue of ramification. To this end, I have collected some ideas and findings which investigators should consider when they try to clarify their own ideas about ramification.

Sources of Cognitive Linkages

An obvious place to start the discussion is to review very briefly some prominent sources of cognitive linkages. These sources represent ways in which isolated elements can become linked.

1. *Affective attributes* (e.g., Heider, 1958; Scott, 1963). Distinctions between preferences and aversions are among the earliest discriminations which persons make, and this experience often affects the linkage process. Elements may become linked because they share the same affective sign.

2. *Instrumental efficacy* (e.g., Katz, 1960; Katz & Stotland, 1959; Rosenberg, 1956; Smith, Bruner, & White, 1956). One element may lead to the attainment or blockage of another element or two elements may have shared instrumental relevance to a consequence. By virtue of instrumentality, the elements become linked positively or negatively. The consistency of the linkage depends upon the evaluative signs attached to the elements.

3. *Temporal contiguity* (e.g., Dillehay, Insko, & Smith, 1966; McGuire, 1960c). Isolated elements often become linked when they are evoked in close temporal proximity. This form of linkage is potentially crucial because most consistency experiments confront subjects with several cognitions in a short span of time, and the effects of temporal proximity and consistency are difficult to separate.

4. *Common authoritative source* (e.g., Rokeach, 1960). If persons are sensitive to authorities because they control rewards and punishments and not because they are credible communicators, then isolated elements may "be related to each other by virtue of their common origin in authority, rather than by virtue of intrinsic connections" (Rokeach, 1960, p. 62).

5. *Responsibility* (e.g., Brehm & Cohen, 1962; Feather, 1964b). If two unrelated elements are elicited situationally so as to suggest volitional responsibility of one for the other, linkage may be induced. An interesting example is compliance under low coercion, wherein the self-element may become linked with a particular action because of perceived responsibility.

6. *Psychological implications* (e.g., Bramel, Chapter 26; Brehm & Cohen, 1962; Festinger, 1957; McGuire, 1960c). When a person holds a given cognition, there may be other cognitions which 'follow from,' or are implied by the original cognitions. If these expected elements already exist in the system, linkages should be formed. If the elements do not exist, the person should be more willing to incorporate them.

7. *Concept exemplars* (e.g., Abelson & Carroll, 1965; Lott, 1955; Scott, 1965). Isolated elements may be related when they can be subsumed under a single more generic concept through processes of stimulus generalization,

response generalization, or mediated stimulus generalization (Manis, 1966). This basis for linkage is exemplified in Christiansen's (1959) finding that persons respond to international conflicts in ways that are similar to their responses to everyday conflicts.

8. *Grouping mechanisms* (e.g., Heider, 1958; Wertheimer, 1923). Cognitive elements may become linked because of their proximity, similarity, common fate, common boundary, good form, and cause-and-effect. While these bases for linkage derive mostly from studies of visual perception, it seems probable that with closer attention, these sources of unit relations may be incorporated more directly and less loosely into consistency theories.

9. *Causal attribution* (e.g., Heider, 1944, 1958). The notion of causal attribution states that persons establish order and coherence among isolated elements by referring them to invariant properties such as motives or intentions. Thus, isolated cognitive elements may become linked when they are interpreted as instances of a common invariant disposition. A possible example of this linkage is the finding noted earlier that persons tend to generalize from interpersonal images to images of international relationships.

Some Determinants of Ramification

The preceding nine sources of cognitive linkage describe only *potential* sources of connection. We have not yet discussed variables which determine whether the linkage will actually occur, how permanent the linkage will be, and the extent to which a given linkage will ramify and induce additional linkages. These considerations will be examined in this section.

1. *Strong initial linkage.* If the source of the original link is intense, then it is probable that the linkage will be more permanent and available for subsequent ramification and also that there will be greater pressures toward ramification. For example, links that are mediated by instrumental efficacy should exhibit greater ramification as the values which are implemented become more important and as the perceived instrumentality increases (Rosenberg, 1956).

Aside from the several relationships for the probability of ramification which can be derived from this intensity principle and the preceding list of linkage sources, there are other variables which cut across all sources of linkage and may affect the extent to which any linkage will ramify.

2. *Differentiation.* Perhaps the most common determinant of ramification discussed in consistency theories is differentiation (e.g., Abelson, 1959; Asch, 1946; Lewin, 1951; Rokeach, 1960; Scott, 1963). Differentiation is variously described as the "distinctiveness of elements" (Scott, 1963, p. 277), the extent to which elements are "distinguishable" (Lewin, 1951, p. 116), the "richness of detail in elements" (Rokeach, 1960, p. 37), or the extent to which separate meanings of a single element are dissociated (Abelson, 1959, p. 345). Differentiation is commonly treated both as a structural property of cognitive systems and as a process. Both emphases have relevance for the issue of ramification.

Differentiation, viewed as a property of cognitive structure, commonly means independence among elements and may be assessed by the amount of information which a person has concerning a specific element (Rokeach, 1960, p. 38). As information and distinctiveness increase, it should be easier to add new elements to a structure because there is a higher probability that there are existing elements to which they can be related. Scott (1965) argues, for example, that the greater the independence among a set of attributes (differentiation), the more they can be selectively associated with or dissociated from an image (p. 86). Conversely, if attributes are highly correlated, the impact of new elements cannot be localized. For this reason, Scott also hypothesizes that when attributes are not differentiated, both contravaluant *and* neutral information will be avoided. Neutral information is potentially aversive for undifferentiated structures because it is not affectively congruent with existing elements, and to incorporate the information, some dimension other than affect must be activated to make the neutral element meaningful.

If differentiation is viewed as a process, there are additional implications for the issue of ramification. When an element is differentiated to establish balance, meanings proliferate and become more refined, and these additional meanings may be viewed as new linkages. One way in which differentiation proceeds has been described by Abelson (1959). "One element is differentiated into two parts, a new part and an old part. The old part retains the relation with the other element in the structure, but the affect toward it is changed. The new part on the other hand, retains the old affect toward the differentiated element, but the sign of the relation with the other element is changed" (p. 346). Thus, if a person dislikes politicians but a prestigeful source glorifies them, differentiation occurs when a person distinguishes between statesmen (associative bond between source and politician is retained, but affect is changed to positive valence) and "wardheelers" (associative bond is changed because prestigeful source obviously does not glorify these persons, and the original negative affect is maintained).

3. *Cognitive skills.* Even though differentiation provides a means to extend linkages, it may be used infrequently because "it requires intellectual ability, flexibility, and because when there is strong affect toward a cognitive object, it is not easily split apart" (Abelson, 1959, p. 348). Furthermore, for a differentiation to be maintained, the two meanings must be strongly dissociated and this may be difficult if the meanings have overlapping attributes.

4. *Rewards for cognitive activity.* Ramification should also be influenced by the extent to which persons have been rewarded in the past for cognitive elaboration of their affective preferences and aversions (Rosenberg, 1965, p. 298). As rewards for elaboration increase, structures should become more differentiated and linkages should be extended rather than narrowed.

5. *Bolstering.* Another mechanism that affects ramification is bolstering, a process that has been discussed by Festinger (1957); Brehm and Cohen (1962, see especially the discussion of behavioral commitment); and Abelson (1959). Bolstering occurs when new elements are related in a balanced manner to one element in the original inconsistent pair. The classic example is the smoker who is anxious about lung cancer and 'swamps' this potential imbalance by adding elements such as smoking is enjoyable, it is relaxing, it aids social life, etc. The original elements remain intact, but one of them receives additional support through an increment in linkages. Repeated uses of bolstering should lead to the addition of new links and to the affirmation of links which already exist.

Given that bolstering may be an important means of extending linkages, it becomes essential to know the conditions that produce bolstering. Abelson (1959) suggests that within an inconsistent pair of elements the more cathected element will be bolstered; that elements which are socially supported will be bolstered; but that bolstering will not occur if only unbalanced new elements are available. Brehm and Cohen (1962) suggest that bolstering is most likely to occur when both dissonant elements are resistant to change. "There are numerous ways in which the individual can justify engaging in the [discrepant] behavior. Almost anything that he can make relevant to the particular behavior in which he has engaged can be used in justifying it. Thus the individual may reduce his dissonance by finding and/or changing the magnitude of one or more such justifications" (Brehm & Cohen, 1962, p. 113). Intensified behavioral commitment to produce consonant linkages is also discussed by Kelman (1962) and by Deutsch, Krauss, and Rosenau (1962).

Bolstering has some interesting properties of especial importance for ramification. It demands less 'cognitive work' than does differentiation and can be implemented by behavioral changes. For these reasons bolstering should serve as a fairly prominent mechanism of ramification.

6. *Memory processes.* One of the better known formulations concerning memory is Bartlett's (1932) investigation of qualitative changes in traces that occur over time. Recent extensions and methodological refinements of Bartlett's ideas (Papageorgis, 1963; Papageorgis & Tyler, 1966) suggest that inconsistent elements tend to be reorganized with the passage of time and to become more consistent with the subject's "culture and existing cognitive categories."

While social psychologists have recently become more interested in the effects of time on consistency (e.g., Freedman, 1965b; McGuire, 1964; Walster, 1964; Chapters 54-58) there still exists in many formulations the somewhat primitive notion that as time passes, traces left by the original inconsistency simply decay. For a complete picture of linkage mechanisms to emerge, it would seem essential to pay greater attention to the dynamic changes that occur over time. If memory traces become organized in a manner that is internally consistent, this means that cognitive systems should become both homogeneous and maximally linked as time passes. However, since organization takes time, we would also expect that shortly after a communication, elements are remembered accurately, even if they are mildly inconsistent and unlinked. (The presence of strong inconsistency may, on the other hand, reduce the accuracy of immediate memory, as suggested in studies by Steiner and Rogers [1962] and Rokeach and Vidulich [1960], among others.) Thus, if we observe a cognitive system immediately after exposure to inconsistent information, we should ordinarily find that elements are minimally linked. But, as time passes and the content becomes reorganized, new linkages may emerge and persons may appear to maximize linkages. It may be that the question of whether persons maximize or minimize linkages can be answered only if the span of time following exposure to information is specified.

7. *Fluidity of barriers.* A substantial portion of Lewinian research (Lewin, 1935, 1951) concerns conditions under which boundaries between interdependent systems become more or less permeable. Evidence suggests that fatigue, satiation, and failure increase fluidity between systems. Extended to the present discussion, it appears possible that as boundaries between sets of elements are rendered more fluid, linkages should increase.

8. *Situational ambiguity.* A prominent hypothesis in theories of ego-involvement (e.g., Allport, 1961; Sherif & Cantril, 1947; Sherif, Sherif, & Nebergall, 1965) is that as situations become more ambiguous, persons re-

spond more in terms of personal dispositions. To the extent that personality tends to be organized in a consistent manner (see Allport, 1961 and Child, 1963 for evidence on this point), we would expect that linkages which are formed in ambiguous situations would be sensitive to personality needs, and therefore would reflect efforts to maximize consistency. As situational pressures become more explicit, linkages are more apt to be limited, especially if the situation has contradictions built into it.

9. *Inertia.* McGuire (1960c) and especially Atkinson and Cartwright (1964) have recently argued that investigators should pay greater attention to the fact that whenever information is presented, some form of behavior is already underway and these inertial tendencies must be overcome if the new information is to have any impact. There may be a delay in the acceptance of new elements or new elements may never be incorporated if ongoing activities are of sufficient strength. These two possibilities are theoretically important because if persons fail to add new elements and linkages, this may be less a property of their cognitive systems and more a function of the dynamics of goal-oriented behavior. Persons may be quite willing to add new elements if inertial tendencies (the persistence of an unsatisfied motive, Atkinson & Cartwright, 1964, p. 586) are slight or if these tendencies can be satisfied by substitute activity directed toward the new stimuli.

10. *Search priorities.* When persons process information, they tend to compare new elements with sets of existing elements in some kind of systematic sequence. Rokeach (1960) hypothesizes that before accepting new information, a person first determines whether it is compatible with primitive notions concerning the self and the physical world (central region of beliefs); then the information is compared against existing beliefs about the nature of valued authorities (intermediate belief region); and only if both 'tests' are passed is the information then filed in the 'peripheral region' which consists of beliefs that derive from authorities. Notice that if information processing proceeds like this, new elements might seem to be consistent with peripheral beliefs and thus acceptable, but fail to be incorporated because they do not meet tests associated with the first two stages of the review process. Conversely, apparently contradictory elements might be accepted because they pass the earlier tests even though they seem to be incompatible with other peripheral beliefs.

The notion of search priorities also suggests that different meanings of an element become salient at different points in time. In Rokeach's model, for example, the first test concerns the fit of new elements with existing notions about the world. If elements do not contain this information they might be passed along for the second test *or* they might be rejected outright. It is important to know which outcome actually occurs because if the element is not rejected and is passed along, then it is probable that a much more heterogeneous, unlinked set of elements would be found in the peripheral region than if information had to meet all tests before it was placed in the peripheral region. If all new elements must meet all tests, then it is more likely that persons would appear to maximize linkages. However, if testing can be short-circuited, then it might be easier for persons to minimize linkages among elements.

11. *Emotion and cue utilization.* A generalization of considerable importance for discussions of linkage has been proposed by Easterbrook (1959).

He argues that "emotional arousal acts consistently to reduce the range of cues that an organism uses, and ... the reduction in range of cue utilization influences action in ways that are either organizing or disorganizing, depending on the behavior concerned" (p. 183). It is proposed that as arousal increases, the number of cues to which a subject orients declines. As the decline in cue utilization proceeds, task-irrelevant cues (peripheral) are excluded before task-relevant cues (central). When all irrelevant cues are excluded, then relevant cues also begin to drop out.

If these notions are extrapolated to the issue of ramification, some interesting implications emerge. When arousal is low and irrelevant cues are noticed, linkages involving heterogeneous elements may be formed. As arousal increases, the range of elements which are added should narrow, but there is a greater likelihood that those which remain will either be actively incorporated or actively rejected. Thus under conditions of high arousal, persons may act in ways which suggest that they minimize linkages. These actions, however, represent not so much an attempt to avoid inconsistency, as they do an inability to incorporate all of the stimuli which are presented.

12. *Incomplete structures*. An important wedge into the question of ramification is found in a recent study by Morrissette, Jahnke, and Baker (1966) which deals with the assumption that cognitive structures tend toward a state of completeness (Harary, 1959) or closure (Hartmann, 1935). Morrissette *et al.* argue that there is a conflict between the assertion that cognitive structures tend toward completeness and the fact that an incomplete structure can be balanced. (Balance is thusly assessed by Harary's [1959] criterion: All semicycles in a graph theoretic representation of the structure are positive.) The conflict occurs because if a structure is balanced, there should be no remaining tension to produce completion.

To test whether incompleteness or imbalance created the greater tension, Morrissette *et al.* created hypothetical situations which contained all possible combinations of balance and completeness, and had subjects rate the amount of discomfort they associated with each structure. The actual ratings of discomfort were compared against two hypothetical orderings of the situations, one which assumed that incomplete structures could be balanced and one which assumed that all incomplete structures were imbalanced. The ratings were predicted more accurately by the formula which permitted balance in incomplete structures. In every case where a structure would generate different amounts of tension depending on the assumptions about completeness, the model which permitted incomplete balance was the most accurate. It was concluded that the completeness hypothesis is not supported and, therefore, either needs to be dropped or revised.

These findings suggest that it is possible under some circumstances for persons to restrict or even sever linkages and still maintain balanced structures. It is difficult to abandon the theoretical possibility, however, that incomplete structures sometimes invite further ramification—as a kind of Zeignarik effect, or perhaps as a search for novelty, if not for the achievement of tension reduction.

CONCLUSION

In the absence of data specifically pointed to the question, do persons tend to maximize or minimize linkages among cognitive elements, we have compiled what amounts to a do-it-yourself discussion. Assorted findings and theoretical distinctions which seem to converge on this question have been gathered and some of their more obvious implications noted. It remains for the individual investigator to select from these sources those which seem of greatest relevance. It seems clear, however, that conceptual slippage in consistency formulations has been sizeable, and consistency theorists must become more explicit in their thinking about cognitive linkages.

Concerning the specific question, do persons try to maximize consistency by maximizing linkages or minimize inconsistency by minimizing linkages, it is possible to make a crude assessment of the preceding discussion to see which point of view tends to be favored.

We have claimed that persons might be expected to expand or maximize linkages: when their structures have strong linkages but are highly differentiated; when they are skilled at cognitive ramification operations and have been rewarded for performing them; when sufficient cognitions are present to facilitate bolstering; if sufficient time is available to permit memory reorganization; if barriers between cognitive subsystems are rendered more fluid; when situations are ambiguous; if ongoing activities can be abandoned with little effort or if there exist distinct opportunities for their eventual resumption; when several stringent stages in information processing are consistently performed; if the prevailing level of emotional arousal is of low or moderate intensity; and possibly also when cognitive structures are incomplete. One or more of these conditions may be present in most consistency manipulations, and for this reason, we would anticipate that linkages would appear to ramify. Such a conclusion is consistent with the Gestalt assumption that systems tend toward closure and good form. The conclusion is also consistent with the general property of systems that "the dimensionality of the output of a system is always less than the dimensionality of the input" (Miller, 1955, p. 529). Selective attention and selective organization have long been bulwarks of psychology, and to the extent that these findings are relevant to systems of cognitive elements, we would expect to observe people trying to maximize consistency.

However, it would certainly be premature to conclude that this is the way people act. If we simply take the opposite of each point listed above, then it is possible to argue that as conditions approach these opposing states, people will tend to restrict cognitive links. And, as we have tried to show, it is distinctly possible that several of these opposing states will occur when inconsistent cognitions are activated.

It seems clear that ramification is a concept that cuts across most consistency formulations, it is relevant to issues of induction and reduction of inconsistency, and so far the concept has received little attention. Until more is known about ramification, consistency theories will remain somewhat cryptic and incomplete.

CHAPTER 47

A Programmable Theory of Cognition and Affect in Individual Personal Belief Systems

Kenneth Mark Colby

Department of Computer Science
Stanford University

PROGRAMMABLE THEORIES

To simulate a system is to build a model which imitates the behavior of the system. If a model behaves as an acceptable imitation, then the principles embodied in the model exemplify a theory which explains how a system operates. To construct a theory of some aspect of human behavior, the best hypotheses available, having some degree of animal, experimental, clinical, and everyday evidence in their favor, are combined or synthesized into a single theory. In computer simulation a model for this conjunction of hypotheses is then constructed in the form of a computer program. The steps in this complicated construction have been described in detail by Abelson (1968). The computer program is gradually improved by subjecting it to tests of consistency, correspondence to real-life situations, and pragmatic usefulness. Increasing explicitness and consistency develop from repeated computer runs of the program. Running a program generates near and remote consequences of the program's postulates. Certain of these consequences on artificial data are then compared with real-life data. When the resemblance between these two sets of data is unsatisfactory, the program or the theory must be revised. Working back and forth between theory, program, and data, one hopes to develop understanding; in this case, of how belief systems operate—how they are maintained, how they change and resist change in the face of inconsistencies, and how they can be revised by input from external sources.

In the following description of the theory, many hypotheses are stated as postulates. It is not claimed that these hypotheses have been confirmed and established. They are assumed as postulates in order to discover the consequences of their conjunction. Given these postulates, a program can test only their consistency, completeness, and independence. Tests of their confirmability remain an empirical matter. Hence the theory proposed must be viewed as tentative and provisional in nature.

This research is supported by Grant MH-06645 from the National Institutes of Health.

520

THE SYSTEM

A system is defined as a set of interacting elements. The elements of a belief system are assumed to consist of (a) units which are concepts organized to form *belief propositions,* and (b) *processes* which handle these belief propositions to give rise to an output of belief statements in a language. Some of the statements describe the information being processed (cognitions) while others describe how the system is functioning (affects). This theory postulates highly interdependent cognitive-affective elements interacting with one another by means of feedback loops which amplify or attenuate the activity of a goal-seeking system. A model of the theory has been constructed in the form of a computer program written in Balgol and currently running on an IBM 7090. For a description of the program see Colby (1965).

BELIEF PROPOSITIONS

A belief proposition, hereafter termed "belief," is a postulated mental state which can be represented by a natural language expression, e.g., "I am afraid of women," "my father is critical of me," or "I feel dissatisfied." A personal belief system possessed by an individual consists of a domain of propositions limited to beliefs regarding persons, including the self, and their conduct, feelings, thoughts, and interrelations. Individual systems differ in semantic and quantitative aspects of their beliefs, in the concepts available, and to some degree, in the order and detailed nature of their processing.

A belief represents a unit in turn made up of concepts organized in a sequential order pattern. For example, the belief "I avoid women" consists of the ordered string of concepts "I," "avoid," and "women." Concepts are linked together by bonds in a directed graph to form beliefs. The full 'meaning' of a concept lies in all the interconnections it has through bonds with other concepts in the graph.

Besides concepts and beliefs there is a third group of units called "implications." An implication connects two or more belief constructions containing "variables." A belief might be "I want to marry Jane" while an implication might be "X is a man and Y is a woman and X loves Y implies X wants to marry Y." In this implication X and Y are variables which can take on values.

A given belief in the system can have other beliefs supporting it as reasons. An implication has beliefs which exemplify it. A belief which serves as a reason for another belief gains this function by way of an implication which can warrant one belief justifying another. A more extensive discussion of the justification of beliefs can be found in Toulmin (1964). Suppose a belief was "I avoid women." The implication "X disturbs Y implies Y avoids X" serves as substitution rule to join the held belief "women disturb me" to "I avoid women" yielding the construction "I avoid women because women disturb me." Implications function not only to construct reasons, but also to detect conflict between beliefs.

Three types of beliefs are distinguished. (a) Fact-beliefs which contain factual information, e.g., "my brother is tall," (b) wish-beliefs, e.g., "I want to marry Joan," and (c) value-beliefs' e.g., "I ought to help my father."

In addition to their semantic components, beliefs possess quantitative components or weights. Two kinds of weights are postulated, credence and charge. The credence of a belief represents its credibility to the individual system, a form of personal or subjective probability. Charge on a belief represents its degree of import or personal interest for the individual belief system. Two types of charges are assumed, one a fixed charge which changes slowly, if at all, in time; and the second, a current charge which can increase or decrease rapidly. Both credence and charge fluctuate over time depending on what happens to a belief during processing.

These weights are assigned to beliefs according to a number of rules. Two sets of core beliefs are postulated, one a credence-core set and the other a charge-core set. The credence-core set consists of beliefs whose credibility is so strong as to be virtually certain. A credence for each belief is assigned according to the amount of evidence which can be found for or against it and as a function of the credences in the credence-core set of its supporting reasons. The charge-core set consists of beliefs assumed to be of greatest import or concern in the system. Charges are assigned to a belief depending upon (a) how many of the charge-core beliefs it is relevant to, (b) how many beliefs in the total system it can support as a reason, and (c) how many beliefs in the system it is relevant to.

PROCESSING

The units thus far described represent the static data-structures of a belief system. They become the operands of the operating system when it progresses through cycles of dynamic processing.

A cycle begins with the formation of a pool of beliefs. A charge-core belief with the highest current charge in the system is selected as the nucleus of a pool. Around this nucleus is collected a group of beliefs relevant to it such that a nucleus and relevant beliefs constitute the pool. Criteria for relevance depend on the semantic components of a belief and there exist various degrees of relevance. Given the belief "I want sex with a girl," a belief containing only the component "I" (e.g. "I like dogs") would be of very low relevance while a belief containing several identical components (e.g. "I fear sex with a girl") would be highly relevant. The belief "My brother is stupid" would have zero relevance while the belief "Men have sex with women" would be of moderate relevance. The belief in the pool with the highest current charge is selected for output. It is termed a regnant. Before the regnant can be expressed it is matched against other beliefs in the pool in a search for conflict.

Conflict is defined as a type of inconsistency, discrepancy, or dissonance which exists between two beliefs when they evoke one or more implications with contradictory consequences. For example, the belief "I want sex with a girl" would conflict with "Sex with a girl disturbs me" if the following implications were present in the system: "X disturbs Y implies Y avoids X"; "Y wants X implies Y seeks X." Substituting the terms of the belief for the variables in the implication, a conflict is found to exist between these two beliefs because of the contradiction between avoiding sex and seeking sex. This use of implication for the detection of conflict is quite similar to Festinger's concept of dissonance (Festinger, 1957).

A fluctuating conflict-threshold determines the fate of a regnant. If the degree of conflict aroused in a pool by a regnant is less than the current conflict-threshold, the regnant belief can be expressed. If the degree of conflict a regnant arouses in a pool exceeds the current-threshold, the regnant must undergo a semantic transformation. For example, "I hate my father" might become transformed into "I hate my brother," or more drastically, into "My father hates me." The beliefs created by such transformations represent semantic distortions of the original regnant. An early description of such transformations in paranoia can be found in Freud (1911). The nature and degree of the transformation selected depend on the current state of affect processes, as described in more detail in Colby and Gilbert (1964). Affects are conceptualized as monitors which survey the overall functioning of the system.

The affect process involves monitors, such as anxiety, satisfaction, esteem, excitation, and well-being, which have quantitative values and thresholds. Changes in these values result from an evaluation of the processing of the system. Similar hypotheses can be found in Tomkins (1962), in Engel (1963), and in Arnold (1960). When monitor values are within optimal ranges, the system continues its current activity. Nonoptimal values signal that a change or discontinuation must be undertaken.

Each affect postulated represents a monitoring of the states of the pool during ongoing processing. Anxiety is a function of the degree of conflict, and excitation is a function of the total charge in the pool. Satisfaction reflects whether or not wish-beliefs are being gratified and whether or not optimal values of well-being are being registered. Esteem is a function of whether or not factual or wish-beliefs conflict with value-beliefs. Well-being represents an overall evaluation of other monitors. Prolonged well-being, above a threshold, besides feeding back into satisfaction as mentioned above, also raises the conflict-threshold so that higher degrees of conflict can be handled with processes other than distorting transformations. Conversely prolonged well-being below this threshold lowers the conflict-threshold.

Monitors representing affect thus function as both dependent and independent variables in the system. For example, the level of anxiety is raised when conflict in the pool is found. The level of anxiety then in part determines the transformations of the regnant selected. If the transformed belief does not conflict in the pool, it is expressed and anxiety is lowered. The level of anxiety influences the level of well-being and in return well-being determines the conflict-threshold which when exceeded raises the level of anxiety. These interactions are characteristic of cybernetic systems in which the processes are closely interdependent and in which a variable is independent under some conditions and dependent under others.

When a regnant belief undergoes transformation, semantic conceptual components of the belief are changed in a copy of the regnant until conflict aroused by it in the pool is less than the conflict-threshold. For example, beginning with the original regnant, "I hate my father," it might be transformed into "My father hates me" which is the belief expressed. The original regnant leaves the pool but remains as one of the beliefs in the system. The newly constructed substitute is added to the system if it is not already present. A belief strongly relevant to the constructed substitute is then chosen to replace the original regnant in the pool. Thus the constituents of the pool change in time but continuity in output expression is maintained by the relevance relation holding between beliefs leaving and entering the pool.

When a regnant belief elicits a degree of conflict in the pool below the current conflict-threshold, the belief is expressed but the system, recognizing some degree of inconsistency, evaluates the belief in an attempt to change its charge, credence, or semantic components. These processes represent mind-changing procedures which can have far-reaching consequences for the organization of the system. For example, when evidence is weighed for a given belief and the negative evidence outweighs positive evidence, its credence is lowered. The converse also holds. This type of weighing evidence is also postulated in the program of Abelson and Carroll (1965). The fixed charge on a belief is lowered when it cannot serve as a good reason for any belief in the pool. If the credence of a belief takes on values above or below an upper or lower threshold, its fixed charge is raised or lowered accordingly. Thus at extremes of credence, credibility and import interact. If credence falls below a lower threshold, a negation of the belief is constructed.

The status of a belief in the system is a function of both its credence and charge. Low values of these parameters lead to a belief not being selected for entry into a pool. Thus although it exists in the system, a low-status belief will have little effect in processing. No belief is ever entirely erased, but its effect can be null.

The regnant of a pool is expressed in its original form or transformed; it also may be subjected to processes which can change its credence or its fixed charge. When a belief is expressed, the value of its current charge is lowered. If the expressed belief is a transformed substitute, both its charge and the charge on its original regnant are lowered. The expression of each belief from the pool leads to an output statement containing semantic information regarding the belief and regarding the states of the affect monitors. Report of the semantic components of a belief might read "My father criticizes me" and a report from a monitor at this moment might read "I feel anxious." Thus each output contains combinations of cognitive and affective elements which can be selected for description by statements in the output language.

After a single output of this sort another belief in the pool is selected as the regnant and the same sequence of processing is attempted. A cycle of processing continues with beliefs entering and leaving a pool until one of two conditions develops which leads to a switching off of a particular pool cycle.

Either interest in the beliefs of the pool, as indicated by an excitation monitor, drops below a threshold, or the well-being monitor indicates that a repetition of distress is becoming too great. The value of the well-being monitor is a function of the values of other affect monitors. When it registers repeated values on a negative or nonoptimal side of a threshold, processing of the current pool is switched off, another charge-core belief is selected as a nucleus, a new pool is formed, and a new cycle begins. Cycle after cycle in pool after pool occurs in the absence of extrasystemic input. Current charges on beliefs not in a pool slowly build up in time so that eventually a belief will gain entry into a pool.

Entry of a belief into a pool is a type of intrasystemic input. The processes which deal with this input are also available for extrasystemic input, e.g., a belief from another person. It is assumed that all extrasystemic input is accepted as credible unless an inconsistency can be found in a pool or unless the credibility and positive affection for the source of input, is low. Since this description of the theory is limited to an outline of broad principles of organization of belief systems without considering the problem of extrasystemic input, I shall conclude the description at this point.

CHAPTER 48

Discussion: Minimalist vs. Maximalist Positions on Cognitive Structure

Robert P. Abelson

The reader of the preceding four chapters probably has been struck by their heterogeneity. In part this may be due to the very wide range of backgrounds and interests of the four authors, but in part it results also from very different assumptions about the role and nature of cognitive systems.

In writing about cognitive constructs, many social psychologists, particularly those adopting the Gestalt tradition, regard beliefs and attitudes as dependent variables worthy of study in their own right. Others, notably those influenced by dissonance theory, find cognitive activity really interesting only insofar as it may mediate behavioral consequences. Thus Freedman, for example, analyzes the role of cognitive consistency tendencies in terms of whether they account for much of "the total variance in behavior" (p. 497), though he nods to older tradition by appending, "and even attitudes." De Soto and Albrecht, on the other hand, argue the importance of simple ordering tendencies with appeal to such phrases as "foremost intellectual traps" and "man's great framing conceptions about what he is," rather than by direct appeal to behavioral outcomes. Weick occupies a position somewhere in between, while Colby emphasizes yet another terminal point for cognitive events, namely their expressive purpose. For Colby, furthermore, affective states such as anxiety and well-being are also important dependent variables.

The reader should not be distracted by the fact that the contributors between them point variously to affective, behavioral, or cognitive consequences as the proof of the structural pudding. This represents temperamental heterogeneity rather than intrinsic theoretical difference. Cognitive processes may play roles at many different levels simultaneously, and each man may simply emphasize a different level.

It is toward the nature, rather than the role, of cognitive systems that the real differences in point of view seem to exist. Freedman's position is apparently that cognitive systems are only rarely exercised to any extent, in 'special situations.' De Soto and Albrecht also regard the scope of cognitive systems as typically relatively modest, focusing on simple structures if not special situations. These papers express the two 'minimalist' positions among the four papers in the section. I should like to remark on certain other aspects of these papers before discussing the 'maximalist' positions.

There is much in Freedman's outlook with which I would heartily agree, but his trichotomous classification of stimulus environments into "special situations," "ordinary situations," and "nonsituations" is rather unashamedly biased in favor of the dissonance theory style of experimentation, and possibly misleading. In particular, when Freedman dismisses data from 'nonsituations' (i.e., questionnaires about imagined situations) because they may greatly overestimate the degree to which subjects are logical, he omits an important point. Questionnaires about imagined situations (cf. Abelson & Rosenberg, 1960; Newcomb, Chapter 2) are not designed to expose *how much* logic subjects use, but rather *what kind* of logic. Even if cognitive consistency forces operate importantly only in 'special' situations, it is necessary to know what is subjectively consistent or inconsistent with what. As I have tried to point out in Chapter 5, if the 'follows from' relationship of dissonance theory is really unambiguously clear to the dissonance theorist, naive subjects ought to be able to report instances of this relationship in imagined situations. To carry the above argument to an ironic extreme (as Bem has done in Chapter 14), one might even contend that the subject supposedly 'behaving' in the special dissonant situation is merely acting in accord with what he judges a detached observer of the situation would consider reasonable. In short, Freedman has in my opinion begged the question of the value of 'nonsituations.'

The De Soto and Albrecht paper leaves open a number of interesting problems, among them what other 'good figures' exist besides balanced groupings and linear orderings. My usage of the term 'implicational molecules' in Chapter 5 is roughly comparable to their 'good figures,' thus the other simple principles suggested there would presumably qualify as suitable additional examples. (In Weick's chapter also, there is a list of suggested principles.) On another point, the authors engage in a paradoxical speculation. They say (p. 512) that "scientists and scholars may be more prone to this kind of simplistic thinking than less meditative people." But what sort of thinking, then, do less meditative people do if it is not simplistic? Something more complicated? It is an empirical question, surely, whether in fact scholars are more compelled than other people by very simple ordering principles, but supposing for the moment that this might be true, a conceptual distinction would be needed to resolve the paradox. The distinction I would propose is between organized simplicity and disorganized simplicity. It is indeed conceivable for individuals (whether scholars or not) to think simplistically by using an unpredictable, desultory collection of half-baked ideas. Picture an individual applying to any given situation the first cliché to come to mind. The result would be simple-minded thinking not necessarily consistent with 'good conceptual figures.' Many clichés might even be considered *bad* conceptual figures, for example, "That's the exception that proves the rule." Thus one can imagine a Man in the Street who avoids compelling, simple cognitive organization not by recourse to complex organization but rather to simple 'mishmash'—a Man in the Street who, for example, on the Vietnam question can be a hawk and a dove simultaneously not because he has worked the issue through but precisely because he has not.

Turning now to the maximalist positions, we note that Weick (like McGuire in Chapter 6) considers it natural under many specified circumstances for individuals to increase the interconnectedness of their cognitive structures, to reach the state he calls high ramification. High ramification is said to be in the interests of psychological economy. Again, with this paper a further clarification is brought about by an extra distinction, this time between organized and disorganized complexity. For Weick, a ramified cognitive structure is a big one, with many elements and links (thus complex) but with very little inconsistency (thus well-organized). However, in a few cases on Weick's evocative list of possible determinants of high ramification, it would seem that disorganized rather than organized complexity might be the predicted end state. For example, under low emotional arousal, heterogeneity and inconsistency might be sought for stimulation or curiosity value, whence the linkages introduced would produce some disorder instead of pure ramification in the author's sense. Perhaps one might argue that temporary disorder functions in the service of subsequent order. In any case, Weick's list of variables bears reconsideration with the present distinction in mind.

Colby also assumes a busy cognitive scene with many interrelated processes and interdependent elements. His simulation model is a very explicit exemplification of a cognitive system embodying organized complexity. A word of qualification is necessary, however. Colby is concerned with highly charged personal belief systems, and his model has no necessary bearing upon systems of less charged and more remote beliefs. It is certainly possible for individuals with maximal systems of personal beliefs to have minimal systems of social beliefs. (See Section III B for discussions of the role of the self concept in cognitive consistency.) In my own present work in the computer simulation of complex systems of social beliefs, I am increasingly coming to believe that highly ramified cognitive structures are relatively rare, occurring mainly among those with a heavy ideological or personal investment in the particular belief area. In this latter case, incidentally, the details of my simulation model are in many ways similar to those of Colby's model. (For a comparative treatment, see Abelson [1968] or Loehlin [1968].) In the case of social belief systems which are minimal, however, it is not easy to construct simulation models because the lack of structure defies structural imitation.

On one basic point, all four papers agree: that there are tendencies toward organization in cognitive structures. The differences concern the frequency and extent of such tendencies. The author's images of cognitive structures vary metaphorically from large, intricate lattices all the way down to scattered croutons floating in undifferentiated cognitive soup. Of course, the presumption that Man is a Meaning-Seeker lies at the heart of the cognitive theoretical approach to social attitudes and behavior. The progress of this approach very much depends upon the success with which the details of cognitive structure and process can be illuminated both by minimalists and maximalists. Among the other sections in this volume addressed in part to issues of cognitive structure are Sections IV B and IV C.

G. SOCIAL AND HISTORICAL PERSPECTIVES ON CONSISTENCY

It is psychologists who have been primarily concerned of late with problems of consistency—or at any rate the kinds of it that are considered in this volume. Not surprisingly, therefore, the contributions that precede and that follow the present section deal with intraindividual processes—what goes on 'in people's heads'—and with their antecedents and their consequences. But here we branch out into larger, social scenes.

The following papers are all concerned with collectivities of human individuals—groups, societies, or nations. The paper by Clinton De Soto and Frank Albrecht is, in a way, an interstitial one; it is concerned as previous and later papers are with individuals' propensities in cognitive structuring, but the special object of structuring in this paper is human groups. The cognitive principle upon which they dwell is the "predilection for linear orderings," not often treated in the consistency literature, yet similar in spirit to other consistency tendencies. Seymour Mandelbaum, from the totally different perspective of the study of human history, points to some parallels between psychologists' and historians' problems of "simple-order" concepts vs. empirical complexity. James Davis, a sociologist, raises in his paper the question whether actually observed "objective" social structures are so organized as to reflect hypothetical preferences for consistency on the part of their members. And, finally, Donald Campbell and Robert LeVine present hypotheses, together with data, about an analogous question: the modal attitudes within different societies toward one another.

CHAPTER 49

Cognition and Social Orderings

Clinton De Soto

The Johns Hopkins University

and

Frank Albrecht

Hollins College

In this chapter we shall discuss the relation between certain tendencies of human thought and social structures. We will avoid the position sometimes taken by psychologists—that social structures have no existence apart from people's conceptions of them. We will also avoid the position sometimes taken by sociologists and anthropologists, that social structures exist entirely apart from people's conceptions of them, or that people's conceptions serve at best only as clues to properties of the real social structure. Our view is that people's conceptions of a social structure in part determine or create the social structure and in part are reports about it, and that in either case attention to cognitive tendencies or predilections can be rewarding.

By 'social structure' we refer to the joint relations among several people, and we will be discussing such relations rather than the subtleties of dyadic relations. Our procedure will be to state some general cognitive principles and then to trace implications of these principles for social structures and people's conceptions of them, elaborating the principles along the way.

SOME COGNITIVE PRINCIPLES

1. People have a predilection for linear orderings. By a linear ordering, we mean a set of elements with a relation between them which is asymmetric (if A bears the relation to B, then B does not bear the relation to A), transitive (if A bears the relation to B, and B bears the relation to C, then A bears the relation to C), and complete (for every pair, A and B, either A bears the relation to B or B bears the relation to A). Such a structure can also be called a simple ordering, a complete ordering, or a chain. It stands in contrast to such structures as the partial ordering, in which completeness is lacking, exemplified by the family tree; or the dominance structure, in which transitivity is lacking, exemplified by dominance structures among birds, in which A may dominate B, B dominate C, and C dominate A. (For evidence supporting this principle, see De Soto, 1960; De Soto & Bosley, 1962; and De Soto & Albrecht, Chapter 45.)

This work was supported in part by Grant GS-653 from the National Science Foundation.

2. People have a predilection for single orderings. The preceding predilection is accompanied by a predilection for a single ordering of a set of elements as opposed to multiple discrepant orderings of the set, which people find uncongenial or aversive (De Soto, 1961; De Soto, London, & Handel, 1965).

3. People end-anchor orderings. People seek in particular to identify the extreme elements in an ordering, attaching special significance to them, and they are relatively tolerant of uncertainty about the location of internal elements (De Soto & Bosley, 1962; De Soto, London, & Handel, 1965).

4. An end-anchored, single, linear ordering is a conceptual good figure in the sense of the Gestalt psychologists. By this we mean that it is an organization toward which thought tends as conditions permit and foster it, not in any sense an inevitable conceptual organization. We further imply that it is a lure or trap primarily when people are engaging in rationalistic, intellective behavior as opposed to nonintellective behavior such as affective and sensory behavior. As thinkers, therefore, scientists and scholars may be more, not less, vulnerable than other men to its appeal. More specifically, it will entrap people

    a. when they cannot see how things are, are thinking more than perceiving;

    b. when they attempt to think of more than they can grasp;

    c. when a linear ordering has somehow been suggested.

For additional discussion of conceptual good figures, see De Soto and Albrecht (Chapter 45).

SMALL INFORMAL GROUPS

Small, informal, face-to-face groups have the peculiar characteristic, not shared by large groups and societies, that the activities and interactions of the members are *visible* to the group and to an outside observer. Direct observation can tell fairly well whether or not the group is structured as a linear ordering.

What has such observation told? It is probably safe to say that the majority of studies of small groups have found linear orderings of status, prestige, or influence. Indeed, some investigators go so far as to search for a status ranking as the test of whether a group truly exists. Sherif, White, and Harvey (1955), for example, in studying experimentally formed boys' groups, say that groups existed by the seventh day, the "criterion being that observers could place the various members in their own status positions with relatively little disagreement, especially at the upper and lower levels, on the basis of such behavior as initiative attempted and accepted, choices in activities, etc." And in the study of natural groups, from Whyte's (1943) classic *Street Corner Society* to Sherif and Sherif's recent *Reference Groups* (1964), a recurring theme has been the importance of status orderings in these groups.

These orderings are generally described as end-anchored and essentially linear, except for vagueness of relations in the middle, as in the above quotation from Sherif, White, and Harvey (1955). It is possible that some investigators go too far in treating these structures as linear orderings. For example, Whyte (1943) consistently speaks of his group, the Nortons, as if it had a linear ordering, with Frank and Alex on the bottom. Yet his chart shows

Frank and Alex at the bottom of one branch of the tree-like partial ordering. We suspect that this group was partially ordered, and there is a good reason why it should have been. The group was originally formed out of several distinct cliques grouped around the leadership of one man. It is reasonable to suppose that these cliques would to some extent retain their old structure in the larger group, and, in fact, on Whyte's chart the old cliques correspond to the various branches of the partial ordering.

These small-group structures are generally described further as tending strongly to be single orderings. The various ordering traits important to the group are seen as correlated. Power and influence are correlated with status and prestige; they depend on one another and induce one another. In fact the predilection for single orderings is so powerful that members of small groups can be observed actively bringing discrepant orderings into line, as when the Nortons forced bowling scores to correlate with status in the group by appropriate encouragement and heckling (Whyte, 1943). Equally impressive are the distortions of judgments group members exhibit because of the predilection, as when Sherif, White, and Harvey (1955) found a correlation of .74 between status and judged performance in handball throwing (although the actual correlation was about zero). In recent years there has been increasing recognition of the cognitive strain and distress people suffer when discrepant orderings of their group are evident to them. For reviews of some of this work on what has been variously referred to as status congruence, status consistency, and status equilibration, see De Soto (1961) and Sampson (1963).

As with the tendency toward linear ordering of small groups, we can safely say about the tendency toward single ordering that it is real. It is based on convincing observational and experimental evidence. It is not something that exists alone in the thinking of the group members or of the scientist-observer, even though it results from cognitive tendencies on the part of the members.

We have, however, suggested that members may overestimate the extent to which their group has a single ordering. What about the scientist? Presumably, to the extent he bases his statements on careful observation, he is less likely to make such a mistake. But if he departs from data, he may, as a more rationalistic person, be even more prone to make the mistake. Evidence to prove this assertion seems unavailable, although one gets an impression that often the social scientist's urge to speak of a single status ranking exceeds even that of his subjects. Possibly the exceptions—scientists like Newcomb (1960), who study group structure intensively but say little about status orderings—are capturing the more significant aspects.

Finally, we would like to quarrel briefly with the functionalistic explanations sometimes given for the occurrence of the phenomena we have been discussing. We refer to arguments that social organizations have these characteristics because they are necessary to their smooth functioning, without regard to cognitive predilections. As counterexamples, we can cite animal societies, which have smoothly functioning social organizations minimally disturbed by cognitive predilections (Brown, 1965). Such societies seem much freer of tendencies toward linear and single orderings. Dominance among birds, which we mentioned earlier, exhibits asymmetry and completeness, but also failures of transitivity which would be distressing to a human group because of the human cognitive predilection for a linear ordering.

Another counterexample is dominance and leadership relations among goats, which have been found to be entirely uncorrelated (Scott, 1958, p. 172)— again, something that would be distressing to a human group because of the human predilection for single cognitive orderings.

FORMAL ORGANIZATIONS

In the informal groups we have discussed, the members are free to shape the group structure according to their cognitive predilections. In a formal organization, in contrast, other exigencies powerfully shape the structure. For one thing, a formal organization characteristically has goals and activities which require much more division of labor, much more specialization of members' activities, than is found in an informal group. This specialization of activities means that certain people need to communicate with one another and influence one another more than others. An appropriate descriptive structure, based on either communication or influence, can hardly be a chain.

As C. P. Snow (1959) puts it, speaking of industrial organizations,

> The personal relations in a productive organisation are of the greatest subtlety and interest. They are very deceptive. They look as though they ought to be the personal relations that one gets in any hierarchical structure with a chain of command, like a division in the army or a department in the civil service. In practice they are much more complex than that, and anyone used to the straight chain of command gets lost the instant he sets foot in an industrial organisation.

While questioning how adequately the "hierarchical structure" conception characterizes even the army or the civil service, we heartily concur that it is a poor representation of a working industrial organization. Yet, it is clearly a tempting one. We agree with Homans (1950, pp. 104–105), though we will not attempt to document it here, that organization charts are always too neat, usually emphasizing vertical interactions at the expense of vital lateral interactions and other kinds of interaction. The urge to see the organization as a linear ordering, or as a collection of linear orderings, is strong, and less likely to be justifiable than in the small, informal, 'unorganized' group.

LARGE SOCIETIES

We have pointed out that formal organizations can hardly be understood simply as linear orderings, despite the predilections of those who plan and chart them, because the specialization of members' activities requires a more complicated system of relations among them.

What about the large societies often studied by social scientists, such as an urban community or even a nation, which can hardly be called formal not even an organization chart? Do the members of such a society somehow organizations because they have no clear goals, only dubious planning, and form a single, linear ordering?

We will argue no, that it makes even less sense to attribute such a structure to them than to the members of a formal organization. In particular, we wish to raise questions about stratification theory, the doctrine of social classes or socioeconomic status. From Aristotle on, most social scientists have held the view that society has such an ordering or hierarchy

(Lenski, 1954). Most sociology texts today have a chapter on stratification. Dissidents have been few. Can such a widely held conception be erroneous? We believe that it is, that the dissidents are probably correct.

Let us draw again on the principles we listed at the beginning. The cognitive predilections we gave—end-anchoring, linear ordering, single ordering—can hold especial sway over thought about large societies because in contrast to small groups and even formal organizations, large societies can be only dimly perceived, they are too big to grasp in thought, and there is a long history of suggestion that they fulfill the predilections. Indeed, probably for these reasons, social scientists often act as though status in a large society is clearer and more real than status in a small group. At the same time, there is less reason to suppose that societies truly fulfill the predilections because—again, in contrast to small groups and formal organizations—they are too big and unwieldly, too diffuse and invisible, too lacking in over-all planning for members to bring their predilections to realization as did the Nortons. And it is far from clear that other mechanisms can operate to fulfill them.

Let us concede immediately that there *are* variables by which members of society can be ordered. Some of the variables which supposedly determine social status clearly yield a linear ordering, at least of classes of people (a weak linear ordering). Education does. Wealth does. Income does.

Other variables which are often identified with social status are, as we shall see, doubtful ordering variables: power, religion, occupational prestige, residential location, race, nationality. It is also evident that a true ordering variable, such as wealth, has ends in the technical sense that somebody has the most and somebody has the least, but it is not clear that there is notable additional significance in this fact apart from the human cognitive tendency to end-anchor.

The predilection for single orderings. We will first comment on the workings of the predilection for single orderings, particularly in the minds of social scientists. The problem here is the tendency to act as though various variables by which members of society can be ranked somehow reduce to a single variable rather than yielding discrepant rankings.

There are two ways in which the reduction to a single ordering is commonly done. One, discussed by Benoit-Smullyan (1944), is to insist that only one of the ordering variables is important, the others being only direct or indirect expressions or consequences of it. Thus a Marxist might say that what counts in Western society is wealth, and power and prestige are merely derivatives of wealth. Pareto might say instead that wealth is only the material expression of social power.

The second method of reduction, more popular today, is to assign each subject a status score by averaging his scores on the several variables, often weighting the variables. Lenski (1954) and Rose (1958) have argued that this involved procedure loses much and gains nothing. We share their view and will shortly cite evidence supporting it.

We must admit that ordering variables of the sort social scientists discuss are in fact correlated. Indeed, in what is probably the definitive study of the intercorrelations among stratification variables, Kahl and Davis (1955) applied factor analysis to the correlations among 19 variables and found only one or possibly two common factors. But what does this show? The length, height, and width of an assortment of pasteboard boxes are likely to be so highly intercorrelated that one could conclude they are not primary dimensions, that the only primary dimension is size (Overall, 1964). Obviously, this would be a seriously misleading conclusion. The search for factors when one has obvious meaningful primary variables is quite a different endeavor from the old search for *g* or common factors in intelligence, which made sense precisely because it was *not* clear what the various subtests of intelligence individually measured and it was reasonable to suppose that they were impure measures of an underlying factor or factors. In contrast, income, education, and other stratification variables are perfectly meaningful variables in their own right; there is no reason to view them as impure measures of a single ill-defined underlying factor.

It should be no surprise that the stratification variables are correlated. Low education leads to low income; higher education leads to higher income. And, to reverse it, parental income, especially in past years, determines education. It is just such processes which Benoit-Smullyan (1944) calls "status equilibration." But the correlations produced by such processes do not imply that the correlated variables are indexes of the same thing. Education remains education, and income remains income. A central task for sociology and social psychology would seem to be to study the processes whereby the correlations observed by Kahl and Davis and others come about. Instead of trying to defend and advocate social class as an explanatory device which is an artificial composite of more meaningful variables, sociologists could perform the service, probably better than any other social or behavioral scientists, of investigating the interplay and effects of these disparate variables. Especially would we urge that they be watchful for the workings of principles of thought of the sort we have described, both in their subjects and in themselves, in their investigation of social systems.

It is not hard to point to examples—even if relatively few—of the benefits to be gained when social scientists recognize and avoid the predilection for single orderings and cease speaking of social class. One recent study (Dunham, Phillips, & Srinivasan, 1966) seriously questions the view originated by Hollingshead and Redlich (1958)—and largely upheld since then—that social class determines the incidence of psychoses, specifically that membership in the lower classes tends somehow to induce psychoses. Dunham, Phillips, and Srinivasan, working with schizophrenia, effectively separated the variables of education and occupational status, and concluded that schizophrenia is cause, not effect. It lowers occupational status, presumably because it interferes with securing and performing a job, but it does not lower educational achievement. Other investigators evidently failed to come up with this entirely plausible and commonsense finding because they leaped too hastily from the separate variables to a composite index of social class.

In a quite different vein, Goldberg (1959) has shown the questionability of an even older and more widely held belief about social class: that lower social classes are more fertile. He found that this "effect" is almost entirely attributable to the simple fact that farm families have more children than do urban families and continue to do so for a generation after they migrate to a city, during which time they also tend to earn low scores on the variables plugged into the social class index, such as occupation, income, and education. Correcting for rural-urban origin wipes out the so-called differential fertility.

The predilection for linear orderings and end-anchoring. The preceding discussion and examples illustrate how social scientists can be trapped by their predilections in thinking about variables which admittedly do order people, such as income and education. Possibly even more dangerous is the temptation to treat variables as ordering variables when in fact they do not yield linear orderings at all.

Just as in small groups, power and influence relations in large societies tempt the cognitive predilections, perhaps with even more misleading consequences. Without dwelling on this problem, we would like to point out that our sympathies would lie with Polsby (1963) in his attack on the stratification theorists who dominate the current literature on community power. This theorizing manifests all the predilections we have discussed, ranging from the notion that power relations form linear orderings, that they correspond to social class (the single ordering), with especial emphasis on the upper class as a power elite (end-anchoring). Polsby shows that this theorizing flies in the face of both logic and empirical evidence. He shows that power relations can form loops or intransitivities. Consider, as an example, a community in which the mayor has power over the police, the police have power over the Negroes, but the Negroes, as a solid voting bloc (p. 53) have power over the mayor. He shows the lack of completeness of power relations; he shows their instability; he shows the fallacy of equating wealth and power, or prestige and power; he shows the fallacy of the supposition that there is a single leader or a single power elite. Where he has difficulty is in accounting for the popularity of the stratification theory of power (pp. 98–111). For us, this popularity is less surprising, inasmuch as the theory so nicely fulfills strong cognitive predilections.

Even occupational prestige, perhaps the most widely used single index of social status, is questionable as an ordering variable. It might seem unassailable, inasmuch as prestige is *imputed* by people, and it would surely seem that people can impute a simple ranking. But even with prestige there are serious difficulties (Gusfield & Schwartz, 1963). One is that there is a considerable amount of disagreement among respondents even though average ratings are stable over time. The other is that occupational characteristics—like skills required, honesty, and others—seem to loom more important in people's thinking about occupations than what could fairly be called prestige, and contribute in subtle ways to what are taken to be prestige ratings.

On the members' conception of their society. Until the last paragraph, this section on large societies has emphasized the scientist-observer's view of things, rather than the members'. One reason for this emphasis is that members' conceptions of large societies are relatively less meaningful than their conceptions of small groups. They cannot perceive as well what goes on in the large society nor can they ordinarily create or manipulate its structure effectively. As a corollary, their conceptions of large societies are more likely to be derived from teachings of social scientists, mere echoes of the scientists' accounts, than are their conceptions of small groups.

But the members' conception of their society becomes critically important when the scientist bases his own conception on it, as in studies which conclude that social classes exist because people say they do (see Brown, 1965, pp. 115–120) or that top leaders exist because people can name them (Polsby, 1963, pp. 47 ff.). Our suspicion—and it is only a suspicion because we know of no direct evidence—is that people in general are less victimized by the cognitive predilections than are social scientists. By *not* attempting to arrive at an overall structure for society, the nonscientist may in some ways be more free to see things as they really are—complicated, inelegant, badly figured. Some support for this notion might be drawn from descriptions of the difficulty interviewers often have in getting respondents to volunteer information about social orderings (Brown, 1965; Polsby, 1963). Many respondents stubbornly speak of society as composed of different kinds of people rather than different ranks, and it is not to the credit of the social scientist that he insists on transforming their simple grouping into a ranking.

CONCLUDING STATEMENTS

After our far too brief survey of the vast literature on social groups we can hardly conclude that the end-anchored, single, linear ordering is never seen as an intellectual trap. But we think we can fairly argue that it too rarely is. As a cognitive good figure it seems to have a subtle appeal more difficult to recognize and overcome even than the appeal of the simple grouping (De Soto & Albrecht, Chapter 45; Kuethe & De Soto, 1965). It would be easy to point to numerous warnings about the temptations of classifying, categorizing, stereotyping, but hard to point to corresponding warnings about ordering.

We think too that our survey supports the merits of the general approach we advocated, that is, to admit that people's predilections in themselves, as well as other processes, can indeed bring about orderings, but that these genuine tendencies toward ordering are subject to many qualifications. We have illustrated the importance of separating the scientist's predilections from his subject's, and indicated that the special appeal of the linear ordering may make the scientist more, not less, susceptible to this particular kind of oversimplification than other people. We have illustrated the distinctions between variables which are inherently orderings, such as education; variables which may be created as orderings by people, such as prestige; and variables which are unlikely to be orderings even though perceived to be, such as power. We have shown the value of treating such variables separately rather than succumbing to the temptation to identify or pool them. We have examined some of the conditions which bear on the existence and on the perception or misperception of orderings, such as size of group or society.

Much of what we have said could be construed as an admonition against simplification, a plea for complication. In a degree this is true, and to that degree we are subject to the argument that statistical and practical considerations demand simplification, that the scientist must ignore some of the complexities and subtleties of the world if he is to make headway.

We believe, however, that arguments for simplification in science should be viewed with great caution. Sometimes they may merely be rationalizations for conceptual good figures, hindering the development of alternative conceptions which may be more valid yet simple enough to pose no technical problems. The explanation of differential fertility as a function of rural vs. urban origin is fully as 'simple' as the stratification explanation. The pluralist conception of community power espoused by Polsby (1963) does not seem inherently more complicated than the stratification theory. The trouble with such alternative conceptions of the social world would seem to be that they lack cognitive appeal, not that they are complex.

But above all we insist that attention to principles of cognition is a necessity, not a luxury, for the understanding of social structures.

CHAPTER 50

Consistency, Creativity, and Modernization

Seymour J. Mandelbaum
University of Pennsylvania

Students of the great social changes which have transformed the world in the last 400 years vary widely in interests and temperament. Some are excited by psychological propositions; others prefer to take their political, economic, social, and intellectual history without dosages of personality, child-rearing, and attitude change (Moore & Hagan, 1963). If you press a macrotheorist, however, he is likely to join a general consensus that the gross process called modernization has involved important changes through time in the modal personality and fundamental patterns of behavior of large populations. The disagreements among theorists are largely about the allocation of psychological variables into dependent, independent, or mediating boxes.

The dimensions used to measure these changes or, more precisely, speculate about them, are often those which engage the contemporary experimental interests of consistency theorists and their critics. Some psychologists will find substantive clues in this intellectual convergence; others will note only that scholars are bedeviled by the same issues which trouble them.

The consensus about modernization would run roughly something like this: In traditional societies, both East and West, large masses of the population believed at one and the same time that the universe was closely ordered and infinitely mysterious. The paradox apparent in this belief found its best known expression in the Christian idea of the Trinity; its most general form in pantheistic peasant religions. The perspectives of men in traditional societies upon social behavior were similar to their cosmologies. Social behavior was ordered and, in a sense, rational, but was not subject to a self-conscious analysis and manipulation which would encroach upon the sacred mysteries of life (Sjoberg, 1952).

The intellectual historians of complex traditional societies—medieval Europe, for example—are quite properly insistent that these theological, cosmological, and social attitudes be treated seriously as ideas to which both the real world and other ideas were forced to accommodate themselves. Traditional societies with any sort of stability were able to adjust to some changes. Most anomalous experiences or dissident persons and ideas were,

539

however, rejected. The rejection could occur at several levels: staying at home, throwing stones, burning or, as intellectual historians note, serious discussion which enveloped the idea or experience in familiar words. Norman Cantor's treatment (1960) of the lay investiture conflict of the Eleventh Century—to offer one illustration of this last effect—describes how old terms were used to allow contestants to debate new issues in a manner which was possible for them, but confusing to later historians.

Risking some measure of overstatement, the exponents of consistency theory seem to be describing behavior characteristic of men in medieval Europe or traditional China and India. In contrast, the images of man developed by the critics of consistency theory should be familiar to analysts of modernization. Modernization has seemed to depend upon men who are curious about the world, eager to discover new relationships, willing to innovate in intellectual, technical, and social behavior, and unhappy with stable social forms, particularly those legitimated solely by age. The search for 'varied experience' seems to be the essence of modernity.

Until recently, historians have been reluctant to accept explanations of change which assume that men are fundamentally different in one period than in another. That reluctance has now been considerably weakened and there is a growing body of literature which attempts to describe and explain modernization as a process which involves basic psychological change. The historical-psychological literature takes several different forms. Most of it simply posits that behind a gross pattern of exploration and innovation, scientific rationalism, and universalistic ethic, stand a group of men who are in a new way exploratory, innovative, rational, and universalistic. What we have in effect is a microreading of macroevents. David McClelland (1961) and his students have cut one step below this sort of microreading. Their studies of shifts in need achievement relate gross economic changes to readings of the values apparent in naive verbal and plastic expressions such as ballads, urns, and school texts. Erik Erikson's *Young Man Luther* (1958) is the best example of another genre of psychological history. Erikson delineates an individual psychodrama and hints that Luther's appeal lay in the relevance of his 'solution' to the personal dilemmas of a great number of men in his era.

The new development of a psychologically oriented history would certainly benefit from an even more sophisticated infusion of psychological theory. It may even be of considerable interest to psychologists. This history suggests that the personality types noted in the population of college sophomores are not necessarily static. The distribution has changed through time and this change has been a very critical one in human history. In another way, however, this literature is not very revealing. It is directly addressed to the contrasting models of man offered by the consistency theorists and their critics and assumes that both are true. In a sense, the historical literature argues that it is necessary to increase the complexity of our model of man before we can understand the important varieties of human behavior.

Eclectic psychological theorists, unhappy with this argument, would like to proceed with the exploration of a simple model which preserves the drive towards consistency and reduction of dissonance, but can explain search, exploration, and the drive for variety. Here the intellectual historian skilled in the intensive analysis of the thought of a small group of very articulate people, rather than the social historian, may be of some aid to the psychologist. Two phenomena noted by intellectual historians of the scientific revolution may be consistent with consistency theory and lend aid and comfort. First, historians have observed that the new 'scientific' world view of the 17th and 18th centuries was much more comprehensive in its vision of orderliness than any of the data available to contemporaries (or to later scientists) was able to support. Secondly, fundamental scientific revolutions have involved what Thomas Kuhn (1962) calls "paradigm shifts," a reorientation of the questions asked and the model of reality assumed by scientists. These shifts are relatively rare and many anomalous findings have to accumulate before they occur. Theories are in fact much more stubborn than facts (cf. Hall, 1956). These two observations suggest that scientific inquiry, the area of creative behavior most important to modernization, can be looked upon as an attempt to reduce dissonance. True believers in the ideas of order, relationship, and knowability are discomfited when they confront a disorderly, unrelated, unknown world. They seek ways to induce order, to search behind chaos, to reduce anomaly. Only when they accumulate a great many anomalous findings which do not fit the preconceived order or model of reality do they shift a fundamental paradigm. (Panofsky's essay [1955] on "The First Page of Giorgio Vasari's *Libro*" is a model study of the operation of the effect of the idea of order in the world of art.)

Analysis of three separate episodes in the history of scientific thought suggests that this shift, when it occurs, is very disturbing, even agonizing. Signs of extreme intellectual discomfort appeared in the initial movement from a mysterious to an orderly scientific world view in the 17th century. They appeared again in the change from a mechanical to an organic conception of the universe in the late Eighteenth and early Nineteenth Centuries. Finally, they are apparent in the Twentieth Century with a shift to indeterminacy and the conception of science itself as a heuristic rather than as a replication of reality. (See Willey, 1942; Hazard, 1953; Gillespie, 1960; Hughes, 1958.)

Analyses of the agonies of change suggest a pattern which may be of interest to consistency theorists. In all three cases, the data that were anomalous or unexplained assumed this character, at least in part, because they had been satisfactorily explained in a preceding and abandoned paradigm. The organic rebellion against mechanism described by Charles Gillespie saved the relationship between inner consciousness and universal mystery which appeared to have been lost in Newton's mechanics and Lavoisier's chemistry. The rebels against positivism described by Stuart Hughes in the same way saved the conception of consciousness and complexity missing in physiologically based psychology, Comtean sociology, and Maxwellian physics, but which was present in early nineteenth-century conceptions of human behavior and the universal order.

The inherently abstract character of ordering conceptions or paradigms must apparently slight some portion of reality. In the process of replacing one paradigm with another, some emotionally charged values and some data are left unexplained and unsatisfied. As a result there is a bundle of dissatisfactions which helps to define as anomalous some phenomena which the new view hopes to explain. The 'rediscovery' of old ideas seems to be inherent in memory and in the partial character of all abstractions.

When we go beyond intellectual history, particularly the history of science, to a broader social history, we encounter much more difficult problems of analysis. The actors are not as articulate as the elite intellectuals and because there are so many of them it is difficult to characterize their views. Nevertheless, some recent social history suggests that the model developed by intellectual historians may have general import. Neil Smelser has described the agonizing effects upon Lancashire cotton workers of what was essentially a shift in social paradigms. The flexible patterns of organization and personal behavior which the workers had developed by 1840 were the popular complement of an innovative scientific structure (Smelser, 1959).

A union of intellectual and social history suggests possibilities which consistency theorists may find interesting. The paradigm shifts which engage analysts and engineers of modernization seem, on their face, to expand the search for information and the development of new knowledge. This face is not deceptive but it does obscure the tactics of the shift, which often involve the differentiation of phenomena and the limitation of the scope of an hypothesis or model. A new paradigm is often useful because it requires less information than an old one in order to yield satisfying results.

Such shifts are inherent in the metaphysics of science and are equally striking, though perhaps not logically necessary, in the development of general social thought and behavior. Several of the most critical developments in the process of modernization restricted the amount of information individuals required to act effectively. Learning early closure had, in effect, socially creative functions.

The two most striking examples of these functions are the development of the price system and of egalitarian patterns of behavior. In a community in which all men know one another, it is clearly impossible, indeed absurd, to treat all men equally. Hierarchical and individualized patterns of thought and behavior yield anomalous results, however, when a series of changes introduces new personnel into the community or into the life experiences of single individuals. Men who 'deserve' deference do not get it; men who do not deserve it, do. The development of egalitarian patterns of behavior limits severely the amount of information you need to know about a man before you can deal with him. The development of the price system has similar characteristics. All you have to know is price and quantity. If you have to worry about your workers as whole men, rather than as inputs of production, you become involved in a host of criteria which inhibit rapid manipulation of the units of production and clearly do not maximize at least short-run profits.

The realization that social anomalies are often resolved by paradigm shifts which reduce cognizance may help to explain why it is so difficult to convince traditional peoples that modernization is worth the winning. They must be convinced not only to accept new knowledge but also to adopt poses of ignorance. They must learn to treat people equally who they know are not equal. They must learn to treat men as units of production who they know are fathers, caste members, and neighbors.

The amount of search activity supported by a particular social or high intellectual paradigm seems, then, to have profound social implications. We cannot assume, however, that extended search is always socially creative. Scholars who do not know when to call a halt to research never write books. Peasants who must be 'sure' about their environment never leave their village. If the definition of creativity has a major sociological dimension, then the polarization assumed by the critics of consistency theory need not hold. Dissonance-reducing activities can be creative; the search for varied experience and information can support traditional paradigms.

At this stage in the development of consistency theory, only a naive historian would triumphantly try to apply the fruits of experiment to the past. This brief essay has simply tried to suggest that the psychologist may benefit from an understanding that the dilemmas which perplex him are central to an understanding of some very important historical changes. He may also gain comfort from the knowledge that there are some bodies of historical literature which develop a dynamic perspective on his own work in a manner which may suggest experimental resolutions of troubling issues.

CHAPTER 51

Social Structures and Cognitive Structures

James A. Davis
Dartmouth College

Consistency theories of the Abelson and Rosenberg (1958), Cartwright and Harary (1956), Heider (1946, 1958), Newcomb (1953), and Osgood and Tannenbaum (1955) genre, as compared with the Festinger (1957) genre, are especially interesting to sociologists because they are not truly theories about consistency. There is no literal inconsistency (contradiction) in liking Sam, who is despised by one's friend Bill. Rather, this painful contretemps is presumed to be a departure from normal tendencies in small-scale, sentimental social structures. If so, any sociologist curious about normal tendencies in small-scale, sentimental social structures must become interested in consistency theories.

The situation is not without irony. Consider the classical psychophysical experiment in which some lawful physical stimulus is varied and human reactions plotted. That the two variables are not generally related in a linear fashion is the central postulate of perceptual psychology, whose rebellious offspring, Gestalt psychology, is the parent (or maybe grandparent) of consistency theories. Because it is a legitimate descendant of psychophysics, one might expect consistency research to proceed in a roughly similar fashion, exposing subjects to lawful variation in social structures and finding out whether they 'get it right.' As we all know, this is hardly the case, for most consistency research consists of exposing subjects to purely hypothetical social stimuli whose structure is determined by the experimenter. The situation is not unlike a psychophysical experiment in which subjects are seated in a dark room and asked to guess what would happen to a light bulb if the electricity were to be turned on.

I wish I could say that this turn of events stems from the psychologists' ignorance of the laws of social structure, but the actual situation is quite the reverse. Sociological knowledge of the laws of small-scale social struc-

The research reported here was supported by National Institutes of Mental Health Grant K3-MH-25, 412-01, and by National Science Foundation Research Grant GS-1286. At the time of the research the author was affiliated with the National Opinion Research Center, University of Chicago.

tures is so slight that we are turning to consistency studies for theories, rather like physicists getting hypotheses from data on sophomores' opinions about how the lights work.

A review of the literature is called for at this point, although it will not detain us long. To my knowledge there are only three published studies which ask whether actual interpersonal sentiments conform to a consistency model. Kogan and Tagiuri (1958) showed that Heider's hypotheses are supported among the sociometric choices in a group of 22 naval enlisted men. White (1961) used the Abelson and Rosenberg theory to describe the sociometric choices of a group of 16 industrial executives. Newcomb's (1961) study of college students in an experimental residence showed that after a few weeks intrapair attraction became correlated with agreement on sentiments toward various issues and toward third parties; and that over time triads, tetrads, and larger high-attraction subgroups tended to develop. Both results are implied by the consistency models. There are, of course, many consistency studies which use sociometric data as part of the design. However, most such studies use perceived sentiments (Festinger & Hutte, 1954; Tagiuri, 1959; Wiest, 1965) as the dependent variable, not extant interpersonal sentiments.

I predict, though, that the literature will swell, and the absence of completed studies allows me freedom to speculate on their outcome. The remainder of this essay will be a string of such speculations. The ruminations are organized around the following questions: (a) Which model shall we use? (b) How must it be modified? (c) Will it work? (d) If it works, why does it work? (e) If it works, what consequences are implied?

WHICH MODEL SHALL WE USE?

Of the various consistency theories, I suspect that the four listed in the first lines of this chapter will be of more interest to sociologists simply because interpersonal content is built into them, while Festinger's theory does not specify any content at all. Among the four, differences are largely a matter of style, since it has been shown that their mathematical structures are fundamentally the same. I suspect, nevertheless, that the Newcomb and Osgood and Tannenbaum versions will find more use in studies of social relationships and attitudes, while the Abelson and Rosenberg model and Cartwright and Harary extension of Heider will be more used in studies of interpersonal relationships *per se*.

Comparing the latter pair, their main difference is that the Abelson and Rosenberg model is algebraic, while Cartwright and Harary use graph theory. I have been told that, over the long haul, the algebraic approach has greater potentialities for the mathematically sophisticated sociologist, of whom there are perhaps three in the profession. Graph theory, nevertheless, is much more accessible to most sociologists and one may argue that it 'feels' more sociological. Note the obvious analogy between a graph and a sociogram, and how close graph theory is to the everyday concepts of 'circle of acquaintances,' 'eternal triangles,' 'good connections,' etc., in contrast with the great gap between the algebraic and commonsense meanings of 'group,' 'ring,' 'power,' etc. Hence graph theory may be more productive of empirical applications. The fairest statement, perhaps, is that my own work draws on the Cartwright and Harary paper which I have found extremely useful.

HOW MUST IT BE MODIFIED?

Having said that I believe the Cartwright and Harary model to be particularly useful in applying consistency theory to small-scale sentimental structures, I must add my opinion that two modifications are required.

First, the heart of their theory, the "structure theorem," states that in a group of three or more persons, Heider's original propositions about *Person, Other*, and X (here assuming X to be a third person) imply that the group will be divided into exactly two unambiguous cliques (if there are negative as well as positive sentiments) such that relationships within each clique are all positive and relationships between persons in different cliques are all negative.

This remarkable theorem is the starting point for applying consistency theory to social structure, but reflection suggests that it is not literally true of the empirical social world. The two clique hypotheses may be plausible for cognitions, e.g., a tendency to see the social world as consisting of 'we' and 'they,' blurring the fact that 'they' are not a single group. However, a recent cognitive study (De Soto, Henley, & London, 1968) suggests that clusterable (more than two cliques) structures are as easily learned as balanced structures, which casts some doubt on the idea. Certainly one may doubt that all of mankind is split into exactly two cliques. Even if we lower our sights to limited groups such as neighborhoods, offices, or schools, the common impression is that while people do tend to form cliques, multiple cliques are as frequent as polarization. It is difficult to go beyond common impression because we lack an unambiguous procedure for locating cliques in sociometric data. (The too-numerous proposals to do this lead to the suspicion that clique identification is a Gordian knot to be cut rather than unravelled.)

I have discussed the problem in another article (Davis, 1967) and have proposed a theorem to supplement the structure theorem. If we define as *clusterability* a division into *two or more* cliques (as defined by a difference in quality of internal and external relationships), it can be proven that *a graph is clusterable if and only if it has no cycles containing a single negative line.* (The reader unfamiliar with graph theory can find an excellent explanation of cycles, lines, etc., in Cartwright and Harary, 1956.) The original structure theorem says that *a graph is divided into two cliques (balanced) if and only if it has no cycles with an odd number of negative lines.* Since one is an odd number, it follows that balance is a special case of clusterability.

Such a theoretical development does not in itself lead to research findings. Before empirical research can take place, a second modification is required, a translation from deterministic to probabilistic language. Both the structure theorem and the clusterability theorem allow no exceptions, and graphs in which only one of thousands of cycles fail to meet the criterion are as 'wrong' as those with numerous exceptions. Obviously empirical data will never lack exceptions, and therefore we must develop probabilistic models to assess the degree of clusterability or balance. The exact details of these models take us beyond the scope of this chapter, but Harary

(1959) has proposed one, and I have sketched some others in an unpublished memorandum which is summarized in a review chapter (Abelson, 1967b).

A probabilistic approach, while necessary for technical reasons, also has substantive implications. If social relationships only tend toward balance (or clusterability) then there will be (a) some friendships between persons in otherwise hostile cliques; (b) some enmities within otherwise all-positive cliques; and (c) some relationships that are pulled in different directions by contradictory structural pressures. Each situation is of some interest since persons involved in the first constitute "liaison persons" (Ross & Harary, 1955) who act as bridges between cliques; relationships in the second situation constitute "faults" which may be sources of stress and eventual change in cliques; and relationships in the third situation provide an interpersonal application of the sociological theory of "cross pressures" (Berelson et al., 1954; Davis, 1963) which predicts that such relationships will tend to become "null" rather than positive or negative. The identification of such persons and their characteristics opens lines for structural research, as does the notion that a group which only tends toward balance (clusterability) will gradually shift toward greater structural perfection (Davis, 1967; Levinson, 1964).

In sum, the prediction is that the Cartwright and Harary model can be usefully modified to (a) separate the clique property *per se* from tendencies toward a particular number of cliques; and (b) develop a probabilistic approach which will be practical for research and will enable one to examine liaison persons, faults within a clique, the cross-pressure hypothesis, and structural dynamics.

WILL IT WORK?

The most important question is whether empirical evidence will support the hypothesis, even when loosened into a probabilistic clusterability form. As noted above, the published literature tells us little. I am at the beginning stages of a project which seeks answers to the question, but at this writing all that can be reported is that reanalysis of several hundred sociograms culled from various sources is encouraging.

Despite one's parental commitment to a hypothesis, I suspect that even if it works the results will not be as strong as they have been in psychological consistency research. The grand theme of perceptual studies is that while man's sensory apparatus is quite limited in terms of extreme values of particular stimuli (infrared rays, high-frequency sounds, etc.) it is excellent— indeed too good—at detecting structures. The propensity for humans to infer clearer structures than their sensory input would warrant is the great theme of Gestalt psychology, and if anything the principle should be doubled in spades for interpersonal stimuli. The Kogan and Tagiuri (1958) study provides direct support for this hypothesis, and indirect support comes from the numerous studies of "assumed similarity" (Fiedler, 1958).

In sum, the prediction is that empirical research applying consistency models to interpersonal relations will show that actual sentiments tend toward such structures, but not as strongly as data about cognitions. This leads to some social psychological problems about the consequences, if it is the case that people behave as if their social world were more crisply structured than it really is.

IF IT WORKS, WHY DOES IT WORK?

Continuing to forge a firm chain of pure conjecture, let us assume that the data will support the modified models. If so, one asks, "Why?" Should such tendencies be considered as 'laws' or can they be explained by other variables and relationships?

The question is wide open, but one may speculate about other variables which, at the least, might contribute to structural trends.

First, it is quite probable that social *categories* play a part in forming sentimental groups, in addition to structural (relational) principles. An example will make the point. Numerous studies have shown that among high school students sociometric choices tend to be concentrated heavily within sex and grade level. If one were to analyze a sociogram which included an entire high school, it would undoubtedly show tendencies toward clusterability, even if choices within a sex and grade subgroup were totally random. So many other social categories (race, religion, socioeconomic status, values, and interests, etc.) leap to mind that one is wary of asserting structural consistency as a completely autonomous principle.

Secondly, it is also probable that the well-established relationship between social interaction and interpersonal sentiments (Homans, 1950) is involved in clusterability. Philip Bonacich, in a personal communication, has suggested that unbalanced sentimental triangles (those with two positive and one negative relationship) may be unstable precisely for this reason. Consider a triad in which there are positive (friendly) relationships between A and B and between A and C, but enmity between B and C. Following Homans' principle, both B and C will seek to interact with A who will indeed seek them both out; but when both are in A's company, they will be thrown together, a situation which Homans claims to be uncomfortable.

An alternative Homansian approach to clusterability involves his notion of the "external system" (Homans, 1950, p. 90), the interpersonal relations which any group develops in order to survive in its environment, i.e., how it organizes to get its work done. One may conjecture that such arrangements almost always produce clusters of social interaction. Soldiers are organized into squads that interact more with each other than with outsiders; children are organized into classrooms which concentrate interaction within subgroups; factories organize work groups; homes cluster family interaction; etc. If social interaction tends to clusterability prior to the development of the interpersonal sentiments which Homans calls the "internal system" (Homans, 1950, p. 109) and if interaction generates positive sentiments, then it is possible that sentimental clusterability can be explained by a prior principle—the clusterability of social relationships. Homans puts it this way: "At whatever level we look at the web of interaction, it always shows certain thin places and the lines between groups fall there" (Homans, 1950, p. 85).

A number of studies show that even apparently trivial differences in the microecology of interaction have a strong effect on sentiments (Blake *et al.*, 1956; Byrne & Buehler, 1955; Caplow & Forman, 1950; Festinger *et al.*, 1950; Gullahorn, 1952; Merton, 1948; Whyte, 1956). Together with Homans' theory, they suggest that careful attention must be given to the role of the external system in molding small-scale social structures.

In sum, the expectation is that if tendencies toward clusterability can be established, rather than satiating interest in the problem the results will stimulate sociologists to explore the social categories and interaction variables which contribute to or explain the generalization.

IF IT WORKS, SO WHAT?

Throwing all caution to the winds, we speculate on the most remote question of them all. There are not so many well-documented regularities in sociology that we can afford to be patronizing toward any of them, but one is still led to ask whether—if it can be established that clusterability (balance) is a common tendency in interpersonal relationship—it is an isolated generalization or one which leads to others. In a previous paper (Davis, 1963) I sketched 56 sociological hypotheses which seemed to flow from Heiderian theory, but here I should like to consider some implications of the clusterability theorem.

If sentimental networks have any important consequences, the most likely is that they serve as channels for the flow of something. There is considerable empirical evidence that information flows along sentimental networks (Coleman et al., 1957; DeFleur & Larsen, 1958; Erbe, 1962; Festinger et al., 1948; Katz, 1958; Larsen & Hill, 1958; Rogers, 1962) and the whole tradition of small group studies supports the claim that influence and attitude change do too, although unequivocal documentation is rarer than one would think outside the laboratory. Such findings, though, merely set the stage for a much more difficult problem: if something flows through networks of sentiment, can we show that different sorts of networks produce different sorts of flows? We do have some rather sophisticated theories (Bailey, 1957; Ford & Fulkerson, 1962; French, 1956) but the clusterability principle generates additional hypotheses.

It seems plausible that in interpersonal flows of most any sort the probability that 'whatever it is' will flow from person i to person j is (a) directly proportional to the number of all-positive (friendship) paths connecting i and j; and (b) inversely proportional to the length of such paths (e.g., one is more likely to be influenced by a friend than by the friend-of-a-friend and even less likely by a friend-of-a-friend-of-a-friend). Now if we consider a clusterable (highly cliquish) social structure we find that each member is connected to the others in his clique directly or by a large number of very short paths. Hence, in contrast to a random structure, flow effects within the clique should be quite powerful. At the same time, members will be connected to those in other cliques by few paths, if any, and the paths will typically be quite long. Hence, in contrast to a random structure, flows between cliques should be quite small. The net result, as it were, is a paradox: very strong flow effects within cliques and very weak ones between cliques. In sociological terms we may expect strong social control within subgroups, but weak integration of the total group. Support for the hypotheses is anecdotal at best, but three studies may be cited.

Regarding the tighter flow of social control within a sentimental cluster we have Elizabeth Bott's well-known study, *Family and Social Network* (1957). Bott, who studied married couples in London, calls a network in which the people known by a family know each other "tightly connected." It can be shown (Davis, 1967) that this is mathematically equivalent to clusterability, since situations where the opposite holds (persons who both know *A* but do not know each other) constitute cycles (triangles) with a single negative side. Bott writes (1957):

> When many of the people a person knows interact with one another
> ... the members of his network tend to reach consensus on norms and
> they exert consistent informal pressure on one another to conform to
> the norms, to keep in touch with one another, and if need be, to help
> one another (p. 60).

Regarding the weak integration of a total group with strong cluster-ability, we have two relevant studies. A discussion of strike rates (Kerr & Siegel, 1954) explains the high rates of industrial conflict among miners, longshoremen, sailors, and loggers, as follows:

> Industries will be highly strike prone when the workers (i) form a
> relatively homogeneous group which (ii) is unusually isolated from
> the general community and which (iii) is capable of cohesion (p.
> 195).

The situation seems equivalent to claiming that miners, longshoremen, sailors, and loggers tend to develop interpersonal clusters.

DeFleur and Larsen (1958), who studied the diffusion of messages in the form of pamphlets dropped from airplanes on cities of various sizes, advance a hypothesis consistent with ours in order to explain why the rate of diffusion does not increase with increasing size of city. They write:

> It is hypothesized that ... when a city reaches a certain critical size,
> the interaction of individuals and groups no longer forms a single or-
> ganized pattern but tends to break up into smaller patterns following
> the "nucleated structure" or ecological patterning of metropolitan
> areas. That is, for some communication purposes, it appears that a large
> city consists of a loosely integrated set of small centers or towns (pp.
> 50–51).

In social science three studies do not a proposition make (although one study sometimes does), but the three examples illustrate the theme of this essay: while the cognitive consistency models of social psychology de-veloped independently of sociological knowledge about actual structures of interpersonal relations, they provide important models which can lead to re-search of at least three types. (a) After suitable modification, the models can be used to study whether the normal tendencies of small-scale social structures are as predicted. If this general hypothesis is supported, they can lead to (b) studies of other social and interpersonal variables which generate, increase, or retard these tendencies, and (c) studies of the consequences of such structures for the flow of influence and information in interpersonal channels.

CHAPTER 52

Ethnocentrism and Intergroup Relations

Donald T. Campbell

Northwestern University

and

Robert A. LeVine

University of Chicago

Theories of cognitive and affective balance, of dissonance, and of belief-system congruity inevitably make predictions concerning intergroup attitudes. Some of these are surveyed here. The setting envisaged for the predictions comes from an ongoing cross-cultural study of ethnocentrism, in which cooperating anthropologists ascertain the traditional relationships and attitudes of a given group (here called the 'ingroup') toward 15 or so neighboring and more remote outgroups. In this setting, three kinds of predictions are asked of each theory examined (Campbell & LeVine, 1965): (a) What kinds of ingroups will be most ethnocentric, most hostile to their neighbors, etc.? (b) For any given ingroup, toward which outgroups will the greatest ethnocentric hostility be directed? (c) What will be the content of stereotypes about outgroups? For balance and congruity theory, it is the second type of question which is most relevant, and which will be treated in the first two sections that follow.

SIMILARITY AND THE LIKING OF OUTGROUPS

Basic to balance theories (e.g., Heider, 1958; Newcomb, 1959, 1961; Harary, Norman, & Cartwright, 1965; Davis, 1963) is the triad *ABX* where *A* and *B* are two actors, valuers, or believers (tribes in our setting, persons in Newcomb's analysis of friendship and values, which we parallel at the group level), and where *X* is some object, value, item of belief, etc., toward which *A* and *B* have evaluative attitudes or identifications. *X* can be another tribe (person, actor) in which case its reciprocal valuings can be considered. This is taken up in the subsequent section on Balanced Relations. In the present section, *X* is to be regarded as an item of culture, as a custom, belief,

Prepared during the authors' joint stay at the Center for Advanced Study in the Behavioral Sciences, Summer, 1966. The Cross-Cultural Study of Ethnocentrism is supported by a grant from the Carnegie Corporation of New York to Northwestern University. An expanded version of this paper will appear as a chapter on "Cognitive Congruity Theories" in D. T. Campbell and R. A. LeVine, *Ethnocentrism and Intergroup Relations: Propositions and Illustrations*, New York: Wiley, in preparation. The authors are indebted to Marilynn Bolt Brewer for several of the points presented.

or artifact. Liking between A and B occurs when their valuing of X is similar, i.e., when both are positive toward it, or when both are negative toward it. Disliking accompanies dissimilar attitudes toward X. All of these instances of liking and disliking are balanced. Other possible relations are imbalanced, unlikely, and unstable. In the pure balance form of the model, there is no causal asymmetry, the attitude of A toward B being as likely to 'cause' his attitude toward X as his attitude toward X to cause his attitude toward B. Attention here focuses on the latter type, however. Considering the many X's about which A and B both have attitudes, we can infer net degrees of liking as a product of likings induced by the many covalued X's. The resulting prediction is that, from the point of view of any ingroup, *the more similar an outgroup is in customs, values, beliefs, and general culture, the more liked it will be.* Social distance and friendly commerce may be included among symptoms of liking.

Rokeach (1960, pp. 293–331) has proposed this for intergroup relations, and has tested it for intergroup attitudes among religious bodies in the United States. He finds a strong relationship between dissimilarity and rejection. He further finds that shifts of church membership, choice of denomination of college, and frequency of interfaith marriages are directly related to similarity. In subsequent research he and others have sustained the claim that even in Negro-white relationships in the United States, it is belief-disparity more than skin color or biological race that is the target of the hostility (e.g., Rokeach & Mezei, 1966; Stein, Hardyck, & Smith, 1965). In a study of the attitudes of Dutch children, Jaspers, van de Geer, Tajfel, and Johnson (1965) found the perceived similarity of another nation to The Netherlands to be strongly related to liking for that country. While perceived similarity rather than more independently assessed similarity was an issue, the same balance principle is involved.

In our own research arena, intertribal attitudes, strong confirmation is also already present. Mitchell (1956) studied social distance among workers from 20 tribes in Zambia. Of several principles emerging, cultural similarity (matrilineal vs. patrilineal organization) was the strongest factor. Gordon Wilson (1961) has surveyed the attitudes of 12 tribal areas of Kenya toward each other, presenting data making possible a secondary analysis on this problem. We have selected three pairs of questions for this purpose, selected because presented in both positive and negative form: "Which of the above tribal groups do you feel will present the greatest [least] problem to internal security after independence?" "Which of the above tribal groups do you feel are the most friendly [unfriendly] people?" "If you were forced to leave your own tribal group for some reason, among which of the above tribal groups would you most [least] like to live, other than your own?" In each area there were interviewed 100 persons, 93 per cent male, predominantly urban and small town, only 15 per cent with no education, only 7 per cent self-employed in agriculture. As the main pooled index of attitude, the average percentage giving the favorable response (Wilson, 1961, Tables 8B, 9A, 10A) less the average percentage giving the unfavorable response (Tables 8A, 9B, 10B) has been used. These values are presented in Table 1.

Groups have been classified in three degrees of similarity. Thus for the Kikuyu, the Meru and Embu were judged similar (S), all other Bantu groups (Abaluhya, Coast, Kamba, Kisii, Taita) as intermediate (I), and

TABLE 1

Net Favorability Toward Outgroups by Each of Twelve Tribes

	Groups Chosen											
Voting By	Kikuyu	Kamba	Meru	Embu	Luo	Kisii	Abaluhya	Kalenjin	Masai	Taita	Coast	Somali
Kikuyu		− 2	9	15	8	3	− 8	−25	−27	15	−10	−13
Kamba	32		2	3	2	0	− 2	− 6	−42	11	2	−18
Meru	28	12		22	0	0	− 1	−13	−30	22	−16	−32
Embu	34	1	21		0	0	0	−13	−22	28	−13	−36
Luo	18	3	0	0		10	5	−16	−47	14	2	− 9
Kisii	− 8	− 4	− 4	− 2	− 6		28	− 6	−20	6	2	− 4
Abaluhya	−69	4	1	0	−13	9		13	− 1	1	10	1
Kalenjin	−62	0	− 1	− 1	−14	2	39		2	0	10	0
Masai	−18	− 3	0	0	− 8	0	10	7		3	10	− 7
Taita	−37	1	− 1	− 1	−27	0	5	8	− 7		32	0
Coast	−45	7	0	0	−30	0	10	7	− 8	40		− 1
Somali	−12	− 2	5	5	−19	− 1	12	2	−10	5	21	

the Luo, Masai, Kalenjin, and Somali as dissimilar (D). For the Luo and Somali, all other groups were classified as dissimilar and they thus do not contribute as judges to this analysis. The Masai and Kalenjin were judged of intermediate similarity to each other, with no similar groups present for either. Among the other Bantu groups there were two similarity pairs: Coast and Taita, and Kisii and Abaluhya. From the viewpoint of the Kamba, the Meru, Embu, and Kikuyu were judged similar, other Bantu groups intermediate, and the non-Bantu groups dissimilar. Linguistic grounds and

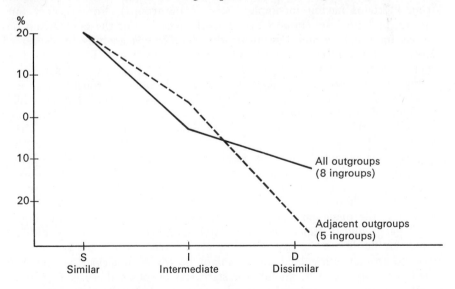

FIGURE 1. Average net favorability to outgroups as a function of cultural similarity (secondary analysis of data from Wilson, 1961).

belief in common origin were primary bases of classification, other cultural factors supporting these.

Figure 1 portrays the outcome, with results that dramatically support the principle of liking and similarity. The "all outgroups" line is an average of averages. For each ingroup, the average percentage of mentions for outgroups of each degree of similarity has been computed. These three values have then been averaged for the eight ingroups having outgroups of all three levels of similarity. The result is a strikingly consistent effect of similarity. Of the 24 opportunities for reversal (8 of $S < I$, 8 of $S < D$, 8 of $I < D$) only 1 occurs (an $I < D$). There are two other comparisons available ($I > D$) for Masai and Kalenjin, and both of these are confirmatory.

Another prime interest in the analysis was the effect of regional proximity. While degree of proximity produces no clear-cut trends when similarity is controlled, there is a special interest in adjacent outgroups, for which interaction should have made attitudes more stable. For five ingroups, all three levels of similarity were available in the adjacent outgroups. Figure 1 presents these averages, too, again confirming the principle.

There are a number of weaknesses in this analysis which could obscure relationships or create spurious ones. Most conspicuous is the great variability in number of mentions received by various outgroups due to fame, visibility, or generally shared beliefs. Thus on the first question the number of mentions received from the sum of all other tribes varies from 0 to 454 (for the Kikuyu). In an effort to correct this, an analysis was done in terms of votes received rather than votes given, so that in any given direct comparison, all attitudes were being expressed about the same outgroup. This analysis used columns from Table 1 whereas the Net Favorability analysis used rows.

The Received Votes analysis confirms, although with less clarity, the similarity-liking correlation, as shown in Table 2, which also reports on the number of instances of inequalities in a given direction (including instances from ingroups having incomplete sets of outgroups). For adjacent outgroups, both analyses support a direct relationship. For the comparison between Intermediate and Dissimilar, the All Groups analysis by Received Votes finds no difference, actually a slight reverse trend. For this analysis there is a trend toward an interaction between adjacency and similarity: remote groups are better liked if they are dissimilar. Probably this is a product of the then current political alliances, as discussed below, which produced favorable images of the Luo and Kalenjin (dissimilar to most judges) on the part of remote groups which would not otherwise have known of them at all.

Another potential weakness, although not one which we believe invalidates the clear-cut finding, is the recurrence of the same target group in the same location for a number of ingroups. Thus in the adjacent outgroups analyses, for those five ingroups having all three levels of similarity among adjacents, the dissimilar outgroup is always the Masai, due to the Masai's great geographical dispersion. The Masai, moreover, are generally disliked. This may be due to the fact that they are so strikingly dissimilar, in which case no artifact is involved. But it might be for an irrelevant reason, here multiply represented. Certainly for statistical purposes there is a great reduction in effective degrees of freedom through this repetition. Because of the ambiguity on such points, we have not attempted the probability statements to which the tallies of inequalities point.

TABLE 2

Similarity and Favorable Attitudes: Three Indices

Index	Average Attitude Index Values			Inequalities		
	Similar	Intermediate	Dissimilar	S>I	S>D	I>D
Net Favorable: All	23	—1	—10	8/8	8/8	9/10
Net Favorable: Adj.	22	5	—26	5/5	6/6	6/7
Received Votes: All	22	—1	0	8/8	8/8	7/10
Received Votes: Adj.	22	10	—4	4/5	6/6	7/7

As to the political party alliances current at that time, these, of course, may be regarded as products of attitudes, but it is also clear to any Kenya expert looking at Table 1 that attitudes have been caused by them too. At this time, the KANU party was headed by the Kikuyu-Luo alliance, unpredictable on similarity grounds, but showing up in favorable attitudes. The competing KADU alliance was formed by smaller tribes out of fear of domination by the two largest, and it too cut across similarity lines, allying, in its leadership, the Bantu Abaluhya and Coast with the Nilohamitic Kalenjin and Masai. Of the high similarity relations, only Kisii (belatedly KANU) and Abaluhya fall into separate camps. In general, the effect of political alliance works more against the similarity-liking hypothesis than for it, accounting for a bulk of the exceptions.

BALANCED PATTERNS OF INTERGROUP RELATIONS

One use of balance theory, particularly as developed in the signed graph tradition (e.g., Harary, Norman, & Cartwright, 1965; Flament, 1963; Davis, 1963, 1967; Chapter 51) is to predict patterns of interpoint relationships where the relationship can take the values of positive (e.g., liking), negative (e.g., disliking), and absent. While such theory is usually applied to persons as points, it can readily be applied to relationships among groups, as Harary (1961) has done in a model prediction of international attitudes in the Middle East. The presentation here is essentially nonmathematical, and depends heavily upon Davis (1963).

The basic prediction is that *regional patterns of intergroup relations will be 'balanced.'* From the mathematical statement of the balance concept, these commonsense statements about triads follow:

> *An ally of an ally will be an ally.*
> *An enemy of an ally will be an enemy.*
> *An ally of an enemy will be an enemy.*
> *An enemy of an enemy will be an ally.*

To give further relevance to the problems this abstract algebra attempts to cover, we can quote from an amazing chapter on "Political Geometry" in Zimmer's (1951) survey of the philosophy of ancient India.

> The principal Hindu formula for the arrangement of foreign alliances and coalitions is based on a pattern of concentric rings of natural enemies and allies. Each king is to regard his own realm as located at the center of a kind of target, surrounded by 'rings' (*mandalas*) which represent, alternately, his natural enemies and his natural allies. The enemies are represented by the first surrounding ring; these are his immediate neighbors, all alert to pounce. The second ring then is that of his natural friends, i.e., the kings just to the rear of his neighbors, who threaten them in turn through the very fact of being neighbors. Then beyond is a ring of remoter danger, interesting primarily as supplying reinforcement to the enemies directly at hand. Furthermore, within each ring are subdivisions signifying mutual natural animosities; for since each kingdom has its own mandala, an exceedingly complicated set of stresses and cross-stresses must be understood to exist. Such a plan of mutual encirclement is to be cast, carefully weighed, and then used as a basis for action. It delineates and brings into manifestation a certain balance and tension of natural powers, as well as touching off periodic, terrific outbursts of widely spreading conflict. Taken for granted as a universal social principle is the propensity of neighbors to be unfriendly, jealous, and aggressive, each biding his hour of surprise and treacherous assault (pp. 114–115).

In this, an assumption that the relations of immediate neighbors are hostile is combined with balance considerations. These do not combine readily, as

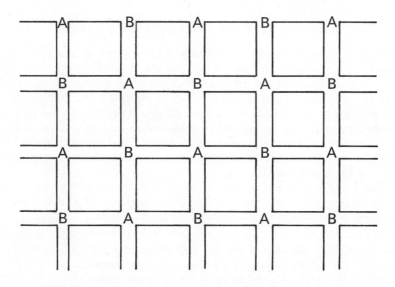

FIGURE 2. Balanced mandala of hypothetical street gangs centered at intersections of city blocks. Type A gangs are enemies of type B gangs, and allies of other type A gangs.

the middle sentences indicate, and under usual circumstances, the alternative rings of enemies and allies will not be balanced.

If we take from the mandala theory an ingroup, one of its immediate neighbors, and the group on the far side of that neighbor, balance holds, for the enemy's enemy is an ally and the ally's enemy is an enemy. But this balance does not hold for an ingroup and two adjacent immediate outgroups. For these, if the mandala ring is to hold for each in turn, the two outgroups being adjacent to each other would be enemies, and an unbalanced all-negative triad would result, for the enemy's enemy would be an enemy.

There is perhaps but one regular pattern providing both balance and mandala circles. This is one in which each ingroup has but four adjacent outgroups, contacts at the 'corners' not counting as adjacency. While such a territorial pattern is unlikely, it could exist for street gangs organized around intersections,[1] as in Figure 2. For adjacent outgroups numbering more than four, balanced mandala circles seem to be unavailable.

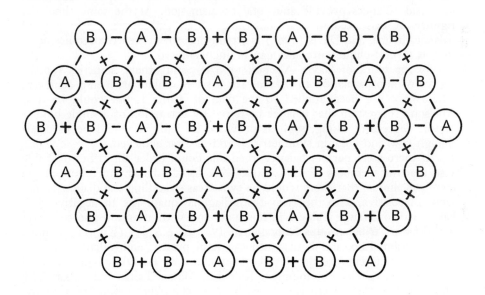

FIGURE 3. A quasi-mandala pattern of intergroup relations. (Pluses represent positive relations; straight lines are minuses, representing negative relations.)

Figure 3 illustrates the nearest approach we have developed to a balanced mandala-like ring pattern for six outgroups. In it, all *A*s are surrounded by hostile *B*s. The *B*s, twice as numerous, have as immediate neighbors half *A*s and half other *B*s (i.e., half friendly, half hostile). For the *A*s, their closest allies (other *A*s) lie beyond the immediate ring of *B*s and conform to the enemy's enemy rule. Half of those in this second ring are, however, enemy *B*s. The very uneven sizes and shapes of actual group boundaries make such ideal types of little practical value.

Balance theory in its simplest algebra predicts that all positive fields

[1] We are indebted to Robert Abelson for this point.

(that is, all ally fields in which every group loves every other) should be more likely than all negative fields (in which each group hates each other). The former are balanced, the latter are unbalanced. The prediction of all positive fields goes so against common observation that balance theorists have not paid much attention to it. All negative fields, in which each in-group distrusts all foreigners, seem more likely, and even to be predicted in the standard presentations of ethnocentrism (e.g., Sumner, 1906). Heider in his original presentation hedged on this point, and trends in the modification of balance theory are to score such patterns as acceptable (Davis, 1967; Chapter 51).

Given that there is a mixture of positive and negative valences between groups, the classical balance theory prediction is that the *groups will fall into but two cliques*, with friendly relations within each and hostile relations between. This condition is illustrated in Figures 2 and 3, and in the mandala-circles concept, in which the odd-numbered concentric circles would be one clique, the even-numbered and the ingroup, another. Bipolar tendencies in world alliances provide anecdotal confirmation. At the same time, the rigidity of this prediction is something of an embarrassment to applied balance theory, and Davis (1967) is attempting to weaken the requirements so that several-clique outcomes can be incorporated.

In the work of Davis, Abelson (1967b), and others, statistics for the degree of approximation to balance for a set of points are being achieved. These have not been applied to the data of Table 1, but could be. For Abelson's suggestion that balance be tested by extraction of a single bipolar factor, degrees of liking, such as provided in Table 1, could be used, al-though row and column symmetry should be first achieved.

If there were perfect balance, then one could order the tribes of Table 1 so that the members of each clique were listed adjacent to fellow clique members, and so that there would be two areas straddling the diagonals that were all positive, with the away-from-diagonal quadrants all negative. We have tried to arrange Table 1 in this way, and with attention also to party. The first six tribal groups belonged in 1961 to KANU (Kikuyu, Kamba, Meru, Embu, Luo, and Kisii) with the Kisii present ambivalently because of their felt closeness to the KADU Abaluhya. The KADU group are listed next, Abaluhya (late in joining), Kalenjin, Masai, Taita, and Coast. The uniformity of the pattern is reduced by the very general popularity of the Taita and the very general unpopularity of the Masai and the Somali. The degree of balance would be somewhat increased if the Kisii were moved to the KADU group. If this were done, and if the Somalis were assimilated to that group too, some 76 per cent of the signs would be in accord with balance (84/110, omitting zeros).

In the simplest balance theory, the valence between two points is $+$ or $-$, a single value relating A to B and B to A. In fuller treatment e.g., Harary, Norman, & Cartwright, 1965) A's valuation of B is treated separately from B's valuation of A. Such is actually the case for Table 1, where the valence of each tribe for the other is recorded separately. In this situation, balance theory predicts that *reciprocal attitudes will tend to agree in sign*. When one examines Table 1 for this, eliminating pairs where either of the values is 0, 66 per cent of the remaining 42 pairs are in agreement. Of the 23 pairs where both percentages are $\pm$ 5 or larger, 74 per cent of the pairs agree.

From balance theory also come predictions, illustrated by Harary (1961), *that wishes as to intergroup relations will show more balance than will actual relations*, and that *perceptual distortions will be in the direction of greater balance*. One area of major differences among the various balance models is the relative emphasis on intrapersonal, perceived balance or interpersonal, objective structural balance. Heider's theory is purely intrapersonal, Cartwright and Harary's primarily interpersonal, and Newcomb's *A-B-X* model is presented in both forms, a distinction being made between intra-individual and collective "systems of orientation" (Newcomb, 1959, 1963). Newcomb emphasizes the role of communication in mediating the two types of balance. Since in our data analyses we have been concerned with perceived rather than actual relations, our results may conform to the balance principle more than would data on specific acts of friendship and hostility. The latter type of data is certainly of interest, but very difficult to come by.

DEGREES OF ETHNOCENTRISM

A basic class of predictions sought from social science theories in the ethnocentrism study asks which group is, or what kinds of groups are, most ethnocentric. Such predictions do not come as directly from balance theory as do those of the previous sections, but they are available. In addition, dissonance theory, so far not considered specifically, makes still other predictions.

Some such predictions come from the application of balance theory at the level of persons to clique formation (e.g., Davis, 1963, 1967) and then translating 'cliques' for our purposes as ingroups and outgroups. Given that all persons have some negative and some positive interpersonal valences, and treating a pool of persons including ingroup and outgroup members, the following prediction results: *The more mutual liking there is within the ingroup, the more ethnocentric the group will be* if ethnocentrism is defined for this purpose as degree of hostile attitudes toward outgroups. The causation could be in any direction. Thus, the presence of threatening hostile outgroups hated in parallel by all threatened ingroup members, induces positive interpersonal attitudes among ingroup members. In thus predicting more ingroup solidarity under greater outgroup threat, balance theory concurs in one of the most ubiquitous of social science predictions, one we have treated under "Realistic Group Conflict" (Campbell & LeVine, 1965; Campbell, 1965, pp. 288–289; Coser, 1956; Sherif & Sherif, 1953).

Another prediction of this same type is the following: *The more homogeneous the belief-systems of the ingroup members, the more homogeneously hostile toward outgroups will be these members.* Internal agreement on belief systems represents parallel valuing of a large number of 'objects' or Xs. These parallel valuings induce balancing positive interpersonal bonds. These positive intragroup bonds force all the hostilities or negative valencings by ingroup members (given that there are some) on to outgroup members.

At the group level, we can predict that *in any local set of groups, the most dissimilar ingroup will show the most hostility toward outgroups.* This is but an application to the "which ingroup" question of the similarity-and-liking principles of the first section above. In that presentation we spoke as though similarity were causal of liking, but balance theory allows balance to be achieved through adjustments in any direction. Sumner hypothesizes a reverse causal relationship, from hostility to cultural uniqueness: "Ethnocentrism leads a people to exaggerate and intensify everything in their own folkways which is peculiar and which differentiates them from others. It therefore strengthens the folkways" (Sumner, 1906, p. 13). Leach (1954) has presented in detail a social system in which historically arbitrary linguistic differences are preserved for such purposes.

DISSONANCE THEORY

Many, perhaps all, of the above predictions could also have been derived from dissonance theory (Festinger, 1957). In these terms it is a dissonant cognition to recognize that a liked and respected person disagrees with you about some third object,[2] or about your valuation of self. Changing your attitudes toward the objects, or changing your valuation of the person, are obviously ways of reducing cognitive dissonance. Dissonance theory makes additional predictions which we might not arrive at from the balance model. These are presented here in terms of the "which ingroups" or "what kinds of ingroups" question.

One aspect of dissonance theory is an emphasis upon congruity between the valuation of an attitude object and the effort of sacrifice made in the service of the object. Thus a group is more valued the more cruel and painful the initiation rite, that high value being required to achieve congruity with the pain endured (e.g., Aronson & Mills, 1959). This leads to the prediction that *the more suffering, cost, and effort that members have endured in association with their group membership, the more loyal and ingroup-esteeming they will be.* This principle has often been noted. Hitler, for example, believed that World War I had "welded together" the German people (Walser, 1964, p. 38). The principle seems separate conceptually from the effects of external threat, although in actual situations external threat and subsequent suffering for the ingroup often will be confounded.

Even more frequent in dissonance research is the forced compliance, fait accompli effect (e.g., Brehm & Cohen, 1962). Several studies suggest that when economic and political conditions change so as to increase both the scope and intensity of coordinated activity, cognitive aspects of ethnocentrism (group labels and stereotypes) subsequently become consistent with the new boundaries implicit in the new forms of coordination; when economic or political conditions change in the reverse direction, however, group labels and stereotypes consistent with the wider coordination are retained.

Our own investigations in Kenya reveal that the territorially separate and autonomous peoples, whose only interethnic contacts were intermittent ones with the immediately adjacent peoples, did not develop full-blown stereotypes of most of the groups in their region, despite sharp discontinuities in language and culture, until they began to be incorporated into the superordinate economic and political system imposed by the British; they then developed rich stereotypes similar in many respects to those of modern

---

[2] Technically speaking, this situation has dubious theoretical status as a dissonance. See Chapter 5, pp. 000–000.—Ed.

societies like the United States. Other observations (e.g., Mitchell, 1956; Colby & Van den Berghe, 1961) indicate that the incorporation of diverse tribal peoples into a modern, urban occupational status system gives the formerly perceived labels and boundaries new stereotype content based on the new status categories. Moerman (1965) found that in northern Thailand, where linguistic and cultural variations are considerable but with no sharp and mutually congruent boundaries, contemporary ethnic labels appear to be derived from a series of defunct states, each with its capital city, which once integrated (at the political level) diverse populations.

This type of evidence might be accounted for in terms of cognitive dissonance, as in the following two hypotheses:

1. *When a population has imposed upon it economic or political structures that entail compliance to a new set of organizational demands entailing an alteration in boundaries between groups or statuses, then group labels and stereotypes will be altered so as to be concordant with the newly established boundary conditions.*

2. *When such economic or political structures decay without being replaced by organizations making new demands, group labels and stereotypes concordant with the defunct structures will persist.*

In terms of dissonance theory, the key point is the compliance involved. When a state develops in or is imposed on a formerly stateless population, the members of the population, whatever benefits of security they may derive from the new organization, find themselves having to comply with a whole new set of regulations concerning law and order, military service, taxation, and deference to authority. At the same time the state, or its leadership, has to define who must comply and who need not, i.e., the boundaries of the state. Members of the new state are faced with the dissonance between their own compliance and the noncompliance of those who are not included. Why should they comply with the state's onerous demands when others need not, and when in fact they themselves did not in the recent past? They reduce this dissonance by defining themselves primarily as members of the state, diminishing the salience of their other group identities (e.g., those based on kinship, language, culture) and by exalting the state and membership in it so that nonmembership is seen as inferiority. Should the state disappear there is no need to alter the identity until it is replaced by another agency requiring similar compliance. The persistence of an identity based on former state membership is particularly likely where, as in northern Thailand, all other bases for identity are inconsistent with one another.

It also follows from this line of argument that once state boundaries are firmly established and the state is exalted as an entity, other bases of group loyalty (e.g., those based on the primordial ties of language, kinship, religion, etc.), not congruent with state boundaries because they include outsiders, would be seen to be as dissonant with the state membership as ethnic identity, and efforts would be made to eliminate them and homogenize the population. This would predict that states would move more rapidly in the direction of linguistic and cultural homogenization than stateless societies.

If the imposition of a superordinate state on diverse ethnic groups occurs simultaneously with the introduction of a modern occupational system, however, it is possible to reduce the dissonance more easily by reinterpreting old linguistic and cultural differences in terms of occupational status, especially if ethnic groups have differential access to occupations (Campbell & LeVine, 1965). The boundaries that formerly defined ethnic identity come increasingly to define status differentiation within a single state-bounded nation. Since status differentiation is not dissonant with the modern state, on the contrary is perhaps even required by it, the simultaneous development of the state and the modern occupational system will promote the perpetuation of reinterpreted ethnic boundaries. In this situation, unless there is rapid incorporation of the bulk of the population into the modern occupational structure, instability is likely to occur, for groups finding themselves rated low in the new status system before they have given up their traditional occupations will find it more dissonance-reducing to redefine themselves as autochthonous tribesmen desiring secession and a state of their own. Only when they have complied with modern occupational demands to such an extent that there is no going back will they look for a means of reducing the dissonance of their new-found low-status position within the new polyethnic state rather than in a tribalist retreat.

This cognitive dissonance between the traditional and modern evaluations of groups and their political attempts to reduce it are dramatically illustrated in the phenomenon of nation-building in contemporary Africa. The rapid establishment of new states with boundaries embracing a multitude of recently autonomous tribes—all of which are called upon to participate in the national polity—has been accompanied by the slow and uneven incorporation of the population into modern occupations. It is typically those groups that have a strong traditional basis for high self-esteem, but did not become educationally and economically modernized during the colonial period, that experience the most intense dissonance between traditional self-evaluation and low evaluation by other groups in the new nation. Such groups often become the dissident regionalists and secessionists in the African states and represent threats (of varying magnitude) to their fragile national integration.

The Masai of East Africa, for example, have long been noted for the pride they take in their own pastoral way of life, despising their agricultural neighbors and others who eat vegetable foods. In recent years, however, they have found themselves not only dominated by their more politically active agricultural neighbors in the new states of Kenya and Tanzania, but also despised in turn as backward nonparticipants in national status systems based on literacy, education, and ability to take advantage of modern occupational opportunities. In a 1965 survey organized by the authors, the Masai were most frequently mentioned by other Kenya groups as being not only the most backward and uncivilized but also the most dirty and stupid. (In northern Tanzania, the Masai and Gogo—another pastoral group—were most frequently named.) By refusing to climb the new status ladders, they have—in the eyes of those who have climbed—come to occupy the bottom rung.

The Masai have not accepted this new evaluation of themselves. Despite the famine and impoverishment that have afflicted them in recent years, Masai respondents to the survey in both Kenya and Tanzania named their own group as "most wealthy." This judgment must be based on number of cattle owned, their traditional measure of wealth, in which they still exceed their more prosperous (by any other standard) neighbors. Thus they reduce the dissonance between their traditionally high evaluation of themselves and the low evaluation they receive in modern economic and social terms (which they can hardly fail to perceive) by adhering rigidly to traditional standards of evaluation by which they rank highest. The majority of Masai are still able to put this into action by remaining pastoralists and refusing to enter the modern occupational system, thus protecting themselves from dissonant self-evaluations. Those that have become educated and are more involved in the national life both economically and politically have produced proposals for a Masai state, uniting the Masai of Kenya and Tanzania and reasserting independence of the other ethnic groups. These proposals for opting out of a national unit in which a modernized status system prevails can be seen as efforts to reduce the extreme dissonance incurred by the contempt which the Masai and other pastoralists experience in the new states.

Another illustration of this phenomenon can be found in Nigeria, where the preparations for independence were seriously threatened by the refusal of certain groups to accept political subordination that their lack of educational and occupational modernization would tend to give them (Coleman, 1958; Sklar, 1964). The Hausa-Fulani of Northern Nigeria had strong sources of pre-colonial pride in their successful conquest states and their Islamic orthodoxy. The colonial administration protected their high self-evaluation by treating their traditional rulers with respect, granting them authority, and keeping missionary influence and modern education (sources of countervailing norms) to a minimum. At the end of the colonial period the Hausa-Fulani were far behind the Southern Nigerians in education and occupational modernization and were regarded by the Christian Southerners as unsophisticated, backward people. The dissonance between the subordinate status they would have in a society dominated by Southerners and their own untarnished sense of religious and cultural superiority led the Hausa-Fulani rulers to refuse to go into a federation unless they could dominate it. Since they controlled a majority of the Nigerian population (albeit the least politically active segment), their claims were stronger than those of minorities like the Masai in other African nations. The Northern leaders insisted on a federal structure in which direct economic and political competition between Northerners and Southerners would be minimized, so that the Hausa-Fulani could reduce the dissonance between their high evaluation of themselves and the low evaluation they would have experienced when measured by the modern standards of Southern Nigeria.

It must be emphasized that, from the viewpoint of dissonance theory, the regionalist and secessionist tendencies of groups like the Masai and the Hausa-Fulani are not due simply to the dissonance in group evaluation but determined also by these groups not having developed a strong commitment to modern occupational roles (even if low status ones) prior to national self-government. Our interpretation of dissonance theory predicts that groups whose members have moved en masse into the modern structure (although in low positions dissonant with their traditional self-image) will attempt to reduce dissonance by efforts to move up *within* the structure rather than to separate themselves from it. Hagen (1962) has developed an elaborate theoretical formulation based on this idea and presents many historical examples.

In Nigeria, before independence, groups like the Ibo seemed to exemplify this phenomenon,[3] and other examples as well suggest that the general hypothesis that when a relatively disadvantaged ethnic group faces the prospect of national self-government before modernization, they will lean toward secession or regional autonomy as a means of dissonance reduction, whereas if they experience occupational modernization first, they will prefer to reduce dissonant evaluations of group status by increased competition within the national framework.

SUMMARY

This chapter has attempted to survey the various points at which cognitive consistency theories impinge upon problems of ethnocentrism and intergroup relations. A number of such predictions have been presented, and have been italicized for scanning in the text. One hypothesis, that the more similar the outgroup the more it is liked, has been given extensive review including new, albeit secondary, data analysis. Other hypotheses receiving more than brief mention deal with the balance among regional sets of intergroup valences, the effects of forced compliance in the colonial and postcolonial organization of territories upon group identification, and the resolution of incongruities in group esteem produced by contact with modern economic systems.

---

[3] The Biafran secession of 1967, more than six years after independence, cannot be understood in these terms, but only in terms of the escalation of ethnic and regional conflict in Nigeria during the revolutionary changes of 1966.

CHAPTER 53

Comment: Parallels Between Individual and Collective Tendencies

Theodore M. Newcomb

Individuals' preferences in ordering cognitions apply to the psychological structuring of their social worlds. Furthermore, 'real' structuring of the latter often corresponds more or less closely to what we would predict from these psychological propensities. Such is the general import of the papers in this section. All of them deal with questions of existence of such parallelisms with the conditions under which they are found, or with the processes by which they develop and are maintained.

It is a rather well-established psychological fact that most individuals have definite preferences for certain ways of ordering cognitions, which they often impose on an objective world that does not always correspond to these predilections. Going on from there, De Soto and Albrecht suggest that social scientists may be more susceptible to such distortions than other people, and point to some reasons for their being particularly so 'victimized.' It is hard to deny that social scientists share the frailties of other humans, and insofar as they rely upon others' reports of how they see their social worlds, their reports are twice affected by the same cognitive predilections. But qua scientists, they operate within a special subculture which may serve to reinforce these same predilections. Modern scientists tend to assume that the basic laws of the universe are essentially simple and that, while phenomena as observed are very complex, they are eventually to be understood by testing single hypotheses with one eye on the law of parsimony. Perhaps the scientist's metatheory of science represents his own special rationalization of his merely human predilection for simple (though not necessarily single) orderings, but for most of them this would be a hard saying indeed. At any rate, the social scientist is particularly susceptible to the kind of "entrapment" that De Soto and Albrecht describe. This warning may well be kept in mind throughout the entire section.

The observation of parallels between individual-psychological and collective phenomena should, these authors plead, lead to questions of processes, mechanisms, and dynamics within groups and societies. Professor Mandelbaum suggests that certain historical movements, or even whole historical epochs, can be viewed as instances of preferring or seeking a simply-ordered world. If so, it is clear that one kind of explanation of the individual-collective parallel will not suffice: the assumption—in itself over-simple—that if units of which a larger system is composed typically behave in a certain way then the larger system will simply show more of the same. That is, if individuals prefer simple structuring, the folklore (or philosophies or scientific viewpoints) of societies will be simply ordered. Mandelbaum himself gives the coup de grace to this explanation, noting that the collective tendency varies in time and space, and that reactions to oversimplicity occur. Hence man's capacities, both for embracing simplicity and for tolerat-ing—even seeking—complexity can express themselves in shared cognitions that emphasize either tendency. After all, even De Soto's child subjects were not unanimous in preferring the simplest structures.

One is reminded of F. H. Allport's distinction (1924) between co-acting and face-to-face groups. In the former, "individuals are primarily occupied with some stimulus other than one another" (p. 260); the latter may be understood in terms of interaction rather than mere coaction. All-port's position was that through social facilitation, which involves interaction through "sights and sounds" if not in other ways, individuals' common be-havior tendencies became intensified in certain collective situations. The point, for present purposes, is that since man does possess both capacities, collective events either toward or away from oversimplification cannot be explained as mere multiplying of 'inherent' individual tendencies. Obviously an adequate explanation of the parallelism must call upon environmental saliencies together with interaction among individuals who may or may not have differing preferences for simple structuring.

Professor Davis notes that, insofar as real social structures correspond to individual-psychological models of consistency, the parallels point to flows of information and influence, which in turn often induce attitude change. His point, of course, is not the truism that information and influence are more likely to be transmitted within the boundaries of groups or or-ganizations than across them, but rather, I assume, that the ties that bind individuals together in social structures are closely related to the processes by which information and influence are exchanged. Models of interpersonal consistency deal with such variables as attraction and similarities or dis-crepancies in cognitions and attitudes and these, in turn, determine and are determined by processes of communication (cf. Festinger et al., 1950; Newcomb, 1953). Thus the individual-collective parallel is mediated by communicative exchange, and required both by psychological forces toward consistency at the individual level and, at the collective level, by functional demands for consensus and group solidarity.

The findings reported by Professors Campbell and LeVine provide impressive support, at the societal and intergroup levels, for predictions derived from individual models of psychological consistency. Their data also make it possible to assess the contribution of other variables to the balance-like sets of attitudes that they report. Of particular interest is the interplay between residential adjacency and distance, on the one hand, and regional alliances on the other. Such propositions as that an ally of an ally will be an ally whereas the enemy of an ally will be an enemy are obviously balance-like. Only under certain conditions do they find that both the principles of balance and those of the mandala circle apply. This is hardly surprising, since propositions usually become harder to confirm as they include more and more variables.

One basis for the increasing complexity of intergroup as compared with interindividual relations is the differing pattern of communication within and between groups. Assuming, for present purposes, that balanced relations (characterized by mutual trust and consensus) are relatively prevalent within such a society as the Kikuyu, such conditions are maintained by daily interdependence and ready access to communicative exchange. As between societies, however—say Kikuyu and Somali—distance not only makes direct communication improbable but thus facilitates cognitive distortion, collectively reinforced within either society by ready communication about the other one, and individually reinforced by preferences for balance ("those people whom we mistrust and who are so different from us"), in the manner of autistic hostility (Newcomb, 1947).

These four papers, in sum, raise questions about parallels between individual and collective tendencies toward consistency. The empirical evidence generally supports the parallelism, but with increasing size, complexity, and spatial dispersion of the collectivities additional variables are introduced. Hopefully, future research will be directed at questions of mechanisms and dynamics by which the parallels, insofar as they appear, develop and persist or change.

IV
Responses
and Consequences

A. THE TEMPORAL COURSE OF INCONSISTENCY REDUCTION

When one examines the processes involved in cognitive consistency, it becomes clear that temporal events are important, if for no other reason than the fact that inconsistency reduction takes time. Moreover, as we shall see, several interesting phenomena occur during this time period. Armed with this bit of hindsight, it is relatively easy to note surprise at the fact that, in the initial statements of consistency theory, time was given little or no consideration. Fortunately, several energetic researchers have begun to investigate this variable in the past few years. And (if I may be forgiven the play on words) it is high time; for the experiments and theorizing that have emerged are not only imaginative and, therefore, of interest in their own right, but they have also led to a reformulation of some of the original ideas on the course of inconsistency reduction.

The following essays include the current ideas on the temporal issue of some of the people who have been most prominent in investigating it. Jon Jecker reviews his recent research and thinking regarding the basic differences between predecisional conflict and postdecisional dissonance. In his essay he makes an interesting distinction between a 'tentative stand' and a full-blown decision—a distinction that bears some resemblance to part of the five-stage model developed by Irving Janis to describe what occurs when a person decides to commit himself to a course of action. In his essay, Janis illustrates this model by presenting some provocative field studies involving real and important decisions. The essay by Norman Miller includes several speculations about temporal events—from the conditions under which dissonance might be reduced *prior* to a decision to the methodological problems presented by the fact that multiple measures of dissonance reduction must take place on a temporal dimension. Finally, Elaine Walster and Ellen Berscheid treat us to a discussion of two important aspects of the temporal problem: (a) the regret phenomenon, originally discovered by Walster, in which the attractiveness of the chosen alternative actually *decreases* immediately after the decision, and (b) the relative permanence of dissonance-reducing behavior—i.e., how long it lasts.

CHAPTER 54

Conflict and Dissonance: A Time of Decision

Jon D. Jecker

The University of Texas

The purpose of this chapter is to summarize some of the work that has given attention to time factors in the arousal and reduction of dissonance, and more importantly to explore and hopefully to clarify general temporal considerations as they impinge on the theory. I believe that the role of time factors in dissonance theory is a relatively simple one.

A major stumbling-block in the path to understanding the role of time in dissonance rests in the generality of the theory. The impact of time on dissonance theory has been studied primarily in decision-making situations, and the results obtained lead one to the conclusion that the occurrence and reduction of dissonance are restricted to postdecision situations. However, in Festinger's (1957) original presentation of the theory, there is no aspect of the *definition* of dissonance which restricts its operation in time: "These two [existant and related cognitive] elements are in a dissonant relation if, considering these two alone, the [contrary] of one element would follow from the other" (p. 13). Dissonance theory applies, or at least is testable, in any instance which satisfies the conditions set by its definition. Dissonance theory is applicable to cognitive situations where no decision, as such, is being made. Many dissonance studies rely on introducing, in a convincing way, information thought by the investigator to be inconsistent with a person's existing cognitions—beliefs, attitudes, feelings, knowledge of past actions, etc. Some studies have employed the technique of inducing a person to act in a manner inconsistent with his previous actions, beliefs, attitudes, or feelings. These situations may or may not involve a *decision* by the person to perform the discrepant act. However, time and its relation to the dynamics of the theory have received virtually no attention across the array of situations which do satisfy the conditions set by the definition. Since time has been the focus of attention and controversy primarily in research involving decision situations, I will focus first on that substantive area.

It becomes clear, while nowhere specifically stated in the original statement of the theory, that with regard to decision situations, dissonance is generated by the occurrence of a decision and is thus postdecisional (Festinger, 1957, pp. 37 ff.). Moreover, none of the latter definitional discussions (Brehm & Cohen, 1962; Cohen, 1964; and Deutsch & Krauss, 1965) of the theory would seem to challenge the statement that, particularly in cases where a relatively clear decision is made at some specific point or brief interval in time, the dynamic drive state called dissonance is a direct consequence of the decision and therefore must be exclusively a postdecision phenomenon. Logically, if dissonance is a postdecision event, attempts at dissonance reduction similarly would not be in evidence until after a decision.

In summary, it would appear that time plays no generally important role in the occurrence and reduction of dissonance *as defined in the theoretical statement*. In practice, however, with regard specifically to decision situations, time *is* very important in predicting cognitive restructuring on the basis of the theory.

Since dissonance theory seems to promise a rather all-encompassing system for understanding cognitive dynamics, the self-imposed temporal limitation in decision situations appears a major compromise with parsimony. Janis (1959), perhaps realizing this, suggested that the notion of dissonance could be incorporated more parsimoniously into a theory of decisional conflict resolution. In essence, he suggested that dissonance was simply postdecision conflict, that dissonance reduction was postdecision conflict resolution, and that the dynamics after decision were essentially the same as those preceding decision. Thus, Janis would have expected that the process of arriving at a decision would be continued after decision until only a tolerable amount of conflict remained, or at least until the conflict could be resolved no further. Were this the case, there certainly would be no need for a new construct, dissonance, in order to pursue an understanding of cognitive dynamics in decision situations.

In response to Janis' equation of the dynamics of predecision conflict and dissonance, the present author and others conducted experiments (Davidson & Kiesler, 1964; Jecker, 1964a; Jecker, 1964b) attempting to demonstrate that the dynamics of dissonance reduction following a decision are quite different from the dynamics of conflict resolution in arriving at decisions. The study by Davidson and Kiesler produced some evidence to support the contention of such a difference, but the results were not immune to an alternative interpretation in terms of a conflict resolution position. Specifically, they found that reevaluation of the attractiveness of specific characteristics of choice alternatives in a dissonance-reduction direction was significantly greater following a decision than preceding one. On the other hand, some evidence of the possibility of reevaluation of a similar nature *was* obtained in a predecision situation where subjects had a relatively long time to consider decision-relevant information. Thus, some evidence was obtained that dissonance-reducing cognitive restructuring may *not* be confined to postdecision periods. In addition, the experiment employed a specific instruction to all subjects to suspend making a decision because 'important' decision-relevant information was to come later. As Festinger (1964b, p. 18) suggests, "It seems quite plausible to argue that ... [the predecision subjects] ... were simply acting as information processors and did not enter a conflict-decision situation until they were asked to make their decision. It is, hence, not surprising that one does not see evidence of much conflict resolution...."

In the present author's first study (Jecker, 1964a) less ambiguous evidence of a difference between conflict and dissonance was obtained. The experiment was designed to allow orthogonal manipulation of degree of conflict and degree of dissonance experienced. Four experimental conditions were employed: High Conflict-Dissonance, High Conflict-No Dissonance, Low Conflict-Dissonance, and Low Conflict-No Dissonance. All experimental conditions allowed a measure of changes in the perceived attractiveness to female high school students of two very desirable objects (phonograph records) from before to after a choice was made between the two. The 'before' measures, taken on a set of 15 popular records, were obtained prior to the subject's awareness that a choice was to be made. The two records to be employed as choice alternatives were then selected by the investigator on the basis of each Ss 'before' ratings of the set of 15. Then, in order to avoid the criticism of the Davidson and Kiesler study suggested by Festinger above (1964b, p. 18), each subject was put into a 'conflict-decision situation' by being instructed that she could have one of the records, possibly both, and that she could choose which record she wanted in case she received only one of them.

The assumption that degree of conflict in making a choice between two desirable objects increases as the probability of receiving both objects diminishes constituted the basis of a manipulation of degree of conflict. Half of the subjects were told, before making their choice, that "19 out of 20" subjects were being given both records; the other half were told that only "1 out of 20" were being given both. It was assumed that subjects receiving the former instruction would experience less conflict in making a choice than those receiving the latter instruction. The effectiveness of this manipulation of degree of conflict was checked and verified by decision time data.

Independently of the level of conflict induced, half of the subjects were placed in a Dissonance condition by receiving, as a result of a rigged drawing, only the record they chose. The other subjects were placed in a No Dissonance situation by receiving both records. Following this manipulation, all subjects rerated the attractiveness of all 15 records.

Analysis of variance of changes in the ratings of the perceived attractiveness of the two choice-alternative records revealed no systematic change that could be attributed to different levels of conflict induced before the choice. The existence of dissonance did systematically influence changes in ratings of attractiveness, and observed differences were consistent with a dissonance reduction hypothesis. Dissonance subjects, regardless of degree of conflict experienced, increased the difference in relative attractiveness of the two records more than No Dissonance subjects.

One possible ambiguity in the Davidson and Kiesler study was that implicit decisions may have been made during conflict in spite of the fact that the experimenters attempted to discourage explicit decision-making. This ambiguity was avoided here by having the dependent measures follow an overt indication of choice in all conditions. Thus, the test of conflict vs. dissonance was not dependent on observing the effect of conflict before a choice was made. If any systematic changes in attractiveness occurred in either the High Conflict-No Dissonance or the Low Conflict-No Dissonance condition, it unambiguously would have been due to conflict resolution since no dissonance was produced by the choice in these conditions.

The only alternative interpretation of these findings in keeping with the "dissonance is postdecision conflict" equation would be the possibility that systematic shifts occur during conflict which are then reversed when no dissonance follows decision. It is complex but not unreasonable to maintain that when both records were received, subjects possibly reversed any systematic shifts in attractiveness which occurred during conflict since such shifts would no longer be psychologically necessary to justify the choice made. To check on this alternative interpretation, three additional experimental conditions were run. In two of these, high or low conflict was manipulated as before, and the dependent measure was taken after choice but *before* subjects discovered whether they would receive one or both records. In the third condition, subjects were simply told they would get one record and asked to choose the one they preferred. If systematic shifts occur during conflict, they should be obtained in all three conditions, though the magnitude of the effects would vary with the amount of conflict. If systematic shifts only occur in postdecision situations involving dissonance, they should only be obtained in the third condition described. Analysis of variance supported the latter expectation, eliminating the alternative conflict resolution interpretation of the earlier results. Where the ramifications and consequences of the choice remain uncertain, systematic changes in the relative attractiveness of the records are not observed regardless of degree of conflict experienced in making the choice.

It would appear, then, that conflict resolution is conducted via some mode other than systematic reevaluation of the attractiveness of choice objects, a mode dissonance theory would expect and which was employed by subjects in dissonance conditions. This research obviously supports the self-imposed limitation of dissonance theory to postdecision situations. Just how serious a limitation is this? Apparently predecisional conflict resolution is not amenable to an analysis by dissonance theory—or is it? To answer these questions, and to explore temporal considerations more generally, this discussion must broaden beyond a consideration of overt choice, or decision.

The term conflict is intuitively applicable to situations that call for decisions, or attitudinal commitments at least—*cognitive action* in a broad sense. The point in time at which a decision is made, or attitudinal commitment is made, is in most cases obscure. It is usually impossible to know exactly when a decision is made, except where one is willing to rely on the report of the person making the decision—someone who undoubtedly knows no more, and possibly less, about the nature of decision-making than the investigator.

Let us take as a hypothetical example a person who is told that we would like him to take a stand concerning some particular issue X, about which he knows nothing. If we then provide him piece by piece with information about that issue, he will probably be motivated to resist taking a tentative stand because he realizes that future incoming information may cause him to change a premature stand. He also may be *able* to resist taking a tentative stand, at least initially. Eventually, and probably still fairly early in the game, the load of information may cease to be amenable to itemization, and our subject will begin to synthesize the information he possesses at that point. It probably is appropriate, though certainly an assumption, to say that the point at which synthesization of information begins marks the occurrence of the first tentative stand. It also probably is true that what most investigators refer to as an attitude on an issue is nothing more or less than a statement of a synthesization, with an emphasis on evaluation, of information relevant to the issue. In any case, once a stand is taken, be it ever so tentative, incoming information which suggests a change in that stand is referred to as inconsistent, contradictory, dissonant, etc.

If it is generally true that processing new information or simply re-calling relevant information about an issue fairly quickly results in taking a tentative stand, and if such a tentative stand occurred in the Jecker study discussed above, why was there no evidence of dissonance reduction in the High Conflict-No Dissonance condition? Even if *no* new information im-pinged following a tentative decision, existing information about favorable aspects of the tentatively rejected alternative should have been sufficient to produce some dissonance. The answer to this question appears to lie in the variety of modes by which dissonance can be reduced.

If conflict is defined in terms of processing information which in part indicates one action and in part another incompatible action, and involves taking a tentative stand, then it may be that the dissonance aroused, *before an overt publicly stated decision*, by information inconsistent with a *tentative* stand is reduced simply by changing to the contraindicated stand. While such choice-switching would not *eliminate* dissonance altogether, it would probably inhibit any systematic reevaluation of the attractiveness of choice alternatives. In the research discussed above, however, the point of choice was taken to be the time at which the subject indicated publicly and overtly to the investigator the object she wanted more, either verbally by naming one of the objects or by pointing to one of them. While it was possible for a subject to change her mind after indicating her choice to the investigator, none did. As Lewin (1952) suggested, overt indication may 'freeze' the choice. This would force the person to resort to other modes of dissonance reduction—reevaluation of choice alternatives in this case.

The possibility that a tentative decision is easily changed (but that overt indication to the investigator is not) is tied directly to discussions else-where (Brehm & Cohen, 1962) of the role of commitment in the occurrence of dissonance. Commitment is obviously a matter of degree, varying from situation to situation and within a situation from individual to individual. The more a person is committed to some stand, due either to public state-ment or to a history of habitual previous adherence to that stand, the more difficult it probably is for him to alter the stand.

Thus I am proposing that existing beliefs, attitudes, and knowledge of past actions, while not being decisions proper, are conceptual equivalents of decisions as they have implications for dissonance theory. Perhaps the term 'tentative decisions' would be a useful way to distinguish them from overt decisions, but degree of commitment seems a better conceptualization of that distinction. The less committed one is to a belief or attitude, the more susceptible that belief or attitude will be to change in the face of inconsistent information. Overt indication of a decision to others involves greater com-mitment and less susceptibility to change, and thus is more likely to force the decision-maker to use other modes of dissonance reduction.

As suggested earlier, the time factor in dissonance is not of great sig-nificance. If the reader will accept the definition of the term *decision* as broadened here to include not only choice among objects or courses of action, but also *choice* among belief, attitudinal, or affective stands, then the relatively simple role time plays in decision situations is that dissonance can only occur *after* at least a tentative decision is made: that is, *after* at least a minimal amount of commitment is felt regarding that decision; and *after* some definite inconsistent information is introduced or recalled.

The foregoing discussion has supported the first of the temporal conditions listed immediately above as necessary ones for the occurrence and reduction of dissonance. That the second condition is necessary is suggested by a finding, mentioned above, of the present author's first experiment (Jecker, 1964a). This finding deserves discussion in its own right. The result is that subjects who had made a decision, as evidenced by an overt indication to the investigator, showed no evidence of dissonance reduction where the *consequences* of the decision were unclear. The specific situation was one in which subjects indicated which object they preferred but performed the second attraction rating before it was determined whether they would get only the object they chose or both objects. Clearly conflict was as much present in this condition as in the others already discussed. The question is, was dissonance? On the one hand, one can say that since the choice had not yet resulted in forfeiting the unchosen alternative, no tangible dissonant elements had been introduced. On the other hand, if only the chosen object is to be obtained, clearly the subject's choice is to be the factor determining which object would be obtained. In addition, Brehm (1960b) has shown that commitment to an action dissonant with one's values is sufficient to result in dissonance-reducing behavior whether or not the dissonant action has yet been performed. However, while commitment was as present in Jecker's study as in Brehm's, certainty about the consequences of the commitment was much lower in Jecker's study.

Additional evidence exists that certainty of consequences plays a role in the arousal and reduction of dissonance. A second study by the present author (Jecker, 1964b), designed to investigate selective exposure to decision-relevant information, contained a similar condition in which a decision was made but the subject remained uncertain of the consequences of the decision. Subsequent to the decision in that condition, subjects spent no more time reading consonant information supporting the decision than dissonant information controverting it. After the decision was made and the subject was given a fixed period of free access to relevant information, recall of the information was obtained from all subjects. In a condition in which there was no uncertainty about the consequences of the decision, recall of the information contained significant distortions in the service of dissonance reduction. No such distortions occurred in the uncertain decision condition. Thus in neither voluntary exposure to, nor recall of, relevant information was there any evidence of dissonance reduction where the consequences of the decision were uncertain. Again, commitment was as present in this study as in Brehm's, and yet the results differ. The major difference in the experiments seems to be the degree of perceived certainty of the consequences of the decision. Brehm's subjects had every reason to believe they would perform the unpleasant act as agreed; Jecker's subjects, on the other hand, had no way of predicting the consequences of their choices.

While intuition may lead us to expect that where an overt decision involving commitment is made, and where that decision clearly *may* result in dissonance, a person should prepare himself for the possible dissonance by employing some of the modes of dissonance reduction. Technically speaking, this would amount to dissonance avoidance. The evidence to date simply does not support such an expectation. Dissonance and its reduction appear to be not only postdecisional, then, but apparently must also wait on the relatively *unambiguous* presence of dissonant information, not the possibility of it.

CHAPTER 55

Stages in the Decision-Making Process

Irving L. Janis
Yale University

This chapter will deal with the stages of decision-making that precede and follow commitment to a plan of action. The theoretical analysis will include both cognitive and motivational concepts. Much of the rigorous experimental research on decision-making during the past 15 years has been limited to simple verbal decisions that are relatively unimportant to the person once he leaves the laboratory. These studies may have given rise to overemphasis on the purely cognitive aspects of decision-making. Relatively little research has dealt with vital personal decisions in adult life, although many clinical studies of neurotic personalities have some bearing on psychological aspects of decision-making and elucidate the personality factors that make for chronic indecisiveness and extreme rigidity. These clinical studies, however, may overemphasize the importance of anxiety and related motivational factors in personal decision-making, since the subjects' neurotic disorders prevented them from making adequate use of their cognitive abilities.

In recent years, my own research has focused on the interplay of motivational and cognitive processes in important personal decisions, such as whether one should undergo a surgical operation recommended by one's physician (Janis, 1958), whether to reduce one's overweight condition by adhering to a low-calorie diet (Sofer, Wishlade, & Janis, 1965), and whether one should give up smoking in order to avoid respiratory diseases (Janis & Terwilliger, 1962; Janis & Mann, 1965; Janis & Kahn, 1966). In Investigating normal people who face these and other such dilemmas, we have obtained observations both before and after the decision was made. Many of the studies are social psychological experiments in which inconsistent cognitions are deliberately made salient at one or another stage in the decision-making sequence by using different types of role-playing procedures, by introducing persuasive communications, or by conducting group discussions.

This paper was written in the fall of 1966, while the author was a Visiting Research Fellow at the Western Behavioral Sciences Institute and Professor of Psychology in Residence at the University of California at San Diego (on leave of absence from Yale University). Preparation of this paper was facilitated by Grant MH-08564 from the National Institute of Mental Health, United States Public Health Service.

The experimental data are supplemented by recordings of the group discussions and intensive individual interviews, which provide some clues to the mediating psychological processes that may account for the outcomes of the experiments. All of these observations have been drawn upon to delineate the stages in decision-making.

STAGES IN ADOPTING A NEW COURSE OF ACTION

What are the stages that a normal person goes through when he successfully adopts a course of action and then, later on, encounters inconsistent information, either from authoritative communications or from direct experiences of frustration and disappointment with regard to the expected consequences of his decision? Five main stages are depicted in the Figure. Each will be described and illustrated mainly by examples from recent research on men and women who have successfully carried out their decision to give up smoking.

Stage 1: Appraisal of a Challenge

The initial step in making a decision to adopt a new course of action is to appraise one or more communications or events that challenge the preexisting attitude. The important feature of a challenge is that it exposes the person to informational inputs about losses to be expected from maintaining his present policy on the issue, whether it has involved taking a definite stand or being indifferent and inactive. These inputs are inconsistent with the person's preexisting cognitions about the desirability of his present policy and generate a temporary personal crisis. Sometimes the crisis arises as a result of a personal life history event whose meaning is interpreted by the person in accordance with prior information or cultural norms (e.g., a person notices that he has developed a chronic cough that gets worse when he starts smoking and this negative feedback induces him to reconsider his policy of smoking a pack of cigarettes each day). The same type of challenge can come from an impressive persuasive communication that offers arguments in favor of a course of action that differs from the person's position (e.g., news stories about the Surgeon General's report on smoking and lung cancer, which presented antismoking information in an authoritative way that was difficult for well-educated smokers to ignore). When momentarily challenged by new information that is inconsistent with expectations concerning the consequences of a current policy, the person initially appraises it in a somewhat biased way to see if he can dismiss it as being untrue, irrelevant to the policy issue, or inapplicable to his own particular circumstances. If he accepts the challenge as being genuine and applicable to himself, he will perceive his present policy as entailing some potential losses that he had not previously taken into account and this will arouse his interest in alternative courses of action.

Stage 2: Appraisal of Recommended Courses of Action

Once the person accepts the challenge, he becomes more interested in finding out about alternative solutions to the threat and he begins to appraise carefully whichever new courses of action are recommended to him. Thus he becomes more attentive to persuasive communications that explicitly or implicitly convey recommendations for coping with the challenge, even

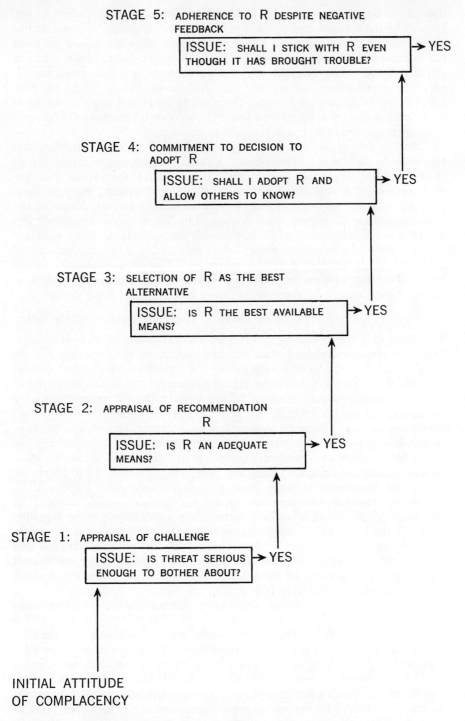

STAGE 5: ADHERENCE TO R DESPITE NEGATIVE
FEEDBACK

ISSUE: SHALL I STICK WITH R EVEN
THOUGH IT HAS BROUGHT TROUBLE? →YES

STAGE 4: COMMITMENT TO DECISION TO
ADOPT R

ISSUE: SHALL I ADOPT R AND
ALLOW OTHERS TO KNOW? →YES

STAGE 3: SELECTION OF R AS THE BEST
ALTERNATIVE

ISSUE: IS R THE BEST AVAILABLE
MEANS? →YES

STAGE 2: APPRAISAL OF RECOMMENDATION
R

ISSUE: IS R AN ADEQUATE
MEANS? →YES

STAGE 1: APPRAISAL OF CHALLENGE

ISSUE: IS THREAT SERIOUS →YES
ENOUGH TO BOTHER ABOUT?

INITIAL ATTITUDE
OF COMPLACENCY

FIGURE.   Stages in making a decision to adhere to a new policy recommended as a
means for coping with a serious threat.

though the recommendations are inconsistent with his present commitments. He will be inclined, of course, to maintain his present policy if possible, but a powerful challenge creates a hunger for information about how to avert the negative consequences which are in the focus of his attention. He will actively try to obtain relevant information by seeking advice from knowledgeable acquaintances concerning the alternatives that might be open to him. Having become vigilant about the possible losses that might ensue from his present policy, the decision-maker will also scan his memory for alternative courses of action he has learned about in the past.

During this phase the decision-maker discards those alternatives that appear to be too unsafe or too costly a means for coping with the threat. (For example, Leventhal and Watts (1966) found that when strongly challenged by a movie depicting the threat of lung cancer, many smokers took seriously the recommendation to stop smoking but they discarded the recommendation to obtain chest X-rays. The latter recommendation was regarded as an inadequate solution, probably because the smokers surmised that if a lung cancer were detected, even at an early stage, the amount of suffering and danger would still be enormous.) The decision-maker ends up by selecting for further consideration those candidates that he judges as having a good chance of averting the losses made salient by the challenge.

Stage 3: Making a Tentative Decision about the Best Available Policy

This phase of decision-making involves intensive scanning of each alternative. Any new recommendation that remains salient in the thinking of the decision-maker is tried out imaginatively for "goodness of personal fit." In addition, there is always one other salient alternative that is also subjected to this same mental process, whether or not it satisfactorily passes the reality testing carried out in Stage 2—the person's current course of action (e.g., continuing to smoke as much as usual). This alternative serves as a point of comparison as well as an attractive choice that one resists relinquishing. As he mentally scans each alternative course of action, the decision-maker becomes aware of anticipated gains and losses. Any alternative for which the anticipated losses are markedly greater than the anticipated gains will be definitely rejected and precluded from his further consideration. (For example, keeping an unlighted cigarette in one's mouth might be regarded as one of the adequate alternatives to smoking, after Stage 2, but it may be promptly rejected in Stage 3 when anticipated ridicule from friends and other negative considerations become salient as the person imagines himself executing this new plan; he may decide that the given means could work for some people but certainly not for him.)

As the person examines the alternatives that survive the initial scanning of consequences, he strives to select one that will provide a net gain with a minimum of losses. When the best candidate is tentatively selected, the final step during this stage is the attempt to minimize the potential negative consequences (e.g., thinking up ways of cutting down on entailed expenditures of time and money, avoiding reactions of social disapproval from family, friends, or other reference groups, and reducing the chances of losing self-esteem from failure to live up to prior commitments). This often leads to working out auxiliary plans and tactics for insuring the success of the new plan (e.g., not telling everyone about it until it is well launched, preparing strong arguments to give to friends who might object, etc.).

Stage 4: Committing Oneself to the New Policy

After the person announces to himself that henceforth he is going to adhere to the new plan of action, he usually takes the first steps to show that he means it and reveals his decision to significant others (e.g., when friends offer him cigarettes he refuses and explains that he has decided to stop smoking). For some embarrassing decisions, this stage may involve a series of substages over a period of many days or weeks as the person partially commits himself more and more, starting by carrying out the decision secretly, next letting a few intimates in on it, and then gradually allowing more and more persons in his social network to know about it. As soon as he has taken the first steps of committing himself, the person anticipates a loss of self-esteem if he fails to carry out the new policy and he begins to consolidate his cognitive framework in a way that enables the new policy to be assimilated with a minimum of cognitive inconsistency. This consolidation process increases as the decision-maker becomes more and more socially committed to his decision. At the same time, each fresh commitment he makes to another person or group becomes an added incentive for sticking with the decision. Throughout this phase, the person deliberately tries to avoid exposing himself to inconsistent information and displays a hearty welcome to communications containing consistent information that will bolster the decision. The tendency to bolster the decision will incline the person to communicate the decision as rapidly as possible to his entire social network if he expects approval or neutral reactions, but it will incline him to keep away from those persons whom he suspects might strongly disapprove.

Stage 5: Adherence to the New Policy Despite Negative Feedback

Obviously the degree of persistence of the attitude changes depends upon the amount and intensity of negative feedback from acting on the new policy. Of central psychological importance is the capacity to tolerate negative feedback. For any given bit of negative feedback, how shaken is the decision-maker? How much negative feedback can he take before the new decision is challenged to the point where the successive stages of decision-making are again activated? In our studies of people who try to stop smoking, the successful cases show a very high threshold in this respect: They verbally refute the arguments offered by opponents; they ignore the minor signs of potential setback and even remain unshaken by relatively severe setbacks. (E.g., many ex-smokers suffer from severe withdrawal symptoms but continue to give themselves moral pep talks to resist the temptation to backslide.) Moreover, they show a tendency to change their values and affiliations so as to minimize postdecisional conflict. (E.g., some ex-smokers avoid friends who tempt them to smoke and despise anyone who ridicules their decision.) In general, they decrease the valuation of those significant persons in their social network who disapprove of the decision and increase the valuation of those who approve.

IMPLICATIONS FOR ATTITUDE CHANGE

Each of the five stages in the decision-making process has some direct implications for attitude change. These implications are summarized in the Table, which postulates gradual changes in eight different attitude components

TABLE

Types of Attitude Change Accompanying Each Stage in Making a Decision to Adhere to a Recommended Policy. (Inferred from Studies of Heavy Smokers Who Decided to Stop Smoking After Being Exposed to Publicity about the Surgeon-General's Report on Smoking and Lung-Cancer.)

Components of Attitude Change New Beliefs, Value Judgments, and Dispositions Toward Recommendation (R)	Initial Attitude of Complacency	Stage 1 Positive Appraisal of Challenge	Stage 2 Positive Appraisal of Recommendation (R)	Stage 3 Selection of R as the Best Alternative	Stage 4 Commitment to Decision to Adopt R	Stage 5 Adherence to R Despite Negative Feedback
	(1)	(2)	(3)	(4)	(5)	(6)
Overt Behavior						
1. Acts in Accordance with R Following Major Challenges to the New Attitude?	No	No	No	No	(?)	Yes
2. Acts in Accordance with R Under Normal Circumstances?	No	No	No	No	Yes	Yes
Verbal Evaluation of R						
3. Feels Willing to Act in Accordance with R?	No	No	No	No	Yes	Yes
4. Believes R is Best Available Means?	No	No	No	Yes	Yes	Yes
5. Believes R is a Satisfactory Means, Worth Considering?	No	No	Yes	Yes	Yes	Yes
6. Selectively Responsive to Subsequent Communications about R? (Accepts Assertions That R is an Effective Means and Rejects Opposing Assertions.)	No	No	Yes	Yes	Yes	Yes
Verbal Evaluation of Threat						
7. Believes the Threat is Serious?	No	Yes	Yes	Yes	Yes	Yes
8. Selectively Responsive to Subsequent Communications about the Threat (Accepts Assertions That the Threat is Serious and Rejects Those That Minimize the Threat.)	No	Yes	Yes	Yes	Yes	Yes

as the decision-maker moves on to each successive stage. One prediction suggested by this analysis is that the various patterns of attitude change shown in the columns of this Table will be found to form a unitary (Guttman) attitude scale. For example, in the earlier stages, we would expect to find a person markedly more receptive to new information about a recommended policy (component No. 6) after he had changed his evaluation of the negative consequences of his present policy (component No. 7) and had become more receptive to new information about the threat (component No. 8). In the later stages, we would not expect to find spontaneous behavioral conformity with the recommendation (components No. 1 and No. 2) unless all the other components (No. 3 to No. 8) had changed from negative to positive.

The scaling implications of the stages, as represented in the Table, have not yet been tested but, in the meantime, the schema has some limited value for analyzing a number of problems concerning the effects of informational inputs that are inconsistent with the person's existing policies, commitments, and expectations. One value of the schema is that it furnishes a set of categories for describing qualitative differences in the attitude changes produced by different types of inputs. For example, an experiment by Janis and Terwilliger (1962), which presented smokers with a pamphlet on smoking and lung cancer, showed that a simple fear-arousing communication mainly succeeded in inducing some subjects to accept the challenge but without carrying any of them beyond Stage 2. In contrast, another experiment that made use of fear-arousing inputs via an emotional role-playing procedure proved to be markedly effective not only in gaining acceptance at the initial challenge stage but in producing changes in successive stages as well.

Janis and Mann (1965) set up a psychodramatic situation in which the subject was asked to play the role of a medical patient who is suffering from the harmful consequences of smoking. During the session, the experimenter, in the role of physician, gave the 'patient' the bad news that the diagnosis was cancer of the lung and required immediate surgery. This role-playing procedure proved to be an extraordinarily disquieting experience for the subjects and produced a relatively high incidence of decisions to stop smoking, as compared with a control condition in which the same information was conveyed without any role-playing.

Some of the role-players spontaneously stated as they were leaving the laboratory that they felt they should throw away their cigarettes and stop smoking altogether (Stage 3). In follow-up interviews, a number of these subjects reported that when they arrived home after the experimental session, they announced their firm intention to cut down on smoking cigarettes to members of the family or friends (Stage 4). Others in the experimental group left the session a bit worried (Stage 1) and went through the subsequent stages at a slower rate, but by one month later had committed themselves to cut down on smoking.

A subsequent follow-up study (Mann & Janis, 1968) revealed that over an 18-month period, the emotional role-players who had participated in the initial experiment continued to report a significantly greater decrease in amount of smoking than the controls, which suggests that a single one-hour session of emotional role-playing succeeded not only in inducing personal commitment to the decision (Stage 4) but also in building up a long-term capacity to persist despite whatever setbacks and counteracting influences the ex-smokers subsequently encountered (Stage 5).

It should be possible to use the five stages as a set of categories to describe different degrees of susceptibility in the audience to specific types of persuasive messages intended to produce adherence to a new policy. In some of our group experiments, conducted in a clinic for persons who want to change their smoking habits, we encounter subjects who are hung up, so to speak, at each of the stages (Janis & Kahn, 1966). Some of the volunteers who come to the clinic merely feel a bit concerned about the unhealthy consequences of smoking and wonder if switching to filtered cigarettes would be a good idea (Stages 1 or 2); whereas others, at the opposite extreme, are chronic ex-exsmokers, who feel convinced that they should quit smoking, have repeatedly committed themselves to do so, but simply cannot tolerate the withdrawal symptoms (Stage 4). All of the volunteers seem to benefit temporarily and move on to the next stage as a result of the added commitment and social support that comes from joining a 'common-problem' group conducted by a psychologist-consultant. Nevertheless, the informational inputs that are especially effective for people at an early stage in the decision-making process are not very effective for persons at a later stage, and vice versa. For example, group members in Stage 1 are likely to resolve to smoke less after they hear a fellow member report glowingly about feeling healthier after cutting down on cigarettes; whereas the members who were recently at Stage 5 and have reverted back to Stage 3 are more likely to be induced to try again when they learn that one other chronic 'addict' in the group has stopped smoking for over a week.

The stage of the decision-making process at which a person is currently located is probably a major determinant of (a) the degree of interest he will have in exposing himself to one or another type of information relevant to the decision and (b) the degree to which he will be positively or negatively influenced by the information if he is exposed to it. The analysis of stages, as presented in the Table, has some obvious implications for receptivity to new information about the positive gains to be expected from adopting the recommended policy. For example, a new bit of antismoking information (such as 'doctors have found that the average person experiences less fatigue if he gives up smoking') will meet with indifference or high resistance before Stage 1 is completed; but if the same new bit of information is presented to the same person when he is at Stage 3 or 4, it will elicit great interest, and will be carefully mulled over and evaluated. If presented at a still later stage (after Stage 4 is completed), it will be highly welcome and promptly assimilated with hardly any critical reflection about it.

An entirely different sequence would be expected from a bit of information that argues in the direction of rejecting the recommendation (e.g., 'doctors have found that most people who give up smoking become chronically overweight'). Before Stage 1, the average smoker would have little interest in such information, but if brought to the focus of his attention in a captive audience, it would be readily assimilated into his cognitive structure. During Stages 2 and 3, the smoker would display much more interest and would evaluate the information in a relatively unbiased way. But then, after Stage 4, the ex-smoker would avoid such information if possible. If he could not escape it, he would be highly skeptical and would try to refute it.

In order to test the generality of the above hypotheses—and of the entire schema of stages presented in the Figure and the Table—it will be necessary to investigate many different types of decisions, in addition to the smoking decision that has furnished most of the empirical basis so far. It seems to me quite likely that we shall find a high degree of generality, in the light of my observations of similar stages in ill persons who were faced with having to decide whether or not to accept their physicians' advice to undergo painful medical treatments (Janis, 1958), and in normal men and women who were in the throes of decisional conflict in connection with marriage or their choice of career (Janis, 1959). Moreover, the schema of stages can be fitted fairly well to descriptive accounts of the sequence of steps in making relatively impersonal decisions, such as those made by scientists and technologists. Kuhn (1962), in his account of the recent history of various scientific theories, calls attention to the resistance of outstanding scientists in physics and chemistry to change in their theories until a crisis is generated by impressively challenging data that are completely incompatible with the paradigm to which they had committed themselves. Original experimental data, according to Kuhn, are likely to be regarded with belittling indifference and disregarded if they go against a long-established theory that has not yet been seriously challenged, but will be given careful scrutiny if they come during the crisis period when none of the new alternative paradigms has been selected. Finally, the experimental findings will meet with least resistance if they are in accord with a new paradigm that has been taken over by research investigators in the entire field (see Chapter 50).

CONSEQUENCES OF FAILING TO 'WORK THROUGH' EACH PHASE

Another suggestive observation that should be mentioned from our studies of would-be-exsmokers pertains to the long-run consequences of 'working through' each successive stage. In contrast to the successful cases who show a high threshold of challenge, there are others who commit themselves to a decision and then, on almost the first occasion when they encounter a bit of negative feedback, fail to adhere to it. There is, of course, a continuum of these failures ranging from weak to very strong adherence. One of the main hypotheses that has grown out of our recent research is that incomplete working through of any of the first four stages of the decision-making process will leave the person vulnerable to negative feedback during the final stage. We are now working on the problem of identifying the types of informational inputs that will induce adequate working through of each successive stage.

The emotional role-playing experiments mentioned earlier (Janis & Mann, 1965; Mann & Janis, 1968) and several recent studies employing similar procedures (Mann, 1967; Elms, 1967; Nowlis & Janis, 1968) suggest that a very impressive confrontation with the negative consequences of one's preexisting policy during the first stage can 'get under one's skin' and create a sustained attitude of personal vulnerability to the threat that will counteract any incipient tendency to backslide during Stage 5. Other observations suggest that the decision-maker is especially vulnerable during Stage 5 to whichever specific bits of negative feedback had not been antici-pated and assimilated during Stages 2 and 3. Any weak link in the chain, resulting from failure to take account of the potential inconsistencies en-gendered by each stage of the decision-making process, may play a deter-mining role in the degree of backsliding the decision-maker will display in response to powerful negative feedback. For example, if Stage 3 is at-tenuated, the decision-maker is especially likely to be shaken during the postdecisional period by rational arguments that are inconsistent with his newly adopted plan and he may revert all the way back to the first stage; whereas, if he has given those same inconsistent considerations some thought beforehand, he would be more likely to regard them as unchallenging by labeling them as 'unimportant,' or as 'already taken into consideration,' and hence remain at Stage 5.

Most people seem to give little thought to certain of the non-utilitar-ian considerations that are unpleasant to dwell on (notably potential social disapproval from reference groups and self-condemnation for violating one's own moral standards and ideals) unless these potential sources of incon-sistency are specifically called to their attention by a friend, counselor, or mentor. Failure to work through any of these sources of potential incon-sistency leaves the person more vulnerable than he otherwise would be, with the result that his new policy might be seriously challenged and re-assessed.

The observations of ex-smokers suggest that if realistic information about potential setbacks and losses that the decision-maker does not know about are presented during Stage 3, before he has fully committed himself to a new policy, the intensity of postdecisional conflicts will be reduced during Stage 5 and hence there will be less likelihood of abandoning the new policy. In other words, tolerance for the negative feedback elicited by acting on a new policy can presumably be built up if appropriate informational inputs are introduced before the new policy goes into operation. This proposition is similar to the conclusions drawn from experimental studies on resistance to counterpropaganda created by two-sided persuasive communications (Lumsdaine & Janis, 1954) and on immunization against persuasive challenges to long-accepted cultural truisms (McGuire, 1968a).

The immunization effects of inducing a 'working through' of negative consequences are suggested by a number of case studies of postdecisional conflicts in ex-smokers and ex-exsmokers, but no systematic investigations have been carried out as yet on this particular type of postdecisional con-flict. Some relevant correlational data, however, have been obtained in stud-ies of surgical patients (Janis, 1958, pp. 274–296). From a survey of several hundred young men who had recently undergone a surgical operation, a number of relationships were observed showing a link between amount of preoperative information (of the type that could be expected to help a person to anticipate and work through the subsequent negative feedback) and tolerance for the frustrations, pains, discomforts, and other stresses of the postoperative period. The negative feedback following acceptance of a physician's advice to undergo surgery is, of course, extremely powerful and makes many patients regret their decision.

The men who were least informed about the unpleasant consequences in store for them were found to have been relatively free from worry before the operation. But then, when subjected to the impact of the stresses of the postoperative period, they became much more upset, angry, and hostile toward the medical staff than the others. These unprepared patients were also less cooperative when the nurses or interns tried to give them an injection or to carry out some other routine postoperative treatment; this uncooperative behavior was tantamount to reversing their earlier decision to allow the hospital staff to take over their medical care.

Egbert, Welsh, and Bartlett (1964) conducted an experiment in order to follow up on this correlational evidence and on the theoretical inferences concerning the increase in subsequent stress tolerance created by 'working through' the major sources of stress in advance. They tested the prediction that a group of surgical patients given appropriate preparatory communications before their operations will show better adjustment to the stresses of the postoperative period than an equivalent group of patients given no special preparatory communications other than the information ordinarily available to any hospitalized patient. This prediction was tested in a carefully controlled field experiment with 97 adult surgical patients at the Massachusetts General Hospital. Neither the surgeons nor the ward nurses were told about this experiment, to make sure that the experimental (informed) and control (uninformed) patients would receive equivalent treatment in all other respects. On the day of the operation both groups required about the same amount of narcotics, but on each of the next five postoperative days, the experimental group required significantly less than the controls. In fact, the requests for medication to relieve their pains were so infrequent from the well-informed patients that their postoperative narcotic requirements were reduced by about one-half, as compared with the uninformed control group. Moreover, 'blind' ratings from an independent observer, which were obtained for slightly more than half of each group, showed that the patients in the experimental group were in better emotional and physical condition than the controls. Further evidence of the more rapid improvement of the well-informed patients is provided by data on duration of hospitalization. Completely unaware of the experimental or control treatments received by the patients, the surgeons decided that the well-informed patients were well enough to be sent home much sooner than the uninformed —an average of 2.7 days earlier. In line with the earlier correlational findings, the investigators also noted that the uninformed controls made many more complaints to the staff.

Thus, the experiment provides systematic evidence in support of the conclusion, derived from the earlier studies, concerning the positive value of advance information about the negative consequences of making a decision to undergo surgery. This is a striking illustration of the general proposition that the more complete the 'work of worrying' during Stages 1–4, the greater the tendency to adhere to the decision when challenging provocations are encountered during Stage 5.

The examples cited in this chapter indicate the range of hypotheses suggested by taking account of the sequence of decision-making stages. One final point is pertinent to the demoralizing state of affairs arising from failure to replicate significant findings in experimental research on attitude change and decision making. Sometimes we wonder if this is a subtractive rather than an additive science, as we encounter contradictory findings from successive experiments that are supposed to be replications, such as those that have given rise to controversies about primacy vs. recency effects in persuasion, the positive vs. negative effects of fear appeals on acceptance of a communicator's recommendations, and the influence of large vs. small monetary rewards in the amount of attitude change induced by role-playing (see Chapter 82). Perhaps if we pay more attention to the micro-processes of each stage of the decision-making process and analyze the data from each attitude-change experiment only after we have sorted the subjects into subgroups corresponding to the five stages, we shall discover interactional effects that help explain some of the apparently inconsistent outcomes. The way a person responds to new arguments and appeals in persuasive messages probably depends partly on whether the informational inputs are challenging his current policy for the first time or are introducing inducements to adopt a new policy at a later stage, when the recipient already feels remorsefully stuck with his old policy and is intensively searching for a more satisfactory alternative.

CHAPTER 56

As Time Goes By

Norman Miller
University of Minnesota

This chapter presents some thoughts about the effect of the passage of time on attempts to cope with conflicting or tension-arousing cognitions. In light of Verplanck's (1957) implication that those who use the word 'cognition' do not know what they are talking about, the chapter can be considered a proliferation of ignorance in that it deals with several facets of cognitive behavior. It considers in varying detail (a) factors which affect the amount of tension-reducing behavior, (b) the effect of decision, (c) the different effects over time for evaluative as opposed to informational elements, and (d) the temporal ordering of measurements. It is frankly speculative at times, presents some kernels of research ideas which await implementation, and, being one of several chapters dealing with this topic, does not attempt systematic coverage.

Experimental psychologists have known for many years that time itself is at best a muddled independent variable, serving primarily as a substitute label for the potpourri of events occurring during its passage. They have emphasized that each bit of learning interferes with the retention of every other bit and have ordered the problem by locating the input of the interfering materials on the time dimension. Thus, they have pointed to two sources of interference: those materials learned before and those learned after the critical elements under study.

FACTORS AFFECTING THE NEED FOR COGNITIVE WORK

The experimental learning psychologist, of course, does not deal with logical or psychological incompatibles. Whereas the social psychologist apparently seems to point to dissimilar elements as generating greatest interference, the experimental psychologist notes greatest interference in the learning process when the competing materials are highly similar (provided

This paper was supported in part by National Science Foundation Grant G-1000 to the University of California. I thank the following colleagues for helpful criticisms and comments: Ellen Berscheid, Donald C. Butler, Linda Fleischer, Ramon Rhine, Paul C. Rosenblatt, Ralph Rosnow, J. Allen Thomas, and Elaine Walster.

589

they require different responses).[1] Thus, to the extent that opposing arguments are highly distinctive and well articulated, we should expect the problem of learning their contents to be minimized and contrariwise, the residual problem of cognitively adjusting their opposing contents to be enhanced. The common techniques for creating cognitive consistency or minimizing inconsistency have been catalogued by others and can be quickly summarized: (a) seeking new information, (b) seeking social support, (c) discrediting the source, (d) misinterpreting the content or 'assimilating' the speaker's position, (e) minimizing the importance of the issue or materials, and (f) forgetting the conflicting material. Since the last mechanism, ignoring any special motivational considerations, increases automatically with the passage of time as a simple consequence of the laws of forgetting, we should expect that, *ceteris paribus*, the need for other mechanisms should decrease as time passes. It is relatively easy to test this obvious proposition by measuring the extent to which the various other techniques are employed at different intervals after the dissonance arousing materials are presented. One objection to any straightforward interpretation of such an experiment is that while time passes, not only may retention of the disturbing elements be impaired, thereby reducing the need for cognitive restructuring, but another process may be simultaneously operating. As time passes, dissonance-arousing elements may not only become unavailable, but also the importance or salience of the issue may have objectively declined. If so, any dissonance-arousing elements that are still available may have little effect. Thus, to be sure that effects are in fact due to forgetting, it would be important to reinstigate the salience of the issue at the time of measurement.

What other factors affect the amount of cognitive work? Some circumstances do not elicit balancing or restructuring processes even though the elements involved are disjunctive. Clearly, there must be individual differences in tolerance for imbalance. Perhaps those with the weak needs for cognitive clarity (Cohen, 1957; Kelman & Cohler, 1959), broad category widths (Pettigrew, 1958), open-mindedness (Rokeach, 1960), or low conceptual differentiation (Gardner & Schoen, 1962) would display greater tolerance for imbalance. The current state of knowledge, however, is unclear regarding the number of dimensions necessary to account for individual differences in cognitive organization and still more tenuous about their relation to variables such as persuasion (Holtzman, 1966; see also Chapter 63). But what additional variables control the need to invoke the peace-of-mind tools listed above? Three factors come to mind, all related to what is meant by commitment, but presumably independently manipulable. These are: personal involvement in the issue, social circumstances that demand display of one's position, and finally, the extent to which a decision or action is demanded. One might indeed ask whether any dissonance reduction techniques would be invoked if none of these three circumstances were present. When strong personal values are involved and attacked by the new materials, one indeed has a problem, whereas for issues we do not care about, it may be possible to withstand conflicting materials without doing

---

[1] This paradoxical contradiction can be resolved by considering the attitude dimension as the stimulus object, and the cognitive representations of two opposing speakers' views as implicit representations of two responses. The situation now becomes analogous to the verbal learning paradigm for creating maximal interference: similar (identical) stimuli and different responses.

much about it. Thus, most of us might feel opposed to an 8:30 curfew for men at Brainbuster College if someone pressed us to assert our position on such an issue. Yet, if for lack of anything better to read we happened to pick up a flyer left in our helicopter seat which strongly and cogently advocated such a stand, we might not engage in any dissonance-reducing techniques because we simply do not care much one way or another about the matter. On the other hand, if our son were attending school there, the situation might well be altered.

But consider the contrast between this situation and the typical social-psychological experiment. One crucial difference is that an experiment always requires a measurement, and most often, the measurement is direct rather than indirect. In other words, the subject is asked to have cognitions and to report them. Under these circumstances, there is the inevitable concern about reactive qualities of the measurement (Campbell & Stanley, 1963). We must consider the fact that the subject knows we are interested in the effect of the treatment. What added effect is produced when the subject knows we are going to ask him for his opinion after he reads the flyer on the helicopter? The requirement that he publicly display a position makes it more necessary for him to cognitively deal with the conflicting materials. In other words, circumstances demanding or implying future display of attitude invoke the dissonance-reducing mechanisms, but in their absence—particularly on uninvolving issues—people may be able to tolerate considerable numbers of conflicting elements as part of the cognitive baggage they constantly tote.

Assuming that greater tension is in fact generated when one knows that at some point in the future he must publicly connect himself to a position, at what point are the tension-reducing mechanisms invoked? Presumably they operate at the time that counterattitudinal materials are presented. But perhaps they are also invoked at the time the respondent is asked "Well, what do you think?" What is the effect of this question itself apart from the effects of the counterattitudinal message and what implications are there for the effect of time? Would equal amounts of dissonance be created for respondents, one of whom is told of our interest in his opinion after he gets off the helicopter, and a second after he returns from his subsequent two-week trip? And, if equal dissonance is created in both situations, will equal amounts of attitude change also occur? The thinking above suggests that the respondent who remains unmeasured until his return will show less change. Not caring about the issue, the counterattitudinal material will have little effect. When his position on the issue is subsequently made important by the measurement operation, the content of the counterattitudinal message will presumably have been forgotten and therefore create less tension and less attitude change.

THE EFFECT OF DECISION

The comments above are relevant to the question of decision. Researchers in the dissonance tradition, at least in part, have formalized the difference between dissonance and conflict theories in terms of the point on the temporal dimension at which one confronts cognitions incompatible with one another (Festinger, 1964b). They argue that dissonance theory predicts discomfort after a decision whereas according to conflict theory the discomfort should be felt prior to any decision and thus accommodation should begin before the decision and facilitate it. Their experimental work has been aimed at showing that the former is indeed the case. The whole issue, however, is probably another of those silly instances where theoretical preferences force polar predictions in so-called crucial experiments. There is probably truth in both statements, i.e., that discomfort is felt before the decision as well as after. The more important empirical task lies in specifying the conditions which heighten or exaggerate the amount of tension, dissonance, or regret experienced both before and after the decision.

In the dissonance theory formulation, something presumably holds the person back, prevents him from reducing dissonance until the decision has been made. That 'something' most likely is the desire to make the best possible decision. But why should this desire keep him from reducing dissonance until after he has decided? Why should the judged favorability of the choice alternatives remain undistorted until after a decision has been made? If one wants to make a good decision, it is usually important to have as much relevant information available as possible. Thus, if the situation is structured so that the possibility of obtaining new relevant information persists up to the very point of decision, it would be foolish to distort or exaggerate the favorability of the respective choice alternatives because new information might support the alternative that has been devalued. On the other hand, if all the relevant information has been accumulated or if there is no possibility of obtaining additional information, distortion should be initiated prior to the point at which an overt choice must be displayed. This is not to say that even in this latter case dissonance-reducing behavior would not occur after the overt choice. The point is that we can probably specify variables which control the extent to which cognitive activity spreads apart choice alternatives both before and after an overt decision.

One important condition generating regret in decision situations is that decisions are often required in circumstances where there is insufficient time to consider adequately all of the ramifications or pros and cons of an issue.[2] It is conceivable that no postdecision dissonance would be experienced if a person were allowed to postpone public action as long as he wished with no possibility of feeling pressured into a decision prematurely because others know that he has not yet made up his mind and it is bad to be indecisive. I suspect that in reality such absence of social pressure is a rare circumstance. To completely avoid social intrusion into the decision process almost requires that no one know about the alternatives with which we are grappling, and further, that no one know our final decision. This position regarding the amount of postdecision dissonance amounts to a strong endorsement of the social comparison notion. In other words, fear of others' evaluation and lack of perfect faith or belief in our ability to make perfect decisions enhances the amount of dissonance or regret experienced after the decision (see Chapter 26). To the extent that a decision is made slowly

---

[2] This point is distinct from and not contradicted by the fact that dissonance produced by a rushed decision can easily be reduced by convincing oneself that the lack of sufficient time to consider the alternatives carefully provides legitimate cause for being less than an infallable decision-maker. The rushed decision can provide an *avenue* of dissonance reduction or rationalization. The point above, however, is that a slow or drawnout decision may generate less dissonance (or a low intensity of dissonance spread over a longer period).

and in vacuo, postdecisional regret will be minimal. If true, further experimentation is nevertheless needed to ascertain the cause of such an effect. Would regret be minimal because slow decisions generate less dissonance or because the dissonance reduction that occurs during their course is more effective and thorough? The effect may be due to commitment. When there is extensive time between the presentation of the choice alternatives and the point of decision, one may feel more committed to one's decision.

Returning now to the more typical circumstances of real life where postdecisional regret is in fact likely to be experienced, what happens to it as time passes? Clearly, regret typically dissipates after time.[3] The important aspect of this point is that counterpersuasive efforts are likely to have maximal effect immediately after a decision (Walster, 1964). Furthermore, the degree to which the decision is involving (has personal consequences), the extent to which it is made under conditions which foreshorten adequate consideration of alternatives, and lastly, the extent to which the correctness of the decision must be evaluated externally (by social rather than personal norms) will all determine the effectiveness of a counterpersuasive appeal.

However, what accounts for the decrease in effectiveness when the counterpersuasive appeal is positioned later in time? Two things contribute to this decrement. The first consideration is that as time passes, the possibility of reversing one's decision typically becomes more remote. Once you have bought the dress, the store is typically less willing to make a refund as time passes. Having decided not to buy the shirt on sale, you are less likely to find it there when you change your mind and come back to buy it. If you accept the fellowship at Pointless State College, the availability of that quarter-time position at Sterling University as janitor's aide may wash out if you wait too long. As time passes, one feels a loss of control over the environment. The rejected alternative action is no longer a possibility. This suggests that if, some weeks considerably after a decision was made, one reintroduced the alternative as a choice which was once again viable, then regardless of how much dissonance reduction had previously occurred, at least some dissonance would be reinstigated.

There are other decisions which can be made more tentatively and which when made, allow one to entertain the possibility of switching. Some even distinctly imply to a 50-50 chance of switching at some later time, as with the expression of a preference as opposed to an actual choice. For this tentative type of decision only a minimal amount of dissonance reduction should occur after the decision. Likewise, for this type of decision the opposite effect would be expected, i.e., when a counterpersuasive appeal is positioned later in time it should be *more* effective.

The second consideration is adaptation. While there is no doubt that dissonance-reducing processes occur over time, adaptation is probably an-

---

[3] Of course this is not always the case. Sometimes the consequences of a decision continually thrust in our face dissonance-arousing features of our poor choice. If a person chooses a second-hand car that is a real lemon, he may experience intense regret with every engine knock. Likewise, the man who marries a shrew may experience dissonance when she nags that is separate from the pain of complying to the content of the nagging tirade. Other decisions to form partnerships also fall into this category (e.g., business partnerships or collaborations in research or book-writing). These exceptions, where recurring exposures to the chosen object repeatedly reinstigate regret, may represent one of the instances where adaptation substitutes for dissonance reduction.

other basic process which reduces the need for dissonance reduction. Experiments on aesthetic judgments suggest that familiarity with a complex stimulus results in increased favorability of response (Child, 1962; Kessen & Munzinger, 1966; Johnson, Thomson, & Frincke, 1960; Shultz, 1965), at least up to a point. Thus, as a sheer consequence of reaffirming one's beliefs—"this is what I believe," or "this is what I said"—or the constant reemphasis of what one did (which often necessarily occurs as a consequence of an act), one might generate more self-tolerance or self-satisfaction. This is not to say that one can come to love the cognition "I am an idiot." Rather, one can confront it with greater equanimity. Yet, while adaptation may indeed have such effect, it does not seem likely that it represents a very powerful source of increased satisfaction.

EVALUATIVE VS. INFORMATIONAL ELEMENTS

Another consideration is the qualitative character of the elements that are in conflict. Are they laden with informational, factual, and logical components, or do they represent evaluational summaries of this more complex and detailed type of content? In most instances, we use evaluational judgments as a mnemonic shorthand for the complex array of informational, factual, and logical content that may have been presented. It is not an uncommon human experience to hear someone say something like "It's a bad idea! I don't know why, but I know I'm right." Scott (1963) has argued that evaluations—distinctions between preferred and aversive stimuli —are among the earliest discriminations which people make. It is important to consider whether the effects for evaluations that are subject to attack at different points on the time dimension are the same as those for factual conglomerates. The well-known laws of forgetting assert that new information must always have the advantage for a while as far as availability is concerned. In terms of the availability of informational elements, a more recent persuasive attempt will triumph over the initial input on the issue. However, if the initial input is not stored as a collection of informational elements but instead is converted into an evaluation or position on the attitude dimension, then the difference in available information favoring the more recent counterpersuasive appeal is no longer as important. One can dismiss the preponderance of informational elements in favor of the new position and maintain one's old stand saying "It may sound good, but it's a bad idea (even if I don't know why)." The point is, one *once* knew why. Having once known why, having summarized it with an evaluation, and having forgotten the elements which produced the evaluation, those elements are no longer available for refutation and the initial attitude remains unscathed by the counterpersuasive appeal. Thus, to the extent that the initial input on the issue is not translated into an evaluative summary, any counterpersuasive attempt will triumph; old information can only maintain parity with new information if the old information is converted into evaluation. But if it is, it tends to become invulnerable. Thus, for some situations, passage of time leads to greater invulnerability against counterpersuasion.

This analysis may account for the conflict in the recency-primacy literature between the outcome for lists of adjectives and personality evaluations as opposed to other types of prose passages. The more frequent outcome of primacy with adjectives may occur because adjectives are char- acteristically evaluational. Prose passages in contrast are less clearly evalua- tional or they are at least in part informational in that they contain support- ing arguments for the stand that is advocated. With informational material, recency is more clearly predicted, and in fact is most often obtained (Miller & Campbell, 1959; Insko, 1964).[4] Furthermore, the effect of familiarity can be incorporated in this same analysis. As Hovland (1958) suggests, and as some data indicate (Rosnow & Lana, 1965), familiarity with the issue under consideration enhances the likelihood of primacy. What happens if one is familiar with an issue? Typically one forms an evaluation regarding the correct position. Thus, once again evaluation is instrumental in producing primacy.[5] Note that as presented above, evaluation is separate from commit- ment. In most definitions, commitment implies some public behavioral act (Hovland, Campbell, & Brock, 1957; Brehm & Cohen, 1962; Kiesler & Sak- umura, 1966) whereas the evaluative act spoken of above is private. Prior research, of course, confirms that commitment makes an attitude or opinion less vulnerable to subsequent counterattacks, but a separate experimental test would be needed to identify the effect of forming an evaluation.

The distinction between informational and evaluative types of elements is related to the previous discussion of decisions. A decision implies an eval- uative choice among the alternatives. Once made, the information upon which it was based need not be stored. This suggests that the argument above also applies to decisions. In other words, one of the reasons why counterpersuasive efforts are increasingly less likely to be effective as time elapses after a decision is that the informational elements on which the de- cision is based become increasingly unavailable. On the other hand, prior to decision, the pro and con supporting arguments are more salient and readily available and therefore additional persuasive arguments on one side of the issue can more readily tip the scale.[6] One implication of this argument is that delayed postdecisional persuasive attempts will be more effective if they rely on social support, consensus, and other *ad hominem* considerations as opposed to information and rational refutation. This should be increas- ingly true as time elapses. The reasons for voting for Will D. Foliate for Commissioner of Parks, all carefully spelled out in the League of Urban

---

[4] The general direction of discrepancy in this literature can also be accounted for in terms of the length of the two competing sets of materials. With longer passages or sets of materials, recency should become increasingly likely. Prose passages are typically lengthier than lists of adjectives and it is with the former that recency is indeed most often obtained.

[5] This presentation may be oversimplified. In one instance evaluation apparently pro- duced the opposite effect (Walster *et al.*, 1966). When both groups were given a nega- tive second evaluation of a person, subjects who had 'held off' on the initial material were affected less than those who initially gave favorable overevaluations. (These results, however, may be due to subjects' response involvement in the task.)

[6] There are other factors, such as commitment, which should produce the same direc- tion of difference between the effectiveness of persuasive attempts introjected before and after a decision. The point is that the quality of the pre- and postdecisional cognitions that are most readily available may be quite different and the difference may have some important consequences. Of course, as previously indicated, there are some decisions for which this distinction does not hold—decisions which produce negative consequences that repeatedly recur. In those cases, with each aversive confrontation the positive rea- sons that initially impelled the decision are likely to be rehearsed and thus be readily available at points in time quite remote from the time of the original decision.

Defilers handout, are no longer available two months after election day. All that one knows is that "he's a good man and I voted for him." When confronted with counterarguments which are rational and informational it is easy to ignore the arguments because one 'knows' that if the facts mentioned by the League could be recalled, they would readily refute the new arguments. In other words, the persuasive appeal can readily be dismissed. In this situation the increasing unavailability of information with the passage of time becomes advantageous. The evaluative decision—"I voted for him" —must carry the burden. To the extent that the highly fallible supporting arguments for the voting decision are unavailable for refutation, the initial evaluation can more readily remain intact. In contrast, an *ad hominem* argument claiming that Pope Paul is against Will D. Foliate might be increasingly effective as the availability of informational counterarguments diminishes.

THE TEMPORAL ORDERING OF MEASUREMENTS

As argued in the opening page of this paper, time is not by itself a satisfactory psychological variable. Its importance or interest rests upon the things that occur during or are confounded with its passage. In social psychological experiments, multiple modes of response measurement are legion and effects stemming from their placement on the time dimension become important.

Consider a single persuasive appeal counter to the subject's current position. In real life such instances are encountered all the time. Typically, there is a balance or positive correlation between the favorability of our evaluation of the source and our agreement with the content. Sometimes of course it becomes necessary for us to differentiate our evaluation of the source in order to maintain this balance. Thus, the well-educated moderate Republican reading some of Einstein's pronouncements concerning peace might say to himself "True, he was a brilliant physicist but it's too bad he was politically so naive." Thus, by differentiating aspects of Einstein, consistency is maintained between negative evaluations of the source and disagreement with the position he advocates even though he generally generates a positive halo. Nevertheless, in cases where there is no prior evaluative feeling about the source, attention is primarily focused on content, and direction of source evaluation probably flops along in consonance with the respondent's reaction to the content (Chapter 3; Osgood & Tannenbaum, 1955).

In experimental studies of attitude change, however, another problem is involved. Quite often we employ two types of response measures, one assessing the effect of the communication on the respondent's own attitude and another tapping the respondent's evaluation or feeling about the communicator. When the communicator (and his stature) is not clearly specified, the position of these two measures on the time dimension may be important (Miller & Levy, 1967). The reason may be related to social-psychological factors invoked by the laboratory setting and may not in fact operate as strongly in real-life situations. Nevertheless, the issue is important if we are to interpret our experiments correctly. In the laboratory, the subject devotes part of his energies toward ascertaining how the experimenter is reacting to him. Speeches to subjects on how 'we only look at group data, etc.' never seem thoroughly to dissipate this concern.[7]

Consider a simple case where a subject is asked to give his opinion on an issue after the experimenter has exposed him to some persuasive materials that are counter to the subject's initial position. In the typical multiple group design with a single treatment for each subject, the subject has no real feeling for the kinds of variables the experimenter may be studying. This remains true even if the experimenter presents some facade beforehand. What is clear to the subject is that 'a psychologist is interested in my opinion on this issue.' The subject feels he is going to be evaluated. This feeling is typically so strong that subjects distort answers in a socially desirable direction even on anonymous questionnaires. This concern with evaluation leads him to search around for cues as to what position on the issue is really correct. In the absence of other hints, the communicator provides one source of such information. Under another experiment (or condition) the subject might be told that his task is to evaluate the communicator. While here, too, the subject might be concerned with 'how do I appear' or 'what does the experimenter think about me,' the emphasis provided by the task casts the subject more in the role of expert. Requesting an evaluation of the source implicitly suggests that the source may possess questionable characteristics. In other words, the task implicitly imposes a more critical stance. Now consider what happens to his attitude under this second condition. If, as usual, attitude and evaluation remain consistent with one another, then less attitude change is an automatic consequence of the fact that our method 'produced' bias toward critical or negative evaluation. Succinctly, while we like to think that the outcome for different response measures reflects the effect of the experimental treatments, different effects found for different response modes may be attributable to their position among other items, since most experimenters do not balance or randomly order the position of response items within treatments. Particularly if the subject does not know in advance that both types of measures are to be obtained, the temporal sequence of source evaluation and own-attitude measurements may determine the primary mode of dissonance reduction or cognitive adjustment that a subject will employ.

As argued above, in an attitude change experiment, the first response item after the treatment might key the subject's perception of what his role within the experiment 'should have been.' Alternatively, it might suggest to him that the experimenter is particularly interested in that mode of response. If so, greater 'demand' would be felt for this item as opposed

---

[7] The problem has been recently emphasized by the numerous examinations of the laboratory experimental situation as a social situation in its own right. The growing concern with the subtle ways in which the experimenter's interaction with his subjects in the laboratory creates compliance or resistance is reflected in Orne's (1962) discussion of "demand characteristics," McGuigan's (1963) *Psychological Bulletin* article on the experimenter, the recent attention to social desirability and acquiescence response sets (Marlowe & Crowne, 1964; Edwards, 1957; Jackson & Messick, 1958), Rosenthal's (1963) recent empirical work on subject-experiment interaction, Zimbardo's (1960) notion of "response involvement" (in contrast to "issue involvement"), Rosenberg's (1965d) recent discussion of "evaluation apprehension," and others. Clearly, the special effects of 'being in an experiment' have to be considered if we have any concern whatsoever for the external validity of our findings.

to other subsequent items. (This type of bias in subjects' responses is of course more likely to occur for questions or choices that are presented verbally rather than printed.) Besides these possible sources of distortion, there is another consideration with multiple response measures. If the tension states generated by one experimental treatment are akin to other drive states such as fear, cathartic effects should occur. Each opportunity to express or reduce dissonance or tension should result in further depletion of the residual. Therefore, when several types of response measures are consecutively administered, the more items that precede any given item, the weaker will be the effect of the experimental treatment on that item. As an example of the potential difficulty this can produce, consider the usual way in which social psychologists study the retention of persuasive material. The researcher typically concludes the experiment by tacking on a measure of retention and then reports that the lack of differences implies that the effects of the experimental treatment on attitudes were not mediated by differences in retention. While the most obvious criticism of this procedure is to question the sensitivity of the measure of recall, an alternative hypothesis is that motivated forgetting is less likely to appear if attempts to measure it are always positioned last.

These comments on the effects of ordering of response measurements are perhaps somewhat less applicable to researchers in the dissonance tradition in that many of them have shown considerable ingenuity in arranging experimental conditions so that only a single mode of dissonance reduction is available to the subject.

CHAPTER 57

The Effects of Time on Cognitive Consistency

Elaine Walster

University of Wisconsin

and

Ellen Berscheid

University of Minnesota

Time dissipates to shining ether the solid angularity of facts. No anchor, no cable, no fences avail to keep a fact a fact.

—Emerson (1865)

In conducting early dissonance studies, some researchers noticed a peculiar phenomenon. When they first started running subjects in an experiment, their reactions as experimenters were naturally somewhat awkward. In particular, after completing their manipulation of the independent variable and before measuring the dependent variable, there were often a number of unintended and annoying delays. Sometimes, for example, the experimenters had to think a moment before they remembered where they had placed their questionnaires. Sometimes they forgot the subjects' pencils. With additional practice, of course, the experimenters began to give a smooth, polished performance. By now the questionnaires for the dependent measure were at their fingertips, sharpened pencils were at each subject's chair, and the experiments moved without interruption. But, curiously enough, researchers found that with the achievement of a polished performance, with the elimination of the awkward pauses, variability in the data often increased.

These researchers came to the reasonable conclusion that dissonance reduction probably takes time. If one is testing a cognitive theory, concerned with what goes on in people's minds, it is plausible to argue that one must give the subjects time to think. And so, a delay between the manipulation of dissonance and the measurement of the resulting dissonance reduction was incorporated into many dissonance studies. Researchers found that such a delay increased their predictive ability. Since time is not itself an independent variable in any of the consistency theories, this delay is not necessary theoretically. But in practice such a delay is often essential. The passage of a certain amount of time seems necessary

---

The preparation of this paper was facilitated by National Science Foundation Grant GS-1056 to the authors.

before dissonance reduction or consistency increase occurs. Data consistent with this notion are available in McGuire (1960a, 1960b).

Time is an important variable only because it allows other variables to operate. In this chapter, consequently, we will be discussing the effect of *events* in time, rather than the effect of time in and of itself, on efforts to achieve and maintain consistency in decision-making situations.

Three aspects of a decision will be crucial to our discussion. The first important aspect of a decision is that it has practical consequences. The decision-maker has a good chance of maximizing his rewards and minimizing his frustrations if he makes a wise choice. The goodness of the potential outcomes of the choice alternatives are always considered in dissonance analyses of decision-making, and, usually, this aspect of the decision is thought to be of prime importance.

There is, however, a second reason why individuals attempt to make wise decisions. People ordinarily want to be considered good decision-makers by themselves and others. When people inquire about our choices, it is embarrassing to confess that we have acquired a house with roaches and silverfish, a bald wife with no teeth, or clothes that disintegrate in the rain. A bad decision says some very negative things about us. There is evidence, in fact, that if one expects to hear that he made a bad decision regardless of what he chooses, he will avoid making a decision altogether (Braden & Walster, 1964).

Finally, a decision is an important point in time for the decision-maker for one more reason. A decision acts to shut the door on one's possibilities. By making a commitment, the decision-maker may move from a state in which all things are possible to a state in which only one thing is possible and other things are impossible. Although the degree to which a decision limits one's opportunities will vary with the strength and type of commitment, it usually—at the very least—makes courses of action other than the one chosen more difficult to follow. Freedom of choice, especially among pleasant alternatives, can be an enjoyable state of affairs, but it ends abruptly when a decision to restrict oneself occurs.

In this chapter we will discuss events which are likely to occur and to affect efforts to achieve consistency within three gross time intervals after the decision: events immediately following a decision, intermediate events, and events which are likely to occur long after a decision has been made.

I. IMMEDIATE POSTDECISION EFFECTS:
REGRET AND SUBSEQUENT DISSONANCE REDUCTION

Dissonance researchers reasoned that in order to reduce postdecision dissonance one must, immediately after a decision, be mainly preoccupied with attending to any existing dissonance. Hence, they hypothesized that as soon as a decision is made all of the negative aspects of the chosen alternative and all of the positive aspects of the rejected alternative become salient for the person. They felt such concentration on dissonance would produce, phenomenally, a feeling of regret in the decision-maker.

Walster (1964) performed an experiment to test this hypothesis. After the subjects in this experiment had made a decision, the attractiveness of the chosen and rejected alternatives were measured at varying intervals of time following the decision. Walster hypothesized that if the regret phenomenon occurs one should find that, in a period soon after the decision, the chosen alternative becomes less attractive and the rejected alternative more attractive than they were before the decision. She further hypothesized that after this, of course, one would obtain the usual evidence of dissonance reduction.

Walster attempted to find a decision situation in which the regret phase of the postdecision process would be likely to be relatively long-lasting. She felt that such a situation would be one in which the subjects were offered a decision between alternatives which had both positive and negative aspects, one which was reasonably important to the subjects, and one in which the decision would have lasting consequences. The situation used met these requirements. Her subjects were men who had just been drafted into the army. Each man was given a choice of which of two occupational specialties he wanted to be assigned to for his two years in the service. In order to make dissonance reduction in this situation rather difficult, the descriptions of the occupational specialties were written so as to emphasize both positive and negative aspects of each alternative. All subjects rated the attractiveness of the jobs predecisionally. One-fourth of the subjects rerated the jobs immediately after they had made their decisions. The other subjects rerated the jobs after an interval of 4 minutes, after an interval of 15 minutes, or after an interval of 90 minutes. Subjects in conditions in which they did not immediately rerate the jobs were sent into a room to wait by themselves and were provided with nothing to help them occupy the time.

In this section we will be concerned only with the results of the first three conditions. The data showed that the subjects who rerated the jobs immediately after making the decision evidenced relatively small and insignificant change in the direction of dissonance reduction. However, those subjects who rerated the jobs after a 4-minute delay showed the opposite of dissonance reduction. In this condition, the chosen alternative decreased somewhat in attractiveness and the rejected alternative increased in attractiveness. There is evidence, then, for the existence of a regret phenomenon in the 4-minute condition. Fifteen minutes after the decision there was no evidence of regret but clear evidence of dissonance reduction. At this time, the chosen alternative was rated as more attractive than it was initially and the rejected alternative was rated as less attractive than it was initially.

The regret finding in the 4-minute condition was supported by the results of another experiment in which it was demonstrated that there is a tendency for people to reverse their decisions immediately after making them (Festinger & Walster, 1964). These studies and a few incidental findings from other studies not designed to directly test the regret hypothesis (Brehm, Cohen, & Sears, 1960; Brehm & Cohen, 1962) suggest that a feeling of regret is indeed often experienced immediately after a decision is made.

Why should regret occur? Let us review the line of deduction which gave rise to the regret hypothesis. The argument went that immediately after a decision is made, the person must necessarily focus his attention on any existing dissonance before he can reduce it: "After all, how else can we expect dissonance to be reduced other than by focusing on, and trying to do something about, the dissonant relations?" (Festinger, 1964b, p. 128). It was further reasoned that one consequence of focusing on the dissonance would be that the dissonant elements would loom larger and seem more important than the consonant elements and, hence, a feeling of regret would result.

This argument is perhaps deceptively simple. Specifically, according to this rationale, what is it that motivates an individual to focus upon the dissonant relationships? He focuses on these relationships because he wants to reduce dissonance. Thus, before he focuses on the relationships, he must already be feeling some dissonance or psychological discomfort. This line of reasoning appears to have the underlying assumption that at the time of making his choice, the individual is only partially aware of the dissonant relations involved in choosing a particular alternative. Thus, after the choice, he is only vaguely aware that something is awry, and, it is this free-floating dissonance which motivates him to seek the source. It is the painful discovery of the cause of discomfort, according to the formulation, that produces regret.

If this explication adequately represents the unstated reasoning of the regret researchers, then we would be led to hypothesize that the situations in which we are most likely to find regret are those in which a person makes a decision which inherently has a great deal of dissonance tied to it, but the person has not had time, predecisionally, to become fully aware of the dissonant relationships. Supporting this line of thinking are the results of several experiments (Davidson & Kiesler, 1964; Jecker, 1964a; Davidson, 1964) which suggest that with a long period of predecisional deliberation of the alternatives, dissonance reduction proceeds rather rapidly after the decision. Whether or not the regret period is bypassed altogether is another question, but one might perhaps speculate that it is.

Though the lack-of-awareness proposition may possibly explain some regret phenomena, it does not seem to be an altogether compelling explanation for the one concrete demonstration of regret we have. Specifically, in the Walster experiment subjects had been given detailed descriptions of both the positive and negative aspects of each alternative. Thus, it seems unlikely that the subjects were not well aware of the negative aspects of the alternatives predecisionally. In addition, the positive and negative aspects were not so numerous as to cause difficulty keeping them clearly in mind and the decision was important enough that we can suspect that subjects studied the alternatives carefully before making a decision. Are there, then, perhaps other explanations of the regret phenomenon?

Some recent work by Brehm suggests another possible determinant of regret. That a state in which one has freedom of behavior is valued by the individual is the basis upon which Brehm (1966) has constructed a theory of psychological "reactance." Brehm deals variously with situations in which a person's alternatives are restricted in a completely fortuitous and impersonal manner, in an apparently intended and personal manner, restricted by a source over which one has little or no power, or by a source over which one has great power. Brehm cites evidence to support his hypothesis that howsoever a person's alternatives are restricted, when an element of choice is eliminated, the person experiences reactance. Reactance is posited to be a state of motivational arousal with a directional quality. Specifically, it is directed toward the reestablishment of whatever freedom is lost, or threatened with loss, and against any further losses of freedom. According to Brehm, reactance manifests itself in part through an increase in the perceived attractiveness of the restricted alternative. This increase is hypothesized and shown to be a direct effect of the alternative's having moved from a position of 'possible' to 'impossible.'

Though Brehm deals with restriction of alternatives in predecisional situations and with restriction through an outside agency, we can see common elements between these reactance situations and the regret situation in which one restricts one's alternatives oneself by making a decision. Perhaps, then, the phenomenon of regret is simply an instance of a phenomenon of wider generality. If this is true, it should be the increase in the attractiveness of the rejected alternative, rather than a decrease in the chosen, which contributes the lion's share to the regret phenomenon. Is there any evidence for this? When we look at the data from the Walster study we find that the amount of increase in the attractiveness of the rejected alternative is, indeed, approximately $2\frac{1}{2}$ times the amount of the decrease in attractiveness of the chosen alternative. Though this is barely suggestive, one might speculate that we would be most likely to find regret in those situations in which one eliminates through choice many alternatives even though the amount of dissonance in the situations was held relatively constant. Situations in which the actual decision especially restricts one's own freedom of behavior, rather than another person's, might also be particularly likely to produce regret.

There is perhaps one additional reason why restricting one's alternatives by making a decision should lead to regret. Very rarely does one's array of choices include the ideal, or perfect, alternative which would most fully maximize one's rewards following the decision. When a professor is trying to decide between a job offer at Podunk, which has good facilities but low salaries, and a job at Nothing U., which promises a high salary but is notorious for its poor facilities, it almost always occurs to him that the whole problem would be solved if only Harvard would offer him a job (Walster, 1964). Once the professor commits himself to the offer from Podunk U. he must finally relinquish hope of receiving that last-minute bid from Harvard. As long as he stays in the predecision state, going to Harvard remains a possibility, remote though it may be. When he makes his commitment, however, the door shuts on Harvard and he must begin to resign himself to life in Podunk. The rejection of ideal alternatives, as well as available alternatives, may contribute to the feeling of regret immediately after the decision.

II. INTERMEDIATE TIME EFFECTS:

GATHERING INFORMATION FROM THE ENVIRONMENT

In the laboratory, a subject's ability to reduce dissonance is limited by his own creative ability. The subject usually has to think of all the dissonance-reducing cognitions himself. In a natural setting, however, and with the passage of a moderate period of time, people are not usually limited to their own resources. For example, much of the dissonance a person experiences may be either reduced or increased by information provided by friends and acquaintances. What these acquaintances think, and whether the information and opinions they provide increase or decrease the dissonance a subject is experiencing, would seem to depend in part on how the dissonance was produced.

When one is irrevocably committed to an important choice, and asks his friends what they think about the choice, we would guess that one's friends would usually be benevolent. There is no point in telling a fellow who has just married the ugliest girl in town that he has made a poor decision, and there is evidence that such gadfly behavior would not be rewarded by the fellow who is experiencing dissonance (Aronson & Ross, 1966).

In addition, important decisions, and thus decisions which by their very nature produce a great deal of dissonance, often bring one into physical contact with people who will aid in reducing dissonance. If one chooses to go to Yale instead of Harvard, he goes to a place where others have made the same decision. Yale students can be expected to have more positive attitudes toward Yale than students who have chosen to attend Harvard. Although fate can always play nasty tricks, and one is never assured that the environment will reduce all the dissonance one experiences from making an important choice, dissonance reduction in such situations is probably the most likely alternative.

There are, however, many dissonance-producing situations in which the people in one's environment could be expected to be malevolent rather than benevolent, insofar as reducing one's dissonance is concerned. For example, one can experience dissonance because he has chosen a course of action that is unacceptable to other people in the immediate environment. The nun who decides the atheistic position has a great deal of merit and the Ford salesman who buys a Pontiac are not likely to receive a great deal of support for their decisions from the people in their environments. In fact, since their deviant stands produce dissonance for their peers, these peers are likely to be anxious to challenge their stands actively (e.g., Schachter, 1951). The prevalence of such a tendency for peers to argue against one's deviant choice is one reason that has been suggested for a possible lack of a relationship between attitude change and subsequent related behavior (Festinger, 1964a).

In any natural setting, then, the opinions of one's peers will be a crucial determinant of whether or not one can reduce dissonance. When individuals ask whether or not dissonance reduction processes maintain themselves over time, they often forget the crucial importance that new information provided by both fate and others will have on efforts to achieve and maintain consistency.

III. LONG-TERM EFFECTS: LOSS OF MEMORY AND CHANGES IN MOTIVATION

It is a common observation that the passage of time has a marked effect on memory. Psychologists have often suggested not only that facts are forgotten in time, but that they are selectively forgotten. Researchers from diverse areas of psychology have proposed and tested the notion that people tend to forget information that does not support their wishes, beliefs, or attitudes. For example, Berelson and Steiner (1965) in their summary of scientific findings conclude, "Representations of the past, as of the present, but even more so, tend to become more simple, more internally consistent, and more 'stable figures' than they are in actuality; they also tend to conform to retroactive expectations and, to some extent, to the wishes of the subject."

Working in a learning-theory framework, Levine and Murphy (1943) tested the hypothesis that a person would be better able to learn and retain material that was congruent with his attitudes than to learn and retain material that was incongruent with his attitudes.

The authors found that consistent material is learned faster and forgotten more slowly than material from the inconsistent passages. Further, they suggest that these retention differences become more marked, though not significantly so, over time. Additional experimental support for the proposal that people remember consistent statements better than inconsistent ones is provided by Edwards (1941), Watson and Hartman (1939), Weiss (1953), and Taft (1954).

In a charming study, Jones and Kohler (1958) suggested an amendment to the simple Levine and Murphy formulation. They agreed that people were biased in their learning of controversial statements. However, they proposed that what kind of argument a person would find especially satisfying to remember would depend on the plausibility of the argument as well as on whether or not the argument supported one's own position. They pointed out that a ludicrously poor argument by one's opposition is something one wants to remember, and that an implausible argument by well-intentioned but unintelligent supporters of one's own position is something one would probably rather forget. It is very comforting to believe that all the wise men are on your side and all the fools are with the opposition. Jones and Kohler demonstrated that one finds it easier to learn plausible arguments supporting his own position than opposing his position, and easier to learn implausible arguments opposing one's own position than supporting one's position.

Waly and Cook (1966) reported three failures to replicate the Jones and Kohler findings and found support for the Levine and Murphy findings in only one of their three replications. If we were to accept the Levine-Murphy results we might be led to conclude that cognitive consistency would tend to *increase* with time. A good argument could be made for this point of view. If a person is motivated to alter the past, it is undoubtedly easier to distort reality systematically when one's memories are distant and vague than when they still possess the 'solid angularity of facts.'

Dissonance researchers have recently conducted some studies which give us a little more evidence concerning the effect that the passage of time has on cognitions that one has previously altered in order to reduce dissonance. In experiments of this type, the investigators have not assumed that consistency would increase in time, but have simply assumed that dissonance-produced effects would be strong enough to endure for a reasonably long period of time. Freedman (1965b), for example, appears to believe that although dissonance-reduction effects are doomed to dissipate to some extent with the passage of time, some residual and measurable effects will even exist after a fair amount of time has elapsed. Two studies are directly relevant to our question as to whether distortions which enhance consistency increase, maintain themselves, or dissipate in time.

According to some dissonance theorists, any time a person abstains from performing a very desirable action he will experience dissonance. The knowledge that he is not performing an act is dissonant with the combined cognitions that it is desirable to perform the act and that he does what is desirable. If the person has some good reason why he abstained from performing the desirable action, he will have little dissonance. For example, the person who is forced to abstain from a pleasurable act, or whose strong moral principles prevented him from performing the act, has a good reason why he did not perform the desirable act, and should experience little dissonance. If, on the other hand, a person has few reasons and little justification for abstaining from a desirable act, and yet he does abstain, he should have a great deal of dissonance and should be strongly motivated to find additional reasons why he did not perform the act. He should try to reduce dissonance, perhaps by convincing himself that there were good reasons for abstaining from it, or perhaps by convincing himself that he did not want to perform the act.

Aronson and Carlsmith (1963) tested the preceding hypothesis with nursery school children. Children were brought into the experimental room, shown some toys, and asked to rank-order them. Then, the experimenter said he was leaving the room and forbade them to play with one of the highly ranked toys while he was gone. In the Severe Threat condition, the children were offered a great deal of justification for not playing with the toy. In the Low Threat condition, children were offered very little justification. Then the experimenter left, leaving the child with the temptation to touch the forbidden toy, and hopefully, to resist the temptation. Finally he returned and asked the children to rank-order the toys. Aronson and Carlsmith measured just one mode of dissonance reduction—the extent to which children derogated the toy they had been tempted to, but refrained from, playing with. The investigators expected Severe Threat children to derogate the forbidden toy less than Mild Threat children, and this hypothesis was supported.

In one portion of the experiment, Aronson and Carlsmith ran each child in either a Mild or Severe Threat condition and obtained a measure of dissonance reduction 45 days later. When we look only at the data from this portion of the experiment, it is possible to compare the dissonance reduction immediately after dissonance was engendered with that still existing 45 days later. Though the number of subjects is now so small that statistical comparisons are impossible, it appears that there is little change in the amount of dissonance reduction children exhibit 45 days after the initial experimental session from that they demonstrated initially. In short, the induced effect appears to persist over time.

A delayed measure of dissonance reduction was also secured by Freedman (1965b) in a tightly controlled replication and extension of Aronson and Carlsmith's study. The Freedman procedure differed from the Aronson procedure in that in addition to Mild Threat and Severe Threat experimental groups, Freedman also added Mild and Severe Threat control groups to this experiment. (In these control conditions, the experimenter did not leave the room; instead he sat down at a nearby desk and did paper work in the experimental room for 10 minutes. Since the experimenter was observing them at all times, children in these conditions were not tempted to play with the toy, and therefore should not have experienced dissonance because they had never made a choice to avoid the desirable toy.) Freedman measured changes in children's ratings of the toys from before to after dissonance was generated. Most important to us, however, is the fact that Freedman also secured a behavioral measure of subject's actual tendency to play with the toys from 23 to 64 days after the original dissonance induction. In these follow-up experimental sessions a woman tester suggested that the children play with some toys while she scored the tests. Among these toys was the previously forbidden toy. Whether or not the child touched the previously forbidden toy was the behavioral measure of dissonance reduction.

Freedman's hypothesis received some support. When we consider children's *ratings* of the avoided toy (which were taken immediately after dissonance was induced), we see that they did not vary significantly among conditions although the changes tended to be in the predicted direction. The delayed behavioral measures of dissonance reduction were significant, however. Children in the Mild Threat experimental condition avoided playing with the forbidden toy more than did children in any other group. Only one-third of the Mild Threat experimental condition children touched the toy. In all other conditions, two-thirds of the children played with the toy.

Unfortunately for our purpose, the rating of the attractiveness of the forbidden toy which was taken immediately after the induction of dissonance and the behavorial measure of attractiveness taken after a 23–64-day delay are not in comparable units. Because of the difference in the dependent variables, it is impossible to tell if the derogation of the toy produced in an attempt to reduce dissonance increased in strength, decreased in strength, or remained the same with the passage in time. All we know is that there is behavioral evidence of dissonance-produced derogation 23–64 days later, even though the immediate measures of dissonance reduction were not significant.

It is clear that the available data provide no definite answer to our question as to whether the consistency of cognitive elements increases, maintains itself, or decreases over time. We can, however, offer some speculations that seem plausible. The passage of time would seem to have two general, and opposite, effects on the maintenance of cognitive consistency. First, as much previous research has demonstrated, time makes specific memory much vaguer. If a person maintains a continuing desire to reduce dissonance, the passage of time and the blurring of memory should make it easier to do so. However, in most of the circumstances in which dissonance is aroused, the desire to reduce dissonance probably does *not* remain at a constant high level over a long time period. For the second effect that time often has is to make decisional outcomes that were important at an earlier time less important and less salient. When you are a very old man, it is probably not too important that you once chose to sign up for a Chemistry 3 afternoon section instead of a morning section, even though the choice between a morning and an afternoon section might have seemed to be a vitally important one at the time you made it. Other events and other choices crowd in on us as time passes. Consequences which were once important are adapted to or altered. After the passage of much time current decisions undoubtedly become more important than previous ones.

We mentioned earlier one possible reason usually not specified in dissonance formulations why it is important for a person to make a good decision. We suggested that one undoubtedly wants to make a good decision because the goodness of a decision provides information to ourselves and others about our capabilities. If this is so, a second reason why past decision and dissonance-producing situations probably lose importance as time passes is because they no longer provide very much information about us. No longer is the information crucial information about how one *is*, but rather it is merely information about how one *was*. It is much easier to admit that you were once a fool than to admit that you currently are one.

Thus, we would speculate that in most real-life dissonance-producing situations, dissonance reduction would markedly decrease in time. It is only in those situations where the elements which produced dissonance initially continue to be important and relatively salient that we would expect dissonance reduction to maintain itself or even increase in time. Consider, for example, two brothers who each buy a used car on the same day, but on very different terms. The first brother pays cash for his car; the second brother, though he has the cash, decides to purchase his car on a long-term payment plan. If at the end of one year we ask the brothers how they feel about their cars, we would expect the all-cash brother to have had a great deal of dissonance about the car at the time he bought the car, but since he has not had a monthly reminder of his decision, the decision should now be forgotten to some extent. He should exhibit less dissonance-reduction than the long-easy-payment brother, who should still be very concerned about his choice. Though his initial dissonance may have been equal to his cash-paying brother's, his motivation to continue reducing dissonance would seem to be greater, since each time he makes a car payment he is forced to think about his choice and to justify his decision to himself.

Ordinarily, then, we would guess that with the passage of time one cares less and less about the issue and forgets more and more the controversy as well as his techniques for reducing dissonance. With the passage of a great deal of time it is likely that the outcomes of previous decisions are now taken into account only as items of information which must be rated objectively in order that new decisions can be made as wisely as possible.

CHAPTER 58

Comment: Time—Past, Present, and Future

Elliot Aronson

The four essays in this section form an interesting fabric—the conceptual and empirical strands cross many areas highlighted primarily by an encouraging degree of agreement and a movement toward similarity among approaches, theories, speculations, and data. In the present discussion I will focus primarily on some of the divergences (real or apparent), not because I feel that the differences are more important than the similarities, but, rather, because I believe that it is more interesting and more profitable to examine differences than merely to describe similarities.

PAST: PREDECISION DISSONANCE?

In distinguishing between conflict and dissonance, Festinger (1964b) stated that people refrain from distorting their evaluations of the alternatives until after they have made a decision. That is, in order to make the best possible decision, the individual must carefully and rationally weigh the alternatives. Any premature distortion of information *before* the decision is made would thwart the goal of making a good decision—a goal which, as Walster and Berscheid note in their essay, is important for two reasons: (a) to ensure the best outcome, and (b) to show ourselves and others that we are good decision-makers. In his contribution to this section, Miller takes issue with this position and suggests situations in which dissonance might be reduced *before* the decision is made.

Miller's speculations would appear to be totally at odds with the approach outlined by dissonance theorists—most specifically, by Jecker in his chapter. Jecker, in reviewing his own elegant experiments, makes it clear that conflict and dissonance are two different processes and that dissonance-reducing behavior (increasing the attractiveness of the chosen alternative, decreasing the attractiveness of the unchosen alternative) does not occur until after the decision has been made. But let us examine this more closely. According to Miller, what are the conditions in which predecisional dissonance-reducing behavior might take place? Miller lists one situational variable: the stoppage of information. He suggests that predecisional distortion might occur when all of the relevant information already had been accumulated—i.e., if the subject had no hope of obtaining additional information, cognitive distortion could no longer interfere with a rational decision and, consequently, the subject could then allow himself the luxury of beginning to reduce dissonance before the decision.

This is an interesting suggestion—but it hinges on the definition of 'decision'; what do we mean when we say 'decision'? In the situation outlined by Miller where all of the information is in, there is nothing to prevent the individual from making a decision to himself—even before an overt decision is called for. To illustrate, suppose I am about to purchase a house and I am vacillating between buying a home in the city and one in the suburbs. If I have collected and examined all of the information about the two alternatives, chances are I will be able to arrive at a decision before I actually sign the papers at the realtor's office. If I know there is no additional information forthcoming, then for all intents and purposes, I have made my decision. Once I decide (to myself) that I will live in the suburbs, I can then begin convincing myself that I love to drive long distances to work every day and that city smog is poisonously harmful—even though the decision is not absolutely final.

What I have suggested above is the kind of phenomenon that Jecker refers to as a "tentative stand" and is similar to the third stage of Janis' more elaborate model. Although I suspect that all of the present contributors might agree that such tentative decisions would never result in as great a degree of cognitive distortion as would follow from an irrevocable commitment, I believe that some distortion would follow a tentative decision in a circumstance like the one Miller describes—i.e., one in which the subject knows that he has all of the available information. I think it is misleading to call what goes on here *pre*decisional behavior.

One might carry this one step further and ask how we could prevent this dissonance-reducing behavior (cognitive distortion of the desirability of the alternatives) in Miller's situation—i.e., where all of the information is already in. The answer is implicit in Jecker's article. Jecker reports data showing that if there is any chance that the individual will actually receive both alternatives, he does not engage in cognitive distortion—even following a full-blown, irrevocable decision. Thus, I might decide to buy the suburban house, but I am not about to convince myself that city smog is poisonously harmful if there is a good chance that my aunt is about to give me her house in the city, thus opening the possibility of my living in both places during alternate months. A portion of Jecker's data (Uncertainty condition) suggests strongly that even when all of the information is in, there will be no cognitive distortion either following a tentative decision or a full-blown decision. This is consistent with Harold Gerard's discussion of commitment (Chapter 38) which he describes as giving something up. According to Gerard, if an individual has reason to believe that, in spite of his decision, he is not really relinquishing anything, he will experience no dissonance. I am sure that Jecker would agree.

PRESENT: IS THE TEMPORAL SEQUENCE OF COGNITIVE BEHAVIOR UNIDIRECTIONAL?

The model presented by Irving Janis is both detailed and intuitively sensible. In five stages, Janis carries the individual from the first challenge directed toward his existing attitude or behavior to his dogged adherence to his changed attitude in the face of deprivation and counterchallenge. Implicit in this model is the assumption of postdecisional unidirectionality of cognitive activity. Once an individual decides on a course of action to meet the challenge—and especially after he commits himself to follow it—all cognitive work seems focused on consolidating and making the best of the decision. This is not to say that there is no backsliding; there is. But such backsliding, according to Janis, is a function of an incomplete 'working through' during the early stages. The *cognitive* activity (especially that involved in successful cases) is unidirectional. Indeed, Janis cites studies which suggest that those who are most impressed by the negative aspects of their prior attitude (the unchosen alternative) show the least tendency toward subsequent backsliding.

The unidirectionality of cognitive activity suggested by Janis' model stands in sharp contrast to the phenomenon of 'regret' discussed by Walster and Berscheid. In their essay they maintain that in order to reduce dissonance, the individual must first attend to it. Thus, soon after making an irrevocable decision, the individual takes a close veridical look at the alternatives and says, in effect, "Oh my God, what have I done!" The act of attending to dissonant elements in order to reduce them carries with it a bit of the flavor of the story about the person who bangs his head against the wall because it feels so good when he stops. Yet the activity need not be as calculated as that. It does seem reasonable to assume (using my earlier example) that before an individual can begin to convince himself that driving long distances can be fun, he must first realize that he is obliged to drive long distances. This and countless other dissonant realizations are what lie behind the regret phenomenon. If one plugs into the postdecisional process at the right point in time, one should be able to observe evidence of regret. And this is exactly what Walster (1964) succeeded in doing. Four minutes after an important and irrevocable decision the regret phenomenon occurred: there was an *increase* in the attractiveness of the unchosen alternative and a *decrease* in the attractiveness of the chosen alternative. Fifteen minutes after the decision, typical dissonance-reducing behavior was in effect.

It might be worthwhile for Janis to attempt to incorporate Walster's findings into his model. Again, while Janis allows that the temptation to backslide (regret?) does occur, he links it with insufficient preparation and equates this with relative failure to resist a countercommunication. But according to dissonance theory, regret is only a temporary phenomenon; moreover, there is no reason to suspect that a high degree of regret experienced immediately after the decision will lead to a less permanent decision (i.e., to actual behavioral backsliding). Indeed, according to the analysis presented by Walster and Berscheid, one might expect just the reverse—the more one attends to the dissonance, the more one will be able to reduce it; and the more effectively one can reduce dissonance, the more permanent the decision.

THE FUTURE: HOW LONG DOES IT LAST?

Both the article by Janis and the one by Walster and Berscheid reflect an interest in the future effectiveness of the process. Janis is principally concerned with resistance to future negative consequences while Walster and Berscheid are interested in long-term attitude change. Janis' data on surgical patients are impressive because of the importance and realness of the decision involved. He reports the results of a correlational study and a field experiment which indicate that the more preoperative information the patient received (concerning unpleasant consequences of the operation), the more tolerant of pain and frustration he was and the smaller was the postoperative recovery period required.

Walster and Berscheid explore evidence on long-lasting postexperimental effects of dissonance reduction. This is a particularly interesting question and one that is somewhat embarrassing for experimental social psychologists who have had to face up to the undeniable fact that most changes brought about in the laboratory barely last until the end of the experiment. For example, if the subject has been told that a high-prestige figure like J. Robert Oppenheimer believes in the feasibility of atomic submarines, he does come to believe that it is true. But four weeks later, most people tend to revert to their previous attitude. How might attitude change be made more permanent? According to the dissonance theory analysis presented by Aronson and Carlsmith (1963), actions performed in the face of insufficient justification should lead to relatively permanent attitude change precisely because the behaviors in question were not performed for an easily identifiable extrinsic reason. In short, the individual comes to believe that X is good because he convinced himself that it is good, not because someone told him that it was good and not because he was rewarded for pretending that he believed it was good. Such belief changes should be difficult to alter because they are not tied to a particular prestige figure or to a specifiable reward. Walster and Berscheid review the experiments on mild vs. severe threats of punishment which, considering the triviality of the issue used in the experiments and its lack of salience in the 'real world,' indicate a degree of permanence that is truly remarkable. This may be merely the beginning. In other words, although dissonance theory has implications for the permanence of attitude change, these implications have just begun to be tested in a systematic fashion. One can only hope for the continuation of this line of research.

B. INDIVIDUAL DIFFERENCES IN REACTIONS TO INCONSISTENCY

This section and the next one, "Modes of Resolution," are addressed to somewhat different aspects of what is essentially the same problem area. There are a number of ways in which people can attempt to cope with cognitive inconsistency, and some consistency theorists have begun to try to separate these ways conceptually from one another, assigning appropriate causal influences to each. Presumably, some of the variance in reactions to inconsistency is attributable to personality factors, some to situational influences, and some to the confluence of personality and situation. In this section are assembled the contributions dealing mainly with personality variables, with consideration of situational variables deferred until the next section. The astute reader will note, however, that this categorical separation does not hold with perfect consistency for all the papers to come, since many of our intrepid contributors do not stay within narrow bounds in this large area. Having thus noted the embarrassing possibility of inconsistent editing in a volume seemingly devoted to the cause of stamping out inconsistency, we may with some trepidation proceed to the substance of the matter.

David Glass considers a number of methodological problems in the study of individual differences in reactions to inconsistency. Reaching into this bag of eels, he finds the contents elusive. Nevertheless he is willing to propose that one of the many extant dichotomies in personality theory is especially relevant to the manner in which individuals cope with bothersome inconsistency. Gerald Miller and Milton Rokeach review a number of studies relating dogmatism and other personality variables to dissonance-reducing or dissonance-avoiding responses, concluding on a note of highly qualified optimism that useful personality distinctions can be made if care is taken in interpreting experimental results.

James Bieri concentrates on 'cognitive complexity,' a stylistic variable which at one pole encompasses individuals cognitively so well-prepared for inconsistency that they might almost be said to welcome it. His approach thus raises a number of issues at seeming variance with the previous two papers. Finally, Ivan Steiner details the difficulties in finding one-one correspondences between general personality styles and specific choices of modes of resolution of inconsistency. Different supposed inconsistencies, he argues, may prove bothersome to different individuals. Further, a given individual may employ several different modes of resolution simultaneously, although the fragmentary literature on this point seems in general to suggest that usages of different modes are negatively correlated, as one would expect if stylistic differences were operative.

CHAPTER 59

Individual Differences and the Resolution of Cognitive Inconsistencies

David C. Glass

Russell Sage Foundation and The Rockefeller University

The purpose of this chapter is to examine the role of individual differences in the arousal and reduction of cognitive inconsistencies. It has been suggested that the predictive accuracy of theories of consistency may be improved by taking into account personality variables that are widely considered to be important determinants of cognition and social behavior (Brehm & Cohen, 1962). Since individual differences may affect different aspects of the inconsistency process, I shall begin with an overview of the kinds of influence that may be exerted by personality variables. In a second part of the paper, I shall discuss some methodological problems involved in relating personality to cognitive inconsistency. The third and final part of the paper will consider the effects of personality variables on the inconsistency process; specifically, the relationship between a person's characteristic style of ego-defense and his preference for modes of reducing one kind of inconsistency—cognitive dissonance. Attention will also be given in this section to some of the situational variables that seem to determine responses to dissonance.

INDIVIDUAL DIFFERENCES AND THE PROCESS OF COGNITIVE INCONSISTENCY

It has been observed repeatedly that people differ in their reactions to inconsistency-arousing situations (Festinger, 1957; Zajonc, 1960; Rosenberg, Hovland et al., 1960; Brehm & Cohen, 1962; Feather, 1964a). Such differences may occur because people perceive the inconsistent situation differently, and it is likely that differential perception is, in part, a function of the individual's personality structure (Harvey, 1965; Neuringer, 1965). Individual differences might also be due to a differential threshold or tolerance limit for inconsistency, and the height of this threshold is undoubtedly affected by a variety of personality factors (Aronson & Festinger, 1958; Bishop, 1965). Aronson and Festinger were among the first to try to construct instruments that would measure tolerance for dissonance, including a

This paper was prepared in conjunction with work supported by Research Grant GS-1354 from the National Science Foundation and by a grant from the Russell Sage Foundation.

personality inventory based on items from tests such as the Minnesota Multiphasic Personality Inventory, the California Personality Inventory, and the California F Scale. Their results were not sufficiently promising, however, to have been followed up in later research.

Hovland and Rosenberg (1960, pp. 215–221) and later Rosenberg (1965b) have also suggested several classes of variables (including personality predispositions), which may influence the intolerance-for-inconsistency threshold. There is some support for their suggestions in studies of social influence, which indicate that a personality pattern characterized by chronic low self-esteem and general passivity disposes the individual to resolve inconsistencies by changing his attitude in the direction advocated by the contrary communication (Hovland & Janis, 1959). Other studies report that high need for affiliation, authoritarianism, and measures of perceptual field dependence correlate positively with general persuasibility (Burdick & Burnes, 1958; Hovland & Janis, 1959). The results of these studies have been interpreted as providing evidence of variability in tolerance for inconsistency as a function of personality variables.

Additional factors responsible for differential reactions to inconsistency are the person's facility in restoring consistency, and his preference for one means of consistency restoration over another. It seems reasonable to assume that characteristic personality patterns are also associated with these factors, and indeed the empirical evidence would seem to support this assumption (cf. Steiner, 1966). I will examine some of this evidence, along with more recent theoretical ideas on the problem, in a later section of this paper. But first let us consider some of the key methodological issues involved in research on personality and cognitive inconsistency.

METHODOLOGICAL ISSUES IN RELATING PERSONALITY TO COGNITIVE CONSISTENCY

The preceding overview suggests that there may be more than one source of difference between people's reactions to inconsistency (see also Adams, Chapter 64). Regardless of the source one decides to emphasize in trying to understand the differences, a major task would be to specify precisely what personality factors influence the inconsistency process. This is often difficult to do, for personality 'explanations' tend to be ad hoc and not theoretically coordinate with the specific inconsistency being manipulated in a particular experiment (Brehm & Cohen, 1962). There is no reason why a randomly chosen personality variable should have implications for reactivity to inconsistent situations. It is absolutely essential, therefore, that an attempt be made to isolate the personality constructs which seem coordinate with the particular cognitions involved in the inconsistency. To select an arbitrary variable from a pool of general personality traits is at best a dubious procedure.

However, an investigator is still confronted with difficulty even where he can isolate relevant personality variables. I refer here to the familiar criticism that the criterion variable, inconsistency, is not directly measurable (Brehm & Cohen, 1962). Thus, the usual procedure is to create a situation containing inconsistent cognitions, and then to infer the existence of inconsistency-produced tension from attempts to restore consistency. Consider, for example, the well-known dissonance experiment by Festinger and

Carlsmith (1959). In this study a subject was induced to accept money for saying something he believed to be untrue. According to theory he should have experienced dissonance. This was determined not by measuring dissonance directly, but by measuring attempts to reduce dissonance. Suppose an experimenter wishes to show that the cognitive style, field dependence, influences the magnitude of dissonance arousal. His first step is to measure the field dependence-independence of a group of subjects. Next, he places each of them in the dissonance situation just described and measures their attempts to reduce dissonance. These measures are then correlated with our index of cognitive style. It is at this point that difficulties begin. First of all, several modes of dissonance reduction are usually operative in any situation. In the example being discussed, this means that subjects could reduce dissonance not only by changing their attitudes toward the experiment, but also by justifying their discrepant behavior. If the only way of measuring dissonance is to measure attempts to reduce it, then clearly, all attempts to reduce it must be measured. Without comprehensive measurement of this kind, it becomes impossible to assess the meaning of the correlation between field dependence and dissonance reduction.

There are, however, a number of problems inherent in trying to measure *all* attempts to reduce inconsistency. Steiner (1966; Chapter 62) has shown that the various modes for restoring consistency are "functional alternatives"—at least in situations involving interpersonal disagreement. People who make predominant use of one mode tend to make little use of other modes of restoration. It may thus be useful to suppress the occurrence of the alternative responses, for otherwise the measurable effect of the experimental manipulations on any one response is likely to be very slight. There is, however, some evidence suggesting that inconsistency-reducing responses under some circumstances may combine additively (for example, Steiner & Johnson, 1964), in which case it may be possible to measure several equally strong responses to a given inconsistency.

Even if all of this could be accomplished, it still would not necessarily be possible to relate the personality measure to the magnitude of stress associated with inconsistency. The correlation may reflect a relationship with factors other than the inconsistency itself. As I noted earlier, and as Brehm and Cohen (1962) have also emphasized, the personality variable may relate, either directly or through a mediating variable, to any of the independent variables controlling the arousal of inconsistency. It may also relate to one or more of the ways in which inconsistency can be reduced, and finally, it may relate to the process by which the mode of inconsistency reduction is selected. It ought to be clear, therefore, that a correlation between a personality variable and attempts to reduce inconsistency does not demonstrate that the personality variable has a direct effect on the magnitude of inconsistency.

An alternative possibility for linking personality to the inconsistency process is to use physiological measures as indicators of the tension produced by inconsistency. Physiological indices have the special utility of permitting the investigator to measure the effects of his manipulations at the time they are applied. Otherwise it is necessary to rely on self-report data at the end of the experiment—a procedure subject to a variety of distortions. On the other hand, there are a number of technical and conceptual difficulties involved in measuring physiological states.

Despite these admittedly fundamental problems, a number of efforts have been made to gauge the magnitude of inconsistency arousal by means of autonomic measurement (Burdick & Burnes, 1958; Brehm, Black, & Bogdonoff, 1964; Steiner, 1964; Zimbardo & Dworkin, 1964). I recently initiated an experiment designed to examine the relationship between psychological stress, dissonance, and physiological reactivity. The independent variable in this study is a threat-arousing film previously used by Lazarus and his colleagues (Lazarus, 1964). The prediction is that skin conductance responses to the film will be affected by experimental instructions in manner consistent with dissonance theory. If a subject voluntarily commits himself to seeing the film he will experience dissonance in inverse proportion to the amount of justification he is given to support his commitment. Dissonance may be reduced in this situation by judging the film as less unpleasant after seeing it in entirety as compared with ratings made after seeing only a brief segment. This cognitive revaluation should be reflected in lower skin-conductance levels relative to a No Dissonance Control condition in which subjects are not given a choice about viewing the entire film. I am suggesting here that the manipulation of cognitions so as to produce dissonance results in a reappraisal of the threatening stimulus as benign, and that this reappraisal is reflected in an autonomic variable like skin conductance. Lazarus (1964) makes an analogous prediction for conditions in which defensive sound tracks accompany the threatening film. The significance of my own experiment lies in specifying how a cognitive process such as dissonance can control autonomic nervous system activity.[1]

RELATIONS BETWEEN PERSONALITY VARIABLES AND COGNITIVE INCONSISTENCY

Despite the methodological problems discussed above, a number of studies of personality and inconsistency have been conducted over the past few years. Steiner (1966) and Glass (1968) have reviewed most of this research, and the reader is referred to these papers for a more comprehensive treatment of the area. Of the several personality and individual difference variables studied in consistency theory experiments, the following have received by far the greatest amount of attention: (a) authoritarianism, dogmatism, and intolerance of ambiguity (Harvey, 1962; Steiner & Johnson, 1964; Newcomb, 1963; Fillenbaum, 1964; Feather, 1964a); (b) cognitive controls, such as concreteness-abstractness (Janicki, 1964; Harvey, 1965) and category width (Rosen, 1961; Steiner & Johnson, 1965); (c) manifest anxiety (Steiner & Rogers, 1963; Kogan & Wallach, 1964); (d) self-esteem (Bramel, 1962, 1963; Secord, Backman, & Eachus, 1964; Silverman, 1964; Glass, 1964; Edlow & Kiesler, 1966; Glass & Wood, 1968); and (e) male-female differences in preferences for dissonance-reducing responses (Brock & Buss, 1962; Steiner & Rogers, 1963; Kogan & Wallach, 1964).

Except for certain interesting aspects of the self-esteem research, the studies mentioned above have been generally unrewarding. Many of the personality variables were too global in character to use in predicting

---

[1] Preliminary analysis of the results showed that skin conductance responses to the stressor film were indeed significantly lower in the Dissonance conditions than in the Control condition.

variability in responses to specific inconsistencies. Another limitation of these studies was that correlations were often carried out between personality predispositions and attempts at inconsistency resolution without regard to whether the focus of interest was on the arousal side or the response side of the inconsistency process. In the remainder of this paper I will concentrate on the reduction aspect of cognitive inconsistency, specifically on personality variables that seem to determine priorities among the different modes of resolution. The conceptual emphasis, moreover, will be on the reduction of cognitive dissonance, both because of my own theoretical persuasion and because the theory has generated more research than other theories of consistency.

AN APPROACH TO THE STUDY OF PREFERENCES AMONG DISSONANCE REDUCING RESPONSES

Several attempts have been made to specify priorities among different modes of dissonance reduction (Festinger, 1957; Brock & Buss, 1962; Pervin & Yatko, 1965), but very little is actually known either about the way dissonance is reduced or the way different modes of reduction interact. Indeed, Brown has suggested that "unless many variables other than dissonance are specified, the theory does not predict one technique" (1962, p. 51). It is not presently clear just what variables lead people to prefer some dissonance-reducing responses over others.[2]

The view proposed here is that responses to dissonance are governed by the same mechanisms people use to resolve 'inner conflict' (Glass, 1965). Certain mechanisms of defense become established over the years as the individual's characteristic reaction to unacceptable impulses aroused by threatening events. It seems reasonable to assume that the prepotent defense against unconscious conflicts can also be used in a wide variety of dissonance situations (cf. Janis, 1959). The dissonance formulation as it now stands makes no assumptions about the person being consciously aware of the cognitive conflict he experiences in order for dissonance to be produced.[3] In terms of the theory, the individual strives to behave in a manner which is consistent with the cognitions he holds about himself. When confronted with information discrepant with some aspect of his self-conception, he experiences dissonance. His attempts to reduce dissonance represent efforts to defend himself against the implications of the discrepant information. In order to account for variation in responses to dissonance, defensive processes may be assumed to occur within the individual which mediate between the arousal of dissonance and observed responses to it. Given this view of dissonance reduction, the theory of ego-defensive behavior, which is directed toward the study of the resolution of unconscious conflict, should permit increased understanding of the way in which dissonance is reduced.

---

[2] As we noted in an earlier section, the problem of response preferences stems, in part, from the fact that most studies usually close off all modes of reduction except the single response in which there is primary interest. An answer to the question of what determines response preferences can only be found in experimental situations that allow a wider range of dissonance-reducing responses than has previously been used.

[3] In 'forced-compliance' experiments (Brehm & Cohen, 1962), however, there is an implicit assumption that the person is aware of his responsibility for his discrepant commitment. [Brock, in Chapter 32, argues that even this implicit assumption assigns too much role to awareness—Ed.]

Clinical conceptions of defense mechanisms stem almost exclusively from psychoanalytic theory. With the advent of the 'new look' in perception, a number of attempts were made to develop categorizations of 'defensive styles' which presumably encompass the diverse mechanisms (Goldstein, 1959; Cohen, 1959; Byrne, 1961). Ego-defensive styles can be divided into two general classes: those based on avoidance of the threatening stimuli and those based on vigilance for threat. Defenses such as intellectualization, projection, and many types of rationalization might be classified as vigilance or sensitizing responses since they involve attempts to reduce tension by approaching or controlling the threatening stimulus and its consequences. Repression and denial, in contrast, represent attempts to avoid recognition of threat and its consequences. Greater repression has been inferred from a variety of behaviors, including (a) relatively higher perceptual recognition thresholds for failure-related words, (b) poorer recall of failures and material associated with painful shock, and (c) lower skin-conductance levels in response to stress-producing films. Greater vigilance implies the opposite behavior on each of these criteria.

The conceptualization of a 'repression-sensitization continuum' implies that ego-defensive processes are predispositions to approach or avoid external events which threaten some aspect of the individual's self-esteem. In accordance with this view, most of the research in this area has been directed toward the development of psychometric devices designed to classify persons as 'repressors' or 'sensitizers.' Among the more frequently used tests is Byrne's (1961) R-S Scale, a 156-item test consisting largely of items from the MMPI. There is general agreement on the high reliability of this scale (Christie & Lindauer, 1963; Byrne, 1964). In whatever ways individuals respond to the R-S items, they do it consistently so that we may safely say the test is measuring a stable personality dimension. The evidence is more equivocal with regard to validity. Some investigators (e.g., Christie & Lindauer, 1963) believe that interpretations based on the face content of R-S items must be considered ambiguous. They argue that the scale probably measures a composite of responses to item content, response sets, social desirability, and possible interactions between them. It may be difficult, therefore, to decide whether subjects who receive high scores (the sensitization end of the continuum) should be classified as 'sensitizers' or 'yeasayers' or low social-desirability people.

This line of reasoning may be correct, yet persons who differ in the degree to which they show response sets and social desirability may also differ in the way in which they characteristically defend against threat. It would not be inconsistent with what is known about psychological defensiveness to classify these people as sensitizers or repressors. A similar position has been taken by Byrne (1964) in his recent review of the construct validity of the R-S scale. He presents data suggesting that something more than social desirability is being measured by tests of ego-defensive style. For example, with scores on the Edwards SD Scale held constant by means of partial correlation, a significant correlation $(-.38)$ was still found between defensive style and ward ratings of anxiety in a group of psychiatric patients.

My own view is to assume that an individual's score on the R-S scale reflects the characteristic way in which he responds to threatening stimuli, and by extrapolation, the way in which he attempts to reduce dissonance.

Repressors will tend to adopt modes of reduction which involve denying or repressing the discrepant information. Sensitizers will tend to ruminate about the discrepant cognitions, verbalize their impact, and thereby neutralize the unpleasant implications. Consider the case of an individual who has high self-esteem and is confronted with information implying he has homosexual tendencies. The man could reduce the resulting dissonance in a number of ways, including denial of the discrepant information and projection of homosexual traits on other persons. If the individual typically defends against a threat to his self-conception by avoiding recognition of the existence of the threat, he is likely to reduce dissonance in this situation by denying the credibility of the discrepant information, thereby effectively blocking the aversive cognitions. If he is the kind of person who characteristically uses the sensitizing class of defense mechanisms, he is likely to reduce dissonance by means of some form of projection. There are, of course, other avenues of dissonance reduction in this situation (e.g., repression of the threatening information), but these too can be classified as either approach or avoidance defenses and therefore are at least theoretically predictable from a person's position on the repression-sensitization continuum.

To my knowledge, the above line of reasoning has not been subjected to empirical test. I am currently engaged in a program of experiments at Rockefeller University designed to implement some of the ideas discussed in this paper. The studies involve the preselection of subjects in terms of their ego-defensive style, the inducement of varying degrees of dissonance using postdecision and 'forced compliance' paradigms (Brehm & Cohen, 1962), and the measurement of attempts to cope with dissonance in situations that permit a number of possible dissonance-reducing responses. The use of preselection devices will of necessity impose limitations on the causal significance of our results. That is, the validity of the hypothesized relationship between defensive style and dissonance reduction will rest largely on correlational findings. Personality variables like defensive style have not been sufficiently studied to permit identification of their essential dynamics, so we must content ourselves with general measures of these variables rather than manipulating them. However, this method will be modified in the course of our research as more promising formulations of the problem arise. A clue to an alternative procedure comes from the work of Lazarus (1964), who has shown that defensive orientations can be induced in subjects by means of verbal instructions.

SITUATIONAL FACTORS FOSTERING SENSITIZING VS.
AVOIDANCE RESPONSES TO DISSONANCE.

This discussion has focused on the role of ego-defensive style in determining the particular method used to reduce dissonance. It is naive to assume, however, that an individual's mode of defense will be the prepotent determiner of responses to any and all sources of dissonance. A given defense mechanism may not be effective in certain types of situations or against certain kinds of stimuli. Thus the nature of the dissonance-arousing stimuli and the context in which they occur must also be considered in predicting modes of dissonance reduction. The question of response preferences for reducing dissonance can be studied by seeing whether subjects with the same characteristic style of defense emphasize the same preferences in different types of situations. There is, however, a prior issue. It is necessary to conceptualize relevant situational variables in a way that permits us to manipulate their effects in a variety of otherwise comparable experimental contexts. It would not do, for example, to compare modes of dissonance reduction used by repressors in two situations involving noncomparable alternatives for dissonance reduction. One must identify those situational factors that can be varied independently of other features of the experimental situation.

One such factor arises from the differential resistance to change of relevant cognitive elements (Festinger, 1957; Brehm & Cohen, 1962). The resistance to change of a cognition is due to its ambiguity and to the difficulty of changing the reality it represents. Cognitions may differ along an ambiguity dimension because the meaning or significance of the event being represented is unclear. Avoidance modes of dissonance reduction are easier to use in an ambiguous area than in one with unequivocal cognitions which make it difficult for the subject to engage in defensive distortion without behaving in a patently unreasonable manner. Studies of attitudes toward smoking and lung cancer are a case in point. Many cigarette smokers would have to give up the habit or tolerate dissonance if the only way to reduce dissonance was to deny the fact of a statistical relationship between smoking and lung cancer. The evidence shows, however, that smokers and nonsmokers do not disagree so much on the fact of a relationship as they do on the interpretation of this fact (Pervin & Yatko, 1965). It is easier for smokers to hold cognitions based on opinions which are not shared by others than it is to hold cognitions reflecting an uncontested, unpleasant fact. Opinions are more ambiguous, hence less responsive to reality. In situations where reality is quite clear, resistance to change of the corresponding cognitions will depend on how difficult it is to change reality. Thus it is easier for a person to correct an erroneous statement he has made than it is to change the fact that he has lost his wristwatch.

Another situational factor that determines how dissonance will be reduced is the amount of effort required to keep dissonance at a minimal level once it has been reduced (Aronson, 1960). The response that involves the least effort in this respect is the one most likely to be adopted by the individual. Take the case of a student who has a strong motivation to succeed but, for some reason, is doing poorly on weekly classroom tests. Dissonance arises from the discrepancy between cognitions that he is doing poorly and that he has a need to do good work. Other things being equal, he could reduce dissonance by convincing himself that he really does not care about doing well, i.e., by minimizing his achievement motivation. Alternatively, he could convince himself that he really cares, but his grades are poor because the tests are unfair or because the teacher dislikes him. We believe that a decrement in achievement motivation would be the preferred technique of reduction, since it requires less subsequent effort to keep dissonance at a minimal level. Once a person manages to reduce his need to achieve success, it will remain reduced. On the other hand, if a person tries to convince himself that his failure is due to the fact that the tests are unfair or that his teacher is prejudiced against him, he would continually need to explain away a series of poor grades. (This prediction is confined to individuals on whom social pressures toward success are low.)

From the preceding considerations there emerge at least three general hypotheses which I am currently investigating at Rockefeller. The first of these is that an avoidance defense, in contrast to a sensitizing defense, is more likely to be used to reduce dissonance, the more ambiguous is the discrepant cognition. The second hypothesis states that the preferred mode of dissonance reduction will depend upon how much effort is required to maintain dissonance at a minimal level once it has been reduced; the less the effort, the greater the preference. The third hypothesis suggests a qualification under which the effort variable affects the method used to reduce dissonance. If the initial cognition is highly resistant to change because of the person's values and standards, dissonance is likely to be reduced not by altering the initial cognition, but by some form of defensive avoidance of the discrepant cognition.

CONCLUDING REMARKS

Any attempt to explore the relationship between personality predispositions and responses to cognitive inconsistency must initially resolve at least two issues. The first is to specify whether it is the arousal or reduction aspects of the inconsistency process to which the personality variables are to be related. Having done this, the next step is to search for personality variables that are theoretically coordinate with the type of inconsistency being studied. In my own research program, I have attempted to satisfy both of these conditions by focusing interest on the reduction side of the dissonance process, and on a personality variable, ego-defensive style, that seems conceptually related to variability in responses to dissonance.

The theoretical relevance of our research program lies, I think, in its extension of our understanding of how people cope with the discomfort occasioned by dissonance. In its present form, dissonance theory contains only one intervening variable, cognitive dissonance, and few explicit assumptions are made about the conditions fostering the use of one rather than another mode of reduction. It is therefore difficult to make a priori predictions about how a specific form of dissonance will be reduced by a given individual. Further development of the theory requires the identification of relevant personality variables, along with selected situational factors, that should be included in the model in order to make more precise predictions about how an individual resolves cognitive inconsistencies. Our own program of studies represents one possible approach to this problem.

CHAPTER 60

Individual Differences and Tolerance for Inconsistency

Gerald R. Miller

and

Milton Rokeach

Michigan State University

Several writers (Frenkel-Brunswik, 1949; Festinger, 1957; Cohen, 1960; Brehm & Cohen, 1962) have suggested that certain personality factors may influence an individual's tolerance for cognitive inconsistency. Generally, discussion of such personality variables has emphasized the possibility of systematic differences in the extent to which persons can endure, or 'live with' inconsistency. Cohen (1960) speculates that a personality construct such as *need for cognitive consistency* might increase the explanatory power of dissonance theory. Brehm and Cohen suggest that "predictions to a range of effects from dissonance theory could be sharpened by taking into account personality variables that are widely considered to be important determinants of cognition, perception, and social interaction" (1962, p. 171). It is thus reasonable to suppose that differences in such personality variables as *authoritarianism* or *dogmatism* may be useful predictors of differential tolerance for inconsistency.

That persons may differ in tolerance is of both theoretical and methodological import. In terms of the development and refinement of consistency theory, the identification of relevant personality factors influencing tolerance for inconsistency would result in more precise generalizations concerning the behavioral consequences of commitments or actions calculated to induce inconsistency. The ability to specify and to control such personality variables should increase the rigor and predictive power of the typical consistency experiment. Such control procedures would offset at least one criticism of some consistency research: the charge that data for certain subjects are often excluded on *post hoc* grounds (Chapanis & Chapanis, 1964). Knowledge of the personality correlates of tolerance for inconsistency would enable the researcher to identify and to measure probable response differences prior to data collection.

Despite the significance of the problem, empirical research dealing with the effects of personality variables on tolerance for inconsistency is not extensive. We shall first discuss several studies dealing more or less directly

---

Preparation of this paper was facilitated by a National Science Foundation research grant to Milton Rokeach.

with relationships between tolerance for inconsistency and the personality variables of authoritarianism and dogmatism. Next, we shall consider whether there is any evidence to suggest that subjects assumed to vary in tolerance for inconsistency behave differently under conditions designed to induce cognitive dissonance.

AUTHORITARIANISM, DOGMATISM, AND TOLERANCE FOR INCONSISTENCY

It is reasonable to assume that authoritarian and dogmatic persons will find it more difficult to tolerate and to withstand cognitive inconsistency. A major characteristic of such persons is their tendency to engage in simple, black-and-white thinking. Frenkel-Brunswik asserts that for the authoritarian "too much existing emotional ambiguity and ambivalence are counteracted by denial and intolerance of cognitive ambiguity. It is as if everything would go to pieces once the existing discrepancies were faced" (1949, p. 134). Similar ideas are expressed by Rokeach (1960), who suggests that closed belief systems are characterized by a relatively high rejection of disbelief systems, by isolation of parts within and between belief and disbelief systems, and by relatively little differentiation within the disbelief system— all indicative of simplistic thinking.

Authoritarian and dogmatic persons should thus seek to structure situations in cognitively consistent and simple ways. Furthermore, inconsistent stimuli should be rejected, distorted, ignored, or denied. By contrast, equalitarian and low dogmatic individuals should be able to tolerate more cognitive inconsistency because of their greater ability to think complexly and in an integrated fashion.

At least four studies (Steiner, 1954; Kenney & Ginsberg, 1958; Harvey, 1962; Steiner & Johnson, 1963) have examined the relationship of tolerance for trait inconsistency to authoritarianism, while one study (Foulkes & Foulkes, 1965) has investigated its relationship to dogmatism. In all of these studies, it was hypothesized that authoritarian or dogmatic persons are less able to entertain the idea that an individual may possess inconsistent traits, for this would disrupt their simple and absolutistic cognitive world. The notion, for example, that a person could be both quick-tempered and lazy or phlegmatic and passionate could be cognitively disconcerting, and the authoritarian or dogmatic individual should be more likely to deny the existence of such incongruence.

Steiner (1954) first pretested sets of trait pairs to determine which pairs were likely and unlikely to occur together. Then, high and low scorers on the California Ethnocentrism Scale were presented trait pairs that had been previously rated as likely to occur (e.g., passionate–quick-tempered) and unlikely to occur (e.g., lazy–quick-tempered). The Ss' task was simply to cross out those pairs whose occurrence they judged as least likely.

The results generally conformed with expectations. High E Ss crossed out a significantly greater number of dissimilar trait pairs than did Low E Ss, leading Steiner to conclude that "high ethnocentrics tolerate less disharmony between their value systems and their perceptual assumptions" (p. 353).

Kenny and Ginsberg (1958), however, found no significant relationship between intolerance for trait inconsistency and authoritarian submission, as measured by a subset of items from the California F Scale. In commenting on this study, Steiner and Johnson (1963) point out that the observed difference may have arisen from a greater heterogeneity of age, educational background, and occupation among Kenny and Ginsberg's Ss. When such heterogeneity was eliminated, Steiner and Johnson found a significant correlation of .26 between F scores and intolerance of trait inconsistency.

These authors further hypothesized that High F Ss faced with a discrepancy between initial trait impressions and subsequent behavior will ignore the latter and retain their initial impressions. In contrast, Low F Ss should respond to the discrepant behavior by reevaluating their initial impressions.

To test these predictions, Steiner and Johnson exposed High and Low F Ss to two confederates, A and B, both initially presented in a favorable light. Pretest ratings indicated that A and B were both perceived favorably. Then, B interacted with the Ss in a manner which was consistent with his initial favorable impression, while A interacted with the Ss in a manner intended to conflict with the earlier impression. Ss then completed posttest ratings of A and B. Steiner and Johnson found, as predicted, that High F Ss did not change their ratings of A or B, while Low F Ss significantly lowered their posttest ratings of A but not B.

In another study dealing with dogmatism and tolerance for trait inconsistency (Foulkes & Foulkes, 1965), high and low scorers on Rokeach's test were first given a series of statements supposedly describing each of four girls, and the Ss' ratings of each girl were obtained. Ss then received additional information intended to reverse the initial impression. They then rated the girls a second time.

Results indicated that High D Ss either changed their original ratings considerably or else showed little change. By contrast, Low D Ss generally showed moderate shifts of personality impression. High D Ss apparently found it more difficult than Low D Ss to tolerate the inconsistency created by the conflicting information, and to reduce it either changed their impressions drastically or else ignored the contradictory information.

In yet another study by Harvey (1962), High and Low F Ss were exposed to inconsistent information about themselves rather than about others. The Ss were provided with two fictitious ratings of themselves, one allegedly prepared by a friend and the other by a stranger. The ratings dealt with such traits as friendliness, sincerity, and considerateness. For some items, the friend's or stranger's ratings were lower than the S's previously obtained self-rating, while for other items the evaluations were identical. The Ss then filled out posttest ratings of themselves, as well as of the friend and stranger.

Harvey found a significant negative correlation: the higher the authoritarianism the less the change in self-ratings. Moreover, authoritarianism correlated positively with: (a) a lowered estimate of how well the source knew the S; (b) a denial that the source was angry with the S; and (c) a denial that the source had made the negative ratings. These various cognitive adjustments apparently enabled those high in authoritarianism to ward off the threatening aspects of the inconsistent information, thus enabling them to retain their initial perceptions.

The studies reviewed above indicate that authoritarian and dogmatic persons possess less tolerance for inconsistency, at least in situations wherein they are required to assess themselves and others. Several ambiguities must, however, be noted. In studies employing correlational measures, it is possible that individual differences other than authoritarianism or dogmatism (e.g., intelligence) may have partially accounted for the differences in results. Furthermore, the ambiguity of the concept *tolerance for inconsistency* makes it difficult to specify the exact nature of the psychological process at work. Is it a process involving differences in threshold or is it rather differences in modes of resolving inconsistency? In either case, the bulk of the evidence would nevertheless suggest that equalitarian and low dogmatic individuals are responding differently than authoritarian and high dogmatic individuals when reacting to incongruous stimuli.

DISSONANCE THEORY AND TOLERANCE FOR INCONSISTENCY

While the preceding studies are more or less directly concerned with the relationship between certain personality variables and tolerance for inconsistency, other studies have dealt with the differential reactions of individuals high and low in authoritarianism or dogmatism to a variety of experimental conditions which are assumed to arouse cognitive dissonance.

Although not explicitly cast in a dissonance theory framework, a study by Paul (1956) investigated the behavior of authoritarian and equalitarian individuals faced with the dissonance-producing effects of a fait accompli. Prior to the 1952 presidential election, Paul obtained personality impressions of Eisenhower and Stevenson from four groups of Ss: Authoritarian, Pro-Eisenhower; Authoritarian, Pro-Stevenson; Equalitarian, Pro-Eisenhower; and Equalitarian, Pro-Stevenson. After the election, measures of the same personality characteristics were again obtained.

Paul reasoned that the additional status and power conferred on Eisenhower as a result of having won the election would lead to more favorable postelection impressions of Eisenhower by all Ss—Pro-Stevenson as well as Pro-Eisenhower. The relatively greater increase of favorableness of impression by the Pro-Stevenson Ss can readily be interpreted from a dissonance viewpoint. The knowledge that one had opposed a particular presidential candidate is dissonant with the knowledge that the candidate was elected. One means of reducing this dissonance is to change to a more favorable perception of the successful candidate.

But as Paul suggests, Pro-Stevenson Ss who are authoritarian should be more susceptible than their equalitarian counterparts to the fait accompli effects of the election. Since the former are assumed to be less tolerant of dissonance, they should be more likely than the latter to reevaluate favorably their impressions of Eisenhower.

Paul's results generally supported these expectations. First, he found that both the Pro-Eisenhower and the Pro-Stevenson Ss perceived Eisenhower more favorably after his election. Secondly, comparison of the post-election ratings of the Pro-Eisenhower and Pro-Stevenson Ss revealed that changes in impressions were greater for the latter. Thirdly, and most relevant to the present discussion, changes in the ratings of Eisenhower by the Authoritarian, Pro-Stevenson group were significantly greater than those obtained for the Equalitarian, Pro-Stevenson group.[1]

---

[1] Very often there are possibilities for regression artifacts in comparisons such as these. In this specific study the Authoritarian Pro-Stevenson subjects rated Eisenhower more extremely negative before the election than did the Equalitarian Pro-Stevenson subjects (Paul, 1956, Table 1), thus throwing any substantive interpretation of differential upward change into doubt—Ed.

In a second study not specifically couched in dissonance theory terms, Vidulich and Kaiman (1961) examined the amount of conformity by High and Low Dogmatic Ss in a situation in which either a high- or a low-status confederate first presented a judgment conflicting with the S's preferred response. Initially, all Ss made 30 judgments of the direction of light movement in an autokinetic situation. The preferred response of each S was determined, and all Ss then engaged in 30 more trials with the confederate. On 80 per cent of these latter trials, the confederate's responses were in the direction least frequently reported by S in his first 30 judgments. One-half of the High and Low Dogmatic Ss were told that the confederate was a college professor experienced in psychological research, while the remaining one-half were told that he was a student at a local high school.

Vidulich and Kaiman predicted that magnitude of conformity would be determined by an interaction of the S's dogmatism and the status of the information source. Specifically, they hypothesized that High Dogmatic Ss paired with a high-status source would show an increase in conformity, while those paired with a low-status source would show a decrease in conformity. Since Low Dogmatic Ss should be less sensitive to status differences, it was expected that their reactions would be similar for high- and low-status information sources.

The findings generally confirmed these predictions. Since the experimental situation was potentially dissonance-producing (i.e., the S made a series of judgments in the face of discrepant information about the direction of light movement), the results seem to indicate less tolerance for dissonance on the part of High Dogmatic Ss. While Low Dogmatic Ss demonstrated a rather moderate degree of conformity, High Dogmatic Ss appear to have reduced dissonance by conforming closely to the judgments of the high-status information source and by offering judgments at odds with those of the low-status source. This conclusion is tempered, however, by the enigmatic finding that Low Dogmatic Ss conformed more readily with the judgments of the low-, rather than the high-status information source.

Turning now to studies which more directly test dissonance theory predictions, we find four studies (Wrenn, 1962; Fillenbaum, 1964; Hunt & Miller, 1965; Kleck & Wheaton, 1967) which have investigated the general hypothesis that High and Low Dogmatic persons behave differently in dissonance-arousing situations. While the results of these investigations are far from conclusive, they all represent attempts to qualify the assumptions, derivations, and empirical generalizations of dissonance theory by suggesting that they may be differentially applicable to persons who vary in degree of dogmatism.

Both Wrenn (1962) and Fillenbaum (1964) propose that High Dogmatic persons are likely to experience more dissonance than Low Dogmatic individuals when induced to commit themselves to, or induced to engage in, actions discrepant with cognitions, and consequently are more likely to engage in behavior designed to reduce dissonance. Data for both the Wrenn and Fillenbaum studies were obtained under experimental conditions similar to those employed by Aronson and Mills (1959). Female Ss were told that they would participate in group discussions dealing with a sexual topic. To induce dissonance, experimental Ss were asked to undergo a severe initiation to qualify as group members, the initiation consisting of reading several vivid sexual passages to *E*. Control group *Ss* either underwent a mild initiation or performed an irrelevant task.

Ss were next asked to listen to a taped discussion, allegedly a discussion which took place within the group they would be joining. What they actually heard was a tape recording in which several females engaged in a dull discussion of secondary sexual characteristics. *Ss* then rated the content of the taped discussion for interest. In line with dissonance theory, it was expected that *Ss* in the Severe Initiation conditions would rate the discussion content as more interesting than would *Ss* in the Control conditions. Also, and of particular interest in the present context, it was hypothesized that this effect would be more marked for High than for Low Dogmatic *Ss*; i.e., because of greater dissonance arousal, or because of less tolerance for dissonance, High Dogmatic *Ss* exposed to the severe initiation should rate the dull discussion more favorably than Low Dogmatic *Ss*.

The results of the Wrenn and Fillenbaum studies provide only equivocal support for the hypothesis. While the differences in the Wrenn study were in the predicted direction—that is, High Dogmatic *Ss* rated the dull discussion more favorably—they were not significant. Furthermore, interpretation of Wrenn's findings is equivocal because there was no significant main effect due to the initiation variable across High and Low Dogmatic groups. Those *Ss* participating in the severe initiation did not rate the discussion as significantly more attractive than control *Ss*. The failure to demonstrate differential dissonance effects makes it difficult to draw conclusions concerning the effects of the dogmatism variable.

Fillenbaum's conclusions are based on a comparison of the product-moment correlations between dogmatism scores and ratings of the discussion's interest for *Ss* in Severe and Mild Initiation conditions. Significant positive relationships between dogmatism and ratings of interest were found for both conditions. The correlation for *Ss* in the Severe condition was .39, but the correlation was even larger—.56—in the Mild condition. The fact that both correlations were significant (and not significantly different from one another) is not in accord with theoretical expectations: a significant correlation was expected in the Severe but not in the Mild condition. Since consistently higher ratings of the dull discussion were obtained from the High Dogmatic *Ss* in both conditions, the correlations may represent some behavioral characteristic distinguishing High Dogmatics from Low Dogmatics that has no direct relevance to dissonance-reducing behavior.

Consider an alternative interpretation. It is reasonable to suppose that High Dogmatic persons, whether in the Severe or Mild Initiation condition, generally will be more reluctant to engage in public discussion of socially taboo topics such as sex. When asked to participate in such a discussion, these individuals should experience more anxiety. Upon discovering that the taped discussion is dull or banal, there is a reduction of anxiety which enhances the attractiveness of the group. Thus, regardless of type of initiation, High Dogmatic *Ss* should evaluate the group more favorably.

The preceding interpretation emphasizes one of the problems involved in research dealing with personality variables assumed to reflect differences in tolerance for dissonance. Care must be taken to specify in what way the personality characteristic is relevant to, or activated by, the particular situation, and reciprocally, to specify pertinent aspects of the situation that should result in differential tolerance for dissonance. It is not clear just which features of the experimental situation employed in the Wrenn and Fillenbaum studies should produce differences in tolerance for dissonance between High and Low Dogmatic persons. Moreover, interpretation is possibly confounded by the presence of other features—such as the emphasis on sex—that might result in behavioral differences that are theoretically unrelated to the issue of tolerance for dissonance.

Two recent studies have reported more clear-cut findings. Kleck and Wheaton (1967) examined responses of High and Low Dogmatic Ss to opinion-consistent and opinion-inconsistent information. Since High Dogmatic Ss should be more motivated than Low Dogmatic Ss to avoid dissonance-producing information, these investigators hypothesized that the former would show: (a) a greater preference for opinion-consistent information, (b) a poorer recall of the opinion-inconsistent information, (c) a less favorable evaluation of opinion-inconsistent information, and a more favorable evaluation of the opinion-consistent information.

Following an attitude pretest on the issue, the Ss were told they could choose to read either an article favoring a minimum age of 18 for obtaining a driver's license or one favoring the established 16-year minimum. The Ss' choices provided a measure of preference for consistent or inconsistent information. Following their choices, all the Ss read both messages and evaluated them. Two weeks later they all completed a test designed to assess their recall of the content of both articles.

All three hypotheses received empirical support. First, High Dogmatic Ss were found to be less willing to expose themselves to inconsistent information, but the difference did not reach statistical significance. Secondly, High Dogmatic Ss recalled significantly less dissonant information than did Low Dogmatic Ss. Since there were no differences between High and Low Dogmatic Ss on total recall of the content of both articles, this finding cannot be attributed to differential intelligence. Finally, High Dogmatic Ss evaluated the opinion-consistent article significantly more favorably than did Low Dogmatic Ss; differences for the inconsistent article were also in the predicted direction, but not significantly so. Kleck and Wheaton conclude that "dogmatism is systematically related to responses to opinion consistent and opinion inconsistent information ... not in terms of differences in selective exposure to that information ... but rather in terms of the cognitive processes initiated subsequent to that exposure" (1967, p. 252).

Further support for this conclusion is found in a study by Hunt and Miller (1965). Their Ss were required to prepare written communications that were discrepant with their beliefs. Rokeach (1960) has presented some evidence which suggests that High Dogmatic individuals generally experience fewer exposures to discrepant beliefs than do Low Dogmatic persons. If this is the case, knowledge that a belief-discrepant communication must be prepared should result in perceptions of greater effort on the part of High Dogmatic individuals, a factor which, as Cohen (1959a) and Aronson (1961) have shown, increases the magnitude of dissonance.

If High Dogmatic persons do indeed experience more dissonance, they should be more likely than Low Dogmatic persons to engage in dissonance-reducing activity. One means of dissonance reduction is for the S to change his attitude so that it becomes more consistent with the position he is to take in the discrepant message. It was thus hypothesized that High Dogmatic Ss who are instructed to write belief-discrepant communications will demonstrate greater attitude change than Low Dogmatic Ss in the direction of the advocated discrepant position.

High and Low Dogmatic Ss were assigned to one of three conditions: (a) a Belief-Discrepant condition wherein Ss were requested to write arguments opposing disarmament, a position at odds with their initial beliefs; (b) a Belief-Congruent condition wherein Ss were requested to write arguments consistent with their prior beliefs; i.e., arguments favoring disarmament; (c) an Irrelevant condition wherein Ss were requested to write arguments dealing with federal aid to education.

The Table summarizes the mean attitude change for the High and Low Dogmatic Ss in the three conditions. As predicted, only the High Dogmatic Ss in the Belief-Discrepant condition changed significantly; i.e., they had a less favorable posttest attitude toward disarmament. These results offer perhaps the best empirical evidence to date for the proposition that individual differences in tolerance for dissonance lead to predictably differential amounts of attitude change in experimental situations designed to induce cognitive dissonance. Even so, the observed changes in opinion do not necessarily permit unambiguous identification of the relevant intervening processes. At least three alternative interpretations come to mind. A discussion of these alternatives should serve to emphasize the ambiguity of the concept *tolerance for dissonance* and to indicate that future research dealing with the role of personality variables in dissonance-reducing behavior should aim at further conceptual refinement.

TABLE

Mean Pretest and Posttest Disarmament Scores and Mean Attitude Change for High and Low Dogmatic Subjects in the Three Conditions

Condition	Group	Pretest	Posttest	Change
Irrelevant	Low-Dogmatic	36.40	35.90	—0.50
	High-Dogmatic	32.58	31.50	—1.08
Belief Congruent	Low-Dogmatic	33.70	34.30	+0.60
	High-Dogmatic	32.82	32.18	—0.64
Belief Discrepant	Low-Dogmatic	31.36	31.07	—0.29
	High-Dogmatic	33.78	27.33	—6.45 *

* Significant beyond .01 level, one-tailed test.

First, it may be argued that Low Dogmatic, as well as High Dogmatic Ss experienced dissonance, but the former group reduced it through means other than attitude change. This line of argument recognizes that there are several avenues through which dissonance may be reduced, and that it is difficult to specify and to measure all possible modes of dissonance reduction. It can thus be contended that some other unidentified means of dissonance reduction may have been employed by the Low Dogmatic Ss.

Secondly, the findings of the Hunt and Miller study can be taken to indicate that in contrast to High Dogmatic Ss, Low Dogmatic Ss did not even experience dissonance. Thus, only High Dogmatic Ss had to behave in some way aimed at reducing it. This interpretation points to a question of central importance to consistency theory: how can one tell whether a given experimental manipulation induces cognitive inconsistency in the first place? The Hunt and Miller study assumes that differences in personality structure may determine whether belief-discrepant behavior induces sufficient dissonance to lead to dissonance-reducing behavior. On the one hand, the High Dogmatic person's general unfamiliarity with opposing beliefs should cause him to experience dissonance in situations requiring him to compose discrepant arguments. By contrast, the Low Dogmatic individual's generally greater familiarity with opposing beliefs should enable him to engage in belief-discrepant behavior without experiencing too much dissonance. Thus, differences in tolerance for dissonance may be largely a result of differences in the extent to which varying personality types have been previously exposed to belief-discrepant stimuli.

Finally, it is possible that Hunt and Miller's Low Dogmatic Ss also experienced dissonance, but were nevertheless able to maintain their original attitudes because they had a greater capacity than the High Dogmatic Ss to tolerate it. While this interpretation is most consistent with the literal meaning of the concept of *tolerance for dissonance*, it poses several difficulties. First, such an interpretation casts doubt upon one of the major assumptions of consistency theories; i.e., that the sheer experience of inconsistency is a necessary and sufficient condition to lead to behavior aimed at reducing it. Secondly, since dissonance is an intervening variable, its presence must be inferred from observation of overt behavior. Unless another independent means of defining dissonance is found, it becomes circular to argue that certain individuals have experienced dissonance, even though they failed to engage in theoretically expected dissonance-reducing behavior. One direction for future research is the development of procedures that would enable investigators to pin down which of the three possible explanations discussed above is the most tenable.

Given the current status of personality and consistency theories, it is doubtful that the conceptual ambiguities discussed here will be quickly resolved. No matter how carefully studies are designed and executed, the exact mediating processes influencing behavior in dissonance-arousing situations may continue to elude us. Such uncertainty should not slow the search for further empirical generalizations linking personality variables with behavioral differences occurring under conditions calculated to induce inconsistency. Such generalizations are of value in their own right, even if the mediating processes which underlie them are not completely understood.

CHAPTER 61

Cognitive Complexity and Judgment of Inconsistent Information

James Bieri

The University of Texas

An analysis of the influence of the cognitive structure of the individual upon his reactions to inconsistent information has several valuable features. Such an approach has merit in that a common conceptual language may be used to define the structure of the stimulus and the structure of the cognitive system, yielding a sharper base upon which to formulate experimental hypotheses. In addition, it becomes clear that both the relative consistency of information *and* its relative dimensionality must be incorporated into an estimate of overall structure. In this paper, a number of studies will be reviewed in which specific predictions were made concerning how one aspect of the structure of a person's cognitive system, its relative complexity-simplicity, affected processing of inconsistent information. Through a consideration of this research we can gain an understanding of the application of structural concepts as well as consider the future value of such an approach in studying how man organizes and uses contradictory information about his social environment.

THE CONCEPT OF STRUCTURE

The notion of *structure*, which provides an 'isomorphic' analysis linking cognitive structure and stimulus information, has received its most explicit impetus from extensions of information theory to the analysis of psychological problems. In particular, the thinking of Garner (1962) concerning structure and information has been provocative. Use of informational concepts in the personality, social, and clinical behavioral realms have been made by Berlyne (1960) and by Bieri, Atkins, Briar, Leaman, Miller, and Tripodi (1966), among others. Put most succinctly, "Structure is *related* uncertainty, ... and to have structure is to have uncertainty" (Garner, 1962, p. 339). In such a definition, of course, Garner is using *uncertainty* in its informational sense to refer to the amount of variability in a system, variability which can be quantified by an informational metric and ex-

Work on this paper was facilitated by research Grant GS-842 from the National Science Foundation.

633

pressed in terms of bits. Amount of structure, then, be it in the stimulus, the response, or the intervening cognitive system of the individual, is specified in terms of the number of events or alternatives present as well as the relation among these events. Let us look at the structure of stimuli in order to amplify these remarks.

THE STRUCTURE OF STIMULI

From a structural viewpoint, information has more structure if it has greater dimensionality and if the manner in which these dimensions are combined is inconsistent (Berlyne, 1960; Tripodi & Bieri, 1964). Consider first information which varies only along one dimension. If a person we had known as *meek* is subsequently presented to us as *timid*, consistency is maximal because both items of information reflect the same or quite close scalar positions on a common dimension such as dominance-submission. If the informational items are at some distance on the same dimension, as when a *meek* individual is subsequently presented as *dominant*, then inconsistency is maximal. It is in the case of such relatively simple, *unidimensional* stimulus information that we may unequivocally speak of inconsistent information as having *more* structure than consistent information. Knowing that a person is meek *and* dominating provides more stimulus alternatives than does the information that a person is meek and timid, or just meek.

Unfortunately, most social stimuli are simply not unidimensional, but when we consider *multidimensional* stimuli the structural distinction between consistent and inconsistent information can be maintained. Multidimensional social information may be consistent if the items it contains are combined in a congruent manner, as when a person is described as both a liberal Democrat and an integrationist. Or, it may be inconsistent, as when the person is described incongruently as a liberal Democrat and a segregationist. In both .cases, the number of stimulus alternatives may be considered the same in that two stimulus elements are combined, however the *mode* of combination leads to either consistent or inconsistent information. In keeping with our assumption that inconsistent information has more structure than consistent information, the liberal Democrat-segregationist information has the greater structure. In short, inconsistent information is assumed to be more structured than consistent information if the relative *dimensionality* of the stimuli is equivalent.

Such considerations may be particularly important when we consider the cognitive structure of the judge. If we assume, as in the discussion below, that the more cognitively complex judge has greater structure in his system of construing others, then he should prefer those social stimuli with greater structure. One implication of this is that holding dimensionality constant, the more cognitively complex judge will prefer inconsistent information over consistent information. For Low Complex judges, greatest preference should be for information which is least structured, i.e., consistent information. Some initial evidence on these matters is presently available, and we shall consider several studies which bear upon these issues.

STRUCTURE AND COGNITIVE COMPLEXITY

Because the more cognitively complex individual has available a greater number of alternative dimensions for judging others' behavior than a less cognitively complex person, we assume this more complex individual has *greater* structure in his system for construing others. Having assessed a person's dimensional versatility, we may study how variation in cognitive complexity influences the judgment of information which differs in amount of structure, including consistent and inconsistent information.

The systematic backdrop for the concept of cognitive complexity was the theory of *personal constructs* developed by G. A. Kelly (1955). Individuals are assumed to invoke personal constructs, defined by a trait *and* its opposite (i.e., a bipolar dimension), in predicting the behavior of others. A number of sources are available for a more detailed consideration of theoretical and empirical issues associated with cognitive complexity (Bieri, 1955, 1961, 1965, 1966, in press; Bonarius, 1965; Crockett, 1965). In contrast with some approaches to cognitive structure (Bieri, in press), cognitive complexity is fairly *specific* in its scope, being concerned with social stimuli only and with the dimensional versatility of the person in his social judgments. Such a specific focus should render the cognitive structure of complexity-simplicity more directly relevant to differences in processing inconsistent information.

As described in more detail elsewhere (Bieri, 1965, 1966), cognitive complexity is most commonly assessed by use of a modified grid or matrix derived from Kelly's Role Construct Repertory Test (1955). A 10 × 10 grid is used in which 10 individuals known to the subject are listed at the top of the columns. Each row is represented by 10 *provided* constructs which are bipolar personal traits, such as friendly-unfriendly, adjusted-maladjusted, and decisive-indecisive. Each of the 10 persons is rated using a six-point scale on each construct row. The similarity in ratings between rows is assessed by a matching procedure. While these basic judgments may be analyzed with different forms of analytic procedures, including factor analysis and multidimensional scaling, Vannoy (1965) has reported this matching procedure to be highly related to more involved analytic methods. In addition, Irwin, Tripodi, and Bieri (1967) report comparable results with the matching procedure when differing forms of stimulus judgments are used.

A variety of studies relating cognitive complexity to the judgment of inconsistent information have been reported. These include studies of the resolution of inconsistent information, inconsistent information and discriminability, certainty, and attribution of conflict.

COGNITIVE COMPLEXITY AND RESOLUTION OF INCONSISTENT INFORMATION

The differences between cognitively High and Low Complex judges in resolving inconsistent information have usually been studied in relation to *sequentially* presented information. For example, in a study couched in terms of primacy and recency effects, Mayo and Crockett (1964) first presented behavior about another that was positive in nature (or negative) and then presented negative (or positive) information. Judgments about the person were made after each presentation. The results indicated that Low Complex judges formed more univalent impressions by changing their initial judgments in the direction of the subsequent contradictory information. Such a recency effect was not found for High Complex judges, who retained both types of information in their final judgments, yielding a more ambivalent impression of the other. Crockett (1965) has also reported two unpublished studies of a similar nature by Rosenkrantz and Supnick. The former investigator obtained effects similar to those of Mayo and Crockett for males but not for females, while the latter obtained results which were inconsistent.

The resolution of inconsistent information was also studied by Leventhal and Singer (1964), who divided subjects into High, Moderate, and Low Complex judges. One of the more interesting results of this study was that High Complex subjects appeared to search for information related to *inner* states such as maladjustment, and Low Complex subjects responded more to surface qualities of behavior. Low Complex subjects were initially more clear about their judgments than High Complex subjects, but the former group became more uncertain after the presentation of inconsistent information. Such findings suggest that the resolution of inconsistent information by subjects differing in cognitive complexity is mediated in part by differential preference for *types* of behavioral information. Preference for more abstract information would appear to facilitate reconciliation of apparently contradictory surface qualities of behavior. Certainly, more study is needed of these phenotypic-genotypic trait preferences in information (Bieri, Bradburn, & Galinsky, 1958).

INCONSISTENT INFORMATION AND DISCRIMINABILITY

In the above studies, there was little systematic analysis of the nature of the inconsistent stimulus information provided the subjects, and it is entirely possible that the relatively detailed information presented in vignettes and interviews about another varied in uncontrolled ways in addition to the overall consistency-inconsistency which was the focus of attention. In part to surmount these uncontrolled stimulus problems, and to broach the issues raised earlier in this paper concerning stimulus inconsistency and multidimensional information, Tripodi and Bieri (1964) specified three properties of stimuli which might relate to differing cognitive complexity of the judge. These include the dimensionality of the stimulus, combining stimulus dimensions in positive (consistent) or negative (inconsistent) ways, and quantity of information.

Tripodi and Bieri had subjects make judgments of pathology based on information which might contain any of the three behavioral dimensions of aggression, body anxiety, and social withdrawal. Judges received information which was either consistently combined or inconsistently combined. In this latter condition, for example, a judge might receive an aggressive stimulus indicating high pathology in combination with a withdrawal stimulus indicative of low pathology. Ability to discriminate among stimuli was measured by means of information measures (Miller & Bieri, 1963; Bieri et al., 1966).

The results for consistent information indicated that there was a significant increase in information transmission when the dimensionality of the stimulus increased from two dimensions to three. However, this increment was greatest for those judges who were *low* in cognitive complexity, suggesting that persons with less cognitive complexity gain more discriminability with an increase in the dimensionality of consistent stimuli than do more complex persons. Such a conclusion would be congruent with the results of Leventhal (1957), who found that Low Complex judges, in comparison with High Complex judges, improved their predictions with increased stimulus information. However, for most stimulus conditions, Tripodi and Bieri (1964) found that the more cognitively complex judges did discriminate better than the less complex judges. In relation to inconsistently combined information, High Complex judges as a group discriminated significantly better than did Low Complex judges. These findings appear to be congruent with those of Mayo and Crockett (1964), who found that High Complex judges were able to integrate contradictory information better than Low Complex judges.

CONFIDENCE AND CERTAINTY

Additional evidence on the differential response of High and Low Complex judges to inconsistent information was obtained by Tripodi and Bieri (1964) when *confidence* judgments were analyzed. It was found that the more cognitively complex judges were *less* confident of their judgments in all stimulus conditions except those involving inconsistent information. For this inconsistent information, High Complex judges had higher confidence ratings than for any of the other types of stimuli they judged, while Low Complex judges gave their lowest confidence judgments to the inconsistent information.

More specific analysis of confidence judgments in this study under consistent vs. inconsistent stimulus conditions when stimulus dimensionality is held constant is instructive. For example, when an aggressive stimulus was combined with a withdrawal stimulus, High Complex judges felt more confident of their judgments if the mode of combination was inconsistent rather than consistent, while Low Complex judges were more confident of the consistent information. Similarly, when two aggressive stimuli were combined, High Complex judges were more confident of the judgments made under the inconsistent mode of combination, while Low Complex judges were more confident when the mode of combination was consistent.

A portion of a more recent study by Tripodi and Bieri (1966) adds further evidence on this issue. Subjects were asked to judge the degree of pathology in information containing aggressive behavior which was combined either in a consistent or an inconsistent manner. Confidence ratings of these judgments indicated that High Complex judges gave certainty ratings for the inconsistent information which were significantly higher than their certainty ratings for consistent information. As in the previous work discussed above, High Complex judges tended to be *less* certain than Low Complex judges when judging consistent information and more certain than the latter when judging inconsistent information. Results reported by Leventhal and Singer (1964) seem to be compatible with these findings. They observed that Low Complex subjects reported initial greater clarity in their judgments than did High Complex judges. However, with the introduction of subsequent inconsistent information, the reported clarity of the Low Complex judges' impressions was significantly reduced.

PERCEIVED CONFLICT AND COGNITIVE COMPLEXITY

The results of the studies reported thus far suggest that those subjects with greater cognitive structure are able to discriminate better among inconsistent stimuli than are those subjects with less cognitive structure. In addition, confidence or certainty ratings of judgments of consistent and inconsistent information support the generalization that more complex judges feel more certain of their judgments of inconsistent information while less complex judges feel more confident of their judgments of consistent information.

Another approach to the study of the relation between differences in cognitive structure and judgment of inconsistent information is possible when the response demanded of the judge is left relatively unstructured. If we assume that the more cognitively complex judge has greater structure in his cognitive system for perceiving others, then it is reasonable that when he is asked to create a story in response to an ambiguous social stimulus, as in a thematic apperception task, this more complex person will project greater structure into his productions. Such response structure can take the form of *conflict*, since as we have noted, a more conflicting response has greater structure than a less conflicting response (Berlyne, 1960).

Evidence on this problem was obtained in the study by Tripodi and Bieri (1966) mentioned earlier. In a task akin to the TAT, subjects were asked to tell stories about imaginary persons in three different social situations. Each subject's productions were scored for the degree of interpersonal conflict they contained. It was found that High Complex subjects perceived significantly more conflict in the relations among the stimulus persons than did the less complex judges. These results are suggestive of a cognitive structural basis for the expression of conflict in fantasy behavior, although it is possible that, as in the study by Tripodi (1967), a tendency for greater pathology in more complex subjects contributes to these findings (Bieri, 1965). The disposition of more cognitively complex subjects to express more conflict in thematic productions is consistent with the finding of Leventhal and Singer (1964) that in an impression formation task High Complex subjects sought information that was related to inner states such as maladjustment, while Low Complex subjects responded more to surface qualities of behavior.

Further elaboration of these relations is found in a study by Tripodi (1966) which analyzed the relation of cognitive complexity to the judgment of the amount of conflict in consistent and inconsistent stimuli and to the certainty of these judgments. Subjects who differed in cognitive complexity were given information about persons which on the basis of prior judgments was combined in either a consistent or an inconsistent manner. Judgments of the amount of conflict *within* the person described indicated that High Complex subjects perceived more conflict in the stimulus individuals than did Low Complex subjects, and that this tendency was significant in the case of one of the two inconsistently described persons. Further, in line with the research of Tripodi and Bieri (1966) described above, it was found that subjects low in cognitive complexity were significantly more confident of their judgments of consistent information than were cognitively complex judges. However, in contrast to the results of Tripodi and Bieri (1966), Low Complex judges tended to be more confident than High Complex subjects of their judgments of inconsistent information, although these differences were not significant.

In order to study the possible interaction of neuroticism and cognitive complexity in relation to judgment of conflict in inconsistent information, scores on Eysenck's neuroticism scale were obtained on all subjects in the study. Significant interaction effects were observed for both judgment of conflict and of certainty. That is, the difference in rated conflict in an inconsistent stimulus was primarily due to differences between High and Low Complex judges who were *high* on neuroticism. Further, the tendency for Low Complex judges to be more certain of their judgments of consistent information was primarily due to those judges who were *low* in neuroticism. We may hypothesize, then, that in predicting the judgments of conflict based on either inconsistent or consistent information, knowledge of both the relative cognitive complexity of the judge and his degree of neuroticism (own conflict) will be of value. High Complex judges who are more neurotic will perceive the greatest conflict in the inconsistent behavior of others. Low Complex judges who are least neurotic will be most certain of their judgments which are based on consistent information.

JUDGMENTS OF POSITIVE AND NEGATIVE STIMULI

Because inconsistent stimuli contain information which has both positive and negative affective value for the judge, it is important also to consider how cognitive structure may be differentially influenced by such negative and positive stimuli. For example, if it can be shown that the *same* number of alternative stimuli with either positive or negative affect for the judge are discriminated to a greater or lesser degree as a function of this affective value, then we may question whether an objective count of the number of positive or negative alternatives in a stimulus is sufficient or adequate when constructing stimuli in studies of inconsistent information. Briefly, two opposing stands may be taken on this issue. Miller and Bieri (1965) posited a *vigilance* hypothesis, which states that greater differentiation will occur among stimuli with negative affect than among stimuli with positive affect. Crockett (1965) has advanced the opposite notion, suggesting that we differentiate more among positive persons with whom we possibly have greater contact.

Irwin, Tripodi, and Bieri (1967) report two studies which examined this issue. In both studies, it was found that using cognitive complexity as a measure of differentiation, persons with whom predominantly negative affect was associated were differentiated significantly more than were persons with whom predominantly positive affect was associated. Further, women differentiated significantly more than men among persons with negative affective value, while among positive persons, men tended to differentiate more than women. In short, as one final complication in research on judgment of inconsistent information, the investigator must be careful in the assumptions he makes concerning equivalence of information which varies in terms of its positive or negative affective value for the individual. To the extent that the affective value of the stimulus is not known for the individual subject, there will be a lack of precision in efforts to specify the nature of inconsistent and consistent information.

FUTURE CONSIDERATIONS

From a variety of empirical efforts, evidence has been presented which on balance supports the general proposition that the structure of the cognitive system of the individual judge, as reflected in a measure of cognitive complexity, will influence his differential reactions to inconsistent and consistent information. Using the concept of structure as a mediating variable, there is evidence that the judge with more structure in his system of perceiving others (i.e., the more cognitively complex judge) will discriminate better among inconsistent stimuli, will prefer and be more certain of his judgments based upon inconsistent information, and will inject greater conflict into his judgments. Certainly, the evidence to date is both tentative and in need of further refinement. In particular, it would appear that because inconsistent information is by definition conflictual, efforts to study internal conflict in the judge in addition to his relative cognitive complexity are called for. The more personally conflicted, High Complex judge could have the greatest structure in his system for perceiving others and could therefore be most sensitive to the discrepancies between consistent and inconsistent information in his social world.

CHAPTER 62

Responses to Inconsistency

Ivan D. Steiner
University of Illinois

In one way or another all consistency models assume that people expect certain events to co-occur, and expect certain other events not to co-occur. Different theories tend to emphasize different expected co-occurrences, but all suggest that disconfirmation of critical expectations constitutes aversive stimulation. When the aversive motivational consequences of disconfirmation exceed some threshold of intensity, the individual is presumed to take steps to restore consistency.

Depending somewhat upon the nature of the expectation that has been violated, a variety of consistency-restoring responses may be feasible. For example, the individual may change his evaluation of the work he has done, the reward he has received, the alternative he has selected, or the attitudinal position he has defended. He may also alter his impression of a friend whose judgments have contradicted his own, minimize the degree of disagreement that has occurred, or devaluate the importance of the issue about which controversy has arisen. All these and other responses have been cited by consistency theorists as techniques for reducing the negative impact of inconsistency. But with few exceptions (e.g., Abelson, 1959; Osgood, 1960), consistency theorists have not attempted to express formal principles that govern the individual's selection of response. As late as 1965, Kelman and Eagly could maintain that the major unresolved issue in balance theory and its derivatives was "the question of what determines the particular mechanism that a person chooses, out of a range of possibilities available to him in a given situation, in order to restore balance or reduce dissonance" (1965, p. 64).

The vast majority of consistency studies have been conducted by persons with little interest in personality variables. The primary aim of most consistency research has been to prove that the average or typical person reacts to disconfirmed expectations in a manner that can be interpreted as restoring consistency. Since what is sought is support for

The author's research on problems relating to alternative modes of response has been supported by Grant M-4460 from the United States Public Health Service, National Institutes of Health.

propositions dealing with typical behavior in particular classes of situations, little attention is given to the problem of individual differences. Situations are systematically varied to determine effects on a particular kind of response measure, but subjects themselves are rarely varied in any deliberate fashion. Individual differences are either ignored or treated as unfortunate complications that obscure fundamental truths about human behavior. This procedure gives scant attention to the possibility that certain kinds of people do not share the expectations that are violated in the research setting, and thus do not experience inconsistency. It also neglects the very real possibility that among those who do experience inconsistency, some are not at all inclined to rely upon the particular consistency-restoring response that is made available to them and measured by the researcher. Many consistency studies appear to reflect rather egocentric assumptions on the part of the experimenter: "Subjects have the same expectations I have; violation of these expectations will distress them as it would me; and they will behave in response to that distress in the same fashion as I would behave." If, as is almost invariably the case, some subjects do not react as anticipated, it is not clear which of these assumptions is incorrect. If, as is less often the case, *most* subjects do not produce the expected response, it is conceivable that many have experienced the hypothesized inconsistency but few have elected to employ the response the experimenter regards as natural or inevitable. In view of the uncertainties that are inherent in this type of research it is regrettable that steps are rarely taken to determine whether (and for whom) inconsistency has been created, or to learn whether some subjects are employing consistency-restoring responses other than the one or two the researcher has elected to study.

Some of the criticisms expressed above could be directed against almost any program of behavioral research. But consistency theorists have been especially prone to prohibit the occurrence of responses that may generally be favored by their subjects, and to avoid serious consideration of individual differences. Consequently, the conclusions generated by consistency research may have limited validity in the broader universe of situations to which they are sometimes generalized. If the implications of the consistency concept are to be fully explored, a new series of investigations is needed. Limitations on subjects' freedom to employ their preferred consistency-restoring strategies should be relaxed, several different responses should be observed and measured in a single study, and efforts should be made to identify the personality determinants of response preferences.

A few attempts have already been made to conduct the kind of research that is needed, but progress has not yet been extensive. Most of the efforts to examine alternative responses have been focused on situations of the type studied by balance theorists rather than by dissonance theorists. Since the two schools of consistency theorists tend to create different kinds of experimental settings and to examine different varieties of response, it is unfortunately not certain that the findings obtained by one approach can be freely generalized to the situations studied by the other.

The remainder of this chapter will be devoted to a brief discussion of research that has examined response strategies under relatively unrestricted experimental conditions. Emphasis will be placed on an examination of the issues that are investigated rather than upon an enumeration of the studies that have been conducted.

If a situation permits several different responses to occur, an individual might conceivably use one response to the virtual exclusion of others, or he might use several simultaneously. Strong use of any one response should restore balance and make additional responses unnecessary. But moderate use of several responses might also eliminate imbalance. Osgood's (1960) law of inverse polarization suggests that, under many circumstances, at least two responses (conformity and rejection of a source) should be expected to occur simultaneously and to have supplementary effects. But Osgood also notes that strong use of certain responses (e.g., "incredulity") may prevent the occurrence of other reactions. Festinger contends that the amount of dissonance created by an interpersonal disagreement is a positive function of (a) the credibility and attractiveness of the communicator, (b) the extent of the discrepancy of opinion, and (c) the importance of, or the involvement in, the cognitive elements in the situation (Festinger, 1957, p. 178). Presumably Festinger would agree that the magnitude of dissonance experienced by an individual can be *reduced* by decreasing the attractiveness of the source (rejection), by minimizing the discrepancy in opinion (conformity to, or underrecall of, the discrepant content of the message), or by lowering one's evaluation of the importance of the issue (devaluation of the issue). But neither Festinger nor Osgood attempts to link response preferences to personality variables. Many personality theories may be interpreted as suggesting that people tend to have favorite response strategies which they apply in situations of the kind under discussion. If this is the case, one may expect that freedom of choice will lead to quite unequal reliance on available alternatives, and that different people will rely upon different balance-restoring strategies.

Evidence on this issue is both sparse and fragmentary. A number of correlational studies have indicated that subjects who make strong use of one response tend to make only slight use of at least one or two others. Thus Festinger and Maccoby (1964) found conformity and rejection to be negatively correlated in three replications of an experiment involving messages concerned with the disadvantages of fraternity life. However, the correlations were significant only when the arguments were accompanied by irrelevant visual material. Kelman and Eagly (1965) obtained a slight negative correlation between conformity and underrecall (positive displacement of message content) when messages were received from positive sources, but the relationship was reversed when sources were negative. Since each of these studies produced somewhat mixed findings concerning only two alternative responses, they leave the issue unresolved. Steiner and Rogers (1963) employed measures of four responses (conformity, rejection, devaluation of the issue, and underrecall) in a single study and noted that only one of the six resulting correlations was positive. Steiner and Vannoy (see Steiner, 1966) repeated certain aspects of this study, adding delayed measures of the responses (taken about one week after interpersonal disagreements had been created) and an index of rationalization (tendency of Ss to conclude that the source had not really attempted to formulate accurate and truthful messages). Not only were correlations between measures of different responses predominately negative *at both of the two points in time*, but changes in scores on any two responses from time one to time two were also negatively correlated. The latter finding suggests that, as time passes, persons who decrease their reliance upon a given response (e.g., rejection of the source) tend to compensate by making increased use of other responses (e.g., conformity or underrecall).

All of the work cited above has been concerned with reactions to interpersonal disagreements; none of it has dealt with postdecision dissonance or problems that arise when people are induced to act in a fashion that conflicts with their attitudes. But the predominance of negative correlations between measured reactions to interpersonal disagreements suggest that (a) the several different responses are functional alternatives, (b) some people favor one alternative and some another, and (c) people who make strong use of any one alternative have comparatively little need to employ others. Whether these conclusions are equally valid for all types of inconsistency-arousing situations remains to be determined.

A number of investigators have employed measures of skin resistance as indexes of autonomic responses to interpersonal disagreements. Smith (1936), Burdick and Burnes (1958), and Gerard (1961) have noted that subjects whose views on an issue are contradicted by a respected source show heightened levels of activation. Although physiological arousal is not always indicative of psychological stress, the GSR data reported by these investigators, together with their observational findings, provide fairly strong support for the contention that interpersonal disagreements represent aversive stimulation. Steiner (1966) has carried the use of skin resistance measures a step further. Subjects heard a prestigeful accomplice's answers to a series of questions before announcing their own replies. To the first 10 questions in the series the accomplice always gave accurate answers, but 11 of his responses to the 22 questions that followed were inaccurate. Measures of conformity, rejection, devaluation of the issue, and underrecall of disagreements were taken; and changes in the subjects' skin resistance were recorded. Analysis of data revealed that the subjects who ranked in the top quarter of the distribution of scores on any one (but only one) of the four consistency-restoring responses showed significantly less decrease in skin resistance than did subjects who did not rank in the top quarter on any of the responses, or who ranked in the top quarter on more than one. These results suggest that strong use of any one of the responses does, in fact, reduce the noxious impact of inconsistency, but that the simultaneous use of more than one may not do so. Unfortunately, the number of subjects using any single response to a high degree was too small to permit a very adequate analysis of differences between those who emphasized one vs. another consistency-restoring strategy. However, it is appropriate to note that the 'underrecallers' showed larger decreases in skin resistance than did those who employed the other three defenses. Perhaps underrecall is a ploy that yields its face-saving rewards only after some period of time has elapsed, whereas conformity, rejection, and devaluation of the issue have more immediate consequences.

The fact that subjects who employed two or more consistency-restoring techniques did not show as much immunity to stress as did those who used only one suggests that the effects of the techniques are not additive. However, a study by Steiner and Johnson (1964) casts doubt on this conclusion. A naive subject was led to believe that he was serving as an accomplice, a role in which he was instructed either to agree or to disagree with the true accomplice's bizarre answers to a number of questions. Half of the subjects who were instructed to conform on these items, and half of those who were instructed to nonconform, were given bogus information about the true accomplice that made rejection of him very improbable. The other half of the subjects in both conformity treatments received bogus information that encouraged rejection. Subjects who were induced to conform *and* reject simultaneously made the least use of conformity (on questions to which they had been instructed to give accurate answers regardless of what the accomplice said), and showed the weakest tendencies to underrecall disagreements and devaluate the issue. Subjects who had been induced to conform *or* reject made moderate use of the three available responses, and subjects who were prohibited from either conforming or rejecting had the highest average scores on the three available alternatives. These findings may be interpreted to indicate that people who use two techniques are more successful in restoring balance than those who use only one. Additional work is needed to determine the conditions under which the effects of simultaneously employed techniques are additive, and the circumstances under which they are, as was implied earlier, disjunctive or even subtractive.

If people tend to have enduring preferences for certain consistency-restoring techniques, it is reasonable to suspect that such preferences are related to personality variables. Indeed, most of the responses studied by consistency research bear a close resemblance to personality 'mechanisms' described by Freud, Horney, Sullivan, Fromm, and others. But contemporary personality theorists appear to be unimpressed by this parallelism, and are content to let social psychologists proceed alone into the murky labyrinth of the consistency cavern. The latter, in turn, are rarely gripped by an overwhelming compulsion to explore the personality implications of the ground they cover.

To be sure, a few attempts have been made to view consistency problems from the perspective of the personality theorist. Harvey, Hunt, and Schroder (1961) described four personality systems that imply special preferences for certain consistency-restoring responses, and Cohen (1959b) emphasized self-esteem as a determinant of people's choice of response strategy. But empirical research has seldom examined more than one response at a time, and the available evidence is exceedingly fragmented. Thus there have been many studies aimed at describing the 'conforming personality,' but few that have dealt with the characteristics of persons who resolve inconsistency by misperceiving, or rationalizing. It is fair to say that serious efforts to link people's personalities to their *preferred* response strategies have almost never been made.

In the case of conformity, the one response that has been examined in great detail, findings are not uniformly encouraging. Although the data of many studies can be interpreted as indicating that certain kinds of persons are predisposed to conform, obtained relationships are generally rather weak and one can usually point to contradictory evidence. In part, this discouraging state of affairs may be attributed to the absence of theory that clearly specifies which of many personality measures should be expected to predict a given preference, and to the marginal validities of most available personality measures. But it is also probable that personality variables interact with situational factors to determine the particular response an individual will employ when confronted by inconsistency. If this is the case, the 'main effects' of personality variables may be negligible when evaluated across many different experimental treatments, but such variables may be implicated in very strong 'interaction effects.' If neglected, personality differences may contribute substantially to unexplained variance and may be responsible for perplexing contradictions between the conclusions of different studies.

It is possible that important relationships between personality variables and response strategies have gone unnoticed because we have not yet developed an adequate taxonomy of response strategies. Thus Hoffman (1957), Deutsch and Gerard (1955), and Kelman (1961) have suggested that not all conformity behaviors have the same psychological meaning. Steiner and Vannoy (1961) investigated the personality correlates of 'two types' of conformity. Subjects who had conformed in a laboratory situation but who had renounced their conforming views in a private session held one week later were compared with subjects who had reasserted their conforming opinions in the private session. During the laboratory experiment the former subjects showed less tendency than did the latter to underrecall disagreements, to devaluate the issue under dispute, and to reject the accomplice. (The finding concerning devaluation was not statistically significant, however.) Personality measures also revealed differences. Subjects who subsequently renounced their conforming responses scored much lower on the Taylor Manifest Anxiety Scale, and significantly higher on a projective measure of aggression, than did those who reaffirmed their compliant views. These findings suggest that the search for the personality correlates of response preferences may require that we create very precise definitions of the responses that are presumed to be useful in restoring consistency. Clearly, conformity that does not persist when social pressures are removed is not the same as conformity that does persist. And the two types of conformity have different relationships to personality variables. Perhaps the same can be said about the other responses to inconsistency.

Another possible implication of personality variables is worthy of consideration. Certain kinds of people may be comparatively immune to the postulated aversive impact of inconsistency. Osgood has often expressed the view that inconsistency is the 'hobgoblin of little minds,' implying that 'big minds' can tolerate disconfirmed expectations without undue hardship. Perhaps they can, but we do not know this to be the truth, and we are ill-prepared to specify what it is that permits a person to have a 'big mind.' That most of the work supporting consistency formulations has been done with college students as subjects suggests that intelligence and high level of education are not sufficient guarantees of big-mindedness. Perhaps some of the existing instruments for evaluating tolerance of inconsistency are appropriate for use in a search for the 'immune personality,' but it is the writer's hunch, buttressed by a recently completed study, that clues bearing on this matter may be uncovered in a variety of ways. Steiner and Spaulding (1966) asked college students to rate the pleasantness of sixteen different interpersonal situations, half of which were balanced and half imbalanced. An index of preference for balance was obtained by subtracting the ratings of imbalanced situations from the ratings of the balanced ones. Subjects who scored high on the Christie Mach scale and on tolerance for ambiguity (Budner) showed greater preference for balance than did subjects with low scores on these variables. These two significant relationships contradicted hypotheses based on the hunch that Machiavellian persons emphasize expediency at the expense of consistency,[1] and that a preference for balance implies a general aversion to ambiguity. First-born females showed a lower preference for balance than did later-born females, but males revealed a weak and nonsignificant reversal of this relationship. In a subsequent study that employed only male subjects, Steiner, Anderson, and Lowe (1968) found that strong preference for balance, as measured by the techniques described above, was significantly associated with conformity to the views of a prestigeful accomplice.

Until more is known about the nature of 'consistency needs,' we should remain tolerant of a wide assortment of hypotheses. Probably it will be ultimately concluded that big-mindedness is somewhat specific to classes of situations, and that the personal characteristics that confer immunity to one variant of inconsistency do not do so for all variants. But this conclusion cannot be asserted until the effects of many combinations of situations and personality variables have been examined. After that has been done, we may be in a position to contend that a major reason why some people do not produce expected responses is that they are not distressed by the class of 'inconsistency' we are producing. If this should prove to be the case we may find it somewhat easier to be big-minded about subjects who violate our own expectations concerning consistency-restoring responses.

---

[1] Recent studies suggest that Machiavellians may confront inconsistency-producing situations on a rather subtle basis. Epstein (1966) found that high scorers on the Mach scale changed their opinions more than low scorers when exposed to a persuasive communication, but when Highs were also asked to role-play the opposing side on the same issue, they showed less opinion change than Lows. In similar vein, Geis & Bogart (in Press) found that Highs could more readily be induced to cheat on a test than Lows when justification was high, but could less readily be induced under low justification. High Machs in both cases act so as to avoid getting 'hooked' in sticky situations, but seem willing to play along with any likely response to situations of mild stress or inconsistency. From this point of view, rating balanced situations as pleasant does not seem an especially un-Machiavellian thing to do—Ed.

CHAPTER 63

Comment: Uncooperative Personality Variables

Robert P. Abelson

Theorizing about the relationships between personality factors and inconsistency reduction reactions courts such great difficulties that the temptation toward simplification is nearly irresistible. In the simplest approach of all, it is assumed that a single personality dichotomy serves to divide individuals into two groups with sharply distinct general modes of handling inconsistencies. Since there are many more than two such modes, some sort of grouping is necessary, and the natural categories seem to be those of 'avoidance modes' and 'coping modes.'

With the former, the individual in some fashion wards off or does not recognize the inconsistency, whereas with the latter type, the individual experiences and somehow deals with the inconsistency. This distinction is by no means completely unambiguously applicable to every mode in every situation, but it has great intuitive appeal, and three of our contributors invoke some version of it. Glass lists repression and denial as mechanisms "based on avoidance of ... threatening stimuli," with intellectualization, projection, and rationalization as "based on vigilance for threat." For Miller and Rokeach, inconsistent stimuli may be either "rejected, distorted, ignored, or denied" on the one hand, or "tolerated" on the other. Bieri, while not manifestly dealing with modes of resolution (since for him inconsistency is not something to be 'resolved,' merely processed), nevertheless refers to "dimensional versatility," with simple univalent cognitive structures as one outcome type and multidimensional ambivalent structures as the opposite type.

On the personality side, it is not at all clear which variable deserves the title of *the* variable in the simple dichotomous approach. Glass invests his faith in Byrne's Represser-Sensitizer scale, Miller and Rokeach place emphasis upon Rokeach's Dogmatism Scale and its cousin the F Scale, and Bieri opts in the context of impression formation studies for the variable of cognitive complexity based on Kelly's Role Rep Test.

All these variables have a certain rather unfortunate evaluative aura about them. Thus, it is the simple, dogmatic, repressive person who uses very primitive defenses to avoid inconsistency, whereas the complex, open-minded, sensitive person ingests the inconsistency and deals with it in more mature fashion. Of course I am not suggesting that our contributors are telling us in so many words to solve the conceptual problem by distinguishing the bad guys from the good guys; nor, that if they were, that such a solution would *necessarily* be incorrect. However, special caution is clearly desirable in reviewing the evidence for relationships between value-laden personality traits and value-laden response variables, since the intuitive presumption of a relationship may be so unduly strong as to override considerable negative evidence.

What adds to one's skepticism, further, is the probable naivete of the single-variable approach to the personality area. Social psychology has a penchant for Univariablism in relation to conformity and attitude change processes, but a review of the repeated attempts to define single, key general personality factors does not inspire confidence. The history of the variables of gullibility, hypnotizability, suggestibility, persuasibility, and various other 'ibilities' conveys the lesson that high hopes invested in single-trait explanations rapidly fade when multiple-factor explanations become required empirically. As interest has been transferred in social psychology from conformity to consistency processes, there seems no reason to believe that personality correlates will be more simply structured in the latter area than in the former.

Just how strong is the evidence for related master dichotomies bridging the personality-consistency process gap? One would have to answer, not very strong. The R-S Scale has not yet really been tried, and the scattering of Dogmatism results are each of rather limited magnitude. The evidence quoted by Bieri is not truly germane to the 'master dichotomies' question, since he is concerned only with the circumscribed domain of impression formation.

The totally simplified approach as just described is not really endorsed by any of our contributors. Their own warnings against oversimplification are indeed abundant, especially in the introductory remarks by Glass and in the deliberately cautious approach of Steiner, who does not even try to lump modes of resolution into two major clusters. Still, it is useful to state the oversimplified approach because several reasons for its potential breakdown are instructive.

Among these reasons are the following: no *definition of inconsistency* insures that what for one individual is an inconsistent situation may not for another be quite normal or easily accounted for; but even if every inconsistency were universal, it is quite probable that reactions to inconsistency vary sharply across *types of inconsistency;* thirdly, even if inconsistencies were universal and of only a single type, individuals would very likely differ in responses to different *contents of inconsistency.* I will now discuss each of these difficulties in turn.

The nongenerality of inconsistency across individuals has been well emphasized by Steiner, and would hardly require further comment were it not for one question: do objective definitions of inconsistency provide for individual differences? For balance and congruity theories the answer is affirmative, since there is explicit provision for sentimental or evaluative relations between persons and objects, and these clearly can differ between individuals. For dissonance theory, the answer has not been entirely clear because the meaning of the crucial 'follows from' relation has seemed ambiguous in general, let alone in connection with the possibility of individual differences. As I have tried to make clear in Chapter 5, however, a reasonable operational definition of dissonant relations is possible, a definition which even allows for individual variation. 'What follows from what' can be elicited separately from different individuals, and the structure of these implications is not going to be perfectly identical for nuns, Red Guards, bookies, and nuclear scientists. There are of course ways to minimize individual variation, particularly by using homogeneous subjects and culturally well-understood situations, such as forced compliance for monetary rewards, as experimenters in the dissonance tradition have done. But Steiner's cautions about the nonuniformity of experienced inconsistency for any given situation are nevertheless well taken. Miller and Rokeach make a similar point in discussing the Hunt and Miller study.

To contemplate various patterns of reaction to different types of inconsistency, it is necessary to spell out what types of inconsistency there might be. Several typologies could be imagined, including classification by different theoretical origin: dissonances vs. imbalances vs. illogical syllogisms, etc. The simplest major division we can propose between types of inconsistencies is that between *puzzles* and *stresses*. Several authors throughout this volume have referred to such a distinction in one way or another. (See, for example, Singer's discussion in Chapter 30.) Without attempting to develop this distinction in great detail here, it suffices to say that by a puzzle I mean an inconsistency with no specifically ego-relevant content but with some interest for the individual, while by a stress I mean an inconsistency with important ego consequences. Now it is easy to imagine that different personality types give different combinations of responses to inconsistencies under these two headings. Some individuals may avoid both stresses and puzzles; others may avoid stresses but welcome puzzles; others may cope with both, but in different ways; and so on. This prospect becomes even more tangled when we realize that the puzzles vs. stresses dichotomy is itself an oversimple division of types of inconsistency.

Finally, the contents of an inconsistency (given that it is recognized as such) apart from type, can trigger different modes of response across individuals because different modes may have been differentially learned. Although dissonance and balance theorists rarely if ever refer to the *learning* of modes of response to inconsistency, there is no reason why standard learning principles should not apply to such responses. Thus, in the presence of particular content cues, a cognitive or behavioral response successful in reducing the (presumed) tension state of dissonance or imbalance will be strengthened for later elicitation in the presence of the same cues. Although some individuals may develop habitual styles of response applying uniformly to many contents, others may develop quite a varied repertoire. Consider the person who rationalizes all bad information about his brother while denying all bad information about his sister, or the person who, after choosing between two vacation spots, primarily enhances the attractiveness of the chosen one, but after choosing between jobs primarily denigrates the unchosen one. There may be satisfactorily reconstructable psychological processes explaining these patterns (e.g., learning histories), but their existence is certain to confound the over-optimistic believer in simple personality-inconsistency relationships.

The straw horse of naivete having been duly flogged, what then is to be done in this area? Surely one would not wish to recommend abandonment of all attempts to relate personality variables to modes of inconsistency reduction, but what then? Apparently there is one reasonable, albeit effortful alternative. It is the course of research action most single-mindedly expressed by Bieri, though our other contributors express it also: to narrow one's focus to a very restricted (though hopefully interesting) experimental task, and to concentrate on aspects of personality appropriate to that task. As Glass says, "It is absolutely essential ... that we try to isolate the personality constructs which seem coordinate with the particular cognitions involved in the inconsistency."

Bieri's primary task involves impression formation in relation to the personality variable of cognitive complexity. That this focus is quite narrow can be appreciated by listing absent features. The task is a puzzle, not a stress, and at that a very special kind of puzzle: the (usually inconsistent) information is about a person, not a group, nor a policy, nor a thing, nor a vacation in Afghanistan. Furthermore, cognitive complexity is typically measured by Bieri in a very particular way concerned with the heterogeneity of spontaneous trait descriptions of familiar people. There are many other ways to measure something that might be called 'cognitive complexity,' and a factor analysis by Vannoy (1965) of some 20 measures has shown that Bieri's measure forms a separate factor with his impression formation task, accounting for less than four per cent of the total variance of the ensemble of cognitive complexity tests.

In spite of this narrowness, however, it seems of interest in its own right to analyze the ways in which individuals deal with trait descriptions. Similarly, it would be worthwhile to explore personality variations in response to other pivotal situations, especially the major dissonance and imbalance paradigms, without any illusion that the personality variables involved need necessarily have wide generality. It is toward these limited goals that all our contributors appear to be painfully progressing.

C. MODES OF RESOLUTION

In this section we continue exploration of the problems raised in the last set of chapters. Many situational factors are proposed here as partial determinants of the mode of resolution of inconsistencies, without necessarily implying that personality-based explanations should be abandoned.

Stacy Adams sets an eclectic tone at the outset with a systematic listing of the many points of entry into the processing of inconsistency. Then three broad analyses of the mode problem are presented, each with a somewhat different basis for classifying the various modes. Bernard Kaplan and Walter Crockett apply the developmentalist's point of view, and then Herbert Kelman and Reuben Baron the functionalist's. Thirdly, Jane Allyn Hardyck and Marcelle Kardush develop an *ad hoc* classification of modes which enables them to organize a wide array of hypotheses about inconsistency resolution. For them, the crucial intervening variable is the importance of the cognitive elements involved in the inconsistency.

Next follow three specialized presentations addressing issues other than the classification of modes. Marc Pilisuk discusses the consequences of inconsistency in terms of the personality layers upon which the dilemma encroaches. The two final chapters of the section treat particular laboratory paradigms with which inconsistency resolution is often studied: Walter Weiss the persuasive communication situation, and Karl Weick the class of experiments which employ insufficient rewards in order to elicit novel justifications or rationalizations for task performance.

In the editorial summary chapter the attempt is made to gather together the mode-of-resolution hypotheses appearing most often in various guises throughout the seven assorted chapters.

CHAPTER 64

A Framework for the Study of Modes of Resolving Inconsistency

J. Stacy Adams
University of North Carolina

Addressing the question of what are the determinants of different modes of resolving inconsistency requires a theoretical and operational framework, and one that will be general enough to accommodate the several theories of inconsistency. This chapter suggests such a framework and is therefore, in a sense, prefatory to the rest of the Section more directly concerned with providing answers to the question.

When a subject adopts one or more of several possible modes of resolving an experienced inconsistency—assuming for the moment that he experiences, not necessarily with awareness, the inconsistency and that he responds so as to resolve it—his behavior is terminal. It is the end link in a hypothetical chain, of which the first link is a theory of inconsistency and of which some intermediate links have the status of intervening variables or of hypothetical constructs. A specification of the links and of their interconnections is useful in the study of modes of resolving inconsistency and, indeed, provides a general, heuristic framework for such study. In the paragraphs that follow, the general framework will be outlined first. Issues relating to modes of inconsistency resolution will then be discussed in relation to the framework.

All theories of inconsistency are sufficiently well articulated to permit a statement of what experimental operations should be productive of a given level of psychological inconsistency, at least on an ordinal scale. This relationship between theory and operational statements of the theory is suggested by the arrow linking the top two boxes in the accompanying figure. The several theories of inconsistency point with varying specificity to the ways in which inconsistency may be resolved. Congruity theory (Osgood & Tannenbaum, 1955), for example, specifies changes in attitude and meaning and is quite precise as regards the direction and magnitude of predicted changes. The theory of cognitive dissonance (Festinger, 1957; Brehm & Cohen, 1962) suggests a broad range of modes of resolution but fails to contain theoretical propositions that permit prediction of which modes will be adopted. Generally, predictions about modes of resolution are based on considerations external to dissonance theory proper. They may rely, for example, on experimental manipulations that are believed to restrict

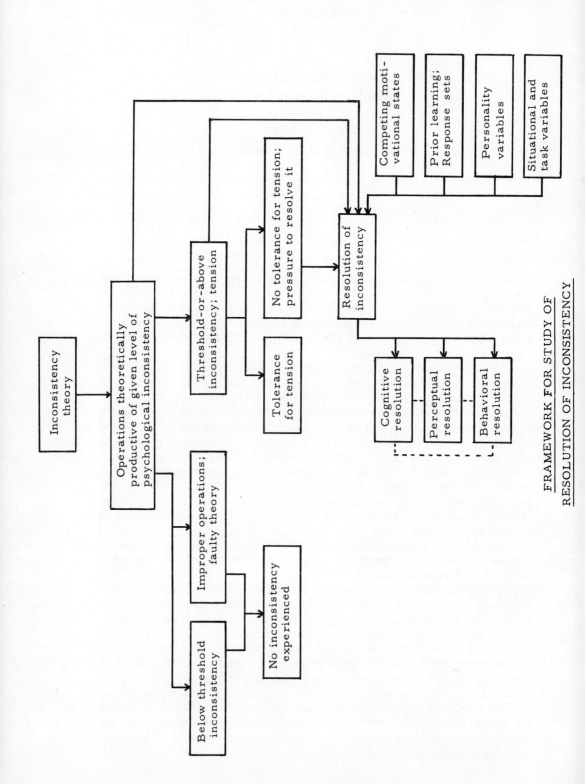

FRAMEWORK FOR STUDY OF
RESOLUTION OF INCONSISTENCY

or to facilitate the adoption of one or more modes; or they may rely on the fine intuition or skill of the experimenter. Whatever the theory, however, once it has been operationalized and an experiment has been designed, *some* form of inconsistency resolution is predicted, though the specific character of the resolution may not always stem from the theory as much as from particular experimental procedures.

Given an operational statement of a theory and a coordinate experimental design and procedures, inconsistency may or may not be experienced[1] by a subject. Inconsistency may fail of realization for two reasons: First, the inconsistency may be of such a small order that it is below the subject's threshold for experiencing it.[2] This is basically a question of individual differences in discrimination. A given level of *manipulated* inconsistency may or may not be discriminated. It should be noted that there is a conceptual difference between the threshold for inconsistency and tolerance for tension produced by inconsistency, though it is probably difficult to differentiate the two operationally without relying on self-reports. Secondly, inconsistency may not be experienced either because the theory per se is faulty, because the operations derived from it are in some manner inadequate or inappropriate, or because the posited inconsistency does not constitute an inconsistency for a particular subject—for example, earning as much as a better qualified worker is not necessarily psychologically inconsistent for every subject, though it may be for most.

If both theory and operations are correct and if the inconsistency attains threshold level for a given subject, inconsistency will be experienced and, according to the several theories, an attendant state of tension will result. A state of tension does not, however, necessarily lead to the arousal of tension-reducing processes, that is, resolution of the inconsistency, though that is explicit or implicit in most theories. It appears meaningful and useful to assume that a subject may tolerate some tension,[3] that there are individual differences in the amount tolerated, and that the maximum amount tolerated assumes a specifiable distribution over a population of subjects. If, then, inconsistency attains a threshold level and the resulting tension is within the limits of tolerance, no pressure or drive to reduce the tension by resolving the inconsistency would be predicted. Conversely, tension beyond the limits of tolerance would motivate inconsistency-resolving behavior.

The assumptions that there is a threshold for experiencing inconsistency which has some population distribution and that, among those who ex-

---

[1] As used here the term 'experience' does not denote, as it does in ordinary usage, awareness.

[2] The threshold value may vary over time. It is also likely to vary as a function of the nature or content importance of the inconsistency. An individual may be more sensitive or more alert to inconsistencies of one kind than another; he may have greater ability to discriminate inconsistencies of one sort than another.

[3] Tolerance level for inconsistency-produced tension may fluctuate over time, partly as a function of the presence or absence of other tensions, if there is a summative tension effect. There is clearly the possibility, however, that the presence of other tensions may increase as well as decrease tolerance for inconsistency-produced tension, for, on the assumption that there is a drive to reduce all tensions attaining a certain magnitude (allowing for recent findings on "complexity" theory, cf. Berlyne, 1965), it may be assumed further that not all may be reduced simultaneously and that there exists an order of priority, demand, or preference for reducing different tensions, provided individuals can discriminate the sources of tensions.

perience inconsistency, there are varying levels of tolerance for the resulting tension force explicit consideration of psychological processes that intervene between experimental operations and terminal, presumably inconsistency-resolving, behavior. And they point up the need for considering individual differences that tend to be overlooked in experiments that focus on between-group differences, despite the fact that inconsistency theories, though usually considered in the province of social psychology, fundamentally make statements about *individual* psychological processes, not group processes.

Resolution of inconsistency has been classified here into three broad categories, cognitive, perceptual, and behavioral. They are interconnected by dotted lines in the Figure to suggest that multiple modes of resolution may be adopted and to suggest, in addition, as Festinger (1963) and Weick (1964) have, that cognitive and perceptual resolutions are probably accompanied or followed by supporting behavioral resolution. Weick (1964), for example, has found support for the assumption that a behavioral mode of dissonance reduction (increased effort on a task) 'validated' a cognitive mode (task evaluation).

Having described a framework for the study of modes of resolving inconsistency, what can be stated about the determinants of modes of resolution? At the most general level, it may be stated that modes of resolution will be affected by variables and events that are intrinsic to the process modeled by the framework and by others that are extrinsic to it. This is reflected in the Figure. Beginning with determinants that are intrinsic to the process, it may be said first that the particular operations chosen to produce inconsistency may largely or in part influence the modes of resolution. Obviously, an experiment in which, for example, a person is confronted with a persuasive communication at variance with his personal opinion limits the modes of inconsistency resolution that may be used, assuming that inconsistency was experienced. The same would apply in an experiment in which a person was made to believe that a close friend reacted oppositely to a third person. And it would apply to a variety of experiments having dissonance theory as a source. Such restraints on possible modes of inconsistency resolution stem from the focal interest of the experiment. Other operational restraints result from tactical procedural choices made by the experimenter. An experimenter intent upon maximizing the opportunity to demonstrate the effects of the arousal of inconsistency upon attitude change may block off or severely limit the operation of all modes of resolving inconsistency, except attitude change. He may, for example, block off discreditation of the communicator as a mode of resolution by imputing high prestige, trustworthiness and expertise to the communicator. Quite different tactical procedures may give all modes of resolving inconsistency full freedom to operate; thus, they impose no restraints in the sense used above. They may, however, limit the ability of the experimenter to measure reliably the incidence of the use of various modes of resolution, particularly when the inconsistency-produced tensions are of small magnitude.

The magnitude of tension produced by inconsistency influences the choice of mode of resolving inconsistency. Working in the context of dissonance theory, Aronson, Turner, and Carlsmith (1963), for example, have shown that in exposures to a mildly credible communicator the probability of derogating the communicator increased and that of changing attitude decreased as the extent of discrepancy between subject and communicator increased, extent of discrepancy presumably being positively correlated with tension. In the realm of congruity theory, Osgood and Tannenbaum (1955) have postulated a credulity factor to account for the fact that people resist attitude change if there is a large discrepancy between their evaluations of attitude object and source. In effect, then, they hypothesize different modes of resolving inconsistency as tension increases. Steiner and Johnson (1964) have reported that different modes of reducing dissonance may sometimes combine additively, thus permitting greater dissonance reduction than when one mode is used. From this it might be hypothesized more generally that as tension increases the probability of adopting more than one mode of inconsistency resolution will increase. It might be further hypothesized that as tension increases behavioral modes of resolution will be increasingly required to support cognitive modes of resolution, for cognitive changes in response to large inconsistencies should be particularly unstable.

Variables that affect modes of resolution and are extrinsic to the inconsistency process described earlier have been arbitrarily classified into four groups, as shown in the lower right of the figure. They are: competing motivational states, prior learning and response sets, personality variables, and situational and task variables. At any time a person experiences inconsistency and its attendant tension, he may also be subject to tensions of different origin. The latter may be so dominant as to require prior reduction, but, aside from dominance, they may compete for responses that would be appropriate for resolving inconsistency. A simple illustration is provided in an experiment by Adams and Jacobsen (1964), in which some subjects were induced to believe that the piecework wage rate they would earn would result in their being inequitably overpaid. These subjects were predicted to reduce the inequity (the inconsistency) by producing fewer work units of higher quality than control subjects who were paid the same piecework rate but were induced to believe the rate was equitable. Most subjects behaved as predicted; one or two, however, produced large quantities of units of relatively low quality. The latter, it was found, were economically deprived and 'needed the money badly' and behaved accordingly, though they recognized the inequity of their wage rate. In sum, it appeared that economic motivation was dominant and that it required a form of response that was antagonistic to resolving the wage-rate-produced inconsistency. The question of competing motivations has been discussed in a somewhat different, but nevertheless relevant, context by Aronson (1966c), who focuses on the controversy aroused by the Festinger and Carlsmith (1959) forced compliance experiment. In that experiment, it will be recalled, subjects evaluated a very boring task more highly if given little justification than if given much justification. Seemingly contradictory findings have occurred which may be explained by an incentive theory (Janis & Gilmore, 1965; Rosenberg, 1965d). Though his argument is long and complex, Aronson (1966c) states in effect that the contradictory results may be explained by the fact that in a forced compliance situation of the Festinger-Carlsmith type two motivations are present, the motivation produced by the monetary incentives and that resulting from dissonance. If the magnitude of dissonance is small, due to low commitment, for example, the motivation due to the incentives will be dominant, and, as a consequence, the task offering greater justification will be rated more highly. In essence, then, Aronson is stating that the relative strengths of different motivations influence the relative availability of modes of resolving inconsistency.

When suggesting that prior learning and response sets influence modes of resolving inconsistency, it is meant that individuals have experienced inconsistencies of various kinds on many occasions in the past and that, in the process, they have learned effective ways of resolving them. As a result, they may have acquired preferred modes of resolution and, indeed, a preference hierarchy of modes. There is no evidence bearing directly on preferred modes of resolution, but the fact that persons vary in persuasibility when confronted by persuasive communications (Hovland & Janis, 1959) suggests stable response patterns to at least one class of inconsistency situations. If such stable response patterns exist, they may be classifiable under personality variables that influence modes of resolution. In the realm of personality, Pilisuk (1962) has suggested and found support for the idea that inconsistencies between an aspect of the self and an external event will be resolved in part as a function of the extent to which the aspect of self is central and highly valent. More generally, he has stated that "where alternatives to change in central attitudes are possible, they will be selected" (p. 102; see also Chapter 68).

Situational and task variables that may influence the adoption of modes of resolution are many. A few examples will serve to illustrate the operation of this class of variables. In the aforementioned study by Pilisuk the fact that the critical experimental partner was a stranger or a close friend determined whether inconsistency was resolved by rejection or rationalization. High communicator credibility will result in more attitude change and less derogation than low credibility (Aronson, Turner, & Carlsmith, 1963). Aggression toward an attractive person will lead to attitude change toward aggression, whereas aggression toward a person who is not strongly liked will result in attitude change toward the victim (Glass & Wood, 1968). Workers overpaid on an hourly basis reduce inconsistency by increasing their productivity, whereas men overpaid on a piecework basis reduce inconsistency by improving the quality of their work (Adams & Rosenbaum, 1962; Adams & Jacobsen, 1964).

The framework offered for the study of the determinants of modes of resolving inconsistency points up the need to consider a complete process from arousal of inconsistency to its resolution, through a series of intervening phases, together with consideration of variables extrinsic to the process that may influence modes of resolution. The framework, in addition, implies a need to develop measures of inconsistency thresholds, tolerance for inconsistency and tension. The development of such measures would be a substantial contribution to the growth and testing of inconsistency theories.

CHAPTER 65

Developmental Analysis of Modes of Resolution

Bernard Kaplan and Walter H. Crockett

Clark University

I

If one examines the usages of the term "development" and its derivatives in the various areas of inquiry in which those terms have been employed (cf. Harris, 1957), one becomes aware that the same word is taken, even by a single investigator, to represent quite different conceptions. In some contexts, 'development' is merely a synonym for changes in some entity or 'organism'[1] over time: irrespective of the nature of these changes, an entity is said to have undergone development if it reveals some modification relative to an earlier state. In other instances, where it is presumed that the entity in question follows a natural course toward a certain end-state, development is taken to occur whenever a change in the entity brings it closer to that end-state. In still other cases, development is predicated of an organism only insofar as there is a qualitative change in the 'structure' governing its functions or activities: here, only certain changes over time are regarded as developmental ones, while other changes (e.g., increase in size) are taken as nondevelopmental. Finally, there are instances in which development is said to take place only when the structural changes are assumed to promote certain qualities in the functioning of the organism that are regarded as approximating some ideal of organization (e.g., maximum differentiation or internal division of labor among the constituents, increased flexibility and stability of the entity under markedly changed circumstances, greater autonomy, and so on).

As has been discussed elsewhere (Kaplan, 1966, 1967) it is this last concept of development—somewhat alien to the American psychological tradition—that is manifested, in varying degrees of fullness and explicitness, in the writings of Freud, Anna Freud, Piaget, Wallon, and Werner, among others. Essentially, this concept of development utilizes organizational rather

---

A part of the research that is reported in this paper was supported by Grant MH-12370-01 from the National Institute of Mental Health.

[1] The term 'organism' as used here refers to any system or subsystem considered as a unity of parts, and thus applies to societies, institutions, groups, etc., as well as to so-called real individuals (see Pepper, 1942; F. H. Allport, 1961).

than temporal criteria to assess the developmental status of an entity. It is an easy step from this viewpoint to apply developmental analysis to entities that are historical contemporaries or of the same chronological age, thus methodologically freeing the concept of development from the concept of time (Kaplan, 1964). In other words, characteristic "ways of doing things" (Mair, 1962, p. 8) determine whether an organism is developmentally more 'primitive' or 'advanced,' irrespective of *when* these modes of operation are brought into play (Werner & Kaplan, 1956). It should be clear that when 'development' is thus conceptualized as an ideal ordered sequence of modes of functioning, developmental analysis can be applied not only to changes over time (e.g., ontogenesis, history), but also to the performances of different organisms of the same age or the 'same' organism in different states or under different conditions.

II

Like the term 'development,' the phrase 'cognitive consistency' is open to multiple interpretations. For some, consistency is linked to notions of rationality or logical cotenability (cf. Schick, 1963): one's belief system reveals consistency only to the degree that the various statements to which one subscribes are cotenable. For others, cognitive consistency seems to be independent of considerations of rationality: one may experience 'inconsistency' between beliefs that are, from the logical point of view, fully compatible, or 'consistency' between beliefs that are logically incompatible. A strain toward 'cognitive consistency,' from this perspective, would simply be a movement toward the reduction of psychological tension or disequilibrium. For still others, cognitive consistency appears to occupy some middle ground between rationality and subjective equilibrium: the individual is credited with some tendency to bring his system of beliefs into a coherent order, but he may well conclude that he has attained coherence and logical cotenability when this is not the case objectively.

III

If one takes 'cognitive consistency' in either the second or third of the above-mentioned senses, then it is clear that the problem of such consistency is not a new one to developmental psychologists. Thus, it may be argued that the psychoanalysts, as one group of developmental psychologists (cf. Rapaport, 1960), have, almost from the outset, concerned themselves with the variety of means ('mechanisms of defense') by which human beings reconcile imperative desires and internalized attitudes incompatible with the realization of such desires. To be sure, psychoanalysts have generally concentrated on the vicissitudes of various mechanisms of defense in the histories of particular individuals. On occasion, however, there have been attempts to delineate some gross sequence in the emergence of the various mechanisms in the course of normal ontogenesis (cf. Anna Freud, 1946); and one can envision the possibility of considering the diverse modes of dealing with conflict in terms of some standard of 'adaption to reality,' ordering them accordingly, and thus arriving at a time-free 'developmental sequence,' in which certain modes of resolving conflict are more advanced than others.

From a somewhat different angle, the work of Piaget and his associates (see Flavell, 1963) may be construed as showing how an absence of conflict among experiences at one period in ontogenesis is felt as conflict or 'inconsistency' at later periods, these inconsistencies being resolved or reconciled through the introduction of new systems of rules for the organization of reality. For example, a young child may find no incongruity in the fact that a certain quantity of water poured from a narrow, tall glass into a wide, short glass is now 'less' (or 'more') than before. Later, however, he recognizes some incompatibility between his sense of the constancy of the quantity and his perception of change, and subsequently reconciles the 'incongruity.' Here again, it may be pointed out, one can disentangle the different systems of rules for the organization of experience from their manifestations in different periods of ontogenesis, and order these systems of rules in an atemporal 'developmental sequence,' in which certain systems of functioning are more advanced than others solely on the basis of organizational criteria.

Finally, it may be noted that Werner (1961, pp. 17–19), in disengaging the concept of levels of functioning from actual history or ontogenesis, has implicitly distinguished and ordered such levels or systems in terms of the cognitive means that are employed to bring order and coherence into one's world. Thus, generally speaking, a primitive level of functioning, relative to an advanced one, homogenizes or fuses diversity—does not differentiate contents—or segregates contents (isolation) without any hierarchic integration. In other words, an organism operating at a primitive level of functioning will achieve 'consistency' in a qualitatively different manner than an organism (perhaps the same one) operating at a more advanced level of functioning.

IV

Although it should be clear from the preceding discussion that the problem of cognitive consistency, in a broad sense, is not a new one for developmental psychologists, it must be acknowledged that, except for the psychoanalysts, there has been relatively little attention directed to the elucidation of the genesis of cognitive consistency with respect to social objects; and, as noted above, even the psychoanalysts have rarely focused on the problem of ordering the different ways of attaining cognitive consistency, irrespective of the time of occurrence of such modes in the careers of individual persons. True, there is the early work of Piaget (1932) and the later work of Kohlberg (1963) on the ontogenesis of the resolution of moral conflicts. Again there is the work done under Brunswik's direction (1959) relating the modes of resolution of incongruity in children to those found in adults under 'microgenetic' conditions and to those found in earlier periods of culture history. In the main, however, there is a dearth of research on the *ways* in which children of different ages or adults of the same age but of different mental status go about recognizing and reconciling discrepant attitudes or discrepant information about social objects.

We have neither the space nor temerity to attempt here a detailed a priori analysis of the development of cognitive consistency.[2] On the other

---

[2] The general lines of such an analysis are, however, indicated below. This analysis is "a priori" in the sense that it orders the various ways of attaining 'consistency' irrespective of who it is that manifests such ways. Certain ways are thus taken as primitive or advanced in terms of organizational rather than temporal criteria.

hand, the sparseness of empirical evidence precludes any inductive generalizations concerning a fixed sequence of modes of resolving inconsistency as a function of age. In this light, it seems to us the better part of valor to focus on one study, still in progress, pertaining to the reconciliation of incongruous information about a person. Our discussion of this study will serve to illustrate the nature of a developmental approach to cognitive consistency not only with respect to subjects of different ages but also with regard to subjects of the same age who, on independent grounds, are distinguishable in their characteristic modes of cognitive functioning. In the process of presenting this study, we shall introduce, where relevant, material from other sources, hoping thus to suggest that several lines of thought and inquiry indicate the burgeoning of a new area of *developmental social psychology*, in which structure and organization are central categories.

v

In this study (Crockett, Gonyea, & Leichtman, in preparation), the main experimental procedure employed was the following: a subject is given eight short descriptions of a person ("John G."), each description being attributed to a distinct individual who is understood to have known that person well. In these descriptions, each one paragraph in length, the person is described variously as "loyal to his friends," "responsible," "generous," "fair," "inconsiderate," "sarcastic," "unenthusiastic," or "stubborn." The subject is given ample time to read and digest each of these characterizations. He is then asked to arrive at an impression of the person, and to communicate this impression in writing to someone else. It will be recognized that this procedure is quite similar to one introduced by Asch more than 20 years ago (1946), and often used since. However, in contrast to the usual concern, in many studies using this kind of technique, with final outcome or achievement measures, the principal interest here is with the *ways* in which the subject's written description deals with the incongruity or inconsistency in these diverse characterizations of a person.

This concern with the *modes* of resolving incongruity rather than with the mere *attainment* of congruity, balance, or consistency (see Werner, 1937) leads one to the recognition that the various attempts at resolution are not all of one piece. But beyond this recognition of qualitative differences in mode of resolution, a developmental orientation prompts one to attempt an ordering of the various modes of resolution in a rational sequence, the more primitive modes reflecting a lesser differentiation and hierarchic integration than the more advanced modes.

The attempt made below to provide such a rational sequence of modes of conflict resolution is not without precursors. For example, Gollin (1954) presented college-age adults with five film shots in which a particular girl was shown alternately engaged in a socially condemned, socially admired, or socially neutral activity (e.g., soliciting as a prostitute, helping an older person on subway steps). The task of the subjects was to form an impression of the girl on the basis of the information presented in the various shots. Using a Wernerian framework, Gollin subjected the students written impressions to a developmental analysis, distinguishing three modes of resolving incongruity. In the most primitive mode ("univalent"), subjects appeared to blind themselves either to the positive or negative material, assimilating all the information to one global-affective impression; one might speak here of a lack of differentiation of parts within a whole. In the intermediate mode ("aggregation"), the 'positive' and 'negative' aspects were differentiated, but no constructs were introduced to bring them into a coherent system. In the advanced mode ("integration"), the information was not only differentiated but, in addition, there was a transcendence of the information presented through the introduction of hypothetical motives or circumstances that would make the varied behaviors more "consistent" with each other. In a subsequent study, using an appropriately modified but essentially similar kind of presentation for children of various ages, Gollin (1958) demonstrated that univalent modes of resolution characterized the impressions of the younger children (10:7), while integrated modes were manifested more often by the older children (16:6).

Another attempt at what might be considered a developmental analysis —although not explicitly advanced as such—is that by Abelson (1959). On the basis of purely theoretical considerations, Abelson delineated four 'mechanisms' for resolving belief dilemmas: *denial, bolstering, differentiation,* and *transcendence.* In *denial,* one or another set of attributes is not considered in the resolution; in *bolstering,* new elements on the same level as the original attributes are introduced ad hoc to support one or another side of the ambivalent information; in *differentiation,* one element, hitherto taken as homogeneous, is differentiated into several elements with distinct meaning; finally, in *transcendence,* higher-level constructs are introduced which provide an account of the more manifest imbalanced traits. Abelson himself notes that these mechanisms can be ordered into a 'hierarchy' of resolution attempts: denial and bolstering are more primitive, while differentiation and transcendence are more advanced means.

Acute and informative as these analyses may be, they were not carried far enough to suit our purposes. Thus, Gollin, although utilizing a developmental framework, did not feel called upon, in the context of his inquiries, to distinguish the different modes of organizing activity that we have found it necessary to delineate. On the other side, Abelson, operating within a different theoretical framework, did not proceed to relate all of his 'mechanisms' to one or another of those two fundamental operations, *differentiation* and *integration* that we, as developmentalists, take as ingredient in all modes and at all levels of organizational activity.

Back, therefore, to the previously mentioned situation and our analysis of modes of resolving incongruity. Recall the task of a subject: on the basis of eight independent and at least moderately incompatible assessments of a particular person, each subject was asked to form and communicate an impression of that person to another, who, like the subject, had no acquaintance with that individual. It will be seen that the situation here is a special case of one in which the 'end' is that of forming a judgment about a social object, and in which there are various means or routes to the end, without any one necessarily insuring a greater 'correctness' or 'veridicality' than the others. An analysis and genetic ordering of these means must, therefore, ignore the secondary, and here nonadjudicable, issue of veridicality or correctness, and concern itself with the ways in which subjects organize information to arrive at a judgment—the ways in which they differentiate, weight, and integrate the diverse factors pertinent to the formation of such a judgment.

A little reflection suggests that there are at least six factors that one might consider in forming an impression of the personality of another on the basis of various properties ascribed to him (predicates asserted of him). Two of these pertain primarily to the *source* of the characterizations; two pertain primarily to the *language* (trait-names) used in the characterizations; and two pertain primarily to the *person being characterized*. Thus, with regard to source, one might consider (a) the *number of sources* responsible for the characterizations, and (b) the factor of *perspectival selectivity* in any characterization of one individual by another, that is, a possible one-sidedness due to the nature of the source and the limited relationships between the source and the one being described. With regard to the language used in characterizing the person, one may take into account (a) the *congruity (or incongruity) of the ascribed traits*, and (b) the factor of *linguistic indeterminacy of trait-names*, that is, the indefiniteness as to contexts and meanings intended by such words. Finally, with regard to anyone who is an object of a characterization or personality-impression, one might consider (a) the factor of *contextual variation* in an individual's normal behavior, that is, the likelihood that a person will behave differently at different times, in different situations and with respect to different individuals; and (b) the factor of *personality stratification*, that is, the dependence of manifest behaviors of an individual in different circumstances upon nonmanifest, 'deeper-lying' dispositions which may provide a coherent account of 'surface' diversity.

It will be recognized that two of these 'factors' are, so to speak, given to the subject in our experimental situation: he is told that the various characterizations come from different sources, eight distinct individuals who knew "John" well; and it seems prima facie clear that there is some incompatibility among the traits ascribed to "John" by these different sources. A subject may or may not exploit this information in forming his judgment. The other factors are not 'given' in the experimental situation, and if a subject is to make use of them in forming his impression, he must 'go beyond the information given' and conjure them up from his knowledge about people and his understanding of how language is used. The following provisional delineation of modes of dealing with incongruity is based on whether, and how, a subject utilizes the factors alluded to above. The modes are presented under three headings: primitive, intermediate, and advanced.

Primitive Modes of Resolution

The more primitive modes of resolution are characterized by an exclusive concern with a single, 'given,' factor, namely, the various attributes that are asserted of the person. There is no consideration of the multiplicity of sources and hence, in effect, there is a dedifferentiation or globalization of the sources. *A fortiori*, there is no consideration of the possibility of perspectival selectivity. Nor is there any utilization of other nonmanifest factors that might play a role. Three modes of resolution may be grouped here.

1. *Simple aggregation.* The impression is formed solely through the juxtaposition of the traits that are attributed to the person. There is no explicit recognition of incompatibility and hence no appeal to any factor to resolve incompatibility of traits.

2. *Simple univalence.* The impression is formed solely on the basis of traits possessing a certain affective tone, the traits of opposing affective tonality being ignored. There is no ground given for this 'denial' of a portion of the information. In such instances, the person is typically characterized in evaluative rather than descriptive or 'explanatory' terms, e.g., "he's a wonderful person," "he's a louse."

3. *Rejection of task.* Here, the subject recognizes trait-incompatibility, but exaggerates incompatibility into contrariety. The hyperdifferentiation leads to a segregation of the traits into two irreconcilable camps. No attempt at resolution is made via an appeal to the factor of sources or to any of the other factors that might be brought into play. A typical response falling under this mode is the following: "I cannot report an impression of this person because I am asked to believe that he is both generous and inconsiderate, fair, and sarcastic."

Intermediate Modes of Resolution

The intermediate modes of resolution are characterized by a 'going beyond the information given,' an appeal to one other factor to resolve the manifest incompatibility of traits. Typically, at this level, the appeal has an ad hoc flavor and does not serve to account specifically for the traits attributed to the person. Four modes of resolution may be grouped under this heading.

1. *Univalence through linguistic reinterpretation.* Here the subject recognizes the prima facie incompatibility of the characterizations, but eliminates the incompatibility by making use of the factor of *linguistic indeterminacy*. Thus terms which are normally applied to express a positive evaluation or to suggest some positive action on the part of an individual are reinterpreted to suggest something negative and vice versa. For example, the trait of 'responsibility' may be construed by one bent on a negative impression to mean an 'overly great concern with picayune detail.' Although the outcome here, as in simple univalence, is a one-sided impression which, in effect, 'denies' some of the traits and 'bolsters' a primary affective impression, there is at least an initial recognition of an 'apparent' incompatibility before the subject assimilates one part of the information to the dominant part of the whole.

2. *Resolution through grossly differentiated sources.* Here the subject accounts for the different and incompatible traits attributed to the person on the basis of a split in the *sources*. For example, the sources are arbitrarily divided into those who know the person well and those who do not know him well, or those who 'really know' him and those who are jealous of him. The upshot is again univalent, one set or the other of the traits 'rejected' arbitrarily because of the unreliability or prejudice of the sources. For example, one subject remarked: "Those who really know John see his good points; special pleaders and those who are jealous of him report negatively."

3. *Resolution via pseudo-explanatory personality trait.* Here again, there is a recognition of trait-incompatibility, positive and negative traits being segregated into two camps. The subject, however, does not openly reject the task but accounts for the incompatibility-become-contrariety in terms of some 'split' within the person. The invocation of this factor is, in effect, simply a recognition of the incompatibility of the traits, but it is introduced as if it accounts for that incompatibility. Moreover, the 'dis-

position' invoked does not even indicate a recognition of the specific traits, and could be brought in to account for any discrepancy in characterizations. In one sense, what is involved here is a more advanced, attenuated, form of 'rejection of the task,' since the subject does not really arrive at a resolution of the incompatibility of the traits. As an illustration, one subject remarked: "John has a split personality."

4. *Resolution via contextual variability.* Here, there is a recognition that the incompatible characterizations may have come about because a person behaves differently in different contexts. No attempt is made, however, to give an account of this variability in terms of some 'deeper lying' factor. The statement of variability is taken as sufficient, the unity of the person being, at best, implicit. It will be recognized that, in one sense, we have here a more advanced form of aggregation. It will also be recognized, perhaps, that this mode of resolution is a transitional form to more advanced modes, since there is the implicit invocation of such factors as *linguistic indeterminacy* and *perspectival selectivity*—the contexts of the application of a term being specified and the specific characterizations being attributed to different sources, each of whom sees the person in only some of his aspects.

Advanced Modes of Resolution

In the more advanced modes of resolution, explicit consideration is given to a multiplicity of factors other than those directly given. Thus the subject explicitly brings into play the contextual variability of behavior, the perspectival selectivity of sources, deeper lying personality factors to account for the variability with respect to the sources, etc. Moreover, these factors are not simply brought in side by side, but are considered with respect to each other, so that the sources and contexts likely to evoke the behavior eliciting a particular characterization are more highly articulated than in less advanced modes. This general description should suffice. No further breakdown need be given here.

The ordered set of categories just presented—as provisional as it is— is meant to demonstrate the character of a developmental analysis of modes of achieving consistency. Although the construction of the categories may be informed by a consideration of actual modes of dealing with inconsistency, it is, in a sense, logically independent of such empirical considerations. It can thus be disentangled from the particular individuals who use the modes, the particular conditions under which the various modes are used by different people, or perhaps, the same person at different times, and so on. Once abstracted from such considerations, the utilization of different modes of resolution of inconsistency may be examined with respect to a host of empirical variables. For example, on the assumption that the course of cognitive change in ontogenesis is developmental in nature, one would expect that the order of emergence of modes in ontogenesis would follow the order of modes articulated in our 'a priori' developmental analysis. Again, one might consider on other grounds, that cognitive structures in some adults are more 'primitive'—diffusely and syncretically organized (cf. Werner, 1961)—than in other adults, and expect that the former would reveal more primitive modes of resolution than the latter. Thus, with complexity of the interpersonal constructs an individual uses to describe his associates taken as an index of advanced mental status, it has been shown that there is a positive correlation between this index and mode of impression formation (Crockett, 1965; Rosenkrantz & Crockett, 1965). Even more complex relationships may be examined. For example, there is some indication that the 'advantages' of cognitive complexity with regard to mode of impression-formation wash out when the traits attributed to another person are incongruent with the central values of the subject (Meltzer, Crockett, & Rosenkrantz, 1966)—a phenomenon that can be attested to by listening to a discussion in a faculty lounge concerning political personalities.

We have focused in this paper on the problem of cognitive consistency with regard to the special area of person perception; let it be clear, however, that we believe that developmental analyses of the kind we have presented are appropriate and useful in all areas of social cognition. As attention shifts in social psychology from a concern with achievement to a focus on the processes that underlie various achievements (Werner, 1937), we look forward to an advanced mode of integration between the now too often segregated domains of social and developmental psychology.

CHAPTER 66

Determinants of Modes of Resolving Inconsistency Dilemmas: A Functional Analysis

Herbert C. Kelman

The University of Michigan

and

Reuben M. Baron

Wayne State University

In this chapter, we attempt a systematic categorization of different modes of handling inconsistency, in terms of our functional analysis (see Chapter 22); and we put forth some hypotheses about the conditions under which these different modes are likely to be utilized.

MODES OF HANDLING INCONSISTENCY

The Table presents a list (by no means exhaustive) of modes of handling inconsistency, classified in terms of two dichotomies: (a) the nature of the process used in handling the inconsistency—whether it is primarily one of avoiding the inconsistency and its implications, or one of actively confronting it; and (b) the nature of the outcome achieved—whether the inconsistency is handled in a way that leads to its reduction, or in a way that leads to its maintenance. We have previously indicated (Chapter 22) that inconsistency-maintenance modes, as well as inconsistency-reduction modes, represent reactions to inconsistencies that are perceived to have functional significance. The Table does not include those cases in which an inconsistency is seen—upon closer examination—as irrelevant to goal achievement, and is therefore ignored.

Inconsistency-reduction modes. The first row of the Table lists those reactions that involve a refusal on the part of the individual to accept or tolerate the inconsistency with which he has been presented. He handles the inconsistency, essentially, by eliminating it—by removing or changing one of the incompatible elements in such a way that the different elements are no longer inconsistent with one another.

Inconsistency-reduction can take one of two general forms. On the one hand, the individual may avoid the implication of the inconsistency by perceiving or interpreting the discrepant element in such a way that it no longer appears to be inconsistent with the potentially challenged

This chapter is a product of a research program on social influence and behavior change supported by Public Health Service Research Grant MH-07280-06 from the National Institute of Mental Health.

TABLE

Modes of Handling Inconsistency Differentiated by (a) the Nature
of the Process Used and (b) the Nature of the Outcome Achieved.

| | | Process | |
		Avoidance of Inconsistency	Confrontation of Inconsistency
Outcome	Inconsistency-Reduction	Denial Distortion Rationalization Derogation of source	Change in attitude Change in action Change in standard Influence attempt

	Inconsistency-Maintenance	Compartmentalization
		Institutionalized
		  insulation
		Compensatory
		  ritualism
			Bolstering
			Differentiation
			Transcendence

element. At the most primitive level, he may deny the very existence of the inconsistent element or of the inconsistent relationship between the two elements. Or else, he may perceive the inconsistent element in distorted fashion; for example, he may perceive the opinions of someone he admires as closer to his own (assimilation) or the opinions of someone he despises as farther removed from his own (contrast) than they actually are. He may rationalize the inconsistent element; for example, if he has engaged in an action that violates one of his values, he may persuade himself that this action was in fact different from what it may appear to have been—that it had a different intent, or a different effect, or that it was not freely chosen—and that it is, therefore, not really inconsistent with his values. Finally, he may derogate the source of the inconsistent information, thus neutralizing its challenging impact. What all of these mechanisms have in common is that they remove inconsistency by allowing the person to recode discrepant information so as to avoid recognition of its implications.

On the other hand, the individual may actively confront the inconsistency and remove it by changing one (or both) of the incompatible elements and bringing them back into line with each other. Thus, he may change his attitude, in order to bring it into line with discrepant information about the attitude object, or about the attitudes of attractive others, or about his own actions. The change in attitude may be a change in the direction of affect toward the object; it may also, however, be a change (increase or decrease) in the intensity of feeling engendered by the object, or in the importance attached to it, or in the person's involvement with it. Another mode of inconsistency-reduction following upon active confrontation of the inconsistency is change in action; for example, if a person finds himself acting in a way that violates his values, he may attempt to reverse or undo his action, or to take steps that would prevent similar violations in the future. A related mechanism involves change in the standard governing the person's behavior; for example, if his attitudes or actions turn out to diverge from those of his reference group, he may shift to another group as a source of comparison and/or support. Finally, he may attempt to remove inconsistency by acting on the environment; for example, he may try to persuade the others whose opinions differ from his own, or to change the reality that is discrepant from his wishes. In all of these mechanisms, the individual confronts the challenge represented by inconsistency and takes corrective action designed to enhance his ability at goal-achievement. The corrective action leads to a reduction in the inconsistency that originally signaled the existence of shortcomings in the person's coping processes.

A central characteristic of all the modes of inconsistency-reduction— whether it be through avoidance or through confrontation—is that the person rejects one (or occasionally both) of the incompatible elements. In the case of avoidance, rejection takes the form of a refusal to recognize the disturbing element or its implication; in the case of confrontation, re- jection takes the form of changing his relationship to that element. In both cases, by rejecting one of the elements, the person sacrifices or endangers the satisfactions and adaptive contributions inherent in that element. This is obvious on the confrontation side: he gives up an attitude, action pref- erence, or standard that has presumably had some functional significance for him; or, by attempting to influence his environment, he risks the stability provided by the status quo. On the avoidance side, the rejected element is information about physical or social reality or the feedback from the person's own actions. In rejecting this element, the person may remove an immediate threat to his equanimity, but he is abandoning a de- gree of reality control and sacrificing the long-run contributions that the rejected information may have made to his coping ability.

Inconsistency-maintenance modes. The second row of the Table lists ways of coming to grips with bothersome inconsistency—of reducing the tensions engendered by it—without eliminating the inconsistency itself. The outcome of these mechanisms is such that the original inconsistency is still in force and the person is at least potentially aware of its existence. The inconsistency is made less disturbing by reducing its salience, or by 'drown- ing it out'—to use Abelson's (1959) term—or by transcending it. Neither of the two inconsistent elements, however, is rejected—either in perception, or in action—and they continue to maintain their inconsistent relationship to one another. Thus, the person does not sacrifice or endanger the satis- factions and adaptive contributions inherent in the two elements, although he does sacrifice some of the satisfactions that derive from consistency as such (coherence, predictability, etc.). Tension is reduced, not by adjusting the inconsistent relationship itself, but by adjusting the larger context with- in which this relationship is embedded.

Again, inconsistency-maintenance can take two general forms. One set of mechanisms allows the person to maintain the inconsistency by avoiding sharp confrontation between the two incompatible elements—by keeping them apart or by blunting the impact of the inconsistency when they cannot be kept apart. Avoidance here differs from avoidance in the case of inconsistency-reduction in that the person does not eliminate the inconsistent element, by perceiving or interpreting it out of existence. He does not avoid recognition of it in its own right, but he avoids bringing it into salience in situations dominated by the incompatible element. Mech- anisms in this category tend to involve more manipulation of the social situation and less manipulation at the cognitive level.

The most characteristic mechanism of this type is compartmentaliza- tion; a person may continue to hold two incompatible beliefs, or to act in ways that contradict his values, by keeping different areas of his life apart from each other. While he may well be aware of the existence of these two inconsistent elements, he thus manages to avoid confrontation between them. Often a person will find support for this separation in certain institutionalized patterns that *prescribe* behavior different from his usual behavior whenever he acts in the context of a particular role. For example, a judge is expected to deal with his friends according to universalistic principles, even though he may be inclined to do otherwise; or a soldier is expected to kill the enemy, even though in general killing is inconsistent with his basic values.[1] In these cases, then, the inconsistent behavior—by being institutionalized—can more easily be insulated from the rest of the person's values and he can thus avoid a confrontation. Institutionalized patterns may not only prescribe inconsistent behavior, but they may also, in certain situations, serve as a buffer against the emergence of inconsistent elements. For example, being sexually attracted by the nude body of a woman is inconsistent with the proper performance of the physician's role. While he cannot physically avoid exposure to nude women in the course of his work, he is helped—by certain institutionalized attitudes, behaviors, and environmental trappings—to insulate himself against sexual feelings when examining his patients.

Finally, a person may be able to avoid a sharp confrontation between two incompatible elements and thus maintain the inconsistent relationship between them by engaging in certain ritual behaviors that hide the inconsistency without removing it. Such mechanisms are particularly likely to come into play when there is a conflict between what a person knows he ought to do and what he is able or prepared to do. Rituals allow him to do what he ought to do—in a highly visible and often dramatic fashion—but, by being routinized and formalized, his actions are drained of their emotional impact. For example, a person may avoid active confrontation of the fact that an important relationship—such as his marriage, or a friendship—has 'gone sour' by paying exaggerated attention to the rituals that are presumed to symbolize such a relationship; he can thus pretend (to himself and others) that the relationship is intact without making the emotional investment of which he has become incapable. An executive may avoid confrontation of the fact that he no longer has a valid function in his organization by compensating, through ritual behaviors, for the emptiness of reality. A military man may avoid his doubts about the dehumanizing aspects of his life by emphasizing the rituals of military honor. In all of these cases, the inconsistency is not removed and the person is aware of it at some level. Its impact is blunted, however, through compensatory behavior that lowers the salience of the inconsistent element.

A second set of mechanisms allows the person to maintain the inconsistency by actively confronting it and cognitively restructuring the context within which the inconsistent elements are seen. Confrontation here differs from confrontation in the case of inconsistency-reduction in that the person does not change the incompatible elements, but changes the envelope that surrounds them. The original inconsistency remains and is at least potentially recognizable. But, given its embeddedness in a new context, the individual is able to tolerate it. Mechanisms in this category are

---

[1] This mechanism may shade over into a form of transcendence, to be discussed below.

similar to the compartmentalization, insulation, and ritualism that we have just discussed, in that adjustments are made not in the inconsistent relationship itself, but in its context. They differ, however, in that these adjustments involve active steps in restructuring one's conception of the context and adding new elements to it, rather than defensive maneuvers designed to forestall a clash.

The three mechanisms of this type listed in the Table are taken from Abelson's excellent discussion (1959), although with some modifications. By bolstering we refer, essentially, to the same mechanism that Abelson describes. While the person accepts the inconsistency between, let us say, his behavior and his knowledge of its probable consequences (e.g., smoking and the probability of cancer), and is aware of the negative motivational implications of this behavior, he adds new elements into the picture that are quite consistent with the behavior. For example, he persuades himself "that smoking is extremely enjoyable, good for his nerves, and socially necessary" (Abelson, 1959, p. 345), thus 'bolstering' the inconsistent behavior by stressing its positive motivational implications. In short, the inconsistency remains; the person continues to smoke *and* to be aware of its negative consequences. The overall picture is changed, however; the negative consequences have been made acceptable because they are overshadowed, 'drowned out,' by positive ones.

We use the term differentiation more narrowly than Abelson, to refer to the separating out of different components or dimensions of an object, each of which may be evaluated differently. Differentiation may help a person accept inconsistency in a way that is quite similar to bolstering. For example, a person may be confronted with the disturbing information that his friend is a liar. He may accept the negative implications of this information and yet maintain his friendship by developing a more differentiated image of this friend, according to which he is indeed a liar, but he is many other things as well. While the person may recognize that lying is an unattractive quality in his friend, that it is inconsistent with friendship, and that it poses problems for the future, he may feel that the friend's positive qualities outweigh this negative one. Thus, differentiation, like bolstering, introduces new cognitive elements that allow a person to tolerate inconsistency by drowning it out.

The third mechanism, transcendence, is particularly interesting and has many ramifications. It involves the introduction of a superordinate principle, which serves as the context for evaluating the inconsistent relationship. The two elements, when viewed in their own terms, remain inconsistent with one another. This very inconsistency, however, is required by a higher principle that transcends the two elements, and it thus becomes acceptable or even desirable. A prime example of this mechanism can be noted in the social legitimization of otherwise unacceptable behavior, such as killing in time of war. The soldier may be quite aware of the inconsistency between his action in taking the lives of others and his values regarding the sanctity of human life. This inconsistency, however, is viewed in the context of a transcendent principle, such as that of defending one's country and way of life. When viewed in that context, the inconsistent behavior is required, acceptable, and even noble. To forego one's scruples, to do 'what has to be done,' even though you find it personally objectionable and distasteful— in short, to be inconsistent—is in itself virtuous in this context. Thus, neither the inconsistent elements nor the relationship between them are changed, but they are embedded in a different context which gives a different meaning to the inconsistent behavior.[2]

In similar fashion, ruthlessness toward the class-enemy in a revolutionary movement is seen as virtuous because actions are not judged in their immediate interpersonal context, but in the context of larger historical forces. In some religious sects, the deliberate commitment of sinful acts is endowed with holiness, in that it is seen as representing a struggle with evil forces. The sinful nature of the actions is not denied or rationalized; it is their very sinfulness that is essential to the transcendent purpose they are designed to meet. At a more mundane level, transcendence also operates in interpersonal relations. For example, a person may find disagreement with a close friend on certain issues quite acceptable by subsuming it under the higher principle that some degree of attitudinal discrepancy makes for a more meaningful relationship. Reference to long-run considerations may be a form of transcendence: A person may tolerate certain inconsistencies— e.g., the knowledge that he is working hard but receiving minimal reward— because he is convinced that such short-run sacrifices are directly conducive to long-run benefits. Finally, the acceptance of inconsistency may itself be the superordinate principle that makes transcendence possible. Thus, a person may tolerate inconsistent behavior or values in himself because he is philosophically resigned to the notion that such inconsistencies are inherent in the nature of man. To some degree, he may even relish inconsistency because it makes him a more interesting and colorful person and because a foolish consistency, after all, is "the hobgoblin of little minds."

All of the inconsistency-maintenance mechanisms that we have discussed lead to a reduction in tension. This tension-reduction is accomplished, however, in a way that allows the two inconsistent elements themselves to remain unchanged and to continue in their inconsistent relationship. The inconsistency-maintenance mechanisms based on avoidance do this by reducing the salience of the inconsistency; those based on confrontation do it by adding consistent relationships. It may be argued that what we have described as inconsistency-maintenance does indeed involve inconsistency-reduction as well as tension-reduction, since the ratio of inconsistent to consistent elements has been reduced. The important difference, however, between these mechanisms and those we have designated as inconsistency-reduction is that the focal inconsistency is maintained. This difference is likely to have some consequences for the future course of events—e.g., for the probability that inconsistency between the two elements will again become troublesome, and the conditions under which it will do so. Moreover, we would expect to find systematic differences between the conditions conducive to the choice of consistency-reduction mechanisms and those

---

[2] Other mechanisms are likely to come into play in this situation, such as rationalization. The soldier may perceive his action, not as killing another, but as self-defense; or he may see the enemy as subhuman and thus not covered by the prohibition against killing. While such mechanisms may be associated with transcendence, they differ from it in that they involve a reduction of inconsistency through an alteration of one of the elements. To the extent that we are dealing with transcendence, the person recognizes that he has intentionally killed another human being and that this is inconsistent with one of his basic values, but he accepts this inconsistency—with some pride, even if mixed with ambivalence—because killing other human beings *is* consistent with the superordinate principle by which the present situation is defined.

conducive to the choice of consistency-maintenance mechanisms. It is to these differences that we shall now direct our attention.

SELECTION AMONG DIFFERENT MODES OF HANDLING INCONSISTENCY

The greatest potential value of a functional analysis is that it can help us predict the specific modes of handling inconsistency that a person is likely to utilize in a given situation by identifying the type of coping process that has been brought into play and the motivational problems with which the person is grappling. Ultimately, a functional approach should yield hypotheses about the conditions under which the handling of an inconsistency dilemma will eventuate in inconsistency reduction as against inconsistency maintenance (top vs. bottom row of the Table); the conditions under which the implications of the inconsistency will be handled through defensive avoidance as against active confrontation (left-hand vs. right-hand column of the Table); and the conditions determining the choice of a specific mode within any one of the four cells. We are not prepared at this point to offer detailed hypotheses, systematically derived from a limited set of concepts. We shall, however, in the brief sections that follow, attempt to provide some hints about the form that such hypotheses might eventually take.

Inconsistency-reduction vs. inconsistency-maintenance. Let us imagine the case of an accountant who is highly motivated to be a successful professional, and to be perceived as such by himself and by others. If he is also passionate about golf, he may be confronted with an inconsistency, because success in his career may require single-minded attention to his business. The inconsistency arises from the fact that behavior supportive of goal B (e.g., spending a lot of time on the golf course) is disruptive of goal A, and vice versa. In other words, the two inconsistent elements are linked to *different* goals and their conflicting demands. If the same accountant, however, considers accounting to be a low-status activity, then we are dealing with a very different kind of situation. In that case, the inconsistency arises from the fact that behavior supportive of goal A is at the same time disruptive of goal A. The harder he works and the more established he becomes as an accountant, the more he commits himself to a career that he devalues. Behavior designed to help him succeed in his profession has, at the same time—given his attitude toward accounting—the effect of interfering with his goal of being a 'successful professional.' In other words, the two inconsistent elements are linked to the *same* goal and have conflicting implications for it.

When the two inconsistent elements are predominantly linked to a single motivational system, any evaluation or action associated with the relevant goal object or goal state inevitably brings both of these elements into play. The very same cognition or behavior is simultaneously consistent and inconsistent with the goal—supportive and disruptive of its achievement. The inconsistency thus introduces a self-defeating quality into all efforts at goal achievement. We propose that *to the extent to which the two inconsistent elements are linked to the same goal, rather than to two different goals, they are most likely to be handled by the use of inconsistency-reduction mechanisms.*

Intraattitudinal inconsistencies, which involve discrepancies between

different components of a single attitude, exemplify—almost by definition—
the case of two inconsistent elements linked to the same goal, and are,
therefore, more likely to be handled through inconsistency-reduction. Take,
for example, affective-cognitive inconsistencies, as investigated by Rosenberg (1960a and 1960b). These are cases in which a person has negative
affect toward an object that he believes to be instrumental to the attainment
of important values, or positive affect toward an object that he believes
to be blocking the attainment of important values. In a series of imaginative
studies, Rosenberg created such inconsistencies by hypnotically altering
his subjects' affect toward a particular social issue, e.g., the question of
Negroes moving into white neighborhoods. He found that these affect
changes were accompanied by a cognitive reorganization that restored the
balance between feelings and beliefs.

In terms of the present analysis, Rosenberg created an inconsistency
between two elements linked to the same goal. Any evaluation or action
with respect to the issue of Negroes moving into white neighborhoods
inevitably brings both elements into play. For example, a person who believes that residential integration is instrumental to the attainment of his
values but, at the same time, is repelled by the idea, is caught in a self-
defeating bind. If, in line with his beliefs, he speaks and acts in support of
integration, then the negative affect that he experiences whenever he engages in these activities is likely to interfere with their effectiveness. Nor
is it possible to be effective by putting the negative feelings out of his
mind, because the very conditions that generate and result from effective
action are calculated to bring the negative affect into salience. If, on the
other hand, the individual gives expression to his negative feelings, then
he finds himself in a situation in which he cannot defend or justify these
feelings, since they are not matched by his beliefs. Along with Rosenberg,
therefore, we would predict that affective-cognitive inconsistencies with
respect to the same attitude object are likely to be unstable and to be
handled through inconsistency-reduction[3] (see Chapter 4).

In interattitudinal inconsistencies it may also happen (though perhaps
more rarely) that the two inconsistent elements are linked to the same goal.
Whether this happens and whether, therefore, we would predict the use
of inconsistency-reduction mechanisms, will depend on the type of motivational orientation that serves to define the situation. Take, for example, the
case in which there is an incongruity between the person's attitude toward
the source of a communication and his attitude toward the message. In
discussing such situations, Kelman and Eagly (1965) distinguish two orienta-

---

[3] According to our functional analysis, the likelihood that inconsistency-reduction will
actually occur depends on the degree to which the person anticipates the necessity for
action vis-à-vis the attitude object, particularly in the interpersonal sphere. We would
speculate that cognitive reorganization following upon attitude change represents an attempt by the person to build up supporting arguments in preparation for a possible defense and justification of his newly acquired position. It follows, from this assumption,
that cognitive reorganization is more likely to occur among individuals who foresee the
necessity of defending their position than among those who foresee no such problem.
For example, individuals whose original position was anchored in their relationship to
important reference persons are likely to be concerned that their new affective orientation might be challenged by these others and might alienate them. Thus, as a preparatory
device, they are likely to change their beliefs so that it would become easier to justify
their new feelings and perhaps to persuade the others to change their attitudes as well.

tions that a person may bring to them: source orientation and content orientation. They define *source orientation* as "an approach to the communication situation in which the relation of the source to the person's self-definition has the greatest motivational significance. ... When source orientation prevails, the person is primarily concerned with the implications of any communication from the other for his own relationship to him. Given this set, he is unable to separate the content of the communication from the source. All communications are treated as emanations from the other and as parts of him ..." (p. 75).

When a person is source-oriented, then—either because of the nature of his relationship to the source, or because of situational demands, or because of personality predispositions—he is likely to perceive an inconsistent message as threatening his relationship to the source and hence his own self-definition, which is anchored in that relationship. In other words, under these circumstances the two inconsistent elements are both linked to the same goal—maintaining the self-defining relationship to the other—and have conflicting implications for it. We would, therefore, predict that one or more inconsistency-reduction mechanisms would come into play—either attitude change, in the form of identification (cf. Kelman, 1961); or such avoidance mechanisms as perceptual displacement of the message, or re-interpretation of it, or refusal to believe that it was correctly ascribed to the source. By contrast, these mechanisms are unlikely to be utilized when the person is content-oriented.

Let us turn now to those cases of inconsistency in which the two inconsistent elements are linked to *different* goals and their conflicting demands. In these cases it is much easier for the person to maintain the inconsistency. The ambitious accountant who is also a passionate golfer can act effectively in both domains without confronting the inconsistency. The two pursuits do not necessarily impinge on one another in the short run, though they may well do so in the long run. It is thus possible for him, at least in the short run, to compartmentalize the two, to put golf out of his mind while engaged in business pursuits, and vice versa. In the long run, he may maintain the inconsistency by some form of bolstering or transcendence: for example, he may become convinced that, while golf does take him away from his work, this kind of diversion benefits his business because it allows him to make potential business contacts, or because it helps to keep him in condition.

Another example can be taken from the situation of source-message incongruity discussed above. When *content orientation* prevails in this type of situation, "the person is primarily concerned with the implications of the particular content of the communication for his efforts at goal achievement and value maximization. While his attitude toward the source determines how seriously he takes the communication, he is perfectly capable of separating content from source" (Kelman & Eagly, 1965, p. 76). For the content-oriented individual, in contrast to the source-oriented one, the two inconsistent elements are linked to two different goals. He is thus better able to maintain the inconsistency—for example, by utilizing such mechanisms as differentiation. He can more readily accept the fact that a person whom he generally respects holds the 'wrong' views on certain specific issues, or that a person whom he generally dislikes has some 'right' opinions.

So far we have said that inconsistency-maintenance mechanisms are more readily *available* when the two inconsistent elements are linked to different goals than when they are linked to a single goal. What can we say, however, about the conditions under which a person would be particularly *motivated* to utilize these mechanisms? We propose that *inconsistency-maintenance is motivated to the extent that the two goals to which the two inconsistent elements are linked are independently important to the individual, particularly if they are of more or less equal importance.*[4] Under these circumstances, the person is concerned with safeguarding the values or satisfactions associated with each of the elements. Inconsistency-reduction would require a sacrifice in at least one of the elements—a resolution that he would prefer to avoid. He is, thus, highly motivated to find some way of handling the discomfort generated by the inconsistency that would, at the same time, permit him to keep the two inconsistent elements intact.

For example, a scientist who is strongly committed to the examination of evidence in his professional activities may be a loyal member of a political group that requires him to accept its program on faith. He may be aware of the inconsistency between these two commitments and bothered by it at some level. However, insofar as these are both important roles for him, with independent roots in his life history, he will be *motivated* to keep them intact, despite their inconsistency; and, insofar as these two domains of his life can be kept apart from one another and he is not forced to make a choice between loyalty to science and loyalty to his political group, he will be *able* to do so. To take another example, a young man who strongly believes in equality of sacrifice may accept a student deferment from the draft, even though he recognizes the inconsistency inherent in this decision. He is likely to find ways of tolerating this inconsistency to the extent to which both his commitment to the principle of equality and his desire to stay out of the army represent central values for him.

Avoidance vs. confrontation. To a considerable degree, the choice between mechanisms in the left-hand column and those in the right-hand column of the Table depends on the *availability* of avoidance mechanisms. In some situations it is relatively easy to deny or misperceive the inconsistent element because the stimuli are ambiguous; or to derogate the source because his status is low; or to compartmentalize because the two inconsistent elements are linked to two separate role domains. In other situations the individual is more sharply confronted with the inconsistency and is forced by reality, as it were, to grapple with it actively. Availability is a function not only of situational factors but also of personality predispositions: some individuals (e.g., high authoritarians or 'levelers') have a greater 'capacity' than others to deny inconsistencies, or to put them out of their minds.

In addition to considerations of availability, however, the choice between avoidance and confrontation mechanisms depends on the particular implications of the inconsistency for the person's goal achievement. *To the*

---

[4] This proposition is quite similar to Newcomb, Turner, and Converse's (1965) proposition about the conditions under which imbalance in an attitude system will be handled by "a breaking up of the system through some form of dissociation or differentiation," i.e., in our terminology, through certain forms of inconsistency-maintenance. They state that such an outcome "becomes more likely as the objects involved in the imbalance are more nearly equated in their centrality for the individual" (p. 149).

extent to which the inconsistency raises questions about the achievement of short-term goals and the person is primarily concerned with preserving the status quo ante, avoidance mechanisms are likely to be utilized. To the extent to which the inconsistency raises questions about the achievement of long-term goals and the person is primarily concerned with preparing himself for future actions and interactions, confrontation mechanisms are likely to be utilized.

Take, for example, the situation in which a person has yielded to situational pressures and said something contrary to his beliefs. If he has misrepresented his beliefs about a very specific, isolable event that he has never faced before and does not anticipate facing in the future, such as the experimental task in the Festinger and Carlsmith (1959) study, then his primary concern is presumably the maintenance of his self-image as a truthful person. Under these circumstances, it is both easy and functional for him to simply distort his memory or interpretation of the event. The immediate threat to his self-image is thus avoided, and there is no reason to expect any future repercussions. On the other hand, if the person has misrepresented his beliefs about an issue that has significance outside of the immediate situation—for example, his political beliefs—then he can usually expect that he will have to defend to others the stand he has taken, that he will be subjected to demands for other actions in line with his pronouncements, and that he will face repeated reminders of his guilt. Under these circumstances, he would be motivated to change his attitude toward the issue, or to seek out a new reference group, or to undo his discrepant action.

Similar considerations apply in the choice between avoidance and confrontation mechanisms designed to maintain inconsistency. A man may find, upon returning to his old neighborhood for a rare visit, that he falls into patterns of speech and action that are inconsistent with those required by his new environment. He is likely to be concerned with maintaining the pleasantness of this temporary interlude without threatening the long-term adjustment that he has achieved in the 'outside' world. Under these circumstances, it is both easy and functional for him to compartmentalize the two situations and to rely on the insulation, both in time and space, of his visits home from his daily life. On the other hand, a public official who finds himself committed to policies that are inconsistent with deeply held private beliefs may be concerned about his ability to function effectively in office in the long run and, at the same time, he may anticipate the future necessity of justifying his actions to himself and his intimate friends. He is likely to search actively for ways of redefining the context of his public actions so that the inconsistency would be overshadowed or transcended.

In Chapter 22 we mentioned that inconsistency may signal either a threat to the individual's ability to achieve certain of his goals, or an occasion to enhance his ability to achieve such goals. In general, it can probably be said that to the extent to which the implications of the inconsistency are predominantly threatening, avoidance mechanisms are likely to be utilized, since the person tends, under these circumstances, to adopt a short-term time perspective and to react defensively. To the extent to which the predominant implications of the inconsistency are for the existence of new opportunities, confrontation mechanisms are likely to be utilized, since the person tends to take a long-term time perspective and to prepare for future eventualities. However, the relationship of threat vs.

opportunity to avoidance vs. confrontation is by no means of a one-to-one nature.

Choice of a specific mode. Within any one of the four cells of the Table, the specific mechanism chosen by an individual should also depend on functional considerations. Given the fact, for example, that a person who has engaged in an attitude-discrepant action is motivated to reduce inconsistency via confrontation, whether he does so by changing his attitude or by attempting to reverse his action ought to be a function of the specific adjustment problem that the inconsistency has brought to the fore. Relatively speaking, however, we would assume that mechanisms within a given cell are more readily interchangeable than mechanisms located in different cells. Thus, we would also expect that if a study made available and measured the entire range of mechanisms—as Steiner and Rogers (1963) and Steiner and Johnson (1964) did for inconsistency-reduction mechanisms—we would find positive correlations between mechanisms within the same cell (e.g., denial and distortion) and negative correlations between mechanisms in different cells (e.g., denial and attitude change, or denial and transcendence).[5]

The interchangeability of mechanisms even within the same cell is only relative, though, and we are particularly interested in the conditions that favor one specific mechanism over others. In discussing the choice between inconsistency-reduction and maintenance, and between avoidance and confrontation, we indicated that it depends in part on the *availability* of these different classes of mechanisms—on the degree to which it is possible (in a given situation and for a given individual) to act effectively despite the presence of inconsistency, or to avoid a confrontation between the inconsistent elements. It seems to us that an analysis in terms of the relative availability of different mechanisms is particularly fruitful, at this stage, for dealing with the question of choice of a specific mode within any one cell.

Other things being equal, we would expect a person to use that mechanism which is most available in that it requires the least adjustment in his perceptions and overall attitudes. Thus, within the reduction-avoidance cell, if a disagreeable message is attributed to a highly attractive source, it would be much easier for the person to use rationalization (cf. Pilisuk, 1962) or, if at all possible, to deny the accuracy of the attribution, than it would be to derogate the source. Again, within the reduction-confrontation cell, we would predict, along with Newcomb, Turner, and Converse (1965), that "balance-restoring change is more likely to occur in attitudes toward objects that are less rather than more central" (p. 149). Thus, a discrepancy between a person's own attitude and that of his reference group is more readily reduced by attitude change if the group is very central for him, and by shifting reference groups if the attitude is very central.

---

[5] This statement must be qualified in line with some important methodological considerations raised by Eagly (1965). The prediction of a positive correlation between mechanisms in the same cell should only hold true if correlations are computed for the entire population. If correlations are computed separately for individuals who tend to use a particular cell (e.g., 'avoiders-reducers'), then we may find a negative correlation between any pair of mechanisms. In other words, compared to the population as a whole, those who use some denial are also more prone to use some distortion; among those who use these types of mechanisms, however, those who rely very heavily on denial are less likely to use distortion, and vice versa.

Availability depends on situational factors such as the ambiguity of relevant events and communications, which determines the range of possible perceptions and interpretations; and the nature of the social norms that are operative, which determines the range of possible actions. Availability also depends, as we have seen, on the strength and centrality of the different attitudes or beliefs that are being challenged. Finally, it depends on personality predispositions. If we assume, for example, that transcendence requires greater cognitive flexibility and a richer store of cognitive categories than bolstering, then we would predict that, for high authoritarians or for levelers, bolstering is a more readily available mechanism than transcendence.

Any analysis in terms of the availability of various mechanisms needs to be linked to a functional analysis.[6] Since we assume that resolving the inconsistency is not an end in itself but a by-product of the person's attempt to deal with the adjustment problem signaled by the inconsistency, the crucial issue for us is not *whether* the inconsistency has been handled, but *how*. It may well be that a person selects a particular mechanism precisely because it is so readily available, while others are more difficult to use. This mechanism, however—even though it 'handles' that inconsistency—may not really deal with the adjustment problem at issue, or may deal with it only in the short run but not in the long run. To analyze the 'adequacy' of a resolution and thus predict its future fate requires an examination of functional considerations in addition to those of availability.

This view leads us to question seriously the use of laboratory procedures that close off all but one mode of handling inconsistency. If one assumes, as we do, that the nature of the available mechanisms helps to define the nature of the situation and its functional significance, then this kind of experimental procedure may change the situation that the investigator has tried to produce or at least create a unique situation and thus limit the range of situations to which the findings can be generalized. For example, forced compliance in a situation in which attitude change is the only mode of dissonance reduction available may well have very different functional implications for the individual than forced compliance usually has. The behavior observed may, therefore, be unique to situations structured in this special way. The conditions controlling the amount of attitude change in this situation may be quite different from those operative in more usual situations. Attitude change, in fact, may have an entirely different meaning when it is the only mechanism available. Under these circumstances, if the relationships found conform to certain 'nonobvious predictions,' one wonders whether this might be due to the fact that a 'nonobvious' situation has been created.

There are, of course, circumstances under which it is completely reasonable to use a laboratory situation in which all mechanisms are closed off except one. The investigator may be especially interested in this type of

---

[6] These two types of analysis often merge into one another. The relative availability of various mechanisms may be determined by and may in turn determine the functional significance of the inconsistency to the individual—i.e., the nature of the problem that he faces. For example, if an individual's attitudes on a peripheral issue diverge from those of a very important group, then attitude change is more functional and hence more readily available than shifting reference groups. Conversely, if the source of a disturbing message is unimpeachable (making derogation unavailable as a mechanism for reducing inconsistency), then the individual may be faced with the problem of accepting the implications of the message.

situation; or he may wish to check out whether a particular set of manipulations produces any effects at all before proceeding to study the exact form of these effects; or he may use this as a standard situation for a series of parametric studies. If this kind of procedure is used, however, it is essential to keep in mind that it does represent a special situation and to take its unique features into account. Above all, it must be recognized that, whatever else it may accomplish, this procedure cannot help us identify the determinants of specific modes of handling inconsistency dilemmas. To answer questions about the selection among different modes we must develop laboratory situations that allow a range of mechanisms to emerge and, furthermore, that allow us to conceive these mechanisms along a time dimension. We submit that these are the important questions to ask if the consistency models are to develop and to contribute to the understanding of social-psychological phenomena.

CHAPTER 67

A Modest Modish Model for Dissonance Reduction

Jane Allyn Hardyck

University of Pennsylvania

and

Marcelle Kardush

San Francisco State College

One of the major problems for dissonance theory is that of predicting which of the many possible avenues an individual will take in attempting to reduce dissonance. We know that subjects in experiments will generally engage in behavior that looks like dissonance reduction if we have previously employed manipulations designed to create dissonance for them. In the majority of studies, however, interest has centered not on the mode of dissonance reduction that will be chosen, but rather on the amount of dissonance reduction that will occur within a given mode when others have been made difficult or impossible to use. Thus our knowledge concerning preferences for one mode of dissonance reduction over another as a function of intrapersonal and situational variables is scanty.

In this paper, we will attempt, first, to present a very general categorization of modes of dissonance reduction. We will then go on to discuss a proposed ordering of these general categories in terms of preference. Next we will present a modest model that is intended as a first step in the direction of some precise prediction of which mode will actually be used under given circumstances. Finally, we will discuss restrictions on the model as a function of individual difference variables.

We assume that a definition of dissonance in this volume would be superfluous. We do wish to stress, however, that at this primitive stage in our thinking we are attempting to deal only with dissonance between two single cognitions and its mode of resolution, not with the total amount of dissonance in a system, defined as the number of dissonant elements divided by the number of consonant elements, each weighted for its importance. Hopefully, once the implications of the model have been fully worked out, generalization to the larger problem will be possible.

A major problem in developing a categorization of modes of dissonance reduction is that dissonance can result from such a myriad of situations: decision making, counterattitudinal advocacy, disconfirmation of expectancy, 'forced compliance,' listening to a persuasive communication, etc. One must always attempt to be highly precise in pin-pointing the two cognitions that are in the dissonant relationship ... in asking oneself "Exactly what's dissonant with what?" One must also be precise in identifying what behaviors will be assumed to be indicative of dissonance-reducing activity. Once one has forced oneself to be precise, we are convinced, the many different modes of reducing dissonance can be grouped into three broad categories: "*stopping thinking*," *changing one element of the two* that are in the dissonant relationship, and *restructuring*. A fourth mode of handling but not of reducing dissonance is that of simply *tolerating* it. This must be viewed as a temporary, stop-gap measure used only when all else fails (or, by some individuals, when the cognitions are so unimportant that little dissonance is aroused).

Let us expand for a moment on exactly how we would fit the commonly discussed modes of dissonance reduction into our category system. "Stopping thinking" (a phrase used by Rosenberg and Abelson, 1960) requires little elaboration. The individual in this case reduces the dissonance either by passively forgetting about it or by a more active process of suppression. We see 'passive forgetting' as a characteristic way of handling highly unimportant dissonant relationships, such as minor disagreements with friends over matters of taste. Suppression is more likely to be used when the dissonance is between highly important cognitions. Most cigarette smokers, for example, seem, when they can, to suppress the whole question of the connection between lung cancer and smoking. (This is made much more difficult of late by that nasty statement on the pack or box.) We will discuss the variable of importance at length later, when we present the model per se.

The category of changing one of the two cognitions includes the great majority of measures of dissonance reduction commonly used: opinion change, rejection of the source of a communication, denial of responsibility for one's behavior, and distortion of the content of dissonance-producing messages. A great deal needs to be said, of course, concerning *which* of the two cognitions will be more likely to change if changing one of them is the opted mode. We will go into that, also, when discussing the model.

Finally, restructuring includes on the one hand what Rosenberg and Abelson refer to as "differentiation," which essentially means increasing the complexity of *cognitions concerning the two cognitions* in the dissonant relationship. For example, "When my friend says he is against the war in Vietnam, he means we should never have gotten involved in it in the first place. When I say I am for it, I mean we shouldn't just pull out, now that we are there. We are not essentially in disagreement." It also includes the response of adding more consonant cognitions or making salient consonant cognitions already present in the cognitive structure, and that of reshuffling the connections between cognitions so that dissonant relationships are seen as irrelevant relationships and consonant cognitions are brought together.

It is hypothesized that *when any mode of reducing dissonance may be employed*, stopping thinking will be the preferred mode; when, for any number of reasons to be discussed below, this possibility is ruled out, simple change in one of the two cognitions in the dissonant relationship will be preferred; when simple change is impossible, restructuring of one type or another will be tried. Our reasoning is based on two considerations. The first of these is the simple-minded notion of least effort. Ceasing to think about one connection between two cognitions can cause no perturbations in whatever cognitive structure exists. It cannot, therefore, introduce new dissonance into the system and, besides, it requires little cognitive work. Changing one of the two cognitions in the dissonant relationship, on the other hand, may well introduce new dissonance into the system. What of other cognitions to which that to-be-changed cognition is related? Furthermore, there is a certain 'inertia' to be overcome when one changes a cognition, and this requires work. Restructuring of almost any sort requires even more thinking than does changing one cognition (although there may be some exceptions). Seeking new consonant cognitions, for example, may easily result in introducing new dissonance, and it requires a good deal of thinking, reading, and talking. Making new connections, seeing new complexities, etc., all involve work ... and, again, the making of such new connections may introduce further dissonance.

A second consideration is that of the efficiency of the respective modes for actually reducing the dissonance. Stopping thinking effectively gets rid of dissonance (although, admittedly, the solution may be only temporary) as does changing one of the two cognitions in the dissonant relationship. Most of the forms of restructuring, however, have the deficiency of only reducing the relative amount of dissonance in the system, not completely eliminating the dissonance between the two specific cognitions. Thus restructuring should be the least preferred way of reducing dissonance, since it has both of the drawbacks we have discussed.

We carefully introduced our proposed hierarchy of preference with the phrase *when any mode of reducing dissonance may be employed*. We turn now to a discussion of several variables that can restrict such free choice. First, there are situational restrictions. Reminders from other people or the extreme salience of a connection between two dissonant cognitions may prevent one from stopping thinking. Much as a patient may wish to ignore the obvious connection between some irrational behavior of his and some consequences of that behavior, a persistent therapist may prevent him from doing so. Or, turning once again to the smoker, as he lights each cigarette he is faced with the statement, "Cigarette smoking may be hazardous to your health." The patient after the hour and the smoker after laying down the box may both subsequently stop thinking; while in the immediate situation, however, it is difficult. Similarly, undeniable physical reality may make it impossible to change either of the two cognitions in the dissonant relationship. If one simultaneously observes that the grass is green and clearly hears one's friend state that it is red, one has great difficulty in changing either cognition. Anyone not himself color blind in this situation is likely to resort to the use of restructuring (by making a reevaluation of the friend's sanity, sobriety, seriousness, etc.).

Most studies testing derivations from dissonance theory have, of course, attempted *experimentally* to restrict the subjects' use of other modes of dissonance reduction than those the investigator has chosen to measure. One source of problems in such studies has been those subjects who appear not to use the suggested mechanisms. The experimenter simply does not know what is happening with these individuals. Has the manipulation failed somehow to introduce dissonance? Or is the subject perhaps simply 'tolerating' the dissonance? We suggest that one problem is that it is nearly (if not completely) impossible to block off restructuring as a mode of dissonance reduction, since so much of it can go on inside the head of the individual and since individuals can engage in so many creative types of restructuring. The category 'simply tolerating it' thus becomes an impossible one to demonstrate; one can never prove that the individual has *not* engaged in restructuring.

The model to be presented assumes that situational restrictions on the choice of mode of dissonance reduction such as those discussed are absent. The independent variable to be considered in relationship to choice of mode is that of the importance of the two cognitions entering into the dissonant relationship. We define importance loosely as relevance to the self. By relevance to the self we do not wish to include merely relevance to the self concept but, more generally, relevance to the person's ability to function effectively in his day-to-day activities. Thus we are able to include also cognitions about the way the physical world operates, e.g., physical constructs such as gravity. In using this definition we are more or less adopting Rokeach's central-peripheral belief dimension (Rokeach, 1960).

Our speculative theoretical curves of amount of use of the three categories of modes of dissonance reduction are presented in the Figure. The ordinate indicates the degree of use. The abscissa represents the dimension of importance, increasing from left to right, for each of the two dissonant cognitions. The curves for stopping thinking and for restructuring present no real problem in understanding. However, when one reads the Figure considering the increase in the importance of cognition X as being represented on the abscissa, the curve for 'change of one cognition' must be interpreted as 'change in X'; conversely, when considering cognition Y, the same curve is read as 'change in Y.'

In making predictions from the graph, one locates each cognition on the abscissa and notes the height of the curves at each of the two points. When the cognitions are widely spaced along the continuum (e.g., one at C and one at G), there is no ambiguity with regard to the prediction. One simply invokes the general hierarchy of preference mentioned earlier. In the example given, then, the prediction would be that the cognition at C would be changed, since changing one cognition is preferred over restructuring as a general rule. That is, when one cognition falls in an area of the graph in which use of a more preferred mode is clearly dominant, that mode will be used.

A special consideration concerning the use of 'stopping thinking' as a mode of reducing dissonance must be kept in mind; namely, 'stopping thinking' cannot be used in combination with either of the other two modes. Either one stops thinking or one does not. If one does not, it is conceivable that one may use any one or a combination of the other modes: a change in X, a change in Y, or restructuring. Thus, the first step in making a prediction from the graph should be to determine whether either of the two cognitions is of such low importance that stopping thinking should be preferred. (Of course, if either cognition is of zero importance—falls at point A—by definition there is no dissonance and the person will stop thinking about the elements involved.) If neither cognition falls at A, but both are of low importance, one *sums* the amount of use of stopping thinking for the two cognitions. If this sum exceeds the degree of changing or of restructuring for *either* of the two individual cognitions, then the prediction is that the individual will stop thinking. This will be the prediction if *both* cognitions fall below C on the continuum or above H.

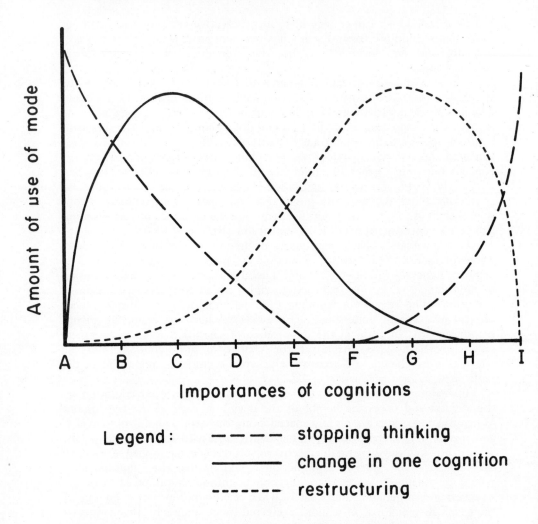

FIGURE.   The model for prediction of mode of dissonance-reduction as a function of the importance of the two cognitions. (Both axes are arbitrarily scaled)

Another restriction concerning the 'stopping thinking' curve is that the curve below F and that above F must be treated separately. We have treated the category of 'stopping thinking' as one, but the dynamics underlying the use of it at low importance and at high importance differ. When either cognition is of low importance one stops thinking by passive forgetting, basically because it is not worth the effort to think about it. When both cognitions are of high importance, one stops thinking by suppression because the tension is very high and one cannot reduce the dissonance in any other way. The representation of the curve as discontinuous is made intentionally to underscore this difference. Similarly, its lack of symmetry is based on the fact that the point at which the self becomes centrally involved is represented in our model at F. This point will be discussed later when parallels will be drawn between our model and congruity theory (Osgood & Tannenbaum, 1955).

A problem for prediction from the model arises when cognitions X and Y are of equal or nearly equal importance. Our present hunch is that it is under these conditions that several modes of dissonance reduction may be employed. For example, if one cognition falls at C and another at D, both cognitions would be expected to change, with the less important one changing more. If one falls at E and the other at F, the cognition falling at E would be changed a little, the cognition falling at F would be changed even less, and restructuring would also be used. In fact, when both cognitions fall in the middle range of the continuum, say, from D to F, we see the most likely mode of resolution, specifically, to be differentiation as Rosenberg and Abelson (1960) use the term—restructuring involving some change in the "judgment of the object"; this process essentially involves some change and some restructuring. Even if the two cognitions are close together in importance, if they both fall above F no problem in prediction is encountered. General restructuring will occur, up to the point beyond H, at which suppression will take over.

We mentioned earlier in the paper that under some circumstances, the situation prevents an individual from using his preferred mode. One special case is the experimental situation: the subject in the laboratory is essentially prevented from using "stopping thinking" by the demands of the experimenter for a response. For the model to be useful in laboratory situations, then, it must be simplified to omit the stopping thinking curve. It will then consist of two ogives; that is, the "change in one cognition" curve will continue to rise below C and the restructuring curve will continue to rise above G. In this form, with the addition of one further assumption, the model can be used to predict the findings obtained by those working within the "congruity" framework (see Chapter 3). This assumption is that importance as we have defined it is highly correlated with the degree of polarization of a concept as measured on the semantic differential evaluative dimension, with zero polarization falling at A on our continuum, $+1$ and -1 at C, $+2$ and -2 at E, and $+3$ and -3 at G. (We conceive of cognitions that fall beyond F on the continuum of importance as having a very high degree of relevance of the self. Since, as Smith states in Chapter 27, "Osgood and Tannenbaum's [1955] congruity model ... in effect excludes the self ...," we have placed the range of measures they use in the lower and middle ranges of our model.)

The consistent findings of the 'congruity' group are that changes in the two cognitions linked by an assertion are inversely proportional to their valence, up to the point at which the valence of both becomes extremely high, at which the subject refuses to believe the assertion (the 'incredulity effect'). This 'incredulous' response is clearly an example of restructuring, and in our model restructuring begins to be used consistently beyond point E (which we have identified with $+2$ and -2 on the polarity dimension used by the 'congruity' group).

There are, of course, a multitude of variables that might be expected to modify the predictions we would make from our model. These are organismic or individual difference variables and we turn, finally, to a discussion of them. We see them as making modifications in our predictions in one of two ways. First, certain variables may place restrictions on the use of certain modes just as do situational constraints. Secondly, other variables may stretch or shrink the areas covered by one or another of the curves, thus changing the points on the continuum of importance at which an individual may be expected to shift from one mode to another.

Variables of the first type include chronological and mental age. Allport (1937) and Lewin (1951) both suggest that the very young child is characterized by very minimal cognitive differentiation and organization. In Lewin's terms, young children (and also the feeble-minded of any age) have fewer and more rigidly bounded regions in their cognitive structures. In Allport's terms, the attitudes of the young child are undifferentiated and lack integration; attitude objects are seen as all good or all bad. As the child develops through adolescence, his cognitive structure becomes more differentiated (comes to include a larger number and variety of subparts, in Lewin's terms) and also develops more integration among the elements.

In the light of Piaget's work (1950) on abstract reasoning ability, it is reasonable to assume that this process is at least in part determined by the child's actual capacity even to *see* complexities and contradictions in a given cognitive area. In Piaget's observations of children's responses to questions concerning conservation of weight and volume, for example, he notes that the youngest appear to concentrate on one attribute (e.g., height of the container) in making their judgments. Somewhat older children alternate between considering one of two attributes; only quite late is the child able to integrate the information coming from the two dimensions. To us this suggests that the sequence of development of modes of handling inconsistencies might also move from (very early) the ability to use only stopping thinking, through the development of the additional mode of simple changes in one cognition (e.g., rejection of information that a 'bad' object has a good aspect) to, finally, the ability to use not only these two modes but also cognitive restructuring. Thus very young (both chronologically and mentally) subjects would be completely *unable* to use restructuring as a mode of dissonance resolution, no matter how important the cognitions entering into the dissonant relationship.

Variables of the second type—those that change the area covered by the curves of the Figure—include cognitive complexity, amount of formal education, and various types of cognitive controls. We will not attempt to deal with a general personality variable of complexity, since it is doubtful that a strong general predisposition to complexity in all cognitive areas actually exists. [But for an extended discussion of complexity, see Bieri, Chapter 61—Ed.] Rather, our discussion will center on the effects of complexity within a given content area. When we refer to cognitive controls, we are using the clinician's category of "conflict-free adaptive mechanisms" that have generally been studied in connection with perception (Gardner, Holzman, Klein, Linton, & Spence, 1959). 'Conflict' in this definition implies that the deeper aspects of the self are involved; when this occurs, cognitive controls supposedly break down and defense mechanisms take over. Cognitive controls are seen as serving the functions for the individual of categorizing and evaluating incoming information and of fitting this information into his existing cognitive structure. Various dimensions of cognitive controls have been studied separately and as combined into cognitive styles.

The consideration of these variables leads us to an important problem not dealt with in the model. The model assumes equal inputs for individuals, i.e., equal levels of dissonance arousal. Clearly this is unrealistic in terms of actual experimental manipulations. More dissonance should be aroused, for example, in an individual who employs the cognitive control of 'sharpening' than for one who uses 'leveling' of the same complex persuasive communication, since the 'sharpener' attends to more of the incoming information. Similarly, a cognitively more simple person is likely to have more total dissonance as a result of incoming inconsistent information than is a cognitively complex individual, because there will be a greater change in the ratio of dissonant to consonant cognitions. Disregarding this problem, however, and assuming for the moment equal arousal of dissonance for all individuals, what will be the modifications in the model necessary to cope with the influence of degrees of cognitive complexity and styles of cognitive control?

The variable of complexity, we suggest, is related to the width of the area covered by the restructuring curve in the Figure. For the cognitively complex individual, the area of the restructuring curve will be extended down to cognitions of less importance, and there will be corresponding shrinking of the areas covered by the curves for change in one cognition and the lower portion of the 'stopping thinking' curve. For the cognitively simple individual, the reverse will be true; the curves for stopping thinking and change in one cognition will extend farther up the continuum of importance and the area covered by the restructuring curve will be reduced. Remember that we are referring to cognitive complexity within a given area; however, amount of formal education should be related to complexity so that those with little formal education would be expected to be less complex in many, although not all, areas (e.g., work- or hobby-related areas might be highly differentiated). Thus in general we would make the same predictions concerning the variable of formal education with regard to modifications in the model as we do for the variable of within-area complexity.

There are, of course, several other variables that are frequently confounded with complexity. Two of these are importance and knowledgeability. One is generally most complex in those areas that one considers to be important and in which one has the most knowledge. And we would have to predict that as importance and knowledgeability increase, change of *own* opinion is less likely. However, one would *not* expect an increase on either of these variables to be associated with a decrease in the rejection of incoming inconsistent information. Above all, we would expect that as complexity increases the use of change in *either* cognition would decrease in favor of the use of restructuring.

We also expect preference for a particular cognitive control to shift the area covered by the curves in the graph. For example, the 'leveler' supposedly deals with inconsistent incoming information by not seeing it. One might assume that, if it gets in, he would have a predisposition first for forgetting it, secondly for changing it, and, finally, when the control breaks down and defense mechanisms take over, for repressing it (the upper half of the 'stopping thinking' curve). The hypothetical set of curves for the 'leveler,' then, would have more area at each end of the scale covered by the two 'stopping thinking' curves and much less area, if any, devoted to the restructuring curve. Similar changes in the areas covered by the curves would be suggested for those characterized as high or low on other control dimensions. Those high on flexibility, for example, might be expected to employ restructuring over a larger range than would the average individual. Those high on 'tolerance for unrealistic experiences' might be expected to have their curves for both change and restructuring shifted up on the continuum, so that more area is covered by the 'passive forgetting' curve. Or they may be individuals who actually 'tolerate' dissonance, at low levels, where most people employ forgetting. The dimensions that have been discussed under the general rubric of cognitive controls are varied and overlapping, and no consistent categorizations have as yet been generally accepted. Thus we mention only a few suggested relationships rather than going into an exhaustive list of predictions.

Many problems remain unanswered by this first attempt at a model. First, when *do* individuals actually 'tolerate' dissonance, without either forgetting it or restructuring? We have suggested that such behavior is rare, yet we all know individuals who claim to like a certain degree of inconsistency. Certainly, 'toleration' for any length of time should occur only at low levels of importance, but when and for whom does it occur? And what does it mean, not only for the model but also for the theory when a person says he *enjoys* some dissonance?

Secondly, the model provides little help in the way of predicting data such as Steiner's (Steiner & Johnson, 1964; Steiner & Rogers, 1963) that show the use of combinations of modes of dissonance reduction. We have made a few suggestions along this line but no solid predictions. It is not easy to see, for example, the logic of how some change in one's own opinion in the direction of the opinion of the communicator *plus* some derogation of the communicator can effectively reduce dissonance. In part this problem stems from the 'all or none' characteristic of dissonance as the theory originally presented it; degrees of dissonance (except as a function of importance) are not theoretically possible, yet the distance of the position of a communicator from one's own position, for example, is clearly a variable influencing the amount of dissonance aroused independent of importance.

Thirdly, the model has nothing specific to say concerning what kind or how much restructuring will occur, if restructuring is the mode of dissonance reduction employed. Clearly, this choice will be influenced not only by the variable of importance but also by personality predispositions such as cognitive styles. A great deal more research is needed concerning exactly what kinds of cognitive realignments are indeed employed in the service of dissonance reduction.

Finally, there is the practical problem of measurement. Clearly we do not wish to judge the importance of a cognition on the basis of an individual's subsequent dissonance-reducing behavior. But obtaining an accurate independent measure of 'self-relevance' of cognitions may prove to be extremely difficult. At the extremes of the scale there is little problem. One can assume that cognitions directly pertaining to central portions of an individual's self-image (e.g., sex role, identity) will be highly important, as will cognitions pertaining to immutable physical laws (e.g., the sun rises in the East). Similarly, one can be relatively certain that certain cognitions completely unrelated to the self will have low importance. However, we generally deal with cognitions that fall in the middle ranges of importance, and how to measure the relative degree of importance of cognitions in this range is a major problem for practical application of the model.

CHAPTER 68

Depth, Centrality, and Tolerance in Cognitive Consistency

Marc Pilisuk

The University of California at Berkeley

Titchener never fully succeeded in his task of describing the elements of experience. One of the blessings of cognitive consistency theories within the past decade is that they have enabled us to bypass the thorny problem of just what the units of cognitive experience should be while describing lawful relationships among them. We still know very little about the boundaries, functions, and compositions of those distinguishable elements of experience which are related by inconsistency theories.

When we note an incongruity between a student's liking his father and disliking his father's meddling in his (the student's) career choice, we can carefully reduce the relevant elements to entities (or to dimensions) which fit neatly into one or another paradigm. This we can do without a good grasp of the significance of what is a father, a dislike, or meddling from the view of the particular student in question. The usefulness of this short cut is demonstrated by the number of interesting theories dealing with cognitive processing of incompatibles and by a wealth of research generated. The difficulties in gaining a completely satisfactory handle on human cognitive experience, however, remain to disturb both the models and the research findings.

A major problem emerging from research findings is that, however the incongruity is conceived, some persons in some situations tolerate it or even prefer it. A study by Freedman (1965c), for example, showed that 17 of 18 subjects chose to request dissonant information in preference to information supporting their own opinions. The author points to a list of possible factors to account for this. The dissonant information may have been more useful. The information may have been more interesting. A confident subject is more prone to seek dissonance especially in areas which are not controversial. These are additions and not original parts to the theory of dissonance. Analogous additions to the theory of cognitive balance are used by Price, Harburg, and Newcomb (1966) to explain why subjects fail to report the anticipated end-state when presented with certain particular balanced (or imbalanced) situations. Specifically, subjects found dissatisfaction with situations involving a negative evaluation of another person although these situations presented apparently balanced states (see

Chapter 2 for a detailed review of these findings). The authors suspect that implicit assumptions of reciprocity in relationships may vary from one situation to another. Similarly, emotional ambivalence or uncertainty (from a weak description of the other person) may affect the postulated relationship. Last, the degree of engagement (or concern) with the cognitive elements being considered may also play a part in determining the tension coming from a particular incongruity.

What the 'additions to theory' in these studies seem to suggest is: (a) that some things just do not matter to people enough to make them uncomfortable regardless of how incongruous the information in the thoughts might appear to an outsider, (b) that a certain amount of incongruity may be preferred, and (c) that some thoughts are not easily described because we do not comprehend their connotations, associations, or unit relationships. The disparities between models—some establishing congruity among beliefs, some among attitudes, some between decision-commitments and behavior, others between logical premises of ideas, and still others between affect and ideation—suggest some elements of a basic dilemma. We still have relatively few cues into what has deeper meaning for individuals and will thus resist change. And we still have few cues into the units which comprise experience and which therefore must be related in incongruity theories.

DEPTH

One place to begin the search for what matters most, among thought processes, is to examine what developed first. The earliest perceptual distinctions appear to be evaluative and relevant only to the question of whether a particular object is or is not edible. Shortly thereafter the evaluation is between who can and who cannot be trusted. Evidently, this same gross evaluative dimension remains a first principle for the categorization of later concepts (cf. Osgood, Suci, & Tannenbaum, 1957).

A second glimpse at early cognition is provided by the speculations of Fairbairn and of H. S. Sullivan with regard to certain early and apparently ill-defined representations of a "good mother" or "bad mother" and a rather amorphous "me." Sullivan even adds a "not me" and leaves room for other objects as well. Fairbairn refers to such representational images as "internal objects" which may be either in tension or at rest with regard to one another (Fairbairn, 1952a, 1952b). Although the rules for establishing congruity are not formalized in Fairbairn's theory, his examples suggest a primitive mechanism of Heiderian balance acting among these ill-defined precursors of later cognition. It is also noted that gross incongruities or tensions occurring at this time fall upon an infant ill adapted to the tasks of rationalization, separation, or postdecision dissonance reduction. Neither can the infant resolve incongruity by reversing his attitudes either toward his parents or toward his own limited pleasures. Lacking such modes of handling incongruity, the infant incurs grave implications for his further development from early incongruous experiences. The double-bind theory suggests, for example, that incongruity between the overt and covert meanings conveyed to the infant by the mother is a cause of schizophrenia (Bateson et al., 1964).

In some instances, then, the tension deriving from incongruity is not tolerable and is indicative of severe breakdown in the ordering of the world of experience. For the infant, at least, the intolerable incongruities involve the salient components of his life space, evaluation of a significant other by self, evaluation of self by a significant other, and probability of receiving nurturance. Later cognitions which represent symbolically the self, significant attributes of the self concept, and significant others hold associations to these earlier preconscious experiences. Especially where undue tension has blocked new learning, the original representations remain in unconscious storage retaining a degree of immunity from later (linguistically differentiated) experience. This immunity, in the case of incongruities, means a source of perpetual tension for the individual whose earliest representations stood in incongruous relationships. Hence, whether or not individuals "naturally" differ in gross tolerance for the tensions of incongruity, they will have, at the deepest levels of thought, a source of individual difference in ongoing tension levels. Moreover, undue tension could be aroused by an apparently superficial incongruity, in apparently normal people, if the particular incongruous attitudes are bound to earlier and more vulnerable representations.

The first distinction I would wish to see made when discussing incongruous components is the psychological 'depth' of the component. Without trying to develop a methodology for projective assessment, it will suffice here to point out the need for including in one's model a way of telling whether one or more of the elements to an incongruity is so deeply represented in an individual's experience that incongruities in its arousal indicate not minor tension but rather intense anxiety. This would give some insights not only into individual differences in managing incongruity but also into the relative tenacity of certain beliefs related to self and significant others. [See Colby's concept of the "charge" of a belief in Chapter 47—Ed.]

CENTRALITY

Even among attitudes and beliefs which are accessible to the individual, there are major differences in their functional significance. I should like to assume in a model of the cognitive field that it is structured with a self at the center immediately surrounded by a set of 'self-relevant' objects or events. These central entities are tied to each other by statements of probability (beliefs) and of evaluation (attitudes).[1] The more central regions will contain strong ties among beliefs and high probabilities that self-relevant activities will lead to positively evaluated outcomes. Such stable anchorages are useful in retaining a reserve of congruous, self-affirming information.

The argument is that people believe, with reasonably high probabilities, that their bases of self-respect will be met. The beliefs and attitudes relevant to the fulfillment of self concept attributes are likely to remain intransigent in the face of incongruity, while the more peripheral attributes are likely to change. While this seems obvious, it does raise certain questions.

First, is there an independent way of judging self-relevance or is the

---

[1] The distinction between belief and attitude and the rationale for the definitions used for each is developed in an article by Fishbein (1965).

theory tautological? In other words, can we only infer self-relevance from observations of what actually refuses to yield under conditions of incongruity? I tend to believe that independent assessment of self-relevance or centrality is possible although it may present unusual difficulties.

Secondly, this formulation would appear to argue that self-criticism is shunned or that significant others and stable parts of the environment are always protected from damaging incongruity. Certainly, this is not always the case. Nevertheless, incongruity involving both a self-attribute and a significant other does seem to be a particularly difficult incongruity to tolerate (Pilisuk, 1962). When I wish to illustrate the balance principle in classroom discussions, I ask people first to identify the worst conceivable act, then their most loved or liked friend, and then their reaction to the information that the friend has committed the act. In hundreds of instances I have never found the imbalance to be simply tolerated.

The point to be made, however, is that the relative invulnerability of some beliefs and attitudes to change is a matter which not only forces resolution of incongruity among central entities but also permits the entertaining of certain other incongruities that are more free from tension.

Anyone can assimilate criticism better from an insignificant adversary than from a trusting friend. But is it easier to tolerate criticism from an uncertain friend than from a sure one? Here the issue would seem to hinge upon the centrality of the criticism. It seems easier to take peripheral criticism from the true friend because one suspects that the friendship is not threatened but is rather helped by the integrity of the exchange.[2] Some models of inconsistency resolution have placed heavy emphasis upon the number of incongruities to be assuaged (or aggravated) by a particular resolution or upon the number of reinforcing assertions supporting a particular attitude. The illustration above was intended to suggest that some indication of functional significance of any particular inconsistency should also be noted. The works of Rosenberg (1956) and of Carlson (1956) suggest particular significance for beliefs and attitudes which are instrumental to the needs of the self.

The same illustration, of criticism from a friend, raises the issue of the *implications* which one belief or attitude may hold for another. If O dislikes something I have done, he may or may not dislike me also. If O expresses a view which shares my estimation of some candidate, this may or may not implicate my estimates of O's more disturbing habits. This, in turn, may or may not implicate my attitude toward another close friend who likes O but does not like the candidate. From the myriad of potential congruous and incongruous beliefs some are implicated and others are not when incongruity is aroused. Mere storage of inconsistent information does not seem to produce tension. A model of cognitive operations should have

---

[2] A difficult problem for a researcher comes from the fact that the centrality of the criticism may be less a function of the message content than of the intentions attributed to the source (Iwao, 1963). Here again is the dilemma of independent assessments of component elements in an incongruous situation. If a person is likely to see two ostensibly equal messages as different (as in prestige studies), then it is possible that the dissonance attributed in the situation appears stronger to the experimenter than to the subject. An interesting study by Kelman and Eagly (1965) deals with this problem of attribution in message contents.

some room for the insulation of components. Ideally, it should be able also to predict the type of implications to be aroused when an individual perceives a given incongruity.

TOLERANCE

J. McV. Hunt has argued that slight degrees of incongruity are sought by the child in accord with his ability to accommodate them. The concept is that moderate incongruity presents challenge and opportunity for mastery (Hunt, 1960). [See also Chapters 16 and 31.] Such opportunities are likely to meet with varying degrees of success as persons go on to develop different capacities and/or interest in the meeting of new incongruities. Harvey (1965) suggests a definite personality constellation with a more differentiated and complex system for judging information and more tolerance for incongruous circumstances. Driver, similarly, postulates a General Incongruity Adaptation Level (GIAL) below which incongruity is sought and above which it is avoided (Driver & Streufert, 1965). These are promising breaks into the question of who tolerates what degree of incongruity. But intense exploration into the content of cognitive elements and their functional significance to the self will surely compound the difficulties in these attempts (see Chapter 63).

Psychotherapists speak frequently of false cures, or flights into reality which sometimes occur with the first blush of transference phenomena. The patient gains a verbal but nonetheless superficial capacity to discuss the inconsistencies of his own life even in matters of apparently deep personal sensitivity. The therapist recognizes a level at which the patient's acceptance of the incongruities in the patient's self concept have not really been assimilated. Here we are faced with the problem of a superficiality in tolerance for inconsistency which persons may assume for purposes of impressing therapists, friends, research psychologists, or even themselves.

A general index of tolerance for incompatibles must sample, from an unknown population, potential attitude-belief incongruities. If we do not know what is deep or shallow, central or peripheral to the individual's view of his own well being, it is quite conceivable that we have either sampled only the peripheral or that we have engaged our subjects to different degrees with our instruments. It is possible that some of our high GIAL people have had their own areas of sensitivity bypassed by the instrument or that some persons are able to treat more of the world with marginal involvements and are hence able to manage incongruities under a wider set of circumstances. Many measures of incongruity tolerance permit the individual to respond as an 'ideal self.' In our measures of an aspect of an ideal self, we may be obtaining reflections of an 'ideal culture,' a culture in which deep, or at least enduring commitment is suspect and the 'cool' accommodator is admired.

The work of Vannoy (1965) suggests that various measures of cognitive complexity do not measure the same thing. Some of the measures used in that factor analytic study were clearly related to ability to deal with incongruity. Even among those most relevant measures, the factor structure differed greatly from one measure to another. It would seem that a model capable of dealing with individuality in dissonance tolerance would have to make distinctions among the regions of experience in which the incongruities are admitted.

THE MODEL

I would like to suggest the outlines of a model of cognitive systems in which the component elements lie at three different removes from the self. The self, at the core, maintains an indisputable belief in the probability of its continued being and in its essential positiveness. When the self is not so depicted, the cognitive system has broken down.

The self is ringed by a region of commitment, then by a region of interest, and lastly by a sphere of transient attention. Interconnectives link objects or events within the same or adjacent regions to one another. The interconnectives are statements of probability of association (beliefs), e.g., O expects a sunny day, or statements of evaluation (attitudes), e.g., O likes the sunshine. The several different types of incongruities described in the literature are possible whenever there are at least three units with common connections. As one moves from central to peripheral areas, the ratio of attitudes to beliefs declines.

To complicate the pattern further, an individual has two (at least two) such systems. They are the simpler, deeper subconscious system and a more differentiated conscious one. Interconnectives between the systems are possible and indeed likely among similar objects represented at both levels. Imbalance or incongruous relations among deeper entities are a source of continuous tension. This tension is either constrained by consistency operations working upon the connections with the surface level phenomena or borne as anxiety.

I think that most of what we measure as a recurring form of intolerance for incongruity or dissonance is to be found in the surface system in the area in which one of the component elements (the unyielding one) is in the region of commitment and another (the one which changes) is in the region of interest. Where we are likely to find some tolerance for inconsistency or to find reliable individual differences in such tolerance is in the region of interests. The tolerance would be found most among inconsistencies which are not strongly evaluative and which are not tied by numerous beliefs and attitudes to the region of commitment. The area of transient attention, I would guess, offers little opportunity for incongruity tolerance except, perhaps, under those highly simplified environments in which the slightest stimulation providing a contrast from adaptation level is sought.

One function, not the only one, of ordering the cognitive field is to provide the image of a self and a near environment worthy and capable of need satisfaction. Cognitive imbalance involving, let us say, a mother image and self-attribute (feeding) is a source of anxiety, not only for the infant but for the adult who has long since superimposed a more complex set of concepts upon his cognitive field. Symbolic associations may sensitize the individual, especially the neurotic individual, to treat imbalances among surface phenomena as if they represented earlier, more central imbalances.

I think that the healthy individual has very strong commitments, to his ideas, his skills, and to people. He is not easily swayed in these attitudes. The evaluative ties which link his committed concepts to his self or to each other tend to resist change. Since evaluative judgments are inherently subjective, this involves no major distortion except perhaps in the perception of the evaluations by others of oneself.

Here, it may be useful to depart from the Heiderian formulations which treat ego's attitudes essentially like attitudes of other persons. The role of others' attitudes in a cognitive system seems to involve a belief component as well as an evaluative one. A person attaches a probability to the other person's actually holding the particular evaluative orientation. In the matter of beliefs, the healthy person would probably be more tolerant of incongruities, even in the region of commitment, than his less healthy counterpart. He might either accept them or else make finer distinctions which indicate the probability of association under more precise conditions.

The problem then, in predicting the outcome of any particular cognitive inconsistency, is to know where on the cognitive map of the particular individual one is landing. The methodological implication of this is that at least some of our studies should pose cognitive inconsistencies among objects, events, or constructs which the subject himself has contributed and pegged for us in his own field of experience. For example, one might pose a subject with inconsistencies among constructs which he has supplied in George Kelley's Role Construct Repertory Test or in concepts alluded to in repeated tests of association.

The second implication is that in some studies we should permit a wide latitude of responses to the handling of incongruity. It is possible that a person uses one style of incongruity resolution in his region of interest and still another where the concepts hit closer to home. In the Unpleasant Situation Test (Pilisuk, 1963a) which presented individuals with some dozen imbalanced situations involving themselves, eight separate categories of answers were offered. All were used. Obviously we cannot let the subject define both independent and dependent variables in the same study and still expect interpretable measurement. But we might, for example, present TAT cards 'doctored' with additional incongruities and try to develop the resolution modes from a scoring of open-ended responses.

The third and final implication for methodology is that we devote some of our studies to a deeper familiarity with our subjects as they go about making cognitive constructions and appraisals of the meaningful parts of their social world. Newcomb's work (1961) on acquaintance suggests that principles may be found which govern transitions from depth to superficiality as in the course of therapeutic relationships (Pilisuk, 1963b).

Our paradigms of incongruity have sensitized us to the mechanisms of information handling. What we still need are better schema to tell us what is central and what peripheral, what is deep and what shallow, what is intolerable and what welcome among the ingredients of the human experience.

CHAPTER 69

Modes of Resolution and Reasoning in Attitude Change Experiments

Walter Weiss

Hunter College of the City University of New York

In general, the object of theory and empirical analysis is to seek explanations for the effects of selected antecedents or systematically arranged test conditions. While this generic purpose is relatively obvious, it is easy to forget that the manner of formulating the instigating conditions and the kinds of effects to be examined can have a decisive influence not only on the style and substance of the theoretical explanation of the observed relationship but on the nature of the relationship itself. This is particularly so, when the designation of the antecedent requires something more than an assertion of objective characteristics, instead involving, implicitly or explicitly, the subject's conception or interpretation of a complex stimulus condition.

For example, consider the situation where a well vs. poorly regarded source delivers a communication that is congruent with vs. discrepant from the initial attitudes in his audience. The set of four stimulus conditions may be described merely in terms of the combinations of the two characteristics of regard for the source and discrepancy from initial attitudes. The effects will then tend to be identified by descriptive terms that are theoretically neutral and that are applicable to the consequents of all four instigating conditions. However, the stimulus relations may also be coordinated to the conceptual dimension of consistency-inconsistency and described in such language. Although this type of location could represent no more than a semantic change, it is usually taken to imply that the subject perceived the theoretically identified inconsistency and reacted in terms of this motivating characteristic. (A more direct test of this primary assumption, at least involving assessment of the subject's *expectation* of a source's position, in advance of exposure to a communication, is often omitted in research.) From this perspective, effects are designated and thereby construed as modes of resolving the inconsistency. In consequence, research so guided will tend to focus on those effects which can be taken to serve such a function and on those conditions which contain or stim-

Preparation of this paper was aided by funds from the Office of Naval Research under Contract NONR 4309

ulate inconsistencies to be resolved. Also, on this formulation, if the inconsistency can be resolved or is resolved by a particular behavior mode, the occurrence of a second effect which could also be construed as having this property would be redundant and presumably psychologically wasteful. Hence, the assumption follows naturally that modes of resolution tend to be alternatives to each other; if one mode solves the problem of the inconsistency then a second need not be used or would at best be only lightly used. But which modes take precedence with what relative effectiveness in an *open* situation has yet to receive adequate empirical analysis or even close and continuous attention.

Unfortunately, conceiving of effects as modes of resolving inconsistencies can lead the unaware to the natural but mistaken inference that the effects resolve the instigating inconsistency, i.e., produce a consequent consistency or remove the inconsistency. At best, research indicates merely a reduction in the extent of the initial degree of inconsistency, with considerable residual inconsistency remaining. Also, the degree of residual inconsistency observed for a given subject, presumably the resultant of the operation of one or more modes of resolution, may very well be comparable to the original degree of inconsistency faced by another subject which presumably would still require reduction via some mode of resolution. To cope with these occurrences and the not infrequent absence of any discernible reduction of inconsistency, some concept relating to a threshold for tolerance of inconsistency becomes necessary. However, the independent assessment of this concept by direct or inferential procedures is rarely to be found in research, with the result that theory-based predictions are more readily preserved against seeming disconfirmations.

In contrast to the foregoing, if outcomes are merely referred to as effects, then these primary assumptions are unlikely to be maintained as theoretical prejudgments; rather, if such statements *were* made, they would reflect inductions from adequate empirical evidence. In addition, it would be expected that a variety of effects could occur and therefore should be examined, rather than that a limitation be imposed to a particular one or two that are made possible by the conditions and tested by the procedure of the experiment. Since some of these effects may be related to presumed mediating processes, this would mean that internal evidence would be available to bear upon critical links in a theory which utilizes a sequential mediating formula of stimulus condition(s) → mediating process(es) or response(s) → effects. Additionally, if conceptually similar types of responses are found regardless of whether consistency or inconsistency obtains or is perceived, the conceptualization of responses evidenced when inconsistency occurs would be set in a new light (cf. Nuttin, 1966); and the need for a different conceptual base for interpreting responses to inconsistency vs. consistency would be obviated. That is, a danger of the implied prejudgment inherent in special labeling of responses to a conceptually discriminated class of antecedents is that it may preclude or impede the development of a more general theory of attitude change by overlooking similarities of responses across a wider class of antecedents. (It is worth noting that there is relatively little experimental research on the effects of communications that are *congruent* with the initial positions of the recipients. A particular aspect of this problem has been studied by McGuire [e.g., 1964].) Essentially, there is a need to examine a wide variety of effects and to note their interrelations without constrictive prejudgment concerning which ones are primary or what the interrelations are, in order to understand better the impact of potential attitude-change experiences. Finally, since in the ordinary, open environment a diversity of responses can and usually does occur, wider generalizability of experimental results would be better served by the examination of varied and naturally occurring effects.

There are many kinds of effects that can be related to exposure to a communication or to an attitude-change experience. Among them are those connected to the principal meaning of the concept of attitude, such as evaluative responses toward the attitude object; those descriptive of related aspects of attitude, such as informational support, saliency, time perspective, policy orientation (cf. Smith, Bruner, & White, 1956); and those reflecting psychological processes considered relevant to, if not mediators of, attitude change, such as comprehension, retention, affective arousal, judgment. Of particular significance, but unfortunately imposing formidable methodological problems of assessment, are the naturally occurring, implicit responses elicited *during* the communication experience. No implication is intended in any of the foregoing that all of these effects or responses should be assessed in every study, although if this were feasible the generation of a matrix of such information would be invaluable in respect to theory; rather, what is suggested is that several should be examined to determine their interrelations over studies and to determine if they are differentially responsive to change in relation to different kinds of instigating conditions, as well as to determine their relationship to the primary measure of attitude. Of particular importance is the inclusion of those responses which are taken to reflect processes that are often used to explain the obtained and predicted connections between antecedents and effects. Their value is especially evident in respect to testing *post hoc* analyses of unanticipated or unpredicted effects.

It should be apparent that I favor the more open heuristic, systematically empirical approach, with theory of the 'grand' variety used as a lightly controlling guide to research. Perhaps some indication of this personally preferred strategy can be given by a brief description of a few of the findings and resultant conjectures from a portion of my current research, which seeks to encompass a variety of effects of persuasive communications.

It is customarily assumed as a primary postulate that the recipient of a communication is not passive psychologically during a communication experience. A variety of reactions, besides those minimal ones related to comprehending and attending to the communication, are likely to occur from time to time. Of particular relevance to an understanding of communication effects, but difficult to assess directly, are those continuous reactions which may be suitably labeled 'cognitive work.' That is, communication stimuli may bring to mind arguments, even if only in vague and incomplete outline, that support a recipient's position (if, indeed, he has one) and rebut or buttress points made by the communicator (Hovland, Lumsdaine, & Sheffield, 1949). A reasonable assumption would be that, other things equal, the attitude change effectiveness of a communication will be inversely related to such communication-stimulated rehearsal of reasons supporting the recipient's original attitude and directly related to the time lapse between exposure to a communicated argument and its implicit rebuttal. (The necessary changes in respect to an attitude-supporting communication are relatively obvious.) In other words, the attitudinal impact of a message point (and the message as a whole) is likely to be reduced if it is quickly counterattacked by a self-generated argument of some cogency. (This effect is separate from diversion of attention which can also occur.) Conversely, self-actuated recall and thinking about or mulling over one or more of the communicator's points may increase the communication's attitude change effectiveness.

On the premise that the recipient's regard for a communicator probably affects such reactions, the reasonable assumption can be drawn that, other things equal, favorableness of regard for the communicator is inversely related to the thinking of direct counterarguments and attitude-supporting reasons for one's own position and directly related to the lapse of time before doing so. Additionally, favorable regard should be directly related to continued, self-induced thinking about the communicator's assertions. However, such effects may occur whether or not a change of attitude follows from exposure to the communication. That is, pondering the source's viewpoint and considering the arguments supporting one's own position may be only loosely linked to or have only a modest influence on attitude change; for the latter may very well be induced more by the connection, for example, between assertions and salient values or goals than by mere thinking about arguments and reasons. Nevertheless, this kind of implicit responding can be considered in its own right as a significant ongoing reaction to a communication. One testable inference pertaining to this reaction is that evaluation of the communicator should differentially affect the variety or kinds of reasons people offer in defense of their own attitudes on an issue. That is, the cognitive work induced by exposure to a communication (even if it is only rethinking a position) ought to be revealed in the kinds of reasons offered in support of one's own position, if these are examined shortly after the communication experience. Reason-giving yields not only an unconstrained manifold of responses but reflects the assimilation and selective utilization of information and arguments, and not merely their learning and retention. An additional source of highly suggestive information can be obtained from questions concerning action intentions, i.e., the subject's willingness to engage in certain kinds of attitude-related public behavior.

Space limitations permit only brief mention of a few suggestive findings, based on the data of several studies (Weiss, 1964; Weiss & Solomon, 1965, 1966), concerning the effects of communications and sources on the reasons people offer in support of their own positions on an issue and on their willingness to engage in attitude-relevant actions. Regardless of the varying strengths of the patterns or the appearance of some in more than one study, all require additional confirmation. Nevertheless, they should illustrate some of the subtle effects that can occur and whose examination may be fruitful for theory. For convenience, exemplifications will be drawn principally from Weiss and Solomon (1966).

Contrary to what might be expected, people who were initially favorable to the communicated viewpoint that Communist China should be admitted to the UN decreased mention of positive consequences of this policy. Although this type of reason was given some prominence in the communication and was frequently noted by control subjects, its significance may have been inadvertently reduced by the communication's considerable emphasis on the primary argument that the UN should contain all nations. This assumption implies that the organization or structure of a communication can narrow the cognitive support considered worth mentioning by favorable recipients. However, in partial compensation for this reduction, the *very* favorable subjects increased their mention of uncommon or idiosyncratic supporting reasons; this effect was somewhat greater when the source was poorly regarded than when well regarded. The latter difference suggests the conjecture that the very favorable subjects may have been seeking to establish a basis of difference between themselves and the negative source, by indicating that they had other or a wider range of reasons to support their position (cf. Birch, 1945). In contrast, attitudinal congruence with the positive source may have released the very favorable subjects from having to focus on obvious reasons and stimulated them to note less ordinary ones. Essentially, these speculations imply that the nature of the source induced differing motivations for the increased mention of less common reasons by the very favorable subjects.

In respect to recipients who were opposed to the communicator's viewpoint, the well regarded source, in comparison with other sources, produced an overall decrease in mention of reasons supporting the subjects' own views on the issue. This kind of effect was not very simply related to a change of attitude on the issue, although among the moderately opposed it may have signified a weakening of adherence to their original positions or an induced uncertainty about the cogency of their positions, to which other influences could contribute to produce attitude change. The implied assumption that this kind of cognitive effect, resulting from the pressure of a cogent communication, is somewhat independent of attitude change receives some support from the reactions of the *very* unfavorable subjects. These recipients evidenced an increase in mention of the 'bad' characteristics of Communist China as a reason for opposing her admission into the UN, a reason which may be taken to counter implicitly the dominant argument in the communication that all nations should be in the UN; but, they mentioned less frequently uncommon or idiosyncratic supporting reasons. It is as though they were narrowing the cognitive support for their attitudes, following a forceful attack, by giving less consideration to uncommon reasons of uncertain strength and, instead, concentrating on ones considered to be strong and fundamental.

Expressed action intentions (involving willingness to distribute literature, convince a friend, and sign a petition) of the initially favorable subjects were not modified by the communication favoring the admission of Communist China into the UN. (These action intentions were not requested by the communicator but were merely assessed in the posttest questionnaire.) However, this lack of overall effect masked divergent patterns of response: the communication increased the willingness of the very favorable subjects to engage in such actions in support of the communicator's viewpoint and decreased their unwillingness to do so, but had a somewhat reverse effect on the moderately favorable subjects. Separate from these overall effects was the finding that the poorly regarded source increased the *un*willingness of the initially favorable subjects to engage in actions supporting the communicator's viewpoint. This adverse effect was found mainly among the moderately favorable subjects, rather than among the very favorable. However, this negative effect on behavioral intentions occurred in the absence of an adverse effect on general position on the issue (cf. Weiss, 1957, 1964). What this suggests is that being made aware of attitudinal congruence with a disliked person or group may not cause a person to change his mind on the issue, but if he is not one of the strong adherents of this viewpoint, it may weaken his willingness to take public actions in support of it.

In general, the communication decreased the willingness of the initially moderately *or* very unfavorable subjects to engage in actions *opposing* the communicator's viewpoint. This effect was least when the source was of low prestige and greatest when of high prestige. Also, the communication increased the willingness of the moderately unfavorable subjects to undertake actions supporting the communicator's viewpoint, probably owing to the greater attitude change effect on these subjects. Perhaps, a general effect of a cogent countercommunication is to induce sufficient uncertainty that the normal congruence between attitude and attitude-supporting action intentions is weakened, as evidenced primarily by increased inhibition against engaging in actions opposing the communicator's viewpoint. This inhibition effect may be decreased if the source is poorly regarded and increased if well regarded. Evidently, an increase in willingness to support the communicator's viewpoint behaviorally requires a marked shift toward his position on the issue.

The patterns of effects permit the general conjecture that behavioral *intentions* may be more responsive to communication stimuli or more labile than is general regard for the attitude object or general position on an issue. This position is based on the several occurrences of change in expressed intentions without a coordinate change in measured position. Obviously, further research is necessary to establish the validity and generality of this surmise and to bring under experimental analysis the effects of communication experiences on overt, attitude-related behavior.

CHAPTER 70

The Panglossian World of Self-Justification

Karl E. Weick
University of Minnesota

Candide's durable tutor Dr. Pangloss, reflecting on an apparently frightful set of experiences, remarks with typical calm,

> There is a chain of events in this best of all possible worlds: for if you had not been turned out of a beautiful mansion at the point of a jackboot for the love of Lady Cunegonde, and if you had not been involved in the Inquisition, and had not wandered over America on foot, and had not struck the Baron with your sword, and lost all those sheep you brought from Eldorado, you would not be here eating candied fruits and pistachio nuts (Translation of Voltaire by Butt, 1947).

Small consolation for Candide perhaps, but then who could ever hope to dissuade Dr. Pangloss?

Amusing as the optimistic Dr. Pangloss may appear, he provides an uncommonly accurate model of subject behavior in studies of self-justification. For even in the laboratory, no matter what fate befalls the subject, he often winds up convinced that this is indeed the best of all possible worlds. Such behavior, however, compounds problems for the researcher studying self-justification or other modes of cognitive escape from painful realities. Despite the best intentions to channel justification into specific areas and to create troublesome dilemmas by reducing justification, investigators have found it difficult to stabilize justification sufficiently so that lawful relationships can be detected. It is perhaps one of the ironies of dissonance research that one of its more enduring findings is also one of the least surprising, namely, when justification is reduced, persons try to increase it. There are some studies of self-justification which suggest that investigators can successfully sabotage the Panglossian world of subjects and learn something about how it works, although the degree of such external control must be regarded as limited.

Preparation of this chapter was facilitated by the National Science Foundation Grant GS-1042.

A PROTOTYPIC SELF-JUSTIFICATION EXPERIMENT

I propose to illustrate the difficulties of studying modes of dissonance reduction by focusing on the self-justification paradigm, concentrating on settings *other than* counterattitudinal advocacy. My interest is in those experiments wherein subjects do something besides argue, with varying amounts of support, that some belief contrary to theirs is correct. [For discussion of counterattitudinal advocacy, see Section IV F.]

The prototypic justification experiment is actually quite simple in its basic design. The subject arrives anticipating that he will perform some task; the reasons for his continuing with the activity are rendered more equivocal either because unanticipated negative features are added (e.g., a person is evaluated negatively by his peers, as in Kiesler & Corbin, 1965) or positive features are reduced (e.g., subjects are told their results are of less than normal value, as in Freedman, 1963); the subject commits himself to continue with the exercise, now aware of the unattractive working conditions; and then he performs some activity which presumably enables him to generate additional justification.

Departures from this basic design are considerable. The principal activity which the subject performs may be the means for him to restore justification (Weick, 1964) or it may be the means to further reduce justification (Aronson & Mills, 1959). In the latter case, evaluations of the activity are obtained at its conclusion. Commitment may also be handled in several ways. The subject may be given an explicit choice to continue with the activity (Pallak, 1966), commitment may be varied by the amount of behavior which he must perform (Brehm, 1960b) or the visibility of the behavior (Walster & Prestholdt, 1966), or commitment may never be raised as an issue (Freedman, 1963). While efforts to increase justification are usually measured by retrospective evaluation, they may be assessed through other behaviors such as reaction time (Cottrell, 1965), underrecall (Johnson, 1966), conformity (Gerard, 1965), quality of performance (Adams & Jacobsen, 1964), quantity of performance (Lawler & O'Gara, 1966), learning (Ferdinand, 1965), projection (Edlow & Kiesler, 1966), exposure to information (Freedman, 1965c), subsequent choices (Freedman, 1965b), or GSR reactivity (Zimbardo, Cohen, Weisenberg, Dworkin, & Firestone, 1966). Typically, more than one dependent measure is obtained and occasionally these measures are correlated to determine whether several resolutions were used simultaneously (Steiner & Johnson, 1964).

With this brief outline in mind and with some suggestion of the domain of studies regarded as relevant to this discussion, it is now possible to look more closely at some problems in these investigations.

PROBLEMS OF INTERPRETATION

Several properties of justification studies render interpretation quite difficult and it is the purpose of this section to indicate some of these problems. Few topics pose quite the measurement problem that the study of self-justification does. The investigator essentially wants to learn how the subject has reconstructed his world in the absence of sufficient justification, but to do so, he often must ask leading questions which suggest resolutions that may not have occurred to the subject. While there have been some attempts to bypass this problem through the measurement of behavioral change, even these measures may suggest resolutions.

Behavioral measures also produce other problems. When they are obtained, changes in belief are also often recorded. Some studies show simultaneous belief and behavior change while other studies suggest that there is an inverse relationship between these two avenues of resolution (e.g., Weick, 1966). One explanation which has been offered for these puzzling findings is that when a person can use any of several resolutions, his actual choice is determined by dispositional factors. This assumes that all resolutions are equally apparent to the subject, an assumption which is questionable given the differential prompts that are embedded in measures. On commonsense grounds it would seem probable that behavioral changes should be accompanied by some cognitive changes, if for no other reason than that persons represent their behavior cognitively. Perhaps investigators have simply assessed an inappropriate set of beliefs. But, it is also possible that there is a complex interaction among intensity and kind of inconsistency and the mode of resolution that is used, a point of view that recently has been detailed by Johnson (1966).

It is also unclear how subjects react when they are confronted by several possible resolutions to restore justification. An abundance of resolutions could be confusing and occasion haphazardness in implementation. Another possibility is that when several sources of justification are present, each source becomes less important and, therefore, subjects are less committed to a single resolution. If this were to occur, probably no single resolution would show significant differences even though several are actually used. An abundance of resolutions might constitute an approach-approach conflict situation. From what is known concerning these dilemmas (e.g., Cofer & Appley, 1964), any slight preference for a specific resolution should result in its prompt implementation. However, if the resolutions constitute an approach-avoidance situation, we would expect to find much more vacillation in the use of a single resolution. Perhaps the most complex possibility is that when an array of resolutions are available, and one must be chosen, there could be lingering dissonance once the choice is made because the person has rejected other attractive resolutions.

Aside from the fact that measures suggest resolutions, studies of self-justifications often suffer because subjects are resourceful in justifying their actions in ways that were not anticipated when the study was designed or in ways that were unsuccessfully blocked. Some idea of the diversity of rationales available to subjects with insufficient justification is found in a stimulating paper by Garfinkel (1960) which details 14 separate, commonsense rationales which persons can use to justify their actions. This paper is valuable because it details potential resolution processes in an orderly format, but it is also sobering because relatively few of these potential rationales have been measured in studies of self-justification.

Inadequate justification is typically produced by a sudden removal of usual supports for activities. A growing body of research in learning theory has examined the effects on performance of sudden shifts in reward (e.g., Logan & Wagner, 1965, pp. 43–46). These studies suggest that when a high level of reward is suddenly reduced, performance drops *below* that of a group which has continually experienced low reward. Lawson (1965) has discussed recent research (e.g., Reynolds, 1961) which demonstrates the possible existence of behavioral contrast effect. This phenomenon can be demonstrated in a free-operant situation where a pigeon is reinforced equally for pecking, sometimes at a green key and sometimes at a red key. Training is continued until stable and equal rates of responding are obtained for both keys. If the rate of reinforcement for one of the keys is drastically reduced, the rate of responding for that key drops sharply. But the fascinating result is that the rate of responding for the other key *increases* over its previous level although none of the procedures in the presence of the stimulus have changed at all. While the mechanisms for these contrast effects are unclear and the findings are based largely on infrahuman species, it seems clear that unanticipated changes in reward do affect performance, and since most studies of self-justification involve such changes, their effects must be considered when investigators try to explain the effects of insufficient justification.

One final problem within justification studies should be noted. Manipulations may interact with dispositional variables in such a way that the experimental outcomes, even when significant, are produced by a small subsample of subjects. For example, when persons agree to perform a meaningless task under varying amounts of coercion, choice may have the effect of differentially motivating those subjects who are high on need achievement (e.g., Atkinson, 1964). High need-achievers might expend considerable effort to perform a task which they have chosen. The presence within the experimental group of a subsample of highly motivated need achievers could inflate the experimental mean sufficiently so that it would look like the experimental group as a whole worked harder to justify their decision. What really happened, however, was that only part of them worked harder, and they did so for reasons other than dissonance reduction. While this possible interaction between choice and disposition is not a problem confined to justification studies, it is a distinct possibility in studies which employ behavioral measures.

The preceding points, all mostly methodological, exemplify problems in studying self-justification. Next, we propose to look more closely at some neglected distinctions and resolutions in justification research.

INVISIBLE ACTORS IN JUSTIFICATION STUDIES

The purpose of this section is to suggest several commonplace ways to handle insufficient justifications which investigators have failed to assess. Our intent is to suggest that there are several dimensions relevant to justification which have been neglected, but which, if examined, could increase our understanding of the justification process. To describe these dimensions, we have distinguished seven different strategies of resolution which should be evident, but which apparently have been overlooked so far.

1. The calm apologist. Some persons, who find themselves in an unattractive situation for insufficient reason, frankly admit that they were wrong or plead that there were extenuating circumstances for their behavior. While these persons are clearly discomforted by the insufficient justification, their admission of wrongdoing should be sufficient to reduce any need for further justification. It is not uncommon for persons to make faulty decisions and it would seem that investigators may underestimate the

extent to which persons are accustomed to this occurrence. A related point
is that the calm apologist may make an implicit appeal to the experimenter
for some understanding and sympathy regarding his plight, and when he
fails to receive such assurance, may become indignant and more indifferent
about what he does. The measures employed in most justification studies
seem to be insensitive to this resolution and some theories of self-justification
would be hard-pressed to incorporate the psychology of apology.

2. *The assertive defender.* Faced with a situation of inadequate justification, a person might be content simply to maintain that his decision was
acceptable, but he might also act in ways intended to convince, to overwhelm, or to silence the audience (whatever it may be) which regards his
decision with some suspicion. While many studies of self-justification do
contain measures which reflect variations in the intensity of a resolution,
these distinctions are crude. They do not take account of the audience
toward which the justification is directed, nor do they indicate whether the
intensity of justification extends beyond some point of sufficiency.

3. *The man of propriety.* Resolutions vary in their appropriateness for
a given situation. Persons are sensitive to these standards, yet in assessing the
avenues of justification which subjects employ, investigators have sometimes
overlooked these implicit standards. A person who behaves with propriety
is one for whom the standards of what is socially acceptable in conduct are
salient. That propriety may intrude into self-justification studies is demonstrated by Brock and Buss' (1962) findings that even in the laboratory,
men can be gallant. When male subjects, opposed to the use of shock in
experiments, found themselves by choice in a situation where they were
administering painful electric shock to other subjects, they tended to
minimize the painfulness of the shock if it was being administered to other
males. But if males shocked females, they tended not to minimize painfulness,
but rather to argue that they were "forced" to act in this manner. To be
sure this is a somewhat maverick way to demonstrate courtesy and consideration, but it does indicate that standards of social conduct may influence
a resolution in ways not anticipated by the investigator.

4. *The patient vindicator.* Earlier we noted that a person might
apologize for his presence in a situation of inadequate justification and let it
go at that, but here we are interested in a more extended response, namely
delayed justification. This is an intricate process but some idea of its form
can be found in Garfinkel's (1960) description. "Grounds of a person's
choice may be those which he quite literally *finds* through retrospectively
interpreting a present outcome. For example, in the effort to determine what
was 'really' decided at a prior time, a person may realize such grounds in the
course of historicizing an outcome. Thus, if a present datum is treated as
an-answer-to-some-question, the datum may motivate the original question.
Selecting, arranging, and unifying the historical context of an action after
its occurrence so as to present a publicly acceptable or coherent account of
it is a familiar meaning of 'rationalization' " (p. 74).

Investigators who have been concerned with the sequence of events in
which a decision produces consistent actions have neglected the opposite
sequence in which actions produce a decision in retrospect.

5. *The responsible citizen.* The variable of commitment has taken on
added importance in justification studies largely through the impetus of
Brehm and Cohen (1962). Concern with commitment has led investigators

to focus more closely on what happens when a person feels *responsibility* for his actions, when he feels accountable for his conduct. However, when a person is capable of determining his own acts, he is also "capable of being deterred by consideration of sanctions of consequences" (Webster, 1966, p. 1935), and it would seem that investigators have neglected this latter emphasis. It is assumed that if the person is committed he will take whatever has happened more seriously, but what has been overlooked is that fact that in responding to the situation, the person may *also* take the consequences of his actions more seriously. If he does so, this should have an effect on resolution processes. The responsible citizen should be less willing to engage in capricious actions which, unfortunately, some forms of justification seem to require; he should be more cautious and deliberate in justifying his actions; he may judge the resolutions in terms of their acceptability; and he should avoid actions with negative consequences. This line of analysis suggests a reinterpretation of the common finding (e.g., Glass, 1964) that laboratory subjects hesitate to make negative assessment of others in order to justify their actions. When an investigator successfully manipulates choice, he clearly heightens commitment, but in doing so he may also sensitize persons to the social consequences of their actions.

6. *The compulsive typesetter.* Anyone who has ever tried to type a manuscript and maintain a right-hand margin of standard width knows that this is virtually impossible. Number then, among one of life's trivial yet intriguing mysteries, how is it that persons who set type for published manuscripts have such uncommonly good luck to have every line be precisely the same length? The answer is that every typesetting machine has a 'justification space' which in the jargon of printing means a space with no predetermined width that is set by striking a spacebar of a keyboard typesetting machine. Thus lines of type can be expanded or narrowed to fit precise space requirements by using the justification space. It would be hard to find a more appropriate model to describe some aspects of 'justification.'

One of the more intriguing formats in which justification has been studied is what we might call a *behavioral vacuum*. What happens essentially is that a person is given some cognition which is inappropriate in his present setting and his problem is to justify why he apparently feels the way he does. Thus, a subject may find that he is highly aroused sexually by pictures of a turtle, cup, or rosebush (Brehm & Behar, 1966) or that he is fearful when exposed to innocuous pictures of smiling Russian students (Bramel, Bell, & Margulis, 1965).

An important common feature of these studies is that *two* points are specified, the cognition and the environment, and it is the subject's task to interpolate between the two (e.g., Bartlett, 1958), and to get from one to the other in a meaningful way, like the compulsive typesetter. This is quite distinct from a problem in which one point is specified and the subject can move from it in any direction in order to justify his actions. While there are usually two points in most justification experiments which the subject must somehow accommodate, these points vary greatly in the clarity with which they are stated and by implication, in the ease with which the subject can move from one point to another in a distinct way. In the absence of clear boundaries, it is probable that justifications would become more heterogeneous, but this question has not been addressed.

7. *The logical masochist.* Strength, resilience, endurance, all are often

regarded as commendable virtues. If this holds true outside of the laboratory, it should also hold true inside. If a person is confronted by a discomforting situation created by insufficient justification, this might provide an opportunity to demonstrate, not only to himself but to another prestigeful individual (the experimenter), that he can tolerate rather intense discomfort without falling apart. This person neither apologizes for his actions, nor is he tolerant in the hope that eventually his judgment will be vindicated. Instead he endures the full brunt of the discomfort. While this person may make some attempts to increase justification, these actions should be limited because they rob him of the rationale for his action, namely, "I am building character." The finding (e.g., Brock & Buss, 1962) that tolerance for shock is inversely related to the amount of justification, may reflect something other than a reorganization of cognitions about painfulness. Tolerance of shock could serve to reaffirm that a person is strong. Such reaffirmation could be quite important in studies where behaving compliantly for minimal reward may be interpreted as a sign of weakness. If a person has engaged in unwarranted compliance, he can accomplish two things by enduring the full force of the accompanying discomfort. He is acting in a responsible manner because he accepts the consequences of his actions (namely, discomfort), and furthermore he offsets his moment of weakness with moments of strength. Again this possibility complicates the life of the person who wishes to study self-justification, but this chain of events seems sufficiently common that we would expect it to occur in the laboratory.

HOPEFUL TRENDS

Several investigators have apparently followed the lead of Candide who replied, after hearing Pangloss' glorious reconstruction of their journeys, "That's true enough ... but we must go and work in the garden" (Butt, 1947, p. 144).

Optimism is whetted by the growing body of literature (e.g., Cohen, Greenbaum, & Mansson, 1963; Zimbardo et al., 1966) which demonstrates that motive intensity may be revised in order to justify actions. It is perhaps one of the ironies of justification research that subjects seem to do much more or much less than experimenters expect. They either engage in a highly specific form of justification which may be missed if questionnaire items are too limited or they engage in rather extensive revisions of basic dispositions. Studies of motive revision, however, are attractive because more refined dependent measures often are available to assess the course of justification.

Another important trend in recent studies is that justification is treated as only one of several resolutions. In this approach, it is argued that as conditions change, other resolutions can be more or less economical than self-justification. Walster (1965b), for example, has proposed that as a person inflicts increasing amounts of harm on another individual, the harm-doer will initially try to compensate the victim, but at that point where compensation is perceived as inadequate, the harm-doer will justify his actions by increased derogation of the victim. Alterations in person perception seem to be an especially prominent avenue of justification (e.g., Aronson, Turner, & Carlsmith, 1963; Sherif, Sherif, & Nebergall, 1965), that offers the possibility of increased clarity of interpretation because changes in perception of another person limit sharply the number of additional resolutions that can be used. Therefore, it is easier for the investigator to establish mutually exclusive resolutions and obtain more explicit information about the process of justification, *if* personal evaluations are used. For example, in the Aronson, Turner, and Carlsmith (1963) study, the principal competing sources of justification were attitude change and derogation. These two sources tend to be mutually exclusive, i.e., the more one derogates a person, the less likely he is to be influenced by him. When such pairs of incompatible responses are built into an experiment, the subject is forced to make a more explicit choice, and this choice should be more apparent to the observant investigator.

Recent advances in analyzing the components of experimental tasks may improve the quality of self-justification research. Shaw (1963) recently scaled and factor analyzed the components of 104 experimental group tasks. The six independent dimensions on which tasks were reliably discriminated included difficulty, cooperation requirements, solution multiplicity, intellectual-manipulative requirements, intrinsic interest, and population familiarity. The intriguing possibility raised by Shaw's analysis is that dimensions on which a particular task has high loadings may direct the resolution. For example, if a person consents to perform a task for insufficient reward, and the task has a high loading on solution multiplicity (the degree to which there is more than one 'correct' answer; Shaw, 1963, p. 19), then the person may convince himself that solution multiplicity is noteworthy and important. If this resolution were adopted, we might expect that subsequent actions would become consistent with this requirement (e.g., the person would attempt to generate several solutions rather than a single one); he would prefer other tasks which load highly on this factor to those which do not; and if he were forced to perform a different second task, he would evaluate it in terms of its adequacy along this dimension and might tend to ignore other, potentially more attractive properties. It seems evident that social psychologists have ignored the ways in which tasks might channel resolutions. This oversight is not surprising since there has been little systematic work directed toward explicating the dimensions of tasks. Fortunately, further advances in this problem are now being made (e.g., Posner, 1964).

Task analyses may be important in other ways. When an investigator predicts that persons will justify unwarranted compliance by task enhancement, the probability that this resolution will actually be used should be influenced by the extent to which the task loads on the dimension of 'intrinsic interest.' Tasks with high intrinsic interest may produce the predicted resolution. But if intrinsic interest is less salient than some other dimension, then it is more likely that something *other than* interest will be enhanced. Thus if an investigator apparently fails to confirm a hypothesis about self-justification, this failure may be only apparent because the task which he used did not permit the predicted resolution to unfold or else made an alternative resolution somewhat easier.

The resurgence of interest in the concept of level of aspiration (Atkinson, 1964; Moulton, 1965; Starbuck, 1963) may be of considerable importance to self-justification research. It now is fairly clear that liking for a task is directly related to level of success on the task (Feather, 1966; Locke, 1965, 1966). This finding, straightforward as it may appear, implies that a prominent source of justification may be in the hands of any subject, namely his aspirations for success on the experimental task. If goals are set and exceeded, the task becomes more attractive, and to the degree that the person feels that he has spent his time working on an attractive task, justification should be restored (Weick, 1963). Several studies of self-justification involve tasks in which it is difficult for the subject to experience success and when this avenue is blocked, others may appear unnoticed to the experimenter. When the experimental tasks *do* permit the subject to gauge his success (Weick, 1966), it seems likely that subjects may actually restore justification by a subtle pattern of success on the assigned task, although the experimenter concludes that little justification took place.

When justification is decreased it is possible that subsequent behavior is placed under the control of a new set of reinforcers. If this happens then insight into the course of a resolution should increase if these new reinforcers are taken into account. Weick and Prestholdt (1968) have found recently that when persons consent to perform a task for insufficient monetary reward, they subsequently avoid reinforcement contingencies which involve money and are significantly more responsive to reinforcement schedules that involve feedback about performance. Persons who perform the same task for adequate or excessive amounts of money show the opposite set of preferences. These findings suggest that processes of justification can be observed by noting the sensitivity of behavior to various sets of reinforcers. There is also the interesting implication that the content of a resolution should be different depending on whether insufficient justification was produced by adding negative features or reducing positive ones. If negative features are added, the positive reinforcers which originally controlled task performance probably remain intact (although there is some possibility of interference from the negative stimuli). However, if positive features are removed, reinforcements for behavior may change with the result that subsequent resolutions come under the control of more idiosyncratic personal dispositions. The argument here is essentially that task performance is typically controlled by a fairly stable set of reinforcements. If these reinforcements remain untouched by a manipulation, performance changes probably will not occur. Either the accustomed level of performance will be executed and interpreted as justifiable, or some additional cognitions that do not directly affect performance will be adduced. More diffuseness in resolutions should occur when familiar sets of reinforcers are removed.

Additional optimism is occasioned by a recent investigation conducted by Penner (1965). Shortly after the attempt by Lawrence and Festinger (1962) to argue that partial reward phenomena could be handled more adequately by dissonance theory than by existing learning formulations, Mowrer (1963) published a strong rejoinder to this conclusion. He argued that resistance to extinction following partial reward was not due to the fact that the subject has discovered 'extra attractions' to justify his performance during training, but rather to the fact that the subject became adapted to the experience of frustration during training and, therefore, did not find extinction to be very painful. Since the notion of counterconditioning had been in the literature for some time, it was argued that the dissonance explanation was superfluous. Penner was able to create a surprisingly simple, yet tightly controlled situation in which dissonance theory and counterconditioning theory made exactly *opposite* predictions concerning the outcome. The results showed that all differences among groups were highly significant, that every result supported the dissonance interpretation, and that GSR measures obtained during task performance followed predicted differences in tension according to the dissonance model and not those predicted by Mowrer. This particular study is important, not only because of its findings, but also because it demonstrates that justification phenomena can be preserved in more tightly controlled investigations. Zimbardo's (Zimbardo & Dworkin, 1964) research involving delayed auditory feedback, Knight's (1963) usage of the venerable "water jars" problem, and Cottrell's (1965) investigations of disconfirmed expectancy within the framework of reaction time all represent impressive attempts to stabilize justification processes, to tighten controls, and to obtain more reliable dependent measures. The important property of these studies is that they do not seem to sacrifice a great deal of validity in the interest of control. The form which justification takes in these studies does not differ substantially from the form it takes in other more 'realistic' studies, and the outcomes are sufficiently more explicit that it is possible to see more clearly what is important in the world of justification.

CONCLUSION

Throughout this chapter we have been concerned with the troublesome fact that subjects who participate in self-justification studies exhibit uncommon (and exasperating) resourcefulness in viewing laboratory life as the best of all possible worlds. Experimenters persist in trying to convince the subjects that this 'just isn't so.' There is some hope, as was indicated in the final section, that methodological and conceptual refinements may yet enable investigators to penetrate the Panglossian world of subjects. If this occurs, then it may yet turn out that self-justification is the best of all possible concepts.

CHAPTER 71

A Summary of Hypotheses on Modes of Resolution

Robert P. Abelson

In the seven contributions to this section, a large number of hypotheses about modes of resolution have been stated. Here I shall try to gather the recurring themes in these statements. Almost all the hypotheses concern either the *personal functionality* or the *situational convenience* of particular modes of resolution of inconsistency. Under the heading of personal functionality are three major subheadings: *ego-centrality*, *goal attainment*, and *cognitive style*. Within the situational category lie the variables of *task characteristics* and of *social context*. Hypotheses pertinent to each of these five factors will be discussed in turn.

Several of our contributors invoke the ego-centrality or self-relevance of the cognitions implicated in an inconsistency. Pilisuk, especially, builds his analysis on the "regions of self" at varying distances from the central core. His key statement is, "Beliefs and attitudes relevant to the fulfillment of self concept attributes are likely to remain intransigent in the face of incongruity." Adams, referring to the work of Pilisuk among others, refers simply to the reluctance of individuals to change their central values. Translating this idea into a mode of resolution hypothesis yields the prediction that *the least important of two inconsistent cognitions will change*. Hardyck and Kardush, in stating this proposition, define "importance" as "relevance to the self's ability to function effectively." (These latter authors broaden somewhat the simple notion that the least central of two inconsistent cognitions will change by postulating that when *both* cognitions are low in importance, the inconsistency will tend to be ignored; when both are moderately important, the least important will change; when both are rather high in importance, "restructuring" rather than single change will occur; and when both are extremely important, suppression or repression may occur.) This proposition seems so self-evident as to need no further inquiry into its psychological basis. Nevertheless the cognitive mechanism by which central cognitions are protected at the expense of peripheral cognitions is not explicitly clear. One very plausible possibility is a "least effort" principle, since a change in a single central value would ordinarily create many new dislocations and discrepancies in the rest of the cognitive system. This is the principle suggested quite a while ago by Rosenberg and

Abelson (1960). Although *cognitively* adequate to explain the centrality effect, least effort seems too bland a principle to capture the motivational intensity associated with the defense of central values. Further, it is an open question whether the ego-centrality of a cognition is necessarily coordinate with extensive cognitive interconnectedness. Quite probably a number of different dimensions of centrality and importance can be conceptually and empirically distinguished.

Among the specific exemplifications of the centrality principle is the familiar proposition given by Kelman and Baron: under strong persuasive pressure from a group, an individual will change his own attitude if the group is central to him, but shift group membership if the attitude is central. A more subtle realization of the principle is implied by Weick in his discussion of the type of experiment in which the subject finds himself administering shocks to another person: an individual committed to engage in a marginally unethical act will change his attitude in favor of the act, but if committed to a clearly unacceptable act, he will deny that he is responsible for it. A great many other realizations of the principle exist or are imaginable, thus the principle could be very powerful with increased clarity of the definition of centrality.

In some contrast to enduring ego-centrality is the idea of immediate motivational relevance. Kelman and Baron emphasize the pursuit of goals rather than the maintenance of central values. Their key hypothesis is that *when inconsistent cognitive elements are linked to the same goal, a "reduction" mode will be used; when linked to different goals, a "maintenance" mode.* Among the reduction modes they suggest are denial, rationalization, and change. Among the maintenance modes are compartmentalization, differentiation, and transcendence. It is interesting to note that when self-image preservation is the single goal in a given situation, the previous hypothesis becomes a particularized case of the present hypothesis. That is, one threat to the self-image may be pitted against another, with inconsistency reduction rather than maintenance the consequence, as in the contest between feelings of weakness and shame in experiments on forced aggression. (The resolutions suggested above for these situations would both qualify as 'reductions' in the sense used by Kelman and Baron.) But when the goals involve external rewards rather than self-enhancement, the previous hypothesis may not be especially helpful. Kelman and Baron remind us, as does Adams, that modes of resolution may be chosen because they satisfy motives extraneous or additional to the defined inconsistency. One possible example of this point is the use of the mechanism of denigration of an inconsistency-arousing communication source when for some reason apart from the inconsistency, the audience member feels personally hostile toward the source. Other examples emphasizing hedonic gain and loss independent of the achievement of cognitive balance have been given by Rosenberg and Abelson (1960), and in many chapters throughout this volume. (Cf. Chapters 1 and 19.)

Kelman and Baron's second major hypothesis separating mode choices on the basis of motive considerations is that *emphasis on short-term goals or threats will generate 'avoidance' modes; emphasis on long-term goals or opportunities will generate 'confrontation' modes.* Among the former are denial and insulation, and among the latter, attitude change and transcendence. This second mode dimension is very similar to my distinction in

Chapter 63 between avoidance and coping modes.

Personal style as a basis for choice of mode of resolution suggests a further broad class of hypotheses. The most compelling dimension relevant to style seems to be the developmental dimension invoked by Kaplan and Crockett. Modes of resolution are said to vary from the most primitive modes in which only a portion of the cognitive material available to the individual is used, to the most advanced in which as much information as possible is taken into account. Denial is an example of the former and differentiation of the latter. The general distinction is close to Kelman and Baron's between avoidance and confrontation modes, although this simple parallel does not do justice to Kaplan and Crockett's excellent detailed analysis of the developmental mode dimension in the context of impression formation.

It is hypothesized that *the mode of resolution is selected appropriately to the developmental level of the individual.* Two independent variables determining developmental level are *age* and *cognitive complexity*, the latter attributable to a bundle of ability and personality factors. Age limitations on resolution capabilities are richly depicted by Pilisuk, and other contributors refer *en passant* to the style complexity variable treated at length in Section IV B. One other independent variable which merits a theoretical connection with developmental level is *tension*, harking back to the old Lewinian idea that situational tension dedifferentiates the cognitive field. None of our contributors advances this general notion explicitly, although Adams cites derogation and incredulity ("primitive" modes) as probable outcomes of certain high tension situations. Interestingly, Weiss describes a "cognitive narrowing" phenomenon in the very pressureful situation in which a highly favorable communication source advocates a position highly discrepant from the recipient's initial opinion: Weiss' subjects in this condition depended heavily and rigidly on one or two safe arguments in defending their positions. Presumably Kaplan and Crockett would classify this cognitive behavior as primitive.

While the developmental dimension for resolution modes is an intriguing one, indiscriminate application of this dimension to all situations is no more apt to be comprehensively satisfactory than the tentative single-variable approaches of Section IV B. Wisely, Kaplan and Crockett apply their analysis in a tractable research context—impression formation—the same well-controllable area chosen by Bieri in Chapter 61 (and Anderson in Chapter 75, among others).

The situational category of hypotheses about resolution modes presents greater conceptual difficulties than the personal functionality category. As Weick points out in his chapter, we do not presently have a very incisive vocabulary for discussing laboratory tasks and situations, much less for stating precise predictions about their effects. One of the additional frustrations for the theorist is that it is not explicit what is meant by 'blocking off' certain modes of resolution experimentally. (This will be recognized as the familiar phraseology of the dissonance tradition.) Nor is there a prescription for how to conceptualize the 'availability' of modes. Nevertheless the intuitive understanding of which modes are blocked and which are specially available plays a very important part in a number of the predictions in the several chapters.

One way to summarize these situational effects is first to note that certain cognitive elements are especially resistant to change, and others notably vulnerable to change, and then to state the proposition: *the resolution mode involving change of the most vulnerable cognitive element will be most preferred, that involving change of the most resistant element the least preferred.* Of course, for this proposition not to be completely empty, it must at least be usefully exemplified, even though its key terms, as noted above, have eluded precise definition. Here, then, are some exemplifications paraphrased from Chapters 64–70.

(a) *Vulnerable elements:*

Ambiguous stimuli encourage misperception (Kelman & Baron).

Low prestige sources are readily denigrated (Adams; Kelman & Baron; Weick).

An accidentally hurt party deserves compensation (Adams; Weick).

A task allowing success is easy to like (Weick).

Unwelcome supportive argumentation spurs invention of different arguments (Weiss).

Overpayment should be returned in kind (Adams).

(b) *Resistant elements:*

Physical realities prevent illusion and avoidance (Hardyck & Kardush; Kelman & Baron).

Social reminders block 'not thinking' (Hardyck & Kardush).

High prestige sources cannot be dismissed (Adams; Kelman & Baron; Weiss).

An overly harmed victim is beyond sympathy (Adams; Weick).

The hardy reader is invited to search through the remainder of this volume for the further examples which exist in abundance. Such a search is perhaps not too appealing a prospect, as the examples may seem insufficiently solid and overly heterogeneous. If one thing is certain, however, it is that these examples cannot in general be subsumed under the earlier centrality and goal-attainment hypotheses: the weaknesses or strengths of the elements in question inhere preponderantly in the stimulus rather than in the cognitive system of the organism; it would be extremely clumsy to claim, for example, that the incontrovertible expertness of a communication source makes him immune to derogation because it is a central value of individuals that they not derogate experts. The conceptual distinction here is akin to the opposition of stimulus incentive and organismic drive. Vulnerable and resistant elements assume the roles of positive and negative *incentives of varying magnitudes* in respectively impelling or repelling modes of resolution of inconsistency, albeit the motive state of the individual be held constant. Without intending to be carried away by this analogy between inconsistency and older motivational constructs (indeed, in Section III A, several of the contributors warn against this analogy), I nevertheless wish to emphasize that we cannot do without *two* classes of mode-of-resolution hypotheses: one motive-oriented, the other incentive-oriented.

The importance of hidden incentive factors is brought out very clearly in Weick's novel essay. Though he does not advertise it, the theme running through most of his thumbnail descriptions of types of resolutions is that the *social context* within which the inconsistency occurs may well determine the resolution. The key proposition (which embodies no more than common sense, though one must have the foresight to think of it) is that *the differential appeal of resolution modes is a function of the identity and perceived attitudes of the people present in the inconsistency-arousing situation.* Again, it is only by exemplification that the proposition can be given interesting content. Some of the examples suggested by Weick and the last one by Pilisuk from laboratory contexts (each with an obvious non-laboratory analogue) are the following:

If the experimenter seems sympathetic, apology may appear an appropriate way to redress a foolish or socially undesirable act.

If the presence of an audience of peers would render the undoing of a dubious action embarrassing, self-justification or vindication will be preferred.

If it seems important to impress the experimenter with one's vigor or stamina, the endurance of pain or stress may become a prepotent response.

If the experimental situation is such as to enhance the sense of personal responsibility the subject bears for his actions (e.g., if the atmosphere is sober or the experiment is presented as especially important), the subject will behave cautiously and avoid seemingly frivolous modes of resolution.

If the measuring instruments encourage self-idealization, subjects will adopt humbly favorable poses, i.e., will 'play it cool.'

As with the previous types of situational factors, the list of such social influences could be extended at length, and indeed would include all the things that now come under the heading of 'demand characteristics' (Orne, 1962). Prominent in this list would be the factors of suspicion arousal and also 'evaluation apprehension,' hypothesized as possible social artifacts interfering with the interpretations dissonance theorists would like to apply to forced compliance experiments (Janis & Gilmore, 1965; Rosenberg, 1965d; see also Section IV F).

Task and social incentives influencing resolution mode can either be studied in their own right or carefully controlled (and, if conceivable, eliminated from the experimental situation) by investigators. This choice is a matter of temperament and theoretical inclination, and the consistency theory area needs both these styles of approach. What should not lightly be done anymore, however, is to proceed with inconsistency studies in innocence of the multiplicity of potential response determinants such as those sketched in this section.

D. RESPONSES TO HETEROGENEOUS STIMULUS AGGREGATES

The ultimate behavioral referent of social psychology is the action of one person toward another. Among the variables that are commonly understood as influencing such action is the person's *attitude* toward the other; and this, in turn, is understood as a product either of experiences with that other person or with communications about him or about the groups to which he 'belongs.'

This simple model is also an old one. Thus, long before the consistency approach reached its present vogue the basic question posed in this section had been formulated and was being explored in experimental research. That question is: How do our impressions of the separate attributes and actions of a person combine to yield an overall and stable orientation toward him?

In his past work on this problem the guiding principle employed by Triandis has been the *additive* one elaborated by his associate Fishbein from a common model employed earlier, and for a somewhat different purpose, by Woodruff and Di Vesta (1948), Smith (1949), and others. Here he reports an interesting cross-cultural study from which he concludes that the additive approach and two separate versions of an *averaging* approach are about equally effective in producing accurate predictions of evaluative responses to complex, adjectival characterizations of hypothetical persons.

Anderson deftly advances, as he has in a large number of earlier articles, his *weighted averaging* model. In so doing he recounts a number of studies which, taken in sequence, produce the effect of ever-increasing clarity in a research area that is burdened with many difficult problems of operationalization and of artifactual contamination.

Feldman addresses himself to the possibility of adjudicating the summation-averaging controversy. Extrapolating from some of his earlier studies he hypothesizes that the additive resolution will occur when the stimulus elements have overlapping meaning while the averaging resolution will be more likely when the elements are independent of one another.

Rosenbaum and Schmidt eschew theoretical commitments and proclaim themselves eclectic empiricists. The program of experimental studies that they report here seems to provide many useful leads about variables that influence the evaluative outcomes of confrontation with complex stimulus aggregates.

The chapters touch upon many important issues and, taken together, seem to point the way toward a more sophisticated and efficient theory. The limits of that theory and the kind of theory that might be required beyond those limits (i.e., in the analysis of attitude change rather than of initial impression formation) are examined in the discussion chapter at the end of this section.

CHAPTER 72

Some Cross-Cultural Studies of Cognitive Consistency

Harry C. Triandis
University of Illinois

The focus of this chapter is on understanding how multiple inputs combine to produce a single judgment. For example, consider the stimulus person 'a female Negro physician.' Each of the elements of this stimulus may be thought to determine a single point in a multidimensional space in which all response continua for making judgments about people are potential dimensions. Suppose we knew the nature of this space. Suppose that it consists of 100 dimensions. Then 'female' will occupy one point in this 100-dimensional space; 'Negro' will occupy a different point; 'physician' will occupy still another point. The basic question is: Can we predict the point that is to be occupied by the complex stimulus person from the knowledge of the position of the points occupied by the elements that constitute it?

When the question is posed in this way, it is difficult to answer. However, when only one dimension of the multidimensional space is considered (e.g., the evaluation of the stimulus) and we know the projections of the three stimuli on that dimension, there are several theoretical approaches to answering the question. Osgood and Tannenbaum (1955) offered the *congruity* principle; Fishbein offered the *summation* principle (Triandis & Fishbein, 1963), Anderson (1965a) discussed *averaging* vs. *adding* models, Rokeach and Rothman (1965) offered the principle of *belief congruence* and Manis, Gleason, and Dawes (1966) the *weighted average* principle. Tests of the first two of these principles are now available with subjects from Greece and the United States (Triandis & Fishbein, 1963) and India, Japan, and the United States (Triandis, Tanaka, & Shunmugam, 1966).

The congruity principle averages the elements that enter into a complex judgment by weighing them according to their relative polarizations. It has provided good predictions in the case of word mixtures (Osgood,

The empirical work reported in this paper was supported by the contract to study Communication, Cooperation, and Negotiation in Culturally Heterogeneous Groups between the University of Illinois and the Advanced Research Projects Agency and the Office of Naval Research (Contract NR 177-472, Nonr 1834(36); Fred E. Fiedler, Lawrence M. Stolurow, and Harry C. Triandis, Principal Investigators). An earlier version of this manuscript was improved by the critical comments of Robert P. Abelson, Earl E. Davis, Martin Fishbein, and Uriel G. Foa.

Suci, & Tannenbaum, 1957) and perceptual signs (Tanaka, 1964). The latter study was done cross-culturally. Improved predictions were made when individual differences were considered, which were based on the Harvey, Hunt, and Schroder (1961) theory of personality (Janicki, 1964).

The summation principle, on the other hand, involves summation with a weighing of the elements by their probability of association with the complex stimulus. It has been found to be more predictive of the judgments of complex person stimuli than the congruity principle, by Triandis and Fishbein (1963), Fishbein and Hunter (1964), L. Anderson and Fishbein (1965), and others.

Another problem concerning cognitive consistency involves the relationships among the dimensions in the hypothetical 100-dimensional space mentioned above. Suppose we consider the evaluation of the 'female Negro physician' (how *good*, *kind*, *honest*, and *clean* is she?) and some behavioral dimension (e.g., would the S admit or exclude this person from his neighborhood?). Perfect cognitive consistency would require that highly evaluated stimuli be admitted to the neighborhood, yet prejudiced white Americans will consistently give a positive evaluation of Negro physicians and simultaneously indicate that they would exclude them from the neighborhood (Triandis & Triandis, 1962). Triandis, Loh, and LeVine (1966) found that with prejudiced Americans race controlled only 3 per cent of the variance on the evaluative factor of the Semantic Differential (Osgood et al., 1957), but 80 per cent of the variance of social distance scores. Thus, on some dimensions one of the characteristics of the complex stimulus persons determines most of the variance; but on another dimension another of the characteristics determines most of the variance. In other words, knowing how Ss combine the inputs on a particular dimension may not permit us to know how they will combine them on another dimension, because there may be no consistency in the laws of input combination from dimension to dimension.[1]

CULTURAL DETERMINATION OF COGNITIVE INTERACTION

The evidence obtained thus far suggests that there are no cultural differences in the relative effectiveness of the congruity and summation principles (Triandis & Fishbein, 1963; Triandis, Tanaka, & Shanmugam, 1966).

A brief description of the second of the above two studies will illustrate the basis for this statement. About 300 Ss, 100 from each of three countries (United States, South India, Central Japan) were asked to respond to 12 Semantic Differential and 16 Behavioral Differential (Triandis, 1964) scales. The stimuli employed in the study were: physician, carpenter, male, female, old, middle aged, young, person of the same religion as you, person of a different religion than you. In addition, all possible combinations of the above mentioned stimuli were utilized. These combinations were generated from a complete factorial design varying the occupation, sex, age, and religion of the complex stimuli. Thus, the Ss responded to the complex stimuli, as well as the single elements that constituted them, on 28 Semantic and Behavioral Differential scales.

---

[1] [This statement is perhaps too strong—the *laws* of combination might be the same, but the numerical values of the *parameters* may differ from dimension to dimension—Ed.]

The correlations between the Semantic Differential scales were factor analyzed and three factors, controlling about three-fourths of the total variance, were obtained in each culture. They were variations of the Osgood *evaluation* (nice, good, familiar), *potency* (big, powerful, strong), and *activity* (fast, alive) factors. In relation to the other two samples the Japanese factors showed clear variations. For example, *nobility* (happy, strong, good, brave, active) and *sedateness* (lonely, heavy, plain) replaced the *evaluation* and *potency* factors. The correlations among the Behavioral Differential scales yielded three factors in each of the three cultures. They were *Respect* (admire character, believe, obey), *Friendship Acceptance* (gossip with, accept as intimate friend, permit to do me a favor), and *Marital Acceptance* (fall in love with, marry). After the factor analyses, composite scores for the three Semantic and three Behavioral Differential factors were computed for all the stimuli.

Predictions of the scores of the complex stimuli from the knowledge of the scores of the single stimuli were undertaken. These predictions were computed on the basis of (a) the congruity principle, (b) the summation principle, and (c) the weighted average principle. The weights for the latter principle were obtained from analyses of variance in which the percentage of variance accounted by the occupation, sex, age, and religion components of the complex stimulus persons were computed. These percentages were used as the weights.

Thus, for every one of the 300 Ss, we could predict the way he would judge 24 complex stimuli from the way he judged 9 simple stimuli. Since we tested three theoretical principles we made 3 times 24 times 300 predictions. For every S, and for every principle, the predicted scores were correlated with the obtained scores (N of 24, the number of stimuli). These correlations were then tabulated as in Table 1, which shows the median correlations between predicted and obtained scores for a selected set of combinations of culture-factor-theoretical principle, in order to conserve space. Each of these medians summarizes about 50 correlations, since there were about 50 same-sex Ss in each culture.

Some further explanations about Table 1 are required. First, it should be noted that if the individual S utilized weights identical to those used by the *average* S in his culture, the predictions obtained by the weighted average principle would be mathematically identical to the predictions obtained from multiple regression equations. Second, the weighted average principle is not a truly a priori principle, since it utilizes information about the way a cultural group weighs the four characteristics; the weights are then applied to every individual member of that group. The congruity and summation principles, on the other hand, are truly a priori.

In order to obtain an impression of the effectiveness of the three principles, Table 1 also shows the multiple correlations obtained when predicting the complex stimulus person judgments from the individual S's judgments of the elements that enter the stimulus. These multiple correlations reflect the S's 'cognitive internal consistency.' They give an indication of the upper limit of prediction, given the reliability of the procedures employed.

Table 1 shows that the median multiple correlation for all cultures and all dimensions is .64. The median correlations between the predictions and the observations obtained from the three principles are about .40 for the

TABLE 1

Median Correlations for each S-sample on each
Semantic Differential Factor, for Three Theoretical Models

Sample	Factor	Multiple R	Congruity	Summation	Weighted Average
Amer.	Evaluation	.64	.29	.35	.28
Males	(familiar, nice)				
(N=49)	Potency	.64	.48	.49	.47
	(big, strong)				
	Activity	.68	.44	.44	.48
	(fast, alive)				
Amer.	Evaluation	.62	.36	.35	.40
Fem.	(familiar, nice)				
(N=48)	Potency	.65	.49	.50	.49
	(strong, big)				
	Activity	.63	.45	.47	.45
	(fast, alive)				
Jap.	Nobility	.66	.44	.40	.40
Males	(brave, strong)				
(N=55)	Sedateness vs.				
	Colorfulness	.72	.48	.52	.46
	(heavy, plain)				
	Familiarity	.61	.10	.12	.08
	(probable, familiar)				
Jap.	Nobility	.68	.37	.38	.44
Fem.	(strong, brave)				
(N=57)	Potency	.65	.32	.29	.27
	(heavy)				
	Sedateness	.65	.40	.36	.41
	(plain, lonely)				
Median of each column		.64	.42	.39	.42

Semantic Differential factors. Table 2 presents the same information for the factors obtained from the Behavioral Differential. Here the multiple correlations have a median of .72 and the three principles have median correlations of the order of .55. The higher correlations obtained from the Behavioral Differential reflect the higher reliabilities of this instrument, as compared to the Semantic Differential (Davis & Triandis, 1965). There is no evidence of differential effectiveness of the three principles. There is also no evidence of cultural differences in the operation of the three principles.

Triandis, Tanaka, and Shanmugam (1966) also examined the effectiveness of the three principles by computing matched t tests, between the predicted and the obtained scores, for each of the principles. The weighted average principle was slightly superior in this analysis, since 32 per cent of the t tests computed with scores derived from this principle were nonsignificant, while only 22 per cent and 23 per cent of the t tests computed on the scores derived from the other two principles were nonsignificant. These percentages are an indication that all three models fall far short of perfection. The ideal principle would have resulted in 95 per cent of the tests being nonsignificant. Again, there was no evidence of better prediction in one culture as opposed to another.

In conclusion, the evidence so far shows no cultural differences in the

TABLE 2

Median Correlations for each *S*-sample on each Behavioral
Differential Factor for Three Theoretical Models

Sample	Factor	Multiple R	Congruity	Summation	Weighted Average
Amer. Males (N=49)	Respect (admire, believe)	.77	.54	.57	.53
	Friendship (gossip with, intimate friend)	.81	.60	.62	.60
	Marital (love, marry)	.73	.59	.68	.70
Amer. Fem. (N=48)	Respect (be commanded by, admire)	.80	.51	.58	.64
	Friendship (gossip with, intimate friend)	.70	.39	.43	.44
	Marital (love, marry)	.73	.63	.67	.65
Jap. Males (N=55)	Subord. with Respect (be commanded, obey)	.70	.27	.34	.44
	Friendship (admire, gossip with)	.60	.23	.32	.27
	Marital (love, marry)	.75	.57	.65	.60
Jap. Fem. (N=57)	Respect (be commanded, obey)	.51	.23	.20	.20
	Friendship (admire, permit to do favor)	.63	.37	.32	.42
	Marital (love, marry)	.78	.60	.71	.66
Median of each column		.72	.52	.58	.56

effectiveness of the three principles. Apparently, cognitive interaction is not influenced by culture. Of course, it is possible that the procedures used here were too crude and that subtle effects do in fact exist. It is also possible that the cultural differences occur in that portion of the variance that is not predicted by the principles, so that the principles are truly universal. Perhaps subtle effects involving cultural differences in cognitive interaction would be observed only if we were able to predict more of the variance.

CULTURAL DIFFERENCES IN THE CONSISTENCY OF THE DIMENSIONS OF JUDGMENT

Table 3 shows the correlations between the dimensions of judgment obtained from the Semantic Differential and those obtained from the Behavioral Differential. Low correlations between the factors of a single instrument should be expected since they are correlations between composite scores computed on orthogonal factors. However, the correlations across instruments, though small, are not artifactually small. The consistency of the results across cultures is impressive. *Good* people are seen as *potent*, *active*, and *young;* such people receive *respect, friendship,* and *marital acceptance.* Slight cultural differences can be seen. For example, the Indian potency factor appears to be different from the potency factors of the other cultures.

Though the correlations of Table 3 are stable across cultures and because of their large N they are highly significant, their size does not

TABLE 3

The Relationship between the Subcomponents of Interpersonal Attitudes

Factor	Sample	N	Semantic Differential			Behavioral Differential		
			Potency	Activity	Age	Respect	Friendship	Marital
Evaluation	Amer. Male	1715	.25	.56	−.14	42	.38	.18
	Amer. Fem.	1680	.31	.64	−.16	.48	.31	.39
	Ind. I	1750	−.14	.42	−.08	.23	.18	.13
	Ind. II	1715	.03	.68	−.12	.31	.09	.11
	Jap. Male	1925	.65	.24	−.24	.24	.31	.27
	Jap. Fem.	1995	.02	.04	−.05	.08	.16	.16
Potency	Amer. Male	1715		.33	−.21	.11	.22	−.16
	Amer. Fem.	1680		.48	−.30	.13	.05	.35
	Ind. I	1750		−.15	.17	−.02	−.06	−.01
	Ind. II	1715		.01	.13	.16	.04	−.07
	Jap. Male	1925		.26	−.25	.16	.29	.15
	Jap. Fem.	1995		.60	−.27	.24	.19	.26
Activity	Amer. Male	1715			−.39	.18	.31	.23
	Amer. Fem	1680			−.41	.34	.28	.36
	Ind. I	1750			−.16	.22	.17	.06
	Ind. II	1715			−.18	.20	.07	.11
	Jap. Male	1925			−.39	−.05	−.06	.18
	Jap. Fem.	1995			−.42	.02	.15	.16
Age	Amer. Male	1715				.08	−.37	−.43
	Amer. Fem.	1680				−.01	−.31	−.43
	Ind. I	1750				.03	−.07	−.02
	Ind. II	1715				.03	−.06	−.08
	Jap. Male	1925				.01	−.06	−.39
	Jap. Fem.	1995				.12	−.11	−.36
Respect	Amer. Male	1715					.40	.04
	Amer. Fem.	1680					.36	.29
	Ind. I	1750					.35	.20
	Ind. II	1715					.22	.15
	Jap. Male	1925					.36	.24
	Jap. Fem.	1995					.43	.30
Friendship	Amer. Male	1715						.32
	Amer. Fem.	1680						.32
	Ind. I	1750						.26
	Ind. II	1715						.04
	Jap. Male	1925						.21
	Jap. Fem.	1995						.37

Notes: These data were obtained by Triandis, Tanaka and Shanmugam (1966). They are correlations obtained from approximately 50 same sex *S*s from each culture. The Indian sample has two samples of males. The *S*s responded to 35 stimulus persons, and the N of the correlations is based on approximately 35 x 50 ≡ 1750 observations. The exact number is shown under the N column. A correlation of .06 is significant at p <.01.

suggest a large degree of cognitive consistency across the dimensions of judgment. The median correlation between *evaluation* and *respect* is only .27; between *evaluation* and *friendship* .26; between *evaluation* and *marital acceptance* barely .17. Thus, the Ss utilize 'practically' independent (though statistically significantly correlated) dimensions in making their judgments. Furthermore, the Ss appear to be equally complex, in all three of the cultures studied. In other words, there is more within culture variance in cognitive complexity than there is between culture variance on this trait as far as can be ascertained by the present procedures.

CULTURAL DIFFERENCES IN THE WEIGHTS GIVEN TO THE CHARACTERISTICS OF STIMULUS PERSONS

There is strong evidence that in different cultures Ss assign different weights to the characteristics of stimulus persons. For example, Triandis and Triandis (1960, 1962) found that Americans give a very large weight to the characteristic *race* when they make social distance judgments, a smaller weight to *occupation*, an even smaller weight to *religion*, and an insignificant weight to the *nationality* of the stimulus persons. On the other hand, Greeks (Triandis & Triandis, 1962) assign much weight to the *religion* of the stimulus person in making their social distance judgments; Germans and Japanese (Triandis, Davis, & Takezawa, 1965) assign much weight to the *occupational* component and lesser weights to the other components when making social distance judgments.

Similarly, Triandis, Tanaka, and Shanmugam (1967) found that Americans give about equal weights to the *occupation* and *religion* of a stimulus person, when they judge him on the Evaluative scales of the Semantic Differential. But, the Indians give *religion* a proportionately much larger weight; the Japanese respond to the corresponding Nobility factor by giving much weight to both *religion* and *age*. On the Respect factor of the Behavioral Differential the percentages of variance on the part of American males were 78 per cent for *occupation*, 11 per cent for *religion*, and 4 per cent for *sex*. The Indian males gave *occupation* only 12 per cent, *religion* 38 per cent, *sex* 13 per cent, and *age* 7 per cent, with interactions accounting for the remaining variance. The Japanese males gave *occupation* 51 per cent, *religion* 26 per cent, *sex* 3 per cent, and *age* 4 per cent. These 'profiles' are quite different.

DISCUSSION

The evidence accumulated to date suggests that cultural differences are of no importance as far as the three principles of cognitive interaction studied so far are concerned. These principles account for only about half the nonrandom variance in our studies. They do not differ in their relative effectiveness.

People do utilize a number of judgment continua that are related to each other in roughly comparable ways across the cultures studied so far. People from different cultures combine simple stimuli to make complex judgments in roughly similar ways. On the other hand, they do utilize different weights for various characteristics.

The above statements must be qualified by the realization that all the studies reviewed above utilized highly Westernized, sophisticated high school or college students in the cultures under study. The West has been heavily influenced by Aristotelian logic, and cognitive consistency is the cornerstone of this logic. Before we may be sure that we have examined the problem in complete fairness, we should test nonliterate Ss who are uninfluenced by the West.

On the other hand, it seems intuitively obvious that if there are cultural differences in the responses to cognitive consistency these will be related to differences in personality. The evidence on differences in basic personality and child training experiences, across cultures, is very poor. There are few rigorous studies. In some of these it is clear that the within culture variance is much larger than the between culture variance. For example, Triandis and Lambert (1961) factor analyzed the responses of mothers of six cultures to a lengthy child training structured interview. Except for the Americans, the mothers were usually illiterate and lived in rural environments. The researchers found that on all their factors the within culture variance was larger than the between culture variance. On one of their factors only 5 per cent of the variance was between cultures, while 95 per cent of the variance was within culture variance. If the same situation prevails for cognitive consistency, then it seems unlikely that culturally determined differences in cognitive consistency tendencies are going to be discovered in the future.

CHAPTER 73

A Simple Model for Information Integration

Norman H. Anderson
University of California, San Diego

Many situations require a judgment or decision based on several pieces of information. Evaluating applicants to graduate school, voting, writing a paper, changing one's mind, or just watching a movie, all involve integration of information.

Over the past several years, my students and I have been engaged in an extensive program of research on certain parts of this general problem. Much of the work has used a personality impression task in which the subject judges the likability of a person described by a set of personality-trait adjectives. Collateral work has been done with judgments of life events, meals, sets of books, and other simple experimental tasks. From these beginnings, recent work has been led in two directions: toward more complex tasks involving inconsistent or heterogeneous information, for instance, and toward very simple, psychophysical type stimuli.

This research has placed strong emphasis on experimental analysis. Nearly all of it, however, concerns the testing and development of a simple mathematical model for information integration. In general form, this is a linear model that has been considered in one way or another by a variety of workers. Since much of both the empirical work and the mathematical analysis is indifferent to the special cases of this general linear model, it is taken as basic in what follows.

There are two special cases of this general linear model that have attracted the particular interest of various investigators. These arise from the question of whether the subject adds or averages the stimulus information. Of course, this will depend in part on the nature of the task and there are tasks to which some kind of adding process would clearly be appropriate.

My own initial involvement in this area was with an averaging formulation. This resulted partly from formal mathematical considerations, partly from a conception of the organism as an analog computer of stimulus averages. This view seems appropriate for many of the tasks used in social psychological experiments, and it underlies much of the work reported here. It is, of course, too early by far to believe that any simple model will hold

This work was supported by NSF Grant GB-3913.

even for simple tasks. However, the averaging model has received some critical experimental support at the qualitative level, and it has been fairly successful in quite exacting quantitative tests.

This paper gives a brief overview of this approach to information integration, with special reference to the problem of inconsistency resolution. Necessarily, much has been glanced at or omitted, and I wish to apologize to the many people whose work I have not been able to discuss adequately here.

LINEAR MODEL

The basic assumption of the present approach is about as simple as possible. It is supposed that the subject has or receives a set of stimuli or pieces of information from which he is to reach some judgment. In very general form, the judgment based on the set is assumed to be a linear function of the values of the items:

$$J = C + \Sigma w_k s_k, \tag{1}$$

where J is the judgment, C a constant, and s_k and w_k are the value and weight of the kth item in the set.

In one form or another, Equation 1 has been considered by a variety of writers for different kinds of tasks involving information integration. Among the earlier reports, those of Spence and Guilford (1963), Asch (1946), Hammond (1955), Johnson (1955), Osgood and Tannenbaum (1955), Peak (1955), Rimoldi (1956), Hoffman (1960), Meehl (1960), Willis (1960), Abelson (1961), Yntema and Torgerson (1961), Young and Christensen (1962), and Helson (1964) may be specifically noted. A formal classification of such models has been given by S. Rosenberg (1968). Somewhat surprisingly, there is very little evidence on the validity of such models, owing in part to the lack of a test of goodness of fit in many reports. However, a general review is beyond the scope of this article.

Implicit in the statement of Equation 1 is the assumption that the dependent variable is numerical. The analysis of categorical choices and decisions would thus require some additional development (e.g., Anderson, 1964b). More directly, of course, the use of such a model requires a theoretically adequate scale of measurement. The scaling problem has been resolved elsewhere (Anderson, 1962a, b, c) and it may here be simply noted that the use of a numerical response has been central to the present work. The test of goodness of fit provides a joint test of the model and the scale of measurement, and the success of the model establishes the validity of the scale.

Equation 1 also assumes that each stimulus item can be represented by two parameters, s and w. Of these, s represents the value of the item along the dimension of judgment, and w represents the weight or importance of that item in the overall judgment.

Both parameters are needed. Scale values will vary both with item and with dimension of judgment. The s-value of *forgetful* may be near zero in a college professor, but would be quite negative in a lawyer or pilot.

The w-value of an item will depend even more strongly on task variables. For instance, the reliability of a source of information could be manipulated experimentally, and this would reflect itself in the subjective weight of the item. A more complete discussion is given elsewhere (Anderson & Jacobson, 1965), and the use of differential weighting to account for inconsistency resolution as well as order effects in serial presentation is considered below.

For experimental analysis, the stimulus items would ordinarily be externally controllable. This need not be true in general, however, and some or all of the pieces of information may be subject-constructed as when a person is evaluating the desirability of some action in terms of its probable consequences. The difficulties of testing the model in this case are great, however, and the present approach has concentrated on experimental analysis.

One special instance of an internal stimulus is important, however. A person may have some initial opinion on a given topic, prior to the presentation of any experimental stimuli. This would be the case in many opinion change studies. This notion of an initial opinion, which is represented by parameters s_0 and w_0, becomes important in accounting for the 'set size effect' both with serial and with simultaneous presentation.

In use, Equation 1 is ordinarily restricted in various ways. Assumptions of parameter constancy are often appropriate for tests of fit as discussed below. Here two special cases of the model are considered, one deriving from a substantive consideration, the other from a task variable. For simplicity, the constant term in Equation 1 is taken to be zero.

From a psychological point of view, it seems important to distinguish whether the subject is adding the stimulus values or whether he is averaging them. The substantive problem is discussed below. Mathematically, an averaging model is obtained from Equation 1 by requiring the weights to sum to unity. In practice, it is often convenient to use unrestricted weights in intermediate steps and then divide each weight by the sum of all the weights. These normalized weights then sum to unity as illustrated in connection with Table 1 and as used in Equation 4.

The second special case of Equation 1 is a formulation that is applicable when the stimuli are presented sequentially, as in attitude change experiments. It is then assumed, at least in the simplest applications, that each new stimulus is integrated with the then current opinion to yield a revised opinion for the next stage. The model may then be written,

$$J_k = c_k s_k + (1 - c_k) J_{k-1}, \tag{2}$$

where J_k and J_{k-1} are the values of the judgment after and before presentation of the kth stimulus, s_k is the scale value of the kth stimulus, and c_k is the change parameter.

Equation 2 is an averaging model since c_k and $1 - c_k$ function as the respective weights associated with the presented stimulus and the current opinion. This model has been used in the discussion of order effects (Anderson & Hovland, 1957), and in an experiment on attitude change (Anderson, 1959).

From a formal standpoint, Equation 2 may be classed as a linear operator model like those used in learning theory (Bush & Mosteller, 1955). However, the mathematical analysis (Anderson, 1961, 1964a, b; Rouanet & S. Rosenberg, 1964) is considerably different because of the use of a numerical response in Equation 2. In addition, the change parameter, c_k, which is analogous to the learning rate, is allowed to vary from one stimulus presentation to the next. This property is vital in the kinds of experiments under consideration.

There is also an interesting relation between the change parameters of Equation 2 and the weights of Equation 1 (Anderson, 1964b). From Equation 2 it can be shown that the last judgment to a series of stimuli is a weighted average of the scale values of the stimuli and the initial impression. The c_k and w_k are related by the equation,

$$c_k = w_k / \sum_0^k w_j. \tag{3}$$

Constant change parameters would correspond to a steady increase of w_k over trials, a recency effect. On the other hand, equal weighting of the stimuli would require quasiharmonic decreases in the change parameter.

Goodness of Fit

A proper test of a quantitative model ordinarily requires a test of goodness of fit. High correlations between the observed data and the model predictions can be encouraging but bypass the central question. It is still necessary to assess the discrepancies between observed and predicted.

Goodness of fit may be tested in various ways, but usually certain additional assumptions are made. The most common of these is the constancy assumption, that the value and weight of any stimulus are essentially the same in all sets. With this, or some equivalent assumption, it is often possible to reduce the test of fit to an ordinary analysis of variance.

This technique may be illustrated with the simple example of Table 1 where A, B, P, and Q represent four stimulus items with scale values, s_A, s_B, s_P, and s_Q. These values are arbitrary, but it is assumed that the row stimuli, A and B, have the same weight, w_1, and the column stimuli, P and Q, also have equal weight, w_2.

TABLE 1

A 2×2 Stimulus Design with Predicted Response Given in
Terms of Scale Value (s) and Weight (w) of the Stimuli in Each Set

	P (s_P, w_2)	Q (s_Q, w_2)
A (s_A, w_1)	$\dfrac{w_1 s_A + w_2 s_P}{w_1 + w_2}$	$\dfrac{w_1 s_A + w_2 s_Q}{w_1 + w_2}$
B (s_B, w_2)	$\dfrac{w_1 s_B + w_2 s_P}{w_1 + w_2}$	$\dfrac{w_1 s_B + w_2 s_Q}{w_1 + w_2}$

The 2×2 arrangement of Table 1 yields four sets of stimuli, AP, BP, AQ, and BQ. Let $R(AP)$ denote the judgment based on the set, AP, etc. Then the model requires that the test score,

$$I = R(AP) - R(AQ) - R(BP) + R(BQ),$$

be zero except for sampling fluctuation. The proof is straightforward and will be indicated only for the averaging model in the case when only the two external stimuli need to be considered. The theoretical response to each set is then as listed in the appropriate cell of Table 1, and substitution of these into the above expression yields a theoretical *I*-score of zero.

The observed *I*-scores will therefore be distributed around zero if the behavior obeys the model, and the evaluation of this prediction constitutes the test of goodness of fit. Significance of the observed discrepancy may be tested nonparametrically if so desired, but the *I*-score is just the algebraic value of the interaction. The analysis of variance may thus be applied directly, and has the advantage of providing estimates of the scale values (Anderson, 1962b).

A simple graphical test of goodness of fit may be used with any two-way factorial design. As is well known, zero interaction then implies that the data plot as parallel curves as illustrated in Anderson (1966).

This example illustrates a general result, that use of a factorial design for constructing the stimulus sets permits a powerful and direct test of fit. If the stimulus parameters are independent of context, then the linear model implies that all interactions of the design are zero. However, this test of fit also allows for context effects if these themselves are linear, a question of some theoretical concern (Anderson, 1966, 1967a).

The general linear model places no restrictions on the weights, but the test of fit for the averaging model does depend on having the same weight for all the stimulus items within any factor of the design. Thus in Table 1, if the weights of B and Q were interchanged, then the interaction would be nonzero unless the weights were equal. In this case, the averaging model makes a different prediction than a summative model (Anderson, 1965a).

This test of goodness of fit is made directly on the raw data and is parameter-free in not requiring explicit estimation of parameters. The use of a factorial design may seem roundabout, of course. The obvious procedure would be to choose two stimuli, A and P, of equal weight, get separate estimates of s_A and s_P, and compare their sum or mean with the observed judgment to the set. However, faulty estimates of s_A and s_P would fail even a correct model. This difficulty does not arise with the present procedure which has other advantages as well. Of course, if the model passes the test of fit, then it may be used to validate independent estimates of the scale values.

A striking property of this test of goodness of fit is that it can be applied to tasks in which the stimuli are presented in serial order. In this case, the serial positions correspond to the factors of the design, and the main effects then yield a serial position curve (Anderson, 1964b, c, 1967a). Some interesting problems of design arise in such experiments since from six to ten serial positions would not be unusual.

Empirical Evidence

One of the first serious tests of the linear model (Anderson, 1962a) used a personality impression task based on that introduced by Asch (1946). Subjects judged on a 1-20 scale how much they thought they would like hypothetical persons described by sets of three adjectives. Each subject judged 27 sets formed from a 3^3 design. To avoid bias in set construction, the adjectives were chosen at random from lists classed as high, medium, or low in normative value (cf. Anderson, 1968b). To obtain generality, six different adjective replications were made and two subjects were run under each replication. To allow a test of the model at the level of the single subject, each subject was run through the design on five successive days. Although this might seem to invite response stereotypy, no difficulty was experienced, possibly because of the high interset similarity.

An adequate test of the model rests on the adequacy of the numerical rating scale data. The adequacy of the data rests squarely on the experimental procedure, and a few precautions deserve specific mention. The first two sessions were considered as practice during which the subject could establish his frame of reference and hopefully adapt out preferences for round numbers, etc. Warmup sets were given at the beginning of each day and these included end-anchor sets which later evidence (Anderson, 1967b) indicates are important in helping ensure that the relevant data come from the interior of the scale. The experimenter read the adjectives of each set to the subject, and the subject then read them aloud in the reverse order. This was intended to minimize possible effects of order of presentation (since true simultaneous presentation was not possible); it was also intended to compel the subject to pay equal attention to each adjective, which would help assure the assumption of equal weighting that was employed. For this same purpose the instructions told the subject to consider that all adjectives were equally important and that each had been contributed by a different acquaintance of the person, attempting thereby to minimize unequal weighting that would be caused by any redundancy or inconsistency in the set.

A separate analysis was run for each subject using the data from the last three sessions. The mean correlation between predicted and observed judgments was .967, a value that has been typical of subsequent work. For a variety of reasons, such correlations do not mean much, in particular because they do not evaluate the discrepancies from prediction. In the test of goodness of fit, 3 of the 12 subjects showed significant discrepancies. These discrepancies were small, however, and the data were interpreted as supporting an averaging model. In one sense, this conclusion was premature since the experimental design did not allow a distinction between the general linear model and the averaging model.

Later experiments using simultaneous presentation of trait-adjectives have given much the same picture (Anderson, 1965a, 1966; Anderson & Jacobson, 1965; Lampel & Anderson, 1968). The model always fits the data quite well, but there are almost always small, significant discrepancies. Inspection of the data has failed to reveal the origin of the discrepancies; they may reflect some fundamental error in the model, or they may result from remaining shortcomings in the experimental technique.

When heterogeneous stimuli are used, with each set containing different kinds of information, a simple model may not hold. In the Lampel and Anderson (1968) experiment, females rated as dates males described by two adjectives and a photograph. Although the adjectives combined in an approximately linear manner, they interacted strongly with the photograph, their effect increasing as the desirability of the photograph increased. It was noted that this result could be accounted for within the general model in terms of differential weighting, however. In Sidowski and Anderson (1967), judgments of city-occupation combinations showed a marked one-point interaction involving one occupation and one city, and this was interpreted as reflecting a corresponding cognitive interaction.

Other early work that may be mentioned here includes the reports of Abelson (1961), Weiss (1963), and Levy and Richter (1963). In Weiss' experiment, persons were described by three opinion statements about capital punishment, and subjects rated their judgment of that person's opinion. Weiss employed an analysis of variance to test, in effect, a linear model with equal weights, but found marked discrepancies. Abelson used real voting data and sociological variables in an analysis of variance test. Levy and Richter had subjects make judgments of groups based on photographs of the group members and used a chi-square test of fit. Neither report found significant discrepancies and both were interpreted as favoring a summative model for the given situations. Both reports used dichotomous rather than numerical judgments so that it is difficult to compare them to the above cited work on personality impression formation.

A special question of considerable interest is whether the subject adds or averages the stimulus information. As long as the sets contain the same number of stimuli, the difference between these two combination rules is usually small. A clear difference seems to emerge when set size is varied while keeping the value of the single stimuli constant. Since the average value of the stimuli is then constant over set size, a simple averaging model would predict no set size effect. However, such an effect was observed for simultaneous presentation by Willis (1960) and Weiss (1963), both of whom concluded that a simple averaging model was inadequate. This point has been pursued by Fishbein and Hunter (1964), discussed below, who use it as the main evidence for a summation rule.

That a summation rule is not adequate was shown in a critical test (Anderson, 1965a) in which mildly favorable or unfavorable information was added to highly favorable or unfavorable information, respectively. A summation rule would predict that the added information would increase the response polarity whereas the opposite result was obtained. Hendrick (1967) has corroborated this finding.

Other failures of a summation rule to account for impression data, together with a hypothesis as to where such a combination rule might be applicable, are given in Anderson (1965a, 1967b). It perhaps deserves explicit mention that getting a decrease in response polarity in the above critical test requires a sufficient difference in scale values. With small or zero differences, the averaging model actually predicts an increase in response polarity. This is the case for the set size effect which will now be considered.

To disprove one model does not prove another, of course, and the inadequacies of a summation rule do not prove that subjects average. However, the use of an initial or neutral impression, to be averaged in with the externally presented stimuli, gave at least a qualitative account of the data. The appropriate equation for simultaneous presentation is,

$$J_k = \frac{kws + (1 - w)s_0}{kw + (1 - w)},\tag{4}$$

where J_k is the judgment of a set of k adjectives each of scale value s and weight w. The term s_0 represents the initial or neutral impression of the subject as he begins the set. This term arises in a natural way with serial presentation, but may seem odd with simultaneous presentation. One way of looking at it is as a neutral impression, based on lack of information (Anderson, 1965a). Its relative importance in the overall impression is $(1 - w)/[kw + (1 - w)]$, which decreases as more information is added.

From Equation 4, it can be seen that the magnitude of the judgment is an increasing function of set size, at least as long as $(1 - w)$ is not zero. This agrees with the data, and more recent work has obtained good quantitative support for this formulation (Anderson, 1967b). An interesting alternative explanation in terms of numerosity has been given by Manis, Gleason, and Dawes (1966). This gives a qualitative account of the set size effect with simultaneous presentation though it has not yet been tested quantitatively.

The experiments discussed above have used simultaneous presentation of the stimuli. Serial presentation is more realistic, of course, but introduces the problem of order effects. This is a complex topic (cf., e.g., Lana, 1964; McGuire, 1966a; Rosnow, Holz, & Levin, 1966) on which only a couple brief remarks will be made here. A discussion of the primacy effect in impression formation will also be given later.

An initial attempt to treat order effects using a linear operator model (Anderson & Hovland, 1957) met with mixed success in an attitude change experiment (Anderson, 1959). The data indicated that the opinion consisted of two components, basal and superficial, and so required a more complex representation than the model provided. However, one rather straightforward property of the model that was qualitatively verified was that attitude should change according to a growth curve as additional pieces of information are presented. This constitutes a set size effect for serial presentation. The data of Fishbein and Hunter (1964) thus appear to be in accord with an averaging formulation since they used essentially a serial procedure, as in Asch (1946), though complicated in various respects such as describing three different persons concurrently.

Later mathematical generalizations of the linear operator model (Anderson, 1961, 1964a, b) have led to the present weighted average model for serial presentation, together with the test of goodness of fit noted above. However, this model has not yet been seriously tested at a quantitative level in attitude or impression experiments, though an experiment on sequential number-averaging (Anderson, 1964c) showed promising results.

The weighted average model is applicable outside of the area of impression and opinions, and the writer has recently begun a program of research on integration of psychophysical stimuli. In one report (Anderson, 1967a), subjects judged the average heaviness of a sequence of six lifted weights. The model fit quite well and the data showed a recency effect as with the serial number-averaging task (Anderson, 1964c). In the case of simultaneous presentation, the model fit quite well for number stimuli again, but some discrepancies were found with spatial position stimuli (Anderson, 1968a).

The study of psychophysical integration is of interest in its own right. Moreover, the greater simplicity of these stimuli may help pin down the cause of the discrepancies from the model that have been obtained with semantic stimuli.

COMPARATIVE ANALYSIS

The purpose of the present section is to propose an experimental paradigm for comparing the present formulation with balance theory (Heider, 1958; M. Rosenberg & Abelson, 1960) and congruity theory (Osgood & Tannenbaum, 1955). The paradigm may be considered a 'thought experiment' since it illuminates the basic theoretical assumptions.

The experimental paradigm is based on the use of impression-dyads, and a schematic version would be as follows. Two hypothetical persons, A and B, are each described by sets of personality-traits, and the subject forms an impression of each. The subject is then informed additionally that A likes B, or that A dislikes B, or some similar relation. The subject is then asked again to say how much he thinks he himself would like A and B.

To experimentalize this paradigm would be straightforward though a number of technical problems would require careful consideration. In particular, it may be desirable to avoid judging A and B twice in close succession. However, these problems will not be considered here.

At the theoretical level, this paradigm involves two problems. The first is how the initial impressions of A and B are formed, based on the two independent sets of traits. This problem has formed the main ground of the present theoretical formulation as already discussed. Congruity theory, as it has been applied to this problem, yields quantitative predictions but it has been uniformly inadequate (e.g., Triandis & Fishbein, 1963; Fishbein & Hunter, 1964; L. R. Anderson & Fishbein, 1965). To conceptualize this task in terms of the triads of balance theory seems awkward at best, and not useful without quantitative development that would allow explicit predictions. However, a related model proposed by Abelson (1963) would seem to be applicable. This turns out to be a summation model which accordingly has special theoretical interest, although it is not entirely in agreement with the data cited above.

The second theoretical question posed by the impression-dyad paradigm centers on the changes in the subject's impressions upon learning of the relation between A and B. This question is the main concern of this section.

In the framework of congruity theory, A likes B would mean that A is the source, B the concept, and likes a positive assertion. In the framework of balance theory, A, B, and the subject form one of Heider's (1958) triads, with sentiment relations between each pair of persons. It may also be noted that A and B, together with the relation between them, form a "band" in the terminology of M. Rosenberg and Abelson (1960).

To obtain a critical experiment, consider the following three impression dyads.

TABLE 2

Impression-Dyads Based on Sets of High (*H*) or
Low (*L*) Personality-Trait Adjectives

	Person *A*	Relation	Person *B*
Impression-Dyad 1	H	likes	H
Impression-Dyad 2	H	dislikes	H
Impression-Dyad 3	H	dislikes	L

Here H is used to denote any person described by a set of favorable traits, and L any person described by a set of unfavorable traits. The several Hs represent different persons, but it is assumed that A and B are described by equally favorable sets of traits in Dyad 1, and similarly in Dyad 2. It is also assumed that the subject's initial impressions of A and B in Dyad 3 are equal and opposite. These restrictions can, of course, be imposed by suitable experimental procedure.

The congruity principle predicts that no change will occur in Dyads 1 or 3 when the subject learns of the relation between A and B. In Dyad 1, A and B are equal in value, and hence are completely congruent when the positive relation is established between them. In Dyad 3, A and B are equal and opposite in value, and hence completely congruent when the negative relation is established between them.

Dyads 1 and 3 are critical for the theory, and there are two other impression-dyads that are also congruent. In each case, the congruity principle predicts zero change. Any observed change, therefore, is evidence against the applicability of congruity theory. It is assumed here that no correction is needed for an "assertion constant" (Osgood & Tannenbaum, 1955) in these impression-dyads. However, the experimental status of this correction is not completely clear, and the use of symmetric dyads such as "A and B like each other" might be preferable. From the theoretical standpoint, it should be noted, use of such a correction would require the use of some principle in addition to the principle of congruity. However, the addition of a principle like information integration, for instance, would probably render the principle of congruity superfluous.

There are also incongruent impression-dyads as exemplified by Dyad 2. Here the theory predicts that the impressions of A and B should both decrease toward zero. These incongruent dyads will not be considered here, but a clear presentation and evaluation of the theory can be found in S. Rosenberg (1968).

The predictions of balance theory are up to a point parallel to those of congruity theory. For the subject to like A and B, who themselves are positively related, is a completely balanced state of affairs. A balance principle consequently affords no basis on which to predict any change in the triad corresponding to Dyad 1. The same can readily be seen for Dyad 3, and there are two other such dyads. These four dyads, it may be noted, correspond directly to the balanced bands of M. Rosenberg and Abelson (1960).

Dyad 2 corresponds to an unbalanced triad, and there are three other such cases. As has been noted (M. Rosenberg & Abelson, 1960; S. Rosenberg, 1968), balance theory here predicts that something will change but, except for a least-effort principle, provides no clue about what will change or how much. Accordingly, these unbalanced dyads will not be considered here.

One important difference between congruity and balance theories should be noted. Congruity theory makes the explicit prediction that no change will occur in any of the four congruent dyads. To find such change would accordingly discredit the theory. In contrast, although the balance principle as it has been used does not provide a basis for predicting any change, balance theory itself need not rule out that such changes might occur. Of course, some additional principle would be needed to explain them.

One possible principle has been suggested by Abelson (1963). Essentially this postulates that each component of a two-element sentence changes in value, either positively or negatively, according as the other component is positive or negative in value. In Dyad 1, this would predict that both *A* and *B* increase in value which seems reasonable. However, the postulate is based on a change from the band concept (M. Rosenberg & Abelson, 1960), and takes the two components of a sentence to be, in effect, the subject, and the verb-object combination. Thus, the two components in Dyad 2 are *H* and *dislikes L*. This apparently leads to indeterminate or anomalous predictions, as can be readily verified. [An attempt to remove these anomalies is made by Abelson in Chapter 5—Ed.]

An approach based on information integration provides a rather different analysis than either balance or congruity theories. The initial impressions of persons *A* and *B* result from the integration of the information in the separate sets of personality-traits. According to the evidence cited above, these initial impressions obey an averaging model. When the subject is then told that *A* likes *B*, this is simply an additional piece of information; it presumably is integrated into the initial impression much as though an additional trait had been presented.

At a general level, a principle of information integration seems adequate to handle the impression-dyad task. In particular, it has the potentiality of handling the interpersonal relation in a quantitative way. Thus, different degrees of liking of *B* by *A* would mean different scale values of the corresponding piece of information. The need for such quantification has been widely recognized, of course, but not much progress has been made.

The present approach seems straightforward and plausible enough at a general level, but it is only fair to point out that getting down to specifics may cause trouble. Perhaps the most serious of these is that the value of the relation information is itself relational. Suppose for instance that *H* dislikes *L*. To dislike may be undesirable in itself, but to dislike a bad person may not be without merit, all the more so if the disliker is likable himself. Sometimes, it is evident, the value and weight of the relation will depend on the total dyad configuration. This is the subject's privilege, to be sure, but it does set limits to the usefulness and testability of any simple model. Whether the subject is simply averaging the relation information in with the initial impression may be difficult to test if the value is configurally determined.

R. P. Abelson has suggested in private conversation that balance theory would be able to handle the impression-dyad task by employing a more general conception of balance than has been used in the definition of balanced bands. I see no reason, in principle, that the idea of balance could not be so developed, though I suspect that the attempt will render the balance principle largely unnecessary. Be this as it may, I wish to emphasize that the interest of the argument should not obscure that the focus of this section is primarily on the value of an incisive experimental base for theoretical development, only secondarily on critical tests per se.

In 1960, M. Rosenberg and Abelson noted that balance theory had not yet evoked much research. Although the experimental work that they reported was quite outstanding, not much has happened since (S. Rosenberg, 1968). Indeed, Abelson and Kanouse (1966) have recently remarked, in a striking metaphor, that balance theory is "foundering on the shoals of insufficient detail," a state of affairs that may validate Zajonc's (1960a) diagnosis that no one has really tried to disprove the theory. This in turn seems to stem from lack of an experimental task that would provoke theoretical explication.

The impression-dyad paradigm has no great novelty, of course. Its formal structure corresponds directly to a triad or band in balance theory, and an early empirical use of such a paradigm was made by Jordan (1953). However, the potentialities in combining the personality impression task with the band format do not seem to have been recognized. The combination provides theoretical power along with very great experimental flexibility.

INCONSISTENCY RESOLUTION

The present formulation provides a direct approach to the consistency problem. As yet, it is in rudimentary quantitative form and is, moreover, limited in scope. Thus, higher order cognitive processes of the sort considered by Heider (1958) and Abelson (1959) are not within the present purview. Unresolvable inconsistencies that prevent integration of the information are also important but will not be considered here.

Within the present framework, a partial definition of inconsistency may be obtained as follows. To resolve an inconsistency in a set of information items, the subject must change his apprehension of the items in some way. The model allows just two possibilities: change in the scale value, and change in the weight. Accordingly, such change is taken as a necessary condition for inconsistency. It is not a sufficient condition since such changes may occur for other reasons. For instance, a redundant item would tend to be given a reduced weight.

In this definition, information integration need not involve any notion of consistency. In the impression task, for instance, suppose a person is described by one very favorable adjective, *wise*, and either one slightly favorable or one slightly unfavorable adjective, such as *punctual* or *unpunctual*. Neither conjunction need trouble anyone, in which case the model would take the impression to be an average of the values of the separate stimuli. No problem of consistency would be involved. Thus, no special principle, such as balance or congruity, is required simply from having items of different value, even of opposite polarity.

Much the same remark applies to attitude change. A communication that argues for a position different from one's own does not necessarily create inconsistency. In the serial averaging model, the scale value of the communication is simply averaged in with the current opinion. This remains true, incidentally, when the communication is relevant to two or more opinions simultaneously. Thus, a spectrum of effects from a single communication, as in the syllogisms used by McGuire (1960), might be handled in a simple manner.

Of course, some sets of information will contain inconsistencies. In the above example, the subject may well feel unpunctuality to be lacking in wisdom, and so lower the scale value of *wise* in that set. In contrast, the inconsistency in the set {*dependable, honest, unreliable*} would presumably be resolved by decreasing the weights of the words. There is relatively little evidence, however, on how people do resolve such inconsistencies, at least in the personality impression task.

Work on the primacy effect in personality impressions is relevant to this question. The competing explanations are that the later words assimilate in value toward the earlier words, a hypothesis due essentially to Asch (1946), and that the later adjectives receive lower weight. The latter interpretation is uniformly favored by the results of a series of experiments (Anderson & Barrios, 1961; Anderson & Hubert, 1963; Anderson & Norman, 1964; Anderson, 1965b; Stewart, 1965) though the question cannot be considered settled.

A change in meaning of the later words would presumably reflect inconsistency resolution, but decreases in their weights could arise from other causes. Thus, the above cited work has been interpreted in terms of attention decrement. However, the recent work with psychophysical stimuli has yielded recency effects in experiments that used comparable presentation times. This is contrary to an attention decrement explanation and emphasizes the possibility that a discounting process (Anderson & Jacobson, 1965) is involved in the primacy effects that are obtained.

Of course, the obvious way to test for change of meaning is to ask what the word means in different contexts. This may be done using a component rating procedure (Anderson & Lampel, 1965; Anderson, 1966). The subject first formed an impression of a person described by three trait-adjectives presented together, and then rated the likability of one of the separate traits of that person. Both experiments yielded large positive context effects, with the rating of each single trait moving toward the values of the other traits of the set.

However, to interpret this context effect as a change in meaning involves a delicate methodological question (Anderson & Norman, 1964). The component may not have separate existence in the overall impression, and the subject, required to make some response, may produce a composite of its context-free value and the impression of the person. Indeed, an averaging model based on this idea gave a rather good account of the data.

A somewhat different approach is to incorporate obvious inconsistencies, such as in {*honest, deceitful, gloomy*}, into the stimulus set and observe the effect on the overall impression. The results of this work (Anderson & Jacobson, 1965) favored the discounting hypothesis that inconsistent adjectives receive reduced weight. The amount of discounting varied with instructions, as would be expected. Somewhat surprisingly, affective and semantic inconsistencies seemed to be nearly equal in effectiveness.

This result suggests that component weight ratings may be useful in consistency analysis. Hopefully, they would not suffer from the difficulty with component value ratings noted above, and would then be a valuable tool in the parametric analysis of inconsistency resolution. Work on this is in progress.

The theory of information integration that has been outlined here is still in the process of development. However, it has done well in a number of demanding experimental tests, both qualitative and exact, and is able to handle a moderately complex body of data in a conceptually simple manner. Integration theory has, moreover, considerable generality since it applies not only to attitude change and impression formation, but to decision making and psychophysical judgment. It is too soon to make any firm evaluation of this approach, but the present outlook is promising.

CHAPTER 74

What Do You Think of a *Cruel, Wise* Man?
The Integrative Response to a Stimulus Manifold

Shel Feldman

University of Pennsylvania

One problem to which the consistency theories address themselves is the relation between: (a) the response to a multiplicity of stimuli presented simultaneously; and (b) those responses that would be made to each of the stimuli, if presented separately. After describing the problem, and previous solutions, I attempt to develop a general approach to its solution and to discuss some related issues.

THE PROBLEM

At any given moment, the individual is faced with a multiplicity of potential stimuli. Only certain of these will actually elicit a response. According to Hullian theory (e.g., 1951), the particular potential stimuli that do elicit a response will be those whose stimulus intensities or incentive values are high, or those particularly relevant to an ongoing drive state.

Often, only one stimulus complex in the situation need be noted, whether because of its intensity, its incentive value, or its drive value. There are, however, many situations in which more than one stimulus complex affects behavior. Still, this may present no particular problem. First, the responses appropriate to different aspects of the stimulus manifold may be completely independent of one another. Second, the individual may have learned a particular response to the combination of stimuli that is different from the responses to the root stimuli. Third, even if no new response is learned and the appropriate responses do overlap, they may still be performed *seriatim*, with no effect of the one upon that following. In none of these cases is there any particular problem for consistency theory.

Nonetheless, much behavior occurs in which the individual is faced with a stimulus manifold, more than one aspect of which elicits a response

I wish to extend my appreciation to Dr. Robert P. Abelson and to Dr. Martin Fishbein for their comments and suggestions on earlier drafts of this paper. I also wish to thank the Annenberg School of Communications, University of Pennsylvania, for support of the study described on p. 749; Dr. Charles Schultz for providing the use of his class; Mr. Lewis C. Winters for serving as the first experimenter; and Mrs. Eve Feldman and Mr. Tulsi B. Saral for preparing the booklets and analyzing the data.

—at least one aspect overlaps with at least one other, to which only one response—not already learned—can be made. For example, a diner may examine the menu in a new restaurant, and find many never-before-tasted dishes. The appropriate response has not been learned; only one order is possible; the ordering of dishes overlaps in that the choice of one entree effectively precludes the choice of another that same night. The usual decision-making study, having come thus far, would proceed to examine the expected subjective utility of each dish, and would endeavor to predict the diner's choice through knowledge of his previous ordering of beef, mussels, sole, veal, etc., and the subjective likelihood of obtaining a reasonable dish of each, based on the reputation of the restaurant. This usual analysis fails to allow the possibility that the diner may reconstruct the alternatives available to him. There is no reason to assume that he might not order three appetizers, strategically chosen to include different types of food, in place of the usual entree (in some restaurants such sampler plates may even be institutionalized and on the menu). This last type of response, which is simultaneously appropriate to several aspects of the stimulus manifold, is what may be called the integrative response (IR).

Let us now take leave of our sated diner, however, and concern ourselves with integrative responses to *verbal* stimuli. Given the fractional nature of the meaning response (Osgood, 1952; 1953, pp. 695–698), it should be far easier to integrate verbal responses than other, more manifest, responses (such as trying to finish three large appetizers). The subject's greater ease in responding verbally allows the study of his responses to several different problems in a single experimental session, so that some regularities of behavior, as measured by evaluative semantic differential scales, can be observed and described.

PREVIOUS SOLUTIONS

Insofar as the earlier literature has dealt with IRs, two different approaches seem to have been taken. The first, a Gestalt approach, is exemplified by Asch (1946); the second, a stimulus-response approach, is exemplified by Hull (1945).

In a series of studies that has become the paradigm for the investigation of IRs in social psychology, Asch presented his subjects with a list of adjectives purporting to describe the personality of some other individual. When manipulating whether the set of stimulus elements contained "warm" or "cold," Asch found greater differences in other adjectives checked as describing the individual than he did when manipulating the elements "polite" and "blunt." From this, and other similar evidence, Asch concluded that there is a dynamic quality to the stimulus manifold, with some elements being more central than others; that the IR actually elicited is not any simple summative function of the root responses (RRs) that would have been elicited by the stimulus elements presented alone.

In Hull's (1945) discussion of responses to stimulus manifolds, he also argues that it is incorrect to expect a simple summative IR. Rather, if no new response has been conditioned to the manifold, one should, he suggests, following Pavlov (1927, p. 70), expect the IR to arise from reciprocal inhibition of the RRs as a function of the root habit strengths involved. There is certainly no reason, in principle, why the weighting of elements cannot be incorporated into a model asserting the possibility of mapping RRs into IRs, thus taking account of the effects of centering, order, contrast, and other parameters isolated by Asch.

It would seem that it is such a weighted reciprocal inhibition model, applied to the meaning response, that is at the base of the congruity hypothesis of Osgood and Tannenbaum (1955). The IR is expected to be a weighted average of the RRs called forth by the stimulus manifold; each RR inhibits the other in proportion to its share of the total response strength elicited, where response strength is indexed by polarity. (Other averaging theories are discussed by, e.g., Agarie, 1961; N. Anderson, 1962; Campbell, 1961; Rimoldi, 1956; and Weiss, 1963.)

At present, the major alternative to some weighted average model of the IR remains a summative model. Such a model has been discussed most fully in recent years by Fishbein (L. Anderson & Fishbein, 1965; Fishbein & Hunter, 1964; Triandis & Fishbein, 1963; cf. also Gulliksen, 1956; Hammond, 1955). Essentially, Fishbein's argument would seem to be that RRs that are not antagonistic should not necessarily inhibit one another: rather, they should be mutually reinforcing, and the IR should be stronger in the given direction than either of the RRs. (RRs in this model *are* weighted, since it is postulated that each contributes to the IR in proportion to its probability of being evoked—its belief strength in Fishbein's [1961, 1963, 1965] model. No proportionality factor is introduced, however, thus yielding a straight summation.) Furthermore, the strength of the IR will be affected by the *amount* of overlap between the RRs: they will summate when they are nonantagonistic, except as they are identical—though even here, they will appear to summate, as belief strength is increased.[1]

TOWARD A MODEL RESOLVING AVERAGING AND SUMMATIVE THEORIES

The model of the IR proposed in this paper arises from an S-R point of view. Basically, it is hypothesized that the IR is the outcome of a response conflict, and that this outcome may be an averaging of the RRs, *or* a summation of them, depending upon their degree of overlap. In this section the development of the response conflict model is described. Beginning with a weighted average model, I suggest that the weighting factor is arousal. From this, and the argument that the factor that is weighted is habit strength, I proceed to the notion that two response potentials have been simultaneously evoked. I attempt to expand the response conflict model, finally, to encompass the possibilities of summative IRs as well as averaging IRs.

As suggested above, the Osgood and Tannenbaum congruity hypothesis is a weighted average model. In it, the weight accorded each RR is identical with its polarity. It is clear, however, that some highly polarized elements are not terribly arousing, while some less polarized elements may be so. In order to investigate empirically what some of the correlates of the weight of an element in a weighted average model might be, the study (Feldman, 1962; Feldman & Abelson, 1962) described below was carried out.

Twenty-five evaluative, personality-related adjectives were chosen as the universe of study. Each of these adjectives was relatively familiar to

---

[1] Martin Fishbein, personal communication, 1966.

subjects and was relatively neutral on potency and activity scales. Each had only one clear personality-related sense, and no obvious slang meanings.

Each of 75 Yale undergraduates rated each adjective in the standard context, "He is an (*adjective*) man," on a nine-point *good-bad* scale. Each subject also rated a balanced subset of 175 of the possible 625 adjective-adjective combinations (AACs) on that evaluative scale, in the same context.[2]

The ratings were pooled across subjects and a portion of the total data matrix was utilized to obtain least square estimates of the weight accorded each adjective in its combinations with other adjectives.[3] These weights or 'modifying capacities' are listed in Table 1. The obtained weights correlated quite well with each other in different noun contexts (*r* ranges from .75 to .95, with all 25 adjectives). Furthermore, these estimates yielded satisfactory prediction of both ratings in the previously unexamined section of the data matrix and ratings of the same AACs in the other noun contexts.

TABLE 1

Modifying Capacities of 25 Adjectives
(From Feldman, 1962)

Adjective	Modifying Capacity	Adjective	Modifying Capacity
Heartless	1.013	Tolerable	.315
Unscrupulous	.906	Normal	.279
Unprincipled	.817	Decent	.266
Immoral	.722	Wise	.261
Cruel	.701	Moderate	.257
Horrid	.656	Interesting	.249
Nice	.486	Clean	.230
Lovable	.474	Holy	.206
Depraved	.439	Sincere	.192
Corrupt	.437	Refined	.187
Crude	.420	Dirty	.186
Average	.396	Ignorant	.157
Scholarly	.366		

Given that the index of weight (w_i) accorded single adjectives (or RRs) in AAC impression formation was reliable and valid, its correlates were investigated. Among the hypotheses examined was that of Osgood and Tannenbaum, that the evaluative polarity of an adjective is identical with its weight. Other hypotheses were derived from Berlyne's (1960) discussion

---

[2] In order to test the generality of the results, two other contexts were also used; viz., "person" and "astronaut" were substituted for "man," and additional ratings were gathered. In all contexts, the order of adjectives within an AAC was varied to test for order effects. Except for a few combinations (in which one adjective seemed amenable to amalgamation with the following noun when that adjective was placed in the second position, as in "an (*adjective*), *holy* man"), no order effect was found. (See Feldman, 1962, pp. 15–19; cf. N. Anderson & Barrios, 1961, who found order effects for combinations of six adjectives [thus replicating Asch, 1946], but did not find such an effect for pairs of adjectives.) The results discussed herein are based, therefore, on ratings pooled across orders (save for amalgamation-prone AACs).

[3] The least square solution (Feldman, 1962, pp. 47–50) was kindly provided by Dr. Robert P. Abelson.

of collative variables as determinants of arousal: identifying arousal with attention paid a stimulus element, and thus, with its weight in determining an IR to a manifold in which it appears, it was hypothesized that w_i should be related to such variables as the novelty, surprisingness, and potency ratings of each adjective.

An intercorrelation matrix (see Table 2) showed that each of these variables is significantly related to the weighting index. It will be noted that evaluative polarity is highly related to w_i, as Osgood and Tannenbaum contend; however, it is neither the only, nor the strongest, correlate of that index. An analysis of variance showed that a significant amount of the variance of w_i was accounted for by other variables, and the beta weights for regressing the other variables onto w_i showed that evaluative polarity was far from the most important single variable.

TABLE 2

Correlations For 25 Adjectives Between Modifying Capacity and Selected Variables
(From Feldman, 1962)

| | Selected Correlates | | | | |
Variable	Evaluative Polarity	Evaluation	Potency[a]	Log Frequency[b]	Surprisingness[c]
Modifying capacity	.53	−.69	.70	−.50	.54
Evaluative polarity		−.36	.40	−.24	.71
Evaluation			−.87	.45	−.68
Potency				−.28	.59
Log Frequency					−.50

[a] Ratings on a nine-point *soft-hard* scale.
[b] Logarithm of G, summary index of word frequency (Thorndike & Lorge, 1944).
[c] Rankings from an independent group of judges (see Feldman, 1962, p. 13).

The conclusion suggested by the study reviewed above is that the weight of an RR in determining an IR is a function of its arousal value. Both potency and the collative variables were explicitly chosen because of their relation to arousal value. Furthermore, it would seem reasonable to consider even evaluative polarity as an index related to arousal—the degree to which an element is able to arouse strong affect, the degree to which it stands out from a bland ground (thus, related to Berlyne's notion of surprisingness as relative novelty, though with respect to affect, not frequency). It may be noted, however, that the study described is purely correlational. Unless the relationship between the arousal value of an RR and the resultant IR can be demonstrated experimentally as well, it might be argued that this relationship is somehow mediated through evaluative polarity.

In a later study (Feldman, 1966a), therefore, the effect of *manipulating* the surprisingness of an adjective upon the rating of AACs in which it appeared was investigated. Prior exposure to a communication repeating an adjective or words related to it should decrease its surprisingness. If its surprisingness were thus mitigated, the adjective should carry less weight in determining the IR to an AAC in which it is involved than if it were not so manipulated. Subjects seeing the prior communication should therefore rate a related AAC closer to the other member of the pair than subjects not seeing it.

Accordingly, several one-page communications were prepared. One used 'corruption' several times in a report on the importance of studying municipal corruption. A second communication discussed the stress on 'scholarship' in colleges. A third communication belabored the importance of 'honesty' in human relationships. Each communication was made to appear as an excerpt from a newspaper or magazine story.

Any effect of the communications upon the evaluative ratings of the adjective forms themselves ('corrupt,' 'scholarly,' and 'honest') would, of course, affect their evaluative polarity, and would thus allow for differential predictions between exposed and nonexposed groups, according to the congruity hypothesis. Care was taken in the writing, therefore, to argue that the stress upon the importance of the problem ('corruption,' 'scholarship,' or 'honesty') was not intended to condone, extol, or disparage the quality itself. Subsequent evaluative ratings of the critical adjectives showed that this requirement was fulfilled: there were no differences between the evaluative ratings of the critical adjectives by groups exposed to the communications and by those not exposed.

Each of 53 summer students at the University of Pennsylvania read two of the communications (thus serving as exposed groups for two of the critical adjectives and as a control, nonexposed group for the third) in what they were told was a study of newspaper stories. They were then asked to participate in what was supposedly a separate study, run by a different experimenter. There, the subjects first rated a number of adjectives singly, and then 60 AACs, including 16 critical ones—pairing 'corrupt,' 'scholarly,' or 'honest' with a word of opposed evaluative meaning.

TABLE 3

Evaluative Ratings of Critical AACs, as Affected by Manipulation of Surprisingness of Elements
(After Feldman, 1966a)

Negative Adjective (and Rating When Alone)	Mean Rating of AAC with *Honest*		Difference in Predicted Direction	Mean Rating of AAC with *Scholarly*		Difference in Predicted Direction
	Exposed Ss	Unexposed Ss		Exposed Ss	Unexposed Ss	
Corrupt (1.69)	3.06	4.00	.94	2.92	3.00	.08
Cruel (1.81)	3.59	3.79	.20	3.20	3.33	.13
Unscrupulous (2.12)	4.00	3.86	−.14	3.51	3.11	−.40
Immoral (2.31)	4.18	4.50	.32	3.29	4.25	.96
Sinful (2.80)	3.29	5.07	1.78	3.32	4.08	.76

Positive Adjective (and Rating When Alone)	Mean Rating of AAC with *Corrupt*		Difference in Predicted Direction
	Exposed Ss	Unexposed Ss	
Honest (7.69)	4.00	3.23	.77
Sincere (7.69)	3.31	3.26	.05
Lovable (7.35)	3.58	3.22	.36
Wise (6.73)	3.15	2.89	.26
Intelligent (6.38)	2.96	2.78	.18
Scholarly (6.35)	2.88	3.00	−.12

Ratings were made on nine-point *good-bad* scales, with 1 = bad.
For the basis of the 'predicted direction' of difference, see text.

The prediction, it will be recalled, is that groups exposed to prior communications utilizing a word related to the adjective will rate an AAC containing that adjective more like their rating of the other adjective alone than will a group not exposed to the prior communication. Thus, those reading the communication about 'corruption' will rate a *wise, corrupt* man more like a *wise* man—more positively—than will those not exposed to that communication. Similarly, those reading a communication about 'scholarship' will rate a *scholarly, immoral* man more like an *immoral* man —more negatively—than those not exposed. Table 3 shows the results; the prediction is borne out in 13 out of 16 cases $Z = 2.53$, ($p < .05$, by size-and-sign test). It may be concluded, therefore, that manipulating surprising-ness does affect ratings of AACs, even with evaluative polarity held constant.

Given both the correlational evidence discussed earlier, and the experimental confirmation of the relationship between arousal and weighting of RRs entering into an IR, it is possible to proceed with the discussion of arousal value or attention as a determinant of the IR, and with the discussion of the implications of this assumption for the development of a model for predicting the response to a stimulus manifold.

The Simple Response Conflict Model

The development of a model may be begun by setting up an equation that postulates the integrative response to be a weighted average of two root responses elicited in an AAC. This model is similar in form to that used by Osgood and Ferguson (in Osgood, Suci, & Tannenbaum, 1957, pp. 275–284; cf. the generalization in Feldman, 1962, p. 44):

$$(1) \qquad IR = \frac{w_1 RR_1 + w_2 RR_2}{w_1 + w_2},$$

where w_1 and w_2 are the weights attached to RR_1 and RR_2, respectively.

Next, on the basis of the studies discussed above, we may identify w with arousal value. We assume, further, that each stimulus in the stimulus manifold does have some arousal value; that it is equivalent to the Hullian (but internalized) stimulus-intensity dynamism, v; and that this arousal value is specific to the habits elicited by that stimulus. (A more complete discussion of internalized motivational responses may be found in Feldman, 1966c; cf. also Logan, Olmsted, Rosner, Schwartz, & Stevens, 1955, pp. 19–23.)

Following this logic, let us postulate that IR and RR_i correspond to some aspect of the internalized habit strengths, h_m and h_i, of the integrative response to the stimulus manifold and of the response to a given root stimulus, respectively. It may be argued that the traditional concepts of habit strength and response hierarchies permit us to conceive of a distribution of habit strength over a response continuum, so long as the responses vary in a single dimension (as they do when evaluations of persons on semantic differential scales are considered, in the studies discussed herein). From this may be derived the possibility of using h to define the *content* of the response that will be made to a stimulus. That is, here h will refer to the evaluative rating that is most probable for a root stimulus, given the distribution of response strengths over the evaluative dimension. Making the appropriate substitutions, then, the initial equation is transformed into:

(2) $$b_m = \frac{v_1 b_1 + v_2 b_2}{v_1 + v_2}.$$

This translation of a general weighted average model into Hullian terms suggests that the integrative response is the resultant of a response conflict. The numerator on the right of Equation (2) is readily interpretable as the sum of two response potentials, where each is a function of both the internalized habit, b, and the internalized dynamism, v, of the stimulus-response association. The denominator may be interpreted, in turn, as the total dynamism present in the stimulus manifold. The fraction thus implies that the contribution of the habit of each RR to that of the IR is proportional to the dynamism of that stimulus-response connection relative to the total dynamism found in reactions to the stimulus manifold:

(3) $$b_m = b_1 \left(\frac{v_1}{v_1 + v_2} \right) + b_2 \left(\frac{v_2}{v_1 + v_2} \right).$$

In other words, different responses have been evoked by different elements of the stimulus manifold. Each competes with the other, but an all-or-none choice between those responses is not made. Rather, an integrative response to the stimulus manifold is made, and it is a function of the habit associated with each root stimulus, the arousal value of the association, and the total arousal value of the competing responses.

Complication of the Response Conflict Model

The formulation presented above fits the averaging theories of the IR referred to earlier. Both the theory and the data presented by Fishbein (L. Anderson & Fishbein, 1965; Fishbein & Hunter, 1964; Triandis & Fishbein, 1963), however, argue that, at least in certain cases, RRs seem to summate rather than to average. It may be asked, therefore, whether the present formulation can be extended to include summative effects. In answer, two complications of the model presented thus far may be considered: The first leaves the theories opposed, but it leads to a second which suggests a more general model embracing both averaging and summative effects.

Let us consider the RRs elicited as a set, S. With each element of that set, s_i, is associated the habit involved, b_i, its dynamism, v_i, and its response potential, e_i. Habit strength and dynamism are functions defined directly on each element, s_i, by some measurement technique. Response potential might be defined, however, as the product of the relevant habit strength with the *total dynamism in the set.*

(4) $$e_i = b_i \sum_j v_j.$$

If we then replace $b_i v_i$ in our earlier equations by $b_i \sum_j v_j$, we obtain:

(5) $$b_m = \frac{b_1 (v_1 + v_2) + b_2 (v_1 + v_2)}{v_1 + v_2}.$$

This last equation, of course, reduces to:

(6) $$b_m = b_1 + b_2,$$

which would render stimulus dynamism irrelevant as a determinant of the integrative response and yield a pure additive theory (where, it should be noted, h may still be weighted—by its probability, or belief strength), with no proportionality involved.

This solution relies on the assumption that the dynamism of each stimulus affects not only the RR it elicits, but all others as well. It is common to assume that drives or incentives multiply all RRs aroused, and multiplying a given h_i by the total drive or total incentive in a situation may be eminently sensible. Such motivational forces as affect all RRs may be laid aside, however, in order to concentrate upon those peculiar to specific stimuli (cf. Feldman, 1966c). Furthermore, it is not clear why stimulus-intensity dynamism, as here considered, *should* affect other RRs.

In contrast to the total dynamism assumption, one might assert that only the *relevant dynamism* energizes the habit:

(7) $$e_i = h_i v_i.$$

The use of this assumption in predicting IR is readily recognized as yielding that solution already given in Equation (2)—a pure averaging model, which seems questionable in light of Fishbein's studies, cited above.

Thus, the adding vs. averaging controversy can be expressed in terms of a set-theoretic model, as here developed. In the present form of the model, however, neither the use of a complete set of v_i nor that of only the single appropriate dynamism can resolve the controversy. Let us therefore proceed to further complications of the model.

A number of authors (including Carlson, 1956; Fishbein, 1961, 1963, 1965; Peak, 1955; Rosenberg, 1956; Smith, 1947; Woodruff & DiVesta, 1948; and Zajonc, 1960) have discussed the relation of evaluative habits to cognitions about, or subresponses to, the stimulus involved. It would seem that, according to this approach, a given subresponse could be associated with more than one stimulus. If so, it would then follow that the evaluative response to a stimulus is composed of a subset of subresponses unique to that stimulus *and* a subset that is also common to other stimuli in the manifold:

(8) $$h_1 = u_1 + c_{1,2}, \text{ and}$$
$$h_2 = u_2 + c_{1,2},$$

where u_1 and u_2 denote the subresponses unique to stimuli 1 and 2, respectively, and $c_{1,2}$ denotes the subresponses common to both.

It follows that:

(9) $$h_1 + h_2 = u_1 + u_2 + 2c_{1,2}.$$

We may then define $m_{1,2}$, the mutuality, or overlap, between the responses h_1 and h_2, and $1 - m_{1,2}$, the nonmutuality, as follows:[4]

(10) $$m_{1,2} = \frac{2c_{1,2}}{u_1 + u_2 + 2c_{1,2}};$$

---

[4] The definition of mutuality given here precludes the assumption that overlap of stimuli is directly related to the evaluative similarity of the stimuli, as assumed by, e.g., Dustin and Baldwin (1966). It is necessary, rather, to measure the overlap of the subresponses, or associates, of the stimuli—the pairs 'honest' and 'trustworthy' and 'honest' and 'lovable' are both similar to one another evaluatively, but the first is clearly less independent than the second (cf. the study presented below).

$$(11) \qquad 1 - m_{1,2} = \frac{u_1 + u_2}{u_1 + u_2 + 2c_{1,2}}.$$

It is now proposed that: (a) the nonmutually-shared portion of the internalized habits evoked is multiplied only by the arousal associated with the particular stimulus-response connection; but also, (b) the mutually-shared portion is affected by the total arousal evoked by the stimulus manifold—the dynamism of each stimulus is a multiplier of the proportion of subresponses that are shared. Thus, combining Equations (2) and (6), as suggested:

$$(12) \qquad h_m = (1 - m) \frac{h_1 v_1 + h_2 v_2}{v_1 + v_2} + m(h_1 + h_2).$$

It is obvious from this equation that complete overlap ($m = 1$; h_1 identical with h_2; $u_1 = u_2 = 0$) yields pure summation, and complete independence ($m = 0$; $c_{1,2} = 0$) yields pure averaging. In other words, the similarity of response implications of stimuli in a manifold should yield a polarization of response: the evocation of common subresponses should reinforce their expression. In contrast, complete independence of response implications should lead to averaging or integration. (It is assumed that the responses are in the same mode; in general, responses that are independent —in that they occur in different modes—should not interact, for there would be no reason to suppose either reciprocal inhibition or mutual reinforcement.) This model, then, can predict either averaging or summation and it will generally predict a combination of them dependent upon the overlap of the response sets evoked by the stimuli.

Two further refinements seem necessary, however, before we may be content with this model. First, it is likely that completely overlapping response sets do not reinforce one another completely. The respondent may feel, for example, that the repetition of the information is not useful: a *sincere, sincere* man is not twice as good as a *sincere* man. The respondent might also feel that the person described is being "damned with faint praise," and rate him *lower* than if the information were not repeated (Feldman, 1962): an *average, average* man may be seen as less good than an *average* man. [Chalmers (1964) has documented these deleterious effects of repetition—Ed.] It should be possible to solve this problem by defining $d_{1,2}$, the degree to which mutuality is reinforcing to the subresponses involved, as a multiplier[5] of m. For simple additivity (the integrative response being as great or greater than the larger of the RRs), then, $m > 0$, $0 < d \le 1$. It is also possible to have subtractivity, $m > 0$, $-1 \le d < 0$, as in the case of the *average, average* man.[6] Furthermore, it should be possible to manipulate the value of d; for example, by varying the surprisingness of the stimulus mani-

---

[5] In essence, this is to assert that adjectives behave similarly to the adverbial multipliers discussed by Cliff (1959, 1960), and Howe (1962), except that whereas true (content-less) adverbs have a constant reinforcing effect, adjectives have a reinforcing effect that varies with the extent to which they relate to one another (and, it would be expected, to the nouns they modify).

[6] This is meant to apply to any $m > 0$; not only to $m = 1$. While few studies in the literature have reported subtractivity (possibly because few have attempted to investigate a very large number of AACs), there is definite evidence of its occurrence, in the Feldman (1962) study cited.

fold, the credibility of the AAC, the demands on the respondent for certainty, etc.

The second refinement of Equation (12) is to note that the sign of d must be variable. A pair of overlapping negative words, such as 'cruel' and 'heartless,' must be additive in the negative direction, rather than in the positive. That is, a *cruel, heartless* man may be worse than either a *cruel* man or a *heartless* man. This problem may be dealt with by postulating that not only is the range of d from -1 to $+1$, but that it is multiplied in turn by a sign function that can take either the value $+1$ or the value -1, depending upon the sign of the unique subresponses elicited. Thus, the equation may be rewritten as follows:

$$(13) \qquad h_m = (1 - m) \frac{v_1 h_1 + v_2 h_2}{v_1 + v_2} + dm_+ (h_1 + h_2) - dm_- (h_1 + h_2),$$

where m_+ and m_- refer to the mutuality of positive subresponses and negative subresponses, respectively.

The model thus completed permits derivation of either adding or averaging, depending upon overlap, with an appropriate correction term for noncomplete mutual reinforcement of overlapping responses. What remains is the necessity to test the model against empirical data.

One such study, just completed, tested the derivation from Equations (12) and (13) that the greater the overlap between adjectives, the more likely that the rating of the AAC will seem to be summative. Size of overlap, derived from a word association study (Feldman, 1966b; cf. Deese, 1962; Laffal & Feldman, 1962, 1963) was compared with the likelihood of finding additivity in negative-negative AACs (using the data of Feldman, 1962). It was found that additive combinations *are* significantly more likely to have high overlap, both by a test of association (see Table 4), $\chi^2_c = 4.26$, $p < .05$, and by a test of the difference between means, $t = 3.41$, $df = 53$, $p < .05$. Further studies, including attempts to manipulate m and d, are now in progress.

TABLE 4

Association Between Overlap Score for Negative-Negative AAC
and Rating of AAC

Rating of AAC[a]	Overlap score between adjectives[b]	
	High[c]	Low
Additive	22	13
Nonadditive	6	14

[a] Data from Feldman (1962).
[b] Data from Feldman (1966b).
[c] Based upon median split. Number of cases in each cell refers to number of different AACs.

SUMMARY

It has been argued that prediction of the response to a stimulus manifold from the responses to the elements of that manifold presents an important problem for consistency theorists. While many have argued that an averaging model is most appropriate, others have argued for an additive model. In this paper, studies using a weighted average model and identifying the weighting function as arousal value were described. These results were utilized in developing a model of the problem as involving a response conflict. That model was shown to be capable of yielding either averaging or additive solutions, depending upon assumptions regarding how internal habits are multiplied by arousal values. By postulating that overlapping subresponses add, and that independent ones average, a more general model was derived; some of its implications were considered, and some empirical support for one of its corollaries was presented.

CHAPTER 75

Whither Pooling Models?
Some Additional Variables

Milton E. Rosenbaum

University of Iowa

and

Charles F. Schmidt

Rutgers University

As will be seen, the view we hold concerning the appropriate model for pooling of disparate information is unformalized and largely embryonic. Our bent, consistent with our Midwest location, is empirical. The availability of stated models serves for us as an embarkation point for the design of studies that may provide tests of the models or offer clues to important, neglected variables.

The area to which we have been attracted is the formation of impressions of persons. We will recount our efforts to evaluate the simply formulated models for averaging and adding. We will summarize two endeavors to deal with relationships within stimulus sets. A series of experiments will be described in which the value of the introduction of a new variable, the source of impression information, is assessed. Finally, we shall attempt to state the position to which we have been led by our empirical activities.

The presence of *inconsistency* in the impression formation literature provided the impetus for our initial venture into the study of impression formation. On the one hand, simple and elegant contrasting hypotheses were available to account for the integration of impression stimuli. On the other hand, ambiguous and contradictory data were presented, derived from diverse and frequently contaminated experimental procedures. We decided to charge in like the 'White Knight' to clear things up. The absence of comparable procedures, measures, and even statistical assessment in these studies precluded any direct comparison of the results which were relevant to the *additive* vs. *averaging* hypotheses.

We planned to expose the dirt to be cleaned out and to provide a basis for a direct comparison of these contrasting hypotheses by conducting three identical and simultaneous experiments varying only in the dependent measures employed. The design of the experiments included list length (three vs. six adjectives), variability of value of stimulus items (homogeneous vs. heterogeneous stimuli), polarity of the adjectives (positive vs. negative) and order of evaluation (first vs. second). In each experiment

Charles F. Schmidt was formerly at the University of Iowa.

208 Ss participated for a total of 624. It may be seen that we intended to clean house.

Two of the three dependent measures used were ones that have been frequently employed in the literature, and the third was homemade. We employed a simple 8-point favorability scale ranging from extremely favorable to extremely unfavorable. We also constructed a check list similar to that used by Asch (1946) and Podell and Podell (1963). Wishner (1960) had indicated the potential difficulty with this measure due to the possible presence of previously acquired language associations between particular stimulus items and particular response items in the dependent measure. We invented the Add-a-Word measure in which Ss simply wrote a word that embraced their impression. This required posthoc scaling to obtain numerical values. The invented scale was derived from rather nonspecific notions concerning an associative basis for impression formation.

The result of our cleaning venture was to mess things up more than ever. The three different measures did not appear to be at fault in that relatively consistent results were obtained across the three experiments. But the results were not entirely consistent with the available literature. We failed to find support for the additive hypothesis in that six-adjective lists did not yield significantly more polarized impressions than three-adjective lists (see the discussion in Chapter 73 of the 'set size effect') but in most cases the trend was in this direction. This was not a very clean result.

Podell and Podell (1963) had found that heterogeneous lists elicited more polarized responses than did homogeneous lists. We found no significant difference as a function of variability but the trend of the data was opposite to the direction found by Podell and Podell (1963). Things were getting messier than ever. The only apparently clean result was a significant contrast effect. Responses to second sets of stimuli were significantly more polarized than to first sets, i.e., a more positive response was given to a positive set of adjectives if it followed a negative set than if it occurred first and similarly for negative sets. Of course, positive never followed positive nor negative, negative in our design and so statistical significance is not necessarily cleanliness or godliness, for that matter.

We were daunted but not stopped in our desire for purification. In juxtaposition to Anderson's (1965a) study supporting averaging, the strongest support for a summation rule is provided by the Fishbein and Hunter (1964) study which we felt could stand a clean replication employing better measures and controls. Four experiments were conducted with 60 Ss in each experiment. Repeated measures designs were employed each allowing 255 degrees of freedom. The basis for four separate experiments with identical designs was the utilization of separately scaled positive and negative adjectives for males and for females. The adjectives were carefully selected using as criteria the variability and scale distance of the items. Actually, each S participated in two successive subexperiments. In all cases, Ss were exposed to adjective lists presented visually that varied in length, i.e., one, two, four, and eight adjectives. The adjective materials and lengths were counterbalanced for Ss by employing a Graeco-Latin Square design. The adjectives were always listed in the order of increasing neutrality.

Booklets were employed for the presentation of stimuli and the response measures. In the subexperiment presented in the first booklet the simple 8-point favorability scale served as the response measure. For the second subexperiment, Fishbein and Raven's (1962) A scales appeared.

Briefly, the results for the first booklet in each of the four experiments support adding, although a weighted average model which utilizes the construct of initial impression (Anderson, 1965a) may also be consistent with these results. The results for the second booklet support averaging. Just what influence the order of two booklets has on the response obtained is not at all clear.

For us, the effort to contribute to the resolution of the adding vs. averaging controversy was clearly not fruitful. The several contributions of Anderson, Fishbein, the Podells, and others which support one or the other hypothesis remain before us. We are still dismayed by the inconsistency in the findings. In addition to other events, what our venture did produce is a keen awareness that the factors that affect impression formation extend well beyond the number of stimulus components and the valuation of the adjectives employed.

Perusal of the details of our data and the stimuli that produced them led us to consider the potential effects of additional aspects of the communications upon the impression response. One such variable of potential theoretical importance for the question of information integration is the redundancy or the degree of relatedness present in the stimulus materials employed. For example, Dustin and Baldwin (1966) have suggested that when the stimulus materials are highly related an averaging rule may best describe the S's response, whereas when the materials are unrelated an additive rule may be the best predictor. [This is exactly opposite to the claim in the preceding chapter!—Ed.] The manner in which relatedness of stimulus materials is construed is, of course, somewhat problematic.

Two different attempts at providing some evidence relevant to the question of the effect of relatedness upon the S's judgment have been carried out at Iowa. In one, Chalmers (1964) investigated, among other variables, the effects of repetition of a descriptive adjective within an information set. Logically such a manipulation is the case of complete redundancy. However, proceeding from a learning theoretic point of view exemplified by Staats and Staats (1958), Chalmers reasoned that the effect of a given trait adjective upon the judgment response should increase with number of pairings of the trait adjective with the person to be judged. When the impression responses to sets containing repeated information were compared with those obtained to sets containing the same adjectives but not repeated, a less favorable judgment was always obtained to sets containing repeated information. That is, repeated positive sets were judged less favorably than nonrepeated positively valued sets, and repeated negatively valued sets were also judged less favorably than nonrepeated negatively valued sets. Thus, it would appear that repetition in general added a negative component to Ss' judgments. The negative component seems to arise from impressions of lack of variability in the personality components of the judged person. In a postexperimental questionnaire, Ss' responses suggested that the imposition of variability on the specific information presented served as an additional contribution to the impression. In order to avoid this extraexperimental intrusion on the assessment of the effects of relationships within stimulus sets, Schmidt (1966) studied the effects of relatedness upon the impression response without introducing repetition or complete redundancy. In this study sentence materials were used and re-latedness was now defined utilizing specifiable linguistic relations between sentences within a set of information. To accomplish this, two general types of sentences were employed.

The first type, termed trait (T) sentence, was a simple attributive sentence of the form *Mr. X is T adjective*. The sentence *Mr. X is intelli-gent* and *Mr. X is kind* are examples of this type of sentence. The second type of sentence, termed instance (I) sentences, were derived from T sentences in one of two ways. For one case, a T adjective was used as an adverb of manner, e.g., *Mr. X does his work intelligently*. For the other, the T adjective was used as part of the verb, e.g., *Mr. X is kind to Mr. Y*.

Using these types of materials, two types of sets were constructed. The first type, the related sets, contained an I sentence which was derived from a T sentence also in the set. The second type, the unrelated sets, contained an I sentence comparable in valuation, but unrelated to any T sentence within the set. When the judgments of these types of sets were compared it was found that the related set was judged less favorably than the unrelated set for positively valued materials. However, when this same comparison was made for negatively valued materials, no difference in the judgment responses was obtained.

Relating these findings to the adding and averaging pooling models is somewhat difficult, since neither of the models have been extended to account for relatedness. In the additive model presented by Fishbein (Fish-bein & Hunter, 1964) the effect of an information item is assumed to be proportional to degree of belief by S that the information component is associated with the person described. This degree of belief is generally identified as the S's estimated subjective probability that the information is in fact characteristic of the person to whom it is attributed. Thus, a straightforward application of the construct of belief would predict an increase in response polarity with increasing relatedness (L. Anderson & Fishbein, 1965). This was not obtained in either the Chalmers or the Schmidt studies. A simple average model also clearly would not account for these findings. However, a proportional change model (Anderson, 1959) would account for the data quite well if the change parameters were dependent upon the degree of independence of the stimulus components. The direc-tion of the effect of relatedness upon the judgment response may well depend, however, on whether or not memory factors are involved. For example, with long and complex stimulus materials or delay between stimulus presentation and judgment assessment, related information may have a greater effect upon the judgment response than unrelated material. Although no firm interpretation of these results involving information relatedness can be offered here, they do suggest the possibility that suffi-cient control of this source of variance may considerably clarify the question of the appropriateness of adding or averaging pooling models.

Another empirical departure concerns the substantive quality of the information provided for impression formation. Although derived from a different conceptualization, Fishbein's (Fishbein, 1963; Triandis & Fish-bein, 1963; L. Anderson & Fishbein, 1965) attempt to deal with belief or credibility, as the operations seem to indicate, is related to our attempts to treat the source of the information utilized for impression formation. The work of Hovland and his associates (Hovland, 1954; Hovland, Janis,

& Kelley, 1953) was provocative in delineating as two crucial variables, the characteristics of the communicator and the character of the message. Impression formation research has concentrated on message variables but no attention has been given to the information source.

We employed as sources of information persons designated by occupational titles. The titles were drawn from the *Dictionary of Occupational Titles* (United States Employment Service, 1965) and scaled by a student population for "value as an informant concerning the characteristics of persons with whom they associate." High value sources such as social worker, dean, and doctor, were differentiated from medium-valued sources such as physicist, artist, and notary public, and low-valued sources such as piano tuner, meter reader, and seamstress. Sentences reading "Mr. A has been described by a (source) as (adjective, adjective, adjective)" were constructed. In a first study, it was found that the higher the value of the source, the more polarized was the evaluation of the described person, with direction of evaluation dependent on the positive or negative quality of the adjective information. Tangentially, it should be noted that neither a simple average nor a simple adding model can account for this finding. A weighted average model would do so if written for the purpose.

Later studies employing source value have utilized the device of two contradictory information messages in order to evaluate the approximate weighting of differentially valued sources. For example, a high value source presents positive information and a low value source presents negative information concerning the person to be evaluated. By manipulating the amount of information offered by high or low value sources, the weight of the source in the impression response may be determined. In initial studies, when the number of information items was equal, the value of the source overwhelmed the impression, independent of the value of the adjectives. If the high value source presented positive information, the impression was clearly positive and for negative information the impression became more negative. When the number of information items was 1 vs. 3 or 3 vs. 6, with higher value sources presenting less information, the impression was in the direction of the information presented by the lower valued source. However, control groups served to indicate that even in the differential amount of information situation, the presence of a high value source decreased the influence of the greater amount of information by the opposing source.

In the Figure, the results of a study in which the amount of information offered by a high valued source was varied are presented. In each stimulus set, low valued sources contributed five adjectives, either all negative or all positive. The curves depict the mean response to sets in which high value sources presented contrary information via one to five adjectives that were positive (HP-LN) or negative (HN-LP). Although the experimental design included variations in order of presentation of sources and adjectives, this factor was not relevant to the present context and is not represented in the Figure.

It may be seen that as single adjectives are added to the sets presented by high value sources, the impression increases or decreases in favorability depending on the positive or negative value of the adjectives offered by the high value source. Inspection of these curves suggests that negative growth and negative decay functions would fit the obtained data points

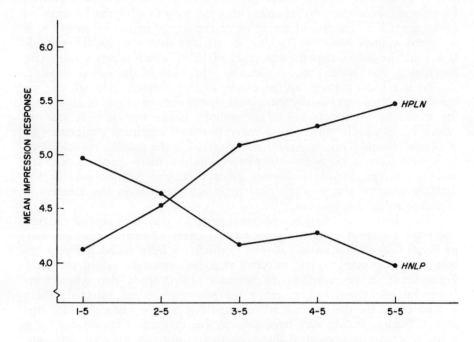

MEAN IMPRESSION RESPONSE

Number of Adjectives Presented by H
Five Adjectives Presented by L

quite well. Such functions are consistent with an assumption that the weighting of the stimuli decreases linearly with the ordinal position of the adjective within the information set (Anderson, 1965b).

A last study of the contribution of sources to impression formation considered the possibility that when the number of adjectives presented by a high and by a low value source were equal, the contribution to the impression response of the low value source will be discounted (Anderson & Jacobson, 1965). In order to examine this hypothesis, Ss were presented with two sets of adjectives describing a person. One set was highly positive (P plus) and the other set was moderately positive (P minus). In one treatment, one high value source presented a highly positive set and another high value source presented a moderately positive set (HP plus-HP minus), and in a second treatment a high value source presented the highly positive set while a low value source presented the moderately positive set (HP plus-LP minus). If discounting occurs the HP plus-LP minus set will elicit a more positive impression, but if averaging takes place the reverse is predicted. The design was completed by presenting LP plus-HP minus and LP plus-LP minus. In all cases the extreme set of the description (P plus) was followed by the moderate set (P minus) of the description. The results for all four sets of adjectives clearly supported averaging and not discounting in that the order of conditions in terms of mean favorability was HP plus-HP minus, HP plus-LP minus, LP plus-HP minus, and LP plus-LP minus.

Again, the relationship of these findings involving the source as a variable in impression formation to the various pooling models is not completely clear. This variable could be incorporated into a weighted average formulation quite easily by assuming that the weighting of the information components is a function of the value of the source of the information. A weighted additive model might also be extended to encompass this variable if it could be shown that the construct of belief which serves a weighting function in the Fishbein model varies as a function of the source variable.

As is evident throughout the course of this chapter, although our interest in the area was initially stimulated by the formalizations of an averaging model by Anderson and of an additive model by Fishbein, our research has gradually shifted to a more low-level empirical exploration of additional variables not originally incorporated in the pooling models. Such extensions form a necessary complement to the more rigorous tests involving the quantitative evaluation of a particular formulation for the understanding of the psychological processes involved in the integration of interpersonal information.

The elaboration of these additional variables may take several courses, and some comment concerning potential avenues of further research may be helpful. In several aspects of our research we have found different results using negatively valued materials than for positively valued materials. For example, it was noted in the Schmidt (1966) study that whereas information relatedness had an effect for positively valued materials, there was no effect for this variable when negatively valued materials were employed. Such a finding may have considerable theoretical importance since it has generally been assumed that positive and negative materials are combined in the same manner by the S. [Note, however, that in Table 1 of Feldman's Chapter 74, negative adjectives have much higher modifying capacities than positive adjectives—Ed.]

Investigation of possible differential effects of information about another person's behavior with respect to other people as contrasted with information about his behavior with respect to impersonal objects may also prove illuminating. Thus, if a person's likelihood of associating with another is a function of the reward value of the other, then information about the other's interpersonal behavior should be most relevant and most influential in the judgment process.

With respect to the source materials, the scaling of occupational titles allows for the investigation of a variety of social psychological questions through the manipulation of who says what about whom. For example, information offered by a cleaning woman about a physicist may appear less credible than information offered by a physicist about another physicist.

However, if these extensions and comparisons of the various pooling models are to finally converge to a general solution, more care must be taken to use comparable procedures and dependent measures. The presence of this type of inconsistency in the research literature of the impression formation area has for us had a most disruptive effect upon our attempts to pool and to integrate the various research findings. However, this simply highlights the need for additional research which will allow for a consistent resolution to these questions.

CHAPTER 76

Discussion: Impression Processing and the Evaluation of New and Old Objects

Milton J. Rosenberg

The experimental studies reported in the four preceding chapters add up (or should one say average out?) to a clear judgmental conclusion. Linear models of the impression formation process seem to be applicable to predicting the final evaluation that a person will make after exposure to information about an object that has not heretofore been evaluated or closely cognized.

However, with this said, a number of issues remain open. The questions that seem most important to me and that I shall attempt to examine here are these: Can one presently make a choice as to whether the additive or the averaging formulation is the more valid? Are the linear models applicable to understanding how we process information about objects toward which attitudes have already been formed and stabilized? If, as I tend to think, the linear models in their present form do not provide adequate explanation or prediction in this latter realm, what other approach might do the job better? And what might such an approach learn or borrow from the models and experimental techniques that have been presented in this section?

Concerning the first of these issues—the comparative validity of the two models—one who has not been partisan to the debate might ask whether a debate is actually required. Some choice between the two approaches would be necessary if they generated strongly opposed predictions. But do they?

In the study reported by Triandis we find that the averaging and additive predictions work out equally well, each yielding a median correlation of about .40 with the evaluative judgments of the stimuli.[1] Triandis does not directly report the correlations between the averaging and additive predictions; but unless they control separate but equal portions of the total variance in evaluative judgments, one tends to conclude that they are highly correlated.

---

[1] That better correlations are obtained with the behavior differential than with the semantic differential does not bear upon the present issue, though it may be evidence that it is a better measure of attitude toward hypothetical persons.

As Anderson has pointed out (1965a) it is possible to show that the two principles produce related rather than opposed predictions under certain circumstances. Particularly, this will be so when the object to be evaluated originally elicits a neutral judgment and that judgment is averaged with the separate evaluations of the ascribed adjectives. For example, as the number of positive adjectives increases the original neutral impression contributes proportionately less to the average and thus the value of the average will rise.

It was Fishbein (1961; Fishbein & Hunter, 1964; L. Anderson & Fishbein, 1965) who first contended that the additive and averaging principles are mutually antithetical. In support of this contention he pitted his version of a weighted additive model against the congruity model of Osgood and Tannenbaum (1955) which employs a rather special kind of averaging formula. His demonstration that the former did a better job of prediction than the latter he then generalized into a conclusion that *all* consistency theories were inadequate when compared to his own conceptualization of attitude dynamic processes. This latter assertion brought to the summation vs. averaging controversy a drama and ostensible relevance that it otherwise might not have possessed.

Unfortunately Fishbein, and some of those who were influenced by his work, failed to recognize some important restrictions. One of these was, of course, the rather special nature of the congruity model and the fact that it cannot stand as a representative of an averaging principle that is supposedly built into other consistency theories. Indeed, one finds it difficult to understand just how Festinger's dissonance theory, my own affective-cognitive consistency approach, or even the many derivatives of Heiderian balance theory can be properly viewed as employing the averaging principle.[2] However, the averaging principle that Fishbein rejects *does* exist (paradoxically, he may have helped force it into fuller existence, or at least toward the lucid elaboration it has received from Anderson and others) and his claims have pointed the way toward its further experimental exploration.

A fair portion of the work that followed is summarized in this section. Now that much experimental data has accumulated we find, as is often the case in such matters, that the victory cannot be assigned to either side; that the two opposing principles are not always clearly opposed; and that whether the one or the other comes closer to confirmation seems to depend upon many other variables, many other aspects of the stimulus aggregate, of the task definition and perhaps even of the stimulus elements themselves. Anderson in his studies, Feldman in his, and Rosenbaum and Schmidt in theirs have all provided many valuable leads that could guide the construction of a theory that would account for both the separate and overlapping provenances of the two prediction principles.

However, rather than attempting further analysis or integration in this area, I shall turn to some other related matters that have not been discussed by the present authors. In so doing I shall be arguing that, quite apart from the averaging and summation approaches, there is at least one other useful way of conceptualizing the formation and alteration of im-

---

[2] In a recent publication (1967) Fishbein has altered his earlier view to the extent of explicitly exempting my affective-cognitive consistency model; but he still asserts that "most theories based on a notion of 'consistency' would predict that attitudes and attitude change are functions of the *mean* amount of affect associated with an individual's beliefs."

pressions and evaluations; and that in one important realm this alternative conceptualization is perhaps more applicable than are either the averaging or additive models.

The realm to which I refer is that in which newly received information refers to *real* rather than *hypothetical* objects or, one might say, to 'old' rather than 'new' ones. A correlate difference between these two realms is that impressions and judgments of persons whom one actually knows and deals with (or of social issues on which one has already taken some position) are likely to require something more organized and structured than a simple liking-disliking evaluative response; while in the realm defined by most of the studies reviewed in the foregoing chapters, a simple positive or negative evaluation (and some indication of its extremity) is all that is usually elicited.

In their experimental work in this latter realm, the present authors appear to have demonstrated that there is a linear and *continuous* relation between the information received about the hypothetical object and the judgment of that object. (Whether these demonstrations are to be taken as completely definitive depends upon the level and content of one's methodological *angst*.)[3] Add a new attractive fact about a hypothetical person (say, a Professor of Social Psychology who does good research and always pays his APA dues on time) and the subject's judgment of that person gets somewhat more positive; add a new unattractive fact (he never pays his APA dues on time) and the judgment gets a bit more negative.

But if the actual friend in the office next door to mine is a Professor of Social Psychology who does good research (and towards whom I have a stable positive attitude) what will happen if a functionary at APA headquarters confides to me that he never pays his dues on time? There is good reason, both from phenomenological observation and from attitude change research (e.g., Carlson, 1956) to predict that my overall evaluation of my colleague will not really move toward the negative in linear relationship (i.e., in an additive or averaging way) to the negative import of the new bit of information.

In such a real-life case involving an old attitude object, the relationship between new information and evaluation change will usually not be a continuous one, will not involve an automatic, invariant rectification of evalua-

---

[3] Here is an example of what one *could* worry about: In the typical impression formation experiment the subject, having received some rather brief information about the hypothetical person, is then asked to judge that person. Given the ambiguity inherent in the underdefined and rather artificial experimental situation, it is quite possible that the subject will construe the situation as one in which his responses will reflect upon his 'intelligence' or 'cooperativeness' or his ability to solve problems. Working only with the scant information the experimenter has supplied, the subject might inadvertently be forced toward defining his task as rendering a judgment that best summarizes, or that is most closely coordinated to, the affectively loaded information he has already received. Thus a sort of evaluation apprehension artifact may induce a linearity (across subjects given stimuli with different affective loadings, or within the same subject given different stimuli across a series of judgments) that is more typical of this sort of experimental situation than of the 'real life' processes it attempts to duplicate. To raise this possibility is to suggest that impression formation researchers would profit by using control and postexperimental inquiry procedures to check for contamination due to the self-presentation problems that they may be rousing in their subjects. That such procedures have rarely, if ever, been used must be considered a serious, but remediable, fault.

tion. To the contrary, the most likely reaction will be an absence of reaction—that is to say, a ready *tolerance* of the inconsistency that has been induced. For my attitude toward the colleague in the next office, or toward any other person, institution, or policy which engages my behavior and my self-definition, serves me (in all the ways clarified by such functionalists as Smith, Bruner, and White, 1956; and Katz, Sarnoff, and McClintock, 1956) in the maximization of effective adaptation. On this and other grounds one develops tolerance for intra-attitudinal inconsistency; and in consequence the affective core of an attitude will often be observed to remain remarkably stable in the face of new, discrepant information, even when that information is credited by the attitude holder.

Yet tolerance has its limits. Elsewhere I have suggested (Rosenberg, 1960a, 1960c; see also Chapter 4) that for any attitude in any person in any situation one can conceive of a threshold of reaction to intra-attitudinal inconsistency. What happens when that threshold is transcended, is violated by a rush of disturbing new information about the attitude object? What happens in my cognitive-evaluative processes if I am informed that my friend the competent researcher next door has inducted some of his students into the psychedelic cult and goes kleptomaniacal when he thinks he is unobserved in the university bookstore?

Probably my tolerance for inconsistency will be exceeded and the total inner structure, as well as the affective-evaluative index, of my attitude will undergo change. However, will the outcome of the process produce a new evaluation that could have been estimated by either an additive or averaging version of the linear model? The complexity of the psychological processes that would ensue after receipt of the new information, and that would mediate the outcome, is not, I fear, captured by the linear mathematical models that we have before us.

A person caught in the sort of suprathreshold inconsistency dilemma that I have described would be less likely to resort to an inner computation of sum or average than to various other available strategems of defense and, where these fail, to attitude reorganization.

Often, as a first line of defense, he will attempt to discount or render unacceptable the previously accepted new information. Where the incredulity response (Osgood & Tannenbaum, 1955) cannot be managed a host of secondary mechanisms are typically available. To employ Abelson's (1959) concepts, "bolstering" or "differentiation" or "transcendence" may be attempted. Under certain circumstances one or the other of these mechanisms may succeed and the attitude, though altered in its detailed cognitive content, will retain its original affective sign and magnitude. Where such mechanisms cannot be successfully employed (and this depends upon the intractability of the new information, upon the person's cognitive processing skills and also upon his functional investment in the maintenance of the original attitude) full attitude change in the sense of a significant shift in the affective component may take place.

It is conceivable, in fact it is sometimes observable, that the affective shift may seem to mirror an approximate kind of algebraic summation or averaging process. That is, to return to my hypothetically real colleague, I may move from a strongly positive evaluation to a weakly positive or negative one and I may justify this by cognizing him as "a mixture of good and bad" or by saying that "if you take all his qualities on average he's really a fairly decent—or a somewhat unacceptable—character after all."

However, whether one can settle for such an internally inconsistent structure will probably depend upon the importance in one's life, or for one's self-definition, of the attitude object. Lower thresholds of intolerance for inconsistency will probably prevail for objects of greater importance (such as one's spouse, one's profession, one's ethnic or religious group, one's idealized political hero). And even for such objects of intermediate significance as one's colleague there may be strong demands toward achieving a univalent attitudinal structure once intolerance for inconsistency has been aroused; clearly individual differences in inconsistency tolerance play an important role in such matters.

What I have so far attempted here might be characterized and summarized in these terms: The view advanced by the four contributors to this section is of a linear, continuous relationship in which evaluation of an object is directly regulated to fit new information about that object. In contrast I am suggesting that such regulation is not so much continuous as spasmodic; that it commences only when the accretion of inconsistent elements has reached a motivating level; and that the outcome of this regulatory process tends to run not so much in the direction of additive or averaging compromise as in the direction of reorganization toward univalence or toward what the gestalt school would call 'good form' and 'configural coherence.'

This latter view I take to be a sort of summation of the spirit, if not the diverse detail, of the view of the attitude change process that follows not only from my own affective-cognitive consistency model (Rosenberg, 1960a) but also from balance theories such as those of Heider (1958), Newcomb (1953), Cartwright and Harary (1956), and Abelson and Rosenberg (1958). While I have provided only a loose and general characterization of this view, aspects of it are capable of more precise and qualified statement (cf. Abelson, 1959; Rosenberg, 1960a, 1960c). However nothing as formally elegant as the mathematical treatments provided in this section by Anderson and Feldman has yet been attempted. The barrier that would stand in the way is that of providing formal symbolic representation of the many variables and functions that are involved in the processes that mediate between receipt of inconsistency-arousing communications, the activation of intolerance for inconsistency, the ensuing cognitive operations and the final attainment of a reorganized attitude structure. The linear models, assuming as they do a near automatic resonance of evaluation to changing information inputs, do not face this sort of difficulty.

One further point requires strong emphasis. If there is any true opposition between the additive and averaging versions of the linear approach this is because they have both been focused upon the same substantive realm; namely, the formation of impressions and evaluations out of diverse bits of information. But between the linear approach as a whole and the noncontinuous, spasmodic reorganization view that I have outlined here, there need be no such competition. This latter view, as I have suggested, is relevant to analyzing and predicting what happens to judgments of 'old' objects when new discrepant information is received; the linear view, whatever aspirations its spokesmen may have for it, has in large part been tested only in connection with the generation of evaluative responses toward 'new' (that is previously nonattitudinal) objects.

That the linear models do seem to work for new objects could be readily incorporated as part of the theoretical explanation of original attitude acquisition and could thus provide a useful complement to the different line of theorizing that seems to be required in accounting for how attitudes, once stabilized, undergo subsequent change. Anderson himself seems to have suspected long ago (Anderson, 1959) that two quite different lines of analysis would be required for what he called the 'superficial' and 'basal' components of opinion.

For me, one of the redeeming features of linear models is that they may apply not only in impression-formation studies but also to the sort of pseudo-attitudinal processes that I have elsewhere (Rosenberg, 1965c) interpreted as due to the deflection of uncertain public opinion toward "perceived public consensus."

Survey specialists and others interested in political psychology have often pondered why public opinion, as gauged by pollsters, is often so readily influenced by the latest stream of official pronouncements; why it so often reflects the most recent mass media 'truths' about some important but factually obscure issue; why prominently featured reports on public opinion sometimes affect public opinion itself.

A basic answer may be that for issues that evoke implicit apathy and confusion because they touch upon psychologically distant matters, the nonattentive publics tend to coordinate their stated opinions (whether elicited by a pollster, an inquiring friend, or a polling booth) to what little 'authoritative' information they have recently received. Under such circumstances the relation between evaluation and information may well be linear; at any rate it does, indeed, seem to show the sort of facile continuousness that the linear models predict.

Out of this sort of process there may eventually emerge some true attitudes (i.e., comparatively stable and cognitively anchored evaluative orientations such as those that, by mid-1967, had shaped into the 'hawk' and 'dove' positions on the Viet Nam war). But for many other issues, particularly those that, though in the realm of public affairs, do not touch upon the individual's perception of his own welfare or upon his own normatively based loyalties, what is frequently observed is a kind of endless and fickle shifting up and down the evaluative scale.

An important question, then, that would be readily available for controlled research is whether the linear models could predict the directional turns and magnitude jumps that characterize this fickleness; and whether, as I would expect, these models would lose their predictive accuracy as the public issue acquired (or, in experimental terms, was made to acquire) more stable cognitive content, richer inner organization, or greater functional value in the maintenance of the subject's social identity.

In summary, I have tried to show why a spasm model may be more useful than a linear one in explaining or predicting the results of inconsistency-arousal focused upon 'old' objects. But at the same time I would urge that we seriously examine the relevance of the linear approach to those familiar personal and political objects which remain 'new' by virtue of the fact that, behind the ostensible show of involvement, they are apprehended with essential indifference.

E. SELECTIVE EXPOSURE TO INFORMATION

The selective exposure hypothesis and related predictions regarding perceptual distortion, selective learning, biased recall, etc., arose long before consistency theories became popular and continue to be derived from a wide variety of approaches. This prediction that one defends oneself against receipt of belief-discrepant material does, however, constitute one of the half dozen most central predictions of consistency theory. Behind this biased scanning prediction lies a logically more fundamental and noncontroversial assumption that one's receptive capacities are limited, thus making some selection necessary.

It would be etymologically correct to apply this term 'selective exposure' to any kind of nonrandom biased attention on the part of the receiver. In this broad sense the concept would then include biased attention governed by such considerations as set, drive states, values, prior reinforcements, etc. However, the term has come to be used in a much more restrictive sense, referring to biased attention specifically programmed to seek out information that confirms one's preconceptions and avoid information that is discrepant with one's initial belief, thus minimizing the introduction of inconsistencies into one's belief system. It is in this traditionally restricted sense that the investigators use the term in this section. It should be noted that there is a double prediction in the selective exposure hypothesis: a selective seeking of belief-supportive information and a selective avoidance of information contrary to one's beliefs. Each of these tendencies would increase cognitive consistency.

Even before consistency theories became popular a great deal of research had been done on the selective exposure hypothesis, and in recent years the amount of this work has been increasing steadily. In spite of all this research, or perhaps because of it, one can hardly claim that nature has spoken out univocally regarding the validity of this prediction. Still, frequent disconfirmations and even apparent reversals of the prediction have not discouraged its proponents, perhaps because the assumption is central to the consistency theories and a number of other theories as well and because somehow the hypothesis seems to deserve to be true.

To provide the reader with an unbiased exposure to the range of perspicacious thinking on this issue, we have asked three researchers who represent diverse viewpoints to contribute to the present section. Two of the contributors, David Sears and Judson Mills, have investigated the selective exposure hypothesis primarily under laboratory conditions. The results of their own research and their analyses of the findings of others have led them to somewhat different interpretations, with Sears taking a rather negative stance and Mills a more sympathetic one regarding the validity of the selective avoidance prediction. (In general, the selective seeking aspect of the hypothesis has been less controversial than the selective avoidance aspect.) The third contributor, Elihu Katz, has studied the hypothesis more by survey research in natural settings than by laboratory manipulations and, like Mills, recognizes the weakness of the prediction, or at least the difficulty of demonstrating it, but continues to feel that the hypothesis should not at this point be rejected.

CHAPTER 77

Interest in Supporting and
Discrepant Information

Judson Mills
University of Missouri

Theories of cognitive consistency lead to the general expectation that people will be more interested in receiving consistent information than inconsistent information. This expectation has been most explicit in Festinger's (1957) theory of cognitive dissonance and most of the relevant research has been done in the context of dissonance theory. Recently the hypothesis that consistent or supporting information is preferred to inconsistent or discrepant information has been severely questioned. In their review of research on selective exposure to information, Freedman and Sears (1965a) concluded that, "Laboratory evidence does not support the hypothesis that people prefer to be exposed to supportive as opposed to non-supportive information" (p. 94).

When evaluating evidence concerning the hypothesis that people tend to prefer supporting information, it is necessary to keep in mind that there are also many other factors which affect exposure to information. For example, if men would rather read discrepant material containing pictures of beautiful women than supporting material without such pictures, this would certainly not provide evidence against the hypothesis. As Heider noted in discussing his balance hypothesis, "there are many cases which, at least if taken at their face value, do not fit the hypothesis. This in itself, however, is no ground for discarding the hypothesis. There can be many reasons for these discrepancies. First of all, it is possible that the exceptions are the result of additional factors which have nothing to do with the hypothesis. The fact that birds fly does not prove they are not attracted by the earth" (Heider, 1958, p. 210).

Additional factors which could explain the results were present in four of the five studies which Freedman and Sears list as showing a preference for nonsupportive information, i.e., the studies by Brodbeck (1956), Rosen (1961, negative articles only), Freedman (1965c), and Sears (1965a). Freedman and Sears mention that in Brodbeck's study only 20.2 per cent of the subjects chose to listen to someone who shared their opinion on wiretapping,

Preparation of this paper was aided by a grant by the National Science Foundation.

although by chance alone 42.9 per cent of the subjects would have chosen to listen to someone of like belief. Brodbeck's procedure necessitated publicly identifying the opinion of each subject in the group. The experimenter explained that this would be done "so that they could make their choices intelligently" (Brodbeck, 1956, p. 168). This explanation could easily have lead the subjects to think the experimenter expected them to choose to listen to someone on the opposite side of the issue. This could account for their apparent preference for discrepant information.

In his replication of the study by Mills, Aronson, and Robinson (1959), Rosen (1961) included two new article descriptions. "Negative information was introduced by having two of the six references read as follows: 'These authors present some evidence that students who prefer essay exams generally do a lot better on objective tests,' and 'the results of this study suggest that students who like objective tests would probably do much better to switch to essay.' Article descriptions were counterbalanced by using two lists differing in the substitution of the word 'objective' for the word 'essay' and vice versa" (Rosen, 1961, p. 189). Rosen found that subjects who chose an essay exam preferred to read the article about students who prefer essay exams and students who chose an objective exam preferred the article about students who like objective tests. This can be explained by the plausible assumption that people prefer to read articles about people like themselves more than articles about dissimilar people. This tendency could well have been strong enough in this situation to outweigh the tendency to prefer supporting information.

Freedman (1965c) found that subjects preferred to read an evaluation of an interviewee which disagreed with their rating of him based on a short one-sided interview. In interpreting his results, Freedman commented that, "it is possible that the dissonant evaluation (i.e., the evaluation that disagreed with the subject) was expected to contain more new information than the consonant evaluation, and the former was, consequently, expected to be more useful in improving performance on the future decisions" (1965c, p. 288). Since Freedman and Sears point out that, "it is essential to hold utility constant in order to provide a rigorous, unambiguous test of the selective exposure hypothesis" (1965a, p. 83), it is difficult to understand why they include this study as evidence against the hypothesis. Certainly Freedman's study does not show that the dissonant information was preferred because it was expected to increase dissonance.

Sears (1965a) found that subjects who had read one-sided synopses of two different murder trials, one favoring conviction and the other acquittal, preferred to receive summations by the attorneys on the opposite side of the cases from the bias of the synopses. This result can be attributed to a tendency for people, when they know there are two opposing sides, to want to be familiar with both of them. As Sears mentioned, "By tradition and by law, jury trials are structured as adversary proceedings, in which each side must have its say" (1965a, p. 374). The existence of a tendency to want to be familiar with both sides does not preclude the existence of a tendency to prefer supporting information.

The other result which Freedman and Sears list as showing a preference for nonsupportive information is from a study by Feather (1962). Feather reported that smokers were more interested in an article about the relationship between smoking and cancer which disagreed with their beliefs than one which agreed with their beliefs. However, there was a trend in the opposite direction for nonsmokers. Neither Feather nor Freedman and Sears offered any reason why the relationship should be different for smokers and nonsmokers. When they are combined there is no particular relationship between beliefs and information preferences. Furthermore, there was no report of a relationship between beliefs and information preferences among smokers by Feather in a repetition of his study (1963).

It should also be mentioned that additional factors which could explain the results were present in two of the four published studies which Freedman and Sears list as showing a preference for supportive information, i.e., the study by Ehrlich, Guttman, Schonbach, and Mills (1957) and the study by Adams (1961). Ehrlich et al. found that new car owners read advertisements of their own cars more frequently than advertisements of other cars. In recent studies (Mills, 1965a, b) a strong positive relationship has been found between the desirability of products and interest in reading ads about the products. Since the new car owners in the Ehrlich et al. study probably regarded their own cars as more desirable than the other cars, this could account for their greater interest in advertisements about their own cars. Adams (1961) found that mothers preferred to hear a talk which agreed with their beliefs about the relative importance of hereditary and environmental factors in child development rather than a talk which disagreed with their beliefs. Freedman and Sears note that, "All but six of the one hundred subjects tested believed a child's behavior to be 'mostly learned' rather than 'mostly inborn.' Hence, the apparent preference for supportive information actually represents a preference for the 'environmental' talk, which may have been more useful to mothers who have little control over the hereditary endowment of their children" (1965a, p. 63).

In the other two published studies listed by Freedman and Sears as showing a preference for supportive information, Mills, Aronson, and Robinson (1959) and Rosen (1961) found that students who had chosen to take either an essay or objective examination preferred to read articles giving positive information about the kind of examination they had chosen rather than articles giving positive information about the rejected examination. In the Mills, Aronson, and Robinson study, articles giving negative information about the chosen examination were equally preferred to articles giving negative information about the rejected examination. Mills et al. explained their results in terms of the combined operation of the tendency to prefer information supporting the choice and the tendency to seek more information about the chosen alternative. For the articles giving positive information about the particular exam, both tendencies would operate in the same direction and yield a strong preference for articles about the chosen examination. For the articles giving negative information, the two tendencies would work in opposite directions and could have cancelled each other so that there was no preference one way or the other. It is very difficult to account for the results of the Mills et al. and Rosen studies unless one assumes that people prefer supporting information.

Additional studies showing that supporting information is preferred to discrepant information have been published since Freedman and Sears wrote their review. Brock (1965) found that when subjects expected they would actually read the articles, smokers preferred an article entitled, "Smoking does not lead to lung cancer," to an article entitled, "Smoking leads to lung cancer." Nonsmokers were more interested in reading the article, "Smoking leads to lung cancer," than the article, "Smoking does not lead to lung cancer."[1] Brock and Balloun (1967) found that smokers worked more to improve aural reception of a message disputing the link between smoking and cancer than to improve reception of a message affirming the smoking-cancer link. The opposite was true for nonsmokers. Lowin (1967a) found greater interest in receiving brochures containing plausible arguments for the preferred Presidential candidate than in receiving brochures containing plausible arguments for the opposition candidate. Interest in receiving implausible arguments for the opposition candidate was greater than interest in receiving implausible arguments for the preferred candidate. The latter finding is consistent with the hypothesis that supporting information is preferred to discrepant information since stupid or silly arguments for the opposition candidate will provide more support for the preferred candidate than will stupid arguments for the preferred candidate.

Mills (1965a) found that when differences due to the desirability of the products were eliminated from measures of interest in advertisements for chosen and rejected products, interest in advertisements for the chosen product was positive. Interest in advertisements for the rejected product was negative, that is, less than would be expected solely from the desirability of the product. In addition to showing that people seek supporting information, this study provides evidence, which was previously lacking, that discrepant or dissonant information is actively avoided. To summarize the current status of the hypothesis that people prefer supporting information to discrepant information, there are a number of studies which corroborate the hypothesis and there are none which provide substantial evidence against the hypothesis.

In their review, Freedman and Sears also concluded that, "The evidence does not support the hypothesis that the greater the magnitude of cognitive dissonance the greater will be the relative preference for exposure to supportive as opposed to nonsupportive information" (1965a, p. 94). In a study published after the Freedman and Sears review was written, Mills (1965b) manipulated certainty about the correctness of a choice by allowing some subjects to choose between products they had ranked about equal in desirability and others between products they had ranked very differently and found that interest in advertisements for the chosen product was greater when certainty was low than when it was high. Interest in advertisements for the rejected product was not affected by amount of certainty about the choice. This study provides evidence that interest in supporting or consonant information is greater, the greater the amount of dissonance. At the same time it indicates that avoidance of dissonant information is not determined by amount of dissonance. The difference for interest in consonant information makes it very difficult to argue that amount of dissonance was not successfully varied or, since interest in consonant and dissonant information was measured in the same way, that interest in dissonant information was not adequately measured.

As previously noted, Festinger's theory of cognitive dissonance has

---

[1] Brock's comparison of the interest of smokers and nonsmokers in the article, "Smoking leads to lung cancer," is contaminated by the greater relevance and utility which articles concerning smoking have for smokers.

been the stimulus for most of the research concerning interest in supporting and discrepant information. However, the findings can also be explained by a theory based on the assumption that people want to be certain when they take an action that it is better than the alternatives, that it will lead to the most favorable consequences for motive satisfaction. If they are not certain the action is the best one, they will try to increase their certainty; the lower their certainty, the stronger will be their desire to increase it. They will also avoid decreasing their certainty. Information supporting the chosen action will increase their certainty that it is the best, while information favoring the other alternatives will decrease their certainty. From these assumptions it follows that people will prefer information supporting the chosen action and that this tendency will be greater, the less certain they are the action is the best one.

This theory leads to some predictions which cannot be made from dissonance theory. One kind of prediction concerns behavior prior to a choice. Dissonance theory does not make predictions about prechoice behavior since, according to the theory, dissonance is not created until a choice is made.[2] On the other hand, the desire to be certain about the correctness of one's action should influence behavior in a predecision situation. People may try to be certain that a particular alternative is the best before they commit themselves (see Chapter 55). If they are not committed and are completely uncertain about which alternative is best, information favoring any of the alternatives will increase their certainty. However, if they are somewhat certain that one is best, information favoring that alternative will increase their certainty while information favoring the other alternatives will decrease it. Thus, choice certainty theory predicts that when people are not committed, the more certain they are an alternative is the best one, the more they will prefer information supporting that alternative. This prediction was confirmed in a study by Mills and Ross (1964) who also found, as predicted by both of the rival theories, that when people are highly committed to an alternative, the less certain they are it is the best one, the more they will prefer supporting information.

In another study of prechoice behavior based on the same theoretical position, Mills (1965c) found evidence supporting the prediction that prior to a choice persons who are uncertain about which alternative is best will be more interested in information favoring one of the alternatives than will persons who are certain that alternative is not the best one. Information favoring one of the alternatives would increase the certainty of those who are uncertain but would decrease the certainty of those who are certain that alternative is not the best one. That information expected to decrease certainty is actively avoided was demonstrated in a follow-up study by Mills and Jellison (1968). Persons who were certain that a particular alternative was not the best spent less time reading information favoring that alternative than persons who were faced with a comparable choice which did not include the alternative.

In summary, the current evidence concerning interest in supporting and discrepant information warrants the conclusion that people tend to seek out supporting information and avoid discrepant information. There is evidence that interest in supporting information is greater, the lower the certainty

---

[2] However, see Jecker, Chapter 54—Ed.

about the correctness of a choice. Avoidance of discrepant information does not appear to be affected by amount of certainty about a choice. The findings concerning interest in supporting and discrepant information can be explained by a theory based on the assumption that people want to be certain when they take an action that it is better than the alternatives. This theory of choice certainty can predict some results which can not be predicted from cognitive dissonance theory.

CHAPTER 78

The Paradox of De Facto Selective Exposure
Without Preferences for Supportive Information

David O. Sears

University of California, Los Angeles

In this paper the plan is to (A) present the basic hypotheses about selective exposure and review briefly the most recent research evidence on them, (B) consider whether or not this evidence may be trusted, (C) suggest some implications of these outcomes for attitude change and consistency theory, and (D) attempt to reconcile the results of laboratory and field findings on selective exposure.

A. BASIC HYPOTHESES AND RECENT RESEARCH

Four basic propositions have been tested in experimental work on selective exposure. They are these: (1) people seek supportive information; (2) people avoid nonsupportive information; (3) both tendencies occur more frequently with greater cognitive dissonance; and (4) both tendencies occur more frequently when the individual has little confidence in his initial opinion.

Freedman and Sears (1965a) reviewed relevant research published through mid-1965, and concluded that available evidence did not favor any of these four propositions. First let us briefly consider whether or not subsequent research forms a more conclusive picture.

Four studies have tested whether or not people seek supportive information. One by Brock (1965) on smoking and lung cancer indicated they do, as did one of three conducted by Mills (1965a, b) in a market survey situation. The same studies provide evidence on whether or not people avoid nonsupportive information. Mills reports significant avoidance in two experiments (Mills, 1965a) but not in a third (1965b), and Brock (1965) found no evidence for avoidance. So in each case only two of the four relevant studies yielded positive evidence. It might be noted parenthetically that most experiments theoretically designed to test separately

Preparation of this manuscript was facilitated by a National Science Foundation grant to the author. Many of the ideas presented in this paper were developed in collaboration with Jonathan Freedman.

'seeking' and 'avoiding' tendencies have not successfully done so, due to the absence of an adequate neutral baseline (Rhine, 1967a).

Relative preferences for supportive and nonsupportive information were also tested in three studies by Lowin (1967a, b) and in studies by Lowe and Steiner (1968) and Thayer (1968). In each case no significant preference emerged. In two other studies (Clarke and James, 1967b), the data are potentially relevant to this question (and supportive information appears to have been preferred somewhat) but the necessary significance tests are not given. All in all, the picture seems to remain a mixed one.

Several attempts have been made at manipulating cognitive dissonance. In three studies, Mills attempted to vary the revocability, importance, and difficulty of making a decision (1965a, b). Selectivity increased with greater decision difficulty in one case (1965b), but his other four variations had no effect. Lowe and Steiner (1968) varied the revocability and importance of a decision and found increased importance actually *decreased* selectivity, while revocability had no effect. Rhine (1967b) varied the similarity of candidates' positions in the 1964 campaign to the subjects' perceptions of their positions (though this variation would appear not to be as directly relevant to dissonance arousal, since the subjects' own positions and candidate preferences were not considered). Avoidance of dissonant information increased with greater dissonance, but the seeking of consonant information did not. A surprising finding in this study was that selectivity was actually lower in the Dissonance-Arousal experimental groups than in the No-Dissonance control group. Also, some evidence is produced for a curvilinear relationship between dissonance arousal and selectivity, which Rhine elsewhere (1967a) argues is the more appropriate derivation from dissonance theory. Nevertheless, the data on the effects of dissonance arousal remain essentially ambiguous.

The fourth proposition has received the most attention. It predicts an interaction between confidence in one's initial opinion and selectivity. Highly confident people are supposed to seek nonsupportive information, confident that they can refute it. People with little confidence should avoid nonsupportive information and seek the reassurance conveyed by supportive information. The corollary is that among difficult-to-refute arguments, supportive information should be preferred to nonsupportive information. Among easily refuted arguments, nonsupportive information should be preferred (Lowin, 1967a, b).

The evidence on this fourth notion again is mixed, unfortunately. Canon (1964) and Freedman (1965a) conducted virtually identical studies manipulating confidence; Canon obtained the predicted interaction, but Freedman found no trace of it, though obtaining similar results to Canon's in other respects. Mills (1965a, b) varied the ease of making a choice, and hence presumably the confidence with which it was made. In one case there were no differences, while in the second confidence affected preference for supportive information but not avoidance of nonsupportive information. Lowin (1967a) and Thayer (1968) varied the subject's confidence in his own judgment, but both found that this variation did not affect subsequent selectivity.

The corollary hypothesis, dealing with message refutability or message strength, has met with more success. In one experiment, greater preference for supportive information was obtained under conditions of high communicator credibility than under low credibility (Lowin, 1967a). And in a mail survey during the 1964 election campaign, Lowin (1967b) found strong supportive and weak nonsupportive messages preferred to strong nonsupportive and weak supportive messages. In a second mail survey, though, the hypothesis was supported in only one of four comparisons (Lowin, 1967b).

Of the eight relevant studies, therefore, two support the confidence hypothesis, two are mixed, and the remaining four fail to support it. It should be noted, however, that no study has yet obtained the converse; i.e., a *positive* relationship between manipulated confidence and selectivity.

In sum, recent research offers no grounds for modifying the conclusions reached in the earlier review. The evidence does not systematically favor any of the four propositions listed.

B. THE INSENSITIVITY POSSIBILITY

It has been repeatedly noted that people are primarily exposed to supportive information in nature, and that most audiences do in fact overrepresent those who initially agree with the communicator. This state of affairs may be termed 'de facto selectivity.' The problem is to reconcile these observations with the apparent burden of the experimental research reviewed above.

There are two obvious possibilities. First, the experimental work may have been badly done, and simply be insensitive to the true differences that are there. Second, there may in fact be no general preference for supportive information, whether under neutral, high-dissonance, or low-confidence conditions. That is, the experimental work may accurately reflect a true state of no differences. Let us consider these two possibilities in turn. First, what grounds might there be for thinking that the experimental work has overlooked true differences?

1. Stimulus Situation

It would be hard to fault the theoretical relevance of stimulus materials that have been used. However, one general problem is insuring that the subject really believes he will be exposed to his choice. Brock (1965) has found greater selectivity with actual exposure choices than with abstract 'interest' ratings. Lowin (1965), on the other hand, obtained approximately the same results from ratings-in-the-abstract and actual requests for information. In previous studies, one or the other procedure has been used, but it is not obvious that one systematically induced more selectivity than the other. Thus the point does not seem to account for the general lack of selectivity in experimental studies. However, it is a useful criticism; exposure choices have often been quite artificial.

2. Confoundings

The supportiveness of a particular exposure alternative has often been confounded with other very obvious factors. Perhaps the most common confounding is with practical utility. A given piece of information often is of practical utility when it is supportive, and of little utility when nonsupportive. Experiments done in market research settings (cf. Mills, 1965a, b) are particularly prone to this confounding, and may artifactually produce selectivity. However, it is not clear that selectivity has generally been *blocked* by confoundings.

3. Self-consciousness

Most people do not like to think they are unwilling to hear 'the other side of the argument.' Thus to maximize the chance of obtaining selectivity, one should not ask the subject's opinion and then his exposure preference immediately thereafter. The subject is likely to resist claiming too strong a preference for anything bolstering his beliefs. Ideally the two should be measured in separate sessions. This precaution has almost never been taken, however. Lowin (1967b) did, but at the expense of obtaining exposure preferences in mail surveys, thus getting a rather small return. Sears and Freedman (1963) measured opinions privately. The norm has been, however, to take both measures publicly and more or less contiguously—thus probably suppressing some selectivity.

4. Sampling Distortions

In the grand tradition of American psychology, the subjects in laboratory exposure experiments have almost invariably been lower division college students drawn from introductory psychology classes. The obvious danger of this selection is that something special may be working against selectivity in this population. And there is good reason to fear such a bias. A major explicit goal of undergraduate education is to train students to view supportive and nonsupportive information alike with a critical but informed eye. It is regarded as cowardice to avoid discrepant information, and as a sign of intellectual maturity the ability to take it in and argue it down. This obviously ought to work against getting selective exposure effects.

However, few researchers have attempted to draw upon other populations, and even these have generally wound up with college-educated and other staunchly middle class groups (Ehrlich *et al.*, 1957; Adams, 1961; Freedman & Sears, 1963). Still, there is some evidence in favor of this interpretation. These latter field studies have been more inclined to report selectivity than have laboratory studies with college student subjects.

As a final note, that old bugaboo of research on dissonance theory, the mystery of the disappearing sample, plagues even research on selective exposure. Brock (1965) found that he had to reject 37 per cent of his subjects, while Lowin (1965), using a mail return technique, lost 76 per cent of his respondents. Normally sample shrinkage is lamented mainly for form; we are so accustomed to using bizarre samples (college sophomores) that the bizarreness of our subsamples hardly seems important, particularly when the selection seems unsystematic across conditions. It may be more important in exposure research, however. Lowin (1965) found strong partisans more selective *and* more likely to return their questionnaires; hence the drop-out rate may determine one's final results.

5. Conclusion

In the absence of compelling reasons to the contrary, one would normally conclude that available data provide the best key to some underlying truth. However there might seem to be special reasons in this case for mistrusting available data. Too many of the methodological shortcomings of this research would seem to operate in a single direction: to minimize selective exposure. This might give grounds for feeling that additional research, conducted in a more thorough and careful manner, would present quite a different picture.

This argument, a common one in psychology when intuitively pleasing hypotheses are not supported, raises a more basic question of statistical inference, however. Normally we assume that probability values are based on what would probably happen if a given experiment were replicated many times; i.e., what would happen in the long run. Yet what in fact do we assume if a series of studies obtain no differences, and finally one does support the hypothesis? The norm seems to be to reject the prior series as having been poorly conducted, with inadequate manipulations, impotent designs, poor sampling, etc. This occurs whether the prior series were 'pilots' of our own or others' finished products. The final study is accepted as finally having proven the point, and the others are rejected as not having been fair tests.

Obviously, though, there must come a point when one starts to take negative results seriously. The question comes down to how many well-conducted studies obtaining positive results will be required to balance the numerous less well-conducted studies already completed and obtaining negative results (and journal editors' not unreasonable biases against negative results must be considered in the balancing).

C. IMPLICATIONS: THE TRUE NULL HYPOTHESIS POSSIBILITY

The second general possibility is that in fact little or no preference for supportive information exists, whether under neutral, high-dissonance, or low-confidence conditions. If this were true, what implications would it have for the three most relevant research areas: attitude change, motivation, and mass communications?

1. Defending Commitments

In the context of consistency theory, selective exposure is thought of as one of the many ways in which people protect themselves from disagreeable information. It has an especially prominent place in this list of mechanisms because it is clearly the most primitive and least adaptive. Rebellious children place their hands over their ears and flout their angry parents, claiming they can hear not a word of scolding. News photographs of the aftermath of a disaster often portray the relatives of dead persons holding their hands over their eyes as if the tragedy would not be real if unseen. In hysteria the sense organ responsible for offensive stimulation is symptomatically closed off, as in hysterical blindness or anesthesia. These are cases in which persons use extraordinarily primitive defenses.

There are other defenses that block veridical reception of information. The most commonly noted are selective perception, selective learning, and selective retention. It is interesting that the same empirical problems arise with these mechanisms as with selective exposure. For example, there is currently some doubt that the early selective learning findings are replicable. In six recent experiments, Waly and Cook (1966) and Greenwald and Sakumura (1967) failed to find any tendency for subjects to learn supportive arguments more easily than nonsupportive arguments. And it has not been difficult at all to find conditions under which nonsupportive material is learned more readily than supportive material. Jones and Aneshansel (1956) found this to occur when subjects expected to be required to produce counterarguments or debate an opponent. Later, Canon (1964) and Freedman (1965c) found exposure to dissonant arguments preferred when the subject expected to be required to counter an unknown set of dissonant arguments. Similarly, Jones and Kohler (1958) anticipated Lowin's (1967a, b) exposure findings by showing that implausible discrepant arguments were learned more readily than implausible supportive arguments (though Waly and Cook, 1966, have failed to replicate this finding).

Efforts to demonstrate that perceptual distortions operate in the service of affective preferences have also met with relatively little success throughout psychology. Methodological artifacts have been difficult to surmount (cf. Solomon & Howes, 1951). In communications research, distortion effects have been obtained, and often in the predicted direction. However, they usually have been of discouragingly minor magnitude (Hovland, Harvey, & Sherif, 1957; Manis, 1961a), and have not been responsive to such straightforward variations as the discrepancy (Harvey, Kelley, & Shapiro, 1957) or ambiguity (Manis, 1961b) of the informational input.

So the empirical data on all these 'avoidance' defenses appear to share a common set of problems: counterexamples are easily found, methodological problems abound, and the magnitude of effect often seems minor. This might lead to a tentative conclusion that the 'avoidance' defenses are relatively unpopular mechanisms for defending beliefs and behavioral commitments. Presumably they are commonly used to defend the organism against severe forms of psychological stress, such as the threat of death, bodily violation, or the loss of a love object (Janis, 1958; Greenstein, 1965). The indicated empirical question has not been posed: When will threat produce the avoidance of veridical information processing, and when will it induce mechanisms involving cognitive or affective change? That is, what distinguishes between the conditions for selective learning, perception, and exposure, and the conditions for opinion change, source derogation, etc?

If the tentative conclusion is accepted, that in everyday life people do not generally utilize information-avoidance techniques as a way of softening the impact of unpleasant information, then two additional directions for further research are indicated. One is added attention to the dynamics of influence resistance. If people resist influence by confronting information and rejecting it, the important questions have to do with the process by which that happens.

Brock and Balloun's (1967) ingenious experiments on attention to persuasive communications seem to represent a productive approach in this respect. Another is increased attention to nondefensive information seeking. Research on exposure has been excessively sterile because of a preoccupation with selectivity in the service of partisan preferences. Thus little is known about what actually contributes to information seeking. The major exposure problem faced by public affairs communicators is not in reaching their enemies, but in reaching anyone at all. Low absolute rates of exposure, rather than widespread selectivity, are the primary obstacles to influence. And little is known about the determinants of variations in absolute rates of exposure.

2. Homeostatic Hedonism

In common with numerous other psychological theories, the consistency theories seem to rest on an assumption that tension-reduction or minimization of stimulation is a major aim of the human organism. Thus the organism is supposed to avoid stimulating or tension-inducing kinds of information, and seek information that reduces tension. In studies on exposure this simple-minded view clearly does not hold; there seem to be just as many instances in which the stimulation-increasing information is preferred.

It may well be that the wrong question is being asked. Implicitly the question of a general preference for supportive information pits man's defensiveness against his curiosity. Which one has won out in his nature is of little interest, because both are obviously strong (see Chapter 16). This conclusion seems likely not to be altered no matter how many subsequent studies are done. The more important question is what determines which tendency will be dominant under any given set of conditions. Similarly, to ask whether or not the organism will respond defensively when threatened, as has been done in varying dissonance arousal, simply misses the point. It would be astonishing if the organism did not respond to threat. The challenge is to try to predict what *kind* of defense will be stimulated.

One qualification should be imposed on this general criticism, however. There may be some cultural value in knowing what specific kinds of choices people generally make, just as it is of some interest to know whether Americans prefer Bonanza to Shakespeare. It tells us something about our culture. This may be especially relevant for our thinking about a democratic political system, since we are accustomed to assuming that the voter prepares to exercise his franchise by informing himself about each alternative.

3. De Facto Selectivity

In nature, the pattern appears to be, in general, one of people being exposed primarily to positions with which they already agree. The usual explanation is that people actively seek supportive information and avoid nonsupportive information. If this hypothesis is rejected as inconsistent with experimental data, what explanations for de facto selectivity remain?

a. De facto selectivity doesn't exist either. One possibility is that de facto selectivity has also been oversold as a general characteristic of communication situations. Sears and Freedman (1967) have critically examined some of the most widely cited data on this point, and indeed it turns out not to be as overwhelming an effect as often suggested. The effect often occurs for one set of partisans but not the other, to be based upon rather small differences, or to be explicable by invoking other variables known to be strongly correlated with exposure (e.g., education). Nevertheless, it appears that de facto selectivity occurs often enough that it deserves additional attention (see Chapter 79).

b. Public economic control. A more sophisticated version of the original selective exposure hypothesis might hold that people use their economic power, whether consciously or unconsciously, to reward their friends and punish their enemies. For example, a community may impose its political beliefs on its newspapers by failing to subscribe to or patronize the advertisers of deviationist newspapers. The trouble with this idea is that it takes too simple-minded a view of the economics of mass communication. The 'loser' in economic competition usually merges with a paper of virtually identical editorial policy. What is eliminated most easily is redundancy rather than diversity. In any event this hypothesis depends upon the psychological hypothesis we have rejected, so no more need be said about it here.

    c. Sycophantic communicators. A related idea, ingeniously tested by Zimmerman and Bauer (1956), is that communicators choose only to tell their audiences what the audience wishes to hear. No doubt this principle accounts for the variations in communications addressed by a given communicator to several audiences. The trouble is that such variations are too small to account for de facto selectivity. The President may emphasize one aspect of a policy before one audience and another before a second, but he supports the same policy alternative in both cases. Billy Graham does not suddenly turn agnostic when he addresses a sophisticated college student audience. Fluctuations from audience to audience are simply not gross enough to account for de facto selectivity. So this explanation is inadequate.

    d. Asymmetric availabilities. Perhaps people are always selecting information from a skewed set of alternatives. That is, the typical information choice may be from a set of many supportive and a few nonsupportive communications. Even random sampling from such a skewed set of alternatives would produce de facto selectivity. Why might supportive generally be much more readily available than nonsupportive information? Two reasons seem especially salient.

    The first reason involves the *ubiquity of consensus.* As Henessey has pointed out, "... most people agree with most other people about most things" (1965, p. 154). This in itself makes it more difficult to find nonsupportive than supportive communications. This general consensus holds in a broad sense for mankind in general on a great many issues; e.g., regarding the assertion that the world is round. On more controversial issues, consensus is no less impressive, though it tends to be limited to our immediate social and informational environment. It would be much harder for most of us to find pro-Soviet information, or information on the opposite side of the race issue from our own, than supportive views on these issues. Each of us lives in what is largely a supportive environment, even on the most divisive and controversial of issues. Hence we are rarely given a 'fair chance' to select nonsupportive information.

    The main reason for this is that we get most of our opinions from our immediate environments. Hence they are bound to reflect the biases of our environments (Greenwald & Sakumura, 1967; Zajonc, 1965). A person growing up in Alabama is likely to form a favorable opinion of Governor Wallace, while the same person, if raised in Massachusetts, would be likely not to. Since the environment was biased in favor of one position prior to opinion formation, the best guess is that it will be biased in the same way afterwards. And the information alternatives from which the individual samples should be skewed in the same way, producing almost by necessity greater availability of supportive than nonsupportive alternatives.

    Diabolical manipulators also maximize de facto selectivity. Some especially powerful communicators can deliberately structure the individual's information alternatives such that his opportunity to choose nonsupportive information is slight indeed. Examples of this kind come to mind easily. The most extreme are totalitarian regimes: the Mainland Chinese regime has severely restricted deviationist literature throughout its period in office; the Roman Catholic Church has made various sporadic efforts over the years to prevent its parishoners from coming into contact with non-Catholic or anti-Catholic ideas (cf. the *Index Librorum Prohibitorum*); even the not altogether totalitarian United States government often restricts public exposure to embarrassing information.

People with considerably less power over communication channels also may effect some restrictions. Conservative merchants attempt to place their newspaper advertising in the place that will both do the most for sales and strengthen the hand of conservative communicators; liberally oriented intellectuals tend to restrict the exposure of college students to nonliberal ideas, and so forth. Apparently much more benign censors are the timid parents who prevent sadistic, cynical, or erotic literature from falling into the hands of small children. Small children in America therefore are rather naive (Easton & Dennis, 1965) about the realities of social existence, given this continuing diet of supportive information. Each of these examples, then, represents a group of communicators who are able to control the exposure alternatives of particular individuals, specifically restricting them to a choice among numerous supportive alternatives mixed with only occasional nonsupportive possibilities.

e. Confounding supportiveness with other attractions. Many information alternatives are overchosen because of attractive features which are irrelevant to, but systematically associated with, their supportiveness. These other attractions are of course many; the following are a few examples of the more important ones.

First, the *perceived truth value* of supportive communications is greater than that of nonsupportive material. Presumably one of the major reasons why people seek information is to find out what is true. The more likely a communication is to indicate the truth, the more attractive it should be. On controversial issues there are two ideal guides. One is a source who is invariably on the side of the good, and the other is a source who invariably chooses the more iniquitous alternative. For example, John F. Kennedy and Robert Welch served these two functions for Democratic subjects in 1963 (Sears, 1965a). If both kinds of sources were equally common, then supportive and nonsupportive communicators would be equally valuable as guides to truth.

As it happens, however, there seem to be more positive guides than negative guides. Numerous Democratic politicians were regarded by Democratic subjects in 1963 as reliable indicators of the correct side of issues, whereas only an occasional Republican politician was regarded as an equally infallible guide to the *incorrect* side. The bulk of Republican leaders (and the Republican Party as a whole) were regarded as sometimes right and sometimes wrong, and therefore as uninformative about the correct side of an issue in most specific instances (Sears, 1965b). Many supportive communicators (Democrats) were useful guides, but only a few nonsupportive communicators (Republicans) were useful. And as a general rule, therefore, the individual who is seeking truth or a correct position is better off sampling sources of information who are generally supportive than sampling sources who are generally nonsupportive.

Another obvious feature is *practical utility*. A mother offered a choice between a speech on how environment affects children's personalities (a position with which she agrees) and one arguing the importance of heredity (with which she disagrees) will certainly choose the former (Adams, 1961). Why? Because information about the environment's impact may be of some practical help to her. Similarly, a choice between information about a product one owns and a product one does not own surely will result in preference for the former (Mills, 1965a, b). The more one knows about a new possession the better, from a practical standpoint. This apparently holds even before the choice: one wants to read about a product one soon will choose, and thus possess, more than about a product one soon will reject, and thus not possess (Mills, 1965c). And when expecting to debate, discuss one's views with others, or transmit one's views to others, supportive information is likely to be sought more than when expecting to read privately about the issue or receive someone else's views (Clarke & James, 1967; Brock & Fromkin, in press). The reason is that one wants to gather information that will help in the task of the moment, not that one needs to shore up a shaky position. These are likely not to be isolated exceptions; rather, examples of a general correlation in nature between utility and supportiveness.

The ways in which propagandistic appeals are distributed in society cause people with certain general kinds of *taste* to be exposed to certain kinds of political views, willy-nilly. An ex-Texan who listens to hillbilly music in Los Angeles is likely to be exposed to right-wing propaganda; the college professor who listens to classical music on FM is going to hear more liberal appeals. Upper middle-class business and professional people subscribe to the New York *Times* rather than the *Daily News*, or the Los Angeles *Times* rather than the *Herald-Examiner*, for obvious social and informational reasons. However, it is doubtful that these decisions rest much on editorial policy. Rather, they rest on long-term habits of taste and preference, normally irrelevant to (but empirically correlated with) political and social opinions.

Finally, the *practical details of self-exposure* are usually less complicated for supportive information. One is more likely to be informed of supportive mass meetings, transportation and companionship are usually easier to arrange, and so on. Just in the normal course of the day's events, without departing from the normal routine, it is easier to be advised of when supportive meetings or TV programs are available, where meetings are, and so on.

Numerous other variables could be mentioned. These seem to be among the most important reasons, however, why supportive information is particularly attractive, quite aside from its ability to reassure or bolster beliefs.

D. CONCLUSIONS

1. There is considerable evidence indicating that in nature, exposure is generally somewhat greater to supportive than to nonsupportive information.

2. There is no empirical evidence indicating a general preference for supportive information over nonsupportive information, regardless of whether the test is conducted under neutral, high-dissonance, or low-confidence conditions.

3. Attempts to explain the ineffectiveness of mass communications in field settings should concentrate upon low absolute rates of exposure and upon resistance to communications the individual processes more or less accurately, and deemphasizes barriers to accurate reception based upon active avoidance of disagreeable information.

4. The most probable explanations for de facto selectivity have to do with the unusual availability of supportive information, and with the likelihood that supportiveness is, in nature, correlated with other attractive features of information; e.g., truthfulness, usefulness, and so on.

CHAPTER 79

On Reopening the Question of Selectivity in
Exposure to Mass Communications

Elihu Katz
University of Chicago and
Hebrew University of Jerusalem

The notion of selective exposure is basic to theory and research on the flow of mass communications. It appears as a major explanatory factor in attempts to account for the repeatedly observed fact that the mass media do not easily persuade people to change their attitudes or practices. Communications campaigns—this argument holds—reach the already-converted; others simply tune out. Hence the generalization that the mass media typically reinforce people in their attitudes and practices, but rarely convert them.

In this sense, selectivity is one of a series of ideas that have led to a reformulation of the image of the relationship between the mass media and their audiences. Whereas the media had been thought capable of impressing their message on the defenseless masses, it now appears as if the audience has quite a lot of power of its own. Indeed, the fashion in research nowadays is not to ask "what the media *do to* people" but "what people *do with* the media," or at least to be sure to ask the second question before the first. This shift in emphasis represents a shift of interest away from the study of mass media 'campaigns' in favor of the study of the 'uses' or the 'gratifications' which people derive from exposure to the media. This shift makes the concept of selectivity all the more important, insofar as the attempt now is to explain selectivity in terms of the functional contribution of exposure to some social or psychological need, of which selectivity for the purpose of attitude-reinforcement may be only a particular case.

It is more than a little dissonance-producing, therefore, to read Freedman and Sears' (1965a) conclusion that neither experimental nor field studies provide convincing evidence of the operation of this sort of motivated selectivity. There is no question that selectivity exists—i.e., that individuals are disproportionately exposed to communications which are congenial to their attitudes. The question is whether there is a motivated choice involved, one that is specifically associated with the quest for reinforcement, as

---
I should like to thank Miss Mady Wechsler for research assistance in this project, and the Social Science Research Committee of the University of Chicago for financial aid.

distinct from the expression of 'interest' or the search for 'utility,' or the like, and as distinct from de facto selectivity whereby circumstances, rather than motives, conspire to expose people to congenial communications.

The objective of what follows is to look again, in the light of the question raised by Freedman and Sears, at the evidence from mass communications studies. We shall try, at the same time, to respond to the Freedman-Sears call to go beyond the specific notion of selectivity-for-the-purpose-of-obtaining-support and to examine other bases of selective exposure. It is probably correct that some of these are considerably more important than 'supportive selectivity' and may set the conditions under which the latter does or does not take place. Nevertheless, we shall argue that 'supportive selectivity'—at least as far as field studies of mass communications bear witness—is still a factor to be reckoned with.

SUPPORTIVE SELECTIVITY AMONG MASS MEDIA AUDIENCES

To restate the argument somewhat more carefully, we will be concerned with the hypotheses (a) that an individual self-censors his intake of communications so as to shield his beliefs and practices from attack; (b) that an individual seeks out communications which support his beliefs and practices; and (c) that the latter is particularly true when the beliefs or practices in question have undergone attack or the individual has otherwise been made less confident of them. Propositions (a) and (c) derive from Festinger's (1957) theory of dissonance. But, say Freedman and Sears, the "experimental evidence does not demonstrate that there is a general psychological tendency to avoid nonsupportive and to seek out supportive information" (p. 69), "nor the more specific hypothesis that whatever preference there is for supportive information will be greater under high than under low dissonance" (p. 75).

When Freedman and Sears turn from the laboratory evidence to the evidence from the (mostly nonexperimental) field studies of mass media campaigns, their argument necessarily changes. They do not say that these studies disprove the hypothesis of selectivity-for-the-purpose-of-obtaining-support but rather that other, more parsimonious, explanations have not been ruled out. Thus, they warn that field studies must take account of the relative availability of different kinds of information before concluding that supportive selectivity has taken place. Equally cogently, they insist that socioeconomic status be controlled before inferring supportive selectivity from findings such as that persons favorable to the United Nations were disproportionately exposed to a UN information campaign. This kind of finding, they rightly maintain, may reflect nothing more than the well-known fact that better-educated individuals are more likely to be in the audience for any communication in the field of public affairs and that better-educated individuals are probably more internationally minded.

While the criticism is sobering, a second look at the admittedly far-from-adequate evidence leaves one wondering whether it is really necessary to change one's bet.

The voting studies are the first to come to mind. Even after Freedman and Sears weight the selective exposure by Democrats and Republicans by the greater availability of Republican information in Erie County, Ohio (Lazarsfeld et al., 1948), there remains very clear evidence of selectivity on the part of the minority party. The same thing holds true—if one weights selectivity by availability in the later Elmira study (Berelson, Lazarsfeld, & McPhee, 1954, p. 245), though the authors do not make the claim themselves. A similar finding turns up in an English election study (Trenaman & McQuail, 1961, p. 87).

The latter, it should be pointed out, presents a stronger case for de facto than for 'motivated' selectivity inasmuch as the correlation between partisanship and selective exposure to party *broadcasts* is only very weak while the relationship between partisanship and choice of partisan *newspapers* is strong. Our inference that this makes a better case for de facto selectivity is based on the assumption that the newspaper can be selected for a large variety of reasons other than political compatibility while the choice of a political broadcast is much more likely to reflect a desire to hear what one of the political parties has to say. Still, it is quite possible—and an interesting subject for comparative study—that Britons seek partisanship in print but fair-play and neutrality in radio and television. It is possible, in other words, that certain arenas are expected to be partisan while others are defined in terms of the expectation of 'equal time.'

Altogether, one must beware—as Mills also points out in Chapter 77—of the bias introduced in the search for selectivity in precisely those arenas where fair play and the hearing of both sides is a fundamental norm, such as in elections, jury trials, debates, and the like. Indeed, these institutions were virtually created to ensure exposure to both sides. Perhaps we should be surprised, therefore, to find any selective exposure at all.

The televised series of Kennedy-Nixon debates is a good example of this. The evidence from several studies (summarized in Katz and Feldman, 1962) indicates that an equally high proportion of members of both parties were in the audience—at least for the first debate. (Subsequent debates tended to include greater numbers of Nixon supporters, probably by virtue of their higher education.) It is particularly interesting, therefore, that there were proportionately more Catholics than Protestants in the audience, despite the generally higher educational and occupational status of the Protestants. Indeed, one of the studies (Deutschmann, 1962) found that those Protestants who mentioned religion as "the most important issue of the campaign" were far less likely to be in the viewing audience. This seems to be a real example of selective avoidance, though the number of cases involved is very small. Moreover, this same study demonstrates that after listening to the debate, listeners sought out somebody to talk with, and, overwhelmingly, this was somebody who shared the listener's initial political predisposition. While it is quite likely that this is another case of 'de facto' selectivity, it is interesting to see how people move back and forth—within the same substantive realm—between partisan and non- or bipartisan exposures.

But if the audiences for political communications tend to be affected by norms of fair-play and de facto selectivity, neither of these factors seems important in the area of religious communications. It is almost too obvious to point out that not only do people attend the church of their choice, they also attend, very selectively, the religious broadcasts of their choice. In a study of the audience for religious broadcasting in New Haven, Parker, Barry, and Smythe (1955, p. 207) found that the audience for 5 Catholic programs was predominantly Catholic while the audience for 11 Protestant programs was mostly Protestant.[1] Or, to tell the story more exactly, the Catholics are strongly oriented to religious radio broadcasts, the Protestants are not. To the extent that Protestants listen at all (14 per cent do), they listen in equal numbers to Protestant and to Catholic programs while a very large proportion of Catholics (41 per cent) listen to Catholic programs, and only a small proportion (4 per cent) to Protestant programs. Yet, since the total audience of the Protestant programs is small, and the number of religious listeners among the Catholics is very large, the small proportion of Catholics which listens to Protestant programs is enough to constitute a sizable minority. Note that the religious listeners among the Protestants act something like the Republicans in Erie County and Elmira, exposing themselves almost equally to both 'parties,' while the Catholics, like the Democrats, are much more strongly selective. There is a suggestion here that the 'minority group' (in terms of the availability of supporting messages, not in terms of numbers in the population) exercises greater selectivity.

Are these people seeking support for their beliefs? It is difficult to imagine why else they are listening and, in the case of the Catholics, why they focus their attention on their own programs. Freedman and Sears say that church attendance may be motivated by factors other than the desire for reinforcement of belief, but even if this is so, the latent functions of attending to religious broadcasts are surely fewer. It is quite likely that such listening partakes of the feeling that one is in touch with one's 'own' and that the mass media are duly recognizing one's belief culture, but these notions are very difficult to separate from the notion of seeking reinforcement.

Another of the studies on which the evidence for selective exposure rests is the classic field experiment reported by Hyman and Sheatsley (1947) in "Some Reasons Why Information Campaigns Fail." Respondents on a national survey were asked whether they had heard a given piece of news (the joint English-French-American announcement denouncing the Franco regime, and the proposal of an Anglo-American Committee that the United States aid in keeping order in Palestine). All respondents—whether they said they had heard or not—were given the substance of the news items by the interviewer (preceded by "As you remember . . ." in the case of those who claimed they had heard). Respondents were then asked whether or not they favored each of the proposals. The finding that those who had heard previously were more favorable than those who had not is presented in support of the selective exposure hypothesis. It may be rightly objected that educational level should have been controlled since it is possible that persons of higher education would have been more likely both to have heard the news and to agree with these two policies. But assuming—and it is not unreasonable—that the finding would stand up under controls, it represents rather strong evidence in support of the 'supportive' hypothesis whether one chooses to regard it as selective exposure or selective retention.

But the notion of selectively seeking support does not appear only in

---

[1] The Catholic programs were not all explicitly such; content analysis confirmed the arbitrary assignment to categories (i.e., the programs designated Catholic had more Catholic content). Although the local audience for Protestant programs was quite small, there were a large number of such programs on the air.

studies of the diffusion of information; it appears in studies of other uses of the mass media as well. A well-known example, though it is based on impressionistic evidence, is Warner's (1948) study of the soap opera, *Big Sister*. Warner argues that the program was so successful among its housewife listeners because it offered them reinforcement for their status in the person of an effective and influential housewife-heroine. In a world in which the housewifely role is challenged as uncreative and unworthy, these programs—so the argument goes—help to reduce the dissonance.

The evidence presented to this point is full of shortcomings and is certainly not conclusive, but it does seem to offer good reason for keeping the hypothesis alive. These studies and the ones criticized by Freedman and Sears (Star & Hughes, 1950; Cartwright, 1949; and others) were not designed, in general, to test the hypothesis that support is sought selectively in the mass media, and they cannot really prove it. The relationships are often weak, the formulations are not really tight, alternative explanations have not been ruled out, and the prevailing norms governing exposure are typically overlooked. These shortcomings are exacerbated by the fact that the kind of selective exposure in evidence in these studies is associated with the second, and least interesting, of the three hypotheses listed at the head of this section. In other words, the studies deal primarily with the observed correspondence between a person's attitudes and the communications to which he exposes himself and are virtually silent on whether individuals actively avoid communications that negate their beliefs, and whether the search for reinforcement is accelerated under conditions of dissonance. But the situation need not remain this way. The methodological possibilities of the panel (repeated interviews with the same respondents) or the field experiment, both of which add a time dimension to mass communications research, would certainly lend themselves to the design of more conclusive research in this area.

UTILITY AS A BASIS OF SELECTIVITY

Even if the hypothesis of supportive selectivity stands up to genuine testing, as I suspect it will, it is very likely that other factors will prove more important as bases for selectivity in exposure to mass communications. Freedman and Sears are correct in calling for more serious attention to some of these other factors and to the psychological dynamics implicit in them.

Thus, Freedman and Sears emphasize the motive of "utility," suggesting that people want information when it answers a felt need or serves a practical purpose. When nonsupportive information is useful, the authors suggest, people will prefer it to less useful information that is supportive.

Freedman and Sears appear to mean by utility any piece of information that helps in the performance of a role or the successful completion of a task. In other words, the notion of utility in this broader sense is nothing short of a functional approach to mass media exposure. It asks, "What do people do with the media?" or, more exactly, "What patterns of communications behavior can be predicted from a knowledge of the needs of different kinds of people?"

Thus, Feldman (1965), for example, indicates that women are more exposed than men to health information—particularly the sort of information that has to do with symptoms of disease—and this despite the lower interest of women in many other substantive areas. Indeed, the difference in the degree of health knowledge between women and men is already evident in the ninth grade. Feldman suggests that these differences in knowledge, interest, and exposure have to do with the fulfillment of role expectations: health information is 'useful' to women in anticipating and carrying out their roles. The same sorts of expectations are directed to educated people and constitute one of the explanations why education is so consistently related to high levels of exposure to all sorts of information, particularly in the realm of public affairs. It also explains why opinion leaders selectively attend to those media which bring information in their own spheres of influence but not to others (Katz, 1958).

Some kinds of exposure, however, are 'useful' precisely because they are 'useless' in that they permit people to avoid, or escape, the performance of a task or a role (cf. Katz & Foulkes, 1962). For example, the less one has of whatever it is that one's schoolmates happen to value (grades, athletic prowess, money), the more heavily one is exposed to the media, particularly to popular expressions of adolescent protest and alienation (Johnstone, 1961).

But 'useful' information can also be rejected—even when it seems to answer an objectively defined need—if one perceives oneself as useless. Thus, in an extremely interesting series of studies, Seeman (1966) has demonstrated that individuals who rank themselves near the 'powerlessness' end of a scale manage to avoid learning information which would be of use to them in their specific situations (reformatory, hospital, workers' organizations) although they do not differ from others on the learning of information unrelated to the exercise of control in their environments. These are studies of selective learning rather than selective exposure, but their import seems very much the same. Indeed, they are very closely related to the finding (Schramm, Lyle, & Parker, 1961) that the greater the disparity between a child's own aspirations and the perceived aspirations for him of parents and peers (where the latter are higher than the former), the greater the exposure to "fantasy-oriented" media and the lower the exposure to "reality-oriented" media. In other words, it appears as if beliefs can sometimes override utility as a selective factor in exposure, bringing the argument full circle.

INTEREST AS A BASIS OF SELECTIVITY

Apart from the quest for support and for utility, mere interest would seem to be an important factor in selectivity. The desire to see one's self-reflection is part of this. So is the desire to keep watch over things in which one has invested one's ego. Thus, moviegoers identify with screen stars of similar age and sex (Handel, 1950; Maccoby & Wilson, 1957); one reads in the newspaper about an event in which one personally participated; one reads advertisements for the product one purchased (Ehrlich et al., 1957; Mills, 1965a); political partisans immerse themselves in political communications regardless of its source; smokers choose to read material supporting the smoking-lung cancer relationship no less than material disclaiming the relationship, and much more avidly than nonsmokers (Feather, 1963); after one has been introduced to a celebrity one notices (or 'follows') his name in print even more frequently.

But while the examples just cited suggest that 'interest' as a basis of selective exposure is a different sort of thing than exposure on the basis of seeking support (interest leads to exposure to *both* sides of the argument), it is not as easy as it sounds to separate interest from utility and support-seeking. Indeed, some of the examples themselves are used as arguments for supportive selectivity. The problem of distinguishing between the two processes arises as soon as one postulates that interest is, or leads to, ego-involvement. And, if one then hypothesizes—in the spirit of dissonance theory—a continual quest for assurance that one's ego is worthy or well-cathected, the seeing of oneself or one's interests reflected and validated in the mass media is a kind of supportive selectivity—even when such communications are negative.[2] The famous public relations slogan sums this up very well: "Don't mind what they say about you, just as long as they mention your name." Narcissism, in other words, may have some built-in dissonance, and the consequent quest for external validation may not be easily distinguishable from ego-involvement. But this, of course, is simply another example of the overall problem of isolating the supportive motive in selective exposure. In principle, however, the distinction is clear: interest, or investment of the ego, may be followed by the desire for validation, and either or both of these may lead to selective exposure.

There is another aspect to the relationship between interest and support as bases of selectivity. We tend to think of opinions as consisting of a component of general interest in a subject, and a component of specific partisanship. Thus, we think of political partisans as having interest in politics in general and a specific partisan commitment. But many opinions or commitments do not work this way. It may well be, for example, that individuals do not have much interest in religion in general, but only in their own denominations. Or, to take another example, it may well be that general interest in a subject—Franco Spain, for example, to hark back to the Hyman-Sheatsley (1947) example—is manifested only by those who are on one side (opponents of the regime, in this case) and that there simply is no 'other side' among those who are interested. There are many issues which have enthusiasts on only one side, while all the rest are disinterested (and, by definition, nonpartisan). Studies of selective exposure on a given issue should take account of the empirical relationship between interest and partisanship. Thus, the pro-Franco respondents who had missed the anti-Franco message, according to Hyman and Sheatsley, may have missed the message not because they disagreed but because they were uninterested. And the anti-Franco people, for their part, may have caught the message because they were interested rather than because they were partisan, and would have been equally aware of a pro-Franco communiqué. Methodologically, this argument is exactly analogous to Freedman and Sears' call for holding educational level constant in tests of the supportiveness hypothesis. Interest and utility must be added to the list of factors to control. In any given case, however, it may turn out that selective exposure on the basis of interest and selective exposure on the

---

[2] I assume here that we are dealing with persons who have high self-esteem (highly positive self concepts) in the area under discussion. This would exclude situations such as those in the Aronson and Carlsmith (1962) study where subjects were purportedly behaving so as to obtain information confirming their low opinions of themselves (see also McGuire, 1966a, pp. 498–500 and Section III E of this volume).

basis of seeking support may be indistinguishable because interest in a subject may be identical with partisanship.

ADDITIONAL NOTES AND CONCLUSIONS

The hypothesis that individuals seek information that will support their beliefs and practices and avoid information that challenges them still seems viable from the vantage point of mass communications research. Reexamination of the evidence in the wake of the objections raised by Freedman and Sears, however, reveals how little evidence is required for an hypothesis to be accepted as 'proven.'

Studies are cited from the fields of public affairs, voting, religion, etc., in support of the hypothesis, though none of them can be considered conclusive or a really strict test. Echoing Freedman and Sears, we have been underlining the importance of holding certain other factors constant before concluding that partisanship is the motivating factor in selective exposure.

But it is not easy to test the hypothesis, especially in a field situation. An ideal test requires (a) the taking account of time, in order to demonstrate that partisanship causes selective exposure rather than vice versa; and (b) a situation in which communications are available on both sides of an issue, and where there is a corresponding division of opinion. But this does not solve the problem of how to demonstrate in the field that people avoid uncongenial information, independent of their preference for congenial information. Some adaptation of the Hyman-Sheatsley (1947) method to include 'neutral' communications might prove effective here, in much the way that Mills (1965a) compares the degree of interest expressed by respondents in reading about accepted and rejected products and other products which are neither accepted nor rejected.

Further thought must also be given to field-testing the hypothesized relationship between the extent of support-seeking and the magnitude of dissonance. An attempt in this direction was made by Troldahl (1963) in a field experiment which predicted, among other things, that there would be greater advice-giving and greater advice-seeking in interpersonal communication under conditions of inconsistency between a message and previous beliefs. Unfortunately, however, the experimental message, 'planted' in an agricultural bulletin directed to suburban farmers, failed to arouse much interest, and consequently there was hardly enough interpersonal communication to test the hypothesis.

An even more basic methodological problem to which attention must be given in field studies has to do with the operational definition of selective exposure itself. What are the mechanisms by means of which individuals recognize that they are in the presence of supportive or discrepant information: Do they scan headlines? Do they anticipate what the content of a communication is likely to be from its source? How, in other words, does an individual select among communications according to the supportiveness principle without being exposed to them? In the laboratory, the subject is asked, typically, whether he would like to read a pamphlet or an advertisement taking a stand for or against his opinion or behavior, or he is shown a list of titles from which to choose. Intuitively, this would seem to be the rough equivalent of headline-reading as a means of selectivity, but is it? And how does this work in the case of TV programs? or conversation?

Altogether, this paper argues that the supportive selectivity hypothesis is, in part, a special case of an approach to the problem of exposure in terms of 'uses' or 'gratifications,' i.e., in functional terms. Some of the evidence for selective exposure on the basis of utility is reviewed, and the concept of 'use' is considerably broadened. It is suggested that a conflict over whether to attend to a communication which includes both nonsupportive and useful elements may be resolved either way. Interest, or ego-involvement, is also discussed as a basis for selective exposure.

The discussion of utility and interest, and to a certain extent, the discussion of supportiveness itself, indicates that the problem of selectivity is not limited to the sphere of mass media information. It relates equally to entertainment and other forms of mass media content, and, indeed, to exposure to the mass media per se (regardless of content). Concern with the notion of utility reflects the overall shift in mass media research away from studies of short-run changes of information and attitude as a result of mass media campaigns to studies of different ways in which mass media messages serve the social and psychological needs of their audiences.

CHAPTER 80

Selective Exposure: A Summing Up

William J. McGuire

The three authors in this section have evaluated the considerable research on the selective exposure hypothesis and, while differing on a few details of the scoring procedure, have agreed that the evidence for the critical selective avoidance aspect of the prediction is quite poor. Yet none of the three is quite ready to reject finally this postulate (though Sears comes close to such abandonment). Once again in psychology, a hypothesis that somehow seems to deserve to be true manages to keep surfacing despite submergence in a sea of empirical disconfirmation.

Experimental nonsupport. The data regarding selective avoidance seem to this editor impressively negative. The contributors provide scorecards showing that even published results give the selective avoidance hypothesis a very poor batting average. Indeed, some of the outcomes are significantly in the direction opposite to that predicted. This poor ratio of confirmation is particularly worrisome to those of us who have become sensitized to the prevalence of experimenter bias, since most of the researchers have been proponents of the postulate and thus the disconfirmations have occurred despite possible biases to the contrary. Further worry arises when one considers that, as Steiner (1962) has pointed out, a number of purportedly supportive studies show when examined more closely that the reported confirmation is in terms of a subtle interaction effect while the main effect is in a direction opposed to the selective avoidance prediction. What must the total research effort indicate, when this published portion is so unfavorable to the prediction? It seems reasonable to expect that the published results on a prediction stemming from any postulate are heavily biased in the direction of overpublication of positive results. Underneath this rather unimpressive ratio of confirming published results, one suspects there lies the massive accumulation of unpublished nonsupportive data that make up the chilling mass of this iceberg of research.

Continued promulgation. In view of the paucity of supportive findings, it is rather touching to witness the tenacity with which the selective avoidance 'principle' has been asserted early and late by many behavioral scientists. Nearly twenty years ago, Klapper (1949) stated that "... Self-selection might well be called the most basic process thus far established by research on the effects of mass media." As recently as 1962, the Behavioral Science Subpanel of the President's Science Advisory Committee (1962) cited as one of its behavioral science findings worthy of the Chief Executive's attention the principle that "... Individuals engage in selective exposure. ... If a new piece of information would weaken the existing structure of their ideas and emotions, it will be shunned." Perhaps some will find solace in this day of concern about security that one may publish the results of his research rather freely in the professional journals and still hope to keep his secret intact from professional colleagues.

Improper disconfirmations? This lingering faith of the contributors is not due to any rigorous practice of Comte's "cerebral hygiene." These cognoscenti make clear that they are aware of the disconfirming evidence, but manage to keep the faith by supposing that the selective exposure postulate is not really dead but simply hiding out amidst some confounding variables. Each contributor, even Sears, who is the least sympathetic to the postulate, has argued that selective avoidance may indeed occur as a trend which is often submerged and even reversed due to the operation of confounding variables. The three contributors have, jointly or singly, managed to suggest an impressive number of plausible confounding variables which I shall for convenience assemble here.

Some of the failures to confirm, they conjecture, may have been due to methodological shortcomings. Sears and Mills point out that the test for exposure is often quite artificial (though Sears notes that the outcome has not been more favorable for the selective avoidance prediction when more realistic tests have been used). This artificiality gives some force to Katz's suggestion that the selective avoidance postulate should fare better in field than in laboratory research. Furthermore, as the two laboratory researchers have pointed out, in some of the studies there is no good evidence that the experimenter succeeded in manipulating the crucial interaction variable such as confidence or commitment. The contributors also cite cases where the demand character of the experiment went against the selective avoidance postulate. For example, some of the experimental situations were such that any subject with sensitivity to the demands of fair play and open-mindedness, or any proneness to making socially desirable responses, would find it difficult to refuse to hear the opposition side. A somewhat related point is that rather restricted, highly educated samples have been used almost invariably in this research, even when performed outside the university laboratory. It might well be that education lowers usage of selective avoidance and hence the negative results are not generalizable to the less-educated sectors of the population who may make more use of this relatively primitive defensive tactic.

Besides these methodological difficulties, the contributors claim that there are several intrinsic factors that tend to stack experiments against the selective avoidance hypothesis. The most commonly cited in this regard is the utility consideration: information about one's own side or one's chosen alternative tends to have utility for the individual. Hence, given the choice between even bad information about one's own side or about the other side, the utility consideration might submerge the defensive avoidance tendency and result in a net preference for the fuller though detrimental information about one's own side. Or instead of utility, other factors such as familiarity, comprehensibility, relevance, etc., could override defensive avoidance in some cases. Or, as Katz points out, simple narcissism could be involved, in that perhaps the person wants to see his own name or his side's name in print, even if it is dealt with in an uncomplimentary manner.

The investigators also excuse some of the negative results on grounds that the selective avoidance tendency is only one of several modes of handling belief-discrepant information. Some of the negative results may simply reflect situations in which the person finds it more appropriate to master the opposition arguments to prepare himself for a more vigorous subsequent onslaught against his belief. Or he may anticipate that these particular opposition arguments might be easy to refute, and hence he will even seek out this discrepant material in the expectation that he will actually gain confidence by demolishing it. All these conjectures demonstrate anew that with determination and a little ingenuity one can survive experimental disconfirmations with one's hypothesis still intact. More charitably, it also shows that disconfirmation serves the perspicacious researcher almost as well as confirmation in developing his theory.

Spurious confirmations. If, as just reviewed, friends of the selective exposure postulate have no difficulty in finding excuses for failures of confirmations, so also its enemies find it easy to attribute the occasional confirmations to spurious factors. Indeed, some of the excuses for failure to find selective avoidance serve to raise questions about the validity of those supposed confirmations that do occur. Most of these alternative explanations for apparent selective exposure posit a sociological, rather than psychological, basis for the behavior. Thus the finding that a person has more information supporting his own side than the other side is attributed, not to his motivated seeking out of information supporting his own side and defensively avoiding information for the other side, but rather to the social system's being structured to promote this seeming bias. It is pointed out, for example, that on most issues there is such community consensus that almost all the information available is supportive. Also, ingratiating communicators tell the listener what they think he wants to know. It is also possible that communication gate keepers try to keep their followers ignorant of the opposition side. Communicators tend to seek out audiences that would naturally be sympathetic to them by communicating over channels to which their adherents are likely to be tuned. Moreover, availability of information is something less than ideal even in the modern technological society, so that it is often difficult to get information even on one's own side and it is almost inevitably more demanding to find information on the opposition side should one ever be motivated to look for it. For all these reasons and others, the contributors point out that even were the obtained results overwhelmingly in accord with the selective exposure hypothesis (which in fact they are not) there might still be some doubt as to whether these results indicated that there is any motivated tendency to seek out supportive and avoid discrepant material.

There are indeed two theories whose heuristic powers are receiving growing recognition which predict a tendency quite the opposite to selective avoidance. One of these is what might be called 'complexity' theory, in rough opposition to present 'consistency' theories, though it goes under other rubrics also, such as exploratory or curiosity drive, stimulus hunger, alternation behavior, etc. It has already been pointed out (McGuire, 1966b) that this theoretical orientation tends to make predictions opposite to those of consistency theories. (Section II of this volume contains discussions by Berlyne and by Maddi of this opposition.) The second theoretical approach with a rather opposite prediction to that of consistency theory on this selective exposure issue is satiation theory (Lambert & Jakobovits, 1960; Amster & Glasman, 1966). While its main attention is on the response rather than the stimulus side, the flavor is to suggest that the person would tend, at least temporarily, to avoid the overfamiliar, supportive data to which he is being constantly exposed.

General implications. The contributors dutifully confine themselves largely to the specific question of selective exposure. But inevitably they touch occasionally on the closely related phenomena of distorted perception, biased learning, prejudiced retention, etc. The questionable empirical status of the selective exposure hypothesis is paralleled by empirical doubts regarding these related phenomena. Conjectures about motivated distortions in these cognitive processes have long been with us, but after some encouraging results obtained a quarter century ago, these predictions have not fared well experimentally. The current state of the question is well demonstrated by the recent program of Stuart Cook (Cook & Selltiz, 1964) on indirect measures of ethnic prejudice. It seems to this editor that the doubts regarding the validity of the selective exposure effect should extend to these related phenomena.

The nonconfirming results reviewed by the three contributors need not indicate that this extended research program on selective exposure has been futile. At worst, it may have served to demonstrate that the selective exposure postulate is invalid. Indeed, the survival of the human race for a period that even the most conservative estimators place at a minimum of 6000 years suggests that people select out information on some basis less primitive than seeking support of what they already know and avoiding any surprises. The effort to confirm the selective exposure postulate has also refined our thinking on information-encoding strategies and has suggested the new principles mentioned above, which in many cases are more interesting than the original postulate they were devised to salvage.

Where do we go from here? Mills suggests a new formulation which he calls "certainty" theory. It might be pursued, though it seems to me that this theory is only very slightly different from the earlier theory which it supplements and is subject to the same empirical embarrassments. Elihu Katz suggests that more research be done in natural settings where the selective exposure tendency might be more operative. Indeed the time does seem to be ripe for more work in natural settings as has been discussed in detail elsewhere (McGuire, 1967). Sears, after some years of confronting humans ingeniously avoiding information in the classroom, wryly wonders if we should ask not how the source gets to his enemy, but how he reaches anyone at all. My own feeling is that we are left with our initial assumption that the information encoding capacity of the individual is quite limited, so that considerable selectivity necessarily occurs. A study of such selectivity would be a fruitful field of research but it seems that defensive avoidance is not a very powerful factor in individual selective strategy. The time has come, I think, to turn to the broader question of which are, in fact, the tactics of perceptual selectivity, and discontinue the current excessive preoccupation with this one possible tactic of defensive avoidance.

F. COUNTERATTITUDINAL BEHAVIOR AND ATTITUDE CHANGE

The substantive question before us in this section is: What really happens inside a person, and ultimately, what happens to some one of his attitudes, when he engages in counterattitudinal performance for sufficient as compared to insufficient reasons? The basic theoretical positions engaged are, on the one hand, dissonance theory and, on the other, various formulations which generate the opposed or 'incentive' prediction: i.e., the greater the justification or reward for open-minded counterattitudinal performance, the greater the consequent attitude change.

But, as will be seen in the following pages, the debate has entered an advanced phase. Imperial monolithic claims have begun to fade in face of the compelling fact that both the dissonance and incentive relationships have been obtained in experiments conducted in recent years. Thus, Merrill Carlsmith (a dissonancer), Irving Janis (an incentivist), and Barry Collins (a questing eclectic) are found to have something in common. They are aware of, and perhaps even troubled by, the complexity of mediating processes; and they show some sensitivity to the problem of the undiscerned, intrusive variables that often bedevil the manipulative elicitation of counterattitudinal behavior.

What is particularly encouraging is that they seem to be working toward the same basic goal: the development of a differentiated understanding of how motivational and perceptual processes are involved in mediating the various outcomes of counterattitudinal performance. That their conclusions are, nevertheless, not identical is a matter of no great surprise. In the role of theorist one does not abandon one's theory; where necessary one defends it by amending it.

On the other hand, a pleasant obligation of the editorial role is the presumption of a judicial function. Thus, in the concluding pages of this section the editor (who is not, to be sure, a totally disinterested party to the present debate) will hazard a few conclusions about the contested theoretical issues and about the ways in which still unrevealed truths might be rescued from the mediational murk that has hitherto obscured them.

CHAPTER 81

Varieties of Counterattitudinal Behavior

J. Merrill Carlsmith

Stanford University

There can be little question that one of the most effective ways to change a person's attitudes is to induce him to engage in behavior inconsistent with those attitudes. Whether he is asked to write arguments counter to his own position, argue for the opposite side, write confessions about behaviors he did not perform, make public speeches denying his position, or perform some behavior which implies that he holds beliefs contrary to his real ones, his attitude will change. Thus the discrepancy between his attitudes and his behavior is reduced. The wide range of behaviors producing this effect suggests that there may be more than a single mechanism responsible for the changes. I will argue below that much of the disagreement about the exact nature of these changes results from an attempt to place all counterattitudinal behavior within some single framework.

The question of major theoretical concern has been the relationship between the amount of inducement offered to attract counterattitudinal behavior and the amount of attitude change produced. There are two points to be noted here. First, concern centers on the amount of positive or negative reward offered to *induce* the person to engage in the behavior. Only those positive or negative aspects which are made clear to the subject before he makes his decision to engage in the behavior are really relevant. Experiments like those of Scott (1959), while important for a more general understanding of the process, are not relevant to the discussion of incentive magnitude and attitude change. Secondly, although many experiments have tried to vary inducement by offering different amounts of money to achieve counterattitudinal behavior, there is no need to limit discussion to just that kind of manipulation. In fact, money may function in a different manner; it may not simply act as an incentive.

Then what can we say about the relationship between incentive and attitude change? There are two simplistic answers to the question: dissonance theory holds that the greater the inducement to engage in counterattitudinal

Preparation of this manuscript was aided by Grant GS-1115 from the National Science Foundation.

behavior, the less the resulting attitude change; "incentive theory" holds that the greater the inducement, the greater should be the attitude change.

Consider first the position of dissonance theory. The argument is straightforward and generally familiar. A person who engages in counter-attitudinal behavior holds two cognitions: "I believe X" and "I am engaging in behavior which implies that I believe *not-X*." Under most circumstances (I will return to this point later) these two cognitions will produce dissonance. The most obvious method of reducing dissonance is to change the belief in the direction of the behavior. Any incentive for performing the behavior produces a third cognition: "I will receive Y for engaging in the behavior." If the person does engage in the behavior, then this latter cognition is consonant with the behavior and will reduce the total amount of dissonance in the situation; it will also reduce the total amount of attitude change. The more Y, the more consonance and the less dissonance.

Support for this position is, I think, truly impressive. As soon as one allows incentive to mean something besides money, there are a large number of studies which are completely in line with the reasoning. At least three experiments can be cited in which the person is asked to say or write something inconsistent with his beliefs and money is the incentive (Festinger & Carlsmith, 1959; Cohen, as reported in Brehm and Cohen, 1962; Carlsmith, Collins, & Helmreich, 1966). An excellent example of the same process is provided by Freedman (1963) who manipulated incentive in another way. In his experiment some subjects were told that their behavior (generating random numbers) was very important; other subjects were given a low incentive or justification for performing the task, being told that their behavior would produce data which were worthless. This experiment, incidentally, shows the importance of presenting incentives before a decision is made. A dissonance effect was observed only when subjects were given justification for performing the behavior before they decided to do it; the opposite result was observed when justification was presented after the task. When the counterattitudinal behavior involves *not* doing something that is otherwise desirable, and when the inducement is varied by varying the strength of the threat for not performing the behavior, results are again in line with dissonance predictions (Aronson & Carlsmith, 1963; Freedman, 1965b; Turner & Wright, 1965). There are several other experiments which are slightly farther removed from this line of reasoning but still quite consistent with it (e.g., Marlowe, Frager, & Nuttall, 1965). However, I think that these are enough to suggest that in a wide variety of situations, the greater the incentive one has for acting against his beliefs, the less will be his opinion change.

We are prevented from simply listing this as a general conclusion by two experiments which are similar in appearance to those described above, but which have failed to find the same effect (Janis & Gilmore, 1965; Elms & Janis, 1965). Two additional experiments (Rosenberg, 1965d; Carlsmith, Collins, & Helmreich, 1966) have reported results in exactly the opposite direction. Let us postpone interpretation of results until after we have discussed the reasons why they do not present evidence counter to dissonance predictions.

There are many situations in which a person engages in behavior which is counter to his attitudes and yet experiences no dissonance. The argument here is that those experiments which have failed to find results in line with dissonance predictions, or have found results which appear directly opposite, may be in that class of situations in which dissonance is not aroused. To see this, let us go back to the definition of dissonance. Two cognitions are said to be dissonant when the opposite of one follows psychologically from the other. It is simply not the case that *any* counterattitudinal behavior leads to dissonance. Consider the following example. On some moderately controversial issue I say to a subject: "Do there exist arguments which favor an attitude somewhat different from your own?" After he responds affirmatively, I ask him whether, as a reasonable, open-minded person, he would mind listing several of them for me. His cognition "I hold attitude X" is not dissonant with his cognition "There exist some arguments against that position which I am listing to show that I am not narrow-minded about the issue." Now the existence of the arguments may arouse dissonance. Considering only the two cognitions "Here is an argument favoring *not-X*" and "I hold attitude X," dissonance will be aroused. For it does follow psychologically for most people that (again considering *only* these two cognitions) "Here is an argument favoring *not-X*" implies "I hold attitude *not-X*." But the important point is that the *behavior* of listing the arguments need not be dissonant with holding the opposite attitude.

I think this point gains support from the empirical observation that all experiments which have failed to find a dissonance effect have asked the subject to write essays contrary to his own position. Typically, in these studies, there is the clear implication that the experimenter understands the subject holds an opposing position but, for one reason or another, the experimenter wants to see some arguments on the other side.[1] The argument I am making then is this: there are many situations in which a person engages in counterattitudinal behavior and yet no dissonance is aroused—at least no dissonance about *engaging* in the behavior. A prime example of this occurs when a person is asked to list a set of arguments counter to his own position, the implication being that this is a purely intellectual task.

It would be desirable to be able to list more generally the classes of situations which will and will not produce dissonance. Yet even an experiment which is able to produce both a dissonance effect and an 'incentive' effect (Carlsmith, Collins, & Helmreich, 1966) does not completely solve the problem. There existed in that experiment a multitude of differences between the condition (essay) in which an incentive effect was obtained and the condition (face-to-face role-playing) in which a dissonance effect was obtained.

Although it is not possible at this time to give an exhaustive listing of those situations which will produce dissonance, I think it is possible to list at least three general classes of counterattitudinal behaviors that are likely to produce dissonance. In this regard, it must be emphasized that in any given situation it is imperative to go back to the basic definition of dissonance— that the opposite of one cognition follows psychologically from the other—

---

[1] The one troublesome experiment in any analysis such as this is the study by Cohen reported by Brehm and Cohen (1962). Cohen did ask subjects to write essays, and his experiment appears very similar to that of Rosenberg (1965d). However, Cohen obtained a clear dissonance effect. Unfortunately, the description of the Cohen experiment is extremely sketchy; any attempt to decide whether or not dissonance was aroused depends on a knowledge of more detail than is presented in his description. For this reason, I will not attempt to reconcile that experiment in this discussion.

to be sure that dissonance is involved. Nevertheless, it is reasonable that the following general classes of situations will usually produce dissonance.

The first situation, which is typical of many of the early dissonance experiments (e.g., Festinger & Carlsmith, 1959), involves public espousal of the position which is opposed to one's beliefs. If a person is induced to make a public statement to an audience that is unaware of his motivation in making that statement, and he cares about the opinion of the audience, dissonance is likely to be aroused. The cognition "I am saying X to some people whom I care about and who do not know why I am saying X" is dissonant with the cognition "I believe $not\text{-}X$." Perhaps the nature of this dissonance is best exemplified by the behavior of one subject in the experiment by Festinger and Carlsmith (1959). In this experiment, subjects were induced to tell a waiting confederate that the experiment which the confederate was about to take part in was fun, interesting, and exciting. In fact, as the subject well knew, it was extremely dull. One subject did tell the waiting confederate that it was interesting, but immediately upon the conclusion of this statement demanded the confederate's phone number, saying he would call her and then saying that he would wait until she had finished the experiment in order to talk to her and explain something very important. An obvious interpretation is that he wished to explain the reasons for his behavior, hoping to reduce his dissonance by changing the situation into one in which the observer understood why he had behaved that way. In general, then, any time a person makes some statement counter to his attitudes, and a listener (whose opinion is important to the speaker) is unaware of both the speaker's attitudes and his motivation for speaking against these attitudes, dissonance will be aroused.

Another general class of events that may be expected to arouse dissonance occurs when a subject is induced to engage in counterattitudinal behavior for unacceptable reasons. Even though any observer may realize that the behavior is counter to the subject's attitudes, the subject will still experience dissonance if he feels that he has been 'bought.' Suppose we say to the subject "I understand that you believe X, but I am prepared to offer you $20 to say that you believe $not\text{-}X$. Other reasons for doing this are not acceptable, but I am offering you enough money to overcome that." (The contrast here is with an experiment like that of Festinger and Carlsmith [1959], where the reasons given to the subject for engaging in the behavior [e.g., helping the experimenter] may be acceptable, but the person hearing the subject is not aware of these reasons.) In this situation, we imagine that everyone knows the reasons for the behavior, but that the reasons (aside from the incentive) provide no justification. Here there is clearly dissonance between the cognition "I believe X" and the cognition "I am saying $not\text{-}X$ for intellectually unacceptable reasons."

The final general class of situations, and perhaps the most common, involves conditions wherein the behavior itself is unpleasant. Perhaps this is best exemplified in the experiment by Freedman (1963). In this study, subjects were induced to generate random numbers for 15 minutes. This behavior was presumably inconsistent with the belief that such behavior was dull and boring. In contrast to situations where the counterattitudinal behavior is in itself innocuous (e.g., simply saying something), this behavior is inherently unpleasant. Along the same line, subjects in the Aronson and Carlsmith (1963) experiment find themselves executing a behavior that is basically unpleasant and therefore contrary to their attitudes. In this experiment, children chose to ignore a toy which they clearly thought was desirable. Again, the behavior itself (not playing with the desirable toy) is unpleasant, and dissonance will be present.

These three general classes of situations, then, describe at least some of the cases in which we can expect the relation between incentive magnitude and attitude change to be negative. When the subject experiences dissonance between cognitions about his behavior and cognitions about his attitudes, we expect that the greater the incentive for performing the behavior, the less the dissonance and the less the attitude change.

If dissonance is not present, however, how do we explain the 'incentive' effect? To answer this question, we should consider how any attitude change resulting from counterattitudinal behavior is to be explained—irrespective of variation with incentive—when no dissonance is present between the behavior and the attitude. There are several possible answers. From the point of view of dissonance theory, there is dissonance between the cognition "I believe X" and the cognition "There are the following good arguments for *not-X*." Various learning theory explanations of attitude change would provide the same kind of argument. Given the existence of good arguments for the opposite position, it is reasonable that the subject's attitude would move toward that position.

But why should the subject's attitude change more with greater incentive? One general class of reasons relies on the notion that the subject works harder for a larger incentive and thus produces better arguments. Such a solution would be ideal except for one fact—the majority of studies do not report significantly better arguments, or more arguments, or in fact any significant qualitative difference in arguments between those subjects offered a large incentive and those subjects offered a small incentive. True, the difference usually tends to be in the direction of more or better arguments with a larger incentive, but that finding is by no means as reliable as the finding of more attitude change with larger incentive. If there were better arguments with a larger incentive, our problem would be simple. A dissonance analysis (more dissonance produced by better arguments) and a learning analysis (more learning of better arguments leading to more attitude change) would both lead to the prediction that higher incentive and better arguments would lead to more attitude change. However, although one might argue that this could be the case in some situations, the fact remains that in most laboratory studies there is no relationship between incentive and production (see Carlsmith, Collins, & Helmreich, 1966) despite the positive relation between incentive and attitude change.

I would like to argue that one reason for the relation between incentive magnitude and attitude change is the subject's differential *perception* of high quality in his arguments under high incentive, even though the actual quality may be no different than under low incentive. Consider a subject who has been offered $10 to produce arguments in favor of some position. Let us imagine two possible outcomes: either he is able to produce some set of reasonable arguments, or he is unable to produce anything convincing. In either case, he must resolve the quality of his arguments with the fact that he was paid a large sum of money to produce them. If he is able to produce a reasonable set of arguments, we may assume that his cognition that he was paid a large sum of money to produce them will imply that they are really awfully good. Either it is the case that good arguments were hard to come by, and thus he was offered a lot of money for them, which implies that any reasonable arguments he is able to present are good, or it is true that the offer of a lot of money aims to produce the *best* possible arguments—again good arguments will lead to the perception that they are awfully good. On the other hand, if good arguments are hard for the subject to produce, the gift of a large sum of money for producing good arguments may lead to a very awkward psychological position. If one cannot resolve the contrast between the amount of money given for the arguments and the quality of the arguments by saying that the arguments are good, then a very drastic alternative solution is required. The most likely solution is to change one's attitudes to contradict the original attitude, saying in essence—"if I cannot defend this attitude for a large sum of money, the attitude must be incorrect."

In essence, I am arguing that the defense of some attitude for a large sum of money places one in a peculiar position. Either one must say that the arguments are extremely good in order to justify the payment (and this will occur when reasonable arguments can be brought forth) or one must deny that the position was defensible. The first, I suggest, is likely to occur in those situations which have produced an "incentive effect." Typically, the subject in these experiments has been faced with a situation where he is asked to produce arguments in opposition to his own position, and where several good arguments (known to the subject) exist on this opposite side. If the subject concludes that his arguments are good, then he will be faced with more dissonance between these good arguments and his original position and will change his attitude more.

Some evidence for this analysis is provided in a recent experiment by Mark Lepper and myself. In this study, we asked subjects to argue for a position which they initially favored. Some of the subjects were presented with a communication opposed to their own position—a communication designed to undercut any arguments they might have in favor of their position. We assume that these subjects find it difficult to marshall any arguments supporting their position. Half of each group of subjects was offered a large amount of money for arguments supporting their own position. Half were offered a small sum.[2]

What can we expect to happen here? Since all subjects are defending their own position, we cannot see any movement toward that position when they are able to produce good arguments. But those subjects who are unable to produce effective arguments (because of having read a communication which effectively undercuts those arguments), and who are paid a lot of money to try to produce arguments, are in an awkward position. The easiest way for them to deal with the fact that they were unable to produce good arguments is to change their attitudes. (If they no longer believe the position they are trying to argue for, then the dissonance about not being able to produce arguments has been reduced.) This is exactly

---

[2] Actually, I have simplified the description of this experiment. To control for the effects of reading the strong communication opposing the subject's initial position, some subjects were asked to write their own arguments and then read the communication. Others were asked to read the communication and then write their arguments (the crucial group for this discussion). A third group merely wrote arguments.

what happened. The only change observed was in those subjects who were paid a large amount of money and who first read a communication which made it difficult to produce arguments. They changed their attitudes away from their original position. Again, however, no difference could be observed between arguments produced for the large and the small incentives. A very similar result was reported as an incidental finding by Nuttin (1965).

The basic argument I have tried to present here is a simple one: not all counterattitudinal behavior arouses dissonance. When behavior is such that we may reasonably expect dissonance to be aroused, there will be an inverse relationship between the amount of incentive offered for the behavior and the amount of attitude change produced. This prediction is well substantiated. When dissonance is not aroused (specifically, dissonance between the behavior and the attitude), then other processes may operate—processes which I think are not so well understood at this time.

CHAPTER 82

Attitude Change via Role Playing

Irving L. Janis

Yale University

Role playing, although only recently brought into the experimental social psychology laboratory, frequently occurs in daily life and may be one of the main ways in which people encounter cognitive inconsistencies that lead them to decide to adopt new courses of action. Social scientists have long taken account of the strong social pressures that are exerted on men and women to live up to the demands of prescribed norms whenever they enter a new occupational role, advance to a more responsible position in an organizational hierarchy, or acquire a new social status in the community. It has been observed that many people, when complying with role demands, express the prescribed attitudes and values even though they do not privately accept them. A transformation from outer to inner compliance seems to be a central feature of role adaptation—a gradual change whereby the person comes to accept privately the beliefs and value judgments that he has expressed publicly while playing the expected social role.

A number of experimental studies have presented systematic evidence concerning the effects of role playing on attitude change. Janis and King (1954; King & Janis, 1956) found that when college students were induced to improvise a talk in order to fulfill the demands of a public-speaking task requiring them to express opinions that differed from their private beliefs, they showed more opinion change than an equivalent control group exposed to the same informational content. Kelman (1953) found a similar increase in opinion change when school children were given a mild incentive to write essays in support of an arbitrarily assigned position; but he observed no such gain in an equivalent group of children put under strong pressure to conform with the role-playing task, many of whom showed signs of constriction, resentment, and negativism.

A "conflict" model can be used as a theoretical basis for a "self-persuasion" hypothesis to explain role-playing effects (Janis, 1959; Janis & Mann, 1968). Decisional conflicts are conceptualized in terms of a balance sheet containing weighted positive and negative values corresponding to the potential gains (positive incentives) and potential losses (negative incentives) that are anticipated by the decision maker when he evaluates each alternative open to him.

Janis and Gilmore (1965) point out that this theoretical approach specifies several conditions for inducing maximal attitude change via role playing that are quite different from those specified by dissonance theory:

> ... when a person accepts the task of improvising arguments in favor of a point of view at variance with his own personal convictions, he becomes temporarily motivated to think up all the good positive arguments he can, and at the same time, suppresses thoughts about the negative arguments which are supposedly irrelevant to the assigned task. This "biased scanning" increases the salience of the positive arguments and therefore increases the chances of acceptance of the new attitude position. A gain in attitude change would not be expected, however, if resentment or other interfering affective reactions were aroused by *negative* incentives in the role-playing situation. Among the obvious instances of negative incentives would be information that lowers the prestige of the sponsor or that leads to his being perceived as a manipulative person who is trying to influence people for his own personal aggrandizement or for other alien purposes. Any signs of exploitative intentions in the behavior of the sponsor would also be expected to operate as negative incentives, evoking responses that conflict with the positive incentive value of improvising arguments in support of the conclusion assigned by the sponsor.

According to conflict theory, the amount of attitude change will depend largely on the degree to which the role player is induced to engage in intensive "biased scanning" of genuine positive incentives that he can accept into his own personal balance sheet. The role player will change his attitude only if he makes the following two types of verbal responses while carrying out the role-playing task: (a) recalling or inventing arguments that are capable of functioning as positive incentives for accepting a new attitude position, and (b) appraising the recalled or improvised arguments with a psychological set that fosters open-minded cognitive exploration of their positive incentive value, rather than a negativistic set of the type engendered by the arousal of hostility, resentment, or suspicion (Elms & Janis, 1965). If the first type of response is made, but not the second, no attitude change would be expected from a role-playing performance. For example, many intelligent American soldiers who were captured by the Chinese Communists during the Korean War could comply with the role-playing demands of their despised 'brain-washing' captors and nevertheless remain uninfluenced: While verbalizing 'good' pro-Communist arguments, the prisoners could privately label all the improvised arguments with negative epithets or could think of counterarguments to refute the statements they were overtly verbalizing (see Lifton, 1961; Schein, 1956).

It should also be noted that role playing would not be expected to bring about attitude change unless the new incentives that emerge when the subjects engage in biased scanning are powerful enough to create a challenge to their present position (Stage 1 in the model of decision-making stages; see Chapter 55). A case in point is the study of Stanley and Klausmeir (1957) in which midwestern isolationists complied with the role-playing instructions to give short talks advocating world government, but showed no evidence of attitude change. It would be extremely improbable that, merely by engaging in a bit of biased scanning in a single experimental session, the subjects would generate a new set of incentives sufficiently powerful not only to seriously challenge their present position in favor of U.S. national autonomy but to reject it in favor of the new alternative. On the other hand, when experimenters set up the necessary conditions for bringing about sufficient challenge to induce at least a slight amount of attitude change (e.g., by selecting a less deeply held attitude or by first introducing an effective persuasive message) the use of the role-playing technique can alter each subject's personal balance sheet of positive and negative incentives sufficiently to produce a much greater amount of attitude change in the role players than in equated control subjects who are passively exposed to the same informational inputs.

The effectiveness of a role-playing procedure would also be expected to depend upon the type of arguments the person is asked to give. For example, if he is instructed to play the role of a person with whom he has little in common, and argues in terms of values and goals that are not his own, he will engage in very little biased scanning of incentives that enter into his own private balance sheet, with the result that none of his anticipations of gains or losses will be altered. In contrast, if the subject is instructed to play the role of someone who shares his values and to make up good arguments that would be convincing to persons like himself, the chances are greatly increased that some new incentives will enter into his private balance sheet and give rise to a change in his position on the issue.

Two specific variables can be singled out which enable predictions to be made that are opposite to those made by dissonance theorists:

1. The amount of attitude change produced by role playing, according to conflict theory, will be a positive function of the degree to which subjects engage in *overt* role playing by verbalizing arguments in support of the assigned position on the issue. Mere *commitment* to play the role could, of course, induce some degree of attitude change (particularly if the subjects engage in implicit role playing in anticipation of executing the task); but actually carrying out the task of verbalizing new arguments in support of the objectionable position would elicit more biased scanning and increase the salience of new incentives, thus increasing the likelihood of attitude change—provided that no strong interfering responses are evoked by unfavorable sponsorship or by other unfavorable conditions. According to a dissonance-theory analysis by Brehm and Cohen (1962), the mere fact that a person commits himself to play any such role, before he executes it, "should be sufficient to produce the attitude-changing dissonance" (pp. 254–255). They cite evidence from a study in which no difference was found between two groups, one of which wrote essays in which the dissonant position was overtly verbalized while the other merely agreed to write the essays (Rabbie, Brehm, & Cohen, 1959).

2. Role playing will be more successful in inducing attitude changes, according to conflict theory, if the sponsor is perceived as someone whose affiliations are benign and whose intentions are public-spirited than if he is perceived as someone whose affiliations and purposes are commercial, exploitative, or immoral. The opposite prediction would be made by a dissonance-theory explanation of role-playing effects, which postulates that "dissonance [among cognitive elements] gives rise to pressures to reduce the dissonance and to avoid increases in dissonance" (Festinger, 1957,

p. 31). According to this theory, the crucial factor in role playing is that it creates dissonance between the person's private opinion and his awareness of what he is overtly saying and doing when he conforms with the sponsor's demands; "the changes in private opinion which ensue are the end result of a process of attempting to reduce or eliminate this dissonance" (Festinger, 1957, p. 112). The total magnitude of dissonance is assumed to decrease as the number and importance of the pressures and justifications which induce the person to say things he does not privately believe are increased (see Brehm & Cohen, 1962, pp. 252–255). Consequently, the prediction would be that more dissonance and therefore more attitude change will result from role playing if the sponsor is perceived as having objectionable affiliations or purposes than if he is perceived as having goals consonant with the subjects' own values—provided, of course, that the subjects can be induced to conform to his role-playing instructions.

For the purpose of testing the opposing predictions from conflict theory and from dissonance theory, two experiments were carried out (Janis & Gilmore, 1965; Elms & Janis, 1965). In both experiments we compared the effects of a positive sponsorship condition that was consonant with the subjects' values with a negative sponsorship condition that was relatively dissonant. We also included, as a matter of secondary interest, the effects of large vs. small monetary payments for the role-playing performance, taking account of the controversial evidence on this variable from the experiments by Festinger and Carlsmith (1959), Brehm and Cohen (1962), and Rosenberg (1965d). The third variable investigated was overt role playing vs. implicit role playing.

In order to include the third variable, we ran into a technical problem concerning the use of 'priming' questions as part of the overt role-playing procedure. During extensive pretesting, we noted that subjects had some difficulty in carrying out the role-playing task, which involved writing an essay as an advocate of a new policy with which they personally disagreed. We found it necessary to use some neutral 'priming' questions to get them thinking about what issues they might discuss. Without these neutral questions most of the essays were devoid of content and the overt role-playing variable we were trying to investigate obviously was not being successfully manipulated. Some brief checks indicated that these neutral questions alone had no effect on attitudes and hence we did not consider them as persuasive communications. We also tried out some priming questions with subjects in the non-overt role-playing condition (who were given the role-playing instructions and then, before carrying out the task, were given the attitude questionnaire). Here we ran into trouble because when the priming questions were combined with the role-playing instructions, we found that the subjects immediately began thinking up good arguments, even though we gave them no chance to write them down, and this threatened to make the differences between the overt and non-overt role-playing conditions so slight that this variable might not be well represented in the experiment. Accordingly, we arrived at the following compromise: In one of the experiments (Janis & Gilmore, 1965) we decided to avoid the risk of failing to manipulate the overt vs. covert role-playing variable by allowing the priming questions to be confounded with the overt role-playing condition and so we withheld the priming questions from the non-overt role players. (It should be noted here that dissonance theorists have argued that this confounding may have introduced a differential amount of new persuasive material and thus might account for the negative findings concerning dissonance theory predictions.) In the other experiment (Elms & Janis, 1965), we avoided the risks associated with differentially introducing the priming questions by giving the priming questions in exactly the same way in both the overt and non-overt conditions, at the risk of losing the opportunity to study the effects of overt vs. non-overt role playing.

For both experiments, a three dimensional factorial design was used in order to test the hypotheses about attitude change as a function of (a) unfavorable vs. favorable sponsorship of the role-playing task; (b) small vs. large monetary rewards (paid in advance, before carrying out the task); and (c) overt vs. non-overt role playing. The two experiments, however, used different topics and different instances of positive and negative sponsorship.

In the Janis and Gilmore experiment, the subjects wrote essays in favor of an unpopular educational policy (that of requiring all college undergraduates in the United States to have additional courses in mathematics and science). Less personal approval of the role-played position was found under Unfavorable Sponsorship conditions (E presenting himself as a representative of a commercial company that was hiring Ss to help prepare advertising copy to promote the sale of science textbooks) than under Favorable Sponsorship conditions (E presenting himself as a representative of a public welfare organization that was hiring Ss to help prepare for a nationwide educational survey). These findings tend to support conflict theory and contradict dissonance theory since they show that overt role playing was more effective when the sponsors' affiliations and goals were regarded by Ss as consonant with their own values than when they were regarded as being relatively dissonant. Additional findings from the same experiment showed that (a) under Favorable Sponsorship conditions, overt role playing (actually writing an essay in which S improvises arguments in favor of an opposed point of view) was more effective in inducing attitude change than non-overt role playing (merely agreeing to write such an essay without actually having the opportunity to do so); and (b) there were no significant differences between role players who were paid $20 in advance and those paid $1 in advance for writing the essays (although the maximum amount of attitude change occurred in the subgroup given the larger amount of money under Favorable Sponsorship conditions).

In the Elms and Janis experiment, college students were asked to invent arguments in favor of a counter-norm proposal, allegedly put forth by the Soviet Union, to allow American students to go to Russia for their entire four-year college education. In the Unfavorable Sponsorship condition, Ss were informed by the interviewer that the Soviet government had hired his firm to collect the materials needed to produce a pamphlet which representatives of the Soviet Union would distribute to all U.S. college campuses, presenting arguments in favor of the proposed program that would be appealing and convincing to American students. The Ss in the Favorable Sponsorship condition, after being given exactly the same background information, were told that the interviewer's firm had a contract with the U.S. State Department to carry out a survey of the attitudes of

American students toward the program; relevant arguments were now being collected as a first step toward preparing survey questions, which would ask students whether they agreed or disagreed.

Analysis of variance of attitude-change scores showed a significant triple interaction effect: a high degree of acceptance of the counter-norm proposal occurred only under conditions of *overt* role playing when *acceptable* justification and *large* rewards were given. The largest amount of attitude change thus occurred in the overt role-playing group that was exposed to the *least dissonant* condition, i.e., favorable sponsorship with large monetary reward.

The results from the two experiments are similar in that the findings from both indicate that when role-playing conditions are relatively consonant with the subjects' values, they show more attitude change than when the conditions are dissonant. In the Elms and Janis study the sponsorship variable alone was found to have a positive effect on the amount of attitude change among the overt role-playing groups, but this effect was subordinate to the interaction of favorable sponsorship with the large monetary reward. This outcome, although somewhat different from that of the other experiment, bears out the prediction that a large monetary reward will have a positive effect on attitude change only when the role-playing task is sponsored by an acceptable group and is oriented toward a goal perceived by S as being consonant with his own; but the same large reward will tend to create suspicion, guilt, or other interfering responses that make for less attitude change when the role-playing task is sponsored by a distrusted sponsor and is perceived as having a purpose antithetical to one's own values.

Although the findings from the two experiments just described support conflict theory rather than dissonance theory, there is in the literature a great deal of seemingly contradictory evidence from other role-playing experiments concerning the effects of large vs. small monetary inducements, which appear to support dissonance theory. Alternative explanations in terms of conflict theory have been suggested elsewhere (Elms & Janis, 1965; Elms, 1967) to account for the findings that appear to show dissonance effects (e.g., large payments may have unfavorable incentive effects when E is regarded by the subjects with suspicion after he asks them to lie to a fellow student). But this is a long story that requires detailed analysis of the incentive conditions employed in each relevant experiment. Suffice to say that relatively large monetary inducements evoke so many mixed reactions that this may be an unproductive type of incentive variable to continue investigating. As McGuire (1966a) puts it, research on this variable has burgeoned into a widespread "twenty-dollar misunderstanding."

Conflict theory, along with other theories of cognitive inconsistency, can be expected to add its two-cents worth to the twenty-dollar questions. Some of the important questions that need to be answered by analytic experiments pertain to the crucial conditions under which relatively strong inducements for role playing will have negative rather than positive effects on attitude change. One obvious prediction from conflict theory has already been alluded to: We would expect that when people are uncertain about the covert intentions of someone who is trying to induce them to advocate a new policy, their suspicion that they are being manipulated will be aroused and will interfere with their open-minded exploration of the cognitions that might lend support to the new policy. Under these conditions, a strong inducement—whether in the form of money, social pressure, or the threat of a penalty—would be relatively ineffective; whereas a milder inducement, which makes for more open-minded exploration of new considerations, could result in more gain from biased scanning and hence produce more attitude change.

There are also more subtle interacting factors suggested by a conflict-resolution model, some of which could be used to extend and modify the promising hypothesis put forth by McGuire (1966a) in an attempt to reconcile the conflict theory explanation of role-playing effects with the dissonance explanation. McGuire's hypothesis is that when role playing is actually carried out, the more reward the person is given for advocating a new point of view, the more adequate his performance will be and hence the greater the chances of self-persuasion; but when the person has merely committed himself to perform the role-playing task and has not yet executed it, his sense of commitment will be greater if he is given only a relatively small reward, which will incline him to justify himself by internalizing the new attitude position, as dissonance theory predicts.

One of the implications of this hypothesis is that whenever a person complies with a request to advocate a new attitude he does not personally accept, he will acquire a new incentive to accept that new attitude insofar as he has the *illusion* that he has committed himself voluntarily to comply with the request. It seems likely that this new incentive, which mainly involves anticipated social disapproval for subsequent reversal of the apparent commitment, would sometimes play a *determining* role, under certain very restricted conditions. One important condition specified by McGuire is that the committed role player has not yet been given the opportunity to carry out the role-playing performance. But even when the role-playing performance has already been carried out, the illusion of commitment to the new position could still play a determining role if certain other conditions were present, such as the following:

1. *Low interest in the issue:* If the decision, attitude, or judgment has little inherent interest to the person because it does not implicate any potential gains or losses that would make for ego involvement, the person is unlikely to think up any new relevant incentives no matter how conscientiously he tries to execute the role-playing task. Strong inducements to perform a role-playing task conscientiously can increase the degree of self-persuasion only when the role player can draw upon a cognitive repertoire to produce relevant arguments and appeals. There will be little or no self-persuasion when the role player is asked to advocate a counterattitudinal position on an issue for which he has only a meager cognitive repertoire, as is the case when he cannot see any ramifications related to his social values, his personal goals, or his previously acquired knowledge. For example, if the role player is instructed to tell others that it was enjoyable to work on a dull experimental task (that is now over and done with) he can easily comply by saying that he liked it, but he is likely to think up relatively few self-convincing arguments. Consequently, at the end of the role-playing session, the role player's personal balance sheet would not change very much from self-persuasion, whether or not he had been strongly motivated to try to think up good arguments. The main source of attitude change to be ex-

pected from this type of role playing would be that resulting from the new incentive added by the illusion of commitment, which requires a low pressure inducement.

The lower the subject's interest and ego involvement in the issue, the more likely that any attitude changes observed following a role-playing performance will be based on the illusion of commitment and not on the salience of self-persuading arguments. Thus an interaction effect would be predicted such that when initial interest in the attitude issue is low, small rewards and weak justifications will be relatively more effective than stronger inducements; whereas, when initial interest is high, large rewards and strong positive justifications will be relatively more effective than weaker inducements—provided, of course, that a significant amount of attitude change can be produced by the role-playing procedure (which must be unusually effective in order to overcome all the sources of resistance that make it difficult to change highly ego-involving attitudes).

2. *Low opportunity for genuine contemplation of the issue during the role-playing performance:* If the role-playing procedure is one that gives the person little time to think about the issue or introduces a source of distraction that prevents him from evaluating the arguments he is mouthing, no new incentives would be introduced into the person's internal balance sheet from self-persuasion. Under these restrictive conditions, the only way that a role-playing performance could give rise to attitude change would be by creating the illusion of commitment, which is fostered when the subject is offered very small rewards and weak justifications for complying. But we would expect strong inducements for performing conscientiously to be relatively more effective whenever the procedures allow the role player ample opportunity to draw upon his cognitive repertoire to think up good arguments in support of the counterattitudinal position he is advocating. Under these nonrestrictive conditions, biased scanning of self-persuading arguments can be a powerful impetus to attitude change, whether or not the subject acquires the illusory belief that he has publicly committed himself to the new position. Thus, here again an interaction effect is predicted: mild inducements will be more effective than strong ones when the role-playing task offers little opportunity for genuine contemplation of the issue; but strong positive inducements will be relatively more effective than mild ones when the task entails little distraction and allows the role players sufficient time to think up supporting arguments. The latter difference is especially likely to emerge when the role-playing performance does not involve public commitment (as when the role player is guaranteed anonymity or is assured that no one outside the research team will know what he said in his written essay or in his tape-recorded speech) since under these conditions there is little opportunity to develop an illusion of commitment.

The two hypotheses concerning variables that interact with large vs. small rewards could readily explain the apparent dissonance effects in the Festinger and Carlsmith (1959) experiment and in several others that used similar attitude issues of meager personal relevance for the subjects. They might also furnish an explanation for the double outcome in the Carlsmith, Collins, and Helmreich (1966) experiment, which showed that low payments were more effective than higher payments when subjects had to tell fellow students face-to-face that a dull experimental task was interesting, whereas the high payments were more effective than low payments when the subjects had to write anonymous essays (which probably gave them more opportunity to think up one or two arguments and created little social commitment).

In role-playing experiments that ask subjects to think up good arguments in the counterattitudinal direction on more interesting ego-involving issues, the gains from self-persuasion (fostered by large rewards and strong positive justifications) would tend to outweigh the gains from creating an illusion of commitment (fostered by small rewards and weak justifications). Thus, when students are asked to write essays on moderately ego-involving topics—such as whether American students should be permitted to go to the Soviet Union for their college education (Elms & Janis, 1965) or whether their victorious college football team should be prohibited from playing in the Rose Bowl game (Rosenberg, 1965d)—we would expect that strong positive inducements for writing good essays will lead to more attitude change than weak ones, just as the results of these experiments show.

Some additional experiments will obviously be necessary to see if the type of issue (ego-involving vs. non-ego-involving) and the type of role-playing procedure (low vs. high opportunity for thinking up effective new arguments) influence the outcome as interacting variables and thus make a crucial difference on the effects of weak vs. strong inducements. It will also be relevant to investigate similar interactions of these two variables with active participation (improvised role playing) vs. passive participation (merely reciting someone else's arguments) since the same explanatory hypotheses might also account for the apparent inconsistencies in experimental findings on this variable (Janis & King, 1954; Jansen & Stolurow, 1962; King & Janis, 1956; McGuire, 1966a; Zimbardo, 1965).

If the various interaction effects predicted from the conflict-theory analysis of counterattitudinal role playing are confirmed, we shall be able to conclude that attitude changes are fostered by strong inducements when the role-playing task allows opportunities for self-persuasion and that the dissonance outcome is limited to the special conditions where the only dominant incentive for attitude change is the illusion of voluntary commitment. But if the predicted interactions are not confirmed, the negative evidence will greatly reduce the presumption that conflict theory will account for all types of attitude change. In the meantime, considerable controversy is to be expected, especially since some of the experimental results already reported by dissonance theorists (e.g., Cohen's experiment described in Brehm & Cohen, 1962, pp. 73–78) remain quite recalcitrant both to the reconciliatory hypothesis offered by McGuire and the above elaborations of it based on the conflict model.

CHAPTER 83

The Mediation of Change Due to
Counterattitudinal Behavior

Barry E. Collins

University of California, Los Angeles

An overt response can be said to be a function of (a) certain factors intrinsic to the individual such as current drives, habits, and personal convictions, and (b) pressure from the environment. In the situations discussed here, where the response is an overt expression of an opinion, the overt expression is a function of (a) a 'latent attitude,' and (b) pressures in the environment which facilitate or inhibit overt utterance. The latent attitude or private opinion is only a hypothetical construct because it cannot be directly observed—although we may be willing to infer the existence of a certain latent attitude from an overt expression (e.g., a response to a paper and pencil attitude item) *if* we assume that environmental pressure had no impact on the overt response. In that case the overt expression would be entirely a function of the latent attitude.

A counterattitudinal response is a response made in the presence of environmental pressure which would not be made in the absence of external pressure. Counterattitudinal expression of an attitude has been demonstrated in the laboratory by applying pressure to produce a particular overt expression and then noting that another (inconsistent) overt expression is made whenever the pressure is removed (Kelman, 1953; McBride, 1954; Burdick, 1955).

Typically, a person makes a 'pretest' response (presumably) without external pressure, a 'counterattitudinal' or inconsistent response elicited by external pressures, and then a third response in the posttest—again (presumably) without external pressure. In some cases it has been observed that the third, or posttest, response differs from the first, or pretest, response such that the posttest has changed in the direction of the second, or counterattitudinal, response.

To the extent to which we are willing to infer latent attitudes from the pretest and posttest responses, this phenomenon constitutes a feedback loop from the overt counterattitudinal expression to the latent attitude. Although dominated by other factors, the latent attitude is one of the factors influencing the overt, counterattitudinal response. Then the process of eliciting the overt counterattitudinal response somehow feeds back to produce a modification of the latent attitude. The changed latent attitude then will, in turn, have a changed impact on future overt expressions (i.e., the posttest).

I want to take this opportunity to emphatically disavow something I am *not* saying. Some behaviorists talk about attitudinal responses as if there were an isomorphism between overt responses and private conviction. This position, perhaps attributable to a few remaining behaviorists, maintains that the attitude and the verbal expression of the attitude are one and the same thing. Such a position is patently untenable (it would imply a breed of George Washingtons who, literally, could not tell a lie); but I fear that it has been used as a naive oversimplification by overenthusiastic behavioristic evangelists and as a straw man by cognitive theorists. In the Festinger and Carlsmith (1959) experiment, for example, the subjects are paid to overtly *state* that the task is fun and interesting. They are not paid to *think* that the task is fun and interesting. In fact, the import of the instructions to the subjects are that they are to deliberately make an overt statement unrelated to their own attitudes. A reinforcement delivered for the overt statement (most behavior theorists would object to the use of the word 'reinforcement' or 'incentive' to describe money delivered *before* the response is emitted) might increase the net strength of the overt statement. But, without the assumption that the overt statement and the latent attitude are inexorably bound together, reinforcement theory does not predict that the latent attitude would be affected in any way. I personally suspect that many of the people who find that the dissonance prediction tested in the Festinger and Carlsmith experiment is counterintuitive fail to make the necessary distinction between the latent attitude and the overt, behavioral expression of the attitude. While it is true that, under some circumstances, the latent attitude may be inferred from the overt response, I will maintain a strong distinction between the two. In particular, not all posttest attitudinal responses are uninfluenced by external pressure; and an incentive for the overt expression is not necessarily an incentive for the latent attitude.

Most of the thinking and research in this general area has centered on the effect of large and small amounts of the environmental pressure which are used to evoke counterattitudinal behavior. Typically, psychologists have been willing to assume that a dissonance-reduction mechanism must account for the changed latent attitude if small pressure leads to the most change. Similarly, many of us have been willing to assume that a behavioristically influenced theory (such as that of Hovland, Janis, & Kelley, 1953) accounts for changes in the latent attitude when high pressure produces the most attitude change. Again I must demur. Since both the positive and the negative relationship can each be explained by several alternate mechanisms, the mere fact of a positive or negative relationship does not, by itself, give any compelling information about the specific mechanism which might have mediated the change.

MECHANISMS WHICH PRODUCE A NEGATIVE RELATIONSHIP

1. Dissonance reduction. The fact that greater attitude change is sometimes observed in low justification conditions is by far the strongest argument that dissonance reduction is (one of) the mediating mechanism(s) by which counterattitudinal behavior is internalized into private acceptance. Strong support for the dissonance interpretation would be provided by experiments which manipulate high and low justification and, *in addition*, some other variable which is theoretically a necessary prerequisite for dissonance production. One such experiment might be a simple 2×2 factorial in which there are two levels of justification or pressure for compliance and two levels of 'commitment.' Commitment might be manipulated by giving the subjects their choice whether to emit the counterattitudinal behavior vs. requiring them to perform the act as a part of a classroom or laboratory obligation. Commitment might also be manipulated by making some counterattitudinal behaviors conspicuously public and others anonymous. Dissonance theory predicts that low justification should produce more attitude change only when the *S* is committed to the counterattitudinal behavior. There should be no difference between the low and high justification conditions in the low commitment condition (or at least only an attenuated negative relationship in the event that the experimenter is not clever enough to eliminate all commitment). Although Aronson has argued that the crucial facet of the 'shotgun' manipulation in Carlsmith, Collins, and Helmreich (1966) is the greater amount of commitment in the face-to-face confrontation condition than in the anonymous essay condition, the Carlsmith *et al.* manipulation is multidimensional and is subject to many alternate interpretations. A successful experiment of this kind, using choice rather than commitment as the second variable, has been reported by Linder, Cooper, and Jones (1967).

While it is not strongly predicted by dissonance theory, the analogy between dissonance and drive is one possible place to look for evidence that dissonance mechanisms do mediate attitude change in studies which find a negative relationship. *If* dissonance is associated with a phenomenal or physiological tension and *if* this tension could be observed to increase following the dissonance manipulation and to decrease at a time when we infer that attitude change has occurred, then we would have evidence that dissonance reduction was at work.

2. Implicit labeling. A second mechanism which could produce a negative relationship between justification and attitude change is the implicit labeling mechanism discussed by Hovland, Janis, and Kelley (1953). This mechanism produces the internalization of the counterattitudinal behavior because the individual gets confused and ascribes the counterattitudinal statements to himself. Any number of factors might lead an individual to attribute counterattitudinal behavior to himself. The improvisation instructions in the Janis studies (Hovland, Janis, & Kelley, 1953; Janis & King, 1954; King & Janis, 1956), for instance, require the *S* to present the material in his own words—a procedure which could well blur the distinction between "what he made me do" and "what I did on my own." If we assume that an *S* paid only $1 is more likely to attribute aspects of his counterattitudinal advocacy to himself than an *S* paid $20, then the implicit labeling mechanism would produce more attitude change in the low justification condition. Some light might be shed on this question if experimenters in counterattitudinal advocacy asked such questions as "How much of the speech did you make up yourself?" or "How many of those ideas were ones you thought up yourself?"

It is difficult to design a manipulation which would facilitate implicit labeling without increasing dissonance (a fact which casts some doubt on the distinctiveness of the two mechanisms). Choice, the most obvious manipulation to blur the distinction between 'their' ideas and 'my' ideas, turns out to be the classical dissonance manipulation. More generally, *any* manipulation which leads the *S* to feel that "I, on my own initiative, said those inconsistent things" will, theoretically, lead to more dissonance.

3. *Overt expression as information about latent attitudes.* Rather than argue that an individual blurs the distinction between latent attitude and overt expression through implicit labeling, Bem (1965, 1967) has argued that the overt expression is the evidence from which an individual infers (or describes) his own latent attitudes. Since counterattitudinal behavior emitted with high choice or low justification is most useful for inferring the content of a latent attitude, Bem argues that the individual is more likely to internalize the implications of a counterattitudinal act under conditions of high choice or low incentive. He does provide evidence that people are more likely to infer the existence of a latent attitude consistent with the overt behavior of another person when the behavior was emitted for low incentive or high choice. If, as Bem argues, the individual uses his own behavior as a cue to the content of his own latent attitudes, then this process would predict a negative relationship between attitude change and pressure for compliance.

4. *Discombobulation.* Several investigators (Kelman, 1953; Janis & Gilmore, 1965), for instance, have suggested that high justifications or incentives create suspicion, hostility, interfering responses, or negative affects which so confuse and disrupt normal cognitive functioning that there is no opportunity for the counterattitudinal behavior to feed back to the implicit, private attitude.

Most of these criticisms have centered on the 'extraordinarily large reward' of $20 used in the Festinger and Carlsmith study, and Janis and Gilmore (1965) do report evidence of suspicion among their $20 subjects. But, since they do not find less attitude change in the $20 condition, we must be careful about generalizing the suspicion found in the study that did not find a difference to one that did. Furthermore, Janis and Gilmore's data fail to confirm the discombobulation theory; since they found suspicion in the $20 condition, the theory predicts less attitude change in that condition. In fact, there was no significant difference in attitude change between the $1 condition and the $20 condition.

Two experiments (Cohen in Brehm & Cohen, 1962; Carlsmith, Collins, & Helmreich, 1966) have found dissonance results with much smaller amounts of money than $20. While it is difficult to attribute discombobulation to the $1.50 *per se* in Carlsmith *et al.*, it is still possible that the magnitude of money could have interacted with the experimental conditions. The rationale for the face-to-face confrontation was appreciably more hectic and 'crisis-like' than the rationale for the essay condition, and the total amount of deception was also much higher. It is just possible that the larger amount of money, *combined with* the crisis atmosphere and higher deception could have inhibited such mechanisms as biased scanning and improvisation, mechanisms said to be crucial in self-persuasion.

5. *Counterattitudinal pressures on the posttest response.* Answers to the posttest constitute observable, overt behavior, and posttest responses are

no more *inevitably* a reflection of the latent attitude than the counterattitudinal behavior induced by the experimenter. Rosenberg (1965d) has suggested two possible pressures on the posttest response which might produce differences as a function of justifications for counterattitudinal behavior. The first is evaluation apprehension. Rosenberg argues that Ss are strongly motivated to achieve a positive evaluation from the scientist-psychologist, and that they develop hypothesis about how to win positive evaluation from the experimenter in the context of an experiment. He suggests that

> "in certain dissonance experiments the use of surprisingly large monetary rewards for eliciting counterattitudinal arguments ... may suggest [to the S] that he is being treated disingenuously .... He may be led to hypothesize that the experimental situation is one in which his autonomy, his honesty, his resoluteness in resisting a special kind of bribe, are being tested" (p. 29). The subject then tries to win the positive evaluation of the experimenter by indicating that his private attitudes remain unaltered by the counterattitudinal behavior Rosenberg also suggests a somewhat simpler mechanism in which the large amount of money makes the S angry at the experimenter because of the latter's perceptible manipulative intent, and the S "provoked to hostility ... may find emotional release in refusing to show the response (attitude change) that he perceives the experimenter to be after" (p. 30).

Rosenberg suggests that these artifacts can be removed by having the posttesting done by someone unconnected with the pressure for the original counterattitudinal behavior, and he reports a positive relationship for counterattitudinal essays when the posttester and E are different people. But since the posttester in the Carlsmith, Collins, and Helmreich study was clearly separated from the experimenter, and since the $1.50 was probably a reasonable amount of money in a context where the Ss were paid $2.50 for participating in the rest of the experiment, it might be difficult to argue that the dissonance effect of that particular study can be accounted for by the Rosenberg mechanisms. Although this makes it difficult to argue that all negative relationships are mediated by these mechanisms, it does not reduce the possibility that some negative relationships are mediated in this manner.

A mechanism closely related to those discussed by Rosenberg arises from the assumption that people tend to give a consistent social presentation. So long as the audience for the posttest is the same as the audience for the counterattitudinal behavior, the S may continue to play the assigned counterattitudinal role while responding to the posttest items. If we add the additional assumption (supported by Bem's data) that a reversion to the latent attitude would be more inconsistent if the counterattitudinal behavior were emitted with little justification or high choice, then we predict that there will be less reversion (i.e., more attitude change) in the low justification condition.

Some weak, post hoc support for the consistency mechanism is provided by Hornbeck (1967). Ss were asked to write essays to the effect that popular music is not as good as electronic music. Some did not sign their names and were assured that only the experimenter would see the essay; others were told that their essays would be posted on the school bulletin board. This public-private manipulation produced no significant effect when the posttest was administered by the experimenter. But public Ss, who wrote favorable essays, indicated more favorable attitudes toward electronic music when an 'independent' posttest was administered by the music teachers in the school (i.e., by someone who was in the potential 'audience' for the public essays but not the private essays).

MECHANISMS WHICH PRODUCE A POSITIVE RELATIONSHIP

For two of the mechanisms which might produce a positive relationship between justification and attitude change, it is assumed that the change in the latent attitude is mediated by differences in overt counterattitudinal behavior; i.e., higher justification produces more effort or higher quality in the counterattitudinal behavior and these behavioral differences feed back to and produce differences in the latent attitude.

1. Dissonance theory (effort). The dissonance formulation predicts that greater effort invested in counterattitudinal behavior produces more attitude change (e.g., Zimbardo, 1965). A dissonance mechanism which would produce more attitude change in the High Justification condition would be composed of two parts and both of these are testable: (a) the typical high-justification manipulation increases the amount of effort and (b) this greater effort investment in the counterattitudinal behavior produces more change in the latent attitude.

These effects of effort work in the opposite direction from other dissonance predictions, and this may be the reason why many studies in forced compliance done by dissonance theorists provide minimal opportunity for individual differences in the amount of effort expended. For example, the Festinger and Carlsmith procedure, in which the S transmits a relatively prescribed message in a short period of time, provides much less opportunity for individual differences in effort than the situation used by Janis, where Ss spoke from a prepared outline after being given time for preparation prior to delivery of the counterattitudinal speech. Scott's (1957, 1959) procedures provide even more room for differential effort since the Ss presumably conducted research to support their counterattitudinal speeches.

2. Biased scanning. Again the prediction is made in two parts: (a) high justification motivates the subject to engage in 'better' or more sincere biased scanning and (b) this better biased scanning is reflected in increased changes in the latent attitude.

The evidence for these behavior-mediated mechanisms is poor indeed. First, the preponderance of the evidence does not support the notion that the typical 'justification' manipulations have any *measureable* effect on the overt counterattitudinal behavior; and, secondly, when the justification manipulations do affect the overt behavior, the behavior differences seldom parallel changes in latent attitudes. Finally, the correlations between measures of the counterattitudinal behavior and attitude change reveal a confusing pattern.

Rosenberg (1965d) finds that there were more words written in the $1 condition than the $.50 condition, but there were no differences in *attitude* between these two conditions. Although there was greater attitude change in the $5 condition than the $1 condition, the essays in the $5 condition did not contain more words. However, Rosenberg does report that the most *persuasive* (as independently judged) essays were associated with the most attitude change, and the essays in the $5 condition were, on the average, more persuasive. Carlsmith, Collins, and Helmreich—after a detailed examination of both essays and transcripts of the face-to-face confrontation—were unable to find any evidence that counterattitudinal behaviors differ as a function of the justification manipulation; and there were no correlations between these measures of behavior and posttest attitude. Elms and Janis (1965) do find that $10 Ss wrote more words than the $.50 Ss in both the Favorable and Unfavorable Sponsorship conditions, but the High Justification subjects indicate more attitude change only in the Favorable Sponsorship condition. Janis and Gilmore (1965) also report higher quality essays in the $20 than in the $1 condition—but these results again fail to parallel the attitude change results.

A study by Collins and Helmreich (1966) casts further doubt on the generality of any simple mechanism which assumes that better, effortful, sincere, counterattitudinal behaviors are associated with greater changes in the latent attitude. Although the justification manipulation failed to produce any differences in either attitude change or quality of essay, both variables differed between two groups which had been given different instructions for writing their essays. While Ss given 'process' instructions evidenced the most attitude change, their essays were judged to be significantly inferior to essays written by Ss given 'consequence' instructions. Furthermore, while the correlation between quality and attitude change was positive in the process condition (+.85), it was negative (−.50) in the consequence condition. These results merely sample from a much longer list of studies which fail to find behavioral differences which parallel attitude change differences.

Janis has further elaborated the biased scanning position. He argues (Janis & Gilmore, 1965) that increased attitude change in the High Pressure condition "would not be expected . . . if resentment or other interfering affective reactions were aroused by negative incentives in the role playing situation" (p. 18). He suggests that lowering the prestige of the sponsor or giving signs of exploitive intentions on the part of the experimenter might produce such interfering negative affective reactions. Elms and Janis (1965) do find the predicted interaction. The differences among the $.50, $1.50, and $10 conditions are negligible for the negative sponsorship condition, but the attitude change means for the positive sponsorship condition are +0.9, −0.1, and +2.4. The change in the $10 condition is significantly different from the $.50 condition. While the (unpredicted) drop from $.50 to $1.50 is not statistically significant, it does extend over a full scalar point and is fully two-thirds of the significant (and predicted) increase from $.50 to $10. But, if the troublesome $1.50 condition is ignored, the Elms and Janis experiment illustrates the way in which a third variable can be used to gain insight into the mechanisms which mediate both positive and negative relationships between justification and attitude change.

3. *Extraneous reinforcement.* A third mechanism which would predict a positive relationship between attitude change and justifications is a theory based on 'extraneous' reinforcement. Such a theory would hold that any response which is being made just prior to the administration of a 'reward' will gain in strength. Very few of the studies on counterattitudinal behavior administer the justification manipulation immediately following the counterattitudinal behavior. Even if they did, we would be left with the

problem of how an increase in strength of the overt, counterattitudinal behavior is converted into a change of the latent attitude.

Several studies indicate empirical operations of extraneous reinforcements in studies of attitude change (Razran, 1940; Janis, Kaye, & Kirschner, 1965; Dabbs & Janis, 1965; Rosnow & Russell, 1963; Rosnow, 1965; Corrozi & Rosnow, 1968). Rosnow (1966) reports both proactive and retroactive effects of both reward and punishment in a role-playing study. The demonstration of the proactive impact of reinforcement is particularly important because (a) most reinforcement theories predict that reinforcements affect prior rather than subsequent behaviors and (b) the 'justification' or 'reinforcement' effects in most studies of counterattitudinal behavior are forward acting or proactive.

Whatever the empirical validity of extraneous reinforcements the theoretical mechanism remains unspecified. For instance, what leads the individual to make implicit counterattitudinal responses in the first place? The justifications force compliance only on the overt response. Since a response must occur before it can be reinforced, we need a mechanism by which the pressure for compliance produces implicit, attitude-like responses, in addition to the required overt response. Secondly, why should the extraneous reinforcement not strengthen the previously dominant implicit responses associated with the latent attitude rather than the counterattitudinal implicit response? These questions should serve to illustrate that learning theory formulations must be further developed before they can predict a change in the *latent* attitude when reinforcements are delivered for the overt counterattitudinal behavior.

4. Differential demand characteristics. A fourth, and also unelaborated, mechanism which would produce more attitude change with high justification begins with the assumption that the justifications or incentives motivate the S to please the experimenter. If we also assume that the S thinks the experimenter would be pleased by a change in the S's attitude ("why else would he ask me to say or write these counterattitudinal things?"), then high justifications would act to produce more attitude change. This theory has the unique feature that the counterattitudinal behavior is, itself, irrelevant to the attitude change mechanism. The *request* for counterattitudinal behavior serves only to drop the subtle hint that the experimenter would like to see the S change his attitude. Any other method, such as an 'inadvertently' dropped comment, would define the demand characteristics of the experiment; so according to this explanation, greater attitude change would be observed in the High Justification condition without any counterattitudinal behavior at all!

CHAPTER 84

Discussion: On Reducing the Inconsistency Between Consistency Theories

Milton J. Rosenberg

In my introduction to this section I spoke of the debate between dissonance theory and other forms of consistency analysis as having "entered an advanced phase."

The three foregoing chapters are illustrative of the transformed situation. A limited area of agreement has now developed and it is clear that, more than anything else, it has been achieved through a partial narrowing of the claims of the dissonance school. This has not been a yielding to the arguments and exhortations of critics. Instead, the leading members of the dissonance group (excepting Festinger who lately has turned to quite different research interests) seem to be responding to some recent experimental studies showing that counterattitudinal advocacy does not always lead to greater attitude change when it is undertaken for weaker justification.

Carlsmith's chapter is clearly illustrative of this trend. He is by no means ready to drown the dissonance baby in the bath of dissonance-disconfirming data. (The same could be said of Aronson [1966c and Chapter 1] and other dissonance theorists.) Instead, he is engaged in revising the theory, restating his conception of the conditions necessary for the generation of greater attitude change through lesser justification for counterattitudinal behavior.

Essentially, Janis is attempting to do the same though he is focusing upon the complementary question: Under what conditions will greater justification for counterattitudinal behavior lead to greater attitude change? Collins accepts the reality of both forms of relationship and offers some exciting speculations about the various types of mediation that might account for each of them. Predictably (since, as dissonance theory itself suggests, prior commitment tends to affect evaluative processes) the amount of residual enthusiasm for the dissonance approach is distributed in a descending order from Carlsmith to Collins to Janis.

In these comments I shall focus upon what I take to be their most important convergences and contrasts and the theoretical interpretations with which these are approached.

Both Janis and Carlsmith seem to be sensitive to the distinction between simple and complex forms of counterattitudinal behavior. By implication

Janis seems willing to concede that the direct concrete assertion of an attitude opposite to one's own, or the assertion of a willingness to argue against one's own attitude, is likely to lead to attitude change in inverse proportion to the degree of justification for the counterattitudinal behavior. But for him, the relevant and more interesting case is that in which the person undertakes true counterattitudinal advocacy: i.e., develops and articulates new arguments, new percepts, in support of the counterattitudinal position.

Drawing upon his own studies on role playing, and also upon studies by Rosenberg (1965d) and Carlsmith, Collins, and Helmreich (1966), he concludes, as he did earlier (Janis & Gilmore, 1965), that where there is more favorable or more positive justification for counterattitudinal advocacy, greater attitude change will be likely to result. This he interprets as due to a mediating process in which high justification produces more biased scanning than low, and also fosters more self-persuasive elaboration and rehearsal of positive and negative incentives.[1]

While (like Collins) Carlsmith is more doubtful than Janis that High Justification conditions actually have been shown to produce more persuasive counterattitudinal advocacy (i.e., more effective biased scanning) he is, nevertheless, willing to concede that high justification for the counterattitudinal performance will often lead to greater attitude change than under Low Justification conditions. But for Carlsmith, demonstrations of this sort of relationship (as in the studies by Janis & Gilmore, 1965; Elms & Janis, 1965; Rosenberg, 1965d; Carlsmith, Collins, & Helmreich, 1966) are not truly in conflict with dissonance theory. They are obtained only in situations that elicit counterattitudinal behavior in a general 'low dissonance' context.

In the development of this point Carlsmith specifies three separate conditions at least one of which must be met if counterattitudinal behavior is to actually arouse a state of dissonance. The first of these is "commitment," in the sense that the subject believes that those to whom he is addressing his counterattitudinal assertion or advocacy perceive him as believing what he is saying; i.e., they do not know "his (true) motivation in making that statement." In the second basic dissonance arousing condition, commitment of this sort is absent but no "intellectually acceptable reason" (one assumes that Carlsmith means ethically acceptable, as well) is visible to the observer to account for the subject's performing an act that the observer knows to be counterattitudinal. The last dissonance-generating condition is, simply, that the counterattitudinal behavior is an "unpleasant" one.

Any attempt to delimit the range of phenomena or situations to which dissonance analysis might apply should be welcomed. A main problem with dissonance theory till now, at least as seen by such critics as Brown (1965) and Chapanis and Chapanis (1964) has been the absence of such criteria. But do the limits suggested by Carlsmith order the presently available data? Do the studies in which the dissonance relationship has been obtained meet

---

[1] This view is closely parallel to one that I have presented (Rosenberg, 1965d, 1966) in the alternative language of my own affective-cognitive consistency model. I note the similarity here as a way of alerting the reader to the preferences that inform some of these comments; true judicial impartiality may be possible in the courtroom, but in volumes such as this the commentator almost inevitably is an erstwhile advocate and his commentary ought to be 'scanned' with a concern for the influence of *his* 'bias.'

any one or more of the three conditions that are supposed to be necessary for the generation of dissonance; do the studies in which the incentive relationship has been obtained not meet any of these conditions?

The subjects in Cohen's well-known albeit sketchily reported counter-attitudinal essay experiment (in Brehm & Cohen, 1962) were not 'committed' (in the special sense in which Carlsmith uses that term). They had some justification other than the promised financial reward (i.e., they were helping a legitimate agency that was conducting an attitude survey) and there is no reason to think that the writing of the brief essay was painful to them. Thus they would appear to have been in the sort of 'low dissonance' situation in which Carlsmith would have to predict an incentive effect, with the highly paid subjects showing more change than the poorly paid subjects. Nevertheless, a dissonance type of effect was obtained.[2]

In the Janis and Gilmore experiment the subjects who wrote counter-attitudinal essays under the Unfavorable Sponsorship condition would seem to have met Carlsmith's second specification for dissonance arousal; that is, there was no intellectually or ethically acceptable reason for this counter-attitudinal behavior—the regnant motive was the subjects' interest in receiving the promised monetary payment. Thus a dissonance relationship should have been observed with the poorly paid subjects showing greater attitude change than the well-paid subjects. In fact, no significant difference was obtained between these two groups though the trend is in the incentive rather than dissonance direction.

In a recent and previously unreported study that I conducted all subjects were 'committed' in the specific sense that after their participation in a dull experimental task they attempted to persuade the 'next subject' that the task was, in fact, an interesting and enjoyable one. With such commitment present, subjects were paid either $.50 or $2.50 for a counterattitudinal advocacy performance which was restricted to either 1½ or 6 minutes of performance time. Between the Low and High Justification cells in the 6-minute treatment an incentive effect is obtained on the postmeasures asking how pleasant and how interesting they found the original dull task. These and related data are treated in greater detail in Chapter 4. Suffice it to say here that they seem to call into question Carlsmith's prediction that counter-attitudinal advocacy undertaken with commitment (and thus in a dissonance-generating context) will necessarily produce that inverse relationship between justification and change that is predicted by dissonance theory.

In another recent study Collins set up 'committed' and 'uncommitted' groups.[3] According to his account the former "were told not to sign their essay and were instructed to mail it in an envelope to Dr. Collins, who will

---

[2] However, as I have suggested elsewhere (Rosenberg, 1965d), these findings may have been due to an unsuspected evaluation apprehension process. My own altered replication of this study, designed to remove the suspected systematic bias, yielded a significant incentive relationship. More recently Linder, Cooper, and Jones (1967) have reported a study on the basis of which they reject my reinterpretation of the Cohen study. But the crucial portion of their study involves a manipulation that seems likely to have given the subjects the impression that the counterattitudinal advocacy task was an illegitimate one which the experimenter could not endorse. This may well have induced one of the types of interference with counterattitudinal self-persuasion posited by Janis; i.e., introjection of the content of one's biased scanning would be impeded if the task of counter-attitudinal advocacy is initially devalued.

[3] Private communication to the author; May, 1967.

not know who you are!" The latter "signed their essays and were told that they would be shown to personal friends scheduled later on in the experiment." According to Collins' summary: "While there is some evidence of higher order interactions, there are no dissonance effects, and there is a positive relationship between incentive and attitude change in nearly every condition."

Studies such as these should be taken as having at least cautionary, if not definitive, bearing upon the problem. The complexity of counterattitudinal research designs and the related possibility of setting off unsuspected and unplanned mediating processes (a problem that Collins delineates with devastating clarity) require that Carlsmith's hypotheses not be hastily put aside. Certainly it does seem quite possible that though the incentive relationship may occur even under the conditions that are supposed to foster a dissonance relationship, it will be found to be a more reliable and common outcome when these conditions are absent. At any rate the question is eminently researchable and should be subjected to closer experimental scrutiny now that it has been raised in this useful form.

However, even if Carlsmith's predictions were proved basically right, one cannot simply relegate to a wastebasket residual category those experiments and phenomena in which, in the absence of his three specific conditions, the incentive relationship prevails. A person who improvises and elaborates a set of counterattitudinal arguments without representing them to another as his true beliefs, and who does this for reasons acceptable to himself and without any accompanying experience of psychic pain is, as Carlsmith himself admits (p. 803), still subject to dissonance, albeit in a presumed less important form. Thus Carlsmith is required to explain the case in which such self-generated inconsistency produces attitude change in direct, rather than inverse, relation to the strength of the incentive by which advocacy was elicited. To do this he invokes a rather elaborate speculation. He asserts that the counterattitudinal arguments produced by subjects are really equally good under low and high reward, but that the highly rewarded subjects think their arguments better because otherwise they would not have been paid so much for them. Thinking the arguments better, they therefore change attitudes more, thus handling the 'argumental dissonance.'

It is heartening to see dissonance theorists grappling valiantly at last with certain phenomena of self-persuasion that they have heretofore neglected; for the burden of the available data certainly does seem to be that true counterattitudinal advocacy (when, as Janis posits, it is undertaken in a situation that allows the person to think up, elaborate, and attend to new arguments) produces more attitude change when it is elicited by stronger rather than weaker incentives. However, Carlsmith's interpretation of this sort of "incentive effect," though it has the virtue of fitting the effect back into the narrow and classic version of dissonance theory, has the disadvantage of turning attention away from a set of findings that enable a more parsimonious account of the mediating process. I have in mind the finding as in my own studies (Rosenberg, 1965d; Chapter 4) that persons paid more for counterattitudinal advocacy produce better, more persuasive arguments—and sometimes a larger number of arguments as well.

Data of this sort suggest that a non-dissonance interpretation (whether in terms of the Janis conflict theory, my own affective-cognitive consistency model, or other balance theory formulations) is, in fact, more parsimonious

—at least for the case in which true counterattitudinal advocacy is undertaken for stronger rather than weaker incentives.[4] It is on these grounds that I would judge Carlsmith's treatment of counterattitudinal advocacy as not fully persuasive: endeavoring to explain *everything* by dissonance-reduction, invoking form *B* where form *A* fails, is an unsatisfactory epicyclic way to try to achieve theoretical parsimony.

What may be required instead is a further restriction of the dissonance view of attitude change. Carlsmith, Aronson, and others, in their commendable attempts to reduce their theory's ambiguity while conserving its unique and compelling insights, have not yet taken a step that seems increasingly to be required. This would be to recognize that dissonance itself ought to be redefined as the sort of particular cognitive dilemma that occurs when a direct and limited (which is not to say unimportant) counterattitudinal (or counterexpectational) act has been committed for comparatively insufficient reasons. This would rule out the other kind of cognitive dilemma upon which dissonance theory has tended to flounder; i.e., that due to the generation of inconsistency (whether by oneself as in counterattitudinal advocacy or by others as in persuasive communication) within the structured affective-cognitive content of an attitude.

The results of such a redefinition would probably be salutary in many directions. It would, I think, reinvigorate the study, from the dissonance point of view, of the intricate and fascinating effects that follow from the elicitation of inauthentic acts, whether they be attitudinal assertions, poorly motivated choices, or lapses from moral standards. At the same time it would facilitate the study of the more complex, cognitively oriented types of persuasion at an analytic level more appropriate to such phenomena. The pertinent approaches for that level I take to be the various other consistency theories, the expanded version of the Yale school sort of conflict analysis that Janis has developed, as well as the functionalist approach (Smith, Bruner, & White, 1956; Katz, 1960; Katz, Sarnoff, & McClintock, 1956).

A basic and exciting problem that lies in the way is to disentangle, in each type of counterattitudinal performance, the pseudo instances from the real ones. Surely there are occasions, or experiments, in which the ostensible commission of the simple counterattitudinal act is accompanied by the private development and rehearsal of justificatory counterattitudinal cognitions. These may account for many of the instances in which the basic dissonance prediction fails though we have reason to expect its confirmation. Similarly there are likely to be occasions, or experiments, in which, despite some ostensible show of counterattitudinal advocacy, the person is in fact

---

[4] As I noted earlier Carlsmith is, of course, aware of this possibility; but he is able to reject it on the ground that in such studies as his own (Carlsmith, Collins, and Helmreich, 1966) subsidiary content analysis did not show more or better argumentation for higher than for lower rewards. However, my own studies in this realm (Rosenberg, 1965d; Chapter 4) *have* disclosed such a relationship. I would suggest that whether this relationship is or is not observed often depends upon the precision and detail of the blind coding techniques that are employed. In passing it should also be noted that by reducing the intertheory difference to the question of whether high reward subjects produce discernibly better counterattitudinal arguments, Carlsmith tends to slight some subtler aspects of the non-dissonance approaches. Thus, high reward can also lead to greater rehersal of, and greater attention to, one's own counterattitudinal arguments; and these latter mediating considerations are also more easily encompassed by the conflict or affective-cognitive consistency theories than by the dissonance approach.

engaging in what he himself would classify as merely a limited, non-elaborated assertion of the counterattitudinal position. Or, though going through the motions of counterattitudinal advocacy, he may be well insulated against having to take any of his own counterattitudinal arguments seriously. Under such circumstances, it would be the *fact* that he has argued counterattitudinally rather than the *content* of his arguments that is producing a motivating inconsistency; and this may account for most of the instances in which the incentive or affective-cognitive prediction (of positive relationship between degree of change and justification) will fail where we have reason to expect its confirmation.

In connection with this last point I would like to enter a strong endorsement of a basic distinction drawn by Janis; namely, that between the kinds of psychological situations in which counterattitudinal advocacy does and does not lead to "appraising the recalled and improvised arguments with a psychological set that fosters open-minded cognitive exploration of their potential incentive value."

Any theory that attempts to comprehend the process of self-persuasion through counterattitudinal advocacy (or, for that matter, any other type of cognitively oriented persuasion) must take realistic note of the fact that individuals are ordinarily motivated to conserve and defend their attitudes against change. However, certain specifiable conditions will determine whether or not this motivational barrier will be circumvented. Janis has suggested two of these: The first is comparatively strong inducement when there is high ego-involvement in the issue. High inherent interest in the attitude topic will facilitate the person being able to "think up ... new relevant incentives," but will produce a greater tendency to reject out of hand any of the counterattitudinal arguments that one has developed. Under these conditions, strong justifications and other positive inducements to carry out the role-playing task conscientiously will be needed to augment the facilitation of attitude change.

The second facilitating condition that Janis suggests is that there be sufficient "opportunity for genuine contemplation of the issue during role-playing performance." With this I would fully agree, though I would add that we do not yet have a thorough list of the particular variables which foster such contemplation in a way that both generates new arguments and facilitates their introjection. Certainly the variables Janis suggests (adequate time for counterattitudinal thinking, absence of distraction) are relevant. But many others are also conceivable. As I have suggested elsewhere (Rosenberg, 1966), one of these may be the kind of task set with which counterattitudinal advocacy is undertaken. Where the advocate defines his task as to deceive another, he is not likely to be as open to positive evaluation of the quality of his own counterattitudinal arguments as when he defines his task as 'exploring the other side of the issue' or as 'giving the opposite view a fair and objective examination.' Where he is set to 'persuade' another person through counterattitudinal advocacy the outcome for his own private attitude may well depend on whether he is led to code his task as 'deception' or as 'rational exploration.'

Incidentally, these last comments can lead us a little closer toward understanding the meaning of a fact that I have already alluded to; namely, that just as certain types of ostensibly simple counterattitudinal action undertaken for low and high justification do not confirm the dissonance prediction, certain types of counterattitudinal advocacy do not confirm the incentive prediction. The latter case can now be more clearly comprehended as one in which there is an absence of those supporting variables that lead the person into actually considering the import and value of the arguments that he has developed. With Janis I would agree that under these special circumstances low justification may lead to greater attitude change because it does generate a greater need to rationalize the commitment to the counterattitudinal position than when high justification has been provided.

This problem is illustrative also of a more general failing in the research and theorizing that have so far been focused upon the effects of counterattitudinal performance. Workers in this field have been far too ready to trust their manipulative operations and to depend upon the construct validity strategy. In fact, we often have reason to doubt that we are creating the states of motivation, the perceptual and conflictual contents that our research designs require. Still more disturbing and troublesome is the usual absence of an operationalized (as opposed to a merely speculative) inquiry into the mediational processes that intervene between the experimental manipulations and the subjects' final attitudinal responses.

Collins, to whose valuable contribution I have not given sufficient attention, has outlined a number of plausible mediational sequences through which both the dissonance and incentive relationships might be generated. Empirical penetration to that deeper level is long overdue. Many techniques are available or conceivable that could be added to almost any experiment in counterattitudinal performance and that would thereby deepen our understanding of what is happening inside our subjects before, during, and after their engagement in simple counterattitudinal action or complex counterattitudinal advocacy.

Among these techniques are more extensive employment of post-experimental inquiry and the "sacrifice design" advocated by Rosenthal (1966) in which subjects are interrupted at crucial junctures in the experimental scenario and interviewed about their present perceptual interpretations of the experimental task and of the experimenter's intentions. Bem's (1967) strategy for role-played replications of reported experiments could also be usefully adapted to the task of illuminating the mediational level of counterattitudinal effects.

At the same time, a great deal more could be accomplished by new manipulative experiments which attempt to produce systematic variation in conditions that have been hypothesized as fostering either the incentive or dissonance outcomes of counterattitudinal performance.

While many important questions remain unresolved, this section makes clear that the research accumulation in this area has grown rich enough to have facilitated entry into a postimperial phase in which once opposed theories are now approaching some sort of conciliation—even if that can be achieved only through rational 'division of the spoils.' How well this division will work in facilitating the development of a general theory of consistency dynamics in attitude change should be clear in a few more years, if research of these problems continues at its current pace and level of competitive vigor.

BIBLIOGRAPHY

ABEL, L. Is there a tragic sense of life? *Commentary*, 1964 (December), 35–40.

ABELSON, R. P. Modes of resolution of belief dilemmas. *Journal of Conflict Resolution*, 1959, *3*, 343–352.

ABELSON, R. P. Computer simulation of "hot" cognition. In S. S. Tomkins & S. Messick (Eds.), *Computer simulation of personality*. New York: Wiley, 1963. Pp. 277–298.

ABELSON, R. P. Computerizing public opinion: Predicting the unpredictable. Paper presented at the convention of the American Psychological Association, Washington, D.C., September, 1967. (a)

ABELSON, R. P. Mathematical models in social psychology. In L. Berkowitz (Ed.), *Advances in experimental social psychology*, Vol. 3. New York: Academic Press, 1967. Pp. 1–54. (b)

ABELSON, R. P. Computer simulation of social behavior. In G. Lindzey & E. Aronson (Eds.), *Handbook of social psychology*. Reading, Massachusetts: Addison-Wesley, 1968.

ABELSON, R. P. & CARROLL, J. D. Computer simulation of individual belief systems. *American Behavioral Scientist*, 1965, *8*, 24–30.

ABELSON, R. P. & KANOUSE, D. E. Subjective acceptance of verbal generalization. In S. Feldman (Ed.), *Cognitive consistency*. New York: Academic Press, 1966. Pp. 171–197.

ABELSON, R. P. & ROSENBERG, M. J. Symbolic psycho-logic: A model of attitudinal cognition. *Behavioral Science*, 1958, *3*, 1–13.

ADAMS, E. W. & FAGOT, R. F. A model of riskless choice. *Behavioral Science*, 1959, *4*, 1–10.

ADAMS, J. S. Reduction of cognitive dissonance by seeking consonant information. *Journal of Abnormal and Social Psychology*, 1961, *62*, 74–78.

ADAMS, J. S. Toward an understanding of inequity. *Journal of Abnormal and Social Psychology*, 1963, *67*, 422–436.

ADAMS, J. S. Inequity in social exchange. In L. Berkowitz (Ed.), *Advances in experimental social psychology*, Vol. 2. New York: Academic Press, 1965. Pp. 267–300.

ADAMS, J. S. & JACOBSEN, P. R. Effects of wage inequities on work quality. *Journal of Abnormal and Social Psychology*, 1964, *69*, 19–25.

ADAMS, J. S. & ROSENBAUM, W. B. The relationship of worker productivity to cognitive dissonance. *Journal of Applied Psychology*, 1962, *46*, 161–164.

ADORNO, T. W., FRENKEL-BRUNSWICK, E., LEVINSON, D. J., & SANFORD, R. N. *The authoritarian personality*. New York: Harper & Row, 1950.

AGARIE, N. Effects of verbal contexts on meaning. Unpublished doctoral dissertation. Yale University, 1961.

ALLEN, V. Uncertainty of outcome and postdecision dissonance reduction. In L. Festinger (Ed.), *Conflict, decision, and dissonance*. Stanford: Stanford University Press, 1964. Pp. 34–42.

ALLPORT, F. H. *Social psychology*. New York: Houghton Mifflin, 1924.

ALLPORT, F. H. The contemporary appraisal of an old problem. *Contemporary Psychology*, 1961, *6*, 195–196.

ALLPORT, G. W. *Personality: A psychological interpretation*. New York: Holt, 1937.

ALLPORT, G. W. The historical background of modern social psychology. In G. Lindzey (Ed.), *Handbook of social psychology*. Cambridge, Massachusetts: Addison-Wesley, 1954.

ALLPORT, G. W. Attitudes. In C. M. Murchison (Ed.), *Handbook of social psychology*. Worcester, Massachusetts: Clark University Press, 1955. Pp. 798–844.

ALLPORT, G. W. The open system in personality theory. *Journal of Abnormal and Social Psychology*, 1960, *61*, 301–310.

ALLPORT, G. W. *Pattern and growth in personality*. New York: Holt, Rinehart & Winston, 1961.

AMSEL, A. & ROUSSEL, J. Motivational properties of frustration: I. Effects on a running response of the addition of frustration to the motivational complex. *Journal of Experimental Psychology*, 1952, *43*, 363–368.

AMSTER, H. & GLASMAN, L. D. Verbal repetition and connotative change. *Journal of Experimental Psychology*, 1966, *71*, 389–395.

ANDERSON, L. R. & FISHBEIN, M. Prediction of attitude from the number, strength, and evaluative aspect of beliefs about the attitude object: A comparison of summation and congruity theories. *Journal of Personality and Social Psychology*, 1965, *2*, 437–443.

ANDERSON, N. H. Test of a model for opinion change. *Journal of Abnormal and Social Psychology*, 1959, *59*, 371–381.

ANDERSON, N. H. Two learning models for responses measured on a continuous scale. *Psychometrika*, 1961, *26*, 391–404.

ANDERSON, N. H. Application of an additive model to impression formation. *Science*, 1962, *138*, 817–818. (a)

ANDERSON, N. H. Application of an additive model to impression formation. Paper presented at a meeting of the Psychonomic Society, St. Louis, 1962. (b)

ANDERSON, N. H. On the quantification of Miller's conflict theory. *Psychological Review*, 1962, *69*, 400–414. (c)

ANDERSON, N. H. Linear models for responses measured on a continuous scale. *Journal of Mathematical Psychology*, 1964, *1*, 121–142. (a)

ANDERSON, N. H. Note on weighted sum and linear operator models. *Psychonomic Science*, 1964, *1*, 189–190. (b)

ANDERSON, N. H. Test of a model for number-averaging behavior. *Psychonomic Science*, 1964, *1*, 191–192. (c)

ANDERSON, N. H. Averaging versus adding as a stimulus-combination rule in impression formation. *Journal of Experimental Psychology*, 1965, *70*, 394–400. (a)

ANDERSON, N. H. Primacy effects in personality impression formation using a generalized order effect paradigm. *Journal of Personality and Social Psychology*, 1965, *2*, 1–9. (b)

ANDERSON, N. H. Component ratings in impression formation. *Psychonomic Science*, 1966, *6*, 279–280.

ANDERSON, N. H. Application of a weighted average model to a psychophysical averaging task. *Psychonomic Science*, 1967, *8*, 227–228. (a)

ANDERSON, N. H. Averaging model analysis of set size effect in impression formation. *Journal of Experimental Psychology*, 1967, *75*, 158–165. (b)

ANDERSON, N. H. Averaging of space and number stimuli with simultaneous presentation. *Journal of Experimental Psychology*, 1968, in press. (a)

ANDERSON, N. H. Likableness ratings of 555 personality-trait adjectives. *Journal of Personality and Social Psychology*, 1968, in press. (b)

ANDERSON, N. H. & BARRIOS, A. A. Primacy effects in personality impression formation. *Journal of Abnormal and Social Psychology*, 1961, *63*, 346–350.

ANDERSON, N. H. & HOVLAND, C. I. The representation of order effects in communication research. In C. I. Hovland (Ed.), *The order of presentation in persuasion*. New Haven: Yale University Press, 1957. Pp. 158–169.

ANDERSON, N. H. & HUBERT, S. Effects of concomitant verbal recall on effects in personality impression formation. *Journal of Verbal Learning and Verbal Behavior*, 1963, *2*, 379–391.

ANDERSON, N. H. & JACOBSON, A. Effect of stimulus inconsistency and discounting instructions in personality impression formation. *Journal of Personality and Social Psychology*, 1965, *2*, 531–539.

ANDERSON, N. H. & LAMPEL, A. K. Effect of context on ratings of personality traits. *Psychonomic Science*, 1965, *3*, 433–434.

ANDERSON, N. H. & NORMAN, A. Order effects in impression formation in four classes of stimuli. *Journal of Abnormal and Social Psychology*, 1964, *69*, 467–471.

ANDREW, R. J. The origin and evolution of the calls and facial expressions of the primates. *Behaviour*, 1963, *20*, 1–109.

ANGYAL, A. *Foundations for a science of personality*. New York: The Commonwealth Fund, 1941.

ANOKHIN, P. K. *Vnutrenne tormozhenie kak problema fiziologii*. (Internal inhibition as a physiological problem.) Moscow: Medgiz, 1958.

ANSCOMBE, G. E. M. *Intention*. Oxford, England: Blackwells, 1957. (Republished: Ithaca, New York: Cornell University Press, 1963.)

ARNOLD, M. B. *Emotion and personality*. New York: Columbia University Press, 1960.

ARONSON, E. The cognitive and behavioral consequences of the confirmation and discon-firmation of expectancies. Unpublished manuscript. Harvard University, 1960.

ARONSON, E. The effect of effort on the attractiveness of rewarded and unrewarded stimuli. *Journal of Abnormal and Social Psychology*, 1961, *63*, 375–380.

ARONSON, E. Avoidance of inter-subject communication. *Psychological Reports*, 1966, *19*, 238. (a)

ARONSON, E. Problem: To find evidence of discomfort as a function of "dissonant" suc-cess. In *Methodological problems of social psychology* for the XVIII International Congress of Psychology, 34th Symposium, Moscow, August, 1966. (b)

ARONSON, E. The psychology of insufficient justification: An analysis of some conflicting data. In S. Feldman (Ed.), *Cognitive consistency: Motivational antecedents and be-havioral consequences*. New York: Academic Press, 1966. Pp. 109–133. (c)

ARONSON, E. & CARLSMITH, J. M. Performance expectancy as a determinant of actual per-formance. *Journal of Abnormal and Social Psychology*, 1962, *65*, 178–182.

ARONSON, E. & CARLSMITH, J. M. Effect of the severity of threat on the valuation of for-bidden behavior. *Journal of Abnormal and Social Psychology*, 1963, *66*, 584–588.

ARONSON, E. & CARLSMITH, J. M. Experimentation in social psychology. In G. Lindzey & E. Aronson (Eds.), *Handbook of social psychology*. (Rev. ed.) Reading, Massa-chusetts: Addison-Wesley, 1968, in press.

ARONSON, E., CARLSMITH, J. M., & DARLEY, J. M. The effects of expectancy on volunteer-ing for an unpleasant experience. *Journal of Abnormal and Social Psychology*, 1963, *66*, 220–224.

ARONSON, E. & FESTINGER, L. Some attempts to measure tolerance for dissonance. USAF WADC Technical Report, 1958, No. 58-942.

ARONSON, E. & GERARD, E. Beyond Parkinson's law. *Journal of Personality and Social Psychology*, 1966, *3*, 336–339.

ARONSON, E. & LINDER, D. Gain and loss of esteem as determinants of interpersonal at-tractiveness. *Journal of Experimental Social Psychology*, 1965, *1*, 156–171.

ARONSON, E. & MILLS, J. The effect of severity of initiation on liking for a group. *Journal of Abnormal and Social Psychology*, 1959, *59*, 177–181.

ARONSON, E. & ROSS, A. The effect of support and criticism on interpersonal attractive-ness. Unpublished data, 1966.

ARONSON, E., TURNER, J., & CARLSMITH, J. M. Communicator credibility and communi-cation discrepancy as determinants of opinion change. *Journal of Abnormal and Social Psychology*, 1963, *67*, 31–36.

ARROWOOD, A. J. & ROSS, L. Anticipated effort and subjective probability. *Journal of Per-sonality and Social Psychology*, 1966, *4*, 57–64.

ASCH, S. E. Studies in the principles of judgments and attitudes: II. Determination of judgements by groups and by ego standards. *Journal of Social Psychology*, 1940, *12*, 433–465.

ASCH, S. E. Forming impressions of personality. *Journal of Abnormal and Social Psy-chology*, 1946, *41*, 258–290.

ASCH, S. E. The doctrine of suggestion, prestige and imitation in social psychology. *Psy-chological Review*, 1948, *55*, 250–276.

ASCH, S. E. Effects of group pressures upon the modification and distortion of judgments. In M. H. Geutzkow (Ed.), *Groups, leadership, and men*. Pittsburgh: Carnegie Press, 1951. Pp. 117–190.

ASCH, S. E. Studies of independence and conformity: I. A minority of one against a unanimous majority. *Psychological Monographs*, 1956, 70 (9, Whole No. 416).

ASRATIAN, E. A. *Compensatory adaptations, reflex activity and the brain*. Oxford and New York: Pergamon Press, 1965.

ATKINSON, J. W. *An introduction to motivation*. Princeton, New Jersey: D. Van Nostrand, 1964.

ATKINSON, J. W. & CARTWRIGHT, D. Some neglected variables in contemporary concep-tions of decision and performance. *Psychological Reports*, 1964, *14*, 575–590.

ATTNEAVE, F. Some informational aspects of visual perception. *Psychological Review*, 1954, *61*, 183–193.

AXELROD, J. The relationship of mood and of mood shift to attitude. Unpublished technical report to the Office of Naval Research, University of Rochester, 1959.

BACK, K. W. & GERGEN, K. J. Apocalyptic and serial time orientations and the structure of opinions. *Public Opinion Quarterly*, 1963, 27, 427–442.

BACKMAN, C. & SECORD, P. The effect of perceived liking on interpersonal attraction. *Human Relations*, 1959, 12, 379–384.

BACKMAN, C. & SECORD, P. Liking, selective interaction, and misperception in congruent interpersonal relations. *Sociometry*, 1962, 25, 321–335.

BAILEY, N. T. J. *The mathematical theory of epidemics*. London: Charles Griffin & Company, 1957.

BANDURA, A. & WALTERS, R. H. *Social learning and personality development*. New York: Holt, Rinehart & Winston, 1963.

BARBER, T. X. Hypnosis as perceptual-cognitive restructuring: IV. "Negative hallucinations." *Journal of Psychology*, 1958, 46, 187–201.

BARTLETT, F. C. *Remembering*. New York: Macmillan, 1932.

BARTLETT, F. C. *Thinking*. New York: Basic Books, 1958.

BATESON, G., JACKSON, D. D., HALEY, J., & WEAKLAND, J. Toward a theory of schizophrenia. In W. G. Bennis, E. H. Schein, D. E. Berlew, & F. J. Steele (Eds.), *Interpersonal dynamics: Essays and readings on human interaction*. Homewood, Illinois: Dorsey, 1964. Pp. 141–161.

BEHAVIORAL SCIENCE SUBPANEL, PRESIDENT'S SCIENCE ADVISORY COMMITTEE. Report to the President: Strengthening the behavioral sciences. *Behavioral Science*, 1962, 7, 275–288.

BEM, D. J. An experimental analysis of self-persuasion. *Journal of Experimental Social Psychology*, 1965, 1, 199–218.

BEM, D. J. Inducing belief in false confessions. *Journal of Personality and Social Psychology*, 1966, 3, 707–710.

BEM, D. J. Self perception: An alternative interpretation of cognitive dissonance phenomena. *Psychological Review*, 1967, 74, 183–200.

BENOIT-SMULLYAN, E. Status, status types, and status interrelations. *American Sociological Review*, 1944, 9, 151–161.

BERELSON, B. R., LAZARSFELD, P. F., & McPHEE, W. N. *Voting*. Chicago: University of Chicago Press, 1954.

BERELSON, B. R. & STEINER, G. *Human behavior: An inventory of scientific findings*. New York: Harcourt, Brace, and World, 1965.

BERGIN, A. Personality interpretations as dissonant persuasive communications. Unpublished doctoral dissertation, Stanford University, 1960.

BERKOWITZ, L. The judgmental process in personality functioning. *Psychological Review*, 1960, 67, 130–142.

BERKOWITZ, L. *Aggression: A social psychological analysis*. New York: McGraw-Hill, 1962.

BERKOWITZ, L. The concept of aggressive drive: Some additional considerations. In L. Berkowitz (Ed.), *Advances in experimental social psychology*, Vol. 2. New York: Academic Press, 1965. Pp. 301–329. (a)

BERKOWITZ, L. Cognitive dissonance and communication preferences. *Human Relations*, 1965, 18, 361–372. (b)

BERKUN, M. M. Factors in the recovery from approach-avoidance conflict. *Journal of Experimental Psychology*, 1957, 54, 65–73.

BERKUN, M. M., BRALEK, H. M., KERN, R. P., & YOGI, K. Experimental studies of psychological stress in man. *Psychological Monographs*, 1962, 76 (Whole No. 534).

BERLYNE, D. E. Novelty and curiosity as determinants of exploratory behavior. *British Journal of Psychology*, 1950, 41, 68–80.

BERLYNE, D. E. An experimental study of human curiosity. *British Journal of Psychology*, 1954, 45, 256–265. (a)

BERLYNE, D. E. A theory of human curiosity. *British Journal of Psychology*, 1954, 45, 180–191. (b)

BERLYNE, D. E. The arousal and satiation of perceptual curiosity in the rat. *Journal of Comparative and Physiological Psychology*, 1955, 48, 238–246.

BERLYNE, D. E. Uncertainty and conflict: A point of contact between information theory and behavior theory. *Psychological Review*, 1957, *64*, 329–339.

BERLYNE, D. E. *Conflict, arousal, and curiosity*. New York: McGraw-Hill, 1960.

BERLYNE, D. E. Conflict and the orientation reaction. *Journal of Experimental Psychology*, 1961, *62*, 476–483.

BERLYNE, D. E. Uncertainty and epistemic curiosity. *British Journal of Psychology*, 1962, *53*, 27–34.

BERLYNE, D. E. Motivational problems raised by exploratory and epistemic behavior. In S. Koch (Ed.), *Psychology: A study of science*, Vol. 5. New York: McGraw-Hill, 1963.

BERLYNE, D. E. Emotional aspects of learning. *Annual Review of Psychology*, 1964, *15*, 115–142.

BERLYNE, D. E. *Structure and direction in thinking*. New York: Wiley, 1965.

BERLYNE, D. E. Curiosity and exploration. *Science*, 1966, *153*, 25–33. (a)

BERLYNE, D. E. The delimination of cognitive development. *Monographs of the Society for Research in Child Development*. Serial No. 107, 1966, Vol. 31, No. 5, 71–81. (b)

BERLYNE, D. E. Arousal and reinforcement. In D. Levine (Ed.), *Nebraska symposium on motivation, 1967*. Lincoln, Nebraska: University of Nebraska Press, 1967.

BERLYNE, D. E. Laughter, humor and play. In G. Lindzey & E. Aronson (Eds.), *Handbook of social psychology* (2nd ed.). Cambridge, Massachusetts: Addison-Wesley, 1968.

BERLYNE, D. E. The reward value of indifferent stimulation. In J. Tapp (Ed.), *Reinforcement*. New York: Academic Press, in press.

BERLYNE, D. E. & BORSA, D. M. On certainty and the orientation reaction. *Perception and Psychophysics*, 1967, 1968, *3*, 77–79.

BERLYNE, D. E., CRAW, M. A., SALAPATEK, P. H., & LEWIS, J. L. Novelty, complexity, incongruity, extrinsic motivation and the GSR. *Journal of Experimental Psychology*, 1963, *66*, 560–567.

BERLYNE, D. E., KOENIG, I. D. V., & HIROTA, T. Novelty, arousal and reinforcement of diversive exploration in the rat. *Journal of Comparative and Physiological Psychology*, 1966, *62*, 222–226.

BERLYNE, D. E. & LEWIS, J. L. Effects of heightened arousal on human exploratory behavior. *Canadian Journal of Psychology*, 1963, *17*, 398–410.

BERLYNE, D. E. & McDONNELL, P. Effects of stimulus complexity and incongruity of duration of EEG desynchronization. *Electroencephalography and Clinical Neurophysiology*, 1965, *18*, No. 2, 156–161.

BERLYNE, D. E., SALAPATEK, P. H., GELMAN, R. S., & ZENER, S. L. Is light increment really rewarding the rat? *Journal of Comparative and Physiological Psychology*, 1964, *58*, 148–151.

BIDERMAN, A. D. *March to calumny: The story of American POW's in the Korean war*. New York and London: MacMillan, 1963.

BIERI, J. Cognitive complexity-simplicity and predictive behavior. *Journal of Abnormal and Social Psychology*, 1955, *51*, 263–268.

BIERI, J. Complexity-simplicity as a personality variable in cognitive preferential behavior. In D. W. Fiske & S. R. Maddi (Eds.), *Functions of varied experience*. Homewood, Illinois: Dorsey, 1961. Pp. 355–379.

BIERI, J. Cognitive complexity: Assessment issues in the study of cognitive structure. Paper presented at the meeting of the American Psychological Association, 1965.

BIERI, J. Cognitive complexity and personality development. In O. J. Harvey (Ed.), *Flexibility, adaptability, and creativity*. New York: Spring, 1966.

BIERI, J. Cognitive structures in personality. In H. M. Schroder & P. Suedfeld (Eds.), *Information processing: A new perspective in personality theory*. New York: Ronald, in press.

BIERI, J., ATKINS, A. L., BRIAR, S., LEAMAN, R. L., MILLER, H., & TRIPODI, T. *Clinical and social judgment: The discrimination of behavioral information*. New York: Wiley, 1966.

BIERI, J., BRADBURN, W. M., & GALINSKY, M. D. Sex differences in perceptual behavior. *Journal of Personality*, 1958, *26*, 1–12.

BINDRA, D. *Motivation: A systematic reinterpretation*. New York: Ronald, 1959.

BIRCH, H. G. The effect of socially disapproved labeling upon a well-structured attitude. *Journal of Abnormal and Social Psychology*, 1945, *40*, 301–310.

BISHOP, F. V. The anal character: A rebel in the dissonance family. Paper presented at the meeting of the American Psychological Association, Chicago, Illinois, September, 1965.

BISHOP, F. V. The anal character: A rebel in the dissonance family. *Journal of Personality and Social Psychology*, 1967, *6*, 23–36.

BLAKE, R. R., RHEAD, C. C., WEDGE, B., & MOUTON, J. S. Housing architecture and social interaction. *Sociometry*, 1956, *19*, 133–139.

BLUM, G. S. *A model of the mind.* New York: Wiley, 1961.

BONARIUS, J. C. J. Research in the personal construct of George A. Kelly: Role construct repertory test and basic theory. In B. A. Maher (Ed.), *Progress in experimental personality research*, Vol. 2. New York: Academic Press, 1965.

BONCHEK, V. Commitment, communicator, credibility and attitude change. Unpublished doctoral dissertation, New York University, 1966.

BOTT, E. *Family and social network: Roles, norms, and external relationships in ordinary urban families.* London: Tavistock Publications, 1957.

BRADEN, M. & WALSTER, E. The effect of anticipated dissonance on predecision behavior. In L. Festinger, *Conflict, decision and dissonance.* Stanford, California: Stanford University Press, 1964. Pp. 145–151.

BRAMEL, D. A disssonance theory approach to defensive projection. *Journal of Abnormal and Social Psychology*, 1962, *64*, 121–129.

BRAMEL, D. Selection of a target for defensive projection. *Journal of Abnormal and Social Psychology*, 1963, *66*, 318–324.

BRAMEL, D., BELL, J. W., & MARGULIS, S. T. Attributing danger as a means of explaining one's fear. *Journal of Experimental Social Psychology*, 1965, *1*, 267–281.

BREHM, J. W. Post-decision changes in the desirability of alternatives. *Journal of Abnormal and Social Psychology*, 1956, *52*, 384–389.

BREHM, J. W. Increasing cognitive dissonance by a fait accompli. *Journal of Abnormal and Social Psychology*, 1959, *58*, 379–382.

BREHM, J. W. A dissonance analysis of attitude-discrepant behavior. In M. J. Rosenberg, C. I. Hovland, W. J. McGuire, R. P. Abelson & J. W. Brehm, *Attitude organization and change: An analysis of consistency among attitude components.* New Haven: Yale University Press, 1960. Pp. 198–232. (a)

BREHM, J. W. Attitudinal consequences of commitment to unpleasant behavior. *Journal of Abnormal and Social Psychology*, 1960, *60*, 379–383. (b)

BREHM, J. W. Motivational effects of cognitive dissonance. *Nebraska Symposium on Motivation, 1962.* Lincoln, Nebraska: University of Nebraska Press, 1962. Pp. 51–77.

BREHM, J. W. Comment on 'Counter-norm attitudes induced by consonant versus dissonant conditions of role-playing.' *Journal of Experimental Research in Personality*, 1965, *1*, 61–64.

BREHM, J. W. *A theory of psychological reactance.* New York: Academic Press, 1966.

BREHM, J. W. & BEHAR, L. B. Sexual arousal, defensiveness, and sex preference in affiliation. *Journal of Experimental Research in Personality*, 1966, *1*, 195–200.

BREHM, J. W. & COHEN, A. R. Choice and chance relative deprivation as determinants of cognitive dissonance. *Journal of Abnormal and Social Psychology*, 1959, *58*, 383–387. (a)

BREHM, J. W. & COHEN, A. R. Re-evaluation of choice alternatives as a function of their number and qualitative similarity. *Journal of Abnormal and Social Psychology*, 1959, *58*, 373–378. (b)

BREHM, J. W. & COHEN, A. R. *Explorations in cognitive dissonance.* New York: Wiley, 1962.

BREHM, J. W., COHEN, A. R., & SEARS, D. Persistence of post-choice dissonance reduction effects. Unpublished data, 1960.

BREHM, M. L., BACK, K. W., & BOGDONOFF, M. D. A physiological effect of cognitive dissonance under stress and deprivation. *Journal of Abnormal and Social Psychology*, 1964, *69*, 303–310.

BROADBENT, D. E. Information processing in the nervous system. *Science*, 1965, *150*, 457–462.

BROCK, T. C. Cognitive restructuring and attitude change. *Journal of Abnormal and Social Psychology*, 1962, *64*, 264–271.

BROCK, T. C. Effects of prior dishonesty on postdecision dissonance. *Journal of Abnormal and Social Psychology*, 1963, *66*, 325–331.

BROCK, T. C. Commitment to exposure as a determinant of information receptivity. *Journal of Personality and Social Psychology*, 1965, *2*, 10–19.

BROCK, T. C. & BALLOUN, J. L. Behavioral receptivity to dissonant information. *Journal of Personality and Social Psychology*, 1967, *6*, 413–428.

BROCK, T. C. & BECKER, L. A. Volition and attraction in everyday life. *Journal of Social Psychology*, 1967, *72*, 89–97.

BROCK, T. C. & BUSS, A. H. Dissonance, aggression, and evaluation of pain. *Journal of Abnormal and Social Psychology*, 1962, *65*, 197–202.

BROCK, T. C. & BUSS, A. H. Effects of justification for aggression and communication with the victim on postaggression dissonance. *Journal of Abnormal and Social Psychology*, 1964, *68*, 403–412.

BROCK, T. C., EDELMAN, S. K., EDWARDS, D. C., & SCHUCK, J. R. Seven studies of performance expectancy as a determinant of actual performance. *Journal of Experimental Social Psychology*, 1965, *1*, 295–310.

BROCK, T. C. & FROMKIN, H. L. Cognitive tuning set and behavioral receptivity to discrepant information. *Journal of Personality*, 1968, *36*, 108–125.

BROCK, T. C. & GRANT, L. D. Dissonance, awareness, and motivation. *Journal of Abnormal and Social Psychology*, 1963, *67*, 53–60.

BROWN, J. S. *The motivation of behavior*. New York: McGraw-Hill, 1961.

BROWN, J. S. & FARBER, I. E. Emotions conceptualized as intervening variables with suggestions toward a theory of frustration. *Psychological Bulletin*, 1951, *48*, 465–493.

BROWN, R. Models of attitude change. In R. Brown, E. Galanter, B. H. Hess, & G. Mandler (Eds.), *New directions in psychology*. New York: Holt, Rinehart & Winston, 1962. Pp. 1–85.

BROWN, R. *Social Psychology*. Glencoe, Illinois: The Free Press, 1965.

BROWNFIELD, C. A. *Isolation: Clinical and experimental approaches*. New York: Random House, 1965.

BRUNER, J. S. Freud and the image of man. *American Psychologist*, 1956, *11*, 463–466.

BRUNER, J. S. On perceptual readiness. *Psychological Review*, 1957, *64*, 123–152.

BRUNER, J. S., GOODNOW, J. J., & AUSTIN, G. A. *A study of thinking*. New York: Wiley, 1956.

BRUNER, J. S. & OLVER, R. P. Development of equivalence transformations in children. *Monographs of the Society for Research in Child Development*, 1963, *28*, 125–143.

BRUNSWIK, E. The conceptual focus of some psychological systems. *Journal of Unified Science*, 1939, *8*, 36–49.

BRUNSWIK, E. The conceptual framework of psychology. *International Encyclopedia of Unified Science*, Vol. I, No. 10, 1952.

BRUNSWIK, E. Ontogenetic and other developmental parallels to the history of science. In H. M. Evans (Ed.), *Men and moments in the history of sciences*. Seattle, Washington: University of Washington Press, 1959.

BRYAN, J. H. & LICHTENSTEIN, E. Effects of subject and experimenter attitudes in verbal conditioning. *Journal of Personality and Social Psychology*, 1966, *3*, 182–189.

BUCKHOUT, R. Changes in heart rate accompanying attitude change. *Journal of Personality and Social Psychology*, 1966, *4*, 695–699.

BUGELSKI, B. R. *An introduction to the principles of psychology*. New York: Holt, Rinehart & Winston, 1960.

BUNKER, G. L. Self-role congruence and status congruence as interacting variables in dyadic behavior. Unpublished doctoral dissertation, University of California, Berkeley, 1965.

BURCHARD, W. W. Role conflicts of military chaplains. *American Sociological Review*, 1954, *19*, 528–535.

BURDICK, H. The compliant behavior of deviates under conditions of threat. Unpublished doctoral dissertation, University of Minnesota, 1955.

BURDICK, H. A. & BURNES, A. J. A test of "strain toward symmetry" theories. *Journal of Abnormal and Social Psychology*, 1958, *57*, 367–369.

BURNSTEIN, E. Sources of cognitive bias in the representation of simple social structures: Balance, minimal change, positivity, reciprocity, and the respondent's own attitude. *Journal of Personality and Social Psychology*, 1967, 7, 36–48.

BUSH, R. R. & MOSTELLER, R. *Stochastic models for learning*. New York: Wiley, 1955.

BUSS, A. H. *The psychology of aggression*. New York: Wiley, 1961.

BUTLER, R. A. Curiosity in monkeys. *Scientific American*, 1954, *190*, 70–75.

BUTT, J. *Translation of Voltaire's Candide or optimism*. Baltimore: Penguin, 1947.

BYRNE, D. Interpersonal attraction and attitude similarity. *Journal of Abnormal and Social Psychology*, 1961, *62*, 713–715. (a)

BYRNE, D. The repression-sensitization scale: Rationale, reliability, and validity. *Journal of Personality*, 1961, *29*, 334–349. (b)

BRYNE, D. Repression-sensitization as a dimension of personality. In B. A. Maher (Ed.), *Progress in experimental personality research*, Vol. I. New York: Academic Press, 1964. Pp. 169–220.

BYRNE, D. & BUEHLER, J. A. A note on the influence of propinquity upon acquaintanceships. *Journal of Abnormal and Social Psychology*, 1955, *51*, 147–148.

CAMPBELL, A. A., CONVERSE, P. E., MILLER, W. E., & STOKES, D. E. *The American Voter*. New York: Wiley, 1960.

CAMPBELL, D. T. Conformity in psychology's theories of acquired behavioral dispositions. In I. A. Berg & B. M. Bass (Eds.), *Conformity and deviation*. New York: Harper & Row, 1961. Pp. 101–158.

CAMPBELL, D. T. Social attitudes and other acquired behavioral dispositions. In S. Koch (Ed.), *Psychology: A study of a science*, Vol. 6. *Investigations of man as socius: Their place in psychology and the social sciences*. New York: McGraw-Hill, 1963.

CAMPBELL, D. T. Ethnocentric and other altruistic motives. In D. Levine (Ed.), *Nebraska Symposium on Motivation: 1965*. Lincoln, Nebraska: University of Nebraska Press, 1965. Pp. 283–311.

CAMPBELL, D. T., HUNT, W. A., & LEWIS, N. A. The effects of assimilation and contrast in judgments of clinical materials. *American Journal of Psychology*, 1957, *70*, 347–360.

CAMPBELL, D. T. & LeVINE, R. A. A proposal for cooperative cross-cultural research on ethnocentrism. *Journal of Conflict Resolution*, 1961, *5*, 82–108.

CAMPBELL, D. T. & LeVINE, R. A. Propositions about ethnocentrism from social science theories. Unpublished manuscript, Northwestern University, March, 1965. To be published, revised as *Ethnocentrism and intergroup relations: Propositions and illustrations*. New York: Wiley, in preparation.

CAMPBELL, D. T. & STANLEY, J. C. Experimental and quasi-experimental designs for research on teaching. In N. L. Gage (Ed.), *Handbook of research on teaching*. Chicago: Rand McNally, 1963. Pp. 171–246.

CANON, L. Self-confidence and selective exposure to information. In L. Festinger, *Conflict, decision, and dissonance*. Stanford: Stanford University Press, 1964. Pp. 83–96.

CANTOR, N. R. The crises of western monasticism. *American Historical Review*, 1960, *66*, No. 1, 47–67.

CAPLOW, T. & FORMAN, R. Neighborhood interaction in a homogeneous community. *American Sociological Review*, 1950, *15*, 357–366.

CARLSMITH, J. M. & ARONSON, E. Some hedonic consequences of the confirmation and disconfirmation of expectancies. *Journal of Abnormal and Social Psychology*, 1965, *66*, 151–156.

CARLSMITH, J. M., COLLINS, B. E., & HELMREICH, R. L. The effect of incentives on face-to-face counter-attitudinal role playing and essay writing. Unpublished data, 1965.

CARLSMITH, J. M., COLLINS, B. E., & HELMREICH, R. L. Studies in forced compliance: I. The effect of pressure for compliance on attitude change produced by face-to-face role playing and anonymous essay writing. *Journal of Personality and Social Psychology*, 1966, *4*, 1–13.

CARLSON, E. R. Attitude change through modification of attitude structure. *Journal of Abnormal and Social Psychology*, 1956, *52*, 256–261.

CARTER, R. F. Communication and affective relations. *Journalism Quarterly*, 1965, *42*, 203–212.

CARTWRIGHT, D. Some principles of mass persuasion. *Human Relations*, 1949, *2*, 253–267.

CARTWRIGHT, D. Of what does consistency consist? Review of Rosenberg, Hovland, *et al.*, *Attitude organization and change in Contemporary Psychologist*, 1962, 7, 43–45.

CARTWRIGHT, D. & HARARY, F. Structural balance: A generalization of Heider's theory. *Psychological Review*, 1956, *63*, 277–293.

CASSIRER, E. *Substance and function.* Chicago: Open Court, 1923.

CASSIRER, E. The concept of group and the theory of perception. *Philosophy and Phenomenological Research*, 1944, *5*, 1–35.

CHALMERS, D. K. Repetition of information and order of presentation in personality impression formation. Unpublished doctoral dissertation. University of Iowa, 1964.

CHAPANIS, N. P. & CHAPANIS, A. Cognitive dissonance: Five years later. *Psychological Bulletin*, 1964, *61*, 1–22.

CHILD, I. L. A study of esthetic judgment. Mimeographed report of Cooperative Research Project No. 669, Office of Education, U.S. Department of Health, Education, and Welfare, 1962.

CHILD, I. L. Problems of personality and some relations to anthropology and sociology. In S. Koch (Ed.), *Psychology: A study of a science*, Vol. 5. New York: McGraw-Hill, 1963. Pp. 593–638.

CHRISTIANSEN, B. *Attitudes toward foreign affairs as a function of personality.* Oslo: University of Oslo, 1959.

CHRISTIE, R. & LINDAUER, F. Personality structure. In P. R. Farnsworth, O. McNemar, & Q. McNemar (Eds.), *Annual review of psychology*, Vol. 1. Palo Alto, California: Annual Reviews, Inc., 1963. Pp. 201–230.

CLARKE, P. & JAMES, J. The effects of situation, attitude intensity and personality on information-seeking. *Sociometry*, 1967, *30*, 235–245.

COCHRAN, W. G. Analysis of convariance: Its nature and its uses. *Biometrics*, 1957, *13*, 261–281.

COFER, C. N. & APPLEY, M. H. *Motivation: Theory and research.* New York: Wiley, 1964.

COHEN, A. R. Need for cognition and order of communication as determinants of opinion change. In C. I. Hovland (Ed.), *The order of presentation in persuasion.* New Haven: Yale University Press, 1957. Pp. 79–97.

COHEN, A. R. Communication discrepancy and attitude change: A dissonance theory approach. *Journal of Personality*, 1959, 27, 386–396. (a)

COHEN, A. R. Some implications of self-esteem for social influence. In C. I. Hovland & I. L. Janis (Eds.), *Personality and persuasibility.* New Haven: Yale University Press, 1959. Pp. 102–120. (b)

COHEN, A. R. Attitudinal consequences of induced discrepancies between cognitions and behavior. *Public Opinion Quarterly*, 1960, *24*, 297–318.

COHEN, A. R. An experiment on small rewards for discrepant compliance and attitude change. In J. W. Brehm & A. R. Cohen, *Explorations in cognitive dissonance.* New York: Wiley, 1962. Pp. 73–78.

COHEN, A. R. *Attitude change and social influence.* New York: Basic Books, 1964.

COHEN, A. R., BREHM, J. W., & FLEMING, W. H. Attitude change and justification for compliance. *Journal of Abnormal and Social Psychology*, 1958, *56*, 276–278.

COHEN, A. R., BREHM, J. W., & LATANE, B. Choice of strategy and voluntary exposure to information under public and private conditions. *Journal of Personality*, 1959, 27, 63–73.

COHEN, A. R., GREENBAUM, C. W., & MANSSON, H. H. Commitment to social deprivation and verbal conditioning. *Journal of Abnormal and Social Psychology*, 1963, *67*, 410–421.

COHEN, A. R., TERRY, H. I., & JONES, C. B. Attitudinal effects of choice in exposure to counter-propaganda. *Journal of Abnormal and Social Psychology*, 1959, *58*, 388–391.

COHEN, A. R. & ZIMBARDO, P. G. An experiment in avoidance motivation. In J. W. Brehm & A. R. Cohen, *Explorations in cognitive dissonance.* New York: Wiley, 1962. Pp. 143–151.

COLRY, B. N. & VAN DEN BERGHE, P. L. Ethnic relations in southeastern Mexico. *American Anthropologist*, 1961, *vol. 63.*

COLBY, K. M. Computer simulation of neurotic processes. In R. W. Stacey & B. Waxman (Eds.), *Computers in biomedical research*. New York: Academic Press, 1965.

COLBY, K. M. & GILBERT, J. P. Programming a computer model of neurosis. *Journal of Mathematical Psychology*, 1964, *1*, 405–417.

COLEMAN, J. S. *Nigeria: Background to nationalism*. Berkeley and Los Angeles: University of California Press, 1958.

COLEMAN, J. S., KATZ, E., & MENZEL, H. The diffusion of an innovation. *Sociometry*, 1957, *20*, 253–270.

COLLINS, B. E. An experimental study of satisfaction, productivity, turn-over, and comparison levels. Unpublished manuscript, Northwestern University, 1963.

COLLINS, B. E. & HELMREICH, R. L. Studies in forced compliance: II. Contrasting mechanisms of attitude change produced by public-persuasive and private-true essays. Unpublished manuscript, 1966.

CONLON, E. T. Performance as determined by expectation of success or failure. Unpublished doctoral dissertation, Columbia University, 1965.

COOK, S. W. & SELLTIZ, C. A multiple-indicator approach to attitude measurement. *Psychological Bulletin*, 1964, *62*, 36–55.

COOLEY, C. H. *Human nature and the social order*. New York: Scribner, 1902.

COOMBS, C. H. A theory of data. *Psychological Review*, 1960, *67*, 143–159.

COOMBS, C. H. *A theory of data*. New York: Wiley, 1964.

CORROZI, J. F. & ROSNOW, R. L. Consonant and dissonant communications as positive and negative reinforcements in opinion change. *Journal of Personality and Social Psychology*, 1968, *8*, 27–30.

COSER, L. A. *The functions of social conflict*. Glencoe, Illinois: Free Press, 1956.

COTTRELL, N. B. Performance expectancy as a determinant of actual performance: A replication with a new design. *Journal of Personality and Social Psychology*, 1965, *2*, 685–691.

COTTRELL, N. B. The effects of expectancy-performance dissonance upon reaction time performance. Paper presented at a meeting of the Midwestern Psychological Association, April, 1965.

COX, D. R. *Planning of experiments*. New York: Wiley, 1958.

CROCKETT, W. H. Cognitive complexity and impression formation. In B. A. Maher (Ed.), *Progress in experimental personality research*, Vol. 2. New York: Academic Press, 1965.

CRONBACH, L. J. The two disciplines of scientific psychology. In M. T. Mednick & S. A. Mednick (Eds.), *Research in personality*. New York: Holt, Rinehart and Winston, 1963. Pp. 3–21.

DABBS, J. M. & JANIS, I. L. Why does eating while reading facilitate opinion change?—An experimental inquiry. *Journal of Experimental Social Psychology*, 1965, *1*, 133–144.

DAS, J. P. & NANDA, P. C. Mediated transfer of attitudes. *Journal of Abnormal and Social Psychology*, 1963, *66*, 12–16.

DAVENPORT, W. Nonunilinear descent and descent groups. *American Anthropologist*, 1959, *61*, 557–572.

DAVIDSON, J. R. Cognitive familiarity and dissonance reduction. In L. Festinger, *Conflict, decision and dissonance*. Stanford: Stanford University Press, 1964. Pp. 45–60.

DAVIDSON, J. R. & KIESLER, S. Cognitive behavior before and after decisions. In L. Festinger, *Conflict, decision, and dissonance*. Stanford: Stanford University Press, 1964. Pp. 10–21.

DAVIS, E. E. & TRIANDIS, H. C. An exploratory study of inter-cultural negotiations. Urbana, Illinois, Group Effectiveness Laboratory, Technical report No. 26, 1965.

DAVIS, J. A. Structural balance, mechanical solidarity, and interpersonal relations. *American Journal of Sociology*, 1963, *68*, 442–462.

DAVIS, J. A. Clustering and structural balance in graphs. *Human Relations*, 1967, *20*, 181.

DAVIS, K. E. & JONES, E. E. Changes in interpersonal perception as a means of reducing cognitive dissonance. *Journal of Abnormal and Social Psychology*, 1960, *61*, 402–410.

DAVIS, R. C., BUCHWALD, A. M., & FRANKMANN, R. W. Autonomic and muscular responses and their relation to simple stimuli. *Psychological Monographs*, 1955, *69* (Whole No. 405).

DEESE, J. On the structure of associative meaning. *Psychological Review*, 1962, *69*, 161–175.

DeFLEUR, M. L. & LARSON, O. N. *The flow of information*. New York: Harper and Brothers, 1958.

DEMBER, W. N. Response by the rat to environmental change. *Journal of Comparative and Physiological Psychology*, 1956, *49*, 93–95.

DEMBER, W. N. Alternative behavior. In D. W. Fiske & S. R. Maddi (Eds.), *Functions of varied experience*. Homewood, Illinois: Dorsey, 1961.

DEMBER, W. N. & EARL, R. W. Analysis of exploratory, manipulatory and curiosity behaviors. *Psychological Review*, 1957, *64*, 91–96.

DENO, S. L. & JENKINS, J. J. Semantic generalization of a voluntary response: Effects of responding in training and rate of presentation. Unpublished manuscript, University of Minnesota, 1965.

DE SOTO, C. B. Learning a social structure. *Journal of Abnormal and Social Psychology*, 1960, *60*, 417–421.

DE SOTO, C. B. The predilection for single orderings. *Journal of Abnormal and Social Psychology*, 1961, *62*, 16–23.

DE SOTO, C. B. & BOSLEY, J. J. The cognitive structure of a social structure. *Journal of Abnormal and Social Psychology*, 1962, *64*, 303–307.

DE SOTO, C. B., HENLEY, N. M., & LONDON, M. Balance and the grouping schema. *Journal of Personality and Social Psychology*, 1968, *8*, 1–7.

DE SOTO, C. B. & KUETHE, J. L. Subjective probabilities of interpersonal relationships. *Journal of Abnormal and Social Psychology*, 1959, *59*, 290–294.

DE SOTO, C. B., LONDON, M., & HANDEL, S. Social reasoning and spatial paralogic. *Journal of Personality and Social Psychology*, 1965, *2*, 513–521.

DEUTSCH, K. *Nationalism and social communication*. New York: Wiley, 1953.

DEUTSCH, M. The pathetic fallacy: An observer error in interpersonal perception. *Journal of Personality*, 1960, *22*, 317–322.

DEUTSCH, M. The interpretation of praise and criticism as a function of their social context. *Journal of Abnormal and Social Psychology*, 1961, *62*, 391–400.

DEUTSCH, M. & COLLINS, M. E. *Interracial housing*. Minneapolis: University of Minnesota Press, 1951.

DEUTSCH, M. & GERARD, H. B. A study of normative and informational social influence upon individual judgment. *Journal of Abnormal and Social Psychology*, 1955, *51*, 629–636.

DEUTSCH, M. & KRAUSS, R. M. *Theories in social psychology*. New York: Basic Books, 1965.

DEUTSCH, M., KRAUSS, R. M., & ROSENAU, N. Dissonance or defensiveness? *Journal of Personality*, 1962, *30*, 16–28.

DEUTSCH, M. & SOLOMON, L. Reactions to evaluations by others as influenced by self-evaluation. *Sociometry*, 1959, *22*, 93–112.

DEUTSCHMANN, P. Viewing, conversation, and voting intentions. In S. Kraus (Ed.), *The great debates*. Bloomington, Indiana: University of Indiana Press, 1962.

DICKHOFF, H. Reactions to evaluations by another person as a function of self-evaluation and the interaction context. Unpublished doctoral dissertation, Duke University, 1961.

DILLEHAY, R. C., INSKO, C. A., & SMITH, M. B. Logical consistency and attitude change. *Journal of Personality and Social Psychology*, 1966, *3*, 646–654.

DiVESTA, F. J., MEYER, D. L., & MILLS, J. Confidence in an expert as a function of his judgments. *Human Relations*, 1964, *17*, 235–242.

DOBY, J. T. *Introduction to social psychology*. New York: Appleton-Century-Crofts, 1966.

DOOB, L. The behavior of attitudes. *Psychological Review*, 1947, *54*, 135–156.

DRISCOLL, J. M., TOGNOLI, J. J., & LANZETTA, J. T. Choice conflict and subjective uncertainty in decision making. *Psychological Reports*, 1966, *18*, 427–432.

DRIVER, M. J. & STREUFERT, S. The 'General incongruity adaption level' (GIAL) hypothesis: An analysis and integration of cognitive approaches to motivation. Institute for Research in the Behavioral, Economic, and Management Sciences, Paper 114, Krannert Graduate School, Purdue University, 1965.

DUFFY, E. *Activation and behavior*. New York: Wiley, 1963.

DULANY, D. E. Hypotheses and habits in verbal operant conditioning. *Journal of Abnormal and Social Psychology*, 1961, *63*, 251–263.

DUNHAM, H. W., PHILLIPS, P. & SRINIVASAN, B. A research note on diagnosed mental illness and social class. *American Sociological Review*, 1966, *31*, 223–227.

DURKHEIM, E. *The division of labor in society*. New York: MacMillan, 1933.

DUSTIN, D. S. & BALDWIN, P. M. Redundancy in impression formation. *Journal of Personality and Social Psychology*, 1966, *3*, 500–506.

EAGLY, A. H. Involvement as a determinant of response to discrepancy. Unpublished doctoral dissertation, University of Michigan, 1965.

EASTERBROOK, J. A. The effect of emotion on cue utilization and the organization of behavior. *Psychological Review*, 1959, *66*, 183–201.

EASTON, D. & DENNIS, J. The child's image of government. *Annals of the American Academy of Political and Social Science*, 1965, *361*, 40–57.

EBBINGHAUS, H. *Abrisa der psychologie*. Leipzig: Voit, 1908.

EDLOW, D. W. & KIESLER, C. A. Ease of denial and defensive projection. *Journal of Experimental Social Psychology*, 1966, *2*, 56–69.

EDWARDS, A. L. Political frames of reference as a factor influencing recognition. *Journal of Abnormal and Social Psychology*, 1941, *38*, 507–517.

EDWARDS, A. L. *The social desirability variable in personality research*. New York: Dryden, 1957.

EGBERT, L., BATTIT, G., WELCH, C., & BARTLETT, M. Reduction of post-operative pain by encouragement and instruction of patients. *New England Journal of Medicine*, 1964, *270*, 825–827.

EHRLICH, D., GUTTMAN, I., SCHONBACH, P., & MILLS, J. Post-decision exposure to relevant information. *Journal of Abnormal and Social Psychology*, 1957, *54*, 98–102.

ELMS, A. C. The influence of fantasy ability on attitude change through role-playing. *Journal of Personality and Social Psychology*, 1966, *4*, 36–43.

ELMS, A. C. & JANIS, I. L. Counter-norm attitudes induced by consonant versus dissonant conditions of role-playing. *Journal of Experimental Research in Personality*, 1965, *1*, 50–60.

EMERSON, R. W. *Essay: First series*. New York: Houghton Mifflin, 1865.

ENGEL, G. L. Toward a classification of affects. In P. Knapp (Ed.), *Expression of the emotions in man*. New York: International Universities Press, 1963.

ENGEL, M. The stability of the self-concept in adolescence. *Journal of Abnormal and Social Psychology*, 1959, *58*, 211–215.

EPSTEIN, G. F. Machiavellianism, dissonance, and the devil's advocate. Unpublished doctoral dissertation, Columbia University, 1966.

EPSTEIN, S. & LEVITT, H. The influence of hunger on the learning and recall of food related words. *Journal of Abnormal and Social Psychology*, 1962, *64*, 130–135.

ERBE, W. Gregariousness, group membership, and the flow of information. *American Journal of Sociology*, 1962, *67*, 502–516.

ERIKSEN, C. W. (Ed.) *Behavior and awareness*. Durham: Duke University Press, 1962.

ERIKSON, E. H.. The problem of ego identity. *Journal of the American Psychoanalytic Association*, 1956, *4*, 56–121.

ERIKSON, E. H. *Young man Luther: A study in psychoanalysis and history*. New York: Norton, 1958.

ESTES, W. K. Stimulus-response theory of drive. In M. R. Jones (Ed.), *Nebraska symposium on motivation, 1958*. Lincoln, Nebraska: University of Nebraska Press, 1958. Pp. 35–69.

FAIRBAIRN, W. R. D. *Psychoanalytic studies of the personality*. London: Tavistock Publications, 1952. (a)

FAIRBAIRN, W. R. D. Theoretical and experimental aspects of psychoanalysis. *British Journal of Medical Psychology*, 1952, *25*, 122–127. (b)

FEATHER, N. T. Cigarette smoking and lung cancer: A study of cognitive dissonance. *Australian Journal of Psychology*, 1962, *14*, 55–64.

FEATHER, N. T. Cognitive dissonance, sensitivity, and evaluation. *Journal of Abnormal and Social Psychology*, 1963, *66*, 157–163.

FEATHER, N. T. Acceptance and rejection of arguments in relation to attitude strength, critical ability, and intolerance of inconsistency. *Journal of Abnormal and Social Psychology*, 1964, *69*, 127–136. (a)

FEATHER, N. T. A structural balance model of communication effects. *Psychological Review*, 1964, *71*, 291–313. (b)

FEATHER, N. T. Effects of prior success and failure on expectations of success and subsequent performance. *Journal of Personality and Social Psychology*, 1966, *3*, 287–298.

FELDMAN, J. J. The dissemination of health information: A case study of adult learning. Unpublished doctoral dissertation, University of Chicago, 1965.

FELDMAN, S. Evaluative ratings of adjective-adjective combinations predicted from ratings of their components. Unpublished doctoral dissertation, Yale University, 1962.

FELDMAN, S. The effect of manipulating "surprisingness" of components on the evaluative ratings of adjective-adjective combinations. Unpublished manuscript, University of Pennsylvania, 1966. (a)

FELDMAN, S. Measuring the overlap between associates of adjectives: A comparison of results obtained under different instructional sets. Unpublished manuscript, University of Pennsylvania, 1966. (b)

FELDMAN, S. Motivational aspects of attitudinal elements and their place in cognitive interaction. In S. Feldman (Ed.), *Cognitive consistency: Motivational antecedents and behavioral consequents*. New York: Academic Press, 1966. Pp. 75–108. (c)

FELDMAN, S. & ABELSON, R. P. Test of a model for predicting ratings of word combinations. *American Psychologist*, 1962, *17*, 362. (Abstract)

FENICHEL, O. *The psychoanalytic theory of neuroses*. New York: Norton, 1945.

FERDINAND, P. R. The effect of forced compliance on recognition. Paper presented at a meeting of the Midwestern Psychological Association, 1965.

FESTINGER, L. Informal social communication. *Psychological Review*, 1950, *57*, 271–282.

FESTINGER, L. A theory of social comparison processes. *Human Relations*, 1954, *7*, 117–140.

FESTINGER, L. *A theory of cognitive dissonance*. Evanston, Ill.: Row, Peterson, 1957.

FESTINGER, L. The motivating effect of cognitive dissonance. In G. Lindzey (Ed.), *Assessment of human motives*. New York: Grove Press, 1958.

FESTINGER, L. Behavioral support for opinion change. Paper presented at the convention of the American Psychological Association, Philadelphia, 1963.

FESTINGER, L. Behavioral support for opinion change. *Public Opinion Quarterly*, 1964, *28*, 404–417. (a)

FESTINGER, L. *Conflict, decision and dissonance*. Stanford: Stanford University Press, 1964. (b)

FESTINGER, L. & ARONSON, E. The arousal and reduction of dissonance in social contexts. In D. Cartwright & A. Zander (Eds.), *Group Dynamics*, (2nd ed.). Evanston, Illinois: Row-Peterson, 1960. Pp. 214–231.

FESTINGER, L., BACK, K., SCHACHTER, S., KELLEY, H. H., & THIBAUT, J. *Theory and experiment in social communication*. Ann Arbor, Michigan: Institute for Social Research, University of Michigan, 1950.

FESTINGER, L. & BRAMEL, D. The reactions of humans to cognitive dissonance. In A. Bachrach (Ed.), *The experimental foundations of clinical psychology*. New York: Basic Books, 1962. Pp. 254–279.

FESTINGER, L. & CARLSMITH, J. M. Cognitive consequences of forced compliance. *Journal of Abnormal and Social Psychology*, 1959, *58*, 203–210.

FESTINGER, L., CARTWRIGHT, D., BARBER, K., FLEISCHL, J., GOOTSDANKER, J., KEYEN, A., & LEAVITT, G. A study of rumor: Its origin and spread. *Human Relations*, 1948, *1*, 464–468.

FESTINGER, L. & FREEDMAN, J. L. Dissonance reduction and moral values. In P. Worchel & D. Byrne (Eds.), *Personality change*. New York: Wiley, 1964. Pp. 220–243.

FESTINGER, L. & HUTTE, H. An experimental investigation of the effect of unstable interpersonal relations in a group. *Journal of Abnormal and Social Psychology*, 1954, *49*, 513–522.

FESTINGER, L. & MACCOBY, N. On resistance to pursuasive communications. *Journal of Abnormal and Social Psychology*, 1964, *68*, 359–366.

FESTINGER, L., RIECKEN, H., & SCHACHTER, S. *When prophecy fails*. Minneapolis: University of Minnesota Press, 1956.

FESTINGER, L., SCHACHTER, S., & BACK, K. W. *Social pressures in informal groups*. New York: Harper, 1950.

FESTINGER, L. & WALSTER, E. Post-decision regret and decision reversal. In L. Festinger (Ed.), *Conflict, decision and dissonance*. Stanford: Stanford University Press, 1964. Pp. 97–111.

FIEDLER, F. E. *Leader attitudes and group effectiveness*. Urbana, Illinois: University of Illinois Press, 1958.

FILLENBAUM, S. Dogmatism and individual differences in reduction of dissonance. *Psychological Reports*, 1964, *14*, 47–50.

FIRESTONE, I. Insulted and provoked: The effects of choice and provocation on hostility and aggression. Unpublished doctoral dissertation, New York University, 1966.

FISHBEIN, M. An investigation of the relationships between beliefs about an object and the attitude toward that object. Unpublished Technical Report, Office of Naval Research, Contract Number N6 onr-233 (54), 1961. (a)

FISHBEIN, M. A theoretical and empirical investigation of the relationships between beliefs about an object and the attitude toward that object. Unpublished doctoral dissertation, University of California at Los Angeles, 1961.

FISHBEIN, M. An investigation of the relationships between beliefs about an object and the attitude toward that object. *Human Relations*, 1963, *16*, 233–239.

FISHBEIN, M. A consideration of beliefs, attitudes, and their relationships. In I. D. Steiner & M. Fishbein (Eds.), *Current studies in social psychology*. New York: Holt, Rinehart and Winston, 1965. Pp. 107–120.

FISHBEIN, M. & HUNTER, R. Summation versus balance in attitude organization and change. *Journal of Abnormal and Social Psychology*, 1964, *69*, 505–510.

FISHBEIN, M. & RAVEN, B. H. The *AB* scales: An operational definition of belief and attitude. *Human Relations*, 1962, *15*, 35–44.

FISKE, D. W. Effects of monotonous and restricted stimulation. In D. W. Fiske & S. R. Maddi (Eds.), *Functions of varied experience*. Homewood, Illinois: Dorsey, 1961.

FISKE, D. W. & MADDI, S. R. (Eds.) *Functions of varied experience*. Homewood, Illinois: Dorsey, 1961.

FLAMENT, C. *Applications of graph theory to group structure*. Englewood Cliffs, New Jersey: Prentice Hall, 1963.

FOLLET, M. *Creative experience*. New York: Longman, Green, 1924.

FOOTE, N. & COTTRELL, L. J., JR. *Identity and interpersonal competence*. Chicago: University of Chicago Press, 1955.

FORD, L. R., JR. & FULKERSON, D. R. *Flows in networks*. Princeton: Princeton University Press, 1962.

FOULKES, D. & FOULKES, S. H. Self-concept, dogmatism and tolerance of trait inconsistency. *Journal of Personality and Social Psychology*, 1965, *2*, 104–111.

FOWLER, H. Response to environmental change: A positive replication. *Psychological Reports*, 1958, *4*, 506.

FOWLER, H. *Curiosity and exploratory behavior*. New York: MacMillan, 1965.

FREEDMAN, J. L. Attitudinal effects of inadequate justification. *Journal of Personality*, 1963, *31*, 371–385.

FREEDMAN, J. L. Involvement, discrepancy, and change. *Journal of Abnormal and Social Psychology*, 1964, *69*, 290–295.

FREEDMAN, J. L. Confidence, utility, and selective exposure: A partial replication. *Journal of Personality and Social Psychology*, 1965, *2*, 778–780. (a)

FREEDMAN, J. L. Long-term behavioral effects of cognitive dissonance. *Journal of Experimental Social Psychology*, 1965, *1*, 145–155. (b)

FREEDMAN, J. L. Preference for dissonant information. *Journal of Personality and Social Psychology*, 1965, *2*, 287–289. (c)

FREEDMAN, J. L. & SEARS, D. O. Voters' preferences among types of information. *American Psychologist*, 1963, *18*, 375. (abstract)

FREEDMAN, J. L. & SEARS, D. O. Selective exposure. In L. Berkowitz (Ed.) *Advances in experimental social psychology*, Vol. 2. New York: Academic Press, 1965. Pp. 58–98. (a)

FREEDMAN, J. L. & SEARS, D. O. Warning, distraction and resistance to influence. *Journal of Personality and Social Psychology*, 1965, *1*, 262–265. (b)

FREEDMAN, J. L. & STEINBRUNER, J. D. Perceived choice and resistance to persuasion. *Journal of Abnormal and Social Psychology*, 1964, *68*, 678–681.

FRENCH, J. R. P., JR. A formal theory of social power. *Psychological Review*, 1956, *63*, 181–194.

FRENCH, J. R. P., JR. & RAVEN, B. H. The bases of social power. In D. Cartwright (Ed.), *Studies in social power*. Ann Arbor: University of Michigan Press, 1959.

FRENCH, J. R. P., JR. & SHERWOOD, J. J. Self-actualization and self-identity theory. Paper No. 107, Institute for Research in the Behavioral, Economic, and Management Sciences, Purdue University, 1965.

FRENKEL-BRUNSWIK, E. Dynamic and cognitive categorization of qualitative material: II. Application to interviews with the ethnically prejudiced. *Journal of Psychology*, 1948, *25*, 261–277.

FRENKEL-BRUNSWIK, E. Intolerance of ambiguity as an emotional and perceptual personality variable. In J. S. Bruner & D. Krech (Eds.), *Perception and personality: A symposium*. Durham: Duke University Press, 1949. Pp. 108–143.

FREUD, A. *The ego and the mechanisms of defense*. New York: International Universities Press, 1946.

FREUD, S. Triebe und Triebschicksale. *Inter. Z. f. ärztl. Psychoanal.* [Instincts and their vicissitudes. In S. Freud, *Collected papers*, Vol. IV. London: Hogarth, 1925.]

FREUD, S. Character and anal eroticism. In *Collected papers*, Vol. II. London: Hogarth, 1949. Pp. 45–50. (a)

FREUD, S. Further recommendations in the technique of psychoanalysis. On beginning the treatment. The question of first communication. The dynamics of the cure. In *Collected papers*, Vol. II. London: Hogarth, 1949. Pp. 342–365. (b)

FREUD, S. On the mechanism of paranoia. In *Psychoanalytic notes on an autobiographical account of a case of paranoia*. (1911) Standard Edition of Complete Psychological Works of Sigmund Freud. London: Hogarth, 1958.

FULTON, R. L. The clergyman and the funeral director: A study in role conflict. *Social Forces*, 1961, *39*, 317–323.

GAILON, A. K. & WATTS, W. A. The time of measurement parameter in studies of dissonance reduction. *Journal of Personality*, 1967, *35*, 521–534.

GARDNER, M. The eerie mathematical art of Maurits C. Escher. *Scientific American*, 1966, *214* (4), 110–121.

GARDNER, R. W., HOLTZMAN, P. S., KLEIN, G. S., LINTON, H. B., & SPENCE, D. P. Cognitive control: A study of individual consistencies in cognitive behavior. *Psychological Issues*, 1959, *1*, No. 4, 1–185.

GARDNER, R. W. & SCHOEN, R. A. Differentiation and abstraction in concept formation. *Psychological Monographs*, 1962, *76* (560).

GARFINKEL, H. The rational properties of scientific and common sense activities. *Behavioral Science*, 1960, *5*, 72–83.

GARNER, W. R. *Uncertainty and structure as psychological concepts*. New York: Wiley, 1962.

GARNER, W. R. & CLEMENT, D. E. Goodness of pattern and pattern uncertainty. *Journal of Verbal Learning and Verbal Behavior*, 1963, *2*, 446–452.

GARNER, W. R., HAKE, H. W., & ERIKSEN, C. W. Operationism and the concept of perception. *Psychological Review*, 1956, *63*, 149–159.

GEIS, F. LINDAUER & BOGART, K. No dissonance for Machiavellians? In F. L. Geis and R. Christie (Eds.) *Studies in Machiavellianism*. New York: Academic Press, in press.

GERARD, H. B. Disagreement with others, their credibility, and experienced stress. *Journal of Abnormal and Social Psychology*, 1961, *62*, 554–564.

GERARD, H. B. Conformity and commitment to the group. *Journal of Abnormal and Social Psychology*, 1964, *68*, 209–211.

GERARD, H. B. Deviation, conformity, and commitment. In I. D. Steiner & M. Fishbein (Eds.), *Current studies in social psychology*. New York: Holt, Rinehart and Winston, 1965. Pp. 263–277.

GERARD, H. B. Choice difficulty, dissonance, and the decision sequence. *Journal of Personality*, 1967, *35*, 91–108.

GERARD, H. B., BLEVANS, S. A., & MALCOLM, T. Self-evaluation and the evaluation of choice alternatives. *Journal of Personality,* 1964, *32,* 395–410.

GERARD, H. B. & MATHEWSON, G. C. The effects of severity of initiation on liking for a group: A replication. *Journal of Experimental Social Psychology,* 1966, *2,* 278–287.

GERGEN, K. The effects of interaction goals and personalistic feedback upon the presentation of the self. *Journal of Personality and Social Psychology,* 1965, *1,* 413–424.

GIESE, P. The logic of 'symbolic psycho-logic.' *Behavioral Science,* 1967, *12,* 391–395.

GILL, M. The present state of psychoanalytic theory. *Journal of Abnormal and Social Psychology,* 1959, *58,* 1–8.

GILLISPIE, C. G. *The edge of objectivity: An essay in the history of scientific ideas.* Princeton: Princeton University Press, 1960.

GILSON, C. & ABELSON, R. P. The subjective use of inductive evidence. *Journal of Personality and Social Psychology,* 1965, *2,* 301–310.

GLANZER, M. Curiosity, exploratory drive, and stimulus satiation. *Psychological Bulletin,* 1958, *55,* 302–315.

GLANZER, M. & CLARK, W. H. Accuracy of perceptual recall: An analysis of organization. *Journal of Verbal Learning and Verbal Behavior,* 1962, *1,* 289–299.

GLASS, D. C. Changes in liking as a means of reducing cognitive discrepancies between self-esteem and aggression. *Journal of Personality,* 1964, *32,* 531–549.

GLASS, D. C. Individual and situational differences in the resolution of cognitive discrepancies. Unpublished manuscript, Columbia University, 1965.

GLASS, D. C. Theories of consistency and the study of personality. In E. F. Borgatta & W. W. Lambert (Eds.), *Handbook of personality theory and research.* Chicago: Rand McNally, 1968.

GLASS, D. C. & WOOD, J. D. Self esteem, aggression, and cognitive dissonance. In P. G. Zimbardo (Ed.), *The cognitive control of motivation.* Chicago: Scott, Foresman, 1968.

GLASS, L. B. & BARBER, T. X. A note on hypnotic behavior, the definition of the situation and the placebo effect. *Journal of Nervous and Mental Disease,* 1961, *132,* 539–541.

GOFFMAN, E. *The presentation of self in everyday life.* Garden City, New York: Doubleday, 1959.

GOFFMAN, E. *Encounters: Two studies in the sociology of interaction.* Indianapolis: Bobbs-Merrill, 1961.

GOLDBERG, D. The fertility of two-generation urbanites. *Population Studies,* 1959, *12,* 214–222.

GOLDBERG, P. A. Expectancy, choice, and the other person. *Journal of Personality and Social Psychology,* 1965, *2,* 685–691.

GOLDSTEIN, K. *Human nature in the light of psychopathology.* Cambridge: Harvard University Press, 1947.

GOLDSTEIN, M. J. The relationship between coping and avoiding behavior and response to fear-arousing propaganda. *Journal of Abnormal and Social Psychology,* 1959, *58,* 247–252.

GOLLIN, E. S. Forming impressions of personality. *Journal of Personality,* 1954, *23,* 65–76.

GOLLIN, E. S. Organizational characteristics of social judgment: A developmental investigation. *Journal of Personality,* 1958, *26,* 139–154.

GOODE, W. J. The theory of role-strain. *American Sociological Review,* 1960, *25,* 483–496.

GORDON, C. M. Some effects of information, situation, and personality on decision-making in a clinical setting. *Journal of Consulting Psychology,* 1966, *30,* 219–224.

GOSLING, J. Mental causes and fear. *Mind,* 1962, *71,* 289–306.

GOULDNER, A. W. The norm of reciprocity: A preliminary statement. In E. P. Hollander & R. G. Hunt (Eds.), *Current perspectives in social psychology.* New York: Oxford University Press, 1963. Pp. 436–447.

GRANT, V. The development of a theory of heredity. *American Scientist,* 1956, *44,* 158–179.

GREEN, R. F. & NOWLIS, V. A factor analytic study of the domain of mood with independent experimental validation of the factors. Paper presented at a convention of the American Psychological Association, 1957.

GREENBERG, B. Performance and message consequences of encoding behavior under cognitive stress. Unpublished doctoral dissertation, University of Wisconsin, 1961.

GREENBERG, B. & TANNENBAUM, P. H. Communicator performance under cognitive stress. *Journalism Quarterly*, 1962, *39*, 169–178.

GREENSTEIN, F. I. College students' reactions. In B. Greenberg & E. Parker (Eds.), *The Kennedy assassination and the American public*. Stanford: Stanford University Press, 1965.

GREENWALD, A. G. & SAKUMURA, J. S. Attitude and selective learning: Where are the phenomena of yesteryear? *Journal of Personality and Social Psychology*, 1967, *7*, 387–397.

GREENWALD, H. J. The involvement controversy in persuasion research. Unpublished manuscript, Columbia University, 1965.

GRINKER, J. The control of classical conditioning by threat and cognitive dissonance. Unpublished doctoral dissertation, New York University, 1967.

GROSS, E. & STONE, G. P. Embarrassment and the analysis of role requirements. *American Journal of Sociology*, 1964, *70*, 1–15.

GROSS, N., McEACHERN, A. W., & MASON, W. S. *Explorations in role analysis*. New York: Wiley, 1958.

GULLAHORN, J. Distance and friendship as factors in the gross interaction matrix. *Sociometry*, 1952, *15*, 123–124.

GULLIKSEN, H. Measurement of subjective values. *Psychometrika*, 1956, *21*, 229–244.

GUSFIELD, J. R. & SCHWARTZ, M. The meanings of occupational prestige. *American Sociological Review*, 1963, *28*, 265–271.

HAAS, H. & MAEHR, M. Two experiments on the concept of self and the reaction of others. *Journal of Personality and Social Psychology*, 1965, *1*, 100–105.

HAGAN, E. *On the theory of social change: How economic growth begins*. Homewood, Illinois: Dorsey, 1962.

HALL, A. R. *The scientific revolution* (2nd ed.). Boston: Beacon Press, 1956.

HAMMOND, K. R. Probalistic functioning and the clinical method. *Psychological Review*, 1955, *62*, 255–262.

HAMPSHIRE, S. & HART, H. L. A. Decision, intention, and certainty. *Mind*, 1958, *67*, 1–12.

HANDEL, LEO. *Hollywood looks at its audience*. Urbana, Illinois: University of Illinois Press, 1950.

HARARY, F. On the measurement of structural balance. *Behavioral Science*, 1959, *4*, 316–323.

HARARY, F. A structural analysis of the situation in the Middle East in 1956. *Journal of Conflict Resolution*, 1961, *5*, 167–178.

HARARY, F., NORMAN, R., & CARTWRIGHT, D. *Structural models*. New York: Wiley, 1965.

HARBURG, E. & NEWCOMB, T. M. Psychological balance in situations of negative interpersonal attitudes. *Journal of Personality and Social Psychology*, 1966, *3*, 265–270.

HARDYCK, J. A. Consistency, relevance, and resistance to change. *Journal of Experimental Social Psychology*, 1966, *2*, 27–41.

HARDYCK, J. A. & BRADEN, M. Prophecy fails again: A report of a failure to replicate. *Journal of Abnormal and Social Psychology*, 1962, *65*, 136–141.

HARE, A. P. *Handbook of small group research*. Glencoe, Illinois: Free Press, 1962.

HARLOW, H. R. Mice, monkeys, men, and motives. *Psychological Review*, 1953, *60*, 23–32.

HARRINGTON, G. M. & LINDER, W. K. A positive reinforcing effect of electrical stimulation. *Journal of Comparative and Physiological Psychology*, 1962, *55*, 1014–1015.

HARRIS, D. B. (Ed.) *The concept of development*. Minneapolis: University of Minnesota Press, 1957.

HART, H. L. A. & HONORE, A. M. *Causation in the law*. Oxford: Clarendon Press, 1959.

HARTSMANN, G. W. *Gestalt psychology*. New York: Ronald Press, 1935.

HARVEY, O. J. Personality factors in the resolution of conceptual incongruities. *Sociometry*, 1962, *25*, 336–352.

HARVEY, O. J. (Ed.) *Motivation and social interaction*. New York: Ronald Press, 1963.

HARVEY, O. J. Some situational and cognitive determinants of dissonance resolution. *Journal of Personality and Social Psychology*, 1965, *1*, 349–354.

HARVEY, O. J. & CLAPP, W. Hope, expectancy, and reactions to the unexpected. *Journal of Personality and Social Psychology*, 1965, *2*, 45–52.

HARVEY, O. J., HUNT, D., & SCHRODER, H. *Conceptual systems and personality organization*. New York: Wiley, 1961.

HARVEY, O. J., KELLEY, H., & SHAPIRO, M. M. Reactions to unfavorable evaluations of the self made by other persons. *Journal of Personality*, 1957, *25*, 393–411.

HAYS, W. L. *Statistics for psychologists*. New York: Holt, Rhinehart & Winston, 1963.

HAYWOOD, H. C. Novelty-seeking behavior as a function of manifest anxiety and physiological arousal. *Journal of Personality*, 1962, *30*, 63–74.

HAZARD, P. *The European mind*. London: Hollis & Carter, 1953.

HEBB, D. O. *The organization of behavior*. New York: Wiley, 1949.

HEBB, D. O. Drives and the C.N.S. (conceptual nervous system). *Psychological Review*, 1955, *62*, 243–254.

HEIDER, F. Ding und Medium. *Symposium*, 1927, *1*, 109–157.

HEIDER, F. Dies Leistung des Wahrnehmungssystems, *Zeitschrift fur Psychologie*, 1930, *114*, 371–394.

HEIDER, F. Social perception and phenomenal causality. *Psychological Review*, 1944, *51*, 358–374.

HEIDER, F. Attitudes and cognitive organizations. *Journal of Psychology*, 1946, *21*, 107–112.

HEIDER, F. *The psychology of interpersonal relations*. New York: Wiley, 1958.

HEIDER, F. On perception and event structure, and the psychological environment. *Psychological Issues*, 1959, *1* (3), 1–123.

HEIDER, F. The gestalt theory of motivation. In M. R. Jones (Ed.), *Nebraska symposium on motivation*, Vol. VIII, 1960. Lincoln, Nebraska: University of Nebraska Press, 1960. Pp. 145–172.

HEIDER, F. & SIMMEL, M. An experimental study of apparent behavior. *American Journal of Psychology*, 1944, *57*, 243–259.

HELMREICH, R. & COLLINS, B. Studies in forced compliance: Commitment and magnitude of inducement to comply as determinants of opinion change. *Journal of Personality and Social Psychology*, in press.

HELSON, H. *Adaptation-level theory*. New York: Harper-Row, 1964.

HENDRICK, C. Comment on Waterman and Ford's dissonance reduction or differential recall. *Journal of Personality and Social Psychology*, 1966, *3*, 706–707.

HENDRICK, C. Unpublished doctoral dissertation. University of Missouri, Columbia, Missouri, 1967.

HENNESSEY, B. *Public opinion*. Belmont, California: Wadsworth, 1965.

HERNANDEZ-PEON, R. Psychiatric implications of neurophysiological research. *Bulletin of the Menninger Clinic*, 1964, *28*, 165–185.

HERSHKOWITZ, A. Reported in Jordan, N., Research Paper p-178, Institute for Defense Analysis, Economic and Political Studies Division, Arlington, Virginia, 1966.

HESS, E. H. & POLT, J. M. Pupil size as related to interest value of visual stimuli. *Science*, 1960, *132*, 349–350.

HILGARD, E. R. What becomes of the input from the stimulus? In C. W. Eriksen (Ed.), *Behavior and awareness*. Durham, North Carolina: Duke University Press, 1962. Pp. 46–72.

HINDE, R. A. Unitary drives. *Animal Behavior*, 1959, *7*, 130–141.

HINDE, R. A. Energy models of motivation. *Symposia of Society of Experimental Biology*, 1960, *14*, 199–213.

HOFFMAN, M. L. Conformity as a defense mechanism and a form of resistance to genuine group influence. *Journal of Personality*, 1957, *25*, 412–424.

HOFFMAN, P. J. The paramorphic representation of clinical judgment. *Psychological Bulletin*, 1960, *57*, 116–131.

HOFFMAN, P. J., FESTINGER, L., & LAWRENCE, D. Tendencies toward group comparability in competitive bargaining. *Human relations*, 1954, *7*, 141–159.

HOLT, E. B. *The Freudian wish*. New York: Holt, 1915.

HOLTZMAN, W. H. Personality structure. In P. R. Farnsworth (Ed.), *Annual Review of Psychology*, 1965, *16*, 119–156.

HOMANS, G. C. *The human group*. New York: Harcourt, Brace & Co., 1950.

HOMANS, G. C. Social behavior as exchange. In E. P. Hollander & R. G. Hunt (Eds.), *Current perspectives in social psychology*. New York: Oxford University Press, 1963. Pp. 436–447.

HORNBECK, F. W. Studies in forced compliance: IX. The effects of deception, commitment, and incentive on attitude change produced by the writing of a counterattitudinal essay. Paper presented at the meeting of the Western Psychological Association, 1967.

HOVLAND, C. I. Effects of mass media of communication. In G. Lindzey (Ed.), *Handbook of social psychology*, Vol. II. Cambridge, Massachusetts: Addison-Wesley, 1954. Pp. 1062–1103.

HOVLAND, C. I. The role of primacy and recency in persuasive communication. In N. Maccoby, T. M. Newcomb, & E. L. Hartley (Eds.), *Readings in social psychology*. New York: Holt, 1958.

HOVLAND, C. I., CAMPBELL, E. H., & BROCK, T. The effects of "commitment" on opinion change following communication. In C. I. Hovland (Ed.), *The order of presentation in persuasion*. New Haven: Yale University Press, 1957. Pp. 23–32.

HOVLAND, C. I., HARVEY, O. J., & SHERIF, M. Assimilation and contrast effects to communication and attitude change. *Journal of Abnormal and Social Psychology*, 1957, *55*, 244–252.

HOVLAND, C. I. & JANIS, I. L. (Eds.), *Personality and persuasibility*. New Haven: Yale University Press, 1959.

HOVLAND, C. I., JANIS, I. L., & KELLEY, H. H. *Communication and persuasion*. New Haven: Yale University Press, 1953.

HOVLAND, C. I., LUMSDAINE, A. A., & SHEFFIELD, F. D. *Experiments on mass communication*. Princeton: Princeton University Press, 1949.

HOVLAND, C. I. & PRITZKER, H. A. Extent of opinion change as a function of amount of change advocated. *Journal of Abnormal and Social Psychology*, 1957, *54*, 257–261.

HOVLAND, C. I. & ROSENBERG, M. J. Summary and further theoretical issues. In M. J. Rosenberg, C. I. Hovland, W. J. McGuire, R. P. Abelson, & J. W. Brehm. *Attitude organization and change: An analysis of consistency among attitude components*. New Haven: Yale University Press, 1960. Pp. 198–232.

HOVLAND, C. I. & WEISS, W. The influence of source credibility on communication effectiveness. *Public Opinion Quarterly*, 1951, *15*, 635–650.

HOVLAND, C. I. & WEISS, W. Transmission of information concerning concepts through positive and negative instances. *Journal of Experimental Psychology*, 1953, *45*, 175–182.

HUGHES, H. S. *Consciousness and society: The reorientation of European social thought, 1890–1930*. New York: Knopf, 1958.

HULL, C. L. *Principles of behavior*. New York: Appleton-Century, 1943.

HULL, C. L. The discrimination of stimulus configurations and the hypothesis of afferent neural interaction. *Psychological Review*, 1945, *52*, 133–142.

HULL, C. L. *Essentials of behavior*. New Haven: Yale University Press, 1951.

HUNT, J. McV. Experience and the development of motivation: Some reinterpretations. *Child Development*, 1960, *35*, 489–504.

HUNT, J. McV. Motivation inherent on information processing and action. In O. J. Harvey (Ed.), *Motivation and social interaction*. New York: Ronald Press, 1963. Pp. 35–94.

HUNT, J. McV. Intrinsic motivation and its role in psychological development. In D. Levine (Ed.), *Nebraska symposium on motivation, 1965*. Lincoln, Nebraska: University of Nebraska Press, 1965.

HUNT, M. R. & MILLER, G. R. Open- and closed-mindedness, belief-discrepant communication behavior, and tolerance for dissonance. Paper presented at the convention of the Speech Association of America, New York, 1965.

HYMAN, H. & SHEATSLEY, P. B. Some reasons why information campaigns fail. *Public Opinion Quarterly*, 1947, *11*, 412–423.

INSKO, C. A. Primacy versus recency in persuasion as a function of the timing of arguments and measures. *Journal of Abnormal and Social Psychology*, 1964, *69*, 381–391.

INSKO, C. A. *Theories of attitude change*. New York: Appleton-Century-Crofts, 1967.

IRWIN, M., TRIPODI, T., & BIERI, J. Affective stimulus value and cognitive complexity. *Journal of Personality and Social Psychology*, 1967, *5*, 444–448.

IWAO, S. Internal vs. external criticism of group standards. *Sociometry*, 1963, *26*, 410–421.

JACKSON, D. N. & MESSICK, S. Content and style in personality assessment. *Psychological Bulletin*, 1958, *55*, 243–252.

JAMES, W. *Principles of psychology*, Vol. I. New York: Holt, 1890.

JANICKI, W. P. Effect of disposition on resolution of incongruity. *Journal of Abnormal and Social Psychology*, 1964, *69*, 579–584.

JANIS, I. L. *Psychological Stress*. New York: Wiley, 1958.

JANIS, I. L. Motivational factors in the resolution of decisional conflicts. In M. R. Jones (Ed.), *Nebraska symposium on motivation, 1959*. Lincoln, Nebraska: University of Nebraska Press, 1959. Pp. 198–231.

JANIS, I. L. & GILMORE, J. B. The influence of incentive conditions on the success of role playing in modifying attitudes. *Journal of Personality and Social Psychology*, 1965, *1*, 17–27.

JANIS, I. L. & KAHN, M. Factors influencing tolerance for deprivation. Unpublished progress report, NIMH Grant No. MH-08564, December, 1966.

JANIS, I. L., KAYE, D., & KIRSCHNER, P. Facilitating effects of "eating while reading" on responsiveness to persuasive communications. *Journal of Personality and Social Psychology*, 1965, *1*, 181–186.

JANIS, I. L. & KING, B. T. The influence of role playing on opinion-change. *Journal of Abnormal and Social Psychology*, 1954, *49*, 211–218.

JANIS, I. L. & MANN, L. Effectiveness of emotional role-playing in modifying smoking habits and attitudes. *Journal of Experimental Research in Personality*, 1965, *1*, 84–90.

JANIS, I. L. & MANN, L. A conflict-theory approach to attitude change and decision making. In A. Greenwald, T. Brock, & T. Ostrom (Eds.) *Psychological foundations of attitudes*. New York: Academic Press, 1968.

JANIS, I. L. & TERWILLIGER, R. An experimental study of psychological resistances to fear-arousing communications. *Journal of Abnormal and Social Psychology*, 1962, *65*, 403–411.

JANSEN, M. J. & STOLOROW, L. M. An experimental study in role playing. *Psychological Monographs*, 1962, *76*, No. 31.

JASPERS, J. M. F., VAN DE GEER, J. P., TAJFEL, H., & JOHNSON, N. *On the development of international attitudes*. Leiden: Psychological Institute, University of Leiden, Rapport E. S. P. No. 001-65, 1965.

JECKER, J. D. The cognitive effects of conflict and dissonance. In L. Festinger, *Conflict, decision and dissonance*. Stanford: Stanford University Press, 1964. Pp. 21–32. (a)

JECKER, J. D. Selective exposure to new information. In L. Festinger, *Conflict, decision and dissonance*. Stanford: Stanford University Press, 1964. Pp. 65–82. (b)

JOHNSON, D. M. *The psychology of thought and judgment*. New York: Harper, 1955.

JOHNSON, H. H. Some effects of discrepancy level on responses to negative information about one's self. *Sociometry*, 1966, *29*, 52–67.

JOHNSON, H. H. & STEINER, I. C. Effort and subjective probability. *Journal of Personality and Social Psychology*, 1965, *1*, 365–368.

JOHNSON, R. C., THOMPSON, C. W., & FRINCKE, G. Word values, word frequency, and visual duration thresholds. *Psychological Review*, 1960, *67*, 332–342.

JOHNSTONE, J. W. C. Social structure and patterns of mass media consumption. Unpublished doctoral dissertation, University of Chicago, 1961.

JONES, E. E. *Ingratiation: A social psychological analysis*. New York: Appleton-Century-Crofts, 1964.

JONES, E. E. & ANESHANSEL, J. The learning and utilization of contravaluent material. *Journal of Abnormal and Social Psychology*, 1956, *53*, 27–33.

JONES, E. E., GERGEN, K., & DAVIS, K. E. Some determinants of reactions to being approved or disapproved as a person. *Psychological Monographs*, 1962, 76 (2), (Whole No. 521).

JONES, E. E. & KOHLER, R. The effects of plausibility on the learning of controversial statements. *Journal of Abnormal and Social Psychology*, 1958, *57*, 315–320.

JONES, R. G. Forced compliance dissonance predictions: Obvious, nonobvious, or nonsense? Paper presented at the meeting of the American Psychological Association, New York, September, 1966.

JONES, S. C. Some determinants of interpersonal evaluating behavior. *Journal of Personality and Social Psychology*, 1966, *3*, 397–403.

JORDAN, N. Behavioral forces that are a function of attitudes and of cognitive organization. *Human Relations*, 1953, *6*, 273–287.

JORDAN, N. Cognitive balance, cognitive organization, and attitude change: A critique. *Public Opinion Quarterly*, 1963, 27, 123–132.

JORDAN, N. The cognitive psychology of Fritz Heider. Unpublished manuscript, N-339 (R), The Institute for Defense Analyses, Arlington, Virginia, 1966.

KAHL, J. A. & DAVIS, J. A. A comparison of indexes of socio-economic status. *American Sociological Review*, 1955, *20*, 317–325.

KANOUSE, D. E. & ABELSON, R. P. Language variables affecting the persuasiveness of simple communications. *Journal of Personality and Social Psychology*, 1967, 7, 158–163.

KAPLAN, B. Development aspects of the representation of time. Paper presented at the meeting of the New England Psychological Association, November, 1964.

KAPLAN, B. The comparative developmental approach and its application to symbolization and language in psychopathology. In S. Arieti (Ed.), *American handbook of psychiatry*, Vol. III. New York: Basic Books, 1966. Pp. 659–688.

KAPLAN, B. Meditations on genesis. *Human Development*, 1967, *10*, 65–87.

KARMOS, G., GRASTYAN, E., LOSONCZY, H., VERECKEY, L., & GROSZ, J. The possible role of the hippocampus in the organization of the orientation reaction. *Acta Physiologica*, 1965, *26*, 131–141.

KATZ, D. The functional approach to the study of attitudes. *Public Opinion Quarterly*, 1960, *24*, 163–204.

KATZ, D., SARNOFF, I., & McCLINTOCK, C. Ego-defense and attitude change. *Human Relations*, 1956, *9*, 27–45.

KATZ, D. E. STOTLAND, E. A preliminary statement to a theory of attitude structure and change. In S. Koch (Ed.), *Psychology: A study of a science*, Vol. 3. New York: McGraw-Hill, 1959. Pp. 423–475.

KATZ, E. The two-step flow of communication: An up-to-date report on an hypothesis. *Public Opinion Quarterly*, 1958, *21*, 61–78.

KATZ, E. & FELDMAN, J. J. The Kennedy-Nixon debates: A survey of surveys. In S. Kraus (Ed.), *The great debates*. Bloomington, Indiana: University of Indiana Press, 1962.

KATZ, E. & FOULKES, D. On the use of the mass media as "escape": Clarification of a concept. *Public Opinion Quarterly*, 1962, *26*, 377–388.

KELLER, F. S. *The definition of psychology*. New York: Appleton-Century-Crofts, 1937.

KELLY, G. A. *The psychology of personal constructs*. New York: Norton, 1955.

KELMAN, H. C. Attitude change as a function of response restriction. *Human Relations*, 1953, *6*, 185–214.

KELMAN, H. C. Compliance, identification, and internalization: Three processes of opinion change. *Journal of Conflict Resolution*, 1958, *2*, 51–60.

KELMAN, H. C. Processes of opinion change. *Public Opinion Quarterly*, 1961, *25*, 57–78.

KELMAN, H. C. The induction of action and attitude change. In G. Nielson (Ed.), *Proceedings of the XIV International Congress of Applied Psychology*, Vol. 2. *Personality research*. Copenhagen: Munksgaard, 1962. Pp. 81–110.

KELMAN, H. C. & COHLER, J. Reactions to persuasive communications as a function of cognitive needs and styles. Paper presented at a meeting of the Eastern Psychological Association, Atlantic City, New Jersey, 1959.

KELMAN, H. C. & EAGLY, A. H. Attitude toward the communicator, perception of communication content, and attitude change. *Journal of Personality and Social Psychology*, 1965, *1*, 63–78.

KELMAN, H. C. & HOVLAND, C. I. "Reinstatement" of the communicator in delayed measurement of opinion change. *Journal of Abnormal and Social Psychology*, 1953, *48*, 327–335.

KENNY, D. T. & GINSBERG, R. The specificity of intolerance of ambiguity measures. *Journal of Abnormal and Social Psychology*, 1958, *56*, 300–304.

KERR, C. & SIEGEL, A. The interindustry propensity to strike: An international comparison. In A. Kornhauser *et al.* (Eds.), *Industrial conflict*. New York: McGraw-Hill, 1954. Pp. 189–212.

KERRICK, J. News pictures, captions, and the point of resolution. *Journalism Quarterly*, 1959, *36*, 183–188.

KESSEN, W. & MUNZINGER, H. Stimulus variability and cognitive change. *Psychological Review*, 1966, *73*, 164–179.

KIESLER, C. A. Attraction to the group and conformity to group norms. *Journal of Personality*, 1963, *31*, 559–569.

KIESLER, C. A. Conformity and commitment. *Trans-action*, 1967 (June), 32–35. (a)

KIESLER, C. A. Group pressure and conformity. In J. Mills (Ed.), *Experimental social psychology*. New York: MacMillan, 1967. (b)

KIESLER, C. A., COLLINS, B. E., & MILLER, N. *Attitude change: A critical analysis of theoretical approaches*. New York: Wiley, 1968.

KIESLER, C. A. & CORBIN, L. H. Commitment, attraction, and conformity. *Journal of Personality and Social Psychology*, 1965, *2*, 890–895.

KIESLER, C. A., KIESLER, S., & PALLAK, M. S. The effect of commitment on reactions to norm violations. Unpublished manuscript, Yale University, 1967.

KIESLER, C. A., PALLAK, M. S., & KANOUSE, D. E. The interactive effects of commitment and dissonance. *Journal of Personality and Social Psychology*, 1968, *8*, 331–338.

KIESLER, C. A. & SAKUMURA, J. A test of a model for commitment. *Journal of Personality and Social Psychology*, 1966, *3*, 349–352.

KIESLER, C. A., ZANNA, M., & DESALVO, J. Deviation and conformity: Opinion change as a function of commitment, attraction, and presence of a deviate. *Journal of Personality and Social Psychology*, 1966, *3*, 458–467.

KIMBERLY, J. C. A theory of status equilibration. In J. Berger, M. Zelditch, & B. Anderson (Eds.), *Sociological theories in progress*. Boston: Houghton-Mifflin, 1966. Pp. 213–226.

KIMBLE, G. A. *Hilgard and Marquis' conditioning and learning*. New York: Appleton-Century-Crofts, 1961.

KING, B. & JANIS, I. L. Comparison of the effectiveness of improvised vs. non-improvised role playing in producing opinion changes. *Human Relations*, 1956, *9*, 177–186.

KLAPPER, J. T. *The effects of the mass media*. New York: Columbia University Bureau of Applied Social Research, 1949.

KLECK, R. E. & WHEATON, J. Dogmatism and responses to opinion consistent and opinion inconsistent information. *Journal of Personality and Social Psychology*, 1967, *5*, 249–253.

KNIGHT, K. E. Effect of effort on behavioral rigidity in a Luchins water jar task. *Journal of Abnormal and Social Psychology*, 1963, *66*, 190–192.

KOCH, S. Epilogue. In S. Koch (Ed.), *Psychology: A study of a science*, Vol. 3. New York: McGraw-Hill, 1959. Pp. 729–788.

KOESTLER, A. *The act of creation*. New York: MacMillan, 1964.

KOFFKA, K. *Principles of gestalt psychology*. New York: Harcourt, Brace, 1935.

KOGAN, N. & TAGIURI, R. Interpersonal preference and cognitive organization. *Journal of Abnormal and Social Psychology*, 1958, *56*, 113–116.

KOGAN, N. & WALLACH, M. A. *Risk taking: A study in cognition and personality*. New York: Rinehart & Winston, 1964.

KOHLBERG, L. The development of children's orientations toward a moral order. I: Sequence in the development of moral thought. *Vita Humana*, 1963, *6*, 11–33.

KOHLER, W. *Gestalt psychology*. New York: Liveright, 1947.

KOROBOW, N. Reactions to stress: A reflection of personality trait organization. *Journal of Abnormal and Social Psychology*, 1955, *51*, 464–468.

KRASNER, L. Studies of the conditioning of verbal behavior. *Psychological Bulletin*, 1958, *55*, 148–170.

KEUTHE, J. L. Social schemas. *Journal of Abnormal and Social Psychology*, 1962, *64*, 31–38.

KEUTHE, J. L. & DE SOTO, C. B Grouping and ordering schemata in competition. *Psychonomic Science*, 1964, *1*, 115–116.

KUHN, T. S. *The structure of scientific revolutions*. Chicago: University of Chicago Press, 1962.

LACEY, J. I. Somatic response patterning and stress: Some revisions of activation theory. Paper presented at a symposium on "Issues in Stress", York University, Toronto, Ontario, Canada, May, 1965.

LAFFAL, J. & FELDMAN, S. The structure of single word and continuous word associations. *Journal of Verbal Learning and Verbal Behavior*, 1962, *1*, 54–61.

LAFFAL, J. & FELDMAN, S. The structure of free speech. *Journal of Verbal Learning and Verbal Behavior*, 1963, 2, 498–503.

LAMB, P. & SINGER, J. E. Pleasant and unpleasant experiences. Research Bulletin 66-13. Princeton, New Jersey: Educational Testing Service, 1966.

LAMBERT, R. M. An examination of the consistency characteristics of Abelson and Rosenberg's 'symbolic psycho-logic.' *Behavioral Science*, 1966, *11*, 126–130.

LAMBERT, W. E. & JAKOBOVITS, L. A. Verbal satiation and changes in the intensity of meaning. *Journal of Experimental Psychology*, 1960, *60*, 376–383.

LAMPEL, A. K. & ANDERSON, N. H. Combining visual and verbal information in an impression formation task. *Journal of Personality and Social Psychology*, 1968, *9*, 1–60.

LANA, R. E. Three interpretations of order effects in persuasive communications. *Psychological Bulletin*, 1964, *61*, 314–320.

LANZETTA, J. & DRISCOLL, J. Preference for information about an uncertain but unavoidable outcome. *Journal of Personality and Social Psychology*, 1966, *3*, 96–102.

LARSEN, O. N. & HILL, R. J. Social structure and interpersonal communication. *American Journal of Sociology*, 1958, *63*, 497–505.

LAWLER, E. E., III, & O'GARA, P. The effects of inequity produced by underpayment on work output, work quality, and attitudes toward work. Unpublished manuscript, Yale University, 1966.

LAWSON, R. *Frustration: The development of a scientific concept.* New York: MacMillan, 1965.

LAWRENCE, D. H. & FESTINGER, L. *Deterrents and reinforcement.* Stanford: Stanford University Press, 1962.

LAZARSFELD, P., BERELSON, B., & GAUDET, H. *The people's choice.* New York: Columbia University Press, 1948.

LAZARUS, R. S. A laboratory approach to the dynamics of psychological stress. *American Psychologist*, 1964, *19*, 400–411.

LAZARUS, R. S. *Psychological stress and the coping process.* New York: McGraw-Hill, 1966.

LAZARUS, R. S. & ALFERT, E. Short circuiting of threat by experimentally altering cognitive appraisal. *Journal of Abnormal and Social Psychology*, 1964, *69*, 195–205.

LAZARUS, R. S., SPEISMAN, J. C., MORDKOFF, A. M., & DAVISON, L. A. A laboratory study of psychological stress produced by a motion picture film. *Psychological Monographs*, 1962, *76* (Whole no. 553).

LEACH, E. R. *Political systems of highland Burma.* London: Bell, 1954.

LECKY, P. *Self-consistency: A theory of personality.* New York: Island Press, 1945.

LENSKI, G. E. Status crystallization: A non-vertical dimension of social status. *American Sociological Review*, 1954, *19*, 405–413.

LEPENDORF, S. The effects of incentive value and expectancy on dissonance resulting from attitude-discrepant behavior and disconfirmation of expectancy. Unpublished doctoral dissertation, State University of New York at Buffalo, 1964.

LEVENTHAL, H. Cognitive processes and interpersonal predictions. *Journal of Abnormal and Social Psychology*, 1957, *55*, 176–180.

LEVENTHAL, H. & SINGER, D. L. Cognitive complexity, impression formation, and impression change. *Journal of Personality*, 1964, *32*, 210–226.

LEVENTHAL, H. & WATTS, J. C. Sources of resistance to fear-arousing communications on smoking and lung cancer. *Journal of Personality*, 1966, *34*, 155–175.

LEVINE, J. M. & MURPHY, G. The learning and forgetting of controversial material. *Journal of Abnormal and Social Psychology*, 1943, *38*, 507–517.

LEVINE, R. A. Socialization, social structure, and intersocial images. In H. Kelman (Ed.), *International behavior: A social psychological analysis.* New York: Holt, Rinehart & Winston, 1965. Pp. 45–69.

LEVINE, R. A. *Dreams and deeds.* Chicago: University of Chicago Press, 1966.

LEVINSON, B. Status and prospects of panel analysis. Unpublished doctoral dissertation, Columbia University, 1964.

LEVY, L. *Psychological interpretation.* New York: Holt, Rinehart and Winston, 1963.

Levy, L. H. Group variance and group attractiveness. *Journal of Abnormal and Social Psychology*, 1964, *68*, 661–664.

Levy, L. H. & Richter, M. L. Impressions of groups as a function of the stimulus values of their individual members. *Journal of Abnormal and Social Psychology*, 1963, *67*, 349–354.

Lewin, K. *A dynamic theory of personality*. New York: McGraw-Hill, 1935.

Lewin, K. Frontiers in group dynamics. *Human Relations*, 1947, *1*, 2–38.

Lewin, K. *Field theory in social science*. New York: Harper, 1951.

Lewin, K. Behavior and development as a function of the total situation. In L. Carmichael (Ed.), *Manual of child psychology*. New York: Wiley, 1954. Pp. 918–970.

Lewin, K. Group decision and social change. In G. Swanson, T. Newcomb, & E. Hartley (Eds.), *Readings in social psychology*. New York: Holt, Rinehart and Winston, 1958. Pp. 197–212.

Lewis, M. Some nondecremental effects of effort. *Journal of Comparative and Physiological Psychology*, 1964, *57*, 367–372.

Lieberman, S. The effects of changes in roles on the attitudes of role occupants. *Human Relations*, 1956, *9*, 385–402.

Lifton, R. J. *Thought reform and the psychology of totalism: A study of "brainwashing" in China*. New York: Norton, 1961.

Linder, D. E., Cooper, J., & Jones, E. E. Decision freedom as a determinant of the role of incentive magnitude in attitude change. *Journal of Personality and Social Psychology*, 1967, *6*, 245–254.

Lindsley, D. B. Emotion. In S. S. Stevens (Ed.), *Handbook of experimental psychology*. New York: Wiley, 1951.

Linton, R. *The study of man*. New York: Appleton-Century, 1936.

Linton, R. *The cultural background of personality*. New York: Appleton-Century-Crofts, 1945.

Lippman, W. *Public opinion*. New York: Harcourt-Brace, 1922.

Locke, E. A. The relationship of task success to task liking and satisfaction. *Journal of Applied Psychology*, 1965, *49*, 379–385.

Locke, E. A. Relationship of task success to task liking: A replication. *Psychological Reports*, 1966, *18*, 552–554.

Loehlin, J. C. *Computer models of personality*. New York: Random House, 1968.

Logan, F. A., Olmsted, D. L., Rosner, B. S., Schwartz, R. D., & Stevens, C. M. *Behavior theory and social science*. New Haven: Yale University Press, 1955.

Logan, F. A. & Wagner, A. R. *Reward and punishment*. Boston: Allyn & Bacon, 1965.

Lott, A. J. & Lott, B. E. Group cohesiveness as interpersonal attraction: A review of relationships with antecedent and consequent variables. *Psychological Bulletin*, 1965, *64*, 259–309.

Lott, B. E. Attitude formation: The development of a color preference response through mediated generalization. *Journal of Abnormal and Social Psychology*, 1955, *50*, 321–326.

Lovejoy, A. O. *The great chain of being*. Cambridge, Massachusetts: Harvard University Press, 1936.

Lowe, R., Hays, R., Steiner, I. D. Some effects of the reversibility and consequences of decisions on postdecision information prefernces. *Journal of Personality Psychology*, 1968, *8*, 172–180.

Lowin, A. Information selectivity as a function of agreement with message and ease of message refutation. Unpublished doctoral dissertation, Columbia University, 1965.

Lowin, A. Approach and avoidance: Alternative modes of selective exposure to information. *Journal of Personality and Social Psychology*, 1967, *6*, 1–9. (a)

Lowin, A. On the choice between supportive and non-supportive information. Paper presented at the convention of the American Psychological Association, Washington, D.C., 1967. (b)

Lowin, A. & Epstein, G. F. Does expectancy determine performance? *Journal of Experimental Social Psychology*, 1965, *1*, 248–255.

Luchins, A. S. Experimental attempts to minimize the impact of first impressions. In C. I. Hovland (Ed.), *The order of presentation in persuasion*. New Haven: Yale University Press, 1957. Pp. 62–75.

LUMSDAINE, A. & JANIS, I. Resistance to "counterpropaganda" produced by a two-sided "propaganda" presentation. *Public Opinion Quarterly*, 1953, *17*, 311–318.

LURIA, A. R. *The nature of human conflicts*. New York: Liveright, 1932.

LYNCH, M. D. Modes of resolution of cognitive inconsistency and mood-stress through communication activity. Unpublished doctoral dissertation, University of Wisconsin, 1963.

MACCOBY, E. E. & WILSON, W. C. Identification and observational learning from films. *Journal of Abnormal and Social Psychology*, 1957, *55*, 76–87.

MACCOBY, E. E., WILSON, W. C., & BURTON, R. V. Differential movie-viewing behavior of male and female viewers. *Journal of Personality*, 1958, *26*, 259–267.

MADDI, S. R. Affective tone during environmental regularity and change. *Journal of Abnormal and Social Psychology*, 1961, *62*, 338–345. (a)

MADDI, S. R. Exploratory behavior and variation-seeking in man. In D. W. Fiske & S. R. Maddi (Eds.), *Functions of varied experience*. Homewood, Illinois: Dorsey, 1961. Pp. 253–277. (b)

MADDI, S. R. Unexpectedness, affective tone, and behavior. In D. W. Fiske & S. R. Maddi (Eds.), *Functions of varied experience*. Homewood, Illinois: Dorsey, 1961. Pp. 380–401. (c)

MADDI, S. R. The pursuit and avoidance of variety. Unpublished manuscript. Chicago, 1968. (a)

MADDI, S. R. Personality theories: A comparative analysis. Homewood, Illinois: Dorsey Press, 1968. (b)

MADDI, S. R. & ANDREWS, S. L. The need for variety in fantasy and self-description. *Journal of Personality*, 1966, *34*, 610–626.

MADDI, S. R. & BERNE, N. Novelty of productions and desire for novelty as active and passive forms of the need for variety. *Journal of Personality*, 1964, *32*, 270–277.

MADDI, S. R. & PROPST, B. S. Activation and personality. Paper presented at a meeting of the American Psychological Association, Philadelphia, 1963.

MADDI, S. R., PROPST, B. S., & FELDINGER, I. Three expressions of the need for variety. *Journal of Personality*, 1965, *33*, 82–98.

MAEHR, M., MENSING, J., & NAFZGHER, S. Concept of self and the reaction of others. *Sociometry*, 1962, *25*, 353–357.

MAIR, L. *Primitive government*. Baltimore: Penguin, 1962.

MALEWSKI, A. The influence of positive and negative self-evaluation on postdecisional dissonance. *Polish Sociological Bulletin*, 1962, *3–4*, 39–49.

MALEWSKI, A. Some limitations of the theory of cognitive dissonance. *Polish Sociological Bulletin*, 1964, No. 1, 6–15.

MALMO, R. B. Measurement of drive: An unsolved problem in psychology. In M. R. Jones (Ed.), *Nebraska symposium on motivation*. Lincoln, Nebraska: University of Nebraska Press, 1958. Pp. 229–265.

MALMO, R. B. Activation: A neurophysiological dimension. *Psychological Review*, 1959, *66*, 367–386.

MANDLER, G., MANDLER, J. M., KREMEN, I., & SHOLITON, R. D. The response to threat: Relations among verbal and physiological indices. *Psychological Monographs*, 1961, *75* (Whole No. 513).

MANDLER, G. & SARASON, S. B. The study of anxiety and learning. *Journal of Abnormal and Social Psychology*, 1952, *47*, 166–173.

MANIS, M. The interpretation of opinion statements as a function of message ambiguity and recipient attitude. *Journal of Abnormal and Social Psychology*, 1961, *63*, 76–81. (a)

MANIS, M. Interpretation of opinion statements as a function of recipient attitude and source prestige. *Journal of Abnormal and Social Psychology*, 1961, *63*, 82–86. (b)

MANIS, M. *Cognitive processes*. Belmont, California: Wadsworth, 1966.

MANIS, M., GLEASON, T. C., & DAWES, R. M. The evaluation of complex social stimuli. *Journal of Personality and Social Psychology*, 1966, *3*, 404–419.

MANN, L. The effects of emotional role-playing on desire to modify smoking habits. *Journal of Experimental Social Psychology*, 1967, *3*, 334–348.

MANN, L. & JANIS, I. L. A follow-up study on the long range effects of emotional role playing. *Journal of Personality and Social Psychology*, 1968, *8*, 339–342.

MANSER, A. Pleasure. *Proceedings of the Aristotelian Society*, 1960–61, *61*, 223–238.

MANSSON, H. H. The cognitive control of thirst motivation: A dissonance approach. Unpublished doctoral dissertation, New York University, 1965.

MARCANTONIO, C. Performance expectancy as a determinant of actual performance: With particular reference to individual difference variables. Unpublished doctoral dissertation, State University of New York at Buffalo, 1966.

MARCH, J. & SIMON, H. *Organizations.* New York: Wiley, 1958.

MAREK, J. Technological development, organization, and interpersonal relations. *Acta Sociologica,* 1966, in press.

MARLOWE, D. & CROWNE, D. P. *The approval motive.* New York: Wiley, 1964.

MARLOWE, D., FRAGER, R., & NUTTALL, R. L. Commitment to action-taking as a consequence of cognitive dissonance. *Journal of Personality and Social Psychology,* 1965, *2*, 864–867.

MASLOW, A. H. A dynamic theory of human motivation. *Psychological Review,* 1943, *50*, 370–396.

MASLOW, A. H. Toward a psychology of being. Princeton: Van Nostrand, 1962.

MAYO, C. W. & CROCKETT, W. H. Cognitive complexity and primacy-recency effects in impression formation. *Journal of Abnormal and Social Psychology,* 1964, *68*, 335–338.

McBRIDE, D. The effects of public and private changes of opinion on intra-group communication. Unpublished manuscript, University of Minnesota, 1954.

McCLELLAND, D. C. *The achieving society.* Princeton: Princeton University Press, 1961.

McCLELLAND, D. C., ATKINSON, J. W., CLARK, R. W., & LOWELL, E. L. *The achievement motive.* New York: Appleton-Century-Crofts, 1953.

McDOUGALL, W. *An introduction to social psychology.* Boston: J. W. Luce, 1923.

McGUIGAN, F. J. The experimenter: A neglected stimulus object. *Psychological Bulletin,* 1963, *60*, 421–428.

McGUIRE, W. J. Cognitive consistency and attitude change. *Journal of Abnormal and Social Psychology,* 1960, *60*, 345–353. (a)

McGUIRE, W. J. Direct and indirect effects of dissonance-producing messages. *Journal of Abnormal and Social Psychology,* 1960, *60*, 354–358. (b)

McGUIRE, W. J. A syllogistic analysis of cognitive relationships. In M. J. Rosenberg, C. I. Hovland, W. J. McGuire, R. P. Abelson, & J. W. Brehm, *Attitude organization and change.* New Haven: Yale University Press, 1960. Pp. 65–111. (c)

McGUIRE, W. J. Inducing resistance to persuasion. In L. Berkowitz (Ed.), *Advances in experimental social psychology,* Vol. I. New York: Academic Press, 1964. Pp. 191–229.

McGUIRE, W. J. Attitudes and opinions. *Annual Review of Psychology,* 1966, *17*, 475–514. (a)

McGUIRE, W. J. The current status of cognitive consistency theories. In S. Feldman (Ed.), *Cognitive consistency: Motivational antecedents and behavioral consequents.* New York: Academic Press, 1966. (b)

McGUIRE, W. J. Some impending reorientations in social psychology. *Journal of Experimental Social Psychology,* 1967, *3*, 124–139.

McGUIRE, W. J. *Immunization against persuasion.* New Haven: Yale University Press, 1968. (a)

McGUIRE, W. J. The nature of attitudes and attitude change. In G. Lindzey & E. Aronson (Eds.), *Handbook of social psychology.* Reading, Massachusetts: Addison-Wesley, 1968. (b)

McGUIRE, W. J. & MILLMAN, S. Anticipatory belief lowering following forewarning of a persuasive attack. *Journal of Personality and Social Psychology,* 1965, *2*, 471–479.

McGUIRE, W. J. & PAPAGEORGIS, D. The relative efficacy of various types of prior belief-defense in producing immunity against persuasion. *Journal of Abnormal and Social Psychology,* 1961, *62*, 327–337.

McKINNON, D. W. The personality correlates of creativity: A study of American architects. *Proceedings of the XIX International Congress of Applied Psychology,* 1962.

McNULTY, J. A. & WALTER, R. H. Emotional arousal, conflict, and susceptibility to social influence. *Canadian Journal of Psychology,* 1962, *16*, 211–220.

MEAD, G. H. *Mind, self, and society*. Chicago: University of Chicago Press, 1934.

MEEHL, P. E. The cognitive activity of the clinician. *American Psychologist*, 1960, *15*, 19–27.

MELTZER, B., CROCKETT, W. H., & ROSENKRANTZ, P. S. Cognitive complexity, value incongruity, and the integration of potentially incompatible information in impressions of others. *Journal of Personality and Social Psychology*, 1966, *4*, 338–343.

MERTON, R. K. Bureaucratic structure and personality. *Social Forces*, 1940, *18*, 560–568.

MERTON, R. K. The social psychology of housing. In W. Dennis (Ed.), *Current trends in social psychology*. Pittsburgh: University of Pittsburgh, 1948. Pp. 203–209.

MERTON, R. K. *Social theory and social structure*. New York: The Free Press of Glencoe, 1957.

MERTON, R. K. & KITT, A. S. Contributions to the theory of reference group behavior. In R. K. Merton & P. F. Lazarsfeld (Eds.), *Studies in the scope and method of "The American soldier."* Glencoe, Illinois: Free Press, 1950.

MILLER, D. R. The study of social relationships: Situation, identity, and social interaction. In S. Koch (Ed.), *Psychology: A study of a science*, Vol. 5. New York: McGraw-Hill, 1963. Pp. 639–737.

MILLER, G. A. The magical number seven plus or minus two: Some limits on our capacity for processing information. *Psychological Review*, 1956, *63*, 81–97.

MILLER, G. A., GALANTER, E., & PRIBRAM, K. H. *Plans and the structure of behavior*. New York: Henry Holt, 1960.

MILLER, H. & BIERI, J. An informational analysis of clinical judgment. *Journal of Abnormal and Social Psychology*, 1963, *67*, 317–325.

MILLER, H. & BIERI, J. Cognitive complexity as a function of the significance of the stimulus object being judged. *Psychological Reports*, 1965, *16*, 1203–1204.

MILLER, J. G. Toward a general theory for the behavioral sciences. *American Psychologist*, 1955, *10*, 513–531.

MILLER, N. Involvement and dogmatism as inhibitors of attitude change. *Journal of Experimental Social Psychology*, 1965, *1*, 121–132.

MILLER, N. & CAMPBELL, D. T. Recency and primacy in persuasion as a function of the timing of speeches and measurements. *Journal of Abnormal and Social Psychology*, 1959, *59*, 1–10.

MILLER, N. & LEVY, B. J. Defaming and agreeing with the communicator as a function of emotional arousal, communication extremity and evaluative set. *Sociometry*, 1967, in press.

MILLER, N. E. Experimental studies of conflict. In J. McV. Hunt (Ed.), *Personality and the behavioral disorders*. Vol. I. New York: Ronald Press, 1944.

MILLER, N. E. Experiments on motivation. *Science*, 1957, *126*, 1271–1278.

MILLER, N. E. Liberalization of basic S-R concepts: Extensions to conflict, behavior, motivation and social learning. In S. Koch (Ed.), *Psychology: A study of a science*, Vol. 2. New York: McGraw-Hill, 1959.

MILLER, N. E. Analytical studies of drive and reward. *American Psychologist*, 1961, *16*, 739–754.

MILLER, N. E. & DOLLARD, J. *Social learning and imitation*. New Haven: Yale University Press, 1941.

MILLS, J. Changes in moral attitudes following temptation. *Journal of Personality*, 1958, *26*, 517–531.

MILLS, J. Avoidance of dissonant information. *Journal of Personality and Social Psychology*, 1965, *2*, 589–593. (a)

MILLS, J. Effect of certainty about a decision upon post decision exposure to consonant and dissonant information. *Journal of Personality and Social Psychology*, 1965, *2*, 749–752. (b)

MILLS, J. The effect of certainty on exposure to information prior to commitment. *Journal of Experimental Social Psychology*, 1965, *1*, 348–355. (c)

MILLS, J., ARONSON, E., & ROBINSON, H. Selectivity in exposure to information. *Journal of Abnormal and Social Psychology*, 1959, *59*, 250–253.

MILLS, J. & JELLISON, J. M. Avoidance of discrepant information prior to commitment. *Journal of Personality and Social Psychology*, 1968, *8*, 59–62.

MILLS, J. & Ross, A. Effects of commitment and certainty upon interest in supporting information. *Journal of Abnormal and Social Psychology*, 1964, *68*, 552–555.

MILTON, G. A. The effects of sex-role identification upon problem solving skill. *Journal of Abnormal and Social Psychology*, 1957, *55*, 208–212.

MISCHEL, T. Personal constructs, rules, and the logic of clinical activity. *Psychological Review*, 1964, *71*, 180–192.

MITCHELL, J. C. *The Kalela dance.* Rhodes-Livingston Institute, Paper No. 27. Manchester: Manchester University Press, 1956.

MITRA, S. Letter to the editors. *Behavioral Science*, 1962, 7, 107.

MITTMAN, L. R. & TERRELL, G. An experimental study of curiosity in children. *Child Development*, 1964, *35*, 851–855.

MOERMAN, M. Ethnic identification in a complex civilization: Who are the Luo? *American Anthropologist*, 1965, *67*, 1215–1230.

MONTGOMERY, K. C. The role of exploratory drive in learning. *Journal of Comparative and Physiological Psychology*, 1954, *47*, 60–64.

MOORE, W. E. & HAGAN, E. E. On the theory of social change. *American Sociological Review*, 1963, *28*(2), 296.

MORGAN, W. J. & MORTON, A. B. The distortion of syllogistic reasoning produced by personal convictions. *Journal of Social Psychology*, 1944, *20*, 39–59.

MORRISSETTE, J. O. An experimental study of the theory of structural balance. *Human Relations*, 1958, *11*, 239–254.

MORRISSETTE, J. O., JAHNKE, J. C., & BAKER, K. Structural balance: A test of the completeness hypothesis. *Behavioral Science*, 1966, *11*, 121–125.

MOULTON, R. W. Effects of success and failure on level of aspiration as related to achievement motives. *Journal of Personality and Social Psychology*, 1965, *1*, 399–406.

MOWRER, O. H. *Learning theory and personality dynamics.* New York: Ronald Press, 1950.

MOWRER, O. H. Cognitive dissonance or counterconditioning? A reappraisal of certain behavioral "paradoxes." *Psychological Record*, 1963, *133*, 197–211.

MURDOCK, P. H. J. The effects of categorization style and cognitive risk upon judgment response language. Unpublished masters thesis, University of North Carolina, 1965.

MURRAY, E. J. & BERKUN, M. M. Displacement as a function of conflict. *Journal of Abnormal and Social Psychology*, 1955, *51*, 47–56.

NEWCOMB, T. M. Autistic hostility and social reality. *Human Relations*, 1947, *1*, 69–86.

NEWCOMB, T. M. *Social Psychology.* New York: Dryden, 1951.

NEWCOMB, T. M. Attitude development as a function of reference groups: The Bennington study. In G. E. Swanson, T. M. Newcomb & E. L. Hartley (Eds.), *Readings in social psychology* (2nd ed.). Holt, Rinehart and Winston, 1952.

NEWCOMB, T. M. An approach to the study of communicative acts. *Psychological Review*, 1953, *60*, 393–404.

NEWCOMB, T. M. Individual systems of orientation. In S. Koch (Ed.), *Psychology: A study of a science*, Vol. 3. New York: McGraw-Hill, 1959. Pp. 384–422.

NEWCOMB, T. M. Varieties of interpersonal attraction. In D. Cartwright & A. Zander (Eds.), *Group dynamics: Research and theory.* Harper & Row, 1960.

NEWCOMB, T. M. *The acquaintance process.* New York: Holt, Rinehart and Winston, 1961.

NEWCOMB, T. M. Stabilities underlying changes in interpersonal attraction. *Journal of Abnormal and Social Psychology*, 1963, *66*, 376–386.

NEWCOMB, T. M., TURNER, R. H., & CONVERSE, P. E. *Social psychology.* Holt, Rinehart and Winston, 1965.

NICKI, R. M. The reinforcing effect of uncertainty reduction on a human operant. Unpublished doctoral dissertation, University of Toronto, 1968.

NORRIS, E. L. Belief change and stress reduction as modes of resolving cognitive inconsistency. Unpublished doctoral dissertation, University of Wisconsin, 1964.

NOWLIS, G. & JANIS, I. L. Factors influencing the effectiveness of emotional role-playing in modifying attitudes and actions. Unpublished manuscript, Yale University, 1968.

NOWLIS, V. The development and modification of motivational systems in personality. *Nebraska symposium on motivation, 1953.* Lincoln, Nebraska: University of Nebraska Press, 1953. Pp. 114–138.

NOWLIS, V. Some dimensions of mood and their interaction. Paper presented at the Symposium on Psychobiological Approaches to Social Behavior, Harvard University, 1963.

NUTTIN, J. M., JR. Dissonant evidence about dissonance theory. Paper presented at the Second Conference of Experimental Social Psychologists in Europe, Frascati, Italy, 1964.

NUTTIN, J. M., JR. Attitude change after rewarded dissonant and consonant "forced compliance." *International Journal of Psychology*, 1966, *1*, 39–57.

ORNE, M. T. On the social psychology of the psychological experiment: With particular reference to demand characteristics and their implications. *American Psychologist*, 1962, *17*, 776–783.

OSGOOD, C. E. The nature and measurement of meaning. *Psychological Bulletin*, 1952, *49*, 197–237.

OSGOOD, C. E. *Method and theory in experimental psychology*. New York: Oxford University Press, 1953.

OSGOOD, C. E. Motivational dynamics of language behavior. In M. R. Jones (Ed.), *Nebraska symposium on motivation, 1957*. Lincoln, Nebraska: University of Nebraska Press, 1957.

OSGOOD, C. E. Cognitive dynamics in the conduct of human affairs. *Public Opinion Quarterly*, 1960, *24*, 341–365.

OSGOOD, C. E., SAPORTA, S., & NUNNALLY, J. C. Evaluative assertion analysis. *Litera*, 1956, *3*, 47–102.

OSGOOD, C. E., SUCI, G. J., & TANNENBAUM, P. H. *The measurement of meaning*. Urbana, Illinois: University of Illinois Press, 1957.

OSGOOD, C. E. & TANNENBAUM, P. H. The principle of congruity in the prediction of attitude change. *Psychological Review*, 1955, *62*, 42–55.

OSSORIO, P. G. *Persons*. Boulder, Colorado: Linguistic Research Institute, 1966.

OSSORIO, P. G. & DAVIS, K. E. The self, intentionality, and reactions to evaluations of the self. In C. Gordon & K. J. Gergen (Eds.), *Self in society*. New York: Wiley, 1968.

OSTROM, T. M. Perspective as an intervening construct in the judgment of attitude statements. *Journal of Personality and Social Psychology*, 1965, *3*, 135–145.

OSTROM, T. M. & BROCK, T. C. A cognitive model of attitudinal involvement. Unpublished manuscript. Ohio State University, 1968.

OVERALL, J. E. Note on the scientific status of factors. *Psychological Bulletin*, 1964, *61*, 270–276.

PALLAK, M. S. Task performance and dissonance reduction processes. Unpublished manuscript, Yale University, 1966.

PAPAGEORGIS, D. Bartlett effect and the persistence of induced opinion change. *Journal of Abnormal and Social Psychology*, 1963, *67*, 61–67.

PAPAGEORGIS, D. & TYLER, C. Bartlett's retention revisited. *Psychological Reports*, 1966, *18*, 723–729.

PARDUCCI, A. & MARSHALL, L. M. Assimilation vs. contrast in the anchoring of perceptual judgments of weights. *Journal of Experimental Psychology*, 1962, *63*, 426–437.

PARKER, E. C., BARRY, D. W., & SMYTHE, D. W. *The television-radio audience and religion*. New York: Harper, 1955.

PAUL, I. H. Impressions of personality, authoritarianism, and the *fait accompli* effect. *Journal of Abnormal and Social Psychology*, 1956, *53*, 338–344.

PAVLOV, I. P. *Conditioned reflexes*. Trans. by G. V. Anrep. London: Oxford University Press, 1927.

PEAK, H. Problems of objective observation. In L. Festinger & D. Katz (Eds.), *Research methods in the behavioral sciences*. New York: Dryden, 1953. Pp. 243–299.

PEAK, H. Attitude and motivation. In M. Jones (Ed.), *Nebraska symposium of motivation, 1955*. Lincoln, Nebraska: University of Nebraska Press, 1955. Pp. 149–188.

PEAK, H. Psychological structure and person perception. In R. Tagiuri & L. Petrullo (Eds.), *Person perception and interpersonal behavior*. Stanford: Stanford University Press, 1958. Pp. 337–352. (a)

PEAK, H. Psychological structure and psychological activity. *Psychological Review*, 1958, *65*, 325–347. (b)

PEAK, H. The effect of aroused motivation on attitudes. *Journal of Abnormal and Social Psychology*, 1960, *61*, 463–468.

PECKHAM, M. *Man's rage for chaos*. Philadelphia: Chelton, 1965.

PENNER, D. D. An experimental test of cognitive dissonance vs. counterconditioning as predictors of resistance to extinction. Paper presented at a meeting of the Midwestern Psychological Association, May, 1966.

PENNER, D. D., FITCH, G., & WEICK, K. E. Dissonance and the revision of choice criteria. *Journal of Personality and Social Psychology*, 1966, *3*, 701–705.

PENROSE, L. S. & PENROSE, R. Impossible objects: A special type of visual illusion. *British Journal of Psychology*, 1958.

PEPITONE, A. *Attraction and hostility*. New York: Atherton Press, 1964.

PEPITONE, A. Some conceptual and empirical problems of consistency models. In S. Feldman (Ed.), *Cognitive consistency*. New York: Academic Press, 1966. Pp. 257–297.

PEPITONE, A. & FESHBACH, S. A theoretical analysis of conflict. In N. Washburne (Ed.), *Decisions, values and groups*, Vol. II. Oxford: Pergamon, 1962. Pp. 440–452.

PEPITONE, A., McCAULEY, C., & HAMMOND, P. Change in attractiveness of forbidden toys as a function of severity of threat. *Journal of Experimental Social Psychology*, 1967, *3*, 221–229.

PEPPER, S. *World hypotheses*. Berkeley: University of California Press, 1942.

PERVIN, L. A. & YATKO, R. J. Cigarette smoking and alternative methods of reducing dissonance. *Journal of Personality and Social Psychology*, 1965, *2*, 30–36.

PETERMANN, B. *The gestalt theory and the problem of configuration*. London: Routledge & Kegan Paul, 1950.

PETERS, R. S. *The concept of motivation*. London: Routledge & Kegan Paul, 1958.

PETERS, R. S. Emotions, passivity, and the place of Freud's theory in psychology. In B. Wolman & E. Nagel (Eds.), *Scientific psychology*. New York: Basic Books, 1965.

PETTIGREW, T. F. The measurement and correlates of category width as a cognitive variable. *Journal of Personality*, 1958, *26*, 532–544.

PFAFFMAN, C. The pleasures of sensation. *Psychological Review*, 1960, *67*, 253–268.

PHILLIPS, J. L. A model for cognitive balance. *Psychological Review*, 1967, *74*, 481–495.

PIAGET, J. *The moral judgment in the child*. London: Kegan Paul, 1932.

PIAGET, J. *The psychology of intelligence*. New York: Harcourt Brace, 1950.

PILISUK, M. Cognitive balance and self-relevant attitudes. *Journal of Abnormal and Social Psychology*, 1962, *65*, 95–103.

PILISUK, M. Anxiety, self acceptance and open-mindedness. *Journal of Clinical Psychology*, 1963, *19*, 387–391. (a)

PILISUK, M. Cognitive balance, primary groups, and the patient-therapist relationship. *Behavioral Science*, 1963, *8*, 137–145. (b)

PLATT, J. R. Beauty: Pattern and change. In D. W. Fiske & S. R. Maddi (Eds.), *Functions of varied experience*. Homewood, Illinois: Dorsey, 1961.

PLAYBOY INTERVIEW: Miles Davis—candid conversation. *Playboy*, 1962, *9*, 57.

PODELL, H. A. & PODELL, J. E. Quantitative connotation of a concept. *Journal of Abnormal and Social Psychology*, 1963, *67*, 509–513.

PODELL, J. E. & PODELL, H. A. Effect of number of trait referent adjectives on impressions of persons. Paper presented at the meeting of the Western Psychological Association, April, 1963.

POLEZHAEV, E. F. The role of the orientation reflex in the co-ordination of the cerebral cortex. In L. G. Voronin *et al.* (Eds.) *Orientirovochny refleks i orientirovochno-issledovatel 'skaia deiatelnost.' (The orienting reflex and exploratory behavior.)* Moscow: Academy of Pedagogical Science, 1958.

POLSBY, N. W. *Community power and political theory*. New Haven: Yale University Press, 1963.

POSNER, M. I. Information reduction in the analysis of sequential tasks. *Psychological Review*, 1964, *71*, 491–504.

POSTMAN, L. & TOLMAN, E. C. Brunswik's probalistic functionalism. In S. Koch (Ed.), *Psychology: A study of a science*, Vol. 1. New York: McGraw-Hill, 1959. Pp. 502–564.

PRELINGER, E. Extension and structure of the self. *Journal of Psychology*, 1959, *47*, 13–23.

PREMACK, D. Reinforcement theory. In D. Levine (Ed.), *Nebraska symposium on motivation, 1965*. Lincoln, Nebraska: University of Nebraska Press, 1965.

PRICE, K. O., HARBURG, E., & NEWCOMB, T. M. Psychological balance in situations of negative interpersonal attitudes. *Journal of Personality and Social Psychology*, 1966, *3*, 265–270.

RABBIE, J. M. Differential preference for companionship under threat. *Journal of Abnormal and Social Psychology*, 1963, *67*, 188–190.

RABBIE, J. M., BREHM, J. W., & COHEN, A. R. Verbalization and reactions to cognitive dissonance. *Journal of Personality*, 1959, *27*, 407–417.

RAPAPORT, C. Character style, anxiety and social affiliation. Unpublished doctoral dissertation, New York University, 1963.

RAPAPORT, D. The structure of psychoanalytic theory: A systematizing attempt. In S. Koch (Ed.), *Psychology: A study of a science*, Vol. 3. New York: McGraw-Hill, 1959. Pp. 55–183.

RAPAPORT, D. Psychoanalysis as a development psychology. In B. Kaplan & S. Wapner (Eds.), *Perspectives in psychological theory*. New York: International Universities Press, 1960.

RAZRAN, G. H. S. Conditioned response changes in rating and appraising sociopolitical slogans. *Psychological Bulletin*, 1940, *37*, 481.

REBERT, C. S., MCADAM, D. W., KNOTT, J. R., & IRWIN, D. A. Slow potential change in human brain related to level of motivation. *Journal of Comparative and Physiological Psychology*, 1967, *63*, 20–23.

REISEN, A. H. Stimulation as a requirement for growth and function in behavioral development. In D. W. Fiske & S. R. Maddi (Eds.), *Functions of varied experience*. Homewood, Illinois: Dorsey, 1961.

RESTLE, F. A metric and an ordering on sets. *Psychometrika*, 1959, *24*, 207–220.

REYNOLDS, G. S. Behavioral contrast. *Journal of Experimental and Analytical Behavior*, 1961, *4*, 57–71.

RHEES, R. Can there be a private language? *Proceedings of the Aristotelian Society*, 1954, Supplement V, *28*, 77–99.

RHINE, R. J. Some problems in dissonance theory research on information selectivity. *Psychological Bulletin*, 1967, *68*, 21–28. (a)

RHINE, R. J. The 1964 presidential election and curves of information seeking and avoiding. *Journal of Personality and Social Psychology*, 1967, *5*, 416–423. (b)

RIMLAND, B. *Infantile autism: The syndrome and its implications for a theory of behavior*. New York: Appleton-Century-Crofts, 1964.

RIMOLDI, H. J. A. Prediction of scale values for combined stimuli. *British Journal of Statistical Psychology*, 1956, *9*, 29–40.

RODRIGUES, A. The psycho-logic of interpersonal relations. Unpublished doctoral dissertation, University of California, Los Angeles, 1966.

RODRIGUES, A. Effects of balance, positivity, and agreement in triadic social relations. *Journal of Personality and Social Psychology*, 1967, *5*, 472–476.

ROGERS, C. A. A theory of therapy, personality, and interpersonal relationships, as developed in the client-centered framework. In S. Koch (Ed.), *Psychology: A study of a science*, Vol. 3. New York: McGraw-Hill, 1959. Pp. 184–256.

ROGERS, E. M. *Diffusion of innovations*. New York: The Free Press of Glencoe, 1962.

ROKEACH, M. *The open and closed mind*. New York: Basic Books, 1960.

ROKEACH, M. & MEYER, L. Race and shared belief as factors in social choice. *Science*, 1966, *151*, 167–172.

ROKEACH, M. & ROTHMAN, G. The principle of belief congruence and the congruity principle as models of cognitive interaction. *Psychological Review*, 1965, *72*, 128–142.

ROKEACH, M. & VIDULICH, R. N. The formation of new belief systems: the roles of memory and the capacity to entertain. In M. Rokeach, *The open and closed mind*. New York: Basic Books, 1960. Pp. 196–214.

ROSE, A. M. The concept of class and American sociology. *Sociological Resumes*, 1958, *25*, 53–69.

ROSEN, S. Postdecision affinity for incompatible information. *Journal of Abnormal and Social Psychology*, 1961, *63*, 188–190.

ROSENBERG, M. J. Cognitive structure and attitudinal affect. *Journal of Abnormal and Social Psychology*, 1956, *53*, 367–372.

ROSENBERG, M. J. An analysis of affective-cognitive consistency. In M. J. Rosenberg, C. I. Hovland, W. J. McGuire, R. P. Abelson, & J. W. Brehm, *Attitude organization and change*. New Haven: Yale University Press, 1960. Pp. 15–64. (a)

ROSENBERG, M. J. Cognitive reorganization in response to the hypnotic reversal of attitudinal affect. *Journal of Personality*, 1960, *28*, 39–63. (b)

ROSENBERG, M. J. A structural theory of attitude dynamics. *Public Opinion Quarterly*, 1960, *24*, 319–340. (c)

ROSENBERG, M. J. Simulated man and the humanistic criticism. In S. S. Tomkins & S. Messick (Eds.), *Computer simulation of personality*. New York: Wiley, 1963. Pp. 113–124.

ROSENBERG, M. J. Images in relation to the policy process. In H. C. Kelman (Ed.), *International behavior*. New York: Holt, Rinehart & Winston, 1965. Pp. 278–334. (a)

ROSENBERG, M. J. Inconsistency arousal and reduction in attitude change. In I. D. Steiner & M. Fishbein (Eds.), *Current studies in social psychology*. New York: Holt, Rinehart & Winston, 1965 . Pp. 121–134. (b)

ROSENBERG, M. J. Some content determinants of intolerance for attitudinal inconsistency. In S. S. Tomkins & C. I. Izard (Eds.), *Affect, cognition and personality*. New York: Springer, 1965. Pp. 130–147. (c)

ROSENBERG, M. J. When dissonance fails: On eliminating evaluation apprehension from attitude measurement. *Journal of Personality and Social Psychology*, 1965, *1*, 28–42. (d)

ROSENBERG, M. J. Some limits of dissonance: Toward a differentiated view of counter-attitudinal performance. In S. Feldman (Ed.), *Cognitive consistency: Motivational antecedents and behavioral consequent* New York: Academic Press, 1966. Pp. 135–170.

ROSENBERG, M. J. & ABELSON, R. P. An analysis of cognitive balancing. In M. J. Rosenberg, C. I. Hovland, W. J. McGuire, R. P. Abelson, & J. W. Brehm, *Attitude organization and change*. New Haven: Yale University Press, 1960. Pp. 112–163.

ROSENBERG, M. J. & GARDNER, C. W. Some dynamic aspects of post-hypnotic compliance. *Journal of Abnormal and Social Psychology*, 1958, *57*, 351–366.

ROSENBERG, M. J., HOVLAND, C. I., McGUIRE, W. J., ABELSON, R. P., & BREHM, J. W., *Attitude organization and change*. New Haven: Yale University Press, 1960.

ROSENBERG, S. Mathematical models of social behavior. In G. Lindzey & E. Aronson (Eds.), *Handbook of social psychology*. Reading, Massachusetts: Addison-Wesley, 1968.

ROSENKRANTZ, P. S. & CROCKETT, W. H. Some factors influencing the assimilation of disparate information in impression formation. *Journal of Personality and Social Psychology*, 1965, *2*, 397–402.

ROSENTHAL, R. On the social psychology of the psychological experiment: The experimenter's hypothesis as an unidentified determinant of experimental results. *American Scientist*, 1963, *51*, 268–283.

ROSENTHAL, R. The effects of the experimenter on the results of psychological research. In B. A. Maher (Ed.), *Progress in experimental personality research*, Vol. I. New York: Academic Press, 1964. Pp. 79–114.

ROSENTHAL, R. *Experimenter effects in behavioral research*. New York: Appleton-Century-Crofts, 1966.

ROSNOW, R. L. A delay-of-reinforcement effect in persuasive communication? *Journal of Social Psychology*, 1965, *67*, 39–43.

ROSNOW, R. L. "Conditioning" the direction of opinion change in persuasive communication. *Journal of Social Psychology*, 1966, *69*, 291–303.

ROSNOW, R. L., HOLZ, R. F., & LEVIN, J. Differential effects of complementary and competing variables in primacy-recency. *Journal of Social Psychology*, 1966, *69*, 135–147.

ROSNOW, R. L. & LANA, R. E. Complementary and competing order effects in opinion change. *Journal of Social Psychology*, 1965, *66*, 201–207.

ROSNOW, R. L. & RUSSELL, G. Spread of effect of reinforcement in persuasive communication. *Psychological Reports*, 1963, *12*, 731–735.

Ross, I. C. & Harary, F. Identification of the liason persons of an organization using the structure matrix. *Management Science*, 1955, *1*, 251–258.

Rouanet, H. & Rosenberg, S. Stochastic models for the response continuum in a determinate situation: Comparisons and extensions. *Journal of Mathematical Psychology*, 1964, *1*, 215–232.

Runkel, P. J. & Peizer D. B. The two-valued orientation of current equilibrium theory. *Behavioral Science*, 1968, *13*, 56–65.

Russell, B. *In praise of idleness*. New York: W. W. Norton, 1935.

Ryle, G. *The concept of mind*. London: Hutchinson & Co., 1949.

Ryle, G. *Dilemmas*. Cambridge: Cambridge University Press, 1954.

Sampson, E. E. Status congruence and cognitive consistency. *Sociometry*, 1963, *26*, 146–152.

Sampson, E. E. & Insko, C. A. Cognitive consistency and performance in the auto-kinetic situation. *Journal of Abnormal and Social Psychology*, 1964, *68*, 184–192.

Sampson, E. E. & Sibley, L. B. A further examination of the confirmation or nonconfirmation of expectancies and desires. *Journal of Personality and Social Psychology*, 1965, *2*, 133–137.

Sarbin, T. R. Role theory. In G. Lindzey (Ed.), *Handbook of social psychology*, Vol. I. Cambridge, Massachusetts: Addison-Wesley, 1954. Pp. 223–258.

Sarbin, T. R. Role theoretical interpretation of psychological change. In P. Worchel & D. Byrne (Eds.), *Personality change*. New York: Wiley, 1964. Pp. 176–219.

Sarbin, T. R. & Allen, V. L. Role theory. In G. Lindzey & E. Aronson (Eds.), *Handbook of social psychology* (rev. ed.). Reading, Massachusetts: Addison-Wesley, 1968.

Sargent, S. S. Conceptions of role and ego in contemporary psychology. In J. H. Rohrer & M. Sherif (Eds.), *Social psychology at the crossroads*. New York: Harper, 1951. Pp. 355–370.

Sarnoff, I. Psychoanalytic theory and social attitudes. *Public Opinion Quarterly*, 1960, *24*, 251–279. (a)

Sarnoff, I. Reaction formation and cynicism. *Journal of Personality*, 1960, *28*, 129–143. (b)

Sarnoff, I. *Personality dynamics and development*. New York: Wiley, 1962.

Sarnoff, I. The experimental evaluation of psychoanalytic hypotheses. *Transactions of the New York Academy of Sciences*, 1965, *28*, 272–289.

Sarnoff, I. & Katz, D. The motivational basis of attitude change. *Journal of Abnormal and Social Psychology*, 1954, *49*, 115–124.

Sarnoff, I., Katz, D., & McClintock, C. Attitude-change procedures and motivating patterns. In D. Katz, D. Cartwright, S. Eldersveld, & A. M. Lee (Eds.), *Public opinion and propaganda*. New York: Dryden, 1954.

Schachter, S. Deviation, rejection and communication. *Journal of Abnormal and Social Psychology*, 1951, *46*, 190–207.

Schachter, S. *The psychology of affiliation*. Stanford: Stanford University Press, 1959.

Schachter, S. The interaction of cognitive and physiological determinants of emotional state. In L. Berkowitz (Ed.), *Advances in experimental social psychology*, Vol. 1. New York: Academic Press, 1964. Pp. 49–80.

Schachter, S. & Singer, J. E. Cognitive, social, and physiological determinants of emotional state. *Psychological Review*, 1962, *69*, 379–399.

Schein, E. H. The Chinese indoctrination program for prisoners of war: A study of attempted "brain washing". *Psychiatry*, 1956, *19*, 149–172.

Schein, E. H. *Coercive persuasion: A socio-psychological analysis of "brainwashing" of American civilian prisoners by the Chinese Communists*. New York: Norton, 1961.

Schildkraut, J. J. & Kety, S. S. Biogenic amines and emotion. *Science*, 1967, *156*, 21–30.

Schlachet, P. The effects of dissonance arousal on the recall of failure stimuli. *Journal of Personality*, 1965, *33*, 443–461.

Schick, F. Consistency and rationality. *Journal of Philosophy*, 1963, *55*, 5–19.

Schmidt, C. F. Some effects of linguistic relations in personality impression formation. Unpublished doctoral dissertation, University of Iowa, 1966.

Schramm, W., Lyle, J., & Parker, E. B. *Television in the lives of our children*. Stanford: Stanford University Press, 1961.

SCHULTZ, D. P. *Sensory restriction.* New York: Academic Press, 1965.

SCOTT, J. P. *Animal behavior.* Chicago: University of Chicago Press, 1958.

SCOTT, W. A. Attitude change through reward of verbal behavior. *Journal of Abnormal and Social Psychology,* 1957, *55,* 72–75.

SCOTT, W. A. Attitude change by response reinforcement: Replication and extension. *Sociometry,* 1959, *22,* 328–335.

SCOTT, W. A. Conceptualizing and measuring structural properties of cognition. In O. J. Harvey (Ed.), *Motivation and social interaction.* New York: Ronald Press, 1963. Pp. 266–288.

SCOTT, W. A. Psychological and social correlates of international images. In H. C. Kelman (Ed.), *International behavior.* New York: Holt, Rinehart & Winston, 1965. Pp. 71–103.

SCRIVEN, M. A study of radical behaviorism. In H. Feigl & M. Scriven (Eds.), *Minnesota studies in philosophy of science,* Vol. 1. Foundations of science and the concepts of psychology and psychoanalysis. Minneapolis: University of Minnesota Press, 1956. Pp. 88–131.

SEARS, D. O. Biased indoctrination and selectivity of exposure to new information. *Sociometry,* 1965, *28,* 363–376. (a)

SEARS, D. O. Effects of the assassination of President Kennedy on political partisanship. In B. S. Greenberg & E. B. Parker, Eds.), *The Kennedy assassination and the American public.* Stanford: Stanford University Press, 1965. Pp. 305–326. (b)

SEARS, D. O. The influence of opposition parties and leaders. *American Psychologist,* 1965, *20,* 540 (abstract). (c)

SEARS, D. O. & FREEDMAN, J. L. Commitment, information utility, and selective exposure. United States Navy Technical Reports, ONR, Nonr-233 (54), No. 12, August, 1963.

SEARS, D. O. & FREEDMAN, J. L. Selective exposure to information: A critical review. *Public Opinion Quarterly,* 1967, *31,* 194–213.

SECORD, P. F. & BACKMAN, C. W. Personality theory and the problem of stability and change in individual behavior: An interpersonal approach. *Psychological Review,* 1961, *68,* 21–32.

SECORD, P. F. & BACKMAN, C. W. *Social psychology.* New York: McGraw-Hill, 1964.

SECORD, P. F. & BACKMAN, C. W. An interpersonal approach to personality. In B. A. Maher (Ed.), *Progress in experimental personality research,* Vol. 2. New York: Academic Press, 1965. Pp. 91–125.

SECORD, P. F., BACKMAN, C. W., & EACHUS, H. T. Effects of imbalance in the self-concept on the perception of persons. *Journal of Abnormal and Social Psychology,* 1964, *68,* 442–446.

SEEMAN, M. Alienation, membership, and political knowledge. *Public Opinion Quarterly,* 1966, *30,* 353–367.

SHAW, M. E. Scaling group tasks: A method for dimensional analysis. University of Florida, Technical Report No. 1, 1963.

SHEFFIELD, F. D. & CAMPBELL, B. A. The role of experience in the "spontaneous" activity of hungry rats. *Journal of Comparative and Physiological Psychology,* 1954, *47,* 97–100.

SHEPARD, R. N. The analysis of proximities: Multidimensional scaling with an unknown distance function. I. *Psychometrika,* 1963, *27,* 125–140.

SHERIF, C. W., SHERIF, M., & NEBERGALL, R. W. *Attitude and attitude change.* Philadelphia: Saunders, 1965.

SHERIF, M. *The psychology of social norms.* New York: Harper, 1936.

SHERIF, M. & CANTRIL, H. *The psychology of ego-involvements.* New York: Wiley, 1947.

SHERIF, M., HARVEY, O. J., WHITE, B. J., HOOD, W. R., & SHERIF, C. W. *Intergroup conflict and cooperation:* The robbers cave experiment. Norman, Oklahoma: University Book Exchange, 1961.

SHERIF, M. & HOVLAND, C. I. *Social judgment.* New Haven: Yale University Press, 1961.

SHERIF, M. & SHERIF, C. W. *Groups in harmony and tension.* New York: Harper, 1953.

SHERIF, M. & SHERIF, C. W. *Reference groups.* New York: Harper & Row, 1964.

SHERIF, M., TAUB, D., & HOVLAND, C. I. Assimilation and contrast effects of anchoring stimuli on judgments. *Journal of Experimental Psychology,* 1958, *55,* 150–155.

SHERIF, M., WHITE, B. J., & HARVEY, O. J. Status in experimentally produced groups. *American Journal of Sociology*, 1955, *60*, 370–379.

SIDOWSKI, J. B. & ANDERSON, N. H. Judgments of city-occupation combinations. *Psychonomic Science*, 1967, 7, 279–280.

SILVERMAN, I. Self-esteem and differential responsiveness to success and failure. *Journal of Abnormal and Social Psychology*, 1964, *69*, 115–119.

SILVERMAN, I. & MARCANTONIO, C. Demand characteristics vs. dissonance-reduction as determinants of failure-seeking behavior. *Journal of Personality and Social Psychology*, 1965, *2*, 882–884.

SINGER, J. E. Motivation for consistency. In S. Feldman (Ed.), *Cognitive consistency: Motivational antecedents and behavioral consequents*. New York: Academic Press, 1966. Pp. 47–73.

SJOBERG, G. Folk and 'feudal' societies. *American Journal of Sociology*, 1952, *58* (3), 231–239.

SKLAR, R. *Nigerian political parties*. Princeton: Princeton University Press, 1964.

SKINNER, B. F. *Science and human behavior*. New York: MacMillan, 1953.

SKINNER, B. F. *Verbal behavior*. New York: Appleton-Century-Crofts, 1957.

SMELSER, N. J. *Social change in the industrial revolution*. Chicago: University of Chicago Press, 1959.

SMELSER, W. T. Dominance as a factor in achievement and perception in cooperative problem solving interactions. *Journal of Abnormal and Social Psychology*, 1961, *62*, 535–542.

SMITH, C. E. The autonomic excitation resulting from the interaction of individual opinion and group opinion. *Journal of Abnormal and Social Psychology*, 1936, *30*, 138–164.

SMITH, E. E. The power of dissonance techniques to change attitudes. *Public Opinion Quarterly*, 1961, *25*, 626–639.

SMITH, F. T. An experiment in modifying attitudes toward the Negro. *Teachers College Contributions to Education*, 1943, No. 887.

SMITH, M. B. The personal setting of public opinions: A study of attitudes toward Russia. *Public Opinion Quarterly*, 1947, *11*, 507–523.

SMITH, M. B. Personal values as determinants of a political attitude. *Journal of Psychology*, 1949, *28*, 477–486.

SMITH, M. B. Attitude change. In *International Encyclopedia of the Social Sciences*. New York: MacMillan Company & The Free Press, 1968.

SMITH, M. B. The phenomenological approach in personality theory: Some critical comments. *Journal of Abnormal and Social Psychology*, 1950, *45*, 516–522.

SMITH, M. B., BRUNER, J. S., & WHITE, R. W. *Opinions and personality*. New York: Wiley, 1956.

SMOCK, C. D. The influence of psychological stress on the "intolerance of ambiguity." *Journal of Abnormal and Social Psychology*, 1955, *50*, 177–182.

SNOW, C. P. *The two cultures and the scientific revolution*. New York: Cambridge University Press, 1959.

SOFER, C., WISHLADE, L., & JANIS, I. L. Social and psychological factors in changing food habits. In J. Yudkin & J. McKenzie (Eds.), *Changing food habits*. London: MacGibbon & Kee, 1964. Pp. 90–108.

SOLOLOV, E. N. *Vospriiate i uslovny refleks*. Moscow: University of Moscow Press, 1958. (Republished: *Perception and the conditioned* reflex. New York: MacMillan, 1963).

SOLOMON, R. L. Extension of control group design. *Psychological Bulletin*, 1949, *46*, 137–150.

SOLOMON, R. L. & Howes, D. W. Word frequency, personal values, and visual duration thresholds. *Psychological Review*, 1951, *58*, 256–270.

SONTAG, S. *Against interpretation*. New York: Farrar, Straus and Giroux, 1961.

SPEISMAN, J. C., LAZARUS, R. S., MORDKOFF, A., & DAVISON, L. Experimental reduction of stress based on ego-defense theory. *Journal of Abnormal and Social Psychology*, 1964, *68*, 367–380.

SPENCE, K. W. Theoretical interpretations of learning. In S. S. Stevens (Ed.), *Handbook of experimental psychology*. New York: Wiley, 1951.

SPENCE, K. W. & GOLDSTEIN, H. Eyelid conditioning performance as a function of emotion-producing instructions. *Journal of Experimental Psychology*, 1961, *62*, 291–294.

SPENCE, W. & GUILFORD, J. P. The affective values of combinations of odors. *American Journal of Psychology*, 1933, *45*, 495–501.

SPERRY, R. W. Neurology and the mind-brain problem. *American Scientist*, 1952, *40*, 291–312.

SPIELBERGER, C. D. *The role of awareness in verbal conditioning*. In C. W. Eriksen (Ed.), *Behavior and awareness*. Durham, North Carolina: Duke University Press, 1962. Pp. 73–101.

SPIELBERGER, C. D., BERNSTEIN, I. H., & RATLIFF, R. G. The information and incentive value of the reinforcing stimulus in verbal conditioning. *Journal of Experimental Psychology*, 1966, *71*, 26–31.

SPIELBERGER, C. D., SOUTHARD, L. D., & HODGES, W. F. The effects of awareness and threat of shock on verbal conditioning. *Journal of Experimental Psychology*, 1966, *72*, 434–438.

SPITZER, S. P. Consensual states and communicative behavior. *Sociometry*, 1964, *27*, 510–515.

STAATS, A. W., STAATS, C. K., & HEARD, W. G. Language conditioning of meaning using a semantic generalization paradigm. *Journal of Experimental Psychology*, 1959, *57*, 187–192.

STAATS, C. K. & STAATS, A. W. Effect of number of trials on the language conditioning of meaning. *American Psychologist*, 1958, *13*, 415 (abstract)

STANLEY, J. C. & KLAUSMEIR, H. J. Opinion constancy after formal role playing. *Journal of Social Psychology*, 1957, *47*, 11–18.

STARBUCK, W. H. Level of aspiration theory and economic behavior. *Behavioral Science*, 1963, *8*, 128–136.

STEIN, D. D., HARDYCK, J. A., & SMITH, M. B. Race and belief: An open and shut case. *Journal of Personality and Social Psychology*, 1965, *1*, 281–289.

STEINER, I. D. Ethnocentrism and tolerance of trait "inconsistency." *Journal of Abnormal and Social Psychology*, 1954, *49*, 349–354.

STEINER, I. D. Receptivity to supportive versus nonsupportive communications. *Journal of Abnormal and Social Psychology*, 1962, *65*, 266–267.

STEINER, I. D. Galvanic skin resistance and responses to interpersonal disagreements. Unpublished progress report, United States Health Service Grant M-4460, University of Illinois, August, 1964.

STEINER, I. D. Personality and the resolution of interpersonal disagreements. In B. A. Maher (Ed.), *Progress in experimental personality research*. New York: Academic Press, 1966. Pp. 195–239.

STEINER, I. D., ANDERSON, J., & HAYS, R. Immediate and delayed reactions to interpersonal disagrements; Some effects of the type of issue and the order of response. *Journal of Experimental Social Psychology*, 1967, *3*, 206–219.

STEINER, I. D. & JOHNSON, H. H. Authoritarianism and "tolerance of trait inconsistency." *Journal of Abnormal and Social Psychology*, 1963, *67*, 388–391.

STEINER, I. D. & JOHNSON, H. H. Relationship among dissonance reducing responses. *Journal of Abnormal and Social Psychology*, 1964, *68*, 38–44.

STEINER, I. D. & JOHNSON, H. H. Category width and responses to interpersonal disagreements. *Journal of Personality and Social Psychology*, 1965, *2*, 290–292.

STEINER, I. D. & PETERS, S. C. Conformity and the A-B-X model. *Journal of Personality*, 1958, *26*, 229–242.

STEINER, I. D. & ROGERS, E. D. Alternative responses to dissonance. *Journal of Abnormal and Social Psychology*, 1963, *66*, 128–136.

STEINER, I. D. & SPAULDING, J. Preference for balanced situations. Technical report No. 1, Grant 4460, United States Public Health Service, University of Illinois, 1966.

STEINER, I. D. & VANNOY, J. S. Personality correlates of two types of conformity behavior. *Journal of Personality and Social Psychology*, 1967, 1966, *4*, 307–315.

STEVENSON, M. W. & ODEM, R. D. Visual reinforcement with children. *Journal of Experimental Child Psychology*, 1964, *1*, 248–255.

STEWART, R. H. Effect of continuous responding on the order effect in personality impression formation. *Journal of Personality and Social Psychology*, 1965, *1*, 161–165.

STOCHOWIAK, J. & MOSS, C. Hypnotic alterations of social attitudes. *Journal of Personality and Social Psychology*, 1965, *2*, 77–83.

STRAWSON, P. *Individuals*. New York: Anchor Books, 1963.

SULLIVAN, H. S. *The interpersonal theory of psychiatry*. New York: Norton, 1953.

SUMNER, W. G. *Folkways*. New York: Ginn, 1906.

SUPPES, P. & ZINNES, J. L. Basic measurement theory. In R. D. Luce, R. R. Bush, & E. Galanter (Eds.), *Handbook of mathematical psychology*. New York: Wiley, 1963. Pp. 1–76.

SUTTON, S., BRAREN, M., ZUBIN, J., & JOHN, E. R. Evoked-potential correlates of stimulus uncertainty. *Science*, 1965, *150*, 1187–1188.

SUTTON, S., TUETING, P., ZUBIN, J., & JOHN, E. R. Information delivery and the sensory evoked potential. *Science*, 1967, *155*, 1436–1439.

TAFT, R. Selective recall and memory distortion of favorable and unfavorable material. *Journal of Abnormal and Social Psychology*, 1954, *49*, 23–28.

TAGIURI, R. Social preference and its perception. In R. Tagiuri & L. Petrullo (Eds.), *Person perception and interpersonal behavior*. Stanford: Stanford University Press, 1959.

TAJFEL, H. Value and the perceptual judgment of magnitude. *Psychological Review*, 1957, *64*, 192–204.

TANAKA, Y. *A test of the congruity hypothesis across three language-culture communities*. Tokyo: Gakushuin Sedei Gakubu Kenkyn Nembo, No. 9, 1964. (In English)

TANNENBAUM, P. H. Attitudes toward source and concept as factors in attitude change through communications. Unpublished doctoral dissertation, University of Illinois, 1953.

TANNENBAUM, P. H. Color as a code for connotative communication. *Penrose Annual*, 1966, *59*, 115–120. (a)

TANNENBAUM, P. H. Mediated generalization of attitude change via the principle of congruity. *Journal of Personality and Social Psychology*, 1966, *3*, 493–499. (b)

TANNENBAUM, P. H. The congruity principle revisited: Studies in the reduction, induction and generalization of persuasion. In L. Berkowitz (Ed.), *Advances in experimental social psychology*, Vol. 3. New York: Academic Press, 1967. Pp. 271–320.

TANNENBAUM, P. H. & GENGEL, R. W. Generalization of attitude change through congruity. *Journal of Personality and Social Psychology*, 1966, *3*, 229–304.

TANNENBAUM, P. H., MACAULAY, J. R., & NORRIS, E. L. The principle of congruity and reduction of persuasion. *Journal of Personality and Social Psychology*, 1966, *3*, 233–238.

TANNENBAUM, P. H. & NORRIS, E. L. Effects of combining congruity principle strategies for the reduction of persuasion. *Sociometry*, 1965, *28*, 145–157.

TAYLOR, C. C. W. Pleasure. *Analysis Supplement*, 1963, *23*.

THAYER, S. Confidence and postjudgment exposure to consonant and dissonant information in a free-choice situation. *Journal of Social Psychology*, 1968, in press.

THIBAUT, J. W. & KELLEY, H. H. *The social psychology of groups*. New York: Wiley, 1959.

THOMPSON, W. R. & SCHAEFFER, R. Early environmental stimulation. In D. W. Fiske & S. R. Maddi (Eds.), *Functions of varied experience*. Homewood, Illinois: Dorsey, 1961.

TINBERGEN, N. *The study of instinct*. Oxford: Oxford University Press, 1951.

TINKLEPAUGH, O. L. An experimental study of representational factors in monkeys. *Journal of Comparative and Physiological Psychology*, 1928, *8*, 197–236.

TIPPETT, J. S. & SILBER, E. Self-image stability: The problem of validation. *Psychological Reports*, 1965, *17*, 323–329.

TOBY, J. Some variables in role conflict analysis. *Social Forces*, 1952, *30*, 323–327.

TOLMAN, E. C. *Purposive behavior in animals and men*. New York: Century, 1932.

TOLMAN, E. C. & BRUNSWIK, E. The organism and the causal texture of the environment. *Psychological Review*, 1935, *42*, 43–77.

TOLMAN, E. C., HALL, C. W., & BRETNALL, L. P. A disproof of the law of effect and a substitution of the law of emphasis, motivation, and disruption. *Journal of Experimental Psychology*, 1932, *15*, 601–614.

TOMKINS, S. *Affect imagery consciousness*. New York: Springer, 1962.

TOULMIN, S. E. *The uses of argument*. London: Cambridge University Press, 1964.

TOYNBEE, A. A study of history. New York and London: Oxford University Press, 1947–1957.

TRENAMAN, J. & McQUAIL, D. *Television and the political image*. London: Methuen and Co., 1961.

TRIANDIS, H. C. Exploratory factor analyses of the behavioral component of social attitudes. *Journal of Abnormal and Social Psychology*, 1964, *68*, 420–430.

TRIANDIS, H. C., DAVIS, E. E., & TAKEZAWA, S. I. Some determinants of social distance among American, German, and Japanese students. *Journal of Personality and Social Psychology*, 1965, *2*, 540–551.

TRIANDIS, H. C. & FISHBEIN, M. Cognitive interaction in person perception. *Journal of Abnormal and Social Psychology*, 1963, *67*, 446–453.

TRIANDIS, H. C., LOH, W., & LEVIN, L. A Race, status, quality of spoken English and opinions about civil rights as determinants of interpersonal attitudes. *Journal of Personality and Social Psychology*, 1966, *3*, 468–472.

TRIANDIS, H. C., TANAKA, Y., & SHANMUGAM, A. V. Interpersonal attitudes among American, Indian, and Japanese students. *International Journal of Psychology*, 1966, 177–206.

TRIANDIS, H. C. & TRIANDIS, L. M. Race, social class, religion, and nationality as determinants of social distance. *Journal of Abnormal and Social Psychology*, 1960, *61*, 110–118.

TRIANDIS, H. C. & TRIANDIS, L. M. A cross-cultural study of social distance. *Psychological Monographs*, 1962, *76*, No. 21 (Whole No. 540).

TRIANDIS, L. M. & LAMBERT, W. W. Pancultural factor analyses of reported socialization practices. *Journal of Abnormal and Social Psychology*, 1961, *62*, 631–639.

TRIPODI, T. The relationship of characteristics of the judge to his perception of conflict in others. Unpublished manuscript, University of California at Berkeley, 1966.

TRIPODI, T. Cognitive complexity and the perception of conflict: A partial replication. *Perceptual and Motor Skills*, 1967, *25*, 543–544.

TRIPODI, T. & BIERI, J. Information transmission in clinical judgments as a function of stimulus dimensionality and cognitive complexity. *Journal of Personality*, 1964, *32*, 119–137.

TRIPODI, T. & BIERI, J. Cognitive complexity, perceived conflict and certainty. *Journal of Personality*, 1966, *34*, 114–153.

TROLDAHL, V. C. Mediated communication and personal influence. Unpublished doctoral dissertation, University of Minnesota, 1963.

TURNER, E. A. & WRIGHT, J. Effects of severity of threat and perceived availability on the attractiveness of objects. *Journal of Personality and Social Psychology*, 1965, *2*, 128–132.

UNITED STATES EMPLOYMENT SERVICE, *Dictionary of occupational titles*. Washington, D.C.: U.S. Government Printing Office, 1965.

UPSHAW, H. S. A linear alternative to assimilation and contrast: A reply to Manis. *Journal of Abnormal and Social Psychology*, 1964, *68*, 691–693.

UPSHAW, H. S. The effect of variable perspectives on judgments of opinion statements for Thurstone scales: Equal-appearing intervals. *Journal of Personality and Social Psychology*, 1965, *2*, 60–69.

UPSHAW, H. S. Attitude measurement. In H. M. Blalock & A. B. Blalock (Eds.), *Methodology in social research*. New York: McGraw-Hill, 1968. Pp. 60–111.

VANNOY, J. S. Generality of cognitive complexity-simplicity as a personality construct. *Journal of Personality and Social Psychology*, 1965, *2*, 385–396.

VERNON, P. E. Personality assessment: A critical survey. London: Methuen, 1964.

VERPLANCK, W. S. A glossary of some terms used in the objective science of behavior. *Psychological Review Supplement*, 1957, *64*, 1–42.

VIDEBECK, R. Self-conception and the reaction of others. *Sociometry*, 1960, *23*, 351–359.

VIDULICH, R. N. & KAIMAN, I. P. The effects of information source status and dogmatism upon conformity behavior. *Journal of Abnormal and Social Psychology*, 1961, *63*, 639–642.

Voronin, L. A. & Sokolov, E. N. Cortical mechanisms of the orientating reflex and its relation to the conditioned reflex. *Electroencephalography and Clinical Neurophysiology*, 1960 (Supplement 13), 335–346.

Waller, W. W. *The sociology of teaching.* New York: Wiley, 1932.

Walser, M. A German mosaic. *Encounter*, 1964, 22, 33–38.

Walster, E. The temporal sequence of post-decision processes. In L. Festinger, *Conflict, decision and dissonance.* Stanford: Stanford University Press, 1964. Pp. 112–127.

Walster, E. The effect of self-esteem on romantic liking. *Journal of Experimental Social Psychology*, 1965, 1, 184–197. (a)

Walster, E. The effect on one's subsequent behavior of treating another unjustly. Unpublished manuscript, University of Minnesota, 1965. (b)

Walster, E., Berscheid, E., & Barclay, A. M. A determinant of preference among modes of dissonance reduction. *Journal of Personality and Social Psychology*, 1967, 7, 211–216.

Walster, E. & Festinger, L. Decisions among imperfect alternatives. In L. Festinger, *Conflict, decision and dissonance.* Stanford: Stanford University Press, 1964. Pp. 129–143.

Walster, E. & Prestholdt, P. The effect of misjudging another: Overcompensation or dissonance reduction? *Journal of Experimental Social Psychology*, 1966, 2, 85–97.

Walster, E. & Walster, B. Effect of expecting to be liked on choice of associates. *Journal of Abnormal and Social Psychology*, 1963, 67, 402–404.

Walster, E., Walster, B., Abrahams, D., & Brown, Z. The effect on liking of underrating and overrating another. *Journal of Experimental Social Psychology*, 1966, 2, 70–84.

Walters, R. H. & Parke, R. D. Social motivation, dependency, and susceptibility to social influence. In L. Berkowitz (Ed.), *Advances in experimental social psychology*, Vol. I. New York: Academic Press, 1964. Pp. 231–276.

Waly, P. & Cook, S. W. Attitude as a determinant of learning and memory: A failure to confirm. *Journal of Personality and Social Psychology*, 1966, 4, 280–288.

Ward, W. D. & Sandvold, K. D. Performance expectancy as a determinant of actual performance: A partial replication. *Journal of Abnormal and Social Psychology*, 1963, 67, 293–295.

Warner, W. L., The radio daytime serial: A symbolic analysis. *Genetic Psychology Monographs*, No. 37, 1948.

Waterman, A. S. & Ford, L. H. Performance expectancy as a determinant of actual performance: Dissonance reduction or differential recall? *Journal of Personality and Social Psychology*, 1965, 2, 464–467.

Watson, W. S. & Hartman, G. W. The rigidity of a basic attitudinal frame. *Journal of Abnormal and Social Psychology*, 1939, 34, 314–335.

Watts, W. A. Cognitive reorganization following a disconfirmed expectancy. *Journal of Personality and Social Psychology*, 1965, 2, 231–241.

Watts, W. A. Commitment under conditions of risk. *Journal of Personality and Social Psychology*, 1966, 3, 507–515.

WEBSTER'S THIRD NEW INTERNATIONAL DICTIONARY OF THE ENGLISH LANGUAGE. Springfield, Massachusetts: Merriam, 1966.

Weick, K. E. Reduction of cognitive dissonance through task enhancement and effort expenditure. *Journal of Abnormal and Social Psychology*, 1964, 68, 533–539.

Weick, K. E. When prophecy pales: The fate of dissonance theory. *Psychological Reports*, 1965, 16, 1261–1275.

Weick, K. E. Task acceptance dilemmas: A site for research on cognition. In S. Feldman (Ed.), *Cognitive consistency: Motivational antecedents and behavioral consequents.* New York: Academic Press, 1966. Pp. 225–255.

Weick, K. E. & Prestholdt, P. Realignment of discrepant reinforcement value. *Journal of Personality and Social Psychology*, 1968, 8, 180–187.

Weiss, W. A "sleeper" effect in opinion change. *Journal of Abnormal and Social Psychology*, 1953, 58, 173–180.

Weiss, W. Opinion congruence with a negative source on one issue as a factor influencing agreement on another issue. *Journal of Abnormal and Social Psychology*, 1957, *34*, 180–186.

WEISS, W. Scale judgments of triplets of opinion statements. *Journal of Abnormal and Social Psychology*, 1963, *66*, 471–479.

WEISS, W. The influence of a source on responses to a persuasive communication. Technical Report No. 1, Office of Naval Research, Contract NONR 4309 (00), December, 1964.

WEISS, W. & SOLOMON, H. The effects of knowledge of source before vs. after exposure to a communication. Technical Report No. 4, Office of Naval Research, Contract NONR 4309 (00), September, 1965.

WEISS, W. & SOLOMON, H. Effects of sources, placement of sources, and persuasive communication on attitude, reason giving and action intentions. Technical Report No. 7, Office of Naval Research, Contract NONR 4309 (00), March, 1966.

WELKER, W. I. Escape, exploratory, and food seeking responses of rats in a novel situation. *Journal of Comparative and Physiological Psychology*, 1959, *52*, 96–111.

WELKER, W. I. An analysis of exploratory and play behavior in animals. In D. W. Fiske & S. R. Maddi (Eds.), *The functions of varied experience*. Homewood, Illinois: Dorsey, 1961. Pp. 175–226.

WERNER, H. Process and achievement. *Harvard Educational Review*, 1937, 7, 353–368.

WERNER, H. *Comparative psychology of mental development*. New York: Science Editions, 1961.

WERNER, H. & KAPLAN, B. The developmental approach to cognition: Its relevance to the psychological interpretation of anthropological and ethnolinguistic data. *American Anthropology*, 1956, *58*, 866–880.

WERTHEIMER, M. Untersuchungen zur Lehre von der Gestalt. II. *Psychologische Forschung*, 1923, *4*, 301–350.

WHITE, A. R. *Attention*. Oxford: Blackwell, 1964.

WHITE, B. J. & HARVEY, O. J. Effects of personality and own stand on judgment and production of statements about a central issue. *Journal of Experimental Social Psychology*, 1965, *1*, 334–347.

WHITE, H. Management conflict and sociometric structure. *American Journal of Sociology*, 1961, *67*, 185–199.

WHITE, R. W. Motivation reconsidered: The concept of competence. *Psychological Review*, 1959, *66*, 297–333.

WHYTE, W. F. *Street corner society: The social structure of an Italian slum*. Chicago: University of Chicago Press, 1943.

WHYTE, W. H. *The organization man*. New York: Simon and Schuster, 1956.

WIEST, W. M. A quantitative extension of Heider's theory of cognitive balance applied to interpersonal perception and self-esteem. *Psychological Monographs*, 1965, *79*(14), (Whole No. 607).

WILLEY, B. *Seventeenth century background*. New York: Columbia University Press, 1942.

WILLIS, R. H. Stimulus pooling and social perception. *Journal of Abnormal and Social Psychology*, 1960, *60*, 365–373.

WILSON, D. T. Ability evaluation, postdecision dissonance, and co-worker attractiveness. *Journal of Personality and Social Psychology*, 1965, *1*, 486–489.

WILSON, G. *Tribalism in Kenya*. Nairobi: Marco Surveys, Report No. 8, 1961.

WINER, B. J. *Statistical principles in experimental design*. New York: McGraw-Hill, 1962.

WISHNER, J. Reanalysis of "Impressions of personality." *Psychological Review*, 1960, *67*, 96–112.

WITKIN, H. A., LEWIS, H. B., HERTZMAN, M., MACHOVER, K., MEISSNER, P. B., & WAPNER, S. *Personality through perception*. New York: Harper, 1954.

WOODRUFF, A. D. & DIVESTA, F. J. The relationship between values, concepts and attitudes. *Educational and Psychological Measurement*, 1948, *8*, 645–660.

WRENN, R. L. The resolution of cognitive dissonance in open and closed belief systems. Unpublished doctoral dissertation, Ohio State University, 1962.

WUNDERLUCH, R. A., YOUNISS, J., & DE SOTO, C. B. Schemas and kinship. *Psychological Reports*, 1962, *11*, 495–498.

Name Index

Abelson, R. P., xv, 4, 24, 63, 79, 81–2, 89, 112–39, 141–2, 158, 169, 182, 187, 206–8, 214, 266, 277, 283–4, 290, 339, 341, 369–70, 384, 387–8, 395, 399, 497–8, 513–5, 520, 524, 526–8, 544–5, 547, 557n, 558, 641, 648–51, 665, 672, 674, 685, 689, 716–20, 723n, 732, 737, 739, 740–2, 744, 746, 747n, 766, 767

Adams, J. S., 190, 324, 333, 616, 653, 655–60, 707, 718, 719, 773, 780, 786

Adorno, T. W., xvi, 97

Agarie, N., 746

Albrecht, F., 114, 495, 504–11, 526–7, 529, 531–8, 565

Allen, V. L., 166, 201–9, 275, 282–4, 286, 459, 461

Allport, F. H., 661n

Allport, G. W., 274, 351, 516–7, 566, 690

Amsel, A., 244

Amster, H., 800

Anderson, J., 647

Anderson, L., 724, 739, 746, 751, 759, 764

Anderson, N. H., 59, 96, 122, 145, 647, 718, 721, 723, 731–43, 746, 747n, 757, 758, 759, 761, 764, 767, 768

Andrew, R. J., 260

Andrews, S. L., 269, 271

Aneshansel, J., 782

Angyal, A., 173, 313

Anokhin, P. K., 259

Appley, M. H., 304, 307, 308

Ariete, 162

Aristotle, 145, 509

Arnold, M. B., 523

Aronson, E., 3, 5–27, 104–6, 125–6, 129, 131, 135, 255, 273, 281, 284, 355, 358–9, 370, 397, 401, 407, 464–7, 469–78, 479–83, 485, 487–9, 491–3, 500–1,

560, 604, 606, 609–12, 615, 622, 628, 630, 658, 659–60, 707, 712–3, 772, 773, 794n, 804, 806, 821, 827, 831

Arrowood, A. J., 398, 474

Asch, S. E., 216, 285, 427, 461–2, 514, 644, 732, 735, 738, 745–6, 747n, 757

Astratian, E. A., 257

Atkins, A. L., 633

Atkinson, J. W., 329, 363, 478, 517, 709, 713

Attneave, F., 259

Austin, G. A., 224

Axelrod, J., 77

Back, K., 5, 261, 301, 311–8, 343–4, 432, 441, 618

Backman, C., 73, 618

Bailey, N. T. J., 549

Baker, K., 518

Baldwin, P. M., 752n, 758

Balloun, J. L., 773, 782

Bandura, A., 308

Barber, T. X., 415

Barclay, A. M., 16

Baron, J., 445, 718, 719

Baron, R. M., 302, 331–6, 344–5, 433, 653, 670–83

Barrios, A. A., 743, 747n

Barry, D. W., 790–1

Bartlett, F. C., 516, 711

Bartlett, M., 587

Bateson, G., 694

Bauer, R., 784

Beach, F., 304

Becker, L. A., 414

Behar, L. B., 711

Bell, J. W., 711

Bem, D. J., 167, 244, 246–56, 275, 286–7, 290–2, 527, 822, 823, 833

Bem, S. L., 246
Benoit-Smullyan, E., 535–6
Berelson, B. R., 547, 604, 790
Bergin, A. E., 199, 466
Berkowitz, L., 212, 301, 303–10, 343, 345, 391, 400–7, 426, 432
Berkun, M. M., 243, 417
Berlyne, D. E., 161, 167, 207, 220, 244, 257–66, 269, 271, 273, 275, 287, 290, 293–5, 363, 392, 402–10, 478, 633, 634, 638, 657, 747, 800
Berne, N., 269
Bernstein, I. H., 410
Berscheid, E., 16, 569, 589n, 599–608, 609, 611–2
Biderman, A. D., 371
Bieri, J., xvii, 613, 633–40, 648, 651, 690, 718
Bindra, D., 304
Birch, H. G., 704
Bishop, F., 196–7, 200, 615
Blake, R. R., 548
Blevans, S. A., 306, 355–6, 460, 465
Blum, G. S., 413
Bogart, K., 647n
Bogdonoff, M. D., 5, 317, 432, 441, 618
Bonarius, J. C. J., 635
Bonchek, V., 199, 548
Borsa, D. M., 262
Bosley, J. J., 506, 531
Bott, E., 549–50
Bradburn, W. M., 636
Braden, M., 473, 600
Bralek, H. M., 417
Bramel, D., 5, 195, 198, 347, 355–65, 370, 386–92, 397, 444, 492, 513, 618, 711
Brehm, J. W., 5–6, 14, 16–7, 102–5, 181, 186, 193, 214–6, 234, 248, 252–3, 255, 265, 278, 285–6, 309–10, 321–2, 361–2, 364, 368–9, 392, 397, 400–7, 410, 412–9, 425, 429, 432, 439, 441, 448–9, 456, 458, 480, 485, 488–9, 493, 513, 515, 560, 571, 575, 576, 595, 601, 602–3, 615, 616, 617, 618, 619, 621–2, 624, 655, 707, 710, 711, 804, 805n, 812–3, 818, 822, 829
Brehm, M. L., 5, 317, 432, 441, 618
Bretnall, L. P., 223
Briar, S., 633

Brodbeck, M., 771–2
Broadbent, D. E., 133
Brock, T. C., 23, 98, 208, 332, 347, 359, 373–83, 386, 392, 401, 408–16, 432, 435, 441, 443, 446, 450, 471, 476, 482, 595, 618, 619, 710, 712, 773–4, 777, 779, 780, 783
Brown, J. S., 244, 260, 303, 322
Brown, R. W., xvi, 54, 73, 82, 101, 105, 116, 129, 179, 214, 355, 533, 538, 619, 828
Brownfield, C. A., 269
Bruner, J., 156, 180, 220, 222, 224, 410, 513, 702, 766
Brunswik, E., 204, 220, 222, 355, 663
Bryan, J. H., 410
Buchwald, A. M., 430
Buck, R. W., 308
Buckhout, R., 432
Buehler, J. A., 548
Bugelski, B. R., 479
Bunker, G. L., 205
Burchard, W. W., 206
Burdick, H. A., 305, 616, 618, 644, 819
Burnes, A. J., 305, 616, 618, 644
Burnstein, E., 40–2, 117–8, 181, 339, 342, 505
Bush, R. R., 733
Buss, A. H., 332, 370, 443, 618–9, 710, 712
Butler, D. C., 589n
Butt, J., 712
Byrne, D., 305–6, 548, 620, 648
Byron, L., 268

Campbell, B. A., 307
Campbell, D. T., 186, 212, 241, 529, 551–64, 566, 591, 595
Campbell, E. H., 450
Canon, L., 26, 401–2, 778, 782
Cantor, N., 540
Cantril, H., 373–9, 516
Caplow, T., 548
Carlsmith, J. M., 5, 7, 11, 17, 19–20, 22, 24–5, 102, 104–8, 110, 125, 130–1, 181, 194, 196, 207, 243–4, 246, 249–54, 281, 284, 332, 354–5, 358–9, 370, 397, 407, 466–7, 469–73, 480–4, 485–91, 493, 500–1, 606, 612, 617, 658, 659,

660, 680, 712–3, 794n, 801, 803–9, 813, 817, 820, 821, 822, 823, 824, 825, 827, 828–31, 831n

Carlson, E. R., 76, 380, 696, 752, 765

Carlyle, T., 411

Carroll, J. D., 136, 513, 524

Carter, R. F., 63

Cartwright, D., 41, 74, 76, 112, 114, 141, 158, 169, 174, 176, 277, 283, 289, 506, 517, 544, 545–6, 547, 551, 555, 558, 559, 767, 792

Cassirer, E., xvii, 174

Chalmers, D. K., 753, 758

Chapanis, A., 11–2, 18, 27, 101, 104, 195, 296, 305, 314, 474, 624, 828

Chapanis, N., 11–2, 18, 27, 101, 104, 195, 269, 305, 314, 474, 624, 828

Chein, I., 289

Child, I. L., 517, 594

Christensen, K. R., 732

Christianson, B., 514

Christie, R., 620, 647

Clark, R. W., 363, 478

Clark, W. H., 504–5

Clarke, P., 778, 786

Clement, D. E., 504

Cliff, N., 753n

Cochran, W. G., 424

Cofer, C. N., 304, 307, 708

Cohen, A. R., 5, 16–7, 19, 102–3, 105, 181, 186, 193, 205, 234, 248, 252–3, 255, 265, 278, 309–10, 321–2, 361–2, 364, 368–9, 392, 400–7, 410, 413–6, 425, 441–3, 446, 448–9, 456, 458, 480, 485, 489, 513, 515, 560, 571, 575, 590, 595, 601, 615–7, 619, 620–2, 624, 630, 645, 655, 707, 710, 712, 804, 805n, 812–3, 818, 822, 829, 829n

Cohler, J., 590

Colby, K. M., 396, 495, 520–5, 526, 528, 695

Coleman, J. S., 549, 563

Collins, B. E., 19–20, 76, 104, 106–8, 110, 118, 124, 143, 167, 181, 240–5, 271, 275, 286–7, 289–91, 354, 398, 801, 804, 805, 806, 817, 819–26, 827, 828–30, 831n, 833

Conlon, E. T., 471, 477

Converse, P. E., 305, 307, 679n, 681

Cook, S. W., 605, 781, 782, 800

Cooley, C. H., 202

Coombs, C. H., 510

Cooper, J., 20–1, 821, 829n

Corbin, L. H., 452, 707

Corrozi, J. F., 826

Coser, L. A., 559

Cottrell, L. J., 315

Cottrell, N. B., 24, 359, 470–1, 476, 482–3, 707, 715

Cox, D. R., 424

Craw, M. A., 262

Crockett, W. H., 635–7, 639, 653, 661–9, 718

Cronbach, L., 196

Crowne, D. P., 597

Dabbs, J. M., 826

Darley, J. M., 359, 467, 472, 476, 480, 491

Darwin, C., 240

Das, J. P., 66

Davenport, W., 510

Davidson, J. R., 14, 572–3, 602

Davis, E. E., 723n, 726, 729

Davis, J. A., 529, 535–6, 544–50, 551, 555, 558–9, 566

Davis, K. E., 124, 207, 301, 327–30, 343

Davis, M., 506–7, 509

Davis, R. C., 430

Dawes, R. M., 59, 723, 738

Deese, J., 754

DeFleur, M. L., 549, 550

Dember, W. N., 260, 268–9

Dennis, J., 785

DeSalvo, J., 452

Descartes, R., 142

De Soto, C. B., 40, 114, 339, 495, 504–11, 526–7, 529, 531–8, 546, 565–6

Deutsch, K., 316

Deutsch, M., 76, 207, 306, 355, 357, 363, 369, 461–2, 475, 516, 571, 646

Deutschman, P., 790

Dillehay, R. C., 151–3, 183, 513

DiVesta, F. J., 74, 341, 721, 752

Doby, J. T., 73

Dollard, J., 258

Doob, L., 66, 207, 241, 289

Dorfman, D., 308

Driscoll, J. M., 259

Driver, M. J., 697
Duffy, E., 268, 303
Dulany, D. E., 414
Dunham, H. N., 536
Durkheim, E., 202
Dustin, D. S., 752n, 758
Dworkin, L., 441, 618, 707, 715

Eachus, H. T., 618
Eagly, A. H., 641, 643, 677–8, 681n, 696n
Earl, R. W., 260, 268
Easterbrook, J. A., 308, 517–8
Easton, D., 785
Ebbinghaus, E., xv
Edelman, S. K., 358–9, 471
Edlow, D. W., 707
Edwards, A. L., 597, 605
Edwards, D. C., 358–9, 471
Egbert, L., 587
Ehrlich, D., 23, 773, 780
Elms, A., 19, 104, 207, 585, 804, 811, 813–5, 818, 828
Emerson, R. W., 268, 599
Engel, G. L., 523
Engel, M., 349
Epstein, G. F., 359, 647n
Epstein, S., 131, 308, 470–1, 482–3
Epting, F., 373
Erbe, W., 549
Eriksen, C. W., 221, 229, 410, 415
Erikson, E., 540
Escher, M., 177
Estes, W. K., 308

Fairbairn, W. R. D., 694
Farber, I. E., 244, 260, 322
Feather, N. T., 401, 615, 619, 713, 772–3, 793
Feldinger, I., 269
Feldman, E., 744
Feldman, S., 59, 61, 179, 278, 721, 744–55, 762, 764, 767, 790, 792–3
Fenichel, O., 403
Ferdinand, P. R., 707
Feshbach, S., 322
Festinger, L., 5–6, 19–22, 26, 102, 104–5, 107, 125, 130, 158, 169, 181–2, 186,

192–200, 202, 230, 243–6, 249–55, 261, 265, 277, 279, 281, 284, 321, 323, 332, 337, 341–2, 354–5, 361, 364, 368–9, 391, 394, 396, 398, 412, 416, 426–7, 430, 432, 447–9, 454, 456, 458, 463, 469, 473–80, 485, 489, 493, 497, 513, 515, 522, 544, 545, 548–9, 560, 566, 571–3, 591, 601–2, 604, 609, 615–6, 619, 622, 624, 643, 655, 658–9, 680, 714, 771, 774, 789, 804, 806, 812–3, 817, 820, 822, 824, 827
Fiedler, F., 547, 723n
Finkelstein, J., 107
Fillenbaum, S., 618, 628–30
Firestone, I., 441, 443, 446, 707
Fishbein, M., 58, 96, 123, 695n, 723, 723n, 724, 737, 738, 739, 744, 746, 751, 752, 757, 758, 759, 762, 764, 764n
Fiske, D. W., 268–9, 272–3
Fitch, G., 216
Flament, C., 114, 555
Flavel, J., 663
Fleischer, L., 589n
Fleming, W. H., 252
Foa, U. G., 723n
Follet, M., 189
Foote, N., 315
Ford, L. H., 359, 471, 482
Ford, L. R., 549
Forman, R., 548
Foulkes, D., 625–6, 793
Foulkes, S. H., 625–6
Fowler, H., 269
Frager, R., 228–38, 804
Frankmann, R. W., 430
Freedman, J. L., 5, 7, 18, 22, 24, 131, 337, 374, 377, 382, 401–2, 404, 450, 467, 485–90, 493, 495–503, 516, 526–7, 605–7, 693, 707, 771, 772–3, 774, 777, 778, 780, 782, 783, 788–9, 792, 794, 804, 806
French, J. R. P., 180, 367–8, 549
Frenkel-Brunswik, E., xvi, 624, 625
Freud, A., 661, 662
Freud, S., 182, 189, 193, 196, 199–200, 258, 282, 406, 413, 523, 645, 661
Frincke, G., 594
Fromkin, H. L., 408, 786
Fromm, E., 645

Fulkerson, D. R., 549
Fulton, R. L., 206

Gailon, A. K., 474–6, 478
Galanter, E., 226, 338
Gardner, R. W., 338, 590, 690
Gardner, M., 76, 177
Garfinkel, H., 708, 710
Garner, W. R., 221, 229, 259, 504
Geis, F. Lindauer, 620, 647n
Gelman, R. S., 257
Gengel, R. W., 64, 192
Gerard, H. B., 7, 11–3, 18, 306, 355–6,
    392, 425–32, 434, 437, 448, 456–63,
    465–6, 610, 644, 646 ,707
Gergen, K. J., 317
Giese, P., 114
Gilbert, J. P., 523
Gill, M., 304
Gillespie, C., 541
Gilmore, J. B., 19, 103, 106, 181, 195,
    204, 659, 720, 804, 811, 813–4, 822,
    825, 828–9,
Gilson, C., 138
Glanzer, M., 504–5
Glasman, L. D., 800
Glass, D. C., 306, 357, 613, 615–23,
    648–9, 660
Glass, L. B., 415, 710
Gleason, T. C., 723, 738
Goffman, E., 201–2, 350, 354
Goldberg, P. A., 359, 472, 476, 480–1,
    536
Goldstein, H., 441
Goldstein, K., 173, 320
Goldwater, B., 136
Gollin, E. S., 664–5
Gonyea, A., 664
Goode, W. J., 208
Goodnow, J. J., 224
Gordon, C. M., 199
Gouldner, A. W., 333
Grant, L. D., 408, 412–7, 441, 446
Grant, V., 510
Grastyan, E., 260
Green, R. F., 417–24
Greenbaum, C. W., 408, 413–4, 416,
    443, 712
Greenberg, B., 420–1, 423

Greenstein, F, I., 782
Greenwald, H. J., 374, 377–8, 382, 781,
    784
Grinker, J., 441, 446
Gross, E., 206, 351
Guilford, J. P., 732
Gullahorn, J., 548
Gulliksen, H., 746
Gusfield, J. R., 537
Guttman, I., 23, 773

Haas, H., 349
Hagan, E. E., 539, 563
Hake, H. W., 221, 229
Hall, A. R., 541
Hall, C. W., 223
Hammond, K. R., 732, 746
Hammond, P., 131
Handel, S., 506, 632, 793
Harary, F., 41, 112, 114, 141, 158, 169,
    174, 176, 277, 283, 289, 506, 518,
    544, 545–7, 551, 555, 558, 559, 767
Harburg, E., 32, 36–7, 39, 42, 44, 192,
    306, 418, 693
Hardyck, J. A., 473, 552, 653, 684–92,
    716, 719
Hare, A. P., 452
Harlow, H. F., 268
Harrington, G. M., 257
Harris, D. B., 661
Hart, H. L. A., 329
Hartmann, G. W., 518, 605
Harvey, O. J., 212, 227, 352–3, 477,
    615, 618, 625, 626, 645, 697, 724, 782
Hays, R., 647
Hays, W. L., 236
Haywood, H. C., 405
Hazard, P., 541
Heard, W. G., 66
Hebb, D. O., 220, 222, 226, 268, 338,
    363, 407, 478
Heider, F., xvi-xvii, 28–33, 78, 112–4,
    120, 128, 135, 141, 158, 166, 169–78,
    189, 202, 216–7, 275–8, 283, 289, 293,
    319, 341, 367, 370–1, 391, 394, 463,
    497, 504, 506, 513–4, 544–6, 551, 558,
    559, 694, 699, 739, 742, 764, 767, 771
Helmreich, R. L., 19–20, 104, 106–8,
    110, 181, 354, 804, 805, 806, 817, 821,
    822, 823, 825, 828, 831n

Helson, H., 212, 227, 732
Hendrick, C., 471, 482, 737
Henley, N. M., 505, 511, 546
Hennessey, B., 784
Hernandez-Péon, R., 338
Hershkowitz, A., 42, 45–6
Hess, E. H., 431
Hilgard, E. R., 410
Hill, R. J., 549
Hinde, R. A., 303–4, 308
Hirota, T., 262
Hodges, W. F., 410
Hoffman, P. J., 646, 732
Hollingshead, A. B., 536
Holt, E. B., 189
Holtzman, P. S., 690
Holtzman, W. H., 590
Holz, R. S., 738
Homans, G., 333, 352, 534, 548
Honoré, A. M., 329
Hood, W. R., 352
Hopkins, G. M., 268
Hornbeck, F. W., 823
Horney, K., 645
Hovland, C. I., 53, 89, 159, 207, 212,
    371, 374, 391, 450, 500, 595, 615, 616,
    660, 702, 759–60, 782, 820, 821
Howe, E. S., 753n
Howes, D. W., 782
Hubert, S., 743
Hughes, H. S., 541, 792
Hull, C. L., 244, 744, 745, 751
Hunt, D., 477, 724
Hunt, J. McV., 260, 402, 628, 632,
    645, 650, 697
Hunt, W. A., 212
Hunter, R., 58, 96, 724, 737, 738, 739,
    746, 751, 757, 759, 764
Hutte, H., 545
Hyman, H., 791, 794–5

Insko, C. A., 73, 116, 151–4, 183, 418,
    513, 595
Irwin, M., 635, 639
Iwao, S., 423

Jackson, D. N., 597
Jacobsen, P. R., 659, 660, 707

Jacobson, A., 733, 736, 743, 761
Jahnke, J. C., 518
Jakobovits, L. A., 800
James, J., 778
James, W., 167, 291, 351, 367
Janicki, W. P., 618, 724
Janis, I., 19, 103–4, 106, 110, 181, 195,
    204, 207, 248, 369, 569, 577–88, 610,
    611, 612, 616, 619, 659, 660, 720, 759–
    60, 782, 804, 810–18, 820, 821, 822,
    825, 826, 827–33, 829n
Jansen, M. J., 818
Jaspers, J. M. F., 552
Jecker, J. D., 14, 459–61, 569, 571–6,
    602, 609, 610, 775n
Jellison, J. M., 775
Johnson, D. M., 732
Johnson, H. H., 474, 476, 552, 594,
    617, 618, 625, 626, 644, 659, 681, 692,
    707
Johnstone, J. W. C., 793
Jones, E. E., 20–1, 207, 350, 782, 821,
    829n
Jones, R. G., 252
Jones, S. C., 32
Jordan, N., 29, 34–6, 42–4, 47, 143, 166,
    169–78, 275–8, 282–3, 288, 306, 313,
    384, 400, 742

Kahl, J. A., 535–6
Kahn, M., 575, 584
Kaiman, I. P., 628
Kanouse, D. E., 138, 450, 741
Kant, I., 173
Kaplan, B., 653, 661–9, 718
Kardush, M., 653, 684–92, 716, 719
Karmos, G., 260
Katz, D., 66, 88, 143, 159, 166, 169,
    179–91, 275–6, 278–80, 282, 284, 287,
    290, 410, 513, 766
Katz, E., 549, 770, 788–96, 799, 831
Kaye, V., 826
Keller, F. S., 240
Kelley, H. H., 66, 212, 215, 759–60,
    782, 820, 821
Kelly, G. A., 55, 267, 273, 635, 648, 699
Kelman, H. C., 180–1, 302, 331–6, 344–
    5, 433, 500, 516, 590, 641, 643, 646,
    670–83, 696n, 719, 810, 819, 822

Kenny, D. T., 625, 626
Kern, R. P., 417
Kerr, C., 550
Kerrick, J. S., 58
Kessen, W., 594
Kety, S. S., 434
Keuthe, J. L., 339, 505–6, 538
Kiesler, C. A., 118, 437, 448–55, 457–8, 465–6, 707
Kiesler, S. B., 14, 453, 572, 573, 595, 602
Kimberly, J. C., 313
Kimble, G. A., 244
King, B. T., 248, 810, 818, 820
Kitt, A. S., 212
Kirschner, P., 826
Klapper, J. T., 797
Klausmeir, H. J., 811
Kleck, R. E., 628, 630
Knight, K. E., 715
Koch, S., 309–10
Koenig, I. D. V., 262
Koestler, A., 315–6
Koffka, K., 504–5
Kogan, N., 30, 340, 545, 547, 618
Kohlberg, L., 663
Kohler, R., 782
Kohler, W., 504–5, 605
Korobow, N., 417
Krasner, L., 410
Krauss, R. M., 207, 306, 355, 363, 369, 475, 516, 571
Kremen, I., 417
Kuhn, T. S., 510, 541, 585

Lacey, J. L., 304
Laffal, J., 754
Lamb, P., 359–97
Lambert, R. M., 114
Lambert, W. E., 800
Lambert, W. W., 730
Lampel, A. K., 736, 743
Lana, R. E., 595, 738
Lanzetta, J. T., 259
Larsen, O. N., 549–50
Latane, B., 405
Lawler, E. E., iii, 707
Lawrence, D. H., 5, 243–4, 255, 355, 400, 432, 714

Lawson, A. R., 708
Lazarsfeld, P., 789–90
Lazarus, R. S., 310, 418–9, 422, 433, 618, 621
Leach, E. R., 560
Leaman, R. L., 633
Leavitt, H., 308
Lecky, P., 206, 267, 320, 367
Lehrer, T., 394
Leichtman, M., 664
Lenski, G. E., 535
Lependorf, S., 19
Lepper, M., 808
Leventhal, H., 580, 636, 637
Levin, J., 738
Levin, K., xvi–xvii, 195, 240, 289, 512, 514
Levin, L. A., 724
Levine, J. M., 605
LeVine, R., 529, 551–64, 566
Levinson, B., 547
Levi-Strauss, C., 162
Levy, L., 199, 306, 737
Lewin, K., 575, 690
Lewis, J. L., 262, 402, 404–5
Lewis, M., 7
Lewis, N. A., 212
Lichtenstein, E., 410
Lieberman, S., 204
Lifton, R. J., 371, 811
Lindauer, F., 620
Linder, D., 20–1, 821, 829n
Linder, W. K., 257
Lindsley, D. B., 303
Linton, H. B., 690
Linton, R., 202, 305, 283
Lippmann, W., 320
Locke, E. A., 713
Loehlin, J., 528
Logan, F. A., 708, 750
Loh, W., 724
London, M., 505–6, 532, 546
Lott, B. E., 513
Lovejoy, A. O., 510
Lowell, E. L., 363, 478
Lowenherz, L., 85
Lowin, A., 359, 470–1, 778–9, 780
Lumsdaine, A., 586, 702
Lyle, J., 793
Lynch, M. D., 421, 423–4

Maccoby, E. E., 643, 793

Madaras, G. R., 246

Maddi, S. R., 161, 167, 207, 244, 267–75, 293–6, 363, 407, 800

Maehr, M., 349, 353

Mair, L., 662

Malcolm, T., 306, 355–6, 460, 465

Malewski, A., 306, 355–6

Malmo, R. B., 303–4, 418

Mandelbaum, S., 529, 539–43, 565, 566

Mandler, G., 417

Mandler, J. M., 417

Manis, M., 59, 514, 723, 738, 782

Mann, L., 575, 583, 585, 810

Mansing, J., 353

Mansson, H. H., 408, 413–4, 416, 441, 443, 446, 712

Marcantonio, C., 359, 479, 482–3

March, J., 190

Marek, J., 176

Margulis, S. T., 711

Marlowe, D., 228–38, 288, 597, 804

Marshall, L. M., 212–3

Maslow, A. H., 188, 313

Mathewson, G. C., 7, 11–3, 18

May, E., 439

Mayo, C. W., 635, 636, 637

McBride, D., 819

McCanley, C., 131

Macaulay, J. R., 70

McClelland, D. C., 259, 363, 407, 478, 540

McClintock, C., 410, 766, 831

McDonnell, P., 262

McDougall, W., 220

McGuigan, F. J., 597

McGuire, W. J., 4–5, 10, 67, 69–71, 118–9, 140–62, 169, 182–3, 255, 275–97, 301, 307–8, 343, 368–71, 384, 395, 411, 416, 469, 475, 498, 500, 513, 516–7, 528, 586, 600, 701, 738, 742, 794n, 797–800, 815–6, 818

McKinnon, D. W., 315

McNulty, J. A., 418

McPhee, W. N., 790

McQuail, E., 790

Mead, H., 202, 204

Meehl, P. E., 732

Meltzer, B., 669

Meno, 151

Merton, R. K., 201, 204, 548

Messick, G., 597

Meyer, D. L., 341

Meyer, L., 552

Miles, R., 329

Miller, D. R., 367

Miller, G. A., xvi, 226, 338, 519

Miller, G. R., 613, 624–32, 648, 650

Miller, H., 633, 636, 639

Miller, N., 118, 374, 378, 382, 569, 589–98, 609, 610

Miller, N. E., xvi, 243–5, 258, 305, 308–9

Millman, S., 475

Mills, J., 7, 11, 18, 23, 26, 125, 341, 401, 426, 480, 488–9, 493, 499, 560, 628, 707, 770, 771–6, 777, 780, 786, 790, 793, 795, 800

Milton, G. A., 205

Milton, J., 444

Mitchell, J. C., 552, 561

Mitra, S., 114

Mittman, L. R., 265

Moerman, M., 561

Montgomery, K. C., 268

Moore, O. K., 145

Morgan, W. J., 384

Morrissette, J., 41–2, 114, 341–2, 518

Morton, A. B., 384

Moss, C., 77

Mosteller, F., 733

Moulton, R. W., 713

Mowrer, O. H., 303, 714

Munzinger, H., 594

Murdock, P. H. J., 212

Murphy, G., 605

Murray, E. J., 243

Nafzgher, S., 353

Nanda, P. C., 66

Nebergall, R. W., 212, 371, 374, 516, 712

Neuringer, C., 615

Newcomb, T. M., xv–xvii, 3, 28–51, 118, 127, 169, 188, 192, 201–2, 277, 283, 305–7, 340, 418, 527, 533, 544–5, 551, 559, 565–6, 567, 618, 679n, 681, 693, 699, 766

Nichols, M., 439

Nicki, R. M., 262, 265

Norman, A., 743
Norman, R., 551, 555, 558
Norris, E. L., 70, 392, 399, 417–24, 432–5
Nowlis, G., 585
Nowlis, V., 392, 399, 417
Nunnally, J. C., 113, 118
Nuttall, R. L., 228–38, 804
Nuttin, J. M., 19, 104, 181, 701, 809

O'Connell, D. W., 156
Odom, R. D., 257
O'Gara, P., 707
Olmsted, D. L., 750
Oltman, P., 83
Olver, R. P., 222
Orne, M., 66, 82, 200, 206, 368, 470, 480–8, 597
Osgood, C. E., xvii, 4, 52–4, 56, 78, 113, 118–9, 122, 186, 188, 202, 216, 230, 248, 266, 277, 320, 369–70, 391, 394, 398–9, 418, 497, 505, 544, 545, 596, 641, 643, 646, 655, 659, 688, 689, 694, 723, 724–5, 732, 739, 745, 746, 747, 748, 764, 766
Ossorio, P. G., 327
Ostrom, T. M., 98, 212–3, 347, 373–83, 386
Overall, J. E., 536

Panofsky, E., 541
Papageorgis, D., 500, 516
Parducci, A., 212–3
Parke, R. D., 303
Parker, C. E., 790
Parker, E. B., 793
Paul, I. H., 627
Peak, H., 76, 167, 218–39, 275, 286–8, 290, 732
Peckham, M., 316
Peizer, D. P., 115
Penner, D. D., 216, 714
Penrose, L. S., 177
Penrose, R., 177
Pepitone, A., 63, 128, 131, 301, 319–26, 345–6, 357, 385
Pepper, S., 661n
Pervin, L. A., 619, 622

Petermann, B., 505
Peters, R. S., 202, 329
Peters, S. C., 477
Peterson, K. M., 246
Pettigrew, T. F., 338, 590
Pfaffman, C., 407
Phillips, J. L., 119
Piaget, J., 162, 661, 662–3, 690
Pilisuk, M., 273, 653, 660, 681, 693–9, 716, 718, 720
Plato, 174
Platt, J. R., 269, 271, 274
Podell, M. A., 59, 757, 758
Podell, J. E., 59, 757, 758
Polezhaev, E. F., 260
Polsby, N. W., 537, 538
Polt, J. M., 431
Posner, M. I., 713
Prelinger, E., 351–2
Premack, D., 257
Prestholdt, P., 707, 714
Pribram, K., 226
Price, K. O., 32, 36–7, 39, 42, 44, 192, 418, 693
Pritzker, H. A., 500
Propst, B. S., 269

Rabbie, J. M., 252, 406, 811
Raven, B. H., 180, 758
Rapaport, C., 445
Rapaport, D., 129, 413, 662
Ratliff, R. G., 410
Razran, G. H. S., 826
Rebert, C. S., 262
Redlich, F., 536
Reisen, A. H., 269
Reynolds, G. S., 709
Rhine, R. J., 589n, 778
Richter, M. L., 737
Riecken, H., 5, 473
Rimland, B., 316
Rimoldi, H. J. A., 732, 746
Robinson, H., 26, 401, 480, 772, 773
Rodin, A., 147
Rodrigues, A., 33–5, 36–40, 42–7
Rogers, C. A., 268
Rogers, E. D., 692
Rogers, E. M., 307, 477, 516, 549
Rokeach, M., 58, 97, 368, 513–4, 516–7,

552, 590, 613, 624–32, 648, 650, 687, 723

Rose, A. M., 535

Rosen, S., 401, 480, 771, 772

Rosenau, N., 207, 306, 355, 363, 369, 475, 516

Rosenbaum, M., 756-62, 764

Rosenbaum, W. B., 191, 660, 721, 756–62

Rosenberg, M. J., xv, 4, 19–20, 63, 73–113, 115, 117–8, 121–2, 141, 158, 169, 181–2, 187, 195, 207, 266, 269, 277, 283, 339, 341, 353, 369–70, 376–7, 380, 384–9, 391, 395, 398–9, 413, 481, 483, 513–5, 527, 544–5, 677, 685, 689, 696, 716, 717, 720, 739, 740–1, 752, 763–8, 804, 805n, 813, 818, 823, 824, 827–33.

Rosenberg, S., 152, 732, 733, 740

Rosenblatt, P., 589n

Rosenkrantz, P. S., 636, 669

Rosenthal, R., 66, 200, 483, 492, 833

Rosner, B. S., 750

Rosnow, R., 589n, 595, 738, 826

Ross, A., 775

Ross, I. C., 547

Ross, L., 26, 398, 474

Rothman, G., 58, 723

Rouanet, H., 733

Roussel, J., 244

Runkel, P. J., 115

Russell, B., 315

Russell, G., 826

Ryle, G., 247

Sakumura, J., 448–51, 453–4, 457–8, 465–6, 595, 781, 784

Salapatek, P. H., 257, 262

Sampson, E. E., 359, 418, 472, 476, 506, 533

Saporta, S., 113, 118

Saral, T. B., 734

Sarason, S. B., 417

Sarbin, T. R., 201–2, 205

Sargent, S. S., 201

Sarnoff, I., 143, 166, 180, 192–200, 275–6, 280–2, 294, 410, 415, 766, 831

Schachter, S., 5, 247, 323, 332, 345, 396, 406, 417–8, 473, 604

Schaeffer, R., 269

Schein, E. H., 371, 811

Schick, F., 662

Schildkraut, J. J., 434

Schlachet, P., 442

Schmidt, C. F., 722, 756–62

Schoen, R. A., 590

Schonbach, P., 23, 773

Schopler, J., 210

Schramm, W., 793

Schroder, H., 477, 645, 724

Schuck, J. R., 358–9, 471

Schultz, C., 744

Schultz, D., 263, 594

Schwartz, M., 537

Schwartz, R. D., 750

Scott, W. A., 21, 85, 204, 248, 375, 513–4, 534, 594, 803, 824

Scriven, M., 247

Sears, D. O., 207, 337, 401, 404, 426, 499, 501, 601, 770, 771, 772–3, 774, 777–87, 788–9, 792, 794, 797, 800

Secord, P. F., 73, 347, 349–54, 385f, 618

Seeman, M., 793

Selltiz, C. A., 800

Shanmugan, A. V., 723, 724, 726, 729

Shapiro, M. M., 782

Shaw, M. E., 713

Sheatsley, P. B., 791, 794–5

Sheffield, F. D., 307, 702

Shepard, R., 155, 221

Sherif, C., 212, 352, 371, 374, 516, 532, 559, 712

Sherif, M., 155, 212, 215, 227, 285, 323, 352, 371, 373–6, 382–3, 516, 532, 533, 559, 712, 782

Sherwood, J. J., 367–8

Sholiton, R. D., 417

Sibley, L. B., 359, 472, 476

Sidowski, J. B., 736

Siegel, A., 550

Silber, E., 349

Silverman, I., 359, 467, 470, 479–84, 491–2, 618

Simmel, M., 170

Simon, H. A., 190

Singer, J. E., 247, 337–42, 345, 391, 393–9, 432–4, 636, 637, 638, 650

Sjoberg, G., 539

Skinner, B. F., 167, 247, 291

Sklar, R., 563
Smelser, N., 205, 542
Smith, E. E., 17
Smith, F. T., 76
Smith, M. B., 74, 151–3, 180, 183, 347, 366–72, 385f, 410, 513, 552, 644, 681, 702, 721, 752, 766, 831
Smith, W. P., 82
Smock, C. D., 403
Smythe, D. W., 790–1
Snow, C. P., 534
Socrates, 151
Sofer, C., 577
Sokolov, E. N., 259, 261
Solomon, H., 703
Solomon, L., 357
Sontag, S., 268
Southard, L. D., 410
Spaulding, J., 36–8, 47, 646
Speisman, J. C., 310
Spence, D. P., 690
Spence, K. W., 244, 441
Spence, W., 732
Sperry, R. W., 261
Spielberger, C. D., 410
Spinoza, 171, 173, 308, 319
Spitzer, S. P., 404
Srinivasan, B., 536
Staats, A. W., 66, 758
Staats, C. K., 66, 758
Stanley, J. C., 591, 811
Starbuck, W. H., 713
Starr, S., 792
Stein, D. D., 552
Steinbruner, J. D., 450
Steiner, I. D., 36–8, 47, 207, 307, 309, 474, 476, 516, 604, 613, 616–8, 625, 626, 641–7, 649, 659, 683, 692, 707, 778, 797
Stevens, C. M., 750
Stevenson, M. W., 257
Stewart, H., 743
Stochowiack, J., 77
Stolurow, L. M., 732n, 818
Stotland, E., 88, 180, 513
Streufert, S., 697
Suci, G. J., 52, 230, 248, 418, 694, 724
Sullivan, H. S., 645, 694
Sumner, W. G., 558, 560
Supnick, L. E., 636

Suppes, P., 211
Sutton, S., 636

Taft, R., 605
Taguiri, R., 30, 340, 545, 547
Tajfel, H., 212, 552
Takezawa, S. I., 729
Tanaka, Y., 723, 724, 726, 729
Tannenbaum, P. H., 4, 52–72, 78, 119, 122–3, 182, 186, 192, 202, 216, 230, 248, 266, 277, 283, 320, 343–6, 369–70, 391, 394, 398–9, 417–8, 432–5, 497, 544, 545, 596, 655, 659, 688, 689, 694, 723, 724, 732, 739, 746, 747, 748, 764, 766
Taub, D., 212
Terrell, G., 265
Terwillinger, R., 575, 583
Thibaut, J. W., 212, 215
Thistlewaite, D. L., 145
Thomas, J. A., 589n
Thompson, W. R., 269
Thomson, C. W., 594
Tinbergen, N., 303
Tinkelpaugh, O. L., 479, 484
Tippett, J. S., 349
Titchener, E. B., xvii, 693
Toby, J., 208
Tognoli, J. J., 259
Tolman, E. C., 220, 223, 243, 355
Tolstoy, L., 509
Tomkins, S., 523
Torgerson, W., 732
Toulmin, S. E., 521
Toynbee, A., 316
Trenamen, J., 790
Triandis, H. C., 58, 723–30, 739, 746, 750, 759, 763
Triandis, L. M., 729, 730
Tripodi, T., 633, 634, 635, 636, 637, 638, 639
Troldahl, V. C., 795
Turner, E. A., 7, 17, 22, 658, 804
Turner, J., 466, 500, 712–3
Turner, R. H., 305, 307, 679n, 681
Twain, M., 396
Tyler, C., 516

Upshaw, H. S., 166, 210–7, 275, 282, 284–6

Van de Geer, J. P., 552
van den Berghe, P. L., 561
Vannoy, J. S., 635, 643, 646, 651, 697
Vernon, P. E., 399
Verplanck, W. S., 589
Vidulich, R. N., 516, 628
Vigotsky, L. S., 155
Voltaire, 706
Voronin, L. A., 259

Wagner, A. R., 708
Wallach, M. A., 618
Waller, W. W., 306
Wallon, H., 661
Walser, M., 560
Walster, E., 16, 306, 475, 478, 516, 569,
   589n, 593, 595, 599–608, 609, 611,
   612, 707
Walster, W., 306
Walters, R. H., 308, 418
Waly, P., 605, 781, 782
Ward, W. D., 359, 470, 482–3
Warner, W. L., 792
Waterman, A. S., 359, 471, 482
Watts, W. A., 467–78, 487, 489, 491–2,
   580
Webster, 711
Wechsler, M., 788
Weick, K. E., 179, 216, 512–9, 526–8,
   653, 706–15, 718, 719, 720
Weisenberg, M., 441, 707
Weiss, W., 43, 53, 159, 371, 545, 605,
   653, 700–5, 718, 719, 737, 746
Welker, W. I., 269, 272
Welsh, C., 587
Werner, H., 661, 662, 663, 664, 668,
   669
Wertheimer, M., 171–2, 504, 614
Wheaton, J., 628, 630
White, B. J., 212, 352, 532

White, R. W., 180, 268, 403, 410, 513,
   702, 766, 831
Whyte, W., 532, 533, 548
Willey, B., 541
Willis, R. H., 59, 732, 737
Wilson, D. T., 358
Wilson, G., 552
Wilson, W. C., 793
Winer, B. J., 109, 424
Winters, L. C., 744
Wishlade, L., 575
Wishner, J., 757
Witkin, H. A., 338
Wood, J. D., 618
Woodruff, A. D., 74, 720, 752
Wrenn, R. L., 628, 629, 630
Wright, J., 7, 22, 804
Wunderluch, R. A., 510
Wylie, R. C., 366

Yaryan, R. B., 398, 474
Yatko, R. J., 619, 622
Yogi, K., 417
Yntema, D., 732
Young, P. T., 407, 732
Youniss, J., 510

Zanna, M. P., 452
Zajonc, R. B., 25–6, 33–5, 40–2, 119,
   134, 179, 181, 305, 308, 339, 342, 375,
   391, 406, 505, 615, 741, 784
Zener, S. L., 257
Ziegler, H. P., 304
Zimbardo, P. G., 7, 17, 198–9, 205,
   286, 309–10, 363, 371, 377–8, 437–47,
   464–6, 480, 597, 618, 707, 712, 715,
   818, 824
Zimmer, H., 556
Zimmerman, C., 784
Zinnes, J. L., 211

Subject Index

Action, 218
  attitude discrepant, 332–34
  goal directed, 219
  intentional, 328–29
  see also, Behavior
Activation, definition of, 222
Activation theory, 218–39, 275, 287–88, 304
  basic constructs of, 220–28
  behavior and, 222
  choice, 237–38
  cognitive dissonance and, 228–38
  postulates of, 222–24
  psychological structure and, 220–22
Adaptation level, 212
Adding vs. averaging models, 723
Affective-cognitive consistency, 73–111, 398
  and post-hypnotic suggestion, 76–77
  and persuasive communications, 85
  cognitive index and, 75–76
  model, 767
  relation of attitude change to, 75
  restoration of, 98–99
Affective-cognitive structure, inauthenticity and, 101–11
Affective response, modification of, 77–78
Affiliation, 406
Aggression
  catharsis theory of, 309–10
  social, 443
  see also Frustration
Ambiguity, intolerance of, xvi, 97
Anal character, attitude change and, 196–97
Animal learning, 241, 289
Anxiety, 417–24
  see also Psychological stress
Approval, need for, 195, 281

Arousal, 261, 304, 402–03
  collative variables and, 261–63
  increment in, 263–64
  level of, 405–07
  reticular formation and, 261
  potential, 263
  see also Cognitive dissonance, Complexity theories
Assertion constant
  see Congruity principle
Associative vs. dissociative relations
  see Psycho-logic
Attractiveness
  effort and, 487
  see also Postdecisional dissonance, Dissonance reduction, Interpersonal balance
Attribution, of causality, 514
Attitudes, xvi
  and unit relations, 34
  as cognitive structures, 395
  behavioristic conceptions of, 241–42
  conceptual conflict and, 264
  ego defenses and, 180, 195
  function of, 180
  implications of, 696–97
  interpersonal, 721
  motivational bases of, 179
  self-judgment of, 252
  see also Attitude change
Attitude change, 17, 801
  and classical conditioning, 66
  and learning theory, 66
  awareness and, 435
  behavioral intentions, 705
  brainwashing and, 371
  commitment and, 450–51, 812
  discrepancy and, 285, 500
  involvement vs., 371, 379–80
  effects of role enactment on, 205–09

ego involvement and, 373–83
experimental studies
    methods of, 596–98
functional approach to, 178–91
incentive and, 196
judgment theory analysis of, 213–14
modes of resolution and reasoning
    in, 700–705
persuasive communications and,
    152–53
psychoanalytic theory and, 195
Socratic method of, 148, 151–53
related effects, 702–05
temporal decay of, 153–54
via informational content, 66
via role playing, 810–18
volition and, 125
see also Congruity principle, Cognitive dissonance, Affective-cognitive consistency, Evaluative induction
Attitudinal vacuity, 87
    detection of, 82–89
Autokinetic effect, 323
Autonomy, 173
Awareness, 208, 280, 345, 408–16
    wants and, 329–30
    learning vs. performance and, 415–16
see also Verbal conditioning

Balance, xvi
    and negative reference groups, 33
    and sentiment relations, 29
    categories of, 35–38
    cognitive, xvi, 169–78, 187
        and unit relations, 29, 174–76, 277–78, 505–06
        autism and, 316
        Gestalt analysis of, 169–78, 276–78
        interpersonal attraction and, 305–06
        liking relations and, 174–76, 277–78
        physiological correlates of, 316–17
        preference for positive, 280
        stability of, 190–91
    definition of, 29
    harmony and, 173–74, 277

interpersonal, 28–51
    principles of, 29–31
    psychological nature of, 31–34
    structural, 169
    vacuous, 176
Balance theory, xvi, 28, 141, 319–20, 463, 551–52
    see also Consistency, Behavior theory vs. Congruity theory, 739–42
Behavior, 15
    attitude-discrepant, 354
    blocking of, 227–28
    cognitive mediation and, 133
    communication, 404
        under stress, 420–21
    complexity-seeking, 293–95
    epistemic, 265
    human, xvi, 102, 174, 276
        adaptive aspects of, 240–41
        see also Variety
    inauthentic, 101
    incentive-reinforcement theory of, 240–45, 275, 287
    incompatible responses and, 397–98
    interpersonal social, 283
    intrapersonal cognitive, 283
    modernization, 539–43
    outcomes of, 227–28
    reactivation of, 227
    relation between attitudes and, 289–90
    role-discrepant, 283
    aggressive, 357
    self-evaluative, 349–51
    self-referent, 349–54
        types of, 349–52
    social, 201–09
    stimulus-seeking, 400–07
Behavioral implication, 457
Behavior episode, definition of, 219
Behaviorism, see Cognitive dissonance
Behavior theory, 240–45, 289–90
    attitude change and, 241
    balance and, 242–43
    cognitive dissonance and, 243–44
Belief, 5, 185
    conceptual conflict and, 264
    conflict, 522
    congruence, 58, 723

dilemmas, resolving, 665
propositions, 521
systems, 141–42, 148, 396, 521–25,
    528
  organization of, 187–88, 520–25
transformation, 522–23
Bernoulli theorem, 236
Bolstering, 119–24, 515–16
Boomerang effect, 333
Boyle's law, 280, 295
Brainwashing, 371

California F scale, 340, 616
  California Personality Inventory,
    616
Charles' law, 280, 295
Choice, see Cognitive dissonance
  commitment and, 448
  freedom of, 456–57
Classical conditioning, 257–58, 441
  see also Attitude change
Cognition, 91, 113, 264, 312–13, 497–99
  and social orderings, 531–38
  dissonance conception of, 243
  effect of role enactment on, 204
  hypnotic manipulation of, 76–77,
    412–14, 445–46
  relation to meaning, 62–63
Cognitions, 5, 28
  conflicting
    effect of decision, 591–94
    effects of time on, 589–98
    evaluative vs. informational ele-
      ments, 594–96
    modes of response measurement,
      596
    source evaluation, 596
  consonant, 6
  overriding, 21–22, 126–27, 135
  perceptual distinctions, 694
  underlying, 21–22
  see also, ideas, beliefs, opinions
Cognitive activity, 131–34, 501
  rewards for, 515
  see also, Conceptual activity
Cognitive camel, 439–40
Cognitive clusters, 59
Cognitive complexity, xvii
  and judgment of inconsistent infor-
    mation, 633–40

and resolution of inconsistent infor-
    mation, 635–36
concept of structure, 633–34
measures of, 697–98
perceived conflict and, 637–39
structure and, 635–36
Cognitive consistency, xv, 140
  and adaptation to reality, 662
  and defence mechanisms, 662
  effects of time on, 599–608, 609–12
  eliciting stimuli and, 308–10
  functional approach to, 179–91
  homeostatic mechanism of, 345
  immediate postdecision effects,
    600–03
  importance of, 497–503
  incongruities in, 693–94, 697
  intermediate effects, 603–08
  interpretation of, 662
  judgmental analysis of, 213–16
  motivation and, 319–26
  need for, 327–30
  predecision dissonance, 609–10
  protective anchoring and, 214
  stimulus processing and, 337–42
  syllogistic analysis of, 395, 411
  wants and, 327–30
  see also, Consistency, Inconsistency
Cognitive dissonance, 178–91, 321–23
  and attitude change, 15, 125
  anxiety and, 365
  arousal of, 8–9, 310, 408–09, 457, 486
    behavior theory and, 244
    commitment and, 462
    frustration and, 361–62
  as drive state, 5, 409
  awareness and, 408–16
  behaviorism and, 246–56
  commitment and, 16, 20–21, 106,
    186, 369, 401, 454–63
  conflict and, 14, 243–45, 322, 425–26
  control of human motivation, 439–47
  decisions and, 6, 13–14, 243–45, 306,
    425, 458–62, 485–90
    see also Postdecisional dissonance
  definition of, 6
  effort and, 7, 16
  ego defenses and, 197–98
  expectancy and, 9, 22–26, 355–65,
    469–78

experimental methodology, 10–13
'follows from' relation and, 125–28, 255–58, 324, 488
guilt, shame and, 361–63
 see also Psychoanalytic theory
hedonic vs. moral, 332–34
 attitude change and, 332–34
inauthenticity and, 101–11
information-seeking and, 401–02, 424
incompetence vs. immorality, 359–61
justification and, 7, 309–10, 413–14, 437, 441–47, 456, 486–87
psychoanalytic theory and, 192–200, 281–82, 410
 comparative scope of, 193
 contentions between, 193–96
radical behaviorism and, 246–56, 290–92
reduction of, 6, 12–17, 207, 307
 failure at, 26
 individual differences in, 193
role theory and, 204–05
selective exposure and, 337
self concept and, 22–26, 355–65
severity of threat and, 7, 131
theory of, 5–27
volition and, 17, 369, 444–47
volunteering and, 234–36, 252
Cognitive elements, 113, 287
 resistance to change of, 448–49
 see also, Commitment
 self concept and, 352–53
Cognitive implication, 4, 322, 345
Cognitive inertia, 158
Cognitive interaction
 cultural determination of, 724–25
Cognitive links, 512–19
 sources of, 513–14
Cognitive mapping, 155
Cognitive microprocesses, 82, 121, 387–88
Cognitive organization, xvi, 278, 290
 deductive and coercive principles of, 114
 equilibrium and, 314
Cognitive ramification, 512–19
 determinants of, 514–18

Cognitive response, modification of, 77
Cognitive structure, 4, 113, 141–42
 and social structures, 544–50
 assumptions about, 495–519
 completeness of, 518
 components of, 288
 ego involvement and, 374–76
 learning of, 338–40
 minimalist vs. maximalist positions, 526–28
 subjective validity of, 323
Cognitive system, 512
 components of, 144–45
 equilibrium point of, 147–48
 structure of, 225, 287
 laws of, 145–47
 model, 698–99
Cognitive validity, 323–26
 hypotheses concerning, 324–26
 need for, 323
Cognitorium, attitudinal, 79–81
Collative variables, 257–66, 293–95, 403
 information theory and, 259
Commitment, 346, 448–55
 as a mediating variable, 437–66
 behavioral, 473–76, 515
 decision-making and, 448
 definition of (Gerard), 457
 definition of (Kiesler), 448
 motivational components of, 450–51, 453–54
 reward-cost implications of, 457–62
 to consonant behavior, 449–51
 to future interactions, 451–53
 volition and, 456–58
 voluntariness and, 456–62
 see also, Cognitive dissonance
Communication, 15, *see also* Selective exposure
 discrepancy, 466
 acceptance of, 116
 counterattitudinal, 292
 situation, 54 *see also*, Congruity principle, Persuasion
Communicator, 15
 credibility, 15, 17, 248–49, 253, 466
 see also, Source, Attitude change
Comparison level, 212, 215

Compartmentalization, 451
  see also, ego defenses
Complexity theories, 119, 161, 292–97
Compliance, 291–92, 371
  see also, Forced-compliance
Computer simulation, 4, 125, 136–39,
    520–25
  strategy of, 136
Conceptual activity, 140
Conceptual good figures, 504–11,
    527–32
  linear orderings as, 506–07
  linear vs. partial order, 507–08
Conceptual network, activation of,
    224–26
Conflict, xvi, 257–66, 522
  cognitive, 181–82
  collative variables and, 257–66
  conceptual, 264–66, 403–07
  conditions for arousal of, 185–86
  decision-making and, 13–14
  functional analysis of, 189–90
  incompatible responses and, 260
  motivating properties of, 322
  postdecisional, 186, 243–45, 290,
    570–76
  psychological, xvi
  social, 556–60
  theory, 369, 425–26, 815
  variety and, 271
  see also, Complexity theories
Conformity, 426, 472
Congruity principle, 52–72, 78, 122–23,
    320–21, 398, 435, 723–24
  and attitude change, 53–56
    generalization of, 63–66, 434
  assertion constant, 56, 67
  communication situations and, 54
  correction for incredulity, 55
Congruity, self-role, 205
Congruity theory
  vs. balance theory, 739–42
Consistency, xv, 28
  maximization of, 140
  need for, 140–41
  pursuit of, 267–74
  usage, xv
  model, 545
  motivation, 341
  theories, 3, 544

and attitude change, 777
  failure of, 185–90
  motivational level and, 181–83
  role theory and, 202–04
  structure theorem, 546
  variety and, 270–74
  see also Balance
Correction for incredulity
  see Congruity principle
Counterattitudinal advocacy, 19, 105–
    06, 131, 268, 466, 827–33
  see also Role playing
Counterattitudinal assertion, 105–06
Counterattitudinal behavior, 801, 819–
    26, 827
  biased scanning, 824
  definition, 819
  differential demand characteristics,
    826
  dissonance theory, 824
  extraneous reinforcements, 825
  varieties, 803–09
Creativity, 315–16
  see also Complexity theories
Cue utilization, 517–18
  Curiosity, 262
  perceptual, 263, 265
  epistemic, 265, 403

Decision-making, 190, 200, 426, 428–
    30, 467–94
  definition of, 610
  justifications for, 444
  psychology of, 431
  satisficing criterion and, 190
  see also Cognitive dissonance, con-
    flict, Self-concept
  stages in the process of, 577–88
    attitude change, 581–85
    unpleasant consequences, 585–88
Demand characteristics, 82, 287, 350,
    368, 470, 476–77, 480–81
Denial, 119–20
  of motivation, 447
  see also, Ego defenses
Dictionary of Occupational Titles, 760
Discrepancy, 331
  cognitive, 186
  see also, Inconsistency, Attitude

change, Cognitive dissonance,
    Involvement, Social comparison
Dissonance
  avoidance, 576
  intolerance for, 698–99
  predecision, 609–10
  sensitizing vs. avoidance responses
    situational factors, 621–23
Dissonance reduction, 6, 821–24
  categorization of modes, 684–92
  choice of modes of, 477, 684–92
  influence of biological drives,
    440–47
  influence of social motives, 440–47
  modes
    difficulties in studying, 707
  physiological effects of, 309, 317
  physiological measures of, 440–47
  preparation and, 473–76
  projection as means of, 198, 397
  self-esteem and, 370
  see also, Cognitive dissonance
Dissonance theory, 815, 824, 827–33
Distributive justice, 333
Dogmatism, 97
Dominance relation, see Psycho-logic
Drive, 258
  curiosity, 388
  generalized, 303–05
  secondary, 258
  see also, Cognitive dissonance
Drive-reduction, 257–66, 293–94,
    307–10

EEG, 263
Effort, see Cognitive dissonance, Sub-
    jective probability, Attractive-
    ness
Ego, 113
  defenses, 193
  involvement, 373, 395, 397, 475
    centrality and, 375, 385
  see also, Attitude change, Cognitive
    dissonance
Equity, 324, 333
Ethnocentrism
  and intergroup relations, 551–64
  and dissonance theory, 560–64
  degree, 562

Ethology, 303–04
Evaluation apprehension, 82, 102, 377,
    483
Evaluative assertion analysis, 113
Evaluative transfer, definition of, 121
Evaluative induction, 121–25
  attitude change and, 124–25
Expectancy, disconfirmed, 356–59,
    467–94
  choice of negative alternatives,
    479–84
  conditioned emotional response and,
    362–64
  reactions to, 469–78
  recall as a result of, 471, 482–83
Expectation
  volunteering as a function of, 472
  see also, Role theory, Cognitive dis-
    sonance, Self
Experimenter bias, 483

Fait accompli, 485, 488, 490
Fenwick study, 81–82, 115–18, 384
Forced-compliance studies, 249–50,
    450, 501–02
  interpersonal simulation of, 250–55
  see also, Cognitive dissonance
Free fatty acids, 5, 317, 432, 441
Frustration, 446
  and aggression, 444
Functional theory, 177–91, 278–80
  motivational aspects of, 179–91, 278–
    80

Generalization, of attitude change
  see Congruity principle
Generalization, empirical, 246, 255
Gestalt, see Psychology
Goal responses, 479
Graph theory, 545–46
Groups, formal, 534
Groups, large, 534–37
  co-acting, 567
  face-to-face, 567
Groups, small, 532, 596
  clusterability, 546–50
GSR, 262, 441, 446, 464

Hedonic satisfaction, 117
Hedonism, 73, 89–101
Human experience, 276
Human thought, 140, 511
  connectedness of, 142–43
  definition of, 144
  internal coherence of, 141–42
  logicality of, 156–62
  process simulation of, 157
  product simulation of, 157–58
  nonrational needs and, 159
  structure of, 140

Ideas, 5
Imbalance, 30–33
  definition of, 31
  Cognitive balance and, 171–73,
    175–77, 266
  Cognitive dissonance and, 126–28
  see also Nonbalance
  tolerance for, 590
Implicational molecules, definition of,
  133
  learning in relation to, 134
  see also, Psychological implication
Implicational principles, 134
  systems of, 135–39
Impression formation, 59, 338
Incentive, 17, 102–11, 290–92
  theory, 17–21, 103
  see also, Behavior, Conflict, Reward
Inconsistency
  and importance, 396
  as a bothersome state, 393–99
    factors influencing, 395–98
  as a motivational construct, 301–02
  as a psychological state, 331–36
  cognitive, 393–94
    discomfort of, 400–07
    mediational responses to, 425–31
  functional implications of, 332–36
  modes of resolution, 613, 716
    determinants of, 670–83
      inconsistency maintenance,
        672–76
      inconsistency reduction,
        670–72
      inconsistency reduction vs. in-
        consistency maintenance,
        676–83

advanced, 668–69
  centrality principle, 717
  intermediate, 667, 668, 678, 679
  primitive, 666, 667
negative affect and, 394
psychological, 7–10
reactions to, 305–07, 641–47
  consistency-restoring responses,
    641–47
  dissonance-reducing responses,
    619–21
  effects of personality variables,
    618–19, 641
  individual differences in, 613,
    615–23
  kinds of influence, 615–16
  methodological issues, 616–18
reduction, 564
  and personality factors, 648–51
resolution of, 119–21, 188–90,
    334–36, 653–720
  competing motivation, 659
  desire for, 329–30
  developmental analysis of modes
    of, 661–69
  hydraulic model of, 309
  role theory and, 207
  stimulus-processing and, 340
state of, 299
tolerance of, xvi, 89, 207
  authoritarianism and, 625–27
  dissonance theory and, 627–32
  dogmatism and, 625–27
  general-personal content and,
    91–94
  hedonic-antihedonic assertions,
    91–94
  individual differences and, 624–32
  see also Hedonic satisfaction
  thresholds for, 97
  wish fulfillment and, 91
Individual differences, 22–23, 615–32
  stimulus processing and, 342
  see also Cognitive dissonance, Inter-
    personal balance
Influence, 180
Information
  belief-discrepant material, 769,
    771–76, 777, 799
  biased recall, 769

belief-supportive, 769, 771–76, 777, 797, 798, 799
disparate, 756–62
  additive vs. averaging, hypotheses, 756, 763–64, 767–68
  impression response, 758–59
  heterogeneous lists, 757
  pooling models, 756–62
  summation rule, 757
  tolerance, 765–66
perceptual distortion, 769
selective avoidance, 769
selective exposure, 769, 777
selective exposure hypothesis, 769
selective learning, 769
Information integration, 731–43
  experimental analysis, 731
  linear model, 732–38, 763, 765, 767–8
  personality impression task, 731
  spasm model, 768
Information processing, xvi, 157, 159, 279, 290, 345
  channel capacity and, xvi, 133, 519
Information-seeking, 430
  see also, Cognitive consistency, Selective exposure
Information theory, 294
Ingratiation, 350
Inoculation theory, 69, 71, 500–01
Instrumental conditioning, 257
Intergroup relations, 551–55
  and dissonance theory, 560–64
  balanced patterns, 555–60
Interpersonal attraction, see Cognitive balance
Interpersonal balance
  and individual differences, 49–50
  empirical studies of, 34–46
Interpersonal relations, xvi
  dyads, xvi, 29–32
  psychology of, xvi, 171
  triads, xvi, 29–32
Involvement, definition of, 373–74
  attitudinal, 373–83
  a model of, 374–76
  types of, 371
  value-bonding and, 379–83

Judgment, 210–12

assimilation and, 212–14
contrast and, 212–14
effect of cultural differences on consistency, 727–29
perceptual, 285
psychophysical, 210–12
  errors of, 211
reference scale and, 211
social comparison and, 426–28
standards of, 212
see also, Psychology
Justification, 441, 464
  of wasted preparation, 475–76
  see also, Cognitive dissonance, Decision-making, Self-justification

Kennedy-Nixon debates, 790

Learning theory, 308
  see also, Behavior theory
Least-effort principle, 59, 395, 716
  see also, Psycho-logic
Logic, xv, 144

Machiavellianism, 131, 647n
Mandala circles, 556–57
Meaning, need for, 291
Memory, long-term, 134
Message, 53
  uniformity, 67
  see also, Communication
Minnesota Multiphasic Personality Inventory 616, 620
Modeling effects, see Experimenter bias
Mood adjective check list, 399, 417, 433–34
  use in consistency studies, 420–24
Motivation, 257–66, 281, 296
  cognitive, 313–14
  epistemic, 291
  equilibrium as, 311–18
  goal-state and, 219, 278
  learning and, 441
  see also Activation theory, Cognitive consistency, Cognitive dissonance, Functional theory

Motivational hierarchy, 197
Motivational states, cognitive control
    of, 309–10
    see also Thirst, Pain tolerance

Need, concept of, 327–29
Needs, 13
    reduction of, 313–14
    see also Cognitive consistency
Negro-white relationships, 552
Nonbalance, 31–33
Novelty, *see* Uncertainty

Opinions, 5
Opinion change, *see* Attitude change
Orientation reaction, 260–61
Organizations
    formal, *see* Groups
    industrial, 534

Pain tolerance
Perception
    interpersonal, 247
    of personal power, 214–15
    person, 170
    see also Self-perception
Perceptual organization, Gestalt laws
    of, 170
Personality, xvi
    authoritarian, xvi
    development of, 194
    dynamics of, 194
    forces in, 296
    individual differences in, 192
    organization, xvi
    see also Cognitive dissonance
Persuasion
    communication and
    resistance to, 69, 500–01
        forewarning and, 501
        strategies for, 69–71
    see also Attitude change, Inocula-
        tion theory, Affective-cognitive
        consistency
Phenomenal causality, xvi, 171
Phi phenomenon, 227
Play, 314–16, 318
Playboy, 506, 509

Pleasure, 315, 318
Pleasure principle, 12, 282
Positivity principle, 117
Postdecisional dissonance, 369, 393–94,
    412–13, 456, 459–60
    selective attention and, 430–31
    physiological measures of, 429–30
Postdecisional regret, 457, 475–76
P-O-X paradigm, 29–33, 175–76,
    388–89
    and ease of learning, 40–42
    and engagement, 33, 42
    and lateral symmetry, 41
    and pleasantness ratings, 34
    and preference for positivity, 42–43,
        117
    and unpleasantness ratings, 35–36
    preference for changed relations, in
        39–40
    relevance of X in, 46–47
    valence of O and X in, 45–46
    see also Balance, Psycho-logic
Pragnänz, law of, 172, 174, 177, 277,
    320, 504
Predecision dissonance, *see* Cognitive
    consistency
Proattitudinal advocacy, 451, 458
Protestant ethic, 324
Psychoanalytic theory, 192–200,
    280–82
    see also, Attitude change
Psycho-logic, xv, 79, 81, 112–15, 141,
    182, 384
    associative vs. dissociative relations
        and, 113
    criticisms of, 118–19
    dominance relation and, 113
    least-effort principle and, 115
    P-O-X triads and, 115–16
    reciprocity principle and, 117
    rivalry principle and, 128
Psychological, xvi
    conflict, xvi
    implication, 112–39, 142–48, 244,
        287–88, 449, 456, 513
        implicational molecules and,
            133–35
        Naive Question Game, 128–30
        operationalization of, 128–32
        negation, 277–78

processes, 29
stress, 391–435
  as a mediator, 433
  changes in, 420–21
  physiological measures of, 418, 426–31
  verbal indices of, 417–24
structure, 220
  association and, 221
  similarity-difference and, 221
  see also, Activation theory
Psychology
  cognitive, 169–78
  Gestalt, 169–71, 177, 227, 275, 312, 463, 504–07, 532, 544, 547
  of inference, 290
  of judgment, 210–17, 275, 282, 284–86
  of personal constructs, 267
Psychophysics, 210, 544
Psychosexual fixation, 196–97

Radical behaviorism, 247, 275, 290–92
Reaction formation, see Ego defenses
Reason, 112, 312–13
  age of, 312
Reciprocity, 333
  see also, Psycho-logic
Reinforcement, see Behaviorism, Incentive
Regret phenomenon, 569
Relative deprivation, 212
Reward, 17
  theory, 17–21
  see also, Incentive
Role conflict, 204–06, 283
  resolution of, 206
Role distance, concept of, 354
Role playing, 341–42, 828
  attitude change, 810–18
  counterattitudinal, 79, 102–11
Role theory, 201–09, 275, 282–84
  expectation and, 202–04, 206–07, 283
R-S scale, 620

Salience, 396–97
  commitment and, 286
  issue vs. response, 286

Satiation theory, 800
Selectivity
  interest as a basis of, 793–95
  utility as a basis of, 792–93
Schemata, definition of, 338
Schizophrenia, 316, 328
Selective attention, 519
  see also Selective exposure, Postdecisional dissonance
Selective exposure, 401–07, 499, 777–87, 788–96, 797–800
  confoundings, 779–80
  de facto selectivity, 783, 790
  defending commitments, 781
  defensive avoidance, 800
  homeostatic hedonism, 783
  mass communications, 788, 795, 796, 798
  mass media audiences, 789, 798
  motivated, 790
  'neutral' communications, 795
  null hypothesis possibility, 781
  sampling distortions, 780
  self-consciousness, 780
  self-exposure, 786
  selective avoidance, 797, 798, 799
  stimulus situation, 779
  supportive selectivity, 789–92, 795
  see also Communication, Cognitive dissonance
Self, 206
  consistency process and, 347–90
  status congruence and, 352–53
Self-actualization, 173, 313
Self concept, 97, 202, 345–46, 384–89
  changes in, 368
  decision-making and, 306–07
  see also, Cognitive dissonance, Self
Self-consistency, 206
Self esteem, 180, 281, 283, 306, 385, 471
  theory, 475
Self-evaluation, 350–51
Self-justification, 465, 706–15
  behavioral measures, 707–12
    counter conditioning, 714
    inadequate justification, 708–09
  need for, 291
  Panglossian model, 706
Self-perception, 367, 387–88
  functional analysis of, 247–56

Self-persuasion, 248–49, 446
Self-presentation, 350–51
Self-reports, 417–24
Semantic combination, 56
    additivity vs. summation, 58
    and mediation theory, 60
Semantic differential, 4, 53, 59, 63, 248,
        418
    and evaluative factor, 53
Sentiment relations, 113, 171–73
    see also, Balance
Shame, 195, 281
Social approval, 413–14, 443
Social communication, xvii
Social comparison, xvii, 323, 406,
        426–28
    discrepancy and, 426–27
Social ecology, 202
Social objects, perception of, 170
Social perception, *see* Perception
Social power, sources of, 180
Social rejection, 364–65
Social schemata, 339, 505–11
    grouping of, 505–06
    learning of, 505, 511
Social structure, 531
    and cognitive structures, 544–50
Socratic effect, 182
    see also, Attitude change
Society, 202–03
Source, of communication, 54
    see also, Communicator
Sour grapes, 16
S-R psychology, 133, 241, 511
Status equilibration, 536
Stereotyping, 320
Stimuli, 744
    as motivational forces, 258
    complication of, 751

response conflict model, 750
responses to stimulus manifolds, 749
verbal, 745
Stimulus processing, *see* Cognitive
        consistency
Structure matrix, 114
Subincision, 420
Subjective probability, as function of
        effort, 474–75
Subjective rationality, 112
Subjective stress scale, 417–18
Summation principle, 723

Tension reduction, 313–14, 335, 518

Uncertainty, 259
    aversiveness of, 262–63
    novelty and, 259
Unit relations, 113, 171–75
    see also Balance
USSR, 257

Variety, human behavior and, 267–74
    need for, 275, 295–96, 388
    personality research and, 269–70
Verbal conditioning, 413, 442–43
    awareness and, 414
Volition, *see* Cognitive dissonance

Weighted average principle, 723
Wishful thinking, 150, 159, 384

Zeigarnik effect, 394, 518

Printed in the U.S.A.